8-2 (b) Net accounts receivable, Jan. 31, $461,280

8-3 (a) Probable expense from uncollectible accounts, $6,740

8-4 (a) May 26. Cash from discounting Davis note, $72,712

8-5 No key figure

8-6 (c) One-year interest charge originally included in face amount of note, $6,240

8-7 (b) June 30. Interest accrued, Patten Co. note payable, $100

8-8 (c) Total current assets, $21,595

8-9 (b) Credit Interest Revenue, $79

Case 8-1 No key figure

Case 8-2 (a) Net income, $17,700

Appendix A

A-1 No key figure

A-2 No key figure

A-3 (a) Payroll taxes expense, $2,618

A-4 (b) Payroll taxes expense, $1,478.40

A-5 (b) FICA taxes deducted from earnings of employees, $8,022.21

9-1 (a) Gross profit percentage, Year 1, 43%

9-2 (a) (1) Inventory, fifo, $74,980

9-3 (a) Gross profit rate for Year 3, 25%

9-4 (a) (1) Fifo, $188,300; (b) Gross profit on sales, lifo, $300,625

9-5 (b) Inventory, Jan. 7, $20,400

9-6 (b) Cost of goods sold for May, $1,385

9-7 (b) Cost percentage, 75%

9-8 (a) Cost of goods sold, Year 9, $503,000

Case 9-1 (b) Gross profit, $9,800

Case 9-2 No key figure

10-1 Depreciation for Year 2: (a) $9,000; (b) $12,000; (c) $12,000

10-2 Depreciation for Year 2: (b) $70,400; (c) $72,000; (d) $114,000

10-3 Depreciation for Year 2: (a) $3,200; (b) $7,980

10-4 Depreciation expense, Year 2, $6,800

10-5 (a) Accumulated depreciation, Machines A, B, and C, Dec. 31, Year 5, $168,030

10-6 (b) Land, $60,000

10-7 (a) Depreciation, Year 3: (1) $7,000; (2) $9,000; (3) $22,940

10-8 (a) (2) Loss on trade-in of plant assets, $3,000; (d) New truck, basis for income tax purposes, $14,300

10-9 (c) Accumulated depletion, $2,127,600

10-10 Adjusted net income, $15,600

Case 10-1 (a) Total depreciation for first three years, Bay Company, $37,500; Cove Company, $68,463

Case 10-2 (b) Revised earnings, Company X, $52,800; (c) Price to be offered for Company X, $383,040

11-1 (b) Withdrawals, $12,300

11-2 (a) (4) Share to Martin, $34,000

11-3 (a) Share to Partner B, $184,000

11-4 (b) Total assets, $187,000

11-5 Stockholders' equity, (a) $189,000; (b) $1,390,000

11-6 (b) Stockholders' equity, $827,500

11-7 (a and c) Stockholders' equity, $7,170,000

11-8 (b) Total assets, $997,000

11-9 No key figure

Case 11-1 No key figure

Case 11-2 (b) Share to Ramirez, first year, $7,000

12-1 Income before extraordinary items, $1,500,000

12-2 Income before extraordinary items, $2,360,000

12-3 (b) Retained earnings, Jan. 1, Year 9, as restated, $364,000

12-4 No key figure

12-5 Book value per share, July 21, $42

12-6 (b) Stockholders' equity, $4,849,500

12-7 (a) Total paid-in capital, $2,800,000; (b) Retained earnings, $369,000

12-8 (a) Net income, $700,000

Case 12-1 No key figure

Case 12-2 (a) Joseph's share of net assets, $480,000

(continued on back flap)

FINANCIAL ACCOUNTING

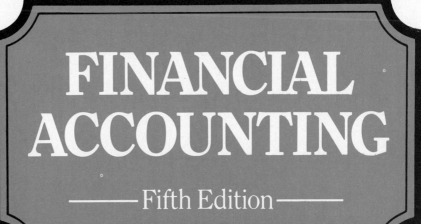

FINANCIAL ACCOUNTING

—Fifth Edition—

Walter B. Meigs
UNIVERSITY OF SOUTHERN CALIFORNIA

Robert F. Meigs
SAN DIEGO STATE UNIVERSITY

McGRAW-HILL BOOK COMPANY

NEW YORK ST. LOUIS SAN FRANCISCO AUCKLAND BOGOTÁ HAMBURG JOHANNESBURG LONDON
MADRID MEXICO MONTREAL NEW DELHI PANAMA PARIS SÃO PAULO SINGAPORE
SYDNEY TOKYO TORONTO

1234567890VNHVNH89876

ISBN 0-07-041631-1

This book was set in ITC Clearface by Progressive Typographers, Inc.
The editors were Jim DeVoe, Elisa Adams, and Edwin Hanson;
the production supervisor was Phil Galea.
The drawings were done by Fine Line Illustrations, Inc.
Part-opening photo credits: Parts 1 and 5, Ed Spiro;
Part 2, Craig Hammell/The Stock Market of N.Y.;
Part 3, Richard Steedman/The Stock Market of N.Y.;
Part 4, Erich Hartmann/Magnum Photos.
Von Hoffmann Press, Inc., was printer and binder.

Library of Congress Cataloging-in-Publication Data

Meigs, Walter B.
    Financial accounting.

    Includes index.
    1. Accounting.   I. Meigs, Robert F.   II. Title.
HF5635.M492   1986   657   85-17074
ISBN 0-07-041631-1

Contents

Preface   xv

Part One   The accounting cycle

Chapter 1   Accounting: the language of business   3
            What is accounting?

            THE PURPOSE AND NATURE OF ACCOUNTING   4

            *The functions of an accounting system. Communicating accounting information —
            who uses accounting reports? Accounting information is user-oriented. The distinc-
            tion between accounting and bookkeeping. The work of accountants. Public
            accounting. Private accounting. Governmental accounting. Development of account-
            ing standards — the FASB. Two primary business objectives. Accounting as the basis
            for business decisions. Internal control. Forms of business organization.*

            FINANCIAL STATEMENTS: THE STARTING POINT IN THE STUDY OF
            ACCOUNTING   15

            *The balance sheet. Assets. Liabilities. Owners' equity. What is capital stock? The
            accounting equation. Effects of business transactions upon the balance sheet. Effect
            of business transactions upon the accounting equation.*

            USE OF FINANCIAL STATEMENTS BY OUTSIDERS   26

            Bankers and other creditors. Owners. Others interested in financial information.

Chapter 2   Recording changes in financial position   40
            The role of accounting records. The use of "accounts" for recording transactions.

            THE LEDGER   41

            *Debit and credit entries. Recording transactions in ledger accounts: illustration.
            Running balance form of ledger account. The normal balance of an account.
            Sequence and numbering of ledger accounts.*

THE JOURNAL   49

Why use a journal? The general journal: illustration of entries. Posting. Ledger accounts after posting.

THE TRIAL BALANCE   56

Uses and limitations of the trial balance. Locating errors. Dollar signs. The accounting cycle: an introduction. Manual and computer-based systems: a comparison.

Chapter 3   Measuring business income   76

Profits: public image versus economic function. Retained earnings. Net income. CASE IN POINT. *Revenue. Expenses. Dividends. Debit and credit rules for revenue and expense.*

RECORDING REVENUE AND EXPENSE TRANSACTIONS: ILLUSTRATION   83

The journal. The ledger. The trial balance. Recording depreciation at the end of the period. The adjusted trial balance. Financial statements. The income statement. Statement of retained earnings. The balance sheet. Income statement and retained earnings statement: a link between two balance sheets.

CLOSING THE ACCOUNTS   95

After-closing trial balance. Sequence of procedures in the accounting cycle. Accounting procedures in a computer-based system. Dividends — declaration and payment. Accrual basis of accounting versus cash basis of accounting.

Chapter 4   Completion of the accounting cycle   120

Accounting periods and financial statements. Transactions affecting more than one accounting period.

ADJUSTING ENTRIES   121

Types of adjusting entries. Characteristics of adjusting entries. Apportioning recorded costs. Apportioning unearned revenue. Recording unrecorded expenses. Recording unrecorded revenue. Adjusting entries and the accrual basis of accounting.

THE WORK SHEET   130

Preparing the work sheet. Uses for the work sheet. Work sheets in a computer-based system. The accounting cycle. Preparing monthly financial statements without closing the accounts. Reversing entries. Reversing entries in a computer-based system.

Part Two   Merchandising concerns, internal control, and accounting systems

Chapter 5   Merchandising transactions and internal control   166

MERCHANDISING COMPANIES   167

Revenue from sales. Sales returns and allowances. Credit terms. Sales discounts. Cost of goods sold. The perpetual inventory system. The periodic inventory system. Beginning inventory and ending inventory. Cost of merchandise purchased for resale. The Transportation-in account. F.O.B. shipping point and F.O.B. destination. Inventory theft and other losses. Income statement for a merchandising company. Work sheet for a merchandising business. Financial statements. Closing entries. Sales taxes. Classified financial statements. The purpose of balance sheet classification. Classification and format of income statements.

THE SYSTEM OF INTERNAL CONTROL   187

The meaning of internal control. Strong internal control now required by law.

GUIDELINES TO STRONG INTERNAL CONTROL   188

Organization plan to establish responsibility for every function. Control of transactions. Subdivision of duties strengthens internal control. Specific methods of achieving internal control. Limitations and cost of internal control.

INTERNAL CONTROLS OVER THE PURCHASE AND SALE OF MERCHANDISE   192

Business documents and procedures. Purchase orders. Invoices. Debit and credit memoranda (debit memos, credit memos). Recording purchase invoices at net price.

Chapter 6   Accounting systems: manual and computer-based   213
Streamlining the accounting process.

MANUAL ACCOUNTING SYSTEMS   214

Sales journal. Controlling accounts and subsidiary ledgers. Purchases journal. Cash receipts journal. Cash payments journal. The general journal. Subsidiary ledger accounts. Ledger accounts. Reconciling subsidiary ledgers and controlling accounts. Variations in special journals. Direct posting from invoices. Unit record for each transaction.

COMPUTER-BASED ACCOUNTING SYSTEMS   235

Advantages of computer-based systems. CASE IN POINT. *Internal control and the computer. Organizational controls.* CASE IN POINT. *Security controls.* CASE IN POINT. *Input controls. Program controls. Accounting applications of the computer.*

Part Three   Current assets and current liabilities

Chapter 7   Cash and marketable securities   258

CASH   258

Management responsibilities relating to cash. Basic requirements for internal control over cash. Internal control over cash receipts. CASE IN POINT. *Internal control over cash disbursements.* CASE IN POINT. *The voucher system. Petty cash. Control features of bank checking accounts. Bank statements. Reconciling the bank account.*

INVESTMENTS IN MARKETABLE SECURITIES   274

Securities exchanges. Marketable securities as current assets. Accounting for investments in marketable securities. Gains and losses from sale of investments in securities. Balance sheet valuation of marketable securities. Lower of cost or market (LCM). The argument for valuation at market value. Presentation of marketable securities in financial statements.

Chapter 8   Receivables and payables   297

ACCOUNTS RECEIVABLE   298

The credit department. Uncollectible accounts receivable. Reflecting uncollectible accounts in the financial statements. The Allowance for Doubtful Accounts. Estimating uncollectible accounts expense. Two methods of estimating uncollectible accounts expense. Writing off an uncollectible account receivable. Recovery of an account receivable previously written off. Direct charge-off method of recognizing uncollectible accounts expense. Credit card sales. Credit balances in accounts receivable. Analysis of accounts receivable. Internal controls for receivables.

NOTES RECEIVABLE   309

Definition of a promissory note. Nature of interest. Accounting for notes receivable. Discounting notes receivable. Classification of receivables in the balance sheet.

CURRENT LIABILITIES   315

NOTES PAYABLE   316

*Notes payable issued to banks. Notes payable with interest charges included in the
face amount. Comparison of the two forms of notes payable. The concept of present
value applied to long-term notes. An illustration of notes recorded at present value.
Installment receivables.*

APPENDIX A. PAYROLL ACCOUNTING   340

Internal control over payrolls. CASE IN POINT. *Deductions from earnings of employees. Social security taxes (FICA).* CASE IN POINT. *Federal income taxes. Other
deductions from employees' earnings. Employer's responsibility for amounts
withheld. Payroll records and procedures. Payroll taxes on the employer. Distinction between employees and independent contractors.*

Chapter 9   Inventories   350
*Inventory defined. Periodic inventory system versus perpetual inventory system.
Inventory valuation and the measurement of income. Importance of an accurate
valuation of inventory. Taking a physical inventory. Pricing the inventory. Cost
basis of inventory valuation. Inventory valuation methods. Consistency in the
valuation of inventory. The environment of inflation. Inventory profits. Disclosing
the effects of inflation. The lower-of-cost-or-market rule (LCM). Estimating ending
inventory and cost of goods sold. Gross profit method. The retail method of
estimating ending inventory. Internal control.* CASE IN POINT. *Perpetual inventory
system. Internal control and perpetual inventory systems.* CASE IN POINT. *Perpetual
inventory records.*

Part Four   Operating assets, long-term liabilities, and owners' equity

Chapter 10   Plant and equipment, depreciation, natural resources, and intan-
             gible assets   390

PLANT AND EQUIPMENT   390

*Plant and equipment represent a stream of services to be received. Major categories
of plant and equipment. Determining the cost of plant and equipment. Capital
expenditures and revenue expenditures.* CASE IN POINT.

DEPRECIATION   395

Allocating the cost of plant and equipment over the years of use. Depreciation not a process of valuation. Accumulated depreciation does not consist of cash. Causes of depreciation. Methods of computing depreciation. Revision of depreciation rates. Depreciation and income taxes. Accelerated Cost Recovery System (ACRS). Inflation and depreciation. Historical cost versus replacement cost. Disclosure of replacement cost.

DISPOSAL OF PLANT AND EQUIPMENT   404

Gains and losses on disposal of plant and equipment. Gains and losses for income tax purposes. Trading in used assets on new.

NATURAL RESOURCES   408

Accounting for natural resources.

INTANGIBLE ASSETS   409

Characteristics. Operating expenses versus intangible assets. Amortization. Goodwill. Patents. Trademarks and trade names. Franchises. Copyrights. Other intangibles and deferred charges. Research and development (R&D) costs.

Chapter 11   Forms of business organization   429

SINGLE PROPRIETORSHIPS   430

Accounting for the owner's equity in a single proprietorship. Closing the accounts. Financial statements for a single proprietorship.

PARTNERSHIPS   432

Significant features of a partnership. Advantages and disadvantages of a partnership. Limited partnerships. The partnership contract. Partnership accounting. Partnership profits and income taxes. Alternative methods of dividing partnership income. Other aspects of partnership accounting.

CORPORATIONS   439

What is a corporation? Advantages of the corporate form of organization. Disadvantages of the corporate form of organization. Formation of a corporation. Authorization and issuance of capital stock. Par value. No-par stock. Preferred stock and common stock. Characteristics of preferred stock. Market price of preferred stock. CASE IN POINT. *The underwriting of stock issues. Market price of common stock.*

Stock issued for assets other than cash. Subscriptions to capital stock. Donated capital. Stockholder records in a corporation. Retained earnings or deficit. Balance sheet for a corporation illustrated.

Chapter 12   Corporations: a closer look   467

Public misconceptions of the rate of corporate earnings. Developing predictive information. Discontinued operations. Extraordinary items. Earnings per share (EPS). Presentation of earnings per share in the income statement. Primary and fully diluted earnings per share. Cash dividends. Dividend dates. Liquidating dividends. Stock dividends. Stock splits. Retained earnings. Prior period adjustments to the Retained Earnings account. Statement of retained earnings. Appropriations and restrictions of retained earnings. Treasury stock. Recording purchases of treasury stock. Reissuance of treasury stock. Restriction of retained earnings when treasury stock is acquired. Book value per share of common stock. Illustration of stockholders' equity section.

APPENDIX B. INVESTMENTS FOR PURPOSES OF CONTROL   503

The equity method.

CONSOLIDATED FINANCIAL STATEMENTS   505

Parent and subsidiary companies. Financial statements for a consolidated economic entity. Principles of consolidation. Consolidation at the date of acquisition. Intercompany eliminations. Acquisition of subsidiary's stock at a price above book value. Less than 100% ownership in subsidiary. Consolidated income statement. Purchase method and pooling-of-interests method: two types of business combination. When should consolidated statements be prepared?

APPENDIX C. INTERNATIONAL ACCOUNTING AND FOREIGN CURRENCY
TRANSLATION   519

What is international accounting? Foreign currencies and exchange rates.

ACCOUNTING FOR TRANSACTIONS WITH FOREIGN COMPANIES   523

Currency fluctuations: who wins and who loses?

CONSOLIDATION OF FOREIGN SUBSIDIARIES   528

Translating financial statement amounts. Accounting principles: the quest for uniformity.

Chapter 13   Bonds payable, leases, and other liabilities   533

BONDS PAYABLE   533

Issuance of bonds payable. Tax advantage of bond financing. Accounting entries for a bond issue. The concept of present value. The present value concept and bond prices. CASE IN POINT. *Bond prices and maturity dates.* CASE IN POINT. *Bonds sold at a discount. Amortization of bond discount. Bonds sold at a premium. Year-end adjustments for bond interest expense. Straight-line amortization: a theoretical shortcoming. Effective interest method of amortization. Amortization of bond discount or premium from the investor's viewpoint. Retirement of bonds payable. Bond sinking fund. Conversion of bonds payable into common stock. Conversion of bonds from the investor's viewpoint.* CASE IN POINT.

LEASES   552

Operating lease. Capital lease.

OTHER LIABILITIES   553

Mortgage notes payable. Pension plans. Estimated liabilities. Loss contingencies. CASE IN POINT.

APPENDIX D. APPLICATIONS OF PRESENT VALUE   567

The concept of present value. Present value tables. Selecting an appropriate discount rate. Discounting annual cash flows. Discount periods of less than one year. Accounting applications of the present value concept.

Part Five   Making use of accounting information

Chapter 14   Accounting principles and concepts: effects of inflation   578

Need for recognized accounting standards. Generally accepted accounting principles. The conceptual framework project. Authoritative support for accounting principles. The accounting entity concept. The going-concern assumption. The time period principle. The monetary principle. The objectivity principle. Asset valuation: the cost principle. Measuring revenue: the realization principle. Measuring expenses: the matching principle. The consistency principle. The disclosure principle. Materiality. Conservatism as a guide in resolving uncertainties. CPA's opinion on published financial statements.

INFLATION—THE GREATEST CHALLENGE TO ACCOUNTING   590

*Profits—fact or illusion? Two approaches to "inflation accounting." FASB
Statement No. 33—disclosing the effects of inflation in financial statements.
Original disclosure requirements for constant dollars and current costs. Net income
measured in constant dollars. Interpreting the constant dollar income statement.
Gains and losses in purchasing power. Interpreting the net gain or loss in purchasing power. Net income on a current cost basis. Interpreting a current cost income
statement. Reduction in the amount of required disclosure.*

Chapter 15   Statement of changes in financial position: cash flows   614

STATEMENT OF CHANGES IN FINANCIAL POSITION   615

*"Funds" defined as working capital. Sources and uses of working capital. Funds
flow: a simple illustration. Effect of transactions on working capital. Working
capital provided by operations. Funds flow: a comprehensive illustration.*

CASH FLOW ANALYSIS   630

Preparation of a cash flow statement. Cash flow from operations.

Chapter 16   Analysis and interpretation of financial statements   650
What is your opinion of the level of corporate profits? CASE IN POINT. *Some specific
examples of corporate earnings . . . and losses. Sources of financial information.
Comparative financial statements. Tools of analysis. Dollar and percentage
changes.* CASE IN POINT. *Trend percentages. Component percentages. Ratios. Comparative data in annual reports of major corporations. Standards of comparison.
Quality of earnings. Quality of assets and the relative amount of debt.* CASE IN
POINT. *Impact of inflation. Illustrative analysis for Seacliff Company. Analysis by
common stockholders. Return on investment (ROI). Leverage. Analysis by long-term
creditors. Analysis by preferred stockholders. Analysis by short-term creditors.
Summary of analytical measurements.*

Chapter 17   Income taxes and business decisions   689
*Tax planning versus tax evasion. The critical importance of income taxes. The
federal income tax: history and objectives. Classes of taxpayers.*

INCOME TAXES: INDIVIDUALS   692

*Cash basis of accounting for income tax returns. Tax rates. Tax rate schedules. The
steeply progressive nature of income taxes. Marginal tax rates compared with
average tax rates. Income taxes and inflation. Income tax formula for individuals.
Total income and gross income. Deductions to arrive at adjusted gross income.
Deductions from adjusted gross income (itemized deductions). Personal exemptions.
Taxable income — individuals. Capital gains and losses. The tax liability. Quarterly
payments of estimated tax. Tax returns, tax refunds, and payment of the tax. Tax
tables. Computation of individual income tax illustrated. Partnerships.*

INCOME TAXES: CORPORATIONS   708

*Taxation of corporations. Corporation tax rates. Computation of taxable income of
corporations. Illustrative tax computation for corporation. Accounting income
versus taxable income. Alternative accounting methods offering possible tax
advantages. Interperiod income tax allocation.*

TAX PLANNING   713

Form of business organization. Tax planning in the choice of financial structure.
CASE IN POINT. *Tax shelters.*

APPENDIX E. FINANCIAL STATEMENTS OF A PUBLICLY OWNED COMPANY   732

Index   747

Preface

A new edition provides authors with an opportunity to add new material, to condense the coverage of topics that have declined in relative importance, to reorganize portions of the book to improve instructional efficiency, and to refine and polish the treatment of basic subject matter. We have tried to do all these things in this fifth edition, the most extensive revision in the history of the text.

The environment of accounting is changing fast, and the shift toward computers, the increasing public interest in income tax policies, and the growing importance of international business activity affect the goals and content of an introductory text in accounting. In order to function intelligently as a citizen as well as in the business community, every individual needs more than ever before an understanding of basic accounting concepts. Our goal is to present accounting as an essential part of the decision-making process for the voter, the taxpayer, the government official, the business manager, and the investor.

This edition, like the preceding one, is designed for use in the first college-level course in accounting. In this course, instructors often recognize three groups of students: those who stand at the threshold of preparation for a career in accounting, students of business administration who need a thorough understanding of accounting as an important element of the total business information system, and students from a variety of other disciplines who will find the ability to use and interpret accounting information a valuable accomplishment. During the process of revision, we have tried to keep in mind the needs and interests of all three groups.

NEW FEATURES IN THIS EDITION

In the text

1 A short preview of each chapter, introducing students to both the educational goals and the technical content of the chapter.
2 Each step in the accounting cycle clearly explained for both manual and computer-based accounting systems.
3 Over 100 new exercises and problems. In addition, virtually all exercises and problems carried forward from the prior edition have been carefully revised.
4 A new category of problem material — Cases for Analysis — emphasizing the use and interpretation of accounting information in interesting yet practical business situations.
5 A new appendix with an introductory-level discussion of international accounting and foreign currency translation, complete with problem material.

6 A new appendix on payroll accounting, with emphasis upon internal control.
7 Frequent use of real business examples — termed Cases in Point — to illustrate key accounting concepts.
8 Increased emphasis upon accounting theory and generally accepted accounting principles throughout the text.
9 Increased emphasis upon the relationship of many accounting practices to the need for achieving adequate internal control.

In the supplemental package

1 Computer software enabling students to work most of the exercises in the textbook on a personal computer.
2 An Electronic Study Guide, with chapter highlights and self-testing material, designed for use on a personal computer.
3 A computer-based practice set, also suited to personal computers.
4 The Financial Accounting Test Bank — a printed manual providing instructors with a wealth of multiple-choice questions and short exercises organized on a chapter-by-chapter basis.
5 EXAMINER and MicroEXAMINER, the computer-based versions of the test bank, now available for use on personal as well as mainframe computers.

FEATURES CARRIED FORWARD FROM PRIOR EDITIONS

Special qualities that are carried forward from prior editions include:

1 Depth of coverage. Topics are covered in a depth that will qualify the student for subsequent course work in accounting.
2 Accuracy in all problem material and solutions. All problems, solutions, and examination materials have been developed and tested first-hand by the authors in their own classes for introductory accounting students. This personal attention to accuracy is supplemented by independent testing by other accounting faculty.
3 Perspective — careful effort throughout the text and problems to utilize current and realistic prices, interest rates, and profit levels.
4 People-oriented problems which depict the complex decisions that must be made by men and women acting as managers, investors, and in other roles.
5 For each chapter, a demonstration problem, a glossary of key terms introduced or emphasized in the chapter, and an abundance of problem material.
6 Emphasis on the impact of inflation upon accounting information.
7 The concept of present value, presented in clear and understandable terms, integrated into the discussions of the valuation of assets and liabilities.
8 Careful integration into the text and problems of the latest pronouncements of the Financial Accounting Standards Board.
9 The most comprehensive package of supplementary materials available for any financial accounting textbook.

NEW AND EXTENSIVELY REVISED CHAPTERS

Many new topics are discussed in this fifth edition. For example, the first four chapters, presenting the basic accounting cycle, now explain the accounting procedures applied in computer-based accounting systems as well as those used in manual systems. Chapter 3, "Measuring Business Income," also includes new discussions of the accounting principles of realization and matching. In addition, Chapter 4 has been extensively revised to explain more clearly and more thoroughly the nature and mechanics of adjusting entries.

Chapter 6, on accounting systems, has been revised to provide up-to-date coverage of computer-based accounting systems. Emphasis is placed upon means of achieving internal control in the EDP environment.

Chapter 8, on receivables and payables, and Chapter 9, covering inventories, both include new material on the relationships between accounting procedures and the objectives of internal control. Internal control is also the emphasis of the new appendix on payroll accounting which follows Chapter 8.

Chapter 10, on plant assets, includes a new section explaining why gains and losses on disposals of plant assets often differ for income tax purposes and financial reporting purposes. Also revised is the discussion of exchanges of plant assets.

Chapter 12, "Corporations: A Closer Look," is now followed by two appendixes. The first covers investments made for purposes of control and includes an introduction to consolidated financial statements. The second appendix, new to this fifth edition, introduces the emerging topics of international accounting and foreign currency translation.

Our last chapter, on income taxes, has been thoroughly revised to incorporate the many recent changes in income tax laws.

In summary, this fifth edition is the most extensive revision we have prepared. In addition to the changes in chapter content, there are many new Cases in Point — real business examples illustrating key accounting concepts. Also, the extent of revision in the end-of-chapter material is virtually without precedent in a financial accounting textbook. There are over 100 new exercises and problems, and a new category of problem material — Cases for Analysis — emphasizing the use and interpretation of accounting information. Essentially all the exercises and problems carried forward from prior editions have been revised to reflect today's price-levels, interest rates, and business environment.

SUPPLEMENTARY MATERIALS

A full assortment of supplementary materials accompanies this text:

1 *Solutions manual.* A comprehensive manual containing answers to all review questions, exercises, problems, and Cases for Analysis contained in the text, along with a complete solution to the practice set.

   In the development of problem material for this book, special attention has been given to the inclusion of problems of varying length and difficulty. By referring to the time estimates, difficulty ratings, and problem descriptions in the *Solutions Manual,* instructors can choose problems that best fit the level, scope, and emphasis of the course they are offering.

2 *An instructor's guide.* This separate manual includes the following three sections for each chapter of the textbook:

a A brief topical outline of the chapter listing in logical sequence the topics the authors like to discuss in class.

b An assignment guide correlating specific exercises and problems with various topics covered in the chapter.

c Comments and observations.

The "Comments and observations" sections indicate the authors' personal views as to relative importance of topics and identify topics with which some students have difficulty. Specific exercises and problems are recommended to demonstrate certain points. Many of these sections include "Asides," introducing real-world situations (not included in the text) that are useful in classroom discussions.

Also included in the Instructor's Guide are sample assignment schedules, ideas for using each element of the supplemental package, and solutions to the parallel sets of Achievement Tests and Comprehensive Examinations.

3 Two parallel sets of **Achievement Tests** and **Comprehensive Examinations.** Each set consists of four Achievement Tests with each test covering three or four chapters; the Comprehensive Examination covers the entire text and may be used as a final examination.

4 The **Financial Accounting Test Bank.** With its abundance of multiple-choice questions and exercises arranged on a chapter-by-chapter basis, this booklet is a most valuable resource for instructors who prefer to assemble their own examinations. In its new format, this supplement represents one of the largest test banks ever to accompany a financial accounting textbook.

The questions and exercises contained in the Text Bank booklet also are available in two computer test-generating programs: EXAMINER, designed for mainframe computers, and the new MicroEXAMINER, designed for personal computers. These, and all other computer-based supplements that accompany this text, assume no prior experience with computers on the part of instructors or students. All computer supplements are available for use on popular microcomputers.

5 *A self-study guide.* The **Study Guide** enables students to measure their progress by immediate feedback. This self-study guide includes an outline of the most important points in each chapter, an abundance of objective questions, and several short exercises for each chapter. In the back of the self-study guide are answers to questions and solutions to exercises to help students evaluate their understanding of the subject. The self-study guide will also be useful in classroom discussions and for review by students before examinations.

6 *An Electronic Study Guide.* An electronic version of the print Study Guide enabling students to review chapter highlights and to test themselves using a personal computer.

7 *Working papers.* A soft-cover book of *partially filled-in working papers* for the problem material is published separately from the text. On these work sheets, the problem headings and some preliminary data have been entered to save students much of the mechanical pencil-pushing inherent in problem assignments.

8 *Manual practice set.* The practice set available with the preceding edition has been completely revised and significantly shortened. Designed for use after completing Chapter 6 of the text, the Candlelight Restaurant Supply, Inc. practice set is bound

in two separate books, making it easy for students to journalize transactions, post entries, and prepare financial statements. The purpose of the manual practice set is to acquaint students with the flow of information through an accounting system and to allow them to personally perform each step in the accounting cycle.

9 *Computerized practice set.* A computer-based version of the Candlelight Restaurant Supply, Inc., practice set accompanies this fifth edition. The computerized practice set is based upon the same narrative as the manual practice set but allows students to experience hands-on operation of a computer-based accounting system.

   This computerized practice set has a unique instructional feature that identifies any erroneous input. If an error is made in analyzing a transaction, the computer responds with hints and help statements until the transaction is recorded correctly. Thus, any printed computer output generated by the student represents a correct solution to the practice set. The practice set is accompanied by a special instruction booklet for the student.

10 *Computer-based exercises.* A new computer supplement, Computerized Applications in Financial Accounting, enables students to work the exercises from the textbook on a personal computer.

11 *Checklist of key figures for problems.* This list appears on the front and back inside covers of this book. The purpose of the checklist is to aid students in verifying their problem solutions and in discovering their own errors.

12 *Transparencies of problem solutions.* This is a visual aid prepared by the publisher for the instructor who wishes to display in a classroom the complete solutions to any or all problems, and selected exercises.

13 *Additional transparencies for classroom illustrations.* A large number of transparencies have been produced for use in the classroom to illustrate various accounting concepts and procedures. These transparencies all differ from the illustrations appearing in the textbook and are enhanced by the use of color.

CONTRIBUTIONS BY OTHERS

We want to express our sincere thanks to the many users of the preceding editions who offered helpful suggestions for this edition. Especially helpful was the advice received from the following reviewers: Sarah L. Adams, California State University, Chico; Andrew H. Barnett, San Diego State University; Rosie Bukics, Lafayette College; Harold L. Cannon, State University of New York, Albany; Marlene Hartman, Loyola Marymount University; Orville Keister, University of Akron; G. Kenneth Nelson, Pennsylvania State University; Bernard Newman, Pace University; Mohamed Onsi, Syracuse University; Barbara Parrish, Wichita State University; Victoria S. Rymer, George Mason University; Kenneth Schwartz, Boston University; Gail Sergenian, Pace University; and Robert Trezevant, California State University, Chico.

We are most appreciative of the expert attention given this book and its many supplements by the editorial staff of McGraw-Hill, especially Jim DeVoe, Elisa Adams, and Ed Hanson.

Our special thanks go to Professor Elizabeth Darr, Marquette University, and Professor Robert Zwicker, Pace University, for assisting us in the proof stages of this edition by reviewing the end-of-chapter problems and text examples for accuracy.

The assistance of Jill Adams and Dave Berg was most helpful in preparation of the manuscript.

We also are grateful to the Financial Accounting Standards Board which granted us permission to quote from FASB Statements, Discussion Memoranda, Interpretations, and Exposure Drafts. All quotations are copyrighted © by the Financial Accounting Standards Board, High Ridge Park, Stamford, Connecticut 06905, U.S.A. and are reprinted with permission. Copies of the complete documents are available from the FASB.

Walter B. Meigs
Robert F. Meigs

FINANCIAL
ACCOUNTING

Part One	The accounting cycle
Chapter 1	Accounting: the language of business
Chapter 2	Recording changes in financial position
Chapter 3	Measuring business income
Chapter 4	Completion of the accounting cycle

In these first four chapters, the continuing example of Greenhill Real Estate is used to illustrate the concepts of accrual accounting for a small, service-type business. Accounting for a merchandising concern will be introduced in Part Two.

Chapter 1
Accounting: the language of business

This introductory chapter explores the nature of accounting information and the environment in which it is developed and used. We emphasize the uses of accounting reports, the services performed by accountants, and the institutions which influence accounting practice. A basic financial statement — the balance sheet — is illustrated and discussed. We explain the nature of assets, liabilities, and owners' equity; and why a balance sheet always "balances." Attention is focused upon the set of standards called generally accepted accounting principles. Specific accounting principles introduced in Chapter 1 are the concept of the business entity, the cost principle, objectivity, and the going-concern assumption. We also introduce Greenhill Real Estate, a company used as a continuing example throughout the first four chapters. In Chapter 1, the activities of Greenhill illustrate the effects of business transactions upon the balance sheet.

After studying this chapter you should be able to:

✓ Explain the role of accounting in making business decisions.
✓ Define the phrase, "generally accepted accounting principles."
✓ Describe the work of CPAs and other accountants.
✓ Explain the function of the FASB.
✓ State two basic financial objectives of every profit-oriented business.
✓ Explain the objectives of a system of internal control.
✓ Describe a balance sheet; define assets, liabilities, and owners' equity.
✓ Discuss the accounting principles involved in asset valuation.
✓ Indicate the effects of various transactions upon the accounting equation and the balance sheet.

3

What is accounting?

Many people think of accounting as a highly technical field which can be understood only by professional accountants. Actually, nearly everyone practices accounting in one form or another on an almost daily basis. Accounting is the art of measuring, communicating, and interpreting financial activity. Whether you are preparing a household budget, balancing your checkbook, preparing your income tax return, or running General Motors, you are working with accounting concepts and accounting information.

Accounting has often been called the "language of business." In recent years, corporate profits have become a topic of considerable public interest. What are "corporate profits"? What levels of corporate profits are necessary to finance the development of new products, new jobs, and economic growth? One cannot hope to answer such questions without understanding the accounting concepts and terms involved in the measurement of income.

Since a language is a means of social communication, it is logical that a language should change to meet the changing needs of society. In accounting, too, changes and improvements are continually being made. For example, as society has become increasingly interested in measuring the profitability of business organizations, our accounting concepts and techniques have been changing to make such measurements more meaningful and more reliable.

We live in an era of accountability. Although accounting has made its most dramatic progress in the field of business, the accounting function is vital to every unit of our society. An individual must account for his or her income, and must file income tax returns. Often an individual must supply personal accounting information in order to buy a car or home, to qualify for a college scholarship, to secure a credit card, or to obtain a bank loan. Large corporations are accountable to their stockholders, to governmental agencies, and to the public. The federal government, the states, the cities, the school district: all must use accounting as a basis for controlling their resources and measuring their accomplishments. Accounting is equally essential to the successful operation of a business, a university, a fraternity, a social program, or a city.

In every election the voters must make decisions at the ballot box on issues involving accounting concepts; therefore, some knowledge of accounting is needed by all citizens if they are to act intelligently in meeting the challenges of our society. The objective of this text is to help you develop your knowledge of accounting and your ability to use accounting information in making economic and political decisions.

THE PURPOSE AND NATURE OF ACCOUNTING

The underlying purpose of accounting is to provide financial information about an economic entity. In this book the economic entity which we will be concentrating upon is a business enterprise. The financial information provided by an accounting system is needed by managerial decision makers to help them plan and control the activities of the economic entity. Financial information is also needed by **outsiders**—owners, creditors, potential investors, the government, and the public—who have supplied money to the business or who have some other interest in the business that will be served by information about its financial position and operating results.

The functions of an accounting system

An accounting system consists of the methods, procedures, and devices used by an entity to keep track of its financial activities and to summarize these activities in a manner useful to decision makers. To accomplish these objectives, an accounting system may make use of computers and video displays as well as handwritten records and reports printed on paper. In fact, the accounting system for any sizable business is likely to include all these records and devices. Regardless of whether the accounting system is simple or sophisticated, three basic steps must be performed as data concerning financial activities is collected and processed—the data must be *recorded, classified,* and appropriately *summarized.*

Step 1—recording financial activity. The first function of an accounting system is to create a systematic record of the daily business activity, in terms of money. For example, goods and services are purchased and sold, credit is extended to customers, debts are incurred, and cash is received and paid out. These *transactions* are typical of business events which can be expressed *in monetary terms,* and must be entered in accounting records. The mere statement of an intent to buy goods or services in the future does not represent a transaction. The term *transaction* refers to a completed action rather than to an expected or possible future action.

The recording of a transaction may be performed in many ways, such as writing with a pen or pencil, entering data through a computer keyboard, or passing machine-readable price tags over an optical scanner.

Of course, not all business events can be objectively measured and described in monetary terms. Therefore, we do not record in the accounting records such events as the death of a key executive or a threat by a labor union to call a strike.

Step 2—classifying data. A complete record of all business activities usually amounts to a huge volume of data—too large and diverse to be useful to decision makers such as managers and investors. Therefore, the data must be classified into related groups or categories of transactions. For example, grouping together those transactions in which cash is received or paid out is a logical step in developing useful information about the cash position of a business.

Step 3—summarizing the data. To be useful to decision makers, accounting data generally must be highly summarized. A complete listing of the sales transactions of a company such as Sears, for example, would be too long for anyone to read. The employees responsible for ordering merchandise need sales information summarized by product. Store managers will want sales information summarized by department, while Sears' top management will want sales information summarized by store. Outsiders, such as the company's stockholders and the Internal Revenue Service, probably will be most interested in a single sales figure which represents the total sales of the entire company.

These three steps we have described—recording, classifying, and summarizing—are the means of creating accounting information. However, the accounting process includes more than the *creating* of information. It also involves *communicating* this information to interested parties and *interpreting* accounting information to help in the making of specific business decisions.

Often we will want to compare the financial statements of Company A with those of Company B. From this comparison, we can determine which company is the more profitable, which is financially stronger, and which offers the better chance of future success. You can benefit personally by making this kind of analysis of a company you are considering investing in — or going to work for.

Communicating accounting information — who uses accounting reports?

An accounting system must provide information to managers and also to a number of outsiders who have an interest in the financial activities of the business enterprise. The major types of accounting reports which are developed by the accounting system of a business enterprise and the parties receiving this information are illustrated in the following diagram:

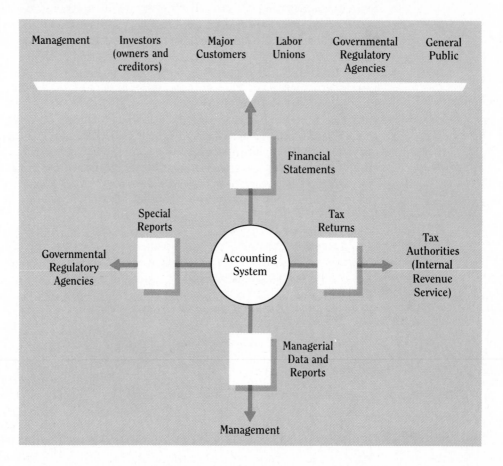

Accounting information is user-oriented

The persons receiving accounting reports are termed the **users** of accounting information. The type of information that a specific user will require depends upon the kinds of decisions that person must make. For example, managers need detailed information about daily operating costs for the purpose of controlling the operations of the business and setting reasonable selling prices. Outsiders, on the other hand, usually need summarized information concerning resources on hand and information on operating results for the past year to use in making investment decisions, imposing income taxes, or making regulatory decisions.

Since the information needs of various users differ, it follows that the accounting system of a business entity must be able to provide various types of accounting reports. The information in these reports must be presented in accordance with certain "ground rules" and assumptions, so that users of the reports will be able to interpret the information properly. For example, if a report indicates that a business owns land with an accounting value of $90,000, what does this dollar amount represent? Is it the original cost of the land to the business, the current market value of the land, or the assessed value for purposes of levying property taxes? Obviously the user of any accounting report needs to understand the standards and assumptions which have been used in preparing that report. In turn, the standards employed in the preparation of an accounting report must relate to the information needs of the user.

Financial statements. Among the most important and most widely used of all accounting reports are financial statements. *Financial statements* are the main source of financial information to persons outside the business organization and also are useful to management. These statements are very concise, summarizing in three or four pages the activities of a business for a specified period of time, such as a month or a year. They show the *financial position* of the business at the end of the time period and also the *operating results* by which the business arrived at this financial position.

The basic purpose of financial statements is to assist decision makers in evaluating the financial strength, profitability, and future prospects of a business. Thus, managers, investors, major customers, and labor all have a direct interest in these reports. Every large corporation prepares annual financial statements which are distributed to all owners of the business. In addition, these statements are filed with various governmental agencies and become a matter of public record.

Generally accepted accounting principles (GAAP). The accounting standards and concepts used in the preparation of financial statements are called *generally accepted accounting principles.* Some of these principles have been established by official standard-setting bodies such as the Financial Accounting Standards Board, while others have simply gained acceptance through widespread use. The various ideas, concepts, and accounting methods that make up generally accepted accounting principles continually change and evolve in response to changes in the business environment.

There is no comprehensive list of generally accepted accounting principles, yet accountants and users of financial statements must know which accounting concepts are acceptable and which are not. Helping you to develop an awareness of the accounting principles and concepts which are "generally accepted" is one of the major objectives of this textbook.

Developing accounting information in conformity with generally accepted accounting principles is called *financial accounting,* because this information summarizes the financial position and operating results of a business entity. In this textbook, we will emphasize financial accounting concepts rather than income tax rules, internal reports to management, or reports to regulatory agencies. As we shall see, financial accounting concepts apply to all types and sizes of business organizations.

Income tax returns. The Internal Revenue Service, as well as certain state and local tax authorities, requires businesses and individuals to file annual income tax returns designed to measure taxable income. *Taxable income* is a legal concept defined by laws originating in Congress (or in state legislatures). Since Congress uses the income tax laws to achieve various social objectives as well as to finance the government, income tax laws are frequently modified or changed. Thus the rules used in preparing income tax returns may vary from one year to the next. In general, however, there is a close parallel between income tax laws and financial accounting concepts.

Managerial data and reports. Management needs much detailed accounting data (in addition to financial statements) for use in planning and controlling the daily operations of the business. Management also needs specialized information for long-range planning and for major decisions such as the introduction of a new product or the modernizing of an older plant. Accounting information provided to managers need not be presented in accordance with generally accepted accounting principles. Rather, it should be tailored to meet the managers' specific information needs.

Reports to regulatory agencies. The activities of many business enterprises are regulated by governmental agencies. These regulatory agencies often require special types of accounting information specifically tailored to their needs. For example, when making a decision whether to allow a rate increase by an electric company, a state utilities commission might request information about the cost to the company of producing electricity and the company's need to accumulate funds to provide service to outlying areas. In large part, however, reports to regulatory agencies are based upon generally accepted accounting principles.

Using accounting information. Accounting extends beyond the process of creating records and reports. The ultimate objective of accounting is the *use* of this information, its analysis and interpretation. Accountants are concerned with the significance of the figures they produce. They look for relationships between business events and financial results; they study the effect of various alternatives, such as buying or leasing a new store building; and they search for significant trends that suggest what may happen in the future.

If managers, investors, creditors, and government officials are to make effective use of accounting information, they too must have some understanding of how the figures were put together and what they mean. An important part of this understanding is to recognize clearly the limitations of accounting reports. A business manager or other decision maker who lacks an understanding of accounting may not appreciate the extent to which accounting information is based upon *estimates* rather than upon precisely accurate measurements.

The distinction between accounting and bookkeeping

Persons with little knowledge of accounting may fail to understand the difference between accounting and bookkeeping. **Bookkeeping** means the recording of transactions, the record-making phase of accounting. The recording of transactions tends to be mechanical and repetitive; it is only a small part of the field of accounting and probably the simplest part. Accounting includes not only the maintenance of accounting records, but also the design of efficient accounting systems, the performance of audits, the development of forecasts, income tax work, and the interpretation of accounting information. A person might become a reasonably proficient bookkeeper in a few weeks or months; however, to become a professional accountant requires several years of study and experience.

The work of accountants

Accountants tend to specialize in a given subarea of the discipline just as do attorneys and members of other professions. In terms of career opportunities, the field of accounting may be divided into three broad areas: (1) the public accounting profession, (2) private accounting, and (3) governmental accounting.

Public accounting

Certified public accountants are independent professional persons comparable to attorneys or physicians, who offer accounting services to clients for a fee. The **CPA certificate** is a license to practice granted by the state on the basis of a rigorous examination and evidence of practical experience. All states require that candidates pass an examination prepared and graded on a national basis twice each year by the American Institute of Certified Public Accountants. Requirements as to education and practical experience differ somewhat among the various states.

Auditing. The principal function of CPAs is auditing. How do people outside a business entity — owners, creditors, government officials, and other interested parties — know that the financial statements prepared by a company's management are reliable and complete? In large part, these outsiders rely upon **audits** performed by a CPA firm which is **independent** of the company issuing the financial statements.

To perform an audit of a business, a firm of certified public accountants makes a careful study of the company's accounting system and gathers evidence both from within the business and from outside sources. This evidence enables the CPA firm to express its professional **opinion** as to the fairness and reliability of the financial statements. Persons outside the business, such as bankers, and investors who rely upon financial statements for information, attach great importance to the annual **audit report** by the CPA firm.

Income tax services. An important element of decision making by business executives is consideration of the income tax consequences of each alternative course of action. The CPA is often called upon for "tax planning," which will show how a future transaction such as the acquisition of new equipment may be arranged in a manner that will hold income taxes to a minimum amount. The CPA is also frequently retained to prepare the federal and state income tax returns. To render tax services, the CPA must have extensive knowledge of tax statutes, regulations, and court decisions, as well as a thorough knowledge of accounting.

Management advisory services. Many CPA firms offer their clients a wide range of management consulting services. For example, a CPA firm might be engaged to study the feasibility of installing a computer-based accounting system, of introducing a new product line, or of merging with another company. The fact that business executives often seek their accountants' advice on a wide range of business problems illustrates the relevance of accounting information to virtually all business decisions.

Private accounting

In contrast to the CPA in public practice who serves many clients, an accountant in private industry is employed by a single enterprise. The chief accounting officer of a medium-sized or large business is usually called the *controller,* in recognition of the fact that one of the primary uses of accounting data is to aid in controlling business operations. The controller manages the work of the accounting staff. He or she is also a part of the top management team charged with the task of running the business, setting its objectives, and seeing that these objectives are met.

The accountants in a private business, large or small, must record transactions and prepare periodic financial statements from accounting records. Within this area of general accounting, a number of specialized phases of accounting have developed. Among the more important of these are:

Design of accounting systems. Although the same basic accounting principles are applicable to all types of business, each enterprise requires an individually tailored *financial information system.* This system includes accounting forms, records, instruction manuals, flow charts, computer programs, and reports to fit the particular needs of the business. Designing an accounting system and putting it into operation constitute a specialized phase of accounting.

Cost accounting. Knowing the cost of a particular product is vital to the efficient management of a business. For example, an automobile manufacturer needs to know the cost of each type of car produced. Knowing the cost of each manufacturing process (such as painting an automobile) or the cost of any business operation (such as an employee training program) is also essential to making sound business decisions. The phase of accounting concerned with collecting and interpreting cost data is called *cost accounting.*

Financial forecasting. A financial forecast (or budget) is a plan of financial operations for some future period expressed in monetary terms. By using a forecast, management is able to make comparisons between *planned operations* and *actual results achieved.* A forecast is thus an attempt to preview operating results before the actual transactions have taken place. A forecast is a particularly valuable tool for the controller because it provides each division of the business with a specific goal, and because it gives management a means of measuring the efficiency of performance throughout the company.

Income tax accounting. As income tax rates have gone up and the determination of taxable income has become more complex, both internal accountants and independent public accountants have devoted more time to problems of taxation. Although many companies rely largely on CPA firms for tax planning and the preparation of income tax returns, large companies also maintain their own tax departments.

Internal auditing. Most large corporations maintain staffs of *internal auditors* with the responsibility of evaluating the efficiency of operations and determining whether company policies are being followed consistently in all divisions of the corporation. The internal auditor, in contrast to the independent auditor or CPA, is not responsible for determining the overall fairness of the company's annual financial statements.

Management accounting. Keep in mind that the accounting system provides information for both external and internal use. The external reporting function has already been touched upon in our discussion of a CPA firm's independent audit of annual financial statements. The *internal* reporting function of an accounting system gives managers information needed for daily operations and also for long-range planning. Developing the types of information most relevant to specific managerial decisions, and interpreting that information, is called *management accounting* or *managerial accounting.* This topic will be emphasized in the second accounting course.

Management accounting uses the techniques of cost accounting and forecasting to help executives formulate both short-range and long-range plans. Management accounting also helps executives (1) to measure success in carrying out these plans, (2) to identify problems requiring executive attention, and (3) to choose among alternative methods of attaining company objectives. At every organizational level of a company, specific problems arise for which accounting is needed to help define the problem, identify alternative courses of action, and make a choice among these alternatives.

Certificate in Management Accounting. The Institute of Management Accounting offers a program leading to a Certificate in Management Accounting. This certificate is a recognition of an individual's knowledge and competence in management accounting. To qualify, one must pass a professional examination and meet specified standards as to education and professional experience.

Governmental accounting

Government officials rely on financial information to help them direct the affairs of their agencies just as do the executives of corporations. Many governmental accounting problems are similar to those applicable to private industry. In other respects, however, accounting for governmental affairs requires a somewhat different approach because the objective of earning a profit is absent from public affairs. Every agency of government at every level (federal, state, and local) must have accountants in order to carry out its responsibilities. Universities, hospitals, churches, and other not-for-profit institutions also follow a pattern of accounting that is similar to governmental accounting.

Internal Revenue Service. One of the governmental agencies which perform extensive accounting work is the Internal Revenue Service (IRS). The IRS handles the millions of income tax returns filed by individuals and corporations, and frequently performs auditing functions relating to these income tax returns and the accounting records on which they are based.

Securities and Exchange Commission. Another governmental agency deeply involved in accounting is the Securities and Exchange Commission (SEC). The SEC establishes requirements regarding the content of financial statements and the reporting standards to be followed. All corporations which offer securities for sale to the public must file annually with the SEC audited financial statements meeting these requirements.

Development of accounting standards — the FASB

Research to develop accounting principles and practices which will keep pace with changes in the economic and political environment is a major activity of professional accountants and accounting educators. In the United States four groups influential in the improvement of financial reporting and accounting practices are the Financial Accounting Standards Board, the American Institute of Certified Public Accountants, the Securities and Exchange Commission, and the American Accounting Association.

Of special importance in establishing generally accepted accounting principles is the Financial Accounting Standards Board, known as the FASB. The FASB consists of seven full-time members, including representatives from public accounting, industry, and accounting education. In addition to conducting extensive research, the FASB issues *Statements of Financial Accounting Standards,* which represent authoritative expressions of generally accepted accounting principles.

Note that the FASB is part of the private sector of the economy and not a government agency. The development of accounting standards in the United States has traditionally been carried on in the private sector although the government, acting through the SEC, has exercised great influence on the FASB and other groups concerned with accounting research and standards of financial reporting.

The contribution of the FASB and the other groups mentioned above will be considered in later chapters. At this point we merely want to emphasize that accounting is not a closed system or a fixed set of rules, but a constantly evolving body of knowledge. As we explore accounting principles and related practices in this book, you will become aware of certain problems and conflicts for which fully satisfactory answers are yet to be developed. The need for further research is apparent despite the fact that present-day American accounting practices and standards of financial reporting are by far the best achieved anywhere at any time.

Two primary business objectives

The management of every business must keep foremost in its thinking two primary objectives. The first is to earn a profit. The second is to stay solvent, that is, to have on hand sufficient cash to pay debts as they fall due. Profits and solvency, of course, are not the only objectives of business managers. There are many others, such as providing jobs for people, protecting the environment, creating new and improved products, and providing more goods and services at a lower cost. It is clear, however, that a business cannot hope to accomplish these objectives unless it meets the two basic tests of survival — operating profitably and staying solvent.

A business is a collection of resources committed by an individual or group of individuals, who hope that the investment will increase in value. Investment in any given business, however, is only one of a number of alternative investments available. If a business does not earn as great a profit as might be obtained from alternative investments, its owners will be well-advised to sell or terminate the business and invest elsewhere. A business that continually operates at a loss will eventually exhaust its resources and be forced out of existence. Therefore, in order to operate successfully and to survive, the owners or managers of an enterprise must direct the business in such a way that it will earn a reasonable profit.

Business concerns that have sufficient cash to pay their debts promptly are said to be *solvent.* In contrast, a company that finds itself unable to meet its obligations as they fall due is called *insolvent.* Solvency must also be ranked as a primary objective of any enterprise, because a business that becomes insolvent may be forced by its creditors to stop operations and end its existence.

Accounting as the basis for business decisions

How do business executives know whether a company is earning profits or incurring losses? How do they know whether the company is solvent or insolvent, and whether it probably will be solvent, say, a month from today? The answer to both these questions in one word is *accounting.* Accounting is the process by which the profitability and solvency of a company can be measured. Accounting also provides information needed as a basis for making business decisions that will enable management to guide the company on a profitable and solvent course.

For specific examples of these decisions, consider the following questions. What prices should the firm set on its products? If production is increased, what effect will this have on the cost of each unit produced? Will it be necessary to borrow from the bank? How much will costs increase if a pension plan is established for employees? Is it more profitable to produce and sell product A or product B? Shall a given part be made or be bought from suppliers? Should an investment be made in new equipment? All these issues call for decisions that should depend, in part at least, upon accounting information. It might be reasonable to turn the question around and ask: What business decisions could be made intelligently *without* the use of accounting information? Examples would be hard to find.

In large-scale business undertakings such as the manufacture of automobiles or the operation of nationwide chains of retail stores, the top executives cannot possibly have close physical contact with and knowledge of the details of operations. Consequently, these executives must depend to an even greater extent than the small business owner upon information provided by the accounting system.

We have already stressed that accounting is a means of measuring the results of business transactions and of communicating financial information. In addition, the accounting system must provide the decision maker with *predictive information* for making important business decisions in a changing world.

Internal control

The topic of internal control goes hand-in-hand with the study of accounting. We have stressed that business decisions of all types are based at least in part upon accounting information. How do the decision makers know that the accounting information they receive is accurate and reliable? This assurance comes, in large part, from the company's **system of internal control.**

A system of internal control consists of all the measures taken by an organization for the purpose of (1) protecting its resources against waste, fraud, and inefficiency; (2) ensuring accuracy and reliability in accounting and operating data; (3) securing compliance with company policies; and (4) evaluating the level of performance in all divisions of the company. In short, a system of internal control includes all of the measures designed to assure management that the entire business operates according to plan.

A basic principle of internal control is that no one person should handle all phases of a transaction from beginning to end. When business operations are so organized that two or more employees are required to participate in every transaction, the possibility of fraud is reduced and the work of one employee gives assurance of the accuracy of the work of another. The principal reason for many business documents and accounting procedures is to achieve strong internal control. Therefore, we shall discuss various internal control concepts and requirements throughout our study of accounting.

Forms of business organization

A business enterprise may be organized as a **single proprietorship**, a **partnership**, or a **corporation**.

Single proprietorship. A business owned by one person is called a single proprietorship. Often the owner also acts as the manager. This form of business organization is common for small retail stores and service enterprises, for farms, and for professional practices in law, medicine, and public accounting. The owner is personally liable for all debts incurred by the business. From an accounting viewpoint, however, the business is an entity separate from the proprietor.

Partnership. A business owned by two or more persons voluntarily associated as partners is called a partnership. Partnerships, like single proprietorships, are widely used for small businesses and professional practices. As in the case of a single proprietorship, a partnership is not legally an entity separate from its owners; consequently, a partner is personally responsible for the debts of the partnership. From an accounting standpoint, however, a partnership is a business entity separate from the personal activities of the partners.

Corporation. A business organized as a separate legal entity with ownership divided into transferable shares of capital stock is called a corporation. Capital stock certificates are issued by the corporation to each stockholder showing the number of shares he or she owns. The stockholders are free to sell all or part of these shares to other investors at any time, and this ease of transfer adds to the attractiveness of investing in a corporation.

Persons wanting to form a new corporation must file an application with state officials for a corporate charter. When this application has been approved, the corporation comes into existence as a *legal entity* separate from its owners. The important role of the corporation in our economy is based on such advantages as the ease of gathering large amounts of money, transferability of shares in ownership, limited liability of owners, and continuity of existence.

Accounting principles apply to all three forms of business organization, but are most carefully defined to aid corporations in making satisfactory financial reports to public investors. In this book we shall use the corporate form of organization as our basic model, along with some specific references to single proprietorships and partnerships.

FINANCIAL STATEMENTS: THE STARTING POINT IN THE STUDY OF ACCOUNTING

The preparation of financial statements is not the first step in the accounting process, but it is a convenient point to begin the study of accounting. The financial statements are the means of conveying to management and to interested outsiders a concise picture of the profitability and financial position of the business. Since these financial statements are in a sense the end product of the accounting process, the student who acquires a clear understanding of the content and meaning of financial statements will be in an excellent position to appreciate the purpose of the earlier steps of recording and classifying business transactions.

The two most widely used financial statements are the *balance sheet* and the *income statement*.[1] Together, these two statements (perhaps a page each in length) summarize all the information contained in the hundreds or thousands of pages comprising the detailed accounting records of a business. In this introductory chapter and in Chapter 2, we shall explore the nature of the balance sheet, or statement of financial position, as it is sometimes called. Once we have become familiar with the form and arrangement of the balance sheet and with the meaning of technical terms such as *assets, liabilities,* and *owners' equity,* it will be as easy to read and understand a report on the financial position of a business as it is for an architect to read the blueprint of a proposed building. (We shall discuss the income statement in Chapter 3.)

The balance sheet

The purpose of a balance sheet is to show the financial position of a business *at a particular date.* Every business prepares a balance sheet at the end of the year, and most companies prepare one at the end of each month. A balance sheet consists of a listing of the assets and liabilities of a business and of the owners' equity. The following balance sheet portrays the financial position of Westside Cleaners, Inc., at December 31.

---

[1] A third financial statement, called a *statement of changes in financial position,* will be discussed later.

WESTSIDE CLEANERS, INC.
Balance Sheet
December 31, 19__

Balance sheet shows
financial position at
a specific date

Assets		Liabilities & Stockholders' Equity		
Cash	$ 20,500	Liabilities:		
Accounts receivable	65,000	Notes payable		$ 26,000
Supplies	1,500	Accounts payable		36,000
Land	68,000	Income taxes payable		18,000
Building	133,500	Total liabilities		$ 80,000
Cleaning equipment	39,000	Stockholders' equity:		
Delivery equipment	22,500	Capital stock	$225,000	
		Retained earnings	45,000	270,000
Total	$350,000	Total		$350,000

Note that the balance sheet sets forth in its heading three items: (1) the name of the business, (2) the name of the financial statement "Balance Sheet," and (3) the date of the balance sheet. Below the heading is the body of the balance sheet, which consists of three distinct sections: assets, liabilities, and stockholders' equity. The remainder of this chapter is largely devoted to making clear the nature of these three sections.

Another point to note about the form of a balance sheet is that cash is always the first asset listed; it is followed by receivables, supplies, and any other assets that will soon be converted into cash or consumed in operations. Following these items are the more permanent assets, such as land, buildings, and equipment.

The liabilities of a business are always listed before the owners' equity. Each type of liability (such as notes payable, accounts payable, and income taxes payable) should be listed separately, followed by a total figure for liabilities.

The business entity. The illustrated balance sheet refers only to the financial affairs of the business entity known as Westside Cleaners, Inc., and not to the personal financial affairs of the owners. Individual stockholders may have personal bank accounts, homes, automobiles, and investments in other businesses; but since these personal belongings are not part of the cleaning company business, they are not included in the balance sheet of this business unit.

In brief, *a business entity is an economic unit which enters into business transactions that must be recorded, summarized, and reported. The entity is regarded as separate from its owner or owners;* the entity owns its own property and has its own debts. Consequently, for each business entity there should be a separate set of accounting records. A balance sheet and an income statement are intended to portray the financial position and the operating results of a single business entity. If the owners were to intermingle their personal affairs with the transactions of the business, the resulting financial statements would be misleading and would fail to describe clearly the activities of the business entity.

Assets are economic resources which are owned by a business and are expected to benefit future operations. Assets may have definite physical form such as buildings, machinery, or merchandise. On the other hand, some assets exist not in physical or tangible form, but in the form of valuable legal claims or rights; examples are amounts due from customers, investments in government bonds, and patent rights.

One of the most basic and at the same time most controversial problems in accounting is determining the dollar values for the various assets of a business. At present, generally accepted accounting principles call for the valuation of assets in a balance sheet at cost, rather than at market values. The specific principles supporting cost as the basis for asset valuation are discussed below.

The cost principle. Assets such as land, buildings, merchandise, and equipment are typical of the many economic resources that will be used in producing income for the business. The prevailing accounting view is that such assets should be recorded at their cost. When we say that an asset is shown in the balance sheet at its *historical cost,* we mean the dollar amount originally paid to acquire the asset; this amount may be very different from what we would have to pay today to replace it.

For example, let us assume that a business buys a tract of land for use as a building site, paying $100,000 in cash. The amount to be entered in the accounting records as the value of the asset will be the cost of $100,000. If we assume a booming real estate market, a fair estimate of the sales value of the land 10 years later might be $250,000. Although the market price or economic value of the land has risen greatly, the accounting value as shown in the accounting records and on the balance sheet would continue unchanged at the cost of $100,000. This policy of accounting for assets at their cost is often referred to as the *cost principle* of accounting.

In reading a balance sheet, the user should bear in mind that the dollar amounts listed do not indicate the prices at which the assets could be sold, nor the prices at which they could be replaced. One useful generalization to be drawn from this discussion is that a balance sheet does *not* show "how much a business is worth."

The going-concern assumption. It is appropriate to ask *why* accountants do not change the recorded values of assets to correspond with changing market prices for these properties. One reason is that the land and building used to house the business are acquired for *use* and not for resale; in fact, these assets ordinarily cannot be sold without disrupting the business. The balance sheet of a business is prepared on the assumption that the business is a continuing enterprise, a "going concern." Consequently, the present estimated prices at which the land and buildings could be sold are of less importance than if these properties were intended for sale.

The objectivity principle. Another reason for using cost rather than current market values in accounting for assets is the need for a definite, factual basis for valuation. The cost for land, buildings, and many other assets purchased for cash can be rather definitely determined. Accountants use the term *objective* to describe asset valuations that are factual and can be verified by independent experts. For example, if land is shown on the balance sheet at cost, any CPA who performed an audit of the business would be able to find objective evidence that the land was actually valued at the cost incurred in acquiring it. Estimated market values, on the other hand, for assets such as buildings and specialized machinery are not factual and objective. Market values are constantly changing and estimates of the prices for which assets could be sold are largely a matter of personal opinion. Of course at the date an asset is acquired, the cost and market value are usually the same because the buyer would not pay more than the asset was worth and the seller would not take less than current market value. The bargaining process which results in the sale of an asset serves to establish both the current market value of the property and the cost to the buyer. With the passage of time, however, the current market value of assets is likely to differ considerably from the cost recorded in the owner's accounting records.

Accounting for inflation. Severe worldwide inflation in recent years has raised serious doubts as to the adequacy of the conventional cost basis in accounting for assets. When inflation becomes very severe, historical cost values for assets simply lose their relevance as a basis for making business decisions. Proposals for adjusting recorded dollar amounts to reflect changes in the value of the dollar, as shown by a price index, have been considered for many years. However, stronger interest is being shown at present in balance sheets which would show assets at *current appraised values* or *replacement costs* rather than at historical cost. The British government has experimented extensively with the revision of corporate accounting to reflect inflation. The British approach proposes that year-end balance sheets show assets at their current value rather than at historical or original cost. Also in the Netherlands, many companies are now using some form of current-value accounting. In the United States, the Financial Accounting Standards Board requires that large corporations disclose the *current replacement cost* of certain assets as *supplementary information* to conventional cost-based financial statements.

Accounting concepts are not as exact and unchanging as many persons assume. To serve the needs of a fast-changing economy, accounting concepts and methods must undergo continuous evolutionary change. As of today, however, the cost basis of valuing assets is still the generally accepted method.

The problem of valuation of assets is one of the most complex in the entire field of accounting. It is merely being introduced at this point; in later chapters we shall explore carefully some of the valuation principles applicable to the major types of assets.

Liabilities

Liabilities are debts. All business concerns have liabilities; even the largest and most successful companies find it convenient to purchase merchandise and supplies on credit rather than to pay cash at the time of each purchase. The liability arising from the purchase of goods or services on credit is called an *account payable,* and the person or company to whom the account payable is owed is called a *creditor.*

A business concern frequently finds it desirable to borrow money as a means of supplementing the funds invested by the owners, thus enabling the business to expand more rapidly. The borrowed funds may, for example, be used to buy merchandise which can be sold at a profit to the firm's customers. Or, the borrowed money might be used to buy new and more efficient machinery, thus enabling the company to turn out a larger volume of products at lower cost. When a business borrows money for any reason, a liability is incurred and the lender becomes a creditor of the business. The form of the liability when money is borrowed is usually a **note payable,** a formal written promise to pay a certain amount of money, plus interest, at a definite future time.

An **account payable,** as contrasted with a **note payable,** does not involve the issuance of a formal written promise to the creditor, and it does not call for payment of interest. When a business has both notes payable and accounts payable, the two types of liabilities are shown separately in the balance sheet, with notes payable listed first. Another important form of liability for corporations is **income taxes payable.** This type of liability does not appear in the balance sheet of a single proprietorship or partnership because an unincorporated business is not a taxable entity. A figure showing the total of the liabilities should also be inserted, as shown in the balance sheet on page 16.

The creditors have claims against the assets of the business, usually not against any particular asset but against the assets in general. The claims of the creditors are liabilities of the business and have priority over the claims of owners. Creditors are entitled to be paid in full even if such payment should exhaust the assets of the business, leaving nothing for the owners.

Owners' equity

The owners' equity in a corporation is called **stockholders' equity.** In the following discussion, we will use the broader term "owners' equity" because the concepts being presented are equally applicable to the ownership equity in corporations, partnerships, and single proprietorships.

The owners' equity in a business represents the resources invested by the owners. The equity of the owners is a **residual claim** because the claims of the creditors legally come first. If you are the owner of a business, you are entitled to whatever remains after the claims of the creditors are fully satisfied. Thus, owners' equity is equal to the total assets minus the liabilities. For example:

Westside Cleaners, Inc., has total assets of	$350,000
And total liabilities amounting to	80,000
Therefore, the owners' equity must equal	$270,000

Suppose that Westside Cleaners, Inc., borrows $20,000 from a bank. After recording the additional asset of $20,000 in cash and recording the new liability of $20,000 owed to the bank, we would have the following:

Westside Cleaners, Inc., now has total assets of	$370,000
And total liabilities are now	100,000
Therefore, the owners' equity still is equal to	$270,000

It is apparent that the total assets of the business were increased by the act of borrowing money from a bank, but the increase in total assets was exactly offset by an increase in liabilities, and the owners' equity remained unchanged. The owners' equity in a business *is not increased* by the incurring of liabilities of any kind.

Increases in owners' equity. The owners' equity in a business comes from two sources:

1 Investment by the owners
2 Earnings from profitable operation of the business

Only the first of these two sources of owners' equity is considered in this chapter. The second source, an increase in owners' equity through earnings of the business, will be discussed in Chapter 3.

Decreases in owners' equity. Decreases in owners' equity also are caused in two ways:

1 Distribution of cash or other assets by the business to its owners
2 Losses from unprofitable operation of the business

Both causes of decreases in owners' equity will be considered in Chapter 3.

Owners' equity in corporations and single proprietorships. The ownership equity of a corporation consists of two elements: capital stock and retained earnings, as shown in the following illustration:

For a Corporation

Equity of stock-
holders . . .

Stockholders' equity:	
Capital stock	$1,000,000
Retained earnings	278,000
Total stockholders' equity	$1,278,000

The $1,000,000 shown under the caption *capital stock* represents the amount invested in the business by its owners. The $278,000 of *retained earnings* represents the portion of owners' equity which has been accumulated through profitable operation of the business. The corporation has chosen to retain this $278,000 in the business rather than to distribute these earnings to the stockholders as *dividends.* The total earnings of the corporation may have been considerably more than $278,000, because any earnings which were paid to stockholders as dividends would not appear on the balance sheet. The term *retained earnings* describes only the earnings which were *not* paid out in the form of dividends.

A single proprietorship is not required to maintain a distinction between invested capital and earned capital. Consequently, the balance sheet of a single proprietorship will have only one item in the owners' equity section, as illustrated below:

For a Single Proprietorship

. . . equity of a
single proprietor

Owner's equity:	
John Smith, capital	$30,000

What is capital stock?

As previously mentioned, the caption *capital stock* in the balance sheet of a corporation represents the amount invested by the owners of the business. When the owners of a corporation invest cash or other assets in the business, the corporation issues in exchange shares of capital stock as evidence of the investor's ownership equity. Thus, the owners of a corporation are termed **stockholders.**

The basic unit of capital stock is called a **share,** but a corporation may issue capital stock certificates in denominations of 1 share, 100 shares, or any other number. The total number of shares of capital stock outstanding at any given time represents 100% ownership of the corporation. Outstanding shares are those in the hands of stockholders. The number of shares owned by an individual investor determines the extent of his or her ownership of the corporation.

Assume, for example, that Draper Corporation issues a total of 5,000 shares of capital stock to investors in exchange for cash. If we assume further that Thomas Draper acquires 500 shares of the 5,000 shares outstanding, we may say that he has a 10% interest in the corporation. Suppose that Draper now sells 200 shares to Evans. The total number of shares outstanding remains unchanged at 5,000, although Draper's percentage of ownership has declined to 6% and a new stockholder, Evans, has acquired a 4% interest in the corporation. The transfer of 200 shares from Draper to Evans had **no effect** upon the corporation's assets, liabilities, or amount of stock outstanding. The only way in which this transfer of stock affects the corporation is that the list of stockholders must be revised to show the number of shares held by each owner.

The accounting equation

A fundamental characteristic of every balance sheet is that the total figure for assets always equals the total of liabilities plus owners' equity. This agreement or balance of total assets with the total of liabilities and owners' equity is one reason for calling this financial statement a **balance sheet.** But **why** do total assets equal total equities? The answer can be given in one short paragraph:

The dollar totals on the two sides of the balance sheet are always equal because these two sides are **merely two views of the same business property.** The listing of assets shows us what things the business owns; the listing of liabilities and owners' equity tells us who supplied these resources to the business and how much each group supplied. Everything that a business owns has been supplied to it by the creditors or by the owners. Therefore, the total claims of the creditors plus the claims of the owners equal the total assets of the business.

The equality of assets on the one hand and of the claims of the creditors and the owners on the other hand is expressed in the equation:

Fundamental accounting equation

$$\text{Assets} = \text{Liabilities} + \text{Owners' Equity}$$
$$\$350,000 = \$80,000 + \$270,000$$

The amounts listed in the equation were taken from the balance sheet illustrated on page 16. A balance sheet is simply a detailed statement of this equation. To emphasize this relationship, compare the balance sheet of Westside Cleaners, Inc., with the above equation.

To emphasize that the owners' equity is a residual element, secondary to the claims of creditors, it is often helpful to transpose the terms of the equation, as follows:

Alternative form of accounting equation

$$\text{Assets} - \text{Liabilities} = \text{Owners' Equity}$$
$$\$350,000 - \$80,000 = \$270,000$$

Every business transaction, no matter how simple or how complex, can be expressed in terms of its effect on the accounting equation. A thorough understanding of the equation and some practice in using it are essential to the student of accounting.

Regardless of whether a business grows or contracts, this equality between the assets and the claims against the assets is always maintained. Any increase in the amount of total assets is necessarily accompanied by an equal increase on the other side of the equation, that is, by an increase in either the liabilities or the owners' equity. Any decrease in total assets is necessarily accompanied by a corresponding decrease in liabilities or owners' equity. The continuing equality of the two sides of the balance sheet can best be illustrated by taking a brand-new business as an example and observing the effects of various transactions upon its balance sheet.

Effects of business transactions upon the balance sheet

Assume that John Green, Susan Green, and R. J. Hill organized a corporation called Greenhill Real Estate. A charter was obtained from the state authorizing the new corporation to issue 18,000 shares of capital stock with a par value of $10 a share.[2] John and Susan Green each invested $72,000 cash and R. J. Hill invested $36,000. The entire authorized capital stock of $180,000 was therefore issued as follows: 7,200 shares to John Green, 7,200 shares to Susan Green, and 3,600 shares to R. J. Hill. The three stockholders each received a stock certificate as evidence of his or her ownership equity in the corporation.

The planned operations of the new business call for obtaining listings of houses and commercial property being offered for sale by property owners, advertising these properties, and showing them to prospective buyers. The listing agreement signed with each property owner provides that Greenhill Real Estate shall receive at the time of sale a commission equal to 6% of the sales price of the property.

The new business was begun on September 1 with the deposit of $180,000 in a bank account in the name of the business, Greenhill Real Estate. The initial balance sheet of the new business then appeared as follows:

GREENHILL REAL ESTATE
Balance Sheet
September 1, 19__

Assets		Stockholders' Equity	
Cash	$180,000	Capital stock	$180,000

Beginning balance sheet of a new business

Purchase of an asset for cash. The next transaction entered into by Greenhill Real Estate was the purchase of land suitable as a site for an office. The price for the land was $141,000, and payment was made in cash on September 3. The effect of this transaction on the balance sheet was twofold: first, cash was decreased by the amount paid out; and

---

[2] Par value is the amount assigned to each share of stock in accordance with legal requirements. The concept of par value is more fully explained in Chapter 11.

second, a new asset, Land, was acquired. After this exchange of cash for land, the balance sheet appeared as follows:

GREENHILL REAL ESTATE
Balance Sheet
September 3, 19__

Assets		Stockholders' Equity	
Cash	$ 39,000	Capital stock	$180,000
Land	141,000		
Total	$180,000	Total	$180,000

Balance sheet totals unchanged by purchase of land for cash

Purchase of an asset and incurring of a liability. On September 5 an opportunity arose to buy a complete office building which had to be moved to permit the construction of a freeway. A price of $36,000 was agreed upon, which included the cost of moving the building and installing it upon Greenhill Real Estate's lot. As the building was in excellent condition and would have cost approximately $60,000 to build, it was considered a very fortunate purchase.

The terms provided for an immediate cash payment of $15,000 and payment of the balance of $21,000 within 90 days. Cash was decreased $15,000, but a new asset, Building, was recorded at cost in the amount of $36,000. Total assets were thus increased by $21,000, but the total of liabilities and owners' equity was also increased as a result of recording the $21,000 account payable as a liability. After this transaction had been recorded, the balance sheet appeared as follows:

GREENHILL REAL ESTATE
Balance Sheet
September 5, 19__

Assets		Liabilities & Stockholders' Equity	
Cash	$ 24,000	Liabilities:	
Land	141,000	Accounts payable	$ 21,000
Building	36,000	Stockholders' equity:	
		Capital stock	180,000
Total	$201,000	Total	$201,000

Totals increased equally by purchase of building on credit

Note that the building appears in the balance sheet at $36,000, its cost to Greenhill Real Estate. The estimate of $60,000 as the probable cost to construct such a building is irrelevant. Even if someone should offer to buy the building from Greenhill for $60,000 or more, this offer, if refused, would have no bearing on the balance sheet. Accounting records are intended to provide a historical record of *costs actually incurred;* therefore, the $36,000 price at which the building was purchased is the amount to be recorded.

Sale of an asset. After the office building had been moved to Greenhill Real Estate's lot, the company decided that the lot was larger than was needed. The adjoining business, Carter's Drugstore, wanted more room for a parking area; so, on September 10, Greenhill sold a small, unused corner of the lot to Carter's Drugstore for a price of $11,000. Since the selling price was computed at the same amount per foot as the corporation had paid for the land, there was neither a profit nor a loss on the sale. No down payment was required, but it was agreed that the full price would be paid within three months. By this transaction a new asset in the form of an account receivable was acquired, but the asset Land was decreased by the same amount; consequently, there was no change in the amount of total assets. After this transaction, the balance sheet appeared as shown below:

GREENHILL REAL ESTATE
Balance Sheet
September 10, 19__

Assets		Liabilities & Stockholders' Equity	
Cash	$ 24,000	Liabilities:	
Accounts receivable	11,000	Accounts payable	$ 21,000
Land	130,000	Stockholders' equity:	
Building	36,000	Capital stock	180,000
Total	$201,000	Total	$201,000

No change in totals by sale of land at cost

In the illustration thus far, Greenhill Real Estate has an account receivable from only one debtor and an account payable to only one creditor. As the business grows, the number of debtors and creditors will increase, but the Accounts Receivable and Accounts Payable accounts will continue to be used. The additional records necessary to show the amount receivable from each debtor and the amount owing to each creditor will be explained in Chapter 6.

Purchase of an asset on credit. A complete set of office furniture and equipment was purchased on credit from General Equipment, Inc., on September 14 for $5,400. As the result of this transaction the business owned a new asset, Office Equipment, but it had also incurred a new liability in the form of Accounts Payable. The increase in total assets was exactly offset by the increase in liabilities. After this transaction the balance sheet appeared as follows:

GREENHILL REAL ESTATE
Balance Sheet
September 14, 19__

Assets		Liabilities & Stockholders' Equity	
Cash	$ 24,000	Liabilities:	
Accounts receivable	11,000	Accounts payable	$ 26,400
Land	130,000	Stockholders' equity:	
Building	36,000	Capital stock	180,000
Office equipment	5,400		
Total	$206,400	Total	$206,400

Totals increased by acquiring asset on credit

Collection of an account receivable. On September 20, cash in the amount of $1,500 was received as partial settlement of the account receivable from Carter's Drugstore. This transaction caused cash to increase and the accounts receivable to decrease by an equal amount. In essence, this transaction was merely the exchange of one asset for another of equal value. Consequently, there was no change in the amount of total assets. After this transaction the balance sheet appeared as follows:

GREENHILL REAL ESTATE
Balance Sheet
September 20, 19__

	Assets		Liabilities & Stockholders' Equity	
Totals unchanged by collection of a receivable	Cash	$ 25,500	Liabilities:	
	Accounts receivable	9,500	Accounts payable	$ 26,400
	Land	130,000	Stockholders' equity:	
	Building	36,000	Capital stock	180,000
	Office equipment	5,400		
	Total	$206,400	Total	$206,400

Payment of a liability. On September 30 Greenhill paid $3,000 in cash to General Equipment, Inc. This payment caused a decrease in cash and an equal decrease in liabilities. Therefore the totals of assets and equities were still in balance. After this transaction, the balance sheet appeared as follows:

GREENHILL REAL ESTATE
Balance Sheet
September 30, 19__

	Assets		Liabilities & Stockholders' Equity	
Totals decreased by paying a liability	Cash	$ 22,500	Liabilities:	
	Accounts receivable	9,500	Accounts payable	$ 23,400
	Land	130,000	Stockholders' equity:	
	Building	36,000	Capital stock	180,000
	Office equipment	5,400		
	Total	$203,400	Total	$203,400

The transactions which have been illustrated for the month of September were merely preliminary to the formal opening for business of Greenhill Real Estate on October 1. During September no sales were arranged by the company and no commissions were earned. Consequently, the stockholders' equity at September 30 is shown in the above balance sheet at $180,000, unchanged from the original investment on September 1. September was a month devoted exclusively to organizing the business and not to regular operations. In succeeding chapters we shall continue the example of Greenhill Real Estate by illustrating operating transactions and considering how the net income of the business can be determined.

Effect of business transactions upon the accounting equation

The balance sheet of a business is merely a detailed expression of the accounting equation, Assets = Liabilities + Owners' Equity. To emphasize the relationship between the accounting equation and the balance sheet, let us now repeat the September transactions of

Greenhill Real Estate to show the effect of each transaction upon the accounting equation. Briefly restated, the seven transactions were as follows:

Sept. 1 Issued capital stock in exchange for $180,000 cash invested in the business by the stockholders.
       3 Purchased land for $141,000 cash.
       5 Purchased a building for $36,000, paying $15,000 cash and incurring a liability of $21,000.
      10 Sold part of the land at a price equal to cost of $11,000, collectible within three months.
      14 Purchased office equipment on credit for $5,400.
      20 Received $1,500 cash as partial collection of the $11,000 account receivable.
      30 Paid $3,000 on accounts payable.

The table below shows the effects of each of the September transactions on the accounting equation. The final line in the table corresponds to the amounts in the balance sheet at the end of September. Note that the equality of the two sides of the equation was maintained throughout the recording of the transactions.

	Assets					=	Liabilities	+	Owners' Equity
	Cash	+ Accounts Receivable	+ Land	+ Building	+ Office Equipment	=	Accounts Payable	+	Capital Stock
Sept. 1	+$180,000								+$180,000
Sept. 3	−141,000		+$141,000						
Balances	$ 39,000		$141,000						$180,000
Sept. 5	−15,000			+$36,000			+$21,000		
Balances	$ 24,000		$141,000	$36,000			$21,000		$180,000
Sept. 10		+$11,000	−11,000						
Balances	$ 24,000	$11,000	$130,000	$36,000			$21,000		$180,000
Sept. 14					+$5,400		+5,400		
Balances	$ 24,000	$11,000	$130,000	$36,000	$5,400		$26,400		$180,000
Sept. 20	+1,500	−1,500							
Balances	$ 25,500	$ 9,500	$130,000	$36,000	$5,400		$26,400		$180,000
Sept. 30	−3,000						−3,000		
Balances	$ 22,500 +	$ 9,500 +	$130,000 +	$36,000 +	$5,400 =		$23,400 +		$180,000

USE OF FINANCIAL STATEMENTS BY OUTSIDERS

Through careful study of the financial statements of a company, it is possible for an outsider with a knowledge of accounting to obtain a fairly complete understanding of the financial position of the business and to become aware of significant changes that have occurred since the date of the preceding balance sheet. Bear in mind, however, that financial statements have limitations. As stated earlier, only those factors which can be reduced to monetary terms appear in the balance sheet. Let us consider for a moment some important business factors which are not set forth in financial statements. Perhaps a competing store has just opened for business across the street; the prospect of intensified competition in the future will not be described in the balance sheet. As another example, the health, experience, and managerial skills of the key people in the management group are extremely important in the success of a business, but these qualities cannot be measured and expressed in dollars in the balance sheet.

Bankers and other creditors

Bankers who have loaned money to a business or who are considering making such a loan are vitally interested in the balance sheet of the business. By studying the amount and kinds of assets in relation to the amount and payment dates of the liabilities, a banker can form an opinion as to the ability of the business to pay its debts promptly. The banker gives particular attention to the amount of cash and of other assets (such as accounts receivable) which will soon be converted into cash, and then compares the amount of these assets with the amount of liabilities falling due in the near future.

The banker is also interested in the amount of the owners' equity, as this ownership capital serves as a protecting buffer between the banker and any losses which may befall the business. Bankers seldom are willing to make a loan unless the balance sheet and other information concerning the prospective borrower offer reasonable assurance that the loan can and will be repaid promptly at the maturity date.

Another important group making constant use of balance sheets consists of the credit managers of manufacturing and wholesaling firms, who must decide whether prospective customers are to be allowed to buy merchandise on credit. The credit manager, like the banker, studies the balance sheets of customers and prospective customers for the purpose of appraising their debt-paying ability. Credit agencies such as Dun & Bradstreet, Inc., make a business of obtaining financial statements from virtually all business concerns and appraising their debt-paying ability. The conclusions reached by these credit agencies are available to business managers willing to pay for credit reports about prospective customers.

Owners

The financial statements of corporations listed on the stock exchanges are eagerly awaited by millions of stockholders. A favorable set of financial statements may cause the market price of the company's stock to rise dramatically; an unfavorable set of financial statements may cause the bottom to fall out of the market price. Current dependable financial statements are one of the essential ingredients for successful investment in securities. Of course, financial statements are equally important in a business organized as a single proprietorship or as a partnership. The financial statements tell the owners just how successful the business has been and also summarize in concise form its present financial position.

Others interested in financial information

In addition to owners, managers, bankers, and merchandise creditors, other groups making use of accounting data include financial analysts, governmental agencies, employees, investors, and writers for business periodicals. Some very large corporations have more than a million stockholders; these giant corporations send copies of their annual financial statements to each of these many owners. In recent years there has been a definite trend toward wider distribution of financial statements to all interested persons, in contrast to the attitude of a few decades ago when many companies regarded their financial statements as confidential material. This trend reflects an increasing awareness of the impact of corporate activities on all aspects of our lives and of the need for greater disclosure of information about the activities of business corporations.

The purpose of this discussion is to show the extent to which a modern industrial society depends upon accounting. Even more important, however, is a clear understanding at the outset of your study that accounting does not exist just for the sake of keeping a record or in order to fill out income tax returns and various other regulatory reports. These are but auxiliary functions. If you gain an understanding of accounting concepts, you will have acquired an analytical skill essential to the field of professional management. *The prime and vital purpose of accounting is to aid decision makers in choosing among alternative courses of action.*

Key terms introduced in chapter 1

Accounting equation. Assets equal liabilities plus owners' equity. $A = L + OE$.

American Institute of Certified Public Accountants (AICPA). The national professional association of certified public accountants (CPAs). Carries on extensive research and is influential in improving accounting standards and practices.

Assets. Economic resources owned by a business which are expected to benefit future operations.

Audit report. A report issued by the CPA firm expressing an independent professional opinion on the fairness and reliability of the financial statements of a business.

Auditing. The principal activity of a CPA firm. Consists of an independent examination of the accounting records and other evidence relating to a business to support the expression of an impartial expert opinion about the reliability of the financial statements.

Balance sheet. A financial statement which shows the financial position of a business entity by summarizing the assets, liabilities, and owners' equity at a specific date.

Business entity. An economic unit that enters into business transactions. For accounting purposes, the activities of the entity are regarded as separate from those of its owners.

Certificate in Management Accounting (CMA). A designation granted to persons who have demonstrated competence in management accounting by passing an examination and meeting educational requirements.

Certified Public Accountants (CPAs). Independent professional accountants licensed by a state to offer auditing and accounting services for a fee.

Corporation. A business organized as a separate legal entity and chartered by a state, with ownership divided into transferable shares of capital stock.

Cost accounting. A specialized field of accounting concerned with determining and controlling the cost of particular products or processes.

Cost principle. The widely used concept of valuing assets for accounting purposes at their original cost to the business.

Creditor. The person or company to whom a liability is owed.

Dividend. A distribution of cash by a corporation to its stockholders.

Financial accounting. The area of accounting which emphasizes measuring and reporting the financial position and operating results of a business entity in conformity with generally accepted accounting principles.

Financial Accounting Standards Board (FASB). An independent group which conducts research in accounting and issues authoritative statements as to proper accounting principles and methods for reporting financial information.

Financial statements. Reports which summarize the financial position and operating results of a business (balance sheet and income statement).

Generally accepted accounting principles (GAAP). The accounting concepts, measurement techniques, and standards of presentation used in financial statements. Examples include the cost principle, the going-concern assumption, and the objectivity principle.

Going-concern assumption. An assumption by accountants that a business will continue to operate indefinitely unless specific evidence to the contrary exists, as, for example, impending bankruptcy.

Internal control. All measures used by a business to guard against errors, waste, and fraud; to assure the reliability of accounting data; to promote compliance with all company policies; and to evaluate the level of performance in all divisions of the company.

Liabilities. Debts or obligations of a business. The claims of creditors against the assets of a business.

Management accounting. The area of accounting which emphasizes developing and interpreting accounting information relevant to specific managerial decisions.

Notes payable. Liabilities evidenced by a formal written promise to pay a certain amount of money plus interest at a future date. Usually arise from borrowing.

Owners' equity. The excess of assets over liabilities. The amount of the owners' investment in a business plus profits from successful operations which have been retained in the business.

Partnership. A business owned by two or more persons voluntarily associated as partners.

Retained earnings. That portion of stockholders' equity resulting from profits which have been retained in the business rather than distributed as dividends.

Securities and Exchange Commission (SEC). A governmental agency which reviews the financial statements and other reports of corporations which offer securities for sale to the public. Works closely with the FASB and the AICPA to improve financial reporting practices.

Single proprietorship. An unincorporated business owned by one person.

Solvency. Having enough money to pay debts as they fall due.

Stockholders' equity. The owners' equity in a corporation.

Transactions. Business events which can be measured in money and which are entered in accounting records.

Demonstration problem for your review

The accounting data (listed alphabetically) for Crystal Auto Wash as of August 31, 19___, are shown below. The figure for Cash is not given but it can be determined when all the available information is assembled in the form of a balance sheet.

Accounts payable	$ 9,000	Land	$40,000
Accounts receivable	800	Machinery & equipment	85,000
Buildings	60,000	Notes payable	29,000
Capital stock	50,000	Retained earnings	99,400
Cash	?	Supplies	400
Income taxes payable	3,000		

On September 1, the following transactions occurred:

(1) Additional capital stock was issued for $15,000 cash.
(2) The accounts payable of $9,000 were paid in full. (No payment was made on the notes payable.)
(3) One-quarter of the land was sold at cost. The buyer gave a promissory note for $10,000. (Interest applicable to the note may be ignored.)
(4) Washing supplies were purchased at a cost of $2,000, to be paid for within 10 days. Washing supplies were also purchased for $600 cash from another car-washing concern which was going out of business. These supplies would have cost $1,000 if purchased through regular channels.

Instructions

a Prepare a balance sheet at August 31, 19___.
b Prepare a balance sheet at September 1, 19___.

Solution to demonstration problem

a
CRYSTAL AUTO WASH
Balance Sheet
August 31, 19___

Assets		Liabilities & Stockholders' Equity		
Cash	$ 4,200	Liabilities:		
Accounts receivable	800	Notes payable		$ 29,000
Supplies	400	Accounts payable		9,000
Land	40,000	Income taxes payable		3,000
Buildings	60,000	Total liabilities		$ 41,000
Machinery & equipment	85,000	Stockholders' equity:		
		Capital stock	$50,000	
		Retained earnings	99,400	149,400
Total	$190,400	Total		$190,400

b
CRYSTAL AUTO WASH
Balance Sheet
September 1, 19___

Assets		Liabilities & Stockholders' Equity		
Cash	$ 9,600	Liabilities:		
Notes receivable	10,000	Notes payable		$ 29,000
Accounts receivable	800	Accounts payable		2,000
Supplies	3,000	Income taxes payable		3,000
Land	30,000	Total liabilities		$ 34,000
Buildings	60,000	Stockholders' equity:		
Machinery & equipment	85,000	Capital stock	$65,000	
		Retained earnings	99,400	164,400
Total	$198,400	Total		$198,400

Review questions

1 In broad general terms, what is the purpose of accounting?

2 Why is a knowledge of accounting terms and concepts useful to persons other than professional accountants?

3 What is meant by the term *business transaction?*

4 What are financial statements and how do they relate to the accounting system?

5 Explain briefly why each of the following groups is interested in the financial statements of a business:

   a Creditors

   b Potential investors

   c Labor unions

6 The following questions relate to the term, *generally accepted accounting principles:*

   a What type of accounting reports should be prepared in conformity with these principles?

   b Why is it important for these principles to be widely recognized?

   c Where do these principles come from?

   d List two examples of generally accepted accounting principles which relate to the valuation of assets.

7 Distinguish between *accounting* and *bookkeeping.*

8 What is the principal function of certified public accountants? What other services are commonly rendered by CPA firms?

9 Private accounting includes a number of subfields or specialized phases, of which cost accounting is one. Name four other such specialized phases of private accounting.

10 Is the Financial Accounting Standards Board (FASB) a government agency? What is its principal function?

11 One primary objective of every business is to operate profitably. What other primary objective must be met for a business to survive? Explain.

12 Not all the significant happenings in the life of a business can be expressed in monetary terms and entered in the accounting records. Identify two or more significant events affecting a business which could not be satisfactorily measured and entered in its accounting records.

13 Information available from the accounting records provides a basis for making many business decisions. List five examples of business decisions requiring the use of accounting information.

14 What are the objectives of a company's system of internal control?

15 State briefly the purpose of a balance sheet.

16 Define assets. List five examples.

17 Define liabilities. List two examples.

18 Mint Corporation was offered $500,000 cash for the land and buildings occupied by the business. These assets had been acquired five years ago at a price of $300,000. Mint Corporation refused the offer, but is inclined to increase the land and buildings to a total valuation of $500,000 in the balance sheet in order to show more accurately "how much the business is worth." Do you agree? Explain.

19 Explain briefly the concept of the *business entity.*

20 State the accounting equation in two alternative forms.

21 The owners' equity in a business arises from what two sources?

22 Why are the total assets shown on a balance sheet always equal to the total of the liabilities and the owners' equity?

23 Can a business transaction cause one asset to increase or decrease without affecting any other asset, liability, or the owners' equity?

24 If a transaction causes total liabilities to decrease but does not affect the owners' equity, what change, if any, will occur in total assets?

25 Give examples of transactions that would:

    a Cause one asset to increase and another asset to decrease without any effect on the liabilities or owners' equity.

    b Cause both total assets and total liabilities to increase without any effect on the owners' equity.

Exercises

Ex. 1-1   The balance sheet items of Aspen Corp., at December 31, 19___, are listed below in alphabetical order. You are to prepare a balance sheet (including a complete heading). Use a sequence for assets similar to that in the illustrated balance sheet on page 16.

Accounts payable	$10,200	Land	$57,000
Accounts receivable	29,500	Notes payable	60,000
Building	70,000	Office equipment	35,700
Capital stock	50,000	Retained earnings	85,800
Cash	13,800		

Ex. 1-2   The following balance sheet of Artists' Gallery is incorrect because of improper headings and the misplacement of several accounts. Prepare a corrected balance sheet.

ARTISTS' GALLERY
March 31, 19___

Assets		Owners' Equity	
Retained earnings	$ 26,200	Accounts receivable	$ 37,800
Cash	10,900	Notes payable	68,800
Building	48,000	Supplies	1,400
Capital stock	40,000	Land	27,000
Automobiles	16,500	Income taxes payable	6,600
	$141,600		$141,600

Ex. 1-3   The balance sheet items of the Perez Corporation as of December 31, 19___, are shown below in random order. You are to prepare a balance sheet for the company, using a similar sequence for assets as in the illustrated balance sheet on page 16. You must compute the amount for retained earnings.

Land	$60,000	Office equipment	$ 6,800
Accounts payable	29,200	Building	140,000
Accounts receivable	37,800	Capital stock	50,000
Retained earnings	?	Notes payable	142,400
Cash	24,200	Income taxes payable	7,600

Ex. 1-4   Compute the missing amount in each of the following three lines:

	Assets	Liabilities	Owners' Equity
a	$186,000	$114,000	?
b	?	75,000	$ 50,000
c	410,000	?	190,000

Ex. 1-5   The following transactions represent part of the activities of Malibu Company for the first month of its existence. Indicate the effect of each transaction upon the total assets of the business by use of the appropriate phrase: "increase total assets," "decrease total assets," "no change in total assets."

    a Issued capital stock in exchange for cash.
    b Purchased a typewriter for cash.
    c Purchased a delivery truck at a price of $12,000, terms $2,000 cash and the balance payable in 24 equal monthly installments.
    d Paid a liability.
    e Borrowed money from a bank.
    f Sold land for cash at a price equal to its cost.
    g Sold land on account (on credit) at a price equal to its cost.
    h Sold land for cash at a price in excess of its cost.
    i Sold land for cash at a price less than its cost.
    j Collected an account receivable.

Ex. 1-6   List four column headings on a sheet of notebook paper as follows:

	Total		
Transaction	Assets	Liabilities	Owners' Equity

Next, you are to identify each of the following transactions by letter on a separate line in the first column. Then indicate the effect of each transaction on the total assets, liabilities, and owners' equity by placing a plus (+) for an increase, a minus sign (−) for a decrease, or the letters (NC) for no change in the appropriate column.

    a Purchased office equipment for cash.
    b Collected an account receivable.
    c Distributed cash as a dividend to stockholders.
    d Paid a liability.
    e Returned for credit some of the office equipment previously purchased on credit but not yet paid for.
    f Purchased a typewriter on credit.
    g Issued capital stock to a creditor in settlement of a liability.

As an example, transaction (a) would be shown as follows:

	Total		
Transaction	Assets	Liabilities	Owners' Equity
(a)	NC	NC	NC

Ex. 1-7   For each of the following categories, state concisely a transaction that will have the required effect on elements of the accounting equation.

a Increase an asset and increase a liability.

b Decrease an asset and decrease a liability.

c Increase one asset and decrease another asset.

d Increase an asset and increase owners' equity.

e Increase one asset, decrease another asset, and increase a liability.

Ex. 1-8   Certain transactions relating to Murdock Construction, Inc., are listed below. For each transaction you are to determine the effect on the total assets, total liabilities, and owners' equity of Murdock Construction, Inc. Prepare your answer in tabular form, identifying each transaction by letter and using the symbols (+) for increase, (−) for decrease, and (NC) for no change. An answer is provided for the first transaction to serve as an example. Note that some of the transactions concern the personal affairs of the owner of the business, John Murdock, rather than being strictly transactions of the corporation.

	Total Assets	Liabil- ities	Owners' Equity
a Issued capital stock to John Murdock in exchange for cash	+	NC	+
b Purchased office equipment for cash			
c Purchased construction equipment on credit			
d Distributed cash as dividend to John Murdock, the only stockholder			
e Paid a liability of the business			
f Returned for credit some defective office equipment which had been purchased on credit but not yet paid for			
g Obtained a loan from the bank for business use			
h John Murdock obtained a personal bank loan and used the money to buy additional shares of capital stock in Murdock Construction, Inc.			

Problems

1-1   Preparation of a balance sheet

A list of balance sheet items in random order appears below for Moon Ridge Lodge at October 31, 19__. You are to prepare a balance sheet at October 31 using a sequence for assets similar to that in the balance sheet on page 16. Include a figure for total liabilities. The figure for Cash must be computed.

Accounts payable	$16,750	Snowmobiles	$12,300
Capital stock	80,000	Notes payable	24,380
Buildings	85,025	Equipment	35,000
Accounts receivable	16,875	Land	40,000
Cash	?	Retained earnings	68,050
Income taxes payable	7,620		

1-2   Preparation of another balance sheet

While the accountant for Nelson Company was on vacation, the balance sheet shown below was prepared by the owner of the business, Ken Nelson, who had never studied accounting. Although the totals are in agreement, the balance sheet contains several errors in the location of items and in the heading. You are to prepare a corrected balance sheet using a sequence for assets similar to that shown in the illustrated balance sheet on page 16. Include a figure for total liabilities.

NELSON COMPANY
For the Year Ended December 31, 19___

Land	$ 70,600	Accounts payable	$127,600
Building	50,988	Accounts receivable	64,337
Notes payable	95,328	Notes receivable	60,000
Capital stock	20,000	Office equipment	14,268
Retained earnings	30,102	Delivery truck	6,825
Cash	6,012		
Total	$273,030	Total	$273,030

1-3   Interpreting the effects of business transactions

Five transactions of Campbell Imports, Inc., are summarized below in equation form, with each of the five transactions identified by a letter. For each of the transactions (a) through (e) you are to write a separate sentence explaining the nature of the transaction. For example, the explanation of transaction (a) could be as follows: Purchased office equipment at a cost of $1,400; paid cash.

	Cash	+	Accounts Receiv-able	+	Land	+	Building	+	Office Equip-ment	=	Accounts Payable	+	Capital Stock
					Assets					= Liabil-ities		+	Owners' Equity
Balances	$ 4,200		$6,700		$22,000		$56,500		–0–		$ 9,400		$80,000
(a)	−1,400								+1,400				
Balances	$ 2,800		$6,700		$22,000		$56,500		$1,400		$ 9,400		$80,000
(b)	+12,000												+12,000
Balances	$14,800		$6,700		$22,000		$56,500		$1,400		$ 9,400		$92,000
(c)									+1,800		+1,800		
Balances	$14,800		$6,700		$22,000		$56,500		$3,200		$11,200		$92,000
(d)	−600								+2,600		+2,000		
Balances	$14,200		$6,700		$22,000		$56,500		$5,800		$13,200		$92,000
(e)	+500		−500										
Balances	$14,700	+	$6,200	+	$22,000	+	$56,500	+	$5,800	=	$13,200	+	$92,000

1-4   Recording the effects of business transactions

The items making up the balance sheet of Walnut Square at June 30 are listed below in tabular form similar to the illustration of the accounting equation on page 26.

	Cash	+	Accounts Receiv-able	+	Auto-mobiles	+	Office Equip-ment	=	Notes Payable	+	Accounts Payable	+	Capital Stock
			Assets					=		Liabilities		+	Owners' Equity
Balances	$9,500		$58,400		$9,000		$3,800		$20,000		$25,200		$35,500

During a short period after June 30, Walnut Square had the following transactions.

(1) Paid $1,200 of accounts payable.
(2) Collected $4,000 of accounts receivable.
(3) Bought office equipment at a cost of $5,700. Paid cash.
(4) Borrowed $10,000 from a bank. Signed a note payable for that amount.
(5) Purchased an automobile for $8,000. Paid $3,000 cash and signed a note payable for the balance of $5,000.

Instructions

a List the June 30 balances of assets, liabilities, and owners' equity in tabular form as shown above.

b Record the effects of each of the five transactions in the tabular arrangement illustrated above. Show the totals for all columns after each transaction.

1-5   Preparation of a comprehensive balance sheet

Shown below is a list of balance sheet items in random order for Valencia Farms at September 30, 19__. You are to prepare a balance sheet by using these items and computing the amount of retained earnings. Use a similar sequence of assets as in the illustrated balance sheet on page 16. Include a figure for total liabilities.

Fences & gates	$18,650	Land	$225,000
Irrigation system	22,180	Buildings	42,500
Income taxes payable	6,540	Notes payable	295,000
Cash	8,015	Accounts receivable	11,425
Retained earnings	?	Livestock	67,100
Notes receivable	7,029	Farm machinery	33,872
Accounts payable	43,630	Capital stock	50,000
Property taxes payable	3,875	Wages payable	1,010

1-6   Preparation of a balance sheet; effects of transactions

The balance sheet items for Hernando's Hideaway (arranged in alphabetical order) were as follows at August 1, 19__. (You are to compute the figure for cash.)

Accounts payable	$ 8,100	Income taxes payable	$ 4,300
Accounts receivable	5,630	Land	67,000
Building	84,000	Notes payable	74,900
Capital stock	55,000	Retained earnings	59,300
Cash	?	Supplies	7,000
Furniture	34,500		

During the next two days, the following transactions occurred:

Aug. 2 Additional capital stock was issued for $25,000 cash. The accounts payable were paid in full. (No payment was made on the notes payable or income taxes payable.)

3 Furniture was purchased at a cost of $9,800 to be paid within 10 days. Supplies were purchased for $1,250 cash from a restaurant supply center which was going out of business. These supplies would have cost $1,890 if purchased through normal channels.

Instructions

a Prepare a balance sheet at August 1, 19___.

b Prepare a balance sheet at August 3, 19___.

1-7   Accounting principles

Hollywood Scripts is a service-type enterprise in the entertainment field, and its owner, Bradford Jones, has only a limited knowledge of accounting. Jones prepared the balance sheet below, which, although arranged satisfactorily, contains certain errors with respect to such concepts as the business entity and asset valuation. Note that Hollywood Scripts is a single proprietorship.

HOLLYWOOD SCRIPTS
Balance Sheet
November 30, 19___

Assets		Liabilities & Owners' Equity	
Cash	$ 940	Notes payable	$ 67,000
Notes receivable	2,900	Accounts payable	29,800
Accounts receivable	2,465	Total liabilities	$ 96,800
Land	70,000	Owner's equity:	
Building	54,326	Bradford Jones, capital	63,080
Office furniture	6,848		
Other assets	22,401		
Total	$159,880	Total	$159,880

In discussion with Jones and by inspection of the accounting records, you discover the following facts:

(1) One of the notes receivable in the amount of $700 is an IOU which Jones received in a poker game about two years ago. The IOU bears only the initials B.K. and Jones does not know the name or address of the maker.

(2) Office furniture includes an antique desk purchased November 29 of the current year at a cost of $2,100. Jones explains that no payment is due for the desk until January and therefore this debt is not included among the liabilities.

(3) Also included in the amount for office furniture is a typewriter which cost $525 but is not on hand, because Jones gave it to a son as a birthday present.

(4) The "Other assets" of $22,401 represents the total amount of income taxes Jones has paid the federal government over a period of years. Jones believes the income tax law to be unconstitutional, and a friend who attends law school will help Jones recover the taxes paid as soon as he completes his legal education.

(5) The asset land was acquired at a cost of $34,000, but was increased to a valuation of $70,000 when a friend of Jones offered to pay that much for it if Jones would move the building off the lot.

Instructions

a Prepare a corrected balance sheet at November 30, 19___.

b For each of the five numbered items above, use a separate numbered paragraph to explain whether the treatment followed by Jones is in accordance with generally accepted accounting principles.

Cases for analysis

Case 1-1   Evaluation of financial position

Sun Corporation and Terra Corporation are in the same line of business and both were recently organized, so it may be assumed that the recorded costs for assets are close to current market values. The balance sheets for the two companies are as follows at July 31, 19__:

SUN CORPORATION
Balance Sheet
July 31, 19__

Assets		Liabilities & Stockholders' Equity		
Cash	$ 18,000	Liabilities:		
Accounts receivable	26,000	Notes payable (due in		
Land	37,200	60 days)		$ 12,400
Building	38,000	Accounts payable		9,600
Office equipment	1,200	Total liabilities		$ 22,000
		Stockholders' equity:		
		Capital stock	$60,000	
		Retained earnings .	38,400	98,400
Total	$120,400	Total		$120,400

TERRA CORPORATION
Balance Sheet
July 31, 19__

Assets		Liabilities & Stockholders' Equity		
Cash	$ 4,800	Liabilities:		
Accounts receivable	9,600	Notes payable (due in		
Land	96,000	60 days)		$ 22,400
Building	60,000	Accounts payable		43,200
Office equipment	12,000	Total liabilities		$ 65,600
		Stockholders' equity:		
		Capital stock	$72,000	
		Retained earnings .	44,800	116,800
Total	$182,400	Total		$182,400

Instructions

a Assume that you are a banker and that each company had applied to you for a 90-day loan of $12,000. Which would you consider to be the more favorable prospect? Explain your answer fully.

b Assume that you are an investor considering purchasing all the capital stock of one or both of the companies. For which business would you be willing to pay the higher price? Do you see any indication of a financial crisis which you might face shortly after buying either company? Explain your answer fully. (It is recognized that for either decision, additional information would be useful, but you are to reach your decision on the basis of the information available.)

Case 1-2   Accounting principles

Linda Shields and Mark Ryan own all the capital stock of Valley Property Management, Inc. Both stockholders also work full time in the business. The company performs management services for apartment house owners, including finding tenants, collecting rents, and doing maintenance and repair work.

When the business was organized, Shields and Ryan invested a total of $50,000 to acquire the capital stock. At December 31, Year 1, a partial list of the corporation's balance sheet items included cash of $15,700, office equipment of $6,100, accounts payable of $16,100, and income taxes payable of $2,900. Additional information concerning the corporation's financial position and operations appears in the following six numbered paragraphs. Some of this information should be included in the balance sheet; some should not.

(1) Earlier in Year 1, the corporation purchased an office building from Shields at a price of $42,000 for the land and $67,000 for the building. Shields had acquired the property several years ago at a cost of $25,000 for the land and $50,000 for the building. At December 31, Year 1, Shields and Ryan estimated that the land was worth $47,000 and the building was worth $70,000. The corporation owes Shields a $49,000 note payable in connection with the purchase of the property.

(2) While working, Shields drives her own automobile, which cost $12,600. Ryan uses a car owned by the corporation, which cost $10,200.

(3) One of the apartment houses managed by the company is owned by Ryan. Ryan acquired the property at a cost of $100,000 for the land and $190,000 for the building.

(4) Company records show a $1,900 account receivable from Ryan and $23,400 accounts receivable from other clients.

(5) Shields has a $20,000 bank account in the same bank used by the corporation. She explains that if the corporation should run out of cash, it may use that $20,000 and repay her later.

(6) Company records have not been properly maintained, and the amount of retained earnings is not known. (You can compute this amount as a final step in preparing the balance sheet.)

Instructions

a Prepare a balance sheet for the business entity Valley Property Management, Inc., at December 31, Year 1.

b For each of the notes numbered (1) through (5) above, explain your reasoning in deciding whether or not to include the items on the balance sheet and in determining the proper dollar valuation.

Chapter 2
Recording changes
in financial position

This chapter has two major objectives. The first is to introduce the principles of double-entry accounting. The second is to illustrate the accounting cycle — the procedures used by a business to record, classify, and summarize the effects of business transactions in its accounting records. The activities of Greenhill Real Estate, which were described in Chapter 1, are now recorded in the company's general journal and posted to the general ledger accounts. The preparation of a trial balance also is illustrated, and the uses and limitations of the trial balance are discussed. The chapter concludes by comparing the accounting procedures applied in manual accounting systems with those in computer-based systems.

After studying
this chapter you
should be able to:

✓ Describe a ledger and a ledger account. List the elements that comprise a T account.
✓ State the rules of debit and credit for balance sheet accounts.
✓ Explain the double-entry system of accounting.
✓ Explain the purpose of a journal and its relationship to the ledger.
✓ Prepare journal entries to record common business transactions affecting balance sheet accounts.
✓ Transfer (post) information from the journal to ledger accounts.
✓ Prepare a trial balance and explain its uses and limitations.
✓ Describe the basic steps of the accounting cycle in both manual and computer-based accounting systems.

The role of accounting records

Many business concerns have several hundred or even several thousand business transactions each day. It would not be practical to prepare a separate balance sheet after each transaction, and it is quite unnecessary to do so. Instead, the many individual transactions are recorded in the accounting records, and at the end of the month or other accounting period, a balance sheet is prepared from these records. In this chapter, we shall see how business transactions are analyzed, entered in the accounting records, and stored for use in preparing a balance sheet. In later chapters, we shall also see that the accounting records contain the data necessary to prepare an income statement, income tax returns, and other financial reports.

The use of "accounts" for recording transactions

An accounting system includes a separate record for each item that appears in the balance sheet. For example, a separate record is kept for the asset Cash, showing all the increases and decreases in cash which result from the many transactions in which cash is received or paid. A similar record is kept for every other asset, for every liability, and for every element of owners' equity. The form of record used to record increases and decreases in a single balance sheet item is called an **account,** or sometimes a **ledger account.** All these separate accounts are usually kept in a loose-leaf binder, and the entire group of accounts is called a **ledger.**

Many businesses use computers for maintaining accounting records and store data on magnetic tapes rather than in ledgers. Nevertheless, an understanding of accounting concepts is most easily acquired by study of a manual accounting system. The knowledge gained by working with manual accounting records is readily transferable to any type of automated accounting system. For these reasons, we shall use standard written accounting records, such as ledger accounts, in our study of basic accounting concepts. These written records continue to be used by a great many businesses, but for our purposes they should be viewed as conceptual devices rather than as fixed components of an accounting system.

THE LEDGER

A ledger account is a means of bringing together in one place all the information about changes in a specific asset, a liability, or an element of owners' equity. For example, a ledger account for the asset **cash** provides a record of the amount of cash receipts, cash payments, and the current cash balance. By maintaining a Cash account, management can keep track of the amount of cash available for meeting payrolls and for making current purchases of assets or services. This record of cash is also useful in planning future operations and in advance planning of applications for bank loans.

In its simplest form, an account has only three elements: (1) a title, consisting of the name of the particular asset, liability, or owners' equity; (2) a left side, which is called the **debit** side; and (3) a right side, which is called the **credit** side. This form of account, illustrated below, is called a **T account** because of its resemblance to the letter T. More complete forms of accounts will be illustrated later.

Title of Account

T account: a	Left or debit side
ledger account in	
simplified form	Right or credit side

Debit and credit entries

An amount recorded on the left or debit side of an account is called a *debit*, or a *debit entry;* an amount entered on the right or credit side is called a *credit*, or a *credit entry.* Accountants also use the words debit and credit as verbs. The act of recording a debit in an account is called *debiting* the account; the recording of a credit is called *crediting* the account.

Students beginning a course in accounting often have preconceived but erroneous notions about the meanings of the terms debit and credit. For example, to some people unacquainted with accounting, the word credit may carry a more favorable connotation than does the word debit. Such connotations have no validity in the field of accounting. Accountants use *debit* to mean an entry on the left-hand side of an account, and *credit* to mean an entry on the right-hand side. The student should therefore regard debit and credit as simple equivalents of left and right, without any hidden or subtle implications.

To illustrate the recording of debits and credits in an account, let us go back to the cash transactions of Greenhill Real Estate as illustrated in Chapter 1. When these cash transactions are recorded in an account, the receipts are listed in vertical order on the debit side of the account and the payments are listed on the credit side. The dates of the transactions may also be listed, as shown in the following illustration:

Cash

Cash transactions	9/1		180,000	9/3	141,000
entered in ledger	9/20	22,500	1,500	9/5	15,000
account			181,500	9/30	3,000
					159,000

Note that the total of the cash receipts, $181,500 is in small-size figures so that it will not be mistaken for a debit entry. The total of the cash payments (credits), amounting to $159,000, is also in small-size figures to distinguish it from the credit entries. These *footings,* or memorandum totals, are merely a convenient step in determining the amount of cash on hand at the end of the month. The difference in dollars between the total debits and the total credits in an account is called the *balance.* If the debits exceed the credits the account has a *debit balance;* if the credits exceed the debits, the account has a *credit balance.* In the illustrated Cash account, the debit total of $181,500 is larger than the credit total of $159,000; therefore, the account has a debit balance. By subtracting the credits from the debits ($181,500 – $159,000), we determine that the balance of the Cash account is $22,500. This debit balance is noted on the debit (left) side of the account. The balance of the Cash account represents the amount of cash owned by the business on September 30; in a balance sheet prepared at this date, Cash in the amount of $22,500 would be listed as an asset.

Debit balances in asset accounts. In the preceding illustration of a cash account, increases were recorded on the left or debit side of the account and decreases were recorded on the right or credit side. The increases were greater than the decreases and the result was a debit balance in the account.

All asset accounts normally have debit balances. In fact, the ownership by a business of cash, land, or any other asset indicates that the increases (debits) to that asset have been greater than the decreases (credits). It is hard to imagine an account for an asset such as land having a credit balance, as this would indicate that the business had disposed of more land than it had acquired and had reached the impossible position of having a negative amount of land.

The balance sheets previously illustrated in Chapter 1 showed all the assets on the left side of the balance sheet. The fact that assets are located on the *left* side of the balance sheet is a convenient means of remembering the rule that an increase in an asset is recorded on the *left* (debit) side of the account, and also that an asset account normally has a debit *(left-hand)* balance.

Any Asset Account

(Debit)	(Credit)
Increase	Decrease

Asset accounts normally have debit balances

Credit balances in liability and owners' equity accounts. Increases in liability and owners' equity accounts are recorded by credit entries, and decreases in these accounts are recorded by debits. The relationship between entries in these accounts and their position on the balance sheet may be summed up as follows: (1) Liabilities and owners' equity belong on the *right* side of the balance sheet; (2) an increase in a liability or an owners' equity account is recorded on the *right* side of the account; and (3) liability and owners' equity accounts normally have credit *(right-hand)* balances.

Any Liability Account
or Owners' Equity Account

(Debit)	(Credit)
Decrease	Increase

Liability accounts and owners' equity accounts normally have credit balances

The diagram on page 44 emphasizes again the relationship between the position of an account in the balance sheet and the method of recording an increase or decrease in the account. The accounts used are those previously shown in the balance sheet prepared for Greenhill Real Estate (page 25).

Concise statement of the rules of debit and credit. The rules of debit and credit, which have been explained and illustrated in the preceding sections, may be concisely summarized as follows:

Asset Accounts	Liability & Owners' Equity Accounts
Increases are recorded by debits	Increases are recorded by credits
Decreases are recorded by credits	Decreases are recorded by debits

Mechanics of debit and credit

Balance Sheet Accounts

(Left side of balance sheet) Assets	=	(Right side of balance sheet) Liabilities + Owners' Equity

Cash

(Debit) Increase	(Credit) Decrease

Accounts Payable

(Debit) Decrease	(Credit) Increase

Accounts Receivable

(Debit) Increase	(Credit) Decrease

Capital Stock

(Debit) Decrease	(Credit) Increase

Land

(Debit) Increase	(Credit) Decrease

Building

(Debit) Increase	(Credit) Decrease

Office Equipment

(Debit) Increase	(Credit) Decrease

Equality of debits and credits. Every business transaction affects two or more accounts. The *double-entry system,* which is the system in almost universal use, takes its name from the fact that *equal debit and credit entries are made for every transaction.* If only two accounts are affected (as in the purchase of land for cash), one account, Land, is debited and the other account, Cash, is credited for the same amount. If more than two accounts are affected by a transaction, the sum of the debit entries must be equal to the sum of the credit entries. This situation was illustrated when Greenhill Real Estate purchased a building for a price of $36,000. The $36,000 debit to the asset account, Building, was exactly equal to the total of the $15,000 credit to the Cash account plus the $21,000 credit to the liability account, Accounts Payable. Since every transaction results in an equal amount of debits and credits in the ledger, it follows that the total of *all* debit entries in the ledger is equal to the total of *all* the credit entries.

Recording transactions in ledger accounts: illustration

The procedure for recording transactions in ledger accounts will be illustrated by using the September transactions of Greenhill Real Estate. Each transaction will first be analyzed in terms of increases and decreases in assets, liabilities, and stockholders' equity. Then we shall follow the rules of debit and credit in entering these increases and decreases in T accounts. Asset accounts will be shown on the left side of the page; liability and stockholders' equity accounts on the right side. For convenience in following the transactions into the ledger accounts, the letter used to identify a given transaction will also appear opposite the debit and credit entries for that transaction. This use of identifying letters is for illustrative purposes only and is not used in actual accounting practice.

Transaction (a). The sum of $180,000 cash was invested in the business on September 1, and 18,000 shares of $10 par value capital stock were issued.

	Analysis	Rule	Entry
Recording an investment in the business	The asset Cash was increased	Increases in assets are recorded by debits	Debit: Cash, $180,000
	The stockholders' equity was increased	Increases in stockholders' equity are recorded by credits	Credit: Capital Stock, $180,000

Cash		Capital Stock	
9/1 (a) 180,000			9/1 (a) 180,000

Transaction (b). On September 3, Greenhill Real Estate purchased land for cash in the amount of $141,000.

	Analysis	Rule	Entry
Purchase of land for cash	The asset Land was increased	Increases in assets are recorded by debits	Debit: Land, $141,000
	The asset Cash was decreased	Decreases in assets are recorded by credits	Credit: Cash, $141,000

Cash		
9/1 180,000	9/3 (b) 141,000	

Land	
9/3 (b) 141,000	

Transaction (c). On September 5, Greenhill Real Estate purchased a building from OK Company at a total price of $36,000. The terms of the purchase required a cash payment of $15,000 with the remainder of $21,000 payable within 90 days.

Analysis	Rule	Entry
A new asset, Building, was acquired	Increases in assets are recorded by debits	Debit: Building, $36,000
The asset Cash was decreased	Decreases in assets are recorded by credits	Credit: Cash, $15,000
A new liability, Accounts Payable, was incurred	Increases in liabilities are recorded by credits	Credit: Accounts Payable, $21,000

Purchase of an asset, with partial payment

Cash				Accounts Payable		
9/1 180,000	9/3 141,000				9/5 (c) 21,000	
	9/5 (c) 15,000					

Building	
9/5 (c) 36,000	

Transaction (d). On September 10, Greenhill Real Estate sold a portion of its land on credit to Carter's Drugstore for a price of $11,000. The land was sold at its cost, so there was no gain or loss on the transaction.

Analysis	Rule	Entry
A new asset, Accounts Receivable, was acquired	Increases in assets are recorded by debits	Debit: Accounts Receivable, $11,000
The asset Land was decreased	Decreases in assets are recorded by credits	Credit: Land, $11,000

Sale of land on credit

Accounts Receivable	
9/10 (d) 11,000	

Land	
9/3 141,000	9/10 (d) 11,000

Transaction (e). On September 14, Greenhill Real Estate purchased office equipment on credit from General Equipment, Inc., in the amount of $5,400.

Analysis	Rule	Entry
Purchase of an asset on credit A new asset, Office Equipment, was acquired	Increases in assets are recorded by debits	Debit: Office Equipment, $5,400
A new liability, Accounts Payable, was incurred	Increases in liabilities are recorded by credits	Credit: Accounts Payable, $5,400

Office Equipment		Accounts Payable	
9/14 (e) 5,400			9/5 21,000
			9/14 (e) 5,400

Transaction (f). On September 20, cash of $1,500 was received as partial collection of the account receivable from Carter's Drugstore.

Analysis	Rule	Entry
Collection of an account receivable The asset Cash was increased	Increases in assets are recorded by debits	Debit: Cash, $1,500
The asset Accounts Receivable was decreased	Decreases in assets are recorded by credits	Credit: Accounts Receivable, $1,500

Cash			
9/1 180,000		9/3 141,000	
9/20 (f) 1,500		9/5 15,000	

Accounts Receivable			
9/10 11,000		9/20 (f) 1,500	

Transaction (g). A cash payment of $3,000 was made on September 30 in partial settlement of the amount owing to General Equipment, Inc.

Analysis	Rule	Entry
Payment of a liability The liability Accounts Payable was decreased	Decreases in liabilities are recorded by debits	Debit: Accounts Payable, $3,000
The asset Cash was decreased	Decreases in assets are recorded by credits	Credit: Cash, $3,000

Cash				Accounts Payable			
9/1 180,000		9/3 141,000		9/30 (g) 3,000		9/5 21,000	
9/20 1,500		9/5 15,000				9/14 5,400	
		9/30 (g) 3,000					

Running balance form of ledger account

The T form of account used thus far is very convenient for illustrative purposes. Details are avoided and we can concentrate on basic ideas. T accounts are also often used in advanced accounting courses and by professional accountants for preliminary analysis of a transaction. In other words, the simplicity of the T account provides a concise conceptual picture of the elements of a business transaction. In formal accounting records, however, more information is needed, and the T account is replaced in many manual accounting systems by a ledger account with special rulings, such as the following illustration of the Cash account for Greenhill Real Estate.

Ledger account with a balance column

Date		Explanation	Ref	Debit	Credit	Balance
19–						
Sept	1			18 000 00		18 000 00
	3				14 100 00	3 900 00
	5				1 500 00	2 400 00
	20			150 00		2 550 00
	30				300 00	2 250 00

The **Date** column shows the date of the transaction — which is not necessarily the same as the date the entry is made in the account. The **Explanation** column is needed only for unusual items, and in many companies it is seldom used. The **Ref** (Reference) column is used to list the page number of the journal in which the transaction is recorded, thus making it possible to trace ledger entries back to their source (a journal). The use of a **journal** is explained later in this chapter. In the **Balance** column of the account, the new balance is entered each time the account is debited or credited. Thus the current balance of the account can always be observed at a glance.

Although we shall make extensive use of this three-column running balance form of account in later chapters, there also will be many situations in which we shall continue to use T accounts to achieve simplicity in illustrating accounting principles and procedures.

The normal balance of an account

The running balance form of ledger account does not indicate specifically whether the balance of the account is a debit or credit balance. However, this causes no difficulty because we know that asset accounts normally have debit balances and that accounts for liabilities and owners' equity normally have credit balances.

The balance of any account normally results from recording more increases than decreases. In asset accounts, increases are recorded as debits, so asset accounts normally have debit balances. In liability and owners' equity accounts, increases are recorded as credits, so these accounts normally have credit balances.

Occasionally an asset account may temporarily acquire a credit balance, either as the result of an accounting error or because of an unusual transaction. For example, an account receivable may acquire a credit balance because a customer overpays his account. However, a credit balance in the Building account could be created only by an accounting error.

Sequence and numbering of ledger accounts

Accounts are usually arranged in the ledger in *financial statement order;* that is, assets first, followed by liabilities, owners' equity, revenue, and expenses. The number of accounts needed by a business will depend upon its size, the nature of its operations, and the extent to which management and regulatory agencies want detailed classification of information. An identification number is assigned to each account. A *chart of accounts* is a listing of the account titles and account numbers being used by a given business.

In the following list of accounts, certain numbers have not been assigned; these numbers are held in reserve so that additional accounts can be inserted in the ledger in proper sequence whenever such accounts become necessary. In this illustration, the numbers from 1 to 29 are used exclusively for asset accounts; numbers from 30 to 49 are used for liabilities; numbers in the 50s signify owners' equity accounts; numbers in the 60s represent revenue accounts; and numbers from 70 to 99 designate expense accounts. Revenue and expense accounts are discussed in Chapter 3. The balance sheet accounts with which we are concerned in this chapter are numbered as shown in the following brief chart of accounts.

	Account Title	Account Number
System for numbering ledger accounts	Assets:	
	Cash	1
	Accounts Receivable	4
	Land	20
	Building	22
	Office Equipment	25
	Liabilities:	
	Accounts Payable	32
	Stockholders' Equity:	
	Capital Stock	50
	Retained Earnings	51

In large businesses with many more accounts, a more elaborate numbering system would be needed. Some companies use an eight- or ten-digit number for each account; each of these digits carries special significance as to the classification of the account.

THE JOURNAL

In our preceding discussion, we recorded business transactions directly in the company's ledger accounts. We did this in order to stress the effects of business transactions upon the individual asset, liability, and owners' equity accounts appearing in the company's balance sheet. In an actual accounting system, however, the information about each business transaction is initially recorded in an accounting record called a *journal.* After the transaction has been recorded in the journal, the debit and credit changes in the individual accounts are entered in the ledger. Since the journal is the accounting record in which transactions are *first recorded,* it is sometimes called the *book of original entry.*

The journal is a chronological (day-by-day) record of all business transactions. The information about each transaction that should be recorded includes the date of the transaction, the debit and credit changes in specific ledger accounts, and a brief explanation of the transaction. At convenient intervals, the debit and credit amounts recorded in the journal are transferred to the accounts in the ledger. The updated ledger accounts, in turn, serve as the basis for preparing the balance sheet and other financial statements.

Why use a journal?

Since it is technically possible to record transactions directly in the ledger, why bother to maintain a journal? The answer is that the unit of organization for the journal is the *transaction,* whereas the unit of organization for the ledger is the *account.* By having both a journal and a ledger, we achieve several advantages which would not be possible if transactions were recorded directly in ledger accounts:

1 *The journal shows all information about a transaction in one place and also provides an explanation of the transaction.* In a journal entry, the debits and credits for a given transaction are recorded together, but when the transaction is recorded in the ledger, the debits and credits are entered in different accounts. Since a ledger may contain hundreds of accounts, it would be very difficult to locate all the facts about a particular transaction by looking in the ledger. The journal is the record which shows the complete story of a transaction in one entry.

2 *The journal provides a chronological record of all the events in the life of a business.* If we want to look up the facts about a transaction of some months or years back, all we need is the date of the transaction in order to locate it in the journal.

3 *The use of a journal helps to prevent errors.* If transactions were recorded directly in the ledger, it would be very easy to make errors such as omitting the debit or the credit, or entering the debit twice or the credit twice. Such errors are not likely to be made in the journal, since the offsetting debits and credits appear together for each transaction.

The general journal: illustration of entries

Many businesses maintain several types of journals. The nature of operations and the volume of transactions in the particular business determine the number and type of journals needed. The simplest type of journal is called a *general journal* and is illustrated below. It has only two money columns, one for debits and the other for credits; it may be used for all types of transactions.

The process of recording a transaction in a journal is called *journalizing* the transaction. To illustrate the use of the general journal, we shall now journalize the September transactions of Greenhill Real Estate which have been discussed previously.

General Journal

September journal entries for Greenhill Real Estate

Date		Account Titles and Explanation	LP	Debit	Credit
19__					
Sept.	1	Cash	1	180,000	
		Capital Stock	50		180,000
		Issued 18,000 shares of $10 par value capital stock in exchange for cash.			
	3	Land	20	141,000	
		Cash	1		141,000
		Purchased land for office site.			
	5	Building	22	36,000	
		Cash	1		15,000
		Accounts Payable	32		21,000
		Purchased building to be moved to our lot. Paid part cash; balance within 90 days to Kent Company.			
	10	Accounts Receivable	4	11,000	
		Land	20		11,000
		Sold the unused part of our lot at cost to Carter's Drugstore. Due within three months.			
	14	Office Equipment	25	5,400	
		Accounts Payable	32		5,400
		Purchased office equipment on credit from General Equipment, Inc.			
	20	Cash	1	1,500	
		Accounts Receivable	4		1,500
		Collected part of receivable from Carter's Drugstore.			
	30	Accounts Payable	32	3,000	
		Cash	1		3,000
		Made partial payment of the liability to General Equipment, Inc.			

Efficient use of a general journal requires two things: (1) ability to analyze the effect of a transaction upon assets, liabilities, and owners' equity and (2) familiarity with the standard form and arrangement of journal entries. Our primary interest is in the analytical phase of journalizing; the procedural steps can be learned quickly by observing the following points in the illustrated journal entries:

1 The year, month, and day of the first entry on the page are written in the date column. The year and month need not be repeated for subsequent entries until a new page or a new month is begun.

2 The name of the account to be debited is written on the first line of the entry and is customarily placed at the extreme left next to the date column. The amount of the debit is entered on the same line in the left-hand money column.

3 The name of the account to be credited is entered on the line below the debit entry and is indented, that is, placed about 1 inch to the right of the date column. The amount credited is entered on the same line in the right-hand money column.

4 A brief explanation of the transaction is usually begun on the line immediately below the title of the last account credited. The explanation need not be indented.

5 A blank line is left after each entry. This spacing causes each journal entry to stand out clearly as a separate unit and makes the general journal easier to read.

6 An entry which includes more than one debit or more than one credit (such as the entry on September 5) is called a *compound journal entry.* Regardless of how many debits or credits are contained in a compound journal entry, all the debits are entered before any credits are listed.

7 The LP (ledger page) column just to the left of the debit money column is left blank at the time of making the journal entry. When the debits and credits are later transferred to ledger accounts, the numbers of the ledger accounts are listed in this column to provide a convenient cross reference with the ledger.

In journalizing transactions, remember to use the exact title of the ledger accounts to be debited and credited. For example, in recording the purchase of office equipment for cash, *do not* prepare a journal entry debiting "Office Equipment Purchased" and crediting "Cash Paid Out." There are no ledger accounts with such titles. The proper journal entry would consist of a debit to *Office Equipment* and a credit to *Cash.*

A familiarity with the general journal form of describing transactions is just as essential to the study of accounting as a familiarity with plus and minus signs is to the study of mathematics. The journal entry is a *tool* for *analyzing* and *describing* the impact of various transactions upon a business entity. The ability to describe a transaction in journal entry form requires a complete understanding of the nature of the transaction and its effects upon the financial position of the business.

Posting

The process of transferring the debits and credits from the general journal to the proper ledger accounts is called *posting.* Each amount listed in the debit column of the journal is posted by entering it on the debit side of an account in the ledger, and each amount listed in the credit column of the journal is posted to the credit side of a ledger account.

The mechanics of posting may vary somewhat with the preferences of the individual. The following sequence is commonly used:

1 Locate in the ledger the first account named in the journal entry.

2 Enter in the debit column of the ledger account the amount of the debit as shown in the journal.

3 Enter the date of the transaction in the ledger account.

4 Enter in the reference column of the ledger account the number of the journal page from which the entry is being posted.

5 The recording of the debit in the ledger account is now complete. As evidence of this fact, return to the journal and enter in the LP (ledger page) column the number of the ledger account or page to which the debit was posted.

6 Repeat the posting process described in the preceding five steps for the credit side of the journal entry.

Illustration of posting. To illustrate the posting process, the journal entry for the first transaction of Greenhill Real Estate is repeated below, along with the two ledger accounts affected by this entry.

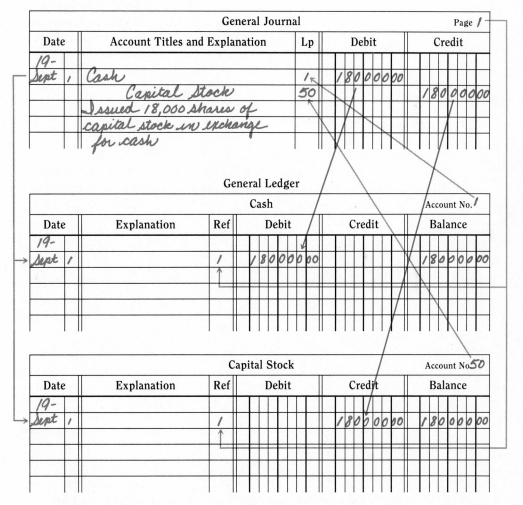

Note that the Ref (Reference) column of each of the two ledger accounts illustrated contains the number 1, indicating that the posting was made from page 1 of the general journal. Entering the journal page number in the ledger account and listing the ledger page in the journal provide a cross reference between these two records. The audit of accounting records always requires looking up some journal entries to obtain more information about the amounts listed in ledger accounts. A cross reference between the ledger and journal is therefore essential to efficient audit of the records. Another advantage gained from entering in the journal the number of the account to which a posting has been made is to provide evidence throughout the posting work as to which items have been posted. Otherwise, any interruption in the posting might leave some doubt as to what had been posted.

Journalizing and posting by hand is a useful method for the study of accounting, both for problem assignments and for examinations. The manual approach is also followed in many small businesses. One shortcoming is the opportunity for error that exists whenever information is being copied from one record to another. In businesses having a large volume of transactions, the posting of ledger accounts is performed by a computer, which speeds up the work and reduces errors. In these more sophisticated systems, transactions may be recorded simultaneously in both the journal and the ledger.

Ledger accounts after posting

After all the September transactions have been posted, the ledger of Greenhill Real Estate appears as follows. The accounts are arranged in the ledger in balance sheet order, that is, assets first, followed by liabilities and stockholders' equity.

To conserve space in this illustration, several ledger accounts appear on a single page. In actual practice, each account occupies a separate page in the ledger.

Ledger showing September transactions

	Cash					Account No. 1	
Date	Explanation	Ref	Debit	Credit	Balance		
19-							
Sept 1		1	18 000 00		18 000 00		
3		1		14 100 00	3 900 00		
5		1		1 500 00	2 400 00		
20		1	150 00		2 550 00		
30		1		300 00	2 250 00		

	Accounts Receivable					Account No. 4	
Date	Explanation	Ref	Debit	Credit	Balance		
19-							
Sept 10		1	1 100 00		1 100 00		
20		1		150 00	950 00		

Land   Account No. 20

Date	Explanation	Ref	Debit	Credit	Balance
19–					
Sept 3		1	141 000 00		141 000 00
10		1		11 000 00	130 000 00

Building   Account No. 22

Date	Explanation	Ref	Debit	Credit	Balance
19–					
Sept 5		1	36 000 00		36 000 00

Office Equipment   Account No. 25

Date	Explanation	Ref	Debit	Credit	Balance
19–					
Sept 14		1	5 400 00		5 400 00

Accounts Payable   Account No. 32

Date	Explanation	Ref	Debit	Credit	Balance
19–					
Sept 5		1		21 000 00	21 000 00
14		1		5 400 00	26 400 00
30		1	3 000 00		23 400 00

Capital Stock   Account No. 50

Date	Explanation	Ref	Debit	Credit	Balance
19–					
Sept 1		1		180 000 00	180 000 00

THE TRIAL BALANCE

Since equal dollar amounts of debits and credits are entered in the accounts for every transaction recorded, the sum of all the debits in the ledger must be equal to the sum of all the credits. If the computation of account balances has been accurate, it follows that the total of the accounts with debit balances must be equal to the total of the accounts with credit balances.

Before using the account balances to prepare financial statements, it is desirable to *prove* that the total of accounts with debit balances is in fact equal to the total of accounts with credit balances. This proof of the equality of debit and credit balances is called a *trial balance*. A trial balance is a two-column schedule listing the names and balances of all the accounts *in the order in which they appear in the ledger.* The debit balances are listed in the left-hand column and the credit balances in the right-hand column. The totals of the two columns should agree. A trial balance taken from the ledger of Greenhill Real Estate appears below.

GREENHILL REAL ESTATE
Trial Balance
September 30, 19___

Cash	$ 22,500	
Accounts receivable	9,500	
Land	130,000	
Building	36,000	
Office equipment	5,400	
Accounts payable		$ 23,400
Capital stock		180,000
	$203,400	$203,400

Trial balance at month-end proves ledger is in balance

Uses and limitations of the trial balance

The trial balance provides proof that the ledger is in balance. The agreement of the debit and credit totals of the trial balance gives assurance that:

1 Equal debits and credits have been recorded for all transactions.
2 The debit or credit balance of each account has been correctly computed.
3 The addition of the account balances in the trial balance has been correctly performed.

Suppose that the debit and credit totals of the trial balance do not agree. This situation indicates that one or more errors have been made. Typical of such errors are (1) the entering of a debit as a credit or vice versa; (2) arithmetical mistakes in balancing accounts; (3) clerical errors in copying account balances into the trial balance; (4) listing a debit balance in the credit column of the trial balance, or vice versa; and (5) errors in addition of the trial balance.

The preparation of a trial balance does *not* prove that transactions have been correctly analyzed and recorded in the proper accounts. If, for example, a receipt of cash were erroneously recorded by debiting the Land account instead of the Cash account, the trial balance would still balance. Also, if a transaction were completely omitted from the ledger, the error would not be disclosed by the trial balance. In brief, *the trial balance proves only one aspect of the ledger, and that is the equality of debits and credits.*

Despite these limitations, the trial balance is a useful device. It not only provides assurance that the ledger is in balance, but it also serves as a convenient stepping-stone for the preparation of financial statements. As explained in Chapter 1, the balance sheet is a formal statement showing the financial position of the business, intended for distribution to managers, owners, bankers, and various outsiders. The trial balance, on the other hand, is merely a working paper, useful to the accountant but not intended for distribution to others. The balance sheet and other financial statements can be prepared more conveniently from the trial balance than directly from the ledger, especially if there are a great many ledger accounts.

Locating errors

In the illustrations given thus far, the trial balances have all been in balance. Every accounting student soon discovers in working problems, however, that errors are easily made which prevent trial balances from balancing. The lack of balance may be the result of a single error or a combination of several errors. An error may have been made in adding the trial balance columns or in copying the balances from the ledger accounts. If the preparation of the trial balance has been accurate, then the error may lie in the accounting records, either in the journal or in the ledger accounts. What is the most efficient approach to locating the error or errors? There is no single technique which will give the best results every time, but the following procedures, done in sequence, will often save considerable time and effort in locating errors.

1 Prove the addition of the trial balance columns by adding these columns in the opposite direction from that previously followed.
2 If the error does not lie in addition, next determine the exact amount by which the schedule is out of balance. The amount of the discrepancy is often a clue to the source of the error. If the discrepancy is *divisible by 9,* this suggests either a *transposition* error or a *slide.* For example, assume that the Cash account has a balance of $2,175, but in copying the balance into the trial balance the figures are *transposed* and written as $2,157. The resulting error is $18, and like all transposition errors is divisible by 9. Another common error is the slide, or incorrect placement of the decimal point, as when $2,175.00 is copied as $21.75. The resulting discrepancy in the trial balance will also be an amount divisible by 9.

To illustrate another method of using the amount of a discrepancy as a clue to locating the error, assume that the Office Equipment account has a *debit* balance of $420 but that it is erroneously listed in the *credit* column of the trial balance. This will cause a discrepancy of two times $420, or $840, in the trial balance totals. Since such errors as recording a debit in a credit column are not uncommon, it is advisable, after determining the discrepancy in the trial balance totals, to scan the columns for an amount equal to exactly *one-half* of the discrepancy. It is also advisable to look over the transactions for an item of the *exact amount* of the discrepancy. An error may have been made by recording the debit side of the transaction and forgetting to enter the credit side.

3 Compare the amounts in the trial balance with the balances in the ledger. Make sure that each ledger account balance has been included in the correct column of the trial balance.

4 Recompute the balance of each ledger account.

5 Trace all postings from the journal to the ledger accounts. As this is done, place a check mark in the journal and in the ledger after each figure verified. When the operation is completed, look through the journal and the ledger for unchecked amounts. In tracing postings, be alert not only for errors in amount but for debits entered as credits, or vice versa.

Dollar signs

Dollar signs are not used in journals or ledgers. Some accountants use dollar signs in trial balances; some do not. In this book, dollar signs are used in trial balances. Dollar signs should always be used in the balance sheet, the income statement, and other formal financial reports. In the balance sheet, for example, a dollar sign is placed by the first amount in each column and also by the final amount or total. Many accountants also place a dollar sign by each subtotal or other amount listed below an underlining. In the published financial statements of large corporations, such as those illustrated in the appendix of this book, the use of dollar signs is often limited to the first and last figures in a column.

When dollar amounts are being entered in the columnar paper used in journals and ledgers, commas and decimal points are not needed. On unruled paper, commas and decimal points should be used. Most of the problems and illustrations in this book are in even dollar amounts. In such cases the cents column can be left blank or, if desired, zeros or dashes may be used.

The accounting cycle: an introduction

The sequence of accounting procedures used to record, classify, and summarize accounting information is often termed the **accounting cycle.** The accounting cycle begins with the initial recording of business transactions and concludes with the preparation of formal financial statements summarizing the effects of these transactions upon the assets, liabilities, and owners' equity of the business. The term "cycle" indicates that these procedures must be repeated continuously to enable the business to prepare new, up-to-date financial statements at reasonable intervals.

At this point, we have illustrated a complete accounting cycle as it relates to the preparation of a balance sheet for a service type business with a manual accounting system. The accounting procedures discussed to this point may be summarized as follows:

1 **Record transactions in the journal.** As each business transaction occurs, it is entered in the journal, thus creating a chronological record of events. This procedure completes the recording step in the accounting cycle.

2 **Post to ledger accounts.** The debit and credit changes in account balances are

posted from the journal to the ledger. This procedure classifies the effects of the business transactions in terms of specific asset, liability, and owners' equity accounts.

3 *Prepare a trial balance.* A trial balance proves the equality of the debit and credit entries in the ledger. The purpose of this procedure is to verify the accuracy of the posting process and the computation of ledger account balances.

4 *Prepare financial statements.* At this point, we have discussed only one financial statement — the balance sheet. This statement shows the financial position of the business at a specific date. The preparation of financial statements summarizes the effects of business transactions occurring through the date of the statements and completes the accounting cycle.

In the next section of this chapter, and throughout this textbook, we shall extend our discussion to include computer-based accounting systems. In Chapters 3 and 4, we shall expand the accounting cycle to include the measurement of business income and the preparation of an income statement.

Manual and computer-based systems: a comparison

In our preceding discussion, we have assumed the use of a manual accounting system, in which all the accounting procedures are performed manually by the company's accounting personnel. The reader may wonder about the relevance of such a discussion in an era when even many small businesses use computer-based accounting systems. However, the concepts and procedures involved in the operation of manual and computer-based accounting systems are *essentially the same.* The differences are largely a question of whether specific procedures require human attention, or whether they can be performed automatically by machine.

Computers can be programmed to perform mechanical tasks with great speed and accuracy. For example, they can be programmed to read data, to perform mathematical computations, and to rearrange data into any desired format. However, computers cannot think. Therefore, they are not able to *analyze* business transactions. Without human guidance, computers cannot determine which events should be recorded in the accounting records, or which accounts should be debited and credited to properly record an event. With these abilities and limitations in mind, we will explore the effects of computer-based systems upon the basic accounting cycle.

Recording business transactions. The recording of transactions requires two steps. First, the transaction must be *analyzed* to determine whether it should be recorded in the accounting records and, if so, which accounts should be debited and credited and for what dollar amounts. Second, the transaction must be *physically entered* (recorded) in the accounting system. As computers do not know which transactions should be recorded, or how to record them properly, these two functions must be performed by accounting personnel in both manual and computerized systems.

Differences do exist, however, in the manner in which data are physically entered into manual and computer-based systems. In manual systems, the data are entered in the form of handwritten journal entries. In a computer-based system, the data will be entered through a keyboard, an optical scanner, or other input device. Also, data entered into a computer-based system need *not* be arranged in the format of a journal entry. The data usually are entered into a *data base,* instead of a journal.

What is a data base? A data base is a warehouse of information stored within a computer system. The purpose of the data base is to allow information that will be used for several different purposes to be entered into the computer system *only once.* Data are originally entered into the data base. Then, as data are needed, the computer refers to the data base, selects the appropriate data, and arranges them in the desired format.

The information that must be entered into the data base is the same as that contained in a journal entry — the date, the accounts to be debited and credited, the dollar amounts, and an explanation of the transaction. However, this information need not be arranged in the format of a journal entry. For example, in a data base, accounts usually are identified by number, rather than by title. Also, abbreviations such as "D" or "C" are used to indicate whether an account should be debited or credited. Once information has been entered in the data base, the computer can arrange this information into any desired format, such as journal entries, ledger accounts, and financial statements.

Posting to ledger accounts. Posting merely transfers existing information from one accounting record to another — a function which can be easily performed by a computer. In a computer-based system, data posted to the ledger accounts come directly from the data base, rather than from the journal.

Preparation of a trial balance. Preparation of a trial balance involves three steps: (1) determining the balances of ledger accounts, (2) arranging the account balances in the format of a trial balance, and (3) adding up the trial balance columns and comparing the column totals. All these functions involve information already contained in the data base and can be performed by the computer.

Preparation of financial statements. The preparation of a balance sheet is similar to the preparation of a trial balance and can be readily performed by the computer. The preparation of an income statement involves additional procedures which will be discussed in Chapter 3.

Summary Computers can eliminate the need for copying and rearranging information which already has been entered into the system. They also can perform mathematical computations. In short, computers eliminate most of the "paper work" involved in the operation of an accounting system. However, they *do not* eliminate the need for accounting personnel who can analyze business transactions and explain these events in conformity with generally accepted accounting principles.

The differences in manual and computer-based systems with respect to the accounting procedures discussed in this chapter are summarized graphically in the following flowcharts. Functions which are performed by accounting personnel are shown in green; tasks which can be performed automatically by the computer are shown in black.

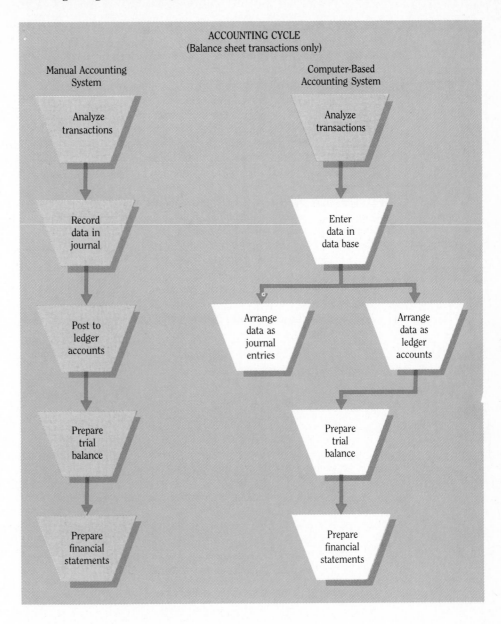

ACCOUNTING CYCLE
(Balance sheet transactions only)

Manual Accounting System

Analyze transactions

Record data in journal

Post to ledger accounts

Prepare trial balance

Prepare financial statements

Computer-Based Accounting System

Analyze transactions

Enter data in data base

Arrange data as journal entries

Arrange data as ledger accounts

Prepare trial balance

Prepare financial statements

Key terms introduced in chapter 2

Account. A record used to summarize all increases and decreases in a particular asset, such as Cash, or any other type of asset, liability, owners' equity, revenue, or expense.

Accounting cycle. The sequence of accounting procedures applied in recording, classifying, and summarizing accounting information. The cycle begins with the occurrence of business transactions and concludes with the preparation of financial statements. This concept will be expanded in later chapters.

Credit. An amount entered on the right-hand side of an account. A credit is used to record a decrease in an asset and an increase in a liability or owners' equity.

Credit balance. The balance of an account in which the total amount of credits exceeds the total amount of debits.

Data base. A storage center of information within a computer-based accounting system. The idea behind a data base is that data intended for a variety of uses may be entered into the computer system only once, at which time the information is stored in the data base. Then, as the information is needed, the computer can retrieve it from the data base and arrange it in the desired format.

Debit. An amount entered on the left-hand side of an account. A debit is used to record an increase in an asset and a decrease in a liability or in owners' equity.

Debit balance. The balance of an account in which the total amount of debits exceeds the total amount of credits.

Double-entry method. In recording transactions, the total dollar amount of debits must equal the total dollar amount of credits.

Footing. The total of amounts in a column.

Journal. A chronological record of transactions, showing for each transaction the debits and credits to be entered in specific ledger accounts.

Ledger. A loose-leaf book, file, or other record containing all the separate accounts of a business.

Posting. The process of transferring information from the journal to individual accounts in the ledger.

Trial balance. A two-column schedule listing the names and the debit or credit balances of all accounts in the ledger.

Demonstration problem for your review

Auto Parks, Inc., was organized on July 1 to operate a parking lot near a new sports arena. The following transactions occurred during July prior to the corporation beginning its regular business operations:

July 1 Issued 20,000 shares of $10 par value capital stock to the owners of the corporation in exchange for their investment of $200,000 cash.

July 2 Purchased land to be used as the parking lot for a total price of $250,000. A cash down payment of $120,000 was made and a note payable was issued for the balance of the purchase price.

July 5 Purchased a small portable building for $36,000 cash. The purchase price included installation of the building on the parking lot.

July 12 Purchased office equipment on credit from Suzuki & Co. for $6,000.

July 28 Paid $2,000 of the amount owed to Suzuki & Co.

The account titles and account numbers used by Auto Parks, Inc., to record these transactions are:

Cash	1	Notes payable	30
Land	20	Accounts payable	32
Building	22	Capital stock	50
Office equipment	25		

Instructions

a Prepare journal entries for the month of July.

b Post to ledger accounts of the three-column running balance form.

c Prepare a trial balance at July 31.

Solution to demonstration problem

a

General Journal   Page 1

Date		Account Titles and Explanations	LP	Debit	Credit
19__					
July	1	Cash	1	200,000	
		Capital Stock	50		200,000
		Issued 20,000 shares of $10 par value capital stock for cash.			
	2	Land	20	250,000	
		Cash	1		120,000
		Notes Payable	30		130,000
		Purchased land. Paid part cash and issued a note payable for the balance.			
	5	Building	22	36,000	
		Cash	1		36,000
		Purchased a small portable building for cash. The price included installation on the company's lot.			
	12	Office Equipment	25	6,000	
		Accounts Payable	32		6,000
		Purchased office equipment on credit from Suzuki & Co.			
	28	Accounts Payable	32	2,000	
		Cash	1		2,000
		Paid part of account payable to Suzuki & Co.			

b

Cash   Account No. *1*

Date		Explanation	Ref	Debit	Credit	Balance
July	1		1	200 000 00		200 000 00
	2		1		120 000 00	80 000 00
	5		1		36 000 00	44 000 00
	28		1		2 000 00	42 000 00

Land   Account No. 20

Date		Explanation	Ref	Debit	Credit	Balance
July	2		1	250 000 00		250 000 00

Building					Account No. 22		
Date	Explanation	Ref	Debit	Credit	Balance		
July 5		1	36 000 00		36 000 00		

Office Equipment					Account No. 25		
Date	Explanation	Ref	Debit	Credit	Balance		
July 12		1	6 000 00		6 000 00		

Notes Payable					Account No. 30		
Date	Explanation	Ref	Debit	Credit	Balance		
July 2		1		130 000 00	130 000 00		

Accounts Payable					Account No. 32		
Date	Explanation	Ref	Debit	Credit	Balance		
July 12		1		6 000 00	6 000 00		
28		1	2 000 00		4 000 00		

Capital Stock					Account No. 50		
Date	Explanation	Ref	Debit	Credit	Balance		
July 1		1		200 000 00	200 000 00		

c

AUTO PARKS, INC.
Trial Balance
July 31, 19___

Cash	$ 42,000	
Land	250,000	
Building	36,000	
Office equipment	6,000	
Notes payable		$130,000
Accounts payable		4,000
Capital stock		200,000
	$334,000	$334,000

Review questions

1 In its simplest form, an account has only three elements or basic parts. What are these three elements? debit, credit, balance

2 What relationship exists between the position of an account on the balance sheet and the rules for recording increases in that account?

3 State briefly the rules of debit and credit as applied to asset accounts. As applied to liability and owners' equity accounts.

4 Is it true that favorable events are recorded by credits and unfavorable events by debits? Explain.

5 Does the term *debit* mean increase and the term *credit* mean decrease? Explain.

6 What requirement is imposed by the double-entry system in the recording of any business transaction?

7 Explain precisely what is meant by each of the phrases listed below. Whenever appropriate, indicate whether the left or right side of an account is affected and whether an increase or decrease is indicated.
   a A debit of $200 to the Cash account
   b Credit balance
   c Credit side of an account
   d A debit of $600 to Accounts Payable
   e Debit balance
   f A credit of $50 to Accounts Receivable
   g A debit to the Land account

8 For each of the following transactions, indicate whether the account in parentheses should be debited or credited, and give the reason for your answer.
   a Purchased a copying machine on credit, promising to make payment in full within 30 days. (Accounts Payable)
   b Purchased land for cash. (Cash)
   c Sold an old, unneeded typewriter on 30-day credit. (Office Equipment)
   d Obtained a loan of $30,000 from a bank. (Cash)
   e Issued 1,000 shares of $25 par value capital stock for cash of $25,000. (Capital Stock)

9 For each of the following accounts, state whether it is an asset, a liability, or owners' equity; also state whether it would normally have a debit or a credit balance: (a) Office Equipment, (b) Capital Stock, (c) Accounts Receivable, (d) Accounts Payable, (e) Cash, (f) Notes Payable, (g) Retained Earnings.

10 List the following four items in a logical sequence to illustrate the flow of accounting information through a manual accounting system:
   a Information entered in journal
   b Financial statements prepared from ledger
   c Occurrence of a business transaction
   d Debits and credits posted from journal to ledger

11 Why is a journal sometimes called the *book of original entry?*

12 Compare and contrast a *journal* and a *ledger.*

13 Which step in the recording of transactions requires greater understanding of accounting principles: (a) the entering of transactions in the journal, or (b) the posting of entries to ledger accounts?

14 What is a *compound* journal entry?

15 What purposes are served by a trial balance?

16 In preparing a trial balance, an accounting student listed the balance of the Office Equipment account in the credit column. This account had a balance of $2,450. What would be the amount of the discrepancy in the trial balance totals? Explain.

17 Are dollar signs used in journal entries? In ledger accounts? In trial balances? In financial statements?

18 A student beginning the study of accounting prepared a trial balance in which two unusual features appeared. The Buildings account showed a credit balance of $20,000, and the Accounts Payable account a debit balance of $100. Considering each of these two abnormal balances separately, state whether the condition was the result of an error in the records or could have resulted from proper recording of an unusual transaction.

19 Since it is possible to record the effects of business transactions directly in ledger accounts, why is it desirable for a business to maintain a journal?

20 List the procedures in the *accounting cycle* as described in this chapter.

21 What is a *data base?* How does a data base relate to the preparation of journal entries and ledger accounts in a computer-based system?

Exercises

Ex. 2-1   Analyze separately each of the following transactions, using the format illustrated at the end of the exercise. In each situation, explain the debit portion of the transaction before the credit portion.

a On April 2, Ginger Denton organized a corporation to conduct business under the name of Vagabond Travel Services, Inc. The corporation issued 16,000 shares of $5 par value capital stock to Denton in exchange for $80,000 cash which she invested in the business.

b On April 11, the corporation purchased an office building in an industrial park for a total price of $128,000, of which $72,000 was applicable to the land and $56,000 to the building. A cash down payment of $34,500 was made and a note payable was issued for the balance of the purchase price.

c On April 21, office equipment was purchased on credit from ADR Company at a price of $6,400. The account payable was to be paid on May 2.

d On April 29, a portion of the office equipment purchased on April 21 was found to be defective and was returned to ADR Company. ADR Company agreed that Vagabond Travel Services would not be charged for the defective equipment, which had cost $950.

e On May 21, the remaining liability to ADR Company was paid in full.

Note: The type of analysis to be made is shown by the following illustration, using transaction (a) as an example:

a (1) The asset Cash was increased. Increases in assets are recorded by debits. Debit Cash, $80,000.

(2) The owners' equity was increased. Increases in owners' equity are recorded by credits. Credit Capital Stock, $80,000.

Ex. 2-2   Enter the following transactions in T accounts drawn on ordinary notebook paper. Label each debit and credit with the letter identifying the transaction. Prepare a trial balance at June 30.

a On June 8, Bluegrass Corporation was organized and issued 8,200 shares of $10 par value capital stock in exchange for $82,000 cash.

b On June 12, land was acquired for $36,000 cash.

c On June 14 a prefabricated building was purchased from E-Z Built Corporation at a cost of $40,800. A cash payment of $10,200 was made and a note payable was issued for the balance.

d On June 20, office equipment was purchased at a cost of $7,100. A cash down payment of $1,100 was made, and it was agreed that the balance should be paid within 30 days.

e On June 26, $3,400 of the amount due E-Z Built Corporation was paid.

Ex. 2-3   The first five transactions of a newly organized company appear in the following T accounts:

Cash		Office Equipment		Accounts Payable	
(1) 57,500	(2) 42,500	(3) 11,250		(5) 6,250	(3) 11,250
	(4) 2,500				
	(5) 6,250				

Land		Delivery Truck		Capital Stock	
(2) 30,000		(4) 10,000			(1) 57,500

Building		Notes Payable	
(2) 45,000			(2) 32,500
			(4) 7,500

For each of the five transactions in turn, indicate the type of accounts affected (asset, liability, or owners' equity) and whether the account was increased or decreased. Arrange your answers in the form illustrated for transaction (1), shown here as an example.

	Account(s) Debited		Account(s) Credited	
Transaction	Type of Account(s)	Increase or Decrease	Type of Account(s)	Increase or Decrease
(1)	Asset	Increase	Owners' equity	Increase

Ex. 2-4   Enter the following transactions in the two-column general journal of Aerobics, Inc. Include a brief explanation of the transaction as part of each journal entry. Do not include in the explanation any amounts or account titles since these are to be shown in the debit-credit portion of the entry.

Aug. 1 Issued an additional 2,600 shares of $5 par value capital stock in exchange for $13,000 cash.

Aug. 3 Purchased an adjacent vacant lot for use as parking space. The price was $31,200, of which $5,200 was paid in cash; a note payable was issued for the balance.

Aug. 12 Collected an account receivable of $4,800 from a customer, Mary Lee Ridgeway.

Aug. 17 Acquired office equipment from DataMax Corp. for $2,210, paying cash.

Aug. 21 Issued a check for $936 in full payment of an account payable to Hampton Supply Co.

Aug. 28 Borrowed $19,000 cash from the bank by signing a 90-day note payable.

Ex. 2-5   Transactions are recorded first in a journal and then posted to ledger accounts. In this exercise, however, your understanding of the relationship between journal and ledger is tested by asking you to study some ledger accounts and determine the journal entries which were probably made by the company's accountant to produce these ledger entries. The following accounts show the first six transactions of the Skyline Corporation. Prepare a journal entry (including written explanation) for each transaction.

Cash			
Nov. 1	60,000	Nov. 8	33,600
		Nov. 25	10,000

Notes Payable			
Nov. 25	10,000	Nov. 8	100,000

Land		
Nov. 8	70,000	
Nov. 30	35,000	

Accounts Payable			
Nov. 21	480	Nov. 15	3,200

Building		
Nov. 8	63,600	

Capital Stock, $10 par value			
		Nov. 1	60,000
		Nov. 30	35,000

Office Equipment			
Nov. 15	3,200	Nov. 21	480

Ex. 2-6   Using the information in the ledger accounts presented in Exercise 2-5, prepare a trial balance for Skyline Corporation at November 30, 19___.

Ex. 2-7   Some of the following errors would cause the debit and credit columns of the trial balance to have unequal totals. For each of the four paragraphs, write a statement explaining with reasons whether the error would cause unequal totals in the trial balance. Include in your explanations the dollar amounts of errors in trial balance totals or ledger account balances. Each paragraph is to be considered independently of the others.

    a An $870 payment for a typewriter was recorded as a debit to Office Equipment of $87 and a credit to Cash of $87.

    b A check for $1,000 issued to pay an account payable was recorded by debiting Accounts Payable $1,000 and crediting Accounts Receivable $1,000.

    c Collection of an account receivable in the amount of $1,200 was recorded by a debit to Cash for $1,200 and a debit to Capital Stock for $1,200.

    d A payment of $695 to a creditor was recorded by a debit to Accounts Payable of $695 and a credit to Cash of $69.

Ex. 2-8   The trial balance prepared by Discount Plumbing Service at June 30 was not in balance. In searching for the error, an employee discovered that a transaction for the purchase of a calculator on credit for $380 had been recorded by a *debit* of $380 to the Office Equipment account and a *debit* of $380 to Accounts Payable. The credit column of the incorrect trial balance has a total of $129,640.

    In answering each of the following five questions, explain fully the reasons underlying your answer and state the dollar amount of the error if any.

    a Was the Office Equipment account overstated, understated, or correctly stated in the trial balance?

    b Was the total of the debit column of the trial balance overstated, understated, or correctly stated?

    c Was the Accounts Payable account overstated, understated, or correctly stated in the trial balance?

   d Was the total of the credit column of the trial balance overstated, understated, or correctly stated?

   e How much was the total of the debit column of the trial balance before correction of the error?

Ex. 2-9   Various steps and decisions involved in the accounting cycle are described in the seven lettered paragraphs below. Indicate which of these procedures are mechanical functions that can be performed by machine in a computerized accounting system, and which require the judgment of people familiar with accounting principles and concepts.

   a Decide whether or not events should be recorded in the accounting records.

   b Determine which ledger accounts should be debited and credited to describe specific business transactions.

   c Arrange recorded data in the format of journal entries.

   d Arrange recorded data in the format of ledger accounts.

   e Prepare a trial balance.

   f Prepare financial statements (a balance sheet).

   g Evaluate the debt-paying ability of one company relative to another.

Problems

2-1   Analysis of transactions; journal entries

The Rent-All Corporation was organized to rent trailers, tools, and other equipment to its customers. The organization of the business began on July 1 and the following transactions occurred in July before the company began regular operations on August 1:

   a On July 1, the corporation issued 20,000 shares of $2 par value capital stock in exchange for $40,000 cash.

   b On July 3, the Rent-All Corporation bought land for use in its operations at a total cost of $25,000. A cash down payment of $15,000 was made, and a note payable (payable within 90 days without interest) was issued for the balance.

   c On July 5, a movable building was purchased for $14,000 cash and installed on the lot.

   d On July 10, office equipment was purchased on credit from Dell Office Equipment at a cost of $2,200. The account payable was to be paid within 30 days.

   e On July 31, a cash payment of $5,000 was made in partial settlement of the note payable issued on July 3.

Instructions

   a Prepare an analysis of the above transactions. The form of analysis to be used is as follows, using transaction (a) above as an example:

   a (1) The asset Cash was increased. Increases in assets are recorded by debits. Debit Cash, $40,000.

      (2) The stockholders' equity was increased. Increases in stockholders' equity are recorded by credits. Credit Capital Stock, $40,000.

   b Prepare journal entries for the above five transactions. Include an explanation as a part of each journal entry.

2-2   Preparation of a trial balance

High-Line Blueprints, Inc., provides fast production and distribution of blueprints and other drawings and documents to customers throughout the city. At September 30, the ledger accounts appear as follows:

Cash	
5,672	1,555
1,684	3,000
7,395	1,785
945	1,080

Notes Payable	
3,000	42,000

Accounts Receivable	
11,394	780
790	165
165	
570	
6,315	

Accounts Payable	
955	692
600	955
1,080	2,670
	801
	1,539

Office Supplies	
4,500	
750	
750	

Capital Stock	
	30,000

Office Equipment	
39,720	

Retained Earnings	
5,000	16,810
	6,053

Delivery Equipment	
18,600	

Instructions Determine the account balances and prepare a trial balance as of September 30, 19___.

2-3   Trial balance and effect of transaction upon a balance sheet
The ledger accounts of Rolling Hills Golf Club at September 30 are shown below in an alphabetical listing.

Accounts payable	$ 5,340	Lighting equipment	$ 52,900
Accounts receivable	1,300	Maintenance equipment	36,500
Building	64,200	Notes payable	340,000
Capital stock	200,000	Notes receivable	24,000
Cash	14,960	Office equipment	1,420
Fences	23,600	Office supplies	490
Golf carts	28,000	Retained earnings	64,060
Land	375,000	Taxes payable	12,970

Instructions

a Prepare a trial balance with the ledger accounts arranged in the usual financial statement order.

b Prepare a balance sheet at September 30, 19___.

c Assume that immediately after the September 30 balance sheet was prepared, a tornado struck the golf course and destroyed the fences, which were not insured against this type of disaster. If the balance sheet were revised to reflect the loss of the fences, explain briefly what other change in the balance sheet would be required.

2-4   Posting and preparation of a trial balance

After several seasons of professional tennis competition, Margo Lane had saved enough money to start her own tennis school, to be known as Rancho Tennis College. During June, while organizing the business, Lane prepared the following journal entries to record all June transactions. She has not posted these entries to ledger accounts. The ledger account numbers to be used are: Cash, 1; Office Supplies, 9; Land, 20; Tennis Courts, 22; Tennis Equipment, 25; Notes Payable, 30; Accounts Payable, 31; and Capital Stock, 50.

Page 1

June	2	Cash	30,000	
		Capital Stock		30,000
		Issued 3,000 shares of capital stock for cash.		
	4	Land	33,200	
		Tennis Courts	72,000	
		Cash		21,600
		Notes Payable		83,600
		Purchased land and tennis courts.		
	7	Tennis Equipment	1,240	
		Accounts Payable		1,240
		Bought equipment on credit from Rackets, Inc.		
	8	Office Supplies	212	
		Accounts Payable		212
		Bought supplies from Miller Supply.		
	13	Tennis Equipment	650	
		Accounts Payable		650
		Bought equipment from Rackets, Inc.		
	18	Accounts Payable	212	
		Cash		212
		Made payment of liability to Miller Supply.		
	23	Accounts Payable	650	
		Cash		650
		Made payment of liability to Rackets, Inc., for purchase of June 13.		

Instructions

a Post the journal entries to ledger accounts of the three-column running balance form.

b Prepare a trial balance at June 30 from the ledger accounts completed in part a.

2-5   Journals, ledgers, and a trial balance

A new business, Beach Properties, Inc., was started on October 1 by Ruth Palmer to provide managerial services for the owners of apartment buildings. The organizational period extended throughout the month of October and included the transactions listed below.

The account titles and account numbers to be used are:

Cash	11	Office equipment	25
Accounts receivable	15	Notes payable	31
Land	21	Accounts payable	32
Building	23	Capital stock	51

Oct. 1 The corporation issued 4,900 shares of capital stock to its owner, Ruth Palmer, in exchange for her investing $49,000 cash in the business.

Oct. 4 Purchased land and an office building for a price of $70,000, of which $33,600 was considered applicable to the land and $36,400 attributable to the building. A cash down payment of $21,000 was made and a note payable for $49,000 was issued for the balance of the purchase price.

Oct. 7 Purchased office equipment on credit from Harvard Office Equipment, $3,850.

Oct. 9 A typewriter (cost $490) which was part of the October 7 purchase of office equipment proved defective and was returned for credit to Harvard Office Equipment.

Oct. 11 Sold to Regent Pharmacy at cost one-third of the land acquired on October 4. No down payment was required. The buyer promised to pay one-half the purchase price of $11,200 within 10 days and the remainder by November 12.

Oct. 18 Paid $1,400 in partial settlement of the liability to Harvard Office Equipment.

Oct. 21 Received cash of $5,600 as partial collection of the account receivable from Regent Pharmacy.

Instructions

a Prepare journal entries for the month of October.
b Post to ledger accounts of the three-column running balance form.
c Prepare a trial balance at October 31.

2-6   More journals, ledgers, and a trial balance

George Harris, after several seasons of professional football, had saved enough money to start his own business, to be known as Number One Auto Rentals, Inc. The following business transactions occurred during March while the new corporation was being organized:

Mar. 1 George Harris invested $210,000 cash in the business, in exchange for which the corporation issued 21,000 shares of its $10 par value capital stock.

Mar. 3 The new company purchased land and a building at a cost of $120,000, of which $72,000 was regarded as applicable to the land and $48,000 to the building. The transaction involved a cash payment of $41,500 and the issuance of a note payable for $78,500.

Mar. 5 Purchased 20 new automobiles at $8,200 each from Fleet Sales Company. Paid $52,000 cash, and agreed to pay another $52,000 by March 26 and the remaining balance by April 15.

Mar. 7 Sold an automobile at cost to Harris's father-in-law, Howard, who paid $3,400 in cash and agreed to pay the balance within 30 days.

Mar. 8 One of the automobiles was found to be defective and was returned to Fleet Sales Company. The amount payable to this creditor was thereby reduced by $8,200.

Mar. 20 Purchased office equipment at a cost of $5,480 cash.

Mar. 26 Issued a check for $52,000 in partial payment of the liability to Fleet Sales Company.

Instructions

a Journalize the above transactions, then post to ledger accounts. Use the running balance form of ledger account rather than T accounts. The account titles and the account numbers to be used are as follows:

Cash	10	Automobiles	22
Accounts receivable	11	Notes payable	31
Land	16	Accounts payable	32
Buildings	17	Capital stock	50
Office equipment	20		

b Prepare a trial balance at March 31, 19__.

2-7   The accounting cycle: a comprehensive problem
Community TV, Inc., was organized in February 19__, to operate as a local television station. The account titles and numbers used by the corporation are listed below:

Cash	11	Telecasting equipment	24
Accounts receivable	15	Film library	25
Supplies	19	Notes payable	31
Land	21	Accounts payable	32
Building	22	Capital stock	51
Transmitter	23		

The transactions for February 19__, were as follows:

Feb.   1 A charter was granted to Paul and Alice Marshal for the organization of Community TV, Inc. The Marshals invested $400,000 cash and received 40,000 shares of stock in exchange.

Feb.   3 The new corporation purchased the land, buildings, and telecasting equipment previously used by a local television station which had gone bankrupt. The total purchase price was $289,000, of which $95,000 was attributable to the land, $88,000 to the building, and the remainder to the telecasting equipment. The terms of the purchase required a cash payment of $189,000 and the issuance of a note payable for the balance.

Feb.   5 Purchased a transmitter at a cost of $225,000 from AC Mfg. Co., making a cash down payment of $67,500. The balance, in the form of a note payable, was to be paid in monthly installments, of $11,250, beginning February 15. (Interest expense is to be ignored.)

Feb.   9 Purchased a film library at a cost of $31,995 from Modern Film Productions, making a down payment of $14,000 cash, with the balance on account payable in 30 days.

Feb. 12 Bought supplies costing $3,425, paying cash.

Feb. 15 Paid $11,250 to AC Mfg. Co. as the first monthly payment on the note payable created on February 5. (Interest expense is to be ignored.)

Feb. 25 Sold part of the film library to City College; cost was $9,000 and the selling price also was $9,000. City College agreed to pay the full amount in 30 days.

Instructions

a Prepare journal entries for the month of February.
b Post to ledger accounts of the three-column running balance form.
c Prepare a trial balance at February 28, 19__.
d Prepare a balance sheet at February 28, 19__.

Cases for analysis

Case 2-1   The accounting cycle in computer-based systems

John Moore is planning to create a computer-based accounting system for small businesses. His system will be developed from a data base program and will be suitable for use on personal computers.

The idea underlying data base software is that data needed for a variety of uses is entered into the data base only once. The computer is programmed to arrange this data into any number of desired formats. In the case of Moore's accounting system, the company's accounting personnel must enter the relevant information about each business transaction into the data base. The program which Moore plans to write will then enable the computer operator to have the information arranged by the computer into the formats of (1) journal entries (with written explanations), (2) three-column running balance form ledger accounts, (3) a trial balance, and (4) a balance sheet.

Instructions

    a Identify the relevant information about each business transaction that the company's accounting personnel must enter into the data base to enable Moore's program to prepare the four types of accounting records and statements described above.

    b As described in this chapter, the accounting cycle includes the steps of (1) analyzing and recording business transactions, (2) posting the debit and credit amounts to ledger accounts, (3) preparing a trial balance, and (4) preparing financial statements (at this stage, only a balance sheet). Indicate which of these functions can be performed automatically by Moore's computer program and which must still be performed by the company's accounting personnel.

Case 2-2   Comparative balance sheets: an introduction to measuring income

David Ray, a college student with several summers' experience as a guide on canoe camping trips, decided to go into business for himself. On June 1, Ray organized Birchbark Canoe Trails by depositing $1,800 of personal savings in a bank account in the name of the business. Also on June 1, the business borrowed an additional $3,000 cash from John Ray (David's father) by issuing a three-year note payable. To help the business get started, John Ray agreed that no interest would be charged on the loan. The following transactions were also carried out by the business on June 1:

    (1) Bought six canoes at a total cost of $5,100; paid $2,000 cash and agreed to pay the balance within 60 days.

    (2) Bought camping equipment at a cost of $4,400 payable in 60 days.

    (3) Bought supplies for cash, $700.

After the close of the season on September 10, Ray asked another student, Sharon Lee, who had taken a course in accounting, to help determine the financial position of the business.

The only record Ray had maintained was a checkbook with memorandum notes written on the check stubs. From this source Lee discovered that Ray had invested an additional $1,400 of savings in the business on July 1, and also that the accounts payable arising from the purchase of the canoes and camping equipment had been paid in full. A bank statement received from the bank on September 10 showed a balance on deposit of $2,910.

Ray informed Lee that all cash received by the business had been deposited in the bank and all bills had been paid by check immediately upon receipt; consequently, as of September 10 all bills for the season had been paid. However, nothing had been paid on the note payable.

The canoes and camping equipment were all in excellent condition at the end of the season and Ray planned to resume operations the following summer. In fact he had already accepted reservations from many customers who wished to return.

Lee felt that some consideration should be given to the wear and tear on the canoes and equipment but she agreed with Ray that for the present purpose the canoes and equipment should be listed in the balance sheet at the original cost. The supplies remaining on hand had cost $80 and Ray felt that these supplies could be used next summer.

Lee suggested that two balance sheets be prepared, one to show the condition of the business on June 1 and the other showing the condition on September 10. She also recommended to Ray that a complete set of accounting records be established.

Instructions

a Use the information in the first paragraph (including the three numbered transactions) as a basis for preparing a balance sheet dated June 1.

b Prepare a balance sheet at September 10. (Because of the incomplete information available, it is not possible to determine the amount of cash at September 10 by adding cash receipts and deducting cash payments throughout the season. The amount on deposit as reported by the bank at September 10 is to be regarded as the total cash belonging to the business at that date.)

c By comparing the two balance sheets, compute the change in owner's equity. Explain the sources of this change in owner's equity and state whether you consider the business to be successful. Also comment on the cash position at the beginning and end of the season. Has the cash position improved significantly? Explain.

Chapter 3
Measuring business income

In Chapter 3 our coverage of the accounting cycle is expanded to include the measurement of business income. Attention is focused on the accounting concepts of revenue, expense, net income, dividends, and retained earnings. Two important accounting principles are introduced — the realization principle and the matching principle. The continuing example of Greenhill Real Estate is then used to show how a business enters revenue and expense transactions and prepares an income statement and statement of retained earnings. As Greenhill Real Estate owns depreciable assets, the concept of depreciation is introduced, and the recording of depreciation expense is illustrated. The procedures for closing the revenue and expense accounts at the end of the accounting period also are illustrated and explained. In summary, this chapter introduces and illustrates the basic concepts of accrual accounting.

After studying
this chapter you
should be able to:

✓ Discuss the role of profits in an expanding economy.
✓ Explain the nature of retained earnings, net income, revenue, expenses, and dividends.
✓ Relate the realization principle and the matching principle to the recording of revenue and expenses.
✓ Apply the rules of debit and credit to revenue and expense transactions.
✓ Define and record depreciation expense.
✓ Prepare an income statement and a statement of retained earnings. Explain how these statements provide a link between two balance sheets.
✓ Prepare closing entries.
✓ Describe the sequence of procedures in the accounting cycle.
✓ Distinguish between the accrual basis and the cash basis of accounting.

In this chapter you will be introduced to the challenge of measuring income. Some people mistakenly assume that measuring income is a matter of simple arithmetic. In fact, no topic in accounting is more complex and controversial than measuring the net income of a specific business for a specific year. We will be concerned with one aspect or another of measuring and reporting income throughout this book.

The earning of net income, or profits, is a major goal of almost every business enterprise, large or small. Profit is the ***increase in the owners' equity resulting from operation of the business.*** This increase usually is accompanied by an increase in total assets. The opposite of profit, a decrease in owners' equity resulting from operation of the business, is termed a ***loss.*** If you were to organize a small business of your own, you would do so with the hope and expectation that the business would operate at a profit, thereby increasing your ownership equity. Individuals who invest in the capital stock of large corporations also expect the business to earn a profit which will increase the value of their investment.

The resources generated by profitable operations may be retained in the business to finance expansion, or they may be distributed as dividends to the stockholders. Some of the largest corporations have become large by retaining their profits in the business and using these profits for growth. Retained profits may be used, for example, to acquire new plant and equipment, to carry on research leading to new and better products, and to extend sales operations into new territories.

Profits: public image versus economic function

The level of business profits often is a controversial issue. Critics may call corporate profits "excessive" and charge that profits are a major cause of high prices. Such charges have received considerable publicity, and as a result some people have come to view business profits as harmful to society. Actually, business profits perform a vital economic function in our economy; a satisfactory level of business profits is necessary to achieve high employment, an improving standard of living, and an expanding national economy.

In a free market economy, profits assist in the efficient allocation of resources. When the demand for a particular product is much greater than the supply, the price that consumers will pay for the product tends to rise. As the price rises, investors are attracted to that industry by the opportunity to earn greater than normal profits. The inflow of capital into the industry results in greater productive capacity, and the supply of the product increases to meet demand.

Corporate profits may be viewed as the "return" to stockholders for having invested their resources in a particular company. When creditors lend money to a company, they expect to earn a reasonable rate of interest. When employees invest their time and labor, they expect to earn a reasonable wage. It is equally logical that stockholders, who supply financial resources to a business, should expect to earn a satisfactory return on their investment.

If business profits were reduced to insignificant levels, prices probably would rise rather than fall. Investors would stop providing capital to those industries in which profit opportunities were unsatisfactory. The resulting capital shortages would leave businesses unable to produce enough goods, causing production shortages, higher prices, and unemployment. Thus, a satisfactory level of business profits is essential to maintaining high levels of production and to financing economic growth.

When competition is restricted, profits may become "excessive." Excessive profits, just as excessive wages or excessive materials costs, can be harmful to the economy. Profits are excessive when they become unreasonably large in relation to the amounts of money invested and the degree of risk being taken by the owners of a business. The risk taken by owners of a business is the chance that future losses may decrease or even wipe out their investment. Once we have completed our study of how business profits are measured, we shall discuss some ways of appraising their adequacy.

Retained earnings

The increase in owners' equity resulting from profitable operations is credited to an account called **Retained Earnings,** which appears in the stockholders' equity section of the balance sheet. If a business has sufficient cash, a distribution of profits may be made to the stockholders. Distributions of this nature are termed **dividends** and decrease both total assets and total stockholders' equity. The decrease in stockholders' equity is reflected by a decrease in the Retained Earnings account. Thus, the balance of the Retained Earnings account represents only the earnings which have **not** been distributed as dividends.

Some people mistakenly believe that retained earnings represent a fund of cash available to a corporation. **Retained earnings is not an asset; it is an element of stockholders' equity.** Although the amount of retained earnings indicates the portion of total assets which were **financed** by earning and retaining net income, it does **not** indicate the **form** in which these resources are currently held. The resources generated by retaining profits may have been invested in land, buildings, equipment, or any other kind of asset. The total amount of cash owned by a corporation is shown by the balance of the Cash account, which appears in the asset section of the balance sheet.

Net income

Since the drive for profits underlies the very existence of business organizations, it follows that a most important function of an accounting system is to provide information about the profitability of a business. Before we can measure the profits of a business, we need to establish a sharp, clear meaning for **profits.** Economists often define profits as the amount by which an entity becomes **better off** during a period of time. Unfortunately, how much "better off" an entity has become is largely a matter of personal opinion and cannot be measured **objectively** enough to provide a useful definition for accountants.

For this reason, accountants usually look to actual business transactions to provide objective evidence that a business has been profitable or unprofitable. For example, if an item which cost a business $60 is sold for $100 cash, we have objective evidence that the business has earned a profit of $40. Since business managers and economists use the word **profits** in somewhat different senses, accountants prefer to use the alternative term **net income,** and to define this term very carefully. **Net income is the excess of the price of goods sold and services rendered over the cost of goods and services used up during a given time period.** At this point, we shall adopt the technical accounting term **net income** in preference to the less precise term **profits.**

To determine net income, it is necessary to measure for a given time period (1) the price of goods sold and services rendered and (2) the cost of goods and services used up. The technical accounting terms for these items comprising net income are **revenue** and *expenses.* Therefore, we may state that *net income equals revenue minus expenses,* as shown in the following income statement:

GREENHILL REAL ESTATE
Income Statement
For the Month Ended October 31, 19__

Income statement for October

Revenue:		
Sales commissions earned		$10,640
Expenses:		
Advertising expense	$ 630	
Salaries expense	7,100	
Telephone expense	144	
Depreciation expense: building	150	
Depreciation expense: office equipment	45	8,069
Net income		$ 2,571

We will show how this income statement is developed from Greenhill's accounting records later in this chapter. For the moment, however, this illustration will assist us in discussing some of the basic concepts involved in measuring business income.

Income must be related to a specified period of time. Notice that Greenhill's income statement covers a *period* of time — namely, the month of October. A balance sheet shows the financial position of a business at a *particular date.* An income statement, on the other hand, shows the results of business operations over a span of time. We cannot intelligently evaluate net income unless it is associated with a specific time period. For example, if an executive says, "My business earns a net income of $10,000," the profitability of the business is unclear. Does it earn $10,000 per week, per month, or per year?

● **CASE IN POINT** ● The late J. Paul Getty, one of the world's first billionaires, was once interviewed by a group of business students. One of the students asked Getty to estimate the amount of his income. As the student had not specified a time period, Getty decided to have some fun with his audience and responded, "About $11,000 . . ." He paused long enough to allow the group to express surprise over this seemingly low amount, and then completed his sentence, ". . . per hour." Incidentally, $11,000 per hour amounts to about $100 million per year.

Every business prepares an annual income statement, and most businesses prepare quarterly and monthly income statements as well. The period of time covered by an income statement is termed the company's *accounting period.* This period may be a month, a quarter of a year, a year, or any other specified period of time.

A 12-month accounting period used by an entity is called its *fiscal year.* The fiscal year used by most companies coincides with the calendar year and ends on December 31. However, some businesses elect to use a fiscal year which ends on some other date. It may be convenient for the business to end its fiscal year during a slack season rather than during a time of peak business activity. The fiscal year of the federal government, for example, begins on October 1 and ends 12 months later on September 30.

Let us now explore the meaning of the accounting terms *revenue* and *expenses*.

Revenue

Revenue is the price of goods sold and services rendered during a given time period. When a business renders services to its customers or delivers merchandise to them, it either receives immediate payment in cash or acquires an account receivable which will be collected and thereby become cash within a short time. The revenue for any given period is equal to the inflow of cash and receivables from sales made in that period. For any single transaction, the amount of revenue is a measurement of the asset values received from the customer.

Revenue causes an increase in owners' equity. The inflow of cash and receivables from customers increases the total assets of the company; on the other side of the accounting equation, the liabilities do not change, but owners' equity is increased to match the increase in total assets. Thus revenue is the gross increase in owners' equity resulting from business activities.

Various terms are used to describe different types of revenue; for example, the revenue earned by a real estate broker might be called ***Sales Commissions Earned,*** or alternatively, ***Commissions Revenue.*** In the professional practice of lawyers, physicians, dentists, and CPAs, the revenue is called ***Fees Earned.*** A business which sells merchandise rather than services (General Motors, for example) will use the term ***Sales*** to describe the revenue earned. Another type of revenue is ***Interest Earned,*** which means the amount received as interest on notes receivable, bank deposits, government bonds, or other securities.

When to record revenue: the realization principle. When is revenue recorded in the accounting records? For example, assume that on May 24, a real estate company signs a contract to represent a client in selling the client's personal residence. The contract entitles the real estate company to a commission equal to 5% of the selling price, due 30 days after the date of sale. On June 10, the real estate company sells the house at a price of $120,000, thereby earning a $6,000 commission ($120,000 × 5%), to be received on July 10. When should the company record this $6,000 commission revenue — in May, June, or July?

The company should record this revenue on June 10 — the day it ***rendered the service*** of selling the client's house. As the company will not collect this commission until July, it must also record an account receivable on June 10. In July, when this receivable is collected, the company must not record revenue a second time. Collecting an account receivable increases one asset, Cash, and decreases another asset, Accounts Receivable. Thus, collecting an account receivable ***does not increase owners' equity*** and does not represent revenue.

Our answer illustrates a generally accepted accounting principle called the ***realization principle.*** The realization principle states that a business should record revenue at the time ***services are rendered to customers*** or ***goods sold are delivered to customers.*** In short, revenue is recorded when it is ***earned,*** without regard as to when the cash is received.

Expenses

Expenses are the cost of the goods and services used up in the process of earning revenue. Examples include the cost of employees' salaries, advertising, rent, utilities, and the gradual wearing-out (depreciation) of such assets as buildings, automobiles, and office equipment. All these costs are necessary to attract and service customers and thereby earn revenue. Expenses are often called the "costs of doing business," that is, the cost of the various activities necessary to carry on a business.

An expense always causes a decrease in owners' equity. The related changes in the accounting equation can be either (1) a decrease in assets, or (2) an increase in liabilities. An expense reduces assets if payment occurs at the time that the expense is recorded or if payment has been made in advance. If the expense will not be paid until later, as, for example, the purchase of advertising services on account, the recording of the expense will be accompanied by an increase in liabilities.

When to record expenses: the matching principle. A significant relationship exists between revenue and expenses. Expenses are incurred for the ***purpose of producing revenue.*** In measuring net income for a period, revenue should be offset by ***all of the expenses incurred in producing that revenue.*** This concept of offsetting expenses against revenue on a basis of "cause and effect" is called the ***matching principle.***

Timing is an important factor in matching (offsetting) revenue with the related expenses. For example, in preparing monthly income statements, it is important to offset this month's expenses against this month's revenue. We should not offset this month's expenses against last month's revenue, because there is no cause and effect relationship between the two.

To illustrate the matching principle, assume that the salaries earned by sales personnel waiting on customers during July are not paid until early August. In which month should these salaries be regarded as an expense? The answer is July, because this is the month in which the sales personnel's services ***helped to produce revenue.***

We previously explained that revenue and cash receipts are not one and the same thing. Similarly, expenses and cash payments are not identical. The cash payment for an expense may occur before, after, or in the same period that an expense helps to produce revenue. In deciding when to record an expense, the critical question is ***"In what period will this expenditure help to produce revenue?"*** not "When did the cash payment occur?"

Expenditures benefiting more than one accounting period. Many expenditures made by a business benefit two or more accounting periods. Fire insurance policies, for example, usually cover a period of 12 months. If a company prepares monthly income statements, a portion of the cost of such a policy should be allocated to insurance expense each month that the policy is in force. In this case, apportionment of the cost of the policy by months is an easy matter. If the 12-month policy costs $240, for example, the insurance expense for each month amounts to $20.

Not all transactions can be so precisely divided by accounting periods. The purchase of a building, furniture and fixtures, machinery, a typewriter, or an automobile provides benefits to the business over all the years in which such an asset is used. No one can determine in advance exactly how many years of service will be received from such long-lived assets. Nevertheless, in measuring the net income of a business for a period of one year or less, the accountant must estimate what portion of the cost of the building and other long-lived assets is applicable to the current year. Since the allocations of these costs are estimates rather than precise measurements, it follows that income statements should be regarded as *useful approximations* of net income rather than as absolutely accurate computations.

For some expenditures, such as those for advertising or employee training programs, it is not possible to estimate objectively the number of accounting periods over which revenue is likely to be produced. In such cases, generally accepted accounting principles require that the expenditure be charged *immediately to expense.* This treatment is based upon the accounting principles of *objectivity* and *conservatism.* Accountants require *objective evidence* that an expenditure will produce revenue in future periods before they will view the expenditure as creating an asset. When this objective evidence does not exist, they follow the conservative practice of recording the expenditure as an expense. Conservatism, in this context, means applying the accounting treatment which results in the lowest (most conservative) estimate of net income for the current period.

Dividends

A dividend is a distribution of assets (usually cash) by a corporation to its stockholders. In some respects, dividends are similar to expenses — they reduce both the assets and the owners' equity in the business. However, *dividends are not an expense, and they are not deducted from revenue in the income statement.* The reason that dividends are not viewed as an expense is that these payments do not serve to generate revenue. Rather, they are a *distribution of profits* to the owners of the business.

Since the declaration and payment of a dividend reduce the stockholders' equity, the dividend could be recorded by debiting the Retained Earnings account. However, a clearer record is created if a separate *Dividends* account is debited for all amounts distributed as dividends to stockholders. The disposition of the Dividends account when financial statements are prepared will be illustrated later in this chapter.

Debit and credit rules for revenue and expense

We have stressed that revenue increases owners' equity and that expenses decrease owners' equity. The debit and credit rules for recording revenue and expenses in the ledger accounts are a natural extension of the rules for recording changes in owners' equity. The rules previously stated for recording increases and decreases in owners' equity were as follows:

Increases in owners' equity are recorded by *credits.*
Decreases in owners' equity are recorded by *debits.*

This rule is now extended to cover revenue and expense accounts:

Revenue increases owners' equity; therefore revenue is recorded by a *credit.*
Expenses decrease owners' equity; therefore expenses are recorded by *debits.*

Ledger accounts for revenue and expenses. During the course of an accounting period, a great many revenue and expense transactions occur in the average business. To classify and summarize these numerous transactions, a separate ledger account is maintained for each major type of revenue and expense. For example, almost every business maintains accounts for Advertising Expense, Telephone Expense, and Salaries Expense. At the end of the period, all the advertising expenses appear as debits in the Advertising Expense account. The debit balance of this account represents the total advertising expense of the period and is listed as one of the expense items in the income statement.

Revenue accounts are usually much less numerous than expense accounts. A small business such as Greenhill Real Estate in our continuing illustration may have only one or two types of revenue, such as commissions earned from arranging sales of real estate and fees earned from managing properties in behalf of clients. In a business of this type, the revenue accounts might be called Sales Commissions Earned and Management Fees Earned.

RECORDING REVENUE AND EXPENSE TRANSACTIONS: ILLUSTRATION

The organization of Greenhill Real Estate during September has already been described in Chapters 1 and 2. The illustration is now continued for October, during which month the company earned commissions by selling several residences for its clients. Bear in mind that the company does not own any residential property; it merely acts as a broker or agent for clients wishing to sell their houses. A commission of 6% of the selling price of the house is charged for this service. During October the company not only earned commissions but incurred a number of expenses.

Note that each illustrated transaction which affects an income statement account also affects a balance sheet account. This pattern is consistent with our previous discussion of revenue and expenses. In recording revenue transactions, we debit the assets received and credit a revenue account. In recording expense transactions, we debit an expense account and credit the asset Cash, or perhaps a liability account if payment is to be made later. The transactions for October were as follows:

Oct. 1 Paid $360 for publication of newspaper advertising describing various houses offered for sale.

	Analysis	Rule	Entry
Advertising expense incurred and paid	The cost of advertising is an expense	Expenses decrease the owners' equity and are recorded by debits	Debit: Advertising Expense, $360
	The asset Cash was decreased	Decreases in assets are recorded by credits	Credit: Cash, $360

Oct. 6 Earned and collected a commission of $2,250 by selling a residence previously listed by a client.

	Analysis	Rule	Entry
Revenue earned and collected	The asset Cash was increased	Increases in assets are recorded by debits	Debit: Cash, $2,250
	Revenue was earned	Revenue increases the owners' equity and is recorded by a credit	Credit: Sales Commissions Earned, $2,250

Oct. 16 Newspaper advertising for October was ordered at a price of $270, payment to be made within 30 days.

	Analysis	Rule	Entry
Advertising expense incurred but not paid	The cost of advertising is an expense	Expenses decrease the owners' equity and are recorded by debits	Debit: Advertising Expense, $270
	An account payable, a liability, was incurred	Increases in liabilities are recorded by credits	Credit: Accounts Payable, $270

Oct. 20 A commission of $8,390 was earned by selling a client's residence. The sales agreement provided that the commission would be paid in 60 days.

	Analysis	Rule	Entry
Revenue earned, to be collected later	An asset in the form of an account receivable was acquired	Increases in assets are recorded by debits	Debit: Accounts Receivable, $8,390
	Revenue was earned	Revenue increases the owners' equity and is recorded by a credit	Credit: Sales Commissions Earned, $8,390

Oct. 30 Paid salaries of $7,100 to employees for services rendered during October.

	Analysis	Rule	Entry
Salaries expense incurred and paid	Salaries of employees are an expense	Expenses decrease the owners' equity and are recorded by debits	Debit: Salaries Expense, $7,100
	The asset Cash was decreased	Decreases in assets are recorded by credits	Credit: Cash, $7,100

Oct. 30 A telephone bill for October amounting to $144 was received. Payment was required by November 10.

	Analysis	Rule	Entry
Telephone expense incurred, to be paid later	The cost of telephone service is an expense	Expenses decrease the owners' equity and are recorded by debits	Debit: Telephone Expense, $144
	An account payable, a liability, was incurred	Increases in liabilities are recorded by credits	Credit: Accounts Payable, $144

Oct. 30 A dividend was declared and paid to the owners of the 18,000 shares of capital stock. The amount of the dividend was 10 cents per share, or a total of $1,800. (As explained on page 82, a dividend is not an expense.)

	Analysis	Rule	Entry
Payment of a dividend	Payment of a dividend decreases the owners' equity	Decreases in owners' equity are recorded by debits	Debit: Dividends, $1,800
	The asset Cash was decreased	Decreases in assets are recorded by credits	Credit: Cash, $1,800

The journal

The journal entries to record the October transactions are as follows:

General Journal   Page 2

	Date		Account Titles and Explanation	LP	Debit	Credit
October journal entries for Greenhill Real Estate Company	19__ Oct.	1	Advertising Expense .... Cash .... Paid for newspaper advertising.	70 1	360	360
		6	Cash .... Sales Commissions Earned .... Earned and collected commission by selling residence for client.	1 60	2,250	2,250
		16	Advertising Expense .... Accounts Payable .... Purchased newspaper advertising; payable in 30 days.	70 32	270	270
		20	Accounts Receivable .... Sales Commissions Earned .... Earned commission by selling residence for client; commission to be received in 60 days.	4 60	8,390	8,390
		30	Salaries Expense .... Cash .... Paid salaries for October.	72 1	7,100	7,100
		30	Telephone Expense .... Accounts Payable .... To record liability for October telephone service.	74 32	144	144
		30	Dividends .... Cash .... Paid dividend to stockholders (18,000 shares at 10 cents per share).	52 1	1,800	1,800

The column headings at the top of the illustrated journal page (*Date, Account Titles and Explanation, LP, Debit,* and *Credit*) are seldom used in practice. They are included here as an instructional guide but will be omitted from some of the later illustrations of journal entries.

The ledger

The ledger of Greenhill Real Estate after the October transactions have been posted is now illustrated. The accounts appear in the ledger in financial statement order, as illustrated.

Cash — Account No. 1

Date		Explanation	Ref	Debit	Credit	Balance
Sept	1		1	180 000 00		180 000 00
	3		1		141 000 00	39 000 00
	5		1		15 000 00	24 000 00
	20		1	1 500 00		25 500 00
	30		1		3 000 00	22 500 00
Oct	1		2		360 00	22 140 00
	6		2	2 250 00		24 390 00
	30		2		7 100 00	17 290 00
	30		2		1 800 00	15 490 00

Accounts Receivable — Account No. 4

Date		Explanation	Ref	Debit	Credit	Balance
Sept	10		1	11 000 00		11 000 00
	20		1		1 500 00	9 500 00
Oct	20		2	8 390 00		17 890 00

Land — Account No. 20

Date		Explanation	Ref	Debit	Credit	Balance
Sept	3		1	141 000 00		141 000 00
	10		1		11 000 00	130 000 00

Building — Account No. 22

Date		Explanation	Ref	Debit	Credit	Balance
Sept	5		1	36 000 00		36 000 00

Office Equipment — Account No. 25

Date	Explanation	Ref	Debit	Credit	Balance
Sept 14		1	5 400 00		5 400 00

Accounts Payable — Account No. 32

Date	Explanation	Ref	Debit	Credit	Balance
Sept 5		1		21 000 00	21 000 00
14		1		5 400 00	26 400 00
30		1	3 000 00		23 400 00
Oct 16		2		270 00	23 670 00
30		2		144 00	23 814 00

Capital Stock — Account No. 50

Date	Explanation	Ref	Debit	Credit	Balance
Sept 1		1		180 000 00	180 000 00

Dividends — Account No. 52

Date	Explanation	Ref	Debit	Credit	Balance
Oct. 30		2	1 800 00		1 800 00

Sales Commissions Earned — Account No. 60

Date	Explanation	Ref	Debit	Credit	Balance
Oct. 6		2		2 250 00	2 250 00
20		2		8 390 00	10 640 00

Advertising Expense — Account No. 70

Date	Explanation	Ref	Debit	Credit	Balance
Oct. 1		2	360 00		360 00
16		2	270 00		630 00

Salaries Expense								Account No. 72	
Date	Explanation	Ref	Debit				Credit		Balance
Oct 30		2	7 1 0 0 00						7 1 0 0 00

Telephone Expense								Account No. 74	
Date	Explanation	Ref	Debit				Credit		Balance
Oct 30		2	1 4 4 00						1 4 4 00

Sequence of accounts in the ledger. Accounts are located in the ledger in financial statement order; that is, the balance sheet accounts first (assets, liabilities, and owners' equity) followed by the income statement accounts (revenue and expenses). The usual sequence of accounts within these five groups is shown by the following list.

Balance Sheet Accounts	Income Statement Accounts
Assets:	Revenue:
01 Cash	60 Commissions earned (fees earned, rent earned, sales, etc.)
02 Marketable securities	
03 Notes receivable	Expenses (No standard sequence of listing exists for individual expense accounts.)
04 Accounts receivable	
08 Inventory (discussed in Chapter 5)	70 Advertising
10 Office supplies (unexpired insurance, prepaid rent, and other prepaid expenses discussed in Chapter 4)	72 Salaries
	74 Rent
	76 Telephone
20 Land	78 Depreciation
22 Buildings	79 Various other expenses
25 Equipment	
26 Other assets	
Liabilities:	
30 Notes payable	
32 Accounts payable	
34 Salaries payable (and other short-term liabilities discussed in Chapter 4)	
Stockholders' equity:	
50 Capital stock	
51 Retained earnings	
52 Dividends	

Why are ledger accounts arranged in financial statement order? Remember that a trial balance is prepared by listing the ledger account balances shown in the ledger, working from the first ledger page to the last. Therefore, if the accounts are located in the ledger in *financial statement order,* the same sequence will naturally be followed in the trial balance, and this arrangement will make it easier to prepare the balance sheet and income statement from the trial balance. Also, this standard arrangement of accounts will make it easier to locate any account in the ledger.

Notice that an account number has been assigned to each account. The number assigned to a particular account depends upon the account's location in the ledger and will not be the same from one company to the next. In a manual accounting system, these account numbers are entered in the *LP* column of the journal to show that an entry has been posted. In a computer-based system, accounts often are identified only by number, thus eliminating the need for the computer operator to enter the entire account title. In addition, the account numbers enable the computer to determine in which financial statement an account should be listed.

The trial balance

A trial balance prepared from Greenhill's ledger accounts is shown below:

GREENHILL REAL ESTATE
Trial Balance
October 31, 19___

Proving the equality of debits and credits

Cash	$ 15,490	
Accounts receivable	17,890	
Land	130,000	
Building	36,000	
Office equipment	5,400	
Accounts payable		$ 23,814
Capital stock		180,000
Dividends	1,800	
Sales commissions earned		10,640
Advertising expense	630	
Salaries expense	7,100	
Telephone expense	144	
	$214,454	$214,454

This trial balance proves the equality of the debit and credit entries in the company's ledger.

Recording depreciation at the end of the period

The trial balance includes all the expenses arising from the October business transactions, but it does not include any *depreciation expense.* Our definition of expense is *the cost of goods and services used up in the process of obtaining revenue.* Some of the goods used up are purchased in advance and used up gradually over a long period of time. Buildings and office equipment, for example, are used up over a period of years. Each year, a portion of these assets *expires,* and a portion of their total cost should be recognized as *depreciation expense.* The term *depreciation* means the *systematic allocation of the cost of an asset to expense over the accounting periods making up the asset's useful life.*

Depreciation expense does not require monthly cash outlays; in effect, it is paid in advance when the related asset is originally acquired. Nevertheless, depreciation is an inevitable and continuing expense. Failure to record depreciation would result in *under-stating* total expenses of the period and consequently *overstating* the net income.

Building. The office building purchased by Greenhill Real Estate at a cost of $36,000 is estimated to have a useful life of 20 years. The purpose of the $36,000 expenditure was to provide a place in which to carry on the business and thereby to obtain revenue. After 20 years of use the building is expected to be worthless and the original cost of $36,000 will have been entirely consumed. In effect, the company has purchased 20 years of "housing services" at a total cost of $36,000. A portion of this cost expires during each year of use of the building. If we assume that each year's operations should bear an equal share of the total cost (straight-line depreciation), the annual depreciation expense will amount to $\frac{1}{20}$ of $36,000, or $1,800. On a monthly basis, depreciation expense is $150 ($36,000 cost ÷ 240 months). There are alternative methods of spreading the cost of a depreciable asset over its useful life, some of which will be considered in Chapter 10.

The journal entry to record depreciation of the building during October follows:

General Journal   Page 2

Date		Account Titles and Explanation	LP	Debit	Credit
19__					
Oct.	31	Depreciation Expense: Building	76	150	
		Accumulated Depreciation: Building	23		150
		To record depreciation for October. Cost of			
		$36,000 ÷ 240 months = $150 a month.			

Recording depreciation of the building

The depreciation expense account will appear in the income statement for October along with the other expenses of salaries, advertising, and telephone expense. The Accumulated Depreciation: Building account will appear in the balance sheet as a deduction from the Building account, as shown by the following illustration of a *partial* balance sheet:

GREENHILL REAL ESTATE
Partial Balance Sheet
October 31, 19__

Showing accumulated depreciation in the balance sheet

Building (at cost)	$36,000	
Less: Accumulated depreciation	150	$35,850

The end result of crediting the Accumulated Depreciation: Building account is much the same as if the credit had been made to the Building account; that is, the net amount shown on the balance sheet for the building is reduced from $36,000 to $35,850. Although the credit side of a depreciation entry *could* be made directly to the asset account, it is customary and more efficient to record such credits in a separate account entitled Accumulated Depreciation. The original cost of the asset and the total amount of depreciation recorded over the years can more easily be determined from the ledger when separate accounts are maintained for the asset and for the accumulated depreciation.

Accumulated Depreciation: Building is an example of a *contra-asset account,* because it has a credit balance and is offset against an asset account (Building) to produce the proper balance sheet amount for the asset.

Office equipment. Depreciation on the office equipment of Greenhill Real Estate must also be recorded at the end of October. This equipment cost $5,400 and is assumed to have a useful life of 10 years. Monthly depreciation expense on the straight-line basis is, therefore, $45, computed by dividing the cost of $5,400 by the useful life of 120 months. The journal entry is as follows:

<table>
<tr><td colspan="7" align="center">General Journal   Page 2</td></tr>
<tr><td colspan="2" align="center">Date</td><td align="center">Account Titles and Explanation</td><td>LP</td><td>Debit</td><td>Credit</td></tr>
<tr><td>19__
Oct.</td><td>31</td><td>Depreciation Expense: Office Equipment ......
   Accumulated Depreciation: Office
     Equipment ....
To record depreciation for October. Cost of
$5,400 ÷ 120 months = $45 a month.</td><td>78

26</td><td>45</td><td>

45</td></tr>
</table>

Recording depreciation of office equipment

No depreciation was recorded on the building and office equipment for September, the month in which these assets were acquired, because regular operations did not begin until October. Generally, depreciation is not recognized until the business begins active operation and the assets are placed in use. Accountants often use the expression *matching costs and revenue* to convey the idea of writing off the cost of an asset to expense during the time periods in which the business uses the asset to generate revenue.

The journal entry by which depreciation is recorded at the end of the month is called an *adjusting entry.* The adjustment of certain asset accounts and related expense accounts is a necessary step at the end of each accounting period so that the information presented in the financial statements will be as accurate and complete as possible. In the next chapter, adjusting entries will be shown for some other items in addition to depreciation.

The adjusted trial balance

After all the necessary adjusting entries have been journalized and posted, an *adjusted trial balance* is prepared to prove that the ledger is still in balance. It also provides a complete listing of the account balances to be used in preparing the financial statements. The following adjusted trial balance differs from the trial balance shown on page 89 because it includes accounts for depreciation expense and accumulated depreciation.

GREENHILL REAL ESTATE
Adjusted Trial Balance
October 31, 19___

Adjusted trial
balance

Cash	$ 15,490	
Accounts receivable	17,890	
Land	130,000	
Building	36,000	
Accumulated depreciation: building		$ 150
Office equipment	5,400	
Accumulated depreciation: office equipment		45
Accounts payable		23,814
Capital stock		180,000
Dividends	1,800	
Sales commissions earned		10,640
Advertising expense	630	
Salaries expense	7,100	
Telephone expense	144	
Depreciation expense: building	150	
Depreciation expense: office equipment	45	
	$214,649	$214,649

FINANCIAL STATEMENTS

Now that Greenhill Real Estate has been operating for a month, managers and outside parties will want to know more about the company than just its financial position. They will want to know the results of Greenhill's operations — whether the company's activities have been profitable or unprofitable. To provide this additional information, we will prepare a more complete set of financial statements, including an income statement, a statement of retained earnings, and a balance sheet.[1]

The income statement

When we measure the net income earned by a business we are measuring its economic performance — its success or failure as a business enterprise. Stockholders, prospective investors, managers, bankers, and other creditors are anxious to see the latest available income statement and thereby to judge how well the company is doing. The October income statement for Greenhill Real Estate appears on the next page.

---

[1] A complete set of financial statements also includes a statement of changes in financial position, which will be discussed in Chapter 15.

GREENHILL REAL ESTATE

Income Statement

For the Month Ended October 31, 19___

Revenue:

Sales commissions earned		$10,640
Expenses:		
Advertising expense	$ 630	
Salaries expense	7,100	
Telephone expense	144	
Depreciation expense: building	150	
Depreciation expense: office equipment	45	8,069
Net income		$ 2,571

This income statement consists of the last six accounts in the adjusted trial balance shown above. It shows that the revenue during October exceeded the expenses of the month, thus producing a net income of $2,571. Bear in mind, however, that our measurement of net income is not absolutely accurate or precise, because of the assumptions and estimates involved in the accounting process.

An income statement has certain limitations. Remember that the amounts shown for depreciation expense are based upon estimates of the useful lives of the company's buildings and office equipment. Also, the income statement includes only those events which have been evidenced by business transactions. Perhaps during October, Greenhill Real Estate has made contact with many people who are right on the verge of buying or selling homes. Good business contacts are an important step toward profitable operations. However, such contacts are not reflected in the income statement because their value cannot be objectively measured until actual transactions take place. Despite these limitations, the income statement is of vital importance and indicates that the new business has been profitable during its first month of operation.

At this point we are purposely ignoring income taxes on corporations. Corporate income taxes will be introduced in Chapter 5 and considered more fully in Chapters 12 and 17.

Alternative titles for the income statement include *earnings statement, statement of operations,* and *profit and loss statement.* However, *income statement* is by far the most popular term for this important financial statement. In brief, we can say that an income statement is used to summarize the *operating results* of a business by matching the revenue earned during a given time period with the expenses incurred in obtaining that revenue.

Statement of retained earnings

Retained earnings is that portion of the stockholders' equity created by earning and retaining net income. The *statement of retained earnings,* which covers the same time period as the related income statement, shows the increases and decreases in retained earnings for the period.

GREENHILL REAL ESTATE
Statement of Retained Earnings
For the Month Ended October 31, 19___

Statement of
retained earnings
for October

Retained earnings, Sept. 30, 19___	$ –0–
Net income for October	2,571
Subtotal	$2,571
Less: Dividends	1,800
Retained earnings, Oct. 31, 19___	$ 771

The ending amount of retained earnings, $771, will appear in Greenhill's October 31 balance sheet. In this example the company had no retained earnings at the beginning of the period. The statement for the following month (November) will show beginning retained earnings of $771.

The balance sheet

In preparing a balance sheet for Greenhill Real Estate at October 31, we can obtain the balances of the asset, liability, and capital stock accounts from the adjusted trial balance on page 92. The amount of retained earnings at October 31 does not appear in the adjusted trial balance, but has been determined in the statement of retained earnings.

Previous illustrations of balance sheets have been arranged in the *account form*, that is, with the assets on the left side of the page and the liabilities and stockholders' equity on the right side. The following balance sheet is presented in *report form*, that is, with the liabilities and stockholders' equity sections listed below rather than to the right of the asset section. Both the account form and the report form are widely used.

GREENHILL REAL ESTATE
Balance Sheet
October 31, 19___

Assets

Balance sheet at
October 31:
report form

Cash		$ 15,490
Accounts receivable		17,890
Land		130,000
Building	$ 36,000	
Less: Accumulated depreciation	150	35,850
Office equipment	$ 5,400	
Less: Accumulated depreciation	45	5,355
Total assets		$204,585

Liabilities & Stockholders' Equity

Liabilities:		
Accounts payable		$ 23,814
Stockholders' equity:		
Capital stock	$180,000	
Retained earnings	771	180,771
Total liabilities & stockholders' equity		$204,585

If we compare the October 31 balance sheet to the one prepared at September 30 (page 25), we see that the stockholders' original investment of $180,000 appears unchanged under the caption of Capital Stock. The amount of retained earnings, however, has changed between the two balance sheet dates. The Retained Earnings account had a zero balance at September 30, but as explained in the statement of retained earnings, it was increased by the $2,571 net income earned during October and decreased by the $1,800 dividend paid, leaving a balance of $771 at October 31. Thus, the amount of retained earnings shown in the October 31 balance sheet is taken from the statement of retained earnings, not from the adjusted trial balance.

The amount of retained earnings at any balance sheet date represents the total earnings of the corporation since it started in business, minus all dividends distributed to its stockholders. One reason for maintaining a distinction between capital stock and retained earnings is that a corporation usually cannot legally pay dividends greater than the amount of retained earnings. The separation of these two elements of ownership also may be informative because it shows how much of the total stockholders' equity resulted from the investment of funds by stockholders and how much was derived from earning and retaining net income.

In the Greenhill Real Estate illustration, we have shown the two common ways in which the stockholders' equity may be increased: (1) investment of cash or other assets by the owners and (2) operating the business at a profit. There are also two common ways in which the stockholders' equity may be decreased: (1) payment of dividends and (2) operating the business at a loss.

Income statement and retained earnings statement: a link between two balance sheets

A set of financial statements becomes easier to understand if we recognize that the balance sheet, income statement, and statement of retained earnings are all *related to one another.* The balance sheet prepared at the end of the previous accounting period and the one prepared at the end of the current period each show the amount of retained earnings at the respective balance sheet dates. The statement of retained earnings summarizes the factors (net income and dividends) which have caused the amount of retained earnings to change between these two balance sheet dates. The income statement explains in greater detail the change in retained earnings resulting from profitable operation of the business. Thus, the income statement and the retained earnings statement provide an informative link between successive balance sheets.

CLOSING THE ACCOUNTS

The accounts for revenue, expenses, and dividends are *temporary owners' equity accounts* used during the accounting period to classify certain changes affecting the owners' equity. At the end of the period, we want to transfer the net effect of these various increases and decreases into retained earnings, which is a permanent owners' equity account. We also want to reduce the balances of the temporary owners' equity accounts to *zero,* so that these accounts will again be ready for use in accumulating information during the next accounting period. These objectives are accomplished by the use of *closing entries.*

Revenue and expense accounts are *closed* at the end of each accounting period by *transferring their balances* to a summary account called *Income Summary.* When the credit balances of the revenue accounts and the debit balances of the expense accounts have been transferred into one summary account, the balance of this Income Summary will be the *net income* or *net loss* for the period. If the revenue (credit balances) exceeds the expenses (debit balances), the Income Summary account will have a credit balance representing net income. Conversely, if expenses exceed revenue, the Income Summary will have a debit balance representing net loss. This is consistent with the rule that increases in owners' equity are recorded by credits and decreases are recorded by debits.

A journal entry made for the purpose of closing the revenue or expense accounts is called a *closing entry.* This term is also applied to the journal entries (to be explained later) used in closing the Income Summary account and the Dividends account into the Retained Earnings account.

A principal purpose of the year-end process of closing the revenue and expense accounts is to reduce their balances to zero. Since the revenue and expense accounts provide information for the income statement of *a given accounting period,* it is essential that these accounts have *zero balances* at the beginning of each new period. The closing of the accounts has the effect of "wiping the slate clean" and preparing the accounts for the recording of revenue and expenses during the succeeding accounting period.

It is common practice to close the accounts only once a year, but for illustration, we shall now demonstrate the closing of the accounts of Greenhill Real Estate at October 31 after one month's operation.

Closing entries for revenue accounts. Revenue accounts have credit balances. Therefore, closing a revenue account means transferring its credit balance to the Income Summary account. This transfer is accomplished by a journal entry debiting the revenue account in an amount equal to its credit balance, with an offsetting credit to the Income Summary account. The debit portion of this closing entry returns the balance of the revenue account to zero; the credit portion transfers the former balance of the revenue account into the Income Summary account.

The only revenue account of Greenhill Real Estate is Sales Commissions Earned, which had a credit balance of $10,640 at October 31. The journal entry necessary to close this account is as follows:

General Journal   Page 3

	Date		Account Titles and Explanation	LP	Debit	Credit
	19__					
	Oct.	31	Sales Commissions Earned	61	10,640	
			Income Summary	53		10,640
			To close the Sales Commissions Earned account.			

Closing a revenue account (margin note)

After this closing entry has been posted, the two accounts affected will appear as shown on the next page. A directional arrow has been added to show the transfer of the $10,640 balance of the revenue account into the Income Summary account.

Closing entries for expense accounts. There are five expense accounts in the ledger of Greenhill Real Estate. Five separate journal entries could be made to close these five

Sales Commissions Earned					61
Date	Exp.	Ref	Debit	Credit	Balance
Oct. 6		2		2,250	2,250
20		2		8,390	10,640
31	To close	3	10,640		–0–

Income Summary					53
Date	Exp.	Ref	Debit	Credit	Balance
Oct. 31		3		10,640	10,640

expense accounts, but the use of one **compound journal entry** is an easier, timesaving method of closing all five expense accounts. A compound journal entry is an entry that includes debits to more than one account or credits to more than one account.

General Journal   Page 3

	Date		Accounts Titles and Explanation	LP	Debit	Credit
Closing the various expense accounts by use of a compound journal entry	19__ Oct.	31	Income Summary	53	8,069	
			Advertising Expense	70		630
			Salaries Expense	72		7,100
			Telephone Expense	74		144
			Depreciation Expense: Building	76		150
			Depreciation Expense: Office Equipment .	78		45
			To close the expense accounts.			

After this closing entry has been posted, the Income Summary account has a credit balance of $2,571, and the five expense accounts have zero balances, as shown on the next page.

Closing the Income Summary account. The five expense accounts have now been closed and the total amount of $8,069 formerly contained in these accounts appears in the debit column of the Income Summary account. The commissions of $10,640 earned during October appear in the credit column of the Income Summary account. Since the credit entry of $10,640 representing October revenue is larger than the debit of $8,069 representing October expenses, the account has a credit balance of $2,571—the net income for October.

The net income of $2,571 earned during October causes the owners' equity to increase. The **credit** balance of the Income Summary account is, therefore, transferred to the Retained Earnings account by the following closing entry:

General Journal   Page 3

	Date		Account Titles and Explanation	LP	Debit	Credit
Net income earned increases the owners' equity	19__ Oct.	31	Income Summary	53	2,571	
			Retained Earnings	51		2,571
			To close the Income Summary account for October by transferring the net income to the Retained Earnings account.			

Expense accounts have zero balances after closing entries have been posted

Income Summary
Account No. 53

Date		Explanation	Ref	Debit	Credit	Balance
19__						
Oct.	31		3		10,640	10,640
	31		3	8,069		2,571

Advertising Expense
Account No. 70

Date		Explanation	Ref	Debit	Credit	Balance
19__						
Oct.	2		2	360		360
	16		2	270		630
	31	To close	3		630	–0–

Salaries Expense
Account No. 72

Date		Explanation	Ref	Debit	Credit	Balance
19__						
Oct.	30		2	7,100		7,100
	31	To close	3		7,100	–0–

Telephone Expense
Account No. 74

Date		Explanation	Ref	Debit	Credit	Balance
19__						
Oct.	30		2	144		144
	31	To close	3		144	–0–

Depreciation Expense: Building
Account No. 76

Date		Explanation	Ref	Debit	Credit	Balance
19__						
Oct.	31		2	150		150
	31	To close	3		150	–0–

Depreciation Expense: Office Equipment
Account No. 78

Date		Explanation	Ref	Debit	Credit	Balance
19__						
Oct.	31		2	45		45
	31	To close	3		45	–0–

After this closing entry has been posted, the Income Summary account has a zero balance, and the net income for October will appear as an increase or credit entry in the Retained Earnings account, as shown below:

		Income Summary				Account No. 53
19__						
Oct.	31	Revenue	3		10,640	10,640
	31	Expenses	3	8,069		2,571
	31	To close	3	2,571		–0–

		Retained Earnings				Account No. 51
19__						
Oct.	31	Net Income for October	3		2,571	2,571

In our illustration the business has operated profitably with revenue in excess of expenses. Not every business is so fortunate. If the expenses of a business are larger than its revenue, the Income Summary account will have a debit balance, representing a **net loss** for the accounting period. In this case, the closing of the Income Summary account requires a debit to the Retained Earnings account and an offsetting credit to the Income Summary account. A debit balance in the Retained Earnings account is referred to as a **deficit;** it is shown as a deduction from Capital Stock in the balance sheet.

Note that the Income Summary account is used only at the end of the period when the accounts are being closed. The Income Summary account has no entries and no balance except during the process of closing the accounts at the end of the accounting period.

Closing the Dividends account. As explained earlier in the chapter, the payment of dividends to the owners is not considered as an expense of the business and, therefore, is not taken into account in determining the net income for the period. Since dividends do not constitute an expense, the Dividends account is **not** closed into the Income Summary account. Instead, it is closed directly to the Retained Earnings account, as shown by the following entry:

	General Journal				Page 3
Date	Account Titles and Explanation	LP	Debit		Credit
19__					
Oct.	31	Retained Earnings	51	1,800	
		Dividends	52		1,800
		To close the Dividends account.			

Dividends account is closed to Retained Earnings

After this closing entry has been posted, the Dividends account will have a zero balance, and the dividends distributed during October will appear as a deduction or debit entry in the Retained Earnings account, as follows:

Dividends   Account No. 52

19__							
Oct.	30	Declaration and payment	2	1,800		1,800
	31	To close	3		1,800	–0–

Retained Earnings   Account No. 51

19__							
Oct.	31	Net income for October	3		2,571	2,571
	31	Dividends	3	1,800		771

The closing process — in summary. The closing of the accounts may be illustrated graphically by the use of T accounts as shown below:

Diagram showing closing of the accounts

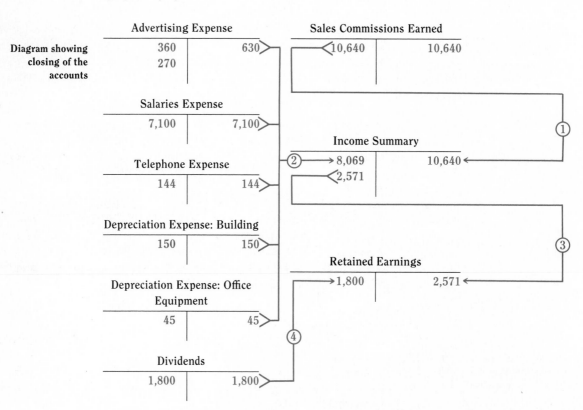

As illustrated in the preceding diagram, the closing process consists of four steps:

1 Close the various revenue accounts by transferring their balances into the Income Summary account.
2 Close the various expense accounts by transferring their balances into the Income Summary account.

3 Close the Income Summary account by transferring its balance into the Retained Earnings account.

4 Close the Dividends account by transferring its balance into the Retained Earnings account.

After-closing trial balance

After the revenue and expense accounts have been closed, it is desirable to prepare an *after-closing trial balance,* which of course will consist solely of balance sheet accounts. There is always the possibility that an error in posting the closing entries may have upset the equality of debits and credits in the ledger. The after-closing trial balance, or *post-closing trial balance* as it is often called, is prepared from the ledger. It gives assurance that the accounts are in balance and ready for the recording of the transactions of the new accounting period. The after-closing trial balance of Greenhill Real Estate follows:

GREENHILL REAL ESTATE
After-Closing Trial Balance
October 31, 19___

Only the balance Cash	$ 15,490	
sheet accounts Accounts receivable	17,890	
remain open Land	130,000	
Building	36,000	
Accumulated depreciation: building		$ 150
Office equipment	5,400	
Accumulated depreciation: office equipment		45
Accounts payable		23,814
Capital stock		180,000
Retained earnings, Oct. 31		771
	$204,780	$204,780

Sequence of procedures in the accounting cycle

The accounting procedures described to this point may be summarized in eight steps, as follows:

1 *Journalize transactions.* Enter all transactions in the journal, thus creating a chronological record of events.

2 *Post to ledger accounts.* Post debits and credits from the journal to the proper ledger accounts, thus creating a record classified by accounts.

3 *Prepare a trial balance.* Prove the equality of debits and credits in the ledger.

4 *Prepare end-of-period adjustments.* Enter adjusting entries in the general journal, and post to ledger accounts.

5 *Prepare an adjusted trial balance.* Prove again the equality of debits and credits in the ledger.

6 *Prepare financial statements.* An income statement shows the results of operation for the period. A statement of retained earnings shows the changes in retained earnings during the period and the closing balance. A balance sheet shows the financial position of the business at the end of the period.

7 *Journalize and post the closing entries.* The closing entries clear the revenue, expense, and dividends accounts, making them ready for recording the events of the next accounting period, and also bring the Retained Earnings account up-to-date.

8 *Prepare an after-closing trial balance.* This step ensures that the ledger remains in balance after posting of the closing entries.

Accounting procedures in a computer-based system

The sequence of procedures performed in computer-based systems is essentially the same as in manual systems. Of course, the computer is programmed to perform a number of these steps automatically. In the preceding list, procedures 1 and 4 both involve the analysis of business transactions and judgmental decisions as to accounts to be debited and credited and the dollar amounts. These two steps in the accounting cycle require human judgment, regardless of whether the data is processed manually or by computer. As mentioned in Chapter 2, a computer-based system may call for recording transactions first in a data base, rather than in a journal. The computer then arranges the data into the format of journal entries, ledger accounts, trial balances, and financial statements.

Procedures such as posting and the preparation of trial balances and financial statements involve the rearrangement of recorded data and may easily be performed by computer. The preparation of closing entries also is a mechanical task, involving the transfer of recorded data from one ledger account to another. Thus, closing entries may be performed automatically in a computer-based system.

Dividends — declaration and payment

Earlier in this chapter the declaration and the payment of a cash dividend were treated as a single event recorded by one journal entry. A small corporation with only a few stockholders may choose to declare and pay a dividend on the same day. In large corporations with thousands of stockholders and constant transfers of shares, an interval of a month or more will separate the date of declaration from the later date of payment.

Assume for example that on April 1 the board of directors of Universal Corporation declares the regular quarterly dividend of $1 per share on the 1 million shares of outstanding capital stock. The board's resolution specifies that the dividend will be payable on May 10 to stockholders of record on April 25. To be eligible to receive the dividend, an individual must be listed on the corporation's records as a stockholder on April 25, the date of record. Two entries are required: one on April 1 for the declaration of the dividend and one on May 10 for its payment, as shown below.

Dividends declared and . . .	Apr. 1	Dividends 1,000,000	
		Dividends Payable	1,000,000
		Declared dividend of $1 per share payable May 10 to stockholders of record Apr. 25.	
. . . Dividends paid	May 10	Dividends Payable 1,000,000	
		Cash	1,000,000
		Paid the $1 per share dividend declared on Apr. 1.	

The Dividends Payable account is a liability which comes into existence when the dividend is declared and is discharged when the dividend is paid.

Accrual basis of accounting versus cash basis of accounting

A business which recognizes revenue in the period in which it is earned and which deducts in the same period the expenses incurred in generating this revenue is using the *accrual basis of accounting.*

The alternative to the accrual basis of accounting is the *cash basis.* Under cash basis accounting, revenue is not recorded until received in cash; expenses are assigned to the period in which cash payment is made. Most business concerns use the accrual basis of accounting, but individuals, professionals (such as physicians and lawyers), and many small service-type companies, usually maintain their accounting records on a cash basis.

The cash basis of accounting does not give a good picture of profitability. For example, it ignores uncollected revenue which has been earned and expenses which have been incurred but not paid. However, the cash basis does offer several advantages in the preparation of income tax returns. Throughout this book we shall be working with the accrual basis of accounting, except for that portion of Chapter 17 dealing with the income tax returns of individuals.

Key terms introduced or emphasized in chapter 3

Accounting period. The span of time covered by an income statement. One year is the accounting period for much financial reporting, but financial statements are also prepared by most companies for each quarter of the year and also for each month.

Accrual basis of accounting. Calls for recording revenue in the period in which it is earned and recording expenses in the period in which they are incurred. The effect of events on the business is recognized as services are rendered or consumed rather than when cash is received or paid.

Accumulated depreciation. A contra-asset account shown as a deduction from the related asset account in the balance sheet. Depreciation taken throughout the useful life of an asset is accumulated in this account.

Adjusted trial balance. A listing of all ledger account balances after the amounts have been changed to include the adjusting entries made at the end of the period.

Adjusting entries. Entries required at the end of the period to update the accounts before financial statements are prepared. Adjusting entries serve to apportion transactions properly between the accounting periods affected and to record any revenue earned or expenses incurred which have not been recorded prior to the end of the period.

After-closing trial balance. A trial balance prepared after all closing entries have been made. Consists only of accounts for assets, liabilities, and owners' equity.

Cash basis of accounting. Revenue is recorded when received in cash and expenses are recorded in the period in which cash payment is made. Fails to match revenue with related expenses and therefore does not lead to a logical measurement of income. Use is limited mostly to individual income tax returns and to accounting records of physicians and other professional firms.

Closing entries. Journal entries made at the end of the period for the purpose of closing temporary accounts (revenue, expense, and dividends accounts) and bringing the Retained Earnings account up-to-date.

Conservatism. The traditional accounting practice of resolving uncertainty by choosing the solution which leads to the lower (more conservative) amount of income being recognized in the current accounting period. This concept is designed to avoid overstatement of financial strength or earnings.

Contra-asset account. An account with a credit balance which is offset against or deducted from an asset account to produce the proper balance sheet valuation for the asset.

Depreciation. The systematic allocation to expense of the cost of an asset (such as a building) during the periods of its useful life.

Dividend. A distribution of cash by a corporation to its stockholders.

Expenses. The cost of the goods and services used up in the process of obtaining revenue.

Financial statement order. Sequence of accounts in the ledger; balance sheet accounts first (assets, liabilities, and owners' equity), followed by income statement accounts (revenue and expenses).

Fiscal year. Any 12-month accounting period adopted by a business.

Income statement. A financial statement showing the results of operations for a business by matching revenue and related expenses for a particular accounting period. Shows the net income or net loss.

Income Summary account. The summary account in the ledger to which revenue and expense accounts are closed at the end of the period. The balance (credit balance for a net income, debit balance for a net loss) is transferred to the Retained Earnings account.

Matching principle. In the measurement of net income, revenue earned during the accounting period is offset with all expenses incurred in generating that revenue whether or not these expenses were paid during the accounting period.

Net income. The excess of revenue earned over the related expenses for a given period.

Realization principle. The generally accepted accounting principle that determines when revenue should be recorded in the accounting records. Revenue is realized when services are rendered to customers or when goods sold are delivered to customers.

Report form balance sheet. A balance sheet in which the sections for liabilities and owners' equity are listed below the section for assets.

Retained earnings. That portion of stockholders' equity resulting from profits earned and retained in the business.

Revenue. The price of goods sold and services rendered by a business. Equal to the inflow of cash and receivables in exchange for services rendered or goods delivered during the period.

Statement of retained earnings. A financial statement showing the changes in the amount of retained earnings over the accounting period.

Temporary owners' equity accounts. The accounts for revenue, expenses, and dividends used during the accounting period to classify changes affecting the owners' equity.

Demonstration problem for your review

Key Insurance Agency was organized on September 1, 19__. Assume that the accounts are closed and financial statements prepared each month. The company occupies rented office space but owns office equipment estimated to have a useful life of 10 years from date of acquisition, September 1. The trial balance for Key Insurance Agency at November 30 is shown on page 105.

Instructions

a Prepare the adjusting journal entry to record depreciation of the office equipment for the month of November.

Cash	$ 3,750	
Accounts receivable	1,210	
Office equipment	4,800	
Accumulated depreciation: office equipment		$ 80
Accounts payable		1,640
Capital stock		6,000
Retained earnings		1,490
Dividends	500	
Commissions earned		6,220
Advertising expense	800	
Salaries expense	3,600	
Rent expense	770	
	$15,430	$15,430

b Prepare an adjusted trial balance at November 30, 19___.

c Prepare an income statement and a statement of retained earnings for the month ended November 30, 19___, and a balance sheet in report form at November 30, 19___.

Solution to demonstration problem

a Adjusting journal entry:

Depreciation Expense: Office Equipment	40	
Accumulated Depreciation: Office Equipment		40

To record depreciation for November ($4,800 ÷ 120 months).

b

KEY INSURANCE AGENCY
Adjusted Trial Balance
November 30, 19___

Cash	$ 3,750	
Accounts receivable	1,210	
Office equipment	4,800	
Accumulated depreciation: office equipment		$ 120
Accounts payable		1,640
Capital stock		6,000
Retained earnings		1,490
Dividends	500	
Commissions earned		6,220
Advertising expense	800	
Salaries expense	3,600	
Rent expense	770	
Depreciation expense: office equipment	40	
Totals	$15,470	$15,470

c

KEY INSURANCE AGENCY
Income Statement
For the Month Ended November 30, 19__

Commissions earned		$6,220
Expenses:		
Advertising expense	$ 800	
Salaries expense	3,600	
Rent expense	770	
Depreciation expense: office equipment	40	5,210
Net income		$1,010

KEY INSURANCE AGENCY
Statement of Retained Earnings
For the Month Ended November 30, 19__

Retained earnings, Oct. 31, 19__	$1,490
Net income for the month	1,010
Subtotal	$2,500
Dividends	500
Retained earnings, Nov. 30, 19__	$2,000

KEY INSURANCE AGENCY
Balance Sheet
November 30, 19__

Assets

Cash		$3,750
Accounts receivable		1,210
Office equipment	$4,800	
Less: Accumulated depreciation	120	4,680
Total assets		$9,640

Liabilities & Stockholders' Equity

Liabilities		
Accounts payable		$1,640
Stockholders' equity:		
Capital stock	$6,000	
Retained earnings	2,000	8,000
Total liabilities & stockholders' equity		$9,640

Review questions

1 What is the meaning of the term **revenue?** Does the receipt of cash by a business indicate that revenue has been earned? Explain.

2 What is the meaning of the term **expenses?** Does the payment of cash by a business indicate that an expense has been incurred? Explain.

3 Explain the effect of operating profitably upon the balance sheet of a business entity.

4 Does the Retained Earnings account represent a supply of cash which could be distributed to stockholders? Explain.

5 A service enterprise performs services in the amount of $500 for a customer in May and receives payment in June. In which month is the $500 of revenue recognized? What is the journal entry to be made in May and the entry to be made in June?

6 When do accountants consider revenue to be realized? What basic question about recording revenue in the accounting records is answered by the realization principle?

7 Late in March, Classic Auto Painters purchased paint on account, with payment due in 60 days. The company used the paint to paint customers' cars during the first three weeks of April. Late in May, the company paid the paint store from which the paint had been purchased. In which month should Classic Auto Painters recognize the cost of this paint as expense? What generally accepted accounting principle determines the answer to this question?

8 Remington Corporation pays dividends regularly. Should these dividends be considered an expense of the business? Explain.

9 Explain the rules of debit and credit with respect to transactions recorded in revenue and expense accounts.

10 Supply the appropriate term (debit or credit) to complete the following statements.

a The Capital Stock account, Retained Earnings account, and revenue accounts are increased by _____ entries.

b Asset accounts and expense accounts are increased by _____ entries.

c Liability accounts and owners' equity accounts are decreased by _____ entries.

11 Supply the appropriate term (debit or credit) to complete the following statements.

a When a business is operating profitably, the journal entry to close the Income Summary account will consist of a _____ to that account and a _____ to Retained Earnings.

b When a business is operating at a loss, the journal entry to close the Income Summary account will consist of a _____ to that account and a _____ to Retained Earnings.

c The journal entry to close the Dividends account consists of a _____ to that account and a _____ to Retained Earnings.

12 How does depreciation expense differ from other operating expenses?

13 Assume that a business acquires a delivery truck at a cost of $9,600. Estimated life of the truck is four years. State the amount of depreciation expense per year and per month. Give the adjusting entry to record depreciation on the truck at the end of the first month, and explain where the accounts involved would appear in the financial statements.

14 All ledger accounts belong in one of the following five groups: asset, liability, owners' equity, revenue, and expense. For each of the following accounts, state the group in which it belongs. Also indicate whether the normal balance would be a debit or a credit.

a Fees Earned
b Notes Payable
c Telephone Expense
d Retained Earnings
e Building
f Depreciation Expense
g Accumulated Depreciation: Building

15 Does a well-prepared income statement provide an exact and precise measurement of net income for the period or does it represent merely an approximation of net income? Explain.

16 For each of the following financial statements, indicate whether the statement relates to a single date or to a period of time:

   a Balance sheet
   b Income statement
   c Statement of retained earnings

17 Which of the following accounts should be closed by a debit to Income Summary and a credit to the account listed?

Dividends	Salaries Expense
Fees Earned	Accounts Payable
Advertising Expense	Depreciation Expense
Accounts Receivable	Accumulated Depreciation

18 Supply the appropriate terms to complete the following statements. _____ and _____ accounts are closed at the end of each accounting period by transferring their balances to a summary account called _____. A _____ balance in this summary account represents net income for the period; a _____ balance represents a net loss for the period.

19 Which of the 10 accounts listed below are affected by closing entries at the end of the accounting period?

Cash	Capital Stock
Fees Earned	Dividends
Income Summary	Accumulated Depreciation
Accounts Payable	Accounts Receivable
Telephone Expense	Depreciation Expense

20 How does the accrual basis of accounting differ from the cash basis of accounting? Which gives a more accurate picture of the profitability of a business? Explain.

Exercises

Ex. 3-1   On October 12, the accountant for Sunray Appliance Company prepared an income statement for the fiscal year ended September 30, 198_. The accountant used the following heading on this financial statement:

SUNRAY CO.
Profit and Loss Statement
October 12, 198_

Instructions

   a Identify any errors in this heading.
   b Prepare a corrected heading.

Ex. 3-2   The following transactions were carried out during the month of August by Rancho Corporation, a firm of real estate brokers. Which of these transactions represented revenue to the firm during the month of August? Explain.

   a Borrowed $12,800 from Century Bank to be repaid in three months.

b Collected cash of $2,400 from an account receivable. The receivable originated in July from services rendered to a client.

c Arranged a sale of an apartment building owned by a client, Stephen Roberts. The commission for making the sale was $14,400, but this amount will not be received until October 20.

d Collected $480 rent for August from a dentist to whom Rancho Corporation rented part of its building.

e Rancho Corporation received $25,000 cash from the issuance of additional shares of its capital stock.

Ex. 3-3 During May the Columbus Company carried out the following transactions. Which of these transactions represented expenses for May? Explain.

a Purchased a copier for $840 cash.

b Paid $92 for gasoline purchases for the delivery truck during May.

c Paid $970 salary to an employee for time worked during May.

d Paid an attorney $560 for legal services rendered in April.

e Declared and paid a $1,000 dividend to shareholders.

f Paid $4,600 in settlement of a loan obtained four months earlier.

Ex. 3-4 Total assets and total liabilities of Mannix Corporation as shown by the balance sheets at the beginning and end of the year were as follows:

	Beginning of Year	End of Year
Assets	$280,000	$390,000
Liabilities	110,000	160,000

Compute the net income or net loss from operations for the year in each of the following independent cases:

a No dividends were declared or paid during the year and no additional capital stock was issued.

b No dividends were declared or paid during the year, but additional capital stock was issued at par in the amount of $50,000.

c Dividends of $20,000 were declared and paid during the year. No change occurred in capital stock.

d Dividends of $10,000 were declared and paid during the year, and additional capital stock was issued at par in the amount of $25,000.

Ex. 3-5 Supply the missing figure in the following independent cases:

a	
Retained earnings at beginning of year	$130,000
Net income for the year	–?–
Dividends for the year	32,000
Retained earnings at end of year	145,500

b	
Retained earnings at beginning of year	$ 91,200
Net income for the year	28,500
Dividends for the year	–?–
Retained earnings at end of year	99,700

c Retained earnings at beginning of year .... –?–
  Net income for the year $189,400
  Dividends for the year 106,000
  Retained earnings at end of year 532,900

d Total stockholders' equity at beginning of year .... $ 74,000
  Additional issuance of capital stock during year 10,000
  Net income for the year 17,500
  Dividends for the year 12,000
  Total stockholders' equity at end of year .... –?–

e Total stockholders' equity at beginning of year $362,500
  Additional issuance of capital stock during year 85,000
  Net income for the year .... –?–
  Dividends for the year 30,000
  Total stockholders' equity at end of year 469,100

Ex. 3-6   Shown below are selected transactions of the law firm of Emmons & Associates, Inc. You are to prepare journal entries to record the transactions in the firm's accounting records. The firm closes its accounts at the end of each calendar year.

Mar. 19   Drafted a prenuptial agreement for C. J. McCall. Sent McCall an invoice for $750, requesting payment within 30 days. (The appropriate revenue account is entitled Legal Fees Earned.)

May 15   Declared a dividend of $60,000, payable on June 30 to stockholders of record on June 10.

May 31   Received a bill from Lawyers' Delivery Service for process service during the month of May, $1,150. Payment due by June 10. (The appropriate expense account is entitled Process Service Expense.)

June 30   Paid the dividend declared on May 15.

Dec. 31   Made a year-end adjusting entry to record depreciation expense on the firm's law library, $2,700.

Ex. 3-7   From the following account balances, prepare first an income statement and then a statement of retained earnings for Chambers Painting Contractors for the year ended December 31, 19__. Include the proper headings on both financial statements.

Retained earnings, Jan. 1, 19__ .	$ 27,200	Salaries Expense	$66,800
Dividends	18,000	Rent Expense	9,600
Painting Fees Earned	140,000	Advertising Expense	3,200
Paint & Supplies Expense	27,500	Depreciation Expense: Painting	
		Equipment	1,200

Ex. 3-8   During the absence of the regular accountant of Sunbelt Center, a new employee, Ralph Jones, prepared the closing entries from the ledger accounts for the year 19__. Jones has very little understanding of accounting and the closing entries he prepared were not satisfactory in several respects. The entries by Jones were:

Entry 1

Sales Commissions Earned	136,800	
Accumulated Depreciation: Building	12,800	
Accounts Payable	43,200	
Income Summary		192,800

To close accounts with credit balances.

Entry 2

Income Summary	130,800	
Salaries Expense		103,200
Dividends		18,000
Advertising Expense		6,400
Depreciation Expense: Building		3,200

To close accounts with debit balances.

Entry 3

Capital Stock	62,000	
Income Summary		62,000

To close Income Summary account.

Instructions

a For each entry, identify any errors which Jones made.

b Prepare four correct closing entries, following the pattern illustrated on pages 96–100.

Problems

3-1 Analysis of transactions; journal entries

The transactions during October for Pacific Electric Company included the following:

(1) On October 1, paid $640 cash for the month's rent.

(2) On October 3, made repairs for First National Bank and collected in full the charge of $1,014.

(3) On October 8, performed repair work for American Home Builders. Sent bill for $1,332 for services rendered.

(4) On October 15, placed an advertisement in the *Tribune* at a cost of $310, payment to be made within 30 days.

(5) On October 21, purchased equipment for $4,000 cash.

(6) On October 30, received a check for $1,332 from American Home Builders.

(7) On October 31, sent check to the *Tribune* in payment of liability incurred on October 15.

(8) On October 31, declared a cash dividend of $5,000 payable on November 30.

Instructions

a Write an analysis of each transaction. An example of the type of analysis desired is as follows:

(1) (a) Rent is an operating expense. Expenses are recorded by debits. Debit Rent Expense, $640.

(b) The asset Cash was decreased. Decreases in assets are recorded by credits. Credit cash, $640.

b Prepare a journal entry (including explanation) for each of the above transactions.

3-2 Journal entries (alternative to problem 3-3)

Bay Plumbers performs repair work on both a cash and credit basis. Credit customers are required to pay within 30 days from date of billing. Among the ledger accounts used by the company are the following:

Cash	Dividends
Accounts receivable	Repair service revenue
Tools	Advertising expense
Notes payable	Rent expense
Accounts payable	Salaries expense
Dividends payable	

Among the June transactions were the following:

June 1 Performed repair work for Arden Hardware, a credit customer. Sent bill for $1,247.
June 2 Paid rent for June, $700.
June 3 Purchased tools with estimated life of 10 years for $1,200 cash.
June 10 Performed repairs for Harris Drugs and collected in full the charge of $510.
June 15 Newspaper advertising to appear on June 18 was arranged at a cost of $250. Received bill from *Tribune* requiring payment within 30 days.
June 18 Received payment in full of the $1,247 account receivable from Arden Hardware for our services on June 1.
June 20 Declared a dividend of $4,500 payable July 15.
June 30 Paid salaries of $3,300 to employees for services rendered during June.

Instructions. Prepare a journal entry (including explanation) for each of the above transactions.

3-3 Journal entries (alternative to problem 3-2)

City Flights provides transportation by helicopter between a major airport and various business centers of a large city. Among the ledger accounts used by the company are the following:

Cash	Passenger fare revenue
Accounts payable	Advertising expense
Dividends payable	Fuel expense
Capital stock	Rent expense
Retained earnings	Repair & maintenance expense
Dividends	Salaries expense

Some of the January transactions of City Flights are listed below.

Jan. 3 Paid $3,200 rent for the building for January.
Jan. 4 Placed advertising in local newspapers for publication during January. The agreed price of $1,080 was payable within 10 days after the end of the month.
Jan. 15 Cash receipts from passengers for the first half of January amounted to $19,300.
Jan. 16 Declared a dividend of $6,000 payable March 15 to stockholders of record March 1.

Jan. 16 Paid salaries to employees for services rendered in first half of January, $11,000.

Jan. 29 Received a bill from Western Oil Co. for fuel used in January, amounting to $3,940, and payable by February 10.

Jan. 31 Paid $3,372 to Stevens Motors for repair and maintenance work during January.

Instructions. Prepare a journal entry (including an explanation) for each of the above transactions.

3-4 Closing entries

At year-end, Oak Creek Park prepared the following adjusted trial balance:

OAK CREEK PARK
Adjusted Trial Balance
December 31, 19__

Cash	$ 12,500	
Accounts receivable	1,800	
Equipment	60,000	
Accumulated depreciation: equipment		$ 18,000
Trucks	30,000	
Accumulated depreciation: trucks		10,000
Capital stock		40,000
Retained earnings, Jan. 1, 19__		32,000
Dividends	25,000	
Admissions revenue		175,000
Advertising expense	12,000	
Rent expense	34,000	
Repairs expense	5,200	
Salaries expense	79,000	
Light & power expense	4,500	
Depreciation expense: equipment	6,000	
Depreciation expense: trucks	5,000	
	$275,000	$275,000

Instructions

a Prepare journal entries to close the accounts. Use four entries: (1) to close the revenue account, (2) to close the expense accounts, (3) to close the Income Summary account, and (4) to close the Dividends account.

b Assume that in the following year, Oak Creek Park again had $175,000 of admissions revenue, but that expenses increased to $190,000. Assuming that the revenue account and all the expense accounts had been closed into the Income Summary account at December 31, prepare a journal entry to close the Income Summary account.

3-5 Closing entries and preparation of financial statements

Ryan Radio Repair was organized on May 1, 19__. The accounts were closed and financial statements prepared each month. An adjusted trial balance as of the succeeding July 31 follows.

RYAN RADIO REPAIR
Adjusted Trial Balance
July 31, 19___

Cash	$ 7,720	
Accounts receivable	4,740	
Land	73,500	
Building	126,000	
Accumulated depreciation: building		$ 1,260
Repair equipment	16,800	
Accumulated depreciation: repair equipment		840
Notes payable		70,000
Accounts payable		2,100
Capital stock		140,000
Retained earnings, June 30, 19___		14,000
Dividends	10,500	
Repair service revenue		23,800
Advertising expense	420	
Depreciation expense: building	420	
Depreciation expense: repair equipment	280	
Repair parts expense	1,820	
Utilities expense	350	
Wages expense	9,450	
	$252,000	$252,000

Instructions

a Prepare journal entries to close the accounts at July 31. Use four entries: (1) to close the revenue account, (2) to close the expense accounts, (3) to close the Income Summary account, and (4) to close the Dividends account.

b Prepare financial statements (income statement, statement of retained earnings, and a balance sheet in report form).

c What were the estimated lives of the building and equipment as assumed by the company in setting the depreciation rates?

3-6 The accounting cycle: end-of-period procedures

The operations of Coast Realty consist of obtaining listings of houses being offered for sale by owners, advertising these houses, and showing them to prospective buyers. The company earns revenue in the form of commissions. The building and office equipment used in the business were acquired on January 1 of the current year and were immediately placed in use. Useful life of the building was estimated to be 30 years and that of the office equipment 8 years. The company closes its accounts monthly; on April 30 of the current year, the trial balance is as shown on page 115.

Instructions. From the trial balance and supplementary data given, prepare the following as of April 30, 19___:

a Adjusting entries for depreciation during April of building and of office equipment.
   (Building: $72,000 cost $\div$ 30 years $\times \frac{1}{12}$ = one month's depreciation)
   (Office equipment: $24,000 cost $\div$ 8 years $\times \frac{1}{12}$ = one month's depreciation)

COAST REALTY
Trial Balance
April 30, 19___

	Debit	Credit
Cash	$ 6,500	
U.S. government bonds	8,000	
Accounts receivable	7,000	
Land	67,000	
Building	72,000	
Accumulated depreciation: building		$ 400
Office equipment	24,000	
Accumulated depreciation: office equipment ..		500
Notes payable		81,000
Accounts payable		10,000
Capital stock		50,000
Retained earnings, Mar. 31, 19___		46,100
Dividends	10,000	
Commissions earned		22,000
Advertising expense	900	
Automobile rental expense	700	
Salaries expense	13,300	
Telephone expense	600	
	$210,000	$210,000

 b An adjusted trial balance.
 c An income statement and a statement of retained earnings for the month of April, and a balance sheet as of April 30.
 d Closing entries.
 e An after-closing trial balance.

3-7 The accounting cycle: a comprehensive problem
Newport Parking System was organized on March 1 for the purpose of operating an automobile parking lot. Included in the company's ledger are the following ledger accounts and their identification numbers.

Cash	11	Dividends	46
Land	21	Income summary	49
Notes payable	31	Parking fees earned	51
Accounts payable	32	Advertising expense	61
Dividends payable	35	Utilities expense	63
Capital stock	41	Salaries expense	65
Retained earnings	45		

The business was organized and operations were begun during the month of March. Transactions during March were as follows:

Mar. 1 The corporation issued 10,000 shares of $10 par value capital stock in exchange for $100,000 cash.

Mar. 2 Purchased land for $140,000, of which $54,000 was paid in cash. A short-term note payable was issued for the balance of $86,000.

Mar. 2 An arrangement was made with the Century Club to provide parking privileges for its customers. Century Club agreed to pay $660 monthly, payable in advance. Cash was collected for the month of March.

Mar. 7 Arranged with Times Printing Company for a regular advertisement in the *Times* at a monthly cost of $114. Paid for advertising during March by check, $114.

Mar. 15 Parking receipts for the first half of the month were $1,836, exclusive of the monthly fee from Century Club.

Mar. 31 Received bill for light and power from Pacific Power Company in the amount of $78, to be paid by April 10.

Mar. 31 Paid $2,720 to employees for services rendered during the month. (Payroll taxes are to be ignored.)

Mar. 31 Parking receipts for the second half of the month amounted to $5,338.

Mar. 31 Declared a dividend of 20 cents per share on the 10,000 shares of outstanding capital stock, payable on June 15 to stockholders of record on April 30.

Mar. 31 Paid $12,000 cash on the note payable incurred with the purchase of land. (You are to ignore any interest on the note. Accounting for interest charges is introduced in Chapter 4.)

Instructions

a Journalize the March transactions.

b Post to ledger accounts. Enter ledger account numbers in the LP column of the journal as the posting work is done.

c Prepare a trial balance at March 31.

d Prepare an income statement and a statement of retained earnings for the month of March, and a balance sheet in report form as of March 31. (Note: No adjusting entries were required for this business at March 31. Therefore, the financial statements may be prepared using the account balances appearing in the trial balance. The figure for retained earnings in the March 31 balance sheet should be taken from the statement of retained earnings.)

e Prepare closing entries and post to ledger accounts.

f Prepare an after-closing trial balance.

3-8 The accounting cycle: another comprehensive problem

On November 1, 19___, Continental Moving Co. was organized to provide transportation of household furniture. During November the following transactions occurred:

Nov. 1 Cash of $800,000 was received in exchange for 80,000 shares of $10 par value capital stock.

Nov. 2 Purchased land for $210,000 and building for $320,000, paying $130,000 cash and signing a $400,000 mortgage payable bearing interest at 9%.

Nov. 3 Purchased six trucks from Willis Motors at a total cost of $432,000. A cash down payment of $200,000 was made, the balance to be paid by January 12.

Nov. 6 Purchased office equipment for cash, $24,000.

Nov. 6 Moved furniture for Mr. and Mrs. Don Fitch from New York to Los Angeles for $8,650. Collected $4,850 in cash, balance to be paid within 30 days (credit Moving Service Revenue).

Nov. 9 Moved furniture for various clients for $32,350. Collected $18,350 in cash, balance to be paid within 30 days.

Nov. 15 Paid salaries to employees for the first half of the month, $17,400.

Nov. 25 Moved furniture for various clients for a total of $37,000. Cash collected in full.

Nov. 30 Salaries expense for the second half of November amounted to $13,250.

Nov. 30 Received a gasoline bill for the month of November from Lucier Oil Company in the amount of $17,500, to be paid by December 10.

Nov. 30 Received bill of $1,250 for repair work on trucks during November by Newport Repair Company.

Nov. 30 Paid $5,000 to the holder of the mortgage payable. This $5,000 payment included $3,000 interest expense for November and $2,000 reduction in the liability.

Nov. 30 Declared an $8,000 dividend, payable December 15.

Estimated useful life of the building was 20 years, trucks 4 years, and office equipment 10 years. The account titles to be used and the account numbers are as follows:

Cash	1	Retained earnings	41
Accounts receivable	3	Dividends	45
Land	11	Income summary	50
Building	12	Moving service revenue	60
Accumulated depreciation: building	13	Salaries expense	70
		Gasoline expense	71
Trucks	15	Repairs & maintenance expense	72
Accumulated depreciation: trucks	16	Interest expense	73
Office equipment	18	Depreciation expense: building	74
Accumulated depreciation: office equipment	19	Depreciation expense: trucks	75
Accounts payable	30		
Dividends payable	31	Depreciation expense: office equipment	76
Mortgage payable, 9%	32		
Capital stock	40		

Instructions

a Prepare journal entries. (Number journal pages to permit cross reference to ledger.)

b Post to ledger accounts. (Number ledger accounts to permit cross reference to journal.)

c Prepare a trial balance at November 30, 19___.

d Prepare adjusting entries and post to ledger accounts.

e Prepare an adjusted trial balance.

f Prepare an income statement for November, and a balance sheet at November 30, 19___, in report form. (A statement of retained earnings is not required.)

g Prepare closing entries and post to ledger accounts.

h Prepare an after-closing trial balance.

Cases for analysis

Case 3-1   Depreciation and cash flow

The Dark Room is a business that develops film within one hour, using a large and expensive developing machine. The business is organized as a single proprietorship and operates in rented quarters in a large shopping center. Sharon Douglas, owner of The Dark Room, plans to retire and has offered the business for sale. A typical monthly income statement for The Dark Room appears below:

Revenue:

Fees earned		$8,900
Operating expenses:		
Wages	$1,600	
Rent	1,850	
Supplies	920	
Depreciation: developing machine	1,510	
Miscellaneous	460	6,340
Net income		$2,560

Revenue is received in cash at the time that film is developed. The wages, rent, supplies, and miscellaneous expenses are all paid in cash on a monthly basis. Douglas explains that the developing machine, which is 12 months old and is fully paid for, is being depreciated over a period of five years. She is using this estimated useful life because she believes that faster and more efficient machines will probably be available at that time. However, if the business does not purchase a new machine, the existing machine should last for 10 years or more.

Dave Berg, a friend of yours, is negotiating with Douglas to buy The Dark Room. Berg does not have enough money to pay the entire purchase price in cash. However, Douglas has offered to accept a note payable from Berg for a substantial portion of the purchase price. The note would call for 18 monthly payments in the amount of $2,500, which would pay off the remainder of the purchase price as well as the interest charges on the note. Douglas points out that these monthly payments can be made "out of the monthly earnings of the business."

Berg comes to you for advice. He feels that the sales price asked by Douglas is very reasonable, and that the owner-financing makes this an excellent opportunity. However, he is worried about turning over $2,500 of the business's earnings to Douglas each month. Berg states, "This arrangement will only leave me with about $60 each month. I figure that my familiy and I need to take about $1,200 out of this business each month just to meet our living expenses." Also, Berg is concerned about the depreciation expense. He does not understand when or to whom the depreciation expense must be paid, or how long this expense will continue.

Instructions

   a Explain to Berg the nature of depreciation expense, including when this expense is paid and what effect, if any, it has upon monthly cash expenditures.

   b Advise Berg as to how much cash the business will generate each month. Will this amount enable Berg to pay $2,500 per month to the former owner and still withdraw $1,200 per month to meet his personal living expenses?

   c Caution Berg about the need to replace the developing machine. Briefly discuss when this expenditure might occur and how much control, if any, Berg has over the timing and dollar amount of this expenditure.

Case 3-2 Accrual versus cash basis

Nancy Jo Hoover, owner of a small business called Imports from India, has accepted a salaried position overseas and is trying to interest you in buying the business. Hoover describes the operating results of the business as follows: "The business has been in existence for only 18 months, but the growth trend is very impressive. Just look at these figures."

	Cash Collections from Customers
First six-month period	$120,000
Second six-month period	160,000
Third six-month period	180,000

"I think you'll agree those figures show real growth," Hoover concluded.

You then asked Hoover whether sales were made only for cash or on both a cash and credit basis. She replied as follows:

"At first we sold both for cash and on open account. In the first six months we made total sales of $200,000 and 70% of those sales were made on credit. We had $80,000 of accounts receivable at the end of the first six-month period.

"During the second six-month period, we tried to discourage selling on credit because of the extra paper work involved and the time required to follow up on slow-paying customers. Our sales on credit in that second six-month period amounted to $70,000, and our total accounts receivable were down to $60,000 at the end of that period.

"During the third six-month period we made sales only for cash. Although we prefer to operate on a cash basis only, we did very well at collecting receivables. We collected in full from every customer to whom we ever sold on credit and we don't have a dollar of accounts receivable at this time."

Instructions

a To assist you in evaluating the performance of Imports from India, prepare a schedule comparing cash collections and sales data for each of the three 6-month periods under review. Use the following column headings:

	(1) Sales on Credit	(2) Collections on Accounts Receivable	(3) Ending Balance of Accounts Receivable	(4) Sales for Cash (5) − (2)	(5) Total Cash Collections from Customers	(6) Total Sales (1) + (4)
First six months					$120,000	
Second six months ...					160,000	
Third six months					180,000	

b Based upon your analysis in part a, do you consider Hoover's explanation of the "growth trend" of cash collections to be a well-founded portrayal of the progress of the business? Explain fully any criticism you may have of Hoover's line of reasoning.

Chapter 4
Completion of the accounting cycle

In Chapter 4 we complete our coverage of the accounting cycle for a service-type business. Emphasis is placed upon steps performed at the end of the cycle, including adjusting entries, preparation of a work sheet, and reversing entries. The continuing example of Greenhill Real Estate is used to illustrate and explain the four basic types of adjusting entries and the preparation of a work sheet. The discussion of reversing entries emphasizes the optional nature of this final step in the accounting cycle. As in our earlier chapters on the accounting cycle, the procedures employed in computer-based accounting systems are compared with those in manual systems.

After studying this chapter you should be able to:

✓ Explain how accounting periods of uniform length are useful in evaluating the income of a business.
✓ State the purpose of adjusting entries and explain how these entries are related to the concepts of accrual accounting.
✓ Describe the four basic types of adjusting entries.
✓ Prepare a work sheet and discuss its usefulness.
✓ Describe the steps in the accounting cycle.
✓ Explain when and why reversing entries may be used.

Accounting periods and financial statements

For the purpose of measuring income and preparing financial statements, the life of a business is divided into accounting periods of equal length. Because accounting periods are equal in length, we can compare the income of the current period with that of prior periods to see if our operating results are improving or declining.

As explained in Chapter 3, the *accounting period* means the span of time covered by an income statement. The usual accounting period for which complete financial statements are prepared and distributed to investors, bankers, and governmental agencies is one year.

However, most businesses also prepare quarterly and monthly financial statements so that management will be currently informed on the profitability of the business from month to month.

Transactions affecting more than one accounting period

Dividing the life of a business into relatively short accounting periods creates the need for *adjusting entries* at the end of each period. Some transactions affect the revenue or expense of only one period. Adjusting entries are *not* required for these types of transactions. Adjusting entries are required, however, for those transactions which affect the revenue or expenses of *more than one accounting period.* For example, assume that a company which prepares monthly financial statements purchases a one-year insurance policy at a cost of $1,200. Clearly, the entire $1,200 does not represent the insurance expense of the current month. Rather, it is the insurance expense for *12* months; only $\frac{1}{12}$ of this cost, or $100, should be recognized as expense in each month covered by the policy. The allocation of this $1,200 cost to expense in 12 separate accounting periods is accomplished by making an adjusting entry at the end of each period.

ADJUSTING ENTRIES

The purpose of adjusting entries is to record certain revenue and expenses that are not properly measured in the course of recording daily business transactions. Thus, adjusting entries help in achieving the goals of accrual accounting — recording revenue when it is *earned* and recording expenses when the related goods and services are *used.* In Chapter 3, the concept of adjusting entries was introduced when Greenhill Real Estate recorded depreciation for the month of October. Adjusting entries are necessary to record depreciation expense, because buildings and equipment are purchased in a single accounting period but are used over many periods. Some portion of the cost of these assets should be allocated to expense in each period of the asset's estimated life. In this chapter, we will see that the use of adjusting entries is not limited to recording depreciation expense. Adjusting entries are needed *whenever transactions affect the revenue or expense of more than one accounting period.*

Types of adjusting entries

A business may need to make a dozen or more adjusting entries at the end of each accounting period. The exact number of adjustments will depend upon the nature of the company's business activities. However, all adjusting entries fall into one of four general categories:

1 *Entries to apportion recorded costs.* A cost that will benefit more than one accounting period usually is recorded by debiting an asset account. In each period that benefits from the use of this asset, an adjusting entry is made to allocate a portion of the asset's cost to expense.

2 *Entries to apportion unearned revenue.* A business may collect in advance for services to be rendered to customers in future accounting periods. In the period in

which these services are actually rendered, an adjusting entry is made to record the portion of the revenue earned during the period.

3 *Entries to record unrecorded expenses.* An expense may be incurred in the current accounting period even though no bill has yet been received and payment will not occur until a future period. Such unrecorded expenses are recorded by an adjusting entry made at the end of the accounting period.

4 *Entries to record unrecorded revenue.* Revenue may be earned during the current period, but not yet billed to customers or recorded in the accounting records. Such unrecorded revenue is recorded by making an adjusting entry at the end of the period.

Characteristics of adjusting entries

It will be helpful to keep in mind two important characteristics of all adjusting entries. First, every adjusting entry *involves the recognition of either revenue or expense.* Revenue and expenses represent changes in owners' equity. However, owners' equity cannot change by itself; there also must be a corresponding change in either assets or liabilities. *Thus, every adjusting entry affects both an income statement account* (revenue or expense) *and a balance sheet account* (asset or liability).

Second, adjusting entries are based upon the concepts of accrual accounting, *not upon monthly bills or month-end transactions.* No one sends us a bill saying, "Depreciation expense on your building amounts to $500 this month." Yet, we must be aware of the need to estimate and record depreciation expense if we are to measure net income properly for the period. Making adjusting entries requires a greater understanding of accrual accounting concepts than does the recording of routine business transactions. In many businesses, the adjusting entries are made by the company's controller or by a professional accountant, rather than by the regular accounting staff.

To demonstrate the various types of adjusting entries, the illustration of Greenhill Real Estate will be continued for November. We shall consider in detail only those November transactions which require adjusting entries at the end of the month.

Apportioning recorded costs

When a business makes an expenditure that will benefit more than one accounting period, the amount usually is debited to an asset account. At the end of each period benefiting from this expenditure, an adjusting entry is made to transfer an appropriate portion of the cost from the asset account to an expense account. This adjusting entry reflects the fact that part of the asset has been used up — or become expense — during the current accounting period.

An adjusting entry to apportion a recorded cost consists of a debit to an expense account and a credit to an asset account (or a contra-asset account). Examples of these adjustments include the entries to record depreciation expense and to apportion the costs of *prepaid expenses.*

Prepaid expenses. Payments in advance are often made for such items as insurance, rent, and office supplies. If the advance payment (or prepayment) will benefit more than just the current accounting period, the cost **represents an asset** rather than an expense. The cost of this asset will be allocated to expense in the accounting periods in which the services or the supplies are used. In summary, **prepaid expenses are assets;** they become expenses only as the goods or services are used up.

Insurance. To illustrate these concepts, assume that on November 1, Greenhill Real Estate paid $600 for a one-year fire insurance policy covering the building. This expenditure was debited to an asset account by the following journal entry:

Expenditure for insurance policy recorded as asset

Unexpired Insurance	600	
Cash		600

Purchased a one-year fire insurance policy.

Since this expenditure of $600 will protect the company against fire loss for one year, the insurance expense applicable to each month's operations is $\frac{1}{12}$ of the annual expense, or $50. In order that the accounting records for November show insurance expense of $50, the following **adjusting entry** is required at November 30:

Adjusting entry. Portion of asset expires (becomes expense)

Insurance Expense	50	
Unexpired Insurance		50

To record insurance expense for November.

This adjusting entry serves two purposes: (1) it apportions the proper amount of insurance expense to November operations and (2) it reduces the asset account to $550 so that the correct amount of unexpired insurance will appear in the balance sheet at November 30.

What would be the effect on the income statement for November if the above adjustment were not made? The expenses would be understated by $50 and consequently the net income would be overstated by $50. The balance sheet also would be affected by failure to make the adjustment: the assets would be overstated by $50 and so would the owners' equity. The overstatement of the owners' equity would result from the overstated amount of net income transferred to the Retained Earnings account when the accounts were closed at November 30.

Office supplies. On November 2, Greenhill Real Estate purchased enough stationery and other office supplies to last for several months. The cost of the supplies was $720, and this amount was debited to an asset account by the following journal entry:

Expenditure for office supplies recorded as asset

Office Supplies	720	
Cash		720

Purchased office supplies.

No entries were made during November to record the day-to-day usage of office supplies, but on November 30 a count was made of the supplies still on hand. This physical count showed unused supplies with a cost of $500. Thus, supplies costing $220 were used during November. On the basis of the November 30 count, an adjusting entry is made debiting an expense account $220 (the cost of supplies consumed during November), and reducing the asset account by $220. The *adjusting entry* follows:

Office Supplies Expense 220
　　Office Supplies 220
To record consumption of office supplies in November.

After this entry is posted the asset account, Office Supplies, will have a balance of $500, representing the cost of office supplies on hand at November 30. The Office Supplies account will appear in the balance sheet as an asset; the Office Supplies Expense account will be shown in the income statement.

How would failure to make this adjustment affect the financial statements? In the income statement for November, the expenses would be understated by $220 and the net income overstated by the same amount. Since the overstated amount for net income in November would be transferred into the Retained Earnings account in the process of closing the accounts, the owners' equity section of the balance sheet would be overstated by $220. Assets also would be overstated because Office Supplies would be listed at $220 too much.

Recording prepayments directly in the expense accounts. In our illustration, payments for insurance and office supplies which are expected to provide benefits for more than one accounting period are recorded by debiting an asset account, such as Unexpired Insurance or Office Supplies. However, some companies follow an alternative practice of debiting these prepayments directly to an expense account such as Insurance Expense. At the end of the period, the adjusting entry would then consist of a debit to Unexpired Insurance and a credit to Insurance Expense for the portion of the insurance cost *which has not yet expired.*

This alternative method leads to the same results in the balance sheet and income statement as does the method used in our Greenhill illustration. Under both procedures, the cost of benefits consumed in the current period is treated as an expense, and the cost of benefits applicable to future periods is carried forward in the balance sheet as an asset.

In this text and in the end-of-chapter problem material, we will follow Greenhill's practice of recording prepayments in asset accounts and then making adjusting entries to transfer these costs to expense accounts as the assets expire.

Depreciation of building. The recording of depreciation expense at the end of an accounting period provides another example of an adjusting entry which *apportions a recorded cost.* The November 30 adjusting entry to record depreciation of the building used by Greenhill Real Estate is exactly the same as the October 31 *adjusting entry* explained in Chapter 3.

Depreciation Expense: Building 150
　　Accumulated Depreciation: Building 150
To record depreciation for November.

This allocation of depreciation expense to November operations is based on the following facts: the building cost $36,000 and is estimated to have a useful life of 20 years (240 months). Using the straight-line method of depreciation, the portion of the original cost which expires each month is $\frac{1}{240}$ of $36,000, or $150.

The Accumulated Depreciation: Building account now has a credit balance of $300 as a result of the October and November credits of $150 each. The book value of the building is $35,700, that is, the original cost of $36,000 minus the accumulated depreciation of $300. The term **book value** means the net amount at which an asset is shown in the accounting records, as distinguished from its market value. **Carrying value** is an alternative term, with the same meaning as book value.

Depreciation of office equipment. The November 30 adjusting entry to record depreciation of the office equipment is the same as the **adjusting entry** for depreciation a month earlier, as shown in Chapter 3.

Adjusting entry. Cost of office equipment gradually converted to expense

Depreciation Expense: Office Equipment   45
     Accumulated Depreciation: Office Equipment   45
To record depreciation for November.

The original cost of the office equipment was $5,400, and the estimated useful life was 10 years (120 months). Depreciation each month under the straight-line method is therefore $\frac{1}{120}$ of $5,400, or $45.

What is the book value of the office equipment at this point? The original cost of $5,400, minus accumulated depreciation of $90 for two months, leaves a book value of $5,310.

Apportioning unearned revenue

In some instances, customers may **pay in advance** for services to be rendered in later accounting periods. For example, a football team collects much of its revenue in advance through the sale of season tickets. Health clubs collect in advance by selling long-term membership contracts. Airlines sell many of their tickets well in advance of a scheduled flight.

For accounting purposes, amounts collected in advance **do not represent revenue**, because these amounts have **not yet been earned.** Amounts collected from customers in advance are recorded by debiting the Cash account and crediting an **unearned revenue** account. Unearned revenue also may be called **deferred revenue.**

When a company collects money in advance from its customers, it has an **obligation** to render services in the future. Therefore, the balance of an unearned revenue account is considered to be a liability; **it appears in the liability section of the balance sheet, not in the income statement.** Unearned revenue differs from other liabilities because it usually will be settled by rendering services, rather than by making payment in cash. In short, it will be **worked off** rather than **paid off.** Of course if the business is unable to render the service, it must discharge this liability by refunding money to its customers.

When the company renders the services for which customers have paid in advance, it is working off its liability to these customers and is earning the revenue. At the end of the accounting period in which the revenue is earned, an **adjusting entry** is made to transfer an appropriate amount from the unearned revenue account to a revenue account. This adjusting entry consists of a debit to a liability account (unearned revenue) and a credit to a revenue account.

To illustrate these concepts, assume that on November 1, Greenhill Real Estate agreed to act as manager of some rental properties for a monthly fee of $300. The owner of the properties, Frank Day, was leaving the country on an extended trip and therefore paid the company for six months' service in advance. The journal entry to record the transaction on November 1 was

Management fee collected but not yet earned

Cash 1,800
    Unearned Management Fees   1,800
Collected in advance six months' fees for management of properties owned by Frank Day.

Remember that Unearned Management Fees is a *liability* account, not a revenue account. This management fee will be earned gradually over a period of six months as Greenhill performs the required services. As the end of each monthly accounting period, Greenhill will make an adjusting entry transferring $\frac{1}{6}$ of this management fee, or $300, from the unearned revenue account to a revenue account. The first in this series of monthly transfers will be made on November 30 by the following *adjusting entry:*

Adjusting entry to recognize earning of a part of management fee

Unearned Management Fees 300
    Management Fees Earned   300
Fee earned by managing Frank Day property during November.

After this entry has been posted, the Unearned Management Fees account will have a $1,500 credit balance. This balance represents Greenhill's obligation to render $1,500 worth of services over the next five months and will appear in the liability section of the company's balance sheet. The Management Fees Earned account will be shown as revenue in the November income statement.

Recording advance collections directly in the revenue accounts. We have stressed that amounts collected from customers in advance represent liabilities, not revenue. However, some companies follow an accounting policy of crediting these advance collections directly to revenue accounts. The adjusting entry then should consist of a debit to the revenue account and a credit to the unearned revenue account for the portion of the advance payments *not yet earned.* This alternative accounting practice leads to the same results as does the method used in our Greenhill Real Estate illustration.

In this text, we will follow the originally described practice of crediting advance payments from customers to an unearned revenue account.

Recording unrecorded expenses

We have already discussed adjusting entries that apportion recorded costs. Such entries recognize expenses stemming from *past* transactions. Hence, the adjusting entry *apportions a cost which has already been recorded in the accounting records.*

We will now describe another type of adjusting entry which also recognizes expenses incurred during the current accounting period. This type of adjusting entry recognizes expenses that will be paid in *future* transactions; thus, no cost has yet been recorded in the accounting records. Salaries of employees and interest on borrowed money are common examples of expenses which accumulate from day to day, but which usually are not recorded until they are paid. These expenses are said to *accrue* over time, that is, to grow or to accumulate. At the end of the accounting period, an adjusting entry should be made to record any expenses which have accrued, but which have not yet been recorded. Since these expenses will be paid at a future date, the adjusting entry consists of a debit to an expense account and a credit to a liability account. We shall now use the example of Greenhill Real Estate to illustrate this type of adjusting entry.

Accrual of interest. On November 1, Greenhill Real Estate borrowed the sum of $3,000 from a bank. Banks require every borrower to sign a *promissory note,* that is, a formal, written promise to repay the amount borrowed plus interest at an agreed future date. (Various forms of notes in common use and the accounting problems involved will be discussed more fully in Chapter 8.) The note signed by John Green, with certain details omitted, is shown below.

Note payable issued to bank

$3,000	Los Angeles, California	November 1, 19___

Three months .... after date ... Greenhill Real Estate ... promises to pay

to the order of .... American National Bank ....

.... ---Three thousand and no/100--- .... dollars

for value received, with interest at ... 12 percent per year ....

Greenhill Real Estate
....

By .... *John Green* ....
President

The note payable is a liability of Greenhill Real Estate, similar to an account payable but different in that a formal written promise to pay is required and interest is charged on the amount borrowed. A Notes Payable account is credited when the note is issued; the Notes Payable account will be debited three months later when the note is paid. Interest accrues throughout the life of the note, but it is not payable until the note matures on February 1.

The journal entry made on November 1 to record the borrowing of $3,000 from the bank was as follows:

Entry when bank loan is obtained

Cash	3,000	
Notes Payable		3,000

Obtained from bank three-month loan with interest at 12% a year.

Three months later, Greenhill Real Estate must pay the bank $3,090, representing payment of the $3,000 note payable plus $90 interest ($3,000 $\times$ .12 $\times \frac{3}{12}$). The $90 is the total interest expense for the three months. Although no payment will be made for three months, one-third of the interest expense ($30) is *incurred* each month, as shown below.

Accrual of interest

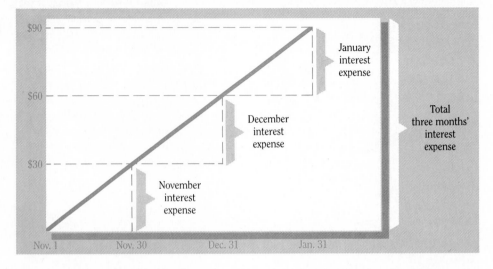

The following *adjusting entry* is made at November 30 to charge November operations with one month's interest expense and also to record the amount of interest owed to the bank at the end of November.

Adjusting entry for interest expense incurred in November

Interest Expense 30
    Interest Payable 30
To record interest expense applicable to November ($3,000 × .12 × $\frac{1}{12}$).

The debit balance in the Interest Expense account will appear in the November income statement; the credit balances in the Interest Payable and Notes Payable accounts will be shown in the balance sheet as liabilities. These two liability accounts will remain in the records until the maturity date of the loan, at which time a cash payment to the bank will wipe out both the Notes Payable account and the Interest Payable account.

Accrual of salary. On November 20, Greenhill hired Carl Nelson as a part-time salesperson whose duties were to work evenings calling on property owners to secure listings of property for sale or rent. The agreed salary was $225 for a five-evening week, payable each Friday; payment for the first week was made on Friday, November 24. Personal income taxes and other taxes relating to payroll are ignored in this illustration.

Assume that the last day of the accounting period, November 30, fell on Thursday. Nelson had worked four evenings since being paid the preceding Friday and therefore had earned $180 ($\frac{4}{5}$ × $225). In order that this $180 of November salary expense be reflected in the accounts before the financial statements are prepared, an *adjusting entry* is necessary at November 30.

Adjusting entry for
salaries expense
incurred but unpaid
at November 30

Salaries Expense 180
    Salaries Payable 180
To record salary expense and related liability to salesperson for last four evenings' work in November.

    The debit balance in the Salaries Expense account will appear as an expense in the November income statement; the credit balance of $180 in the Salaries Payable account is the amount owing to the salesperson for work performed during the last four days of November and will appear among the liabilities in the balance sheet at November 30.

    The next regular payday for Nelson will be Friday, December 1, which is the first day of the new accounting period. Since the accounts were adjusted and closed on November 30, all the revenue and expense accounts have zero balances at the beginning of business on December 1. The payment of a week's salary to Nelson will be recorded by the following entry on December 1:

Payment of salary
overlapping two
accounting periods

Salaries Payable 180
Salaries Expense 45
    Cash 225
Paid weekly salary to salesperson.

    Note that the net result of the November 30 accrual entry has been to split the weekly salary expense between November and December. Four days of the work week fell in November, so four days' pay, or $180, was recognized as November expense. One day of the work week fell in December so $45 was recorded as December expense.

    No accrual entry is necessary for other salaries in Greenhill Real Estate because everyone except Nelson is paid regularly on the last working day of the month.

Recording unrecorded revenue

    A business may earn revenue during the current accounting period but not bill the customer until a future accounting period. This situation is likely to occur if additional services are being performed for the same customer, in which case the bill might not be prepared until all services are completed. Any revenue which has been *earned but not recorded* during the current accounting period should be recorded at the end of the period by means of an adjusting entry. This adjusting entry consists of a debit to an account receivable and a credit to the appropriate revenue account. The term *accrued revenue* often is used to describe revenue which has been earned during the period but which has not been recorded prior to the closing date.

    To illustrate this type of adjusting entry, assume that on November 16, Greenhill Real Estate entered into a management agreement with Angela Clayton, the owner of two small office buildings. The company agreed to manage the Clayton properties for a fee of $240 a month, payable on the fifteenth of each month. No entry is made in the accounting records at the time of signing a contract, because no services have yet been rendered and no change has occurred in assets or liabilities. The managerial duties are to begin immediately, but the first monthly fee will not be received until December 15. The following *adjusting entry* is therefore necessary at November 30:

Adjusting entry for
fees earned but
uncollected

Management Fees Receivable 120
    Management Fees Earned 120
To record accrued revenue from services rendered to Angela Clayton during November.

The debit balance in the Management Fees Receivable account will be shown in the balance sheet as an asset. The credit balance of the Management Fees Earned account, including earnings from both the Day and Clayton contracts, will appear in the November income statement.

The collection of the first monthly fee from Clayton will occur in the next accounting period (December 15, to be exact). Of this $240 cash receipt, half represents collection of the asset account, Management Fees Receivable, created at November 30 by the adjusting entry. The other half of the $240 cash receipt represents revenue earned during December; this should be credited to the December revenue account for Management Fees Earned. The entry on December 15 is as follows:

Management fee
applicable to two ac-
counting periods

Cash 240
    Management Fees Receivable 120
    Management Fees Earned 120
Collected commission for month ended December 15.

The net result of the November 30 accrual entry has been to divide the revenue from managing the Clayton properties between November and December in accordance with the timing of the services rendered.

Adjusting entries and the accrual basis of accounting

Adjusting entries help make accrual basis accounting work successfully. By preparing adjusting entries, we can recognize revenue in the accounting period in which it is *earned* and also recognize expenses which helped to *produce that revenue.* For example, the adjusting entry to record revenue which has been earned but not yet recorded helps achieve our goal of including in the income statement all the revenue *realized* during the accounting period. The adjusting entries which recognize expenses help to achieve the *matching principle* — that is, offsetting revenues with all the expenses incurred in generating that revenue.

THE WORK SHEET

The work necessary at the end of an accounting period includes construction of a trial balance, journalizing and posting of adjusting entries, preparation of financial statements, and journalizing and posting of closing entries. So many details are involved in these end-of-period procedures that it is easy to make errors. If these errors are recorded in the journal and in the ledger accounts, considerable time and effort can be wasted in correcting them. Both the journal and the ledger are formal, permanent records. They may be prepared manually in ink or printed by a computer. One way of avoiding errors in the permanent accounting records and also of simplifying the work to be done at the end of the period is to use a *work sheet.*

A work sheet is a large columnar sheet of paper, especially designed to arrange in a convenient systematic form all the accounting data required at the end of the period. The work sheet is not a part of the permanent accounting records; it is prepared in pencil by accountants for their own convenience. (The use of a computer to prepare a work sheet is discussed later in this chapter.) If an error is made on the work sheet, it may be erased and corrected much more easily than an error in the formal accounting records. Furthermore, the work sheet is designed to reduce errors by automatically bringing to light many types of discrepancies which otherwise might be entered in the journal and posted to the ledger accounts. Dollar signs, decimal points, and commas are not used with the amounts entered on work sheets, although commas are shown in this example. A work sheet for Greenhill Real Estate appears on page 132.

The work sheet may be thought of as a testing ground on which the ledger accounts are adjusted, balanced, and arranged in the general form of financial statements. The satisfactory completion of a work sheet provides considerable assurance that all the details of the end-of-period accounting procedures have been properly brought together. After this point has been established, the work sheet then serves as the source from which the formal financial statements are prepared and the adjusting and closing entries are made in the journal.

Preparing the work sheet

Note that the heading of the work sheet illustrated for Greenhill Real Estate consists of three parts: (1) the name of the business, (2) the title *Work Sheet,* and (3) the period of time covered. The body of the work sheet contains five pairs of money columns, each pair consisting of a debit and a credit column. The procedures to be followed in preparing a work sheet will now be illustrated in five simple steps.

1 Enter the ledger account balances in the Trial Balance columns. The titles and balances of the ledger accounts at November 30 are copied into the Trial Balance columns of the work sheet. In practice these amounts may be taken directly from the ledger. It would be a duplication of work to prepare a trial balance as a separate schedule and then to copy this information into the work sheet. As soon as the account balances have been listed on the work sheet, these two columns should be added and the totals entered.

2 Enter the adjustments in the Adjustments columns. The required adjustments for Greenhill Real Estate were explained earlier in this chapter; these same adjustments are now entered in the Adjustments columns of the work sheet. (See page 133.)

As a cross reference, the debit and credit parts of each adjustment are keyed together by placing a key letter to the left of each amount. For example, the adjustment debiting Insurance Expense and crediting Unexpired Insurance is identified by the key letter (a). The use of the key letters makes it easy to match a debit entry in the Adjustments columns with its related credit. The identifying letters also key the debit and credit entries in the

GREENHILL REAL ESTATE
Work Sheet
For the Month Ended November 30, 19___

1. Enter ledger account balances before adjustments in Trial Balance columns on work sheet

	Trial Balance		Adjustments		Adjusted Trial Balance		Income Statement		Balance Sheet	
	Dr	Cr	Dr	Cr	Dr	Cr	Dr	Cr	Dr	Cr
Cash	21,740									
Accounts receivable	16,990									
Unexpired insurance	600									
Office supplies	720									
Land	130,000									
Building	36,000									
Accumulated depreciation: building		150								
Office equipment	5,400									
Accumulated depreciation: office equipment		45								
Notes payable		3,000								
Accounts payable		23,595								
Unearned management fees		1,800								
Capital stock		180,000								
Retained earnings, Oct. 31, 19___		771								
Dividends	1,500									
Sales commissions earned		15,484								
Advertising expense	1,275									
Salaries expense	9,425									
Telephone expense	1,195									
	224,845	224,845								

GREENHILL REAL ESTATE
Work Sheet
For the Month Ended November 30, 19___

	Trial Balance Dr	Trial Balance Cr	Adjustments* Dr	Adjustments* Cr	Adjusted Trial Balance Dr	Adjusted Trial Balance Cr	Income Statement Dr	Income Statement Cr	Balance Sheet Dr	Balance Sheet Cr
Cash	21,740									
Accounts receivable	16,990									
Unexpired insurance	600			(a) 50						
Office supplies	720			(b) 220						
Land	130,000									
Building	36,000									
Accumulated depreciation: building		150		(c) 150						
Office equipment	5,400									
Accumulated depreciation: office equipment		45		(d) 45						
Notes payable		3,000								
Accounts payable		23,595								
Unearned management fees		1,800	(e) 300							
Capital stock		180,000								
Retained earnings, Oct. 31, 19___		771								
Dividends	1,500									
Sales commissions earned		15,484								
Advertising expense	1,275									
Salaries expense	9,425		(g) 180							
Telephone expense	1,195									
Totals	224,845	224,845								
Insurance expense			(a) 50							
Office supplies expense			(b) 220							
Depreciation expense: building			(c) 150							
Depreciation expense: office equipment			(d) 45							
Management fees earned				(e) 300 / (h) 120						
Interest expense			(f) 30							
Interest payable				(f) 30						
Salaries payable				(g) 180						
Management fees receivable			(h) 120							
Totals			1,095	1,095						

Explanatory footnotes keyed to adjustments

* Adjustments:
(a) Portion of insurance cost which expired during November
(b) Office supplies used during November
(c) Depreciation of building during November
(d) Depreciation of office equipment during November
(e) Earned one-sixth of the commission collected in advance on the Day properties
(f) Interest expense accrued during November on note payable
(g) Salesperson's salary for last four days of November
(h) Rental commission accrued on Clayton contract in November

133

GREENHILL REAL ESTATE
Work Sheet
For the Month Ended November 30, 19___

	Trial Balance Dr	Trial Balance Cr	Adjustments* Dr	Adjustments* Cr	Adjusted Trial Balance Dr	Adjusted Trial Balance Cr	Income Statement Dr	Income Statement Cr	Balance Sheet Dr	Balance Sheet Cr
Cash	21,740				21,740					
Accounts receivable	16,990				16,990					
Unexpired insurance	600			(a) 50	550					
Office supplies	720			(b) 220	500					
Land	130,000				130,000					
Building	36,000				36,000					
Accumulated depreciation: building		150		(c) 150		300				
Office equipment	5,400				5,400					
Accumulated depreciation: office equipment		45		(d) 45		90				
Notes payable		3,000				3,000				
Accounts payable		23,595				23,595				
Unearned management fees		1,800	(e) 300			1,500				
Capital stock		180,000				180,000				
Retained earnings, Oct. 31, 19___		771				771				
Dividends	1,500				1,500					
Sales commissions earned		15,484				15,484				
Advertising expense	1,275				1,275					
Salaries expense	9,425		(g) 180		9,605					
Telephone expense	1,195				1,195					
Totals	224,845	224,845								
Insurance expense			(a) 50		50					
Office supplies expense			(b) 220		220					
Depreciation expense: building			(c) 150		150					
Depreciation expense: office equipment			(d) 45		45					
Management fees earned				(e) 300 (h) 120		420				
Interest expense			(f) 30		30					
Interest payable				(f) 30		30				
Sales salaries payable				(g) 180		180				
Management fees receivable			(h) 120		120					
			1,095	1,095	225,370	225,370				

Enter the adjusted amounts in columns 5 and 6 of work sheet

* Explanatory notes relating to adjustments are the same as on page 133.

134

Adjustments columns to the brief explanations which appear at the bottom of the work sheet.

The titles of any accounts debited or credited in the adjusting entries but not listed in the trial balance should be written on the work sheet below the trial balance. For example, Insurance Expense does not appear in the trial balance; therefore it should be written on the first available line below the trial balance totals. After all the adjustment debits and credits have been entered in the Adjustments columns, this pair of columns must be totaled. Proving the equality of debit and credit totals helps to detect any arithmetical errors and to prevent them from being carried over into other columns of the work sheet.

3 Enter the account balances as adjusted in the Adjusted Trial Balance columns. The work sheet as it appears after completion of the Adjusted Trial Balance columns is illustrated on page 134. Each account balance in the first pair of columns is combined with the adjustment, if any, in the second pair of columns, and the combined amount is entered in the Adjusted Trial Balance columns. This process of combining the items on each line throughout the first four columns of the work sheet requires horizontal addition or subtraction. It is called *cross footing,* in contrast to the addition of items in a vertical column, which is called *footing* the column.

For example, the Office Supplies account has a debit balance of $720 in the Trial Balance columns. This $720 debit amount is combined with the $220 credit appearing on the same line in the Adjustments column; the combination of a $720 debit with a $220 credit produces an adjusted debit amount of $500 in the Adjusted Trial Balance debit column. As another example, consider the Office Supplies Expense account. This account had no balance in the Trial Balance columns but shows a $220 debit in the Adjustments debit column. The combination of a zero starting balance and $220 debit adjustment produces a $220 debit amount in the Adjusted Trial Balance.

Many of the accounts in the trial balance are not affected by the adjustments made at the end of the month; the balances of these accounts (such as Cash, Land, Building, or Notes Payable in the illustrated work sheet) are entered in the Adjusted Trial Balance columns in exactly the same amounts as shown in the Trial Balance columns. After all the accounts have been extended into the Adjusted Trial Balance columns, this pair of columns is totaled to prove that no arithmetical errors have been made up to this point.

4 Extend each amount in the Adjusted Trial Balance columns into the Income Statement columns or into the Balance Sheet columns. Assets and liabilities are entered in the Balance Sheet columns. The owners' equity accounts (Capital Stock, Retained Earnings, and Dividends) are also entered in the Balance Sheet columns. The revenue and expense accounts are entered in the Income Statement columns.

The process of extending amounts horizontally across the work sheet should begin with the account at the top of the work sheet, which is usually Cash. The cash figure is extended to the Balance Sheet debit column. Then the accountant goes down the work sheet line by line, extending each account balance to the appropriate column. The work sheet as it appears after completion of this sorting process is illustrated on page 136. Note that each amount in the Adjusted Trial Balance columns is extended to one *and only one* of the four remaining columns.

GREENHILL REAL ESTATE
Work Sheet
For the Month Ended November 30, 19___

	Trial Balance Dr	Trial Balance Cr	Adjustments* Dr	Adjustments* Cr	Adjusted Trial Balance Dr	Adjusted Trial Balance Cr	Income Statement Dr	Income Statement Cr	Balance Sheet Dr	Balance Sheet Cr
Cash	21,740				21,740				21,740	
Accounts receivable	16,990				16,990				16,990	
Unexpired insurance	600			(a) 50	550				550	
Office supplies	720			(b) 220	500				500	
Land	130,000				130,000				130,000	
Building	36,000				36,000				36,000	
Accumulated depreciation: building		150		(c) 150		300				300
Office equipment	5,400				5,400				5,400	
Accumulated depreciation: office equipment		45		(d) 45		90				90
Notes payable		3,000				3,000				3,000
Accounts payable		23,595				23,595				23,595
Unearned management fees		1,800	(e) 300			1,500				1,500
Capital stock		180,000				180,000				180,000
Retained earnings, October 31, 19___		771				771				771
Dividends	1,500				1,500				1,500	
Sales commissions earned		15,484				15,484		15,484		
Advertising expense	1,275				1,275		1,275			
Salaries expense	9,425		(g) 180		9,605		9,605			
Telephone expense	1,195				1,195		1,195			
Totals	224,845	224,845								
Insurance expense			(a) 50		50		50			
Office supplies expense			(b) 220		220		220			
Depreciation expense: building			(c) 150		150		150			
Depreciation expense: office equipment			(d) 45		45		45			
Management fees earned				(e) 300 (h) 120		420		420		
Interest expense			(f) 30		30		30			
Interest payable				(f) 30		30				30
Sales salaries payable				(g) 180		180				180
Management fees receivable			(h) 120		120				120	
			1,095	1,095	225,370	225,370				

Extend each adjusted amount to columns for income statement or balance sheet

* Explanatory notes relating to adjustments are the same as on page 133.

5 Total the Income Statement columns and the Balance Sheet columns. Enter the net income or net loss as a balancing figure in both pairs of columns, and again compute column totals. The work sheet as it appears after this final step is shown on page 138.

The net income or net loss for the period is determined by computing the difference between the totals of the two Income Statement columns. In the illustrated work sheet, the credit column total is the larger and the excess represents net income:

Income Statement credit column total (revenue)	$15,904
Income Statement debit column total (expenses)	12,570
Difference: net income for period	$ 3,334

Note that the net income of $3,334 is entered in the Income Statement *debit* column as a balancing figure and also on the same line as a balancing figure in the Balance Sheet *credit* column. The caption Net Income is written in the space for account titles to identify and explain this item. New totals are then computed for both the Income Statement columns and the Balance Sheet columns. Each pair of columns is now in balance.

The reason for entering the net income of $3,334 in the Balance Sheet *credit column* is that the net income accumulated during the period in the revenue and expense accounts causes an increase in the owners' equity. If the balance sheet columns did not have equal totals after the net income had been recorded in the credit column, the lack of agreement would indicate that an error had been made in the work sheet.

Let us assume for a moment that the month's operations had produced a loss rather than a profit. In that case the Income Statement debit column would exceed the credit column. The excess of the debits (expenses) over the credits (revenue) would have to be entered in the *credit column* in order to bring the two Income Statement columns into balance. The incurring of a loss would decrease the owners' equity; therefore, the loss would be entered as a balancing figure in the Balance Sheet *debit column.* The Balance Sheet columns would then have equal totals.

Self-balancing nature of the work sheet. Why does the entering of the net income or net loss in one of the Balance Sheet columns bring this pair of columns into balance? The answer is short and simple. All the accounts in the Balance Sheet columns have November 30 balances with the exception of the Retained Earnings account, which still shows the October 31 balance of $771. By bringing in the current month's net income of $3,334 and the Dividends of $1,500, the total owners' equity is brought up to date as of November 30. The Balance Sheet columns now prove the familiar proposition that assets are equal to the total of liabilities and owners' equity.

Uses for the work sheet

Preparing financial statements. Preparing the formal financial statements from the work sheet is an easy step. All the information needed for both the income statement and the balance sheet has already been sorted and arranged in convenient form in the work sheet. For example, compare the amounts on the following income statement with the amounts listed in the Income Statement columns of the completed work sheet.

Completed work sheet

GREENHILL REAL ESTATE
Work Sheet
For the Month Ended November 30, 19___

	Trial Balance		Adjustments*		Adjusted Trial Balance		Income Statement		Balance Sheet	
	Dr	Cr	Dr	Cr	Dr	Cr	Dr	Cr	Dr	Cr
Cash	21,740				21,740				21,740	
Accounts receivable	16,990				16,990				16,990	
Unexpired insurance	600			(a) 50	550				550	
Office supplies	720			(b) 220	500				500	
Land	130,000				130,000				130,000	
Building	36,000				36,000				36,000	
Accumulated depreciation: building		150		(c) 150		300				300
Office equipment	5,400				5,400				5,400	
Accumulated depreciation: office equipment		45		(d) 45		90				90
Notes payable		3,000				3,000				3,000
Accounts payable		23,595				23,595				23,595
Unearned management fees		1,800	(e) 300			1,500				1,500
Capital stock		180,000				180,000				180,000
Retained earnings, Oct. 31, 19___		771				771				771
Dividends	1,500				1,500				1,500	
Sales commissions earned		15,484				15,484		15,484		
Advertising expense	1,275				1,275		1,275			
Salaries expense	9,425		(g) 180		9,605		9,605			
Telephone expense	1,195				1,195		1,195			
Totals	224,845	224,845								
Insurance expense			(a) 50		50		50			
Office supplies expense			(b) 220		220		220			
Depreciation expense: building			(c) 150		150		150			
Depreciation expense: office equipment			(d) 45		45		45			
Management fees earned				(e) 300 (h) 120		420		420		
Interest expense			(f) 30		30		30			
Interest payable				(f) 30		30				30
Sales salaries payable				(g) 180		180				180
Management fees receivable			(h) 120		120				120	
Totals			1,095	1,095	225,370	225,370	12,570	15,904	212,800	209,466
Net income							3,334			3,334
Totals							15,904	15,904	212,800	212,800

* Explanatory notes relating to adjustments are the same as on page 133.

GREENHILL REAL ESTATE
Income Statement
For the Month Ended November 30, 19__

Data taken from Income Statement columns of work sheet

Revenue:		
Sales commissions earned		$15,484
Management fees earned		420
Total revenue		$15,904
Expenses:		
Advertising	$1,275	
Office supplies	220	
Salaries	9,605	
Telephone	1,195	
Insurance	50	
Depreciation: building	150	
Depreciation: office equipment	45	
Interest	30	
Total expenses		12,570
Net income		$ 3,334

As noted in Chapter 3, we are purposely ignoring income taxes on corporations at this stage of our study. Corporate income taxes are introduced in Chapter 5 and considered more fully in Chapters 12 and 17.

The amounts used in the statement of retained earnings to compute the ending balance of retained earnings can be taken directly from the work sheet. Compare the following statement of retained earnings with amounts shown on the completed work sheet for November. The October 31 balance of $771 in retained earnings, the $3,334 of net income earned in November, and the $1,500 of dividends all appear in the balance sheet columns of the work sheet. Together, these amounts comprise the new ending balance of the Retained Earnings account, $2,605, as shown below:

GREENHILL REAL ESTATE
Statement of Retained Earnings
For the Month Ended November 30, 19__

Net income exceeded dividends

Retained earnings, Oct. 31, 19__	$ 771
Net income for November	3,334
Subtotal	$4,105
Less: Dividends	1,500
Retained earnings, Nov. 30, 19__	$2,605

Finally, the Greenhill balance sheet illustrated for the month of November contains the amounts for assets, liabilities, and capital stock listed in the Balance Sheet columns of the work sheet, along with the new balance of retained earnings.

GREENHILL REAL ESTATE
Balance Sheet
November 30, 19—

Assets

Compare these amounts with figures in Balance Sheet columns of work sheet

Cash		$ 21,740
Accounts receivable		16,990
Management fees receivable		120
Unexpired insurance		550
Office supplies		500
Land		130,000
Building	$ 36,000	
Less: Accumulated depreciation	300	35,700
Office equipment	$ 5,400	
Less: Accumulated depreciation:	90	5,310
Total assets		$210,910

Liabilities & Stockholders' Equity

Liabilities:		
Notes payable		$ 3,000
Accounts payable		23,595
Interest payable		30
Salaries payable		180
Unearned management fees		1,500
Total liabilities		$ 28,305
Stockholders' equity:		
Capital stock	$180,000	
Retained earnings	2,605	182,605
Total liabilities & stockholders' equity		$210,910

Recording adjusting entries in the accounting records. After the financial statements have been compiled from the work sheet at the end of the period, adjusting journal entries are prepared to bring the ledger accounts into agreement with the financial statements. This is an easy step because the adjustments have already been computed on the work sheet. The amounts appearing in the Adjustments columns of the work sheet and the related explanations at the bottom of the work sheet provide all the necessary information for the adjusting entries, as shown in the journal illustration on page 141. These adjusting entries are first entered in the journal and then posted to the ledger accounts.

Recording closing entries. When the financial statements have been prepared, the revenue and expense accounts have served their purpose for the current period and should be closed. These accounts then will have zero balances and will be ready for the recording of revenue and expenses during the next fiscal period. The completed work sheet provides in convenient form all the information needed to make the closing entries.

General Journal   Page 5

Date		Account Titles and Explanation	LP	Debit	Credit
19__					
Nov.	30	Insurance Expense		50	
		Unexpired Insurance			50
		Insurance expense for November.			
	30	Office Supplies Expense		220	
		Office Supplies			220
		Office supplies used during November.			
	30	Depreciation Expense: Building		150	
		Accumulated Depreciation: Building			150
		Depreciation for November			
		($36,000 ÷ 240 = $150).			
	30	Depreciation Expense: Office Equipment		45	
		Accumulated Depreciation: Office			
		Equipment			45
		Depreciation for November			
		($5,400 ÷ 120 =$45).			
	30	Unearned Management Fees		300	
		Management Fees Earned			300
		Earned one-sixth of fee collected in advance for			
		management of the properties owned by John Day.			
	30	Interest Expense		30	
		Interest Payable			30
		Interest expense accrued during November on note			
		payable ($3,000 × 12% × $\frac{1}{12}$).			
	30	Salaries Expense		180	
		Salaries Payable			180
		To record expense and related liability to sales-			
		person for last four evenings' work in November.			
	30	Management Fees Receivable		120	
		Management Fees Earned			120
		To record the receivable and related revenue			
		earned for managing properties owned by Angela			
		Clayton.			

The preparation of closing entries from the work sheet may be summarized as follows:

1 To close the accounts listed in the Income Statement credit column, debit the revenue accounts and credit Income Summary.
2 To close the accounts listed in the Income Statement debit column, debit Income Summary and credit the expense accounts.
3 To close the Income Summary account, transfer the balancing figure in the Income Statement columns of the work sheet ($3,334 in the illustration) to the Retained Earnings account. A profit is transferred by debiting Income Summary and crediting the Retained Earnings account; a loss is transferred by debiting the Retained Earnings account and crediting Income Summary.
4 To close the Dividends account, debit the Retained Earnings account and credit the Dividends account.

The entries to close the revenue and expense accounts, as well as the Dividends account, at November 30 are shown below:

General Journal

Page 6

Date		Account Titles and Explanation	LP	Debit	Credit
19__ Nov.	30	Sales Commissions Earned		15,484	
		Management Fees Earned		420	
		Income Summary			15,904
		To close the revenue accounts.			
	30	Income Summary		12,570	
		Advertising Expense			1,275
		Salaries Expense			9,605
		Telephone Expense			1,195
		Insurance Expense			50
		Office Supplies Expense			220
		Depreciation Expense: Building			150
		Depreciation Expense: Office			
		Equipment			45
		Interest Expense			30
		To close the expense accounts.			
	30	Income Summary		3,334	
		Retained Earnings			3,334
		To close the Income Summary account.			
	30	Retained Earnings		1,500	
		Dividends			1,500
		To close the Dividends account.			

Closing entries derived from work sheet

Work sheets in computer-based systems. Most of the steps involved in the preparation of a work sheet are mechanical and can be performed automatically in a computer-based accounting system. The trial balance, for example, is a listing of the account balances contained in the general ledger. Entering the adjustments, on the other hand, requires human judgment and analysis. Someone familiar with generally accepted accounting principles and with the unrecorded business activities of the company must decide what adjustments are necessary and must then enter the adjustment data. Once the adjustments have been entered, the computer can complete the work sheet by computing adjusted account balances, listing these balances in an adjusted trial balance, and extending the account balances into the income statement and balance sheet columns. Totaling the income statement columns to compute net income also is a mechanical function which can be performed by computer.

Some computer-based accounting systems print out the content of the work sheet as a series of separate schedules, rather than as a single document. These separate schedules include the same information as would be contained in a work sheet — namely, a trial balance, a schedule of adjusting entries, an adjusted trial balance, and financial statements.

The accounting cycle

As stated at the beginning of this chapter, the life of a business is divided into accounting periods of equal length. In each period we repeat a standard sequence of accounting procedures beginning with the journalizing of transactions and concluding with an after-closing trial balance.

Because the work sheet includes the trial balance, the adjusting entries in preliminary form, and an adjusted trial balance, the use of a work sheet will modify the sequence of procedures given in Chapter 3, as follows:

1 Journalize transactions. Analyze business transactions as they occur and record them promptly in the journal.

2 Post to ledger accounts. Transfer debits and credits from journal entries to ledger accounts.

3 Prepare a work sheet. Begin with a trial balance of the ledger, enter all necessary adjustments, compute the adjusted account balances, sort the adjusted balances between income statement accounts and balance sheet accounts, and determine the net income or net loss.

4 Prepare financial statements. Utilize the information in the work sheet to prepare an income statement, a statement of retained earnings, and a balance sheet.

5 Adjust and close the accounts. Using the information in the work sheet as a guide, enter the adjusting entries in the journal. Post these entries to ledger accounts. Prepare and post journal entries to close the revenue and expense accounts into the Income Summary account and to transfer the net income or net loss to the Retained Earnings account. Also prepare and post a journal entry to close the Dividends accounts into the Retained Earnings account.

6 Prepare an after-closing trial balance. Prove that equality of debit and credit balances in the ledger has not been upset by the adjusting and closing procedures.

The above sequence of accounting procedures constitutes a complete accounting process. The regular repetition of this standardized set of procedures in each accounting period is often referred to as the ***accounting cycle.*** The procedures of a complete accounting cycle are illustrated on page 145. The white symbols indicate the accounting procedures; the shaded gray symbols represent accounting records, schedules, and statements.

Note that the preparing of financial statements (Step 4) comes before entering adjusting and closing entries in the journal and posting these entries to the ledger (Step 5). This sequence reflects the fact that ***management wants the financial statements as soon as possible.*** Once the work sheet is complete, all information required for the financial statements is available. Top priority then goes to preparation of the financial statements.

In most business concerns the accounts are closed only once a year; for these companies the accounting cycle is one year in length. For purposes of illustration in a textbook, however, it is often convenient to assume that the entire accounting cycle is performed within the time period of one month. The completion of the accounting cycle is the occasion for preparing financial statements and closing the revenue and expense accounts.

Preparing monthly financial statements without closing the accounts

Many companies which close their accounts only once a year nevertheless prepare *monthly* financial statements for managerial use. These monthly statements are prepared from work sheets, but the adjustments indicated on the work sheets are not entered in the accounting records and no closing entries are made. Under this plan, the time-consuming operation of journalizing and posting adjustments and closing entries is performed only at the end of the fiscal year, but the company has the advantage of monthly financial statements. Monthly and quarterly financial statements are often referred to as ***interim statements,*** because they are in between the year-end statements. The annual or year-end statements are usually audited by a firm of certified public accountants; interim statements are usually unaudited.

Reversing entries

Reversing entries are an optional bookkeeping procedure which may be carried out at year-end to simplify the recording of certain routine cash receipts and cash payments in the following period. As the name suggests, a ***reversing entry*** is the exact reverse of an adjusting entry. It contains the same account titles and dollar amounts as the related adjusting entry, but the debits and credits are the reverse of those in the adjusting entry and the date is the first day of the next accounting period.

Let us use as an example a small company on a five-day work week which pays its employees each Friday. Assume that the payroll is $600 a day or $3,000 for a five-day

ILLUSTRATION OF THE ACCOUNTING CYCLE

*Work sheet contains:
Trial balance
Adjustments
Adjusted trial balance
Income statement
Balance sheet

Daily procedures

Business transactions

Journal

1
Journalize
(analyze and
record)

2
Post to
ledger
accounts

Ledger

3
Prepare
a work
sheet

**Work
sheet***

4
Prepare
financial
statements

**Income
statement**

**Statement
of
retained earnings**

Balance sheet

5
Adjust and
close the
accounts

Journal

6
Prepare
after-closing
trial
balance

Ledger

**After-closing
trial balance**

End-of-period procedures

week. Throughout the year, the company's bookkeeper makes a journal entry each Friday as follows:

Regular weekly entry for payroll

Salaries Expense 3,000
    Cash 3,000
To record payment of salaries for the week.

Next, let us assume that December 31, the last working day of Year 1, falls on Wednesday. All expenses of Year 1 must be recorded before the accounts are closed and financial statements prepared at December 31. Therefore, an adjusting entry must be made to record the salaries expense and the related liability to employees for the three days they have worked since the last payday. The adjusting entry for $1,800 (computed as $3 \times \$600$ daily salary expense) is shown below:

Adjusting entry at end of year

Dec. 31 Salaries Expense 1,800
        Salaries Payable 1,800
     To record salaries expense and the related liability to employees
     for last three days worked in December.

The closing of the accounts on December 31 will reduce the Salaries Expense account to zero, but the liability account, Salaries Payable, will remain open with its $1,800 credit balance at the beginning of the new year. On the next regular payday, Friday, January 2, the company's bookkeeper can record the $3,000 payroll by a debit of $1,800 to Salaries Payable, a debit of $1,200 to Salaries Expense, and a credit of $3,000 to Cash. However, splitting the debit side of the entry in this manner ($1,800 to the liability account and $1,200 to expense) requires more understanding and alertness from the bookkeeper than if the entry were identical with the other 51 payroll entries made during the year.

By making a reversing entry as of the first day of the new accounting period, we can simplify the recording of routine transactions and avoid the need for the company's bookkeeper to refer to prior adjusting entries for guidance. The reversing entry for the $1,800 year-end accrual of salaries would be dated January 1, Year 2, and would probably be made under the direction of the accountant responsible for the year-end closing of the accounts and preparation of financial statements. The entry would be as follows:

Reversing entry makes possible . . .

Jan. 1 Salaries payable 1,800
      Salaries Expense 1,800
    To reverse the accrual of salaries made on Dec. 31, Year 1.

This reversing entry closes the Salaries Payable account by transferring the $1,800 liability to the credit side of the Salaries Expense account. Thus, the Salaries Expense account begins the new year with an abnormal credit balance of $1,800. On Friday, January 2, the normal payroll entry for $3,000 will be made to the same accounts as on every other Friday during the year.

. . . regular payroll entry for first payday of new year

Jan. 2 Salaries Expense 3,000
      Cash 3,000
    Paid salaries for week ended Jan. 2, Year 2.

After this January 2 entry has been posted, the ledger account for Salaries Expense will show a debit balance of $1,200, the result of this $3,000 debit and the $1,800 credit from the reversing entry on January 1. The amount of $1,200 is the correct expense for the two workdays of the new year at $600 a day. The results, of course, are *exactly the same* as if no reversing entry had been used and the company's bookkeeper has split the debit side of the January 2 payroll entry between Salaries Payable and Salaries Expense.

The ledger accounts for Salaries Expense and for Salaries Payable are shown below to illustrate the effect of posting the adjusting entry and the reversing entry.

Salaries Expense			Debit	Credit	Balance
Year 1					
Various	(51 weekly entries of $3,000)				153000
Dec	31	Adjusting entry (3 days @ $600)	1800		154800
	31	To close at year-end		154800	-0-
Year 2					
Jan.	1	Reversing entry		1800	1800 cr
	2	Weekly payroll	3000		1200

Salaries Payable			Debit	Credit	Balance
Year 1					
Dec	31	Adjusting entry (3 days @ $600)		1800	1800
Year 2					
Jan	1	Reversing entry	1800		-0-

Which adjusting entries should be reversed? Even when a company follows a policy of making reversing entries, *not all adjusting entries should be reversed.* Only those adjustments which *create an account receivable or a short-term liability* should be reversed. These adjustments will be followed by cash receipts or cash payments within the near future. Reversing these adjusting entries will enable the company's bookkeeper to record the upcoming cash transactions in a routine manner.

An adjusting entry which apportions an amount recorded in the past *should not be reversed.* Thus we do *not* reverse the adjusting entries which apportion recorded costs (such as depreciation), or which record the earning of revenue collected in advance.

In summary, reversing entries may be made for those adjusting entries which record *unrecorded expenses* or *unrecorded revenue.* Reversing entries are *not* made for adjustments which apportion recorded costs or recorded revenue.

Reversing entries in a computer-based system. Reversing entries do not require any analysis of transactions. Rather, they merely involve reversing the debit and credit amounts of specific adjusting entries. The adjusting entries to be reversed can be identified by a simple rule — namely, reverse those adjustments which increase accounts receivable or short-term liabilities. Thus, a computer may be programmed to prepare reversing entries automatically.

Finally, remember that reversing entries are **optional.** They are intended to simplify the accounting process, but they are **not essential** in the application of generally accepted accounting principles or in the preparation of financial statements.

Key terms introduced or emphasized in chapter 4

Accounting cycle. The sequence of accounting procedures performed during an accounting period. The procedures include journalizing transactions, posting, preparation of a work sheet and financial statements, adjusting and closing the accounts, and preparation of an after-closing trial balance.

Accrued expenses. Expenses such as salaries of employees and interest on notes payable which have been accumulating day-by-day but are unrecorded and unpaid at the end of the period. Also called **unrecorded expenses.**

Accrued revenue. Revenue which has been earned during the accounting period but has not been recorded or collected prior to the closing date. Also called **unrecorded revenue.**

Book value. The net amount at which an asset is shown in accounting records. For depreciable assets, book value equals cost minus accumulated depreciation. Also called **carrying value.**

Carrying value. See book value.

~~**Deferred revenue.**~~ See **unearned revenue.** (Liability)

Interim statements. Financial statements prepared at intervals of less than one year. Usually quarterly and monthly statements.

Asset — **Prepaid expenses.** Advance payments for such expenses as rent and insurance. The portion which has not been used up at the end of the accounting period is included in the balance sheet as an asset.

Promissory note. A formal written promise to repay an amount borrowed plus interest at a future date.

Reversing entries. An optional year-end bookkeeping technique consisting of the reversal on the first day of the new accounting period of those year-end adjusting entries which accrue expenses or revenue and thus will be followed by later cash payments or receipts. Purpose is to permit company personnel to record routine transactions in a standard manner without referring to prior adjusting entries.

Unearned revenue. An obligation to render services or deliver goods in the future because of advance receipt of payment. Also called **deferred revenue.**

Unrecorded expenses. See **accrued expenses.**

Unrecorded revenue. See **accrued revenue.**

Work sheet. A large columnar sheet designed to arrange in convenient form all the accounting data required at the end of the period. Facilitates preparation of financial statements and the work of adjusting and closing the accounts.

Demonstration problem for your review

Reed Geophysical Company adjusts and closes its accounts at the end of the calendar year. At December 31, 198_ the following trial balance was prepared from the ledger.

REED GEOPHYSICAL COMPANY
Trial Balance
December 31, 198_

Cash	$12,540	
Prepaid office rent	8,400	
Prepaid dues and subscriptions	960	
Supplies on hand	1,300	
Equipment	20,000	
Accumulated depreciation: equipment		$ 1,200
Notes payable		5,000
Unearned consulting fees		35,650
Capital stock		10,000
Retained earnings, Jan. 1, 198_		12,950
Dividends	7,000	
Consulting fees earned		15,200
Salaries expense	26,900	
Telephone expense	550	
Miscellaneous expenses	2,350	
	$80,000	$80,000

Other data

(1) On January 1, 198_ the Prepaid Office Rent account had a balance of $2,400, representing the prepaid rent for the months from January to June 198_ inclusive. On July 1, the lease was renewed and office rent for one year at $500 per month was paid in advance.

(2) Dues and subscriptions expired during the year in the total amount of $710.

(3) A count of supplies on hand was made at December 31; the cost of the unused supplies was $450.

(4) The useful life of the equipment has been estimated at 10 years from date of acquisition.

(5) Accrued interest on notes payable amounted to $100 at year-end. Set up a separate Interest Expense account.

(6) Consulting services valued at $32,550 were rendered during the year for clients who had made payment in advance.

It is the custom of the firm to bill clients only when consulting work is completed or, in the case of prolonged engagements, at six-month intervals.

(7) December 31, engineering services valued at $3,000 had been rendered to clients but not yet billed. No advance payments had been received from these clients.

(8) Salaries earned by staff engineers but not yet paid amounted to $200 at December 31.

Instructions. Prepare a work sheet for the year ended December 31, 198_.

Solution to demonstration problem

REED GEOPHYSICAL COMPANY
Work Sheet
For the Year Ended December 31, 198_

	Trial Balance Dr	Trial Balance Cr	Adjustments* Dr	Adjustments* Cr	Adjusted Trial Balance Dr	Adjusted Trial Balance Cr	Income Statement Dr	Income Statement Cr	Balance Sheet Dr	Balance Sheet Cr
Cash	12,540				12,540				12,540	
Prepaid office rent	8,400			(a) 5,400	3,000				3,000	
Prepaid dues and subscriptions	960			(b) 710	250				250	
Supplies on hand	1,300			(c) 850	450				450	
Equipment	20,000				20,000				20,000	
Accumulated depreciation: equipment		1,200		(d) 2,000		3,200				3,200
Notes payable		5,000				5,000				5,000
Unearned consulting fees		35,650	(f) 32,550			3,100				3,100
Capital stock		10,000				10,000				10,000
Retained earnings, Jan. 1, 198_		12,950				12,950				12,950
Dividends	7,000				7,000				7,000	
Consulting fees earned		15,200		(f) 32,550 (g) 3,000		50,750		50,750		
Salaries expense	26,900		(h) 200		27,100		27,100			
Telephone expense	550				550		550			
Miscellaneous expenses	2,350				2,350		2,350			
	80,000	80,000								
Rent expense			(a) 5,400		5,400		5,400			
Dues and subscriptions expense			(b) 710		710		710			
Supplies expense			(c) 850		850		850			
Depreciation expense: equipment			(d) 2,000		2,000		2,000			
Interest expense			(e) 100		100		100			
Interest payable				(e) 100		100				100
Consulting fees receivable			(g) 3,000		3,000				3,000	
Salaries payable				(h) 200		200				200
			44,810	44,810	85,300	85,300	39,060	50,750	46,240	34,550
Net income							11,690			11,690
							50,750	50,750	46,240	46,240

* Adjustments:
(a) Rent expense for year
(b) Dues and subscriptions expense for year
(c) Drafting supplies used for year
(d) Depreciation expense for year
(e) Accrued interest on notes payable
(f) Consulting services performed for clients who paid in advance
(g) Services rendered but not billed
(h) Salaries earned but not paid

Review questions

1 What is the purpose of making adjusting entries? Your answer should relate adjusting entries to the goals of accrual accounting.

2 Do all transactions involving revenue or expenses require adjusting entries at the end of the accounting period? If not, what is the distinguishing characteristic of those transactions which do require adjusting entries?

3 Do adjusting entries affect income statement accounts, balance sheet accounts, or both? Explain.

4 Why does the recording of adjusting entries require a better understanding of the concepts of accrual accounting than does the recording of routine revenue and expense transactions occurring throughout the period?

5 Why does the purchase of a one-year insurance policy four months ago give rise to insurance expense in the current month?

6 If services have been rendered during the current accounting period but no revenue has been recorded and no bill has been sent to the customers, why is an adjusting entry needed? What types of accounts should be debited and credited by this entry?

7 What is meant by the term, **unearned revenue?** Where should an unearned revenue account appear in the financial statements? As the work is done, what happens to the balance of an unearned revenue account?

8 At the end of the current year, the adjusted trial balance of the Midas Company showed the following account balances, among others:

Building, $31,600
Depreciation Expense: Building, $1,580
Accumulated Depreciation: Building, $11,060

Assuming that straight-line depreciation has been used, what length of time do these facts suggest that the Midas Company has owned the building?

9 The weekly payroll for employees of Ryan Company, which works a five-day week, amounts to $5,000. All employees are paid up to date at the close of business each Friday. If December 31 falls on Wednesday, what year-end adjusting entry is needed?

10 The Marvin Company purchased a one-year fire insurance policy on August 1 and debited the entire cost of $540 to Unexpired Insurance. The accounts were not adjusted or closed until the end of the year. Give the adjusting entry at December 31.

11 Office supplies on hand in the Melville Company amounted to $642 at the beginning of the year. During the year additional office supplies were purchased at a cost of $1,561 and charged to the asset account. At the end of the year a physical count showed that supplies on hand amounted to $812. Give the adjusting entry needed at December 31.

12 At year-end the adjusting entry to reduce the Unexpired Insurance account by the amount of insurance premium applicable to the current period was accidentally omitted. Which items in the income statement will be in error? Will these items be overstated or understated? Which items in the balance sheet will be in error? Will they be overstated or understated?

13 What is the purpose of a work sheet?

14 In performing the regular end-of-period accounting procedures, does the preparation of the work sheet precede or follow the posting of adjusting entries to ledger accounts? Why?

15 Assume that when the income statement columns of a work sheet are first totaled, the total of the debit column exceeds the total of the credit column by $60,000. Explain how the amount of net income (or net loss) should be entered in the work sheet columns.

16 Does the ending balance of retained earnings appear in the work sheet? Explain.

17 Can each step in the preparation of a work sheet be performed automatically in a computer-based accounting system? Explain.

18 List in order the procedures comprising the accounting cycle when a work sheet is used.

19 Is a work sheet ever prepared when there is no intention of closing the accounts?

20 The weekly payroll of Stevens Company, which has a five-day work week, amounts to $15,000 and employees are paid up to date every Friday. On January 1 of the current year, the Salaries Expense account showed a credit balance of $9,000. Explain the nature of the accounting entry or entries which probably led to this balance.

21 Four basic types of adjusting entries were discussed in this chapter. If reversing entries are made, which of these types of adjusting entries should be reversed? Why?

Exercises

Ex. 4-1 Armored Transport, Inc., provides armored car services to businesses throughout the city. The company has a one-month accounting period. On June 30, adjusting entries were made to record:

a Depreciation expense for the month.

b Revenue earned during the month which has not yet been billed to customers.

c Salaries payable to company personnel which have accrued since the last payday in June.

d The portion of the company's prepaid insurance policies which has expired during June.

e Earning a portion of the amount collected in advance from Rocky Mountain Bank for armored car services.

f Interest expense that has accrued during June.

Indicate the effect of each of these adjusting entries upon the major elements of the company's financial statements—that is, upon revenue, expenses, net income, assets, liabilities, and owners' equity. Organize your answer in tabular form, using the column headings shown below and the symbols + for increase, − for decrease, and NE for no effect. The answer for adjusting entry (a) is provided as an example.

| Adjusting Entry | Income Statement | | | Balance Sheet | | |
	Revenue	Expenses	Net Income	Assets	Liabilities	Owners' Equity
a	NE	+	−	−	NE	−

Ex. 4-2 The Gamblers, a professional football team, prepare financial statements on a monthly basis. Football season begins in August, but in July the team engaged in the following transactions:

a Paid $1,050,000 to the City of Las Vegas as advance rent for daily use of Las Vegas Stadium for the five-month period from August 1 through December 31. This payment was debited to the asset account, Prepaid Rent.

b Collected $2,080,000 cash from sales of season tickets for the team's eight home games. This amount was credited to Unearned Ticket Revenue.

During the month of August, The Gamblers played one home game and two games on the road. Their record was two wins, one loss.

Instructions. Prepare the two adjusting entries required at August 31 to apportion this recorded cost and recorded revenue.

Ex. 4-3   The law firm of Barlow & Cloud prepares its financial statements on an annual basis at December 31. Among the situations requiring year-end adjusting entries were the following:

    a Salaries to staff attorneys are paid on the fifteenth day of each month. Salaries accrued since December 15 amount to $14,300 and have not yet been recorded.

    b The firm is defending R. H. Dominelli in a civil lawsuit. The agreed upon legal fees are $2,000 per day while the trial is in progress. The trial has been in progress for nine days during December and is not expected to end until late January. No legal fees have yet been billed to Dominelli. (Legal fees are recorded in an account entitled Legal Fees Earned.)

Instructions. Prepare the two adjusting entries required at December 31 to record the accrued salaries expense and the accrued legal fees revenue.

Ex. 4-4   On Friday of each week, Lake Company pays its sales personnel weekly salaries amounting to $60,000 for a five-day work week.

    a Draft the necessary adjusting entry at year-end, assuming that December 31 falls on Wednesday.

    b Also draft the journal entry for the payment by Lake Company of a week's salaries to its sales personnel on Friday, January 2, the first payday of the new year. (Assume that the company does not use reversing entries.)

Ex. 4-5   Hill Corporation adjusts and closes its accounts at the end of the calendar year. Prepare the adjusting entries required at December 31 based on the following information. (Not all of these items may require adjusting entries.)

    a A bank loan had been obtained on September 1. Accrued interest on the loan at December 31 amounts to $4,800. No interest expense has yet been recorded.

    b Depreciation of office equipment is based on an estimated life of five years. The balance in the Office Equipment account is $25,000; no change has occurred in the account during the year.

    c Interest receivable on United States government bonds owned at December 31 amounts to $2,300. This accrued interest revenue has not been recorded.

    d On December 31, an agreement was signed to lease a truck for 12 months beginning January 1 at a rate of 35 cents a mile. Usage is expected to be 2,000 miles per month and the contract specifies a minimum payment equivalent to 18,000 miles a year.

    e The company's policy is to pay all employees up to date each Friday. Since December 31 fell on Monday, there was a liability to employees at December 31 for one day's pay amounting to $2,800.

Ex. 4-6   Among the ledger accounts used by Glenwood Speedway are the following: Prepaid Rent, Rent Expense, Unearned Admissions Revenue, Admissions Revenue, Prepaid Printing, Printing Expense, Concessions Receivable, and Concessions Revenue. For each of the following items, write first the journal entry (if one is needed) to record the external transaction and second the adjusting entry, if any, required on May 31, the end of the fiscal year.

    a On May 1, paid rent for six months beginning May 1 at $25,000 per month.

    b On May 2, sold season tickets for a total of $700,000 cash. The season includes 70 racing days: 20 in May, 25 in June, and 25 in July.

    c On May 4, an agreement was reached with Snack-Bars, Inc., allowing that company to sell refreshments at the track in return for 10% of the gross receipts from refreshment sales.

    d On May 6, schedules for the 20 racing days in May and the first 10 racing days in June were printed and paid for at a cost of $9,000.

e On May 31, Snack-Bars, Inc., reported that the gross receipts from refreshment sales in May had been $145,000 and that the 10% owed to Glenwood Speedway would be remitted on June 10.

Ex. 4-7 The trial balances of Fisher Insurance Agency, as of November 30, 19__, before and after the posting of adjusting entries, are shown below:

	Before Adjustments		After Adjustments	
	Dr	Cr	Dr	Cr
Cash	$ 5,980		$ 5,980	
Commissions receivable			850	
Office supplies	600		240	
Office equipment	6,600		6,600	
Accumulated depreciation: office equipment		$ 2,420		$ 2,530
Accounts payable		1,660		1,660
Salaries payable				550
Unearned commissions		400		190
Capital stock		5,500		5,500
Retained earnings, Oct. 31, 19__		2,300		2,300
Commissions earned		3,900		4,960
Salaries expense	3,000		3,550	
Office supplies expense			360	
Depreciation expense: office equipment ..			110	
	$16,180	$16,180	$17,690	$17,690

Instructions. By comparing the two trial balances shown above, it is possible to determine which accounts have been adjusted. You are to prepare the adjusting journal entries which must have been made to cause these changes in account balances. Include an explanation as part of each adjusting entry.

Ex. 4-8 Milo Company closes its accounts at the end of each calendar year. The company operates on a five-day work week and pays its employees up to date each Friday. The weekly payroll is regularly $5,000. On Wednesday, December 31, Year 1, an adjusting entry was made to accrue $3,000 salaries expense for the three days worked since the last payday. The company *did not* make a reversing entry. On Friday, January 2, Year 2, the regular weekly payroll of $5,000 was paid and recorded by the usual entry debiting Salaries Expense $5,000 and crediting Cash $5,000.

Were Milo Company's accounting records correct for Year 1? For Year 2? Explain two alternatives the company might have followed with respect to payroll at year-end. One of the alternatives should include a reversing entry.

Ex. 4-9 The following amounts are taken from consecutive balance sheets of Raymond Corporation at December 31.

	Year 1	Year 2
Unexpired insurance	$ –0–	$900
Unearned rental revenue	2,000	–0–
Interest payable	100	700

The income statement for Year 2 of the Raymond Corporation shows the following items:

Insurance expense	$ 800
Rental revenue	16,000
Interest expense	1,800

Instructions. Determine the following amounts:

a Cash paid during Year 2 on insurance policies.
b Cash received during Year 2 as rental revenue.
c Cash paid during Year 2 for interest.

Problems

4-1 Adjusting entries (alternative to problem 4-3)

Wind River Motel adjusts and closes its accounts once a year on December 31. Most guests of the motel pay at the time they check out, and the amounts collected are credited to Rental Revenue. A few guests pay in advance for rooms and these amounts are credited to Unearned Rental Revenue at the time of receipt. The following information is available as a source for preparing adjusting entries at December 31.

(a) Salaries earned by employees but not yet paid amount to $10,000.

(b) As of December 31 the motel has earned $5,040 rental revenue from current guests who will not be billed until they are ready to check out. (Debit Rent Receivable.)

(c) On December 16, a suite of rooms was rented to a corporation for six months at a monthly rental of $1,600. The entire six months' rent of $9,600 was collected in advance and credited to Unearned Rental Revenue. At December 31, the amount of $800, representing one-half month's rent, was considered to be earned and the remainder of $8,800 was considered to be unearned.

(d) A one-year bank loan in the amount of $90,000 had been obtained on November 1. No interest has been paid and no interest expense has been recorded. The interest accrued at December 31 is $1,800.

(e) Depreciation on the motel for the year ended December 31 was $43,800.

(f) Depreciation on a station wagon owned by the motel was based on a four-year life. The station wagon had been purchased new on September 1 of the current year at a cost of $9,600. Depreciation for four months should be recorded at December 31.

(g) On December 31, Wind River Motel entered into an agreement to host the National Building Suppliers Convention in June of next year. The motel expects to earn rental revenue of at least $15,000 from the convention.

Instructions. For each of the above lettered paragraphs, draft a separate adjusting journal entry (including explanation), if the information indicates that an adjusting entry is needed. One or more of the above paragraphs may not require any adjusting entry.

4-2   Adjusting entries from trial balance
On January 1, 19___, Linda Kane organized Kane Storage Company for the purpose of leasing a large vacant building and renting space in this building to others for storage of various industrial materials. The accounting policies of the company call for making adjusting entries and closing the accounts each month. Shown below is a trial balance and other information needed one month later in making adjusting entries at January 31.

KANE STORAGE COMPANY
Trial Balance
January 31, 19___

Cash	$ 8,990	
Unexpired insurance	3,000	
Office supplies	405	
Office equipment	12,000	
Notes payable		$ 9,000
Unearned storage fees		1,350
Capital stock		10,000
Storage fees earned		8,800
Rent expense	1,800	
Telephone expense	135	
Salaries expense	2,820	
	$29,150	$29,150

Other data

(a) The monthly insurance expense amounted to $300.
(b) The amount of office supplies on hand, based on a physical count on January 31, was $300, indicating that supplies costing $105 had been used in January.
(c) A $9,000 one-year note payable was signed on January 1. At January 31, accrued interest payable amounted to $90.
(d) The useful life of office equipment was estimated at 8 years.
(e) Certain clients chose to pay several months' storage fees in advance. It was determined that $500 of such fees were still unearned as of January 31 and that $850 had been earned.
(f) Several clients neglected to send in storage fees amounting to $1,330 for the month of January. These amounts have not been recorded but are considered collectible.
(g) Salaries earned by employees but not yet paid amounted to $1,500.

Instructions. Based on the above trial balance and other information, prepare the adjusting entries (with explanations) needed at January 31.

4-3   Adjusting entries (alternative to problem 4-1)
North Rim Lodge maintains its accounting records on the basis of a fiscal year ending June 30. The following information is available as a basis for adjusting entries at June 30, 198_. Prepare a separate adjusting journal entry for each of the eight lettered paragraphs which you believe to require an adjustment.

(a) Depreciation on the buildings for the year ended June 30 amounts to $14,125.
(b) A 12-month fire insurance policy had been purchased on June 1 of the current year. The premium of $3,600 for the entire life of the policy had been paid on June 1 and recorded as Unexpired Insurance. The expense allocable to the year ended June 30 is $300.
(c) A portion of the land owned had been leased on June 16 of the current year to a service station operator at a yearly rental rate of $4,800. One year's rent was collected in advance at the date of the lease and credited to Unearned Rental Revenue. Your adjusting entry should show that one-half of one month's rent has been earned at June 30 and should reduce the Unearned Rental Revenue account accordingly.
(d) A small bus to carry guests to and from the airport had been rented early on June 19 from Truck Service, Inc., at a daily rate of $30. No rental payment has yet been made and no accounting entry has been recorded.
(e) Among the assets owned by North Rim Lodge are government bonds with a face amount of $25,000. Accrued interest receivable on the bonds at June 30 was computed to be $975. This interest has not yet been recorded.
(f) A bank loan in the amount of $100,000 had been obtained on June 1. No interest expense has yet been paid or recorded. Interest expense accrued to June 30 is $1,200.
(g) The company signed an agreement on June 30 of the current year to lease a truck from Hill Motors for a period of one year beginning July 1 at a rate of 20 cents a mile and with a clause providing for a minimum monthly charge of $300. No payment has been made and no entry recorded in the accounting records.
(h) The last regular payday of North Rim Lodge was June 28. Since then, the salaries earned by employees but not paid amount to $3,300.

4-4   Analysis of adjusted data

Island Adventures, Inc., operates a large catamaran which takes tourists at several island resorts on diving and sailing excursions. The company adjusts and closes its accounts at the end of each month. Selected account balances appearing on the June 30 *adjusted* trial balance are as follows:

Prepaid rent	$ 4,500	
Unexpired insurance	900	
Catamaran	42,000	
Accumulated depreciation: catamaran		$7,700
Unearned passenger revenue		180

Other data

(1) Four months' rent had been prepaid on June 1.
(2) The unexpired insurance is a 12-month fire insurance policy purchased on January 1.
(3) The catamaran is being depreciated over a 10-year estimated useful life, with no residual value.
(4) The unearned passenger revenue represents tickets good for future rides sold to a resort hotel for $12 per ticket on June 1. During June, 35 of the tickets were used.

Instructions

a Determine
   (1) The monthly rent expense
   (2) The original cost of the 12-month fire insurance policy
   (3) The age of the catamaran in months
   (4) How many $12 tickets for future rides were sold to the resort hotel on June 1
b Prepare the adjusting entries which were made on June 30.

4-5   Format of a worksheet

Pacific Beach Motor Camp obtains revenue from camping fees and also from a concessionaire who sells refreshments on the premises. The books are closed at the end of each calendar year. At December 31 the data for adjustments were compiled and a work sheet was prepared. The first four columns of the work sheet contained the account balances and adjustments shown below.

	Trial Balance		Adjustments*	
	Dr	Cr	Dr	Cr
Cash	12,400			
Unexpired insurance	2,100			(a) 700
Prepaid advertising	1,000			(b) 300
Land	365,000			
Equipment	48,000			
Accumulated depreciation:				
equipment		8,000		(f) 4,000
Notes payable		86,000		
Unearned revenue from concessions		7,500	(d) 5,000	
Capital stock		250,000		
Retained earnings, Jan. 1, 19__		21,800		
Revenue from camping fees ..		174,500		
Advertising expense	5,600		(b) 300	
Water expense	10,500			
Salaries expense	79,700		(e) 1,100	
Repairs and maintenance expense	17,700			
Miscellaneous expense	5,800			
	547,800	547,800		
Insurance expense			(a) 700	
Interest expense			(c) 400	
Interest payable				(c) 400
Revenue from concessions ...				(d) 5,000
Salaries payable				(e) 1,100
Depreciation expense: equipment			(f) 4,000	
			11,500	11,500

* Adjustments:
(a) $700 insurance expired during year
(b) $300 prepaid advertising expired at end of year
(c) $400 accrued interest expense on notes payable
(d) $5,000 concession revenue earned during year
(e) $1,100 of salaries earned but unpaid at Dec. 31, 19__
(f) $4,000 depreciation expense for year

Instructions. Complete the work sheet by listing the appropriate amounts in the remaining six columns. Follow the format of the work sheet illustrated on page 138.

4-6   Work sheet including adjustments
Southern Cross Flying Service was organized on June 1. The company follows the policy of adjusting and closing its accounts each month. At December 31, after seven months of operating experience, the trial balance below was prepared from the ledger.

SOUTHERN CROSS FLYING SERVICE
Trial Balance
December 31, 19___

Cash	$ 40,500	
Prepaid rent	18,000	
Unexpired insurance	15,600	
Prepaid maintenance service	7,500	
Spare parts	19,000	
Aircraft	270,000	
Accumulated depreciation: aircraft		$ 25,920
Unearned passenger revenue		10,000
Capital stock		300,000
Retained earnings, Nov. 30, 19___		17,730
Dividends	5,000	
Passenger revenue earned		55,350
Fuel expense	4,600	
Salaries expense	27,000	
Advertising expense	1,800	
	$409,000	$409,000

Other data

(a) Monthly rent amounted to $3,000.

(b) Insurance expense for December was $1,300.

(c) All necessary maintenance work was provided by Cook Air Services at a fixed charge of $2,500 a month. Service for three months had been paid for in advance on December 1.

(d) Spare parts used in connection with maintenance work amounted to $2,000 during the month.

(e) Depreciation expense for December was computed to be $8,640.

(f) The Chamber of Commerce purchased 2,000 special price tickets for $20,000. Note that the special price per ticket is $10. Each ticket allowed the holder one flight. During the month 400 of these *special price tickets* had been used. (Credit Passenger Revenue Earned for 400 tickets at $10.)

(g) Salaries earned by employees but not paid at December 31 amounted to $1,100.

Instructions. Prepare a 10-column work sheet for the month ended December 31.

4-7   Work sheet and financial statements
Delphi Bureau performs investigations and prepares financial analyses for business organizations and governmental agencies. Much of its work is done through a computer service center for which

payment is made on an hourly basis. The company adjusts and closes its accounts monthly. At September 30, 19___, the account balances were as follows before adjustments were made.

Cash	$ 71,000	
Research fees receivable	-0-	
Prepaid office rent	28,800	
Prepaid computer rental	42,900	
Office supplies	3,000	
Office equipment	25,200	
Accumulated depreciation: office equipment		$ 600
Notes payable		24,000
Accounts payable		8,000
Interest payable		-0-
Salaries payable		-0-
Unearned research fees		114,000
Capital stock		50,000
Retained earnings, Aug. 31, 19___		44,980
Dividends	12,000	
Research fees earned		15,000
Office salaries expense	5,040	
Research salaries expense	60,000	
Telephone expense	2,640	
Travel expense	6,000	
Office rent expense	-0-	
Computer rent expense	-0-	
Office supplies expense	-0-	
Depreciation expense: office equipment	-0-	
Interest expense	-0-	
	$256,580	$256,580

Other data

(a) The amount in the Prepaid Office Rent account represents office rent at $3,600 a month, paid in advance for eight months on September 1 when the lease was renewed. You are to record the September rent expense.

(b) During September, computer time costing $39,600 was used, leaving a balance of $3,300 in the prepaid account at September 30.

(c) Office supplies **on hand** September 30 were determined by count to amount to $1,000.

(d) Office equipment was estimated to have a useful life of seven years from date of purchase, indicating monthly depreciation of $300. You are to record the September depreciation.

(e) Accrued interest on notes payable amounted to $100 on September 30.

(f) Unearned Research Fees of $80,000 were earned during September by services performed for clients who had made payment in advance.

(g) Fees of $35,000 were earned during September through services to clients who had not paid in advance. These fees had not been billed or recorded. You are to record this revenue at September 30. (Debit Research Fees Receivable.)

(h) Salaries earned by research staff but not paid amounted to $5,000 on September 30.

Instructions

a Prepare a 10-column work sheet for the month ended September 30. All necessary accounts are included in the above trial balance.

b Prepare an income statement, a statement of retained earnings, and a balance sheet in report form.

4-8 End-of-period procedures: a comprehensive problem

A trial balance and supplementary information needed for adjustments at September 30 are shown below for Golden Gate Theater. The company follows a policy of adjusting and closing its accounts at the end of each month.

GOLDEN GATE THEATER
Trial Balance
September 30, 19___

Cash	$ 65,500	
Prepaid advertising	15,500	
Prepaid film rental	65,000	
Land	75,000	
Building	210,000	
Accumulated depreciation: building		$ 4,375
Projection equipment	90,000	
Accumulated depreciation: projection equipment		7,500
Notes payable		37,500
Accounts payable		8,500
Capital stock		250,000
Retained earnings, Aug. 31, 19___		164,750
Dividends	10,000	
Revenue from admissions		87,375
Salaries expense	21,250	
Light and power expense	7,750	
	$560,000	$560,000

Other data

(a) Advertising expense for the month, $9,375, leaving a balance of $6,125 in Prepaid Advertising.

(b) Film rental expense for the month, $42,125.

(c) Depreciation expense on building, $875 per month; on projection equipment, $1,500 per month.

(d) Accrued interest on notes payable, $250.

(e) The company's share of revenue from concessions for September, as reported by concessionaire, $8,125. Check should be received by October 6.

(f) Salaries earned by employees but not paid, $3,750.

Instructions. Prepare

a A work sheet for the month ended September 30.

b An income statement.

c A statement of retained earnings.
d A balance sheet.
e Adjusting and closing entries.

4-9   Reversing entries
Financial Press maintains its accounts on the basis of a fiscal year ending March 31. The company works a five-day week and pays its employees up-to-date each Friday. Weekly salaries have been averaging $15,000. At the fiscal year-end, the following events occurred relating to salaries.

Mar. 28 (Friday) Paid regular weekly salaries of $15,000.
Mar. 31 (Monday) Prepared an adjusting entry for accrued salaries of $3,000.
Apr. 1 (Tuesday) Prepared a reversing entry for accrued salaries.
Apr. 4 (Friday) Paid regular weekly salaries of $15,000.

Instructions

a Prepare journal entries (with explanations) for the four above events relating to salaries.
b How much of the $15,000 in salaries paid on April 4 represents an April expense? Explain.
c Assume that no reversing entry had been made by Financial Press; prepare the journal entry for payment of salaries on April 4.

Cases for analysis

Case 4-1   The accounting cycle in computer-based systems
In Case 2-1, Jim Moore used data base software to design a simple accounting system for use on personal computers. Moore's first system prepared only a balance sheet; he is now ready to design an enhanced system which will perform all of the steps in the accounting cycle and will produce a complete set of financial statements. This enhanced system also will utilize data base software.

The idea underlying data base software is that data intended for a variety of different uses must be entered into the data base only once. The computer can then arrange these data into any number of desired formats. It can also combine data and perform mathematical computations using data in the data base.

In Moore's new accounting system, the computer will arrange the data into the following formats: (1) journal entries (with explanations) for all transactions, (2) three-column running balance ledger accounts, (3) a 10-column work sheet, (4) a complete set of financial statements, (5) journal entries for all adjusting and closing entries, (6) an after-closing trial balance, and (7) reversing entries. As each of these records and statements is prepared, any totals or subtotals in the record are included automatically in the data base. For example, when ledger accounts are updated, the new account balances become part of the data base.

Instructions

In Chapter 4, the steps of the accounting cycle were described as follows: (a) journalize transactions, (b) post to ledger accounts, (c) prepare a work sheet, (d) prepare financial statements, (e) adjust and close the accounts, (f) prepare an after-closing trial balance, and (g) prepare reversing entries. For each step in this cycle, briefly describe the types of data used in performing the step. Indicate whether this data is already contained in the data base, or whether the computer operator must enter data to enable the computer to perform the step.

Case 4-2 Accrual versus cash basis

Sam Reed is interested in buying Foxie's, an aerobic dance studio. He has come to you for help in interpreting the company's financial statements and to seek your advice about purchasing the business.

Foxie's has been in operation for one year. The business is a single proprietorship owned by Pam Austin. Foxie's rents the building in which it operates, as well as all of its exercise equipment. As virtually all of the company's business transactions involve cash receipts or cash payments, Austin has maintained the accounting records on a cash basis. She has prepared the following income statement and balance sheet from these cash basis records at year-end:

Income Statement

Revenue:		
Membership fees	$150,000	
Membership dues	30,000	$180,000
Expenses:		
Rent	$ 18,000	
Wages	52,000	
Advertising	20,000	
Miscellaneous	15,000	105,000
Net income		$ 75,000

Balance Sheet
Assets

Cash	$ 25,000

Liabilities & Owner's Equity

Pam Austin, capital	$ 25,000

Austin is offering to sell Foxie's for the balance of her capital account — $25,000. Reed is very enthusiastic and states, "How can I go wrong? I'll be paying $25,000 to buy $25,000 cash, and I'll be getting a very profitable business which generates large amounts of cash in the deal."

In a meeting with you and Reed, Austin makes the following statement: "This business has been very good to me. In the first year of operations, I've been able to withdraw $50,000 in cash. Yet the business is still quite solvent — it has lots of cash and no debts."

You ask Austin to explain the difference between membership fees and membership dues. She responds, "Foxie's is an exclusive club. We cater only to members. This year, we sold 500 five-year memberships. Each membership requires the customer to pay $300 cash in advance and to pay dues of $10 per month for five years. I credited the advance payments to the Membership Fees account and credited the $10 monthly payments to Membership Dues. Thus, all the revenue is hard cash — no 'paper profits' like you see in so many businesses."

You then inquire as to when these five-year memberships were sold. Austin responds, "On the average, these memberships are only six months old. No members have dropped out, so Foxie's should continue receiving dues from these people for another four and one-half years, thus assuring future profitability. Another beneficial factor is that the company hasn't sold any new memberships in the last several months. Therefore, I think that the company could discontinue its advertising and further increase future profitability."

Instructions

a The financial statements of Foxie's were prepared on the cash basis of accounting, not the accrual basis. Prepare a revised income statement and balance sheet applying the concepts of accrual accounting. Remember that only $\frac{1}{10}$ (or $\frac{6}{60}$) of the customers' advance payments for memberships has been earned as of year-end.

b Assume that none of the 500 members drop out of Foxie's during the next year, and that the business sells no new memberships. What would be the amount of the company's expected cash receipts? Assuming that advertising expense is discontinued but that other expenses remain the same, what would be the expected amount of cash payments for the coming year?

c Use the information in your analysis in parts a and b to draft a letter to Reed advising him on the wisdom of purchasing Foxie's for $25,000. Specifically address the issues of whether the business (1) is profitable, (2) has no debts, and (3) is likely to generate sufficient cash to enable the owner to make large cash withdrawals during the coming year.

Part Two	Merchandising concerns, internal control and accounting systems
Chapter 5	Merchandising transactions and internal control
Chapter 6	Accounting systems: manual and computer-based

This part consists of two chapters. In the first, we explain the accounting concepts applicable to merchandising companies and discuss means of achieving internal control over purchases and sales of merchandise. In the second chapter, we explore some of the ways that an accounting system may be modified to handle efficiently a large volume of transactions.

Chapter 5
Merchandising
transactions
and
internal control

In Chapter 5 our discussion of the accounting cycle is expanded to include merchandising concerns — those businesses that sell goods rather than services. We illustrate various types of merchandising transactions, the computation of net sales and the cost of goods sold, and a work sheet and closing entries for a merchandising company. Both the perpetual and periodic inventory methods are described. After this discussion of inventory, the concepts of classified financial statements are illustrated and explained. Our discussion covers single-step and multiple-step income statements, the presentation of income taxes expense, balance sheet classifications, and the computation of working capital and the current ratio. In addition, this chapter introduces the important topic of internal control, with emphasis upon control procedures relating to purchases and sales of merchandise.

After studying
this chapter you
should be able to:

✓ Account for purchases and sales of merchandise.
✓ Determine the cost of goods sold by the periodic inventory method.
✓ Prepare a work sheet and closing entries for a merchandising company.
✓ Prepare a classified balance sheet and either a single-step or multiple-step income statement.
✓ Explain the purpose of the current ratio and the meaning of working capital.
✓ Explain the nature and importance of a system of internal control.
✓ Explain how purchase orders, invoices, receiving reports, and other business documents can be used to maintain internal control over merchandise transactions.
✓ Explain the advantages of recording purchase invoices by the net price method.

MERCHANDISING COMPANIES

The preceding four chapters have illustrated step by step the complete accounting cycle for businesses rendering personal services. Service-type companies represent an important part of our economy. They include, for example, airlines, railroads, hotels, insurance companies, ski resorts, hospitals, and professional sports teams. These enterprises earn revenue by rendering services to their customers. The net income of a service-type business is equal to the excess of revenue over the operating expenses incurred.

In contrast to the service-type businesses, merchandising companies, both wholesalers and retailers, earn revenue by selling goods or merchandise. The term **merchandise** refers to goods acquired for resale to customers. Selling merchandise introduces a new and major cost of doing business — the cost to the company of the merchandise being resold to customers. This cost is termed the **cost of goods sold** and is so important that it is shown separately from operating expenses in the income statement of a merchandising company. Thus, the net income of a merchandising company is the excess of revenue over the sum of (1) the cost of goods sold and (2) the operating expenses of the business. These relationships are illustrated in the following highly condensed income statement of a merchandising concern.

CORNER STORE

Income Statement

For the Year Ended December 31, 19___

Revenue from sales	$1,000,000
Less: Cost of goods sold	700,000
Gross profit on sales	$ 300,000
Less: Operating expenses	250,000
Net income	$ 50,000

In this simplified example of an income statement, Corner Store sold for $1,000,000 goods which cost $700,000. Thus the store earned a $300,000 gross profit on sales. Operating expenses, such as store rent and salaries, are subtracted from the gross profit to produce net income of $50,000.

Notice that the cost of goods sold is deducted from revenue to arrive at a subtotal called gross profit. If a merchandising business is to succeed or even to survive, it must sell its goods at prices higher than it pays to the vendors or suppliers from whom it buys. Gross profit represents the difference between the selling price of merchandise sold during the period and the cost paid by the business to acquire that merchandise. Management and investors are both interested in the amount of gross profit, because it must exceed the company's operating expenses if the business is to earn any net income. If gross profit is less than the operating expenses, the business will incur a net loss. If the level of gross profit is unsatisfactory, management will consider such actions as changing sales prices or selling a different line of merchandise.

Revenue from sales

Revenue earned by selling merchandise is credited to a revenue account entitled **Sales.** The figure shown in our illustrated income statement, however, is the **net sales** for the accounting period. The term net sales means total sales revenue *minus* sales returns and allowances, and sales discounts. To illustrate this concept, let us now illustrate the revenue section of Corner Store's income statement in greater detail:

CORNER STORE
Partial Income Statement
For the Year Ended December 31, 19__

Revenue from sales:		
Sales		$1,012,000
Less: Sales returns and allowances	$8,000	
Sales discounts	4,000	12,000
Net sales		$1,000,000

The $1,012,000 figure labeled "sales" in the partial income statement is sometimes called *gross sales.* This amount represents the total of both cash and credit sales made during the year. When a business sells merchandise to its customers, it either receives immediate payment in cash or acquires an account receivable to be collected at a later date. Cash sales are rung up on cash registers as the transactions occur. At the end of the day, the total shown on all of the company's cash registers represents total cash sales for the day and is recorded by a journal entry, as follows:

Journal entry for cash sales

Cash	900	
Sales		900
To record the sale of merchandise for cash.		

For a sale of merchandise on credit, a typical journal entry would be:

Journal entry for sale on credit

Accounts Receivable	500	
Sales		500
Sold merchandise on credit to Kay's Gift Shop; payment due within 30 days.		

Sales revenue is earned in the period in which the merchandise is *delivered to the customer,* even though payment may not be received for a month or more after the sale. Consequently, the revenue earned in a given accounting period may differ considerably from the cash receipts of that period.

The amount and trend of sales are watched very closely by management, investors, and others interested in the progress of a company. A rising volume of sales is evidence of growth and suggests the probability of an increase in earnings. A declining trend in sales, on the other hand, is often the first signal of reduced earnings and of financial difficulties ahead. The amount of sales for each year is compared with the sales of the preceding year; the sales of each month may be compared with the sales of the preceding month and also with the corresponding month of the preceding year. These comparisons bring to light significant trends in the volume of sales.

Sales returns and allowances

Most merchandising companies allow customers to obtain a refund by returning merchandise which is found to be unsatisfactory. When customers find that merchandise purchased has minor defects, they may agree to keep such merchandise if an allowance is made on the sales price. Refunds and allowances have the effect of reversing previously recorded sales and reducing the amount of revenue earned by the business. The journal entry to record sales returns and allowances is shown below:

Journal entry for sales returns and allowances

Sales Returns and Allowances 100
    Accounts Receivable (or Cash) 100
Made refund for merchandise returned by customer.

At the end of the accounting period, the amount accumulated in the Sales Returns and Allowances account will be shown in the income statement as a deduction from sales, as illustrated on page 168. Sales Returns and Allowances is a **_contra-revenue_** account.

    Why use a separate Sales Returns and Allowances account rather than recording refunds by directly debiting the Sales account? The answer is that using a separate contra-revenue account enables management to see both the total amount of sales and the amount of sales returns. The relationship between these two amounts gives management an indication of customer satisfaction with the merchandise.

Credit terms

For all sales of merchandise on credit, the terms of payment should be clearly stated, so that buyer and seller can avoid any misunderstanding as to the time and amount of the required payment. One common example of credit terms is "net 30 days" or "n/30," meaning that the net amount of the invoice or bill is due in 30 days. Another common form of credit terms is "10 e.o.m.," meaning payment is due 10 days after the end of the month in which the sale occurred.

Sales discounts

Manufacturers and wholesalers often sell goods on credit terms of 30 to 60 days or more, but offer a discount for earlier payment. For example, the credit terms may be "2% 10 days, net 30 days." These terms mean that the authorized credit period is 30 days, but that the customer company may deduct 2% of the amount of the invoice if it makes payment within 10 days. On the invoice, these terms would appear in the abbreviated form "2/10, n/30"; this expression is read "2, 10, net 30." The 10-day period during which the discount is available is called the **_discount period._** Because a sales discount provides an incentive to the customer to make an early cash payment, it is often referred to as a **_cash discount._**

    For example, assume that Adams Company on November 3 sells merchandise for $1,000 on credit to Zipco, Inc., terms 2/10, n/30. At the time of the sale, the seller does not know if the buyer will take advantage of the discount by paying within the discount period; therefore, Adams Company records the sale at the full price by the following entry:

Nov. 3 Accounts Receivable 1,000
        Sales 1,000
    To record sale to Zipco, Inc., terms 2/10, n/30.

The customer now has a choice between saving $20 by paying within the discount period, or waiting a full 30 days and paying the full price. If Zipco mails its check on or before November 13, it is entitled to deduct 2% of $1,000 or $20, and settle the obligation for $980. If Zipco decides to forgo the discount, it may postpone payment an additional 20 days until December 3 but must then pay $1,000.

Assuming that payment is made by Zipco on November 13, the last day of the discount period, the entry by Adams Company to record collection of the receivable is

Nov. 13	Cash	980	
	Sales Discount	20	
	Accounts Receivable		1,000
	Collected from Zipco, Inc., for our sale of Nov. 3, less 2% cash discount.		

If a customer returns a portion of the merchandise before making payment, the discount applies only to the portion of the goods kept by the customer. In the above example, if Zipco had returned $300 worth of goods out of the $1,000 purchase, the discount would have been applicable only to the $700 portion of the order which the customer kept.

Sales Discounts is a *contra-revenue account.* In the income statement, sales discounts are deducted from gross sales revenue along with any sales returns and allowances. This treatment was illustrated in the partial income statement on page 168.

Cost of goods sold

The cost of the merchandise sold during the year appears in the income statement as a deduction from the net sales of the year. The merchandise which is *available for sale but not sold* during the year constitutes the *inventory* of merchandise on hand at the end of the year. The inventory is included in the year-end balance sheet as an asset.

How can a business determine, at the end of a year, a month, or other accounting period, the quantity and the cost of the goods remaining on hand? How can management determine the cost of the goods sold during the period? These amounts must be determined before either a balance sheet or an income statement can be prepared. In fact, the determination of inventory value and of the cost of goods sold may be the most important single step in measuring the profitability of a business. The two alternative approaches to the determination of inventory and of cost of goods sold are called the *perpetual inventory system* and the *periodic inventory system.*

The perpetual inventory system

Automobile dealers and television stores sell merchandise of *high unit value* and make a relatively small number of sales each day. Because sales transactions are few and of substantial amount, it is easy to look up the cost of the individual automobile or television set being sold. Thus a cost figure can be recorded as the *cost of goods sold* for each sales transaction. Under this system, the records show the cost of each article in stock. Units added to inventory and units removed for delivery to customers are recorded on a daily basis — hence the name *perpetual inventory system.* When financial statements are to be prepared, the total cost of goods sold during the accounting period is easily determined by adding the costs recorded from day to day for the units sold.

The perpetual inventory system will be discussed in Chapter 9; at present we are concentrating upon the *periodic inventory system* used by many companies dealing in merchandise of low unit value.

The periodic inventory system

In a business selling a variety of merchandise with low unit prices, the periodic inventory system may be more suitable than attempting to maintain perpetual inventory records of all items in stock. A business such as a drugstore may sell a customer a bottle of aspirin, a candy bar, and a tube of toothpaste. It is not practicable to look up in the records at the time of each sale the cost of such small items. Instead, stores which deal in merchandise of low unit value usually wait until the end of the accounting period to determine the cost of goods sold. To do this, the store must have information on three things: (1) the beginning inventory, (2) the cost of goods purchased during the period, and (3) the ending inventory or cost of goods unsold and on hand at the end of the period. This information enables the store to compute the cost of goods sold during the period as follows:

Computing cost of goods sold

Inventory of merchandise at beginning of year	$ 50,000
Purchases	250,000
Cost of goods available for sale	$300,000
Less: Inventory at end of year	60,000
Cost of goods sold	$240,000

In this example the store had $50,000 of merchandise at the beginning of the year. During the year it purchased an additional $250,000 worth of merchandise. Thus it had available for sale merchandise costing $300,000. By the end of the year all but $60,000 worth of merchandise had been sold. Consequently, the cost of the goods sold during the year must have been $240,000.

In more general terms, we can say that every merchandising business has *available for sale* during an accounting period the merchandise on hand at the beginning of the period *plus* the mechandise purchased during the period. If all these goods were sold during the period, there would be no ending inventory, and cost of goods sold would be equal to the cost of goods available for sale. Normally, however, some goods remain unsold at the end of the period; *cost of goods sold is then equal to the cost of goods available for sale minus the ending inventory of unsold goods.*

The cost of goods sold is an important concept which requires careful attention. To gain a thorough understanding of this concept, we need to consider the nature of the accounts used in determining the cost of goods sold.

Beginning inventory and ending inventory

An inventory of mechandise consists of the goods on hand and available for sale to customers. The goods on hand at the beginning of an accounting period are called the *beginning inventory;* the goods on hand at the end of the period are called the **ending**

inventory. Since a new accounting period begins as soon as the old one ends, the *ending inventory of one accounting period is the beginning inventory of the following period.*

A business using the periodic inventory system will determine the amount of the ending inventory by taking a physical inventory. Taking inventory includes three steps. First, all items of merchandise in the store and stockrooms are counted; second, the quantity of each item is multiplied by the cost per unit; and third, the costs of the various kinds of merchandise are added together to get a total cost figure for all goods on hand.

The cost figure for ending inventory appears as an asset in the balance sheet and as a deduction in the cost of goods sold section of the income statement. It is brought into the accounting records by *a closing entry debiting Inventory and crediting Income Summary.* (This entry will be illustrated and explained more fully later in this chapter.) After the ending inventory has been recorded in the ledger, the Inventory account remains unchanged throughout the next accounting period. It represents both the ending inventory of the completed accounting period and the beginning inventory of the following period. Keep in mind that the Inventory account is not debited or credited as goods are purchased or sold. The balance in the Inventory account during the year shows the amount of goods which were on hand at the beginning of the present period.

Cost of merchandise purchased for resale

Under the periodic inventory system, the cost of merchandise purchased for resale is recorded by debiting an account called Purchases, as shown below.

Journal entry for purchase of merchandise

Nov. 3 Purchases 10,000
        Accounts Payable 10,000
    Purchased merchandise from ABC Supply Co. Credit terms
    2/10, n/30.

The Purchases account *is used only for merchandise acquired for resale;* assets acquired for use in the business (such as a delivery truck, a typewriter, or office supplies) are recorded by debiting the appropriate asset account, not the Purchases account. The Purchases account does not indicate whether the purchased goods have been sold or are still on hand.

At the end of the accounting period, the balance accumulated in the Purchases account represents the total cost of merchandise purchased during the period. This amount is used in preparing the income statement. The Purchases account has then served its purpose and it is closed to the Income Summary account. Since the Purchases account is closed at the end of each period, it has a zero balance at the beginning of each succeeding period.

Purchase discounts. As explained earlier, manufacturers and wholesalers frequently grant a cash discount to customers who will pay promptly for goods purchased on credit. The selling company regards a cash discount as a *sales discount;* the buying company calls the discount a *purchase discount.*

If the $10,000 purchase of November 3 shown above is paid for on or before November 13, the last day of the discount period, the purchasing company will save 2% of the price of the merchandise, or $200, as shown by the following entry:

Nov. 13   Accounts Payable 10,000
                    Purchase Discounts   200
                    Cash   9,800
            Paid ABC Supply Co. for purchase of Nov. 3, less 2% cash
            discount.

The effect of the discount was to reduce the cost of the merchandise to the buying company. The credit balance of the Purchase Discounts account should therefore be deducted in the income statement from the debit balance of the Purchases account.

If the buying company chooses to postpone payment rather than take the discount, it will have the use of $9,800 for an additional 20 days. However, the extra $200 expense is a high penalty to incur for the use of $9,800 for 20 days. (A 20-day period is approximately $\frac{1}{18}$ of a year; 18 times 2% amounts to 36%.[1]) Although interest rates vary widely, most businesses are able to borrow money from banks at an annual interest rate of 15% or less. Well-managed businesses, therefore, generally pay all invoices within the discount period even though this policy necessitates borrowing from banks in order to have the necessary cash available.

Purchase returns and allowances. When merchandise purchased from suppliers is found to be unsatisfactory, the goods may be returned, or a request may be made for an allowance on the price. A return of goods to the supplier is recorded as follows:

Journal entry for return of goods to supplier

Accounts Payable 1,200
        Purchase Returns and Allowances   1,200
To reduce liability to Jet Supply Co. by the cost of goods returned for credit.

It is preferable to credit Purchase Returns and Allowances when merchandise is returned to a supplier rather than crediting the Purchases account directly. The accounts then show both the total amount of purchases and the amount of purchases which required adjustment or return. Management is interested in the percentage relationship between goods purchased and goods returned, because the returning of merchandise for credit is an expensive, time-consuming process. Excessive returns suggest inefficiency in the operation of the purchasing department and a need to find more dependable suppliers.

The Transportation-in account

The cost of merchandise acquired for resale logically includes any transportation charges necessary to bring the goods to the purchaser's place of business. A separate ledger account is used to accumulate transportation charges on merchandise purchased. The journal entry to record transportation charges on inbound shipments of merchandise is as follows:

Journalizing transportation charges on purchases of merchandise

Transportation-in 125
        Cash (or Accounts Payable)   125
Air freight charges on merchandise purchased from Miller Brothers, Kansas City.

---

[1] A more accurate estimate of interest expense on an annual basis can be obtained as follows: ($200 × 18) ÷ $9800 = 36.7%.

Since transportation charges are part of the **delivered cost** of merchandise purchased, the Transportation-in account is combined with the Purchases account in the income statement to determine the cost of goods available for sale.

Transportation charges on inbound shipments of merchandise must not be confused with transportation charges on outbound shipments of goods to customers. Freight charges and other expenses incurred in making deliveries to customers are regarded as selling expenses; these outlays are debited to a separate account entitled Delivery Expense and are not included in the cost of goods sold.

F.O.B. shipping point and F.O.B. destination

The agreement between the buyer and seller of merchandise includes a provision as to which party shall bear the cost of transporting the goods. The term **F.O.B. shipping point** means that the seller will place the merchandise "free on board" the railroad cars or other means of transport, and that the buyer must pay transportation charges from that point. In most merchandise transactions involving wholesalers or manufacturers, the buyer bears the transportation cost. Sometimes, however, as a matter of convenience, the seller prepays the freight and includes this cost in the amount billed to the buyer.

F.O.B. destination means that the seller agrees to bear the freight cost. If the seller prepays the truckline or other carrier, the agreed terms have been met and no action is required of the buyer other than to pay the agreed purchase price of the goods. If the seller does not prepay the freight, the buyer will pay the carrier and deduct this payment from the amount owed the seller when making payment for the merchandise.

Inventory theft and other losses

Under the periodic inventory system, it is assumed that all goods available for sale during the year are either sold or are on hand at year-end for the ending inventory. As a result of this assumption, the cost of merchandise lost because of shoplifting, employee theft, or spoilage will be included automatically in cost of goods sold. For example, assume that a store has goods available for sale which cost $600,000. Assume that shoplifters steal $10,000 worth of goods and that the ending inventory is $100,000. (If the thefts had not occurred, the ending inventory would have been $10,000 larger.) The cost of goods sold is computed at $500,000 by subtracting the $100,000 ending inventory from the $600,000 cost of goods available for sale. The theft loss is not shown separately in the income statement. In reality, cost of goods **sold** was $490,000, and cost of goods **stolen** was $10,000.

Although the periodic inventory system causes inventory losses to be included automatically in cost of goods sold, accountants have devised a method of estimating losses of merchandise from theft. This method is explained in Chapter 9.

Income statement for a merchandising company

To bring together the various concepts discussed thus far in the chapter, we need to look at a classified income statement for a merchandising business. The income statement of Olympic Sporting Goods shown on the next page has three major sections: (1) a revenue section, (2) a cost of goods sold section, and (3) an operating expenses section. We have already discussed the various accounts used in the first two sections. Note that the amount of **gross profit on sales**, $200,000, is determined by subtracting the cost of goods sold from net sales. If the business is to be successful, the gross profit on sales must be sufficient to cover the operating expenses such as salaries, advertising, and depreciation.

The operating expenses in the third major section of the income statement are classified either as selling expenses or as general and administrative expenses. Selling expenses include all expenses of storing and displaying merchandise for sale, advertising, sales salaries, and delivering goods to customers. General and administrative expenses include the expenses of the general offices, accounting department, personnel office, and credit and collection departments.

OLYMPIC SPORTING GOODS
Income Statement
For the Year Ended December 31, Year 11

This income statement consists of three major sections

Revenue:			
Sales			$506,000
Less: Sales returns and allowances		$ 4,000	
Sales discounts		2,000	6,000
Net sales			$500,000
Cost of goods sold:			
Inventory, Jan. 1		$ 60,000	
Purchases	$300,000		
Less: Purchase returns and allowances	$2,000		
Purchase discounts	1,000	3,000	
Net purchases		$297,000	
Add: Transportation-in		13,000	
Cost of goods purchased			310,000
Cost of goods available for sale			$370,000
Less: Inventory, Dec. 31			70,000
Cost of goods sold			300,000
Gross profit on sales			$200,000
Operating expenses:			
Selling expenses:			
Sales salaries		$ 76,000	
Delivery service		4,000	
Advertising		16,000	
Depreciation		9,000	
Total selling expenses			$105,000
General & administrative expenses:			
Office salaries		$ 60,000	
Telephone		2,000	
Depreciation		8,000	
Total general & administrative expenses			70,000
Total operating expenses			175,000
Income from operations			$ 25,000
Income taxes expense			5,000
Net income			$ 20,000

In many companies certain expenses, such as depreciation of the building, need to be divided, part to selling expense and part to general and administrative expenses. Olympic Sporting Goods divided its $17,000 of depreciation expense by allocating $9,000 to selling expenses and $8,000 to general and administrative expenses. This allocation can conveniently be made when the income statement is prepared from the work sheet; thus no additional ledger accounts are required. The account for Telephone Expense, $2,000, was not divided because management did not consider the amount large enough to warrant such treatment.

Note that the final deduction on the income statement is for income taxes expense. A corporation is a legal entity subject to corporation income tax; consequently, the ledger of a corporation must contain accounts for recording income taxes. No such accounts are needed for a business organized as a single proprietorship or partnership. Income taxes are based on a corporation's earnings and are recorded by an adjusting entry such as the following:

Recording corporate income taxes

Income Taxes Expense 5,000
    Income Taxes Payable 5,000
To record income taxes payable.

The account debited in this entry, Income Taxes Expense, is shown as the last deduction on the income statement to arrive at the "bottom line" figure for net income. The account for Income Taxes Payable is a current liability.

Analyzing the income statement. How does this income statement compare in form and content with the income statement of the service-type business presented in preceding chapters? The most important change is the inclusion of the section entitled Cost of Goods Sold. Note how large the cost of goods sold is in comparison with other figures on the statement. The cost of merchandise sold during the year amounts to $300,000, or 60% of the year's net sales of $500,000. Another way of looking at this relationship is to say that for each dollar the store receives by selling goods to customers, the sum of 60 cents represents a recovery of the cost of the merchandise. This leaves a ***gross profit*** of 40 cents from each sales dollar, out of which the store must pay its operating expenses. In our illustration the operating expenses for the year were $175,000, that is, 35% of the net sales figure of $500,000. Therefore, the gross profit of 40 cents contained in each dollar of sales was enough to cover the operating expenses of 35 cents and leave a pretax income of 5 cents from each dollar of sales. After the deduction of income taxes expense, the net income amounted to $20,000, or 4 cents from each dollar of net sales.

Of course the percentage relationship between sales and cost of goods sold will vary from one type of business to another, but in all types of merchandising companies the cost of goods sold is one of the largest elements in the income statement. Accountants, investors, bankers, and business managers in general have the habit of mentally computing percentage relationships when they look at financial statements. Formation of this habit will be helpful throughout the study of accounting, as well as in many business situations.

In analyzing an income statement, we compare each item in the statement with the amount of net sales. The amount of net sales is regarded as 100%, and every other item or subtotal on the statement is expressed as a percentage of net sales. The cost of goods sold in most types of business will be between 60 and 80% of net sales. Conversely, the **gross profit on sales** (net sales minus cost of goods sold) usually will vary between 40 and 20% of net sales.

Work sheet for a merchandising business

A merchandising company, like the service business discussed in Chapter 4, uses a work sheet at the end of the period to organize the information needed to prepare financial statements and to adjust and close the accounts. The new elements in the work sheet for Olympic Sporting Goods on page 178 are the beginning inventory, the ending inventory, and the other merchandising accounts. The inventory accounts are shown in a distinctive color to help focus your attention on their treatment.

Trial balance columns. The Trial Balance columns were prepared by listing the ledger account balances at December 31, Year 11. Notice that the Inventory account in the Trial Balance debit column shows a balance of $60,000, the cost of merchandise on hand at the end of the prior year. No entries were made in the Inventory account during the current year despite the various purchases and sales of merchandise. The significance of the Inventory account in the trial balance is that it shows the amount of merchandise with which Olympic Sporting Goods began operations on January 1 of the current year.

Adjustments on the work sheet. Only two adjustments were necessary at December 31: one to record depreciation of the building and the other to record the income taxes expense for the year. (The amount of income taxes is given as $5,000. We are not concerned at this point with the procedures for computing income taxes expense.) After these two adjustments were recorded, the Adjustments columns were then totaled to prove the equality of the adjustment debits and credits.

Income Statement columns. The accounts to be carried from the Adjusted Trial Balance columns to the Income Statement columns are the revenue accounts, the cost of goods sold accounts, and the expense accounts.

Recording the ending inventory on the work sheet. The key point to be observed in this work sheet is the method of recording the **ending inventory.** On December 31, a physical inventory was taken of all merchandise on hand. The entire inventory, priced at cost, amounted to $70,000. This ending inventory, dated December 31, does not appear in the trial balance; it is therefore written on the first available line below the trial balance totals. The amount of $70,000 is listed in the Income Statement credit column and also in the Balance Sheet debit column. By entering the ending inventory in the Income Statement **credit** column, we are in effect deducting it from the total of the beginning inventory, the purchases, and the transportation-in, all of which are extended from the adjusted trial balance to the Income Statement **debit** column.

OLYMPIC SPORTING GOODS
Work Sheet
For the Year Ended December 31, Year 11

	Trial Balance Dr	Trial Balance Cr	Adjustments* Dr	Adjustments* Cr	Adjusted Trial Balance Dr	Adjusted Trial Balance Cr	Income Statement Dr	Income Statement Cr	Balance Sheet Dr	Balance Sheet Cr
Cash	19,000				19,000				19,000	
Accounts receivable	25,000				25,000				25,000	
Inventory, Jan. 1	60,000				60,000		60,000			
Land	123,000				123,000				123,000	
Building	120,000				120,000				120,000	
Accumulated depreciation: building		61,000		(a) 17,000		78,000				78,000
Notes payable		20,000				20,000				20,000
Accounts payable		30,000				30,000				30,000
Capital stock		150,000				150,000				150,000
Retained earnings, Dec. 31, Year 10		64,000				64,000				64,000
Dividends	10,000				10,000				10,000	
Sales		506,000				506,000		506,000		
Sales returns and allowances	4,000				4,000		4,000			
Sales discounts	2,000				2,000		2,000			
Purchases	300,000				300,000		300,000			
Purchase returns and allowances		2,000				2,000		2,000		
Purchase discounts		1,000				1,000		1,000		
Transportation-in	13,000				13,000		13,000			
Advertising expense	16,000				16,000		16,000			
Sales salaries	76,000				76,000		76,000			
Office salaries	60,000				60,000		60,000			
Telephone expense	2,000				2,000		2,000			
Delivery service	4,000				4,000		4,000			
	834,000	834,000								
Depreciation expense: building			(a) 17,000		17,000		17,000			
Income taxes expense			(b) 5,000		5,000		5,000			
Income taxes payable				(b) 5,000		5,000				5,000
			22,000	22,000	856,000	856,000				
Inventory, Dec. 31								70,000	70,000	
							559,000	579,000	367,000	347,000
Net income							20,000			20,000
Totals							579,000	579,000	367,000	367,000

Note the treatment of the beginning inventory

Note the treatment of the ending inventory

* Adjustments: (a) Depreciation of building during the year.
 (b) To accrue income taxes.

178

One of the functions of the Income Statement columns is to bring together all the accounts involved in determining the cost of goods sold. The accounts with debit balances are the beginning Inventory, Purchases, and Transportation-in; these accounts total $373,000. Against this total the three credit items of Purchase Returns and Allowances, $2,000, Purchase Discounts, $1,000, and ending Inventory, $70,000, are offset. The three accounts with debit balances exceed in total the three credit balances by an amount of $300,000; this amount is the cost of goods sold, as shown in the income statement on page 175.

The ending inventory is also entered in the Balance Sheet debit column of the work sheet, because this inventory of merchandise on December 31 will appear as an asset in the balance sheet bearing this date.

Completing the work sheet. When all the accounts on the work sheet have been extended into the Income Statement or Balance Sheet columns, the final four columns should be totaled. The net income is computed and the work sheet completed in the same manner as illustrated in Chapter 4 for a service business.

Financial statements

The work to be done at the end of the period is much the same for a merchandising business as for a service-type firm. First, the work sheet is completed; then, financial statements are prepared from the data in the work sheet; next, the adjusting and closing entries are entered in the journal and posted to the ledger accounts; and finally, an after-closing trial balance is prepared.[2] This completes the periodic accounting cycle.

The income statement on page 175 was prepared from the information in the income statement columns of the Olympic Sporting Goods work sheet. The statement of retained earnings and the balance sheet appear below and on the next page. Note that the final amount in the statement of retained earnings also appears in the stockholders' equity section of the balance sheet as the new amount of retained earnings.

OLYMPIC SPORTING GOODS
Statement of Retained Earnings
For the Year Ended December 31, Year 11

Retained earnings, Dec. 31, Year 10	$64,000
Net income for Year 11	20,000
Subtotal	$84,000
Less: Dividends	10,000
Retained earnings, Dec. 31, Year 11	$74,000

---

[2] The journalizing of the two adjusting entries for Olympic Sporting Goods is not illustrated here because these entries are similar to those demonstrated in previous chapters.

OLYMPIC SPORTING GOODS
Balance Sheet
December 31, Year 11

Assets

Cash		$ 19,000
Accounts receivable		25,000
Inventory		70,000
Land		123,000
Building	$120,000	
Less: Accumulated depreciation	78,000	42,000
Total assets		$279,000

Liabilities & Stockholders' Equity

Liabilities:		
Notes payable		$ 20,000
Accounts payable		30,000
Income taxes payable		5,000
Total liabilities		$ 55,000
Stockholders' equity:		
Capital stock	$150,000	
Retained earnings	74,000	224,000
Total liabilities & stockholders' equity		$279,000

Closing entries

The entries used in closing revenue and expense accounts have been explained in preceding chapters. The important new elements in this illustration of closing entries for a trading business are the entries showing the *elimination* of the beginning inventory and the *recording* of the ending inventory. The beginning inventory is cleared out of the Inventory account by a debit to Income Summary and a credit to Inventory. A separate entry could be made for this purpose, but we can save time by making one compound entry which will debit the Income Summary account with the amount of the beginning inventory and with the amounts of all temporary owners' equity accounts having debit balances.

The *temporary owners' equity accounts* are those which appear in the income statement. As the name suggests, the temporary owners' equity accounts are used during the period to accumulate temporarily the increases and decreases in the owners' equity resulting from operation of the business. The entry to close out the beginning inventory and temporary owners' equity accounts with debit balances is illustrated below. (For emphasis, the accounts unique to a merchandising business are shown in black.)

Closing temporary owners' equity accounts with debit balances

Dec. 31	Income Summary	559,000	
	Inventory (Jan. 1)		60,000
	Purchases		300,000
	Sales Returns and Allowances		4,000
	Sales Discounts		2,000
	Transportation-in		13,000
	Advertising Expense		16,000
	Sales Salaries Expense		76,000
	Office Salaries Expense		60,000
	Telephone Expense		2,000
	Delivery Service		4,000
	Depreciation Expense		17,000
	Income Taxes Expense		5,000

To close out the beginning inventory and the temporary owners' equity accounts with debit balances.

The preceding closing entry closes all the operating expense accounts and Income Taxes Expense, as well as the accounts used to accumulate the cost of goods sold. It also closes the accounts for Sales Returns and Allowances and for Sales Discounts. Although the accounts for Sales Returns and Allowances and for Sales Discounts have debit balances, they are not expense accounts. In terms of account classification, they belong in the revenue group of accounts because they are offsets to the Sales account and appear in the income statement as deductions from Sales. After this first closing entry, the Inventory account has a zero balance. Therefore, it is time to record in this account the new inventory of $70,000 determined by count at December 31.

To bring the ending inventory into the accounting records after the stocktaking on December 31, we could make a separate entry debiting Inventory and crediting the Income Summary account. It is more convenient, however, to combine this step with the closing of the Sales account and any other temporary proprietorship accounts having credit balances, as illustrated in the following closing entry:

Closing temporary proprietorship accounts with credit balances

Dec. 31	Inventory (Dec. 31)	70,000	
	Sales	506,000	
	Purchase Returns and Allowances	2,000	
	Purchase Discounts	1,000	
	Income Summary		579,000

To record the ending inventory and to close all temporary owners' equity accounts with credit balances.

The remaining closing entries serve to transfer the balance of the Income Summary account to the Retained Earnings account and to close the Dividends account, as follows:

Closing Income Summary account and Dividends account

Dec. 31	Income Summary	20,000	
	Retained Earnings		20,000

To close the Income Summary account.

31	Retained Earnings	10,000	
	Dividends		10,000

To close the Dividends account.

After the preceding four closing entries have been posted to the ledger, the only accounts left with dollar balances will be balance sheet accounts. An after-closing trial balance should be prepared to prove that the ledger is in balance after the year-end entries to adjust and close the accounts.

Sales taxes

Sales taxes are levied by many states and cities on retail sales. Sales taxes actually are imposed upon the consumer, not upon the seller. However, the seller must collect the tax, file tax returns at times specified by law, and remit the taxes collected on all reported sales.

For cash sales, sales tax is collected when the sale is made. For credit sales, the sales tax is included in the amount charged to the customer's account. The liability to the governmental unit for sales taxes may be recorded at the time the sale is made as follows:

Sales tax recorded at time of sale

Accounts Receivable (or Cash)	1,050	
Sales Tax Payable		50
Sales		1,000

To record sale of $1,000 subject to 5% sales tax.

This approach requires a separate credit entry to the Sales Tax Payable account for each sale. At first glance, this may seem to require an excessive amount of bookkeeping. However, today's electronic cash registers can be programmed to automatically record the sales tax liability at the time of each sale.

Instead of recording the sales tax liability at the time of sale, some businesses prefer to credit the Sales account with the entire amount collected, including the sales tax, and to make an adjustment at the end of each period to reflect sales tax payable. For example, suppose that the total recorded sales for the period under this method were $315,000. Since the Sales account includes both the sales price and the sales tax (say, 5%), it is apparent that $315,000 is 105% of the actual sales figure. Actual sales are $300,000 ($315,000 ÷ 1.05) and the amount of sales tax due is $15,000. (Proof: 5% of $300,000 = $15,000.) The entry to record the liability for sales taxes would be

Sales tax recorded as adjustment of sales

Sales	15,000	
Sales Tax Payable		15,000

To remove sales taxes of 5% on $300,000 of sales from the Sales account, and reflect as a liability.

This second approach is widely used in businesses which do not use electronic devices for recording each sales transaction.

Sales of certain products, such as food and cigarettes, are exempt from sales tax. If some of the products being sold are not subject to sales tax, the business must keep separate records of taxable and nontaxable sales.

Classified financial statements

The financial statements illustrated up to this point have been rather short and simple because of the limited number of accounts used in these introductory chapters. Now let us look briefly at a more comprehensive balance sheet for a merchandising business.

In the balance sheet of Skymart Corporation illustrated below, the assets are classified into three groups: (1) current assets, (2) plant and equipment, and (3) other assets. The liabilities are classified into two types: (1) current liabilities and (2) long-term liabilities. This classification of assets and liabilities is virtually a standard one throughout American business.

SKYMART CORPORATION
Balance Sheet
December 31, 19____

Assets

Current assets:			
Cash			$ 145,000
U.S. government bonds			100,000
Notes receivable			124,000
Accounts receivable			261,000
Inventory			352,000
Prepaid expenses			12,000
Total current assets			$ 994,000
Plant and equipment:			
Land		$100,000	
Building	$240,000		
Less: Accumulated depreciation	19,200	220,800	
Store equipment	$ 94,000		
Less: Accumulated depreciation	18,800	75,200	
Delivery equipment	$ 28,000		
Less: Accumulated depreciation	7,000	21,000	
Total plant and equipment			417,000
Other assets:			
Land (future building site)			165,000
Total assets			$1,576,000

Liabilities & Stockholders' Equity

Current liabilities:		
Notes payable		$ 115,000
Accounts payable		180,400
Income taxes payable		20,000
Accrued expenses payable		10,000
Unearned revenue		5,100
Total current liabilities		$ 330,500
Long-term liabilities:		
Mortgage payable (due in 10 years)		250,000
Total liabilities		$ 580,500
Stockholders' equity:		
Capital stock	$600,000	
Retained earnings	395,500	995,500
Total liabilities & stockholders' equity		$1,576,000

The purpose of balance sheet classification

The purpose underlying a standard classification of assets and liabilities is to aid management, owners, creditors, and other interested persons in understanding the financial position of the business. Bankers, for example, would have a difficult time in reading the balance sheets of all the companies which apply to them for loans, if each of these companies followed its own individual whims as to the sequence and arrangement of accounts comprising its balance sheet. Standard practices as to the order and arrangement of a balance sheet are an important means of saving the time of the reader and of giving a fuller comprehension of the company's financial position. Some of the major balance sheet classifications are discussed briefly in the following section.

Current assets. Current assets include cash, government bonds and other marketable securities, receivables, inventories, and prepaid expenses. To qualify for inclusion in the current asset category, an asset must be capable of being converted into cash within a relatively short period without interfering with the normal operation of the business. The period is usually one year, but it may be longer for those businesses having an operating cycle in excess of one year.

The term *operating cycle* means the average time period between the purchase of merchandise and the conversion of this merchandise back into cash. The series of transactions comprising a complete cycle often runs as follows: (1) purchase of merchandise, (2) sale of the merchandise on credit, (3) collection of the account receivable from the customer. The word *cycle* suggests the circular flow of capital from cash to inventory to receivables to cash again. This cycle of transactions in a merchandising business is portrayed in the following diagram:

The operating cycle repeats continuously

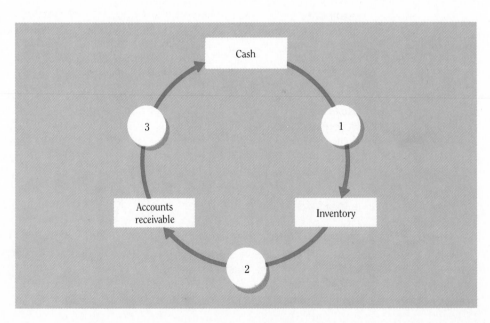

In a business handling fast-moving merchandise (a supermarket, for example) the operating cycle may be completed in a few weeks; for most merchandising businesses the operating cycle requires several months but less than a year.

The sequence in which current assets are listed depends upon their liquidity; the closer an asset is to becoming cash the higher is its liquidity. The total amount of a company's current assets and the relative amount of each type give some indication of the company's short-run, debt-paying ability.

Current liabilities. Liabilities that must be paid within one year or the operating cycle (whichever is longer) are called *current liabilities.* Among the more common types of current liabilities are notes payable, accounts payable, taxes payable, salaries payable, interest payable, and unearned revenue. Notes payable are usually listed first, followed by accounts payable; any sequence of listing is acceptable for other current liabilities.

Settlement of most types of current liabilities requires writing a check to the creditor; in other words, use of the current asset cash. A somewhat different procedure for settlement is followed for the current liability of unearned revenue. As explained in Chapter 4, unearned revenue is a liability which arises when money is received from customers in advance for goods or services to be delivered in the future. To meet such obligations usually will require using up current assets either through delivering merchandise to the customer or making payments to employees or others to provide the agreed services.

The key point to recognize is the relationship between current liabilities and current assets. Current liabilities must be paid in the near future and current assets must be available to make these payments. Comparison of the amount of current liabilities with the amount of current assets is an important step in appraising the ability of a company to pay its debts in the near future.

Current ratio. Many bankers and other users of financial statements believe that for a business to qualify as a good credit risk, the total current assets should be about twice as large as the total current liabilities. In studying a balance sheet, a banker or other creditor will compute the *current ratio* by dividing total current assets by total current liabilities. The current ratio is a convenient measure of the short-run debt-paying ability of a business.

In the illustrated balance sheet of Skymart Corporation the current assets of $994,000 are approximately three times as great as the current liabilities of $330,500; the current ratio is therefore 3 to 1, which would generally be regarded as a very strong current position. The current assets could shrink by two-thirds and still be sufficient for payment of the current liabilities. Although a strong current ratio is desirable, an extremely high current ratio (such as 4 to 1 or more) may signify that a company is holding too much of its resources in cash, accounts receivable, and other current assets and is not pursuing opportunities for growth as aggressively as it might.

Working capital. The excess of current assets over current liabilities is called *working capital;* the relative amount of working capital is another indication of short-term financial strength. In the illustrated balance sheet of Skymart Corporation, working capital is $663,500, computed by subtracting the current liabilities of $330,500 from the current assets of $994,000. The importance of solvency (ability to meet debts as they fall due) was emphasized in Chapter 1. Ample working capital permits a company to buy merchandise in large lots, to carry an adequate stock of goods, and to sell goods to customers on favorable credit terms. Many companies have been forced to suspend business because of inadequate working capital, even though total assets were much larger than total liabilities.

Classification and format of income statements

There are two common forms of income statements: the **multiple-step income statement** and the **single-step income statement.** The multiple-step statement is more convenient in illustrating accounting principles and has been used consistently in our illustrations thus far. The income statement for Olympic Sporting Goods on page 175 is in multiple-step form. It is also a **classified** income statement because the various items of expense are classified into significant groups. The single-step form of income statement is illustrated on page 187.

Multiple-step income statement. The multiple-step income statement is so named because of the **series of steps** in which costs and expenses are deducted from revenue. As a first step, the cost of goods sold is subtracted from net sales to produce an amount for **gross profit** on sales. As a second step, operating expenses are deducted to obtain a subtotal term **income from operations** (or **operating income**). As a final step, income taxes expense is subtracted to determine net income. The multiple-step income statement is noted for its numerous sections and significant subtotals. It is widely used by small businesses.

The operating expenses of Olympic Sporting Goods were classified into two categories: selling expenses and general and administrative expenses. These classifications aid management in controlling expenses by emphasizing that certain expenses are the responsibility of sales executives and that other expenses relate to the business as a whole. Of course, many small companies are not organized into departments; consequently they do not subdivide operating expenses on the income statement.

Income taxes are not included among operating expenses because income taxes do not help to produce operating revenue (sales). Other examples of nonoperating expenses include interest expense and losses on sales of investments. Nonoperating expenses appear in a final section of the income statement after the figure showing **income from operations.** Any nonoperating revenue, such as interest earned and gains on sales of investments, also should be listed in this final section of the income statement.

Single-step income statement. The income statements prepared by large corporations for distribution to thousands of stockholders often are greatly condensed because the public presumably is more interested in a concise report than in the details of operations. The **single-step** form of income statement takes its name from the fact that the total of all expenses (including the cost of goods sold) is deducted from total revenue in a single step. All types of revenue, such as sales, interest earned, and rent revenue, are added together to show the total revenue. Then all expenses are grouped together and deducted in one step without the use of subtotals. A condensed income statement in single-step form is shown below for National Corporation, a large merchandising company.

NATIONAL CORPORATION
Income Statement
For the Year Ended December 31, 19__

Condensed single-step income statement

Revenue:

Net sales		$90,000,000
Interest earned		1,800,000
Total revenue		$91,800,000

Expenses:

Cost of goods sold	$60,000,000	
Selling expenses	14,400,000	
General & administrative expenses	9,750,000	
Income taxes expense	3,150,000	
Total expenses		87,300,000
Net income		$ 4,500,000

Use of the single-step income statement has increased in recent years, perhaps because it is relatively simple and easy to read. A disadvantage of this format is that useful concepts such as the gross profit on sales are not readily apparent.

THE SYSTEM OF INTERNAL CONTROL

The meaning of internal control

In this section we shall round out our discussion of a merchandising business by considering the *system of internal control* by which management maintains control over the purchasing, receiving, storing, and selling of merchandise. Strong internal controls are needed not only for purchases and sales transactions, but for all other types of transactions as well. In fact, the concept of internal control affects all the assets of a business, all liabilities, the revenue and expenses, and every aspect of operations. The purpose of internal control is to provide assurance that the entire business operates in accordance with management's plans and policies.

As defined in Chapter 1, the system of internal control includes all the measures taken by an organization for the purpose of (1) protecting its resources against waste, fraud, and inefficiency; (2) ensuring accuracy and reliability in accounting and operating data; (3) securing compliance with company policies; and (4) evaluating the level of performance in all divisions of the company.

Many people think of internal control as a means of safeguarding cash and preventing fraud. Although internal control is an important factor in protecting assets and preventing fraud, this is only a part of its role. Remember that business decisions are based on accounting data: and the system of internal control provides assurance of the *dependability of the accounting data used in making decisions.*

The decisions made by management are communicated throughout the organization and become company policy. The results of the policies — the consequences of managerial decisions — must be reported back to management so that the soundness of company policies can be evaluated. Among the means of communication included in the system of internal control are organization charts, manuals of accounting policies and procedures, flow charts, financial forecasts, purchase orders, receiving reports, invoices, and many other documents. The term **documentation** refers to all the charts, forms, reports, and other business papers that guide and describe the working of a company's system of accounting and internal control.

Administrative controls and accounting controls. Internal controls fall into two major classes: administrative controls and accounting controls. **Administrative controls** are measures that increase operational efficiency and compliance with policies in all parts of the organization. For example, an administrative control may be a requirement that traveling salespersons submit reports showing the number of calls made on customers each day. Another example is a directive requiring airline pilots to have regular medical examinations. These internal administrative controls have no direct bearing on the reliability of the financial statements. Consequently, administrative controls are not of direct interest to accountants and independent auditors.

Internal accounting controls are measures that relate to protection of assets and to the reliability of accounting and financial reports. An example is the requirement that a person whose duties involve handling cash shall not also maintain accounting records. More broadly stated, the accounting function must be kept separate from the custody of assets. Another **accounting control** is the requirement that checks, purchase orders, and other documents be serially numbered. Still another example is the rule that a person who orders merchandise and supplies should not be the one to receive them and should not sign checks to pay for them.

Strong internal control now required by law

Some American corporations in past years made payments to foreign officials which could have been interpreted as bribes. These payments in many cases were legal under the laws of the countries in which they were made, although they were not in conformity with American business ethics. The top executives of the corporations involved sometimes were not aware that these questionable transactions were taking place.

To put an end to such practices, the United States Congress passed the Foreign Corrupt Practices Act. This act requires every publicly owned corporation in the United States to maintain a system of internal control sufficient to provide reasonable assurance that transactions are executed only with the knowledge and authorization of management. The system of internal control also must limit the use of corporate assets to those purposes approved by management. Finally, the act requires that accounting records of assets be compared at reasonable intervals with the assets actually on hand. Thus a strong system of internal control, long recognized as vital to the operation of a large business, is now required by federal law.

GUIDELINES TO STRONG INTERNAL CONTROL

Organization plan to establish responsibility for every function

An organization plan should indicate clearly the departments or persons responsible for such functions as purchasing, receiving incoming shipments, maintaining accounting records, approving credit to customers, and preparing the payroll. When an individual or department is assigned responsibility for a function, authority to make decisions should also be granted. The lines of authority and responsibility can be shown on an organization chart, as illustrated on the next page.

Control of transactions

If management is to direct the activities of a business according to plan, every transaction should go through four steps: It should be *authorized, approved, executed*, and *recorded*. For example, consider the sale of merchandise on credit. The top management of the company may *authorize* the sale of merchandise on credit to customers who meet certain standards. The manager of the credit and collection department may *approve* a sale of given dollar amount to a particular customer. The sales transaction is *executed* by preparing a sales invoice and delivering the merchandise to the credit customer. The sales transaction is *recorded* in the accounting department by debiting Accounts Receivable and crediting Sales.

Consider for a moment the losses that would probably be incurred if this internal control of transactions did not exist. Assume, for example, that all employees in a store were free to sell on credit any amount of merchandise to any customer, and responsibility for recording the sales transactions was not fixed on any one person or department. The result no doubt would be many unrecorded sales; of those sales transactions that were recorded, many would represent uncollectible receivables.

Subdivision of duties strengthens internal control

The subdivision of duties within a company should be designed so that *no one person or department handles a transaction completely from beginning to end.* When duties are divided in this manner, the work of one employee serves to verify that of another and any errors which occur tend to be detected promptly.

To illustrate the development of internal control through subdivision of duties, let us review the procedures for a sale of merchandise on account by a wholesaler. The sales department of the company is responsible for securing the order from the customer; the credit department must approve the customer's credit before the order is filled; the stock room assembles the goods ordered; the shipping department packs and ships the goods; and the accounting department records the transaction. Each department receives written evidence of the action of the other departments and reviews the documents describing the transaction to see that the actions taken correspond in all details. The shipping department, for instance, does not release the merchandise until after the credit department has approved the customer as a credit risk. The accounting department does not record the sale until it has received documentary evidence that (1) the goods were ordered, (2) the extension of credit was approved, and (3) the merchandise was shipped to the customer.

Accounting function separate from custody of assets. An employee who has custody of an asset or access to an asset should not maintain the accounting record of that asset. The person having custody of an asset will not be inclined to waste it, steal it, or give it away if he or she is aware that another employee is maintaining a record of the asset. The employee maintaining the accounting record does not have access to the asset and

PORTION OF AN ORGANIZATION CHART

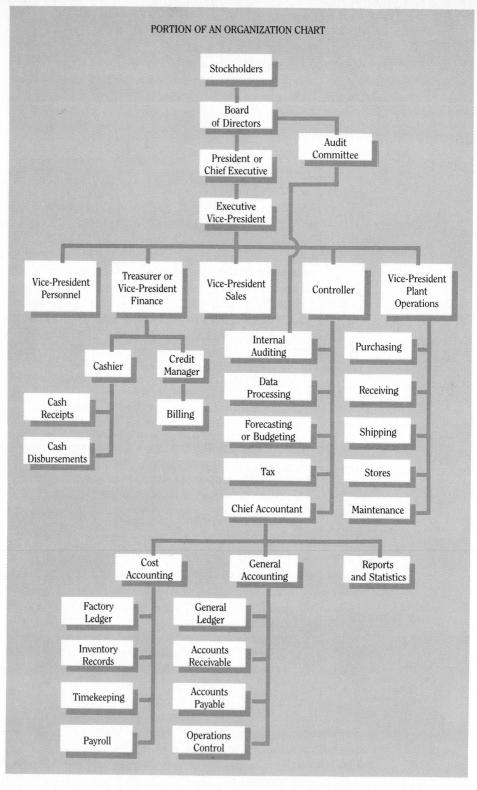

therefore has no incentive to falsify the record. If one person has custody of assets and also maintains the accounting records, there is both opportunity and incentive to falsify the records to conceal a shortage. The diagram that follows illustrates how separation of duties creates strong internal control.

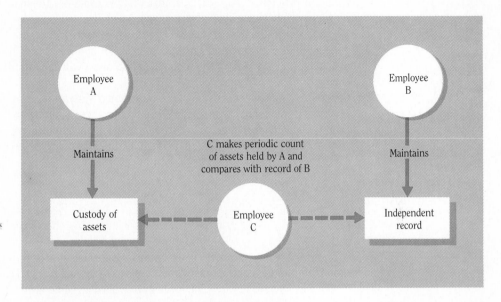

In this diagram Employee A has custody of assets and Employee B maintains an accounting record of the assets. Employee C periodically counts the assets and compares the count with the record maintained by B. This comparison should reveal any errors made by either A or B unless the two have collaborated to conceal an error or irregularity.

Prevention of fraud. If one employee is permitted to handle all aspects of a transaction, the danger of fraud is increased. Studies of fraud cases suggest that many individuals may be tempted into dishonest acts if given complete control of company property. Most of these persons, however, would not engage in fraud if doing so required collaboration with another employee. Losses through employee dishonesty occur in a variety of ways: merchandise may be stolen; payments by customers may be withheld; suppliers may be overpaid with a view to kickbacks to employees; and lower prices may be allowed to favored customers. The opportunities for fraud are almost endless if all aspects of a sale or purchase transaction are concentrated in the hands of one employee.

Specfic methods of achieving internal control

Among the more important internal control devices are the following:

1 *Internal auditing.* Virtually every large organization has an internal auditing staff. The internal auditors study both administrative controls and accounting controls in all units of the organization and prepare reports to top management on their findings.

2 *Financial forecasts.* A plan of operations is prepared each year setting goals for each division of the business, as, for example, the expected volume of sales, amounts of expenses, and future cash balances. Actual results are compared with forecasted amounts month by month. This comparison strengthens actual controls because variations from planned results are investigated promptly and may reveal accounting errors or other breakdowns in company policies.

3 *Serially numbered documents.* The printer should include serial numbers on such documents as checks, purchase orders, and sales invoices. If a document is misplaced or concealed, the break in the sequence of numbers will call attention to the discrepancy.

4 *Competent personnel.* Even the best-designed system of internal control will not work well unless the people using it are competent. Competence and integrity of employees are in part developed through training programs, but they also are related to the policies for selection of personnel, the adequacy of supervision, and the complexity of the system.

Limitations and cost of internal control

Although internal control is highly effective in increasing the reliability of accounting data and in protecting against fraud, no system of internal control is foolproof. Two or more dishonest employees working in collusion can defeat the system — temporarily. Carelessness by employees and misunderstanding of instructions can cause a breakdown in controls. Finally, the question of cost of controls cannot be ignored. Too elaborate a system of internal control may entail greater expense than is justified by the protection gained. For this reason, a system of internal control must be tailored to meet the needs of an individual business.

INTERNAL CONTROLS OVER THE PURCHASE AND SALE OF MERCHANDISE

Business documents and procedures

Carefully designed business documents and procedures for using them are necessary to ensure that all transactions are properly authorized, approved, executed, and recorded. Some of the more important of these business documents and the procedures related to them are shown in the following table:

Business Document	Initiated by	Sent to
Purchase requisition Issued when quantity of goods on hand falls below established reorder point	Departmental sales managers or inventory control department	Purchasing department
Purchase order Specifies prices, quantities, and method of transportation	Purchasing department	Original to selling company (vendor, supplier), copies to buyer's accounting, receiving, and finance departments

Business Document	Initiated by	Sent to
Invoice Confirms that goods have been shipped and requests payment	Seller (supplier)	Accounting department of buying company
Receiving report Based on count and inspection of goods received	Receiving department of buying company	Original to accounting department, copies to purchasing department and to department requisitioning goods
Invoice approval form	Accounting department of buying company	Finance department, to support issuance of check. Returned to accounting department with carbon copy of check

Purchase orders

In many businesses and especially in large organizations, the buying company uses its own purchase order forms. A purchase order of Fairway Pro Shop issued to Adams Manufacturing Company is illustrated below.

Serially numbered purchase order

PURCHASE ORDER   Order No. 999

FAIRWAY PRO SHOP
10 Fairway Avenue, San Francisco, California

To: Adams Manufacturing Company   Date Nov. 10, 19—

19 Union Street   Ship via Jones Truck Co.

Kansas City, Missouri   Terms: 2/10, n/30

Please enter our order for the following:

Quantity	Description	Price	Total
15 sets	Model S irons	$120.00	$1,800.00
50 dozen	X3Y Shur-Par golf balls	14.00	700.00

Fairway Pro Shop

By *D. D. McCarthy*

Several copies of a purchase order are usually prepared. The original is sent to the supplier; it constitutes an authorization to deliver the merchandise and to submit a bill based on the prices listed.

The issuance of a purchase order does not call for any entries in the accounting records of either the prospective buyer or seller. The company which receives an order does not consider that a sale has been made *until the merchandise is delivered.* At that point ownership of the goods changes, and both buyer and seller should make entries to record the transaction.

Invoices

When a manufacturer or wholesaler receives an order for its products, it takes two actions. One is to ship the goods to the customer and the other is to send the customer an invoice. By the act of shipping the merchandise, the seller is giving up ownership of one type of asset, inventory; by issuing the invoice the seller is recording ownership of another form of asset, an account receivable.

An invoice contains a description of the goods being sold, the quantities, prices, credit terms, and method of shipment. The illustration below shows an invoice issued by Adams Manufacturing Company in response to the previously illustrated purchase order from Fairway Pro Shop.

Invoice is basis for accounting entry

INVOICE

ADAMS MANUFACTURING COMPANY
19 Union Street
Kansas City, Missouri

Sold to: Fairway Pro Shop   Invoice no. 782

          10 Fairway Avenue   Invoice date Nov. 15, 19__

          San Francisco, Calif.   Your order no. 999

Shipped to Same   Date shipped Nov. 15, 19__

Terms 2/10, n/30   Shipped via Jones Truck Co.

Quantity	Description	Price	Amount
15 sets	Model S irons	$120.00	$1,800.00
50 dozen	X3Y Shur-Par golf balls	14.00	700.00
			$2,500.00

From the viewpoint of the seller, an invoice is a *sales invoice;* from the buyer's viewpoint it is a *purchase invoice.* The invoice is the basis for an entry in the accounting records of both the seller and the buyer because it evidences the transfer of ownership of goods. At the time of issuing the invoice, the selling company makes an entry debiting Accounts Receivable and crediting Sales. The buying company however, does not record the invoice as a liability until after verifying the following aspects of the transaction:

1 The invoice agrees with the purchase order as to prices, quantities, and other provisions.
2 The invoice is arithmetically correct in all extensions of price times quantity and in the addition of amounts.
3 The goods covered by the invoice have been received and are in satisfactory condition.

Evidence that the merchandise has been received in good condition must be obtained from the receiving department. It is the function of the receiving department to receive all incoming goods, to inspect them as to quality and condition, and to determine the quantities received by counting, measuring, or weighing. The receiving department should prepare a serially numbered report for each shipment received; one copy of this *receiving report* is sent to the accounting department for use in verifying the invoice.

The verification of the invoice in the accounting department is accomplished by comparing the purchase order, the invoice, and the receiving report. Comparison of these documents establishes that the merchandise described in the invoice was actually ordered, has been received in good condition, and was billed at the prices specified in the purchase order.

When these verification procedures have been completed, the invoice is recorded as a liability by an entry debiting the Purchases account and crediting Accounts Payable.

Debit and credit memoranda (debit memos, credit memos)

If merchandise purchased on account is unsatisfactory and is to be returned to the supplier (or if a price reduction is agreed upon), a *debit memorandum* may be prepared by the purchasing company and sent to the supplier. The debit memorandum informs the supplier that his or her account is being debited (reduced) by the buyer and explains the circumstances.

The supplier upon being informed of the return of damaged merchandise (or having agreed to a reduction in price) will issue a *credit memorandum* as evidence that the account receivable from the purchaser is being credited (reduced) by the supplier.

Notice that issuing a credit memorandum has the same effect upon a customer's account as does receiving payment from the customer — that is, the account receivable is credited (reduced). Thus, it is important that an employee with authority to issue credit memoranda *not be allowed to handle cash receipts from customers.* If both of these duties were assigned to the same employee, that person could abstract some of the cash collected from customers and conceal this theft by issuing credit memoranda.

Recording purchase invoices at net price

Most well-managed companies have a firm policy of taking all purchase discounts offered. The recording of purchase invoices at their gross amount and making payment of a reduced amount within the discount period was described earlier in this chapter. Some companies which regularly take advantage of all available purchase discounts prefer the alternative method of recording purchase invoices at the **net amount** after discount rather than at the gross amount. If the amount which the buyer intends to pay is the invoice amount minus a cash discount, why not record this net amount as the liability at the time the invoice is received? For example, if Fairway Pro Shop receives a $10,000 purchase invoice from Gator Sportswear bearing terms of 2/10, n/30, the entry could be

Entry for purchase: net price method

Nov. 3	Purchases	9,800	
	Accounts Payable		9,800
	To record purchase invoice from Gator Sportswear less 2% cash discount available.		

Assuming that the invoice is paid within 10 days, the entry for the payment is as follows:

Entry for payment: net price method

Nov. 13	Accounts Payable	9,800	
	Cash		9,800
	To record payment of $10,000 invoice from Gator Sportswear less 2% cash discount.		

Through oversight or carelessness, the purchasing company occasionally may fail to make payment of an invoice within the 10-day discount period. If such a delay occurred in paying the invoice from Gator Sportswear, the full amount of the invoice would have to be paid rather than the recorded liability of $9,800. The journal entry to record the late payment on, say, December 3, is as follows:

Entry for payment after discount period: net price method

Dec. 3	Accounts Payable	9,800	
	Purchase Discounts Lost	200	
	Cash		10,000
	To record payment of invoice and loss of discount by delaying payment beyond the discount period.		

Under this method the cost of goods purchased is properly recorded at $9,800, and the additional payment of $200 caused by failure to pay the invoice promptly is placed in a special expense account designed to attract the attention of management. The gross price method of recording invoices described earlier in this chapter shows the amount of purchase discounts **taken** each period; the **net price method** now under discussion shows the amount of purchase discounts **lost** each period. The latter method has the advantage of drawing the attention of management to a breakdown in internal control. The fact that a purchase discount has been taken does not require attention by management, but a discount **lost** because of inefficiency in processing accounts payable does call for managerial investigation.

Under the net price method, inefficiency and delay in paying invoices is not concealed by including the lost discounts in the cost of merchandise purchased. The purchases are stated at the net price available if all discounts had been taken; any purchase discounts lost are shown separately in the income statement as an operating expense.

Key terms introduced or emphasized in chapter 5

Beginning inventory. Goods on hand and available for sale to customers at the beginning of the accounting period.

Cash discount. A reduction in price (usually 2% or less) offered by manufacturers and wholesalers to encourage customers to pay invoices within a specified discount period.

Cost of goods sold. A computation appearing as a separate section of an income statement showing the cost of goods sold during the period. Computed by adding net delivered cost of merchandise purchases to beginning inventory to obtain cost of goods available for sale, and then deducting from this total the amount of the ending inventory. Usually equal to between 60 and 80% of net sales.

Credit memorandum. A document issued to show a reduction in the amount owed by a customer because of goods returned, a defect in the goods or services provided, or an error.

Current assets. Cash and other assets that can be converted into cash within one year or the operating cycle (whichever is longer) without interfering with the normal operation of the business.

Current ratio. Current assets divided by current liabilities. A measure of short-run debt-paying ability.

Ending inventory. Goods still on hand and available for sale to customers at the end of the accounting period.

Financial forecast. A plan of operations for a future period with expected results expressed in dollars.

Fraud. Dishonest acts intended to deceive, often involving the theft of assets and falsification of accounting records and financial statements.

Gross profit on sales. Net sales minus cost of goods sold.

Internal auditing. An activity carried on in large organizations by a professional staff to investigate and evaluate the system of internal control on a year-round basis. Also to evaluate the efficiency of individual departments within the organization.

Internal control. All measures used by a business to guard against errors, waste, or fraud and to assure the reliability of accounting data. Designed to aid in the efficient operation of a business and to encourage compliance with company policies.

Inventory (merchandise). Goods acquired and held for sale to customers.

Invoice. An itemized statement of goods being bought or sold. Shows quantities, prices, and credit terms. Serves as the basis for an entry in the accounting records of both seller and buyer because it evidences the transfer of ownership of goods.

Multiple-step income statement. An income statement in which cost of goods sold and expenses are subtracted from revenue in a series of steps, thus producing significant subtotals prior to net income.

Net price method. A policy of recording purchase invoices at amounts net of (reduced by) cash discounts.

Net sales. Gross sales revenue minus sales returns and allowances and minus sales discounts.

Operating cycle. The average time period from the purchase of merchandise to its sale and conversion back into cash.

Periodic inventory system. A system of accounting for merchandise in which inventory at the balance sheet date is determined by counting and pricing the goods on hand. Cost of goods sold is computed by subtracting the ending inventory from the cost of goods available for sale.

Perpetual inventory system. A system of accounting for merchandise that provides a continuous record showing the quantity and cost of all goods on hand.

Physical inventory. The process of counting and pricing the merchandise on hand at a given date, usually the end of the accounting period.

Purchase order. A serially numbered document sent by the purchasing department of a business to a supplier or vendor for the purpose of ordering materials or services.

Purchases. An account used under the periodic inventory system to record the cost of merchandise purchased for resale to customers.

Receiving report. An internal form prepared by the receiving department for each incoming shipment showing the quantity and condition of goods received.

Single-step income statement. An income statement in which the cost of goods sold and all expenses are combined and deducted from total revenue in a single step to determine net income.

Working capital. Current assets minus current liabilities. Another measure of short-run debt-paying ability.

Demonstration problem for your review

Village Supply completed the following merchandising transactions during May. The company's policy calls for taking advantage of all cash discounts available to it from suppliers; purchase invoices are recorded at the *net amount.* In making sales, the company grants credit terms of 2/10, n/30, and strictly enforces the 10-day limitation. The amounts listed as cash sales below are net of sales discounts.

May   3 Sold merchandise to Rich Company for cash, $32,880.

May 16 Sold merchandise on account to Riverside Company, $14,820.

May 16 Purchased merchandise from Hilton Supply Company, $18,900; terms 2/10, n/30 (to be recorded at the net amount).

May 17 Paid transportation charges on goods received from Hilton Supply Company, $726.

May 18 Issued credit memorandum no. 102 to Riverside Company for allowance on damaged goods, $420.

May 24 Purchased merchandise from Pete Construction Co., $17,100; terms 1/10, n/30 (to be recorded at the net amount).

May 25 Returned defective goods with invoice price of $900 to Pete Construction Co., accompanied by debit memorandum no. 122.

May 26 Received cash from Riverside Company in full payment of account.

May 26 Paid Hilton Supply Company account in full.

Instructions

a Journalize the above transactions, recording purchase invoices at the net amount.

b Prepare a partial multiple-step income statement for May showing sales and cost of goods sold (in detail), and gross profit on sales. Assume the inventory at April 30 to be $11,400 and the inventory at May 31 to be $13,920.

c What is the amount of accounts payable at May 31? What would be the amount of accounts payable at May 31 if the company followed a policy of recording purchase invoices at the gross amount?

Solution to demonstration problem

General Journal

May 3	Cash	32,880	
	Sales		32,880
	To record the sale of merchandise for cash.		
16	Accounts Receivable	14,820	
	Sales		14,820
	To record sale to Riverside Company		
16	Purchases	18,522	
	Accounts Payable		18,522
	To record $18,900 purchase invoice from Hilton Supply Company less 2% cash discount available (terms 2/10, n/30).		
17	Transportation-in	726	
	Cash		726
	Paid transportation charges on goods purchased from Hilton Supply Company.		
18	Sales Returns & Allowances	420	
	Accounts Receivable		420
	Issue credit memo no. 102 to customer, Riverside Company for damaged goods.		
24	Purchases	16,929	
	Accounts Payable		16,929
	To record $17,100 purchase invoice from Pete Construction Co., less 1% cash discount available (terms 1/10, n/30).		
25	Accounts Payable	891	
	Purchase Returns & Allowances		891
	To reduce liability to Pete Construction Co., for net amount of defective goods returned. Invoice price $900 − 1% discount = $891 recorded liability. Debit memo no. 122.		
26	Cash	14,112	
	Sales Discount	288	
	Accounts Receivable		14,400
	Collected from Riverside Company for our May 16 sale, $14,820 − return of $420 and 2% discount on balance of $14,400.		
26	Accounts Payable	18,522	
	Cash		18,522
	Paid $18,900 purchase invoice from Hilton Supply Company less 2% discount.		

b

VILLAGE SUPPLY
Partial Income Statement
For the Month Ended May 31, 19—

Gross sales			$47,700
Less: Sales returns & allowances		$ 420	
Sales discounts		288	708
Net sales			$46,992
Cost of goods sold:			
Inventory, Apr. 30, 19—		$11,400	
Purchases	$35,451		
Transportation-in	726		
Delivered cost of purchases	$36,177		
Less: Purchase returns & allowances	891		
Net purchases		35,286	
Cost of goods available for sale		$46,686	
Less: Inventory, May 31, 19—		13,920	
Cost of goods sold			32,766
Gross profit on sales			$14,226

c Accounts payable (net), $16,038; accounts payable (gross), $16,200. Computed as $16,038 ÷ .99 = $16,200, or $17,100 purchase − $900 return = $16,200.

Review questions

1 During the current year, Green Bay Company made all sales of merchandise at prices in excess of cost. Will the business necessarily report a net income for the year? Explain.

2 The income statement for Stereo West showed gross profit on sales of $144,000, operating expenses of $130,000, and cost of goods sold of $216,000. What was the amount of net sales?

3 Valley Mart during its first year of operations had cost of goods sold of $480,000 and a gross profit equal to 40% of net sales. What was the dollar amount of net sales for the year?

4 Is the normal balance of the Sales Returns and Allowances account a debit or a credit? Is the normal balance of the Purchase Returns and Allowances account a debit or a credit?

5 Supply the proper terms to complete the following statements:
   a Net sales − cost of goods sold = ?
   b Beginning inventory + purchases − purchase returns and allowances − purchase discounts + transportation-in = ?
   c Cost of goods sold + ending inventory = ?
   d Cost of goods sold + gross profit on sales = ?
   e Net income + operating expenses = ?

6 During the current year, Davis Corporation purchased merchandise costing $200,000. State the cost of goods sold under each of the following alternative assumptions:
   a No beginning inventory; ending inventory $40,000

    b Beginning inventory $60,000; no ending inventory

    c Beginning inventory $58,000; ending inventory $78,000

    d Beginning inventory $90,000; ending inventory $67,000

7 Zenith Company uses the periodic inventory system and maintains its accounting records on a calendar-year basis. Does the beginning or the ending inventory figure appear in the trial balance prepared from the ledger on December 31?

8 Compute the amount of cost of goods sold, given the following account balances: beginning inventory $40,000, purchases $84,000, purchase returns and allowances $4,500, purchase discounts $1,500, transportation-in $1,000, and ending inventory $36,000.

9 In which columns of the work sheet for a merchandising company does the ending inventory appear?

10 State briefly the difference between the **perpetual** inventory system and the **periodic** inventory system.

11 When the periodic inventory method is in use, how is the amount of inventory determined at the end of the period?

12 What is the purpose of a closing entry consisting of a debit to the Income Summary account and a credit to the Inventory account?

13 Tireco is a retail store in a state that imposes a 5% sales tax. Would you expect to find an account entitled Sales Tax Expense and another account entitled Sales Tax Payable in Tireco's ledger? Explain your answer.

14 Explain the terms **current assets, current liabilities,** and **current ratio.**

15 Madison Corporation has current assets of $540,000 and current liabilities of $300,000. Compute the current ratio and the amount of working capital.

16 Barnes Imports has a current ratio of 3 to 1 and working capital of $60,000. What are the amounts of current assets and current liabilities?

17 What is the purpose of a system of internal control? List four specific objectives which the measures included in a system of internal control are designed to achieve.

18 Suggest a control device to protect a business against the loss or nondelivery of invoices, purchase orders, and other documents which are routed from one department to another.

19 Criticize the following statement: "In our company we get things done by requiring that a person who initiates a transaction follow it through in all particulars. For example, an employee who issues a purchase order is held responsible for inspecting the merchandise upon arrival, approving the invoice, and preparing the check in payment of the purchase. If any error is made, we know definitely whom to blame."

20 Explain why the operations and custodianship functions should be separate from the accounting function.

21 A system of internal control is often said to include two major types of controls: administrative controls and accounting controls. Explain the nature of each group and give an example of each.

22 How does a single-step income statement differ from the multiple-step income statement?

23 Company A sells merchandise to B on credit and two days later agrees that B can return a portion of the merchandise. B does so. What document should Company A issue to record the return? What accounts on Company A's records are affected by this return of merchandise?

24 Name three documents (business papers) which are needed by the accounting department to verify that a purchase of merchandise has occurred and that payment of the related liability should be made.

25 Why should authority to issue credit memoranda relating to accounts receivable from customers not be given to an employee who handles cash collections from these customers? Explain.

Exercises

Ex. 5-1   Hudson Company sold merchandise to River Company for $6,000; terms 2/10, n/30. River Company paid for the merchandise within the discount period. Both companies record invoices at the gross amounts.

   a Give the journal entries by Hudson Company to record the sale and the subsequent collection.
   b Give the journal entries by River Company to record the purchase and the subsequent payment. Assume the account payable is recorded at the **gross** amount.

Ex. 5-2   Some of the items in the income statement of Traders' Market are listed below.

Net sales	$400,000
Gross profit on sales	160,000
Beginning inventory	30,000
Purchase discounts	1,000
Purchase returns & allowances	4,000
Transportation-in	6,000
Operating expenses	80,000
Purchases	250,000

Use the appropriate items from this list as a basis for computing (a) the cost of goods sold, (b) the cost of goods available for sale, and (c) the ending inventory.

Ex. 5-3   This exercise stresses the sequence and relationship of items in a multiple-step income statement for a merchandising business. Each of the five horizontal rows in the table represents a separate set of income statement items. You are to copy the table and fill in the missing amounts. A net loss in the right-hand column is to be indicated by placing brackets before and after the amount, as for example, in line e (25,000).

	Net Sales	Beginning Inventory	Net Purchases	Ending Inventory	Cost of Goods Sold	Gross Profit	Expenses	Net Income or (Loss)
a	200,000	54,000	130,000	44,000	?	60,000	70,000	?
b	500,000	60,000	340,000	?	330,000	?	?	25,000
c	600,000	120,000	?	85,000	390,000	210,000	165,000	?
d	800,000	?	500,000	150,000	?	260,000	205,000	?
e	?	230,000	?	255,000	660,000	240,000	?	(25,000)

Ex. 5-4   The accountant for Village Ski Shop prepared a work sheet at December 31, Year 5. Shown below are the Income Statement columns from that work sheet. Dividends declared by the company during Year 5 amounted to $22,000. Using this information, prepare four separate journal entries to close the accounts at December 31. Use the sequence of closing entries illustrated in this chapter.

	Income Statement	
	Debit	Credit
Inventory, Dec. 31, Year 4	90,000	
Sales		420,350
Sales returns & allowances	8,700	
Sales discounts	2,650	
Purchases	275,000	
Purchase returns & allowances		3,200
Purchase discounts		5,100
Transportation-in	4,300	
Selling expenses	48,000	
General and administrative expenses ....:...............	36,000	
Income taxes expense	7,000	
Inventory, Dec. 31, Year 5		81,000
	471,650	509,650
Net income	38,000	
	509,650	509,650

Ex. 5-5   Use the data from the Village Ski Shop work sheet in Exercise 5-4 to prepare:

a A multiple-step income statement in as much detail as the work sheet data will allow.

b A single-step income statement in condensed form. "Condensed form" means that net sales and the cost of goods sold will each be shown as a single amount, without showing the individual account balances which are used to compute these subtotals.

Ex. 5-6   The Hasagami General Store operates in an area in which a 6% sales tax is levied on all products handled by the store. On cash sales, the salesclerks include the sales tax in the amount collected from the customer and ring up the entire amount on the cash register without recording separately the tax liability. On credit sales, the customer is charged for the list price of the merchandise plus 6%, and the entire amount is debited to Accounts Receivable and credited to the Sales account. On sales of less than one dollar, the tax collected is rounded to the nearest cent.

Sales tax must be remitted to the government quarterly. At March 31 the Sales account showed a balance of $161,650 for the three-month period ended March 31.

a What amount of sales tax is owed at March 31?

b Give the journal entry to record the sales tax liability on the books.

Ex. 5-7   The balance sheet of Hunt Company contained the following items, among others:

Cash	$ 39,600
Accounts receivable	158,000
Inventory	206,400
Store equipment (net)	192,000
Other assets	28,800

Mortgage payable (due in 3 years)	48,000
Notes payable (due in 10 days)	19,200
Accounts payable	142,400
Bob Hunt, capital	220,800

Instructions

a From the above information compute the amount of current assets and the amount of current liabilities.

b How much working capital does Hunt Company have?

c Compute the current ratio.

Ex. 5-8   Sylvia Cole, president of Cole Sportswear, a merchandising business, explains to you how duties have been assigned to employees. Cole states: "In order to have clearly defined responsibility for each phase of our operations, I have made one employee responsible for the purchasing, receiving, and storage of merchandise. Another employee has been charged with responsibility for maintaining the accounting records and for making all collections from customers. I have assigned to a third employee responsibility for maintaining personnel records for all our employees and for timekeeping, preparation of payroll records, and distribution of payroll checks. My goal in setting up this organization plan is to have a strong system of internal control."

You are to evaluate Cole's plan of organization and explain fully the reasoning underlying any criticism you may have.

Ex. 5-9   Taft Company received purchase invoices during July totaling $44,000, all of which carried credit terms of 2/10, n/30. It was the company's regular policy to take advantage of all available cash discounts, but because of employee vacations during July, there was confusion and delay in making payments to suppliers, and none of the July invoices was paid within the discount period.

a What was the amount of the additional cost incurred by Taft Company as a result of the company's failure to take the available purchase discounts?

b Explain briefly two alternative ways in which the amount of Taft Company's purchases might be presented in the July income statement.

c What method of recording purchase invoices can you suggest that would call to the attention of the Taft Company management the inefficiency of operations in July?

Problems

5-1   Journal entries for merchandising transactions

Runners' World deals in a wide variety of low-priced merchandise and uses the periodic inventory system. Purchases are recorded at the full (gross) invoice price. Shown below is a partial list of transactions occurring during May.

May 2 Purchased merchandise (running shoes) on credit from MinuteMan Shoes, $9,600. Terms, 2/10, n/30.

May 3 Paid freight charges of $45 on the shipment of merchandise purchased from MinuteMan Shoes.

May 4 Upon unpacking the shipment from MinuteMan, discovered that some of the shoes were the wrong style. Returned these shoes, which cost $400, to MinuteMan and received full credit.

May 9 Sold merchandise on account to Desert Spa Hotel, $4,100. Terms, 2/10, n/30.

May 11 Paid $22 freight charges on the outbound shipment to Desert Spa Hotel.

May 12 Paid MinuteMan Shoes within the discount period the remaining amount owed for the May 2 purchase, after allowing for the purchase return on May 4.

May 16 Sold merchandise on account to Holiday Sportswear, $2,755. Terms, 2/10, n/30.

May 19 Received check from Desert Spa Hotel within the discount period in full settlement of the May 9 sale.

May 21 Holiday Sportswear returned $650 of the merchandise it had purchased on May 16. Runners' World has a policy of accepting all merchandise returns within 30 days of the date of sale without question. Full credit was given to Holiday for the returned merchandise.

Instructions. Prepare journal entries to record each of these transactions in the accounting records of Runners' World. Include a written explanation for each journal entry.

5-2 Condensed income statement and closing entries

The following accounts relate to the income of Leather Bandit for the three-month period ended March 31, 198X:

Sales	$250,000	Transportation-in	$ 1,700
Sales returns & allowances	5,000	Inventory, Jan. 1, 198X	97,000
Sales discounts	3,700	Inventory, Mar. 31, 198X	102,700
Purchases	160,000	Operating expenses	72,400
Purchase returns & allowances	2,500	Income taxes expense	3,400
Purchase discounts	3,200		

Instructions

a Compute the amount of net sales for the three-month period.

b Compute the cost of goods sold.

c Prepare a **condensed** multiple-step income statement. Show both net sales and the cost of goods sold as "one-line items," without showing the accounts used to compute these amounts. Income taxes expense should be shown after determining income from operations.

d Prepare closing entries for the three-month period ended March 31. Only three closing entries are required, as the company did not declare any dividends during the period.

5-3 Work sheet and closing entries

Westport Landing is a small company maintaining its accounts on a calendar-year basis and using a periodic inventory system. A four-column schedule consisting of the first four columns of a 10-column work sheet appears on the next page.

WESTPORT LANDING
Work Sheet
For the Year Ended December 31, 19___

	Trial Balance		Adjustments	
	Debit	Credit	Debit	Credit
Cash	7,600			
Accounts receivable	19,500			
Inventory, Jan. 1	60,000			
Prepaid rent	4,400			
Equipment	22,000			
Accumulated depreciation:				
equipment		5,700		(a) 1,900
Accounts payable		20,400		
Capital stock		60,000		
Retained earnings		28,400		
Dividends	20,000			
Sales		529,000		
Sales returns & allowances	21,000			
Sales discounts	8,000			
Purchases	368,000			
Purchase returns & allowances ..		18,000		
Purchase discounts		6,000		
Transportation-in	12,000			
Advertising expense	32,000			
Rent expense	25,000			
Salaries expense	68,000			
	667,500	667,500		
Depreciation expense			(a) 1,900	
Income taxes expense			(b) 3,400	
Income taxes payable				(b) 3,400
			5,300	5,300

The completed Adjustments columns have been included in the work sheet to minimize the detail work involved. These adjustments were derived from the following information available at December 31.

(*a*) Depreciation expense for the year on store equipment, $1,900.
(*b*) Income taxes, $3,400.

A physical inventory taken at December 31 showed the ending inventory to be $66,000.

Instructions

a Prepare a 10-column work sheet following the format illustrated on page 178. Include at the bottom of the work sheet a legend consisting of a brief explanation keyed to each adjusting entry.

b Prepare the two journal entries to adjust the accounts at December 31.

c Prepare the necessary journal entries to close the accounts on December 31. (*Suggestion:* Use four separate closing entries. The first entry may be used to close the beginning inventory and all nominal accounts having debit balances; the second entry to record the ending inventory and to close nominal accounts having credit balances; the third entry to close the Income Summary account; and the fourth entry to close the Dividends account.)

5-4   Detailed income statement and closing entries

Mitsui Electronics, a small merchandising business, uses a periodic inventory system and maintains its accounts on a calendar-year basis. The adjusted trial balance of Mitsui Electronics, after all necessary adjustments had been made, appeared as shown below.

MITSUI ELECTRONICS
Adjusted Trial Balance
December 31, 198X

Cash	$ 32,000	
Accounts receivable	77,000	
Inventory, Jan. 1	86,000	
Prepaid insurance	2,700	
Office supplies	3,000	
Furniture & fixtures	40,600	
Accumulated depreciation: furniture & fixtures		$ 3,600
Notes payable		10,000
Accounts payable		64,900
Income taxes payable		10,300
Capital stock		100,000
Retained earnings		57,900
Dividends	30,000	
Sales		880,000
Sales returns & allowances	11,000	
Sales discounts	2,000	
Purchases	575,000	
Purchase returns & allowances		2,600
Purchase discounts		2,400
Transportation-in	30,000	
Sales salaries expense	100,000	
Advertising expense	32,000	
Rent expense	24,000	
Depreciation expense: furniture & fixtures	4,800	
Office salaries expense	64,000	
Office supplies expense	3,400	
Insurance expense	2,400	
Telephone expense	1,500	
Income taxes expense	10,300	
Totals	$1,131,700	$1,131,700

The inventory on December 31, as determined by count, amounted to $108,000.

Instructions

a Prepare a multiple-step income statement for Mitsui Electronics. Use the format illustrated on page 175. Divide operating expenses into two groups: (1) selling expenses and (2) general and administrative expenses. The company allocates rent expense and depreciation expense 75% to selling expense and 25% to general and administrative expense. Insurance expense and telephone expense are considered to be too small to require allocation and are to be classified under general and administrative expenses.

b Prepare the four journal entries required to close the accounts at December 31. Use the sequence of closing entries illustrated in this chapter.

5-5   End-of-period procedures; a comprehensive problem
The trial balance below was prepared from the ledger of Delta Traders at December 31. The company maintains its accounts on a calendar-year basis and closes the accounts only once a year. The periodic inventory system is in use.

DELTA TRADERS
Trial Balance
December 31, 19__

Cash	$ 20,000	
Accounts receivable	76,000	
Inventory, Jan. 1	160,000	
Unexpired insurance	4,000	
Office supplies	1,800	
Land	35,000	
Buildings	100,000	
Accumulated depreciation: buildings		$ 20,000
Notes payable		80,000
Accounts payable		60,000
Capital stock		100,000
Retained earnings		94,800
Dividends	26,000	
Sales		658,000
Sales returns and allowances	42,000	
Sales discounts	16,000	
Purchases	431,000	
Purchase returns and allowances		23,000
Purchase discounts		8,000
Transportation-in	10,000	
Advertising expense	5,000	
Salaries expense	110,000	
Utilities expense	7,000	
Totals	$1,043,800	$1,043,800

Other data

(*a*) The depreciation rate on the building is 4%, based on a 25-year life.
(*b*) Unexpired insurance at the end of the year was determined to be $1,500.
(*c*) Office supplies unused and on hand at year-end amounted to $800, indicating that supplies costing $1,000 had been consumed.
(*d*) Income taxes expense for the year was determined to be $7,500.
(*e*) A physical inventory of merchandise at December 31, showed goods on hand of $140,000.

Instructions

a Prepare a 10-column work sheet at December 31. Use the format illustrated on page 178.
b Prepare a multiple-step income statement for the year. Operating expenses are not to be subdivided between selling expenses and general and administrative expenses. Show income taxes expense after determining income from operations.
c Prepare a statement of retained earnings for the year.
d Prepare a classified balance sheet as of December 31.
e Prepare adjusting and closing entries at December 31.

5-6 Current ratios and working capital
Some of the year-end ledger account balances of Mailorder Warehouse are listed below.

Delivery equipment	$ 26,000
Interest payable	7,180
Advance payments from customers	5,760
Notes payable (due in 90 days)	71,000
U.S. government bonds	19,200
Accounts receivable	90,500
Accounts payable	52,200
Interest receivable	200
Inventory (ending)	144,600
Accumulated depreciation: delivery equipment	3,155
Salaries payable	2,560
Cash	23,000
Land	95,000
Furniture & fixtures	11,200
Mortgage payable (due in 20 years)	60,000
Buildings	250,000

Instructions

a Prepare a partial balance sheet for Mailorder Warehouse consisting of the current asset section and the current liability section *only*. Select the appropriate items from the above list.
b Compute the current ratio and the amount of working capital. Explain how each of these measurements is computed. State with reasons whether you consider the company to be in a strong or weak current position.

5-7 Internal control: case study
At Crown Theater, the cashier is located in a box office at the front of the building. The cashier receives cash from customers and operates a ticket machine which ejects serially numbered tickets.

The serial number appears on each end of the ticket. The tickets come from the printer in large rolls which fit into the ticket machine and are removed at the end of each cashier's working period.

After purchasing a ticket from the cashier, in order to be admitted to the theater, a customer must hand the ticket to a doorman stationed some 50 feet from the box office at the entrance to the theater lobby. The doorman tears the ticket in half, opens the door for the customer, and returns the ticket stub to the customer. The other half of the ticket is dropped by the doorman into a locked box.

Instructions

a Describe the internal controls present in Crown Theater's method of handling cash receipts.
b What steps should be taken regularly by the theater manager or other supervisor to make these internal controls work most effectively?
c Assume that the cashier and the doorman decided to collaborate in an effort to abstract cash receipts. What action might they take?
d On the assumption made in **c** of collaboration between the cashier and the doorman, what features of the control procedures would be most likely to disclose the embezzlement?

5-8   Net price method of recording invoices

Village Hardware completed the following transactions relating to the purchase of merchandise during August, the first month of operation. It is the policy of the company to record all purchase invoices at the **net amount** and to pay invoices within the discount period.

Aug. 1 Purchased merchandise from Lifetime Tools Company, invoice price, $30,000; terms 2/10, n/30.
Aug. 8 Purchased merchandise from Home Products, $36,000; terms 2/10, n/30.
Aug. 8 Merchandise with an invoice price of $3,000 purchased from Lifetime Tools Company on August 1 was found to be defective. It was returned to the supplier accompanied by debit memorandum no. 118, reducing the liability by the **net price** of the goods returned.
Aug. 18 Paid Home Product's invoice of August 8, less cash discount.
Aug. 25 Purchased merchandise from Home Products, $22,800; terms 2/10, n/30.
Aug. 30 Paid Lifetime Tools Company's invoice of August 1, taking into consideration the return of defective goods on August 8. (Remember that the August 1 purchase and the August 8 return were both recorded at **net amount** and not at invoice price.)

The inventory of merchandise on August 1 was $98,880; on August 31, $93,780.

Instructions

a Journalize the above transactions, recording invoices at the net amount.
b Prepare the cost of goods sold section of the income statement.
c What is the amount of accounts payable at the end of August? What would be the amount of accounts payable at the end of August if Village Hardware followed the policy of recording purchase invoices at the gross amount?

5-9   Internal control procedures

Shown below are eight possible errors which might occur in a merchandising business. List the letter (**a** through **h**) designating each of these errors. Beside each letter, place the number indicating the internal control procedure that would prevent this type of error from occurring. If none of the specified control procedures would effectively prevent the error, place "0" after the letter.

Possible Errors

a The cashier conceals the embezzlement of cash by reducing the balance of the ledger account for cash.

b Management is unaware that the company often fails to pay its bills in time to take advantage of the cash discounts offered by its suppliers.

c Paid a supplier for goods that were never received.

d The purchasing department ordered goods from one supplier when a better price could have been obtained by ordering from another supplier.

e Paid an invoice in which the supplier had accidentally doubled the price of the merchandise.

f Paid a supplier for goods that were delivered, but that were never ordered.

g Purchased merchandise which turned out not to be popular with customers.

h Several sales invoices were misplaced and the accounts receivable department is therefore unaware of the unrecorded credit sales.

Internal Control Procedures

1 Use of serially numbered documents

2 Comparison of purchase invoice with the receiving report

3 Comparison of purchase invoice with the purchase order

4 Separation of the accounting function from custody of assets

5 Separation of the responsibilities for approving and recording transactions

6 Use of the net price method of recording purchases

0 None of the above control procedures can effectively prevent this error from occurring.

Cases for analysis

Case 5-1   Internal control: case study

Printing Made Easy sells a variety of printers for use with personal computers. Last April Arthur Doyle, the company's purchasing agent, discovered a weakness in internal control and engaged in a scheme to steal printers. Doyle issued a purchase order for 20 printers to one of the company's regular suppliers, but included a typewritten note requesting that the printers be delivered to 221B Baker Street, Doyle's home address.

The supplier shipped the printers to Baker Street and sent a sales invoice to Printing Made Easy. When the invoice arrived, an accounting clerk carefully complied with company policy and compared the invoice with a copy of the purchase order. After noting agreement between these documents as to quantities, prices, and model numbers, the clerk recorded the transaction in the accounting records and authorized payment of the invoice.

Instructions. What is the weakness in internal control discovered by the purchasing agent to enable him to commit this theft? What changes would you recommend in the company's internal documentation and invoice approval procedures to prevent such problems in the future?

Case 5-2   Purchase of a business: solvency considerations

Megan DeLong, an experienced engineer, is considering buying Eastern Engineering Company at year-end from its current owner, Jack Peterson. Eastern Engineering Company, a single proprietorship, has been a profitable business, earning about $70,000 to $75,000 each year. DeLong is certain she could operate the business just as profitably. The principal activity of the business has been the performance of engineering studies for government agencies interested in the development of air and water pollution control programs.

Peterson has agreed to sell the business for "what he has in it" — namely, $200,000. DeLong comes to you with the balance sheet of Eastern Engineering Company shown below and asks your advice about buying the business.

EASTERN ENGINEERING COMPANY
Balance Sheet
December 31, 19___

Assets		Liabilities & Owner's Equity	
Cash	$ 40,500	Notes payable	$ 60,000
U.S. government contract		Accounts payable	20,600
receivable	110,000	Wages payable	5,400
Other contracts receivable	21,500	J. Peterson, capital	200,000
Equipment			
(net of depreciation)	76,000		
Patents	38,000		
	$286,000		$286,000

DeLong immediately points out, as evidence of the firm's solvency, that the current ratio for Eastern Engineering is 2 to 1. In discussing the specific items on the balance sheet, you find that the patents were recently purchased by Eastern, and DeLong believes them to be worth their $38,000 cost. The notes payable liability consists of one note to the manufacturer of the equipment owned by Eastern, which Peterson had incurred five years ago to finance the purchase of the equipment. The note becomes payable, however, in February of the coming year. The accounts payable all will become due within 30 to 60 days.

Since DeLong does not have enough cash to buy Peterson's equity in the business, she is considering the following terms of purchase: (1) Peterson will withdraw all the cash from the business, thus reducing his equity to $159,500, (2) Peterson will also keep the $110,000 receivable from the U.S. government, leaving his equity in the business at $49,500, and (3) by borrowing heavily, DeLong thinks she can raise $49,500 in cash, which she will pay to Peterson for his remaining equity. DeLong will assume the existing liabilities of the business.

Instructions

a Prepare a classified balance sheet for Eastern Engineering Company as it would appear immediately after DeLong acquired the business, assuming that the purchase is carried out immediately on the proposed terms.

b Compute the current ratio and the working capital position of Eastern Engineering Company after DeLong's purchase of the business.

c Write a memorandum to DeLong explaining what problems she might encounter if she purchases the business as planned.

Chapter 6
Accounting systems: manual and computer-based

In this chapter we address the problem of streamlining an accounting system to handle efficiently a large volume of transactions. Special journals are illustrated and explained, with emphasis upon how such journals reduce the time and effort involved in recording and posting transactions. The use of subsidiary ledger accounts is explained, along with the relationship between a subsidiary ledger and the related controlling account in the general ledger. Computer-based accounting systems also are described, including the use of point-of-sale terminals to record business transactions. Attention is focused upon achieving strong internal control in computer-based systems.

After studying this chapter you should be able to:

✓ Explain the purpose and characteristics of special journals.
✓ Use special journals to record sales on credit, purchases on account, and cash transactions.
✓ Explain the usefulness of a subsidiary ledger and its relationship to a controlling account in the general ledger.
✓ Post entries in special journals to the general ledger and subsidiary ledgers.
✓ Discuss accounting applications of computers and means of achieving internal control in computer-based accounting systems.

Streamlining the accounting process

An accounting system consists of the business documents, journals, ledgers, procedures, and internal controls needed to produce reliable financial statements and other accounting reports. Accounting systems in common use range from simple systems in which accounting records are maintained by hand to sophisticated systems in which accounting records are maintained on magnetic discs. The accounting system to be used in any given company should be especially tailored to the size and to the information needs of the business.

In the early chapters of an introductory accounting book, basic accounting principles can be discussed most conveniently in terms of a small business with only a few customers and suppliers. This simplified model of a business has been used in preceding chapters to demonstrate the analysis and recording of the more common types of business transactions.

The recording procedures illustrated thus far call for recording each transaction by an entry in the general journal, and then posting each debit and credit from the general journal to the proper account in the ledger. We must now face the practical problem of streamlining and speeding up this basic accounting system so that the accounting department can keep pace with the rapid flow of transactions in a modern business.

MANUAL ACCOUNTING SYSTEMS

In a large business there may be hundreds or even thousands of transactions every day. To handle a large volume of transactions rapidly and efficiently, it is helpful to group the transactions into like classes and to use a specialized journal for each class. This will greatly reduce the amount of detailed recording work and will also permit a division of labor, since each special-purpose journal can be handled by a different employee. The great majority of transactions (perhaps as much as 90 or 95%) usually fall into four types. These four types and four corresponding special journals are as follows:

Type of Transaction	Name of Special Journal
Sales of merchandise on credit	Sales journal
Purchases of merchandise on credit	Purchases journal
Receipts of cash	Cash receipts journal
Payments of cash	Cash payments journal

In addition to these four special journals, a **general journal** will be used for recording transactions which do not fit into any of the above four types. The general journal is the same book of original entry illustrated in preceding chapters; the adjective "general" is added merely to distinguish it from the special journals.

Sales journal

Illustrated on the next page is a sales journal containing entries for all sales on account made during November by the Seaside Company. Whenever merchandise is sold on credit, several copies of a sales invoice are prepared. The information listed on a sales invoice usually includes the date of the sale, the serial number of the invoice, the customer's name, the amount of the sale, and the credit terms. One copy of the sales invoice is used by the seller as the basis for an entry in the sales journal.

Notice that the illustrated sales journal contains **special columns** for recording each of these aspects of the sales transaction, except the credit terms. If it is the practice of the business to offer different credit terms to different customers, a column may be inserted in the sales journal to show the terms of sale. In this illustration it is assumed that all sales

Sales Journal

Page 1

Entries for sales on credit during November

Date		Account Debited	Invoice No.	✓	Amount
19__					
Nov	2	John Adams	301	✓	450
	4	Harold Black	302	✓	1,000
	5	Debbie Cross	303	✓	975
	11	H. R. Davis	304	✓	620
	18	C. D. Early	305	✓	900
	23	John Frost	306	✓	400
	29	D. H. Gray	307	✓	11,850
					16,195
					(5)(41)

are made on terms of 2/10, n/30; consequently, there is no need to write the credit terms as part of each entry. *Only sales on credit are entered in the sales journal.* When merchandise is sold for cash, the transaction is recorded in a *cash receipts* journal, which is illustrated later in this chapter.

Advantages of the sales journal. Note that each of the above seven sales transactions is recorded on a single line. Each entry consists of a debit to a customer's account; the offsetting credit to the Sales account is understood without being written, because sales on account are the only transactions recorded in this special journal.

An entry in a sales journal need not include an explanation; if more information about the transaction is desired it can be obtained by referring to the file copy of the sales invoice. The invoice number is listed in the sales journal as part of each entry. The one-line entry in the sales journal requires much less writing than would be necessary to record a sales transaction in the general journal. Since there may be several hundred or several thousand sales transactions each month, the time saved in recording transactions in this streamlined manner becomes quite important.

Every entry in the sales journal represents a debit to a customer's account. Charges to customers' accounts should be posted daily so that each customer's account will always be up-to-date and available for use in making decisions relating to collections and to the further extension of credit. A check mark (✓) is placed in the sales journal opposite each amount posted to a customer's account, to indicate that the posting has been made.

Another advantage of the special journal for sales is the great saving of time in posting credits to the Sales account. Remember that every amount entered in the sales journal represents a credit to Sales. In the illustrated sales journal above, there are seven transactions (and in practice there might be 700). Instead of posting a separate credit to the Sales account for each sales transaction, we can wait until the end of the month and make one posting to the Sales account for the total of the amounts recorded in the sales journal.

In the illustrated sales journal for November, the sales on account totaled $16,195. On November 30 this amount is posted as a credit to the Sales account, and the ledger account number for Sales (41) is entered under the total figure in the sales journal to show that the posting operation has been performed. The total sales figure is also posted as a debit to ledger account no. 5, Accounts Receivable. To make clear the reason for this posting to Accounts Receivable, an explanation of the nature of controlling accounts and subsidiary ledgers is necessary.

Controlling accounts and subsidiary ledgers

In preceding chapters all transactions involving accounts receivable from customers have been posted to a single account entitled Accounts Receivable. Under this procedure, however, it is not easy to look up the amount receivable from a given customer. In practice, businesses which sell goods on credit *maintain a separate account receivable for each customer.* If there are 4,000 customers, this would require a ledger with 4,000 accounts receivable, in addition to the accounts for other assets, and for liabilities, owners' equity, revenue, and expenses. Such a ledger would be cumbersome and un-wieldy. Also, the trial balance prepared from such a large ledger would be a very long one. If the trial balance showed the ledger to be out of balance, the task of locating the error or errors would be most difficult. All these factors indicate that it is not desirable to have too many accounts in one ledger. Fortunately, a simple solution is available; this solution is to divide the ledger into several separate ledgers.

In a business which has a large number of customers and a large number of creditors, it is customary to divide the ledger into three separate ledgers. All the accounts with *customers* are placed in alphabetical order in a separate ledger, called the *accounts receivable ledger.* All the accounts with *creditors* are arranged alphabetically in another ledger called the *accounts payable ledger.* Both of these ledgers are known as *subsidiary ledgers*, because they support and are controlled by the general ledger.

After thus segregating the accounts receivable from customers in one subsidiary ledger and placing the accounts payable to creditors in a second subsidiary ledger, we have left in the original ledger all the revenue and expense accounts and also all the balance sheet accounts except those with individual customers and individual creditors. This ledger is called the *general ledger,* to distinguish it from the subsidiary ledgers.

When the numerous individual accounts receivable from customers are placed in a subsidiary ledger, an account entitled Accounts Receivable continues to be maintained in the general ledger. This account shows the *total amount due from all customers;* in other words, this single *controlling account* in the general ledger represents the numerous customers' accounts which make up the subsidiary ledger. The general ledger is still in balance because the controlling account, Accounts Receivable, has a balance equal to the total of the individual customers' accounts. Agreement of the controlling account with the sum of the accounts receivable in the subsidiary ledger also provides assurance of accuracy in the subsidiary ledger.

A controlling account entitled Accounts Payable is also kept in the general ledger in place of the numerous accounts with creditors which form the accounts payable subsidiary ledger. Because the two controlling accounts represent the total amounts receivable from customers and payable to creditors, a trial balance can be prepared from the general

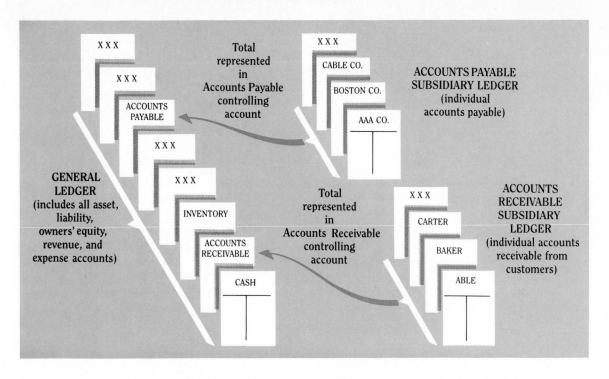

Relationship of subsidiary ledgers to controlling accounts in general ledger

ledger alone. The illustration above shows the relationship of the subsidiary ledgers to the controlling accounts in the general ledger.

Posting to subsidiary ledgers and to controlling accounts. To illustrate the posting of subsidiary ledgers and of controlling accounts, let us refer again to the sales journal illustrated on page 215. Each debit to a customer's account is posted currently during the month from the sales journal to the customer's account in the accounts receivable ledger. The accounts in this subsidiary ledger are usually kept in alphabetical order and are not numbered. When a posting is made to a customer's account, a check mark (✓) is placed in the sales journal as evidence that the posting has been made to the subsidiary ledger.

At month-end the sales journal is totaled. The total amount of sales for the month, $16,195, is posted as a credit to the Sales account and also as a debit to the controlling account, Accounts Receivable, in the general ledger. The controlling account will, therefore, equal the total of all the customers' accounts in the subsidiary ledger.

The diagram below shows the day-to-day posting of individual entries from the sales journal to the subsidiary ledger. The diagram also shows the month-end posting of the total of the sales journal to the two general ledger accounts affected, Accounts Receivable and Sales. Note that the amount of the monthly debit to the controlling account is equal to the sum of the debits posted to the subsidiary ledger.

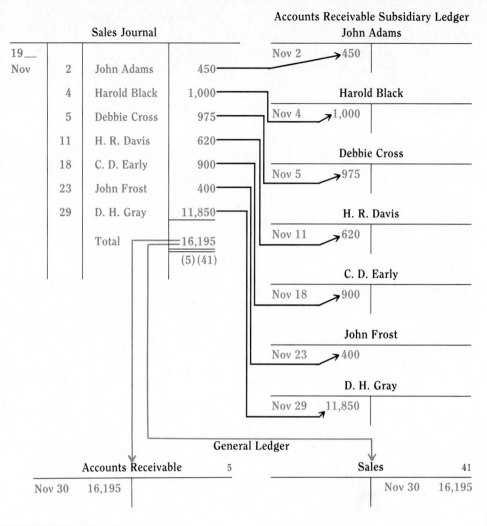

Purchases journal

The handling of purchase transactions when a purchases journal is used follows a pattern quite similar to the one described for the sales journal.

Assume that the purchases journal illustrated on the next page contains all purchases of merchandise on credit during the month by the Seaside Company. The invoice date is shown in a separate column because the cash discount period begins on this date.

The five entries are posted as they occur during the month as credits to the creditors' accounts in the subsidiary ledger for accounts payable. As each posting is completed a check mark (✓) is placed in the purchases journal.

Purchases Journal   Page 1

Date			Account Credited	Invoice Date		✓	Amount
19__				19__			
Nov	2		Alabama Supply Co. (net 30)	Nov	2	✓	3,325
	4		Barker & Bright (2/10, n/30)		4	✓	700
	10		Canning & Sons (net 30)		9	✓	500
	17		Davis Co. (2/10, n/30)		16	✓	900
	27		Excelsior, Inc. (net 30)		25	✓	1,825
							7,250
							(50)(21)

Entries for purchases on credit during November

At the end of the month the purchases journal is totaled and ruled as shown in the above illustration. The total figure, $7,250, is posted to two general ledger accounts as shown on the next page:

1 As a debit to the Purchases account
2 As a credit to the Accounts Payable controlling account

The account numbers for Purchases (50) and for Accounts Payable (21) are then placed in parentheses below the column total of the purchases journal to show that the posting has been made.

Under the particular system being described, the only transactions recorded in the purchases journal are **purchases of merchandise on credit.** The term **merchandise** means goods acquired for resale to customers. If merchandise is purchased for cash rather than on credit, the transaction should be recorded in the cash payments journal, as illustrated on pages 224 and 225.

The diagram on the next page illustrates the day-to-day posting of individual entries from the purchases journal to the accounts with creditors in the subsidiary ledger for accounts payable. The diagram also shows how the column total of the purchases journal is posted at the end of the month to the general ledger accounts, Purchases and Accounts Payable. One objective of this diagram is to emphasize that the amount of the monthly credit to the control account is equal to the sum of the credits posted to the subsidiary ledger.

When assets other than merchandise are being acquired, as, for example, a delivery truck or an office desk for use in the business, the journal to be used depends upon whether a cash payment is made. If assets of this type are purchased for cash, the transaction should be entered in the cash payments journal; if the transaction is on credit, the general journal is used. The purchases journal is not used to record the acquisition of these assets because the total of this journal is posted to the Purchases account and this account (as explained in Chapter 5) is used in determining the cost of goods sold.

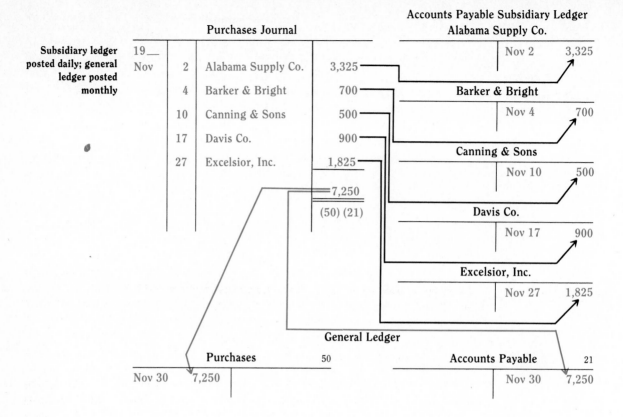

Cash receipts journal

All transactions involving the receipt of cash are recorded in the cash receipts journal. One common example is the sale of merchandise for cash. As each cash sale is made, it is rung up on a cash register. At the end of the day the total of the cash sales is computed by striking the total key on the register. This total is entered in the cash receipts journal, which therefore contains one entry for the total cash sales of the day. For other types of cash receipts, such as the collection of accounts receivable from customers, a separate journal entry may be made for each transaction. The cash receipts journal illustrated on pages 222 and 223 contains entries for selected November transactions, all of which include the receipt of cash.

Nov. 1 R. B. Jones organized Seaside Company by investing $75,000 cash in exchange for 7,500 shares of $10 par value capital stock.

Nov. 4 Sold merchandise for cash, $300.

Nov. 5 Sold merchandise for cash, $400.

Nov. 8 Collected from John Adams for sales invoice of Nov. 2, $450 less 2% cash discount.

Nov. 10 Sold a small portion of land not needed in business for a total price of $7,000, consisting of cash of $1,000 and a note receivable for $6,000. The cost of the land sold was $5,000.

Nov. 12 Collected from Harold Black for sales invoice of Nov. 4, $1,000 less 2% cash discount.

Nov. 20 Collected from C. D. Early for sales invoice of Nov. 18, $900 less 2% cash discount.

Nov. 27 Sold merchandise for cash, $125.

Nov. 30 Obtained $4,000 loan from bank. Issued a note payable in that amount.

Note that the cash receipts journal illustrated on pages 222 and 223 has three debit columns and three credit columns as follows:

Debits:
1 Cash. This column is used for every entry, because only those transactions which include the receipt of cash are entered in this special journal.
2 Sales discounts. This column is used to accumulate the sales discounts allowed during the month. Only one line of the cash receipts book is required to record a collection from a customer who takes advantage of a cash discount.
3 Other accounts. This third debit column is used for debits to any and all accounts other than cash and sales discounts, and space is provided for writing in the name of the account. For example, the entry of November 10 in the illustrated cash receipts journal shows that cash and a note receivable were obtained when land was sold. The amount of cash received, $1,000, is entered in the Cash debit column; the account title Notes Receivable is written in the Other Accounts debit column along with the amount of the debit to this account, $6,000. These two debits are offset by credit entries to Land, $5,000, and to Gain on Sale of Land, $2,000, in the Other Accounts credit column.

Credits:
1 Accounts receivable. This column is used to list the credits to customers' accounts as receivables are collected. The name of the customer is written in the space entitled Account Credited to the left of the Accounts Receivable column.
2 Sales. The existence of this column will save posting by permitting the accumulation of all sales for cash during the month and the posting of the column total at the end of the month as a credit to the Sales account (41).
3 Other accounts. This column is used for credits to any and all accounts other than Accounts Receivable and Sales. In some instances, a transaction may require credits to two accounts. Such cases are handled by using two lines of the special journal, as illustrated by the transaction of November 10, which required credits to both the Land account and to Gain on Sale of Land.

Posting the cash receipts journal. It is convenient to think of the posting of a cash receipts journal as being divided into two phases. The first phase consists of the daily posting of individual amounts throughout the month; the second phase consists of the posting of column totals at the end of the month.

Cash Receipts Journal

	Date		Explanation	Cash	Sales Discounts	Other Accounts Name	LP	Amount
						Debits		
Includes all transactions involving receipt of cash	19__							
	Nov	1	Issued capital stock	75,000				
		4	Cash sales	300				
		5	Cash sales	400				
		8	Invoice Nov. 2, less 2%	441	9			
		10	Sale of land	1,000		Notes Receivable	3	6,000
		12	Invoice Nov. 4, less 2%	980	20			
		20	Invoice Nov. 18, less 2%	882	18			
		27	Cash sales	125				
		30	Obtained bank loan	4,000				
				83,128	47			6,000
				(1)	(43)			(X)

Posting during the month. Daily posting of the Accounts Receivable credit column is desirable. Each amount is posted to an individual customer's account in the accounts receivable subsidiary ledger. A check mark (✓) is placed in the cash receipts journal alongside each item posted to a customer's account to show that the posting operation has been performed. When debits and credits to customers' accounts are posted daily, the current status of each customer's account is available for use in making decisions as to further granting of credit and as a guide to collection efforts on past-due accounts.

The debits and credits in the Other Accounts sections of the cash receipts journal may be posted daily or at convenient intervals during the month. If this portion of the posting work is done on a current basis, less detailed work will be left for the busy period at the end of the month. As the postings of individual items are made, the number of the ledger account debited or credited is entered in the LP (ledger page) column of the cash receipts journal opposite the item posted. Evidence is thus provided in the special journal as to which items have been posted.

Posting column totals at month-end. At the end of the month, the cash receipts journal is ruled as shown above and on page 223. Before posting any of the column totals, it is first important to prove that *the sum of the debit column totals is equal to the sum of the credit column totals.*

After the totals of the cash receipts journal have been crossfooted, the following column totals are posted:

1 Cash debit column. Posted as a debit to the Cash account.
2 Sales Discounts debit column. Posted as a debit to the Sales Discounts account.

Account Credited	Credits				
	Accounts Receivable			Other Accounts	
	✓	Amount	Sales	LP	Amount
Capital Stock, $10 par				30	75,000
			300		
			400		
John Adams	✓	450			
Land				11	5,000 ⎫
Gain on Sale of Land				40	2,000 ⎬
Harold Black	✓	1,000			
C. D. Early	✓	900			
			125		
Notes Payable				20	4,000
		2,350	825		86,000
		(5)	(41)		(X)

3 Accounts Receivable credit column. Posted as a credit to the controlling account, Accounts Receivable.

4 Sales credit column. Posted as a credit to the Sales account.

As each column total is posted to the appropriate account in the general ledger, the ledger account number is entered in parentheses just below the column total in the special journal. This notation shows that the column total has been posted and also indicates the account to which the posting was made. The totals of the Other Accounts columns in both the debit and credit sections of the special journal are not posted, because the amounts listed in the column affect various general ledger accounts and have already been posted as individual items. The symbol (X) is placed below the totals of these two columns to indicate that no posting is made.

Cash payments journal

Another widely used special journal is the cash payments journal, sometimes called the *cash disbursements journal*, in which all payments of cash are recorded. Among the more common of these transactions are payments of accounts payable to creditors, payment of operating expenses, and cash purchases of merchandise.

The cash payments journal illustrated below contains entries for all November transactions of the Seaside Company which required the payment of cash.

Nov. 1 Paid rent on store building for November, $800.
Nov. 2 Purchased merchandise for cash, $500.

Date		Check No.	Explanation	Cash	Purchase Discounts	Other Accounts Name	LP	Amount
19__								
Nov	1	101	Paid November rent	800				
	2	102	Purchased merchandise	500				
	8	103	Invoice of Nov. 4, less 2%	686	14			
	9	104	Bought land and building	70,000		Notes Payable	20	30,000
	17	105	Paid sales salaries	3,600				
	26	106	Invoice of Nov. 17, less 2%	882	18			
	27	107	Purchased merchandise	400				
	28	108	Purchased merchandise	650				
	29	109	Newspaper advertisement	50				
	29	110	Three-year ins. policy	720				
				78,288	32			30,000
				(1)	(52)			(X)

Includes all transactions involving payment of cash

Nov. 8 Paid Barker & Bright for invoice of Nov. 4, $700 less 2%.

Nov. 9 Bought land, $65,000, and building, $35,000, for future use in business. Paid cash of $70,000 and signed a promissory note for the balance of $30,000. (Land and building were acquired in a single transaction.)

Nov. 17 Paid salespeople's salaries, $3,600.

Nov. 26 Paid Davis Co. for invoice of Nov. 16, $900 less 2%.

Nov. 27 Purchased merchandise for cash, $400.

Nov. 28 Purchased merchandise for cash, $650.

Nov. 29 Paid for newspaper advertising, $50.

Nov. 29 Paid for three-year insurance policy, $720.

Note in the illustrated cash payments journal that the three credit columns are located to the left of the three debit columns; any sequence of columns is satisfactory in a special journal as long as the column headings clearly distinguish debits from credits. The Cash column is often placed first in both the cash receipts journal and the cash payments journal because it is the column used in every transaction.

Good internal control over cash disbursements requires that all payments be made by check. The checks are serially numbered and as each transaction is entered in the cash payments journal, the check number is listed in a special column provided just to the right of the date column. An unbroken sequence of check numbers in this column gives assurance that every check issued has been recorded in the accounting records.

The use of the six money columns in the illustrated cash payments journal parallels the procedures described for the cash receipts journal.

Account Debited	Debits				
	Accounts Payable			Other Accounts	
	✓	Amount	Purchases	LP	Amount
Store Rent Expense				54	800
			500		
Barker & Bright	✓	700			
Land				11	65,000 ⎫
Building				12	35,000 ⎭
Sales Salaries Expense				53	3,600
Davis Co.	✓	900			
			400		
			650		
Advertising Expense				55	50
Unexpired Insurance				6	720
		1,600	1,550		105,170
		(21)	(50)		(X)

Posting the cash payments journal. The posting of the cash payments journal falls into the same two phases already described for the cash receipts journal. The first phase consists of the daily posting of entries in the Accounts Payable debit column to the individual accounts of creditors in the accounts payable subsidiary ledger. Check marks (✓) are entered opposite these items to show that the posting has been made. If a creditor telephones to inquire about any aspect of his account, information on all purchases and payments made to date is readily available in the accounts payable subsidiary ledger.

The individual debit and credit entries in the Other Accounts columns of the cash payments journal may be posted daily or at convenient intervals during the month. As the postings of these individual items are made, the number of the ledger account debited or credited is entered in the LP (ledger page) column of the cash payments journal opposite the item posted.

The second phase of posting the cash payments journal is performed at the end of the month. When all the transactions of the month have been journalized, the cash payments journal is ruled as shown above, and the six money columns are totaled. The equality of debits and credits is then proved before posting.

After the totals of the cash payments journal have been proved to be in balance, the totals of the columns for Cash, Purchase Discounts, Accounts Payable, and Purchases are posted to the corresponding accounts in the general ledger. The numbers of the accounts to which these postings are made are listed in parentheses just below the respective column totals in the cash payments journal. The totals of the Other Accounts columns in both the debit and credit section of this special journal are not to be posted, and the symbol (X) is placed below the totals of these two columns to indicate that no posting is required.

The general journal

When all transactions involving cash or the purchase and sale of merchandise are recorded in special journals, only a few types of transactions remain to be entered in the general journal. Examples include the declaration of dividends, the purchase or sale of plant and equipment on credit, the return of merchandise for credit to a supplier, and the return of merchandise by customers for credit to their accounts. The general journal is also used for adjusting and closing entries at the end of the accounting period.

The following transactions of the Seaside Company during November could not conveniently be handled in any of the four special journals and were therefore entered in the general journal.

Nov. 25 A customer, John Frost, was permitted to return for credit $50 worth of merchandise that had been sold to him on Nov. 23.

Nov. 28 The Seaside Company returned to a supplier, Excelsior, Inc., for credit $300 worth of the merchandise purchased on Nov. 27.

Nov. 29 Purchased for use in the business office equipment costing $1,225. Agreed to make payment within 30 days to XYZ Equipment Co.

General Journal

Page 1

	Date		Account Titles and Explanation	LP	Dr	Cr
Transactions which do not fit any of the four special journals	19__					
	Nov	25	Sales Returns and Allowances	42	50	
			Accounts Receivable, John Frost ...	5/✓		50
			Allowed credit to customer for return of merchandise from sale of Nov. 23.			
		28	Accounts Payable, Excelsior, Inc.	21/✓	300	
			Purchase Returns and Allowances ..	51		300
			Returned to supplier for credit a portion of merchandise purchased on Nov. 27.			
		29	Office Equipment	14	1,225	
			Accounts Payable, XYZ Equipment Co.	21/✓		1,225
			Purchased office equipment on 30-day credit.			

Each of the preceding three entries includes a debit or credit to a controlling account (Accounts Receivable or Accounts Payable) and also identifies by name a particular creditor or customer. When a controlling account is debited or credited by a *general journal entry,* the debit or credit must be posted twice: one posting to the controlling account in the general ledger and another posting to a customer's account or a creditor's account in a subsidiary ledger. This double posting is necessary to keep the controlling account in agreement with the subsidiary ledger.

For example, in the illustrated entry of November 25 for the return of merchandise by a customer, the credit part of the entry is posted twice:

1 To the Accounts Receivable controlling account in the general ledger; this posting is evidenced by listing the account number (5) in the LP column of the general journal.
2 To the account of John Frost in the subsidiary ledger for accounts receivable; this posting is indicated by the check mark (✔) placed in the LP (ledger page) column of the general journal.

Showing the source of postings in ledger accounts

When a general journal and several special journals are in use, the ledger accounts should indicate the book of original entry from which each debit and credit was posted. An identifying symbol is placed opposite each entry in the reference column of the account. The symbols used in this text are as follows:

S1   meaning page 1 of the sales journal
P1   meaning page 1 of the purchases journal
CR1 meaning page 1 of the cash receipts journal
CP1 meaning page 1 of the cash payments journal
J1   meaning page 1 of the general journal

Subsidiary ledger accounts

The following illustration shows a customer's account in a subsidiary ledger for accounts receivable.

Name of Customer

Date			Ref	Debit	Credit	Balance
19__						
July	1		S1	400		400
	20		S3	200		600
Aug	4		CR7		400	200
	15		S6	120		320

Subsidiary ledger: accounts receivable

The advantage of this three-column form of account is that it shows at a glance the present balance receivable from the customer. The current amount of a customer's account is often needed as a guide to collection activities, or as a basis for granting additional credit. In studying the above illustration note also that the Reference column shows the source of each debit and credit.

Accounts appearing in the accounts receivable subsidiary ledger are assumed to have debit balances. If one of these customer's accounts should acquire a credit balance by overpayment or for any other reason, the word *credit* should be written after the amount in the Balance column.

The same three-column form of account is also generally used for creditors' accounts in an accounts payable subsidiary ledger, as indicated by the following illustration:

Name of Creditor

Date			Ref	Debit	Credit	Balance
19__						
July	10		P1		625	625
	25		P2		100	725
Aug	8		CP4	725		0
	12		P3		250	250

Subsidiary ledger: accounts payable (margin note)

Accounts in the accounts payable subsidiary ledger normally have credit balances. If by reason of payment in advance or accidental overpayment, one of these accounts should acquire a debit balance, the word **debit** should be written after the amount in the Balance column.

As previously stated, both the accounts receivable and accounts payable subsidiary ledgers are customarily arranged in alphabetical order and account numbers are not used. This arrangement permits unlimited expansion of the subsidiary ledgers, as accounts with new customers and creditors can be inserted in proper alphabetical sequence.

Ledger accounts

The general ledger. The general ledger accounts of the Seaside Company illustrated next indicate the source of postings from the various books of original entry. The subsidiary ledger accounts appear on pages 231–232. To gain a clear understanding of the procedures for posting special journals, you should trace each entry in the illustrated special journals into the general ledger accounts and also to the subsidiary ledger accounts where appropriate. The general ledger accounts are shown in T-account form in order to distinguish them more emphatically from the accounts in the subsidiary ledgers.

Note that the Cash account contains only one debit entry and one credit entry, although there were many cash transactions during the month. The one debit, $83,128, represents the total cash received during the month and was posted from the cash receipts journal on November 30. Similarly, the one credit entry of $78,288 was posted on November 30 from the cash payments journal and represents the total of all cash payments made during the month.

General ledger accounts (margin note)

Cash   1

19__					19__					
Nov	30		CR1	83,128	Nov	30		CP1	78,288

Notes Receivable   3

19__									
Nov	10		CR1	6,000					

Accounts Receivable   5

19__					19__					
Nov	30		S1	16,195	Nov	25		J1	50
						30		CR1	2,350

Unexpired Insurance   6

19__										
Nov	29		CP1	720					

Land   11

19__					19__					
Nov	9		CP1	65,000	Nov	10		CR1	5,000

Building   12

19__										
Nov	9		CP1	35,000					

Office Equipment   14

19__										
Nov	29		J1	1,225					

Notes Payable   20

					19__					
					Nov	9		CP1	30,000
						30		CR1	4,000

Accounts Payable   21

19__					19__					
Nov	28		J1	300	Nov	29		J1	1,225
	30		CP1	1,600		30		P1	7,250

Capital Stock   30

					19__					
					Nov	1		CR1	75,000

Gain on Sale of Land   40

					19__					
					Nov	10		CR1	2,000

Sales   41

						19__					
						Nov	30			CR1	825
							30			S1	16,195

Sales Returns and Allowances   42

19__											
Nov	25			J1	50						

Sales Discounts   43

19__											
Nov	30			CR1	47						

Purchases   50

19__											
Nov	30			CP1	1,550						
	30			P1	7,250						

Purchase Returns and Allowances   51

						19__					
						Nov	28			J1	300

Purchase Discounts   52

						19__					
						Nov	30			CP1	32

Sales Salaries Expense   53

19__											
Nov	17			CP1	3,600						

Store Rent Expense   54

19__											
Nov	1			CP1	800						

Advertising Expense   55

19__											
Nov	29			CP1	50						

Accounts receivable ledger. The subsidiary ledger for accounts receivable appears as follows after the posting of the various journals has been completed.

Customers' accounts

John Adams

19__						
Nov	2		S1	450		450
	8		CR1		450	0

Harold Black

19__						
Nov	4		S1	1,000		1,000
	12		CR1		1,000	0

Debbie Cross

19__						
Nov	5		S1	975		975

H. R. Davis

19__						
Nov	11		S1	620		620

C. D. Early

19__						
Nov	18		S1	900		900
	20		CR1		900	0

John Frost

19__						
Nov	23		S1	400		400
	25		J1		50	350

D. H. Gray

19__						
Nov	29		S1	11,850		11,850

Accounts payable ledger. The accounts with creditors in the accounts payable subsidiary ledger are as follows:

Creditors' accounts

Alabama Supply Co.

19__						
Nov	2		P1		3,325	3,325

Barker & Bright

19__						
Nov	4		P1		700	700
	8		CP1	700		0

Canning & Sons

19__						
Nov	10		P1		500	500

Davis Co.

19__						
Nov	17		P1		900	900
	26		CP1	900		0

Excelsior, Inc.

19__						
Nov	27		P1		1,825	1,825
	28		J1	300		1,525

XYZ Equipment Co.

19__						
Nov	29		J1		1,225	1,225

Reconciling subsidiary ledgers and controlling accounts

At the end of each accounting period, the equality of debits and credits in the general ledger is established by preparation of a trial balance, as illustrated in preceding chapters. When controlling accounts and subsidiary ledgers are in use, it is also necessary to determine that each subsidiary ledger is in agreement with its controlling account. This process is termed *reconciling* the subsidiary ledger with the controlling account.

The first step in reconciling a subsidiary ledger with its controlling account is to prepare a schedule of the balances of the accounts in the subsidiary ledger. The total of this schedule then is compared with the balance of the controlling account. Seaside Company's trial balance and schedules of accounts receivable and accounts payable appear on page 234. Notice that the totals of the accounts receivable and accounts payable ledger schedules agree with the balance of the related controlling accounts.

Reconciling subsidiary ledgers with their controlling accounts is an important internal control procedure and should be performed at least once a month. This procedure may disclose such errors in the subsidiary ledger as failure to post transactions, transposition or slide errors, or mathematical errors in determining the balances of specific accounts receivable or accounts payable. However, this procedure will *not* disclose an entry which was posted to the wrong account within the subsidiary ledger.

Variations in special journals

The number of columns to be included in each special journal and the number of special journals to be used will depend upon the nature of the particular business and especially upon the volume of the various kinds of transactions. For example, the desirability of including a Sales Discounts column in the cash receipts journal depends upon whether a business offers discounts to its customers for prompt payment.

A retail store may find that customers frequently return merchandise for credit. To record efficiently this large volume of sales returns, the store may establish a sales returns and allowances journal. A purchase returns and allowances journal may also be desirable if returns of goods to suppliers occur frequently.

Special journals should be regarded as laborsaving devices which may be designed with any number of columns appropriate to the needs of the particular business. A business will usually benefit by establishing a special journal for any type of transaction that occurs quite frequently.

Direct posting from invoices

In many business concerns the efficiency of data processing is increased by posting sales invoices directly to the customers' accounts in the accounts receivable ledger rather than copying sales invoices into a sales journal and then posting to accounts in the subsidiary ledger. If the sales invoices are **serially numbered,** a file or binder of duplicate sales invoices arranged in numerical order may take the place of a formal sales journal. By accounting for each **serial number,** it is possible to be certain that all sales invoices are included. At the end of the month, the invoices are totaled on a calculator, and a general journal entry is made debiting the Accounts Receivable controlling account and crediting Sales for the total of the month's sales invoices.

Direct posting may also be used in recording purchase invoices. As soon as purchase invoices have been verified and approved, credits to the creditors' accounts in the accounts payable ledger may be posted directly from the purchase invoices.

The trend toward direct posting from invoices to subsidiary ledgers is mentioned here as further evidence that accounting records and procedures can be designed in a variety of ways to meet the individual needs of different business concerns.

SEASIDE COMPANY
Trial Balance
November 30, 19___

<table>
<tr><td>General ledger trial
balance</td><td>Cash ....</td><td>$ 4,840</td><td></td></tr>
<tr><td></td><td>Notes receivable ....</td><td>6,000</td><td></td></tr>
<tr><td></td><td>Accounts receivable (see schedule below) ....</td><td>13,795</td><td></td></tr>
<tr><td></td><td>Unexpired insurance ....</td><td>720</td><td></td></tr>
<tr><td></td><td>Land ....</td><td>60,000</td><td></td></tr>
<tr><td></td><td>Building ....</td><td>35,000</td><td></td></tr>
<tr><td></td><td>Office equipment ....</td><td>1,225</td><td></td></tr>
<tr><td></td><td>Notes payable ....</td><td></td><td>$ 34,000</td></tr>
<tr><td></td><td>Accounts payable (see schedule below) ....</td><td></td><td>6,575</td></tr>
<tr><td></td><td>Capital, stock, $10 par ....</td><td></td><td>75,000</td></tr>
<tr><td></td><td>Gain on sale of land ....</td><td></td><td>2,000</td></tr>
<tr><td></td><td>Sales ....</td><td></td><td>17,020</td></tr>
<tr><td></td><td>Sales returns and allowances ....</td><td>50</td><td></td></tr>
<tr><td></td><td>Sales discounts ....</td><td>47</td><td></td></tr>
<tr><td></td><td>Purchases ....</td><td>8,800</td><td></td></tr>
<tr><td></td><td>Purchase returns and allowances ....</td><td></td><td>300</td></tr>
<tr><td></td><td>Purchase discounts ....</td><td></td><td>32</td></tr>
<tr><td></td><td>Sales salaries expense ....</td><td>3,600</td><td></td></tr>
<tr><td></td><td>Store rent expense ....</td><td>800</td><td></td></tr>
<tr><td></td><td>Advertising expense ....</td><td>50</td><td></td></tr>
<tr><td></td><td></td><td>$134,927</td><td>$134,927</td></tr>
</table>

Schedule of Accounts Receivable
November 30, 19___

<table>
<tr><td>Subsidiary ledgers
in balance with
controlling accounts</td><td>Debbie Cross ....</td><td>$ 975</td></tr>
<tr><td></td><td>H. R. Davis ....</td><td>620</td></tr>
<tr><td></td><td>John Frost ....</td><td>350</td></tr>
<tr><td></td><td>D. H. Gray ....</td><td>11,850</td></tr>
<tr><td></td><td>Total (per balance of controlling account) ....</td><td>$13,795</td></tr>
</table>

Schedule of Accounts Payable
November 30, 19___

<table>
<tr><td>Alabama Supply Co ....</td><td>$3,325</td></tr>
<tr><td>Canning & Sons ....</td><td>500</td></tr>
<tr><td>Excelsior, Inc. ....</td><td>1,525</td></tr>
<tr><td>XYZ Equipment Co. ....</td><td>1,225</td></tr>
<tr><td>Total (per balance of controlling account) ....</td><td>$6,575</td></tr>
</table>

Unit record for each transaction

Our discussion has thus far been limited to a manual accounting system. One of the points we have emphasized is that an *immediate record* should be made of every business transaction. This initial record of each transaction need not be an entry in the accounting records. Rather, the transaction often is first recorded on a business document or form, such as an invoice, a check stub, or a cash register receipt. This concept of making an *individual record* of each transaction is an important one in every type of accounting system. Regardless of whether accounting records are maintained by hand or by electronic equipment, the documentation of each transaction is an essential step in the accounting process.

COMPUTER-BASED ACCOUNTING SYSTEMS

The concepts of special journals and subsidiary ledgers apply to computer-based accounting systems as well as manual systems. In fact, special journals and subsidiary ledgers are far easier to maintain in computerized systems. We have stressed that two purposes of special journals are to reduce the amount of time involved in writing journal entries and posting to ledger accounts. In a computer-based system, the accountant need only enter the data needed for the computer to prepare journal entries. All the writing and all the posting to general ledger and subsidiary ledger accounts is then handled by machine with no further human effort.

Advantages of computer-based systems

The primary advantage of the computer is its incredible speed. The time needed for a computer to post a transaction or determine an account balance is but a few millionths of a second. This speed creates several advantages over manual accounting systems, including the following:

1 *Large amounts of data can be processed quickly and efficiently.* Large businesses may engage in tens of thousands of transactions per day. In processing such a large volume of data, computers can save vast amounts of time in each step of the accounting process, including the recording of transactions, posting to ledger accounts, and preparing of accounting records, schedules, and reports.

   For example, a large department store makes thousands of credit sales each day. To process these transactions manually would require a huge bookkeeping staff. Through devices such as *point-of-sale terminals* (electronic cash registers), a computer can process these transactions automatically as the salesperson rings up the sale.

2 *Account balances may be kept up-to-date.* The speed with which data may be processed by a computer enables businesses to keep subsidiary ledger accounts, perpetual inventory records, and most general ledger accounts continually up-to-date.

3 *Additional information may be developed at virtually no additional cost.* On page 215 we illustrated the type of sales journal that might be prepared in a manual accounting system. A similar journal can be maintained in a computerized system.

However, the computer can also rearrange this information to show daily sales totals for each sales department, for each salesperson, and for specific products. Time and cost considerations often make the preparation of such supplementary information impractical in a manual accounting system.

4 *Instant feedback may be available as transactions are taking place.* In *on-line, real-time (OLRT)* computer systems, the employee executing a transaction may have a terminal which is in direct communication with the computer. Thus, the employee has immediate access to accounting information useful in executing the current transaction.

● **CASE IN POINT** ● The electronic cash registers now found in many department stores are point-of-sale terminals in direct communication with the store's computer system. When a salesperson makes a credit sale to a customer who is using a store credit card, the salesperson enters the credit card number into the terminal. The computer compares this number to a list of cancelled or stolen credit cards and also determines whether the current sales transaction would cause the customer's account balance to exceed a predetermined credit limit. If any of these procedures indicate that credit should not be extended to the customer, the computer notifies the salesperson not to make the credit sale.

5 *Additional internal control procedures may be possible in a computer-based system.* Approval of each credit sale, described in the preceding *Case in point,* is but one example of an internal control procedure that makes use of the unique capabilities of the computer. Such a control procedure may not be practical in a manual system, especially if the accounts receivable subsidiary ledger is not kept continually up-to-date.

Internal control and the computer

Computer hardware itself is highly reliable and the possibility of errors caused by computer malfunction is very small. However, the use of reliable equipment does not entirely eliminate the possibility of errors in accounting records. Human beings create the information which is entered into the computer, and human beings make mistakes. In addition, the computer program may contain errors and, therefore, may process certain transactions improperly. Finally, there is the risk of improper human intervention — someone tampering with the computer programs or the computer-based records for the purpose of deliberately falsifying accounting information.

Thus internal control is just as important in a computer-based system as in a manual accounting system. We shall now discuss some of the most important internal control concepts for computer-based accounting systems.

Organizational controls

We have stressed the need for separation of duties as a means of achieving internal control. This concept is equally important in manual and computer-based accounting systems. An employee with custody of assets should not also have access to accounting records. If these duties are assigned to the same employee, this person has the opportunity to conceal a shortage of assets by falsifying the accounting records.

Separation of duties is also necessary among a company's computer department personnel. The purpose of such separation is to ensure that *no one person is in a position to make unauthorized changes* in programs or computer-based records. Thus, all programs should be tested by someone *other than* the programmer who wrote the program. In addition, the responsibilities for *programming* and actual *operation* of the computer should be assigned to different employees. Several computer-based frauds have occurred when programmers were also responsible for daily computer operations. An individual with this combination of duties is in a position to use the computer to make unauthorized changes in programs. As an additional precaution, the computer should create a log of all instructions given to the machine by the computer operator. This record should be reviewed daily by a computer department control group to determine that the operator has not made any unauthorized changes in programs or files.

● **CASE IN POINT** ● One recent computer fraud in a large company was linked to a well-publicized change in income tax rates. Knowing that employees expected a change in the amount of income taxes withheld from their paychecks, a computer programmer wrote a new payroll program which overstated by a few dollars the income taxes withheld from each employee. The program then added these excess withholdings to the programmer's own paycheck. As a large labor force was involved, the dollar amount of this fraud was quite substantial.

This fraud would not have been possible if the new payroll program had been carefully tested by other employees.

Security controls

The purpose of security controls is to safeguard computer-based records, computer programs, and computer equipment against damage, theft, or unauthorized use. It is essential that only authorized personnel have access to computer programs and accounting records. When programs or records can be accessed from a computer terminal, the user of the terminal should be required to enter *secret passwords* to gain access to the system. The computer should issue a warning to the computer department control group if repeated attempts are made to gain access to the system using incorrect passwords. Computer facilities, programs, and records should be safely locked up after working hours.

● **CASE IN POINT** ● A consultant for a large bank was able to use the bank's electronic funds transfer system to transfer $10 million of the bank's money to his own account at another bank. The consultant had noticed that the "secret" passwords necessary to make wire transfers were posted on the wall beside a computer terminal.

The fraud remained undetected for eight days. In the meantime, the consultant transferred the money to a Swiss bank account and then converted it into diamonds. He might never have been caught, except that he returned to his home state and tried to sell some of the diamonds.

Input controls

Input controls are precautions taken to ensure that the data being entered into the computer are correct. Input controls vary, depending upon whether transactions are being entered into the system as they occur *(online, real-time)*, or whether they are processed periodically in large groups or *batches.*

In an online, real-time *(OLRT)* system, input controls include such concepts as identification numbers and passwords to identify authorized users. In addition, the terminals used for recording specific types of transactions should have only *limited access* to the computer-based records. For example, the point-of-sale terminals in retail department stores are used to record cash sales and credit sales. Therefore, the only entries which need to be made from these terminals are debits to the Cash and Accounts Receivable accounts and credits to the Sales account. These terminals should not have access to other accounts or records.

Another input control in an OLRT system is the use of *machine-readable input.* For example, many items in supermarkets are labeled with machine-readable codes. The cashier passes this merchandise over an optical scanner, which identifies the merchandise to the computer. The computer then determines the price of the item from a master price list and displays this amount for both the cashier and the customer to see. This automatic entry procedure virtually eliminates errors in recording the sales price of merchandise.

Often transactions are processed in periodic batches, rather than as they occur. The preparation of a payroll at the end of each pay period is a common example of *batch processing.* Advance preparation of *control totals* can be an effective input control when data is processed in a batch. A control total represents the total dollar amount of all transactions sent to the EDP department for processing. The computer will add up the total dollar amount of all data processed and print this total as part of the computer output. The predetermined control total may then be compared to the total printed by the computer. This comparison will show whether any data has been added or lost within the EDP department, and also will bring to light such items as transposition errors.

Program controls

Program controls are error-detecting measures built into the computer program. An example of a program control is a *limit test,* which compares every item of data processed by the computer to a specified dollar limit. In the event an amount exceeds the dollar limit, the computer does not process that item and prints out an error report. A limit test is particularly effective in such computer applications as preparing paychecks, when it is known that none of the paychecks should be for more than a specified amount, such as $1,000.

Another example of a program control is an *item count.* The total number of data items to be processed by the computer is determined, and that total is entered as part of the input to the computer. The computer then counts the number of items it processes, and if this number differs from the predetermined total, an error report is printed. This item count ensures that all the data are actually processed by the computer.

Accounting applications of the computer

The use of electronic data processing equipment is possible for virtually every phase of accounting operations. Even a CPA firm, in conducting an annual audit, may use the computer as an audit tool. For this purpose the auditors may employ specially written computer programs to aid in their work of sampling and analyzing data to determine the fairness of the financial statements.

The most common application of the computer, however, is to process large masses of accounting data relating to routine repetitive operations such as recording retail sales, maintaining perpetual inventory records, preparing payroll, and posting to ledger accounts.

Retail sales — accounts receivable and inventory records. The point-of-sale terminals now prominent in many retail establishments greatly reduce the work involved in accounting for sales transactions. Many of these terminals use an optical scanner or other electronic device to "read" magnetically coded labels attached to the merchandise. As the merchandise is passed over the optical scanner, the code is sent instantaneously to the computer. From the code number, the computer is able to identify the item being sold, record the amount of the sale, and transfer the cost of the item from the Inventory account to the Cost of Goods Sold account. If the transaction is a credit sale, the salesclerk enters the customer's credit card number in the electronic register. This number enables the computer to update instantly the customer's account in the subsidiary ledger.

Note that all of the accounting is done automatically as the salesclerk rings up the sale. Thus any number of transactions can be recorded and posted with virtually no manual work. At the end of each day, the computer prints a complete sales journal along with up-to-date balances for the general ledger and subsidiary ledger accounts relating to sales transactions.

Payrolls. In a manual accounting system the preparation of payroll checks is usually separate from the maintenance of records showing pay rates, positions, time worked, payroll deductions, and other personnel data. A computer, however, has the capability of maintaining all records relating to payroll as well as turning out the required paychecks. Payroll processing is usually one of the first accounting operations to be placed on the computer.

The payroll procedure consists of determining for each employee the gross earnings, making deductions, computing net pay, preparing the payroll check, and maintaining a record of each individual's earnings. Also, the company needs a payroll summary for each period and usually a distribution of payroll costs by department, by product, or classified by the various productive processes. The payroll function has become increasingly complex and time-consuming in recent years because of the advent of social security taxes, income tax withholding, and other payroll deductions. Each employee must receive not only a payroll check but a statement showing the gross earnings, deductions, and net pay. The company's records must be designed to facilitate filing regular payroll reports to the federal and state governments showing amounts withheld for income taxes, unemployment insurance, and social security. The time and the expense required to prepare payrolls have risen in proportion to the need for more information.

A computerized payroll system will not only maintain the necessary records, prepare the checks, and print the required reports, but will also keep management informed of the costs of various functions within the business. For example, data can be produced showing the work-hours and labor costs on each job, labor cost by department for each salesclerk, or the time required by different employees to perform similar work. The comparison below illustrates the efficiency of processing payrolls by computer rather than manually:

Payroll may be prepared either manually or by EDP

Function	Payroll Prepared Manually	Payroll Prepared by Computer
1 Timekeeping	Fill in new set of records each period, making extensions manually.	Enter raw data on appropriate forms.
2 Computation of gross pay	Compute gross pay for each employee, perhaps with desk calculator, and enter manually in records.	Performed electronically.
3 Calculation of deductions	For each employee, refer to charts and make computations; enter manually in records.	Performed electronically.
4 Preparation of checks, earnings statements, and payroll register	Write by hand or type checks. Proofread and maintain controls.	Performed electronically.
5 Bank reconciliation	Reconcile payroll bank account per accounting records with monthly bank statement.	Performed electronically.
6 Reports to government	Prepare quarterly reports showing for each employee and in total amounts earned, deducted, and paid. Reconcile individual data with controls.	Performed electronically.
7 Managerial control data	Prepare distribution of hours and labor cost by department or by job. Other analyses may be needed.	Performed electronically.

Computer-based journals and ledgers. As mentioned earlier in this chapter, computers also may be used to maintain the journals and ledgers and to prepare financial statements. Transactions and end-of-period adjustments still must be analyzed by persons possessing a knowledge of accounting principles. However, after these transactions have been analyzed and prepared in computer input form, the computer can be used to print the journals, post to the ledger accounts, and print the financial statements and other financial reports. The advantage of maintaining accounting records by computer is that the possibility of mathematical errors is greatly reduced, and the speed of the computer permits the records to be kept continuously up-to-date.

Other accounting applications of computers include forecasting the profit possibilities inherent in alternative courses of action, analyzing gross profit margins by department or by product line, and determining future cash requirements long in advance. Recent developments of accounting applications of the computer provide much more information about business operations than was available to management in the past.

Key terms introduced or emphasized in chapter 6

Accounts payable ledger. A subsidiary ledger containing an account with each supplier or vendor. The total of the ledger agrees with the general ledger controlling account, Accounts Payable.

Accounts receivable ledger. A subsidiary ledger containing an account with each credit customer. The total of the ledger agrees with the general ledger controlling account, Accounts Receivable.

Batch processing. A method of data processing in which transactions are accumulated into groups for processing at periodic intervals, rather than being processed as the transactions occur. Batch processing is widely used for such applications as payrolls. Contrasts with *online, real-time processing.*

Cash payments journal. A special journal used to record all payments of cash.

Cash receipts journal. A special journal used to record all receipts of cash.

Controlling account. A general ledger account which is supported by detailed information in a subsidiary ledger.

Input controls. Internal control measures to ensure accuracy of data entered into a computer (such as control totals, the total dollar amount of documents to be processed).

Online, real-time (OLRT) processing. Using terminals in direct communication with the computer to process transactions instantaneously as they occur. Airline reservation systems, teller terminals at banks, and point-of-sale terminals are examples of OLRT systems. Contrasts with *batch processing.*

Point-of-sale terminal. Electronic cash registers used for *online, real-time processing* of sales transactions. Widely used in large retail stores.

Program. Instructions to a computer consisting of a series of steps planned to carry out a certain process (such as payroll preparation).

Program controls. Error-detecting measures built into a computer program (such as a limit test setting a maximum dollar amount, or item counts specifying the number of items to be processed).

Purchases journal. A special journal used exclusively to record purchases of merchandise on credit.

Sales journal. A special journal used exclusively to record sales of merchandise on credit.

Security controls. Internal control procedures designed to protect computer programs, records, and equipment against theft, damage, and unauthorized use. The use of secret passwords to gain access to computer-based records is an example of a security control.

Subsidiary ledger. A supplementary record used to provide detailed information for a control account in the general ledger. The total of accounts in a subsidiary ledger equals the balance of the related control account in the general ledger.

Demonstration problem for your review

The Signal Corporation began operations on November 1, 19___. The chart of accounts used by the company included the following accounts, among others:

Cash	10	Purchases	60
Marketable securities	15	Purchase returns & allowances	62
Office supplies	18	Purchase discounts	64
Notes payable	30	Salaries expense	70
Accounts payable	32	Utilities expense	71

November transactions relating to the purchase of merchandise and to accounts payable are listed below, along with selected other transactions.

Nov. 1 Purchased merchandise from Moss Co. for $3,000. Invoice dated today; terms 2/10, n/30.

Nov. 3 Received shipment of merchandise from Wilmer Co. and invoice dated November 2 for $7,600; terms 2/10, n/30.

Nov. 6 Purchased merchandise from Archer Company at cost of $5,600. Invoice dated November 5; terms 2/10, n/30.

Nov. 9 Purchased marketable securities for cash, $1,200.

Nov. 10 Issued check to Moss Co. in settlement of invoice dated November 1, less discount.

Nov. 12 Received shipment of merchandise from Cory Corporation and an invoice dated November 11 in amount of $7,100; terms net 30 days.

Nov. 14 Issued check to Archer Company in settlement of invoice of November 5.

Nov. 16 Paid cash for office supplies, $110.

Nov. 17 Purchased merchandise for cash, $950.

Nov. 19 Purchased merchandise from Klein Co. for $11,500. Invoice dated November 18; terms 2/10, n/30.

Nov. 21 Purchased merchandise from Belmont Company for $8,400. Invoice dated November 20; terms 1/10, n/30.

Nov. 24 Purchased merchandise for cash, $375.

Nov. 26 Purchased merchandise from Brooker Co. for $6,500. Invoice dated today; terms 1/10, n/30.

Nov. 28 Paid utilities, $150.

Nov. 30 Paid salaries for November, $2,900. (Payroll taxes and withholding are to be ignored.)

Nov. 30 Paid $2,600 cash to Wilmer Co. and issued 12%, 90-day promissory note for $5,000 in settlement of invoice dated November 2.

Instructions

a Record the transactions in the appropriate journals. Use a single-column purchases journal and a six-column cash payments journal.

b Indicate how postings would be made by placing ledger account numbers and check marks in the appropriate columns of the journals.

c Prepare a schedule of accounts payable at November 30 to prove that the subsidiary ledger is in balance with the controlling account.

Solution to demonstration problem

a & b   Purchases Journal   Page 1

Date		Account Credited		Invoice Date		✓	Amount
19__				19__			
Nov	1	Moss Co.	(terms 2/10, n/30)	Nov	1	✓	3,000
	3	Wilmer Co.	(terms 2/10, n/30)		2	✓	7,600
	6	Archer Company	(terms 2/10, n/30)		5	✓	5,600
	12	Cory Corporation	(terms net 30)		11	✓	7,100
	19	Klein Co.	(terms 2/10, n/30)		18	✓	11,500
	21	Belmont Company	(terms 1/10, n/30)		20	✓	8,400
	26	Brooker Co.	(terms 1/10, n/30)		26	✓	6,500
							$49,700
							(60)(32)

Cash Payments Journal

| Date | Explanation | Credits | | | | | Account Debited | | Debits | | | |
| | | Cash | Purchase Discounts | Other Accounts | | | | ✓ | Accounts Payable | Purchases | Other Accounts | |
				Name	LP	Amount					LP	Amount
19— Nov												
9	Bought securities	1,200					Marketable Securities				15	1,200
10	Invoice, Nov. 1, less 2%	2,940	60				Moss Co.	✓	3,000			
14	Invoice, Nov. 5, less 2%	5,488	112				Archer Company	✓	5,600			
16	Purchased office supplies	110					Office Supplies				18	110
17	Cash purchases	950								950		
24	Cash purchases	375								375		
28	Paid utilities	150					Utilities Expense				71	150
30	Paid salaries	2,900					Salaries Expense				70	2,900
30	Invoice, Nov. 2, note issued for unpaid balance	2,600		Notes Payable	30	5,000	Wilmer Co.	✓	7,600			
		16,713	172			5,000			16,200	1,325		4,360
		(10)	(64)			(X)			(32)	(60)		(X)

243

c

SIGNAL CORPORATION
Schedule of Accounts Payable
November 30, 19___

Belmont Company	$ 8,400
Brooker Co.	6,500
Cory Corporation	7,100
Klein Co.	11,500
Total (per general ledger controlling account)	$33,500

Review questions

1 What advantages are offered by the use of special journals?

2 100 Flavors, Inc., uses a general journal and four special journals: (a) sales journal, (b) purchases journal, (c) cash receipts journal, and (d) cash payments journal. Which journal should the company use to record (1) the declaration of a dividend, and (2) the later payment of this dividend? Explain the reasoning underlying your answer.

3 The column total of one of the four special journals described in this chapter is posted at month-end to two general ledger accounts. One of these two accounts is Accounts Payable. What is the name of the special journal? What account is debited and what account is credited with this total?

4 Pine Hill General Store makes about 500 sales on account each month, using only a two-column general journal to record these transactions. What would be the extent of the work saved by using a sales journal?

5 When accounts receivable and accounts payable are kept in subsidiary ledgers, will the general ledger continue to be a self-balancing ledger with equal debits and credits? Explain.

6 Explain how, why, and when the cash receipts journal and cash payments journal are cross-footed.

7 During November the sales on credit made by the Hardy Company actually amounted to $41,625, but an error of $1,000 was made in totaling the amount column of the sales journal. When and how will the error be discovered?

8 Considerable copying work may be performed in preparing a sales invoice, a sales journal, and a receivables ledger. Is this step-by-step sequence, with its related opportunity for errors, a characteristic of all types of accounting system? Explain.

9 For a large modern department store, such as a Sears or J. C. Penney, is it necessary to maintain a manual single-column sales journal? Explain.

10 Briefly describe some of the advantages of processing accounting information by computer rather than manually.

11 Explain several factors which may cause accounting information processed by a computer to be in error.

12 What is the purpose of subdividing duties among the personnel of a company's EDP department?

13 A computer usually maintains a log of all instructions given to the computer by the computer operator while data is being processed. What use should be made of this log? Explain.

14 Explain the purpose of security controls in a computer-based accounting system.

15 Explain the meaning of the term *input control* and give an example.

16 Explain the meaning of the term *program control* and give an example.

17 Distinguish between *online, real-time* processing and *batch* processing.

18 In processing the monthly payroll by computer, the gross pay of one employee was accidentally recorded as $1,238 instead of $1,283. Will this error most likely be brought to light by a limit test, an item count, or a control total? Explain.

Exercises

Ex. 6-1   Medical Supply Co. uses a cash receipts journal, a cash payments journal, a sales journal, a purchases journal, and a general journal. Indicate which journal should be used to record each of the following transactions.

a Payment of property taxes
b Purchase of office equipment on credit
c Sale of merchandise on credit
d Sale of merchandise for cash
e Cash refund to a customer who returned merchandise
f Return of merchandise to a supplier for credit
g Adjusting entry to record depreciation
h Purchase of delivery truck for cash
i Purchase of merchandise on account
j Return of merchandise by a customer company for credit to its account

Ex. 6-2   Island Company, a merchandising concern, uses a cash receipts journal, a cash payments journal, a sales journal, a purchases journal, and a general journal.

a In which of the five journals would you expect to find the smallest number of transactions recorded?
b At the end of the accounting period, the total of the sales journal should be posted to what account or accounts? As a debit or credit?
c At the end of the accounting period, the total of the purchases journal should be posted to what account or accounts? As a debit or credit?
d Name two subsidiary ledgers which would probably be used in conjunction with the journals listed above. Identify the journals from which postings would regularly be made to each of the two subsidiary ledgers.
e In which of the five journals would adjusting and closing entries be made?

Ex. 6-3   The accounting system used by Gortex, Inc., includes a general journal and also four special journals for cash receipts, cash payments, sales, and purchases of merchandise. On January 31, after all January posting had been completed, the Accounts Receivable controlling account in the general ledger had a debit balance of $160,000, and the Accounts Payable controlling account had a credit balance of $48,000.

The February transactions recorded in the four special journals can be summarized as follows:

Sales journal .... Total transactions, $96,000
Purchases journal .... Total transactions, $56,000
Cash receipts journal .... Accounts Receivable column total, $76,800 (credit)
Cash payments journal .... Accounts Payable column total, $67,200 (debit)

a What posting would be made of the $76,800 total of the Accounts Receivable column in the cash receipts journal at February 28?

b What posting would be made of the $96,000 total of the sales journal at February 28?

c What posting would be made of the $56,000 total of the purchases journal at February 28?

d What posting would be made of the $67,200 total of the Accounts Payable column in the cash payments journal at February 28?

e Based on the above information, state the balances of the Accounts Receivable controlling account and the Accounts Payable controlling account in the general ledger after completion of posting at February 28?

Ex. 6-4 Pacific Products uses a sales journal to record all sales of merchandise on credit. During July the transactions in this journal were as follows:

Sales Journal

Date		Account Debited	Invoice No.	Amount
July	6	Robert Baker	437	3,600
	15	Minden Company	438	8,610
	17	Pell & Warden	439	1,029
	26	Stonewall Corporation	440	17,500
	27	Robert Baker	441	3,000
				33,739

Entries in the general journal during July include one for the return of merchandise by a customer, as follows:

July	18	Sales Returns and Allowances	500	
		Accounts Receivable, Minden Company		500
		Allowed credit to customer for return of		
		merchandise from sale of July 15.		

a Prepare a subsidiary ledger for accounts receivable by opening a T account for each of the four customers listed above. Post the entries in the sales journal to these individual customers' accounts. From the general journal, post the credit to the account of Minden Company.

b Prepare general ledger accounts in T form as follows: a controlling account for Accounts Receivable, a Sales account, and a Sales Returns and Allowances account. Post to these accounts the appropriate entries from the sales journal and general journal.

c Prepare a schedule of accounts receivable at July 31 to prove that this subsidiary ledger is in agreement with its controlling account.

Ex. 6-5 Keystone Company maintains a manual accounting system with the four special journals and general journal described in this chapter. During September, the following errors were made. For each of the errors you are to list the identifying letter and explain how and when the error will be brought to light.

    a Incorrectly added the debit entries in a customer's account in the accounts receivable subsidiary ledger and listed the total as $950 when it should have been $550.

    b A purchase of merchandise on credit from Rex Company in the amount of $1,000 was erroneously entered in the purchases journal as a $100 purchase.

    c Recorded correctly in the sales journal a $400 sale of merchandise on credit but posted the transaction to the customer's account in the subsidiary ledger as a $40 sale.

    d Made error at September 30 in adding the entries in the purchases journal, determining a total for September purchases of $62,491. The correct total was $52,491.

Ex. 6-6   Trendline Graphics, a wholesaler, follows the practice of posting customers' accounts in the accounts receivable subsidiary ledger directly from duplicate copies of sales invoices rather than copying the invoices into a sales journal. Credit memos also are posted directly to customers' accounts. At month-end, a general journal entry is made for the total of sales invoices issued during the month, and another general journal entry is used to record the total of the credit memos issued.

    During January, the company issued 389 sales invoices totaling $116,420. Also during January, 27 credit memos were issued in the total amount of $2,160. You are to prepare the two general journal entries needed at January 31.

Ex. 6-7   Mission Stores uses electronic registers to record its sales transactions. All merchandise bears a magnetic code number which can be read by an optical scanner. When merchandise is sold, the sales clerk passes each item over the scanner. The computer reads the code number, determines the price of the item from a master price list, and displays the price on a screen for the customer to see. After each item has been passed over the scanner, the computer displays the total amount of the sale and records the transaction in the company's accounting records.

    If the transaction is a credit sale, the sales clerk enters the customer's credit card number into the register. The computer checks the customer's credit status and updates the accounts receivable subsidiary ledger.

    Items *a* through *d* below describe problems which may arise in a retailing business which uses manual cash registers and accounting records. Explain how the electronic registers used by Mission Stores will help reduce or eliminate these problems. If the electronic registers will not help to eliminate the problems, explain why not.

    a A sales clerk is unaware of a recent change in the price of a particular item.

    b Merchandise is stolen by a shoplifter.

    c A sales clerk fails to record a cash sale and keeps the cash received from the customer.

    d A customer buys merchandise on account using a stolen Mission Stores credit card.

Problems

6-1   Subsidiary ledgers and controlling accounts

The accounting system used by Furniture Warehouse includes a general journal and four special journals for daily recording of transactions. Information recorded in these journals is posted to a general ledger and two subsidiary ledgers: one of the subsidiary ledgers contains accounts receivable and the other accounts payable. All three ledgers are in the three-column, running balance form. At September 30, the subsidiary ledger for accounts payable contained the accounts with creditors shown below. Note that postings to these accounts have been made from three different journals.

Raleigh Products, Inc.

Date		Explanation	Ref	Debit	Credit	Balance
19–						
Sept.	1		P1		1 600 00	1 600 00
	20		P1		1 28 00	2 88 00
	21	Returned Mdse.	J2	8 00		2 80 00
	28		CP3	1 52 00		1 28 00

Superior Furniture Co.

Date		Explanation	Ref	Debit	Credit	Balance
19–						
Sept.	22		P1		1 37 60	1 37 60

Traditional Interiors

Date		Explanation	Ref	Debit	Credit	Balance
19–						
Aug.	31	Balance				9 60
Sept	15		CP3	9 60		– 0 –
	16		P1		30 00	30 00
	20		P1		48 00	78 00

Ultra Designs, Inc.

Date		Explanation	Ref	Debit	Credit	Balance
19–						
Aug.	31	Balance				3 52 00
Sept	5	Returned Mdse.	J2	19 20		3 32 80
	20		CP3	2 40 00		9 2 80
	25		P1		16 00	1 08 80

Instructions. You are to prepare the general ledger controlling account, Accounts Payable, corresponding to the above subsidiary ledger accounts for the month of September. Use a three-column running balance form of ledger account. (Remember that a controlling account is posted on a daily basis for transactions recorded in the general journal, but is posted only at the end of the month for the *monthly totals* of special journals such as the purchases journal and the cash payments journal.)

Enter in the controlling account the beginning balance at August 31, the transactions from the general journal during September in chronological order, and the running balance of the account after each entry. Finally, make one posting for all purchases of merchandise on credit during

September and one posting for all cash payments to suppliers during September. For each entry in the controlling account, show the date and source (journal and page number) of the item. Use the symbols shown on page 227 to identify the individual journals.

6-2 Special journals and subsidiary ledgers (without posting)

The accounting system of Springfield Express includes a general journal, four special journals, a general ledger, and two subsidiary ledgers. The chart of accounts includes the following accounts, among others:

Cash	10	Sales	50
Notes receivable	15	Sales returns & allowances	52
Accounts receivable	17	Sales discounts	54
Land	20	Purchases	60
Office equipment	25	Purchase returns & allowances	62
Notes payable	30	Interest revenue	82
Accounts payable	32	Gain on sale of land	85

Transactions in June involving the sale of merchandise and the receipt of cash are shown below, along with certain other selected transactions.

June 1 Sold merchandise to Williams Company for cash, $472.

June 4 Sold merchandise to Bravo Corporation $8,500. Invoice no. 618; terms 2/10, n/30.

June 5 Received cash refund of $1,088 for merchandise returned to a supplier.

June 8 Sold merchandise to Bradley Company for $4,320. Invoice no. 619; terms 2/10, n/30.

June 9 Received a check from Kamtex, Inc., in payment of a $2,400 invoice, less 2% discount.

June 11 Received $1,120 from Olympus Company in payment of a past-due invoice.

June 13 Received check from Bravo Corporation in settlement of invoice dated June 4, less discount.

June 16 Sold merchandise to XYZ Company, $4,040. Invoice no. 620; terms 2/10, n/30.

June 16 Returned $960 of merchandise to supplier, King Industries, for reduction of account payable.

June 18 Purchased office equiment at a cost of $3,040, signing a 9%, 90-day note payable for the full amount.

June 20 Sold merchandise to Armstrong Co. for $7,000. Invoice no. 621; terms 2/10, n/30.

June 21 XYZ Company returned for credit $640 of merchandise purchased on June 16.

June 23 Borrowed $24,000 cash from a local bank, signing a six-month note payable.

June 25 Received payment in full from XYZ Company in settlement of invoice dated June 16, less return and discount.

June 29 Sold land costing $30,400 for $11,200 cash and a note receivable for $33,600. (Credit Gain on Sale of Land for $14,400.)

June 30 Collected from Armstrong Co. amount of invoice dated June 20, less 2% discount.

June 30 Collected $12,992 in full settlement of a $12,800 note receivable held since May 1. (No interest revenue has yet been recorded.)

June 30 Received a 60-day note receivable for $4,320 from Bradley Company in settlement of invoice dated June 8.

Instructions. Record the above transactions in the appropriate journals. Use a single-column sales journal, a six-column cash receipts journal, and a two-column general journal. Foot and rule the special journals and indicate how postings would be made by placing ledger account numbers and check marks in the appropriate columns of the journals.

6-3   Special journals and subsidiary ledgers (including posting)
Appliance City has a chart of accounts which includes the following accounts, among others:

Cash	10	Accounts payable	30
Office supplies	18	Purchases	50
Land	20	Purchase returns & allowances	52
Building	22	Purchase discounts	53
Notes payable	28	Salaries expense	60

The April transactions relating to the purchase of merchandise for resale and to accounts payable are listed below along with selected other transactions.

Apr.   1   Purchased merchandise from Super Cold Refrigerators at a cost of $12,420. Invoice dated today; terms 2/10, n/30.

Apr.   4   Purchased merchandise from Nisson TV for $26,500. Invoice dated April 3; terms 2/10, n/30.

Apr.   5   Returned for credit to Super Cold Refrigerators defective merchandise having a list price of $2,920.

Apr.   6   Received shipment of merchandise from Ranges, Inc., and their invoice dated April 5 in amount of $31,500. Terms net 30 days.

Apr.   8   Purchased merchandise from Modern Maid, $25,000. Invoice dated today with terms 1/10, n/60.

Apr. 10   Purchased merchandise from Hilo Corporation, $16,000. Invoice dated April 9; terms 2/10, n/30.

Apr. 10   Issued check to Super Cold Refrigerators in settlement of balance resulting from purchase of April 1 and purchase return of April 5.

Apr. 11   Issued check to Nisson TV in payment of April 3 invoice.

Apr. 18   Issued check to Hilo Corporation in settlement of invoice dated April 9.

Apr. 20   Purchased merchandise for cash, $1,080.

Apr. 21   Bought land, $72,500, and building, $140,000, for expansion of business. Paid cash of $50,000 and signed a promissory note for the balance of $162,500. (Land and building were acquired in a single transaction from R. M. Wilson.)

Apr. 23   Purchased merchandise for cash, $1,100

Apr. 26   Purchased merchandise from Dry Fast, Inc., for $22,400. Invoice dated April 26; terms 2/10, n/30.

Apr. 28   Paid cash for office supplies, $630.

Apr. 29   Purchased merchandise for cash, $2,590.

Apr. 30   Paid salaries for April, $13,040.

Instructions

a Record the transactions in the appropriate journals. Use a single-column purchases journal, a six-column cash payments journal, and a two-column general journal. Foot and rule the special journals. Make all postings to the proper general ledger accounts and to the accounts payable subsidiary ledger.

b Prepare a schedule of accounts payable at April 30 to prove that the subsidiary ledger is in balance with the controlling account for accounts payable.

6-4   Special journals: cash receipts and cash payments
Backpacker & Co. uses an accounting system that includes multicolumn special journals for cash

receipts and cash payments. These journals are similar to those illustrated on pages 222–223 and 224–225. All the cash transactions during September are described below.

Sept.   1   Cash purchase of merchandise, $6,848.

Sept.   1   Paid Spalding Company invoice, $2,600 less 1% discount.

Sept.   2   Cash sales of merchandise, $5,504.

Sept.   2   Paid inbound freight charges on merchandise from Watkins Company, $326. (Debit Transportation-in.)

Sept.   4   Purchased furniture and fixtures, $5,120, making a down payment of $1,280 and issuing a note payable for the balance.

Sept.   5   Received $960 cash as partial collection of our $3,840 invoice to National Co. Also received a note receivable for the $2,880 balance of this invoice. (Use cash receipts journal.)

Sept.   6   Paid Newcomb Company invoice, $4,500 less 2% discount.

Sept.   9   Paid note payable due today, $9,600, plus interest amounting to $192. (Debit Interest Expense, $192.)

Sept. 15   Cash sales of merchandise, $4,243.

Sept. 15   Paid September rent, $2,080.

Sept. 17   Purchased U.S. government bonds, $6,400. (Debit U.S. Government Bonds.)

Sept. 18   Cash purchase of merchandise, $4,640.

Sept. 20   Received $1,960 cash in full settlement of our $2,000 invoice to Mesa Company after allowing 2% discount.

Sept. 21   Paid Mammoth Co. invoice, $5,200 less 2% discount.

Sept. 23   Paid sales commissions of $2,528 to sales staff.

Sept. 30   Received payment in full settlement of our $5,500 invoice to Presley Company, less 2% discount.

Sept. 30   Paid monthly salaries, $9,000.

Sept. 30   Cash sales of merchandise, $5,105.

Instructions

a   Enter the above transactions in the cash receipts journal and the cash payments journal.

b   Foot and rule the journals.

6-5   Special journals: a comprehensive problem

Four Seasons began business in October and established the following ledger accounts:

Cash	10	Sales	50
Notes receivable	14	Sales returns & allowances	52
Accounts receivable	15	Sales discounts	54
Merchandise inventory	17	Purchases	60
Unexpired insurance	19	Purchase returns & allowances	62
Land	20	Purchase discounts	64
Building	21	Transportation-in	66
Furniture and fixtures	24	Rent expense	70
Notes payable	30	Salaries expense	72
Accounts payable	32	Taxes expense	74
Mortgage payable	36	Supplies expense	76
Capital stock	40	Insurance expense	78
Retained earnings	42	Interest earned	80
Income summary	45	Interest expense	83

The company offers terms of 2/10, n/30 on all sales of merchandise on credit. The transactions during October were as follows:

Oct. 1 Sold capital stock for $80,000, and deposited this amount in the bank under the name Four Seasons.

Oct. 4 Purchased land and building at a total cost of $100,000. Paid $40,000 cash and signed a mortgage for the balance of the purchase price. Estimated value of the land was $45,000, and of the building, $55,000.

Oct. 6 Sold merchandise to Brad Parks, $6,800. Invoice no. 1, terms 2/10, n/30.

Oct. 7 Purchased merchandise from Lakeview Company, $12,000. Invoice dated today; terms 2/10, n/30.

Oct. 7 Sold merchandise for cash, $1,300.

Oct. 7 Paid $486 for a two-year fire insurance policy. (Debit Unexpired Insurance.)

Oct. 10 Paid freight charges of $369 on purchase from Lakeview Company.

Oct. 12 Sold merchandise to ABC Corporation, $8,800. Invoice no. 2; terms 2/10, n/30.

Oct. 13 Purchased merchandise for cash, $2,556.

Oct. 15 Received payment from Brad Parks. Invoice no. 1, dated October 6, less 2% discount.

Oct. 16 Issued credit memorandum no. 1 to ABC Corporation, $800, for goods returned today by ABC Corporation.

Oct. 17 Paid Lakeview Company invoice of October 7, less discount.

Oct. 18 Purchased merchandise from Baker Company, $6,000. Invoice dated today; terms 2/10, n/30.

Oct. 20 A portion of merchandise purchased from Baker Company was found to be substandard. After discussion with the vendor, a price reduction of $200 was agreed upon and a credit memo for this amount was received from Baker Company.

Oct. 22 Received payment from ABC Corporation. Invoice no. 2, less return of merchandise on October 16 and discount on balance.

Oct. 23 Purchased merchandise from Lakeview Company, $7,560. Invoice dated today; terms 2/10, n/60.

Oct. 27 Sold merchandise for cash, $927.

Oct. 28 Borrowed $15,400 from bank, issuing a note payable as evidence of indebtedness.

Oct. 28 Paid Baker Company invoice of October 18, less allowance and discount.

Oct. 30 Paid first installment on mortgage, $900. This payment included interest of $600.

Oct. 30 Purchased merchandise for cash, $1,656.

Oct. 31 Paid monthly salaries of $6,000.

Oct. 31 Sold merchandise to Frank Sullivan, $4,950. Invoice no. 3; terms 2/10, n/30.

Instructions

a Enter the October transactions in the following journals:
   Two-column general journal
   One-column sales journal
   One-column purchases journal
   Six-column cash receipts journal
   Six-column cash payments journal

b Foot and rule all special journals.

c Show how posting would be made by placing the ledger account numbers and check marks in the appropriate columns of the journals. This instruction includes placing ledger account numbers in the LP columns as well as under the totals for the month.

6-6   Special journals: another comprehensive problem
Sand Castle Company uses the following accounts (among others) in recording transactions:

Cash	10	Dividends	53
Notes receivable	14	Sales	60
Accounts receivable	16	Sales returns and allowances	62
Supplies	17	Sales discounts	64
Unexpired insurance	18	Purchases	70
Equipment	26	Purchase returns and allowances	72
Accumulated depreciation:		Purchase discounts	74
equipment	28	Transportation-in	76
Notes payable	30	Salaries expense	80
Accounts payable	32	Supplies expense	84
Dividends payable	34	Insurance expense	86
Mortgage payable	40	Depreciation expense: equipment	88
Capital stock	50	Gain on sale of equipment	90
Retained earnings	52	Interest expense	92

The schedules of accounts receivable and accounts payable for the company at October 31, 19___, are shown below:

Schedule of Accounts Receivable October 31, 19__		Schedule of Accounts Payable October 31, 19__	
Ace Contractors	$20,800	Durapave, Inc.	$30,000
Reliable Builders, Inc.	8,750		
Total	$29,550		

The November transactions of Sand Castle Company were as follows:

Nov. 2 Purchased merchandise on account from Durapave, Inc., $28,000. Invoice was dated today with terms of 2/10, n/30.

Nov. 3 Sold merchandise to Ace Contractors, $16,000. Invoice no. 428; terms 2/10, n/30.

Nov. 4 Purchased supplies for cash, $875. (Debit the asset account, Supplies.)

Nov. 5 Sold merchandise for cash, $5,600.

Nov. 7 Paid the Durapave, Inc., invoice for $30,000, representing October purchases. No discount was allowed by Durapave, Inc., as the discount period had expired.

Nov. 10 Purchased merchandise from Tool Company, $32,500. Invoice dated November 9 with terms of 1/10, n/30.

Nov. 10 Collected from Ace Contractors for invoice no. 428 for $16,000 less 2%, and for October sales of $20,800 on which the discount had lapsed.

Nov. 12 Sold merchandise to Rex Company, $21,750. Invoice no. 429; terms 2/10, n/30.

Nov. 14 Paid freight charges of $2,050 on goods purchased November 10 from Tool Company.

Nov. 14 Sold equipment for $9,000, receiving cash of $1,500 and a 30-day, 10% note receivable for the balance. Equipment cost $20,000 and accumulated depreciation was $13,000. (Debit Accumulated Depreciation: Equipment for $13,000 and credit Gain on Sale of Equipment for $2,000.)

Nov. 15 Issued credit memo no. 38 to Rex Company upon return of $1,000 of merchandise.

Nov. 18 Paid for one-year fire insurance policy, $1,425. (Debit Unexpired Insurance.)

Nov. 18 Purchased merchandise for cash, $7,625.

Nov. 19　Paid the Tool Company invoice dated November 9, less the 1% discount.

Nov. 20　Sold merchandise on account to Vincent Co., $13,650; invoice no. 430. Required customer to sign a 30-day, non-interest-bearing note. (Record this sale by a debit to Accounts Receivable, then transfer from Accounts Receivable to Notes Receivable by means of an entry in the general journal.)

Nov. 22　Purchased merchandise for cash, $4,050.

Nov. 22　Sold merchandise for cash, $4,675.

Nov. 22　Received payment from Rex Company for invoice no. 429. Customer made deduction for credit memorandum no. 38 issued November 15, and a 2% discount.

Nov. 23　Sold merchandise on account to Waite, Inc., $9,950. Invoice no. 431; terms 2/10, n/30.

Nov. 24　Declared a dividend of $37,500 on capital stock, payable December 20, 19__.

Nov. 25　Purchased merchandise from Smith Company, $26,500. Invoice dated November 24 with terms of 2/10, n/60.

Nov. 26　Issued debit memorandum no. 42 to Smith Company in connection with merchandise returned today amounting to $2,125.

Nov. 27　Purchased equipment having a list price of $60,000. Paid $10,000 down and signed a promissory note for the balance of $50,000. (Equipment is for use in the business.)

Nov. 30　Paid monthly salaries of $14,800 for services rendered by employees during November.

Nov. 30　Paid monthly installment on mortgage, $3,500, of which $1,020 was interest.

Instructions

a　Record the November transactions in the following journals:
　　General journal — 2 columns
　　Sales journal — 1 column
　　Purchases journal — 1 column
　　Cash receipts journal — 6 columns
　　Cash payments journal — 6 columns
　Foot and rule all special journals and show how postings would be made by placing ledger account numbers and check marks in the appropriate columns of the journals.

b　Prepare a schedule of accounts receivable and accounts payable as of November 30. You may want to use T accounts to compile the accounts receivable from customers and amounts payable to suppliers at November 30. Begin with the October 31 balances. You can verify your November 30 totals by computing the balances of the controlling accounts determined by posting of totals from the special journals and individual transactions from the general journal.

6-7　Internal control procedures: computer-based systems

Shown below are eight possible errors or problems which might occur in a business. Also listed are several internal control procedures. List the letter (a through h) designating each possible error. Beside this letter, place the number indicating the internal control procedure that should prevent this type of problem from occurring. If none of the specified internal control procedures would effectively prevent the problem, place a "0" opposite the letter. Unless stated otherwise, assume that a computer-based accounting system is in use.

Possible Errors or Problems

a　A sales clerk rings up a sale at an incorrect price.

b　In preparing the monthly payroll, a factory worker's wages of $900 for the two-week pay period are accidentally entered into the computer as $9,000.

c　A shoplifter steals merchandise while the sales clerk is busy with another customer.

d　A credit sale is posted to the wrong account in the accounts receivable subsidiary ledger.

e The cashier of a business conceals a theft of cash by adjusting the balance of the Cash account in the company's computer-based accounting records.

f Through oversight, a credit sale is not posted from the sales journal to the accounts receivable subsidiary ledger. (Assume that a manual accounting system is in use.)

g A department store sales clerk unknowingly makes a credit sale to a customer who is using a store credit card which has been reported stolen.

h While running the program to prepare the monthly payroll, a computer operator inserts data causing the machine to prepare paychecks for five fictitious employees.

Internal Control Procedures

1 The computer prepares a report with separate daily sales totals for each salesperson.

2 Subsidiary ledgers are periodically compared to the balances of the controlling accounts in the general ledger.

3 Employees with custody of assets do not have access to accounting records.

4 All merchandise has a magnetically coded label which can be read automatically by a device attached to the electronic cash register. This code identifies to the computer the merchandise being sold.

5 Credit cards issued by the store have magnetic codes which can be read automatically by a device attached to the electronic cash register. Credit approval and posting to customers accounts are handled by computer.

6 An item count.

7 A limit test.

0 None of the above control procedures can effectively prevent this type of error from occurring.

Cases for analysis

Case 6-1 Special journals — purpose and design

Leisure Clothing is a mail-order company which sells clothes to the public at discount prices. Recently Leisure Clothing initiated a new policy allowing a 10-day free trial on all clothes bought from the company. At the end of the 10-day period, the customer may either pay cash for the purchase or return the goods to Leisure Clothing. The new policy caused such a large boost in sales that, even after considering the many sales returns, the policy appeared quite profitable.

The accounting system of Leisure Clothing includes a sales journal, purchases journal, cash receipts journal, cash payments journal, and a general journal. As an internal control procedure, an officer of the company reviews and initials every entry in the general journal before the amounts are posted to the ledger accounts. Since the 10-day free trial policy has been in effect, hundreds of entries recording sales returns have been entered in the general journal each week. Each of these entries has been reviewed and initialed by an officer of the firm, and the amounts have been posted to Sales Returns & Allowances and to the Accounts Receivable controlling account in the general ledger, and also to the customer's account in the accounts receivable subsidiary ledger.

Since these sales return entries are so numerous, it has been suggested that a special journal be designed to handle them. This could not only save time in journalizing and posting the entries, but also eliminate the time-consuming individual review of each of these repetitive entries by an officer of the company.

Instructions

a How many amounts are entered in the general journal to describe a single sales return transaction? Are these amounts the same?

b Explain why these sales return transactions are suited to the use of a special journal. Explain in detail how many money columns the special journal should have, and what postings would have to be done either at the time of the transaction or at the end of the period.

c Assume that there were 3,000 sales returns during the month. How many postings would have to be made during the month if these transactions were entered in the general journal? How many postings would have to be made if the special journal you designed in b were used? (Assume a one-month accounting period.)

Case 6-2   Special-purpose special journal

At Valley Savings, tellers use computer terminals to record transactions with customers. All cash receipts fall into one of the three categories of transactions described below:

Transaction code

1 Deposits into savings accounts (debit Cash, credit the liability account, Savings Deposits).
2 Deposits into checking accounts (debit Cash, credit the liability account, Demand Deposits).
3 Loan payments collected (debit Cash; credit Notes Receivable for the portion of the payment applied to the principal amount owed, and credit Interest Revenue for any interest charges included in the payment).

To record the receipt of cash from a customer, the teller enters the following information into the computer terminal:

1 A three-digit teller identification number.
2 The transaction code (*1*, *2*, or *3*) indicating the nature of the transaction.
3 The customer's six-digit account number or loan number.
4 The dollar amount received.

Using this information, the computer records the transactions and updates all general ledger and subsidiary ledger accounts. The computer automatically records the date of each transaction. For loan payments received from customers, the computer automatically determines the portion of the payment representing interest revenue and the portion representing a reduction in notes receivable.

Instructions

a On a sheet of blank paper, design the special journal that might be printed by Valley Saving's computer listing the cash receipts recorded by the company's tellers. Your journal should have columns to show the date, teller identification number, a brief description of the transaction (in place of the transaction code), all dollar amounts debited or credited to various ledger accounts, the customer's account number or loan number, and all posting references to subsidiary ledger accounts. (Hint: Valley Savings maintains three subsidiary ledgers which are affected by cash receipts from customers.)

You may use the cash receipts journal on pages 222–223 of your text as a model. However, you will have to make numerous changes in the number of columns and in column headings to accommodate the special needs of Valley Savings.

b Enter the following three transactions in your journal. Each transaction is dated August 19.
(1) Teller no. 012 receives $1,800 for deposit into savings account no. 444444.
(2) Teller no. 004 receives $720 for deposit into checking account no. 666666.
(3) Teller no. 007 receives $641 as a monthly payment on loan no. 999999. (The computer determines that $606 of this payment represents interest revenue and the remaining $35 reduces the note receivable from the customer.)

Part Three	Current assets and current liabilities
Chapter 7	Cash and marketable securities
Chapter 8	Receivables and payables
Appendix A	Payroll accounting
Chapter 9	Inventories

Part Three begins our discussion of the major elements of financial statements. The next three chapters and one appendix emphasize transactions involving current assets and current liabilities. Such transactions encompass much of a company's normal business activity, including purchases and sales of merchandise, payrolls, collections of accounts receivable, and payments of various expenses. All appendixes in this text are designed to provide optional coverage of selected special topics; future chapters do not assume coverage of these appendixes.

Chapter 7
Cash and marketable securities

In this chapter we discuss the two most liquid types of current assets—cash and investments in marketable securities. Our discussion of cash transactions centers around the need for adequate internal control over cash receipts and cash disbursements. We illustrate and explain the use of a voucher system, a petty cash fund, and periodic bank reconciliations as means of achieving internal control over cash transactions. The second half of the chapter focuses upon investments in marketable securities (stocks and bonds). We explain how these securities are bought and sold in organized securities exchanges, and why these assets are almost as liquid as cash itself. We then illustrate how an investor accounts for investment transactions, including purchases of securities, recognition of dividend and interest revenue, gains or losses on sales of securities, and the valuation of equity securities (stocks) at the lower of cost or market.

After studying this chapter you should be able to:

✓ Explain the objectives of efficient cash management.
✓ Discuss means of achieving internal control over cash receipts and disbursements.
✓ Describe the operation of a petty cash fund and of a voucher system.
✓ Prepare a bank reconciliation.
✓ Acccount for investments in stocks and bonds.
✓ Apply the lower-of-cost-or-market rule to a portfolio of marketable equity securities.

CASH

Accountants define cash as money on deposit in banks and any items that banks will accept for immediate deposit. These items include not only coins and paper money, but also checks and money orders. On the other hand, notes receivable, IOUs, and postdated checks are not accepted for immediate deposit and are not included in the accountants' definition of cash.

In the balance sheet, cash is listed first among the current assets, because it is the most current and liquid of all assets. The banker, credit manager, or investor who studies a balance sheet critically is always interested in the total amount of cash as compared with other balance sheet items, such as accounts payable. These outside users of a company's financial statements are not interested, however, in such details as the number of separate bank accounts, or in the distinction between cash on hand and cash in banks. A business that carries checking accounts with several banks will maintain a separate ledger account for each bank account. On the balance sheet, however, the entire amount of cash on hand and cash on deposit with the several banks will be shown as a single amount. One objective in preparing financial statements is to keep them short, concise, and easy to read.

Some bank accounts are restricted as to their use, so that they are not available for making payments to meet normal operating needs of the business. An example (discussed in Chapter 13) is a bond sinking fund, consisting of cash being accumulated by a corporation for the specific purpose of paying off bonded indebtedness at a future date and not available for any other use. A bank account located in a foreign country may also be restricted if monetary regulations prevent the transfer of funds between the two countries. Restricted bank accounts are not regarded as current assets because they are not available for use in paying current liabilities.

Management responsibilities relating to cash

Efficient management of cash includes measures that will:

1 Provide accurate accounting for cash receipts, cash payments, and cash balances
2 Prevent losses from fraud or theft
3 Maintain a sufficient amount of cash at all times to make necessary payments, plus a reasonable balance for emergencies
4 Prevent unnecessarily large amounts of cash from being held idle in bank accounts which produce no revenue

Internal control over cash is sometimes regarded merely as a means of preventing fraud or theft. A good system of internal control, however, will also aid in achieving management's other objectives of accurate accounting for cash transactions and the maintenance of adequate but not excessive cash balances.

Basic requirements for internal control over cash

Cash is more susceptible to theft than any other asset. Furthermore, a large portion of the total transactions of a business involve the receipt or disbursement of cash. For both these reasons, internal control over cash is of great importance to management and also to the employees of a business. If a cash shortage arises in a business in which internal controls are weak or nonexistent, every employee is under suspicion. Perhaps no one employee can be proved guilty of the theft, but neither can any employee prove his or her innocence.

On the other hand, if internal controls over cash are adequate, theft without detection is virtually impossible except through the collusion of two or more employees. To achieve internal control over cash or any other group of assets requires first of all that *the custody of assets be clearly separated from the recording of transactions.* Secondly, the recording function should be subdivided among employees, so that the work of one person is verified by that of another. This ***subdivision of duties*** discourages fraud, because collusion among employees would be necessary to conceal an irregularity. Internal control is more easily achieved in large companies than in small companies, because extensive subdivision of duties is more feasible in the larger business.

The major steps in establishing internal controls over cash include the following:

1 Separate the function of handling cash from the maintenance of accounting records. Employees who handle cash should not have access to the accounting records, and accounting personnel should not have access to cash.

2 Prepare an immediate ***control listing*** of cash receipts at the time and place that the money is received. This initial listing may consist of a cash register tape or serially numbered sales tickets rather than formal entries in the accounting records. A list of incoming checks should be prepared by the employee assigned to open the mail.

3 Require that all cash receipts be deposited daily in the bank.

4 Make all payments by check. The only exception should be for small payments to be made in cash from a petty cash fund. Payments should never be made out of cash receipts. Checks should never be drawn payable to Cash. A check drawn to a named payee requires endorsement by the payee on the back of the check before it can be cashed or deposited. This endorsement provides permanent evidence identifying the person who received the funds. On the other hand, a check payable to Cash can be deposited or cashed by anyone.

5 Require that the validity and amount of every expenditure be verified before a check is issued in payment.

6 Separate the function of approving expenditures from the function of signing checks.

The application of these principles in building an adequate system of internal control over cash can best be illustrated by considering separately the topics of cash receipts and cash disbursements.

Internal control over cash receipts

Cash receipts consist of two major types: cash received over the counter at the time of a sale and cash received through the mail as collections on accounts receivable.

Use of cash registers. Cash received over the counter at the time of a sale should be rung up on a cash register, ***so located that the customer will see the amount recorded.*** Since the customer presumably will not pay more than the amount shown on the register, the use of cash registers provides assurance that an immediate record is made of all cash sales. At the end of the day, the store manager or other supervisor should compare the cash register tape with the total cash collected.

● **CASE IN POINT** ● Many large supermarkets have achieved faster checkout lines and stronger internal control by using electronic scanning equipment to read and record the price of all groceries passing the checkout counters. All of the 12,000 or so grocery items on the shelves bear a product code, consisting of a pattern of thick and thin vertical bars.

At the checkout counter, the code on each item is read by a scanning laser. The code is sent instantaneously to a computer which locates the price and description of the item and flashes that information on a display panel in view of the customer and the checkout clerk. After all of the items have been passed through the scanner, the display panel shows the total amount of the sale. The clerk then enters the amount of cash received from the customer, and the display panel shows the amount of change that the customer should receive.

This system has many advantages. Not only is an immediate record made of all cash receipts, but the risk of errors in pricing merchandise or in making change is greatly reduced. This system also improves inventory control by giving management continuous information on what is being sold moment by moment, classified by product and by manufacturer. Comparison of these sales records with records of purchases will direct attention to any losses from theft or shoplifting.

Use of prenumbered sales tickets. Another means of establishing internal control over cash sales is by writing out a prenumbered sales ticket in duplicate at the time of each sale. The original is given to the customer and the carbon copy is retained. Prenumbered sales tickets are widely used in businesses such as restaurants where one central cashier rings up the sales made by all salespeople.

At the end of the day, an employee computes the total sales figure from these sales tickets and also makes sure that no tickets are missing from the series. This total sales figure is then compared with the cash register tape and the total cash receipts.

Cash received through the mail. The procedures for handling checks and currency received through the mail are also based on the internal control principle that two or more employees should participate in every transaction.

The employee who opens the mail should prepare a list of the checks received. In order that this list shall represent the total receipts of the day, the totals recorded on the cash registers may be added to the list. One copy of the list is forwarded with the cash (currency and checks) to the cashier, who will deposit in the bank all the cash received for the day. Another copy of the list is sent to the accounting department, which will record the amount of cash received.

At the close of business each day, the manager should determine that the total cash receipts recorded that day in the accounting records agree with the amount of the cashier's deposit, and also with the list of total cash receipts for the day.

Cash over and short. In handling over-the-counter cash receipts, a few errors in making change will inevitably occur. These errors will cause a cash shortage or overage at the end of the day, when the cash is counted and compared with the reading on the cash register.

For example, assume that the total cash sales for the day amount to $500 as recorded by the cash register, but that the cash in the drawer when counted amounts to only $490. The following entry would be made to record the day's sales and the cash shortage of $10.

Recording cash shortage

Cash	490	
Cash Over and Short	10	
Sales		500

The account entitled Cash Over and Short is debited with shortages and credited with overages. If the cash shortages during an entire accounting period are in excess of the cash overages, the Cash Over and Short account will have a debit balance and will be shown as miscellaneous *expense* in the income statement. On the other hand, if the overages exceed the shortages, the Cash Over and Short account will show a credit balance at the end of the period and should be treated as an item of miscellaneous *revenue*.

Subdivision of duties. Employees who handle cash receipts should *not have access to the accounting records.* This combination of duties might enable the employee to alter the accounting records and thereby conceal a cash shortage. For example, assume that an employee who serves as both the cashier and bookkeeper of a small business removes $500 from the day's cash sales receipts. By altering the accounting records, the employee could conceal this theft in any number of ways. One approach is simply to record the day's cash sales at $500 less than the actual amount. Another means of concealing the theft is to record cash sales correctly, but then record a fictitious sales return for $500 (debit Sales Returns & Allowances, credit Cash). In either case, the balance of the Cash account will not exceed the amount of cash on hand after the theft.

Employees who handle cash receipts also should *not have authority to issue credit memoranda for sales returns.* This combination of duties might enable the employee to conceal cash shortages by issuing fictitious credit memoranda. Assume, for example, that an employee with these responsibilities collects $100 cash from a customer as payment of the customer's account. The employee might remove this cash and issue a $100 credit memorandum, indicating that the customer had returned the merchandise instead of paying off the account. The credit memoranda would cause the customer's account to be credited. However, the offsetting debit would be to the Sales Returns & Allowances account, not to the Cash account. Thus, the books would remain in balance, the customer would receive credit for the abstracted payment, and there would be no record of cash having been received.

Internal control over cash disbursements

An adequate system of internal control requires that each day's cash receipts be deposited intact in the bank and that *all disbursements be made by check.* Checks should be prenumbered. Any spoiled checks should be marked "Void" and filed in sequence so that all numbers in the series can be accounted for.

Every transaction requiring a cash disbursement should be verified and approved before payment is made. The official designated to sign checks should not be given authority to approve invoices for payment or to make entries in the accounting records. When a check is presented to a company official for signature, it should be accompanied by the approved invoice and voucher showing that the transaction has been fully verified and that payment is justified. When the check is signed, the supporting invoices and vouchers should be perforated or stamped "Paid" to eliminate any possibility of their being presented later in support of another check. If these rules are followed, it is almost impossible for a fraudulent cash disbursement to be concealed without the collusion of two or more persons.

In large companies which issue hundreds or thousands of checks daily, it is not practicable for a company official to sign each check manually. Instead, check-signing machines with various built-in control devices are used. This automation of the check-signing function does not weaken the system of internal control if attention is given to proper use of the machine and to control of the checks both before and after they pass through the check-signing machine.

● **CASE IN POINT** ● A large Boston-based construction company issued a great many checks every day but paid little attention to internal controls over its cash payments. Stacks of unissued checks were kept in an unlocked supply closet along with Styrofoam coffee cups. Because the number of checks issued was too great for the treasurer to sign them manually, a check-signing machine was used. This machine, after signing the checks, ejected them into a box equipped with a lock. In spite of warnings from the company's CPA firm, company officials found that it was "too inconvenient" to keep the box locked. The company also failed to make any use of the check-counting device built into the check-signing machine. Although the company maintained very large amounts on deposit in checking accounts, it did not bother to reconcile bank statements for weeks or months at a time.

These weaknesses in internal control led to a crisis when an employee was given a three-week-old bank statement and a bundle of paid checks and told to prepare a bank reconciliation. The employee found that the bundle of paid checks accompanying the bank statement was incomplete. No paid checks were on hand to support over $700,000 of charges deducted on the bank statement. Further investigation revealed that over $1 million in unauthorized and unrecorded checks had been paid from the corporation's bank accounts. These checks had been issued out of serial number sequence and had been run through the company check-signing machine. It was never determined who had carried out the theft and the money was not recovered.

The voucher system

One widely used method of establishing control over cash payments is the voucher system. The basic idea of this system is that every transaction which will result in a cash payment must be verified, approved in writing, and recorded before a check is issued. A written authorization called a **voucher** is prepared for every transaction that will require a cash payment, regardless of whether the transaction is for payment of an expense, purchase of merchandise or a plant asset, or for payment of a liability. Vouchers are serially numbered so that the loss or misplacement of a voucher would immediately be apparent.

To demonstrate the internal control inherent in a voucher system, consider the way a voucher is used in verifying an invoice received from a supplier. A serially numbered voucher is attached to each incoming invoice. The voucher (as illustrated on page 265) has spaces for listing the data from the invoice and showing the ledger accounts to be debited and credited in recording the transaction. Space is also provided for approval signatures for each step in the verification and approval process. A completed voucher provides a description of the transaction and also of the work performed in verifying the liability and approving the cash disbursement.

Preparing a voucher. To illustrate the functioning of a voucher system, let us begin with the receipt of an invoice from a supplier. A voucher is prepared by filling in the appropriate blanks with information taken from the invoice, such as the invoice date, invoice number, amount, and the creditor's name and address. The voucher with the supplier's invoice attached is then sent to the employees responsible for verifying the extensions and footings on the invoice and for comparing prices, quantities, and terms with those specified in the purchase order and receiving report. When completion of the verification process has been evidenced by approval signatures of the persons performing these steps, the voucher and supporting documents are sent to an employee of the accounting department, who indicates on the voucher the accounts to be debited and credited.

The voucher is now reviewed by an accounting official to provide assurance that the verification procedures have been satisfactorily completed and that the liability is a proper one. After receiving this supervisory approval, the voucher is entered in a journal called a *voucher register.*

Entries in the voucher register indicate the nature of the expenditure by debiting the appropriate asset, expense, or liability accounts. The credit portion of each entry is always to a short-term liability account entitled *Vouchers Payable.* Note that the entry in the voucher register is not made until the liability has been verified and approved.

In the voucher system, the ledger account, Vouchers Payable, replaces Accounts Payable. For purposes of balance sheet presentation, however, most companies continue to use the more widely understood term Accounts Payable.

Paying the voucher within the discount period. After the voucher has been entered in the voucher register, it is placed (with the supporting documents attached) in a tickler file according to the date of required payment. Cash discount periods generally run from the date of the invoice. Since a voucher is prepared for each invoice, the required date of payment is the last day on which a check can be prepared and mailed to the creditor in time to qualify for the discount.

When the payment date arrives, an employee in the accounting department removes the voucher from the unpaid file, draws a check for signature by the treasurer, and records payment of the voucher in a special journal called a *check register.* Since checks are issued only in payment of approved vouchers, every entry in the check register represents a debit to Vouchers Payable and a credit to Cash.

An important factor in achieving internal control is that the employee in the accounting department who prepares the check *is not authorized to sign it.* The unsigned check and the supporting voucher are now sent to the treasurer or other designated official in the finance department. The treasurer reviews the voucher, especially the approval signatures, and signs the check. Thus, the invoice is *approved for payment* in the accounting department, but the actual cash disbursement is made by the finance department. *No one person or department is in a position both to approve invoices for payment and to issue signed checks.*

Once the check has been signed, the treasurer should mail it directly to the creditor. The voucher and all supporting documents are then perforated with a PAID stamp and are

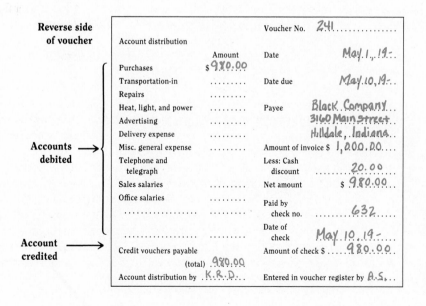

Use of voucher ensures verification of invoice

BROADHILL CORPORATION
Chicago, Illinois

Pay to *Black Company*
3160 Main Street
Hilldale, Indiana

Voucher No. *241* ← **Serial number**
Date *May 1, 19—*
Date due *May 10, 19—*

Date of Invoice *April 30, 19—*   Gross amount $ *1,000.00*
Invoice number *847*   Less: Cash discount   *20.00*
Credit terms *2/10, n 30*   Net amount $ *980.00*

Approval

	Dates	Approved by
Extensions and footings verified	*May 1, 19—*	*RG*
Prices in agreement with purchase order	*May 1, 19—*	*RG*
Quantities in agreement with receiving report	*May 1, 19—*	*RG*
Credit terms in agreement with purchase order	*May 1, 19—*	*RG*
Account distribution & recording approved	*William Cross*	
Approved for payment	*Judith Davis*	

← **Verification procedures**

← **Approved for payment**

Accounting Supervisor

Reverse side of voucher

Account distribution

Voucher No. *241*

	Amount
Purchases	$ *980.00*
Transportation-in	....
Repairs	....
Heat, light, and power	....
Advertising	....
Delivery expense	....
Misc. general expense	....
Telephone and telegraph	....
Sales salaries	....
Office salaries	....
....	
....	
Credit vouchers payable	
(total) *980.00*	
Account distribution by *K.R.D.*	

Accounts debited →

Account credited →

Date *May 1, 19—*

Date due *May 10, 19—*

Payee *Black Company*
3160 Main Street
Hilldale, Indiana

Amount of invoice $ *1,000.00*
Less: Cash discount *20.00*
Net amount $ *980.00*

Paid by check no. *632*
Date of check *May 10, 19—*
Amount of check $ *980.00*

Entered in voucher register by *A.S.*

OPERATION OF A VOUCHER SYSTEM

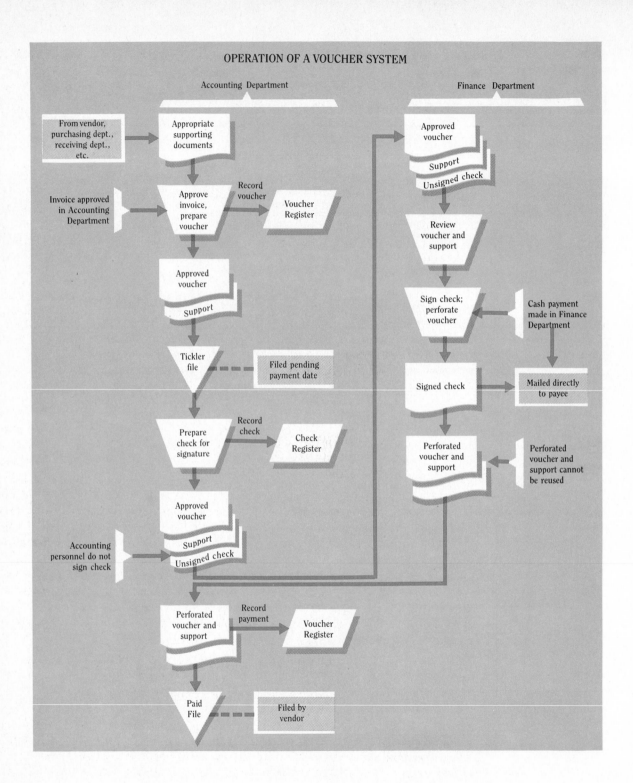

Accounting Department

Finance Department

From vendor, purchasing dept., receiving dept., etc.

Appropriate supporting documents

Invoice approved in Accounting Department

Approve invoice, prepare voucher

Record voucher → Voucher Register

Approved voucher

Support

Tickler file — Filed pending payment date

Prepare check for signature

Record check → Check Register

Approved voucher

Support

Unsigned check

Accounting personnel do not sign check

Approved voucher

Support

Unsigned check

Review voucher and support

Sign check; perforate voucher

Cash payment made in Finance Department

Signed check → Mailed directly to payee

Perforated voucher and support

Perforated voucher and support cannot be reused

Perforated voucher and support

Record payment → Voucher Register

Paid File — Filed by vendor

forwarded to the accounting department, which will note payment of the voucher in the voucher register and file the paid voucher. The operation of a voucher system is illustrated in the flow chart on page 266. Notes have been made on the illustration identifying the most important internal control features in the system.

Petty cash

As previously emphasized, adequate internal control over cash requires that all receipts be deposited in the bank and all disbursements be made by check. However, every business finds it convenient to have a small amount of cash on hand with which to make some minor expenditures. Examples include payments for small purchases of office supplies, postage stamps, and taxi fares. Internal control over these small cash payments can best be achieved through a petty cash fund.

Establishing the petty cash fund. To create a petty cash fund, a check is written for a round amount such as $100 or $200, which will cover the small expenditures to be paid in cash for a period of two or three weeks. This check is cashed and the money kept on hand in a petty cash box or drawer in the office.

The entry for the issuance of the check is:

Creating the petty cash fund

| Petty Cash .... | 200 | |
| Cash .... | | 200 |
To establish a petty cash fund.

Making disbursements from the petty cash fund. As cash payments are made out of the petty cash box, the custodian of the fund is required to fill out a *petty cash voucher* for each expenditure. A petty cash voucher shows the amount paid, the purpose of the expenditure, the date, and the signature of the person receiving the money. A petty cash voucher should be prepared for every payment made from the fund. The petty cash box should, therefore, always contain cash and/or vouchers totaling the exact amount of the fund.

The petty cash custodian should be informed that occasional surprise counts of the fund will be made and that he or she is personally responsible for the fund being intact at all times. Careless handling of petty cash has often been a first step toward large thefts; consequently, misuse of petty cash funds should not be tolerated.

Replenishing the petty cash fund. Assume that a petty cash fund of $200 was established on June 1 and that payments totaling $174.95 were made from the fund during the next two weeks. Since the $200 originally placed in the fund is nearly exhausted, the fund should be replenished. To replenish a petty cash fund means to replace the amount of money that has been spent, thus restoring the fund to its original amount. A check is drawn payable to Petty Cash for the exact amount of the expenditures, $174.95. This check is cashed and the money placed in the petty cash box. The vouchers totaling that amount are perforated to prevent their reuse and filed in support of the replenishment check. The journal entry to record the issuance of the check will debit the expense accounts indicated by inspection of the vouchers, as follows:

<table>
<tr><td>Replenishment of</td><td>Office Supplies Expense ....</td><td>80.60</td><td></td></tr>
<tr><td>petty cash fund</td><td>Freight-in ....</td><td>16.00</td><td></td></tr>
<tr><td></td><td>Postage Expense ....</td><td>45.25</td><td></td></tr>
<tr><td></td><td>Miscellaneous Expense ....</td><td>33.10</td><td></td></tr>
<tr><td></td><td>   Cash ....</td><td></td><td>174.95</td></tr>
</table>

To replenish the petty cash fund.

Note that **expense accounts** are debited each time the fund is replenished. The Petty Cash account is debited only when the fund is first established. There ordinarily will be no further entries in the Petty Cash account after the fund is established, unless the fund is discontinued or a decision is made to change its size from the original $200 amount.

The petty cash fund is usually replenished at the end of an accounting period, even though the fund is not running low, so that all vouchers in the fund are charged to expense accounts before these accounts are closed and financial statements prepared.

Control features of bank checking accounts

We have already emphasized that all significant cash disbursements should be made by check. The use of checking accounts contributes to strong internal control in many ways. For example:

1 Checking accounts eliminate the need to keep large amounts of cash on hand.
2 The board of directors must notify the bank who is authorized to sign checks. Thus, access to cash is limited to those officers or employees designated by the board.
3 The person responsible for each cash disbursement is readily identified by the signature on the check.
4 The bank returns all checks which have been paid from the account. Thus, the depositor has documentary evidence showing the date and amount of each cash payment and the identity of the person who received the cash.
5 A comparison of the monthly **bank statement** with the depositor's accounting records will bring to light any errors made either by the bank or by the depositor in accounting for cash transactions.

Bank statements

Each month the bank will provide the depositor with a statement of the depositor's account, accompanied by the checks paid and charged to the account during the month.[1] As illustrated on the next page, a bank statement shows the balance on deposit at the beginning of the month, the deposits, the checks paid, any other debits and credits during the month, and the new balance at the end of the month. (To keep the illustration short, we have shown a limited number of deposits rather than one for each business day in the month.)

---

[1] Large businesses may receive bank statements on a weekly basis.

STATEMENT OF ACCOUNT WITH

WESTERN NATIONAL BANK

PERIOD ENDING
July 31, 198X

ACCOUNT NO.
501390

Parkview Company
109 Parkview Road
Los Angeles, Calif. 90034

Clip along this line when sending a change of address - See reverse

CHECKS - LISTED IN ORDER OF PAYMENT - READ ACROSS					DEPOSITS	DATE	NEW BALANCE
					30000	7–1	532930
110000					125000	7–2	547930
41520		1000				7–3	505410
102500		9000	3650		118510	7–5	508770
					600	7–8	514770
9600	40000					7–10	465170
137657					102377	7–12	429890
42500						7–15	387390
209575					220000	7–18	397815
8500					10119	7–22	399434
115027					108325	7–24	392732
5025M					50000M	7–30	437707
1200S					63510	7–31	500017

SUMMARY OF ACTIVITY

BALANCE FORWARD	DEBITS		CREDITS		SERVICE CHARGE		NEW BALANCE
	NUMBER	AMOUNT	NUMBER	AMOUNT	ITEMS	AMOUNT	
5029 30	14	8 355 54	10	8 338 41	1	12 00	500017

Please examine this statement at once. If no error is reported in ten days the account will be considered correct. All items are credited subject to final payment.

ER-11 10-76

EXPLANATION OF SYMBOLS
M MISCELLANEOUS ENTRY   S SERVICE CHARGE

Certain items in the bank statement of Parkview Company need explanation and are discussed in the following paragraphs.

NSF checks. Bank deposits made by a business include checks received from customers. Occasionally a customer's check may "bounce"; that is, the bank on which the check is drawn may refuse payment. The most common cause for such refusal is that the customer's bank balance is less than the amount of the check. For example, on July 24

Parkview Company received a check for $50.25 from J. B. Ball, and the check was included in the bank deposit made on that day. The Ball check was returned to Western National Bank by the bank on which it was drawn marked NSF (Not Sufficient Funds), indicating that Ball did not have a sufficient balance on deposit to cover the check. Western National Bank therefore charged the NSF check against Parkview Company's account as shown by the July 30 debit of $50.25. (The letter M alongside this entry stands for Miscellaneous Entry.)

After getting the NSF check back from the bank, Parkview Company should remove this check from the cash classification by a journal entry debiting an account receivable from J. B. Ball and crediting Cash. The NSF check is thus regarded as a receivable until it is collected directly from the maker and redeposited, or is determined to be worthless.

Bank service charges. Under the date of July 31 on the illustrated bank statement is a debit for $12 accompanied by the symbol S. This symbol means Service Charge, a charge made by the bank to cover the expense of handling the account. The amount of the service charge is based upon such considerations as the average balance of the account and the number of checks and deposits. Banks do not usually impose a service charge on large checking accounts. However, a service charge is shown here for illustrative purposes.

When the bank sends the monthly statement and paid checks to the depositor, it will include debit memoranda for service charges and any other charges not represented by checks.

Miscellaneous charges and credit. Other charges which may appear on the bank statement include rental fees for safe deposit boxes, charges for printing checks, collection charges on notes left with the bank for collection, and interest charges on loans from the bank. If the checking account is of the interest-bearing type, a credit for interest earned during the month will also appear on the bank statement.

Reconciling the bank account

The purpose of reconciling the bank account is to assure that the bank and the depositor are in agreement on the amount of money on deposit. Remember that the bank and the depositor are maintaining independent records of the deposits, the checks, and the running balance of the bank account. Once a month an employee prepares a **bank reconciliation** to verify that these two independent sets of records are in agreement. For strong internal control, the employee who prepares the bank reconciliation should not have access to cash or be responsible for recording cash transactions in the accounting records.

The balance shown on the monthly statement received from the bank will usually not agree with the balance of cash shown by the depositor's accounting records. Certain transactions recorded by the depositor will not yet have been recorded by the bank. The most common examples are:

1 Outstanding checks. These are checks written by the depositor and deducted from

the Cash account on the depositor's records but not yet presented to the bank for payment.

2 Deposits in transit. Deposits mailed to the bank are usually not received by the bank and not entered on the bank's records until a day or two later than the cash receipts entry on the depositor's accounting records.

Transactions which may appear on the bank statement but which have not yet been recorded by the depositor include:

1 Service charges
2 Charges for NSF checks
3 Credits for interest earned by the depositor
4 Miscellaneous bank charges and credits

In some cases the bank reconciliation will be complete after such items as outstanding checks, deposits in transit, and miscellaneous bank charges have been taken into account. Other cases may require the correction of errors by the bank or errors in the depositor's accounting records to complete the reconciliation.

Preparing a bank reconciliation. Specific steps to be taken in preparing a bank reconciliation are:

1 Compare the deposits listed on the bank statement with the deposits shown in the company's records. Place check marks in the company's cash records and on the bank statement beside the items which agree. Any unchecked item in the company's records of deposits will be deposits not yet recorded by the bank, and should be added to the balance reported by the bank. Determine that any deposits in transit listed in last month's bank reconciliation are included as deposits in the current month's bank statement.

2 Arrange the paid checks in sequence by serial numbers and compare each check with the corresponding entry in the cash payments journal. (In the case of personal bank accounts for which the only record maintained is the checkbook, compare each paid check with the check stub.) Place a check mark in the depositor's cash payments journal opposite each entry for which a paid check has been returned by the bank. The unchecked entries should be listed in the bank reconciliation as *outstanding checks to be deducted from the balance reported by the bank.* Determine whether the checks listed as outstanding in the bank reconciliation for the preceding month have been returned by the bank this month. If not, such checks should be listed as outstanding in the current reconciliation.

3 Deduct from the balance per the depositor's records any debit memoranda issued by the bank which have not been recorded by the depositor. In the illustrated bank reconciliation on page 273, examples are the NSF check for $50.25 and the $12 service charge.

4 Add to the balance per the depositor's records any credit memoranda issued by the bank which have not been recorded by the depositor. An example in the illustrated bank reconciliation on page 273 is the credit of $500 collected by the bank in behalf

of Parkview Company. Any interest credited to the account by the bank must be added to the balance per the depositor's records.

5 Determine that the *adjusted* balance of the depositor's records is equal to the *adjusted* balance of the bank statement, as in the illustration on the next page.

6 Prepare journal entries for any items on the bank statement which have not yet been recorded in the depositor's accounts.

Illustration of bank reconciliation. The July bank statement prepared by the bank for Parkview Company was illustrated on page 269. This statement shows a balance of cash on deposit at July 31 of $5,000.17. We shall assume that Parkview Company's records at July 31 show a bank balance of $4,182.57. Our purpose in preparing the bank reconciliation is to identify the items that make up the difference of $817.60 and to determine the correct cash balance.

Assume that the specific steps to be taken in preparing a bank reconciliation have been carried out and that the following reconciling items have been discovered:

1 A deposit of $310.90 mailed to the bank on July 31 does not appear on the bank statement.

2 A credit memorandum issued by the bank on July 30 in the amount of $500 was returned with the July bank statement and appears in the Deposits column of that statement. This credit represents the proceeds of a note receivable left with the bank by Parkview Company for the purpose of collection. The collection of the note has not yet been recorded by Parkview Company.

3 Four checks issued in July or prior months have not yet been paid by the bank. These checks are:

Check No.	Date	Amount
801	June 15	$100.00
888	July 24	10.25
890	July 27	402.50
891	July 30	205.00

4 A debit memorandum issued by the bank on July 31 for a $12 service charge was enclosed with the July bank statement.

5 Check no. 875 was issued July 20 in the amount of $85 but was erroneously listed on the check stub and in the cash payments journal as $58. The check, in payment of telephone service, was paid by the bank, returned with the July bank statement, and correctly listed on the bank statement as an $85 charge to the account. The Cash account is overstated because of this $27 error ($85 − $58).

6 No entry has as yet been made in Parkview Company's accounts to reflect the bank's action on July 30 of charging against the account the NSF check for $50.25 drawn by J. B. Ball.

The July 31 bank reconciliation for Parkview Company follows:

PARKVIEW COMPANY
Bank Reconciliation
July 31, 19__

Update and correct the balance per depositor's records	Balance per depositor's records, July 31, 19__		$4,182.57
	Add: Note receivable collected for us by bank		500.00
			$4,682.57
	Less: Service charge	$ 12.00	
	NSF check of J. B. Ball	50.25	
	Error on check stub no. 875	27.00	89.25
	Adjusted balance		$4,593.32
Update and correct the balance per bank statement	Balance per bank statement, July 31, 19__		$5,000.17
	Add: Deposit of July 31 not recorded by bank		310.90
			$5,311.07
	Less: Outstanding checks		
	No. 801	$100.00	
	No. 888	10.25	
	No. 890	402.50	
	No. 891	205.00	717.75
	Adjusted balance (as above)		$4,593.32

The adjusted balance of $4,593.32 is the amount of cash owned by Parkview Company and is, therefore, the amount which should appear as cash in the July 31 balance sheet.

Note that the adjusted balance of cash differs from both the bank statement and the depositor's records. This difference is explained by the fact that neither set of records is up to date as of July 31, and also by the existence of an error on Parkview Company's records.

Adjusting the records after the reconciliation. To make Parkview Company's records up-to-date and accurate, four journal entries affecting the Cash account are necessary for the four items that make up the difference between the $4,182.57 balance per the depositor's records and the adjusted balance of $4,593.32. These four reconciling items call for the following entries:

Cash	500.00	
Notes Receivable		500.00
To record the note receivable collected for us by the bank.		

Miscellaneous Expense	12.00	
Cash		12.00
To record the service charge by the bank.		

Accounts Receivable, J. B. Ball	50.25	
Cash		50.25
To record as a receivable from J. B. Ball the amount of the NSF check returned to us by the bank.		

Telephone Expense 27.00

    Cash 27.00

To correct the error by which check no. 875 for an $85 payment for
telephone service was recorded as $58 ($85 − $58 = $27).

Instead of making four separate journal entries affecting the Cash account, one compound journal entry can be made to record all four of the above items.

INVESTMENTS IN MARKETABLE SECURITIES

The term *marketable securities* refers primarily to U.S. government bonds and the bonds and stocks of large corporations. Because marketable securities can be sold quickly on securities exchanges, an investment in these securities is almost as liquid an asset as cash itself. In fact, investments in marketable securities are often called "secondary cash resources." If cash is needed for any operating purpose, these securities may be converted quickly into cash; in the meantime, investments in marketable securities are preferable to cash because of the interest or dividend revenue which they produce. Most companies watch their cash balances very carefully and invest any cash not needed for current operations in high-grade marketable securities.

When an investor owns several different marketable securities, the group of securities is termed an investment *portfolio.* In deciding upon the securities to include in the portfolio, the investor seeks to maximize return while minimizing risk. Risk often can be reduced by *diversification,* that is, by including in the portfolio a variety of securities, especially securities of companies in different industries.

Some investors own enough of a company's capital stock to influence or control the company's activities through the voting rights of the shares owned. Such large holdings of capital stock create an important business relationship between the investor and the issuing corporation. Since investments of this type cannot be sold without disturbing this relationship, they are not considered marketable securities. *Investments for purposes of control* will be discussed in Appendix B, which follows Chapter 12.

Securities exchanges

The stocks and bonds of most large corporations are listed on organized securities exchanges, such as the *New York Stock Exchange.* An investor may either buy or sell these listed securities through any brokerage firm which is a member of the exchange. The brokerage firm represents the investor and negotiates with other exchange members to buy or sell the securities on behalf of its customer. The price at which the broker negotiates the transaction represents the current market value of the security and is immediately printed on the stock exchange ticker tape for reference by other investors. The financial pages of many newspapers report on a daily basis the highest, lowest, and closing (last) prices at which each listed security is exchanged.

At the time of issuance of stocks or bonds, the transaction is between the investor and the issuing corporation. The great daily volume of transactions in securities, however, consists of the sale of stocks and bonds by investors to other investors. On the New York

Stock Exchange alone, 100 million or more shares of stock often are exchanged on a single day. The stocks and bonds of many smaller companies are not listed on an organized securities exchange, but brokerage firms also arrange for the purchase and sale of these unlisted or *over-the-counter* securities.

Quoted market prices. The market prices of stocks are quoted in terms of dollars per share. Bond prices, however, are quoted as a *percentage* of their face value or *maturity* value, which is usually $1,000. The maturity value is the amount the issuing company must pay to redeem the bond at the date it matures (becomes due). A bond quoted at *102* would therefore have a market price of $1,020 (102% of $1,000). The following line from the financial page of a daily newspaper summarizes the previous day's trading in bonds of American Telephone & Telegraph (AT&T):

What is the market value of this bond?

Bonds	Sales	High	Low	Close	Net Change
ATT 10⅜ 90	145	96	95	95½	−1

This line of condensed information indicates that 145 of AT&T's 10⅜, $1,000 bonds maturing in 1990 were traded. The highest price is reported as 96 or $960 for a bond of $1,000 face value. The lowest price was 95 or $950, for a $1,000 bond. The closing price (last sale of the day) was 95½ or $955. This was one point below the closing price of the previous day, a decrease of $10 in the price of a $1,000 bond.

The primary factors which determine the market value of a bond are (1) the relationship of the bond's interest rate to other investment opportunities and (2) investors' confidence that the issuing company will be able to meet its obligations for future interest and principal payments. A bond selling at a market price greater than its maturity value is said to be selling at a *premium;* a bond selling at a price below its maturity value is selling at a *discount.* As a bond nears its maturity date, the market price of the bond approaches its maturity value. At the maturity date the market price of the bond should be exactly equal to its maturity value, and the issuing corporation will redeem the bond for that amount.

Listed corporations report to a million owners. When a corporation invites the public to purchase its stock and bonds, it accepts an obligation to keep the public informed on its financial condition and the profitability of operations. This obligation of disclosure includes public distribution of financial statements. The Securities and Exchange Commission is the government agency responsible for seeing that corporations make adequate disclosure of their affairs so that investors have a basis for intelligent investment decisions. The flow of corporate accounting data distributed through newspapers and financial advisory services to millions of investors is a vital force in the functioning of our economy. In fact, the successful working of a profit-motivated economy rests upon the quality and dependability of the accounting information being recorded.

Listed corporations are audited by certified public accountants. Corporations with securities listed on organized stock exchanges are required to have regular audits by independent public accountants. The financial statements distributed each year to stockholders are accompanied by a report by a firm of certified public accountants indicating that an audit has been made and expressing an opinion as to the fairness of the company's financial statements. It is the ***independent status*** of the auditing firm that enables investors to place confidence in audited financial statements.

Marketable securities as current assets

A recent balance sheet of International Business Machines Corporation (IBM) shows the following items listed first in the current assets section.

Current assets:
Cash .... $ 208,607,210
Marketable securities, at lower of cost or market 5,947,653,848

The large investment by IBM in marketable securities is in no way unusual; many corporations have large holdings of marketable securities. In the balance sheet, marketable securities are usually listed immediately after the asset Cash, because they are so liquid as to be almost the equivalent of cash.

The Financial Accounting Standards Board (FASB) has stated that a company may separate its marketable securities into two groups: (1) temporary investments classified as current assets, and (2) long-term investments classified as noncurrent assets.[2] Those marketable securities which management intends to hold on a long-term basis may be listed in the balance sheet just below the current asset section under the caption Long-Term Investments. In most cases, however, management stands ready to sell marketable securities whenever company needs or stock market trends make such action advantageous. Consequently, marketable securities generally are viewed as current assets.

Accounting for investments in marketable securities

When securities are purchased, an account entitled Marketable Securities is debited for the entire purchase price, including any commissions to stockbrokers and any transfer taxes. A subsidiary ledger must also be maintained which shows for each security owned the acquisition date, total cost, number of shares (or bonds) owned, and cost per share (or bond). This subsidiary ledger provides the information necessary to determine the amount of gain or loss when an investment in a particular stock or bond is sold.

The principal distinction between the recording of an investment in bonds and an investment in stocks is that interest on bonds accrues from day to day. The interest accrued since the last semiannual interest payment date is paid for by the purchaser and should be recorded separately from the cost of the bond itself. Dividends on stock, however, ***do not accrue*** and the entire purchase price paid by the investor in stocks is recorded in the Marketable Securities account.

Bond interest payments. The amount of interest paid to bondholders is equal to a stated percentage of the bond's maturity value. Thus, the owner of a 12% bond would receive $120 interest (12% of $1,000) every year. Since bond interest usually is paid semiannually, the bondholder would receive two semiannual interest payments of $60 each.

---

[2] *FASB Statement No. 12,* "Accounting for Certain Marketable Securities" (Stamford, Conn.: 1975).

When bonds are purchased between interest dates, the purchaser pays the quoted market price for the bond *plus* the interest accrued since the last interest payment date. By this arrangement the new owner becomes entitled to receive in full the next semiannual interest payment. An account called Bond Interest Receivable should be debited for the amount of interest purchased.

Income on investments in bonds. To illustrate the accounting entries for an investment in bonds, assume that on August 1 an investor purchases ten 9%, $1,000 bonds of Rider Co. which pay interest on June 1 and December 1. The investor buys the bonds on August 1 at a price of 98, plus a brokerage commission of $50 and two months' accrued interest of $150 ($10,000 $\times$ 9% $\times$ $\frac{2}{12}$ = $150). The entry on August 1 to record this investment is:

<table>
<tr><td>**Separate account for accrued bond interest purchased**</td><td>Marketable Securities ....</td><td>9,850</td><td></td></tr>
<tr><td></td><td>Bond Interest Receivable ....</td><td>150</td><td></td></tr>
<tr><td></td><td>Cash ....</td><td></td><td>10,000</td></tr>
</table>

Purchased ten 9% bonds of Rider Co. at 98 plus a brokerage commission of $50 and two months' accrued interest.

On December 1, the semiannual interest payment date, the investor will receive an interest check for $450, which will be recorded as follows:

<table>
<tr><td>**Note portion of interest check earned**</td><td>Cash ....</td><td>450</td><td></td></tr>
<tr><td></td><td>Bond Interest Receivable ....</td><td></td><td>150</td></tr>
<tr><td></td><td>Bond Interest Revenue ....</td><td></td><td>300</td></tr>
</table>

Received semiannual interest on Rider Co. bonds.

The $300 credit to Bond Interest Revenue represents the amount actually earned during the four months the bonds were owned by the investor (9% $\times$ $10,000 $\times$ $\frac{4}{12}$ = $300).

If the investor's accounting records are maintained on a calendar-year basis, the following adjusting entry is required at December 31 to record bond interest earned since December 1:

Bond Interest Receivable 75
    Bond Interest Revenue 75

To accrue one month's interest earned (Dec. 1–Dec. 31) on Rider Co. bonds ($10,000 $\times$ 9% $\times$ $\frac{1}{12}$ = $75).

The $75 in bond interest receivable recorded at December 31 will not be collected until the next semiannual interest payment date, which will be June 1 of the following year. (Assume that the investor does not use reversing entries.) The entry on June 1 will be:

Cash 450
    Bond Interest Receivable 75
    Bond Interest Revenue 375

To record receipt of semiannual interest on Rider Co. bonds and recognize interest earned since December 31 ($10,000 $\times$ 9% $\times$ $\frac{5}{12}$ = $375).

Income on investments in stock. Since dividends do not accrue, they generally are not recognized by the stockholder as revenue until the dividend check arrives. The entry upon receipt of the dividend check consists of a debit to Cash and a credit to Dividend Revenue.

Gains and losses from sale of investments in securities

The sale of an investment in stocks is recorded by debiting Cash for the amount received and crediting the Marketable Securities account for the cost of the securities sold. Any difference between the proceeds of the sale and the cost of the investment is recorded by a debit to Loss on Sale of Marketable Securities or by a credit to Gain on Sale of Marketable Securities.

At the date of sale of an investment in bonds, any interest which has accrued since the last interest payment date (or year-end) should be recognized as interest revenue. For example, assume that 10 bonds of the Elk Corporation carried in the accounts of an investor at $9,600 are sold at a price at 94 and accrued interest of $90. The commission on the sale is $50. The following entry should be made:

Investment in bonds sold at a loss	Cash 9,440	
	Loss on Sale of Marketable Securities 250	
	Marketable Securities	9,600
	Bond Interest Revenue	90

Sold 10 bonds of Elk Corporation at 94 and accrued interest of $90 less broker's commission of $50.

Balance sheet valuation of marketable securities

Although the market price of a bond may fluctuate from day to day, we can be reasonably certain that when the maturity date arrives the market price will be equal to the bond's maturity value. Stocks, on the other hand, do not have maturity values. When the market price of stock declines, there is no way we can be certain whether the decline will be temporary or permanent. For this reason, different valuation standards are applied in accounting for investments in marketable *debt* securities (bonds) and investments in marketable *equity* securities (stocks).

Valuation of marketable debt securities. A short-term investment in bonds is generally carried in the accounting records at *cost* and a gain or loss is recognized when the investment is sold. If bonds are held as a long-term investment and the difference between the cost of the investment and its maturity value is substantial, the valuation of the investment becomes more complex. The valuation of long-term investments in bonds is discussed in Chapter 11.

Valuation of marketable equity securities. The market values of stocks may rise or fall dramatically during an accounting period. An investor who sells an investment at a price above or below cost will recognize a gain or loss on the sale. But what if the investor continues to hold securities after a significant change in their market value? In this case, should any gain or loss be recognized in the financial statements?

The FASB (Financial Accounting Standards Board) ruled that a portfolio of marketable equity securities should be shown in the balance sheet at the *lower* of aggregate cost or current market value. The effect of the *lower-of-cost-or-market (LCM)* rule is to recognize losses from drops in market value without recognizing gains from rising market prices.

Note that this rule does not accord the same treatment to market gains and losses. Accountants traditionally have applied different criteria in recognizing gains and losses. One of the basic principles in accounting is that increases in market value above original cost shall not be recognized until they are *realized,* and the usual test of realization is the sale of the asset in question. Losses, on the other hand, are recognized *as soon as objective evidence indicates that a loss has been incurred.*

Lower of cost or market (LCM)

In applying the lower-of-cost-or-market rule, the total cost of the portfolio of marketable equity securities is compared with its current market value, and the lower of these two amounts is used as the balance sheet valuation. If the market value of the portfolio is below cost, an entry is made to reduce the carrying value of the portfolio to current market value and to recognize an *unrealized loss* for the amount of the market decline. The write-down of an investment in marketable equity securities to a market value below cost is an end-of-period adjusting entry and should be based upon market prices at the balance sheet date.

To illustrate the lower-of-cost-or-market adjustment, assume the following facts for the investment portfolio of Eagle Corporation at December 31, Year 1:

	Cost	Market Value
Capital stock of Adams Corporation	$100,000	$106,000
Capital stock of Barnes Company	60,000	52,000
Capital stock of Parker Industries	200,000	182,000
Other marketable equity securities	25,000	25,000
Totals	$385,000	$365,000

Since the total market value of the securities in our example is less than their cost to Eagle Corporation, the balance sheet valuation would be the lower amount of $365,000. This downward adjustment of $20,000 means that an unrealized loss of $20,000 will be included in the determination of the year's net income. The accounting entry would be as follows:

Year 1
Dec. 31   Unrealized Loss on Marketable Securities   20,000
                Valuation Allowance for Marketable Securities   20,000
            To reduce the carrying value of the investment in marketable
            securities to the lower of cost or market.

The loss from the decline in the market value of securities owned is termed an *unrealized loss* to distinguish it from a loss which is realized by an actual sale of securities.

The valuation account. The Valuation Allowance for Marketable Securities is a *contra-asset* account or *valuation* account. In the balance sheet, this valuation account is offset against the asset Marketable Securities in the same manner as the Accumulated Depreciation account is offset against the asset Building. The following partial balance sheet illustrates the use of the Valuation Allowance for Marketable Securities:

Current assets:

Cash		$ 80,000
Marketable securities	$385,000	
Less: Valuation allowance for marketable securities	20,000	365,000

The valuation account is adjusted every period. At the end of every period, the balance of the valuation account is adjusted to cause marketable equity securities to be shown in the balance sheet at the lower of cost or current market value. If the valuation allowance must be increased because of further declines in market value, the adjusting entry will recognize an additional unrealized loss. On the other hand, if market prices have gone up since the last balance sheet date, the adjusting entry will reduce or eliminate the valuation allowance and recognize an *unrealized gain.*

To illustrate the adjustment of the valuation account, let us assume that by the end of Year 2 the market value of Eagle Corporation's portfolio has increased to an amount greater than cost. Since market value is no longer below cost, the valuation allowance, which has a credit balance of $20,000, is no longer needed. Thus, the following entry would be made to eliminate the balance of the valuation allowance:

Year 2

Dec. 31	Valuation Allowance for Marketable Securities	20,000	
	Unrealized Gain on Marketable Securities		20,000
	To increase the carrying value of marketable securities to		
	original cost following recovery of market value.		

Unrealized gain cannot exceed the former balance of the valuation account

Note that the amount of unrealized gain recognized is limited to the amount in the valuation account. *Increases in market value above cost are not recognized in the accounting records.* In brief, when marketable securities have been written down to the lower of cost or market, they can be written back up *to original cost* if the market prices recover. However, current rules of the FASB do not permit recognition of a market rise above the original cost of the portfolio.

Because the valuation allowance is based upon a comparison of *total* portfolio cost and market value, the allowance cannot be directly associated with individual investments. The valuation allowance reduces the carrying value of the total portfolio but does not affect the individual carrying values of the investments which comprise the portfolio. Lower-of-cost-or-market adjustments, therefore, have *no effect* upon the gain or loss recognized when an investment is sold. When specific securities are sold, the gain or loss realized from the sale is determined by comparing the *cost* of the securities (without regard to lower-of-cost-or-market adjustments) to their selling price.[3]

---

[3] The reader may notice that a decline in the market value of securities owned could be reported in the income statement on two separate occasions: first, as an unrealized loss in the period in which the price decline occurs; and second, as a realized loss in the period in which the securities are sold. However, after securities with market values below cost have been sold, the valuation allowance may be reduced or eliminated. The entry to reduce the valuation allowance involves the recognition of an unrealized gain which offsets the unrealized losses reported in earlier periods.

Income tax rules for marketable securities. The FASB rules described above are not acceptable in determining income subject to income tax. The only gains or losses recognized for income tax purposes are realized gains and losses resulting from sale of an investment.

The argument for valuation at market value

A weakness in the position taken by the FASB is that some increases in the market value of securities owned are recognized in the financial statements while others are ignored. For this reason, many accountants believe that investments in marketable securities should be valued in the balance sheet at current market price regardless of whether this price is above or below cost. Increases and decreases in market value would then be recognized as gains or losses as these changes occur.

Several strong arguments exist for valuing marketable securities at market value:

1 Market value is a better indicator of the current debt-paying ability represented by the securities than is their original cost.
2 Market values may be objectively determined from market price quotations.
3 The market price may be realized at any time without interfering with the normal operations of the business.
4 Changes in market price may constitute a major portion of the economic benefit resulting from investments in marketable securities.

At this point it is important to stress that valuation of marketable securities at current market values which exceed cost is not in accordance with the present accounting practices of most companies.[4] However, the valuation of marketable securities is a controversial issue in the accounting profession and may be an area of forthcoming change in generally accepted accounting principles.

Presentation of marketable securities in financial statements

Gains and losses on the sale of investments, as well as interest and dividend revenue, are nonoperating types of income. These items should be specifically identified in the income statement and shown after the determination of operating income.

Although marketable securities are usually classified as current assets in the balance sheet, they may alternatively be classified as long-term investments if management has a definite intention to hold the securities for more than one year. Regardless of how marketable equity securities are classified in the balance sheet, they are shown at the lower-of-cost-or-market value.

The unrealized gains and losses resulting from application of the lower-of-cost-or-market rule, however, are presented differently in the financial statements depending upon whether the securities portfolio is classified as a current asset or a long-term investment. When the portfolio is viewed as a current asset, the unrealized gains and losses are closed into the Income Summary account and shown in the income statement along with other types of investment income.

---

[4] Companies whose principal business activity includes investing in marketable securities (such as mutual funds and brokerage houses) currently use market values in accounting for their investment portfolios.

The FASB has ruled that holding gains and losses on *long-term* investments should *not* be included in the measurement of the current year's income because management does not intend to sell these securities in the near future. Therefore, any unrealized loss recognized on long-term investments is shown in the balance sheet as a *reduction in stockholders' equity* instead of being closed into the Income Summary account.

Key terms introduced or emphasized in chapter 7

Bank reconciliation. A schedule listing the items which make up the difference between the balance shown on the bank statement and the balance of cash according to the depositor's records.

Bond. A formal certificate (or debt instrument) issued by a corporation to borrow money on a long-term basis.

Check register. A simplified version of the cash payments journal (see Chapter 6) used for recording cash payments when a voucher system is in use.

Deposits in transit. Cash receipts which have been entered in the depositor's accounting records and mailed to the bank or left in the bank's night depository, but which reached the bank too late to be credited to the depositor's current monthly bank statement.

Lower of cost or market. The technique of valuing a portfolio of marketable equity securities in the balance sheet at the lower of cost or current market value. A write-down to a market value below cost involves recognition of an *unrealized loss.*

Marketable securities. A highly liquid type of investment which can be sold at any time without interfering with normal operation of the business. Usually classified as a current asset second only to cash in liquidity.

Maturity value. The amount (usually $1,000 per bond) which the issuing company must pay to redeem its bonds at the date they mature (become due). Bond prices and interest rates are stated as percentages of maturity value.

NSF check. A customer's check which was deposited but returned because of a lack of funds (Not Sufficient Funds) in the account on which the check was drawn.

Outstanding checks. Checks issued by a business to suppliers, employees, or other payees but not yet presented to the bank for payment.

Petty cash fund. A small amount of cash set aside for making minor cash payments for which writing of checks is not practicable.

Portfolio. An investment in various marketable securities which is managed and accounted for as a single unit rather than as a number of separate investments. An investor may have both short-term and long-term investment portfolios.

Realization principle. The principle of recognizing revenue and gains in the accounting records only when the earning process is virtually complete. The usual criterion for realization is a sales transaction.

Unrealized losses and gains. An unrealized loss results from writing down marketable equity securities to a market value below cost. An unrealized gain results from restoring a former write-down because of a recovery in market price. Securities cannot be written up above aggregate cost. Unrealized losses and gains on marketable securities classified as current assets are included in the determination of the year's net income. The net unrealized loss on marketable securities classified as long-term investments is excluded from the determination of net income and is shown in the balance sheet as a reduction in stockholders' equity.

Valuation allowance for marketable securities. The contra-asset account used to reduce the carrying value of marketable equity securities from cost to a market value below cost. Adjusted at each balance sheet date.

Voucher. A document prepared to authorize and describe an expenditure.

Voucher register. A special journal used to record all liabilities which have been approved for payment.

Voucher system. A method of controlling expenditures and the payment of liabilities. Requires that every liability be recorded as soon as it is incurred, and that checks be issued only in payment of approved liabilities.

Demonstration problem for your review

The information listed below is available in reconciling the bank statement for the White River Company on November 30, 19___.

(1) The ledger account for Cash showed a balance at November 30 of $12,761.94; the bank statement at November 30 indicated a balance of $9,734.70.

(2) The November 30 cash receipts of $5,846.20 had been mailed to the bank on that date and did not appear among the deposits on the November bank statement.

(3) The paid checks returned with the November bank statement disclosed two errors in the cash records. Check no. 936 for $504.00 had been erroneously recorded as $50.40 in the cash payments journal, and check no. 942 for $245.50 had been recorded as $254.50. Check no. 936 was issued in payment of advertising expense, and check no. 942 was for the acquisition of office equipment.

(4) Included with the November bank statement was an NSF check for $220 signed by a customer, J. Wilson. This amount had been charged against the bank account on November 30.

(5) Of the checks issued in November, the following were not included among the paid checks returned by the bank:

Check No.	Amount	Check No.	Amount
924	$136.25	944	$ 95.00
940	105.00	945	716.15
941	11.46	946	60.00
943	826.70		

(6) A service charge for $340 by the bank had been made in error against the White River Company account.

(7) A non-interest-bearing note receivable for $1,890 owned by the White River Company had been left with the bank for collection. On November 30 the company received a memorandum from the bank indicating that the note had been collected and credited to the company's account after deduction of a $5 collection charge. No entry has been made by the company to record collection of the note.

(8) A debit memorandum for $12 was enclosed with the paid checks at November 30. This charge covered the cost of printing checks bearing the White River Company name and address.

Instructions

a Prepare a bank reconciliation at November 30, 19___.

b Prepare journal entries required as of November 30, 19___, to bring the company's records up to date. Use one journal entry to record all increases in the Cash account and another journal entry to record all decreases.

Solution to demonstration problem

a

WHITE RIVER COMPANY
Bank Reconciliation
November 30, 19___

Balance per depositor's records, Nov. 30			$12,761.94
Add: Error in recording check no. 942			
for office equipment:			
Recorded as	$254.50		
Correct amount	245.50	$ 9.00	
Note receivable collected by bank, $1,890,			
less collection charge, $5		1,885.00	1,894.00
			$14,655.94
Less: Error in recording check no. 936 for			
advertising expense:			
Correct amount	$504.00		
Recorded as	50.40	$ 453.60	
NSF check, J. Wilson		220.00	
Charge by bank for printing checks		12.00	685.60
Adjusted balance			$13,970.34
Balance per bank statement, Nov. 30			$ 9,734.70
Add: Deposit of Nov. 30 not recorded by bank		$5,846.20	
Service charge made by bank in error		340.00	6,186.20
Subtotal			$15,920.90
Less: Outstanding checks on Nov. 30:			
No. 924		$ 136.25	
No. 940		105.00	
No. 941		11.46	
No. 943		826.70	
No. 944		95.00	
No. 945		716.15	
No. 946		60.00	1,950.56
Adjusted balance (as above)			$13,970.34

General Journal

b

19___

Nov. 30	Cash	1,894.00	
	Miscellaneous Expense	5.00	
	Office Equipment		9.00
	Notes Receivable		1,890.00
	To record increase in Cash account as indicated by bank		
	reconciliation.		

Nov. 30	Advertising Expense	453.60	
	Miscellaneous Expense	12.00	
	Accounts Receivable, J. Wilson	220.00	
	Cash		685.60
	To record decrease in Cash account as indicated by bank reconciliation.		

Review questions

1 In bidding for some surplus property offered at auction by a government agency, the Argus Company on December 28 drew a check for $3,000 and mailed it with the bid. The government agency on January 3 rejected the bid and returned the check. Should the $3,000 be included as cash in the December 31 balance sheet, which was prepared by the Argus Company on January 5 after the check had been returned? Explain.

2 Does the expression "efficient management of cash" mean anything more than procedures to prevent losses from fraud or theft? Explain.

3 Mention some principles to be observed by a business in establishing strong internal control over cash receipts.

4 Explain how internal control over cash transactions is strengthened by compliance with the following rule: "Deposit each day's cash receipts intact in the bank, and make all disbursements by check."

5 Name three internal control practices relating to cash which would be practicable even in a small business having little opportunity for division of duties.

6 With respect to a *voucher system*, what is meant by the terms *voucher, voucher register*, and *check register?*

7 What is the greatest single advantage of the voucher system?

8 Randall Company uses a voucher system to control its cash disbursements. With respect to a purchase of merchandise, what three documents would need to be examined to verify that the voucher should be approved?

9 Suggest an internal control procedure to prevent the documents supporting a paid voucher from being resubmitted later in support of another cash disbursement.

10 Pico Stationery Shop has for years maintained a petty cash fund of $75, which is replenished twice a month.
   a How many debit entries would you expect to find in the Petty Cash account each year?
   b When would expenditures from the petty cash fund be entered in the ledger accounts?

11 Classify each of the numbered reconciling items listed below under one of the following headings: (a) an addition to the balance per depositor's records; (b) a deduction from the balance per depositor's records; (c) an addition to the balance per bank statement; (d) a deduction from the balance per bank statement.
   (1) Deposits in transit
   (2) Outstanding checks
   (3) Customer's check deposited but returned by bank marked NSF
   (4) Bank service charges
   (5) Collection by bank of note receivable left with bank for collection in behalf of depositor

12 A check for $455 issued in payment of an account payable was erroneously listed in the cash payments journal as $545. The error was discovered early in the following month when the paid check was returned by the bank. What corrective action is needed?

13 In the reconciliation of a bank account, what reconciling items necessitate a journal entry in the depositor's accounting records?

14 It is standard accounting practice to treat as cash all checks received from customers. When a customer's check is received, recorded, and deposited, but later returned by the bank marked NSF, what accounting entry or entries would be appropriate?

15 Why are investments in marketable securities usually regarded as current assets?

16 Why should an investor who owns numerous marketable securities maintain a marketable securities subsidiary ledger?

17 If an investor buys a bond between interest dates, he or she pays as a part of the purchase price the accrued interest since the last interest date. On the other hand, if the investor buys a share of common or preferred stock, no "accrued dividend" is added to the quoted price. Explain why this difference exists.

18 Because of a decline in market prices, National Corporation had to write down the carrying value of its investment in marketable securities by $70,000 in the current year. In the determination of net income for the current year, does it make any difference if National Corporation's investment portfolio is classified as a current asset or a long-term investment? Explain fully.

19 In the current asset section of its balance sheet, Delta Industries shows marketable securities at a market value $82,000 below cost. If the market value of these securities rises by $99,000 during the next accounting period, how large an unrealized gain (if any) should Delta Industries include in its next income statement? Explain fully.

20 How does the financial reporting requirement of valuing marketable securities at the lower-of-cost-or-market value compare with income tax rules concerning marketable securities?

21 "To substitute current market value for cost as a basis for valuing marketable securities would represent a departure from traditional accounting practice." Discuss the case for and against using market value consistently as the basis of valuation in accounting for marketable securities.

Exercises

Ex. 7-1 Certain subdivisions of duties are highly desirable for the purpose of achieving a reasonable degree of internal control. For each of the following five responsibilities, explain whether or not assigning the duty to an employee who also handles cash receipts would represent a significant weakness in internal control. Briefly explain your reasoning.

    a Responsibility for issuing credit memoranda for sales returns.

    b Responsibility for preparing a control listing of all cash collections.

    c Responsibility for preparing monthly bank reconciliations.

    d Responsibility for executing both cash and credit sales transactions.

    e Responsibility for maintaining the general ledger.

Ex. 7-2 Some of the following practices are suggestive of strength in internal controls; others are suggestive of weakness. Identify each of the seven practices with the term Strength or the term Weakness. Give reasons for your answers.

    a Checks received through the mail are recorded daily by the person maintaining accounts receivable records.

    b All cash receipts are deposited daily.

    c All payments under $200 are made through a petty cash fund.

    d Any difference between a day's over-the-counter cash receipts and the day's total shown by the cash register is added to or removed from petty cash.

e Each invoice from a supplier is processed individually through a voucher system; no accounts payable subsidiary ledger is maintained.

f Checks for expenditures of less than $50 are drawn payable to "Cash," rather than specifically identifying the payee.

g Vouchers and all supporting documents are perforated with a "Paid" stamp before being sent to the finance department for review and signing of checks.

Ex. 7-3 Beach Corporation maintains a petty cash fund of $200. At December 31, the end of the company's fiscal year, the fund contained the following:

Currency and coins	$ 76.80
Expense vouchers:	
Taxi fares (debit Travel Expense)	37.00
Office supplies expense	46.20
Contributions to Boy Scouts and others	40.00
Total	$200.00

Prepare the entry (in general journal form) to record the replenishing of the petty cash fund.

Ex. 7-4 Columbia Corporation received a bank statement at the end of the month showing a balance of $56,000 on deposit. The reconciling items consisted of outstanding checks totaling $11,600, bank service charges of $12, a deposit in transit of $8,800, and a memorandum showing that a note receivable belonging to Columbia Corporation had been collected in the amount of $4,800 and credited to the company's account.

a What is the adjusted amount of cash which should appear on Columbia Corporation's balance sheet?

b What was the balance per the depositor's records before making adjusting entries?

Ex. 7-5 At September 30 the Cash account in the ledger of Canvasback, Inc., showed a balance of $72,900. The bank statement, however, showed a balance of $87,400 at the same date. The only reconciling items consisted of a $4,800 deposit in transit, a credit for interest earned of $200, and 30 outstanding checks.

a Compute the amount of cash which should appear on the company's balance sheet at September 30.

b Compute the total amount of the oustanding checks.

Ex. 7-6 The information necessary for preparing a bank reconciliation for Chapel School at November 30, 19__, appears below.

(1) As of November 30, cash per the accounting records was $32,496; per bank statement, $27,754.

(2) Cash receipts of $6,244 on November 30 were not deposited until December 1.

(3) Among the paid checks returned by the bank was a stolen check for $1,008 paid in error by the bank after Chapel School had issued a stop payment order to the bank. Note that the bank was at fault.

(4) The following memoranda accompanied the bank statement:

(a) A debit memo for service charges for the month of November, $14.

(b) A debit memo attached to a $778 check of Frank Miller, marked NSF.

(5) The following checks had been issued but were not included in the paid checks returned by the bank: no. 921 for $1,564, no. 924 for $964, and no. 925 for $774.

Instructions. Prepare a bank reconciliation for Chapel School at November 30, 19___, in the form illustrated on page 273.

Ex. 7-7 Yamato Company purchased as a short-term investment $50,000 face value of the 9% bonds of Lorenzo, Inc., on March 31 of the current year, at a total cost of $50,625, including interest accrued since January 1. Interest is paid by Lorenzo, Inc., on June 30 and December 31. On July 31, four months after the purchase, Yamato Company sold the bonds and interest accrued since July 1 for a total price of $50,525.

Prepare in general journal form all entries required in the accounting records of Yamato Company relating to the investment in Lorenzo, Inc., bonds. (Commissions are to be ignored.)

Ex. 7-8 Prepare general journal entries in the accounting records of Axel Masters, Inc., to record the following transactions.

Jan.   7 Purchased as a temporary investment 1,000 shares of Reed Company common stock at a price of $41.50 per share, plus a brokerage commission of $500.
Feb. 12 Received a cash dividend of $2.20 per share on the investment in Reed Company stock.
Aug. 14 Sold 500 shares of Reed Company common stock at a price of $46 per share, less a brokerage commission of $290.

Ex. 7-9 The cost and market value of Edgebrook Corporation's portfolio of marketable securities at the end of Years 1 and 2 are shown below. The marketable securities are viewed as a current asset.

	Cost	Market Value
Year 1	$79,000	$67,800
Year 2	91,000	97,600

Show how the portfolio would appear in the balance sheet at the end of Year 1 and at the end of Year 2. If appropriate, use a valuation account in your presentation.

Problems

7-1 Internal control procedures
Listed below are nine possible errors or problems which might occur in the processing of cash transactions. Also shown is a list of internal control procedures.

Possible Errors or Problems

a An employee steals the cash collected from a customer in payment of an account receivable and conceals this theft by issuing a credit memorandum indicating that the customer returned the merchandise

b The same voucher was circulated through the system twice, causing the supplier to be paid twice for the same invoice.

c Without fear of detection, the cashier sometimes abstracts cash forwarded to him from the mailroom or the sales department instead of depositing these receipts in the company's bank account.

d A purchase invoice was paid even though the merchandise was never received.

e A salesclerk often rings up a sale at less than the actual sales price and then removes the additional cash collected from the customer.

f The cashier conceals a shortage of cash by making an entry in the general ledger debiting Miscellaneous Expense and crediting Cash.

g A salesclerk occasionally makes an error in the amount of change given to a customer.

h The official designated to sign checks is able to steal blank checks and issue them for unauthorized purposes without fear of detection.

i All cash received during the last four days is lost in a burglary on Thursday night.

Internal Control Procedures

1 Periodic reconciliation of bank statements with depositor's accounting records.

2 Use of a Cash Over and Short account.

3 Adequate subdivision of duties.

4 Use of prenumbered sales tickets.

5 Depositing each day's cash receipts intact in the bank.

6 Use of electronic cash registers equipped with optical scanners to read magnetically coded labels on merchandise.

7 Immediate preparation of a control listing when cash is received, and the comparison of this listing to bank deposits.

8 Perforation of voucher and supporting documents with a PAID stamp at time of issuing check to pay the voucher.

9 Requirement that a voucher be prepared as advance authorization of every cash disbursement.

0 None of the above control procedures can effectively prevent this type of error from occurring.

Instructions. List the letters (a through i) designating each possible error or problem. Beside this letter, place the number indicating the internal control procedure that should prevent this type of error or problem from occurring. If none of the specified internal control procedures would effectively prevent the error, place a "0" opposite the letter.

7-2 Operation of a petty cash fund

On September 1 Bay City Graphics established a petty cash fund of $200. The company does not use a voucher system. The petty cash fund was established by writing a check for $200 payable to Petty Cash. This check was cashed and the money placed in a lockbox in the custody of the cashier.

During September small payments from the petty cash fund totaled $176.20, as shown below.

Transportation-in	$ 37.10
Postage expense	72.00
Automobile expense	12.50
Telephone expense	19.00
Parking expense	35.60
Total of petty cash vouchers	$176.20

On September 30 a check was drawn payable to Petty Cash for $176.20 and the fund was replenished.

Instructions

a Prepare a journal entry (in general journal form) to record the establishment of the petty cash fund on September 1.

b Prepare a journal entry to record the replenishment of the petty cash fund at September 30.

c Net income for September for Bay City Graphics amounted to $2,412.80 as shown by the September income statement. What amount of net income would have appeared on the September income statement if Bay City Graphics had failed to replenish the petty cash fund at September 30?

7-3   Bank reconciliation

Information necessary for the preparation of a bank reconciliation and related journal entries for the Stonehenge Corporation at November 30 is listed below:

(1) Cash balance per records of Stonehenge Corporation is $10,423.09.

(2) The bank statement shows a balance of $9,154.57 as of November 30.

(3) Two debit memoranda accompanied the bank statement: one for $13 was for service charges for the month; the other for $864.60 was attached to an NSF check from Thomas Jones.

(4) The paid checks returned with the November bank statement disclosed two errors in the cash records. Check no. 832 for $923.48 had been erroneously recorded as $932.48 in the cash payments journal, and check no. 851 for $66.33 had been recorded as $33.66. Check no. 832 was issued in payment for a store display counter; check no. 851 was for advertising expense.

(5) A collection charge for $100.00 (not applicable to Stonehenge Corporation) was erroneously deducted from the account by the bank.

(6) Cash receipts of November 30 amounting to $625.25 were mailed to the bank too late to be included in the November bank statement.

(7) Checks outstanding as of November 30 were as follows: no. 860 for $160.00, no. 870 for $75.20, and no. 880 for $122.80.

Instructions

a Prepare a bank reconciliation at November 30.

b Prepare the necessary adjusting entries in general journal form.

7-4   Another bank reconciliation

The cash transactions and cash balances of Norfleet Farm for July were as follows:

(1) The ledger account for Cash showed a balance at July 31 of $16,766.95

(2) The July bank statement showed a closing balance of $18,928.12.

(3) The cash received on July 31 amounted to $4,017.15. It was left at the bank in the night depository chute after banking hours on July 31 and was therefore not recorded by the bank on the July statement.

(4) Also included with the July bank statement was a debit memorandum from the bank for $7.65 representing service charges for July.

(5) A credit memorandum enclosed with the July bank statement indicated that a non-interest-bearing note receivable for $4,545 from Rene Manes, left with the bank for collection, had been collected and the proceeds credited to the account of Norfleet Farm.

(6) Comparison of the paid checks returned by the bank with the entries in the cash payments journal revealed that check no. 821 for $835.02 issued July 15 in payment for office equipment had been erroneously entered in the cash payments journal as $853.02.

(7) Examination of the paid checks also revealed that three checks, all issued in July, had not yet been paid by the bank: no. 811 for $861.12; no. 814 for $640.80; no. 823 for $301.05.

(8) Included with the July bank statement was a $180 check drawn by Howard Williams, a customer of Norfleet Farm. This check was marked NSF. It had been included in the deposit of July 27 but had been charged back against the company's account on July 31.

Instructions

    a Prepare a bank reconciliation for Norfleet Farm at July 31.

    b Prepare journal entries (in general journal form) to adjust the accounts at July 31. Assume that the accounts have not been closed.

    c State the amount of cash which should appear on the balance sheet at July 31.

7-5 Bank reconciliation concealing a cash shortage

Rancho Lumber Co. had never given much attention to internal control concepts and the internal controls over cash transactions were not adequate. Donna Jones, the cashier-bookkeeper, handled cash receipts, made small disbursements from the cash receipts, maintained accounting records, and prepared the monthly reconciliations of the bank account.

At April 30, the statement received from the bank showed a balance on deposit of $30,510. The outstanding checks were as follows: no. 7062 for $371.16, no. 7183 for $306.00 no. 7284 for $470.61, no. 8621 for $315.34, no. 8623 for $613.80, and no. 8632 for $311.04. The balance of cash shown by the company's ledger account for Cash was $35,474.96, which included the cash on hand. The bank statement for April showed a credit of $360 arising from the collection of a note left with the bank; the company's accounts did not include an entry to record this collection.

Recognizing the weakness existing in internal control over cash transactions, Jones removed all the cash on hand in excess of $6,025.14, and then prepared the following reconciliation in an attempt to conceal this theft.

Balance per accounting records, Apr. 30		$35,474.96
Add: Outstanding checks:		
No. 8621	$315.34	
No. 8623	613.80	
No. 8632	311.04	1,060.18 ✗
		$36,535.14
Less: Cash on hand		6,025.14
Balance per bank statement, Apr. 30		$30,510.00
Less: Unrecorded credit		360.00
True cash, Apr. 30		$30,150.00

Instructions

    a Determine how much cash Jones took. Prepare a bank reconciliation in a form which first shows the balance per the accounting records after adding the cash from collection of the note and, second, shows an adjusted bank balance after deducting the proper amount for all outstanding checks. The two adjusted balances will not agree; the difference is the amount of undeposited cash which should be on hand. Comparison of the undeposited cash which should be on hand with the actual amount on hand of $6,025.14 will indicate the amount of the cash shortage.

    b Explain how Jones attempted to conceal her theft in the improper bank reconciliation shown on the preceding page. Your explanation may be in the form of a list of dollar amounts which add up to the total cash stolen by Jones.

    c Suggest some specific internal control devices for the Rancho Lumber Co.

7-6   Investment in bonds; interest revenue

On April 1, Year 7, Imperial Motors purchased $60,000 face value of the 10% bonds of Crest Theatres, Inc., at a price of 96 plus accrued interest. The bonds pay interest semiannually on March 1 and September 1.

Instructions

    a In general journal form, prepare the entries required in Year 7 to record:
        (1) Purchase of the bonds on April 1
        (2) Receipt of the semiannual interest payment on September 1
        (3) Adjustment of the accounts at December 31 for bond interest earned since September 1. (Imperial Motors adjusts and closes its accounts annually, using the calendar year.)
    b Assume that on January 31, Year 8, Imperial Motors sells the entire investment in Crest Theatre bonds for $57,850 plus accrued interest. Prepare the entries to:
        (1) Accrue bond interest earned from December 31, Year 7, through the date of sale
        (2) Record the sale of the bonds on January 31

7-7   Valuation of marketable equity securities

In the current asset section of its most recent balance sheet, Affordable Homes, Inc., showed marketable securities as follows:

Marketable securities	$82,400	
Less: Valuation allowance for marketable securities	7,250	$75,150

Shortly after the above balance sheet date, Affordable Homes, Inc., sold for $46,000 marketable securities which had cost $42,600.

Instructions

    a Prepare a journal entry to record the above sale for $46,000 of marketable securities which had cost $42,600.
    b The following numbered items are **independent** assumptions as to the current market value of the equity securities which remain in Affordable Homes, Inc.,'s portfolio at the next balance sheet date after the sale recorded in part a. For each assumption, prepare the journal entry required to adjust the carrying value of the portfolio to the lower of cost or market as of the balance sheet date. Show computations supporting each entry.
        (1) Assume current market value is $30,500.
        (2) Assume current market value is $36,300.
        (3) Assume current market value is $42,000.

7-8   Valuation of stock portfolio: short-term versus long-term

Target Corporation owns marketable equity securities which cost $100,000 and are classified in the balance sheet as a long-term investment. In the current year, the market value of the securities declined from an amount greater than cost to $90,000, and Target Corporation correctly made the following year-end adjusting entry:

Unrealized Loss on Long-Term Investments	10,000	
Valuation Allowance for Long-Term Investments		10,000
To adjust carrying value of long-term investment in equity securities to lower of cost or market.		

Instructions

For each of the financial statement items or relationships listed below, explain what change (if any) would result if the marketable securities were classified as a current asset instead of a long-term investment.

    a Current assets
    b Total assets
    c Current ratio (With the portfolio classified as a long-term investment, current assets total $180,000 and current liabilities total $100,000.)
    d Net income
    e Retained earnings
    f Total stockholders' equity

The type of explanation desired is illustrated below, using item a as an example:

    a Current assets would be increased by $90,000 if the securities were classified as a current asset.

7-9   Stocks and bonds: a comprehensive problem

The marketable securities owned by Bar Harbor Corporation at the beginning of the current year are listed below. Management considers all investments in marketable securities to be current assets.

$60,000 maturity value of Micro Computer Co. 12% bonds due Apr. 30, 1999.	
Interest is payable on Apr. 30 and Oct. 31 of each year. Cost $990 per bond	$59,400
2,000 shares of Ryan Corporation capital stock. Cost $42 per share	84,000

Transactions relating to marketable securities during the current year were as follows:

Jan. 21 Received semiannual cash dividend of $1.10 per share on the 2,000 shares of Ryan Corporation capital stock.

Feb. 8 Purchased 1,000 shares of Gramm Co. capital stock at $39¾ per share. Brokerage commissions amounted to $250.

Apr. 30 Received semiannual interest on Micro Computer Co. 12% bonds. Accrued interest of $1,200 had been recorded on December 31 of last year in the Bond Interest Receivable account.

May 31 Sold $40,000 face value of Micro Computer Co. 12% bonds at a price of 103, plus one month's accrued interest, less a brokerage commission of $200.

July 21 Received cash dividend on 2,000 shares of Ryan Corporation capital stock. Amount of dividend has increased to $1.20 per share.

Oct. 19 Sold 600 shares of Ryan Corporation capital stock at $37 per share, less a brokerage commission of $150.

Oct. 31 Received semiannual interest payment on remaining $20,000 face value of Micro Computer Co. 12% bonds.

At December 31 of the current year, the quoted market prices of the marketable equity securities owned by Bar Harbor Corporation were as follows: Ryan Corporation, $33 per share; Gramm Co., $43 per share.

Instructions

a Prepare journal entries to record the transactions listed above. Include an adjusting entry to record the accrued interest on the remaining Micro Computer Co. bonds through December 31. (Do not consider a lower-of-cost-or-market adjustment in part a.)

b Prepare a schedule showing the cost and market value of the marketable *equity* securities owned by Bar Harbor Corporation at December 31. Prepare the adjusting entry, if one is required, to reduce the portfolio to the lower of cost or market. (At the beginning of the current year, the market value of the portfolio was above cost and the Valuation Allowance for Marketable Securities account had a zero balance.)

7-10 Stocks and bonds (alternative to problem 7-9)

The portfolio of marketable securities owned by Sanford Communications at January 1 of the current year consisted of the three securities listed below. All marketable securities are classified as current assets.

$50,000 maturity value Copper Products Co. 9% bonds due Apr. 30, 2002. Interest is payable on Apr. 30 and Oct. 31 of each year. (Cost $990 per bond)	$49,500
1,500 shares of Aztec Corporation capital stock. (Cost $35 per share)	52,500
800 shares of Donner-Pass, Inc., capital stock. (Cost $55 per share)	44,000

Transactions relating to marketable securities during the current year were as follows:

Jan. 10 Purchased 1,000 shares of Rhodes Co. capital stock at $43 per share. Brokerage commissions paid amounted to $250.

Jan. 21 Received quarterly dividend of $1.50 per share on 800 shares of Donner-Pass, Inc., capital stock.

Mar. 5 Sold 800 shares of Donner-Pass, Inc., capital stock at $58 per share less a brokerage commission of $200.

Apr. 30 Received semiannual interest on Copper Products Co. 9% bonds. Accrued interest of $750 had been recorded on December 31 of last year in the Bond Interest Receivable account.

June 30 Sold $25,000 face value of Copper Products Co. 9% bonds at 93, plus two months' accrued interest, less a commission of $125.

Sept. 24 Sold 1,000 shares of Aztec Corporation capital stock at $40 per share, less a brokerage commission of $150.

Oct. 31 Received semiannual interest payment on remaining $25,000 face value of Copper Products Co. 9% bonds.

At December 31 of the current year, the quoted market prices of the marketable equity securities owned by Sanford Communications were as follows: Aztec Corporation capital stock, $37; and Rhodes Co. capital stock, $31½.

Instructions

a Prepare journal entries to record the transactions listed above. Include an adjusting entry to record accrued interest on the remaining Copper Products Co. bonds through December 31. (Do not consider a lower-of-cost-or-market adjustment in part a.)

b Prepare a schedule showing the cost and market value of the marketable equity securities owned by Sanford Communications at December 31. Prepare the adjusting entry, if one is required, to reduce the portfolio to the lower of cost or market. (At the beginning of the current year, the market value of the portfolio was above cost and the Valuation Allowance for Marketable Securities account had a zero balance.)

Cases for analysis

Case 7-1   Internal control — a short case study

J. K. Panther, a trusted employee of Bluestem Products, found himself in personal financial difficulties and carried out the following plan to steal $1,000 from the company and to conceal the fraud.

Panther removed $1,000 in currency from the cash register. This amount represented the bulk of the cash received in over-the-counter sales during three business days since the last bank deposit. Panther then removed a $1,000 check from the day's incoming mail; this check had been mailed in by a customer, Larry Jansen, in full payment of his account. Panther made no entry in the cash receipts journal for the $1,000 collection from Jansen but deposited the check in Bluestem Products' bank account in place of the $1,000 of over-the-counter cash receipts he had stolen. In order to keep Jansen from protesting when his month-end statement reached him, Panther made a general journal entry debiting Sales Returns and Allowances and crediting Accounts Receivable — Larry Jansen. Panther posted this entry to the two general ledger accounts affected and also to Jansen's account in the subsidiary ledger for accounts receivable.

Instructions

a Did these actions by Panther cause the general ledger to be out of balance or the subsidiary ledger to disagree with the controlling account? Explain.

b Several weaknesses in internal control apparently exist in Bluestem Products. Indicate the corrective actions needed.

Case 7-2   Internal control — a challenging case study

June Davis inherited a highly successful business, Bluestem Products, shortly after her twenty-second birthday and took over the active management of the business. A portion of the company's business consisted of over-the-counter sales for cash, but most sales were on credit and were shipped by truck. Davis had no knowledge of internal control practices and relied implicitly upon the bookkeeper-cashier, J. K. Panther, in all matters relating to cash and accounting records. Panther, who had been with the company for many years, maintained the accounting records and prepared all financial statements with the help of two assistants, made bank deposits, signed checks, and prepared bank reconciliations.

The monthly income statements submitted to Davis by Panther showed a very satisfactory rate of net income; however, the amount of cash in the bank declined steadily during the first 18 months after Davis took over the business. To meet the company's weakening cash position, a bank loan was obtained and a few months later when the cash position again grew critical, the loan was increased.

On April 1, two years after Davis assumed the management of the company, Panther suddenly left town, leaving no forwarding address. Davis was immediately deluged with claims of creditors who stated their accounts were several months past due and that Panther had promised all debts would be paid by April 1. The bank telephoned to notify Davis that the company's account was overdrawn and that a number of checks had just been presented for payment.

In an effort to get together some cash to meet this emergency, Davis called on two of the largest customers of the company, to whom substantial sales on account had recently been made, and asked if they could pay their accounts at once. Both customers informed her that their accounts were paid in full. They produced paid checks to substantiate their payments and explained that Panther had offered them reduced prices on merchandise if they would pay within 24 hours after delivery.

To keep the business from insolvency, Davis agreed to sell at a bargain price a half interest in the company. The sale was made to Helen Smith, who had had considerable experience in the industry.

One condition for the sale was that Smith should become the general manager of the business. The cash investment by Smith for her half interest was sufficient for the company to meet the demands on it and continue operations.

Immediately after Smith entered the business, she launched an investigation of Panther's activities. During the course of this investigation the following irregularities were disclosed:

(1) During the last few months of Panther's employment with the company, bank deposits were much smaller than the cash receipts. Panther had abstracted most of the receipts and substituted for them a number of worthless checks bearing fictitious signatures. These checks had been accumulated in an envelope marked "Cash Receipts — For Deposit Only."

(2) Numerous legitimate sales of merchandise on account had been charged to fictitious customers. When the actual customer later made payment for the goods, Panther abstracted the check or cash and made no entry. The account receivable with the fictitious customer remained in the records.

(3) When checks were received from customers in payment of their accounts, Panther had frequently recorded the transaction by debiting an expense account and crediting Accounts Receivable. In such cases Panther had removed from the cash receipts an equivalent amount of currency, thus subsituting the check for the currency and causing the bank deposit to agree with the recorded cash receipts.

(4) More than $3,000 a month had been stolen from petty cash. Fraudulent petty cash vouchers, mostly charged to the Purchases account, had been created to conceal these thefts and to support the checks cashed to replenish the petty cash fund.

(5) For many sales made over the counter, Panther had recorded lesser amounts on the cash register or had not rung up any amount. He had abstracted the funds received but not recorded.

(6) To produce income statements that showed profitable operations, Panther had recorded many fictitious sales. The recorded accounts receivable included many from nonexistent customers.

(7) In preparing bank reconciliations, Panther had omitted many outstanding checks, thus concealing the fact that the cash in the bank was less than the amount shown by the ledger.

(8) Inventory had been recorded at inflated amounts in order to increase reported profits from the business.

Instructions

a For each of the numbered paragraphs, describe one or more internal control procedures you would recommend to prevent the occurrence of such fraud.

b Apart from specific internal controls over cash and other accounts, what general precaution could June Davis have taken to assure herself that the accounting records were properly maintained and the company's financial statements complete and dependable? Explain fully.

Chapter 8
Receivables
and payables

In this chapter our attention is focused on the measurement of current assets and current liabilities arising from credit transactions. We emphasize the principles of valuing accounts receivable and the related question of measuring uncollectible accounts expense. We also consider the need for internal controls, the nature of interest, and the methods of accounting for notes receivable and notes payable. In the final pages of this chapter, the concept of present value is applied to long-term notes payable. An appendix on payroll accounting, complete with separate problem material, follows Chapter 8.

After studying
this chapter you
should be able to:

✓ Apply the balance sheet approach and the income statement approach to estimating uncollectible accounts expense.

✓ Account for the write-off and reinstatement of an account receivable.

✓ Account for credit card sales.

✓ Compare the allowance method and the direct charge-off method of accounting for uncollectible accounts receivable.

✓ Account for the receipt of notes, accrual of interest, collection or default, and the discounting of notes to banks.

✓ Explain the nature of a discount on a note receivable or note payable.

✓ Discuss the concept of present value.

✓ Account for notes with the interest charges included in the face amount.

One of the key factors underlying the tremendous expansion of the American economy has been the trend toward selling all types of goods and services on credit. The automobile industry has long been the classic example of the use of retail credit to achieve the efficiencies of large-scale output. Today, however, in nearly every field of retail trade it appears that sales and profits can be increased by granting customers the privilege of making payment a month or more after the date of sale. The sales of manufacturers and wholesalers are made on credit to an even greater extent than in retail trade.

ACCOUNTS RECEIVABLE

The credit department

No business concern wants to sell on credit to a customer who will prove unable or unwilling to pay his or her account. Consequently, most business organizations have a credit department which investigates the credit worthiness of each prospective customer. If the prospective customer is a business concern as, for example, a retail store, the financial statements of the store will be obtained and analyzed to determine its financial strength and the trend of operating results. The credit department naturally prefers to rely upon financial statements which have been audited by certified public accountants.

Regardless of whether the prospective customer is a business concern or an individual consumer, the investigation by the credit department will probably include the obtaining of a credit report from a local credit agency or from a national credit-rating institution such as Dun & Bradstreet, Inc. A credit agency compiles credit data on individuals and business concerns and distributes this information to its clients. Most companies that make numerous sales on credit find it worthwhile to subscribe to the services of one or more credit agencies.

Uncollectible accounts receivable

A business that sells its goods or services on credit will inevitably find that some of its accounts receivable are uncollectible. Regardless of how thoroughly the credit department investigates prospective customers, some uncollectible accounts will arise as a result of errors in judgment or because of unexpected developments. In fact, a limited amount of uncollectible accounts is evidence of a sound credit policy. If the credit department should become too cautious and conservative in rating customers, it might avoid all credit losses but, in so doing, lose profitable business by rejecting many acceptable customers.

Reflecting uncollectible accounts in the financial statements

In measuring business income, one of the most fundamental principles of accounting is that **revenue must be matched with the expenses incurred in generating that revenue.**

Uncollectible accounts expense is caused by selling goods on credit to customers who fail to pay their bills; such expenses, therefore, are incurred in the year in which the sales are made, even though the accounts receivable are not determined to be uncollectible until the following year. An account receivable which originates from a sale on credit in Year 1 and is determined to be uncollectible sometime during Year 2 represents an expense of Year 1. Unless each year's uncollectible accounts expense is **estimated** and reflected in the year-end balance sheet and income statement, both of these financial statements will be seriously deficient.

To illustrate, let us assume that Arlington Corporation began business on January 1, Year 1, and made most of its sales on credit throughout the year. At December 31, Year 1, accounts receivable amounted to $200,000. On this date the management reviewed the status of the accounts receivable, giving particular study to accounts which were past due. This review indicated that the collectible portion of the $200,000 of accounts receivable amounted to approximately $190,000. In other words, management estimated that uncollectible accounts expense for the first year of operations amounted to $10,000. The following adjusting entry should be made at December 31, Year 1:

Provision for uncollectible accounts

Uncollectible Accounts Expense	10,000	
Allowance for Doubtful Accounts		10,000
To record the estimated uncollectible accounts expense for Year 1.		

The Uncollectible Accounts Expense account created by the debit part of this entry is closed into the Income Summary account in the same manner as any other expense account. The Allowance for Doubtful Accounts which was credited in the above journal entry will appear in the balance sheet as a deduction from the face amount of the accounts receivable. It serves to reduce the accounts receivable to their *estimated realizable value* in the balance sheet, as shown by the following illustration:

ARLINGTON CORPORATION
Partial Balance Sheet
December 31, Year 1

How much is the estimated realizable value of the accounts receivable?

Current assets:		
Cash		$ 75,000
Accounts receivable	$200,000	
Less: Allowance for doubtful accounts	10,000	190,000
Inventory		300,000
Total current assets		$565,000

The Allowance for Doubtful Accounts

There is no way of telling in advance which accounts receivable will be collected and which ones will prove to be worthless. It is therefore not possible to credit the account of any particular customer to reflect our overall estimate of the year's credit losses. Neither is it possible to credit the Accounts Receivable controlling account in the general ledger. If the Accounts Receivable controlling account were to be credited with the estimated amount of doubtful accounts, this controlling account would no longer be in balance with the total of the numerous customers' accounts in the subsidiary ledger. The only practicable alternative, therefore, is to credit a separate account called Allowance for Doubtful Accounts with the amount estimated to be uncollectible.

The Allowance for Doubtful Accounts often is described as a *contra-asset* account or a *valuation* account. Both of these terms indicate that the Allowance for Doubtful Accounts has a credit balance, which is offset against the asset Accounts Receivable to produce the proper balance sheet value for this asset.

Estimating uncollectible accounts expense

Before the accounts are closed and financial statements are prepared at the end of the accounting period, an estimate of uncollectible accounts expense must be made. This estimate will usually be based upon past experience, perhaps modified in accordance with current business conditions. Since the allowance for doubtful accounts is necessarily an estimate and not a precise calculation, the factor of personal judgment may play a considerable part in determining the size of this valuation account.

Conservatism as a factor in valuing accounts receivable. The larger the allowance established for doubtful accounts, the lower the net valuation of accounts receivable will be. Some accountants and some business executives tend to favor the most conservative valuation of assets that logically can be supported. Conservatism in the preparation of a balance sheet implies a tendency to resolve uncertainties in the valuation of assets by reporting assets *at the lower end of the range of reasonable values* rather than by establishing values in a purely objective manner.

The valuation of assets at conservative amounts is a long-standing tradition in accounting, stemming from the days when creditors were the major users of financial statements. From the viewpoint of bankers and others who use financial statements as a basis for granting loans, conservatism in valuing assets has long been regarded as a desirable policy.

Assume that the balance sheet of Company A presents optimistic, exaggerated values for the assets owned. Assume also that this "unconservative" balance sheet is submitted to a banker in support of an application for a loan. The banker studies the balance sheet and makes a loan to Company A in reliance upon the values listed. Later the banker finds it impossible to collect the loan and also finds that the assets upon which the loan was based had been greatly overstated in the balance sheet. The banker will undoubtedly consider the overly optimistic character of Company A's balance sheet as partially responsible for the loss incurred by the bank. Experiences of this type have led creditors as a group to stress the desirability of conservatism in the valuation of assets.

In considering the argument for balance sheet conservatism, it is important to recognize that the income statement is also affected by the estimate made of uncollectible accounts expense. The act of providing a relatively large allowance for doubtful accounts involves a correspondingly heavy charge to expense. Setting asset values at a minimum in the balance sheet has the related effect of stating the current year's net income at a minimum amount.

Two methods of estimating uncollectible accounts expense

The provision for uncollectible accounts is an estimate of expense sustained in the current year. Two alternative approaches are widely used in making this annual estimate. One method consists of adjusting the valuation account to a new balance equal to the estimated uncollectible portion of the existing accounts receivable. This method is referred to as the *balance sheet* approach and rests on an *aging of the accounts receivable.* The adjusting entry takes into consideration the existing balance in the Allowance for Doubtful Accounts.

The alternative method requires an adjusting entry computed as a percentage of the year's net sales. This method may be regarded as the *income statement* approach to estimating uncollectible accounts expense. This *percentage of sales* method emphasizes the expense side of the adjustment and leaves out of consideration any existing balance in the valuation allowance account. If a substantial balance builds up in the Allowance for Doubtful Accounts year after year, however, a reduction in the percentage figure applied to sales may become necessary. These two methods are illustrated below.

Aging the accounts receivable. A past-due account receivable is always viewed with some suspicion. The fact that a receivable is past due suggests that the customer is either unable or unwilling to pay. The analysis of accounts receivable by age is known as aging the accounts, as illustrated by the schedule below.

Analysis of Accounts Receivable by Age
December 31, 19___

Customer	Total	Not Yet Due	1–30 Days Past Due	31–60 Days Past Due	61–90 Days Past Due	Over 90 Days Past Due
A. B. Adams	$ 500	$ 500				
B. L. Baker	150			$ 150		
R. D. Carl	800	800				
H. V. Davis	900				$ 800	$ 100
R. M. Evans	400	400				
Others	32,250	16,300	$10,000	4,200	200	1,550
Totals	$35,000	$18,000	$10,000	$4,350	$1,000	$1,650
Percentage	100	51	29	12	3	5

If you were credit manager . . .?

This analysis of accounts receivable gives management a useful picture of the status of collections and the probabilities of credit losses. Almost half the total accounts receivable are past due. The question "How long past due?" is pertinent, and is answered by the bottom line of the aging analysis. About 29% of the total receivables are past due from 1 to 30 days; another 12% are past due from 31 to 60 days; about 3% are past due from 61 to 90 days; and 5% of the total receivables consist of accounts past due more than three months. If an analysis of this type is prepared at the end of each month, management will be informed continuously on the trend of collections and can take appropriate action to ease or to tighten credit policy. Moreover, a yardstick is available to measure the performance of the persons responsible for collection activities.

The longer past due an account receivable becomes, the greater the likelihood that it will not be collected in full. In recognition of this fact, the analysis of receivables by age groups can be used as a stepping-stone in determining a reasonable amount to add to the Allowance for Doubtful Accounts. To determine this amount, we estimate the percentage of probable expense for each age group of accounts receivable. This percentage, when applied to the dollar amount in each age group, gives a probable expense for each group. By adding together the probable expense for all the age groups, the required balance in the Allowance for Doubtful Accounts is determined. The following schedule lists the group totals from the preceding illustration and shows how the total probable expense from uncollectible accounts is computed.

Accounts Receivable by Age Groups

	Amount	Percentage Considered Uncollectible	Probable Uncollectible Accounts
Not yet due	$18,000	1	$ 180
1–30 days past due	10,000	3	300
31–60 days past due	4,350	10	435
61–90 days past due	1,000	20	200
Over 90 days past due	1,650	50	825
Totals	$35,000		$1,940

Estimate of probable uncollectible accounts expense

This summary indicates that an allowance for doubtful accounts of $1,940 is required. Before making the adjusting entry, it is necessary to consider the existing balance in the allowance account. If the Allowance for Doubtful Accounts has a credit balance of, say, $500, the adjusting entry should be for $1,440 in order to bring the account up to the required balance of $1,940. This entry is as follows:

Increasing allowance for doubtful accounts

Uncollectible Accounts Expense	1,440	
Allowance for Doubtful Accounts		1,440
To increase the valuation account to the estimated required total		
of $1,940, computed as follows:		
Present credit balance of valuation account	$ 500	
Current provision for doubtful accounts	1,440	
New credit balance in valuation account	$1,940	

On the other hand, if the Allowance for Doubtful Accounts contained a *debit* balance of $500 before adjustment, the adjusting entry would be made in the amount of $2,440 ($1,940 + $500) in order to create the desired credit balance of $1,940. (The circumstances which could lead to a temporary debit balance in the Allowance for Doubtful Accounts will be explained later in this chapter.)

Estimating uncollectible accounts as a percentage of net sales. An alternative approach preferred by some companies consists of computing the charge to uncollectible accounts expense as a percentage of the net sales for the year. The question to be answered is not "How large a valuation allowance is needed to reduce our receivables to realizable value?" Instead, the question is stated as "How much uncollectible accounts expense is associated with this year's volume of sales?" This method may be regarded as the *income statement* approach to estimating uncollectible accounts.

As an example, assume that for several years the expense of uncollectible accounts has averaged 1% of net sales (sales minus returns and allowances and sales discounts). At the end of the current year, before adjusting entries, the following account balances appear in the ledger:

	Dr	Cr
Sales		$1,260,000
Sales returns and allowances	$40,000	
Sales discounts	20,000	
Allowance for doubtful accounts		1,500

The *net sales* of the current year amount to $1,200,000; 1% of this amount is $12,000. The existing balance in the Allowance for Doubtful Accounts *should be ignored in computing the amount of the adjusting entry,* because the percentage of net sales method stresses the *relationship between uncollectible accounts expense and net sales* rather than the valuation of receivables at the balance sheet date. The entry is

Provision for uncollectible accounts based on percentage of net sales

Uncollectible Accounts Expense	12,000	
Allowance for Doubtful Accounts		12,000

To record uncollectible accounts expense of 1% of the year's net sales (.01 × $1,200,000).

If a company makes both cash sales and credit sales, it is better to exclude the cash sales from consideration and to compute the percentage relationship of uncollectible accounts expense to credit sales only.

This approach of estimating uncollectible accounts receivable as a percentage of credit sales is easier to apply than the method of aging accounts receivable. The aging of receivables, however, tends to give a more reliable estimate of uncollectible accounts because of the consideration given to the age and collectibility of the specific accounts receivable at the balance sheet date. Some companies use the income statement approach for preparing monthly financial statements and internal reports but use the balance sheet method for preparing annual financial statements.

Writing off an uncollectible account receivable

Whenever an account receivable from a specific customer is determined to be uncollectible, it no longer qualifies as an asset and should be written off. To *write off* an account receivable is to reduce the balance of the customer's account to zero. The journal entry to accomplish this consists of a credit to the Accounts Receivable controlling account in the general ledger (and to the customer's account in the subsidiary ledger), and an offsetting debit to the Allowance for Doubtful Accounts.

Referring again to the example of Arlington Corporation as shown on page 299, the ledger accounts were as follows after the adjusting entry for estimated uncollectible accounts had been made on December 31, Year 1:

Accounts receivable	$200,000
Less: Allowance for doubtful accounts	10,000

Next let us assume that on January 27, Year 2, customer William Brown becomes bankrupt and the account receivable from him in the amount of $1,000 is determined to be worthless. The following entry should be made by Arlington Corporation:

Writing off an uncollectible account

Allowance for Doubtful Accounts 1,000
  Accounts Receivable, William Brown 1,000
To write off the receivable from William Brown as uncollectible.

The important thing to note in this entry is that the debit is made to the Allowance for Doubtful Accounts and *not* to the Uncollectible Accounts Expense account. The estimated expense of customer credit losses is charged to the Uncollectible Accounts Expense account at the end of each accounting period. When a particular account receivable is later determined to be worthless and is written off, this action does not represent an additional expense but merely confirms our previous estimate of the expense. If the Uncollectible Accounts Expense account were first charged with *estimated* credit losses and then later charged with *proven* credit losses, we would be double counting the actual uncollectible accounts expense.

After the entry writing off William Brown's account has been posted, the Accounts Receivable controlling account and the Allowance for Doubtful Accounts appear as follows:

Accounts Receivable

Both accounts reduced by write-off of worthless receivable

Year 1		Year 2	
Dec. 31	200,000	Jan. 27 (Brown write-off)	1,000

Allowance for Doubtful Accounts

Year 2		Year 1	
Jan. 27 (Brown write-off)	1,000	Dec. 31	10,000

Note that the *net* amount of the accounts receivable was unchanged by writing off William Brown's account against the Allowance for Doubtful Accounts. The write-off reduced the asset account and the allowance account by the same amount.

Before the Write-Off		After the Write-Off	
Net value of receivables unchanged by write-off Accounts receivable	$200,000	Accounts receivable	$199,000
Less: Allowance for doubtful accounts	10,000	Less: Allowance for doubtful accounts	9,000
Net value of receivables	$190,000	Net value of receivables	$190,000

The fact that writing off a worthless receivable against the Allowance for Doubtful Accounts does not change the net carrying value of accounts receivable shows that no loss or expense is entered in the accounting records when an account receivable is written off. This example bears out the point stressed earlier in the chapter. *Credit losses belong in the period in which the sale is made, not in a later period in which the account receivable is discovered to be uncollectible.*

Write-offs seldom agree with previous estimates. The total amount of accounts receivable written off in a given year will seldom, if ever, be exactly equal to the estimated amount previously credited to the Allowance for Doubtful Accounts.

If the amounts written off as uncollectible turn out to be less than the estimated amount, the Allowance for Doubtful Accounts will continue to show a credit balance. If the amounts written off as uncollectible are greater than the estimated amount, the Allowance for Doubtful Accounts will acquire a ***temporary debit balance,*** which will be eliminated by the adjusting entry at the end of the period.

Recovery of an account receivable previously written off

Occasionally a receivable which has been written off as worthless will later be collected in full or in part. Such collections are often referred to as ***recoveries*** of bad debts. Collection of an account receivable previously written off is evidence that the write-off was an error; the receivable should therefore be reinstated as an asset.

Let us assume, for example, that a past-due account receivable in the amount of $400 from J. B. Barker was written off by the following entry:

Barker account considered uncollectible

Allowance for Doubtful Accounts	400	
Accounts Receivable, J. B. Barker		400
To write off the receivable from J. B. Barker as uncollectible.		

At some later date the customer, J. B. Barker, pays the account in full. The entry to restore Barker's account will be

Barker account reinstated

Accounts Receivable, J. B. Barker	400	
Allowance for Doubtful Accounts		400
To reinstate as an asset an account receivable previously written off.		

A separate entry will be made in the cash receipts journal to record the collection from Barker. This entry will debit Cash and credit Accounts Receivable, J. B. Barker.

Direct charge-off method of recognizing uncollectible accounts expense

A few companies do not use a valuation allowance for accounts receivable. Instead of making adjusting entries to record uncollectible accounts expense on the basis of estimates, these companies recognize no uncollectible accounts expense until specific receivables are determined to be worthless. This method makes no attempt to match revenue and related expenses. Uncollectible accounts expense is recorded in the period in which individual accounts receivable are determined to be worthless rather than in the period in which the sales were made.

When the direct charge-off method is in use, the accounts receivable will be listed in the balance sheet at their gross amount, and ***no valuation allowance*** will be used. The receivables, therefore, are not stated at their probable realizable value.

In the determination of taxable income under present federal income tax regulations, both the direct charge-off method and the allowance method of estimating uncollectible accounts expense are acceptable. From the standpoint of accounting theory, the allowance method is much the better, for it enables expenses to be matched with related revenue and thus aids in making a logical measurement of net income.

Credit card sales

Many retailing businesses avoid the risk of uncollectible accounts by making credit sales to customers who use well-known credit cards, such as American Express, Visa, and MasterCard. A customer who makes a purchase using one of these cards must sign a multiple-copy form, which includes a **credit card draft.** A credit card draft is similar to a check which is drawn upon the funds of the credit card company rather than upon the personal bank account of the customer. The credit card company promptly pays cash to the merchant to redeem these drafts. At the end of each month, the credit card company bills the credit card holder for all the drafts it has redeemed during the month. If the credit card holder fails to pay the amount owed, it is the credit card company which sustains the loss.

By making sales through credit card companies, merchants receive cash more quickly from credit sales and avoid uncollectible accounts expense. Also, the merchant avoids the expenses of investigating customers' credit, maintaining an accounts receivable subsidiary ledger, and making collections from customers.

Bank credit cards. Some widely used credit cards (such as Visa and MasterCard) are issued by banks. When the credit card company is a bank, the retailing business may deposit the signed credit card drafts directly in its bank account, along with the currency and personal checks received from customers. Since banks accept these credit card drafts for immediate deposit, sales to customers using bank credit cards are recorded as cash sales.

In exchange for handling the credit card drafts, the bank makes a monthly service charge which usually runs between $1\frac{1}{4}$ and $3\frac{1}{2}$% of the amount of the drafts deposited by the merchant during the month. This monthly service charge is automatically deducted from the merchant's bank account and appears with other bank service charges in the merchant's monthly bank statement.

Other credit cards. When customers use nonbank credit cards (such as American Express, Diners' Club, and Carte Blanche), the retailing business cannot deposit the credit card drafts directly in its bank account. Instead of debiting Cash, the merchant records an account receivable from the credit card company. Periodically, the credit card drafts are mailed to the credit card company, which then sends a check to the merchant. Credit card companies, however, do not redeem the drafts at the full sales price. The agreement between the credit card company and the merchant usually allows the credit card company to take a discount of between $3\frac{1}{2}$ and 5% when redeeming the drafts.

To illustrate the procedures in accounting for these credit card sales, assume that Bradshaw Camera Shop sells a camera for $200 to a customer who uses a Quick Charge credit card. The entry would be

Receivable is from the credit card company

Accounts Receivable, Quick Charge Co.	200	
Sales		200
To record sale to customer using Quick Charge Credit card.		

At the end of the week, Bradshaw Camera Shop mails credit card drafts totaling $1,200 to Quick Charge Co., which redeems the drafts less a 5% discount. When payment is received, the entry is

```
Cash ........................................................  1,140
Credit Card Discount Expense ...................................     60
      Accounts Receivable, Quick Charge Co. ........................         1,200
To record collection of account receivable from Quick Charge Co., less 5%
discount.
```

The expense account, Credit Card Discount Expense, should be included among the selling expenses in the income statement of Bradshaw Camera Shop.

From a theoretical viewpoint, one might argue that the credit card discount expense should be recorded at the date of sale rather than at the date of collection. In this case, the sale of the camera for $200 would have been recorded by debiting Credit Card Discount Expense for $10 and Accounts Receivable, Quick Charge Co. for $190. Although this procedure would be theoretically preferable in terms of matching revenue with related expenses, it requires computing the discount expense separately for each sales transaction. For this reason, it is common practice to record the discount expense at the date of collection. Since the discount expense is relatively small and collection usually occurs shortly after the date of sale, the difference between the two methods does not have a material effect upon the financial statements.

Credit balances in accounts receivable

Customers' accounts in the accounts receivable subsidiary ledger normally have debit balances, but occasionally a customer's account will acquire a credit balance. This may occur because the customer overpays, pays in advance, or returns merchandise previously paid for. Any credit balances in the accounts receivable subsidiary ledger should be accompanied by the notation "Cr" to distinguish them from accounts with normal debit balances.

Suppose that the Accounts Receivable controlling account in the general ledger has a debit balance of $9,000, representing the following individual accounts with customers in the subsidiary ledger:

```
49 accounts with debit balances totaling ...................................  $10,000
1 account with a credit balance .........................................     1,000
Net debit balance of 50 customers' accounts ...............................  $ 9,000
```

One of the basic rules in preparing financial statements is that assets and liabilities should be shown at their gross amounts rather than being netted against each other. Accordingly, the amount which should appear as accounts receivable in the balance sheet is not the $9,000 balance of the controlling account, but the $10,000 total of the receivables with debit balances. The account with the $1,000 *credit balance is a liability* and should be shown as such rather than being concealed as an offset against an asset.

The balance sheet presentation should be as follows:

Current assets:		Current liabilities:	
Accounts receivable	$10,000	Credit balances in customers'	
		accounts	$1,000

Analysis of accounts receivable

What dollar amount of accounts receivable would be reasonable for a business making annual credit sales of $1,200,000? Comparison of the average amount of accounts receivable with the sales made on credit during the period indicates how long it takes to convert receivables into cash. For example, if annual credit sales of $1,200,000 are made at a uniform rate throughout the year and the accounts receivable at year-end amount to $200,000, we can see at a glance that the receivables represent one-sixth of the year's sales, or about 60 days of uncollected sales. Management naturally wants to make efficient use of the available capital in the business, and therefore is interested in a rapid "turnover" of accounts receivable. If the credit terms offered by the business in this example were, say, 30 days net, the existence of receivables equal to 60 days' sales would indicate difficulty in making collections and would warrant investigation. The analysis of receivables is considered more fully in Chapter 16.

Internal controls for receivables

As emphasized in earlier chapters, internal controls are measures that provide **protection of assets** and increase the **reliability of financial statements.** One of the most important principles of internal control is that employees who have custody of cash or other negotiable assets must not maintain accounting records. Documents such as sales invoices and credit memos must be serially numbered and every number in the series accounted for.

In a small business, it is not uncommon to find that one employee has responsibility for handling cash receipts from customers, maintaining the accounts receivable records, issuing credit memos for goods returned by customers, and writing off receivables judged to be uncollectible. Such a combination of duties is a virtual invitation to fraud. The employee in this situation is able to remove the cash collected from a customer without making any record of the collection. The next step is to dispose of the balance in the customer's account. This can be done by issuing a credit memo indicating that the customer had returned merchandise, or by writing off the customer's account as uncollectible. Thus, the employee has the cash, the customer's account shows a zero amount, and the books are in balance.

To avoid fraud in the handling of receivables, some of the most important rules are that employees who maintain the accounts receivable subsidiary ledger must not have access to cash receipts, and employees who handle cash receipts must not have access to the records of receivables. Furthermore, employees who maintain records of receivables must not have authority to issue credit memos or to write off receivables as uncollectible. These are classic examples of incompatible duties.

NOTES RECEIVABLE

Definition of a promissory note

A promissory note is an unconditional promise in writing to pay on demand or at a future date a definite sum of money.

The person who signs the note and thereby promises to pay is called the **maker** of the note. The person to whom payment is to be made is called the **payee** of the note. In the illustration below, G. L. Smith is the maker of the note and A. B. Davis is the payee.

Simplified form of promissory note

$1,000   Los Angeles, California   July 10, 19__

...........One month........... after date.......I.......promise to pay

to the order of ....A. B. Davis...........

-----One thousand and no/100----- ....dollars

payable at ....First National Bank of Los Angeles...........

for value received, with interest at ....12% per annum...........

G. L. Smith

From the viewpoint of the maker, G. L. Smith, the illustrated note is a liability and is recorded by crediting the Notes Payable account. However, from the viewpoint of the payee, A. B. Davis, this same note is an asset and is recorded by debiting the Notes Receivable account. The maker of a note expects to pay cash at the maturity date; the payee expects to receive cash at that date.

Nature of interest

Interest is a charge made for the use of money. A borrower incurs interest expense. A lender earns interest revenue. When you encounter notes payable in a company's financial statements, you know that the company is borrowing and you should expect to find interest expense. When you encounter notes receivable, you should expect interest revenue.

Computing interest. A formula used in computing interest is as follows:

$$\text{Principal} \times \text{Rate of Interest} \times \text{Time} = \text{Interest}$$

(Often expressed as $P \times R \times T = I$)

Interest rates are usually stated on an annual basis. For example, the interest on a $1,000, one-year, 12% note is computed as follows:

$$\$1,000 \times 0.12 \times 1 = \$120$$

If the term of the note were only four months instead of a year, the interest charge would be $40, computed as follows:

$$\$1,000 \times 0.12 \times \tfrac{4}{12} = \$40$$

If the term of the note is expressed in days, the exact number of days must be used in computing the interest. *The day on which a note is dated is not included; the day on which a note falls due is included.* Thus, a note dated today and maturing tomorrow involves only one day's interest. To simplify the computation of interest, we shall assume that a year contains 360 days rather than 365.[1] This assumption applies to illustrations and problems throughout this book. Suppose, for example, that a 60-day, 12% note for $1,000 is drawn on June 10. The interest charge could be computed as follows:

$$\$1,000 \times 0.12 \times \tfrac{60}{360} = \$20$$

The principal of the note ($1,000) plus the interest ($20) equals $1,020, and this amount (the *maturity value*) will be payable on August 9. The computation of days to maturity is as follows:

Days remaining in June (30 – 10; date of origin is not included)	20
Days in July	31
Days in August to maturity date (date of payment is included)	9
Total days called for by note	60

Prevailing interest rates. Interest rates, like the prices of goods and services, are always in a process of change. The Federal Reserve Board has a policy of deliberately causing interest rates to rise or fall in an effort to keep the economy running at a reasonable level of activity. In the early 1980s, the Federal Reserve Board combatted inflation by raising interest rates to record levels (20% and more). Then, as both inflation and business activity declined, the Federal Reserve Board reduced interest rates in an effort to stimulate business activity and increase employment.

The rate of interest you receive by depositing money in a savings account at a bank or a savings and loan association depends on the length of time you agree to leave the deposit untouched. The lowest interest rate (presently 5 or 6% a year) applies to a passbook account which gives you the right to withdraw all or part of your deposit at any time. However, you can earn a higher rate of interest (perhaps 8 to 12% a year) if you agree to leave your money on deposit for, say, six months or a year or more.

If you had obtained a long-term mortgage loan on a residence at the time this book was

---

[1] In calculating interest, banks and other businesses traditionally assumed that a year contained 360 days rather than 365. Consequently, one day's interest was treated as $1/360$ of a year, rather than $1/365$. This assumption causes the interest amount for a short-term note to be slightly higher, but makes interest computations much simpler. In recent years, however, most banks have changed to the use of a 365-day year for interest calculations.

going to press, you would now probably be paying between 11 and 13% as an annual interest rate. A business obtaining a loan from a bank may pay between 10% and 18% a year. Early in the 1980s interest rates were roughly double the rates which prevailed a few years before. The interest rate which banks charge on loans to the largest and strongest corporations is called the *prime rate.* Smaller companies and those not in a strong financial position may have to pay several percentage points more than the prime rate in order to obtain a bank loan.

Many retail stores charge interest on installment accounts at $1\frac{1}{2}$% a month, which is equivalent to 18% a year. Keep in mind that interest rates vary widely depending upon the nature of the loan and the financial strength of the borrower — and upon the fiscal policy of the federal government.

Accounting for notes receivable

In some lines of business, notes receivable are seldom encountered; in other fields they occur frequently and may constitute an important part of total assets. Business concerns that sell high-priced durable goods such as automobiles and farm machinery often accept notes receivable from their customers. Many companies obtain notes receivable in settlement of past-due accounts receivable.

All notes receivable are usually posted to a single account in the general ledger. A subsidiary ledger is not essential because the notes themselves, when filed by due dates, are the equivalent of a subsidiary ledger and provide any necessary information as to maturity, interest rates, collateral pledged, and other details. The amount debited to Notes Receivable is always the *face amount* of the note, regardless of whether or not the note bears interest. When an interest-bearing note is collected, the amount of cash received will be larger than the face amount of the note. The interest collected is credited to an Interest Revenue account, and only the face amount of the note is credited to the Notes Receivable account.

Illustrative entries. Assume that a 12%, 90-day note receivable is acquired from a customer, Marvin White, in settlement of an existing account receivable of $30,000. The entry for acquisition of the note is as follows:

Note received to replace account receivable	Dec. 1	Notes Receivable 30,000	
		Accounts Receivable, Marvin White	30,000
		Accepted 12%, 90-day note in settlement of account receivable.	

At December 31, the end of the company's fiscal year, the interest earned to date on notes receivable should be accrued by an adjusting entry as follows:

Adjusting entry for interest revenue earned in December	Dec. 31	Interest Receivable 300	
		Interest Revenue	300
		To accrue interest for the month of December on Marvin White note ($30,000 \times 12\% \times \frac{1}{12} = \$300$).	

On March 1 (90 days after the date of the note), the note matures. The entry to record collection of the note will be:

<table>
<tr><td>Collection of
principal and
interest</td><td>Mar. 1</td><td>Cash ....</td><td>30,900</td><td></td></tr>
<tr><td></td><td></td><td>Notes Receivable ....</td><td></td><td>30,000</td></tr>
<tr><td></td><td></td><td>Interest Receivable ....</td><td></td><td>300</td></tr>
<tr><td></td><td></td><td>Interest Revenue ....</td><td></td><td>600</td></tr>
</table>

Collected 12%, 90-day note from Marvin White ($30,000 $\times$ 12% $\times \frac{3}{12}$ = $900 interest of which $600 was earned in current year).

The preceding three entries show that interest is being earned throughout the life of the note and that the interest should be apportioned between years on a time basis. The revenue of each year will then include the interest actually earned in that year.

As explained in Chapter 4, some companies follow a policy of using reversing entries at year-end to simplify recording the later collection of interest applicable to two accounting periods. Under this optional policy, the reversing entry on January 1 would consist of a debit to Interest Revenue and a credit to Interest Receivable for the same amount as the prior adjusting entry. Later, when the interest is collected in cash, the collection will be recorded by a debit to Cash and a credit to Interest Revenue for the entire amount of interest received.

When a note is received from a customer at the time of making a sale of merchandise on account, two entries may be made, as follows:

<table>
<tr><td>Sale may be run
through accounts
receivable when note
is received from
customer</td><td>Accounts Receivable, Russ Company ....</td><td>7,500</td><td></td></tr>
<tr><td></td><td>Sales ....</td><td></td><td>7,500</td></tr>
<tr><td></td><td colspan="3">To record sale of merchandise on account.</td></tr>
<tr><td></td><td>Notes Receivable ....</td><td>7,500</td><td></td></tr>
<tr><td></td><td>Accounts Receivable, Russ Company ....</td><td></td><td>7,500</td></tr>
<tr><td></td><td colspan="3">To record receipt of note from customer.</td></tr>
</table>

When this procedure is employed, the account with a particular customer in the subsidiary ledger for accounts receivable provides a complete record of all transactions with that customer, regardless of the fact that some sales may have been made on open account and others may have involved a note receivable. Having a complete history of all transactions with a customer on a single ledger card may be helpful in reaching decisions as to collection efforts or further extensions of credit.

If the maker of a note defaults. A note receivable which cannot be collected at maturity is said to have been *defaulted* by the maker. Immediately after the default of a note, an entry should be made by the holder to transfer the amount due from the Notes Receivable account to an account receivable from the debtor.

Assuming that a 60-day, 12% note receivable for $1,000 from Robert Jones is not collected at maturity, the following entry would be made:

Default of note
receivable

Accounts Receivable, Robert Jones 1,020
    Notes Receivable 1,000
    Interest Revenue 20
To record default by Robert Jones of a 12%, 60-day note.

The interest earned on the note is recorded as a credit to Interest Revenue and is also included in the account receivable from the marker. The interest receivable on a defaulted note is just as valid a claim against the maker as is the principal of the note; if the principal is collectible, then presumably the interest too can be collected.

The transfer of past-due notes receivable into Accounts Receivable accomplishes two things. First, the Notes Receivable account is limited to current notes not yet matured and is, therefore, regarded as a highly liquid type of asset. Second, the account receivable ledger card will show that a note has been defaulted and will present a complete picture of all transactions with the customer.

Discounting notes receivable

Many business concerns which obtain notes receivable from their customers prefer to sell the notes to a bank for cash rather than to hold them until maturity. Selling a note receivable to a bank or finance company is often called *discounting* a note receivable. The holder of the note endorses the back of the note (as in endorsing a check) and delivers the note to the bank. The bank expects to collect the *maturity value* (principal plus interest) from the maker of the note at the maturity date, but if the maker fails to pay, the bank can demand payment from the endorser.

When a business endorses a note and turns it over to a bank for cash, it is promising to pay the note if the maker fails to do so. The endorser is therefore contingently liable to the bank. A *contingent liability* may be regarded as a potential liability which either will develop into a full-fledged liability or will be eliminated entirely by a future event. The future event in the case of a discounted note receivable is the payment (or default) of the note by the maker. If the maker pays, the contingent liability of the endorser is thereby ended. If the maker fails to pay, the contingent liability of the endorser becomes a real liability. In either case the period of contingent liability ends at the maturity date of the note.

The discounting of notes receivable with a bank may be regarded by a company as an alternative to borrowing by issuing its own note payable. To issue its own note payable to the bank would, of course, mean the creation of a liability; to obtain cash by discounting a note receivable creates only a contingent liability.

Computing the proceeds. The amount of cash obtained from the bank by discounting a note receivable is termed the *proceeds* of the note. The proceeds are computed by applying an interest rate (termed the *discount rate*) to the maturity value of the note for the time remaining before the note matures.

To illustrate, assume that on July 1 Retail Sales Company receives a 75-day, 12% note for $8,000 from Raymond Kelly. The note will mature on September 14 (30 days in July,

31 days in August, and 14 days in September). On July 16, Retail Sales Company discounts this note receivable with its bank, which charges a discount rate of 15% a year. How much cash will Retail Sales Company receive? The computation is as follows:

Face of the note	$8,000
Add: Interest from date of note to maturity ($8,000 × .12 × $\frac{75}{360}$)	200
Maturity value	$8,200
Less: Bank discount at 15% for the discount period of 60 days	
(July 16 to Sept. 14) ($8,200 × .15 × $\frac{60}{360}$)	205
Proceeds (cash received from bank)	$7,995

The entry made by Retail Sales Company to record the discounting of the Kelly note would be as follows:

Cash	7,995	
Interest Expense	5	
Note Receivable		8,000

Discounted Raymond Kelly note at bank at 15% annual interest rate.
Maturity value $8,200 minus $205 discount equals proceeds of $7,995.

In this illustration, the cash of $7,995 received from the bank was less than the $8,000 face amount of the note. The proceeds received from discounting a note may be *either more or less* than the face amount of the note, depending upon the interest rates and time periods involved. The difference between the face amount of the note being discounted and the cash proceeds is usually recorded as either Interest Expense or Interest Revenue. If the proceeds are less than the face value, the difference is debited to Interest Expense. However, if the proceeds exceed the face value of the note, the difference is credited to Interest Revenue.

Discounted note receivable paid by maker. Before the maturity date of the discounted note, the bank will notify the maker, Raymond Kelly, that it is holding the note. Kelly will therefore make payment directly to the bank.

Discounted note receivable defaulted by maker. If Kelly should be unable to pay the note at maturity, the bank will give notice of the default to the endorser, Retail Sales Company, which immediately becomes obligated to pay, and will make the following entry to record the payment:

Accounts Receivable, Raymond Kelly	8,200	
Cash		8,200

To record payment to bank of maturity value of discounted Kelly note, defaulted by maker.

Under these assumptions Retail Sales Company's contingent liability to the bank has become a real liability and has been discharged by a cash payment. Retail Sales Company now has an account receivable from the maker of the defaulted note for the amount which it was compelled to pay to the bank.

Classification of receivables in the balance sheet

Accounts receivable from customers ordinarily will be collected within the operating cycle; they are therefore listed among the current assets on the balance sheet. Receivables may also arise from miscellaneous transactions other than the sale of goods and services. These miscellaneous receivables, such as advances to officers and employees, and claims against insurance companies for losses sustained, should be listed separately on the balance sheet and should not be merged with trade accounts receivable. If an account receivable or note receivable from an officer or employee originates as a favor to the officer or employee, efforts at collection may await the convenience of the debtor. Consequently, it is customary to include such receivables in the balance sheet as noncurrent assets under the caption of Other Assets.

Notes receivable usually appear among the current assets; but if the maturity date of a note is more than a year distant and beyond the operating cycle of the business, the note should be listed as noncurrent under a heading such as Long-Term Investments. Any accrued interest receivable at the balance sheet date is a current asset and may be combined on the balance sheet with other accrued items such as accrued rents receivable or royalties receivable.

Disclosure of contingent liabilities. Since contingent liabilities are potential liabilities rather than full-fledged liabilities, they are not included in the liability section of the balance sheet. However, these potential liabilities may affect the financial position of the business if future events cause them to become real liabilities. Therefore, contingent liabilities should be *disclosed in footnotes to the financial statements.* The contingent liability arising from the discounting of notes receivable could be disclosed by the following footnote:

Note 6: Contingencies and commitments

At December 31, 19___, the Company was contingently liable for notes receivable discounted with maturity values in the amount of $250,000.

CURRENT LIABILITIES

Current liabilities are obligations that must be paid within one year or the operating cycle (whichever is longer). A comparison of the amount of current liabilities with the amount of current assets available for paying these debts helps us in judging a company's short-run debt-paying ability.

In accounting for current liabilities, we are especially interested in making certain that all such obligations are included in the balance sheet. Fraud may be concealed by deliberate *omission of a liability.* The omission or understatement of a liability will usually be accompanied by an overstatement of owners' equity or else by an understatement of assets. Depending on the nature of the error, the net income of the business may also be overstated.

A first essential of satisfactory internal control over accounts payable is the segregation of duties so that a cash disbursement to a creditor will be made only after approval of the purchasing, receiving, accounting, and finance departments. All purchase transactions should be evidenced by serially numbered purchase orders, copies of which are sent to the accounts payable department for comparison with receiving reports and vendors' invoices.

Among the more common current liabilities are notes payable, accounts payable, accrued liabilities such as interest and wages, and estimated liabilities such as income taxes. An *estimated* liability is an obligation known to exist but for which the dollar amount is uncertain. In this chapter we shall consider the accounting problems relating to notes payable; the liabilities arising from payrolls will be considered in Appendix A at the end of this chapter.

NOTES PAYABLE

Notes payable are issued whenever bank loans are obtained. Other transactions which may give rise to notes payable include the purchase of real estate or costly equipment, the purchase of merchandise, and the substitution of a note for a past-due account payable.

Notes payable issued to banks

Assume that on November 1 Porter Company borrows $10,000 from its bank for a period of six months at an annual interest rate of 12%. Six months later on May 1, Porter Company will have to pay the bank the *principal* amount of $10,000 plus $600 interest ($10,000 \times .12 \times \frac{6}{12}$.) The owners of Porter Company have authorized John Caldwell, the company's treasurer, to sign notes payable issued by the company. The note issued by Porter Company could read as shown below (omitting a few minor details).

This note is for the principal amount with interest stated separately

> Miami, Florida   November 1, Year 1
>
> Six months .... after this date   Porter Company ....
>
> promises to pay to Security National Bank the sum of $ ....   10,000 ....
>
> with interest at the rate of ....12%.... per annum.
>
> Signed... *John Caldwell* ....
>
> Title   Treasurer ....

The journal entry in Porter Company's accounting records for this borrowing is

Face amount of note

Cash 10,000
          Notes Payable   10,000
Borrowed $10,000 for six months at 12% interest per year.

Notice that no liability is recorded for the interest charges when the note is issued. At the date that money is borrowed, the borrower has a liability *only for the principal amount of the loan;* the liability for interest accrues day by day over the life of the loan. At December 31, two months' interest expense has been incurred, and the following year-end adjusting entry is made:

A liability for interest accrues day by day.

Interest Expense	200	
Interest Payable		200

To record interest expense incurred through year-end on 12%, six-month note dated Nov. 1 ($10,000 × $\frac{2}{12}$ = $200).

If we assume that the company does not use reversing entries, the entry on May 1 when the note is paid will be:

Payment of principal and interest

Notes Payable	10,000	
Interest Payable	200	
Interest Expense	400	
Cash		10,600

To record payment of 12%, six-month note on maturity date and to recognize interest expense incurred since year-end ($10,000 × .12 × $\frac{4}{12}$ = $400).

Notes payable with interest charges included in the face amount

Instead of stating the interest rate separately as in the preceding illustration, the note payable issued by Porter Company could have been drawn to include the interest charge in the face amount of the note, as shown below:

This note shows interest included in face amount of note

Miami, Florida	November 1, Year 1
Six months	after this date Porter Company
promises to pay to Security National Bank the sum of $	$10,600
	Signed *John Caldwell*
	Title Treasurer

Notice that the face amount of this note ($10,600) is greater than the amount borrowed ($10,000). Porter Company's liability at November 1 is only $10,000; the other $600 included in the face amount of the note represents *future interest charges.* As interest expense is incurred over the life of the note, Porter Company's liability will grow to $10,600, just as in the preceding illustration.

The entry to record Porter Company's $10,000 borrowing from the bank at November 1 will be as follows for this type of note payable:

Cash	10,000	
Discount on Notes Payable	600	
Notes Payable		10,600

Issued to bank a 12%, six-month note payable with interest charge included in face amount of note.

The liability account, Notes Payable, was credited with the full face amount of the note ($10,600). It is therefore necessary to debit a *contra-liability* account, **Discount on Notes Payable,** for the future interest charges included in the face amount of the note. Discount on Notes Payable is shown in the balance sheet as a deduction from the Notes Payable account. In our illustration, the amounts in the balance sheet would be Notes Payable, $10,600, minus Discount on Notes Payable, $600, or a net liability of $10,000 at November 1.

Discount on Notes Payable. The balance of the account Discount on Notes Payable represents *interest charges applicable to future periods.* As this interest expense is incurred, the balance of the discount account gradually is transferred into the Interest Expense account. Thus, at the maturity date of the note, Discount on Notes Payable will have a zero balance, and the net liability will have increased to $10,600. The process of transferring the amount in the Discount on Notes Payable account into the Interest Expense account is called *amortization* of the discount.

Amortization of the discount. The discount on *short-term* notes payable usually is amortized by the straight-line method, which allocates the same amount of discount to interest expense for each month the note is outstanding.[2] Thus, the $600 discount on the Porter Company note payable will be transferred from Discount on Notes Payable into Interest Expense at the rate of $100 per month ($600 ÷ 6 months). Notice that $100 of interest expense per month is the same amount we could compute by multiplying the 12% rate stated in the note to the $10,000 principal amount, as follows: $10,000 \times 12\% \times \frac{1}{12} = \$100$.

Adjusting entries should be made to amortize the discount at the end of the year and at the date the note matures. At December 31, Year 1, Porter Company will make the following adjusting entry to recognize the two months' interest expense incurred since November 1:

Interest Expense	200	
Discount on Notes Payable		200

To record interest expense incurred to end of year on 12%, six-month note dated Nov. 1 ($600 discount $\times \frac{2}{6}$).

Notice that the liability for accrued interest is recorded by crediting Discount on Notes

---

[2] When an interest charge is included in the face amount of a long-term note, the effective interest method of amortizing the discount is often used instead of the straight-line method. The effective interest method of amortization is discussed in Chapter 13.

Payable rather than Accrued Interest Payable. The credit to Discount on Notes Payable reduces the debit balance in this contra-liability account from $600 to $400, thereby increasing the **net liability** for notes payable by $200.

At December 31, Porter Company's net liability for the bank loan will appear in the balance sheet as shown below:

Liability shown net of discount

Current liabilities:

Note payable	$10,600	
Less: Discount on notes payable	400	$10,200

The net liability of $10,200 consists of the $10,000 principal amount of the debt plus the $200 interest which has accrued since November 1.

When the note matures on May 1, Year 2, Porter Company will recognize the four months' interest expense incurred since year-end and will pay the bank $10,600. The entry is

Two-thirds of interest applicable to second year

Notes Payable	10,600	
Interest Expense	400	
Discount on Notes Payable		400
Cash		10,600

To record payment of six-month note due today and recognize interest expense incurred since year-end ($10,000 × 12% × $\frac{4}{12}$ = $400).

Comparison of the two forms of notes payable

We have illustrated two alternative methods which Porter Company could use in accounting for its $10,000 bank loan, depending upon the form of the note payable. The journal entries for both methods, along with the resulting balance sheet presentations of the liability at November 1 and December 31, are summarized on page 320. Notice that both methods result in Porter Company recognizing the same amount of interest expense and the same total liability in its balance sheet. The form of the note does not change the economic substance of the transaction.

The concept of present value applied to long-term notes

If you borrow cash by issuing a note payable, you can easily determine whether an interest charge is included in the face amount of the note. For example, if you borrow $9,000 and sign a note payable for $10,000, you know that an interest charge of $1,000 has been included in the face amount of the note. However, if you issue a $10,000 note in exchange for noncash assets, such as land or machinery, the amount of interest (if any) included in the face amount of the note may be less apparent.

If a realistic rate of interest is stated separately in a long-term note, we may assume that no interest charge is included in the face amount. If no interest rate is stated, however, or if the stated interest rate is unrealistically low (such as 2% a year), a portion of the face amount of the note must be assumed to represent an interest charge. When such a note is issued or received, the transaction should be recorded at the **present value** of the note rather than at the face amount.

Note written for $10,000 plus 12% interest

Note written with interest included in face amount

Entry to record borrowing on Nov. 1

Cash	10,000
Notes Payable	10,000

Cash	10,000
Discount on Notes Payable	600
Notes payable	10,600

Partial balance sheet at Nov. 1

Current liabilities:

Notes payable	$10,000

Current liabilities:

Notes payable	$10,600	
Less: Discount on notes payable	600	$10,000

Adjusting entry at Dec. 31

Interest Expense	200
Interest Payable	200

Interest Expense	200
Discount on Notes Payable .	200

Partial balance sheet at Dec. 31

Current liabilities:

Notes payable	$10,000	
Interest payable	200	$10,200

Current liabilities:

Notes payable	$10,600	
Less: Discount on notes payable	400	$10,200

Entry to record payment of note on May 1

Notes Payable	10,000
Interest payable	200
Interest Expense	400
Cash	10,600

Notes Payable	10,600
Interest Expense	400
Discount on Notes Payable .	400
Cash	10,600

The concept of present value is based upon the "time value" of money — the idea that an amount of money which will not be received until some future date is equivalent to a smaller amount of money received today. The present value of a future cash receipt is the amount of money which, if received today, would be considered equivalent to the future receipt. The present value is always less than the future amount, because money available today can be invested to earn interest and thereby become equivalent to a larger amount in the future.

When a note does not call for the payment of interest, the present value of the note is less than its face amount, because the face amount of the note will not be received until the maturity date. The difference between the present value of a note and its face amount should be viewed as an interest charge included in the face amount. Often we can determine the present value of a note by the fair market value of the asset acquired when the note is issued. As an alternative, we can compute the present value by using the mathematical techniques illustrated in Appendix D following Chapter 13.

The **effective rate of interest** associated with a note is that interest rate which will cause the note's present value to increase to the full maturity value of the note by the time the note matures.

An illustration of notes recorded at present value

To illustrate the use of present value in transactions involving long-term notes, let us assume that on September 1, Everts Company buys equipment from Tru-Tool, Inc., by issuing a one-year note payable in the face amount of $230,000 with no mention of an interest rate. It is not logical to assume that Tru-Tool, Inc., would extend credit for one year without charging any interest. Therefore, some portion of the $230,000 face amount of the note should be regarded as a charge for interest. In the accounting records of Everts Company, the amount of this interest charge should be debited to the contra-liability account Discount on Notes Payable, instead of being treated as part of the cost of the equipment.

If Everts Company were to debit Equipment and credit Notes Payable for the full $230,000 face amount of the note, the following errors would result: (1) the cost of the equipment and the amount of the related liability would be **overstated** by the amount of the interest charge included in the face amount of the note; (2) interest expense would be **understated** over the life of the note; and (3) depreciation expense would be **overstated** throughout the estimated service life of the equipment.

Let us assume that the regular sales price of this equipment is $200,000. In this case, the present value of the note is apparently $200,000, and the remaining $30,000 of the face amount represents a charge for interest. The rate of interest which will cause the $200,000 present value of the note to increase to the $230,000 maturity value in one year is 15%. Thus, the face amount of the note actually includes an interest charge computed at the effective interest rate of 15%.

Everts Company should use the present value of the note in determining the cost of the equipment and the amount of the related net liability, as shown by the following journal entry:

```
Equipment .............................................  200,000
Discount on Notes Payable ...............................   30,000
     Notes Payable ......................................             230,000
Purchased equipment for $200,000 by issuing a one-year note payable
with a 15% interest charge included in the face amount.
```

Over the next 12 months, the $30,000 recorded as a discount on the note payable will be amortized into interest expense.

It is equally important for the selling company, Tru-Tool, Inc., to use the present value of the note in determining the amount of revenue to be recognized from the sale. The $30,000 interest charge included in the face amount of the note receivable from Everts Company represents **unearned interest** to Tru-Tool, Inc., and is **not part of the sales price of the equipment.** If Tru-Tool, Inc., were to treat the entire face amount of the note receivable as the sales price of the equipment, the result would be to overstate sales revenue and notes receivable by $30,000, and also to understate interest revenue by this amount over the life of the note. Tru-Tool, Inc., should record the sale at the present value of the note received, as follows:

```
Accounts Receivable, Everts Company .......................  200,000
     Sales ..............................................             200,000
To record sale of equipment to Everts Company.


Notes Receivable ........................................  230,000
     Discount on Notes Receivable ..........................              30,000
     Accounts Receivable, Everts Company ....................             200,000
Obtained from Everts Company a one-year note with a 15% interest
charge included in the face amount.
```

Notice that the interest charge included in the face amount of the note receivable is credited to **Discount on Notes Receivable.** This account represents unearned interest and is a contra-asset account which appears in the balance sheet as a deduction from notes receivable. As the interest is earned, the balance of the discount account will gradually be transferred into Interest Revenue. At December 31, Tru-Tool, Inc., will have earned four months' interest revenue and will make the following entry:

```
Discount on Notes Receivable ...............................   10,000
     Interest Revenue ...................................              10,000
To record interest earned from Sept. 1 through Dec. 31 on Everts Company
note ($200,000 × 15% × 4/12).
```

On September 1 of the following year, when the note receivable is collected from Everts Company, the required entry will be

Cash	230,000	
Discount on Notes Receivable	20,000	
Interest Revenue		20,000
Notes Receivable		230,000

To record collection of Everts Company note and to recognize interest earned since year-end.

In an earlier era of accounting practice, failure to use the concept of present value in recording transactions involving long-term notes sometimes resulted in large overstatements of assets and sales revenue, especially by real estate development companies. In recognition of this problem, the Financial Accounting Standards Board now requires the use of present value in recording transactions involving **long-term** notes receivable or payable which do not bear reasonable stated rates of interest.[3]

When a note is issued for a short period of time, any interest charge included in its face amount is likely to be relatively small. Therefore, the use of present value is not required in recording normal transactions with customers or suppliers involving notes due in less than one year. Notes given or received in such transactions which do not specify an interest rate may be considered non-interest-bearing.

Installment receivables

Another application of present value is found in the recording of **installment sales.** Many retailing businesses sell merchandise on installment sales plans, which permit customers to pay for their credit purchases through a series of monthly payments. The importance of installment sales is emphasized by a recent balance sheet of Sears, Roebuck, and Co., which shows about $6 billion of customer accounts receivable, nearly all of which call for collection in monthly installments.

When merchandise is sold on an installment plan, substantial interest charges are usually added to the "cash selling price" of the product in determining the total dollar amount to be collected in the series of installment payments. The amount of sales revenue recognized at the time of sale, however, is limited to the **present value** of these installment payments. In most cases, the present value of these future payments is equal to the regular sales price of the merchandise. The portion of the installment account receivable which represents unearned finance charges is credited to the contra-asset account, Discount on Installment Receivables. Thus, the entry to record an installment sale consists of a debit to Installment Contracts Receivable, offset by a credit to Discount on Installment Receivables for the unearned finance charges and a credit to Sales for the regular sales price of the merchandise. The balance of the contra-asset account, Discount on Installment Receivables, is then amortized into Interest Revenue over the length of the collection period.

Although the collection period for an installment receivable often runs as long as 24 to

[3] *APB Opinion No. 21,* "Interest on Receivables and Payable," AICPA (New York: 1971).

36 months, such receivables are regarded as current assets if they correspond to customary credit terms of the industry. In published balance sheets, the Discount on Installment Receivables is often called Deferred Interest Income or Unearned Finance Charges. A typical balance sheet presentation of installment accounts receivable is illustrated below:

Trade accounts receivable:		
Accounts receivable		$ 75,040,000
Installment contracts receivable, including $31,000,000 due after one year		52,640,000
		$127,680,000
Less: Deferred interest income ($8,070,000) and allowance for doubtful		
accounts ($1,872,000)		9,942,000
Total trade accounts and notes receivable		$117,738,000

Income tax aspects of installment sales. Current provisions of the federal income tax law permit sellers to spread the recognition of the gross profit from installment sales over the years in which collections are received. The result of this treatment is to postpone the recognition of taxable income and the payment of income tax. In financial statements, however, the entire gross profit from installment sales is recognized *in the period in which the sale occurs.* The method of recognizing gross profit from installment sales for income tax purposes will be illustrated in Chapter 14. There are a number of other more complex issues relating to installment sales; these are covered in advanced accounting courses.

Key terms introduced or emphasized in chapter 8

Aging the accounts receivable. The process of classifying accounts receivable by age groups such as current, past due 1–30 days, past due 31–60 days, etc. A step in estimating the uncollectible portion of the accounts receivable.

Allowance for Doubtful Accounts. A valuation account or contra account relating to accounts receivable and showing the portion of the receivables estimated to be uncollectible.

Contingent liability. A potential liability which either will develop into a full-fledged liability or will be eliminated entirely by a future event.

Contra account. A ledger account which is deducted from or offset against a related account in the financial statements, for example, Allowance for Doubtful Accounts, Discount on Notes Payable, and Discount on Notes Receivable.

Default. Failure to pay interest or principal of a promissory note at the due date.

Direct charge-off method. A method of accounting for uncollectible receivables in which no expense is recognized until individual accounts are determined to be worthless. At that point the account receivable is written off with an offsetting debit to uncollectible accounts expense. Fails to match revenue and related expenses.

Discount on Notes Payable. A contra-liability account representing any interest charges applicable to future periods included in the face amount of a note payable. Over the life of the note, the balance of the Discount on Notes Payable account is amortized into Interest Expense.

Discount on Notes Receivable. A contra-asset account representing any unearned interest included in the face amount of a note receivable. Over the life of the note, the balance of the Discount on Notes Receivable account is amortized into Interest Revenue.

Discounting notes receivable. Selling a note receivable prior to its maturity date.

Effective interest rate. The rate of interest which will cause the present value of a note to increase to the maturity value by the maturity date.

Installment sales. Sales on credit in which the customer agrees to make a series of installment payments, including substantial interest charges.

Interest. A charge made for the use of money. The formula for computing interest is Principal $\times$ Rate of interest $\times$ Time $=$ Interest $(P \times R \times T = I)$.

Maker (of a note). A person or entity who issues a promissory note.

Maturity date. The date on which a note becomes due and payable.

Maturity value. The value of a note at its maturity date, consisting of principal plus interest.

Notes payable. A liability evidenced by issuance of a formal written promise to pay a certain amount of money, usually with interest, at a future date.

Notes receivable. A receivable (asset) evidenced by a formal written promise to pay a certain amount of money, usually with interest, at a future date.

Payee. The person named in a promissory note to whom payment is to be made (the lender).

Present value concept. Based upon the time value of money. The basic premise is that an amount of money which will not be received until a future date is equivalent to a smaller amount of money available today.

Present value of a future cash receipt. The amount of money which an informed investor would pay today for the right to receive that future cash receipt. The present value is always less than the future amount, because money available today can be invested to earn interest and thereby become equivalent to a larger amount in the future.

Principal amount. That portion of the maturity value of a note which is attributable to the amount borrowed, or to the cost of the asset acquired when the note was issued, rather than being attributable to interest charges.

Proceeds. The amount received from selling a note receivable prior to its maturity. Maturity value minus discount equals proceeds.

Demonstration problem for your review

The Monastery, Inc., sells custom wood furniture to decorators and to the general public. Selected transactions relating to the company's receivables and payables for the month of August are shown below. The company uses the allowance method in accounting for uncollectible accounts.

Aug. 1 Borrowed $48,000 from Central Bank by issuing a 90-day note payable with a stated interest rate of 15%.

Aug. 5 Sold merchandise priced at $960 to R. Lucas on the installment plan. Lucas signed an installment contract requiring 12 monthly payments of $90 each, beginning September 5. (Record transaction by debiting Installment Contracts Receivable rather than Accounts Receivable.)

Aug. 8 A $420 account receivable from S. Wilson was determined to be worthless and was written off.

Aug. 10 Sold merchandise to Century Interiors on account, $15,200. It was agreed that Century Interiors would issue a 60-day, 8% note upon receipt of the merchandise and could deduct any freight it paid on the goods.

Aug. 11 Received a 60-day note from StyleCraft Co. in settlement of $3,600 open account. Interest computed at the effective rate of 8% was included in the face amount of the note.

Aug. 13 Received a letter from Century Interiors stating that it had paid $200 freight on the shipment of August 10. Enclosed was a 60-day, 8% note dated August 13 for $15,000.

Aug. 16 Purchased land for $92,000, making a cash down payment of $20,000 and issuing a one-year note payable for the balance. The face amount of the note was $78,480, which included interest computed at an effective rate of 9%.

Aug. 20 Received full payment from J. Porter of a $4,500, 60-day, 12% note dated June 21. Accrued interest receivable of $30 had been recorded in prior months.

Aug. 23 Discounted the Century Interiors note dated August 13 at the bank. The bank discount rate of 9% was applied to the maturity value of the note for the 50 days remaining to maturity.

Aug. 25 An account receivable of $325 from G. Davis had been written off in June; full payment was unexpectedly received from Davis.

Aug. 29 Sales to ExtraCash credit card customers during August amounted to $14,800. (Summarize all credit card sales in one entry. ExtraCash Co. is not a bank.)

Aug. 30 Collected cash from ExtraCash Co. for the August credit card sales, less a 5% discount charged by ExtraCash.

Aug. 31 The Discount on Installment Receivables account is amortized to reflect $3,960 of finance charges earned during August.

Aug. 31 As a result of substantial write-offs, the Allowance for Doubtful Accounts has a debit balance of $320. Aging of the accounts receivable indicates that the allowance account should have a $1,200 credit balance at the end of August.

Instructions. Prepare journal entries to record the transactions listed above and to make any adjusting entries necessary at August 31.

Solution to demonstration problem

General Journal

19__

Aug. 1	Cash	48,000	
	Notes Payable		48,000
	Borrowed $48,000 from Central Bank; issued a 90-day, 15% note payable.		
5	Installment Contracts Receivable, R. Lucas	1,080	
	Discount on Installment Receivables		120
	Sales		960
	Installment sale, due in 12 monthly installments of $90 each.		
8	Allowance for Doubtful Accounts	420	
	Accounts Receivable, S. Wilson		420
	Wrote off uncollectible account from S. Wilson.		
10	Accounts Receivable, Century Interiors	15,200	
	Sales		15,200
	Sale of merchandise on account.		
11	Notes Receivable	3,648	
	Discount on Notes Receivable		48
	Accounts Receivable, StyleCraft Co.		3,600
	Received 60-day note with interest at effective rate of 8% included in face amount in settlement of open account.		

13	Notes Receivable	15,000	
	Delivery Expense ....,........	200	
	Accounts Receivable, Century Interiors		15,200

To record credit to Century Interiors for freight paid by them and receipt of 60-day, 8% note for balance of amount owed.

16	Land	92,000	
	Discount on Notes Payable	6,480	
	Notes Payable		78,480
	Cash		20,000

Purchased land for $92,000, paying $20,000 cash and issuing a one-year note payable with a 9% interest charge included in the face amount.

20	Cash	4,590	
	Notes Receivable		4,500
	Accrued Interest Receivable		30
	Interest Revenue		60

Collected note from J. Porter, including $90 interest.

23	Cash	15,010	
	Notes Receivable		15,000
	Interest Revenue		10

Discounted Century Interiors' note at bank, proceeds computed as follows: Maturity value $15,200 — bank charge of $190 ($15,200 $\times$ .09 $\times \frac{50}{360}$) = $15,010.

25	Account Receivable, G. Davis	325	
	Allowance for Doubtful Accounts		325

To reinstate Davis receivable previously written off.

25	Cash	325	
	Accounts Receivable, G. Davis		325

To record collection of Davis account.

29	Accounts Receivable, ExtraCash Co.	14,800	
	Sales		14,800

To record credit card sales for August.

30	Cash	14,060	
	Credit Card Discount Expense	740	
	Accounts Receivable, ExtraCash Co.		14,800

Collected August credit card sales invoices, less 5%.

31	Discount on Installment Receivables	3,960	
	Interest Revenue		3,960

To record finance charges earned on installment contracts receivable during August.

31 Uncollectible Accounts Expense 1,520
        Allowance for Doubtful Accounts   1,520
    To provide for estimated uncollectibles as follows:
      Balance required $1,200
      Present balance (debit)   320
      Required increase in allowance $1,520

31 Interest Expense 600
        Interest Payable   600
    To record interest expense on note payable to Central
    Bank ($48,000 × 15% × $\frac{30}{360}$).

31 Discount on Notes Receivable 16
        Interest Revenue   16
    To record interest earned through Aug. 31 on
    StyleCraft note receivable ($48 discount × $\frac{20}{60}$ = $16).

31 Interest Expense 270
        Discount on Notes Payable   270
    To amortize discount through Aug. 31 on one-year
    note payable dated Aug. 16 ($6,480 × $\frac{1}{12}$ × $\frac{1}{2}$).

Review questions

1 Jones Company, a retailer, makes most of its sales on credit. In the first 10 years of operation, the company incurred some bad debts or uncollectible accounts expense each year. Does this record indicate that the company's credit policies are in need of change?

2 Company A and Company B are virtually identical in size and nature of operations, but Company A is more conservative in valuing accounts receivable. Will this greater emphasis on conservatism cause A to report higher or lower net income than Company B? Assume that you are a banker considering identical loan applications from A and B and you know of the more conservative policy followed by A. In which set of financial statements would you feel more confidence? Explain.

3 Adams Company determines at year-end that its Allowance for Doubtful Accounts should be increased by $6,500. Give the adjusting entry to carry out this decision.

4 In making the annual adjusting entry for uncollectible accounts, a company may utilize a *balance sheet approach* to make the estimate or it may use an *income statement approach.* Explain these two alternative approaches.

5 At the end of its first year in business, Baxter Laboratories had accounts receivable totaling $148,500. After careful analysis of the individual accounts, the credit manager estimated that $146,100 would ultimately be collected. Give the journal entry required to reflect this estimate in the accounts.

6 In February of its second year of operations, Baxter Laboratories (Question 5 above) learned of the failure of a customer, Sterling Corporation, which owed Baxter $800. Nothing could be collected. Give the journal entry to recognize the uncollectibility of the receivable from Sterling Corporation.

7 What is the *direct charge-off method* of handling credit losses as opposed to the *allowance method?* What is its principal shortcoming?

8 Morgan Corporation has decided to write off its account receivable from Brill Company because the latter has entered bankruptcy. What general ledger accounts should be debited and credited, assuming that the allowance method is in use? What general ledger accounts should be debited and credited if the direct charge-off method is in use?

9 Mill Company, which has accounts receivable of $309,600 and an allowance for doubtful accounts of $3,600, decides to write off as worthless a past-due account receivable for $1,500 from J. D. North. What effect will the write-off have upon total current assets? Upon net income for the period? Explain.

10 Describe a procedure by which management could be informed each month of the status of collections and the overall quality of the accounts receivable on hand.

11 What are the advantages to a retailer of making credit sales only to customers who use nationally recognized credit cards?

12 Alta Mine Co., a restaurant that had always made cash sales only, adopted a new policy of honoring several nationally known credit cards. Sales did not increase, but many of Alta Mine Co.'s regular customers began charging dinner bills on the credit cards. Has the new policy been beneficial to Alta Mine Co.? Explain.

13 Determine the maturity date of the following notes:
   a A three-month note dated March 10
   b A 30-day note dated August 15
   c A 90-day note dated July 2

14 X Company acquires a 9%, 60-day note receivable from a customer, Robert Waters, in settlement of an existing account receivable of $4,000. Give the journal entry to record acquisition of the note and the journal entry to record its collection at maturity.

15 Distinguish between
   a Current and long-term liabilities
   b Estimated and contingent liabilities

16 Does a contingent liability appear on a balance sheet? If so, in what part of the balance sheet?

17 Jonas Company issues a 90-day, 12% note payable to replace an account payable to Smith Supply Company in the amount of $8,000. Draft the journal entries (in general journal form) to record the issuance of the note payable and the payment of the note at the maturity date.

18 Howard Benson applied to the City Bank for a loan of $20,000 for a period of three months. The loan was granted at an annual interest rate of 12%. Write a sentence illustrating the wording of the note signed by Benson if
   a Interest is stated separately in the note.
   b Interest is included in the face amount of the note.

19 With reference to Question 18 above, give the journal entry required on the books of Howard Benson for issuance of each of the two types of notes.

20 Rager Products sold merchandise to Baron Company in exchange for a one-year note receivable. The note was made out in the face amount of $13,189, *including* a 9% interest charge. Compute the amount of sales revenue to be recognized by Rager Products. (Hint: $13,189 equals 109% of sales amount.)

21 Sylmar Industries buys a substantial amount of equipment having an estimated service life of five years by issuing a two-year note payable. The note includes no mention of an interest charge. Explain the errors which will result in the future financial statements of Sylmar Industries if the equipment and related liability are recorded at the face value, rather than the present value, of the note.

22 Maxline Stores sells merchandise with a sales price of $1,260 on an installment plan requiring 12 monthly payments of $120 each. How much revenue will this sale ultimately generate for Maxline Stores? Explain the nature of this revenue and when it should be recognized in the accounting records.

23 With reference to Question 22 above, make the journal entries required in the accounting records of Maxline Stores to record

    a Sale of the merchandise on the installment plan.

    b Collection of the first monthly installment payment. (Assume that an equal portion of the discount is amortized at the time that each installment payment is received.)

Exercises

Ex. 8-1   Meadow Corporation uses the income statement approach to estimating uncollectible accounts. At December 31 the company had accounts receivable of $150,000 and a credit balance of $1,050 in the Allowance for Doubtful Accounts. On this date, the controller estimated that bad debts expense would amount to one-half of 1% of the $900,000 of net sales made during the year. This estimate was entered in the accounts by an adjusting entry at December 31. On January 14, an account receivable of $825 from J. R. Baker was determined to be uncollectible and was written off. However, on July 5, Baker inherited some property and immediately paid the $825 past-due account. You are to prepare four entries in general journal form to record the above events.

Ex. 8-2   At year-end, Clayton Corporation had accounts receivable totaling $294,000. The company uses the balance sheet approach to estimate uncollectible accounts expense. An aging analysis of the receivables showed an estimated loss of $7,320. You are to draft the year-end adjusting entries for uncollectible accounts under each of the following independent assumptions:

    a The Allowance for Doubtful Accounts had a credit balance of $5,280.

    b The Allowance for Doubtful Accounts had a debit balance of $1,776.

Ex. 8-3   Lincoln Corporation's unadjusted trial balance at year-end included the following accounts:

	Debit	Credit
Sales (25% represent cash sales)		$1,152,000
Accounts receivable	$288,000	
Allowance for doubtful accounts		2,184

Compute the uncollectible accounts expense for the current year, assuming that uncollectible accounts expense is determined as follows:

    a Income statement approach, 1% of total sales.

    b Income statement approach, $1\frac{1}{2}$% of credit sales.

    c Balance sheet approach. The estimate based on an aging of accounts receivable is that an allowance of $12,000 will be adequate.

Ex. 8-4   Basin Company has accounts receivable from 100 customers in its accounts receivable subsidiary ledger. The controlling account in the general ledger shows a debit balance of $930,000. The subsidiary ledger shows that 99 of the customers' accounts have debit balances and that one customer has a credit balance of $45,000. How should these facts be shown in the balance sheet? Explain the reason for the treatment you recommend.

Ex. 8-5   The balance sheet of Mayfair, Inc., at the end of last year included the following:

Notes receivable from customers	$ 36,000
Accrued interest on notes receivable	720

Accounts receivable	151,200
Less: Allowance for doubtful accounts and notes	3,600

You are to record the following events of the current year in general journal entries:

a Accounts receivable of $3,456 are written off as uncollectible.

b A customers' note for $990 on which interest of $54 has been accrued in the accounts is deemed uncollectible, and both balances are written off against the Allowance for Doubtful Accounts and Notes.

c An account receivable for $468 previously written off is collected.

d Aging of accounts receivable at the end of the current year indicates a need for a $5,400 allowance to cover possible failure to collect amounts currently outstanding. (Consider the effect of entries for a, b, and c on the Allowance for Doubtful Accounts and Notes.)

Ex. 8-6 Star Company follows the income statement approach to estimating uncollectible accounts expense. For several years the company has computed the charge to uncollectible accounts expense as 1% of net sales. All sales are made on credit. The following data appear in the accounting records at December 31, Year 9, before adjustments.

	Debit	Credit
Sales		5,360,000
Sales returns & allowances	$200,000	
Sales discounts	160,000	
Allowance for doubtful accounts		7,600

On January 12, Year 10, the company wrote off a $4,800 account receivable from John Brown which was determined to be uncollectible.

Prepare journal entries in general journal form to record the estimated uncollectible accounts expense at December 31, Year 9, and the write-off of the Brown receivable on January 12, Year 10.

Ex. 8-7 Three notes receivable, each in the amount of $60,000, were discounted by Micro, Inc., at its bank on May 10. The bank charged a discount rate of 12% per year, applied to the maturity value.

Date of Note	Annual Interest Rate, %	Life of Note
Note A — Apr. 10	12	3 months
Note B — Mar. 31	9	60 days
Note C — Mar. 11	16	90 days

Instructions

From the above date, compute the proceeds of each note. Remember that all interest rates quoted are annual rates. In making interest calculations, assume a 360-day year. Answers should be rounded to the nearest cent wherever necessary.

Ex. 8-8 Hill Corporation on November 1 borrowed $300,000 from a local bank, and agreed to repay that amount plus 12% interest (per year) at the end of six months. (Remember that interest is stated at an annual rate.) Show two different presentations of the liability to the bank on Hill Corporation's December 31 balance sheet, assuming that the note payable to the bank was drawn as follows:

a For $300,000, with interest stated separately and payable at maturity

b With the total interest charge included in the face amount of the note

Ex. 8-9   Dale Motors, an automobile dealer, sold three trucks to Zorro Truck Lines on April 1, Year 1, for a total price of $68,000. Under the terms of the sale, Dale Motors received $20,000 cash and a promissory note due in full 18 months later. The face amount of the note was $53,760, which included interest on the note for the 18 months.

Prepare all entries (in general journal form) for Dale Motors relating to the sales transaction and to the note for the fiscal year ended September 30, Year 1. Include the adjusting entry needed to record interest earned to September 30.

Ex. 8-10   Based upon the information in Exercise 8-9 above, prepare all entries (in general journal form) for Zorro Truck Lines relating to the purchase of the trucks and the note for the fiscal year ended December 31, Year 1. Include the adjusting entries to record interest expense and depreciation expense to December 31. (The trucks are to be depreciated over an 8-year service life by the straight-line method. There is no estimated salvage value.)

Problems

8-1   Aging accounts receivables; write-offs

Torres Company uses the balance sheet approach to estimating uncollectible accounts expense. At year-end an aging of the accounts receivable produced the following classification:

Not yet due	$ 54,000
1–30 days past due	30,000
31–60 days past due	13,000
61–90 days past due	3,000
Over 90 days past due	5,000
Total	$105,000

On the basis of past experience, the company estimated the percentages probably uncollectible for the above five age groups to be as follows: Group 1, 1%; Group 2, 3%; Group 3, 10%; Group 4, 20%; and Group 5, 50%.

The Allowance for Doubtful Accounts before adjustment at December 31 showed a credit balance of $1,800.

Instructions

a   Compute the total probable expense from uncollectible accounts based on the above classification by age groups.

b   Prepare the adjusting entry needed to bring the Allowance for Doubtful Accounts to the proper amount.

c   Assume that on January 10 of the following year, Torres Company learned that an account receivable which had originated on September 1 in the amount of $2,000 was worthless because of the bankruptcy of the customer, Mesa Company. Prepare the journal entry required on January 10 to write off this account.

8-2   Estimating bad debts: balance sheet approach

At December 31 last year, the balance sheet prepared by Pedro Montoya included $504,000 in accounts receivable and an allowance for doubtful accounts of $26,400. During January of the current year selected transactions are summarized as follows:

(1) Sales on account $368,000
(2) Sales returns & allowances 7,360
(3) Cash collections from customers (no cash discounts) 364,800
(4) Account receivable from Acme Company written off as worthless 9,280

After a careful aging and analysis of all customers' accounts at January 31, it was decided that the allowance for doubtful accounts should be adjusted to a balance of $29,280 in order to reflect accounts receivable at net realizable value in the January 31 balance sheet.

Instructions

a Give the appropriate entry in general journal form for each of the four numbered items above and the adjusting entry at January 31 to provide for uncollectible accounts.

b Show the amounts of accounts receivable and the allowance for doubtful accounts as they would appear in a partial balance sheet at January 31.

c Assume that several months after the receivable from Acme Company had been written off as worthless, Acme Company won a large award in the settlement of patent litigation and immediately paid the $9,280 debt to Pedro Montoya. Give the journal entry or entries (in general journal form) to reflect this recovery of a receivable previously written off.

8-3 Estimating bad debts: two methods

Rivero Graphics, owned by Maria Rivero, sells paper novelty goods to retail stores. All sales are made on credit and the company has regularly estimated its uncollectible accounts expense as a percentage of net sales. The percentage used has been $\frac{1}{2}$ of 1% of net sales. However, it appears that this provision has been inadequate because the Allowance for Doubtful Accounts has a debit balance of $3,900 at December 31 prior to making the annual provision. Rivero has therefore decided to change the method of estimating uncollectible accounts expense and to rely upon an analysis of the age and character of the accounts receivable at the end of each accounting period.

At December 31, the accounts receivable totaled $260,000. This total amount included past-due accounts in the amount of $46,000. None of these past-due accounts was considered worthless; all accounts regarded as worthless had been written off as rapidly as they were determined to be uncollectible. After careful investigation of the $46,000 of past-due accounts at December 31, Rivero decided that the probable loss contained therein was 10%. In addition she decided to provide for a loss of 1% of the current accounts receivable.

Instructions

a Compute the probable uncollectible accounts expense applicable to the $260,000 of accounts receivable at December 31, based on the analysis by the owner.

b Prepare the journal entry necessary to carry out the change in company policy with respect to providing for uncollectible accounts expense.

8-4 Journal entries for notes receivable

Union Square, a wholesaler, sells merchandise on 30-day open account, but requires customers who fail to pay invoices within 30 days to substitute promissory notes for their past-due accounts. No sales discount is offered. Among recent transactions were the following:

Mar. 17 Sold merchandise to S. R. Davis on account, $72,000, terms n/30.
Apr. 16 Received a 60-day, 10% note from Davis dated today in settlement of the open account of $72,000.

May 26 Discounted the Davis note at the bank. The bank discount rate was 12% applied to the maturity value of the note for the 20 days remaining to maturity.

June 15 Received notice from the bank that the Davis note due today was in default. Paid the bank the maturity value of the note. Since Davis has extensive business interests, the management of Union Square is confident that no loss will be incurred on the defaulted note.

June 25 Made a $48,000 loan to John Raymond on a 30-day, 15% note.

Instructions

a Prepare in general journal form the entries necessary to record the above transactions. (In making interest calculations, assume a 360-day year.)

b Prepare the adjusting journal entry needed at June 30, the end of the company's fiscal year, to record interest accrued on the two notes receivable. [Accrue interest at 10% per annum from date of default (June 15) on the maturity value of the Davis note.]

8-5 Notes payable; adjusting entries for interest

Arrowhead Corporation engaged in the following transactions involving notes payable during the fiscal year ended October 31. It is the company's policy to use a 360-day year for all interest calculations.

June   6 Borrowed $6,000 from a long-time employee, C. W. Jones. Issued a 45-day, 12% note payable to Jones as evidence of the indebtedness.

July 13 Purchased office equipment from New Company. This invoice amount was $9,000 and the New Company agreed to accept as full payment a 16%, three-month note for the invoiced amount.

July 21 Paid the Jones note plus accrued interest.

Sept. 1 Borrowed $126,000 from Security Bank at an interest rate of 16% per annum; signed a 90-day note with interest included in the face amount of the note.

Oct.   1 Purchased merchandise in the amount of $5,400 from Post Co. Gave in settlement a 90-day note bearing interest at 18%.

Oct. 13 The $9,000 note payable to New Company matured today. Paid the interest accrued and issued a new 30-day, 16% note to replace the maturing note.

Instructions

a Prepare journal entries (in general journal form) to record the above transactions.

b Prepare the adjusting entries needed at October 31, prior to closing the accounts. Use one adjusting entry to accrue interest on the two notes in which interest is stated separately (the Post Co. note and the New Company note). Use a separate adjusting entry to record interest expense accrued on the note with interest included in the face amount (the Security Bank note).

8-6 Analysis of interest revenue

On March 31, Year 8, Monitor Corporation sold merchandise to West Supply Co. in exchange for a note receivable due in **one year.** The note was drawn in the face amount of $58,240, which included the principal amount and an interest charge. In its December 31, Year 8, balance sheet, Monitor Corporation correctly presented the note receivable as follows:

Note receivable, due Mar. 31, Year 9 .... $58,240
Less: Discount on note receivable 1,560 $56,680

Instructions

    a Determine the monthly interest revenue earned by Monitor Corporation from this note receivable. (Hint: The balance in the discount account represents unearned interest as of December 31, Year 8. This is a one-year note with three months remaining before it matures.)

    b Compute the amount of interest revenue recognized by Monitor Corporation from the note during Year 8.

    c Compute the amount of sales revenue recognized by Monitor Corporation on March 31, Year 8, when this note was received.

    d Compute the effective annual rate of interest (stated as a percentage) represented by the interest charge originally included in the face amount of the note.

    e Prepare all journal entries relating to this note in the accounting records of Monitor Corporation for Years 8 and 9. Assume that adjusting entries are made only at December 31, and that the note was collected on the maturity date.

8-7 Notes payable; and interest computations

During the fiscal year ending June 30 and shortly thereafter, Houston Center had the following transactions relating to notes payable.

Feb. 6 Borrowed $10,000 from L. W. Smith and issued a 45-day, 16% note payable.

Mar. 12 Purchased delivery truck from E-Z Company. Issued a 12%, three-month note payable for $15,000, the full cost of the truck.

Mar. 23 Paid the note due today to L. W. Smith plus accrued interest.

May 1 Borrowed the amount of $200,000 for 90 days from First Bank at an interest rate of 14% per year; signed a note payable with the interest included in the face amount of the note.

May 31 Purchased merchandise for $7,500 from Patten Co. Issued a 90-day note bearing interest at 16% annually. (Use two entries: one to record the purchase with a credit to Accounts Payable, and the other to transfer the liability to Notes Payable.)

June 12 The $15,000 note payable to E-Z Company matured today. Paid in cash the interest accrued and issued a new 30-day note bearing interest at 14% per annum to replace the maturing note. (Use one compound journal entry for this transaction.)

June 30 End of fiscal year.

July 12 Paid principal and interest of the 30-day, 14% note to E-Z Company dated June 12 which matured today.

July 30 Paid in full the 90-day note to First Bank dated May 1 and maturing today.

Instructions

    a Prepare journal entries (in general journal form) to record the six transactions dated prior to June 30. All interest rates quoted are annual rates. Use a 360-day year for interest computations.

    b Prepare two adjusting entries at June 30 relating to interest expense. The first entry should accrue interest on the two notes with interest stated separately (the note to Patten Company and the note to E-Z Company). The explanation should include computations showing the amount of interest accrued on each note. The second adjusting entry should record interest on the First Bank note in which interest was included in the face amount.

    c Prepare journal entries for the two transactions occurring in July.

8-8 Receivables, discounting, balance sheet presentation

The following information concerning the receivables of Del Mar Corporation appeared in the accounts on December 1, Year 7. The company uses a 360-day year for all interest calculations.

Accounts receivable:

C. L. Laurence	$ 2,425
E. D. Nemson	3,870
C. A. Shively	6,200
Total	$12,495

Notes receivable:

A. P. Marra, 8%, 45-day note, dated Nov. 4, Year 7	$ 6,000
C. M. Hines, 9%, 90-day note, dated Nov. 30, Year 7	4,000
Total	$10,000
Installment contracts receivable:	
M. Moyers (monthly payment $150)	$ 2,850
Unearned interest on installment contracts:	
Applicable to M. Moyers contract	$ 386

During the month of December, the following additional transactions took place:

Dec. 7 E. D. Nemson paid $870 on account and gave a 30-day, 8% note to cover the balance.

Dec. 12 Received a 60-day, 8% note from C. L. Laurence in full settlement of his account.

Dec. 19 A. P. Marra wrote that he would be unable to pay the note due today and included a check to cover the interest due and a new 30-day, 7% note renewing the old note. No accrued interest has been recorded in prior months.

Dec. 28 Discounted the C. L. Laurence note at the bank. The proceeds on the note amounted to $2,432.

Dec. 31 Received the monthly payment on the M. Moyers contract. The payment of $150 includes $20 of interest revenue earned during December. The interest charges included in the face amount of the installment contract had originally been credited to the contra-asset account, Unearned Interest on Installment Contracts.

Instructions

a Prepare five journal entries (in general journal form) for the five December transactions listed above.

b Prepare an adjusting entry at December 31 to accrue interest receivable on the three notes receivable on hand (the Nemson, Marra, and Hines notes). Include in the explanation portion of the adjusting entry the computations to determine the accrued interest on each of the three notes. Add these three accrued amounts to find the total amount for the adjusting entry.

c Prepare a partial balance sheet for Del Mar Corporation at December 31 showing under the heading of current assets the notes receivable, accounts receivable, installment contracts receivable, unearned interest on installment contracts, and accrued interest receivable. Also add a footnote to disclose the amount of the contingent liability for the discounted note receivable.

8-9 Receivables and payables; a comprehensive problem
During the month of August, Delux Office Supply Co. engaged in the following transactions involving receivables and payables:

Aug. 1 Sold merchandise to C. Reed for $4,500. Reed issued a 90-day, 16% note for the amount of the purchase.

Aug. 4 Received a 60-day, 18% note from Reno Corporation for $6,200 in settlement of open account.

Aug. 11 Issued a 60-day, 15% note payable to Magnum Company for $5,040 in settlement of open account.

Aug. 16 Borrowed $12,000 from First Charter Bank and signed a six-month, 18% note payable which included the interest in the face amount.

Aug. 17 Discounted the Reno Corporation note. The proceeds from the bank amounted to $6,221.

Aug. 21 Sold merchandise to Howard Wright. As payment, Wright issued a 60-day note for a face amount of $5,814, which included an interest charge of $114.

Aug. 24 Received payment from W. Harned of a $4,000, 60-day, 12% note dated June 25. Accrued interest receivable of $48 had been recorded in prior months.

Aug. 26 A long overdue account receivable from J. Bartlett in the amount of $720 was written off as uncollectible against the allowance for doubtful accounts.

Aug. 28 Full payment of a $290 account receivable was unexpectedly received from J. Kievits. This account had been written off as uncollectible several months ago.

Aug. 30 Sales to HandyCharge credit card customers in August amounted to $9,500. (Summarize all credit card sales in one entry. HandyCharge Co. is not a bank.)

Aug. 31 Collected cash from HandyCharge for August credit card sales, less 3% discount charged by HandyCharge.

Aug. 31 An aging of accounts receivable on August 31 indicates the allowance for doubtful accounts should be increased to $1,950. On July 31, the balance in the allowance account had been $1,830. No entries other than those described above have been made in the allowance account during August.

Instructions

a Prepare in general journal form the entries necessary to record the preceding transactions.

b Prepare any adjusting entries needed at August 31. (Hint: Four notes require adjusting entries.)

c Draft the appropriate footnote to the financial statements to disclose the contingent liability relating to the discounted note receivable.

Cases for analysis

Case 8-1   Allan Carter was a long-time employee in the accounting department of Marston Company. Carter's responsibilities included the following:

(1) Maintain the accounts receivable subsidiary ledger.

(2) Prepare vouchers for cash disbursements. The voucher and supporting documents were forwarded to John Marston, owner of the company.

(3) Compute depreciation on all plant assets.

(4) Authorize all sales returns and allowances given to credit customers and prepare the related credit memoranda. The credit memoranda were forwarded to Howard Smith, who maintains the company's journals and general ledger.

John Marston personally performs the following procedures in an effort to achieve strong internal control:

(1) Prepare monthly bank reconciliations.

(2) Prepare monthly trial balances from the general ledger and reconcile the accounts receivable controlling account with the subsidiary ledger.

(3) Prepare from the subsidiary ledger all monthly bills sent to customers and investigate any complaints from customers about inaccuracies in these bills.

(4) Review all vouchers and supporting documents before signing checks for cash disbursements.

Carter became terminally ill and retired. Shortly thereafter, he died. However, he left a letter confessing that over a period of years he had embezzled over $300,000 from Marston Company. As part of his scheme, he had managed to obtain both a bank account and a post office box in the name of Marston Company. He had then contacted customers whose accounts were overdue and offered them a 20% discount if they would make payment within five days. He instructed them to send their payments to the post office box. When the payments arrived, he deposited them in his "Marston Company" bank account. Carter stated in his letter that he had acted alone, and that no other company employees knew of his dishonest actions.

Marston cannot believe that Carter committed this theft without the knowledge and assistance of Howard Smith, who maintained the journals and the general ledger. Marston reasoned that Carter must have credited the customers' accounts in the accounts receivable subsidiary ledger, because no customers had complained about not receiving credit for their payments. Smith must also have recorded these credits in the general ledger, or Marston would have discovered the problem by reconciling the subsidiary ledger with the controlling account. Finally, Smith must have debited some other account in the general ledger to keep the ledger in balance. Thus, Marston is about to bring criminal charges against Smith.

Instructions

a Explain how Carter might have committed this theft without Smith's knowledge and without being detected by Marston's control procedures. (Assume that Carter had no personal access to the journals or general ledger.)

b Which of the duties assigned to Carter should not have been assigned to an employee responsible for maintaining accounts receivable? Would internal control be strengthened if this duty were assigned to the company's cashier? Explain.

Case 8-2   Record House and Concert Sound are two companies engaged in selling stereo equipment to the public. Both companies sell equipment at a price 50% greater than cost. Customers may pay cash, purchase on 30-day accounts, or make installment payments over a 36-month period. The installment receivables include a three-year interest charge (which amounts to 30% of the sales price) in the face amount of the contract. Condensed income statements prepared by the companies for their first year of operations are shown below:

	Record House	Concert Sound
Sales	$387,000	$288,000
Cost of goods sold	210,000	192,000
Gross profit on sales	$177,000	$ 96,000
Operating expenses	63,000	60,000
Operating income	$114,000	$ 36,000
Interest revenue	–0–	$ 10,800
Net income	$114,000	$ 46,800

When Record House makes a sale of stereo equipment on the installment plan it immediately credits the Sales account with the face amount of the installment receivable. In other words, the interest charges are included in sales revenue at the time of the sale. The interest charges included in Record House's installment receivables originating in the first year amount to $72,000, of which $59,100 is unearned at the end of the first year. Record House uses the direct charge-off method to recognize uncollectible accounts expense. During the year, accounts receivable of $2,100 were written off as uncollectible, but no entry was made for $37,200 of accounts estimated to be uncollectible at year-end.

Concert Sound records sales revenue equal to the present value of its installment receivables and recognizes the interest *earned during the year* as interest revenue. Concert Sound provides for uncollectible accounts by the allowance method. The company recognized uncollectible accounts expense of $11,100 during the year and this amount appeared to be adequate.

Instructions

a   Prepare a condensed income statement for Record House for the year, using the same methods of accounting for installment sales and uncollectible accounts as were used by Concert Sound. The income statement you prepare should contain the same seven items shown in the illustrated income statements. Provide footnotes showing the computations you made in revising the amount of sales and any other figures you decide to change.

b   Compare the income statement you have prepared in part a to the one originally prepared by Record House. Which income statement do you believe better reflects the results of the company's operations during the year? Explain.

c   What do you believe to be the key factor responsible for making one of these companies more profitable than the other? What corrective action would you recommend be taken by the less profitable company to improve future performance?

Appendix A
Payroll Accounting

This appendix emphasizes internal control over payrolls with special attention to the need for subdivision of duties. Simple illustrations show the computation and deduction of social security taxes and other items from employees' paychecks. Payroll taxes on the employer are also illustrated, and the distinction between employees and independent contractors is made clear.

After studying
this appendix you
should be able to:

✓ Describe the basic separation of duties in a payroll system and explain how this separation of responsibilities contributes to strong internal control.
✓ Identify the factors involved in computing the amount of (1) social security taxes and (2) federal income taxes withheld from employees' paychecks.
✓ Identify those taxes which are withheld from employees' paychecks and those payroll taxes which are levied upon the employer.
✓ Distinguish between an employee and an independent contractor and explain the significance of this distinction with respect to withholding and payroll taxes.
✓ Account for a payroll, including computation of amounts to be withheld, net pay to employees, and payroll taxes on the employer.

Labor costs and related payroll taxes constitute a large and constantly increasing portion of the total costs of operating most business organizations. In the commercial airlines, for example, labor costs traditionally have represented 40 to 50% of total operating costs.

The task of accounting for payroll costs would be an important one simply because of the large amounts involved; however, it is further complicated by the many federal and state laws which require employers to maintain certain specific information in their payroll records not only for the business as a whole but also for each individual employee. Frequent reports of total wages and amounts withheld must be filed with government agencies. These reports are prepared by every employer and must be accompanied by payment to the government of the amounts withheld from employees and of the payroll taxes levied on the employer.

A basic rule in most business organizations is that every employee must be paid on time, and the payment must be accompanied by a detailed explanation of the computations used in determining the net amount received by the employee. The payroll system must therefore be capable of processing the input data (such as employee names, social security numbers, hours worked, pay rates, overtime, and taxes) and producing a prompt and accurate output of paychecks, payroll records, withholding statements, and reports to government agencies. In addition, the payroll system must have built-in safeguards against overpayments to employees, the issuance of duplicate paychecks, payments to fictitious employees, and the continuance on the payroll of persons who have been terminated as employees.

Internal control over payrolls

Payroll fraud has a long history. Before the era of social security records and computers, payroll records were often handwritten and incomplete. Employees were commonly paid in cash and documentary evidence was scanty. Some specific characteristics of present-day payroll accounting render more difficult the fraudulent manipulation of payroll data. These helpful factors include the required frequent filing of payroll data with the government, and the universal use of employer identification numbers and employees' social security numbers. For example, "padding" a payroll with fictitious names is more difficult when social security numbers must be on file for every employee, individual earnings records must be created, and quarterly reports must be submitted to the Internal Revenue Service, showing for every employee the gross earnings, social security taxes, and income tax withheld.

However, neither automation of the accounting process nor extensive reporting of payroll data to government has caused payroll fraud to disappear. Satisfactory internal control over payrolls still requires separation and subdivision of duties. In an EDP system, this means clear separation of the functions of systems analysts, programmers, computer operators, and control group personnel.

In most organizations the payroll activities include the functions of (1) employing workers, (2) timekeeping, (3) payroll preparation and record keeping, and (4) the distribution of pay to employees. Internal control will be strengthened if each of these functions is handled by a separate department.

Employment (personnel) department. The work of the employment or personnel department begins with interviewing and hiring job applicants. When a new employee is hired, the personnel department prepares records showing the date of employment, the authorized rate of pay, and payroll deductions. The personnel department sends a written notice to the payroll department to place the new employee on the payroll. Changes in pay rates and termination of employees will be recorded in personnel department records. When a person's employment is terminated, the personnel department should conduct an exit interview and notify the payroll department to remove the employee's name from the payroll.

Timekeeping. For employees paid by the hour, the time of arrival and departure should be punched on time cards. A new time card should be placed in the rack by the time clock at the beginning of each week or other pay period. Control procedures should exist to ensure that each employee punches his or her own time card and no other. The timekeeping function should be lodged in a separate department which will control the time cards and transmit these source documents to the payroll department.

The payroll department. The input of information to the payroll department consists of hours reported by the timekeeping department, and authorized names, pay rates, and payroll deductions received from the personnel department. The output of the payroll department includes (1) payroll checks, (2) individual employee records of earnings and deductions, and (3) regular reports to the government showing the earnings of employees and taxes withheld.

Distribution of paychecks. The paychecks prepared in the payroll department are transmitted to the *paymaster,* who distributes them to the employees. The paymaster should not have responsibility for hiring or firing employees, timekeeping, or preparation of the payroll.

Paychecks for absent employees should never be turned over to other employees or to supervisors for delivery. Instead, the absent employee should later pick up the paycheck from the paymaster after presenting proper identification and signing a receipt. The distribution of paychecks by the paymaster provides assurance that paychecks will not continue to be issued to fictitious employees or employees who have been terminated.

The operation of a typical payroll system is illustrated on the flow chart on the next page. Notes have been made indicating the major internal control points within the system.

Weaknesses in internal control. There is seldom justification for paying employees in cash. The use of paychecks provides better evidence that payments were made only to existing employees at authorized rates. Even in companies with numerous small branches, it is urgent that branch managers not be authorized to combine such duties as hiring and firing employees with the preparation of payrolls, or the distribution of paychecks. Much better internal control can be achieved by lodging in the headquarters office the work outlined above relating to employment, pay rates, pay changes, deductions, terminations, payroll preparation, and distribution of paychecks.

● **CASE IN POINT** ● Metals, Inc., a manufacturer with several hundred employees, permitted weaknesses in internal control that led to a large-scale payroll fraud. Supervisors in the factory had access to time cards and they also distributed W-2 forms to employees at the end of each year. This combination of duties enabled the supervisors to maintain more than 20 fictitious names on the payroll. Paychecks for these nonexistent employees were taken by the supervisors and endorsed for their own use.

This fraud was disclosed by chance when a temporary summer employee applied for a college loan and was refused on the grounds of excessive earnings. The employee's parents wrote to the president of Metals, Inc., complaining that the company had reported to the IRS much larger earnings than he had really received. The president of the company ordered an investigation which revealed that a factory supervisor had punched the temporary employee's time card daily, thus keeping him on the payroll after his termination. The supervisor had kept and endorsed the paychecks issued in the student's name.

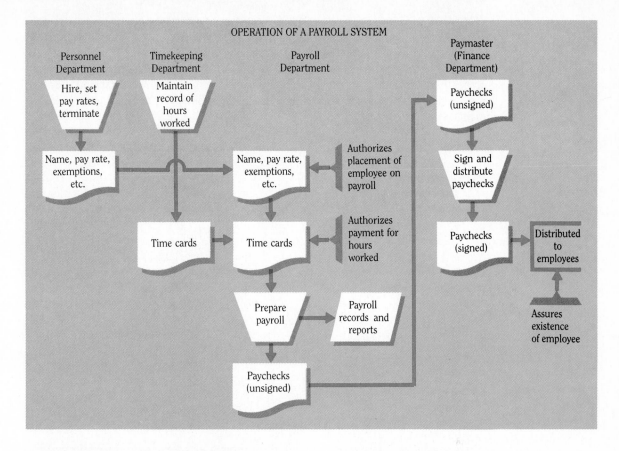

OPERATION OF A PAYROLL SYSTEM

Deductions from earnings of employees

The take-home pay of most employees is much less than the gross earnings. Major factors explaining this difference between the amount earned and the amount received are social security taxes, federal income taxes withheld, and other deductions discussed in the following pages.

Social security taxes (FICA)

Under the terms of the Social Security Act, qualified workers who retire after reaching a specified age receive monthly retirement payments and Medicare benefits. Benefits are also provided for the family of a worker who dies before or after reaching this retirement age. Funds for the operation of this program are obtained through taxes levied under the Federal Insurance Contributions Act, often referred to as FICA taxes, or simply as *social security taxes.*

Employers are required by the Federal Insurance Contributions Act to withhold a portion of each employee's earnings as a contribution to the social security program. A tax at the same rate is levied against the employer. For example, assume that an employee earns $20,000 subject to FICA taxes of 7%. The employer will withhold $1,400

($20,000 × .07) from the employee's earnings. The employer will then pay to the government the amount of $2,800, consisting of the $1,400 withheld from the employee plus an additional $1,400 of FICA tax on the employer.

Two factors are involved in computing the FICA tax: the **base** or amount of earnings subject to the tax, and the **rate** which is applied to the base. Both the **base** and the **rate** have been increased many times in recent years and probably will continue to be changed in future years.

● **CASE IN POINT** ● The enormous increase in social security taxes is revealed in the following table.

Year	Base (Earnings Subject to FICA Tax)	Tax Rate	Amount of Tax
1937	$ 3,000	1.0%	$ 30
1951	3,600	1.5%	54
1966	6,600	4.2%	277
1972	9,000	5.2%	468
1977	16,500	5.85%	965
1983	35,700	6.70%	2,392
1985	39,600	7.05%	2,792
1990	?	?	?

We can see from the table that individuals with earnings greater than the base were required to pay approximately 93 times as much in 1985 as they were in 1937 when the social security plan was started.

These changes in rates and in the base do not affect the accounting principles or procedures involved. For illustrative purposes in this book, we shall assume the rate of tax to be **7%** on both the employee and the employer, applicable to a **base of $40,000** (the first $40,000 of wages received by each employee in each calendar year). This assumption of round amounts for both the tax and the base is a convenient one for the purpose of illustrations and for the solution of problems by the student, regardless of frequent changes in the rate and base.

An example may clarify the expression "subject to FICA tax." Assume that during a year when a $40,000 base prevails, you earn $43,000 in salary. You would have to pay the 7% FICA tax on $40,000 of your salary. You would *not* pay FICA tax on the $3,000 by which your salary exceeded the $40,000 base.

Federal income taxes

Our pay-as-you-go system of federal income tax requires employers to withhold a portion of the earnings of their employees. The amount withheld depends upon the amount of the earnings and upon the number of income tax exemptions claimed by the employee. For each income tax exemption, the employee is entitled to a witholding allowance of $1,000. (Actually the amount was $1,040 at the time this was written, but it is changed each year in accordance with the change in the Consumer Price Index. For convenience, a personal exemption amount of $1,000 is used in all illustrations and problems in this book.) Each withholding allowance thus causes $1,000 of yearly earnings to be exempt from income tax. On a federal income tax return, one exemption is allowed for oneself, one for a spouse, and one for each dependent. Thus a married couple with three dependent children would be entitled to five exemptions and would qualify for five withholding allowances.

Present regulations provide a graduated system of withholding, designed to make the amount of income tax withheld approximate the individual's tax liability at the end of the year. Because persons in higher income brackets are subject to higher rates of taxation, the withholding rates are correspondingly higher for them. There is no ceiling with respect to the amount of salary subject to income tax.

Most states and cities which levy income taxes also require the employer to withhold the tax from employees' earnings. Because such situations involve a variety of rates, they will not be discussed here.

Other deductions from employees' earnings

In addition to the compulsory deductions for taxes, many other deductions are voluntarily authorized by employees. Union dues and insurance premiums already have been mentioned as examples of payroll deductions. Others include charitable contributions, retirement programs, savings bond purchases, and pension plans.

Employer's responsibility for amounts withheld

In withholding amounts from an employee's earnings for either voluntary or involuntary deductions, the employer acts merely as a collection agent. The amounts withheld are paid to the designated organization, such as a government agency or labor union. The employer is also responsible for maintaining accounting records which will enable it to file required reports and make timely payments of the amounts withheld. From the employer's viewpoint, the amounts withheld from employees' earnings represent current liabilities.

Payroll records and procedures

Although payroll records and procedures vary greatly according to the number of employees and the extent of automation in processing payroll data, there are a few fundamental steps common to payroll work in most organizations. One of these steps taken at the end of each pay period is the preparation of a *payroll register* showing for each employee the gross earnings, amounts withheld, and net pay. When the computation of the payroll register has been completed, the next step is to reflect the expense and the related liabilities in the ledger accounts. A general journal entry as shown on the next page may be used to bring into the accounts the information summarized in the payroll register. (This entry does not include payroll taxes on the employer.)

Sales Salaries Expense	4,800	
Office Salaries Expense	3,200	
FICA Tax Payable (7% of $8,000)		560
Liability for Income Tax Withheld		1,370
Liability for Group Insurance Withheld		150
Accrued Payroll		5,920

To record the payroll for the period Jan. 1–Jan. 15.

The two debits to expense accounts indicate that the business has incurred salaries expense of $8,000; however, only $5,920 of this amount will be paid to the employees on payday. The payment will be recorded by a debit to Accrued Payroll and a credit to Cash. The remaining $2,080 (consisting of deductions for taxes and insurance premiums withheld) is lodged in liability accounts. Payment of these liabilities must be made at frequent intervals.

Wage and tax statement. By January 31 each year, employers are required to furnish every employee with a Wage and Tax Statement (Form W-2). This form shows gross earnings for the preceding calendar year and the amounts withheld for FICA tax and income taxes. The employer sends one copy of this form to the federal government, one copy to the state government, and gives three copies to the employee. When the employee files a federal income tax return, he or she must attach a copy of the withholding statement. A copy also must be attached to the state income tax return.

Payroll taxes on the employer

The discussion of payroll taxes up to this point has dealt with taxes levied on employees and withheld from their pay. From the viewpoint of the employing company, such withheld taxes are significant because they must be accounted for and remitted in a timely manner to the appropriate government agencies. However, *payroll taxes are also levied on the employer.* These taxes on the employer are expenses of the business and *are recorded by debits to expense accounts,* just as in the case of property taxes or license fees for doing business.

Social Security (FICA) tax. The employer is taxed to help finance the social security program. The tax is figured at the same rate and on the same amount of earnings used to compute FICA tax on employees. (In all problems and illustrations in this book, the tax is assumed to be 7% on the first $40,000 of gross earnings by each employee in each calendar year.)

Federal unemployment insurance tax. Unemployment insurance is another part of the national social security program designed to offer temporary relief to unemployed persons. The FUTA tax (Federal Unemployment Tax Act) is levied on *employers only* and is not deducted from the wages of employees. The rates of tax and the wage base subject to the tax are changed from time to time. For purposes of illustration in this book, we shall assume that employers are subject to federal unemployment tax at the rate of 6.2% on the first $7,000 of each employee's earnings in each calendar year. However, the employer may take a credit against this tax (not in excess of 5.4% of the first $7,000 of each employee's wages) for amounts that are paid into state unemployment funds. As a result, an employer may be subject to a *federal* tax of only .8% on wages up to $7,000 per employee.

State unemployment compensation tax. All the states participate in the federal-state unemployment insurance program. The usual rate of tax is 5.4% of the first $7,000 of earnings by each employee during the calendar year. Under this provision, the employer actually makes payment of the larger part of the FUTA tax directly to state governments which carry out the federal-state unemployment insurance program. This arrangement means that the FUTA tax is divided into two parts: the larger part, or 5.4%, of the first $7,000 of wages paid going to the state and the remainder (.8%) to the federal government.

Accounting entry for employer's payroll taxes. The entry to record the employer's payroll taxes is usually made at the same time the payroll is recorded. To illustrate, let us use again the $8,000 payroll first used on page 346 in the discussion of amounts withheld from employees; this time, however, we are illustrating taxes levied on the *employer.* (None of the employees has earned over $7,000 since this is the first pay period of the current year.)

Journal entry to	Payroll Taxes Expense 1,056	
record payroll taxes	FICA Tax Payable (7% of $8,000)	560
on employer	State Unemployment Tax Payable (5.4% of $8,000)	432
	Federal Unemployment Tax Payable (0.8% of $8,000)	64

To record payroll taxes on employer for period ended Jan. 15.

Thus the total payroll expense for the employer is $9,056, which consists of wages of $8,000 and payroll taxes of $1,056.

Distinction between employees and independent contractors

Every business obtains personal services from *employees* and also from *independent contractors.* The employer-employee relationship exists when the company paying for the services has a right to direct and supervise the person rendering the services. Independent contractors, on the other hand, are retained to perform a specific task and exercise their own judgment as to the best methods for performing the work. Examples of independent contractors include CPAs engaged to perform an audit, attorneys retained to represent a company in a law suit, and a plumber called in to repair a broken pipe. The *fees* paid to independent contractors, are not included in payroll records and are not subject to withholding or payroll taxes.

Problems

A-1   The "padded" payroll; internal control
A foreman in the factory of Barton Products, a large manufacturing company, discharged an employee but did not notify the personnel department of this action. The foreman then began

forging the employee's signature on time cards. When giving out paychecks, the foreman diverted to his own use the paychecks drawn payable to the discharged worker. What internal control measure would be most effective in preventing this fraudulent activity?

A-2   Internal control over payrolls
Char Burger, a chain of 10 drive-in hamburger stands, is a sole proprietorship owned by Betty Lee. Although Lee has other business interests, she devotes a portion of her time to management of the drive-in chain. A manager is employed at each of the 10 locations and the number of employees at each location varies from six to twelve.

The manager of each unit prepares payroll sheets each week showing hours worked as reported by the employees on time cards which are approved by the manager. Each manager's salary is also listed on the weekly payroll. Upon completion of the payroll, the manager pays all employees and him- or herself in cash. Each employee acknowledges receipt of payment by signing the payroll sheet.

Employees at each branch are employed and terminated by the local managers, who also set wage rates. The salaries of the managers are authorized by Betty Lee.

Each week the payroll sheets are mailed by the managers to Lee, whose secretary prepares individual earnings records for each employee and compiles federal and state tax returns from the weekly payroll sheets.

Instructions

a Write a paragraph evaluating the adequacy of internal controls over payrolls. State the specific practices, if any, which you think should be changed.

b List four specific ways in which payroll fraud could be carried on by the manager of any of the 10 drive-ins.

A-3   Entries for payroll and payroll taxes
Martin earns a salary of $31,200 per year from Arcade Games. Federal income tax withheld during the year amounted to $4,884. Assume that FICA taxes are 7% of wages up to $40,000. Federal unemployment taxes are 6.2% of wages up to $7,000, but a credit against this FUTA tax is permitted for payment to the state of 5.4% of wages up to $7,000. Martin has authorized the withholding of $70 per month throughout the year for group medical insurance.

Instructions

a Prepare two entries (in general journal form) to summarize for the entire year (1) the amounts paid to and withheld from Martin, and (2) the payroll taxes upon Arcade Games relating to employee Martin. (In drafting these summary entries, ignore any payments of tax during the year and let the liability accounts show the total for the year. Credit Cash for the amount paid to Martin.)

b Compute the total cost to Arcade Games during the year, including payroll taxes, of having Martin on the payroll at a salary of $31,200.

A-4   Recording payroll and payroll taxes
During January, Black Sands, Inc., incurred salaries expense of $11,200, classified as follows: $8,000 of salaries expense for the sales force and $3,200 salaries expense for office personnel.

FICA taxes were withheld from employees' earnings at an assumed rate of 7%. Other amounts withheld were $1,500 for federal income taxes and $180 for group insurance premiums.

Instructions

   a Prepare a general journal entry to record the payroll and the deductions from employees' earnings. Do not include payroll taxes on the employer in this journal entry.

   b Prepare a general journal entry to record the payroll taxes on the ***employer*** as a result of the above payroll. Assume an FICA tax of 7%, a state unemployment tax of 5.4%, and a federal unemployment tax of .8% on the entire payroll.

   c What is the total payroll expense of Black Sands, Inc., for January? Show computations.

A-5   Employees' earnings records; payroll taxes

The employees' earnings records of Marine Associates are as follows so far in the current year:

Employee	Cumulative Earnings	Employee	Cumulative Earnings
Axler, C. F.	$ 8,593	Hart, P. W.	$ 5,261
Cox, R. M.	14,121	Kelly, P. T.	41,890
Ford, G. A.	11,530	Loe, S. B.	2,358
Gamble, E. H.	6,701	Pratt, L. M.	26,039

The FICA taxes are assumed to be 7% on the first $40,000 of gross earnings. The rate of federal unemployment tax is assumed to be 6.2% on the first $7,000 of gross earnings, but with credit to the employer for a maximum of 5.4% of gross earnings for state unemployment taxes.

Instructions

   a Prepare a three-column schedule showing for each employee the following accounts: cumulative earnings (as given), earnings subject to unemployment compensation tax, and earnings subject to FICA taxes. As an example, the first line of the schedule would show for Axler, C. F. the following three amounts: $8,593, $7,000, and $8,593.

   b Some payroll taxes are levied on the employee and some on the employer. Use the information shown in part a above to compute the total payroll taxes ***deducted*** from the earnings of the employees as a group. (Income taxes are not involved in this problem.)

   c Compute the total payroll taxes levied on the employer, Marine Associates, and the percentage of the total payroll ($116,493) represented by this payroll tax. Round amounts to the nearest tenth of a percent.

Chapter 9
Inventories

Our first goal in Chapter 9 is to show that determining the valuation of inventory also establishes the cost of goods sold. Thus, the validity of both the balance sheet and the income statement rest on accuracy in the valuation of inventory. A second goal is to stress that inventory is valued at cost, but that several alternative methods are available to measure cost. Four methods (specific identification, average-cost, fifo, and lifo) are illustrated and evaluated. Both the gross profit method and the retail method are introduced as examples of estimating inventory. The chapter concludes by indicating the significance of internal control over inventories and the advantages offered by use of the perpetual inventory system whenever feasible.

After studying this chapter you should be able to:

✓ Explain what goods should be included in inventory.
✓ Describe the effects of an inventory error on the income statements of the current and succeeding years.
✓ Determine the cost of inventory by using (*a*) specific identification, (*b*) average cost, (*c*) fifo, and (*d*) lifo. Discuss the relative merits and shortcomings of these methods.
✓ Define inventory profits and explain why some accountants consider these profits fictitious.
✓ Explain the lower-of-cost-or-market rule.
✓ Estimate ending inventory by the gross profit method and by the retail method.
✓ Explain how a perpetual inventory system operates.

In the previous chapters we have illustrated how the amount of inventory on hand at year-end is recorded in the accounts. Remember that the inventory figure appears in both the balance sheet and the income statement. In the balance sheet, inventory is often the largest current asset. In the income statement, the ending inventory is subtracted from the cost of goods *available* for sale to determine the *cost of goods sold* during the period.

In our previous discussions, the dollar amount of the ending inventory was given with only a brief explanation as to how this amount was determined. The basis for the valuation of inventory, as for most other types of assets, is cost. We are now ready to explore the concept of *cost* as applied to inventories of merchandise.

Inventory defined

One of the largest assets in a retail store or in a wholesale business is the inventory of merchandise, and the sale of this merchandise at prices in excess of cost is the major source of revenue. For a merchandising company, *the inventory consists of all goods owned and held for sale in the regular course of business.* Merchandise held for sale will normally be converted into cash within less than a year's time and is therefore regarded as a current asset. In the balance sheet, inventory is listed immediately after accounts receivable, because it is just one step further removed from conversion into cash than are the accounts receivable.

In manufacturing businesses there are three major types of inventories: *raw materials, goods in process of manufacture,* and *finished goods.* All three classes of inventories are included in the current asset section of the balance sheet.

To expand our definition of inventory to fit manufacturing companies as well as merchandising companies, we can say that inventory means "the aggregate of those items of tangible personal property which (1) are held for sale in the ordinary course of business, (2) are in process of production for such sale, or (3) are to be currently consumed in the production of goods or services to be available for sale."[1]

Periodic inventory system versus perpetual inventory system

The distinction between a periodic inventory system and a perpetual inventory system was explained earlier in Chapter 5. To summarize briefly, a periodic system of inventory accounting requires that acquisitions of merchandise be recorded by debits to a Purchases account. At the date of a sales transaction, no entry is made to record the cost of the goods sold. Under the periodic inventory system, the Inventory account is brought up to date only at the end of the accounting period when all the goods on hand are counted and priced.

The periodic inventory system is likely to be used by a business that sells a variety of merchandise with low unit prices, such as a drugstore or hardware store. To maintain perpetual inventory records in such a business would ordinarily be too time-consuming and expensive.

Companies that sell products of high unit value such as automobiles and television sets usually maintain a perpetual inventory system that shows at all times the amount of inventory on hand. As merchandise is acquired, it is added to an inventory account; as goods are sold, their cost is transferred out of inventory and into a cost of goods sold account. This continuous updating of the inventory account explains the name *perpetual* inventory system.

In the early part of this chapter we will use the periodic inventory system as a point of reference; in the latter part we will emphasize perpetual inventories.

[1] AICPA, *Accounting Research and Terminology Bulletins,* Final Edition (New York: 1961), p. 28.

Inventory valuation and the measurement of income

In measuring the gross profit on sales earned during an accounting period, we subtract the *cost of goods sold* from the total *sales* of the period. The figure for sales is easily accumulated from the daily record of sales transactions, but in many businesses no day-to-day record is maintained showing the cost of goods sold.[2] The figure representing the cost of goods sold during an entire accounting period is computed at the end of the period by separating the *cost of goods available for sale* into two elements:

1 The cost of the goods sold
2 The cost of the goods not sold, which therefore comprise the ending inventory

This idea, with which you are already quite familiar, may be concisely stated in the form of an equation as follows:

Finding cost of goods sold

$$\frac{\text{Cost of Goods}}{\text{Available for Sale}} - \frac{\text{Ending}}{\text{Inventory}} = \frac{\text{Cost of}}{\text{Goods Sold}}$$

Determining the amount of the ending inventory is the key step in establishing the cost of goods sold. In separating the *cost of goods available for sale* into its components of *goods sold* and *goods not sold,* we are just as much interested in establishing the proper amount for cost of goods sold as in determining a proper figure for inventory. Throughout this chapter you should bear in mind that the procedures for determining the amount of the ending inventory are also the means for determining the cost of goods sold. The valuation of inventory and the determination of the cost of goods sold are in effect the two sides of a single coin.

The American Institute of Certified Public Accountants has summarized this relationship between inventory valuation and the measurement of income in the following words: "A major objective of accounting for inventories is the proper determination of income through the process of matching appropriate costs against revenues."[3] The expression "matching costs against revenues" means determining what portion of the cost of goods available for sale should be deducted from the revenue of the current period and what portion should be carried forward (as inventory) to be matched against the revenue of the following period.

Importance of an accurate valuation of inventory

The most important current assets in the balance sheets of most companies are cash, accounts receivable, and inventory. Of these three, the inventory of merchandise is usually much the largest. Because of the relatively large size of this asset, an error in the valuation of inventory may cause a material misstatement of financial position and of net income. An error of 20% in valuing the inventory may have as much effect on the financial statements as would the complete omission of the asset cash.

[2] As explained in Chap. 5, a company that maintains perpetual inventory records will have a day-to-day record of the cost of goods sold and of goods in inventory. Our present discussion, however, is based on the assumption that the periodic system of inventory is being used.

[3] AICPA, op. cit.

An error in inventory will of course lead to other erroneous figures in the balance sheet, such as the total current assets, total assets, owners' equity, and the total liabilities and owners' equity. The error will also affect key figures in the income statement, such as the cost of goods sold, the gross profit on sales, and the net income for the period. Finally, it is important to recognize that *the ending inventory of one year is also the beginning inventory of the following year.* Consequently, the income statement of the second year will also be in error by the full amount of the original error in inventory valuation.

Effects of an error in valuing inventory: illustration. Assume that on December 31, Year 1, the inventory of the Hillside Company is actually $100,000 but, through an accidental error, it is recorded as $90,000. The effects of this $10,000 error on the income statement for Year 1 are indicated in the first illustration shown below, showing two income statements side by side. The left-hand set of figures shows the inventory of December 31, Year 1, at the *proper value of $100,000* and represents a correct income statement for Year 1. The right-hand set of figures represents an incorrect income statement, because the ending inventory is *erroneously listed as $90,000.* Note the differences between the two income statements with respect to net income, gross profit on sales, and cost of goods sold. Income taxes have purposely been omitted in this illustration.

HILLSIDE COMPANY

Income Statement

For the Year Ended December 31, Year 1

		With Correct Ending Inventory		With Incorrect Ending Inventory
Sales		$240,000		$240,000
Cost of goods sold:				
Beginning inventory, Jan. 1, Year 1 ...	$ 75,000		$ 75,000	
Purchases	210,000		210,000	
Cost of goods available for sale	$285,000		$285,000	
Less: Ending inventory, Dec. 31,				
Year 1	100,000		90,000	
Cost of goods sold		185,000		195,000
Gross profit on sales		$ 55,000		$ 45,000
Operating expenses		30,000		30,000
Net income		$ 25,000		$ 15,000

Effects of error in inventory

This illustration shows that an understatement of $10,000 in the ending inventory for Year 1 caused an understatement of $10,000 in the net income for Year 1. Next, consider the effect of this error on the income statement of the following year. The ending inventory of Year 1 is, of course, the beginning inventory of Year 2. The preceding illustration is now continued to show side by side a correct income statement and an incorrect statement for Year 2. The *ending* inventory of $120,000 for Year 2 is the same in both statements and is to be considered correct. Note that the $10,000 error in the beginning inventory of the right-hand statement causes an error in the cost of goods sold, in gross profit, and in net income for Year 2.

HILLSIDE COMPANY
Income Statement
For the Year Ended December 31, Year 2

		With Correct Beginning Inventory	With Incorrect Beginning Inventory
Effects on succeeding year	Sales	$265,000	$265,000
	Cost of goods sold:		
	Beginning inventory, Jan. 1, Year 2 ... $100,000		$ 90,000
	Purchases 230,000		230,000
	Cost of goods available for sale $330,000		$320,000
	Less: Ending inventory, Dec. 31,		
	Year 2 120,000		120,000
	Cost of goods sold	210,000	200,000
	Gross profit on sales	$ 55,000	$ 65,000
	Operating expenses	33,000	33,000
	Net income	$ 22,000	$ 32,000

Counterbalancing errors. The illustrated income statements for Years 1 and 2 show that an understatement of the ending inventory in Year 1 caused an understatement of net income in that year and an offsetting overstatement of net income for Year 2. Over a period of two years the effects of an inventory error on net income will *counterbalance,* and the total net income for the two years together will be the same as if the error had not occurred. Since the error in reported net income for the first year is exactly offset by the error in reported net income for the second year, it might be argued that an inventory error has no serious consequences. Such an argument is not sound, for it disregards the fact that accurate yearly figures for net income are a primary objective of the accounting process. Moreover, many actions by management and many decisions by creditors and owners are based upon *trends* indicated in the financial statements for two or more years. Note that the inventory error has made the Year 2 net income appear to be more than twice as large as the Year 1 net income, when in fact *less* net income was earned in Year 2 than in Year 1. Anyone relying on the erroneous financial statements would be greatly misled as to the trend of Hillside Company's earnings.

To produce dependable financial statements, inventory must be accurately determined at the end of each accounting period. The counterbalancing effect of the inventory error by the Hillside Company is illustrated below:

		With Inventory Correctly Stated	With Inventory at Dec. 31, Year 1, Understated	
			Reported Net Income Will Be	Reported Net Income Will Be Overstated (Understated)
Counterbalancing effect on net income	Net income for Year 1	$25,000	$15,000	$(10,000)
	Net income for Year 2	22,000	32,000	10,000
	Total net income for two years	$47,000	$47,000	$ –0–

Relation of inventory errors to net income. The effects of errors in inventory upon net income may be summarized as follows:

1 When the *ending* inventory is understated, the net income for the period will be understated.
2 When the *ending* inventory is overstated, the net income for the period will be overstated.
3 When the *beginning* inventory is understated, the net income for the period will be overstated.
4 When the *beginning* inventory is overstated, the net income for the period will be understated.

Although single errors in inventory which counterbalance over two years are not uncommon, they are only part of the picture. Some companies (usually small and unaudited) intentionally understate their ending inventory year after year for the purpose of evading income taxes. This type of fraud is discussed further at a later point in this chapter.

Taking a physical inventory

At the end of each accounting period the ledger accounts will show up-to-date balances for most of the assets. For inventory, however, the balance in the ledger account represents the *beginning* inventory, because no entry has been made in the Inventory account since the end of the preceding period. All purchases of merchandise during the present period have been recorded in the Purchases account. The ending inventory does not appear anywhere in the ledger accounts; it must be determined by a physical count of merchandise on hand at the end of the accounting period.

Establishing a balance sheet valuation for the ending inventory requires two steps: (1) determining the quantity of each kind of merchandise on hand, and (2) multiplying the quantity by the cost per unit. The first step is called *taking the inventory;* the second is called *pricing the inventory.* Taking inventory, or more precisely, taking a physical inventory, means making a systematic count of all merchandise on hand.

In most merchandising businesses the taking of a physical inventory is a year-end event. In some lines of business an inventory may be taken at the close of each month. It is common practice to take inventory after regular business hours or on Sunday. By taking the inventory while business operations are suspended, a more accurate count is possible than if goods were being sold or received while the count was in process.

Planning the physical inventory. Unless the taking of a physical inventory is carefully planned and supervised, serious errors are apt to occur which will invalidate the results of the count. To prevent such errors as the double counting of items, the omission of goods from the count, and other quantitative errors, it is desirable to plan the inventory so that the work of one person serves as a check on the accuracy of another.

There are various methods of counting merchandise. One of the simplest procedures is carried out by the use of two-member teams. One member of the team counts and calls the description and quantity of each item. The other person lists the descriptions and quantities on an inventory sheet. (In some situations a tape recorder is useful in recording quantities counted.) When all goods have been counted and listed, the items on the inventory sheet are priced at cost, and the unit prices are multiplied by the quantities to determine the valuation of the inventory.

Goods in transit. Do goods in transit belong in the inventory of the seller or of the buyer? If the selling company makes delivery of the merchandise in its own trucks, the merchandise remains its property while in transit. If the goods are shipped by rail, air, or other public carrier, the question of ownership of the goods while in transit depends upon whether the public carrier is acting as the agent of the seller or of the buyer. If the terms of the shipment are *F.O.B.* (free on board) *shipping point,* title passes at the point of shipment and the goods are the property of the buyer while in transit. If the terms of the shipment are *F.O.B. destination,* title does not pass until the shipment reaches the destination, and the goods belong to the seller while in transit. In deciding whether goods in transit at year-end should be included in inventory, it is therefore necessary to refer to the terms of the agreement with vendors (suppliers) and customers.

At the end of the year a company may have received numerous orders from customers, for which goods have been segregated and packed but not yet shippped. These goods generally should be included in inventory. An exception to this rule is found occasionally when the goods have been prepared for shipment but are being held for later delivery at the request of the customer.

Passage of title to merchandise. The debit to Accounts Receivable and the offsetting credit to the Sales account should be made *when title to the goods passes to the customer.* It would obviously be improper to set up an account receivable and at the same time to include the goods in question in inventory. Great care is necessary at year-end to ensure that all last-minute shipments to customers are recorded as sales of the current year and, on the other hand, that no customer's order is recorded as a sale until the date the goods are shipped. Sometimes, in an effort to meet sales quotas, companies have recorded sales on the last day of the accounting period, when in fact the merchandise was not shipped until early in the next period. Such practices lead to an overstatement of the year's earnings and are not in accordance with generally accepted principles of accounting.

Merchandise in inventory is valued at *cost,* whereas accounts receivable are stated at the *sales price* of the merchandise sold. Consequently, the recording of a sale prior to delivery of the goods results in an unjustified increase in the total assets of the company. The increase will equal the difference between the cost and the selling price of the goods in question. The amount of the increase will also be reflected in the income statement, where it will show up as additional earnings. An unscrupulous company, which wanted to make its financial statements present a more favorable picture than actually existed, might do so by treating year-end orders from customers as sales even though the goods were not yet shipped.

Pricing the inventory

One of the most interesting and widely discussed problems in accounting is the pricing of inventory. Even those business executives who have little knowledge of accounting are usually interested in the various methods of pricing inventory, because inventory valuation may have a significant effect upon reported net income.

Accounting for inventories involves determination of cost and of current fair value or replacement cost. An understanding of the meaning of the term *cost* as applied to inventories is a first essential in dealing with the overall problem of inventory valuation.

Cost basis of inventory valuation

In the words of the AICPA's Committee on Accounting Procedure, "The primary basis of accounting for inventory is cost, which has been defined generally as the price paid or consideration given to acquire an asset. As applied to inventories, cost means in principle the sum of the applicable expenditures and charges directly or indirectly incurred in bringing an article to its existing condition and location."[4] A number of interesting questions arise in determining the *cost* of inventory. For example, should any expenditures other than the invoice price of purchased goods be considered as part of inventory cost? Another provocative question — if identical items of merchandise are purchased at different prices during the year, which of these purchase prices represent the cost of the items remaining in inventory at year-end? We will now address these and other questions involved in determining the cost of inventory.

Inclusion of additional incidental costs in inventory — a question of materiality. From a theoretical point of view, the cost of an item of inventory includes the invoice price, minus any discount, plus all expenditures necessary to place the article in the proper location and condition for sale. Among these additional incidental costs are import duties, transportation-in, storage, insurance of goods being shipped or stored, and costs of receiving and inspecting the goods.

In determining the cost of the ending inventory, some companies add to the net invoice price of the goods a reasonable share of the charges for transportation-in incurred during the year. However, in other lines of business, it is customary and logical to price the year-end inventory *without* adding transportation-in or any other incidental costs because these charges *are not material in amount.* Although this practice results in a slight understatement of inventory cost, the understatement is so small that it does not affect the usefulness or reliability of the financial statements. Thus, the omission of transportation and other incidental charges from the cost of inventory often may be justified by the factors of convenience and economy. Accounting textbooks stress theoretical concepts of cost and income determination. The student of accounting should be aware, however, that in many business situations a close *approximation* of cost will serve the purpose at hand. The extra work involved in developing more precise accounting data must be weighed against the benefits that will result.

To sum up, we can say that in theory a portion of all the incidental costs of acquiring goods should be assigned to each item in the year-end inventory. However, the expense of computing cost in such a precise manner would usually outweigh the benefits to be derived. Consequently, these incidental costs relating to the acquisition of merchandise

---

[4] AICPA, *Accounting Research and Terminology Bulletins,* Final Edition (New York: 1961), p. 28.

are usually treated as expense of the period in which incurred, rather than being carried forward to another accounting period by inclusion in the balance sheet amount for inventory. Thus, the accounting principle of *materiality* may at times take priority over the principle of *matching costs and revenue.*

Inventory valuation methods

The prices of many kinds of merchandise are subject to frequent change. When *identical* lots of merchandise are purchased at various dates during the year, each lot may be acquired at a different cost price.

To illustrate the several alternative methods in common use for determining which purchase prices apply to the identical units remaining in inventory at the end of the period, assume the data shown below.

	Number of Units	Cost per Unit	Total Cost
Beginning inventory	100	$ 80	$ 8,000
First purchase (Mar. 1)	50	90	4,500
Second purchase (July 1)	50	100	5,000
Third purchase (Oct. 1)	50	120	6,000
Fourth purchase (Dec. 1)	50	130	6,500
Available for sale	300		$30,000
Units sold	180		
Units in ending inventory	120		

This schedule shows that 180 units were sold during the year and that 120 identical units are on hand at year-end to make up the ending inventory. In order to establish a dollar amount for cost of goods sold and for the ending inventory, we must make an assumption as to which units were sold and which units remain on hand at the end of the year. There are several acceptable assumptions on this point; four of the most common will be considered. Each assumption made as to the cost of the units in the ending inventory leads to a different method of pricing inventory and to different amounts in the financial statements. The four assumptions (and inventory valuation methods) to be considered are known as (1) specific identification, (2) average cost, (3) first-in, first-out, and (4) last-in, first-out.

Although each of these four methods will produce a different answer as to the cost of goods sold and the cost of the ending inventory, the valuation of inventory in each case is said to be at "cost." In other words, *these methods represent alternative definitions of inventory cost.*

Specific identification method. The specific identification method is best suited to inventories of high-priced, low-volume items. If each item in inventory is different from all others, as in the case of valuable paintings, custom jewelry, estate homes, and most other types of real estate, the specific identification method is clearly the logical choice. This type of inventory presents quite different problems from an inventory composed of large quantities of identical items.

If the units in the ending inventory can be identified as coming from specific purchases, they **may** be priced at the amounts listed on the purchase invoices. Continuing the example already presented, if the ending inventory of 120 units can be identified as, say, 50 units from the purchase of March 1, 40 units from the purchase of July 1, and 30 units from the purchase of December 1, the cost of the ending inventory may be computed as follows:

Specific identifica-
tion method
and . . .

50 units from the purchase of Mar. 1 @ $90	$ 4,500
40 units from the purchase of July 1 @ $100	4,000
30 units from the purchase of Dec. 1 @ $130	3,900
Ending inventory (specific identification)	$12,400

The cost of goods sold during the period is determined by subtracting the ending inventory from the cost of goods available for sale.

. . . cost of goods
sold computation

Cost of goods available for sale	$30,000
Less: Ending inventory	12,400
Cost of goods sold (specific identification method)	$17,600

The specific identification method has an intuitive appeal because it assigns actual purchase costs to the specific units purchased. For decision-making purposes, however, this approach does not always provide the most useful accounting information for a company handling a large volume of identical units.

As a simple example, assume that a coal dealer purchased 100 tons of coal at $60 a ton and a short time later made a second purchase of 100 tons of the same grade of coal at $80 a ton. The two purchases are in separate piles and it is a matter of indifference as to which pile is used in making sales to customers. Assume that the dealer makes a retail sale of one ton of coal at a price of $100. In measuring the gross profit on the sale, which cost figure should be used, $60 or $80? To insist that the cost depended on which of the two identical piles of coal was used in filling the delivery truck is an argument of questionable logic.

A situation in which the specific identification method is more likely to give meaningful results is in the purchase and sale of such high-priced articles as boats, automobiles, and jewelry.

Average-cost method. Average cost is computed by dividing the total cost of goods available for sale by the number of units available for sale. This computation gives a **weighted-average unit cost,** which is then applied to the units in the ending inventory.

Average-cost
method and . . .

Cost of goods available for sale	$30,000
Number of units available for sale	300
Average unit cost	$ 100
Ending inventory (at average cost, 120 units @ $100)	$12,000

Note that this method, when compared with the specific identification method, leads to a different amount for cost of goods sold as well as a different amount for the ending inventory.

Cost of goods available for sale	$30,000
Less: Ending inventory	12,000
Cost of goods sold (average-cost method)	$18,000

When the average-cost method is used, the cost figure of $12,000 determined for the ending inventory is influenced by all the various prices paid during the year. The price paid early in the year may carry as much weight in pricing the ending inventory as a price paid at the end of the year. A common criticism of the average-cost method of pricing inventory is that it attaches no more significance to current prices than to prices which prevailed several months earlier.

First-in, first-out method. The first-in, first-out method, which is often referred to as *fifo,* is based on the assumption that the first merchandise acquired is the first merchandise sold. In other words, each sale is made out of the **oldest** goods in stock; **the ending inventory therefore consists of the most recently acquired goods.** The fifo method of determining inventory cost may be adopted by any business, regardless of whether or not the physical flow of merchandise actually corresponds to this assumption of selling the oldest units in stock. Using the same data as in the preceding illustrations, the 120 units in the ending inventory would be regarded as consisting of the most recently acquired goods as follows:

50 units from the Dec. 1 purchase @ $130	$ 6,500
50 units from the Oct. 1 purchase @ $120	6,000
20 units from the July 1 purchase @ $100	2,000
Ending inventory, 120 units (at fifo cost)	$14,500

During a period of **rising prices** the first-in, first-out method will result in a larger amount ($14,500) being assigned as the cost of the ending inventory than would be assigned under the average-cost method. When a relatively large amount is allocated as cost of the ending inventory, a relatively small amount will remain as cost of goods sold, as indicated by the following calculation:

Cost of goods available for sale	$30,000
Less: Ending inventory	14,500
Cost of goods sold (first-in, first out method)	$15,500

It may be argued in support of the first-in, first-out method that the inventory valuation reflects recent costs and is therefore a realistic value in the light of conditions prevailing at the balance sheet date.

Last-in, first-out method. The last-in, first-out method, commonly known as *lifo,* is one of the most interesting methods of pricing inventories. The title of this method suggests that the most recently acquired goods are sold first, and that **the ending inventory consists of "old" goods acquired in the earliest purchases.** Although this assumption is not in accord with the physical movement of merchandise in most businesses, there is a strong logical argument to support the lifo method.

For the purpose of measuring income, the **flow of costs** may be more significant than the physical flow of merchandise. Supporters of the lifo method contend that the measurement of income should be based upon *current* market conditions. Therefore, current sales revenue should be offset by the *current* cost of the merchandise sold. Under the lifo method, the costs assigned to the cost of goods sold are relatively current, because they stem from the most recent purchases. Under the *fifo* method, on the other hand, the cost of goods sold is based on "older" costs.

Using the same data as in the preceding illustrations, the 120 units in the ending inventory would be priced as if they were the oldest goods available for sale during the period, as follows:

Last-in, first-out method and . . .

100 units from the beginning inventory @ $80	$8,000
20 units from the purchase of Mar. 1 @ $90	1,800
Ending inventory, 120 units (at lifo cost)	$9,800

Note that the lifo cost of the ending inventory ($9,800) is very much lower than the fifo cost ($14,500) of ending inventory in the preceding example. Since a relatively small part of the cost of goods available for sale is assigned to ending inventory, it follows that a relatively large portion must have been assigned to cost of goods sold, as shown by the following computation:

. . . cost of goods sold computation

Cost of goods available for sale	$30,000
Less: Ending inventory	9,800
Cost of goods sold (last-in, first-out method)	$20,200

Comparison of the alternative methods of pricing inventory. We have now illustrated four common methods of pricing inventory at cost; the specific identification method, the average-cost method, the first-in, first-out method, and the last-in, first-out method. By way of contrasting the results obtained from the four methods illustrated, especially during a period of rapid price increases, let us summarize the amounts computed for ending inventory, cost of goods sold, and gross profit on sales under each of the four methods. Assume that sales for the period amounted to $27,500.

Four methods of determining inventory cost compared

	Specific Identification Method	Average-Cost Method	First-In, First-Out Method	Last-In, First-Out Method
Sales	$27,500	$27,500	$27,500	$27,500
Cost of goods sold:				
Beginning Inventory	$ 8,000	$ 8,000	$ 8,000	$ 8,000
Purchases	22,000	22,000	22,000	22,000
Cost of goods available for sale	$30,000	$30,000	$30,000	$30,000
Less: Ending inventory	12,400	12,000	14,500	9,800
Cost of goods sold	$17,600	$18,000	$15,500	$20,200
Gross profit on sales	$ 9,900	$ 9,500	$12,000	$ 7,300

This comparison of the four methods makes it apparent that during periods of *rising prices,* the use of lifo will result in lower reported profits and lower income taxes than would be the case under the other methods of inventory valuation. Perhaps for this reason many businesses have adopted lifo. Current income tax regulations permit virtually any business to use the last-in, first-out method in determining taxable income.[5]

During a period of **declining prices**, the use of lifo will cause the reporting of relatively large profits as compared with fifo, which will hold reported profits to a minimum. Therefore, the choice of an inventory pricing method may significantly affect the amount of income reported during prolonged periods of changing price levels.

Which method of inventory valuation is best? All four of the inventory methods described are regarded as acceptable accounting practices and all four are acceptable in the determination of taxable income. No one method of inventory valuation can be considered as the "correct" or the "best" method. In the selection of a method, consideration should be given to the probable effect upon the balance sheet, upon the income statement, upon the amount of taxable income, and upon such business decisions as the establishment of selling prices for goods.

The specific identification method has the advantage of portraying the actual physical flow of merchandise. However, this method permits manipulation of income by selecting which items to deliver in filling a sales order. Also, the specific identification method may lead to faulty pricing decisions by implying that identical items of merchandise have different economic values.

Identical items will have the same accounting values only under the average-cost method. Assume for example that a hardware store sells a given size nail for 65 cents per pound. The hardware store buys the nails in 100-pound quantities at different times at prices ranging from 40 to 50 cents per pound. Several hundred pounds of nails are always on hand, stored in a large bin. The average-cost method properly recognizes that when a customer buys a pound of nails it is not necessary to know exactly which nails the customer happened to select from the bin in order to measure the gross profit on the sale.

A shortcoming in the average-cost method is that changes in current replacement costs of inventory are concealed because these costs are averaged with older costs. As a result of this averaging, the reported gross profit may not reflect current market conditions. This problem is illustrated in the discussion of **inventory profits** later in this chapter.

The inflation of recent years is a strong argument for the use of the lifo method. When prices are rising drastically, the most significant cost data to use as a guide to sales policies are probably the **current replacement costs** of the goods being sold. The lifo method of inventory valuation comes closer than any of the other methods described to measuring net income in the light of current selling prices and replacement costs.

On the other hand, the use of lifo during a period of rising prices is apt to produce a balance sheet figure for inventory which is far below the current replacement cost of the goods on hand. The fifo method of inventory valuation will lead to a balance sheet valuation of inventory more in line with current replacements costs.

Some business concerns which adopted lifo more than 40 years ago now show a balance sheet figure for inventory which is less than half the present replacement cost of the goods

---

[5] Income tax laws require the use of lifo for financial reporting if it is used for tax purposes.

in stock. An inventory valuation method which gives significant figures for the income statement may thus produce misleading amounts for the balance sheet, whereas a method which produces a realistic figure for inventory on the balance sheet may provide less realistic data for the income statement.

The search for the "best" method of inventory valuation is rendered difficult because the inventory figure is used in both the balance sheet and the income statement, and these two financial statements are intended for different purposes. In the income statement the function of the inventory figure is to permit a matching of costs and revenue. In the balance sheet the inventory and the other current assets are regarded as a measure of the company's ability to meet its current debts. For this purpose a valuation of inventory in line with current replacement cost would appear to be more significant.

Consistency in the valuation of inventory

The **principle of consistency** is one of the basic concepts underlying reliable financial statements. This principle means that once a company has adopted a particular accounting method, that company should follow that method consistently rather than switch methods from one year to the next. Consider the consequences if we were to ignore the principle of consistency in accounting for inventories. A company could cause its net income for any given year to increase or decrease merely by changing its method of inventory valuation. The principle of consistency does not mean that every company in an industry must use the same accounting method; it does mean that a given company should not switch year after year from one accounting method to another.

Bear in mind that a company has considerable latitude in selecting a method of inventory valuation best suited to its needs. The principle of consistency comes into play after a given method has been selected. We have already illustrated in the example on page 361 how different methods can produce differences in reported income. Consequently, a change from one inventory method to another will usually cause reported income to change significantly in the year in which the change is made. Frequent switching of methods would make the income statements undependable as a means of portraying trends in operating results. Because of the principle of consistency, the user of financial statements is able to assume that the company has followed the same accounting methods it used in the preceding year. Thus, the value of financial statements is increased because they enable the user to make reliable comparisons of the results achieved from year to year.

The principle of consistency does not mean that a business can **never** change its method of inventory valuation. However, when a change is made, the effects of the change upon reported net income should be **disclosed fully** in the footnotes accompanying the financial statements.[6] **Adequate disclosure** of all information necessary for the proper interpretation of financial statements is another basic principle of accounting. Even when the same method of inventory pricing is being followed consistently, the financial statements should include a disclosure of the pricing method in use.

---

[6] A change in the method of inventory valuation also requires the approval of the Internal Revenue Service.

The environment of inflation

We have previously discussed the relationship between the valuation of assets in the balance sheet and the recognition of costs and expenses in the income statement. As assets are sold or used up, their cost is removed from the balance sheet and recognized in the income statement as a cost or expense. In the case of inventory, the cost of units sold is transferred from the balance sheet to the income statement as cost of goods sold. In the case of depreciable assets, such as a building, the cost is gradually transferred to the income statement as depreciation expense. This flow of costs is illustrated in the chart below.

Historical costs appear in both balance sheet and income statement

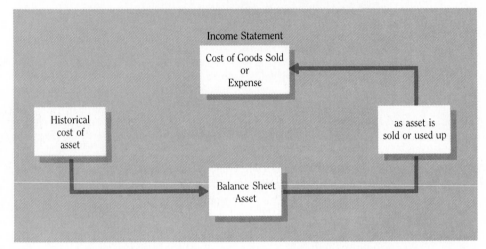

A period of sustained inflation causes some distortion in financial statements which are based upon historical costs. Rising price levels may cause assets to be valued in the balance sheets at amounts substantially below their current replacement cost. Similarly, the cost assigned to the income statement as these assets are sold or used up tends to understate the cost to the business of replacing these assets.

The inflationary policies and high income tax rates of recent years have stimulated the interest of business management in the choice of inventory methods. Although the rate of inflation slowed significantly in the early 1980s, most business executives and government officials expect the trend of rising prices to continue. In other words, an environment of inflation has come to be considered as normal. The lifo method of inventory valuation causes reported net income to reflect the increasing cost of replacing the merchandise sold during the year and also tends to avoid basing income tax payments on an exaggerated measurement of taxable income. Therefore, the existence of inflation is an argument for the lifo method of inventory valuation.

Inventory profits

Many accountants believe that the use of fifo or of average cost during a period of inflation results in the reporting of overstated profits and consequently in the payment of excessive income taxes. Profits are overstated under both the fifo and average-cost methods because the gross profit is computed by subtracting "old" inventory costs rather than current replacement costs from sales revenue. These old costs are relatively low, resulting in a high reported gross profit. However, the company must pay the higher current cost in order to replenish its inventory.

To illustrate this concept, assume that TV Sales Shop has an inventory of 20 television sets which were acquired at an average cost of $270. During the current month, 10 television sets are sold for cash at a sales price of $350 each. Using the average-cost method to value inventory, the company will report the following gross profit for the month:

Sales (10 × $350)	$3,500
Cost of goods sold (10 × $270)	2,700
Gross profit on sales	$ 800

However, TV Sales Shop must replace its inventory of television sets to continue in business. Because of inflation, TV Sales Shop can no longer buy 10 television sets for $2,700. Let us assume that the current replacement cost of television sets is $325 each; TV Sales Shop must pay $3,250 to replenish its inventory. Thus, TV Sales Shop is able to keep only $250 ($3,500 − $3,250) of the reported $800 gross profit; the remaining $550 has to be reinvested in inventory because of the increasing cost of television sets. This $550 would be considered a fictitious profit, or an *inventory profit*, by many accountants and business executives.

The inventory profit included in the reported net income of a business may be computed by deducting the cost of goods shown in the income statement from the *replacement cost* (computed at the date of sale) of these goods.

In periods of rapid inflation, a significant portion of the reported net income of companies using fifo or average cost actually may be inventory profits. The net income of companies using lifo will include much less inventory profit because lifo causes more current costs to be included in the cost of goods sold.

Disclosing the effects of inflation

In an effort to compensate for the distortions in financial statements caused by inflation, the Financial Accounting Standards Board adopted *Statement No. 33*, "Financial Reporting and Changing Prices."[7] This Statement requires large corporations to disclose the extent to which historical costs in both the balance sheet and the income statement understate current price levels. These disclosures can be in a footnote to the historical cost-based financial statements, or in a special set of supplementary financial statements. This information thus *supplements* rather than replaces the use of historical cost as a basis of accounting.

One requirement of Statement No. 33 is that large corporations disclose what it would cost to *replace* their inventories at year-end and what their cost of goods sold would be if computed by using the *current replacement cost* at the date of sale. The disclosure of the cost of goods sold computed on the basis of replacement cost has revealed that a

---

[7] FASB, *Statement No. 33*, "Financial Reporting and Changing Prices" (Stamford, Conn.: 1979).

substantial portion of the net income reported by many large corporations *is actually inventory profit.* In other words, net income tends to be **overstated** when companies rely solely on historical cost values during a period of inflation.

The FASB's action to require disclosure of replacement cost information may prove to be one of the most significant changes in accounting practice in many years. Some accountants view it as a major step away from cost-based accounting toward current-value accounting. At present, only very large corporations are required to make the disclosures called for in Statement No. 33, but the FASB encourages smaller companies to comply on a voluntary basis. Statement No. 33 calls for many disclosures in addition to the replacement cost of inventories and the cost of goods sold. These other disclosure requirements, including current replacement costs of plant assets, are discussed in later chapters of this text.

The lower-of-cost-or-market rule (LCM)

Although cost is the primary basis for valuation of inventories, circumstances may arise under which inventory may properly be valued at less than its cost. If the **utility** of the inventory has fallen below cost because of a decline in the price level, a loss has occurred. This loss may appropriately be recognized as a loss of the current period by reducing the accounting value of the inventory from cost to a lower level designated as **market.** The word **market** as used in this context means **current replacement cost.** For a merchandising company, **market** is the amount which the concern would have to pay at the present time for the goods in question, purchased in the customary quantities through the usual sources of supply and including transportation-in. To avoid misunderstanding, the rule might better read "lower of actual cost or replacement cost."

In the early days of accounting when the principal users of financial statements were creditors and attention was concentrated upon the balance sheet, **conservatism** was a dominant consideration in asset valuation. The lower-of-cost-or-market rule was then considered justifiable because it tended to produce a "safe" or minimum value for inventory. The rule was widely applied for a time without regard for the possibility that although replacement costs had declined, there might be no corresponding and immediate decline in selling prices.

As the significance of the income statement has increased, considerable dissatisfaction with the lower-of-cost-or-market rule has developed. If ending inventory is written down from cost to a lower market figure but the merchandise is sold during the next period at the usual selling prices, the effect of the write-down will have been to reflect a fictitious loss in the first period and an exaggerated profit in the second period. Selling prices do not always drop when replacement prices decline. Even if selling prices do follow replacement prices downward, they may not decline by a proportionate amount.

Because of these objections, the lower-of-cost-or-market rule has undergone some modification and is now qualified in the following respects. If the inventory can probably be sold at prices which will yield a **normal profit,** the inventory should be carried at cost even though current replacement cost is lower. Assume, for example, that merchandise is purchased for $1,000 with the intention of reselling it to customers for $1,500. The replacement cost then declines from $1,000 to $800, but it is believed that the merchandise can still be sold to customers for $1,450. In other words, the normal anticipated profit has shrunk by $50. The carrying value of the inventory could then be written down from $1,000 to $950. There is no justification for reducing the inventory to the replacement cost of $800 under these circumstances.

Another qualification of the lower-of-cost-or-market rule is that inventory should never be carried at an amount greater than **net realizable value,** which may be defined as prospective selling price minus anticipated selling expenses. Assume, for example, that because of unstable market conditions, it is believed that goods acquired at a cost of $5,000 and having a current replacement cost of $4,500 will probably have to be sold for no more than $5,200 and that the selling expenses involved will amount to $1,200. The inventory should then be reduced to a carrying value (net realizable value) of $4,000, which is less than current replacement cost.

Application of the lower-of-cost-or-market rule. The lower of cost or market for inventory is often computed by determining the cost and the market figures for each item in inventory and using the lower of the two amounts in every case. If, for example, item A cost $100 and replacement cost is $90, the item should be priced at $90. If item B cost $200 and replacement cost is $225, this item should be priced at $200. The total cost of the two items is $300 and total replacement cost is $315, but the total inventory value determined by applying the lower-of-cost-or-market rule to each item in inventory is only $290. This application of the lower-of-cost-or-market rule is illustrated by the tabulation shown below:

Application of Lower-of-Cost-or-Market Rule, Item-by-Item Method

		Unit Cost		Total Cost		Lower of Cost or Market
Item	Quantity	Cost	Market	Cost	Market	Market
A	10	$100	$ 90	$ 1,000	$ 900	$ 900
B	8	200	225	1,600	1,800	1,600
C	50	50	60	2,500	3,000	2,500
D	80	90	70	7,200	5,600	5,600
Totals				$12,300	$11,300	$10,600

Pricing inventory at lower of cost or market

If the lower-of-cost-or-market rule is applied item by item, the carrying value of the above inventory would be $10,600. However, an alternative and less rigorous version of the lower-of-cost-or-market rule calls for applying it to the total of the entire inventory rather than to the individual items. If the above inventory is to be valued by applying the lower-of-cost-or-market rule to the total of the inventory, the balance sheet amount for inventory is determined merely by comparing the total cost of $12,300 with the total replacement cost of $11,300 and using the lower of the two figures. Still another alternative method of using the lower-of-cost-or-market concept is to apply it to categories of the inventory rather than item by item. Each of these alternative methods of applying the lower-of-cost-or-market rule is acceptable in current accounting practice, although once a method has been selected it should be followed consistently from year to year.

Estimating ending inventory and cost of goods sold

When the periodic inventory system is being used, a physical inventory must be taken to determine the amount of the ending inventory. However, business managers need monthly financial statements in order to manage a business efficiently. To prepare these monthly financial statements, we need to know the amount of inventory at the end of each month. However, the taking of a physical inventory is too time-consuming and costly a job to be performed every month. Most companies take a physical inventory only once a year. For monthly or quarterly financial statements, these companies use an estimated amount for the ending inventory. One method of *estimating* inventories is the *gross profit method;* another method is called the *retail inventory method.*

Gross profit method

The gross profit method is a quick, simple technique for estimating inventories which can be used in almost all types and sizes of business. In using the gross profit method, we assume that the rate of gross profit earned in the preceding year will remain the same for the current year. (Some companies prefer to use an average of the gross profit rates of recent years.) When we know the rate of gross profit, we can divide the dollar amount of net sales into two elements: (1) the gross profit and (2) the cost of goods sold. We view net sales as 100%. If gross profit, for example, is 40%, the cost of goods sold must be 60%. In other words, the cost of goods sold percentage (cost percentage) is determined by deducting the gross profit percentage from 100%.

When the gross profit percentage is known, the ending inventory can be estimated by the following procedures:

1   Determine the *cost of goods available for sale* from the general ledger records of beginning inventory and net purchases.
2   Estimate the *cost of goods sold* by multiplying the net sales by the cost percentage.
3   Deduct the *cost of goods sold* from the *cost of goods available for sale* to find the estimated ending inventory.

To illustrate, assume that Metro Hardware has a beginning inventory of $50,000 on January 1. During the month of January, net purchases amount to $20,000 and net sales total $30,000. Assume that the company's normal gross profit rate is 40% of net sales; it follows that the cost percentage is 60%. Using these facts, the inventory on January 31 may be estimated as follows:

	Goods available for sale:		
	Beginning inventory, Jan. 1		$50,000
	Net purchases		20,000
Step 1 . . .	Cost of goods available for sale		$70,000
	Deduct: Estimated cost of goods sold:		
	Net sales	$30,000	
Step 2 . . .	Cost percentage (100% − 40%)	60%	
	Estimated cost of goods sold		18,000
Step 3 . . .	Estimated ending inventory, Jan. 31		$52,000

The gross profit method of estimating inventory has several uses apart from the preparation of monthly financial statements. If an inventory is destroyed by fire, the company must determine the amount of the inventory on hand at the date of the fire in order to file an insurance claim. The most convenient way to determine this inventory amount is often the gross profit method.

The gross profit method is also used at year-end after the taking of a physical inventory to confirm the overall reasonableness of the amount determined by the counting and pricing process.

The retail method of estimating ending inventory

The retail method of inventory is widely used by department stores and other types of retail business. To use the retail inventory method, a store must maintain records showing the beginning inventory *at cost* and *at retail*. The term "at retail" means the marked selling prices of all items in the store. The records also must show the purchases during the period both *at cost* and *at retail*. The only other information needed is the net sales for the month. The amount of net sales, of course, is equal to the amount recorded in the Sales revenue account during the period minus any sales returns and sales discounts.

The records described above enable us to know the amount of goods available for sale, stated both at cost and at retail selling prices. (As you know, goods available for sale are the total of beginning inventory and net purchases.) With this information, all we need to do is to deduct the net sales for the month from the retail sales value of the goods available for sale. The result will be the ending inventory at retail selling price. A final step is to convert the ending inventory at retail selling price to a cost basis by multiplying it by the *cost percentage*. The cost percentage is the *ratio of cost to selling price for the current period*. To compute the cost percentage, divide the cost of goods available for sale by the retail sales value of these goods. The end result of these procedures is that we have an estimated cost value for inventory without going through the extensive work of taking a physical inventory.

The following illustration shows the calculation of an ending inventory of $280,000 by the retail inventory method.

	Cost Price	Retail Selling Price
Estimating inventory for monthly financial statements Goods available for sale:		
Beginning inventory	$415,000	$ 560,000
Net purchases	285,000	440,000
Goods available for sale	$700,000	$1,000,000
Cost percentage: $700,000 ÷ $1,000,000 = 70%		
Deduct: Net sales at retail		600,000
Ending inventory at retail selling price		$ 400,000
Ending inventory at cost ($400,000 × 70%)	$280,000	

Reducing a physical inventory to cost by the retail method. A second use for the retail inventory method is to aid in the completion of the annual physical inventory. Goods on sale in retail stores have price tags attached, showing retail prices. When the annual physical inventory is taken, it is more convenient to list the retail prices from the price tags than to look up purchase invoices to find the unit cost of each item in the store. The total of the inventory at retail selling price is then reduced to cost by applying the cost percentage, that is, the ratio between cost and selling price during the current period. The following illustration shows a year-end physical inventory amounting to $235,400 at retail selling price. This amount is reduced to a cost basis of $141,240 by applying the cost percentage of 60%.

Take year-end physical inventory at retail; then reduce it to cost

	Cost Price	Retail Selling Price
Goods available for sale:		
Beginning inventory	$131,000	$220,000
Net purchases	49,000	80,000
Goods available for sale	$180,000	$300,000
Cost percentage: $180,000 ÷ $300,000 = 60%		
Ending inventory at retail selling price (per physical inventory) ...		$235,400
Ending inventory at cost ($235,400 × 60%)	$141,240	

In this illustration we have shown the calculation of inventory by the retail inventory method without going into the complications which would arise from markups and markdowns in the original retail selling prices. Such changes in price are considered in advanced accounting courses.

Although the inventory amount is an estimate, experience has shown this retail inventory method to be a reliable one. An inventory amount established in this manner is acceptable in audited financial statements and also in federal income tax returns.

Internal control

Inventories are usually the largest current asset of a merchandising or manufacturing business. Furthermore, the very nature of inventories makes them subject to theft and to major errors and misstatement. The large dollar amounts involved, coupled with the rapid turnover of inventory items, and the variety of alternative valuation methods make it possible for a major shortage to occur in inventories without attracting immediate attention. Thus, the accountant's approach to inventories should stress an awareness of the possibility of large intentional errors as well as major accidental errors in establishing inventory quantities and amounts. If one or more members of a company's management is determined to evade income taxes, to conceal shortages arising from irregularities, or to mislead absentee owners, inventories constitute the most likely area for such fraudulent action to take place.

To provide the strong internal control procedures needed to protect inventories, the various physical functions involved in acquiring and handling merchandise should be assigned to separate departments. These functions may include purchasing, receiving, storing, issuing, and shipping the items which comprise the inventory. Thus, the organizational structure of a company should include a purchasing department with exclusive authority to make all purchases. All merchandise received by the company should be cleared through a receiving department. This department will count the merchandise received, detect any damaged items, issue a receiving report to the accounts payable department and other departments, and transmit the merchandise to the stores department.

In addition to the protection afforded by extensive subdivision of duties, another important approach to assuring reliability in the amounts reported as inventory and cost of goods sold is an annual audit by a CPA firm. Every independent audit includes firsthand observation of the annual taking of a physical inventory. Such observation by a competent outsider provides assurance that the physical inventory is carefully counted and priced, thus leading to valid amounts for inventory and cost of goods sold in the financial statements. In addition, the independent auditors will study and test the system of internal control.

Many small companies have too few employees to permit the extensive subdivision of duties described above. Moreover, these small concerns usually are unwilling to incur the cost of an annual audit by a CPA firm. Under these circumstances, the amounts shown in the financial statements (especially inventory, cost of goods sold, gross profit, and net income) should be viewed with caution by absentee owners, bankers, creditors, IRS agents, and other outsiders.

● **CASE IN POINT** ● The Internal Revenue Service (IRS) conducts audits of the income tax returns of most business organizations to see that these companies have not understated taxable income and thereby evaded income taxes. The IRS has found that a business which wants to understate its taxable income is likely to do so by understating inventory. Small businesses, in particular, which are not audited by CPA firms, may make a practice of regularly understating the ending inventory year after year in order to understate taxable income. In income tax audits, therefore, the IRS makes it standard practice to verify as fully as possible the determination of the amount of ending inventory. An ending inventory which is quite small in relation to the year's sales volume is a "red flag signal" to the tax auditor.

Perpetual inventory system

Companies which deal in merchandise of high unit cost, such as automobiles, television sets, or expensive jewelry, find a perpetual inventory system worthwhile and efficient. Since inventory is often one of the largest assets in a business and has a rapid rate of turnover, strong internal control is especially important. A perpetual inventory system, if properly designed and operated, can provide the strongest possible internal control over the inventory of merchandise. The key feature of a perpetual inventory system is that the records show continuously the amount of inventory on hand and the cost of goods sold.

Companies with computer-based accounting records including point-of-sale terminals are in a good position to carry on continuous updating of inventory records.

Internal control and perpetual inventory systems

A perpetual inventory system has the potential of providing excellent internal control. However, the fact that perpetual inventory records are in use does not automatically guarantee strong internal control. Such basic internal control concepts as the subdivision of duties, the control of documents by serial numbers, and separation of the accounting function from the custody of assets are essential elements with either the perpetual or periodic inventory systems.

● **CASE IN POINT** ● Par-Flite, a manufacturer of golf equipment, maintained an inventory of several thousand sets of golf clubs. The clubs were kept in a storeroom with barred windows and doors under the supervision of John Adams. Adams was also responsible for maintaining detailed perpetual inventory records of the golf clubs in the storeroom. Another employee acquired an unauthorized key to the storeroom and began stealing large numbers of clubs. Adams discovered that the quantities on hand did not agree with the perpetual records he maintained. Afraid that his records would be criticized as highly inaccurate, he made numerous changes in the records so they would agree with quantities of golf clubs on hand. The theft of clubs continued and large losses were sustained before the inventory shortage came to the attention of management.

If the person maintaining records had not also been responsible for physical custody of the merchandise, there would have been no incentive or opportunity to conceal a shortage by falsifying the records. Satisfactory internal control over inventories requires that the accounting function be separate from the custody of assets. Frequent comparison of quantities of merchandise on hand with the quantities shown by the perpetual inventory records should be made by employees who do not have responsibility either for custody of assets or for maintenance of records.

Perpetual inventory records

The information required for a perpetual system can be processed electronically or manually. In a manual system a subsidiary record card, as shown below, is used for each type of merchandise on hand. If the company has 100 different kinds of products in stock, then 100 inventory record cards will make up the subsidiary inventory record. Shown below is an inventory record card for item XL-2000.

On this card, the quantity and cost of units received will be listed at the date of receipt; the quantity and cost of units sold will be recorded at the date of sale; and after each purchase or sales transaction, the balance remaining on hand will be shown. This running balance will be shown in number of units, cost per unit, and total dollar amount.

The information on the illustrated inventory record shows that the first-in, first-out basis of pricing the inventory is beng used. After the sale of two units on January 7, the

Perpetual inventory record card

Item	XL-2000	Maximum	20
Location	Storeroom 2	Minimum	8

	PURCHASED			SOLD			BALANCE		
Date	Units	Unit Cost	Total	Units	Unit Cost	Total	Units	Unit Cost	Balance
Jan. 1							12	$50.00	$600.00
7				2	$50.00	$100.00	10	50.00	500.00
9	10	$55.00	$550.00				10	50.00	
							10	55.00	1,050.00
12				8	50.00	400.00	2	50.00	
							10	55.00	650.00
31				2	50.00	100.00			
				1	55.00	55.00	9	55.00	495.00

remaining inventory consisted of 10 units at a cost of $50 each. The purchase on January 9 of 10 units carried a unit cost of $55, rather than $50, hence must be accounted for separately. The balance on hand after the January 9 purchase appears on two lines: 10 units at $50 and 10 units at $55. When eight units were sold on January 12, they were treated as coming from the oldest stock on hand and therefore had a cost of $50 each. The balance remaining on hand then consisted of two units at $50 and 10 units at $55. When three units were sold on January 31, the cost consisted of two units at $50 and one unit at $55. The ending inventory of nine units consists of the most recently acquired units with a cost of $55 each.

Perpetual inventory records may also be maintained on a last-in, first-out basis or on an average-cost basis, but these systems involve some complexities which are considered in advanced accounting courses.

Control over the amount invested in inventory can be strengthened by listing on each inventory card the maximum and minimum quantities that should be kept in stock. By maintaining quantities within these limits, overstocking and out-of-stock situations can be avoided.

General ledger entries for a perpetual inventory system. The general ledger controlling account entitled *Inventory* is continuously (perpetually) updated when a perpetual inventory system is in use. This Inventory account controls the many subsidiary record cards discussed above. A continuously updated Cost of Goods Sold account is also maintained in the general ledger.

The purchase of merchandise by a company using a perpetual inventory system requires a journal entry affecting general ledger controlling accounts as follows:

Inventory 1,500
        Accounts Payable, Lake Company   1,500
To record purchase of merchandise on credit.

This purchase transaction would also be recorded in the subsidiary ledger (the perpetual inventory cards) showing the quantity of each kind of merchandise purchased. The $1,500 purchase from Lake Company might affect only one or perhaps a dozen of the subsidiary records, depending on how many types of merchandise were included in this purchase transaction.

For every sales transaction, we can determine the cost of the goods sold by referring to the appropriate perpetual inventory card record. Therefore, at the time of a sale, we can record both the amount of the selling price and the *cost* of the goods sold, as illustrated in the following pair of related entries.

Accounts Receivable, J. Williams 140
        Sales   140
To record the sale of merchandise on credit.

Cost of Goods Sold 100
        Inventory   100
To record the cost of goods sold and the related decrease in inventory.

To avoid making a large number of entries in the general journal, a special column can be entered in the sales journal to show the cost of the goods involved in each sales transaction. At the end of the month the total of this "Cost" column can be posted as a debit to Cost of Goods Sold and a credit to Inventory.

A company maintaining perpetual inventory records will also conduct a physical count of all merchandise once a year and compare the amount of the physical inventory with the perpetual inventory records. An adjusting entry can be made to bring the inventory records into agreement with the physical inventory. For example, if shoplifting or other factors have caused an inventory shortage, the adjusting entry will consist of a debit to the loss account, Inventory Shortage, and a credit to Inventory.

When a perpetual inventory system is in use, the Inventory account is increased by purchases of merchandise. It is decreased by the cost of goods sold, by purchase returns and allowances, and by purchase discounts. At the end of the year the dollar balances of all the subsidiary inventory record cards should be added to see that the total is in agreement with the general ledger controlling account. The only adjustment necessary at year-end will be to correct the Inventory controlling account and the subsidiary records for any discrepancies indicated by the taking of a physical inventory.

The advantages of a perpetual inventory system as indicated in the preceding discussion include:

1 Stronger internal control. By comparing the physical inventory with the perpetual records, management will be made aware of any shortages or errors and can take corrective action.

2 A physical inventory can be taken at dates other than year-end, or it can be taken for different products or different departments at various dates during the year, since the perpetual records always show the amounts which **should** be on hand.

3 Quarterly or monthly financial statements can be prepared more readily because of the availability of dollar amounts for inventory and cost of goods sold in the accounting records.

Key terms introduced or emphasized in chapter 9

Average-cost method. A method of inventory valuation. Weighted-average unit cost is computed by dividing the total cost of goods available for sale by the number of identical units available for sale.

Consistency in inventory valuation. An accounting standard that calls for the use of the same method of inventory pricing from year to year, with full disclosure of the effects of any change in method. Intended to make financial statements comparable.

First-in, first-out (fifo)method. A method of computing the cost of inventory and the cost of goods sold based on the assumption that the first merchandise acquired is the first merchandise sold, and that the ending inventory consists of the most recently acquired goods.

F.O.B. destination. A term meaning the seller bears the cost of shipping goods to the buyer's location. Title to the goods remains with the seller while the goods are in transit.

F.O.B. shipping point. The buyer of goods bears the cost of transportation from the seller's location to the buyer's location. Title to the goods passes at the point of shipment and the goods are the property of the buyer while in transit.

Gross profit method. A method of estimating the cost of the ending inventory based on the assumption that the rate of gross profit remains approximately the same from year to year.

Inventory profits. The amount by which the cost of replacing goods sold (computed at the date of sale) **exceeds** the reported cost of goods sold. Many accountants consider inventory profits to be a "fictitious" profit, because this amount usually must be reinvested in inventories and therefore is not available for distribution to stockholders.

Last-in, first-out (lifo) method. A method of computing the cost of goods sold by use of the prices paid for the most recently acquired units. Ending inventory is valued on the basis of prices paid for the units first acquired.

Lower-of-cost-or-market method. A method of inventory pricing in which goods are valued at original cost or replacement cost (market), whichever is lower.

Net realizable value. The prospective selling price minus anticipated selling expenses. Inventory should not be carried at more than net realizable value.

Perpetual inventory system. Provides a continuous (perpetual) running record of the goods on hand. As goods are sold their cost is transferred to a Cost of Goods Sold account.

Physical inventory. A systematic count of all goods on hand, followed by the application of unit prices to the quantities counted and development of a dollar value for ending inventory.

Retail method. A method of estimating inventory in a retail store based on the assumption that the cost of goods on hand bears the same percentage relationship to retail prices as does the cost of all goods available for sale to the original retail prices. Inventory is first priced at retail and then converted to cost by application of a cost-to-retail percentage.

Specific identification method. A method of pricing inventory by identifying the units in the ending inventory as coming from specific purchases.

Demonstration problem for your review

One of the popular products carried by Auto Sport is an 8-inch speaker unit. The inventory quantities, purchases, and sales of this unit for the current year are summarized below.

	Number of Units	Cost per Unit	Total Cost
Inventory, Jan. 1	900	$10.00	$ 9,000
First purchase (Apr. 3)	1,180	10.20	12,036
Second purchase (July 7)	800	10.35	8,280
Third purchase (Oct. 22)	620	10.70	6,634
Fourth purchase (Dec. 15)	1,000	10.85	10,850
Goods available for sale	4,500		$46,800
Units sold during the year	3,200		
Inventory, Dec. 31	1,300		

Instructions. Compute the cost of the December 31 inventory and the cost of goods sold for the 8-inch speaker units in the current year using:

a The first-in, first-out method
b The last-in, first-out method
c The average-cost method

Solution to demonstration problem

	Units	Unit Cost	Total Cost
Inventory and cost of goods sold:			
a Fifo:			
Inventory:			
Fourth purchase (Dec. 15)	1,000	$10.85	$10,850
Third purchase (Oct. 22)	300	10.70	3,210
Ending inventory, fifo	1,300		$14,060
Cost of goods sold:			
Cost of goods available for sale			$46,800
Less: Ending inventory, fifo			14,060
Cost of goods sold, fifo			$32,740
b Lifo:			
Inventory:			
Beginning inventory	900	$10.00	$ 9,000
First purchase (Apr. 3)	400	10.20	4,080
Ending inventory, lifo	1,300		$13,080
Cost of goods sold:			
Cost of goods available for sale			$46,800
Less: Ending inventory, lifo			13,080
Cost of goods sold, lifo			$33,720

c Average cost:

Inventory:

Total goods available for sale	4,500		$46,800
Average unit cost ($46,800 ÷ 4,500 units)		$10.40	
Ending inventory, weighted average of $10.40 per unit	1,300	$10.40	$13,520
Cost of goods sold, weighted average of $10.40 per unit	3,200	$10.40	$33,280

Review questions

1 Which of the seven items listed below are used in computing the *cost of goods available for sale?*

    a Ending inventory   e Transportation-in
    b Sales   f Purchase returns and allowances
    c Beginning inventory   g Delivery expense
    d Purchases

2 Through an error in counting of merchandise at December 31, Year 4, the Trophy Company overstated the amount of goods on hand by $8,000. Assuming that the error was not discovered, what was the effect upon net income for Year 4? Upon owners' equity at December 31, Year 4? Upon net income for Year 5? Upon owners' equity at December 31, Year 5?

3 Is the establishment of an appropriate valuation for the merchandise inventory at the end of the year more important in producing a dependable income statement, or in producing a dependable balance sheet?

4 Explain the meaning of the term *physical inventory.*

5 Near the end of December, Hadley Company received a large order from a major customer. The work of packing the goods for shipment was begun at once but could not be completed before the close of business on December 31. Since a written order from the customer was on hand and the goods were nearly all packed and ready for shipment, Hadley felt that this merchandise should not be included in the physical inventory taken on December 31. Do you agree? What is probably the reason behind Hadley's opinion?

6 During a prolonged period of rising prices, will the fifo or lifo method of inventory valuation result in higher reported profits?

7 Throughout several years of strongly rising prices, Company A used the lifo method of inventory valuation and Company B used the fifo method. In which company would the balance sheet figure for inventory be closer to current replacement cost of the merchandise on hand? Why?

8 You are making a detailed analysis of the financial statements and accounting records of two companies in the same industry, Adams Company and Bar Company. Price levels have been rising steadily for several years. In the course of your investigation, you observe that the inventory value shown on the Adams Company balance sheet is quite close to the current replacement cost of the merchandise on hand. However, for Bar Company, the carrying value of the inventory is far below current replacement cost. What method of inventory valuation is probably used by Adams Company? By Bar Company? If we assume that the two companies are identical except for the inventory valuation method used, which company has probably been reporting higher net income in recent years?

9 Why do some accountants consider the net income reported by businesses during a period of rising prices to be overstated?

10 Assume that a business uses the first-in, first-out method of accounting for inventories during a prolonged period of inflation and that the business pays dividends equal to the amount of reported net income. Suggest a problem that may arise in continued successful operation of the business. What does this situation have to do with "inventory profits"?

11 The Financial Accounting Standards Board requires large corporations to disclose the cost of replacing their inventories and to disclose what their cost of goods sold would be if computed by using replacement costs. Do you think this policy indicates that corporate profits have tended to be overstated or understated in recent years? Explain.

12 Explain the meaning of the term **market** as used in the expression "lower of cost or market."

13 One of the items in the inventory of Grayline Stores is marked for sale at $125. The purchase invoice shows the item cost $95, but a newly issued price list from the manufacturer shows the present replacement cost to be $90. What inventory valuation should be assigned to this item if Grayline Stores follows the lower-of-cost-or-market rule?

14 Explain the usefulness of the **gross profit method** of estimating inventories.

15 A store using the **retail inventory method** takes its physical inventory by applying current retail prices as marked on the merchandise to the quantities counted. Does this procedure indicate that the inventory will appear in the financial statements at retail selling price? Explain.

16 Estimate the ending inventory by the gross profit method, given the following data: beginning inventory $40,000, net purchases $100,000, net sales $106,667, average gross profit rate 25% of net sales.

17 Summarize the difference between the **periodic system** and the **perpetual system** of accounting for inventory. Which system would usually cost more to maintain? Which system would be most practicable for a restaurant, a retail drugstore, a new car dealer?

18 Identify each of the four statements shown below as true or false. Also, give a brief explanation. In the accounting records of a company using a perpetual inventory system:
   a The Inventory account will ordinarily remain unchanged until the end of an accounting period.
   b The Cost of Goods Sold account is debited with the sales price of merchandise sold.
   c The Inventory account and the Cost of Goods Sold account will both normally have debit balances.
   d The Inventory account and the Cost of Goods Sold account will normally have equal but offsetting balances.

19 A large art gallery has in inventory several hundred paintings. No two are alike. The least expensive is priced at more than $1,000 and the higher priced items carry prices of $100,000 or more. Which of the four methods of inventory valuation discussed in this chapter would you consider to be most appropriate for this business? Give reasons for your answer.

Exercises

Ex. 9-1   Carlox Corporation had two large shipments of merchandise in transit at December 31. One was a $60,000 inbound shipment of merchandise (shipped December 28, F.O.B. shipping point) which arrived at the Carlox receiving dock on January 2. The other shipment was a $40,000 outbound shipment of merchandise to a customer which was shipped and billed by Carlox on December 30 (terms F.O.B. shipping point) and reached the customer on January 3.

In taking a physical inventory on December 31, Carlox counted all goods on hand and priced the inventory on the basis of average cost. The total amount was $360,000. In developing this figure, Carlox gave no consideration to goods in transit.

What amount should appear as inventory on the company's balance sheet at December 31? Explain. If you indicate an amount other than $360,000, state what asset or liability other than inventory would also be changed in amount.

Ex. 9-2   The concept of conservatism sometimes enters into the valuation of inventory. This concept indicates that when some doubt exists about the valuation of merchandise, the accountant should favor the accounting option which produces a lower net income for the current period and a less favorable financial position. For each of the following pairs of options, indicate which is the more conservative practice.

1 a Inventory items are priced at net invoice price plus all additional incidental costs incurred to transport, store, and insure the goods until they reach the place and condition for sale.
   b All incidental costs relating to the purchase of merchandise (such as transportation-in, import duties, storage, and insurance of goods in storage or in transit) are treated as period costs; that is, they are treated as expense of the period in which incurred.
2 a Inventory is priced by the lower-of-cost-or-market rule, applied on an item-by-item basis.
   b Inventory is priced by the lower-of-cost-or-market rule, applied to the inventory as a whole.
3 a During a long period of rising prices, inventory is priced by the average-cost method.
   b During a long period of rising prices, inventory is priced by the first-in, first-out method.

Ex. 9-3   The condensed income statements prepared by Chapel Company for two successive years are shown below:

	Year 2	Year 1
Sales	$1,000,000	$960,000
Cost of goods sold	586,400	609,600
Gross profit on sales	$ 413,600	$350,400
Operating expenses	307,000	298,000
Net income	$ 106,600	$ 52,400

The inventory at the end of Year 1 was understated by $33,600, but the error was not discovered until after the accounts had been closed and financial statements prepared at the end of Year 2. The balance sheets for the two years showed owners' equity of $142,800 at the end of Year 1 and $173,600 at the end of Year 2.

Compute the correct net income figures for Year 1 and Year 2 and the gross profit percentage for each year based on corrected data. What correction, if any, should be made in owners' equity at the end of Year 1 and at the end of Year 2?

Ex. 9-4   The records of Barker, Inc., showed the beginning inventory balance of item T12 on January 1 and the purchases of this item during the current year to be as follows:

Jan. 1 Beginning inventory	1,000 units @ $10.00	$10,000
Feb. 23 Purchase	3,200 units @ $11.00	35,200
Apr. 20 Purchase	2,000 units @ $11.20	22,400
May 4 Purchase	2,000 units @ $11.60	23,200
Nov. 30 Purchase	800 units @ $12,50	10,000
Totals	9,000 units	$100,800

At December 31 the ending inventory consisted of 1,200 units.

Determine the cost of the ending inventory, based on each of the following methods of inventory valuation:

a Average cost
b First-in, first-out
c Last-in, first-out

Ex. 9-5 During the current year, Blue Ridge Supply made several purchases of a small part called a gate valve and made sales of this item daily. The inventory quantities, purchases, and sales for the year are summarized below:

	Number of Units	Cost per Unit	Total Cost
Beginning inventory (Jan. 1)	9,100	$4.00	$ 36,400
First purchase (Feb. 20)	20,000	4.10	82,000
Second purchase (May 10)	30,000	4.25	127,500
Third purchase (Aug. 24)	50,000	4.60	230,000
Fourth purchase (Nov. 30)	10,900	5.00	54,500
Goods available for sale	120,000		$530,400
Units sold during the year	105,000		
Ending inventory (Dec. 31)	15,000		

Compute the cost of the ending inventory of gate valves, using the following inventory valuation methods:

a First-in, first-out
b Last-in, first-out
c Average cost

Ex. 9-6 Spring Corporation sells only one product; sales and purchases occur at a uniform rate throughout the year. The following items appear in the company's financial statements for Year 4:

Purchases	$2,000,000
Cost of goods sold	1,900,000
Inventory, Jan. 1, Year 4 (fifo basis)	520,000
Inventory, Dec. 31, Year 4 (fifo basis)	620,000

A footnote to the financial statements disclosed that the replacement cost of inventory at December 31, Year 4, was $650,000 and that the cost of goods sold computed using replacement costs at the date of sale amounted to $2,150,000.

a Compute the amount of inventory profit included in Spring Corporation's reported income for Year 4.

b Did the number of units in Spring Corporation's inventory increase or decrease during Year 4? Explain your reasoning. (Hint: Was the company's spending for merchandise purchases sufficient to replace the units sold?)

Ex. 9-7 Hale Company has compiled the following information concerning items in its inventory at December 31:

Item	Quantity	Unit Cost Cost (fifo)	Market
A	200	$ 46	$ 50
B	70	160	136
C	62	100	110
D	81	280	290

Determine the total inventory value to appear on Hale Company's balance sheet under the lower-of-cost-or-market rule, assuming (a) that the rule is applied to inventory as a whole and (b) that the rule is applied on an item-by-item basis.

Ex. 9-8 When Helen Long arrived at her store on the morning of January 29, she found empty shelves and display racks; thieves had broken in during the night and stolen the entire inventory. Long's accounting records showed that she had $55,000 inventory on January 1 (cost value). From January 1 to January 29, she had made net sales of $200,000 and net purchases of $141,800. The gross profit during the past several years had consistently averaged 30% of sales. Long wishes to file an insurance claim for the theft loss. You are to use the gross profit method to estimate the cost of her inventory at the time of the theft. Show computations.

Ex. 9-9 Vagabond Shop wishes to determine the approximate month-end inventory using data from the accounting records without taking a physical count of merchandise. From the following information, estimate the cost of the September 30 inventory by the *retail* method of inventory valuation.

	Cost Price	Retail Selling Price
Inventory of merchandise, Aug. 31	$264,800	$400,000
Purchases (net) during September	170,400	240,000
Sales (net) during September		275,200

Ex. 9-10 Santa Cruz Wholesale Company uses a *perpetual inventory system*. On January 1, the Inventory account had a balance of $93,500. During the first few days of January the following transactions occurred:

Jan. 2 Purchased merchandise on credit from Bell Company for $12,500.
Jan. 3 Sold merchandise for cash, $9,000. The cost of this merchandise was $6,300.

a Prepare entries in general journal form to record the above transactions.
b What was the balance of the Inventory account at the close of business January 3?

Ex. 9-11 Coast Bicycle Shop uses the first-in, first-out method of inventory valuation. At the end of the current year the shop had exactly the same number of bicycles in stock as at the beginning of the year, and the same proportion of each model. However, the year had been one of severe inflation and the cost of the ending inventory was shown in the accounts at $36,000 whereas the cost of the beginning inventory had been only $24,000. The net income reported by the shop for the year was $27,000. Comment on the validity of the reported net income and indicate what adjustment might be reasonable to give the owner of this business a realistic picture of the results of the year's operations.

Problems

9-1   Inventory errors: effect on earnings
Financial Fantasy is being offered for sale as a going concern. Its income statements for the last three years include the following key figures:

	Year 3	Year 2	Year 1
Net sales	$430,000	$425,000	$400,000
Cost of goods sold	240,800	243,000	240,000
Gross profit on sales	$189,200	$182,000	$160,000
Gross profit percentage	44%	43%*	40%

* Rounded to nearest full percentage point.

In discussions with prospective buyers, the owners are emphasizing the rising trends of gross profit and gross profit percentage as very favorable factors.

Assume that you are retained by a prospective purchaser of the business to make an investigation of the fairness and reliability of Financial Fantasy accounting records and financial statements. You find everything in order except for the following: (1) The inventory was understated by $12,000 at the end of Year 1 and (2) it was overstated by $21,500 at the end of Year 3. The company uses the periodic inventory system and these errors had not been brought to light prior to your investigation.

Instructions

a Prepare a revised three-year schedule along the lines of the one illustrated above.
b Comment on the trend of gross profit and gross profit percentage before and after the revision.

9-2   Fifo, lifo, average cost
Fluid Power, Inc., derives much of its revenue from the sale of a certain type of valve. During Year 4, the inventory quantities, purchases, and sales of this valve were as follows:

	Number of Units	Cost per Unit	Total Cost
Inventory, Jan. 1, Year 4	8,000	$5.89	$ 47,120
First purchase (Mar. 15)	10,300	6.20	63,860
Second purchase (June 6)	12,400	6.60	81,840
Third purchase (Sept. 20)	9,600	6.80	65,280
Fourth purchase (Dec. 31)	7,700	7.00	53,900
Goods available for sale	48,000		$312,000
Units sold during Year 4	37,200		
Inventory, Dec. 31, Year 4	10,800		

Instructions

a Compute the cost of the December 31, Year 4, inventory and the cost of goods sold for the valves in Year 4 using:
  (1) The first-in, first-out method
  (2) The last-in, first-out method
  (3) The average-cost method

b Which of the three inventory pricing methods provides the most realistic balance sheet valuation of inventory in light of the current replacement cost of the valves? Does this same method also produce the most realistic measure of income in light of the costs being incurred by Fluid Power to replace the valves when they are sold? Explain.

9-3 Gross profit method: fire loss

On May 1 of Year 4, the entire inventory of Sherwood Forest, a wholesaling business, was destroyed by fire. The inventory had been stored in a rented warehouse; the offices occupied by the company were not damaged and the accounting records were intact. Sherwood Forest did not maintain perpetual inventory records, and the last physical inventory taken had been on December 31 of the prior year.

An estimate of the inventory value at May 1, the date of the fire, must be prepared in order to file an insurance claim. The income statement for the prior year is shown below to aid you in estimating the amount of the inventory at the date of the fire. Use the gross profit method.

SHERWOOD FOREST
Income Statement
For the Year Ended December 31, Year 3

Net sales		$738,000
Cost of goods sold:		
Inventory, Jan. 1	$144,000	
Purchases	666,000	
Cost of goods available for sale	$810,000	
Less: Inventory, Dec. 31	234,000	576,000
Gross profit on sales		$162,000
Expenses		72,000
Net income		$ 90,000

Other data. Included in the purchases figure shown in the income statement was $22,500 of office equipment which Sherwood Forest had acquired late in December for its own use from a competing concern which was quitting business. The bookkeeper of Sherwood Forest had not understood the nature of this transaction and had recorded it by debiting the Purchases account. The office equipment, however, was not included in the inventory at December 31, Year 3.

The accounting records revealed the merchandise transactions from December 31, Year 3, to the date of the fire to be: sales, $306,000; sales returns and allowances, $2,700; transportation-in, $1,800; purchases, $196,200; purchase returns and allowances, $3,600.

Instructions

a Prepare a report directed to the insurance adjuster summarizing your findings. Include an estimate of the inventory value as of the date of the fire and a computation of the applicable gross profit rate. (Hint: Make the necessary correction to Year 3 amounts before computing the gross profit percentage for Year 3.)

b Explain how the gross profit method of estimating inventories may be used other than in case of a fire loss.

9-4 Fifo, lifo, average cost: income statement and income tax

Micro Meter, Inc., achieved total sales revenue of $930,000 for the current year. The company sells only one product. The beginning inventory at January 1 of the current year consisted of 15,000 units valued at cost of $112,500. Purchases during the year were as follows: 20,000 units at $7.75; 28,500 units at $8.00; 21,000 units at $8.30; and 15,500 units at $8.40. The ending inventory at December 31 consisted of 22,500 units.

Instructions

a Compute the dollar amount of the year-end (December 31) inventory using:
   (1) The first-in, first-out method
   (2) The last-in, first-out method
   (3) The average-cost method
b Prepare partial income statements for each of the above three methods of pricing inventory. The income statements are to be carried only to the determination of gross profit on sales.
c Which of the three methods of pricing inventory would be most advantageous from an income tax standpoint during a period of rising prices? Comment on the significance of the inventory figure under the method you recommend with respect to current replacement cost.

9-5 Entries for perpetual inventory

Satellite Trackers sells satellite tracking systems for receiving television broadcasts from satellites in outer space. At December 31, Year 1, the company's inventory amounted to $22,000. During the first week of January, the company made only one purchase and one sale. These transactions were as follows:

Jan. 3 Sold one tracking system costing $11,200 to Mystery Mountain Resort for cash, $18,900.
Jan. 6 Purchased merchandise on account from Yamaha, $9,600. Terms, net 30 days.

Instructions

a Prepare journal entries to record these transactions assuming that Satellite Trackers uses the perpetual inventory system. Use separate entries to record the sales revenue and the cost of goods sold for the sale on January 3.
b Compute the balance of the Inventory account on January 7.
c Prepare journal entries to record the two transactions assuming that Satellite Trackers uses the periodic inventory system.
d Compute the cost of goods sold for the first week of January assuming use of a periodic inventory system. Use your answer to part b as the ending inventory.
e Which inventory system do you believe that a company such as Satellite Trackers would probably use? Explain your reasoning.

9-6 Perpetual inventory records in a small business

A perpetual inventory system is used by Gallon-Pak and an inventory record card is maintained for each type of product in stock. The following transactions show the beginning inventory, the purchases, and the sales of product KR9 for the month of May:

May 1 Balance on hand, 20 units, cost $40 each $800
     5 Sale, 8 units, sales price $60 each 480
     6 Purchase, 20 units, cost $45 each 900
    21 Sale, 10 units, sales price $60 each 600
    31 Sale, 15 units, sales price $65 each 975

Instructions

a Record the beginning inventory, the purchases, the cost of goods sold, and the running balance on an inventory record card like the one illustrated on page 373. Use the first-in, first-out method.

b Assume that all sales were made on credit. Compute the total sales and the total cost of goods sold of product KR9 for May. Prepare an entry in general journal form to record these sales and a second entry to record the cost of goods sold for the month of May.

c Compute the gross profit on sales of product KR9 for the month of May.

9-7   Retail inventory method

Madison's, a retail store, carries a wide range of merchandise consisting mostly of articles of low unit price. The selling price of each item is plainly marked on the merchandise. At each year-end, the company has taken a physical count of goods on hand and has priced these goods at cost by looking up individual purchase invoices to determine the unit cost of each item in stock. Stevens, the store manager, is anxious to find a more economical method of assigning dollar values to the year-end inventory, explaining that it takes much more time to price the inventory than to count the merchandise on hand.

By analyzing the accounting records you are able to determine that net purchases of merchandise in Year 4 totaled $1,330,000; the retail selling price of this merchandise was $1,750,000. At the end of Year 4, a physical inventory showed goods on hand priced to sell at $375,000. This represented a considerable increase over the inventory of a year earlier. At December 31, Year 3, the inventory on hand had appeared in the balance sheet at cost of $170,000, although it had a retail value of $250,000.

Instructions

a Outline a plan whereby the inventory can be computed without the necessity of looking up individual purchase invoices. List step by step the procedures to be followed. Ignore the possibility of markups and markdowns in the original retail price of merchandise.

b Compute the cost of the inventory at December 31, Year 4, using the method described in part a.

c Explain how the inventory method you have described can be modified for the preparation of monthly financial statements when no physical count of inventory is taken.

9-8   Effect of cutoff errors on income and owner's equity

The owner's equity as shown in the balance sheets prepared by Ranch Supply for the last three years was as follows: December 31, Year 8, $560,000; December 31, Year 9, $676,500; and December 31, Year 10, $787,800.

The income statements for Years 9 and 10 were as follows:

	Year 10	Year 9
Net sales	$879,500	$835,500
Cost of goods sold:		
Beginning inventory	$123,400	$110,200
Net purchases	540,200	501,200
Cost of goods available for sale	$663,600	$611,400
Ending inventory	140,600	123,400
Cost of goods sold	$523,000	$488,000
Gross profit on sales	$356,500	$347,500
Expenses	245,200	231,000
Net income	$111,300	$116,500

Samuel Peterson, accountant for Ranch Supply, decided early in Year 11 to make a review of the documents and procedures used in taking the physical inventory at December 31, Year 9 and Year 10. His investigation revealed two questionable items as indicated below:

(1) Merchandise shipped to a customer on December 31, Year 9, F.O.B. shipping point, was included in the physical inventory at December 31, Year 9. The cost of the merchandise was $2,800 and the sales price was $4,500. Because of the press of year-end work, the sales invoice was not prepared until January 8, Year 10. On that date the sale was recorded as a January, Year 10, transaction in the sales journal, and the invoice was mailed to the customer.

(2) Merchandise with a cost of $12,200 which had been received on December 31, Year 9, had been included in the inventory taken on that date, although the purchase was not recorded until January 8, Year 10, when the vendor's invoice arrived. The invoice was then recorded in the purchases journal as a January transaction.

Instructions

a Prepare corrected income statements for the periods ended December 31, Year 9 and Year 10. (You may find it helpful to set up T accounts for sales, Year 9, and Sales, Year 10; Purchases, Year 9, and Purchases, Year 10; and Inventory, December 31, Year 9.)

b Compute corrected amounts for owner's equity at December 31, Year 9 and Year 10. (No withdrawals were made by the owner during these two years.)

Cases for analysis

Case 9-1   Specific identification method and managerial decisions

You are the sales manager of Continental Motors, an automobile dealership specializing in European imports. Among the automobiles in Continental Motors' showroom are two Italian sports cars, which are identical in every respect except for color; one is red and the other white. The red car had been ordered last February, at a cost of $13,300 American dollars. The white car had been ordered early last March, but because of a revaluation of the Italian lira relative to the dollar, the white car had cost only $12,000 American dollars. Both cars arrived in the United States on the same boat and had just been delivered to your showroom. Since the cars were identical except for color and both colors were equally popular, you had listed both cars at the same suggested retail price, $18,000.

Smiley Miles, one of your best salesmen, comes into your office with a proposal. He has a customer in the showroom who wants to buy the red car for $18,000. However, when Miles pulled the inventory card on the red car to see what options were included, he happened to notice the inventory card of the white car. Continental Motors, like most automobile dealerships, uses the specific identification method to value inventory. Consequently, Miles noticed that the red car had cost $13,300, while the white one had cost Continental Motors only $12,000. This gave Miles the idea for the following proposal.

"Have I got a deal for you! If I sell the red car for $18,000, Continental Motors makes a gross profit of $4,700. But if you'll let me discount that white car $500, I think I can get my customer to buy that one instead. If I sell the white car for $17,500, the gross profit will be $5,500, so Continental Motors is $800 better off than if I sell the red car for $18,000. Since I came up with this plan, I feel I should get part of the benefit, so Continental Motors should split the extra $800 with me. That way, I'll get an extra $400 commission, and the company still makes $400 more than if I sell the red car."

Instructions

a Prepare a schedule which shows the total revenue, cost of goods sold, and gross profit to Continental Motors if *both* cars are sold for $18,000 each.

b Prepare a schedule showing the revenue, cost of goods sold, and gross profit to Continental Motors if both cars are sold but Miles's plan is adopted and the white car is sold for $17,500. Assume the red car is still sold for $18,000. To simplify comparison of this schedule to the one prepared in part a, include the extra $400 commission to Miles in the cost of goods sold of the part b schedule.

c Write out your decision whether or not to accept Miles's proposal, and explain to Miles why the proposal either would or would not be to the advantage of Continental Motors. (Hint: Refer to your schedules prepared in parts a and b in your explanation.)

Case 9-2   Inventory: target of the IRS

Carla Wilson is an auditor with the Internal Revenue Service. She has been assigned to audit the income tax return of The French Connection, a corporation engaged in selling imported bicycles by mail order. Selected figures from the company's income tax return are shown below.

Sales	$1,200,000
Beginning inventory	30,000
Purchases	885,000
Ending inventory	15,000
Cost of goods sold	900,000
Gross profit	300,000

As Wilson examined these figures, she began to suspect that the income reported by The French Connection had been understated. She sent a letter to the company to arrange a date for performing the tax audit. As part of her preliminary investigation, Wilson then telephoned The French Connection. Pretending to be a customer, she asked what types of bicycles the company had available for immediate delivery. The salesclerk told her that The French Connection had in stock three makes of French bicycles and three lines of Italian bicycles.

Wilson's letter about the tax audit was received by Greg Thomas, the president and owner of The French Connection. The letter made Thomas quite nervous, because over the last five years he had understated the income reported in the company's income tax returns by a total of $100,000. Thomas hurriedly began making his own preparations for the tax audit. These preparations included renting an empty building a few blocks from The French Connection.

When Wilson arrived at The French Connection, she was met by Thomas. Wilson introduced herself and asked to see the company's accounting records. As Thomas was showing her to the company's accounting office, they passed through the bicycle warehouse. Much of the large warehouse was empty, but along one wall were about 50 bicycles. Each had the name "LeMond" written on the frame in bright red letters.

Thomas explained, "Milo LeMond is the finest bicycle maker in all of France. We have the largest selection of his bicycles in the United States."

Wilson asked if the company had more bicycles at another location.

Thomas replied, "No. This is our entire inventory. We stock about 50 bikes. After all, these bikes cost us about $300 each. One of the secrets of success in the mail-order business is not tying up a lot of money in a big inventory. We've cut way back on our inventory over the years — helps keep our costs down."

Wilson's suspicions had been confirmed. She now knew that The French Connection had substantially understated its income. Of course, she would still have to find out by just how much. She felt a little sorry for Thomas. Not only would his company have to face additional taxes and a stiff penalty, but he might be in for a jail sentence. Wilson was sure that the company's understatement of income was no accident — it was a deliberate act of tax evasion, which Thomas was now trying desperately to conceal.

Instructions

a What was it about the figures in The French Connection's income tax return that originally made Wilson suspicious that the company might have understated its income?

b What happened to confirm Wilson's suspicions? Why does she believe that the understatement of income was a deliberate act which Thomas is now attempting to conceal?

c Assume that The French Connection correctly reported all its revenue in its income tax returns. How do you think that Thomas caused the company's income to be understated year after year?

d What do you think Thomas has in the building he rented? Be as specific as possible.

Part Four	Operating assets, long-term liabilities, and owners' equity
Chapter 10	Plant and equipment, depreciation, natural resources, and intangible assets
Chapter 11	Forms of business organization
Chapter 12	Corporations: a closer look
Appendix B	Investments for purposes of control
Appendix C	International accounting and foreign currency translation
Chapter 13	Bonds payable, leases, and other liabilities
Appendix D	Applications of present value

The following section of this text contains four chapters and three appendixes. The four chapters complete our discussion of balance sheet and income statement topics. The appendixes are intended to provide optional coverage of selected special topics. Future chapters do not assume coverage of these appendixes. The chapter on long-term liabilities follows, rather than precedes, the two chapters on owners' equity. This departure from a "balance sheet sequence" of presentation enables us to illustrate the tax advantages of using debt rather than equity to finance expansion.

Chapter 10
Plant and equipment, depreciation, natural resources, and intangible assets

In the first part of Chapter 10, our goal is to define plant and equipment and to explain the principles for determining its cost. Once cost has been recorded, the next step is to allocate this cost of plant and equipment over the years of its use by means of a depreciation program. Various methods of depreciation are then evaluated, as, for example, straight-line, units-of-output, double-declining-balance, and sum-of-the-years'-digits method. The Accelerated Cost Recovery System (ACRS) authorized by the IRS for income tax returns is given special consideration. The final part of the chapter deals with the accounting treatment of natural resources and intangible assets.

After studying
this chapter you
should be able to:
- ✓ Determine the cost of plant assets.
- ✓ Distinguish between capital expenditures and revenue expenditures.
- ✓ Explain the relationship between depreciation and the matching principle.
- ✓ Compute depreciation by the straight-line, units-of-output, declining-balance, sum-of-the-years'-digits, and ACRS methods.
- ✓ Explain why depreciation based upon historical costs may cause an overstatement of profits.
- ✓ Record the sale, trade-in, or scrapping of a plant asset.
- ✓ Account for the depletion of natural resources and the amortization of intangibles.
- ✓ Explain the nature of goodwill and indicate when this asset should appear in the accounting records.

PLANT AND EQUIPMENT

The term *plant and equipment* is used to describe long-lived assets acquired for use in the operation of the business and not intended for resale to customers. Among the more common examples are land, buildings, machinery, furniture and fixtures, office equipment, and automobiles. A delivery truck in the showroom of an automobile dealer is inventory; when this same truck is sold to a drugstore for use in making deliveries to customers, it becomes a unit of plant and equipment.

The term *fixed assets* has long been used in accounting literature to describe all types of plant and equipment. This term, however, has virtually disappeared from the published financial statements of large corporations. *Plant and equipment* appears to be a more descriptive term. Another alternative title used on many corporation balance sheets is *property, plant, and equipment.*

Plant and equipment represent a stream of services to be received

It is convenient to think of a plant asset as a stream of services to be received by the owner over a period of years. Ownership of a delivery truck, for example, may provide about 100,000 miles of transportation. The cost of the delivery truck is customarily entered in a plant and equipment account entitled Delivery Truck, which in essence represents payment in advance for several years of transportation service. Similarly, a building may be regarded as payment in advance for several years' supply of housing services. As the years go by, these services are utilized by the business and the cost of the plant asset is gradually transferred into depreciation expense.

An awareness of the similarity between plant assets and prepaid expenses is essential to an understanding of the accounting process by which the cost of plant assets is allocated to the years in which the benefits of ownership are received.

Major categories of plant and equipment

Plant and equipment items are often classified into the following groups:

1 Tangible plant assets. The term *tangible* denotes physical substance, as exemplified by land, a building, or a machine. This category may be subdivided into two distinct classifications:
   a Plant property subject to depreciation; included are plant assets of limited useful life such as buildings and office equipment.
   b Land. The only plant asset not subject to depreciation is land, which has an unlimited term of existence.
2 Intangible assets. The term *intangible assets* is used to describe assets which are used in the operation of the business but have no physical substance, and are noncurrent. Examples include patents, copyrights, trademarks, franchises, and goodwill. Current assets such as accounts receivable or prepaid rent are not included in the intangible classification, even though they are lacking in physical substance.

Determining the cost of plant and equipment

The cost of plant and equipment includes all expenditures reasonable and necessary in acquiring the asset and placing it in a position and condition for use in the operations of the business. Only *reasonable* and *necessary* expenditures should be included. For example, if the company's truck driver receives a traffic ticket while hauling a new machine to the plant, the traffic fine is *not* part of the cost of the new machine. If the machine is dropped and damaged while being unloaded, the cost of repairing the damage should be recognized as expense in the current period and should *not* be added to the cost of the machine.

Cost is most easily determined when an asset is purchased for cash. The cost of the asset is then equal to the cash outlay necessary in acquiring the asset plus any expenditures for freight, insurance while in transit, installation, trial runs, and any other costs necessary to make *the asset ready for use.* If plant assets are *purchased* on the installment plan or by issuance of notes payable, the interest element or carrying charge should be recorded as interest expense and *not* as part of the cost of the plant assets. However, if a company *constructs* a plant asset for its own use, interest costs incurred *during the construction period* are viewed as part of the cost of the asset.[1]

This principle of including in the cost of a plant asset all the incidental charges necessary to put the asset in use is illustrated by the following example. A factory in Minneapolis orders a machine from a San Francisco tool manufacturer at a list price of $10,000, with terms of 2/10, n/30. Sales tax of $588 must be paid, also freight charges of $1,250. Transportation from the railroad station to the factory costs $150, and installation labor amounts to $400. The cost of the machine to be entered in the Machinery account is computed as follows:

Items included in cost of machine	
List price of machine	$10,000
Less: Cash discount (2% × $10,000)	200
Net cash price	$ 9,800
Sales tax	588
Freight	1,250
Transportation from railroad station to factory	150
Installation labor	400
Cost of machine	$12,188

Why should all the incidental charges relating to the acquisition of a machine be included in its cost? Why not treat these incidental charges as expenses of the period in which the machine is acquired?

The answer is to be found in the basic accounting principle of *matching costs and revenue.* The benefits of owning the machine will be received over a span of years, 10 years, for example. During those 10 years the operation of the machine will contribute to revenue. Consequently, the total costs of the machine should be recorded in the accounts as an asset and allocated against the revenue of the 10 years. All costs incurred in acquiring the machine are costs of the services to be received from using the machine.

Land. When land is purchased, various incidental costs are generally incurred, in addition to the purchase price. These additional costs may include commissions to real estate brokers, escrow fees, legal fees for examining and insuring the title, delinquent taxes paid by the purchaser, and fees for surveying, draining, clearing, and grading the property. All these expenditures become part of the cost of the land.

[1] *FASB Statement No. 34,* "Capitalization of Interest Costs" (Stamford, Conn.: 1979).

Apportionment of a lump-sum purchase. Separate ledger accounts are necessary for land and buildings, because buildings are subject to depreciation and land is not. The treatment of land as a nondepreciable asset is based on the premise that land used as a building site has an unlimited life. When land and building are purchased for a lump sum, the purchase price must be apportioned between the land and the building. An appraisal may be necessary for this purpose. Assume, for example, that land and a building are purchased for a bargain price of $400,000. The apportionment of this cost on the basis of an appraisal may be made as follows:

<table>
<tr><td></td><td>Value per Appraisal</td><td>Percentage of Total</td><td>Apportionment of Cost</td></tr>
<tr><td>Land ....</td><td>$200,000</td><td>40%</td><td>$160,000</td></tr>
<tr><td>Building ....</td><td>300,000</td><td>60%</td><td>240,000</td></tr>
<tr><td>Total ....</td><td>$500,000</td><td>100%</td><td>$400,000</td></tr>
</table>

Apportioning cost between land and building

Sometimes a tract of land purchased as a building site has on it an old building which is not suitable for the buyer's use. The Land account should be charged with the entire purchase price *plus any costs incurred in tearing down or removing the building.* Proceeds received from sale of the materials salvaged from the old building are recorded as a credit in the Land account.

Land improvements. Improvements to real estate such as driveways, fences, parking lots, and sprinkler systems have a limited life and are therefore subject to depreciation. For this reason they should be recorded not in the Land account but in a separate account entitled Land Improvements.

Buildings. Old buildings are sometimes purchased with the intention of repairing them prior to placing them in use. Repairs made under these circumstances are charged to the Buildings account. After the building has been placed in use, ordinary repairs are considered as maintenance expense when incurred.

Capital expenditures and revenue expenditures

Expenditures for the purchase or expansion of plant assets are called *capital expenditures* and are recorded in asset accounts. Expenditures for ordinary repairs, maintenance, fuel, and other items necessary to the ownership and use of plant and equipment are called *revenue expenditures* and are recorded by debits to expense accounts. The charge to an expense account is based on the assumption that the benefits from the expenditure will be used up in the current period, and the cost should therefore be deducted from the revenue of the current period in determining the net income.

A business may purchase many items which will benefit several accounting periods, but which have a relatively low cost. Examples of such items include auto batteries, wastebaskets, and pencil sharpeners. Such items are theoretically capital expenditures, but if they are recorded as assets in the accounting records it will be necessary to compute and record the related depreciation expense in future periods. We have previously mentioned the idea that the extra work involved in developing more precise accounting information should be weighed against the benefits that result. Thus, for reasons of convenience and economy, expenditures which are *not material* in dollar amount are treated in the accounting records as expenses of the current period. In brief, *any material expenditure that will benefit several accounting periods is considered a capital expenditure. Any expenditure that will benefit only the current period or that is not material in amount is treated as a revenue expenditure.*

Many companies develop formal policy statements defining capital and revenue expenditures as a guide toward consistent accounting practice from year to year. These policy statements often set a minimum dollar limit for a capital expenditure (such as $100 or $200).

Effect of errors in distinguishing between capital and revenue expenditures. Because a capital expenditure is recorded by debiting an asset account, the transaction has no immediate effect upon net income. However, the depreciation of the amount entered in the asset account will be reflected as an expense in future periods. A revenue expenditure, on the other hand, is recorded by debiting an expense account and therefore represents an immediate deduction from earnings in the current period.

Assume that the cost of a new delivery truck is erroneously debited to the Repairs Expense account. The result will be to overstate repairs expense, thereby understating the current year's net income. If the error is not corrected, the net income of subsequent years will be overstated because no depreciation expense will be recognized during the years in which the truck is used.

On the other hand, assume that ordinary truck repairs are erroneously debited to the asset account, Delivery Truck. The result will be to understate repairs expense, thereby overstating the current year's net income. If the error is not corrected, the net income of future years will be understated because of excessive depreciation charges based upon the inflated balance of the Delivery Truck account.

These examples indicate that a careful distinction between capital and revenue expenditures is essential to attainment of one of the most fundamental objectives of accounting — the determination of net income for each year of operation of a business.

● **CASE IN POINT** ● During an annual audit of Bowden Company, a CPA firm was reviewing entries in the general journal. An entry that caught the attention of Carol Jones, CPA, consisted of a debit to Office Furniture and a credit to Notes Payable for $52,000. Upon investigation, Jones learned that the transaction involved a hand-carved clock acquired from James Burns, the former president of Bowden Company. Burns's hobby for many years had been the building of hand-carved clocks. At a retirement banquet honoring Burns, Bowden Company had awarded him a $52,000 bonus, represented by the company's 12%, five-year note payable. At the same banquet, Burns had presented Bowden Company with one of his clocks.

Further investigation by Jones indicated that the commercial value of the clock was about $400. Jones therefore advised the company to transfer the $52,000 expenditure out of the Office Furniture account and into Executive Compensation Expense.

DEPRECIATION

Allocating the cost of plant and equipment over the years of use

Plant assets, with the exception of land, are of use to a company for only a limited number of years, and the cost of each plant asset is allocated as expense among the years in which it is used. Accountants use the term *depreciation* to describe this gradual conversion of the cost of a plant asset into expense. Depreciation, as the term is used in accounting, does not mean the decrease in market value of a plant asset over a period of time. *Depreciation means the allocation of the cost of a plant asset to expense in the periods in which services are received from the asset.*

When a delivery truck is purchased, its cost is first recorded as an asset. This cost becomes expense over a period of years through the accounting process of depreciation. On the other hand, when gasoline is purchased for the truck, the price paid for each tankful is immediately recorded as expense. In theory, both outlays (for the truck and for a tank of gas) represent the acquisition of assets. However, since it is reasonable to assume that a tankful of gasoline will be consumed in the accounting period in which it is purchased, we record the outlay for gasoline as an expense immediately. It is important to recognize, however, that *both the outlay for the truck and the payment for the gasoline become expense in the period or periods in which each renders services.*

Depreciation differs from most expenses in that it does not require a cash payment at or near the time it is recorded. The entry to record depreciation (a debit to Depreciation Expense and a credit to Accumulated Depreciation) has no effect on current assets or current liabilities. However, when depreciable assets wear out, a large cash payment must be made in order to replace them.

A separate Depreciation Expense account and a separate Accumulated Depreciation account are generally maintained for each group of depreciable assets such as factory buildings, delivery equipment, and office equipment so that a proper allocation of depreciation expense can be made between functional areas of activity such as sales and manufacturing.

Depreciation not a process of valuation

Accounting records do not purport to show the constantly fluctuating market values of plant and equipment. Occasionally the market value of a building may rise substantially over a period of years because of a change in the price level, or for other reasons. Depreciation is continued, however, regardless of the increase in market value. The accountant recognizes that the building will render useful services for only a limited number of years, and that its full cost must be allocated as expense of those years regardless of fluctuations in market value.

The *book value* or *carrying value* of a plant asset is its cost minus the related accumulated depreciation. Plant assets are shown in the balance sheet at their book values, representing the portion of their cost which will be allocated to expense in future periods. Accumulated depreciation represents the portion of the assets' cost which has already been recognized as expense.

Accumulated depreciation does not consist of cash

Many readers of financial statements who have not studied accounting mistakenly believe that accumulated depreciation accounts represent money accumulated for the purpose of buying new equipment when the present equipment wears out. Perhaps the best way to combat such mistaken notions is to emphasize that a credit balance in an accumulated depreciation account represents the **expired cost** of assets acquired in the past. The amounts credited to the accumulated depreciation account could, as an alternative, have been credited directly to the plant and equipment account. An accumulated depreciation account has a **credit** balance; it does not represent an asset; and it cannot be used in any way to pay for new equipment. To pay for a new plant asset requires cash; the total amount of cash owned by a company is shown by the asset account for cash.

Causes of depreciation

The two major causes of depreciation are physical deterioration and obsolescence.

Physical deterioration. Physical deterioration of a plant asset results from use, and also from exposure to sun, wind, and other climatic factors. When a plant asset has been carefully maintained, it is not uncommon for the owner to claim that the asset is as "good as new." Such statements are not literally true. Although a good repair policy may greatly lengthen the useful life of a machine, every machine eventually reaches the point at which it must be discarded. In brief, the making of repairs does not lessen the need for recognition of depreciation.

Obsolescence. The term **obsolescence** means the process of becoming out of date or obsolete. An airplane, for example, may become obsolete even though it is in excellent physical condition; it becomes obsolete because better planes of superior design and performance have become available.

The usefulness of plant assets may also be reduced because the rapid growth of a company renders such assets inadequate. **Inadequacy** of a plant asset may necessitate replacement with a larger unit even though the asset is in good physical condition. Obsolescence and inadequacy are often closely associated; both relate to the opportunity for economical and efficient use of an asset rather than to its physical condition.

Methods of computing depreciation

There are several alternative methods of computing depreciation. A business need not use the same method of depreciation for all its various assets. For example, a company may use straight-line depreciation on some assets and a declining-balance method for other assets. Furthermore, the methods used for computing depreciation expense in financial statements **may differ** from the methods used in the preparation of the company's income tax return.

Straight-line method. The simplest and most widely used method of computing depreciation is the straight-line method. This method was described in Chapter 3 and has been used repeatedly in problems throughout this book. Under the straight-line method, an equal portion of the cost of the asset is allocated to each period of use; consequently, this method is most appropriate when usage of an asset is fairly uniform from year to year.

The computation of the periodic charge for depreciation is made by deducting the estimated *residual* or *salvage value* from the cost of the asset and dividing the remaining *depreciable cost* by the years of estimated useful life. For example, if a delivery truck has a cost of $20,000, a residual value of $2,000, and an estimated useful life of four years, the annual computation of depreciation expense will be as follows:

$$\frac{\text{Cost} - \text{Residual Value}}{\text{Years of Useful Life}} = \frac{\$20,000 - \$2,000}{4} = \$4,500$$

This same depreciation computation is shown below in tabular form.

<table>
<tr><td>Computing
depreciation by
straight-line method</td><td>Cost of the depreciable asset ....</td><td>$20,000</td></tr>
<tr><td></td><td>Less: Estimated residual value (amount to be realized by sale of asset when it is
      retired from use) ....</td><td>2,000</td></tr>
<tr><td></td><td>Total amount to be depreciated (depreciable cost) ....</td><td>$18,000</td></tr>
<tr><td></td><td>Estimated useful life ....</td><td>4 years</td></tr>
<tr><td></td><td>Depreciation expense each year ($18,000 ÷ 4) ....</td><td>$ 4,500</td></tr>
</table>

The following schedule summarizes the accumulation of depreciation over the useful life of the asset. The amount to be depreciated is $18,000 (cost of $20,000 minus estimated residual value of $2,000).

Depreciation Schedule: Straight-Line Method

Year	Computation	Depreciation Expense	Accumulated Depreciation	Book Value
				$20,000
First	($\frac{1}{4}$ × $18,000)	$ 4,500	$ 4,500	15,500
Second	($\frac{1}{4}$ × $18,000)	4,500	9,000	11,000
Third	($\frac{1}{4}$ × $18,000)	4,500	13,500	6,500
Fourth	($\frac{1}{4}$ × $18,000)	4,500	18,000	2,000
		$18,000		

Constant annual depreciation expense appears in the left margin beside the table.

Depreciation rates for various types of assets can conveniently be stated as percentages. In the above example the asset had an estimated life of four years, so the depreciation expense each year was $\frac{1}{4}$ of the depreciable amount. The fraction "$\frac{1}{4}$" is of course equivalent to an annual rate of 25%. Similarly, a 10-year life indicates a depreciation rate of $\frac{1}{10}$, or 10% and an 8-year life a depreciation rate of $\frac{1}{8}$, or $12\frac{1}{2}$%.

In the preceding illustration we assumed that the company maintained its accounts on a calendar-year basis and that the asset was acquired on January 1, the beginning of the accounting period. If the asset had been acquired sometime during the year, on October 1 for example, it would have been in use for only three months, or $\frac{3}{12}$ of a year. Consequently, the depreciation to be recorded at December 31 would be only $\frac{3}{12}$ of $4,500, or $1,125. Stated more precisely, the depreciation expense in this situation is computed as follows: 25% × $18,000 × $\frac{3}{12}$ = $1,125.

In practice, the possibility of residual value is sometimes ignored and the annual depreciation charge computed by dividing the total cost of the asset by the number of years of estimated useful life. This practice may be justified in those cases in which residual value is not material and is difficult to estimate accurately.

Units-of-output method. For certain kinds of assets, more equitable allocation of the cost can be obtained by dividing the cost (minus salvage value, if significant) by the estimated units of output rather than by the estimated years of useful life. A truck line or bus company, for example, might compute depreciation on its vehicles by a mileage basis. If we assume that the delivery truck in our example has an estimated useful life of 200,000 miles, the depreciation rate per mile of operation is 9 cents ($18,000 ÷ 200,000). This calculation of the depreciation rate may be stated as follows:

$$\frac{\text{Cost} - \text{Residual Value}}{\text{Estimated Units of Output (Miles)}} = \frac{\text{Depreciation per}}{\text{Unit of Output (Mile)}}$$

or

$$\frac{\$20,000 - \$2,000}{200,000 \text{ miles}} = \$0.09 \text{ depreciation per mile}$$

At the end of each year, the amount of depreciation to be recorded would be determined by multiplying the 9-cent rate by the number of miles the truck had operated during the year. This method is suitable only when the total units of output of the asset over its entire useful life can be estimated with reasonable accuracy.

Accelerated depreciation methods. The term *accelerated depreciation* means recognition of relatively large amounts of depreciation in the early years of use and reduced amounts in the later years. Many types of plant and equipment are most efficient when new and therefore provide more and better services in the early years of useful life. If we assume that the benefits derived from owning an asset are greatest in the early years when the asset is relatively new, then the amount of the asset's cost which we allocate as depreciation expense should be greatest in these same early years. This is consistent with the basic accounting concept of matching costs with related revenue. Accelerated depreciation methods are widely used in income tax returns because they reduce the current year's tax burden by recognizing a relatively large amount of depreciation expense.

Declining-balance method. The accelerated depreciation method which allocates the largest portion of the cost of an asset to the early years of its useful life is called *double declining balance*. This method consists of doubling the straight-line depreciation rate and applying this doubled rate to the undepreciated cost (book value) of the asset.

To illustrate, consider our example of the $20,000 delivery truck. The estimated useful life of the truck is four years; therefore, the depreciation rate under the straight-line method would be 25%. To depreciate the automobile by the double-declining-balance method, we double the straight-line rate of 25% and apply the doubled rate of 50% to the book value. Depreciation expense in the first year would then amount to $10,000. In the second year the depreciation expense would drop to $5,000, computed at 50% of the remaining book value of $10,000. In the third year depreciation would be $2,500, and in the fourth year only $1,250. The following table shows the computation of each year's depreciation expense by the declining-balance method:

Depreciation Schedule: Declining-Balance Method

| | | Depreciation | Accumulated | Book |
Year	Computation	Expense	Depreciation	Value
				$20,000
First	(50% × $20,000)	$10,000	$10,000	10,000
Second	(50% × $10,000)	5,000	15,000	5,000
Third	(50% × $ 5,000)	2,500	17,500	2,500
Fourth	(50% × $ 2,500)	1,250	18,750	1,250

Accelerated depreciation: declining-balance

Notice that the estimated residual value of the delivery truck did not enter into the computation of depreciation expense by the declining-balance method. This is because the declining-balance method provides an "automatic" residual value. As long as each year's depreciation expense is equal to only a portion of the undepreciated cost of the asset, the asset will never be entirely written off. However, if the asset has a significant residual value, depreciation should stop at this point. Since our delivery truck has an estimated residual value of $2,000, the depreciation expense for the fourth year should be limited to $500 rather than the $1,250 computed in the table. By limiting the last year's depreciation expense in this manner, the book value of the truck at the end of the fourth year will be equal to its $2,000 estimated residual value.

If the asset in the above illustration had been acquired on October 1 rather than on January 1, depreciation for only three months would be recorded in the first year. The computation would be 50% × $20,000 × $\frac{3}{12}$, or $2,500. For the next calendar year the calculation would be 50% × ($20,000 − $2,500), or $8,750.

Sum-of-the-years'-digits method. This is another method of allocating a large portion of the cost of an asset to the early years of its use. The depreciation rate to be used is a fraction, of which the numerator is the remaining years of useful life (as of the beginning of the year) and the denominator is the sum of the years of useful life. Consider again the example of the delivery truck costing $20,000 having an estimated life of four years and an estimated residual value of $2,000. Since the asset has an estimated life of four years, the denominator of the fraction will be 10, computed as follows:[2] $1 + 2 + 3 + 4 = 10$. For the first year, the depreciation will be $\frac{4}{10}$ × ($20,000 − $2,000), or $7,200. (Notice that we reduced the cost of the truck by the estimated residual value in determining the amount to be depreciated.) For the second year, the depreciation will be $\frac{3}{10}$ × $18,000, or

[2] Alternatively, the denominator may be computed by using the formula $n \left(\dfrac{n+1}{2} \right)$, where n is the useful life of the asset. According to this formula, the sum of the years' digits for an asset with a four-year life is computed as follows: $4 \left(\dfrac{4+1}{2} \right) = 4(2.5) = 10$. Similarly, the sum of the years' digits for an asset with a 10-year life would be computed as follows: $10 \left(\dfrac{10+1}{2} \right) = 10(5.5) = 55$.

$5,400; in the third year $\frac{2}{10} \times$ $18,000, or $3,600; and in the fourth year, $\frac{1}{10} \times$ $18,000, or $1,800. In tabular form, this depreciation program will appear as follows:

Depreciation Schedule: Sum-of-the-Years'-Digits Method

<table>
<tr><th>Year</th><th>Computation</th><th>Depreciation Expense</th><th>Accumulated Depreciation</th><th>Book Value</th></tr>
<tr><td></td><td></td><td></td><td></td><td>$20,000</td></tr>
<tr><td>First ....</td><td>($\frac{4}{10} \times$ $18,000)</td><td>$ 7,200</td><td>$ 7,200</td><td>12,800</td></tr>
<tr><td>Second ....</td><td>($\frac{3}{10} \times$ $18,000)</td><td>5,400</td><td>12,600</td><td>7,400</td></tr>
<tr><td>Third ....</td><td>($\frac{2}{10} \times$ $18,000)</td><td>3,600</td><td>16,200</td><td>3,800</td></tr>
<tr><td>Fourth ....</td><td>($\frac{1}{10} \times$ $18,000)</td><td>1,800</td><td>18,000</td><td>2,000</td></tr>
<tr><td></td><td></td><td>$18,000</td><td></td><td></td></tr>
</table>

Accelerated depreciation: sum of the years' digits

Assume that the asset being depreciated by the sum-of-the-years'-digits method was acquired on October 1 and the company maintains its accounts on a calendar-year basis. Since the asset was in use for only three months during the first accounting period, the depreciation to be recorded in this first period will be for only $\frac{3}{12}$ of a full year, that is, $\frac{3}{12} \times$ $7,200, or $1,800. For the second accounting period the depreciation computation will be:

$\frac{9}{12} \times$ ($\frac{4}{10} \times$ $18,000) $5,400
$\frac{3}{12} \times$ ($\frac{3}{10} \times$ $18,000) 1,350
Depreciation expense, second period $6,750

A similar pattern of allocation will be followed for each accounting period of the asset's life.

Depreciation for fractional periods. When an asset is acquired in the middle of an accounting period, it is not necessary to compute depreciation expense to the nearest day or week. In fact, such a computation would give a misleading impression of great precision. Since depreciation is based upon an estimated useful life of many years, the depreciation applicable to any one year is only an approximation at best.

One widely used method of computing depreciation for part of a year is to round the calculation to the nearest whole month. Thus, if an asset is acquired on July 12, depreciation is computed for the six months beginning July 1. If an asset is acquired on July 16 (or any date in the latter half of July), depreciation is recorded for only five months (August through December) in the current calendar year.

Another acceptable approach, called the **half-year convention,** is to record six months' depreciation on all assets acquired during the year. This approach is based upon the assumption that the actual purchase dates will "average out" to approximately midyear. The half-year convention is widely used for assets such as office equipment, automobiles, and machinery. For buildings, however, income tax rules require that depreciation be computed for the actual number of months that the building is owned.

The half-year convention enables us to treat similar assets acquired at different dates during the year as a single group. For example, assume that an insurance company purchases hundreds of typewriters throughout the current year at a total cost of

$600,000. The company depreciates typewriters by the straight-line method, assuming a five-year life and no residual value. Using the half-year convention, the depreciation expense on all of the typewriters purchased during the year may be computed as follows: $600,000 ÷ 5 years × $\frac{6}{12}$ = $60,000. If we did not use the half-year convention, depreciation would have to be computed separately for typewriters which had been purchased in different months.

Revision of depreciation rates

Depreciation rates are based on estimates of the useful life of assets. These estimates of useful life are seldom precise and sometimes are grossly in error. Consequently, the annual depreciation expense based on the estimated useful life may be either excessive or inadequate. What action should be taken when, after a few years of using a plant asset, it is decided that the asset actually is going to last for a considerably longer or shorter period than was originally estimated? When either of these situation arises, a revised estimate of useful life should be made and the periodic depreciation expense decreased or increased accordingly.

The procedure for correcting the depreciation program is to **spread the remaining undepreciated cost of the asset over the years of remaining useful life.** This correction affects only the amount of depreciation expense that will be recorded in the **current and future periods.** The financial statements of past periods are **not** revised to reflect changes in the estimated useful lives of depreciable assets.

To illustrate, assume that a company acquires a $10,000 asset which is estimated to have a 10-year useful life and no residual value. Under the straight-line method, the annual depreciation expense is $1,000. At the end of the sixth year, accumulated depreciation amounts to $6,000, and the asset has an undepreciated cost (or book value) of $4,000.

At the beginning of the seventh year, it is decided that the asset will last for eight more years. The revised estimate of useful life is, therefore, a total of 14 years. The depreciation expense to be recognized for the seventh year and for each of the remaining years is $500, computed as follows:

Revision of depreciation program

Undepreciated cost at end of sixth year ($10,000 − $6,000)	$4,000
Revised estimate of remaining years of useful life	8 years
Revised amount of annual depreciation expense ($4,000 ÷ 8)	$ 500

Depreciation and income taxes

Different methods of depreciation may be used for the purpose of preparing financial statements and the purpose of preparing income tax returns. Many large corporations use straight-line depreciation in their financial statements, because this permits reporting higher earnings which in turn suggests that management is doing an efficient job. For income tax purposes, however, many businesses use an accelerated depreciation method.

For assets acquired prior to 1981, taxpayers may use such accelerated depreciation methods as double declining balance and sum of the years' digits. For assets acquired after

January 1, 1981, taxpayers are required to use either straight-line depreciation or a special accelerated method called the Accelerated Cost Recovery System in preparing federal income tax returns.

Accelerated Cost Recovery System (ACRS)

ACRS is a depreciation method which allows businesses to depreciate assets in an extremely rapid manner for income tax purposes. By claiming large deductions for depreciation expense in the early years of an asset's life, the business is able to reduce its current income tax burden. Thus, ACRS is intended to create a powerful incentive for businesses to invest in new plant and equipment. This investment, in turn, should create new jobs and stimulate the entire enconomy through higher levels of production.

ACRS speeds up the write-off of the cost of an asset in two ways. First, ACRS designates four "recovery periods" over which the costs of various types of assets are written off. In most cases, these recovery periods are substantially shorter than the useful life of the assets. For example, buildings and land improvements are considered "18-year property," which means that they may be fully depreciated over 18 years. Pipelines, nuclear plants, and amusement parks may be written off over 10 years. Most machinery and equipment is written off over a five-year period. Automobiles, trucks, and some special tools qualify for write-off over only three years.

ACRS also requires the use of an accelerated depreciation rate, similar to the declining-balance rate. The table that follows shows the percentages of an asset's total cost that may be written off in each year of the recovery period.

ACRS Depreciation Rates

	Year	3-Year Property	5-Year Property	10-Year Property	18-Year Property*
Depreciation rates for federal income tax purposes; applicable only to assets purchased after January 1, 1981	1	25%	15%	8%	9%
	2	38	22	14	9
	3	37	21	12	8
	4		21	10	7
	5		21	10	7
	6			10	6
	7			9	5
	8			9	5
	9			9	5
	10			9	5
	11				5
	12				5
	13–18				4
		100%	100%	100%	100%

* Our percentages for 18-year property assume that the asset was purchased in January of the first year. Other tables must be used if the asset was purchased in another month. A complete set of tables is published by the Internal Revenue Service.

To demonstrate the use of the ACRS depreciation table, consider again our example of the delivery truck costing $20,000. We may disregard the estimated four-year useful life; for income tax purposes, trucks are considered three-year property. The depreciation expense that may be reported on the federal income tax return each year is determined as follows:

Truck Depreciation Schedule: ACRS Income Tax Method

Year	Computation	Depreciation Expense	Accumulated Depreciation	Book Value
				$20,000
First	(25% × $20,000)	$ 5,000	$ 5,000	15,000
Second	(38% × $20,000)	7,600	12,600	7,400
Third	(37% × $20,000)	7,400	20,000	– 0 –
		$20,000		

Notice that under ACRS, the truck is depreciated to a book value of zero. ACRS ignores residual values. Also, no fractional-period computations are made in the year of acquisition; the full percentage rate shown in the table is applied regardless of when during the year the asset was acquired.[3] ACRS is used for *income tax purposes only.* If the estimated residual value is material in dollar amount, or if the ACRS recovery period differs substantially from the asset's estimated useful life, the ACRS method is *not acceptable* in financial statements.[4]

Inflation and depreciation

The valuation of plant and equipment on a cost basis and the computation of depreciation in terms of cost will work very well during periods of stable price levels. However, the substantial rise in the price level in recent years has led many government officials and business executives to suggest that a more realistic measurement of net income could be achieved by basing depreciation on the *estimated replacement cost* of plant assets rather than on the original cost of the assets presently in use.

As a specific illustration, assume that a manufacturing company purchased machinery in 1977 at a cost of $1,000,000. Estimated useful life was 10 years and straight-line depreciation was used. During this 10-year period the price level rose sharply. By 1987 the machinery purchased in 1977 was fully depreciated; it was scrapped and replaced by new machinery in 1987. Although the new machines were not significantly different from the old, they cost $3,000,000, or three times as much as the old machinery. Many accountants would argue that the depreciation expense for the 10 years was in reality $3,000,000, because this was the outlay required for new machinery if the company was

---

[3] The depreciation rates shown for the first year in the 3-, 5-, and 10-year property columns of the previous table are based upon the half-year convention. For 18-year property, separate tables are used depending upon the month in which the asset is acquired. Here we illustrate only the table for depreciation of 18-year property acquired in January.

[4] As a matter of convenience, some small businesses use ACRS depreciation in both their income tax returns and their financial statements. In such cases, the financial statements are *not* in conformity with generally accepted accounting principles.

merely to "stay even" in its productive facilities. It also may be argued that reported profits are **overstated** during a period of rising prices if depreciation is based on the lower plant costs of some years ago.

Historical cost versus replacement cost

The above criticism of depreciation accounting based on the historical cost of assets is a convincing one. (**Historical cost** means the cost actually incurred by a company in acquiring an asset, as evidenced by paid checks and other documents.) However, this criticism does not mean that American business is on the verge of abandoning the cost principle in accounting for assets and computing depreciation. To substitute estimated current replacement cost for the historical cost of plant and equipment would create many new difficulties and a great deal of confusion. For many assets, current replacement cost cannot be determined easily or with precision. For example, the current cost of replacing a steel mill with its great variety of complex, made-to-order machinery would involve making many assumptions and unprovable estimates. Or, as another example, consider the difficulty of estimating the replacement cost of a large tract of timber or of a gold mine.

Another difficulty in substituting replacement cost for historical cost of plant assets would be that the whole process of establishing estimated cost data would presumably need to be repeated each year. In contrast, historical cost (which we presently use as the basis of accounting for plant and equipment) is determined at the time of acquiring an asset and remains unchanged throughout the useful life of the asset.

These difficulties connected with the possible adoption of replacement cost as a basis of accounting for assets do not mean that such a change cannot or should not be attempted. However, these difficulties do explain why American business has continued to use historical cost as a primary basis of accounting for assets even during continued inflation.

Disclosure of replacement cost

Persistent inflation has led to criticism that traditional financial statements do not portray adequately the effects of rising prices on earnings or on certain assets. In response, the Financial Accounting Standards Board in **Statement No. 33,** "Financial Reporting and Changing Prices," required large corporations to **disclose** the estimated current replacement cost of plant and equipment.[5] Also required to be disclosed is depreciation expense based on the replacement cost of the assets. **This rule does not mean that replacement cost is to be used instead of historical cost, but rather that additional supplementary information is to be disclosed.** The disclosure can be made in a footnote to the financial statements or as a supplementary section accompanying the financial statements.

DISPOSAL OF PLANT AND EQUIPMENT

When depreciable assets are disposed of at any date other than the end of the year, an entry should be made to record depreciation for the **fraction of the year** ending with the date of

---

[5] *FASB Statement No. 33,* "Financial Reporting and Changing Prices" (Stamford, Conn.: 1979).

disposal. If the half-year convention is in use, six months' depreciation should be recorded on all assets disposed of during the year. In the following illustrations of the disposal of items of plant and equipment, it is assumed that any necessary entries for fractional-period depreciation have been recorded.

As units of plant and equipment wear out or become obsolete, they must be scrapped, sold, or traded in on new equipment. Upon the disposal or retirement of a depreciable asset, the cost of the property is removed from the asset account, and the accumulated depreciation is removed from the related contra-asset account. Assume, for example, that office equipment purchased 10 years ago at a cost of $5,000 has been fully depreciated and is no longer useful. The entry to record the scrapping of the worthless equipment is as follows:

Scrapping fully depreciated asset

Accumulated Depreciation: Office Equipment 5,000
    Office Equipment 5,000
To remove from the accounts the cost and the accumulated depreciation on fully depreciated office equipment now being scrapped. No salvage value.

Once an asset has been fully depreciated, no more depreciation should be recorded on it, even though the property is in good condition and is continued in use. The objective of depreciation is to spread the *cost* of an asset over the periods of its usefulness; in no case can depreciation expense be greater than the amount paid for the asset. When a fully depreciated asset is continued in use beyond the original estimate of useful life, the asset account and the Accumulated Depreciation account should remain in the accounting records without further entries until the asset is retired.

Gains and losses on disposal of plant and equipment

Since the residual value and useful life of plant assets are only estimates, it is not uncommon for plant assets to be sold at a price which differs from their book value at the date of disposal. When plant assets are sold, any gain or loss on the disposal is computed by comparing the *book value with the amount received from the sale.* A sales price in excess of the book value produces a gain; a sales price below the book value produces a loss. These gains or losses, if material in amount, should be shown separately in the income statement in computing the income from operations.

Disposal at a price above book value. Assume that a machine which cost $10,000 and has a book value of $2,000 is sold for $3,000. The journal entry to record this disposal is as follows:

Gain on disposal of - plant asset

Cash 3,000
Accumulated Depreciation: Machinery 8,000
    Machinery 10,000
    Gain on Disposal of Plant Assets 1,000
To record sale of machinery at a price above book value.

Disposal at a price below book value. Now assume that the same machine is sold for $500. The journal entry in this case would be as follows:

Loss on disposal of
plant asset

Cash	500	
Accumulated Depreciation: Machinery	8,000	
Loss on Disposal of Plant Assets	1,500	
Machinery		10,000

To record sale of machinery at a price below book value.

The disposal of a depreciable asset at a price equal to book value would result in neither a gain nor a loss. The entry for such a transaction would consist of a debit to Cash for the amount received, a debit to Accumulated Depreciation for the balance accumulated, and a credit to the asset account for the original cost.

Gains and losses for income tax purposes

Keep in mind that a business may use one depreciation method in its financial statements and another method for income tax purposes. As a result of using different depreciation methods, the asset's book value for income tax purposes may differ from its book value in the financial statements. Since the gain or loss on disposal is determined by comparing the disposal price to the asset's book value, the amount of gain or loss computed for income tax purposes may differ from that reported in the company's financial statements.

To illustrate, assume that a company purchases a small bus for $30,000. For financial statement purposes, the bus will be depreciated over four years by the straight-line method, with an estimated residual value of $10,000. For income tax purposes, however, the bus qualifies as "3-year property" and will be depreciated by the ACRS method. The following schedule indicates the amount of depreciation expense and the book values of the bus at the end of each year for both financial statement purposes and for federal income tax purposes. (The term *basis* is widely used to describe an asset's book value for income tax purposes.)

	For Financial Statements		For Federal Income Taxes	
Date	Depreciation	Book Value	Depreciation	Book Value (or Basis)
Jan. 4, Year 1		$30,000		$30,000
Dec. 31, Year 1	$5,000(1)	25,000	$ 7,500(2)	22,500
Dec. 31, Year 2	5,000	20,000	11,400(3)	11,100
Dec. 31, Year 3	5,000	15,000	11,100(4)	–0–
Dec. 31, Year 4	5,000	10,000	–0–	–0–

(1) ($30,000 − $10,000) × $\frac{1}{4}$
(2) $30,000 × 25% (from ACRS rate table on page 402)
(3) $30,000 × 38%
(4) $30,000 × 37%

Now let us assume that on January 1, Year 3, the bus is sold for $18,000. Since the bus has a book value of $20,000 for financial statement purposes, this transaction results in a $2,000 loss which should be reported in the company's Year 3 income statement. For income tax purposes, however, the bus had a basis (book value) of only $11,100 at December 31, Year 2. Therefore, in the computation of income subject to federal income taxes, the sale of the bus at the beginning of Year 3 for $18,000 results in a $6,900 gain ($18,000 sales price, minus $11,100 basis).

Trading in used assets on new

Certain types of depreciable assets, such as automobiles and office equipment, are customarily traded in on new assets of the same kind. The trade-in allowance granted by the dealer may differ materially from the book value of the old asset. If the dealer grants a trade-in allowance in excess of the book value of the asset being traded in, there is the suggestion of a gain being realized on the exchange. The evidence of a gain is not conclusive, however, because the list price of the new asset may purposely have been set higher than a realistic cash price to permit the offering of inflated trade-in allowances.

For the purpose of determining taxable income, no gain or loss is recognized when a depreciable asset is traded in on another similar asset. The tax regulations provide that *the cost of the new asset shall be the sum of the book value of the old asset traded in plus the additional amount paid or to be paid in acquiring the new asset.*

To illustrate the handling of an exchange transaction in this manner, assume that a delivery truck is acquired at a cost of $8,000. The truck is depreciated on the straight-line basis with the assumption of a five-year life and no salvage value. Annual depreciation expense is ($8,000 ÷ 5), or $1,600. After four years of use, the truck is traded in on a new model having a list price of $10,000. The truck dealer grants a trade-in allowance of $2,400 for the old truck; the additional amount to be paid to acquire the new truck is, therefore, $7,600 ($10,000 list price minus $2,400 trade-in allowance). The **cost basis** of the new truck is computed as follows:

Trade-in: cost of new equipment

Cost of old truck	$8,000
Less: Accumulated depreciation ($1,600 × 4)	6,400
Book value of old truck	$1,600
Add: Cash payment for new truck (list price, $10,000 − $2,400 trade-in allowance)	7,600
Cost basis of new truck	$9,200

The trade-in allowance and the list price of the new truck are not recorded in the accounts; their only function lies in determining the amount which the purchaser must pay in addition to turning in the old truck. The journal entry for this exchange transaction is as follows:

Entry for trade-in

Delivery Truck (new)	9,200	
Accumulated Depreciation: Delivery Truck (old)	6,400	
Delivery Truck (old)		8,000
Cash		7,600

To remove from the accounts the cost of old truck and accumulated depreciation thereon, and to record new truck at cost equal to book value of old truck traded in plus cash paid.

Note that the method used above to record the trade-in of an old productive asset for a new one is different from the usual assumption that the cost of a newly acquired asset is equal to its implied cash price. The reason for not recognizing a gain on a trade-in is that revenue is not realized merely by the act of substituting a new productive asset for an old one. Revenue flows from the production and sale of the goods or services which the productive asset makes possible.[6]

Financial accounting principles and income tax regulations are alike in not recognizing a *gain* on a trade-in, they differ in the case of a trade-in which involves a material *loss.* Tax regulations do not permit recognition of the loss, but for financial statements *the loss should be recognized.* For example, assume that a company received a trade-in allowance of only $10,000 for old machinery which has a book value of $100,000. A journal entry illustrating this situation follows:

Machinery (new)	600,000	
Accumulated Depreciation: Machinery (old)	300,000	
Loss on Trade-in of Plant Assets	90,000	
Machinery (old)		400,000
Cash		590,000

To recognize for financial reporting purposes a material loss on trade-in of machinery. Loss not recognized in determining taxable income.

If a trade-in transaction involved only a very small loss, most companies would probably follow the income tax rules and not recognize the loss. This treatment would eliminate the need for a double record of depreciable assets and depreciation expense; the departure from financial accounting rules would be permissible if the amount of the loss was not material.

NATURAL RESOURCES

Accounting for natural resources

Mining properties, oil and gas reserves, and tracts of standing timber are leading examples of natural resources or "wasting assets." The distinguishing characteristics of these assets are that they are physically consumed and converted into inventory. Theoretically, a coal mine might be regarded as an underground "inventory" of coal; however, such an "inventory" is certainly not a current asset. In the balance sheet, mining property and other natural resources are classified as property, plant, and equipment.

We have explained that plant assets such as buildings and equipment depreciate because of physical deterioration or obsolescence. A mine or an oil reserve does not "depreciate" for these reasons, but it is gradually *depleted* as the natural resource is removed from the ground. Once all of the coal has been removed from a coal mine, for example, the mine is "fully depleted" and will be abandoned or sold for its residual value.

To illustrate the depletion of a natural resource, assume that Rainbow Minerals pays $10,500,000 to acquire the Red Valley Mine, which is believed to contain 10 million tons of coal. The residual value of the mine after all of the coal is removed is estimated to be

[6] *APB Opinion No. 29,* "Accounting for Nonmonetary Transactions, AICPA (New York: 1973).

$500,000. The depletion that will occur over the life of the mine is the original cost minus the residual value, or $10,000,000. This depletion will occur at the rate of $1 per ton ($10,000,000 ÷ 10 million tons) as the coal is removed from the mine. If we assume that 2 million tons are mined during the first year of operations, the entry to record the depletion of the mine would be as follows:

Recording depletion

Depletion of Coal Deposits	2,000,000	
Accumulated Depletion: Red Valley Mine		2,000,000

To record depletion of the Red Valley Mine for the year; 2,000,000 tons mined @ $1 per ton.

Accumulated Depletion is a contra-asset account similar to the Accumulated Depreciation account; it represents the portion of the mine which has been used up (depleted) to date. In Rainbow Mineral's balance sheet, the Red Valley Mine now appears as follows:

Property, Plant, & Equipment:

Mining properties: Red Valley Mine	$10,500,000	
Less: Accumulated depletion	2,000,000	$8,500,000

The Depletion of Coal Deposits account may be viewed as similar to the Purchases account of a merchandising business. This account is added to any other mining costs and any beginning inventory of coal to arrive at the cost of goods (coal) available for sale. If all of the coal has been sold by year-end, these costs are deducted from revenue as the cost of goods sold. If some of the coal is still on hand at year-end, a portion of these costs should be assigned to the ending inventory of coal, which is a current asset.

Percentage depletion versus cost depletion. For the determination of taxable income, the Internal Revenue Code permits a deduction for depletion expense equal to a specified *percentage of the revenue* from production from a few mineral deposits such as gold, silver, lead, and zinc ore. Depletion computed as a percentage of revenue *is used only for income tax purposes, not for financial statements.* In terms of generally accepted accounting principles, depletion is always based on the *cost* of the mine or other natural resource.

Depreciation of buildings and equipment closely related to natural resources. Buildings and equipment installed at a mine or drilling site may be useful only at that particular location. Consequently, such assets should be depreciated over their normal useful lives, or over the life of the natural resource, *whichever is shorter.* Often depreciation on such assets is computed using the units-of-output method, thus relating the depreciation expense to the rate at which units of the natural resource are removed.

INTANGIBLE ASSETS

Characteristics

As the word *intangible* suggests, assets in this classification have no physical substance. Leading examples are goodwill, patents, and trademarks. Intangible assets are classified in the balance sheet as a subgroup of plant assets. However, not all assets which lack physical substance are regarded as intangible assets. An account receivable, for example, or a short-term prepayment is of nonphysical nature but is classified as a current asset and is not regarded as an intangible. In brief, *intangible assets are assets which are used in the operation of the business but which have no physical substance and are noncurrent.*

The basis of valuation for intangible assets is cost. In some companies, certain intangible assets such as trademarks may be of great importance but may have been acquired without the incurring of any cost. An intangible asset should appear in the balance sheet *only* if a cost of acquisition or development has been incurred.

Operating expenses versus intangible assets

Many types of expenditures offer at least a half promise of yielding benefits in subsequent years, but the evidence is so doubtful and the period of usefulness so hard to define that most companies treat these expenditures as expense when incurred. Another reason for charging these outlays to expense is the practical difficulty of separating them from the recurring expenses of current operations.

Examples are the expenditures for intensive advertising campaigns to introduce new products, and the expense of training employees to work with new types of machinery or office equipment. There is little doubt that some benefits from these outlays continue beyond the current period, but because of the uncertain duration of the benefits, it is almost universal practice to treat expenditures of this nature as expense of the current period.

Amortization

The term *amortization* is used to describe the write-off to expense of the cost of an intangible asset over its useful life. The usual accounting entry for amortization consists of a debit to Amortization Expense and a credit to the intangible asset account. There is no theoretical objection to crediting an accumulated amortization account rather than the intangible asset account, but this method is seldom encountered in practice.

Although it is difficult to estimate the useful life of an intangible such as a trademark, it is highly probable that such an asset will not contribute to future earnings on a permanent basis. The cost of the intangible asset should, therefore, be deducted from revenue during the years in which it may be expected to aid in producing revenue. Under the current rules of the Financial Accounting Standards Board, the maximum period for amortization of an intangible asset cannot exceed 40 years.[7] The straight-line method of amortization is generally used for intangible assets.

Goodwill

Business executives used the term *goodwill* in a variety of meanings before it became part of accounting terminology. One of the most common meanings of goodwill in a nonac-

---

[7] *APB Opinion No. 17,* "Intangible Assets," AICPA (New York: 1970), par. 29.

counting sense concerns the benefits derived from a favorable reputation among cus-tomers. To accountants, however, goodwill has a very specific meaning not necessarily limited to customer relations. It means the ***present value of future earnings in excess of the normal return on net identifiable assets.*** Above-average earnings may arise not only from favorable customer relations but also from such factors as superior manage-ment, manufacturing efficiency, and weak competition.

The phrase ***normal return on net identifiable assets*** requires explanation. Net assets means the owners' equity in a business, or assets minus liabilities. Goodwill, however, is not an ***identifiable*** asset. The existence of goodwill is implied by the ability of a business to earn an above-average return; however, the cause and precise dollar value of goodwill are largely matters of personal opinion. Therefore, ***net identifiable assets*** means all assets except goodwill, minus liabilities. A ***normal return*** on net identifiable assets is the rate of return which investors demand in a particular industry to justify their buying a business at the ***fair market value*** of its net identifiable assets. A business has goodwill when investors will pay a higher price because the business earns more than the normal rate of return.

Assume that two businesses in the same line of trade are offered for sale and that the normal return on the fair market value of net identifiable assets in this industry is 15% a year. The relative earning power of the two companies during the past five years is shown below:

	Company X	Company Y
Fair market value of net identifiable assets	$1,000,000	$1,000,000
Normal rate of return on net assets	15%	15%
Average net income for past five years	$ 150,000	$ 190,000
Normal earnings, computed as 15% of net identifiable assets ...	150,000	150,000
Earnings in excess of normal	$ -0-	$ 40,000

An investor would be willing to pay $1,000,000 to buy Company X, because Company X earns the normal 15% return which justifies the fair market value of its net identifiable assets. Although Company Y has the same amount of net identifiable assets, an investor would be willing to pay ***more*** for Company Y than for Company X because Company Y has a record of superior earnings which will presumably continue for some time in the future. The extra amount that a buyer would pay to purchase Company Y represents the value of Company Y's goodwill.

Estimating goodwill. How much will an investor pay for goodwill? Above-average earn-ings in past years are of significance to prospective purchasers only if they believe that these earnings will continue after they acquire the business. Investors' appraisals of goodwill, therefore, will vary with their estimates of the future earning power of the business. Very few businesses, however, are able to maintain above-average earnings for more than a few years. Consequently, the purchaser of a business will usually limit any amount paid for goodwill to not more than four or five times the amount by which annual earnings exceed normal earnings.

Arriving at a fair value for the goodwill of a going business is a difficult and subjective process. Any estimate of goodwill is in large part a matter of personal opinion. The following are several methods which a prospective purchaser might use in estimating a value for goodwill:

1 Negotiated agreement between buyer and seller of the business may be reached on the amount of goodwill. For example, it might be agreed that the fair market value of net identifiable assets is $1,000,000 and that the total purchase price for the business will be $1,180,000, thus providing a $180,000 payment for goodwill.

2 Goodwill may be determined as a multiple of the amount by which average annual earnings exceed normal earnings. Referring to our example involving Company Y, a prospective buyer may be willing to pay four times the amount by which average earnings exceed normal earnings, indicating a value of $160,000 (4 × $40,000) for goodwill. The purchase price of the business, therefore, would be $1,160,000.

The multiple applied to the excess annual earnings will vary widely from perhaps 1 to 10. An investor who pays four times the excess earnings for goodwill must, of course, expect these earnings to continue for at least four years.

3 Goodwill may be estimated by *capitalizing* the amount by which average earnings exceed normal earnings. Capitalizing an earnings stream means dividing those earnings by the investor's required rate of return. The result is the maximum amount which the investor could pay for the earnings and have them represent the required rate of return on the investment. To illustrate, assume that the prospective buyer decides to capitalize the $40,000 annual excess earnings of Company Y at a rate of 20%. This approach results in a $200,000 estimate ($40,000 ÷ .20 = $200,000) for the value of goodwill. (Note that $40,000 per year represents a 20% return on a $200,000 investment.)

A weakness in the capitalization method is that *no provision is made for the recovery* of the investment. If the prospective buyer is to earn a 20% return on the $200,000 investment in goodwill, either the excess earnings must continue *forever* (an unlikely assumption) or the buyer must be able to recover the $200,000 investment at a later date by selling the business at a price above the fair market value of net identifiable assets.

Recording goodwill in the accounting records. Goodwill is recorded in the accounting records *only when it is purchased;* this situation usually occurs only when a going business is purchased in its entirety. After the fair market values of all identifiable assets have been recorded in the accounting records of the new owners, any additional amount paid for the business may properly be debited to an asset account entitled Goodwill. This intangible asset must then be amortized over a period not to exceed 40 years, although a much shorter amortization period usually is appropriate.

Many businesses have never purchased goodwill but have generated it internally through developing good customer relations, superior management, or other factors which result in above-average earnings. Because there is no objective means of determining the dollar value of goodwill unless the business is sold, internally developed goodwill is *not recorded* in the accounting records. Thus, goodwill may be a very important asset of a successful business but may not even appear in the company's balance sheet.

Patents

A patent is an exclusive right granted by the federal government for manufacture, use, and sale of a particular product. The purpose of this exclusive grant is to encourage the invention of new machines and processes. When a company acquires a patent by purchase from the inventor or other holder, the purchase price should be recorded by debiting the intangible asset account Patents.

Patents are granted for a period of 17 years, and the period of amortization must not exceed that period. However, if the patent is likely to lose its usefulness in less than 17 years, amortization should be based on the shorter period of estimated useful life. Assume that a patent is purchased from the inventor at a cost of $100,000, after five years of the legal life have expired. The remaining *legal* life is, therefore, 12 years, but if the estimated *useful* life is only four years, amortization should be based on this shorter period. The entry to be made to record the annual amortization expense would be:

Entry for amortization of patent

Amortization Expense: Patents	25,000	
Patents		25,000

To amortize cost of patent on a straight-line basis and estimated life of four years.

Trademarks and trade names

Coca-Cola's distinctive bottle was for years the classic example of a trademark known around the world. A trademark is a word, symbol, or design that identifies a product or group of products. A permanent exclusive right to the use of a trademark, brand name, or commercial symbol may be obtained by registering it with the federal government. The costs of developing a trademark or brand name often consists of advertising campaigns which should be treated as expense when incurred. If a trademark or trade name is purchased, however, the cost may be substantial. Such cost should be capitalized and amortized to expense over a period of not more than 40 years. If the use of the trademark is discontinued or its contribution to earnings becomes doubtful, any unamortized cost should be written off immediately.

Franchises

A franchise is a right granted by a company or a governmental unit to conduct a certain type of business in a specific geographical area. An example of a franchise is the right to operate a McDonald's restaurant in a specific neighborhood. The cost of franchises varies greatly and often may be quite substantial. When the cost of a franchise is small, it may be charged immediately to expense or amortized over a short period such as five years. When the cost is substantial, amortization should be based upon the life of the franchise (if limited); the amortization period, however, may not exceed 40 years.

Copyrights

A copyright is an exclusive right granted by the federal government to protect the production and sale of literary or artistic materials for the life of the creator plus 50 years.

The cost of obtaining a copyright in some cases is minor and therefore is chargeable to expense when paid. Only when a copyright is purchased will the expenditure be material enough to warrant its being capitalized and spread over the useful life. The revenue from copyrights is usually limited to only a few years, and the purchase cost should, of course, be amortized over the years in which the revenue is expected.

Other intangibles and deferred charges

Many other types of intangible assets are found in the published balance sheets of large corporations. Some examples are formulas, processes, name lists, and film rights.

Intangibles, particularly those with limited lives, are sometimes classified as "deferred charges" in the balance sheet. A **deferred charge** is an expenditure that is expected to yield benefits for several accounting periods, and should be amortized over its estimated useful life. Included in this category are such items as bond issuance costs, plant rearrangement and moving costs, start-up costs, and organization costs. The distinction between intangibles and deferred charges is not an important one; both represent a "stream of services" in the form of long-term prepayments awaiting allocation to those accounting periods in which the services will be consumed.

Research and development (R&D) costs

The spending of billions of dollars a year on research and development leading to all kinds of new products is a striking characteristic of American industry. In the past, some companies treated all research and development costs as expense in the year incurred; other companies in the same industry recorded these costs as intangible assets to be amortized over future years. This diversity of practice prevented the financial statements of different companies from being comparable.

The lack of uniformity in accounting for R&D was ended when the Financial Accounting Standards Board ruled that all research and development expenditures should be charged to expense when incurred.[8] This action by the FASB had the beneficial effect of reducing the number of alternative accounting practices and helping to make financial statements of different companies more comparable. However, the FASB's decision was very controversial. Critics argued that a policy of reducing current earnings for all R&D expenditures might discourage companies from undertaking large R&D programs.

The controversy over the FASB's position on R&D expenditures raises an interesting question about the formulation of accounting standards: Is it possible for accounting standards to **describe** economic activity without also **influencing** that activity?

Key terms introduced or emphasized in chapter 10

Accelerated Cost Recovery System (ACRS). An accelerated depreciation method for depreciating assets acquired after January 1, 1981, for federal income tax reporting. All assets are fully

---

[8] *FASB Statement No. 2,* "Accounting for Research and Development Costs" (Stamford, Conn.: 1974), par. 12.

depreciated over a period of 3, 5, 10, or 18 years. The method is *not* used in financial statements prepared in accordance with generally accepted accounting principles.

Accelerated depreciation. Methods of depreciation that call for recognition of relatively large amounts of depreciation in the early years of an asset's useful life and relatively small amounts in the later years.

Amortization. The systematic write-off to expense of the cost of an intangible asset over the periods of its economic usefulness.

Book value. The cost of a plant asset minus the total recorded depreciation, as shown by the Accumulated Depreciation account. The remaining undepreciated cost is also known as *carrying value*.

Capital expenditure. A cost incurred to acquire a long-lived asset. An expenditure that will benefit several accounting periods.

Declining-balance depreciation. An accelerated method of depreciation in which the rate is a multiple of the straight-line rate, which is applied each year to the *undepreciated cost* of the asset. Most commonly used is double the straight-line rate.

Deferred charge. An expenditure expected to yield benefits for several accounting periods and therefore capitalized and written off during the periods benefited.

Depletion. Allocating the cost of a natural resource to the units removed as the resource is mined, pumped, cut, or otherwise consumed.

Depreciation. The systematic allocation of the cost of an asset to expense over the years of its estimated useful life.

Goodwill. The present value of expected future earnings of a business in excess of the earnings normally realized in the industry. Recorded when a business entity is purchased at a price in excess of the fair value of its net identifiable assets (excluding goodwill) less liabilities.

Half-year convention. The practice of taking six months' depreciation in the year of acquisition and the year of disposition, rather than computing depreciation for partial periods to the nearest month. This method is widely used and is acceptable for both income tax reporting and financial reports, as long as it is applied to *all* assets of a particular type acquired during the year. The half-year convention generally is *not* used for buildings.

Intangible assets. Those assets which are used in the operation of a business but which have no physical substance and are noncurrent.

Natural resources. Mines, oil fields, standing timber, and similar assets which are physically consumed and converted into inventory.

Net identifiable assets. Total of all assets *except goodwill* minus liabilities.

Percentage depletion. For income tax purposes only, a deduction for depletion expense equal to a specified percentage of the revenue from a natural resource. Eliminated or reduced by recent legislation.

Replacement cost. The estimated cost of replacing an asset at the current balance sheet date. Disclosure of such data is required of large companies.

Residual (salvage) value. The portion of an asset's cost expected to be recovered through sale or trade-in of the asset at the end of its useful life.

Revenue expenditure. Any expenditure that will benefit only the current accounting period.

Straight-line depreciation. A method of depreciation which allocates the cost of an asset (minus any residual value) equally to each year of its useful life.

Sum-of-years'-digits depreciation. An accelerated method of depreciation. The depreciable cost is multiplied each year by a fraction of which the numerator is the remaining years of useful life (as of the beginning of the current year) and the denominator is the sum of the years of useful life.

Units-of-output depreciation. A depreciation method is which cost (minus residual value) is divided by the estimated units of lifetime output. The unit depreciation cost is multiplied by the actual units of output each year to compute the annual depreciation expense.

Demonstration problem for your review

The ledger of Cypress Company contained an account entitled Property, which had been used to record a variety of expenditures. At the end of Year 6, the Property account contained the following entries:

Debit entries:

1/10	Purchase for cash of building site	$200,000
2/4	Cost of removing old building from site	8,000
9/30	Paid contract price for new building completed today	560,000
9/30	Insurance, inspection fees, and other costs directly related to construction of new building	18,000
	Total debits	$786,000

Credit entries:

2/4	Proceeds from sale of salvaged material from demolition of old building	$ 3,000	
12/31	Depreciation for Year 6, computed at 4% of balance in Property account ($783,000). Debit was to Depreciation Expense	31,320	
	Total credits		34,320
12/31	Balance in Property account at year-end		$751,680

Instructions

a List the errors made in the application of accounting principles or practices by Cypress Company.

b Prepare a compound correcting journal entry at December 31, Year 6, assuming that the estimated life of the new building is 25 years and that depreciation is to be recognized for three months of Year 6 using the straight-line method. The accounts have not been closed for Year 6.

Solution to demonstration problem

a Errors in accounting principles or practices were:

(1) Including land (a nondepreciable asset) in the same account with building (a depreciable asset)

(2) Using the total of land and building as a base for applying the depreciation rate on building

(3) Recording a full year's depreciation on a new building that was in use only the last three months of the year

(4) Crediting the depreciation for the period directly to the asset account (Property) rather than to a contra-asset account (Accumulated Depreciation: Building)

b   **Correcting Journal Entry**

Year 6

Dec. 31 Land 205,000
         Building 578,000
             Property   751,680
             Accumulated Depreciation: Building   5,780
             Depreciation Expense   25,540
         To correct the accounts reflecting land, building, and
         depreciation in accordance with the computations shown in
         the following schedule:

	Land	Building
Amount paid to acquire building site	$200,000	
Cost of removing old building from site	8,000	
Less: Proceeds from salvaged materials	(3,000)	
Contract price for new building		$560,000
Insurance, inspection fees, and other costs directly related to		
construction of new building		18,000
Totals	$205,000	$578,000

Depreciation: $578,000 \times 4\% \times \frac{3}{12} = \underline{\$5,780}$

Correction of depreciation expense: $31,320 - \$5,780 = \underline{\$25,540}$

Review questions

1 Which of the following characteristics would prevent an item from being included in the classification of plant and equipment? (a) Intangible, (b) limited life, (c) unlimited life, (d) held for sale in the regular course of business, (e) not capable of rendering benefits to the business in the future.

2 The following expenditures were incurred in connection with a large new machine acquired by a metals manufacturing company. Identify those which should be included in the cost of the asset. (a) Freight charges, (b) sales tax on the machine, (c) payment to a passing motorist whose car was damaged by the equipment used in unloading the machine, (d) wages of employees for time spent in installing and testing the machine before it was placed in service, (e) wages of employees assigned to lubrication and minor adjustments of machine one year after it was placed in service.

3 What is the distinction between a *capital expenditure* and a *revenue expenditure?*

4 If a capital expenditure is erroneously treated as a revenue expenditure, will the net income of the current year be overstated or understated? Will this error have any effect upon the net income reported in future years? Explain.

5 Which of the following statements best describes the nature of depreciation?
   a Regular reduction of asset value to correspond to the decline in market value as the asset ages.

  b A process of correlating the carrying value of an asset with its gradual decline in physical efficiency.

  c Allocation of cost in a manner that will ensure that plant and equipment items are not carried on the balance sheet at amounts in excess of net realizable value.

  d Allocation of the cost of a plant asset to the periods in which services are received from the asset.

6 Should depreciation continue to be recorded on a building when ample evidence exists that the current market value is greater than original cost and that the rising trend of market values is continuing? Explain.

7 What connection exists between the choice of a depreciation method used to depreciate expensive new machinery for income tax reporting and the amount of income taxes payable in the near future?

8 Criticize the following quotation:

  "We shall have no difficulty in paying for new plant assets needed during the coming year because our estimated outlays for new equipment amount to only $80,000, and we have more than twice that amount in our depreciation reserves at present."

9 A factory machine acquired at a cost of $94,200 was to be depreciated by the sum-of-the-years'-digits method over an estimated life of eight years. Residual salvage value was estimated to be $15,000. State the amount of depreciation during the first year and during the eighth year.

10 After four years of using a machine acquired at a cost of $15,000, Ohio Construction Company determined that the original estimated life of 10 years had been too short and that a total useful life of 12 years was a more reasonable estimate. Explain briefly the method that should be used to revise the depreciation program, assuming that straight-line depreciation has been used. Assume that the revision is made after recording depreciation and closing the accounts at the end of four years of use of the machine.

11 a Give some reasons why a company may change its depreciation policy for financial reporting purposes from an accelerated depreciation method to the straight-line method.

  b Is it possible for a corporation to use accelerated depreciation for income tax purposes and straight-line depreciation for financial reporting purposes?

12 What is *ACRS?* Can it be applied to all assets? Why is ACRS not generally considered acceptable for use in financial statements? Are there any circumstances under which ACRS would conform to generally accepted accounting principles?

13 Explain two approaches to computing depreciation for the fractional period in the year in which an asset is purchased. (Neither of your approaches should require the computation of depreciation to the nearest day or week.)

14 Explain what is meant by the following quotation: "In periods of rising prices companies do not recognize adequate depreciation expense, and reported corporate profits are substantially overstated."

15 Century Company traded in its old computer on a new model. The trade-in allowance for the old computer is greater than its book value. Should Century Company recognize a gain on the exchange in computing its taxable income or in determining its net income for financial reporting? Explain.

16 Newton Products purchased for $2 million a franchise making it the exclusive distributor of Gold Creek Beer in three western states. This franchise has an unlimited legal life and may be sold by Newton Products to any buyer who meets with Gold Creek Beer's approval. The accountant at Newton Products believes that this franchise is a permanent asset, which should appear in the company's balance sheet indefinitely at $2 million, unless it is sold. Is this treatment in conformity with generally accepted accounting principles, as prescribed by the FASB?

17 Lead Hill Corporation recognizes $1 depletion for each ton of ore mined. During the current

year the company mined 600,000 tons but sold only 500,000 tons, as it was attempting to build up inventories in anticipation of a possible strike by employees. How much depletion should be deducted from revenue of the current year?

18 Define **intangible assets.** Would an account receivable arising from a sale of merchandise under terms of 2/10, n/30 qualify as an intangible asset under your definition?

19 Over what period of time should the cost of various types of intangible assets be amortized by regular charges against revenue? (Your answer should be in the form of a principle or guideline rather than a specific number of years.) What method of amortization is generally used?

20 Several years ago March Metals purchased for $120,000 a well-known trademark for padlocks and other security products. After using the trademark for three years, March Metals discontinued it altogether when the company withdrew from the lock business and concentrated on the manufacture of aircraft parts. Amortization of the trademark at the rate of $3,000 a year is being continued on the basis of a 40-year life, which the owner of March Metals says is required by accounting standards. Do you agree? Explain.

21 Under what circumstances should **goodwill** be recorded in the accounts?

22 In reviewing the financial statements of Digital Products Co. with a view to investing in the company's stock, you notice that net tangible assets total $1 million, that goodwill is listed at $400,000, and that average earnings for the past five years have been $50,000 a year. How would these relationships influence your thinking about the company?

Exercises

Ex. 10-1   Lane Corporation purchased machinery with a list price of $54,000. The vendor's invoice specified credit terms of 2/10, n/30, and included sales tax of $2,646. Lane paid the invoice within the discount period. Lane also paid inbound transportation charges of $645 on the new machines as well as labor cost of $1,140 to install the machines in various locations. During the process of unloading and installation, one of the machines fell from a loading platform and was damaged. The repairs required on the damaged machine cost $3,270.

After the machines had been in operation for three months, they were thoroughly cleaned and lubricated at a cost of $390. You are to prepare a list of the amounts which should be capitalized by debit to the Machinery account. Show the total cost of the new machines.

Ex. 10-2   Identify the following expenditures as capital expenditures or revenue expenditures:

a Purchased new battery at a cost of $40 for two-year-old delivery truck.

b Installed an escalator at a cost of $12,500 in a three-story building which had previously been used for some years without elevators or escalators.

c Purchased a pencil sharpener at a cost of $3.50.

d Immediately after acquiring a new delivery truck at a cost of $5,500, paid $125 to have the name of the store and other advertising material painted on the truck.

e Painted delivery truck at a cost of $175 after two years of use.

f Original life of the delivery truck had been estimated as four years and straight-line depreciation of 25% yearly had been recognized. After three years' use, however, it was decided to recondition the truck thoroughly, including a new engine and transmission, at a cost of $4,000. By making this expenditure it was believed that the useful life of the truck would be extended from the original estimate of four years to a total of six years.

Ex. 10-3   During the current year, Airport Auto Rentals purchased 60 new automobiles at a cost of $9,200 per car. The cars will be sold to a wholesaler at an estimated $3,700 each as soon as they have been driven 50,000 miles. Airport Auto Rentals computes depreciation expense on its automobiles by the units-of-output method, based upon mileage.

Instructions

a Compute the amount of depreciation to be recognized for each mile that a rental automobile is driven.

b Assuming that the 60 rental cars are driven a total of 1,650,000 miles during the current year, compute the total amount of depreciation expense that Airport Auto Rentals should recognize on this fleet of cars for the year.

Ex. 10-4   Machinery with an estimated useful life of five years was acquired by VPI Industries at a cost of $55,000. The estimated residual value of the machinery is $6,000. Compute the annual depreciation on this machinery for each of the five years using the double-declining-balance method. Limit the depreciation recognized in the fifth year to an amount that will cause the book value of the machinery to equal the estimated $6,000 residual value at year-end.

Ex. 10-5   On January 2, Bartel Company acquired a machine at a cost of $14,000. The machine is expected to have a useful life of five years with a residual value of $2,000. You are to compute the annual depreciation on the machine in each of the five years of its useful life using the sum-of-the-years'-digits method. (One full year's depreciation will be taken each year.)

Ex. 10-6   Rex Company traded in an old machine on a similar new one. The original cost of the old machine was $30,000 and the accumulated depreciation was $24,000. The list price of the new machine was $40,000 and the trade-in allowance was $8,000. What amount must Rex pay? Compute the indicated gain or loss (regardless of whether it should be recorded in the accounts). Compute the cost basis of the new machine to be used in figuring depreciation for determination of income subject to federal income tax.

Ex. 10-7   On January 4, Year 1, equipment was acquired at a cost of $40,000. For income tax purposes, the equipment qualifies as "5-year property" and is depreciated by the ACRS method. After three full years of use, the equipment was sold for $19,200. Compute (a) the income tax basis of the equipment at the date of disposal, and (b) the gain or loss on the disposal to be reported for income tax purposes.

Ex. 10-8   On June 3, Year 1, Standard Tire Company purchased equipment at a cost of $300,000. The useful life of the equipment was estimated at six years and the residual value at $30,000. Compute the depreciation expense to be recognized in each calendar year during the life of the equipment under each of the following methods:

a Straight line (round computations for a partial year to the nearest full month)

b Straight line (use the half-year convention)

c Accelerated Cost Recovery System (use the table on page 402; assume the equipment qualifies as three-year property)

Ex. 10-9   A tractor which cost $25,000 had an estimated useful life of five years and an estimated salvage value of $5,000. Straight-line depreciation was used. Give the entry (in general journal form) required by each of the following alternative assumptions:

a The tractor was sold for cash of $15,000 after two years' use.

b The tractor was traded in after three years on another tractor with a list price of $36,000.

Trade-in allowance was $14,600. The trade-in was recorded in a manner acceptable for income tax purposes.

c The tractor was scrapped after four years' use. Since scrap dealers were unwilling to pay anything for the tractor, it was given to a scrap dealer for his services in removing it.

Ex. 10-10   In 198X, Midwest Mining Company purchased the Black Hills Mine for $3,800,000 cash. The mine was estimated to contain 2 million tons of ore and have a residual value of $800,000.

During the first year of mining operations at the Black Hills Mine, 400,000 tons of ore were mined, of which 300,000 tons were sold.

a Prepare a journal entry to record depletion of the Black Hills Mine during the year.

b Show how the mine and accumulated depletion would appear in Midwest Mining Company's balance sheet after the first year of operations.

c Will the entire balance of the account debited in part a be deducted from revenue in determining the income for the year? Explain.

Ex. 10-11   During the past several years the annual net income of Goldtone Appliance Company has averaged $270,000. At the present time the company is being offered for sale. Its accounting records show net assets (total assets minus all liabilities) to be $1,500,000.

An investor negotiating to buy the company offers to pay an amount equal to the book value for the net assets and to assume all liabilities. In addition, the investor is willing to pay for goodwill an amount equal to net earnings in excess of 15% on net assets, capitalized at a rate of 25%.

On the basis of this agreement, what price should the investor offer for Goldtone Appliance?

Problems

10-1   Three depreciation methods

Delta Company acquired new equipment with an estimated useful life of five years. Cost of the equipment was $50,000 and the residual salvage value was estimated to be $5,000.

Instructions. Compute the annual depreciation expense throughout the five-year life of the equipment under each of the following methods of depreciation:

a Straight-line

b Sum-of-the-years'-digits

c Double-declining-balance. Limit the amount of depreciation recognized in the fifth year to an amount that will cause the book value of the equipment to equal the estimated $5,000 residual value at year-end.

10-2   Four depreciation methods, including ACRS

New machinery was acquired by Video Corporation at a cost of $300,000. Useful life of the machinery was estimated to be five years, with residual salvage value of $36,000.

Instructions. Compute the annual depreciation expense throughout the five-year life of the machinery under each of the following four methods of depreciation:

a Straight-line

b Sum-of-the-years'-digits

c Double-declining-balance. Limit the amount of depreciation recognized in the fifth year to an amount that will cause the book value of the machinery to equal the $36,000 estimated residual value.

d ACRS—the income tax method. Use the table on page 402. Assume that the machinery qualifies as "3-year property."

10-3   Disposal of a plant asset

Gourmet Market purchased a delivery truck for $21,000. For financial statement purposes, the truck was depreciated by the straight-line method over an estimated life of five years, with a residual value of $5,000. For income tax purposes, the truck qualified as "3-year property" and was depreciated by the ACRS method. After the truck had been owned for two full years, it was sold for $12,000, on the first day of the third year. No depreciation was taken in the third year either for financial statement purposes or income tax purposes.

Instructions

a For financial statement purposes, compute (1) the book value of the truck at the end of the second year of ownership, and (2) the amount of gain or loss on the sale.

b For income tax purposes, compute (1) the tax basis (book value) of the truck at the end of the second year of ownership, and (2) the amount of gain or loss on the sale. In computing the accumulated depreciation on the truck at the end of the second year, refer to the ACRS depreciation rate table on page 402.

10-4   Revision of depreciation rates

Grain Products uses straight-line depreciation on all its depreciable assets. The accounts are adjusted and closed at the end of each calendar year. On January 4, Year 1, the corporation purchased machinery for cash at a cost of $80,000. Useful life was estimated to be 10 years and residual value $12,000. Depreciation for partial years is recorded to the nearest full month.

In Year 3, after almost three years of experience with the equipment, management decided that the estimated life of the equipment should be revised from 10 years to six years. No change was made in the estimate of residual value. The revised estimate of useful life was decided upon prior to recording depreciation for the period ended December 31, Year 3.

Instructions. Prepare journal entries in chronological order for the above events, beginning with the purchase of the machinery on January 4, Year 1. Show separately the depreciation for Years 1, 2, and 3.

10-5   Depreciation: a comprehensive problem

During the last few years, Sunhill Corporation has acquired four costly machines but has given little consideration to depreciation policies. At the time of acquisition of each machine, a different accountant was employed; consequently, various methods of depreciation have been adopted for the several machines. For machines A and D, assume that the depreciation rate was double the rate under the straight-line method. Information concerning the four machines appears below.

Machine	Date Acquired	Cost	Estimated Useful Life, Years	Estimated Residual Value	Method of Depreciation
A	Jan. 1, Year 4	$145,800	6	None	Declining-balance
B	June 30, Year 4	302,400	8	10%	Straight-line
C	Jan. 1, Year 5	201,600	10	$3,600	Sum-of-the-years'-digits
D	Jan. 1, Year 6	237,600	12	None	Declining-balance

Instructions

a Compute the amount of accumulated depreciation, if any, on each machine at December 31, Year 5. In the year of acquisition, assume that depreciation was computed to the nearest month.

b Prepare a depreciation schedule for use in the computation of the depreciation expense. Use the following column headings:

Machine	Method of Depreciation	Date of Acquisition	Cost	Estimated Residual Value	Amount to Be Depreciated	Useful Life, Years	Accumulated Depreciation, Dec. 31, Year 5	Depreciation Expense Year 6

c Prepare a journal entry to record the depreciation expense for Year 6.

d Using the ACRS rate table on page 402, compute the amount of depreciation (cost recovery) that would be allowed on each machine for income tax reporting in Year 6. Assume that all the machines qualify as "5-year property."

10-6 Errors in accounting for plant assets
Included in the ledger of Angus-Lee was an account entitled Property, which had been used to record a variety of expenditures including the cost of a new building completed on September 30, Year 5, and estimated to have a useful life of 20 years. At the end of Year 5, the Property account showed the following entries:

Debit entries:

4/3 Amount paid to acquire building site	$ 62,500
4/15 Cost of removing old unusable building from site	5,000
9/30 Contract price for new building completed Sept. 30	200,000
9/30 Insurance, inspection fees, and other costs directly related to construction of new building	10,000
Total debits	$277,500

Credit entries:

4/15 Proceeds from sale of old lumber and other material from demolition of old building	$ 7,500	
12/31 Depreciation for Year 5, computed at 5% of balance in Property account ($270,000). Debit was to Depreciation Expense	13,500	
Total credits		21,000
12/31 Balance in Property account at year-end		$256,500

Instructions

a Identify four errors made by Angus-Lee in accounting for plant assets and depreciation.

b Prepare a two-column schedule with column headings of Land and Buildings. Use this schedule to classify properly the debits and credits (other than depreciation) which Angus-Lee entered in its account entitled Property. For example, use the first line of your schedule to show in which account the debit of April 3 should be recorded.

c Prepare a compound journal entry to correct the accounts according to the classification developed in b. This correcting entry should include a credit for $256,500 to close the Property account and replace it with more descriptive accounts. The entry will also include adjustment of the incorrect treatment of depreciation. Estimated life of the new building was 20 years; depreciation should be recognized for the three months the building was in use during the current year, using the straight-line method. The revenue and expense accounts have not been closed for the current year.

10-7   Effect of depreciation methods on net income

On October 4, Year 1, Farm Fresh Foods purchased equipment at a cost of $62,000. The equipment was estimated to have a useful life of six years and a residual value of $20,000. The manager of Farm Fresh is trying to decide upon the appropriate depreciation method for this equipment and wants to see how various methods will affect the company's net income.

Instructions

a Compute the depreciation for each calendar year in which depreciation would be recognized using each of the following methods:
   (1) Straight-line, with depreciation for fractional periods rounded to the nearest full month.
   (2) Sum-of-the-years'-digits, using the half-year convention.
   (3) ACRS, using the table on page 402 and assuming that the equipment qualifies as "3-year property."

b After reviewing your schedule, the manager asks the following questions. Write a brief reply to each question, explaining the reasons for your answer.
   (1) In this situation, would the ACRS method be acceptable for use in the company's financial statements as well as for income tax purposes?
   (2) Which method that is acceptable for financial statement purposes would result in the company's reporting the highest net income during the next three years (Years 1, 2, and 3)?
   (3) Would it be acceptable to apply the half-year convention to only equipment purchased during the first half of the year, and to round the depreciation to the nearest month when the equipment is purchased in the last half of the year?

10-8   Trade-in of plant assets; a comprehensive problem

Hartman Editorial Services has entered into the following two transactions involving trade-ins of plant assets:

   (1) A truck which had cost $12,000 was traded in on a new truck with a list price of $16,800. The trade-in allowance on the old truck was $4,500, and the remaining $12,300 was paid in cash. At the date of the trade-in, the old truck had been fully depreciated to its estimated residual value of $2,000.
   (2) A word processor with a cost of $6,700 was traded in on a new word processor with a list price of $7,900. The trade-in allowance was $500, with the remaining $7,400 cost being paid in cash. At the date of this transaction, the accumulated depreciation on the old word processor amounted to $3,200.

Instructions

a Prepare journal entries to record each of these exchange transactions in accordance with generally accepted accounting principles. Assume all dollar amounts are material. (The asset accounts used for trucks and for word processors are entitled Vehicles and Office Equipment, respectively.)

     b Compute the basis of each of the newly acquired assets for federal income tax purposes.

     c Compute the depreciation expense that Hartman Editorial Services will recognize for financial statement purposes on each of the newly acquired assets in the year of acquisition. Assume that each asset will be depreciated over five years using the straight-line method, with an estimated residual value of $2,000, and with use of the half-year convention.

     d Compute the depreciation for income tax purposes on each of the newly acquired assets in the year of acquisition. For each asset, assume use of the straight-line method, a life of five years, zero residual value, and the half-year convention.

10-9   Depletion of a mine

Early in Year 6, Global Minerals began operations at its Wedding Bells Mine. The mine had been acquired several years earlier at a cost of $6,900,000. The mine is expected to contain 3 million tons of ore and to have a residual value of $1,500,000. Before beginning mining operations, the company installed equipment costing $2,700,000 at the mine. This equipment will have no economic usefulness once the mine is depleted. Therefore, depreciation of the equipment is based upon the estimated number of tons of ore produced each year (units-of-production method).

Ore removed from the Wedding Bells Mine amounted to 500,000 tons in Year 6 and 682,000 tons in Year 7.

Instructions

     a Compute the per-ton depletion rate of the mine and the per-ton depreciation rate of the mining equipment.

     b Make the year-end adjusting entries at December 31, Year 6, and December 31, Year 7, to record depletion of the mine and the related depreciation. (Use separate entries to record depletion of the mine and depreciation of the equipment.)

     c Show how the Wedding Bells Mine should appear in Global's balance sheet at the end of Year 7. (Use "Mineral Deposits: Wedding Bells Mine" as the title of the asset account; show accumulated depletion but do not include the equipment.)

10-10   Intangible assets or operating expense: GAAP

Protein Plus is a processor and distributor of frozen foods. The company's management is anxious to report the maximum amount of net income allowable under generally accepted accounting principles, and therefore uses the longest acceptable lives in depreciating or amortizing the company's plant assets. Depreciation and amortization computations are rounded to the nearest full month.

Near year-end the company's regular accountant was in an automobile accident, so a clerk with limited accounting experience prepared the company's financial statements. The income statement prepared by the clerk indicated a net loss of $45,000. However, the clerk was unsure that he had properly accounted for the following items:

     (1) On April 4, the company purchased a small food processing business at a cost $80,000 above the value of that business's net identifiable assets. The clerk classified this $80,000 as goodwill on Protein Plus's balance sheet and recorded no amortization expense because the food processor's superior earnings are expected to continue indefinitely.

     (2) During the year the company spent $32,000 on a research project to develop a method of freezing avocados. The clerk classified these expenditures as an intangible asset on the company's balance sheet and recorded no amortization expense because it was not yet known whether the project would be successful.

     (3) Two gains from the disposal of plant assets were included in the income statement. One gain, in the amount of $4,300, resulted from the sale of a plant asset at a price above its book value.

The other gain, in the amount of $2,700 on December 31, was based on receiving a trade-in allowance higher than the book value of an old truck that was traded in on a new one.

(4) A CPA firm had determined that the company's depreciation expense for income tax purposes was $51,400, using the ACRS method. The clerk used this figure as depreciation expense in the income statement, although in prior years the company had used the straight-line method of depreciation in its financial statements. Depreciation for the current year amounts to $35,600 when computed by the straight-line method.

(5) On January 4, the company paid $90,000 to purchase a 10-year franchise to become the exclusive distributor in three eastern states for a brand of Mexican frozen dinners. The clerk charged this $90,000 to expense in the current year because the entire amount had been paid in cash.

(6) During the year, the company incurred advertising costs of $22,000 to promote the newly acquired line of frozen dinners. The clerk did not know how many periods would be benefited from these expenditures, so he included the entire amount in the selling expenses of the current year.

Instructions

a For each of the numbered paragraphs, explain whether the clerk's treatment of the item is in conformity with generally accepted accounting principles.

b Prepare a schedule determining the correct net income (or net loss) for the year. Begin with "Net loss originally reported . . . $45,000," and indicate any adjustments that you consider appropriate. If you indicate adjustments for the amortization of intangible assets acquired during the year, round the amortization to the nearest month.

Cases for analysis

Case 10-1   Impact of depreciation methods upon reported earnings

Samuel Slater is interested in buying a manufacturing business and has located two similar companies being offered for sale. Both companies are single proprietorships which began operations three years ago, each with invested capital of $400,000. A considerable part of the assets in each company is represented by a building with an original cost of $100,000 and an estimated life of 40 years, and by machinery with an original cost of $200,000 and an estimated life of 20 years. Residual value is estimated at zero. Each company acquired its building and equipment on January 1 and has recorded three full years of depreciation.

Bay Company uses straight-line depreciation and Cove Company uses declining balance depreciation (double the straight-line rate). In all other respects the accounting policies of the two companies are quite similar. Neither company has borrowed from banks or incurred any indebtedness other than normal trade payables. The nature of products and other characteristics of operations are much the same for the two companies.

Audited financial statements for the three years show net income as follows:

Year	Bay Company	Cove Company
1	$ 62,000	$ 59,000
2	65,200	63,200
3	68,400	66,900
Totals	$195,600	$189,100

Slater asks your advice as to which company to buy. They are offered for sale at approximately the same price, and Slater is inclined to choose Bay Company because of its consistently higher earnings. On the other hand, the fact that Cove Company has more cash and a stronger working capital position is impressive. The audited financial statements show that withdrawals by the two owners have been approximately equal during the three-year life of the two companies.

Instructions

a Compute the depreciation recorded by each company in the first three years. Round off depreciation expense for each year to the nearest dollar.

b Write a memorandum to Slater advising which company in your judgment represents the more promising purchase. Give specific reasons to support your recommendation. Include a recomputation of the earnings of Cove Company by using straight-line depreciation in order to make its income statements comparable with those of Bay Company. Compare the earnings of the two companies year by year after such revision to a uniform basis.

Case 10-2   The best of three: an investor's choice

Ruth Barnes, an experienced executive in retail store operation, is interested in buying an established business in the retail clothing field. She is now attempting to make a choice among three similar concerns which are available for purchase. All three companies have been in business for five years. The balance sheets presented by the three companies may be summarized as follows:

Assets	Company X	Company Y	Company Z
Cash	$ 24,000	$ 24,000	$ 40,000
Accounts receivable	185,600	190,400	217,600
Inventory	352,000	288,000	288,000
Plant assets (net)	110,400	128,000	80,000
Goodwill		4,800	
	$672,000	$635,200	$625,600

Liabilities & Owner's Equity	Company X	Company Y	Company Z
Current liabilities	$284,800	$296,000	$320,000
Owner's equity	387,200	339,200	305,600
	$672,000	$635,200	$625,600

The average net earnings of the three businesses during the past five years had been as follows: Company X, $59,200; Company Y, $51,200; and Company Z, $54,400.

With the permission of the owners of the three businesses, Barnes arranged for a certified public accountant to examine the accounting records of the companies. This investigation disclosed the following information:

Accounts receivable. In Company X, no provision for uncollectible accounts had been made at any time, and no accounts receivable had been written off. Numerous past-due receivables were in the accounts, and the estimated uncollectible items which had accumulated during the past five years amounted to $16,000. In both Company Y and Company Z, the receivables appeared to be carried at estimated realizable value.

Inventories. Company Y had adopted the first-in, first-out method of inventory valuation when first organized but had changed to the last-in, first-out method after one year. As a result of this change in method of accounting for inventories, the present balance sheet figure for inventories was approximately $32,000 less than replacement cost. The other two companies had used the first-in, first-out method continuously, and their present inventories were approximately equal to replacement cost.

Plant and equipment. In each of the three companies, the plant assets included a building which had cost $80,000 and had an estimated useful life of 25 years with no residual scrap value. Company X had taken no depreciation on its building; Company Y had used straight-line depreciation at 4% annually; and Company Z had erroneously depreciated its building for five years by applying a constant rate of 4% to the undepreciated balance. (Note that the depreciation method used by Company Z was not accelerated depreciation, because the straight-line rate was not increased. Company Z merely made a basic error in its attempt to use straight-line depreciation.) All plant assets other than buildings had been depreciated on a straight-line basis (correctly applied) in all companies. Barnes believed that the book value of the plant assets in all three companies would approximate fair market value if depreciation were computed uniformly on a straight-line basis.

Goodwill. The item of goodwill, $4,800, on the balance sheet of Company Y represented the cost of a nonrecurring advertising campaign conducted during the first year of operation.

Barnes is willing to pay for net tangible assets (except cash) at book value, plus an amount for goodwill equal to three times the average net earnings in excess of 10% on the net tangible assets. Cash will not be included in the transfer of assets.

Instructions

a Prepare a revised summary of balance sheet data after correcting all errors made by the companies. In addition to correcting errors, make the necessary changes to apply straight-line depreciation and first-in, first-out inventory methods in all three companies. Round all amounts to the nearest dollar. (In computing the correct amount for net plant assets of Company Z, the following approach may be helpful. First, compute the total depreciation actually taken by Company Z under its erroneous use of straight-line depreciation; next, compute the correct depreciation for the five-year period under straight-line depreciation; finally, compare these two totals and use the difference as an adjustment of the net plant assets of Company Z.)

b Determine revised amounts for average net earnings of the three companies after taking into consideration the correction of errors and changes of method called for in a above.

c Determine the price which Barnes should offer for each of the businesses.

Chapter 11
Forms of business organization

Chapter 11 compares and contrasts the three most common forms of business organization — single proprietorships, partnerships, and corporations. We stress the basic characteristics of each organization, and the accounting for transactions between the business and its owners. Our discussion of single proprietorships and partnerships illustrates the use of owners' capital and drawing accounts. Attention also is focused upon the problem of dividing partnership net income among the partners. The remainder of the chapter emphasizes the nature of corporations and the various elements of stockholders' equity. The concept of par value is explained, and the issuance of capital stock at a price above par is illustrated. Preferred stock is contrasted with common stock. Also covered are such special topics as stock issued for assets other than cash, conversion of preferred stock into common, donated capital, and subscriptions to capital stock.

After studying this chapter you should be able to:

✓ Explain the basic characteristics of a single proprietorship, a partnership, and a corporation.
✓ Account for investments and withdrawals by the owners of an unincorporated business.
✓ Prepare a statement of owner's (or partners') capital.
✓ Prepare a schedule distributing partnership income among the partners.
✓ Explain the rights of stockholders and the roles of corporate directors and officers.
✓ Discuss the features of preferred stock and of common stock.
✓ Account for the issuance of stock in exchange for cash or other assets.
✓ Account for subscriptions to capital stock and for donated capital.

Three types of business organization are common to American business: the single proprietorship, the partnership, and the corporation. When these forms of organization were introduced in Chapter 1, we stressed that most accounting principles apply to all three forms and that the main area of difference lies in accounting for owners' equity. In this chapter, we shall describe briefly the unique characteristics and accounting practices of single proprietorships and partnerships, and then move to a discussion of corporations. Our discussion of the accounting practices of corporations will continue into the following chapter.

SINGLE PROPRIETORSHIPS

Any unincorporated business owned by one person is called a single proprietorship. This form of organization is common among small retail stores, farms, service businesses, and professional practices. In fact, the single proprietorship is the most common form of business organization in our economy. Most of these businesses, however, tend to be relatively small.

An important characteristic of the single proprietorship is that, from a legal viewpoint, the business and its owner are not regarded as separate entities. Thus, the owner is *personally liable* for the debts of the business. If the business becomes insolvent, creditors can force the owner to sell his or her personal assets to pay the business debts.

From an accounting viewpoint, however, a single proprietorship is regarded as an entity *separate from the other affairs of its owner.* For example, assume that Jill Green owns two single proprietorships—a gas station and a shoe store. The assets, liabilities, revenue, and expenses relating to the gas station would not appear in the financial statements of the shoe store. Also, Green's personal assets, such as her house, furniture, and savings account, would not appear in the financial statements of either business entity.

Accounting for the owner's equity in a single proprietorship

A balance sheet for a single proprietorship shows the entire ownership equity as a single dollar amount without any effort to distinguish between the amount originally invested by the owner and the later increase or decrease in owner's equity as a result of profitable or unprofitable operations. A corporation must maintain separate accounts for capital stock and retained earnings, because distributions to owners in the form of dividends cannot legally exceed the earnings of the corporation. In an unincorporated business, however, the owner is free to withdraw assets from the business at any time and in any amount.

The accounting records for a single proprietorship do not include accounts for capital stock, retained earnings, or dividends. Instead of these accounts, a *capital* account and a *drawing* account are maintained for the owner.

The owner's capital account. In a single proprietorship, the title of the capital account includes the name of the owner, as, for example, *John Jones, Capital.* The capital account is credited with the amount of the proprietor's original investment in the business and also with any subsequent investments. When the accounts are closed at the end of each accounting period, the Income Summary account is closed into the owner's capital account. Thus the capital account is credited with the net income earned (or debited with the net loss incurred). Withdrawals by the proprietor during the period are debited to a drawing account, which later is closed into the capital account.

The owner's drawing account. A withdrawal of cash or other assets by the owner reduces the owner's equity in the business and could be recorded by debiting the owner's capital account. However, a clearer record is created if a separate Drawing account is maintained. This drawing account (entitled, for example, *John Jones, Drawing*) replaces the Dividends account used by a corporation.

The drawing account is debited for any of the following transactions:

1 Withdrawals of cash or other assets. If the proprietor of a clothing store, for example, withdraws merchandise for personal use, the Drawing account is debited for the cost of the goods withdrawn. The offsetting credit is to the Purchases account (or to Inventory if a perpetual inventory system is maintained).
2 Payment of the proprietor's personal bills out of the business bank account.
3 Collection of an account receivable of the business, with the cash collected being retained personally by the proprietor.

Withdrawals by the proprietor (like dividends to stockholders) are not an expense of the business. Expenses are incurred for the purpose of generating revenue, and a withdrawal of cash or other assets by the proprietor does not have this purpose.

Closing the accounts

The revenue and expense accounts of a single proprietorship are closed into the Income Summary account in the same way as for a corporation. The Income Summary account is then closed to the proprietor's Capital account, rather than to a Retained Earnings account. To complete the closing of the accounts, the balance of the Drawing account is transferred into the proprietor's Capital account.

Financial statements for a single proprietorship

The balance sheet of a single proprietorship differs from that of a corporation only in the owner's equity section. To see how ownership equity appears in the balance sheet of a single proprietorship and also in the balance sheet of a corporation, you may wish to review the illustration in Chapter 1 (page 20).

A *statement of owner's equity* may be prepared in a form similar to the statement of retained earnings used by a corporation. The statement of owner's equity, however, shows additional investments made by the owner as well as the earnings retained in the business. An illustration follows:

JONES INSURANCE AGENCY
Statement of Owner's Equity
For the Year Ended December 31, 19__

John Jones, capital, Jan. 1, 19__	$ 80,400
Add: Additional investments	10,000
Net income for year	30,500
Subtotal	$120,900
Less: Withdrawals	34,000
John Jones, capital, Dec. 31, 19__	$ 86,900

Note that withdrawals may exceed net income

The *income statement* of a proprietorship differs from that of a corporation in two significant respects. First, the income statement for a single proprietorship does not include any salary expense representing managerial services rendered by the owner. One reason for not including a salary to the owner-manager is the fact that individuals in such a position are able to set their own salaries at any amount they choose. The use of an unrealistic salary to the proprietor would tend to destroy the significance of the income statement as a device for measuring the earning power of the business. It is more logical to regard the owner-manager as working to earn the entire net income of the business than as working for a salary.

The second distinctive feature of the income statement of a single proprietorship is the absence of any income taxes expense. Since a proprietorship is not recognized as a legal entity separate from its owner, the business does not file its own income tax return or pay any income taxes. However, the proprietor must include the income of the business on his or her individual income tax return, along with any taxable income from other sources. (Notice that the proprietor must pay income taxes upon the entire net income of the business, not merely upon the amount withdrawn during the year.) In contrast, a corporation does pay income taxes on its earnings, and income taxes expense will appear in its income statement.

PARTNERSHIPS

A partnership is an unincorporated business that is jointly owned by two or more people. In the professions and in businesses which stress the factor of personal service, the partnership form of organization is widely used. In the fields of manufacturing, wholesaling, and retail trade, partnerships are also popular, because they afford a means of combining the capital and abilities of two or more persons. A partnership is often referred to as a *firm;* the name of the firm often includes the word "company" as, for example, "Adams, Myers, and Company."

Significant features of a partnership

Before taking up the accounting problems peculiar to partnerships, it will be helpful to consider briefly some of the distinctive characteristics of the partnership form of organization. These characteristics (such as limited life and unlimited liability) all stem from the basic point that a partnership is not a separate legal entity in itself but merely a voluntary association of individuals.

Ease of formation. A partnership can be created without any legal formalities. When two or more persons agree to become partners, such agreement constitutes a contract and a partnership is automatically created. The contract should be in writing in order to lessen the chances for misunderstanding and future disagreement.

Limited life. A partnership may be ended at any time by the death or withdrawal of any member of the firm. Other factors which may bring an end to a partnership include the bankruptcy or incapacity of a partner, or the completion of the project for which the partnership was formed. The admission of a new partner or the retirement of an existing member means an end to the old partnership, although the business may be continued by the formation of a new partnership.

Mutual agency. Each partner acts as an agent of the partnership, with authority to enter into contracts. The partnership is bound by the acts of any partner as long as these acts are within the scope of normal operations. The factor of mutual agency suggests the need for exercising great caution in the selection of a partner. To be in partnership with an irresponsible person or one lacking in integrity is an intolerable situation.

Unlimited liability. Each partner is personally responsible for all the debts of the firm. The lack of any ceiling on the liability of a partner may deter a wealthy person from entering a partnership.

A new member joining an existing partnership may or may not assume liability for debts incurred by the firm prior to his or her admission. A partner withdrawing from membership must give adequate public notice of withdrawal; otherwise the former partner may be held liable for partnership debts incurred subsequent to his or her withdrawal. The retiring partner remains liable for partnership debts existing at the time of withdrawal unless the creditors agree to a release of this obligation.

Co-ownership of partnership property and profits. When a partner invests a building, inventory, or other property in a partnership, he or she does not retain any personal right to the assets contributed. The property becomes jointly owned by all partners. Each member of a partnership also has an ownership right in the profits.

Advantages and disadvantages of a partnership

Perhaps the most important advantage of most partnerships is the opportunity to bring together sufficient capital to carry on a business. The opportunity to combine special skills, as, for example, the specialized talents of an engineer and an accountant, may also induce individuals to join forces in a partnership. To form a partnership is much easier and less expensive than to organize a corporation. Members of a partnership enjoy more freedom from government regulation and more flexibility of action than do the owners of a corporation. The partners may withdraw funds and make business decisions of all types without the necessity of formal meetings or legalistic procedures.

Operating as a partnership *may* in some cases produce income tax advantages as compared with doing business as a corporation. The partnership itself is not a legal entity and does not have to pay income taxes as does a corporation, although the individual partners pay taxes on their respective shares of the firm's income.

Offsetting these advantages of a partnership are such serious disadvantages as limited life, unlimited liability, and mutual agency. Furthermore, if a business is to require a large amount of capital, the partnership is a less effective device for raising funds than is a corporation. Many persons who invest freely in common stocks of corporations are unwilling to enter a partnership because of the unlimited liability imposed on partners.

Limited partnerships

In recent years a number of businesses have been organized as "limited partnerships." This form of organization is widely used for businesses which provide tax sheltered income to investors, such as real estate syndications and oil drilling ventures. However, limited partnerships are not appropriate for businesses in which the owners intend to be active managers.

A limited partnership must have at least one *general partner* as well as one or more *limited partners.* The general partners are partners in the traditional sense, with unlimited liability for the debts of the business and the right to make managerial decisions. The limited partners, however, are basically *investors* rather than traditional partners. They have the right to participate in profits of the business, but their liability for losses is limited to the amount of their investment. Also, limited partners do not actively participate in management of the business. Thus, the concepts of unlimited liability and mutual agency apply only to the general partners in a limited partnership.

In this chapter, we emphasize the characteristics and accounting practices of conventional partnerships rather than limited partnerships. Limited partnerships are discussed in depth in courses on business law and federal income taxes.

The partnership contract

Although a partnership can be formed by an oral agreement, it is highly desirable that a written partnership agreement be prepared, summarizing the partners' mutual understanding on such points as:

1 Names of the partners, and the duties and rights of each
2 Amount to be invested by each partner including the procedure for valuing any noncash assets invested or withdrawn by partners
3 Methods of sharing profits and losses
4 Withdrawals to be allowed each partner

Partnership accounting

Partnership accounting is similar to that in a single proprietorship, except that separate capital and drawing accounts are maintained for each partner. A distinctive feature of partnership accounting is that the net income of the business must be divided among the partners in the manner specified by the partnership agreement.

Opening the accounts of a new partnership. When a partner contributes assets other than cash, a question always arises as to the value of such assets. The valuations assigned to noncash assets should be their *fair market values* at the date of transfer to the partnership. The valuations assigned must be agreed to by all the partners.

To illustrate the opening entries for a newly formed partnership, assume that on January 1, John Blair and Melinda Cross, who operate competing retail stores, decide to form a partnership by consolidating their two businesses. A capital account will be opened for each partner and credited with the agreed valuation of the *net assets* (total assets less total liabilities) that partner contributes. The journal entries to open the accounts of the partnership of Blair and Cross are as follows:

Entries for
formation of
partnership

Cash	40,000	
Accounts Receivable	60,000	
Inventory	90,000	
Accounts Payable		30,000
John Blair, Capital		160,000

To record the investment by John Blair in the partnership of Blair and Cross.

Cash	10,000	
Land	60,000	
Building	100,000	
Inventory	60,000	
Accounts Payable		70,000
Melinda Cross, Capital		160,000

To record the investment by Melinda Cross in the partnership of Blair and Cross.

The values assigned to assets in the accounts of the new partnership may be quite different from the amounts at which these assets were carried in the accounts of their previous owners. For example, the land contributed by Cross and valued at $60,000 might have appeared in her accounting records at a cost of $20,000. The building which she contributed was valued at $100,000 by the partnership, but it might have cost Cross only $80,000 some years ago and might have been depreciated on her records to a net value of $60,000. Assuming that market values of land and buildings had risen sharply while Cross owned this property, it is only fair to recognize the *current market value* of these assets at the time she transfers them to the partnership and to credit her capital account accordingly. Depreciation of the building in the partnership accounts will be based on the assigned value of $100,000 at the date of acquisition by the partnership.

Withdrawals and additional investments. Partners may make withdrawals of cash or other partnership assets at any time; there is no need for a formal "declaration" as with dividends paid by a corporation. The amounts withdrawn need not be the same for all partners. The withdrawal of cash or other assets by a partner is recorded by debiting that partner's drawing account. If a partner invests additional assets in the business, the investment is recorded by crediting the partner's capital account.

Closing the accounts at year-end. The revenue and expense accounts of a partnership are closed into the Income Summary account in the same way as for a corporation. The balance of the Income Summary account is then closed into the partners' capital accounts, in accordance with the profit-sharing provisions of the partnership agreement. If the partnership agreement does not specify how profits are to be divided, the law requires that any profits or losses be divided equally among the partners.

Let us assume that Blair and Cross have agreed to share profits equally and that the partnership earns net income of $60,000 during its first year of operations. The entry to close the Income Summary account would be as follows:

<table>
<tr><td>**Closing Income Summary: profits shared equally**</td><td>Income Summary ....</td><td>60,000</td><td></td></tr>
<tr><td></td><td>   John Blair, Capital ....</td><td></td><td>30,000</td></tr>
<tr><td></td><td>   Melinda Cross, Capital ....</td><td></td><td>30,000</td></tr>
</table>

To divide net income for 19___ in accordance with partnership agreement to share profits equally.

The next step in closing the accounts is to transfer the balance of each partner's drawing account to his or her capital account. Assuming that withdrawals during the year amounted to $24,000 for Blair and $16,000 for Cross, the entry at December 31 to close the drawing accounts is as follows:

<table>
<tr><td>**Closing the drawing accounts to capital accounts**</td><td>John Blair, Capital ....</td><td>24,000</td><td></td></tr>
<tr><td></td><td>Melinda Cross, Capital ....</td><td>16,000</td><td></td></tr>
<tr><td></td><td>   John Blair, Drawing ....</td><td></td><td>24,000</td></tr>
<tr><td></td><td>   Melinda Cross, Drawing ....</td><td></td><td>16,000</td></tr>
</table>

To transfer debit balances in partners' drawing accounts to their respective capital accounts.

Income statement for a partnership. The income statement for a partnership differs from that of a single proprietorship in only one respect: a final section may be added to show the division of the net income between the partners, as illustrated below for the firm of Blair and Cross. The income statement of a partnership is consistent with that of a single proprietorship in showing no income taxes expense and no salaries expense relating to services rendered by partners.

BLAIR AND CROSS

Income Statement

For the Year Ended December 31, 19___

<table>
<tr><td>**Note distribution of net income**</td><td>Sales ....</td><td></td><td>$600,000</td></tr>
<tr><td></td><td>Cost of goods sold:</td><td></td><td></td></tr>
<tr><td></td><td>   Inventory, Jan. 1 ....</td><td>$150,000</td><td></td></tr>
<tr><td></td><td>   Purchases ....</td><td>460,000</td><td></td></tr>
<tr><td></td><td>   Cost of goods available for sale ....</td><td>$610,000</td><td></td></tr>
<tr><td></td><td>   Less: Inventory, Dec. 31 ....</td><td>210,000</td><td></td></tr>
<tr><td></td><td>   Cost of goods sold ....</td><td></td><td>400,000</td></tr>
<tr><td></td><td>Gross profit on sales ....</td><td></td><td>$200,000</td></tr>
<tr><td></td><td>Operating expenses:</td><td></td><td></td></tr>
<tr><td></td><td>   Selling expenses ....</td><td>$100,000</td><td></td></tr>
<tr><td></td><td>   General & administrative expenses ....</td><td>40,000</td><td>140,000</td></tr>
<tr><td></td><td>Net income ....</td><td></td><td>$ 60,000</td></tr>
<tr><td></td><td>Distribution of net income:</td><td></td><td></td></tr>
<tr><td></td><td>   To John Blair (50%) ....</td><td>$ 30,000</td><td></td></tr>
<tr><td></td><td>   To Melinda Cross (50%) ....</td><td>30,000</td><td>$ 60,000</td></tr>
</table>

Statement of partners' capitals. The partners will usually want an explanation of the change in their capital accounts from one year-end to the next. A financial statement called a *statement of partners' capitals* is prepared to show this information and is illustrated below for the partnership of Blair and Cross:

BLAIR AND CROSS
Statement of Partners' Capitals
For the Year Ended December 31, 19___

	Blair	Cross	Total
Investment, Jan. 1, 19___	$160,000	$160,000	$320,000
Add: Additional investment	10,000	10,000	20,000
Net income for the year	30,000	30,000	60,000
Subtotals	$200,000	$200,000	$400,000
Less: Drawings	24,000	16,000	40,000
Balances, Dec. 31, 19___	$176,000	$184,000	$360,000

Changes in capital accounts during the year

The balance sheet of Blair and Cross would show the capital balance for each partner, as well as the total capital of $360,000.

Partnership profits and income taxes

Partnerships are not required to pay income taxes. However, a partnership is required to file an information tax return showing the amount of the partnership net income, and the share of each partner in the net income. Each partner must include his share of the partnership profit (after certain technical adjustments) on his individual income tax return. Partnership net income is thus taxable to the partners individually in the year in which it is earned. The income tax rules applicable to investment in a partnership are quite complex; those complexities are appropriate to advanced accounting courses.

Note that partners report and pay tax on their respective shares of the profits earned by the partnership during the year and not on the amounts which they have drawn out of the business during the year. *The net income of the partnership is taxable to the partners each year,* even though there may have been no withdrawals. This treatment is consistent with that accorded a single proprietorship.

Alternative methods of dividing partnership income

In the preceding illustration, the partners divided net income equally. Partners can, however, share net income in any way they wish. Factors that partners might consider in arriving at an equitable plan to divide net income include (1) the amount of time each partner devotes to the business, (2) the amount of capital invested by each partner, and (3) any other contribution by each partner to the success of the partnership. Net income, for example, may be shared in any agreed ratio such as in the ratio of beginning capitals, or in a fixed ratio after an allowance is made to each partner for salary and interest on capital invested.

To illustrate, assume that the partnership of Adams and Barnes earned $97,000 (before interest and salary allowances to partners) in Year 1 and that they had agreed to share net income as follows:

1. Salary allowances of $24,000 per year to Adams and $48,000 per year to Barnes. (Partners' salaries are merely a device for sharing net income and are not necessarily withdrawn from the business.)
2. Interest at 15% on beginning capitals to be allowed to each partner. Beginning capital balances for Adams and Barnes amounted to $100,000 and $40,000, respectively.
3. Any amount in excess of the foregoing salary and interest allowances to be divided equally.

In accordance with the terms of this agreement, the net income of $97,000 would be divided between Adams and Barnes as follows:

Division of Net Income

	Adams	Barnes	Income Allocated
Net income to be divided			$ 97,000
Salaries to partners	$24,000	$48,000	(72,000)
Remaining income after salaries			$ 25,000
Interest on beginning capitals:			
Adams ($100,000 × 15%)	15,000		
Barnes ($40,000 × 15%)		6,000	
Total allocated as interest			(21,000)
Remaining income after salaries and interest			$ 4,000
Allocated in a fixed ratio:			
Adams (50%)	2,000		
Barnes (50%)		2,000	(4,000)
Total share to each partner	$41,000	$56,000	$ –0–

Profit sharing; salaries, interest, and fixed ratio as basis

The journal entry to close the Income Summary account in this case will be:

Income Summary	97,000	
Lynn Adams, Capital		41,000
Dale Barnes, Capital		56,000

To close the Income Summary account by crediting each partner with authorized salary, interest at 15% on beginning capital, and dividing the remaining profits equally.

Authorized salaries and interest in excess of net income. In the preceding example the total of the authorized salaries and interest was $93,000 and the net income to be divided was $97,000. Suppose that the net income had been only $75,000; how should the division have been made?

If the partnership contract provides for salaries and interest on invested capital, these provisions are to be followed even though the net income for the year is less than the total of the authorized salaries and interest. If the net income of the firm of Adams and Barnes amounted to only $75,000, this amount would be divided between the partners as shown below.

Division of Net Income

	Adams	Barnes	Income Allocated
Net income to be divided			$ 75,000
Salaries to partners	$24,000	$48,000	(72,000)
Remaining income after salaries			$ 3,000
Interest on beginning capitals:			
Adams ($100,000 × 15%)	15,000		
Barnes ($40,000 × 15%)		6,000	
Total allocated as interest			(21,000)
Remaining income (loss) after salaries and interest ..			$(18,000)
Allocated in a fixed ratio:			
Adams (50%)	(9,000)		
Barnes (50%)		(9,000)	18,000
Total share to each partner	$30,000	$45,000	$ –0–

Authorized salaries and interest may exceed net income

The residual loss of $18,000 is divided equally because the partnership contract states that profits and losses are to be divided equally after providing for salaries and interest.

Other aspects of partnership accounting

The foregoing discussion of partnership accounting is by no means exhaustive. The admission of a new partner to the partnership, the withdrawal of a partner, and the liquidation of a partnership, for example, may raise some very complex accounting issues. These issues are primarily of interest to advanced accounting students and for that reason are not included in this introductory text.

CORPORATIONS

Nearly all large businesses and many small ones are organized as corporations. There are still more single proprietorships and partnerships than corporations, but in dollar volume of business activity, corporations hold an impressive lead. Why is the corporation the most common form of organization for large businesses? One reason is that corporations obtain their equity capital by issuing shares of capital stock. Since a corporation may issue a vast number of these shares, it may amass the combined savings of a great number of investors. Thus, the corporation is an ideal means of obtaining the capital necessary to finance large-scale operations. Because of the prominent role of corporations in our economy, it is important for everyone with an interest in business, economics, or politics to have an understanding of corporations and their accounting practices.

What is a corporation?

A corporation is a legal entity having an existence separate and distinct from that of its owners. In the eyes of the law, a corporation is an artificial person having many of the rights and responsibilities of a real person.

A corporation, as a separate legal entity, may own property in its own name. Thus, the assets of a corporation belong to the corporation itself, not to the stockholders. A corporation has legal status in court, that is, it may sue and be sued as if it were a person. As a legal entity, a corporation enters into contracts, is responsible for its own debts, and pays income taxes on its earnings.

Advantages of the corporate form of organization

The corporation offers a number of advantages not available in other forms of organization. Among these advantages are the following:

1   *No personal liability for stockholders.* Creditors of a corporation have a claim against the assets of the corporation, not against the personal property of the stockholders. Thus, the amount of money which stockholders risk by investing in a corporation is *limited to the amount of their investment.* To many investors, this is the most important advantage of the corporate form.

2   *Ease of accumulating capital.* Ownership of a corporation is evidenced by transferable *shares of stock.* The sale of corporate ownership in units of one or more shares permits both large and small investors to participate in ownership of the business. Some corporations actually have more than a million individual stockholders. For this reason, large corporations are often said to be *publicly owned.* Of course not all corporations are large. Many small businesses are organized as corporations and are owned by a limited number of stockholders. Such corporations are said to be *closely held.*

3   *Ownership shares are readily transferable.* Shares of stock may be sold by one investor to another without dissolving or disrupting the business organization. The shares of most large corporations may be bought or sold by investors in organized markets, such as the *New York Stock Exchange.* Investments in these shares have the advantage of *liquidity,* because investors may easily convert their corporate ownership into cash by selling their stock.

4   *Continuous existence.* A corporation is a separate legal entity with a perpetual existence. The continuous life of the corporation despite changes in ownership is made possible by the issuance of transferable shares of stock. By way of contrast, a partnership is a relatively unstable form of organization which is dissolved by the death or retirement of any of its members. The continuity of the corporate entity is essential to most large-scale business activities.

5   *Professional management.* The stockholders own the corporation, but they do not manage it on a daily basis. To administer the affairs of the corporation, the stockholders elect a *board of directors.* The directors, in turn, hire a president and other corporate officers to manage the business. There is no mutual agency in a corporation; thus, an individual stockholder has no right to participate in the management of the business unless he or she has been hired as a corporate officer.

Disadvantages of the corporate form of organization

Among the disadvantages of the corporation are:

1 *Heavy taxation.* The income of a partnership or a single proprietorship is taxable only as personal income to the owners of the business. The income of a corporation, on the other hand, is subject to income taxes which must be paid by the corporation. The combination of federal and state corporate income taxes often takes about 50% of a corporation's before-tax income. If a corporation distributes its earnings to stockholders, the stockholders must pay personal income taxes on the amounts they receive. This practice of first taxing corporate income to the corporation and then taxing distributions of that income to the stockholders is sometimes called *double taxation.*

2 *Greater regulation.* A corporation comes into existence under the terms of state laws and these same laws may provide for considerable regulation of the corporation's activities. For example, the withdrawal of funds from a corporation is subject to certain limits set by law. Federal laws administered by the Securities and Exchange Commission require large corporations to make extensive public disclosure of their affairs.

3 *Separation of ownership and control.* The separation of the functions of ownership and management may be an advantage in some cases but a disadvantage in others. On the whole, the excellent record of growth and earnings in most large corporations indicates that the separation of ownership and control has benefited rather than injured stockholders. In a few instances, however, a management group has chosen to operate a corporation for the benefit of insiders. The stockholders may find it difficult in such cases to take the concerted action necessary to oust the officers.

Formation of a corporation

A corporation is created by obtaining a corporate *charter* from the state in which the company is to be incorporated. To obtain a corporate charter, an application called the *articles of incorporation* is submitted to the state corporations commissioner or other designated official. Once the charter is obtained, the stockholders in the new corporation hold a meeting to elect *directors* and to pass *bylaws* as a guide to the company's affairs. The directors in turn hold a meeting at which officers of the corporation are appointed.

Organization costs. The formation of a corporation is a much more costly step than the organization of a partnership. The necessary costs include the payment of an incorporation fee to the state, the payment of fees to attorneys for their services in drawing up the articles of incorporation, payments to promoters, and a variety of other outlays necessary to bring the corporation into existence. These costs are charged to an intangible asset account called Organization Costs. In the balance sheet, organization costs appear under the "Other assets" caption, as illustrated on page 455.

The incurring of these organization costs leads to the existence of the corporate entity; consequently, the benefits derived from these costs may be regarded as extending over the entire life of the corporation. Since the life of a corporation may continue indefinitely, one might argue that organization costs are an asset with an unlimited life. However, present income tax rules permit organization costs to be written off over a period of five years or more; consequently, most companies elect to write off organization costs over a five-year period. Accountants have been willing to accept this practice, because organization costs are not material in amount. The accounting principle of *materiality* permits departures from theoretical concepts on the grounds of convenience if the practice in question will not cause any material distortion of net income.

Rights of stockholders. The ownership of stock in a corporation usually carries the following basic rights:

1 To vote for directors, and thereby to be represented in the management of the business. The approval of a majority of stockholders may also be required for such important corporate actions as mergers and acquisitions, the selection of independent auditors, the incurring of long-term debts, the establishment of stock option plans, or the splitting of capital stock into a larger number of shares.

When a corporation issues both common stock and preferred stock, voting rights generally are granted only to the holders of common stock. These two different types of capital stock will be discussed in detail later in this chapter.

2 To share in profits by receiving *dividends* declared by the board of directors. Stockholders in a corporation cannot make withdrawals of company assets, as an owner of an unincorporated business may do.

3 To share in the distribution of assets if the corporation is liquidated. When a corporation ends its existence, the creditors of the corporation must first be paid in full; any remaining assets are divided among stockholders in proportion to the number of shares owned.

4 To subscribe for additional shares in the event that the corporation decides to increase the amount of stock outstanding. This *preemptive right* entitles stockholders to maintain their percentages of ownership in the company by subscribing, in proportion to their present stockholdings, to any additional shares issued. In many cases, however, stockholders agree to waive their preemptive rights in order to grant more flexibility to management in issuing stock.

Stockholders' meetings are usually held once a year. Each share of stock is entitled to one vote. In large corporations, these annual meetings are usually attended by relatively few persons, often by less than 1% of the stockholders. Prior to the meeting, the management group will request stockholders who do not plan to attend in person to send in *proxy statements* assigning their votes to the existing management. Through this use of the proxy system, management may secure the right to vote as much as, perhaps, 90% or more of the total outstanding shares.

Functions of the board of directors. The primary functions of the board of directors are to manage the corporation and to protect the interests of the stockholders. At this level, management may consist principally of formulating policies and reviewing acts of the officers. Specific duties of the directors include declaring dividends, setting the salaries of officers, reviewing the system of internal control with the internal auditors and with the company's independent auditors, authorizing officers to arrange loans from banks, and authorizing important contracts of various kinds.

The official actions of the board are recorded in minutes of their meetings. The **minutes book** is the source of many of the accounting entries affecting the stockholders' equity accounts.

Functions of corporate officers. Corporate officers usually include a president, one or more vice-presidents, a controller, a treasurer, and a secretary. A vice-president is often made responsible for the sales function; other vice-presidents may be given responsibility for such important functions as personnel, finance, and production.

The responsibilities of the controller, treasurer, and secretary are most directly related to the accounting phase of business operation. The **controller,** or chief accounting officer, is responsible for the maintenance of adequate internal control and for the preparation of accounting records and financial statements. Such specialized activities as budgeting, tax planning, and preparation of tax returns are usually placed under the controller's jurisdiction. The **treasurer** has custody of the company's funds and is generally responsible for planning and controlling the company's cash position. The **secretary** represents the corporation in many contractual and legal matters and maintains minutes of the meetings of directors and stockholders. Another responsibility of the secretary is to coordinate the preparation of the annual report, which includes the financial statements and other information relating to corporate activities. In small corporations, one officer frequently acts as both secretary and treasurer. The following organization chart indicates lines of authority extending from stockholders to the directors to the president and other officers:

Typical corporate organization

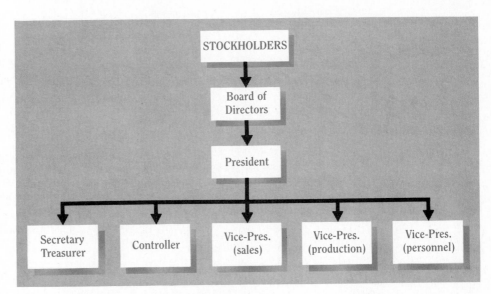

Authorization and issuance of capital stock

In previous chapters we have seen that corporations use separate owners' equity accounts (Capital Stock and Retained Earnings) to represent (1) the capital invested by the stockholders (called **paid-in capital**) and (2) the capital acquired and retained through profitable operations *(earned capital)*. Up to this point we have assumed that all paid-in capital may be recorded in a single ledger account entitled Capital Stock. In this chapter we will see that a corporation may issue several different types of capital stock. In addition, state laws may affect the manner in which the issuance of capital stock is recorded in the accounts. In these situations, additional ledger accounts are necessary to indicate the nature of the capital invested by the stockholders.

The articles of incorporation specify the number of shares of each type of capital stock which a corporation is authorized to issue and the *par value,* if any, per share. Large issues of capital stock to be offered for sale to the general public must be approved by the SEC as well as by state officials. The corporation may choose not to issue immediately all the authorized shares; in fact, it is customary to secure authorization for a larger number of shares than presently needed. In future years, if more capital is needed, the previously authorized shares will be readily available for issue; otherwise, the corporation would be forced to apply to the state for permission to increase the number of authorized shares.

Par value

The chief significance of par value is that it represents the *legal capital* per share, that is, the amount below which stockholders' equity cannot be reduced except by (1) losses from business operations or (2) legal action taken by a majority vote of stockholders. A dividend cannot be declared by a corporation if such action would cause the stockholders' equity to fall below the par value of the outstanding shares. Par value, therefore, may be regarded as a minimum cushion of equity capital existing for the protection of creditors.

Par value may be $1 per share, $5, $100, or any other amount decided upon by the corporation. The par value of the stock is *no indication of its market value;* the par value merely indicates the amount per share to be entered in the Capital Stock account. The par value of most common stocks is relatively low. Polaroid Corporation common stock, for example, has a par value of $1; Sears, Roebuck & Co. common stock has a par value of 75 cents; and Avon Products has a par value of 50 cents per common share. The market value of all these securities is far above their par value.

Issuance of par value stock. The authorization of a stock issue does not bring an asset into existence, nor does it give the corporation any capital. The obtaining of authorization from the state for a stock issue merely affords a legal opportunity to obtain assets through the sale of stock.

When par value stock is *issued,* the Capital Stock account is credited with the par value of the shares issued, regardless of whether the issuance price is more or less than par. Assuming that 10,000 shares of $10 par value stock have been authorized and that 6,000 of these authorized shares are issued at a price of $10 each, Cash would be debited and Capital Stock would be credited for $60,000. When stock is sold for more than par value, the Capital Stock account is credited with the par value of the shares issued, and a separate account, Paid-in Capital in Excess of Par Value, is credited for the excess of selling price over par. If, for example, the issuance price is $15, the entry is as follows:

Stockholders' investment in excess of par value

Cash	90,000	
Capital Stock		60,000
Paid-in Capital in Excess of Par Value		30,000
Issued 6,000 shares of $10 par value stock at a price of $15 a share.		

The amount received in excess of par value *does not represent a profit* to the corporation. It is part of the invested capital and it will be added to the capital stock on the balance sheet to show the total paid-in capital. The stockholders' equity section of the balance sheet is illustrated below. (The existence of $10,000 in retained earnings is assumed in order to have a complete illustration.)

Corporation's capital classified by source

Stockholders' equity:

Capital stock, $10 par value, authorized 10,000 shares, issued and outstanding 6,000 shares	$ 60,000
Paid-in capital in excess of par value	30,000
Total paid-in capital	$ 90,000
Retained earnings	10,000
Total stockholders' equity	$100,000

If stock is issued by a corporation for less than par, the account Discount on Capital Stock should be debited for the difference between the issuance price and the par value. The issuance of stock at a discount is seldom encountered; it is illegal in many states.

No-par stock

In an earlier period of the history of American corporations, all capital stock had par value, but in more recent years state laws have permitted corporations to choose between par value stock and no-par value stock. However, most companies which issue no-par capital stock establish a stated value per share. From an accounting viewpoint, stated value and par value mean the same thing — both terms designate the legal capital per share and the amount to be credited to the Capital Stock account.

Assume that a corporation is organized in a state which permits the board of directors to establish a *stated value* on no-par stock, and that the board passed a resolution setting the stated value per share at $5. If a total of 40,000 shares were issued at $20 per share, the journal entry to record the issuance would be:

Note stated value per share

Cash	800,000	
Capital Stock		200,000
Paid-in Capital in Excess of Stated Value		600,000
Issued 40,000 shares of no-par value capital stock at $20 each.		
Stated value set by directors at $5 per share.		

In the absence of a stated value, the entire proceeds on the sale of stock ($800,000) would be credited to the Capital Stock account and would be viewed as legal capital not subject to withdrawal.

Preferred stock and common stock

In order to appeal to as many investors as possible, a corporation may issue more than one kind of capital stock. The basic type of capital stock issued by every corporation is called *common stock*. Common stock has the four basic rights previously mentioned. Whenever these rights are modified, the term *preferred stock* (or sometimes Class B Common) is used to describe this second type of capital stock. A few corporations issue two or more classes of preferred stock, each class having certain distinctive features designed to interest a particular type of investor. In summary, we may say that every business corporation has common stock; a good many corporations also issue preferred stock; and some companies have two or more types of preferred stock.

Common stock may be regarded as the basic, residual element of ownership. It carries voting rights and, therefore, is the means of exercising control over the business. Common stock has unlimited possibilities of increase in value; during periods of business expansion the market prices of common stocks of some leading corporations may rise to many times their former values. On the other hand, common stocks lose value more rapidly than other types of securities when corporations encounter periods of unprofitable business.

The following stockholders' equity section illustrates the balance sheet presentation for a corporation having both preferred and common stock; note that the item of retained earnings is not apportioned between the two groups of stockholders.

Balance sheet presentation

Stockholders' equity:

12% cumulative preferred stock, $100 par value, authorized 100,000 shares, issued 50,000 shares	$ 5,000,000
Common stock, $5 par value, authorized 3 million shares, issued 2 million shares	10,000,000
Retained earnings	3,500,000
Total stockholders' equity	$18,500,000

Characteristics of preferred stock

Most preferred stocks have the following distinctive features:

1 Preferred as to dividends
2 Preferred as to assets in event of the liquidation of the company
3 Callable at the option of the corporation
4 No voting power

Another important but less common feature is a clause permitting the **conversion** of preferred stock into common at the option of the holder. Preferred stocks vary widely with respect to the special rights and privileges granted. Careful study of the terms of the individual preferred stock contract is a necessary step in the evaluation of any preferred stock.

Stock preferred as to dividends. Stock preferred as to dividends is entitled to receive each year a dividend of specified amount before any dividend is paid on the common stock. The dividend is usually stated as a dollar amount per share. For example, the balance sheet of General Motors Corporation shows two types of preferred stock outstanding, one paying $5.00 a year and the other $3.75 a year, as shown below:

Dividend stated as dollar amount

Capital stock:

Preferred, without par value (authorized 6 million shares):	
$5.00 series; stated value $100 per share, redeemable at $120 per share, outstanding 1,835,644 shares	$183,564,400

> $3.75 series; stated value $100 per share, redeemable at $100 per share,
> outstanding 1,000,000 shares 100,000,000

Some preferred stocks state the dividend preference as a percentage of par value. For example, a 9% preferred stock with a par value of $100 per share would mean that $9 must be paid yearly on each share of preferred stock before any dividends are paid on the common. An example of the percentage method of stating the dividend on a preferred stock is found in the balance sheet of UAL, Inc. (United Airlines).

Dividend stated as percentage of par

> Shareholders' equity:
> 5½% cumulative prior preferred stock, $100 par value; authorized and
> outstanding 71,702 shares $7,170,200

The holders of preferred stock have no assurance that they will always receive the indicated dividend. A corporation is obligated to pay dividends to stockholders only when the board of directors declares a dividend. Dividends must be paid on preferred stock before anything is paid to the common stockholders, but if the corporation is not prospering, it may decide not to pay dividends on either preferred or common stock. For a corporation to pay dividends, profits must be earned and cash must be available. However, preferred stocks in general offer more assurance of regular dividend payments than do common stocks.

Cumulative preferred stock. The dividend preference carried by most preferred stocks is a *cumulative* one. If all or any part of the regular dividend on the preferred stock is omitted in a given year, the amount omitted is said to be *in arrears* and must be paid in a subsequent year before any dividend can be paid on the common stock. Assume that a corporation was organized January 1, Year 1, with 10,000 shares of $4 cumulative preferred stock and 50,000 shares of common stock. Dividends paid in Year 1 were at the rate of $4 per share of preferred stock and $2 per share of common. In Year 2, earnings declined sharply and the only dividend paid was $1 per share on the preferred stock. No dividends were paid in Year 3. What is the status of the preferred stock at December 31, Year 3? Dividends are in arrears in the amount of $7 a share ($3 omitted during Year 2 and $4 omitted in Year 3). On the entire issue of 10,000 shares of preferred stock, the dividends in arrears amount to $70,000.

Dividends in arrears *are not listed among the liabilities of a corporation,* because no liability exists until a dividend is declared by the board of directors. Nevertheless, the amount of any dividends in arrears on preferred stock is an important factor to investors and should always be disclosed. This disclosure is usually made by a note accompanying the balance sheet such as the following:

Footnote disclosure of dividends in arrears

Note 6: Dividends in arrears
As of December 31, Year 3, dividends on the $4 cumulative preferred stock were in arrears to the extent of $7 per share and amounted in total to $70,000.

In Year 4, we shall assume that the company earned large profits and wished to pay dividends on both the preferred and common stocks. Before paying a dividend on the common, the corporation must pay the $70,000 in arrears on the cumulative preferred stock plus the regular $4 a share applicable to the current year. The preferred stockholders would, therefore, receive a total of $110,000 in dividends in Year 4; the board of directors would then be free to declare dividends on the common stock.

For a **noncumulative preferred stock,** any unpaid or omitted dividend is lost forever. Because of this factor, investors view the noncumulative feature as an unfavorable element, and very few noncumulative preferred stocks are issued.

Stock preferred as to assets. Most preferred stocks carry a preference as to assets in the event of liquidation of the corporation. If the business is terminated, the preferred stock is entitled to payment in full of its par value or a higher stated liquidation value before any payment is made on the common stock. This priority also includes any dividends in arrears.

Callable preferred stock. Most preferred stocks include a *call provision.* This provision grants the issuing corporation the right to repurchase the stock from the stockholders at a stipulated *call price.* The call price is usually slightly higher than the par value of the stock. For example, $100 par value preferred stock may be callable at $105 or $110 per share. In addition to paying the call price, a corporation which redeems its preferred stock must pay any dividends in arrears. A call provision gives a corporation flexibility in adjusting its financial structure, for example, by eliminating a preferred stock and replacing it with other securities if future growth of the company makes such change advantageous.

Convertible preferred stock. In order to add to the attractiveness of preferred stock as an investment, corporations sometimes offer a conversion privilege which entitles the preferred stockholders to exchange their shares for common stock in a stipulated ratio. If the corporation prospers, its common stock will probably rise in market value, and dividends on the common stock will probably be increased. The investor who buys a convertible preferred stock rather than common stock has greater assurance of regular dividends. In addition, through the conversion privilege, the investor is assured of sharing in any substantial increase in value of the company's common stock.

As an example, assume that Remington Corporation issued a 10%, $100 par, convertible preferred stock on January 1, at a price of $100 a share. Each share was convertible into four shares of the company's $10 par value common stock at any time. The common stock had a market price of $20 a share on January 1, and an annual dividend of $1 a share was being paid. During the next few years, Remington Corporation's earnings increased, the dividend on the common stock was raised to an annual rate of $4, and the market price of the common stock rose to $40 a share. At this point the preferred stock would have a market value of at least $160, since it could be converted at any time into four shares of common stock with a market value of $40 each. In other words, the market value of a *convertible* preferred stock will tend to move in accordance with the price of the common.

When the dividend rate is increased on the common stock, some holders of the preferred stock may convert their holdings into common stock in order to obtain a higher cash return on their investments. If the holder of 100 shares of the preferred stock presented these shares for conversion, Remington Corporation would make the following journal entry:

Conversion of preferred stock into common

10% Convertible Preferred Stock 10,000
    Common Stock 4,000
    Paid-in Capital in Excess of Par Value 6,000
To record the conversion of 100 shares of preferred stock, par $100, into 400 shares of $10 par value common stock.

Note that the issue price recorded for the 400 shares of common stock is based upon the carrying value of the preferred stock in the accounting records, not upon market prices at the date of conversion.

Participating clauses in preferred stock. Since participating preferred stocks are very seldom issued, discussion of them will be brief. A fully participating preferred stock is one which, in addition to the regular specified dividend, is entitled to participate in some manner with the common stock in any additional dividends paid. For example, a $5 participating preferred stock would be entitled to receive $5 a share before the common stock received anything. After $5 a share had been paid to the preferred stockholders, a $5 dividend could be paid on the common stock. If the company desired to pay an additional dividend to the common, say, an extra $3 per share, the preferred stock would also be entitled to receive an extra $3 dividend. In brief, a fully participating preferred stock participates dollar for dollar with the common stock in any dividends paid in excess of the stated rate on the preferred stock.

It is important to remember that most preferred stocks are *not* participating. Although common stock dividends may increase year after year if the corporation prospers, the dividends on most preferred stocks are fixed in amount. A $6 preferred stock, unless it is participating, *will never pay an annual dividend in excess of $6.*

Market price of preferred stock

Investors buy preferred stocks primarily to receive the dividends that these stocks pay. But what happens to the market price of an 8% preferred stock, originally issued at a par value of $100, if government policies and other factors cause long-term interest rates to rise to, say, 15 or 16%? If investments offering a return of 16% are readily available, investors will no longer pay $100 for a share of preferred stock which provides a dividend of only $8 per year. Thus, the market price of the preferred stock will fall to about half of its original issue price, or about $50 per share. At this market price, the stock offers a 16% return (called the *dividend yield*) to an investor purchasing the stock ($8 per year ÷ $50 = 16%). However, if the prevailing long-term interest rates should again decline to the 8% range, the market price of an 8% preferred stock should quickly rise to approximately par value.

In conclusion, the market price of preferred stock *varies inversely with interest rates.* As interest rates rise, preferred stock prices decline; as interest rates fall, preferred stock prices rise.

● **CASE IN POINT** ● The preceding point is illustrated by the performance of Philadelphia Electric's $9\frac{1}{2}$%, $100 par value, preferred stock as interest rates have fluctuated over recent years:

	Long-Term Interest Rates*	Stock Price
September 1978	$9\frac{1}{2}$%	$99
August 1981	$15\frac{1}{4}$%	60
March 1983	$12\frac{1}{2}$%	76
April 1985	$13\frac{1}{2}$%	68

* The long-term interest rates cited in this example are the market yields of federally insured 30-year fixed rate mortgages.

The underwriting of stock issues

When a large amount of stock is to be issued, the corporation will probably utilize the services of an investment banking firm, frequently referred to as an **underwriter.** The underwriter guarantees the issuing corporation a specific price for the stock and makes a profit by selling the stock to the investing public at a higher price. The corporation records the issuance of the stock at the net amount received from the underwriter. The use of an underwriter assures the corporation that the entire stock issue will be sold without delay, and the entire amount of funds to be raised will be available on a specific date.

Market price of common stock

The preceding sections concerning the issuance of stock at prices above and below par value raise a question as to how the market price of stock is determined. The price which the corporation sets on a new issue of stock is based on several factors including (1) an appraisal of the company's expected future earnings, (2) the probable dividend rate per share, (3) the present financial position of the company, and (4) the current state of the investment market.

After the stock has been issued, the price at which it will be traded among investors will rise and fall in response to all the forces of the marketplace. The market price per share will tend to reflect the progress of the company, with primary emphasis being placed on earnings and dividends. At this point in our discussion, the significant fact to emphasize is that market price is not related to par value, and that it tends to reflect investors' expectations of future earnings and dividends.

Stock issued for assets other than cash

Corporations generally sell their capital stock for cash and use the cash to buy the various types of assets needed in the business. Sometimes, however, a corporation may issue shares of its capital stock in a direct exchange for land, buildings, or other assets. Stock may also be issued in payment for services rendered by attorneys and promoters in the formation of the corporation.

When a corporation issues capital stock in exchange for services or for assets other than cash, the transaction should be recorded at the current *market value* of the goods or services received. Often, the best evidence as to the market value of these goods or services is the market value of the shares issued in exchange. For example, assume that a company issues 10,000 shares of its $1 par value common stock in exchange for land. Competent appraisers may have differing opinions as to the market value of the land. But let us assume that the company's stock is currently selling on a stock exchange for $90 per share. It is logical to say that the cost of the land to the company is $900,000, the market value of the shares issued in exchange.

Once the valuation has been decided, the entry to record the issuance of the stock in exchange for the land is as follows:

How were dollar amounts determined?

Land	900,000	
Common Stock		10,000
Paid-in Capital in Excess of Par Value		890,000

To record the issuance of 10,000 shares of $1 par value common stock in exchange for land. Current market value of stock ($90 per share) used as basis for valuing the land.

Subscriptions to capital stock

Small corporations sometimes sell stock on a subscription plan, in which the investor agrees to pay the subscription price at a future date or in a series of installments. When the subscription contract is signed, Subscriptions Receivable: Common is debited and Common Stock Subscribed is credited. Later, as installments are collected, the entry is a debit to Cash and a credit to Subscriptions Receivable: Common. When the entire subscription price has been collected, the stock certificates are issued. The issuance of the stock is recorded by debiting Common Stock Subscribed and crediting Common stock. The following illustration demonstrates the accounting procedures for stock subscriptions.

In this example, 10,000 shares of $10 par value stock are subscribed at a price of $15. Subscriptions for 6,000 of these shares are then collected in full. A partial payment is received on the other 4,000 shares.

Subscription price above par

Subscriptions Receivable: Common	150,000	
Common Stock Subscribed		100,000
Paid-in Capital in Excess of Par Value		50,000

Received subscriptions for 10,000 shares of $10 par value stock at price of $15 a share.

When the subscriptions for 6,000 shares are collected in full, certificates for 6,000 shares will be issued. The following entries are made:

Certificates issued for fully paid shares

Cash	90,000	
Subscriptions Receivable: Common		90,000

Collected subscriptions in full for 6,000 shares at $15 each.

| Common Stock Subscribed .... | 60,000 | |
| Common Stock .... | | 60,000 |

Issued certificates for 6,000 fully paid $10 par value shares.

The subscriber to the remaining 4,000 shares paid only half of the amount of the subscription but promised to pay the remainder within a month. Stock certificates will not be issued until the subscription is collected in full, but the partial collection is recorded by the following entry:

Partial collection of subscription

| Cash .... | 30,000 | |
| Subscriptions Receivable: Common .... | | 30,000 |

Collected partial payment on subscription for 4,000 shares.

From the corporation's point of view, Subscriptions Receivable is a current asset, which ordinarily will be collected within a short time. If financial statements are prepared between the date of obtaining subscriptions and the date of issuing the stock, the Common Stock Subscribed account is regarded as legal capital and will appear in the stockholders' equity section of the balance sheet.

Donated capital

On occasion, a corporation may receive assets as a gift. To increase local employment, for example, some cities have given corporations the land upon which to build factories. A corporation's total assets and total stockholders' equity are both increased by the market value of the assets received. *No profit is recognized when a gift is received;* the increase in stockholders' equity is regarded as paid-in capital. The receipt of a gift is recorded by debiting asset accounts and crediting an account entitled *Donated Capital.* Donated capital appears as part of the paid-in capital in the stockholders' equity section of the balance sheet, as illustrated on page 455.

Stockholder records in a corporation

A large corporation with shares listed on the New York Stock Exchange usually has millions of shares outstanding and several hundred thousand stockholders. Each day many stockholders sell their shares; the buyers of these shares become new members of the company's family of stockholders. An investor purchasing stock in a corporation receives a *stock certificate* from the company indicating the number of shares acquired. If the investor later sells these shares, this stock certificate must be surrendered to the corporation for cancellation before a new certificate is issued to the new owner of the shares.

A corporation must have an up-to-date record of the names and addresses of this constantly changing army of stockholders so that it can send dividend checks, financial statements, and voting forms to the right people. Also, the corporation must make sure that old stock certificates are cancelled as new ones are issued so that no excess certificates become outstanding.

Stockholders' ledger. When there are numerous stockholders, it is not practical to include a separate account for each stockholder in the general ledger. Instead, a single controlling account entitled Capital Stock appears in the general ledger, and a subsidiary stockholders' ledger is maintained. This ledger contains a page for each individual stockholder. Entries in the stockholders' ledger are made in number of shares rather than in dollars. Thus, each stockholder's account shows the number of shares owned, and the dates of acquisitions and sales. This record enables the corporation to send each stockholder a single dividend check, even though the stockholder may have acquired several stock certificates at different dates.

Stock transfer agent and stock registrar. Companies with shares traded on organized stock exchanges must engage an independent stock transfer agent and stock registrar to maintain their stockholder records and to control the issuance of stock certificates. These transfer agents and registrars usually are large banks or trust companies.[1] When stock certificates are to be transferred from one owner to another, the old certificates are sent to the transfer agent, who cancels them, makes the necessary entries in the stockholders' ledger, and prepares a new certificate for the new owner of the shares. This new certificate then must be registered with the stock registrar before it represents valid and transferable ownership of stock in the corporation.

Small, closely held corporations generally do not use the services of independent registrars and transfer agents. In these companies, the stockholder records usually are maintained by the corporate secretary. To prevent the accidental or fraudulent issuance of an excessive number of stock certificates, even a small corporation should require that each certificate be signed by at least two designated corporate officers.

Retained earnings or deficit

Capital provided to a corporation by stockholders in exchange for shares of either preferred or common stock is called paid-in capital, or contributed capital. The second major type of stockholders' equity is retained earnings. The amount of the Retained Earnings account at any balance sheet date represents the accumulated earnings of the company since the date of incorporation, minus any losses and minus all dividends distributed to stockholders.

For a corporation with $1,000,000 of paid-in capital and $600,000 of retained earnings, the stockholders' equity section of the balance sheet may appear as follows:

Paid-in capital and earned capital

Stockholders' equity:

Capital stock, $10 par value, 100,000 shares authorized, 20,000 shares issued	$ 200,000
Paid-in capital in excess of par value	800,000
Total paid-in capital	$1,000,000
Retained earnings	600,000
Total stockholders' equity	$1,600,000

---

[1] Regulations of the New York Stock Exchange now allow a single bank or trust company to act as both stock transfer agent and stock registrar for the same corporation. Traditionally, these functions were performed by two separate institutions.

If this same company had been unprofitable and incurred losses of $300,000 since its organization, the stockholders' equity section of the balance sheet would be as follows:

Paid-in capital
reduced by losses
incurred

Stockholders' equity:

Capital stock, $10 par value, 100,000 shares authorized, 20,000 shares issued	$ 200,000
Paid-in capital in excess of par value	800,000
Total paid-in capital	$1,000,000
Less: Deficit	300,000
Total stockholders' equity	$ 700,000

This second illustration tells us that $300,000 of the original $1,000,000 invested by stockholders has been lost. Note that the presentation of total paid-in capital in both illustrations remains at the fixed amount of $1,000,000, the stockholders' original investment. The accumulated profits or losses since the organization of the corporation are shown as *retained earnings* or as a *deficit* and are not intermingled with the paid-in capital. The term *deficit* indicates a negative amount of retained earnings.

Balance sheet for a corporation illustrated

A fairly complete balance sheet for a corporation is illustrated on page 455. Note the inclusion in this balance sheet of liabilities for income taxes payable and dividends payable. These liabilities do not appear in the balance sheets of unincorporated businesses. Note also that the caption for each capital stock account indicates the type of stock, the par value per share, and the number of shares authorized and issued. The caption for preferred stock also indicates the dividend rate, call price, and other important features.

Bear in mind that current practice includes many alternatives in the choice of terminology and the arrangement of items in financial statements. Some of these alternatives are illustrated in Appendix E, following Chapter 17.

Key terms introduced or emphasized in chapter 11

Board of directors. Persons elected by common stockholders to direct the affairs of a corporation.

Call price. The price to be paid by a corporation for each share of callable preferred stock if the corporation decides to call (redeem) the preferred stock.

Closely held corporation. A corporation owned by a small group of stockholders. The stock of closely held corporations is not traded on stock exchanges.

Common stock. A type of capital stock which possesses the basic rights of ownership including the right to vote. Represents the residual element of ownership in a corporation.

Corporation. A business organized as a legal entity separate from its owners. Chartered by the state with ownership divided into shares of transferable stock. Stockholders are not liable for debts of the corporation.

Deficit. Accumulated losses incurred by a corporation. A negative amount of retained earnings.

Drawing account. The account used to record the withdrawals of cash or other assets by the owner (or owners) of an unincorporated business. Closed at the end of the period by transferring its balance to the owner's capital account.

DEL MAR CORPORATION
Balance Sheet
December 31, Year 10

Assets

Current assets:

Cash			$ 305,600
Accounts receivable (net of allowance for doubtful accounts)			1,105,200
Subscriptions receivable: Common stock			110,000
Inventories (lower of fifo cost or market)			1,300,800
Short-term prepayments			125,900
Total current assets			$2,947,500

Plant and equipment:

Land		$ 900,000	
Buildings and equipment	$5,283,000		
Less: Accumulated depreciation	1,250,000	4,033,000	4,933,000
Other assets: Organization costs			14,000
Total assets			$7,894,500

Liabilities & Stockholders' Equity

Current liabilities:

Accounts payable		$ 998,100
Income taxes payable		324,300
Dividends payable		109,700
Interest payable		20,000
Total current liabilities		$1,452,100
Long-term liabilities: Bonds payable, 12%, due Oct. 1, Year 20		1,000,000
Total liabilities		$2,452,100

Stockholders' equity:

Cumulative 8% preferred stock, $100 par, callable at $104, authorized and issued 10,000 shares	$1,000,000	
Common stock, $1 par, authorized 1,000,000 shares, issued 600,000 shares	600,000	
Common stock subscribed, 20,000 shares	20,000	
Paid-in capital in excess of par: common	2,070,000	
Donated capital	210,000	
Total paid-in capital	$3,900,000	
Retained earnings	1,542,400	
Total stockholders' equity		5,442,400
Total liabilities & stockholders' equity		$7,894,500

Limited liability. An important characteristic of the corporate form of organization. The corporation as a separate legal entity is responsible for its own debts; the stockholders are not personally liable for the corporation's debts.

Limited partnership. A partnership which has one or more *limited partners* as well as one or more *general partners.* Limited partnerships are used primarily to attract investment capital from the limited partners for such ventures as exploratory oil drilling and real estate development.

Mutual agency. Authority of each partner to act as agent for the partnership within its normal scope of operations and to enter into contracts which bind the partnership.

No-par stock. Stock without par value. Usually has a stated value which is similar to par value.

Organization costs. Costs incurred to form a corporation.

Paid-in capital. The amounts invested in a corporation by its stockholders.

Par value. The legal capital of a corporation. Also the face amount of a share of capital stock. Represents the minimum amount per share to be invested in the corporation when shares are originally issued.

Preferred stock. A class of capital stock usually having preferences as to dividends and in the distribution of assets in event of liquidation.

Single proprietorship. An unincorporated business owned by one person.

Stated capital. That portion of capital invested by stockholders which cannot be withdrawn. Provides protection for creditors. Also called *legal capital.*

Statement of partners' capitals. An annual financial statement which shows for each partner and for the firm the amounts of beginning capitals, additional investments, net income, drawings, and ending capitals.

Stock certificate. A document issued by a corporation (or its transfer agent) as evidence of the ownership of the number of shares stated on the certificate.

Stock registrar. An independent fiscal agent, usually a large bank, retained by a corporation to provide assurance against overissuance of stock certificates.

Stock transfer agent. A bank or trust company retained by a corporation to maintain its records of capital stock ownership and make transfers from one investor to another.

Stockholders' ledger. A subsidiary record showing the number of shares owned by each stock-holder.

Subscriptions to capital stock. Formal promises to buy shares of stock from a corporation with payment at a later date. Stock certificates are delivered when full payment is received.

Underwriter. An investment banking firm which handles the sale of a corporation's stock to the public.

Demonstration problem for your review

At the close of the current year, the stockholders' equity section of the Rockhurst Corporation's balance sheet appeared as follows:

Stockholders' equity:
$1.50 preferred stock, $25 par value, authorized 1,500,000 shares:

Issued	$10,800,000	
Subscribed	5,400,000	$16,200,000
Common stock, no par, $5 stated value, authorized 6,000,000 shares		12,300,000
Paid-in capital in excess of par or stated value:		
On preferred stock	$ 810,000	
On common stock	7,626,000	8,436,000
Retained earnings (deficit)		(600,000)
Total stockholders' equity		$36,336,000

Among the assets of the corporation appears the following item: Subscriptions Receivable: Preferred, $1,123,200.

Instructions. On the basis of this information, write a brief answer to the following questions, showing any necessary supporting computations.

    a How many shares of preferred and common stock have been issued?
    b How many shares of preferred stock have been subscribed?
    c What was the average price per share received (including stock subscribed) by the corporation on its preferred stock?
    d What was the average price per share received by the corporation on its common stock?
    e What is the average amount per share that subscribers of preferred stock have yet to pay on their subscriptions?
    f What is the total paid-in capital including stock subscribed?
    g What is the total legal or stated value of the capital stock including stock subscribed?

Solution to demonstration problem

a Preferred stock issued <u>432,000 shares</u> ($10,800,000 ÷ $25)

    Common stock issued <u>2,460,000 shares</u> ($12,300,000 ÷ $5)

b Preferred stock subscribed <u>216,000 shares</u> ($5,400,000 ÷ $25)

c Preferred stock par value ($10,800,000 + $5,400,000) $16,200,000
    Paid-in capital in excess of par .... <u>810,000</u>
      Total paid-in and subscribed $17,010,000
    Total shares (432,000 + 216,000) 648,000
    Average price per share ($17,010,000 ÷ 648,000 as
      computed in a and b) .... <u>$26.25</u>

d Common stock stated value $12,300,000
    Paid-in capital in excess of par .... <u>7,626,000</u>
      Total paid-in $19,926,000
    Total shares (see a) 2,460,000
    Average price per share ($19,926,000 ÷ 2,460,000) .... <u>$ 8.10</u>

e Subscriptions receivable, preferred .... $ 1,123,200
    Shares subscribed 216,000
    Average price per share ($1,123,200 ÷ 216,000) .... <u>$ 5.20</u>

f Total paid-in capital <u>$36,936,000</u> (preferred $16,200,000 + common $12,300,000 + paid-in capital in excess of par or stated value $8,436,000)

g Total stated capital <u>$28,500,000</u> (preferred $16,200,000 + common $12,300,000)

Review questions

    1 Three types of business organization are common to American business: the single proprietorship, the partnership, and the corporation. Which of these three forms accounts for the largest number of business organization? Which form accounts for the largest dollar volume of business activity?

2 Jane Miller is the proprietor of a small manufacturing business. She is considering the possibility of joining in partnership with Mary Bracken, whom she considers to be thoroughly competent and congenial. Prepare a brief statement outlining the advantages and disadvantages of the potential partnership to Miller.

3 Compare the right of partners to withdraw assets from a partnership with the right of stockholders to receive dividends from a corporation. Explain any significant differences in these rights.

4 Allen and Baker are considering forming a partnership. What do you think are the two most important factors for them to include in their partnership agreement?

5 What is meant by the term *mutual agency?*

6 A real estate development business is managed by two experienced developers and is financed by 50 investors from throughout the state. To allow maximum income tax benefits to the investors, the business is organized as a partnership. Explain why this type of business would probably be a limited partnership rather than a regular partnership.

7 Scott has land having a book value of $50,000 and a fair market value of $80,000 and a building having a book value of $70,000 and a fair market value of $60,000. The land and building become Scott's sole capital contribution to a partnership. What is Scott's capital balance in the new partnership? Why?

8 Partner Susan Reed withdraws $35,000 from a partnership during the year. When the financial statements are prepared at the end of the year, Reed's share of the partnership income is $25,000. Which amount must Reed report on her individual income tax return?

9 What factors should be considered in drawing up an agreement as to the way in which income shall be shared by two or more partners?

10 Is it possible that a partnership agreement containing interest and salary allowances as a step toward distributing income could cause a partnership net loss to be divided so that one partner's capital account would be decreased by more than the amount of the entire partnership net loss? Explain.

11 Partner John Young has a choice to make. He has been offered by his partners a choice between (a) no salary allowance and a one-third share in the partnership income or (b) a salary of $16,000 per year and a one-quarter share of residual profits. Write a brief memorandum explaining the factors he should consider in reaching a decision.

12 Why are large corporations often said to be *publicly owned?*

13 Distinguish between corporations and partnerships in terms of the following characteristics:
a Owners' liability
b Transferability of ownership interest
c Continuity of existence
d Federal taxation on income

14 What are the basic rights of the owner of a share of corporate stock? In what way are these basic rights commonly modified with respect to the owner of a share of preferred stock?

15 Explain the meaning of the term *double taxation* as it applies to corporate profits.

16 Explain the significance of *par value.* Does par value indicate the reasonable market price for a share of stock? Explain.

17 Describe the usual nature of the following features as they apply to a share of preferred stock: (a) cumulative, (b) convertible, and (c) callable.

18 When stock is issued by a corporation in exchange for assets other than cash, accountants face the problem of determining the dollar amount at which to record the transaction. Discuss the factors they should consider and explain their significance.

19 State the classification (asset, liability, stockholders' equity, revenue, or expense) of each of the following accounts:
a Subscriptions receivable
b Organization costs
c Preferred stock
d Retained earnings

    e Capital stock subscribed   g Income taxes payable

    f Paid-in capital in excess of par value

20 If the Retained Earnings account has a debit balance, how is it presented in the balance sheet and what is it called?

21 A professional baseball team received as a gift from the city the land upon which to build a stadium. What effect, if any, will the receipt of this gift have upon the baseball team's balance sheet and income statement? Explain.

22 Explain the following terms:

    a Stock transfer agent   d Minutes book

    b Stockholders' ledger   e Stock registrar

    c Underwriter

EXERCISES

Ex. 11-1 John Stewart owns Steamers & Beer, a seafood restaurant organized as a single proprietorship. Explain what effect, if any, recording the following transactions will have upon the balance of Stewart's capital account and drawing account.

    a Stewart brings his personal computer from home to use full time in the business.

    b Stewart pays a number of his personal bills from the business bank account.

    c Stewart hires his daughter to work in the restaurant while she is home from college during semester break. Her salary, paid from the business bank account, is $800.

    d Stewart writes a check from his personal bank account to pay a liability of the business.

    e At the end of the accounting period, the balance of Stewart's drawing account is closed into his capital account.

Ex. 11-2 A business owned by Megan Rogers was short of cash and Rogers therefore decided to form a partnership with Steve Wilson, who was able to contribute cash to the new partnership. The assets contributed by Rogers appeared as follows in the balance sheet of her business: cash, $900; accounts receivable, $18,900, with an allowance for doubtful accounts of $600; inventory, $36,000; and store equipment, $19,000. Rogers had recorded depreciation of $1,500 during her use of the store equipment in her single proprietorship.

Rogers and Wilson agreed that the allowance for doubtful accounts was inadequate and should be $1,000. They also agreed that a fair value for the inventory was its replacement cost of $42,000 and that the fair value of the store equipment was $15,000. You are to open the partnership accounts by making a general journal entry to record the investment by Rogers.

Ex. 11-3 Redmond and Adams, both of whom are CPAs, form a partnership, with Redmond investing $40,000 and Adams $30,000. They agree to share net income as follows:

    (1) Interest at 15% on beginning capital balances.

    (2) Salary allowances of $50,000 to Redmond and $40,000 to Adams.

    (3) Any partnership earnings in excess of the amount required to cover the interest and salary allowances to be divided 60% to Redmond and 40% to Adams.

The partnership net income for the first year of operations amounted to $120,500 before interest and salary allowances. Show how this $120,500 should be divided between the two partners. Use a three-column schedule with a separate column for each partner and a column for the total income allocated. List on separate lines the amounts of interest, salaries, and the residual amount divided.

Ex. 11-4 BioTech Corporation was authorized to issue 10,000 shares of $100 par value, 10% cumulative preferred stock, and 200,000 shares of no-par common stock with a stated value of $5 per share.

All the preferred stock was issued at par and 140,000 shares of the common stock were sold for $27 per share. Prepare the stockholders' equity section immediately after the issuance of the securities but prior to operation of the company.

Ex. 11-5 Wolfe Company has outstanding two classes of $100 par value stock: 5,000 shares of 9% cumulative preferred and 25,000 shares of common. The company had a $50,000 deficit at the beginning of the current year, and preferred dividends had not been paid for two years. During the current year, the company earned $250,000. What will be the balance in retained earnings at the end of the current year, if the company pays a dividend of $1 per share on the common stock?

Ex. 11-6 A portion of the stockholders' equity section from the balance sheet of Palermo Corporation appears below:

Stockholders' equity:
Preferred stock, 9% cumulative, $50 par, 40,000 shares authorized and issued $2,000,000
Preferred stock, 12% noncumulative, $100 par, 8,000 shares authorized and
  issued   800,000
Common stock, $5 par, 400,000 shares authorized and issued   2,000,000
  Total paid-in capital $4,800,000

Instructions. Assume that all the stock was issued on January 1, 19___, and that no dividends were paid during the first two years of operations. During the third year, Palermo Corporation paid total cash dividends of $736,000.

a Compute the amount of cash dividends paid during the third year to each of the three classes of stock.
b Compute the dividends paid **per share** during the third year for each of the three classes of stock.

Ex. 11-7 The stockholders' equity section of the balance sheet appeared as follows in a recent annual report of Samoa Corporation:

Stockholders' equity:
Capital stock:
  $5.50 cumulative preferred stock; no-par value, 300,000 shares
    authorized, 180,000 shares outstanding, stated at .... $ 18,000,000
  Common stock; no-par value, 5,000,000 shares authorized, 4,300,000
    shares issued, stated at   32,250,000
Retained earnings   75,800,000
  Total stockholders' equity $126,050,000

Instructions. From this information compute answers to the following questions:

a What is the stated value per share of the preferred stock?
b What was the average issuance price of a share of common stock?
c What is the amount of the total legal capital and the amount of the total paid in capital?
d What is the total amount of the annual dividend requirement on the preferred stock issue?
e Total dividends of $5,200,000 were declared on the preferred and common stock during the year. The balance in retained earnings at the beginning of the year amounted to $67,800,000. What was the amount of net income for the year?

Problems

11-1 Single proprietorship: use of capital and drawing account

Dean Engineering is a single proprietorship owned by Sharon Dean. During the month of April, Dean's ownership equity was affected by the following events:

Apr. 7 Dean invested an additional $20,000 cash in the business.

Apr. 15 Dean withdrew $6,500 in cash and used the money to pay her personal income taxes.

Apr. 22 Dean collected from J. Barker an $1,800 account receivable of the business and deposited the money in her personal checking account.

Apr. 30 Dean drew a check payable to herself on the business bank account in the amount of $4,000. She had stipulated this amount as her monthly salary as owner-manager of the business.

Apr. 30 The Income Summary account shows a credit balance of $7,200; the accounts of Dean Engineering are closed monthly.

Instructions

a Prepare journal entries for each of the above events in the accounts of Dean Engineering. Include the entries necessary to close the Income Summary account and Dean's drawing account at April 30.

b Prepare a statement of owner's capital for the month ended April 30. Assume that the balance of Dean's capital account on April 1 was $57,800.

11-2 Division of partnership income

The partnership of L & M Electrical was formed with Lewis investing $40,000 and Martin investing $60,000. During the first year, net income amounted to $55,000.

Instructions

a Determine how the $55,000 net income would be divided under each of the following four independent assumptions as to the agreement for sharing profits and losses. Use schedules of the type illustrated in this chapter to show all steps in the distribution of net income between the partners.

(1) The partnership agreement does not mention profit sharing.

(2) Net income is to be divided in a fixed ratio: 40% to Lewis and 60% to Martin.

(3) Interest at 15% to be allowed on beginning capital investments and balance to be divided equally.

(4) Salaries of $18,000 to Lewis and $28,000 to Martin, interest at 15% to be allowed on beginning capital investments, balance to be divided equally.

b Prepare the journal entry to close the Income Summary account, using the division of net income developed in the last case (a,4) above.

11-3 Another division of partnership income

Research Consultants has three partners—A, B, and C. During the current year their capital balances were: A, $140,000; B, $100,000; and C, $60,000. The partnership agreement provides that partners shall receive salary allowances as follows: A, none, B, $50,000; and C, $38,000. The partners shall also be allowed 12% annually on their capital balances. Residual profits or losses are to be divided: A, $\frac{1}{2}$; B, $\frac{1}{3}$; and C, $\frac{1}{6}$.

Instructions. Prepare separate schedules showing how income will be divided among the three partners in each of the following cases. The figure given in each case is the annual income available for distribution among the partners.

a Income of $490,000
b Income of $67,000
c Loss of $20,000

11-4 Partnerships: comprehensive problem

The partnership of Trees 'n' Stuff, a retail nursery, was formed on July 1, when George Foster and Dinah Moore agreed to invest equal amounts and to share profits and losses equally. The investment of Foster consists of $25,000 cash and an inventory of merchandise valued at $55,000.

Moore also is to contribute a total of $80,000. However, it is agreed that her contribution will consist of the following assets of her business along with the transfer to the partnership of her business liabilities. The agreed values of the various items as well as their carrying values on Moore's records are listed below. Moore also contributes enough cash to bring her capital account to $80,000.

	Investment by Moore	
	Balances on Moore Records	Agreed Value
Accounts receivable	$89,600	$89,600
Allowance for doubtful accounts	3,840	8,000
Inventory	9,600	11,000
Office equipment (net)	12,800	9,000
Accounts payable	27,000	27,000

Instructions

a Draft entries (in general journal form) to record the investments of Foster and Moore in the new partnership.

b Prepare the beginning balance sheet of the partnership (in report form) at the close of business July 1, reflecting the above transfers to the firm.

c On the following June 30 after one year of operation, the Income Summary account showed a credit balance of $74,000 and the Drawing account for each partner showed a debit balance of $32,000. Prepare journal entries to close the Income Summary account and the drawing accounts at June 30.

d Based upon the information developed in parts b and c, prepare a statement of partners' capitals for the year ended June 30. (Begin your statement of partners' capitals with a balance of $80,000 in each partners' capital account as of July 1, 19___. Do not show Moore's initial investment as an "additional investment.")

11-5 Preparation of stockholders' equity section: two short cases

The two cases described below are independent of each other. Each case provides the information necessary to prepare the stockholders' equity section of a corporate balance sheet.

Case A. Baker Company was organized early in Year 3 with authorization to issue 20,000 shares of $5 par value common stock. All the shares were issued at a price of $12 per share. The operations of the company resulted in a net loss of $20,000 for Year 3 and a net loss of $52,000 in Year 4. In Year 5 net income was $21,000. No dividends were declared during the three-year period.

Case B. Street Corporation was formed early in Year 1. Authorization was obtained to issue 100,000 shares of $1 par value common stock and 2,000 shares of $100 par value cumulative preferred stock. All the preferred stock was issued at par and 80,000 shares of the common stock were sold for $10 per share. The preferred stock was callable at $105 per share and was entitled to dividends of 9% before any dividends were paid to common. During the first five years of existence, the corporation earned a total of $560,000 and paid dividends of 20 cents per share each year on common stock.

Instructions. For each of the situations described above, prepare in good form the stockholders' equity section of the balance sheet as of December 31, Year 5. Include a supporting schedule for each case showing your determination of the balance of retained earnings that should appear in the balance sheet.

11-6 Corporations; short comprehensive problem

The following information provides the basis for preparing journal entries and the stockholders' equity section of a corporate balance sheet.

Early in Year 10, Roger Gordon and several friends organized a corporation called Fitness Centers, Inc. The corporation was authorized to issue 50,000 shares of $100 par value, 10% cumulative preferred stock and 400,000 shares of $2 par value common stock. The following transactions (among others) occurred during Year 10:

Jan. 6 Issued for cash 20,000 shares of common stock at $14 per share. The shares were issued to Gordon and 10 other investors.

Jan. 7 Issued an additional 500 shares of common stock to Gordon in exchange for his services in organizing the corporation. The stockholders agreed that these services were worth $7,000.

Jan. 12 Issued 2,500 shares of preferred stock for cash of $250,000.

June 4 Acquired land as a building site in exchange for 15,000 shares of common stock. In view of the appraised value of the land and the progress of the company, the directors of Fitness Centers, Inc., agreed that the common stock was to be valued for purposes of this transaction at $15 per share.

Nov. 15 The first annual dividend of $10 per share was declared on the preferred stock to be paid December 20 of Year 10.

Dec. 20 Paid the cash dividend declared on November 15.

Dec. 31 After the revenue and expenses were closed into the Income Summary account, that account indicated a net income of $90,500.

Instructions

a Prepare journal entries for Year 10 in general journal form to record the above transactions. Include entries at December 31 to close the Income Summary account and the Dividends account.

b Prepare the stockholders' equity section of the balance sheet at December 31, Year 10.

11-7 Convertible preferred stock

Harbor Light, Inc., was authorized to issue 500,000 shares of $10 par value common stock and 20,000 shares of 6% convertible and cumulative, $100 par value, preferred stock. Each share of preferred stock is convertible, at the option of the shareholder, into four shares of common stock. All the preferred stock was issued at $100 per share, and 300,000 shares of common stock were issued at $15 per share. The balance in Retained Earnings at January 1, Year 10, is $670,000, and there are no dividends in arrears.

Instructions

    a Prepare the stockholders' equity section of the balance sheet at January 1, Year 10.
    b Assume that on January 1, Year 10, all the preferred stock is converted into shares of common stock. Prepare a journal entry to record the conversion.
    c Prepare a revised stockholders' equity section of the balance sheet at January 1, Year 10, after the conversion of the preferred stock.

11-8   Issuance of capital stock and stock subscriptions

For several years, Linda Green has operated a successful business organized as a single proprietorship. In order to raise the capital to operate on a larger scale, she decided to organize a new corporation to continue in the same line of business. In January of Year 6, Green organized Malibu Corporation, which was authorized to issue 250,000 shares of $1 par value common stock. During January Malibu Corporation completed the following transactions:

Jan. 10 Issued 10,000 shares of common stock to various investors for cash at $22 per share.
Jan. 10 Issued 30,000 shares of common stock to Green in exchange for assets with a current market value as follows:

Inventory	$120,000
Equipment	50,000
Building	260,000
Land	230,000

Jan. 15 Received an invoice from an attorney for $7,000 for services relating to the formation of Malibu Corporation. The invoice will be paid in 30 days.
Jan. 17 Received subscriptions for 5,000 shares of common stock at $22 per share; 1,000 of the shares were subscribed by Green and 4,000 were subscribed by other investors.
Jan. 31 Collected from Green the full amount of her subscription to 1,000 shares of common stock and issued a stock certificate for these shares. (No collection has yet been made from the subscribers to the other 4,000 shares.)

The corporation will begin operations in February; no revenue was earned and no expenses were incurred during January. No depreciation of plant assets and no amortization of organization cost will be recognized until February when operations get under way.

Instructions

    a Prepare journal entries to record the transactions for January in the accounting records of Malibu Corporation.
    b Prepare a classified balance sheet for the corporation at January 31, Year 6.

11-9   Analysis of stockholders' equity

The year-end balance sheet of J.D. Ross Co. includes the following stockholders' equity section (with certain details omitted):

Stockholders' equity:

$9.50 cumulative preferred stock, $100 par value, callable at $110, authorized 30,000 shares	$ 1,800,000
Common stock, $5 par value, authorized 500,000 shares	2,100,000
Paid-in capital in excess of par: common	6,510,000
Donated capital	500,000
Retained earnings	6,400,000
Total stockholders' equity	$17.310,000

Instructions. On the basis of this information, answer the following questions and show any necessary supporting computations:

a How many shares of preferred stock are outstanding?

b What is the total dollar amount of the annual dividend requirement on preferred stock?

c How many shares of common stock are outstanding?

d What was the average issuance price of a share of common stock?

e What is the total legal capital of the corporation?

f What is the total paid-in (or contributed) capital?

g Total dividends of $1,011,000 were declared on the preferred and common stock during the year, and the balance of retained earnings at the beginning of the year was $5,184,000. What was the amount of net income for the year?

Cases for analysis

Case 11-1 Factors affecting market prices of preferred and common stocks

ADM Labs is a publicly owned company with several issues of capital stock outstanding. Over the past decade, the company has consistently earned modest profits and has increased its common stock dividend annually by 5 or 10 cents per share. Recently the company introduced several new products which you believe will cause future sales and profits to increase dramatically. You also expect a gradual increase in long-term interest rates from their present level of about 11% to, perhaps, 12 or 12½%. Based upon these forecasts, explain whether you would expect to see the market prices of the following three issues of ADM capital stock increase or decrease. Explain your reasoning in each answer.

a 10% preferred stock, $100 par value, (currently selling at $90 per share).

b $5 par value common stock (currently paying an annual dividend of $2.50 and selling at $40 per share).

c 7% convertible preferred stock, $100 par value, (currently selling at $125 per share).

Case 11-2 Developing an equitable plan for division of partnership income

Juan Ramirez and Robert Cole are considering forming a partnership to engage in the business of aerial photography. Ramirez is a licensed pilot, is currently earning $48,000 a year, and has $50,000 to invest in the partnership. Cole is a professional photographer who is currently earning $20,000 a year. He has recently inherited $70,000 which he plans to invest in the partnership.

Both partners will work full time in the business. After careful study, they have estimated that expenses are likely to exceed revenue by $10,000 during the first year of operations. In the second year, however, they expect the business to become profitable, with revenue exceeding expenses by an estimated $90,000. (Bear in mind that these estimates of expenses do not include any salaries or interest to the partners.) Under present market conditions, a fair rate of return on capital invested in this type of business is 20%.

Instructions

a On the basis of this information, prepare a brief description of the income-sharing agreement which you would recommend for Ramirez and Cole. Explain the basis for your proposal.

b Prepare a separate schedule for each of the next two years showing how the estimated amounts of net income would be divided between the two partners under your plan. (Assume that the original capital balances for both partners remain unchanged during the two-year period. This simplifying assumption allows you to ignore the changes which would normally occur in capital accounts as a result of divisions of profits, or from drawings or additional investments.)

c Write a brief statement explaining the differences in allocation of income to the two partners and defending the results indicated by your income-sharing proposal.

Chapter 12
Corporations:
a closer look

Chapter 12 explores special topics relating primarily to the financial statements of large corporations. We illustrate how the results of discontinued operations and other unusual events are presented in the income statement. We also illustrate and explain the presentation of earnings per share, with emphasis upon interpretation of the different per-share amounts. The remainder of the chapter discusses the concept of book value per share and a variety of transactions affecting stockholders' equity, including cash dividends, stock dividends, stock splits, prior period adjustments, treasury stock transactions, and book value per share. Two optional appendixes follow Chapter 12. The first covers investments for purposes of control, including an introduction to consolidated financial statements; the second discusses the special accounting problems of multinational corporations.

After studying
this chapter you
should be able to:

✓ Describe how discontinued operations and extraordinary items are presented in the income statement.
✓ Compute earnings per share.
✓ Distinguish between primary and fully diluted earnings per share.
✓ Account for stock dividends and stock splits, and explain the probable effect of these transactions upon market price.
✓ Define prior period adjustments and explain how they are presented in financial statements.
✓ Account for treasury stock transactions.
✓ Compute book value per share.

The most important aspect of corporate financial reporting, in the view of most stockholders, is the determination of periodic net income. Both the market price of common stock and the amount of cash dividends per share depend to a considerable extent on the current level of earnings (net income). Even more important than the absolute amount of net income is the *trend* of earnings over time. Is net income increasing or decreasing from one year to the next? The common stocks of those companies which regularly achieve higher earnings year after year become the favorite securities of the investment community. Such stature helps greatly in raising new capital, in attracting and retaining highly competent management, and in many other ways.

In this chapter, we will see that the corporate income statement is organized to help investors to evaluate the trend of earnings and to associate total earnings with their ownership shares. In addition, we will discuss transactions that may affect the amount of stockholders' equity and the market price of common stock, but that do not affect net income. Transactions of this nature include cash and stock dividends, stock splits, prior period adjustments, and treasury stock transactions.

Public misconceptions of the rate of corporate earnings

Numerous public opinion surveys indicate that most people mistakenly believe that corporate earnings generally amount to somewhere between 20 and 50% of sales. College and university students should be better informed, but the authors have found, from questioning students in classes at the beginning of the first course in accounting, that college students in guessing at the average rate of corporate earnings usually suggest far higher rates than actually exist. If you will look at the published annual reports of leading corporations, you will find that net income usually falls somewhere between 2 and 10% of sales. Remember that these financial statements have been audited by independent CPA firms, and also reviewed by the SEC. For all manufacturing companies a representative rate of earnings in recent years has been around 4 to 5%. Of course, there are exceptions. In the airline industry, for example, American Airlines, TWA, and Pan American each operated at a net loss for several years during the last decade. This question of the rate of corporate earnings will be considered more fully in Chapter 16.

Developing predictive information

An income statement tells us a great deal about the performance of a company over the past year. For example, study of the income statement makes clear the rate of gross profit on sales, the net income for the year, the percentage of profit per dollar of sales, and the net income earned on each share of common stock. Can we expect the income statement for *next year* to indicate about the same level of performance? If the transactions summarized in the income statement for the year just completed were of a normal recurring nature, such as selling merchandise, paying employees, and incurring other normal expenses, we can reasonably assume that the operating results were typical and that somewhat similar results can be expected in the following year. However, in any business, unusual and nonrecurring events may occur which cause the current year's net income to be quite different from the income we should expect the company to earn in the future. For example, the company may have sustained large losses in the current year from an earthquake or some other event which is not likely to recur in the near future.

Ideally, the results of unusual and nonrecurring transactions should be shown in a separate section of the income statement *after* the income or loss from normal business activities has been determined. Income from *normal and recurring* activities presumably should be a more useful figure for predicting future earnings than is a net income figure which includes the results of nonrecurring events. The problem in creating such an income statement, however, is in determining which events are so unlikely to recur that they should be excluded from the results of "normal" operations.

The question of how unusual an event should be to require separate presentation has long been debated by accountants and other interested parties. Two categories of events that currently require special treatment in the income statement are (1) the results of discontinued operations and (2) extraordinary items. The criteria which define these categories and the related income statement presentation are still being debated and may well change in future years.

Discontinued operations

Virtually all large corporations are engaged in several different types of business activity. For example, Exxon, the oil company, has a division which manufactures office equipment. PepsiCo, known primarily as a soft drink manufacturer, owns and operates the Pizza Hut restaurant chain. Sears Roebuck & Co., in addition to its retail stores, has a variety of business lines, including an insurance company, a stock brokerage, a real estate firm, and a chain of savings and loan companies. Accountants use the term *segment of a business* to describe each distinct type of business activity. Some corporations may have a dozen or more segments.

Sometimes a corporation may sell a segment of its operations to another company. A problem then arises in using past income statements to forecast future earnings because the size and scope of the company's operations change whenever a segment of the business is discontinued. The FASB has accepted the position that the results of a company's *continuing operations* should be reported in the income statement separately from the operating results of any segments discontinued during the year.[1] The income of a discontinued segment (including any gain or loss on the disposal of the segment) is listed separately in the income statement *after* determining the income from continuing operations. The purpose of such separate disclosure is to enable users of financial statements to make better predictive judgments as to the future performance of the company.

For example, assume that Commuter Airways operates both an airline service and a small chain of motels. Near the end of the current year, the company sells all of the motels to a national motel chain. The operating results of Commuter Airways' two business segments for the current year are as follows:

	Airline Operations	Motel Operations*
Net revenue	$12,000,000	$5,000,000
Costs and expenses (including applicable income taxes)	11,200,000	6,100,000
Gain on sale of motels, net of income taxes		500,000

* Revenue and expenses of motel operations are prior to date of sale.

[1] *APB Opinion No. 30,* "Reporting the Results of Operations — Reporting the Effects of Disposal of a Segment of a Business, and Extraordinary, Unusual and Infrequently Occurring Events and Transactions," AICPA (New York: 1973).

The following condensed income statement illustrates the proper presentation of the discontinued motel operations:

COMMUTER AIRWAYS
Condensed Income Statement
For the Current Year

Net revenue	$12,000,000
Cost and expenses (including applicable income taxes)	11,200,000
Income from continuing operations	$ 800,000
Discontinued operations:	
Operating loss from motels, net of income taxes .... $(1,100,000)	
Gain on sale of motels, net of income taxes 500,000	(600,000)
Net income	$ 200,000

Income from continuing operations. Notice that the top section of this income statement includes only the revenue and expenses of the continuing airline operations. This enables us to develop a subtotal, Income from Continuing Operations, which measures the profitability of the ongoing business activities. This subtotal should be helpful in making predictions of the company's future earnings. For example, if we predict no significant changes in the profitability of airline operations, we should expect Commuter Airways to earn a net income of approximately $800,000 next year.

In their annual reports to stockholders, many companies include the income statements from one or more prior years to assist investors in evaluating the trend in earnings. If Commuter Airways includes prior years' income statements in its annual report, these statements should be reorganized to show separately the operating results of the airlines and of the motels. This will further assist investors in evaluating the earnings prospects for the company's ongoing operations.

Presentation of the discontinued operations. After determination of the income from continuing operations, the operating results of the discontinued motel segment are shown in two parts. The first of these parts is the $1,100,000 net operating loss ($5,000,000 revenue, minus $6,100,000 in costs and expenses) incurred during the portion of the year that the motels were owned by Commuter Airways. The second item is the gain or loss resulting from the sale of the motels. Since the motels are no longer owned by Commuter Airways, it is not considered necessary to itemize the revenue and expense items which contributed to the net operating loss for this segment of the business. However, the total revenue earned by the discontinued segment ($5,000,000) should be disclosed in a footnote to the financial statements.

Notice the phrase *net of income taxes* in the discontinued operations section of the income statement. This phrase means that the operating loss on the discontinued segment and the gain on its sale have been adjusted for any applicable income tax effects. For example, Commuter Airways may have realized a $700,000 gain on the sale of the motels, but if this $700,000 gain results in an additional $200,000 in income taxes being owed, the after-tax gain is only $500,000. Similarly, before considering income taxes, the operating loss on the motels may have amounted to $2,000,000 for the year. If this loss results in a $900,000 reduction in income taxes, however, the loss *net of related income taxes* is only $1,100,000.

Income taxes applicable to the airline segment of the business are included among the $11,200,000 in costs and expenses deducted in arriving at the Income from Continuing Operations. Corporate income taxes are discussed further in Chapter 17.

Extraordinary items

The second category of events requiring disclosure in a separate section of the income statements is extraordinary items. An extraordinary item is a gain or loss that is *(1) material in amount, (2) unusual in nature, and (3) not expected to recur in the foreseeable future.* By definition, extraordinary items are extremely rare; hence, they seldom appear in financial statements. Examples of extraordinary items include the effects of unusual casualties (such as earthquakes or tornadoes), expropriation of assets by a foreign government, and gains or losses that may result from a newly enacted law. Gains or losses from such transactions as sales of plant assets, strikes, or settlements of litigation are recurring events in the business environment and do *not* qualify as extraordinary items.

When a gain or loss qualifies as an extraordinary item, it appears at the bottom of the income statement following the subtotal, *Income before Extraordinary Items.* Since the extraordinary item is so unusual, this subtotal is considered necessary to show investors what the net income *would have been* if the unusual event had not occurred. Extraordinary items are shown net of any related income tax effects. The presentation of an extraordinary item is illustrated in the following income statement:

SEAPORT MALL
Income Statement
For the Year Ended December 31, 19__

Net sales		$10,000,000
Costs and expenses:		
Cost of goods sold	$6,000,000	
Selling expenses	1,100,000	
General and administrative expenses	700,000	
Loss from settlement of litigation	200,000	
Income taxes (excluding tax effects of the extraordinary loss).	800,000	8,800,000
Income before extraordinary items		$ 1,200,000
Extraordinary item: Loss from earthquake damage, net of related tax effects		(300,000)
Net income		$ 900,000

Other nonoperating gains and losses. Some transactions are not typical of normal operations but also do not meet the criteria for separate presentation as extraordinary items. Among such events are losses incurred because of strikes and the gains or losses resulting from sales of plant assets. Such items, if material, should be individually listed as items of revenue or expense, rather than being combined with other items in broad categories such as sales revenue or general and administrative expenses.

In the income statement of Seaport Mall illustrated above, the nonoperating loss of $200,000 resulting from the settlement of a lawsuit was disclosed separately in the income statement but was **not** listed as an extraordinary item. This loss was important enough to bring to the attention of readers of the financial statements, but lawsuits are not so unusual or infrequent as to be considered extraordinary items.

The income or loss from a discontinued segment of the business (including any gain or loss on disposal of the segment) is **not** an extraordinary item. When discontinued operations and an extraordinary item appear in the same income statement, the income or loss from the discontinued operations is presented **before** the extraordinary item. Thus, the subtotal Income before Extraordinary Items **includes** the operating results of any segments of the business which have been discontinued during the year.

Earnings per share (EPS)

Perhaps the most widely used of all accounting statistics is **earnings per share** of common stock. Everyone who buys or sells stock in a corporation needs to know the annual earnings per share. Stock market prices are quoted on a per-share basis. If you are considering investing in IBM stock at a price of, say, $120 per share, you need to know the earnings per share and the annual dividend per share in order to decide whether this price is reasonable. In other words, how much earning power and how much dividend income would you be getting for each share you buy?

To compute earnings per share, the annual net income available to the common stockholders is divided by the average number of common shares outstanding. The concept of earnings per share applies **only to common stock;** preferred stock has no claim to earnings beyond the stipulated preferred stock dividends.

Many financial analysts express the relationship between earnings per share and market price per share as a **price-earnings ratio** (p/e ratio). This ratio is computed by dividing the market price per share of common stock by the annual earnings per share.

Weighted-average number of shares outstanding. The simplest example of computing earnings per share is found when a company has issued only common stock and the number of shares outstanding has not changed during the year. In this situation, the net income for the year divided by the number of shares outstanding at year-end equals earnings per share.

In many companies, however, the number of shares of stock outstanding is changed one or more times during the year. When additional shares are issued in exchange for assets during the year, the computation of earnings per share is based upon the **weighted-average** number of shares outstanding.[2]

The weighted-average number of shares for the year is determined by multiplying the number of shares outstanding by the fraction of the year that said number of shares

---

[2] When the number of shares outstanding changes as a result of a stock split or a stock dividend (discussed later in this chapter), the computation of the weighted-average number of shares outstanding should be adjusted *retroactively* rather than weighted for the period the new shares were outstanding. Earnings per share data for prior years thus will be consistently stated in terms of the current capital structure.

outstanding remained unchanged. For example, assume that 100,000 shares of common stock were outstanding during the first nine months of Year 1 and 140,000 shares during the last three months. Assume also that the increase in shares outstanding resulted from the sale of 40,000 shares for cash. The weighted-average number of shares outstanding during Year 1 would be 110,000 determined as follows:

100,000 shares $\times \frac{9}{12}$ of a year	75,000
140,000 shares $\times \frac{3}{12}$ of a year	35,000
Weighted-average number of common shares outstanding	110,000

This procedure gives more meaningful earnings per share data than if the total number of shares outstanding at the end of the year were used in the calculations. By using the weighted-average number of shares, we recognize that the proceeds from the sale of the 40,000 shares were available to generate earnings only during the last three months of the year. The contribution to earnings made by 40,000 shares outstanding during one-fourth of the year is equivalent to that of 10,000 shares outstanding for a full year. In other words, the weighted-average number of shares outstanding consists of 100,000 shares outstanding during the entire year plus the 10,000-share full-year equivalent of the shares issued during the year.

Preferred dividends and earnings per share. When a company has preferred stock outstanding, the preferred stockholders participate in net income to the extent of the preferred stock dividends. To determine the earnings *applicable to the common stock*, we must first deduct from net income the amount of any preferred stock dividends. To illustrate, let us assume that Tanner Corporation has 200,000 shares of common stock and 10,000 shares of $4 preferred stock outstanding throughout the year. Net income for the year totals $480,000. Earnings per share of common stock would be computed as follows:

Net income	$480,000
Less: Dividends on preferred stock (10,000 shares $\times$ $4)	40,000
Earnings applicable to common stock	$440,000
Weighted-average number of common shares outstanding	200,000
Earnings per share of common stock ($440,000 $\div$ 200,000 shares)	$2.20

Presentation of earnings per share in the income statement

All publicly owned corporations are required to present earnings per share data in their income statements.[3] If an income statement includes subtotals for income from continuing operations, or for income before extraordinary items, per-share figures are shown for these amounts as well as for net income. These additional per-share amounts are computed by substituting the amount of the appropriate subtotal for the net income figure in the preceding calculation.

[3] The FASB has exempted closely held corporations (those not publicly owned) from the requirement of computing and reporting earnings per share. See *FASB Statement No. 23*, "Suspension of the Reporting of Earnings per Share and Segment Information by Nonpublic Enterprises" (Stamford, Conn.: 1978).

To illustrate all of the potential per-share computations, we will expand our Tanner Corporation example to include income from continuing operations and income before extraordinary items. We should point out, however, that all of these figures seldom appear in the same income statement. Very few companies have both discontinued operations and an extraordinary item to report in the same year. The following condensed income statement is intended to illustrate the proper format for presenting earnings per share figures and to provide a review of the calculations.

TANNER CORPORATION
Condensed Income Statement
For the Year Ended December 31, 19__

Net sales	$8,000,000
Cost and expenses (detail omitted for illustrative purposes)	7,340,000
Income from continuing operations	$ 660,000
Loss from discontinued operations, net of related tax effects	(60,000)
Income before extraordinary items	$ 600,000
Less: Extraordinary loss from tornado damage, net of related tax effects	(120,000)
Net income	$ 480,000
Earnings per share of common stock:	
Earnings from continuing operations	$3.10[a]
Loss from discontinued operations	(.30)
Earnings before extraordinary items	$2.80[b]
Extraordinary loss	(.60)
Net earnings	$2.20[c]

[a] ($660,000 − $40,000 preferred dividends) ÷ 200,000 shares
[b] ($600,000 − $40,000) ÷ 200,000 shares
[c] ($480,000 − $40,000) ÷ 200,000 shares

For emphasis the three required figures for earnings per share are printed in black. We have shown in color the per-share amounts for the loss from discontinued operations and the extraordinary loss, but these are merely reconciling amounts and sometimes are omitted in a formal income statement. For illustration, we have also shown how the various amounts for earnings per share were computed. These explanatory computations would not be included in an actual income statement.

Interpreting the different per-share amounts. To informed users of financial statements, each of these figures has a different significance. Earnings per share from continuing operations represents the results of continuing and ordinary business activity. This figure is the most useful one for predicting future operating results. *Net earnings* per share, on the other hand, shows the overall operating results of the current year, including any discontinued operations or extraordinary items.

Unfortunately the term *earnings per share* often is used without qualification in referring to various types of per-share data. When using per-share information, it is important to know exactly which per-share statistic is being presented. For example, the price-earnings ratios (market price divided by earnings per share) for common stocks listed on major stock exchanges are reported daily in **The Wall Street Journal** and many other newspapers. Which earnings per share figures are used in computing these ratios? If a company reports an extraordinary gain or loss, the price-earnings ratio is computed using the per-share **earnings before the extraordinary item.** Otherwise, the ratio is based upon **net earnings** per share.

Primary and fully diluted earnings per share

Let us assume that a company has an outstanding issue of preferred stock that is convertible into shares of common stock at a rate of, say, two shares of common for each share of preferred. The conversion of this preferred stock would increase the number of common shares outstanding and might **dilute** (reduce) earnings per share. Any common stockholder interested in the trend of earnings per share will want to know what effect the conversion of the preferred stock would have upon this statistic.

To inform investors of the potential dilution which might occur, two figures are presented for each earnings per share statistic. The first figure, called **primary** earnings per share, is based upon the weighted-average number of common shares actually outstanding during the year. Thus, this figure ignores the potential dilution represented by the convertible preferred stock.[4] The second figure, called **fully diluted** earnings per share, shows the impact that conversion of the preferred stock would have upon primary earnings per share.

Primary earnings per share are computed in the same manner illustrated in our preceding example of Tanner Corporation. Fully diluted earnings per share, on the other hand, are computed on the assumption that all the preferred stock **had been converted into common stock at the beginning of the current year.**[5] (The mechanics of computing fully diluted earnings per share are covered in the intermediate accounting course.)

It is important to remember that fully diluted earnings per share represent a **hypothetical case.** This statistic is computed even though the preferred stock actually was **not** converted during the year. The purpose of showing fully diluted earnings per share is to warn common stockholders of what **could** have happened. When the difference between primary and fully diluted earnings per share becomes significant, investors should recognize the **risk** that future earnings per share may be reduced by conversions of other securities into common stock.

When a company reports both primary and fully diluted earnings per share, the price-earnings ratio shown in newspapers is based upon the primary figure.

Cash dividends

The prospect of receiving cash dividends is a principal reason for investing in the stocks of corporations. An increase or decrease in the established rate of dividends will usually

---

[4] If certain criteria are met, convertible securities qualify as **common stock equivalents** and enter into the computation of primary earnings per share. Common stock equivalents and other complex issues relating to earnings per share are discussed in intermediate accounting courses and in *APB Opinion No. 15,* "Earnings per Share," AICPA (New York, 1969).

[5] If the preferred stock had been issued during the current year, we would assume that it was converted into common stock on the date it was issued.

cause an immediate rise or fall in the market price of the company's stock. Stockholders are keenly interested in prospects for future dividends and as a group are strongly in favor or more generous dividend payments. The board of directors, on the other hand, is primarily concerned with the long-run growth and financial strength of the corporation; it may prefer to restrict dividends to a minimum in order to conserve cash for purchase of plant and equipment or for other needs of the company. Many of the so-called "growth companies" plow back into the business most of their earnings and pay only very small cash dividends.

The preceding discussion suggests three requirements for the payment of a cash dividend. These are:

1 *Retained earnings.* Since dividends represent a distribution of earnings to stockholders, the theoretical maximum for dividends is the total undistributed net income of the company, represented by the credit balance of the Retained Earnings account. As a practical matter, many corporations limit dividends to somewhere near 40% of annual net income, in the belief that a major portion of the net income must be retained in the business if the company is to grow and to keep pace with its competitors.

2 *An adequate cash position.* The fact that the company reports large earnings does not mean that it has a large amount of cash on hand. Earnings may have been invested in new plant and equipment, or in paying off debts, or in acquiring larger inventory. There is no necessary relationship between the balance in the Retained Earnings account and the balance in the Cash account. The traditional expression of "paying dividends out of retained earnings" is misleading. Cash dividends can be paid only "out of" cash.

3 *Dividend action by the board of directors.* Even though the company's net income is substantial and its cash position seemingly satisfactory, dividends are not paid automatically. A formal action by the board of directors is necessary to declare a dividend.

Dividend dates

Four significant dates are involved in the distribution of a dividend. These dates are:

1 *Date of declaration.* On the day on which the dividend is declared by the board of directors, a liability to make the payment comes into existence.

2 *Date of record.* The date of record always follows the date of declaration, usually by a period or two or three weeks, and is always stated in the dividend declaration. In order to be eligible to receive the dividend, a person must be listed as the owner of the stock on the date of record.

3 *Ex-dividend date.* The ex-dividend date is significant for investors in companies with stocks traded on the stock exchanges. To permit the compilation of the list of stockholders as of the record date, it is customary for the stock to go "ex-dividend" three business days before the date of record. A stock is said to be selling ex-dividend on the day that it loses the right to receive the latest declared dividend. A person who buys the stock before the ex-dividend date is entitled to receive the dividend; con-

versely, a stockholder who sells shares before the ex-dividend date does not receive the dividend.

4 **Date of payment.** The declaration of a dividend always includes announcement of the date of payment as well as the date of record. Usually the date of payment comes from two to four weeks after the date of record.

The journal entries to record the declaration and payment of a cash dividend were illustrated in Chapter 3 but are repeated here with emphasis on the date of declaration and date of payment.

Entries made on declaration date and . . .

June 1	Dividends	100,000	
	Dividends Payable		100,000
	To record declaration of a cash dividend of $1 per share on the 100,000 shares of common stock outstanding. Payable July 10 to stockholders of record on June 20.		

. . . on payment date

July 10	Dividends Payable	100,000	
	Cash		100,000
	To record payment of $1 per share dividend declared June 1 to stockholders of record on June 20.		

At the end of the accounting period, a closing entry is required to transfer the debit balance of the Dividends account into the Retained Earnings account. Some companies follow the alternative practice of debiting Retained Earnings when the dividend is declared instead of using a Dividends account. Under either method, the balance of the Retained Earnings account ultimately is reduced by all dividends declared during the period.

Most dividends are paid in cash, but occasionally a dividend declaration calls for payment in assets other than cash. A large distillery once paid a dividend consisting of a bottle of whiskey for each share of stock. When a corporation goes out of existence (particularly a small corporation with only a few stockholders), it may choose to distribute noncash assets to its owners rather than to convert all its assets into cash.

Liquidating dividends

A *liquidating* dividend occurs when a corporation returns to stockholders all or part of their paid-in capital investment. Liquidating dividends are usually paid only when a corporation is going out of existence or is making a permanent reduction in the size of its operations. Normally dividends are paid as a result of profitable operations, and the recipients of a dividend are entitled to assume that the dividend represents a distribution of income unless they are specifically notified that the dividend is a return of invested capital.

Stock dividends

Stock dividend is a term used to describe a distribution of additional shares of stock to a company's stockholders in proportion to their present holdings. In brief, the dividend is payable in *additional shares of stocks* rather than in cash. Most stock dividends consist of additional shares of common stock distributed to holders of common stock, and our discussion will be limited to this type of stock dividend.

A *cash* dividend reduces the assets of a corporation and reduces the stockholders' equity by the same amount. A *stock* dividend, on the other hand, causes no change in assets and no change in the *total* amount of the stockholders' equity. The only effect of a stock dividend on the accounts is to transfer a portion of the retained earnings into the Common Stock account and the Paid-in Capital from Stock Dividends account. In other words, a stock dividend merely "reshuffles" the stockholders' equity accounts, increasing the permanent capital accounts and decreasing the Retained Earnings account. A stockholder who receives a stock dividend will own an increased number of shares, but his or her total ownership equity in the company will be *no larger than before.*

To illustrate this point, assume that a corporation with 2,000 shares of stock is owned equally by James Davis and Susan Miller, each owning 1,000 shares of stock. The corporation declares a stock dividend of 10% and distributes 200 additional shares (10% of 2,000 shares), with 100 shares going to each of the two stockholders. Davis and Miller now hold 1,100 shares apiece, but each still owns one-half of the business. The corporation has not changed; its assets and liabilities and its total stockholders' equity are exactly the same as before the dividend. From the stockholders' viewpoint, the ownership of 1,100 shares out of a total of 2,200 outstanding shares represents no more than did the ownership of 1,000 shares out of a total of 2,000 shares previously outstanding.

Assume that the market price of this stock was $110 per share prior to the stock dividend. Total market value of all the outstanding shares was, therefore, 2,000 times $110, or $220,000. What would be the market value per share and in total after the additional 200 dividend shares were issued? The 2,200 shares now outstanding should have the same total market value as the previously outstanding 2,000 shares, because the "pie" has merely been divided into more but smaller pieces. The price per share should have dropped from $110 to $100, and the aggregate market value of outstanding shares would consequently be computed as 2,200 shares times $100, or $220,000. Whether the market price per share will, in all cases, decrease in proportion to the change in number of outstanding shares is another matter. The market prices of stocks listed on a stock exchange are influenced daily by many different factors.

Reasons for distribution of stock dividends. Many reasons have been given for the popularity of stock dividends; for example:

1 To conserve cash. When the trend of earnings is favorable but cash is needed for expansion, a stock dividend may be an appropriate device for "passing along the earnings" to stockholders without weakening the corporation's cash position.[6]
2 To reduce the market price of a corporation's stock to a more convenient trading range by increasing the number of shares outstanding. This objective is usually present in large stock dividends (25 to 100% or more).
3 To avoid income tax on stockholders. For income tax purposes, stock dividends are not considered as income to the recipient; therefore, no income tax is payable.

[6] For example, the Standard Oil Company of California, in a letter to its stockholders, gave the following reason for the "payment" of a 5% stock dividend: "Payment of this stock dividend recognizes the continuing increase in your stockholders' equity in the Company's assets, resulting from reinvestment of part of the Company's earnings. Reinvestment of earnings has helped to sustain the Company's long-range program of capital and exploratory expenditures and investments aimed to increase future income and enhance further the value of your shareholding."

Entries to record stock dividends. Assume that a corporation had the following stock-holders' equity accounts on December 15, Year 1, just prior to declaring a 10% stock dividend:

Stockholders' equity
before stock dividend

Stockholders' equity:

Common stock, $10 par value, 300,000 shares authorized, 100,000 shares issued and outstanding	$1,000,000
Paid-in capital in excess of par	500,000
Retained earnings	2,000,000
Total stockholders' equity	$3,500,000

Assume also that the closing market price of the stock on December 15, Year 1, was $30 a share. The company declares a 10% stock dividend, consisting of 10,000 common shares (10% $\times$ 100,000 = 10,000). The entry to record the *declaration* of the dividend is as follows:

Stock dividend
declared; note use of
market price of stock

Year 1

Dec. 15 Retained Earnings	300,000	
Stock Dividend to Be Distributed		100,000
Paid-in Capital from Stock Dividends		200,000

To record declaration of a 10% stock dividend consisting of 10,000 shares of $10 par value common stock, to be distributed on Feb. 9, Year 2, to stockholders of record on Jan. 15, Year 2. Amount of retained earnings transferred to permanent capital is based on market price of $30 a share on Dec. 15, Year 1.

The Stock Dividend to Be Distributed account is *not a liability,* because there is no obligation to distribute cash or any other asset. If a balance sheet is prepared between the date of declaration of a stock dividend and the date of distribution of the shares, this account, as well as Paid-in Capital from Stock Dividends, should be presented in the stockholders' equity section of the balance sheet.

The entry to record *distribution* of the dividend shares is as follows:

Stock dividend
distributed

Year 2

Feb. 9 Stock Dividend to Be Distributed	100,000	
Common Stock		100,000

To record distribution of stock dividend of 10,000 shares.

Note that the amount of retained earnings transferred to permanent capital accounts by the above entries is not the par value of the new shares, but the *market value,* as indicated by the market price prevailing at the date of declaration. The reasoning behind this practice is simple: Since stockholders tend to measure the "worth" of a small stock dividend (say, 20 to 25% or less) in terms of the market value of the additional shares issued, then Retained Earnings should be reduced by this amount.

Large stock dividends (for example, those in excess of 20 to 25%) should be recorded by transferring only the par or stated value of the dividend shares from the Retained Earnings account to the Common Stock account. Large stock dividends generally have the effect of proportionately reducing the market price of the stock. For example, a 100% stock dividend would reduce the market price by about 50%, because twice as many shares would be outstanding. A 100% stock dividend is very similar to the 2 for 1 *stock split* discussed in the following section of this chapter.

Stock splits

Most large corporations are interested in as wide as possible a distribution of their securities among the investing public. If the market price reaches very high levels as, for example, $150 per share, the corporation may feel that, by splitting the stock 5 for 1 and thereby reducing the price to $30 per share, the number of shareholders may be increased. The bulk of trading in securities occurs in 100-share lots and an extra commission is charged on smaller transactions. Many investors with limited funds prefer to make their investments in 100-share lots of lower-priced stocks. The majority of leading American corporations have split their stock; some have done so several times. Generally the number of shareholders has increased noticeably after the stock has been split.

A stock split consists of increasing the number of outstanding shares and reducing the par or stated value per share in proportion. For example, assume that a corporation has outstanding 1 million shares of $10 par value stock. The market price is $90 per share. The corporation now reduces the par value from $10 to $5 per share and increases the number of shares from 1 million to 2 million. This action would be called a 2 for 1 stock split. A stockholder who owned 100 shares of the stock before the split would own 200 shares after the split. Since the number of outstanding shares has been doubled without any change in the affairs of the corporation, the market price will probably drop from $90 to approximately $45 a share.

A stock split does not change the balance of any ledger account; consequently, the transaction may be recorded merely by a memorandum notation in the general journal and in the Common Stock account.

Distinction between stock splits and large stock dividends. What is the difference between a 2 for 1 stock split and a 100% stock dividend? There is very little difference; both will double the number of outstanding shares without changing total stockholders' equity, and both will serve to cut the market price of the stock in half. The stock dividend, however, will cause a transfer from the Retained Earnings account to the Common Stock account equal to the par or stated value of the dividend shares, whereas the stock split does not change the dollar balance of any account.

After an increase in the number of shares as a result of a stock split or stock dividend, earnings per share are computed in terms of the increased number of shares. In presenting five- or 10-year summaries, the earnings per share for earlier years are *retroactively revised* to reflect the increased number of shares currently outstanding and thus make the trend of earnings per share from year to year a valid comparison.

Stock splits and stock dividends from the investor's viewpoint. How should an investor account for the additional shares received in a stock split or a stock dividend? These additional shares are *not income* to the investor. Rather, the new shares reduce the investor's cost basis per share, because the original investment is now represented by an increased number of shares. The reduction in the cost basis per share is recorded by a *memorandum entry* in the investor's general journal.

To illustrate, assume that Pat Smith buys 100 shares of Delta Company common stock for $72 per share, a total investment of $7,200. Later Smith receives an additional 20 shares in a 20% stock dividend. Smith's $7,200 investment now consists of 120 shares, indicating a new cost per share of $60. The memorandum entry to be made in Smith's general journal is:

July 10   Memorandum: Received 20 additional shares of Delta Co. common stock as a result of 20% stock dividend. Now own 120 shares with a cost basis of $7,200, or $60 per share.

If Smith later sells any of these investment shares, she will measure her gain or loss by comparing the sales price to the adjusted cost basis per share. For example, if Smith sells 50 shares at a price of $68 per share, the gain on the sale should be computed as follows:

Sales price ($68 × 50 shares)	$3,400
Cost of shares sold ($60 × 50 shares)	3,000
Gain on sale of marketable securities	$ 400

Retained earnings

Throughout this book the term **retained earnings** is used to describe that portion of stockholders' equity derived from profitable operations. Retained earnings is a historical concept, representing the accumulated earnings (including prior period adjustments) minus dividends declared from the date of incorporation to the present. If we assume that there are no **prior period adjustments,** the major sources of entries in the Retained Earnings account will be (1) the periodic transfer of net income (or loss) from the Income Summary account and (2) the debits resulting from the declaration of dividends.

Prior period adjustments to the Retained Earnings account

On occasion, a company may discover that a material error was made in the measurement of net income in a prior year. Since net income is the source of retained earnings, an error in reported net income will cause an error in the amount of retained earnings shown in all subsequent balance sheets. When such an error comes to light, it should be corrected. However, if the error in measuring the net income of a prior year is corrected in the current period's income statement, net income for the current period will be distorted. Therefore, material errors in the amount of net income reported in prior periods are corrected by adjusting the balance of the Retained Earnings account. Such adjustments are called **prior period adjustments.**

Material errors in the financial statements of prior years may arise as a result of mathematical errors, failure to interpret properly the accounting effects of transactions, or the use of inappropriate accounting principles and concepts. Assume, for example, that in Year 10 Vista Corporation is audited for the first time by a firm of certified public accountants. During the audit, the CPAs discover that in Year 6 land costing $220,000 had been written up in Vista Corporation's accounting records to an appraised value of $280,000 and a $60,000 gain had been included in net income. Since land should be valued in accounting records at cost rather than appraised value, the recognition of this $60,000 gain constitutes a material error in Vista Corporation's Year 6 financial statements.

What effect does this error have upon the Vista Corporation's financial statements in Year 10? Since the net income of Year 6 has been closed into the Retained Earnings account, both land and retained earnings are overstated in Year 10 by $60,000. The entry to correct this error is shown below:

Retained Earnings	60,000	
Land		60,000

Prior period adjustment to correct error made in the valuation of land
and recognition of income in Year 6.

Presentation of prior period adjustments in financial statements. Corrections of the operating results of prior years are *not* included in the income statement of the current year. Prior period adjustments are shown in the *statement of retained earnings* as an adjustment to the balance of retained earnings at the beginning of the current year.[7] The amount of the prior period adjustment should be shown net of any related tax effects. The presentation of the prior period adjustment in the statement of retained earnings of Vista Corporation is illustrated on the next page.

Most companies present comparative financial statements; that is, financial statements of the preceding year are presented along with those of the current year. If the financial statements for the year in which the error occurred are being presented for comparative purposes, these statements should be *revised to eliminate the error.* A footnote to the comparative statements should explain that the financial statements for the earlier year have been revised to reflect correction of the error.

Prior period adjustments rarely appear in the financial statements of large, publicly owned corporations. The financial statements of these corporations are audited annually by certified public accountants and are not likely to contain material errors which subsequently will require correction by prior period adjustments. Such adjustments are much more likely to appear in the financial statements of closely held corporations that are not audited on an annual basis.

Statement of retained earnings

In addition to the balance sheet and the income statement, most corporations include a statement of retained earnings and a statement of changes in financial position in their annual reports to stockholders. (The latter statement will be illustrated in Chapter 15.) If a company is audited by a CPA firm, all four of these basic financial statements are covered by the audit report. A simple example of a statement of retained earnings follows:

[7] *FASB Statement No. 16,* "Prior Period Adjustments" (Stamford, Conn.: 1977).

SHORE LINE CORPORATION
Statement of Retained Earnings
For the Year Ended December 31, 19___

Retained earnings at beginning of year	$620,000
Net income for the year	280,000
Subtotal	$900,000
Less: Dividends	100,000
Retained earnings at end of year	$800,000

In the published annual reports of publicly owned corporations, the statement of retained earnings is usually presented in *comparative* form covering two years. This format and the treatment of a prior period adjustment are illustrated below for Vista Corporation.

VISTA CORPORATION
Statement of Retained Earnings
For Years Ended December 31

	Year 10	Year 9
Statement of retained earnings shows prior period adjustments, net income, and dividends		
Retained earnings at beginning of year:		
As originally reported	$ 810,000	$780,000
Prior period adjustment — to correct error in valuation of land		
recorded in Year 6	(60,000)	(60,000)
As restated	$ 750,000	$720,000
Net income	360,000	210,000
Subtotal	$1,110,000	$930,000
Less: Cash dividends on common stock:		
$2.40 per share in Year 10	240,000	
$1.80 per share in Year 9		180,000
Retained earnings at end of year	$ 870,000	$750,000

The error in the Year 6 financial statements was discovered in Year 10 and is shown as a correction to the beginning balance of retained earnings for both Year 10 and Year 9, since both beginning amounts were overstated. The statement of retained earnings thus provides a useful vehicle for the disclosure of prior period adjustments and for the explanation of all changes in retained earnings during the accounting period.

An alternative presentation of net income and retained earnings is used by some companies. The reconciliation of retained earnings may be shown in the body of a *combined statement of income and retained earnings,* as illustrated on the next page for Lacey Corporation.

LACEY CORPORATION
Combined Statement of Income and Retained Earnings
For Years Ended December 31

	Year 5	Year 4
Net sales	$2,900,000	$2,700,000
Cost of goods sold	1,730,000	1,650,000
Gross profit on sales	$1,170,000	$1,050,000
Operating expenses	620,000	590,000
Income before income taxes	$ 550,000	$ 460,000
Income taxes	260,000	215,000
Net income	$ 290,000	$ 245,000
Retained earnings at beginning of year	730,000	665,000
Subtotal	$1,020,000	$ 910,000
Dividends: $1 per share in Year 5 and $0.90 per share in Year 4	210,000	180,000
Retained earnings at end of year	$ 810,000	$ 730,000
Earnings per share of common stock	$1.38	$1.23

The statement for Lacey Corporation emphasizes the close relationship of operating results and retained earnings. Some readers of financial statements, however, object to the fact that net income (or loss) is "buried" in the body of a combined statement of income and retained earnings rather than being prominently displayed as the final figure before reporting earnings per share.

Appropriations and restrictions of retained earnings

A few corporations transfer a portion of their retained earnings into separate accounts called **appropriations.** The purpose of such appropriations is to indicate to users of financial statements that a portion of retained earnings is not available for the declaration of cash dividends. The limitation on cash dividends may be established voluntarily by the board of directors or it may be required by law or contract. An appropriation of retained earnings is recorded by a debit to Retained Earnings and a credit to the appropriation account such as Retained Earnings Appropriated for Contingencies. Appropriation accounts are still a part of total retained earnings, as indicated by the following partial stockholders' equity section which appeared in a recent balance sheet of Wm. Wrigley Jr. Company:

Appropriations in the balance sheet

Stockholders' equity:

Capital stock, no-par value—authorized and issued—2,000,000 shares	$ 19,200,000
Accumulated earnings retained for use in the business	109,130,000
Accumulated earnings appropriated for guarantees under employment assurance contracts	2,000,000

When the restriction on retained earnings is no longer needed, the appropriation account is eliminated by transferring its balance back to the Retained Earnings account.

Instead of establishing appropriations of retained earnings, most corporations disclose restrictions on the declaration of cash dividends in notes accompanying the financial statements.[8] For example, a company with total retained earnings of $10,000,000 might include the following note in its financial statements:

Footnote disclosure of restrictions placed on retained earnings

Note 7: Restriction of retained earnings

As of December 31, 198X, certain long-term debt agreements prohibited the declaration of cash dividends that would reduce the amount of retained earnings below $5,200,000. Retained earnings not so restricted amounted to $4,800,000.

Since the only purpose of appropriating retained earnings is to inform readers of the financial statements that a portion of the retained earnings is "reserved" for a specific purpose and is not available for declaration of cash dividends, this information can be conveyed more directly, with less danger of misunderstanding, by a note accompanying the financial statements.

Treasury stock

Corporations frequently reacquire shares of their own capital stock by purchase in the open market. Paying out cash to reacquire shares will reduce the assets of the corporation and reduce the stockholders' equity by the same amount. One reason for such purchases is to have stock available to reissue to officers and employees under bonus plans. Other reasons may include a desire to increase the reported earnings per share or to support the current market price of the stock.

Treasury stock may be defined as shares of a corporation's own capital stock that have been issued and later ***reacquired by the issuing company,*** but that have not been canceled or permanently retired. Treasury shares may be held indefinitely or may be issued again at any time. Shares of capital stock held in the treasury are not entitled to receive dividends, to vote, or to share in assets upon dissolution of the company. In the computation of earnings per share, shares held in the treasury are not regarded as outstanding shares.

Recording purchases of treasury stock

Purchases of treasury stock should be recorded by debiting the Treasury Stock account with the cost of the stock.[9] For example, if Torrey Corporation reacquires 150 shares of its own $5 par stock at a price of $100 per share, the entry is as follows:

Treasury stock recorded at cost

Treasury Stock 15,000
    Cash   15,000
Purchased 150 shares of $5 par treasury stock at $100 per share.

---

[8] According to a recent issue of *Accounting Trends & Techniques* published by the AICPA, very few of the 600 annual reports surveyed showed appropriated retained earnings while a large majority of the annual reports referred to restrictions on retained earnings.

[9] State laws may prescribe different methods of accounting for treasury stock transactions. In this text, we illustrate only the widely used "cost method." Alternative methods are presented in intermediate accounting courses.

Note that the Treasury Stock account is debited for the **cost** of the shares purchased, not their par value.

Treasury stock not an asset. When treasury stock is purchased, the corporation is eliminating part of its stockholders' equity by paying off one or more stockholders. The purchase of treasury stock should be regarded as a **reduction of stockholders' equity,** not as the acquisition of an asset. For this reason, the Treasury Stock account should appear in the balance sheet **as a deduction in the stockholders' equity section.**[10] The presentation of treasury stock in a corporate balance sheet is illustrated on page 489.

Reissuance of treasury stock

When treasury shares are reissued, the Treasury Stock account is credited for the cost of the shares reissued and Paid-in Capital from Treasury Stock Transactions is debited or credited for any difference between **cost** and the reissue price. To illustrate, assume that 100 of the treasury shares acquired by Torrey Corporation at a cost of $100 per share are now reissued at a price of $115 per share. The entry to record the reissuance of these shares at a price above cost would be:

Reissued at a price above cost

Cash	11,500	
Treasury Stock		10,000
Paid-in Capital from Treasury Stock Transactions		1,500

Sold 100 shares of treasury stock, which cost $10,000, at a price of $115 per share.

If treasury stock is reissued at a price below cost, paid-in capital from previous treasury stock transactions is reduced (debited) by the excess of cost over the reissue price. To illustrate, assume that Torrey Corporation reissues its remaining 50 shares of treasury stock (cost $100 per share) at a price of $90 per share. The entry would be:

Reissued at a price below cost

Cash	4,500	
Paid-in Capital from Treasury Stock Transactions	500	
Treasury Stock		5,000

Sold 50 shares of treasury stock, which cost $5,000, at a price of $90 each.

If there is no paid-in capital from previous treasury stock transactions, the excess of the cost of the treasury shares over the reissue price may be recorded as a debit in any other paid-in capital account. If the company had no paid-in capital in excess of par from any source, the debit would be entered in the Retained Earnings account.

No profit or loss on treasury stock transactions. Note that **no gain or loss is recognized on treasury stock transactions,** even when the shares are reissued at a price above or below cost. A corporation earns profits by selling goods and services to outsiders, not

---

[10] Despite a lack of theoretical support, a few corporations do classify treasury stock as an asset, on the grounds that the shares could be sold for cash just as readily as shares owned in another corporation. The same argument could be made for treating unissued shares as assets. Treasury shares are basically the same as unissued shares, and an unissued share of stock is definitely not an asset.

by issuing or reissuing shares of its own capital stock. When treasury shares are reissued at a price above cost, the corporation receives from the new stockholder a larger amount of paid-in capital than was eliminated when the corporation acquired the treasury shares. Conversely, if treasury shares are reissued at a price below cost, the corporation ends up with less paid-in capital as a result of the purchase and reissuance of the shares. Thus, any changes in stockholders' equity resulting from treasury stock transactions are regarded as changes in *paid-in capital* and are *not* included in the measurement of net income.

Restriction of retained earnings when treasury stock is acquired

If a corporation is to maintain its paid-in capital intact, it must not pay out to its stockholders any more than it earns. As previously stated in the section dealing with dividends, the amount of dividends to be paid must not exceed the corporation's accumulated earnings, or the corporation will be returning a portion of the stockholders' original investment to them.

The payment of cash dividends and the acquisition of treasury stock have a good deal in common. In both transactions, the corporation is disbursing cash to its stockholders. Of course, the dividend payment is spread out among all the stockholders, whereas the payment to purchase treasury stock may go to only a few stockholders, but this does not alter the fact that the corporation is turning over some of its assets to its owners. The total amount which a corporation may pay to its stockholders without reducing paid-in capital is shown by the balance in the Retained Earnings account. Consequently, it is important that a corporation keep track of the total amount disbursed in payment for treasury stock and make sure that this amount plus any dividends paid does not exceed the company's accumulated earnings. This objective is conveniently accomplished by *restricting* the availability of retained earnings for dividends to the extent of the cost of treasury stock held at the balance sheet date. The restriction should be disclosed in a note accompanying the financial statements.

Book value per share of common stock

Since each stockholders' equity in a corporation is determined by the number of shares he or she owns, an accounting measurement of interest to many stockholders is book value per share of common stock. Book value per share is equal to the *net assets* represented by one share of stock. The term *net assets* means total assets minus total liabilities; in other words, net assets are equal to total stockholders' equity. Thus in a corporation which has issued common stock only, the book value per share is computed by dividing total stockholders' equity by the number of shares outstanding.

For example, assume that a corporation has 4,000 shares of capital stock outstanding and the stockholders' equity section of the balance sheet is as follows:

How much is book value per share?

Capital stock, $1 par value	$ 4,000
Paid-in capital in excess of par value	40,000
Retained earnings	76,000
Total stockholders' equity	$120,000

The book value per share is $30; it is computed by dividing the stockholders' equity of $120,000 by the 4,000 shares of outstanding stock. In computing book value, we are not concerned with the number of authorized shares but merely with the outstanding shares, because the total of the outstanding shares represents 100% of the stockholders' equity.

Book value when a company has both preferred and common stock. Book value is usually computed only for common stock. If a company has both preferred and common stock outstanding, the computation of book value per share of common stock requires two steps. First, the redemption value or call price of the entire preferred stock issue and any dividends in arrears are deducted from total stockholders' equity. Second, the remaining amount of stockholders' equity is divided by the number of common shares outstanding to determine book value per common share. This procedure reflects the fact that the common stockholders are the residual owners of the corporate entity.

To illustrate, assume that the stockholders' equity of Video Company at December 31 is as follows:

Two classes of stock 8% preferred stock, $100 par, callable at $110	$1,000,000
Common stock, no-par; $10 stated value; authorized 100,000 shares, issued and outstanding 50,000 shares	500,000
Paid-in capital in excess of par value	750,000
Retained earnings	130,000
Total stockholders' equity	$2,380,000

Because of a weak cash position, Video Company has paid no dividends during the current year. As of December 31, dividends in arrears on the cumulative preferred stock total $80,000.

All the capital belongs to the common stockholders, except the $1.1 million call price ($110 × 10,000 shares) applicable to the preferred stock and the $80,000 of dividends in arrears on preferred stock. The calculation of book value per share of common stock can therefore be made as follows:

Total stockholders' equity		$2,380,000
Less: Equity of preferred stockholders:		
Call price of preferred stock	$1,100,000	
Dividends in arrears	80,000	1,180,000
Equity of common stockholders		$1,200,000
Number of common shares outstanding		50,000
Book value per share of common stock ($1,200,000 ÷ 50,000)		$24

The concept of book value is of vital importance in many contracts. For example, a majority stockholder might obtain an option to purchase the shares of the minority stockholders at book value at a specified future date. Many court cases have hinged on definitions of book value.

Book value is also used in judging the reasonableness of the market price of a stock. However, it must be used with great caution; the fact that a stock is selling at less than its book value does not necessarily indicate a bargain. The disparity between book value and market price per share is indicated by the following data currently available for three well-known corporations: United States Steel, book value $58, market price $24; United Airlines, book value $38, market price $41; Johnson & Johnson, book value $15, market price $49. Current earnings, dividends per share, and prospects for future earnings are usually more important factors affecting market price than is book value.

Book value does *not* indicate the amount which the holder of a share of stock would receive if the corporation were to be dissolved. In liquidation, the assets would probably be sold at prices quite different from their carrying values in the accounts, and the stockholders' equity would go up or down accordingly.

Illustration of stockholders' equity section

The following illustration of a stockholders' equity section of a balance sheet shows a fairly detailed classification by source of the various elements of corporate capital:

Stockholders' Equity

<table>
<tr><td style="text-align:right">**Compare with**
published financial
statements</td><td>Capital stock:</td><td></td><td></td><td></td></tr>
<tr><td></td><td>9% preferred stock, $100 par value, authorized and issued 1,000
    shares ....</td><td style="text-align:right">$100,000</td><td></td><td></td></tr>
<tr><td></td><td>Common stock, $5 stated value, authorized 100,000 shares,
    issued 60,000 shares, of which 1,000 are held in treasury ....</td><td style="text-align:right">300,000</td><td></td><td></td></tr>
<tr><td></td><td>Common stock subscribed, 6,000 shares ....</td><td style="text-align:right">30,000</td><td style="text-align:right">$430,000</td><td></td></tr>
<tr><td></td><td>Additional paid-in capital:</td><td></td><td></td><td></td></tr>
<tr><td></td><td>Paid-in capital from stock dividends ....</td><td style="text-align:right">$ 50,000</td><td></td><td></td></tr>
<tr><td></td><td>Paid-in capital in excess of stated value: common stock ....</td><td style="text-align:right">290,000</td><td></td><td></td></tr>
<tr><td></td><td>Paid-in capital from treasury stock transactions ....</td><td style="text-align:right">5,000</td><td style="text-align:right">345,000</td><td></td></tr>
<tr><td></td><td>Total paid-in capital ....</td><td></td><td style="text-align:right">$775,000</td><td></td></tr>
<tr><td></td><td>Retained earnings (of which $12,000, an amount equal to the cost
  of treasury stock purchased, is unavailable for dividends) ....</td><td></td><td style="text-align:right">162,000</td><td></td></tr>
<tr><td></td><td></td><td></td><td style="text-align:right">$937,000</td><td></td></tr>
<tr><td></td><td>Less: Treasury stock, common, 1,000 shares at cost ....</td><td></td><td style="text-align:right">(12,000)</td><td></td></tr>
<tr><td></td><td>Total stockholders' equity ....</td><td></td><td style="text-align:right">$925,000</td><td></td></tr>
</table>

The published financial statements of leading corporations indicate that there is no one standard arrangement for the various items making up the stockholders' equity section. Variations occur in the selection of titles, in the sequence of items, and in the extent of detailed classification. Many companies, in an effort to avoid excessive detail in the balance sheet, will combine several related ledger accounts into a single balance sheet item. An example of published financial statements appears in Appendix E at the end of this book.

Key terms introduced or emphasized in chapter 12

Book value per share. The stockholders' equity represented by each share of common stock, computed by dividing common stockholders' equity by the number of common shares outstanding.

Comparative financial statements. Financial statements of current year and the preceding year which are presented together to facilitate comparison.

Date of record. The date on which a person must be listed as a shareholder in order to be eligible to receive a dividend. Follows the date of declaration of a dividend by two or three weeks.

Discontinued operations. The net operating results (revenue and expenses) of a segment of a company which has been or is being sold.

Earnings per share (EPS). Net income available to the common stock divided by the weighted-average number of common shares outstanding during the year.

Ex-dividend date. A date three days prior to the date of record specified in a dividend declaration. A person buying a stock prior to the ex-dividend date also acquires the right to receive the dividend. The three-day interval permits the compilation of a list of stockholders as of the date of record.

Extraordinary items. Transactions and events that are material in dollar amount, unusual in nature, and occur infrequently; for example, a large earthquake loss. Such items are shown separately in the income statement after the determination of Income before Extraordinary Items.

Fully diluted earnings per share. Earnings per share computed under the assumption that all convertible securities had been converted into additional common shares at the beginning of the current year. The purpose of this hypothetical computation is to warn common stockholders of the risk that future earnings per share might be diluted by the conversion of other securities into common stock.

Price-earnings ratio. Market price of a share of common stock divided by annual earnings per share.

Primary earnings per share. Net income available to the common stock divided by weighted-average number of common shares outstanding.

Prior period adjustment. A correction of a material error in the earnings reported in the financial statements of a prior year. Prior period adjustments are recorded directly in the Retained Earnings account and are not included in the income statement of the current period.

Restrictions of retained earnings. Action by the board of directors to classify a portion of retained earnings as unavailable for dividends.

Segment of a business. A component of a business. The activities of the component represent a major line of business or class of customer.

Statement of retained earnings. A basic financial statement showing the change in retained earnings during the year.

Stock dividend. A distribution of additional shares to common stockholders in proportion to their holdings.

Stock split. An increase in the number of shares outstanding with a corresponding decrease in par value per share. The additional shares are distributed proportionately to all common shareholders. Purpose is to reduce market price per share and encourage wider public ownership of the company's stock. A 2 for 1 stock split will give each stockholder twice as many shares as previously owned.

Treasury stock. Shares of a corporation's stock which have been issued and then reacquired, but not canceled.

Demonstration problem for your review

The stockholders' equity of Sutton Corporation at December 31, Year 9, is shown below:

Stockholders' equity:

Common stock, $10 par, 100,000 shares authorized, 40,000 shares issued	$ 400,000
Paid-in capital in excess of par: common stock	200,000
Total paid-in capital	$ 600,000
Retained earnings	1,500,000
Total stockholders' equity	$2,100,000

Transactions affecting stockholders' equity during Year 10 are as follows:

Mar. 1 A 5 for 4 stock split proposed by the board of directors was approved by vote of the stockholders.

Mar. 31 Additional shares were distributed to stockholders pursuant to the 5 for 4 split.

Apr. 1 The company purchased 2,000 shares of its common stock on the open market at $37 per share.

July 1 The company reissued 1,000 shares of treasury stock at $45 per share.

July 1 Issued for cash 20,000 shares of previously unissued $8 par value common stock at a price of $45 per share.

Dec. 1 A cash dividend of $1 per share was declared, payable on December 30, to stockholders of record at December 14.

Dec. 22 A 10% stock dividend was declared; the dividend shares to be distributed on January 24, Year 11. The market price of the stock on December 22 was $48 per share.

The net income for the year ended December 31, Year 10, amounted to $177,000, after an extraordinary loss of $35,400 (net of related tax effects).

Instructions

a Prepare journal entries (in general journal form) to record the transactions relating to stockholders' equity that took place during Year 10.

b Prepare the lower section of the income statement for the year ended December 31, Year 10, beginning with the income before extraordinary items and showing the extraordinary loss and the net income. Also illustrate the presentation of earnings per share in the income statement, assuming that earnings per share is determined on the basis of the weighted-average number of shares outstanding during the year.

c Prepare a statement of retained earnings for the year ended December 31, Year 10.

Solution to demonstration problem

a   General Journal

Mar. 1 Memorandum: Stockholders approved a 5 for 4 stock split. This action increased the number of shares of common stock outstanding from 40,000 to 50,000 and reduced the par value from $10 to $8 per share.

31 Common Stock, $10 par	400,000	
Common Stock, $8 par		400,000
Distributed 10,000 additional shares of stock pursuant to 5 for 4 stock split, and reduced par value.		
Apr. 1 Treasury Stock	74,000	
Cash		74,000
Acquired 2,000 shares of treasury stock at $37 per share.		
July 1 Cash	45,000	
Treasury Stock		37,000
Paid-in Capital from Treasury Stock Transactions		8,000
Sold 1,000 shares of treasury stock at $45 per share.		

	1	Cash	900,000	
		Common Stock, $8 par		160,000
		Paid-in Capital in Excess of Par: Common Stock		740,000

Issued 20,000 shares of previously unissued $8 par value
stock for cash of $45 per share.

Dec.	1	Dividends	69,000	
		Dividends Payable		69,000

To record declaration of cash dividend of $1 per share on
69,000 shares of common stock outstanding (1,000 shares in
treasury are not entitled to receive dividends).

Note: Entry to record the payment of the cash dividend is not shown here since the action does not affect the stockholders' equity.

Dec.	22	Retained Earnings	331,200	
		Stock Dividends to Be Distributed		55,200
		Paid-in Capital from Stock Dividends		276,000

To record declaration of 10% stock dividend consisting of
6,900 shares of $8 par value common stock to be distributed
on Jan. 24, Year 11. Excess of fair market value of stock
over par value, $40 ($48 − $8), is credited to Paid-in Capital
from Stock Dividends.

	31	Income Summary	177,000	
		Retained Earnings		177,000

To close Income Summary account.

	31	Retained Earnings	69,000	
		Dividends		69,000

To close Dividends account.

b

SUTTON CORPORATION
Partial Income Statement
For Year Ended December 31, Year 10

Income before extraordinary items	$212,400
Extraordinary loss, net of tax effects	(35,400)
Net income	$177,000

Earnings per share:*

Income before extraordinary items	$3.60
Extraordinary loss, net of tax effects	(0.60)
Net income	$3.00

* On 59,000 weighted-average number of shares of common stock outstanding during Year 10: determined as follows:

Jan. 1–Mar. 31: (40,000 + 10,000 shares issued pursuant to a 5 for 4 split) × ¼ of year	12,500
Apr. 1–June 30: (50,000 − 2,000 shares of treasury stock) × ¼ of year	12,000
July 1–Dec. 31: (50,000 + 20,000 shares of new stock − 1,000 shares of treasury stock) × ½ of year	34,500
Weighted-average number of shares outstanding	59,000

c

SUTTON CORPORATION
Statement of Retained Earnings
For the Year Ended December 31, Year 10

Retained earnings, Jan. 1, Year 10		$1,500,000
Net income		177,000
Subtotal		$1,677,000
Dividends:		
Cash, $1 per share	$ 69,000	
Stock, 10% (to be distributed Jan. 24, Year 11)	331,200	400,200
Retained earnings, Dec. 31, Year 10		$1,276,800

Review questions

1 What is the purpose of arranging an income statement to show subtotals for Income from Continuing Operations and for Income before Extraordinary Items?

2 Define a **segment** of a business and give three examples.

3 Define **extraordinary items.** Give three examples of losses which qualify as extraordinary items and three examples of losses which would not be classified as extraordinary.

4 Briefly describe how each of the following should be reported in the income statement for the current year:
    a Write-off of a large account receivable from a bankrupt customer
    b Large loss from sale of a major segment of a business
    c Large gain from sale of one of many investments in common stock
    d Large write-off of obsolete inventory
    e Large uninsured loss from earthquake

5 Explain how each of the following is computed:
    a Price-earnings ratio
    b Primary earnings per share
    c Fully diluted earnings per share

6 Throughout the year, Gold Seal Co. had 4 million shares of common stock and 120,000 shares of convertible preferred stock outstanding. Each share of preferred is convertible into four shares of common. What number of shares should be used in the computation of (a) primary earnings per share, and (b) fully diluted earnings per share?

7 A financial analyst notes that Baxter Corporation's earnings per share have been rising steadily for the last five years. The analyst expects the company's net income to continue to increase at the same rate as in the past. In forecasting future primary earnings per share, what special risk should the analyst consider if Baxter's primary earnings are significantly larger than its fully diluted earnings?

8 Explain the significance of the following dates relating to dividends: date of declaration, date of record, date of payment, ex-dividend date.

9 Should stock dividends received be considered revenue to an investor? Explain.

10 Distinguish between a **stock split** and a **stock dividend.** Is there any reason for the difference in accounting treatment of these two events?

11 What are **prior period adjustments?** How are they presented in financial statements?

12 What is the purpose of an appropriation of retained earnings? What are the arguments for and against the use of such appropriations?

13 If a statement of retained earnings consisted of only four items, what would these four items most probably be?

14 What is the most effective method of disclosing in financial statements the fact that a portion of the retained earnings is restricted by the terms of a long-term debt agreement and therefore not available for payment of dividends or acquisition of treasury stock?

15 "In a long-established, successful corporation, the Cash account would normally have a dollar balance equal to or larger than the Retained Earnings account." Do you agree with this quotation? Explain.

16 What is *treasury stock?* Why do corporations purchase their own shares? Is treasury stock an asset? How should it be reported in the balance sheet?

17 In many states, the corporation law requires that retained earnings be restricted for dividend purposes to the extent of the cost of treasury shares. What is the reason for this legal rule?

18 What does *book value per share* of common stock represent? Does it represent the amount common stockholders would receive in the event that the corporation were liquidated? Explain briefly.

19 How is book value per share of common stock computed when a company has both preferred and common stock outstanding?

20 What would be the effect, if any, on book value per share of common stock as a result of each of the following independent events: (a) a corporation obtains a bank loan; (b) a dividend is declared (to be paid in the next accounting period); and (c) a corporation issues additional shares of common stock as a stock dividend.

Exercises

Ex. 12-1   The operations of Sailboards, Inc., are summarized below for Year 10:

	From Continuing Operations	From Discontinued Operations
Net sales	$9,600,000	$1,940,000
Cost and expenses (including applicable income taxes)	8,600,000	2,100,000
Loss on disposal of discontinued segment, net of income taxes		290,000

Instructions. Assuming that the company had an average of 200,000 shares of a single class of capital stock outstanding during Year 10, prepare a condensed income statement (including earnings per share).

Ex. 12-2   For the year ended December 31, Union Chemical had net sales of $4,200,000, costs and other expenses (including income taxes) of $3,720,000, and an extraordinary loss (net of income tax) of $690,000. Prepare a condensed income statement (including earnings per share), assuming that 100,000 shares of common stock were outstanding throughout the year.

Ex. 12-3   In the year just ended, Sunshine Citrus earned net income of $9,020,000. The company has issued only one class of capital stock, of which 2 million shares were outstanding at January 1. Compute the company's earnings per share under each of the following *independent* assumptions:

 a No change occurred during the year in the number of shares outstanding.

 b On October 1, the company issued an additional 200,000 shares of capital stock in exchange for cash.

 c On July 1, the company distributed an additional 200,000 shares of capital stock as a 10% stock dividend. (No additional shares are issued on October 1.)

Ex. 12-4 The net income of Carriage Trade Clothiers amounted to $3,840,000 for the current year. Compute the amount of earnings per share under two independent assumptions as to the shares of capital stock outstanding throughout the year:

 a 300,000 shares of $10 par value common stock and no preferred stock.

 b 200,000 shares of 9%, $100 par value preferred stock and 300,000 shares of $5 par value common stock.

Ex. 12-5 Fred Johnson purchased 100 shares of stock in Mills Corporation at the time it was organized. At the end of the first year's operations, the corporation reported earnings (after taxes) of $6 per share, and declared a dividend of $3 per share. Johnson complains that he is entitled to the full distribution of the amount earned on his investment. Is there any reason why a corporation that earns $6 per share may not be able to pay a dividend of this amount? Are there any advantages to Johnson in the retention by the company of one-half of its earnings?

Ex. 12-6 Brass Corporation has 1 million shares of $5 par value common stock outstanding. You are to prepare the journal entries to record the following transactions:

June 1 Declared a cash dividend of 60 cents per share. (Debit Dividends.)
July 1 Paid the 60-cent cash dividend to stockholders.
Aug. 1 Declared a 5% stock dividend. Market price of stock was $19 per share.
Sept. 10 Issued 50,000 shares pursuant to the 5% stock dividend.
Dec. 1 Declared a 50% stock dividend. Market price of stock was $20 per share.

Ex. 12-7 Jiffy Tool Co. has a total of 40,000 shares of common stock outstanding and no preferred stock. Total stockholders' equity at the end of the current year amounts to $3 million and the market value of the stock is $96 per share. At year-end, the company declares a stock dividend of one share for each five shares held. If all parties concerned clearly recognize the nature of the stock dividend, what should you expect the market price per share of the common stock to be on the ex-dividend date?

Ex. 12-8 Cable Transmissions engaged in the following transactions involving treasury stock:

Nov. 10 Purchased for cash 12,500 shares of treasury stock at a price of $20 per share.
Dec. 4 Reissued 5,000 shares of treasury stock at a price of $22 per share.
Dec. 22 Reissued 4,000 shares of treasury stock at a price of $18.50 per share.

Instructions

 a Prepare general journal entries to record these transactions.

 b Compute the amount of retained earnings that should be restricted because of the treasury stock still owned at December 31.

Ex. 12-9 Presented below is the information necessary to compute the net assets (stockholders' equity) and book value per share of common stock for Ringside Corporation:

9% cumulative preferred stock, $100 par (callable at $110)	$200,000
Common stock, $5 par, authorized 100,000 shares, issued 60,000 shares	300,000
Paid-in capital in excess of par	470,800
Deficit	126,800
Dividends in arrears on preferred stock, 2 full years	36,000

Instructions

a Compute the amount of net assets (stockholders' equity).
b Compute the book value per share of common stock.

Problems

12-1 Preparation of an income statement with earnings per share
The operations of Goldrush Financial are summarized below for the year ended December 31:

	From Continuing Operations	From Discontinued Operations
Net sales	$14,000,000	$3,000,000
Costs and expenses (including applicable income taxes)	12,200,000	2,850,000
Loss on disposal of discontinued segment, net of income taxes		450,000
Extraordinary loss, net of income tax effects	660,000	

Instructions. Assuming that the company had an average of 300,000 shares of common stock outstanding during the year, prepare a condensed income statement (including earnings per share).

12-2 Income statement: alternative to Problem 12-1
Coastal Airlines, Inc., operated both an airline service and several motels located near airports. During the year just ended, all motel operations were discontinued and the following operating results were reported:

	Airline Operations	Motel Operations
Net sales	$38,000,000	$4,500,000
Costs and expenses (including applicable income taxes)	34,800,000	5,870,000
Gain on sale of motel properties, net of income taxes		530,000
Extraordinary loss, net of income taxes	900,000	

The extraordinary loss resulted from the expropriation of an airliner by a foreign government.
   Coastal Airlines, Inc., had 300,000 shares of common stock and 80,000 shares of 10%, $100 par value, preferred stock outstanding throughout the year.

Instructions. Prepare a condensed income statement including proper presentation of the discontinued motel operations and the extraordinary loss. Include all appropriate earnings-per-share figures.

12-3 Statement of retained earnings; prior period adjustments

At the end of Year 9, Sandy Boone was hired as the new controller of Garrison Manufacturing, a successful family-owned business. Boone was shown the following comparative statement of retained earnings which had been prepared by the corporation's part-time accountant:

	Year 9	Year 8
Retained earnings, Jan. 1	$545,000	$490,000
Net income	170,000	145,000
Subtotal	$715,000	$635,000
Less: Dividends	100,000	90,000
Retained earnings, Dec. 31	$615,000	$545,000

Because Garrison Manufacturing had never been audited by a CPA firm, Boone decided to make a careful examination of the company's accounting records. Her investigation disclosed the following errors made in prior years:

(1) In Year 4, land costing $165,000 had been written up to an appraised value of $300,000 and a $135,000 "appraisal gain" had been included in net income in that year.

(2) In Year 8, the company had recorded no depreciation expense on new machinery placed in service in June of that year. The unrecorded depreciation expense for Year 8 amounted to $46,000. Depreciation expense for Year 9 was computed and recorded correctly.

Neither of these errors had entered into the computation of the company's income taxes. Thus, income taxes expense had been correctly computed and recorded each year.

Instructions

a Prepare the journal entries necessary at December 31, Year 9, to correct the errors made in Years 4 and 8. (Use a separate journal entry for correcting each error.)

b Prepare a revised comparative statement of retained earnings for Years 8 and 9. Your statement should begin with the balance of retained earnings at the beginning of Years 8 and 9 *as originally reported* and should then show any necessary prior period adjustments to these balances. The net income for Year 8 should be shown at the correct amount. (Hint: The amount of retained earnings reported at the beginning of Year 8 is not affected by the failure to record depreciation during Year 8.)

12-4 Book value of common stock

SwitchMaster builds an excellent product, but the company is poorly managed. Maria Soto wants to acquire enough of the company's voting stock to elect a new board of directors which will hire new management. Soto has entered into contracts with several of SwitchMaster's stockholders to buy their common stock at a price equal to its book value at the end of Year 5. Because SwitchMaster has issued both preferred and common stock, Soto is not certain how the book value per share of common stock should be computed. She has come to you for assistance and has provided you with the following information.

At the end of Year 5, the total stockholders' equity of SwitchMaster is $1,290,000. The company was organized early in Year 1 and immediately issued 5,000 shares of 8%, $100 par, preferred stock and 30,000 shares of $5 par common stock. Except as explained below, there have been no changes in the number of shares outstanding.

Instructions. Compute for Soto the book value per share of common stock at the end of Year 5 under each of the following independent assumptions:

   a The preferred stock was redeemed by SwitchMaster in Year 4 and only the common stock remains outstanding.
   b All shares of preferred and common stock are still outstanding. The preferred stock is callable at $105 and there are no dividends in arrears.
   c The preferred stock is cumulative and callable at $108. The company paid the full preferred dividend in Years 1 and 2, but has paid no dividends in Years 3, 4, or 5.
   d The preferred stock was convertible into common stock at a rate of four shares of common stock for each share of preferred. By the end of Year 5, all 5,000 shares of preferred stock had been converted into common stock.

12-5   Stockholders' equity transactions; book value per share
On January 1, Electric Pump Company has total stockholders' equity of $4,400,000 and 50,000 outstanding shares of a single class of capital stock. During the year, the corporation completes the following transactions affecting its stockholders' equity accounts:

Jan. 10 The board of directors declares a cash dividend of $4.20 per share, payable February 15.
Apr. 30 The capital stock is split, two shares for one.
June 11 The corporation acquires 2,000 shares of its own capital stock at a cost of $56.60 per share.
July 21 All 2,000 shares of the treasury stock are reissued at a price of $61.60 per share.
Nov. 10 A 5% stock dividend is declared and distributed (market value $60 per share).
Dec. 31 Net income of $378,000 (equal to $3.60 per share) is reported for Year 8.

Instructions. Compute the amount of total stockholders' equity, the number of shares of capital stock outstanding, and the book value per share following each successive transaction. Organize your solution as a three-column schedule with separate column headings for (1) Total Stockholders' Equity, (2) Number of Shares Outstanding, and (3) Book Value per Share.

12-6   Treasury stock, cash dividends, and stock dividends
At the beginning of the year, Marco Construction showed the following amounts in the stockholders' equity section of its balance sheet:

Stockholders' equity:
Common stock, $10 par value, 500,000 shares authorized, 191,000 issued .. $1,910,000
Paid-in capital in excess of par   1,540,000
   Total paid-in capital $3,450,000
Retained earnings   986,000
Total stockholders' equity $4,436,000

The transactions relating to stockholders' equity accounts during the year are as follows:

Jan.   3 Declared a dividend of $1 per share to stockholders of record on January 31, payable on February 15. (Debit Dividends.)

Feb. 15 Paid the cash dividend declared on January 3.

Apr. 12 The corporation purchased 3,000 shares of its own capital stock at a price of $32 per share.

May 9 Reissued 2,000 shares of the treasury stock at a price of $36 per share.

June 1 Declared a 5% stock dividend to stockholders of record at June 15, to be distributed on June 30. The market price of the stock at June 1 was $35 per share. (The 1,000 shares remaining in the treasury do not participate in the stock dividend.)

June 30 Distributed the stock dividend declared on June 1.

Aug. 4 Reissued 500 of the 1,000 remaining shares of treasury stock at a price of $30 per share.

Dec. 31 Closed the Income Summary account and the Dividends account into Retained Earnings. The Income Summary account showed net income of $613,500.

Instructions

a Prepare in general journal form the entries to record the above transactions.

b Prepare the stockholders' equity section of the balance sheet at December 31. Include a supporting schedule showing your computation of retained earnings at that date.

c Compute the maximum cash dividend per share which legally could be declared at December 31, without impairing the paid-in capital of Marco Construction. (Hint: The availability of retained earnings for dividends is restricted by the cost of treasury stock owned.)

12-7 Preparation of stockholders' equity section

The Mandella family decided early in Year 1 to incorporate their family-owned vineyards under the name Mandella Corporation. The corporation was authorized to issue 200,000 shares of a single class of $10 par value capital stock. Presented below is the information necessary to prepare the stockholders' equity section of the company's balance sheet at the end of Year 1 and at the end of Year 2.

Year 1. In January the corporation issued to members of the Mandella family 84,000 shares of capital stock in exchange for cash and other assets used in the operation of the vineyards. The fair market value of these assets indicated an issue price of $30 per share. In December, Joe Mandella died, and the corporation purchased 4,000 shares of its own capital stock from his estate at $35 per share. Because of the large cash outlay to acquire this treasury stock, the directors decided not to declare cash dividends in Year 1 and instead declared a 10% stock dividend to be distributed in January of Year 2. The stock price at the declaration date was $35 per share. (The treasury shares do not participate in the stock dividend.) Net income for Year 1 was $475,000.

Year 2. In January the corporation distributed the stock dividend declared in Year 1, and in February, the 4,000 treasury shares were sold to Maria Mandella at $39 per share. In June, the capital stock was split, two shares for one. (Approval was obtained to increase the authorized number of shares to 400,000.) On December 15, the directors declared a cash dividend of $2 per share, payable in January of Year 3. Net income for Year 2 was $542,000.

Instructions. Prepare the stockholders' equity section of the balance sheet at

a December 31, Year 1

b December 31, Year 2

Show any necessary computations.

12-8 Financial statement presentation: a comprehensive review

A new employee of Raytown Electronics improperly prepared the following income statement for Year 5:

RAYTOWN ELECTRONICS
Income Statement
For Year 5

Net sales		$ 9,000,000
Sale of treasury stock in Year 5 (cost, $110,000; proceeds $150,000)		40,000
Excess of proceeds over par value of common stock issued in Year 5		1,300,000
Total revenue		$10,340,000
Less:		
Prior period adjustment to correct valuation of land	$ 400,000	
Cost of goods sold	5,000,000	
Selling expenses	800,000	
General and administrative expenses	1,400,000	
Loss from tornado (net of related tax effects)	260,000	
Dividends declared on capital stock	300,000	
Income taxes (excluding effects of extraordinary loss)	840,000	9,000,000
Net income		$ 1,340,000

The prior period adjustment is to correct the carrying value of land which was erroneously written up to its appraised value in Year 4. At the beginning of Year 5, the company's financial statements showed retained earnings of $2,920,000. However, this retained earnings figure was overstated by $400,000 because of the gain erroneously recorded in Year 4 from the write-up of the land to appraised value. The total income taxes for Year 5 and the tax effects relating to the tornado loss have been correctly estimated by an income tax advisor.

Instructions

a Prepare a corrected income statement for Year 5 using the single-step format illustrated on page 471. Show appropriate earnings per share figures in the income statement. Assume that the company had a weighted average of 200,000 shares of a single class of capital stock (common stock) outstanding during the year.

b Prepare a statement of retained earnings for Year 5. The starting point for your statement should be retained earnings at the beginning of Year 5 as originally reported ($2,920,000).

Cases for analysis

Case 12-1 Interpretation of earning per share

For many years American Studios has produced television shows and operated several FM radio stations. Late in the current year, the radio stations were sold to Times Publishing, Inc. Also during the current year, American Studios sustained an extraordinary loss when one of its camera trucks caused an accident in an international grand prix auto race. Throughout the current year, the company had 3 million shares of common stock and a large quantity of convertible preferred stock outstanding. Earnings per share reported for the current year were as follows:

	Primary	Fully Diluted
Earnings from continuing operations	$8.20	$6.80
Earnings before extraordinary items	$6.90	$5.50
Net earnings	$3.80	$2.40

Instructions

a Briefly explain why American Studios reports fully diluted earnings per share amounts as well as earnings per share computed on a primary basis. What is the purpose of showing investors the fully diluted figures?

b What was the total dollar amount of the extraordinary loss sustained by American Studios during the current year?

c Assume that the price-earnings ratio shown in the morning newspaper for American Studios' common stock indicates that the stock is selling at a price equal to 10 times the reported earnings per share. What is the approximate market price of the stock?

d Assume that you expect both the revenue and expenses involved in producing television shows to increase by 10% during the coming year. What would you forecast as the company's net earnings per share (primary basis) for the coming year under each of the following independent assumptions? (Show your computations and explain your reasoning.)

   (1) *None* of the convertible preferred stock is converted into common stock during the coming year.

   (2) *All* of the convertible preferred stock is converted into common stock at the beginning of the coming year.

Case 12-2   Stock dividends from investor's viewpoint
Near the end of the current year, the board of directors of the Shadetree Corporation is presented with the following statement of stockholders' equity:

Capital stock (120,000 shares issued)	$2,400,000
Paid-in capital in excess of par	1,440,000
Retained earnings	1,920,000
Total stockholders' equity	$5,760,000

Shadetree Corporation has paid dividends of $3.60 per share in each of the last five years. After careful consideration of the company's cash needs, the board of directors declared a stock dividend of 24,000 shares. Shortly after the stock dividend had been distributed and before the end of the year, the company declared a cash dividend of $3 per share.

John Joseph owned 10,000 shares of Shadetree Corporation's stock, acquired several years ago. The market price of this stock before any dividend action in the current year was $60 per share.

Instructions. Based on the information given above, answer each of the following questions, showing all relevant computations:

a What is Joseph's share (in dollars) of the net assets as reported in the balance sheet of the Shadetree Corporation before the stock dividend action? What is his share after the stock dividend action? Explain why there is or is not any change as a result of the 20% stock dividend.

b What are the probable reasons why the market value of Joseph's stock differs from the amount of net assets per share shown in the accounting records?

c How does the amount of cash dividends that Joseph received in the current year compare with dividends received in prior years?

d On the day the stock went ex-dividend (with respect to the 20% stock dividend), its quoted market price fell from $60 to $50 per share. Did this represent a loss to Joseph? Explain.

e If the Shadetree Corporation had announced that it would continue its regular cash dividend of $3.60 per share on the increased number of shares outstanding after the 20% stock dividend, would you expect the market price of the stock to react in any way different from the change described in d? Why?

Appendix B
Investments for purposes of control

This appendix addresses situations in which one corporation owns enough of another corporation's voting stock to influence the operations of the owned company. The first topic discussed is the equity method—an accounting technique employed when the investor is able to influence, but not totally control, the activities of the investee. The major topic of the appendix, however, is the preparation of consolidated financial statements when a parent company owns enough stock in a subsidiary corporation to exercise complete control. Consolidated statements portray the parent company and its subsidiaries as if the affiliated corporations were a single economic entity. A distinction is drawn between purchase accounting and pooling-of-interests as a means of preparing consolidated financial statements.

After studying this appendix you should be able to:

✓ Account for an investment in common stock by the equity method.
✓ Describe how a parent company controls its subsidiaries.
✓ Explain why intercompany transactions must be eliminated as a step in preparing consolidated financial statements.
✓ Prepare a consolidated balance sheet.
✓ Differentiate between the purchase method and the pooling method of accounting for business combinations.
✓ Explain when consolidated statements should be prepared.

As discussed in Chapter 7, a portfolio of marketable securities may include investments in common stock. Marketable securities generally are classified as current assets, and the investor recognizes cash dividends received as investment income. Some investors, however, may own enough of a company's common stock to *influence or control* that company's activities through the voting rights of the shares owned. Such large holdings of common stock create an important business relationship between the investor and the issuing company (called the ***investee***). Since investments of this type cannot be sold without disrupting this relationship, they are not included in the portfolio of marketable securities. Such investments are shown in the balance sheet under the caption Long-Term Investments, which follows the current asset section.

If an investor is able to exercise significant control over the investee's management, dividends paid by the investee may no longer be a good measure of the investor's income from the investment. This is because the investor may control the investee's dividend policy. In such cases, dividends paid by the investee are likely to reflect the ***investor's*** cash needs and income tax considerations, rather than the profitability of the investment.

For example, assume that Sigma Company owns all the common stock of Davis Company. For three years Davis Company is very profitable but pays no dividends, because Sigma Company has no need for additional cash. In the fourth year, Davis Company pays a large cash dividend to Sigma Company despite operating at a loss for that year. Clearly, it would be misleading for Sigma Company to report no investment income while the company it owns is operating profitably, and then to show large investment income in a year when Davis Company incurred a net loss.

The investor does not have to own 100% of the common stock of the investee to exercise a significant degree of control. An investor with much less than 50% of the voting stock may have effective control, since the remaining shares are not likely to vote as an organized block. In the absence of other evidence (such as another large stockholder), ownership of 20% or more of the investee's common stock is considered an investment for purposes of control. In such cases, the investor should account for the investment by using the ***equity method***.[1]

The equity method

When the equity method is used, an investment in common stock is first recorded at cost but later is adjusted each year for changes in the stockholders' equity of the investee. As the investee earns net income, the stockholders' equity in the company increases. An investor using the equity method recognizes his ***proportionate share of the investee's net income*** as an increase in the carrying value of his investment. A proportionate share of a net loss reported by the investee is recognized as a decrease in the investment.

When the investee pays dividends, the stockholders' equity in the company is reduced. The investor, therefore, treats dividends received from the investee as a conversion of the investment into cash, thus reducing the carrying value of the investment. Investments accounted for by the equity method are ***not*** adjusted to the lower of cost or market value. In effect, the equity method causes the carrying value of the investment to rise and fall with changes in the book value of the shares.

Illustration of the equity method. Assume that Cove Corporation purchases 25% of the common stock of Bay Company for $200,000, which corresponds to the underlying book

---

[1] *APB Opinion No. 18,* "The Equity Method of Accounting for Investments in Common Stock," AICPA (New York: 1971).

value. During the following year, Bay Company earns net income of $120,000 and pays dividends of $80,000. Cove Corporation would account for its investment as follows:

Investment in Bay Company	200,000	
Cash		200,000
To record acquisition of 25% of the common stock of Bay Company.		

Investment in Bay Company	30,000	
Investment Income		30,000
To increase the investment for 25% share of net income earned by Bay Company (25% × $120,000).		

Cash	20,000	
Investment in Bay Company		20,000
To reduce investment for dividends received from Bay Company (25% × $80,000).		

The net result of these entries by Cove Corporation is to increase the carrying value of the investment in Bay Company account by $10,000. This corresponds to 25% of the increase reported in Bay Company's retained earnings during the period [25% × ($120,000 − $80,000) = $10,000].

In this illustration of the equity method, we have made several simplifying assumptions: (1) Cove Corporation purchased the stock of Bay Company at a price equal to the underlying book value; (2) Bay Company had issued common stock only and the number of shares outstanding did not change during the year; and (3) there were no intercompany transactions between Cove Corporation and Bay Company. If we were to change any of these assumptions, the computations in applying the equity method would become more complicated. Application of the equity method in more complex situations is discussed in advanced accounting courses.

CONSOLIDATED FINANCIAL STATEMENTS

Parent and subsidiary companies

A corporation which owns **all or a majority** of another corporation's capital stock is called a **parent** company, and the corporation which is wholly owned or majority-held is called a **subsidiary**.[2] Through the voting rights of the owned shares, the parent company can elect the board of directors of the subsidiary company and thereby control the subsidiary's resources and activities. In effect, the **affiliated companies** (the parent and its subsidiaries) function as a **single economic unit** controlled by the directors of the parent company. This relationship is illustrated in the diagram at the top of the next page.

There are a number of economic, legal, and income tax advantages which encourage large business organizations to operate through subsidiaries rather than through a single legal entity. Although we think of Sears, General Electric, or IBM as single companies,

[2] Ownership of a majority of a company's voting stock means holding at least 50% plus one share.

each of these organizations is really a group of affiliated corporations. Since the parent company in each case controls the resources and activities of its subsidiaries, it is logical for us to consider an affiliated group such as IBM as one *economic* entity.

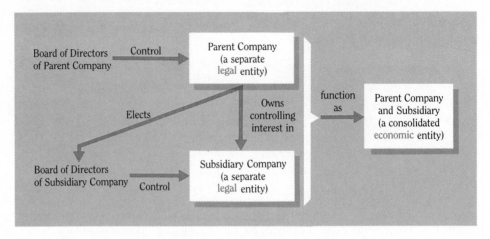

Financial statements for a consolidated economic entity

Because the parent company and its subsidiaries are separate legal entities, separate financial statements are prepared for each company. In the *separate* financial statements of the parent company, the subsidiaries appear only as investments accounted for by the *equity method.* Since the affiliated companies function as a single economic unit, the parent company also prepares financial statements which show the financial position and operating results of the entire group of companies. Such statements are called *consolidated financial statements.*

The distinctive feature of consolidated financial statements is that the assets, liabilities, revenue, and expenses of *two or more separate corporations are combined in a single set of financial statements.* In a *consolidated balance sheet,* the assets of the entire group of affiliated companies are combined and reported as though only a single entity existed. For example, the amount shown as Cash on a consolidated balance sheet is the total of the cash owned by all of the affiliated companies. Liabilities of the various companies also are combined. Similarly, in a *consolidated income statement,* the revenue and expenses of the affiliated companies are combined to show the operating results of the consolidated economic entity.

Stockholders in the parent corporation have a vital interest in the financial results of all operations under the parent company's control, including those conducted through subsidiaries. Therefore, the parent company includes consolidated financial statements in its annual and quarterly reports to stockholders. Most of the companies listed on major stock exchanges are actually parent companies with one or more subsidiaries. Thus anyone using published financial statements will find it useful to understand the basic principles used in preparing consolidated financial statements.

Principles of consolidation

Consolidated financial statements are prepared by combining the amounts that appear in the separate financial statements of the parent and subsidiary companies. In the combining process, however, certain adjustments are made to *eliminate the effects of intercompany transactions* and thus to reflect the assets, liabilities, and stockholders' equity from the viewpoint of a single economic entity.

Intercompany transactions. The term *intercompany transactions* refers to transactions between affiliated companies. These transactions may include, for example, the sale of merchandise, the leasing of property, and the making of loans. When the affiliated companies are viewed separately, these transactions may create assets and liabilities for the individual companies. However, when the affiliated companies are viewed as a single business entity, these assets and liabilities are merely the result of internal transfers within the business organization and should not appear in the consolidated financial statements.

For example, if a subsidiary borrows money from the parent company, a note payable will appear as a liability in the balance sheet of the subsidiary company and a note receivable will appear as an asset in the separate balance sheet of the parent. When the two companies are viewed as a single consolidated entity, however, this "loan" is nothing more than a transfer of cash from one part of the business to another. Transferring assets between two parts of a single business entity does not create either a receivable or a payable for that entity. Therefore, the parent company's note receivable and the subsidiary's note payable should not appear in the consolidated financial statements.

Preparing consolidated financial statements. Separate accounting records are maintained for each company in an affiliated group, but no accounting records are maintained for the consolidated entity. The amounts shown in consolidated financial statements *do not come from a ledger;* they are determined on a *working paper* by combining the amounts of like items on the financial statements of the affiliated companies. For example, the inventories of all the affiliated companies are combined into one amount for inventories. Entries to eliminate the effects of intercompany transactions are made *only* on this working paper. These elimination entries are *not recorded in the accounting records* of either the parent company or its subsidiaries.

Consolidation at the date of acquisition

To illustrate the basic principles of consolidation, we will now prepare a consolidated balance sheet. Assume that on January 1, Year 10, Post Corporation purchases for cash 100% of the capital stock of Sun Company at its book value of $300,000. (The shares are purchased from Sun Company's former stockholders.) Also on this date, Post Corporation lends $40,000 cash to Sun Company, receiving a note as evidence of the loan. Immediately after these two transactions, the separate balance sheet accounts of Post Corporation and Sun Company are as shown in the working paper at the top of the next page.

Intercompany eliminations

Before the balance sheet amounts of Post Corporation and Sun Company are combined, entries are made in the working paper to eliminate the effects of intercompany transactions. Intercompany eliminations may be classified into three basic types:

1 Elimination of intercompany stock ownership
2 Elimination of intercompany debt
3 Elimination of intercompany revenue and expenses

POST CORPORATION AND SUBSIDIARY
Working Paper — Consolidated Balance Sheet
January 1, Year 10 (Date of Acquisition)

	Post Corporation	Sun Company	Intercompany Eliminations Debit	Intercompany Eliminations Credit	Consolidated Balance Sheet
Cash	60,000	45,000			105,000
Notes receivable	40,000			(b) 40,000	
Accounts receivable (net)	70,000	50,000			120,000
Inventories	110,000	95,000			205,000
Investment in Sun Company	300,000			(a) 300,000	
Plant & equipment (net)	210,000	180,000			390,000
Totals	790,000	370,000			820,000
Notes payable		40,000	(b) 40,000		
Accounts payable.......................	125,000	30,000			155,000
Capital stock — Post Corporation	400,000				400,000
Capital stock — Sun Company		200,000	(a) 200,000		
Retained earnings — Post Corporation	265,000				265,000
Retained earnings — Sun Company		100,000	(a) 100,000		
Totals	790,000	370,000	340,000	340,000	820,000

Explanation of elimination:
(a) To eliminate the investment in Sun Company against Sun Company's stockholders' equity.
(b) To eliminate intercompany note receivable against related note payable.

The first two types of eliminations are illustrated in our example of Post Corporation and Sun Company. The elimination of intercompany revenue and expenses will be discussed later in this appendix.

To understand the need for elimination entries, we must adopt the viewpoint of the consolidated entity, in which Post Corporation and Sun Company are regarded as two departments within a single company.

Entry (a): Elimination of intercompany stock ownership. The purpose of entry (a) in the illustrated working paper is to eliminate from the consolidated balance sheet both the asset account and the stockholders' equity accounts representing the parent company's ownership of the subsidiary.

Post Corporation's ownership interest in Sun Company appears in the *separate* balance sheets of both corporations. In the parent's balance sheet, this ownership interest is shown as the asset, Investment in Sun Company. In the separate balance sheet of the subsidiary, the parent company's ownership interest is represented by the stockholders' equity accounts, Capital Stock and Retained Earnings. In the ***consolidated*** balance sheet, however, this "ownership interest" is neither an asset nor a part of stockholders' equity.

From the viewpoint of the single consolidated entity, ***there are no stockholders in Sun Company.*** "Stockholders" are outside investors who have an ownership interest in a business. All of Sun Company's capital stock is "internally owned" by another part of the consolidated entity. A company's "ownership" of its own stock does not create either an asset or stockholders' equity. Therefore the asset account, Investment in Sun Company, and Sun Company's related stockholders' equity accounts must be eliminated from the consolidated balance sheet.

Entry *(b)*: Elimination of intercompany debt. When Post Corporation loaned $40,000 to Sun Company, the parent company recorded a note receivable and the subsidiary recorded a note payable. This "receivable" and "payable" exist only when Post Corporation and Sun Company are viewed as two separate entities. When both corporations are viewed as a single company, this "loan" is merely a transfer of cash from one part of the business to another. Such internal transfers of assets do not create either a receivable or a payable for the consolidated entity. Therefore, entry *(b)* is made to eliminate Post Corporation's note receivable and Sun Company's note payable from the consolidated balance sheet.

After the necessary eliminations have been entered in the working paper, the remaining balance sheet amounts of Post Corporation and Sun Company are combined to determine the assets, liabilities, and stockholders' equity of the consolidated entity. The following consolidated balance sheet is then prepared from the working paper:

POST CORPORATION AND SUBSIDIARY
Consolidated Balance Sheet
January 1, Year 10
Assets

<table>
<tr><td colspan="3">Current assets:</td></tr>
<tr><td>Cash ....</td><td></td><td>$105,000</td></tr>
<tr><td>Accounts receivable (net) ....</td><td></td><td>120,000</td></tr>
<tr><td>Inventories ....</td><td></td><td>205,000</td></tr>
<tr><td>Total current assets ....</td><td></td><td>$430,000</td></tr>
<tr><td>Plant & equipment (net) ....</td><td></td><td>390,000</td></tr>
<tr><td>Total assets ....</td><td></td><td>$820,000</td></tr>
</table>

Note stockholders' equity is that of parent company

Liabilities & Stockholders' Equity

<table>
<tr><td colspan="3">Current liabilities:</td></tr>
<tr><td>Accounts payable ....</td><td></td><td>$155,000</td></tr>
<tr><td colspan="3">Stockholders' equity:</td></tr>
<tr><td>Capital stock ....</td><td>$400,000</td><td></td></tr>
<tr><td>Retained earnings ....</td><td>265,000</td><td></td></tr>
<tr><td>Total stockholders' equity ....</td><td></td><td>665,000</td></tr>
<tr><td>Total liabilities & stockholders' equity ....</td><td></td><td>$820,000</td></tr>
</table>

Acquisition of subsidiary's stock at a price above book value

When a parent company purchases a controlling interest in a subsidiary, it often pays a price for the shares in excess of their book value.[3] We cannot ignore a difference between the cost of the parent company's investment and the underlying book value of these shares. In consolidation, the parent's investment is offset against the stockholders' equity accounts of the subsidiary, and if the two amounts are not equal, we must determine what the difference between them represents.

To illustrate, assume that C Company purchases all of the outstanding shares of D Company for $980,000. At the date of acquisition, D Company's balance sheet shows total stockholders' equity of $700,000, consisting of capital stock of $300,000 and retained earnings of $400,000. In preparing the elimination entry on the working papers for a consolidated balance sheet, we must determine what to do with the $280,000 difference between the price paid, $980,000, and the stockholders' equity of D Company, $700,000.

Why would C Company pay a price in excess of book value for D Company's stock? C Company's management must believe that either (1) the fair market value of certain specific assets of D Company (such as land or buildings) is in excess of book value, or (2) D Company's future earnings prospects are so favorable as to justify paying $280,000 for D Company's unrecorded *goodwill.*

If we assume that the $280,000 represents unrecorded goodwill, the entry in the working papers to eliminate C Company's investment account against the stockholders' equity accounts of D Company would be:

Elimination entry when price paid for shares of subsidiary exceeds their book value

Capital Stock — D Company	300,000	
Retained Earnings — D Company	400,000	
Goodwill	280,000	
Investment in D Company (C Company's asset account)		980,000

To eliminate the cost of C Company's 100% interest in D Company against D's stockholders' equity accounts and to recognize D Company's unrecorded goodwill.

(Although we have shown this entry in general journal form, it actually would be made only in the Intercompany Eliminations columns of the working paper for a consolidated balance sheet.)

The $280,000 of goodwill will appear as an asset in the consolidated balance sheet.[4] This asset will be amortized to expense over its useful life.

Less than 100% ownership in subsidiary

If a parent company owns a majority interest in a subsidiary but less than 100% of the outstanding shares, a new kind of ownership equity known as the *minority interest* will appear in the consolidated balance sheet. This minority interest represents the ownership interest in the subsidiary held by stockholders other than the parent company.

[3] The parent company also might acquire the shares of the subsidiary at a price below book value. This situation will be discussed in an advanced accounting course.

[4] If specific assets of D Company had been undervalued, the $280,000 would be allocated to increase the valuation of those assets in the consolidated working papers. The revaluation of specific assets is beyond the scope of our introductory discussion.

When there are minority stockholders, only the portion of the subsidiary's stockholders' equity owned by the parent company is eliminated. The remainder of the stockholders' equity of the subsidiary is included in the consolidated balance sheet under the caption Minority Interest.

To illustrate, assume that at the end of Year 4, Park Company purchases 75% of the outstanding capital stock of Sims Company for $150,000 cash, an amount equal to the book value of the stock acquired. The working paper to prepare a consolidated balance sheet on the date that control of Sims Company is acquired appears below:

PARK COMPANY AND SUBSIDIARY
Working Paper — Consolidated Balance Sheet
December 31, Year 4 (Date of Acquisition)

	Park Company	Sims Company	Intercompany Eliminations		Consolidated Balance Sheet
			Debit	Credit	
Cash	200,000	50,000			250,000
Other assets	500,000	210,000			710,000
Investment in Sims Company	150,000			(a) 150,000	
Totals	850,000	260,000			960,000
Liabilities	250,000	60,000			310,000
Capital stock — Park Company	500,000				500,000
Capital stock — Sims Company		120,000	(a) 90,000 (b) 30,000		
Retained earnings — Park Company	100,000				100,000
Retained earnings — Sims Company		80,000	(a) 60,000 (b) 20,000		
Minority interest (25% of $200,000)				(b) 50,000	50,000
Totals	850,000	260,000	200,000	(b) 200,000	960,000

Explanation of elimination:
(a) To eliminate Park Company's investment in 75% of Sims Company's stockholders' equity.
(b) To classify the remaining 25% of Sims Company's stockholders' equity as a minority interest.

Entry *(a)* in this working paper offsets Park Company's asset, Investment in Sims Company, against *75%* of Sims Company's capital stock and retained earnings. The purpose of this entry is to eliminate intercompany stock ownership from the assets and stockholders' equity shown in the consolidated balance sheet. Entry *(b)* reclassifies the remaining 25% of Sims Company's capital stock and retained earnings into a special stockholders' equity account entitled Minority Interest. In the consolidated balance sheet, the minority interest appears in the stockholders' equity section as shown below:

Stockholders' equity:	
Minority interest	$ 50,000
Capital stock	500,000
Retained earnings	100,000
Total stockholders' equity	$650,000

Minority interest. Why is the minority interest shown separately in the consolidated balance sheet instead of being included in the amounts shown for capital stock and retained earnings? The reason for this separate presentation is to distinguish between the ownership equity of the controlling stockholders and the equity of the minority stockholders.

The stockholders in the parent company own the controlling interest in the consolidated entity. Because these stockholders elect the directors of the parent company, they control the entire group of affiliated companies. The minority interest, however, has *no control* over any of the affiliated companies. Because they own shares only in a subsidiary, they cannot vote for the directors of the parent company. Also, they can never outvote the majority stockholder (the parent company) in electing the directors or establishing the policies of the subsidiary.[5]

The minority stockholders receive 25% of the dividends declared by Sims Company but do not participate in dividends declared by the parent company. The stockholders of Park Company, on the other hand, receive all the dividends declared by the parent company but do not receive dividends declared by the subsidiary.

Consolidated income statement

A consolidated income statement is prepared by combining the revenue and expense accounts of the parent and subsidiary. Revenue and expenses arising from *intercompany transactions* are eliminated because they reflect transfers of assets from one affiliated company to another and do not change the net assets from a consolidated viewpoint.

Elimination of intercompany revenue and expenses. Some of the more common examples of intercompany items that should be eliminated in preparing a consolidated income statement are:

1 Sales to affiliated companies
2 Cost of goods sold resulting from sales to affiliated companies
3 Interest expense on loans from affiliated companies
4 Interest revenue on loans made to affiliated companies
5 Rent or other revenue received for services rendered to affiliated companies
6 Rent or other expenses paid for services received from affiliated companies

In its separate accounting records, the parent company uses the *equity method* to account for its investment in a subsidiary. Under the equity method, the parent company recognizes as investment income its share of the subsidiary's earnings. Because the individual revenue and expenses of the subsidiary are included in a consolidated income statement, the parent company's Investment Income (from subsidiary) account must be eliminated to avoid double counting this portion of the subsidiary's earnings.

Because of the complexity of the intercompany eliminations, the preparation of a consolidated income statement and a consolidated statement of retained earnings are topics appropriately deferred to an advanced accounting course.

---

[5] Some companies emphasize the limited ownership role of the minority stockholders by showing the minority interest between the liabilities section and the stockholders' equity section of the consolidated balance sheet.

Purchase method and pooling-of-interests method: Two types of business combination

The transaction in which two corporations become affiliated is called a **business combination.** In our discussion of business combinations up to this point, we have assumed that the parent acquired a subsidiary company by paying cash for its shares. This kind of acquisition is accounted for by the **purchase method.** The purchase method is also used for cases in which the parent issues its own bonds payable or capital stock in payment for the subsidiary's shares. The term **purchase method** implies that the parent has acquired the subsidiary by purchase and that the former stockholders in the subsidiary have sold out. In addition to the purchase method which we have been discussing, there is an alternative called the **pooling-of-interests method.** We will now consider the type of business combination for which the pooling-of-interests method may be used.

If the stock of a subsidiary is acquired **in exchange for shares of the parent company's common stock** and if certain other criteria are met, a business combination may be treated as a pooling of interests.[6] A key aspect of such acquisitions is that the stockholders of the subsidiary company **become stockholders of the parent corporation.** The stockholders of the two companies are said to have **pooled their interests,** rather than one ownership group having sold its equity to the other.

When a subsidiary is acquired by a pooling of interests, no ownership interest is severed — in other words, no "purchase" or "sale" of the subsidiary's net assets occurs. Therefore, the net assets of the subsidiary are **not revalued** in the consolidated balance sheet, regardless of the market value of the securities issued in exchange. In the consolidated balance sheet, the assets of the subsidiary appear at their book values and **no goodwill is recorded.** Therefore, no amortization expense relating to goodwill appears in the consolidated income statement.

Another significant difference between the purchase and the pooling-of-interests methods is the treatment in the consolidated income statement of the subsidiary's earnings (revenue and expenses) in the year of affiliation. Under the purchase method, only the subsidiary's earnings **after the date of acquisition** are included in the consolidated income statement. Under the pooling-of-interests method, the consolidated income statement includes the earnings of the subsidiary **for the entire year.**

To illustrate, let us assume that X Company acquired 100% of Y Company's stock on November 1, Year 1, and that each company earned $600,000 during Year 1. Assuming the $600,000 net income of Y Company was earned at a uniform rate during Year 1, the consolidated net income for the two companies under the purchase method would be $700,000 (X Company's $600,000 $+ \frac{2}{12}$ of Y Company's $600,000). However, consolidated net income on a pooling basis would be $1,200,000 even though $500,000 ($\frac{10}{12}$ of $600,000) of the earnings of Y Company were earned before the two companies became affiliated on November 1.

The following brief summary emphasizes some of the points of contrast between treating a corporate acquisition as a **purchase** or as a **pooling of interests.**

---

[6] In addition to the parent company issuing only common stock in exchange for the subsidiary's shares, other specific criteria must be met for the affiliation to qualify as a pooling of interests. For example, at least 90% of the subsidiary's stock must be acquired within one year following the beginning of negotiations. For a more complete discussion of the differences between a purchase and a pooling of interests, see *APB Opinion No. 16,* "Business Combinations," AICPA (New York: 1970).

Purchase Method	Pooling-of-Interests Method
1 If the price paid by the parent for the subsidiary's stock exceeds book value, goodwill is recorded (or the subsidiary's assets are revalued).	No goodwill is recorded and the subsidiary's assets are not revalued, regardless of the market value of the shares issued by the parent company.
2 If goodwill appears in the consolidated balance sheet, consolidated net income in future periods is reduced by amortization expense relating to this asset.	Since no goodwill appears in the consolidated balance sheet, consolidated net income is not reduced by any related amortization expense.
3 Earnings of subsidiary are combined with the earnings of the parent only from the date of the affiliation.	Earnings of subsidiary for the entire year in which the affiliation occurs are included in the consolidated income statement.

In the opinion of the authors, the failure to record goodwill based upon the market value of the shares issued by the parent company is a serious weakness in the pooling-of-interests method. In many cases, the failure to record goodwill results in significant understatement of consolidated assets and an overstatement of consolidated net income.

To illustrate, assume that S Company has total assets and stockholders' equity with a book value of $6 million. (For simplicity, we will assume that S Company has no liabilities.) The *market value* of S Company's assets and stockholders' equity, however, is $10 million, due to the existence of $4 million in unrecorded goodwill.

Now assume that P Company issues $10 million (market value) of its own shares in exchange for 100% of S Company's capital stock. If this acquisition is treated as a purchase, S Company's assets will appear in the consolidated balance sheet at $10 million, including the $4 million in goodwill. As discussed in Chapter 10, goodwill must be amortized over a period of not more than 40 years. Therefore, consolidated net income will be reduced by at least $100,000 per year ($4 million ÷ 40 years) as the goodwill is amortized to expense.

If this affiliation is treated as a pooling of interests, the $4 million in unrecorded goodwill will *not appear* in the consolidated balance sheet, and the assets of S Company will be shown at their book value of $6 million. Also, there will be no amortization of goodwill in the consolidated income statement, thus causing net income to appear at a higher amount.

When should consolidated statements be prepared?

As a general rule, consolidated financial statements are prepared when one corporation owns a *controlling interest* (more than 50% of the voting stock) in one or more subsidiaries. However, the accounts of some subsidiary companies may not be included in consolidated statements. Consolidation of accounts is appropriate only when control over the subsidiary is a continuing situation and when the consolidated statements *give a meaningful picture of financial position.* For example, a subsidiary's accounts should not be consolidated with those of the parent if control is likely to be temporary or if the subsidiary is facing bankruptcy. Similarly, if the assets of a foreign subsidiary cannot be withdrawn by the parent because of restrictions placed on such assets by foreign governments, the accounts should not be consolidated.

In other instances, consolidation may not be appropriate because the activities of the subsidiary are **significantly different** from those of the parent. For example, Sears, Roebuck and Co. does not consolidate its wholly owned subsidiary, Allstate Insurance Company. When the parent company controls a subsidiary but consolidation is not considered appropriate, the **unconsolidated subsidiary** appears in the financial statements as a long-term investment, accounted for by the equity method.

Review questions

1 When should investors use the equity method to account for an investment in common stock?
2 Dividends on stock owned are usually recognized as income when they are received. Does an investor using the **equity method** to account for an investment in common stock follow this policy? Explain fully.
3 Alexander Corporation owns 80% of the outstanding common stock of Benton Company. Explain the basis for the assumption that these two companies constitute a single economic entity operating under unified control.
4 What are consolidated financial statements? Explain briefly how these statements are prepared.
5 List the three basic types of intercompany eliminations which should be made as a step in the preparation of consolidated financial statements.
6 Explain why the price paid to acquire a controlling interest in a subsidiary company may be different from the book value of the equity acquired.
7 The following item appears on a consolidated balance sheet: "Minority interest in subsidiary . . . $620,000." Explain the nature of this item, and where you would expect to find it on the consolidated balance sheet.
8 Briefly explain the differences found in consolidated financial statements when a business combination is viewed as a **pooling of interests** rather than as a **purchase.**
9 As a general rule, when should consolidated financial statements be prepared?
10 The annual report of Superior Manufacturing Company and Subsidiaries included the following note: "Accounts of all subsidiaries in which the Company owns more than 50% of the voting stock are shown on a consolidated basis, with three exceptions: Western Casualty and Indemnity Company, Consumer Credit Corporation, and Superior Manufacturing of Argentina, which are accounted for by the equity method."

Explain the probable reasons for not consolidating these three subsidiaries. Also explain how the investments in these unconsolidated subsidiaries will be shown in the consolidated balance sheet.

Problems

B-1   Equity method
On January 1, Year 1, City Broadcasting purchases 30% of the common stock of News Service, Inc., for $250,000, which corresponds to the underlying book value. News Service, Inc., has issued common stock only. At December 31, Year 1, News Service, Inc., reported net income for the year of $140,000 and paid cash dividends of $60,000. City Broadcasting uses the equity method to account for this investment.

Instructions

a Prepare all journal entries in the accounting records of City Broadcasting relating to the investment during Year 1.

b During Year 2, News Service, Inc., reports a net loss of $110,000 and pays no dividends. Compute the carrying value of City Broadcasting's investment in News Service, Inc., at the end of Year 2.

B-2 Consolidated balance sheet with minority interest

On June 30 of Year 1, P Company *purchased* 70% of the stock of S Company for $420,000 in cash. The separate condensed balance sheets immediately after the purchase are shown below:

	P Company	S Company
Cash	$ 130,000	$ 90,000
Investment in S Company	420,000	
Other assets	2,250,000	710,000
	$2,800,000	$800,000
Liabilities	$ 600,000	$200,000
Capital stock	1,200,000	400,000
Retained earnings	1,000,000	200,000
	$2,800,000	$800,000

Instructions. Prepare a consolidated balance sheet immediately after P Company acquired control of S Company.

B-3 Consolidated balance sheet with goodwill

Condensed balance sheets of Marina Restaurants and Pelican Pier at December 31, Year 1, are shown below:

Assets	Marina Restaurants	Pelican Pier
Current assets	$1,890,000	$240,000
Plant and equipment	1,710,000	660,000
Total assets	$3,600,000	$900,000

Liabilities & Stockholders' Equity		
Current liabilities	$ 640,000	$120,000
Long-term debt	800,000	80,000
Capital stock	1,200,000	360,000
Retained earnings	960,000	340,000
Total liabilities & stockholders' equity	$3,600,000	$900,000

Instructions. Assume that on December 31, Year 1, Marina Restaurants used current assets to purchase all the outstanding capital stock of Pelican Pier for $850,000. The excess of this purchase price over the book value of Pelican Pier shares is regarded as payment for Pelican Pier's unrecorded goodwill. Prepare a consolidated balance sheet for Marina Restaurants and Pelican Pier at the date of acquisition. Show goodwill as a separate asset in the consolidated balance sheet.

B-4   Purchase accounting versus pooling-of-interests
Par Co. is planning to acquire all the shares of Sun Co. at a price of $4,700,000. Sun Co.'s shares have a book value of $3,400,000, but Par Co.'s management believes that the excess of the purchase price over this book value is justified by Sun Co.'s unrecorded goodwill. Payment will be made either in cash or by issuing additional shares of Par Co. common stock with a fair market value of $4,700,000.

The business combination will take place on December 31 of the current year. During the current year, Par Co. earned $2,100,000 and Sun Co. earned $900,000.

Instructions. Compute (1) the amount of goodwill, if any, and (2) the amount of consolidated net income that will appear in the consolidated financial statements for the current year under each of the following independent assumptions:

a Par Co. pays cash for Sun Co.'s shares and accounts for the combination by the purchase method.
b Par Co. issues shares of its own stock to acquire Sun Co.'s shares and accounts for the combination as a pooling of interests.

B-5   Analysis of consolidated balance sheet
The following information relates to Major Company and its subsidiary, the Minor Company:

Assets	Major Company	Minor Company	Consolidated
Cash	$ 120,000	$ 75,000	$ 195,000
Accounts receivable	180,000	100,000	160,000
Merchandise inventory	360,000	230,000	590,000
Investment in Minor Company	900,000		
Other assets	1,200,000	530,000	1,730,000
Goodwill			220,000
Total assets	$2,760,000	$935,000	$2,895,000

Liabilities & Stockholders' Equity			
Accounts payable	$ 165,000	$ 90,000	$ 135,000
Accrued liabilities	30,000	45,000	75,000
Notes payable (long-term)	450,000		450,000
Capital stock	1,000,000	300,000	1,000,000
Paid-in capital in excess of par	365,000	160,000	365,000
Retained earnings	750,000	340,000	750,000
Minority interest			120,000
Total liabilities & stockholders' equity	$2,760,000	$935,000	$2,895,000

Major Company acquired its controlling interest in Minor Company by issuing a combination of notes payable and additional shares of capital stock.

Instructions

   a Was the acquisition of Minor Company viewed as a purchase or a pooling of interests? Why?

   b What percentage of the outstanding stock of Minor Company is owned by Major Company? (Hint: First determine the percentage of Minor Company's stockholders' equity owned by the minority stockholders.)

   c If Minor Company's accounts payable include $85,000 owed to Major Company, how much of Major Company's accounts payable are apparently owed to Minor Company?

   d Explain why $220,000 of goodwill appears in the consolidated balance sheet.

Appendix C
International accounting and foreign currency translation

This appendix addresses the special accounting problems encountered by companies which conduct part of their business in foreign countries or in foreign currencies. Four major issues are discussed. The first is the gain or loss resulting from fluctuations in currency exchange rates when a business has either receivables or payables stated in terms of a foreign currency. The second is the "hedging" techniques that a business might employ to protect itself against losses from currency fluctuations. Next, the nature of a "cumulative translation adjustment" is explained and contrasted with gains and losses from exchange rate fluctuations. Finally, in this appendix we discuss the effort to establish international accounting standards.

After studying this appendix you should be able to:

✓ Translate an amount of foreign currency into the equivalent number of U.S. dollars.
✓ Explain why exchange rates fluctuate and what is meant by a "strong" or a "weak" currency.
✓ Compute the gain or loss on a receivable or payable stated in terms of a foreign currency when exchange rates fluctuate.
✓ Explain how fluctuations in foreign exchange rates affect companies with receivables or with payables stated in terms of foreign currencies.
✓ Describe several techniques for "hedging" against losses from fluctuations in exchange rates.
✓ Define a "cumulative translation adjustment," and explain how this item differs from the gains and losses resulting from exchange rate fluctuations.
✓ Discuss the problems arising from the use of different accounting standards in different countries.

From what geographical area does Bank of America—the largest bank in California—earn most of its revenue? The answer is abroad—that is, from its operations in foreign countries. Bank of America is not alone in its pursuit of business on a worldwide basis.

519

Most large corporations, such as Exxon, IBM, Volkswagen, and Sony, do business in many countries. Coca-Cola, for example, recently announced that it has operations in 155 countries throughout the world. Companies that do business in more than one country often are described as **multinational** corporations. The extent to which foreign sales contributed to the revenue of several well-known multinational corporations in a recent year is shown below:

Company	Headquarters	Total Revenue (in millions)	% Earned from Foreign Operations
Nestles	Switzerland	$13,626	97.2
Sony	Japan	4,528	74.5
Exxon	USA	97,173	71.4
Volkswagen	W. Germany	15,427	67.9
Bank of America	USA	14,955	53.8
British Petroleum	Great Britain	51,353	52.3
IBM	USA	34,364	44.6
Coca-Cola	USA	6,250	42.7

Most large and well-known multinational corporations are headquartered in the highly industrialized countries, such as the United States, Japan, Great Britain, and the countries of Western Europe. Virtually every country, however, has many companies that engage in international business activity.

What is international accounting?

Accounting for business activities that span national borders comprises the field of international accounting. In this appendix, we emphasize accounting for transactions with foreign companies. We also briefly discuss some of the problems of preparing consolidated financial statements for American-based companies with subsidiaries located in foreign countries. Our discussion is limited to basic concepts; the details and complexities of international accounting will be covered in advanced accounting courses.[1]

Foreign currencies and exchange rates

One of the principal problems in international accounting arises because every country uses a different currency. Assume, for example, that a Japanese company sells merchandise to an American corporation. The Japanese company will want to be paid in Japanese currency — yen, but the American company's bank account contains U.S. dollars. Thus, one currency must be converted into another.

Most banks participate in an international currency exchange, which enables them to buy foreign currencies at the prevailing **exchange rate.** Thus, our American corporation can pay its liability to the Japanese company through the international banking system. The American company will pay its bank in dollars. The bank will then use these dollars to

---

[1] For a more thorough discussion of accounting for transactions with foreign companies and consolidation of foreign subsidiaries, see *FASB Statement No. 52*, "Foreign Currency Translation" (Stamford, Conn.: 1981).

purchase the required amount of yen on the international currency exchange and will arrange for delivery of the yen to the Japanese company's bank.[2]

Exchange rates. A currency exchange rate is the ratio at which one currency may be converted into another. Thus, the exchange rate may be viewed as the "price" of buying units of foreign currency, stated in terms of the domestic currency (which for our purpose is U.S. dollars). Exchange rates fluctuate daily, based upon the worldwide supply and demand for particular currencies. The current exchange rate between the dollar and most major currencies is published daily in the financial press. For example, a few of the exchange rates listed in a recent issue of *The Wall Street Journal* are shown below:

Country	Currency	Exchange Rate (in dollars)
Britain	Pound (£)	$1.3025
France	French franc (FF)	.1117
Japan	Yen (¥)	.0040
Mexico	Peso ($)	.0030
West Germany	Deutsche mark (DM)	.3430

Exchange rates may be used to determine how much of one currency is equivalent to a given amount of another currency. Assume that the American company in our preceding example owes the Japanese company 1 million yen (expressed ¥1,000,000). How many dollars are needed to settle this obligation, assuming that the current exchange rate is $.0040 per yen? To restate an amount of foreign currency in terms of the equivalent amount of U.S. dollars, we multiply the foreign currency amount by the exchange rate, as illustrated below.[3]

$$\begin{array}{ccc} \text{Amount Stated} & & \text{Equivalent} \\ \text{in Foreign} & \times \text{Exchange Rate} = & \text{Number of} \\ \text{Currency} & \text{(in Dollars)} & \text{U.S. Dollars} \end{array}$$

$$¥1,000,000 \times \$.0040 \text{ per yen} = \$4,000$$

This process of restating an amount of foreign currency in terms of the equivalent number of dollars is called *translating* the foreign currency.

Why exchange rates fluctuate. An exchange rate represents the "price" of one currency, stated in terms of another. These prices fluctuate, based upon supply and demand, just as do the prices of gold, silver, soybeans, and other commodities. When the demand for a particular currency exceeds supply, the price (exchange rate) rises. If supply exceeds demand, the exchange rate falls.

What determines the demand and supply for particular currencies? In short, it is the

---

[2] Alternatively, the American company may send the Japanese company a check (or a bank draft) stated in dollars. The Japanese company can then arrange to have the dollars converted into yen through its bank in Japan.

[3] To convert an amount of dollars into the equivalent amount of a foreign currency, we would divide the dollar amount by the exchange rate. For example, $4,000 ÷ $.0040 per yen = ¥1,000,000.

quantities of the currency that traders and investors seek to buy or to sell. Buyers of a particular currency include purchasers of that country's exports and foreign investors seeking to invest in the country's capital markets. Sellers of a currency include companies within the country that are importing goods from abroad and investors within the country who would prefer to invest their funds abroad. Thus, two major factors in the demand and supply for a currency are (1) the ratio of the country's imports to its exports, and (2) the real rate of return available in the country's capital markets.

To illustrate the first of these points, let us consider Japan and Great Britain. Japan exports far more than it imports. As a result, Japan's customers must buy yen in the international currency market in order to pay for their purchases. This creates a strong demand for the yen and has caused its price (exchange rate) to rise relative to most other currencies. Great Britain, on the other hand, imports more than it exports. Thus, British companies must sell British pounds in order to acquire the foreign currencies needed to pay for their purchases. This has increased the supply of pounds in the currency markets, and the price of the pound has declined substantially over the last several decades.

The second factor — the international attractiveness of a country's capital markets — depends upon both political stability and the country's interest rates relative to its internal rate of inflation. When a politically stable country offers high interest rates relative to inflation, foreign investors will seek to invest their funds in that country. First, however, they must convert their funds into that country's currency. This demand tends to raise the exchange rate for that currency. High interest rates relative to the internal rate of inflation have been the major reason for the strength of the U.S. dollar during the 1980s.

Exchange rate "jargon." In the financial press, currencies are often described as "strong," "weak," or as rising or falling against one another. For example, an evening newscaster might say that "A strong dollar rose sharply against the weakening British pound, but fell slightly against the Japanese yen and the Swiss franc." What does this mean about exchange rates?

To understand such terminology, we must remember that an exchange rate is simply the price of one currency *stated in terms of another currency.* Throughout this appendix, we refer to the prices of various foreign currencies stated in terms of U.S. dollars. In other countries, however, the U.S. dollar is a foreign currency, and its price is stated in terms of the local (domestic) currency.

To illustrate, consider our table from *The Wall Street Journal,* which shows the exchange rate for the Japanese yen to be $.0040. At this exchange rate, ¥250 is equivalent to $1 (¥250 × $.0040 per yen = $1). Thus, while we would say that the exchange rate for the Japanese yen is $.0040, the Japanese would say that the exchange rate for the U.S. dollar is ¥250.

Now let us assume that the exchange rate for the yen (stated in dollars) rises to $.0042. At this exchange rate, ¥238 is approximately equivalent to $1 (¥238 × $.0042 = $1). In the United States, we would say that the exchange rate for the yen has *risen* from $.0040 to $.0042. In Japan, however, they would say that the exchange rate for the dollar has *fallen* from ¥250 to ¥238. In the financial press, it might be said that "the yen has risen against the dollar," or that "the dollar has fallen against the yen." The two statements mean the same thing — that the yen has become more valuable relative to the dollar.

Now let us return to our original phrase, "A strong dollar rose sharply against the weakening British pound, but fell slightly against the Japanese yen and the Swiss franc." When exchange rates are stated in terms of U.S. dollars, this statement means that the price (exchange rate) of the British pound fell sharply, but the prices of the Japanese yen and the Swiss franc rose slightly.

A currency is described as "strong" when its exchange rate is rising relative to most other currencies and as "weak" when its exchange rate is falling. Both the U.S. dollar and the Japanese yen have been strong currencies over recent years. On any given day, however, one of these currencies may be stronger than the other. Hence, while the exchange rates for both the dollar and the yen might be rising in relation to most other currencies, the exchange rate for the dollar might still fall when stated in yen. The reverse is also true — that is, the exchange rate for the yen might fall when stated in dollars.

ACCOUNTING FOR TRANSACTIONS WITH FOREIGN COMPANIES

When an American company buys or sells merchandise in a transaction with a foreign company, the transaction price may be stipulated either in U.S. dollars or in units of the foreign currency. If the price is stated in **dollars,** the American company encounters no special accounting problems. The transaction may be recorded in the same manner as are similar transactions with domestic suppliers or customers.

If the transaction price is stated in terms of the **foreign currency,** the American company encounters two accounting problems. First, since the American company's accounting records are maintained in dollars, the transaction price must be translated into dollars before the transaction can be recorded. The second problem arises when (1) the purchase or sale is made **on account,** and (2) the exchange rate **changes** between the date of the transaction and the date that the account is paid. This fluctuation in the exchange rate will cause the American company to experience either a gain or a loss in the settlement of the transaction.

Credit purchases with prices stated in a foreign currency. Assume that on August 1 an American company buys merchandise from a British company at a price of 10 thousand British pounds (£10,000), with payment due in 60 days. The exchange rate on August 1 is $1.30 per British pound. The entry on August 1 to record this purchase (assuming use of the periodic inventory system) is shown below:

Purchases	13,000	
Accounts Payable		13,000

To record the purchase of merchandise from a British company for £10,000 when the exchange rate is $1.30 per pound (£10,000 × $1.30 = $13,000).

Let us now assume that by September 30, when the £10,000 account payable must be paid, the exchange rate has fallen to $1.28 per British pound. If the American company had paid for the merchandise on August 1, the cost would have been $13,000. On September 30, however, only $12,800 is needed to pay off the £10,000 liability (£10,000 × $1.28 = $12,800). Thus, the decline in the exchange rate has saved the company $200. This savings is recorded in the accounting records as a *Gain on Fluctuations in Foreign Exchange Rates.* The entry on September 30 to record payment of the liability and recognition of this gain would be:

Accounts Payable	13,000	
Cash		12,800
Gain on Fluctuations in Foreign Exchange Rates		200

To record payment of £10,000 liability to British company and to recognize gain from decline in exchange rate:

Original liability (£10,000 × $1.30)	$13,000
Amount paid (£10,000 × $1.28)	12,800
Gain from decline in exchange rate	$ 200

Now let us assume that instead of declining, the exchange rate had *increased* from $1.30 on August 1 to $1.33 on September 30. Under this assumption, the American company would have to pay $13,300 in order to pay off the £10,000 liability on September 30. Thus, the company would be paying $300 more than if the liability had been paid on August 1. This additional $300 cost was caused by the increase in the exchange rate and should be recorded as a loss. The entry on September 30 would be:

Accounts Payable	13,000	
Loss on Fluctuations in Foreign Exchange Rates	300	
Cash		13,300

To record payment of £10,000 liability to British company and to recognize loss from increase in exchange rate:

Original liability (£10,000 × $1.30)	$13,000
Amount paid (£10,000 × $1.33)	13,300
Loss from increase in exchange rate	$ 300

In summary, having a liability that is fixed in terms of a foreign currency results in a gain for the debtor if the exchange rate falls between the date of the transaction and the date of payment. The gain results because fewer dollars will be needed to repay the debt than had originally been owed. An increase in the exchange rate, on the other hand, causes the debtor to incur a loss. In this case, the debtor will have to spend more dollars than had originally been owed in order to purchase the foreign currency needed to pay the debt.

Credit sales with prices stated in a foreign currency. A company that makes credit sales at prices stated in a foreign currency also will experience gains or losses from fluctuations in the exchange rate. To illustrate, let us change our preceding example to assume that the American company *sells* merchandise on August 1 to the British company at a price of £10,000. We shall again assume that the exchange rate on August 1 is $1.30 per British pound and that payment is due in 60 days. The entry on August 1 to record this sale is:

Accounts Receivable	13,000	
Sales		13,000

To record sale to British company with sales price set at £10,000 (£10,000 × $1.30) = $13,000. To be collected in 60 days.

In 60 days (September 30), the American company will collect from the British company the U.S. dollar equivalent of £10,000. If the exchange rate on September 30 has fallen to $1.28 per pound, the American company will collect only $12,800 (£10,000 × $1.28 = $12,800) in full settlement of its account receivable. Since the receivable had originally been equivalent to $13,000, the decline in the exchange rate has caused a loss of $200 to the American company. The entry to be made on September 30 is:

Cash	12,800	
Loss on Fluctuations in Foreign Exchange Rates	200	
Accounts Receivable		13,000

To record collection of £10,000 receivable from British company and to recognize loss from fall in exchange rate since date of sale:

Original sales price (£10,000 × $1.30)	$13,000
Amount received (£10,000 × $1.28)	12,800
Loss from decline in exchange rate	$ 200

Now consider the alternative case, in which the exchange rate rises from $1.30 at August 1 to $1.33 at September 30. In this case, the British company's payment of £10,000 will convert into $13,300, creating a gain for the American company. The entry on September 30 would then be:

Cash	13,300	
Accounts Receivable		13,000
Gain on Fluctuations in Foreign Exchange Rates		300

To record collection of £10,000 receivable from British company and to recognize gain from increase in exchange rate:

Original sales price (£10,000 × $1.30)	$13,000
Amount received (£10,000 × $1.33)	13,300
Gain from increase in exchange rate	$ 300

Adjustment of foreign receivables and payables at the balance sheet date. We have seen that fluctuations in exchange rates may cause gains or losses for companies with accounts payable or receivable in foreign currencies. The fluctuations in the exchange rates occur on a daily basis. For convenience, however, the company usually waits until the account is paid or collected before recording the related gain or loss. An exception to this convenient practice occurs at the end of the accounting period. An *adjusting entry* must be made to recognize any gains or losses that have accumulated on any foreign payables or receivables through the balance sheet date.

To illustrate, assume that on November 10 an American company buys equipment from a Japanese company at a price of 10 million yen (¥10,000,000), payable on January 10 of the following year. If the exchange rate is $.0040 per yen on November 10, the entry to record the purchase would be:

Equipment	40,000	
Accounts Payable		40,000

To record purchase of equipment from Japanese company at a price of ¥10,000,000, payable January 10 (¥10,000,000 × $.0040 = $40,000).

Now assume that on December 31, the exchange rate has fallen to $.0037 per yen. At this exchange rate, the American company's account payable is equivalent to only $37,000 (¥10,000,000 × $.0037). In *Statement No. 52,* the FASB requires that gains and losses from fluctuations in exchange rates be recognized in the period in which the rate changes. Therefore, the company should make an adjusting entry to reduce the liability to its current dollar-equivalent and to recognize any related gain or loss. This entry, which would be dated December 31, is as follows:

Accounts Payable	3,000	
Gain on Fluctuations in Foreign Exchange Rates		3,000

To adjust balance of ¥10,000,000 account payable to amount indicated by year-end exchange rate:

Original account balance	$40,000
Adjusted balance (¥10,000,000 × $.0037)	37,000
Required adjustment	$ 3,000

Similar adjustments should be made for any other accounts payable or receivable at year-end that are fixed in terms of a foreign currency.

If the exchange rate changes again between the date of this adjusting entry and the date that the American company pays the liability, an additional gain or loss must be recognized. Assume, for example, that on January 10 the exchange rate has risen to $.0038 per yen. The American company must now spend $38,000 to buy the ¥10,000,000 needed to pay its liability to the Japanese company. Thus, the rise in the exchange rate has caused the American company a $1,000 loss since year-end. The entry to record payment of the account on January 10 would be:

Accounts Payable	37,000	
Loss on Fluctuations in Foreign Exchange Rates	1,000	
Cash		38,000

To record payment of ¥10,000,000 payable to Japanese company and to recognize loss from rise in exchange rate since year-end:

Account payable, December 31	$37,000
Amount paid, January 10	38,000
Loss from increase in exchange rate	$ 1,000

Gains and losses from fluctuations in foreign exchange rates should be shown in the income statement following the determination of income from operations. This treatment is similar to that accorded to gains and losses from the sale of plant assets or investments.

Currency fluctuations: who wins and who loses?

Gains and losses from fluctuations in exchange rates are sustained by companies (or individuals) that have either payables or receivables that are *fixed in terms of a foreign currency.* When a foreign exchange rate falls, debtors will gain and creditors will lose. As an exchange rate falls, the foreign currency becomes less valuable. Therefore, debtors will have to spend fewer dollars in order to pay off their foreign liabilities, but creditors will have to watch their foreign receivables become worth fewer and fewer dollars.

When exchange rates rise, this situation reverses. Debtors will lose, because more dollars will be required to pay the foreign debts. Creditors will gain, because their foreign receivables will become equivalent to an increasing number of dollars.

What does this mean to American-based companies? The U.S. dollar has been quite strong in recent years, which means that most foreign exchange rates (stated in dollars) have been falling. Thus, American companies with large foreign liabilities have experienced sizable gains, while companies with large foreign receivables have experienced losses from exchange rate fluctuations.

Strategies to avoid losses from rate fluctuations. There are two basic approaches to avoiding losses from fluctuations in foreign exchange rates. One approach is to insist that receivables and payables be settled at specified amounts of domestic currency. The other approach is called *hedging* and can be accomplished in a number of ways.

To illustrate the first approach, assume that an American company makes large credit sales to companies in Mexico, but anticipates that the exchange rate for the Mexican peso will gradually decline. The American company can avoid losses by setting its *sales prices in dollars.* Then, if the exchange rate does decline, the Mexican companies will have to spend more pesos to pay for their purchases, but the American company will not receive fewer dollars. On the other hand, the American company will benefit from making credit purchases from Mexican companies at *prices stated in pesos,* because a decline in the exchange rate will reduce the number of dollars needed to pay for these purchases.

The interests of the Mexican companies, however, are exactly the opposite of those of the American company. If the Mexican companies anticipate an increase in the exchange rate for the U.S. dollar, they will want to buy at prices stated in pesos and sell at prices stated in dollars. Ultimately, the manner in which the transactions will be priced simply depends upon which company is in the better bargaining position.

Hedging. Hedging refers to the strategy of "sitting on both sides of the fence" — that is, of taking offsetting positions so that your gains and losses tend to offset one another. To illustrate the concept, assume that after a few beers you make a large bet on a football game. Later you have second thoughts about the bet, and you want to eliminate your risk of incurring a loss. You could "hedge" your original bet by making a similar bet on the other team. In this way, you will lose one bet, but you will win the other — your loss will be offset by a corresponding gain.

A company that has similar amounts of accounts receivable and accounts payable in the same foreign currency automatically has a hedged position. A decrease in the foreign exchange rate will cause losses on the foreign receivables and gains on the foreign payables. If the exchange rate rises, the gains on the foreign receivables will be offset by losses on the foreign payables.

Most companies, of course, do **not** have similar amounts of receivables and payables in the same foreign currency. However, they may create this situation by buying or selling foreign currency *future contracts.* These contracts, commonly called *futures,* are the right to receive a specified quantity of foreign currency at a future date. In short, they are accounts receivable in foreign currency. Thus, a company that has only foreign accounts payable may hedge its position by purchasing a similar dollar amount of foreign currency future contracts. Then, if the exchange rate rises, any losses on the foreign payables will be offset by a gain in the value of the future contracts.

A company with only foreign receivables may hedge its position by *selling* future contracts, thus receiving dollars today and *creating a liability* payable in foreign currency.

CONSOLIDATION OF FOREIGN SUBSIDIARIES

In Appendix B, we discussed the principles of preparing consolidated financial statements for an economic entity that conducts all or part of its operations through subsidiaries. These principles apply to foreign subsidiaries as well as those operating within the United States. However, two special accounting problems arise in the mechanical process of combining the financial statements of foreign subsidiaries with those of domestic subsidiaries and the parent company.

The first problem involves currencies. The accounting records of foreign subsidiaries generally are maintained in units of foreign currency. Obviously, we cannot add Mexican pesos, British pounds, and U.S. dollars and come up with a meaningful total. Therefore, the amounts appearing in the foreign subsidiaries' financial statements must be *translated* into U.S. dollars as a preliminary step in the consolidation process.

The second problem involves accounting principles. The generally accepted accounting principles that form the framework for financial reporting in the United States are not in use worldwide. Many countries require that corporations operating within their borders, including subsidiaries of American-based companies, prepare financial statements in accordance with local income tax laws or other unique accounting principles.

Translating financial statement amounts

The mechanics of translating the financial statements of a foreign subsidiary into U.S. dollars are beyond the scope of the introductory accounting course. However, a brief discussion of the topic is appropriate in order to distinguish between *cumulative foreign currency translation adjustments* and gains and losses from fluctuations in foreign exchange rates.

What is a "translation adjustment" and where does it come from? Cumulative Translation Adjustment is an account title found in the stockholders' equity section of the balance sheet of virtually every multinational corporation. The account may have either a debit or credit balance and often is very large in dollar amount.[4]

The most important thing to understand about a cumulative translation adjustment is that it does *not* represent a gain or a loss. Also, it does *not affect* the amount of cash that the company will receive or pay out. In short, the translation adjustment is a "plug figure," resulting from the mechanics of translating the financial statements of a foreign

---

[4] The account tends to have a debit balance when the exchange rates in those countries in which the company has subsidiaries have been falling and a credit balance when these rates have been rising.

subsidiary into U.S. dollars. For most purposes, the translation adjustment is not relevant to the interpretation of the financial statements and may be ignored.

Let us briefly explain the origin of the translation adjustment and why this amount is neither a gain nor a loss. The exchange rate used to translate the assets and liabilities of a foreign subsidiary into U.S. dollars generally is the rate *in effect at the balance sheet date.* If the same rate were also used to translate each element of owners' equity, the balance sheet would remain in balance. However, the owners' equity accounts are *not* translated at this year-end rate. Net income, which represents part of the ending balance of retained earnings, is translated at the *average* exchange rate for the year. The argument for use of the average rate is that revenue was earned and expenses were incurred on a somewhat uniform basis throughout the year. Paid-in capital, on the other hand, is translated using the *historical* exchange rates in effect when the stockholders made their investments.

Since the exchange rates used in translating owners' equity accounts differ from those used in translating assets and liabilities, it follows that the mechanics of the translation process throw the balance sheet out of balance. The cumulative translation adjustment is simply the amount necessary to bring the balance sheet back into balance. It is what accountants call a "plug figure."

Translation adjustments compared to gains and losses from fluctuations in exchange rates. Gains and losses from fluctuations in exchange rates actually *change the number of dollars* that a company will receive or that it must pay out. Hence, these gains and losses cause the company to become either better or worse off and are included in the income statement for the period. Cumulative translation adjustments, on the other hand, result entirely from the mechanics of translating the financial statements of a foreign subsidiary into dollars. These adjustments do not affect the company's cash flows or its economic well-being. Thus, the translation adjustment does not appear in the income statement, but is shown only in the owners' equity section of the balance sheet.

Accounting principles: the quest for uniformity

Unfortunately, accounting standards and principles vary from one country to another. Some countries, such as Italy, require companies to adhere closely to local income tax laws in the preparation of their financial statements. Other countries, such as Brazil and the Netherlands, require greater use of general price-level adjustments and current costs than is allowable under American generally accepted accounting principles.

When consolidated financial statements are prepared for distribution to investors within the United States, these statements should be prepared in conformity with American generally accepted accounting principles. Thus, in consolidating the financial statements of a foreign subsidiary, it usually is necessary to make adjustments in order to bring these statements into conformity with American accounting standards. These adjustments are made on work sheets, not in the subsidiary's accounting records.

Adjusting the information contained in financial statements from one set of accounting standards to another is not as difficult a task as it might seem at first glance. Remember that in the United States, generally accepted accounting principles (GAAP) differ significantly from income tax rules. Yet both financial statements and income tax returns are prepared from the same accounting records. The approach used to convert from GAAP to income tax rules is the same as that used to convert foreign accounting standards to GAAP — that is, entries made on work sheets.

International investors. The lack of international accounting standards poses a greater problem for international investors than for multinational corporations. Investors no longer are limited to investing in the securities of domestic corporations. Through organized capital markets throughout the world, they may invest in the securities of many foreign companies. The financial statements of companies located in different countries, however, may not be directly comparable. Hence, international investors may have difficulty in efficiently allocating their resources.

In the long run, a solution to this problem may lie with the International Accounting Standards Committee (IASC). This committee seeks to develop international accounting standards, and its members include the professional accounting associations of more than 40 countries. As an international organization, however, IASC relies upon voluntary compliance by its members; it has no enforcement power. Nonetheless, IASC's efforts already have enhanced the uniformity of accounting standards among nations. The organization's ultimate goal — an international set of accounting standards — would contribute significantly to the efficient allocation of scarce resources throughout the world.

Review questions

1   Translate the following amounts of foreign currency into an equivalent number of U.S. dollars using the exchange rates in the table on page 521:
    a £300,000
    b ¥275,000
    c DM24,000

2   Assume that an American company makes a purchase from a West German company and agrees to pay a price of 2 million deutsche marks.
    a How will the American company determine the cost of this purchase for the purpose of recording it in the accounting records?
    b Briefly explain how an American company can arrange the payment of deutsche marks to a West German company.

3   A recent newspaper shows the exchange rate for the British pound at $1.2800 and for the yen at $.0043. Does this indicate that the pound is a stronger currency than the yen? Explain.

4   Identify two factors that tend to make the exchange rate for a country's currency rise.

5   Explain how an increase in a foreign exchange rate will affect a U.S. company that makes:
    a Credit sales to a foreign company at prices stated in the foreign currency.
    b Credit purchases from a foreign company at prices stated in the foreign currency.
    c Credit sales to a foreign company at prices stated in U.S. dollars.

6   You are the purchasing agent for an American business that purchases merchandise on account from companies in Mexico. The exchange rate for the Mexican peso has been falling against the dollar and the trend is expected to continue for at least several months. Would you prefer that the prices for purchases from the Mexican companies be specified in U.S. dollars or in Mexican pesos? Explain.

7   Explain two ways in which a company that makes purchases on account from foreign companies

can protect itself against the losses that would arise from a sudden increase in the foreign exchange rate.

8 CompuTech is an American-based multinational corporation. Foreign sales are made at prices set in U.S. dollars, but foreign purchases are often made at prices stated in foreign currencies. If the exchange rate for the U.S. dollar has risen against most foreign currencies throughout the year, would CompuTech have recognized primarily gains or losses as a result of exchange rate fluctuations? Explain.

9 Identify two problems that may arise in consolidating the financial statements of a foreign subsidiary with those of an American-based parent company.

10 Explain why a cumulative translation adjustment may be needed to bring the balance sheet of a multinational company with foreign subsidiaries into balance.

11 Describe how cumulative translation adjustments and the gains and losses from fluctuations in foreign currencies are presented in financial statements.

12 Why does the use of different accounting standards in different countries pose a problem for international investors? What, if anything, is being done to help solve this problem?

Problems

C-1 Gains and losses from fluctuations in exchange rates

Europa-West is an American corporation that purchases automobiles from European manufacturers for distribution in the United States. A recent purchase involved the following events:

Nov. 12 Purchased automobiles from Mercedes-Benz for DM2,000,000, payable in 60 days. Current exchange rate, $.3450 per deutsche mark. (Europa-West uses the perpetual inventory system; debit the Inventory account.)

Dec. 31 Made year-end adjusting entry relating to the DM2,000,000 account payable to Mercedes-Benz. Current exchange rate, $.3620 per deutsche mark.

Jan. 11 Issued a check to World Bank for $716,000 in full payment of the account payable to Mercedes-Benz.

Instructions

a Prepare in general journal form the entries necessary to record the preceding events.

b Compute the exchange rate (price) of the deutsche mark in U.S. dollars on January 11.

c Explain a hedging technique that Europa-West might have used to protect itself from the possibility of losses resulting from a significant increase in the exchange rate for the deutsche mark.

C-2 Gains and loss on rate fluctuations: an alternate to Problem C-1

IronMan, Inc., is an American company that manufactures exercise machines and also distributes several lines of imported bicycles. Selected transactions of the company are listed below:

Oct. 4 Purchased manufacturing equipment from Rhine Mfg. Co., a West German company. The purchase price was DM150,000, due in 60 days. Current exchange rate, $.3500 per deutsche mark. (Debit the Equipment account.)

Oct. 18 Purchased 2,000 racing bicycles from Ninja Cycles, a Japanese company, at a price of ¥80,000,000. Payment is due in 90 days; the current exchange rate is $.0040 per yen. (IronMan uses the perpetual inventory system; debit the Inventory account.)

Nov. 15 Purchased 1,000 touring bicycles from Royal Lion Ltd., a British corporation. The purchase price was £199,500, payable in 30 days. Current exchange rate, $1.33 per British pound.

Dec. 3 Issued check to First Bank for the U.S. dollar-equivalent of DM150,000 in payment of the account payable to Rhine Mfg. Co. Current exchange rate, $.3700 per deutsche mark.

Dec. 15 Issued check to First Bank for dollar-equivalent of £199,500 in payment of the account payable to Royal Lion Ltd. Current exchange rate, $1.30 per British pound.

Instructions

a Prepare entries in general journal form to record the preceding transactions.

b Prepare the December 31 adjusting entry relating to the account payable to Ninja Cycles. The year-end exchange rate is $.0042 per Japanese yen.

C-3 A comprehensive problem on exchange rate fluctuations and "hedging"

Wolfe Computer is an American company that manufactures portable personal computers. Many of the components for the computer are purchased abroad, and the finished product is sold in foreign countries as well as in the United States. Among the recent transactions of Wolfe are the following:

Oct. 28 Purchased from Mitsutonka, a Japanese company, 20,000 disc drives. The purchase price was ¥200,000,000, payable in 30 days. Current exchange rate, $.0042 per yen. (Wolfe uses the perpetual inventory method; debit the Inventory of Raw Materials account.)

Nov. 9 Sold 600 personal computers to the Bank of England for £528,000, due in 30 days. The cost of the computers, to be debited to the Cost of Goods Sold account, was $398,000. Current exchange rate, $1.25 per British pound. (Use one compound journal entry to record the sale and the cost of goods sold. In recording the cost of goods sold, credit Inventory of Finished Goods.)

Nov. 27 Issued a check to Inland Bank for $920,000 in full payment of account payable to Mitsutonka.

Dec. 2 Purchased 10,000 amber monitors from German Optical for DM1,200,000, payable in 60 days. Current exchange rate, $.3600 per deutsche mark. (Debit Inventory of Raw Materials.)

Dec. 9 Collected dollar equivalent of £528,000 from the Bank of England. Current exchange rate, $1.23 per British pound.

Dec. 11 Sold 9,000 personal computers to Computique, a French retail chain, for FF99,000,000, due in 30 days. Current exchange rate, $.1000 per French franc. The cost of the computers, to be debited to Cost of Goods Sold and credited to Inventory of Finished Goods, is $5,970,000.

Instructions

a Prepare in general journal form the entries necessary to record the preceding transactions.

b Prepare the adjusting entries needed at December 31 for the DM1,200,000 account payable to German Optical and the FF99,000,000 account receivable from Computique. Year-end exchange rates, $.3500 per deutsche mark and $.1020 per French franc. (Use a separate journal entry to adjust each account balance.)

c Compute the unit sales price of computers in U.S. dollars in either the November 9 or December 11 sales transactions. (The sales price is the same in each transaction.)

d Compute the exchange rate for the yen, stated in U.S. dollars, on November 27.

e Explain how Wolfe Computer could have hedged its position to reduce the risk of losses from exchange rate fluctuations on (1) its foreign payables, and (2) its foreign receivables.

Chapter 13
Bonds payable,
leases,
and other liabilities

This chapter describes various types of long-term debt. Large corporations borrow vast amounts of money; Exxon Corporation, for example, has debts totaling more than $30 billion. Emphasis is placed upon the issuance of bonds payable — a form of borrowing which enables large corporations to raise hundreds of millions of dollars from thousands of individual investors. Both the straight-line and effective interest methods of amortizing bond discount and premium are illustrated and explained. Corporate bonds also are discussed from the viewpoint of the investor. Other long-term liabilities covered in this chapter include mortgages, lease payment obligations, and pension plans. The chapter concludes with a discussion of loss contingencies — footnote disclosures which may affect the very survival of an apparently healthy business.

After studying this chapter you should be able to:

✓ Describe the typical characteristic of bonds.
✓ Explain the advantages of raising capital by issuing bonds instead of stock.
✓ Discuss the relationship between interest rates and bond prices.
✓ Explain how bond discount or premium effectsthe cost of borrowing.
✓ Account for bond interest payments and year-end adjustments.
✓ Amortize discount or premium by the straight-line and effective interest methods.
✓ Explain the accounting treatment of operating leases and of capital leases.
✓ Define loss contingencies and explain how they are presented in financial statements.

BONDS PAYABLE

Financially sound corporations may arrange some long-term loans by issuing a note payable to a bank or an insurance company. But to finance a large project, such as building a refinery or acquiring a new fleet of jumbo jets, a corporation may need more long-term financing than any single lender can supply. When a corporation needs to raise a large amount of long-term capital — perhaps 10, 50, or 100 million dollars or more — it generally sells additional shares of capital stock or issues **bonds payable.**[1]

The issuance of bonds payable is the equivalent of splitting a large loan into a great many units, called **bonds.** Each bond is, in essence, a long-term interest-bearing note payable, usually in the face amount of $1,000, or a multiple of $1,000. The bonds are sold to the investing public, thus allowing many different investors to participate in the loan. An example of a corporate bond issue is the 8% sinking fund debentures of The Singer Company, due January 15, 1999. With this bond issue, The Singer Company borrowed $100 million by issuing 100,000 bonds of $1,000 each.

Issuance of bonds payable

From the viewpoint of the issuing corporation, bonds payable constitute a long-term liability. Throughout the life of this liability, the corporation makes semiannual interest payments to the bondholders for the use of their money. A bondholder is a creditor of the corporation, not an owner. Therefore, bondholders generally do not have voting rights and do not participate in the earnings of the corporation beyond receiving the contractual, semiannual interest payments.

Authorization of a bond issue. Formal approval by the board of directors and by the stockholders is usually required before bonds can be issued. If the bonds are to be sold to the general public, approval must also be obtained from the SEC, just as for an issue of capital stock which is offered to the public.

The issuing corporation also selects a **trustee** to represent the interests of the bond-holders. This trustee generally is a large bank or trust company. A contract is drawn up indicating the terms of the bond issue and the assets (if any) which are pledged as collateral for the bonds. Sometimes this contract places limitations on the payment of dividends to stockholders during the life of the bonds. For example, dividends may be permitted only when working capital is above specified amounts. If the issuing corporation defaults on any of the terms of this contract, the trustee may foreclose upon the assets which secure the bonds or may take other legal action on behalf of the bondholders.

The role of the underwriter in marketing a bond issue. An investment banker or underwriter is usually employed to market a bond issue, just as in the case of capital stock. The corporation turns the entire bond issue over to the underwriter at a specified price; the underwriter sells the bonds to the public at a slightly higher price. By this arrangement the corporation is assured of receiving the entire proceeds on a specified date.

Transferability of bonds. Corporation bonds, like capital stocks, are traded daily on organized securities exchanges. The holders of a 25-year bond issue need not wait 25 years to convert their investment into cash. By placing a telephone call to a broker, an

---

[1] Bonds payable also are issued by the federal government and by many other governmental units such as states, cities, and school districts. In this chapter, our discussion is limited to corporate bonds, although many of the concepts also apply to the board issues of government agencies.

investor may sell bonds within a matter of minutes at the going market price. This quality of liquidity is one of the most attractive features of an investment in corporation bonds.

Quoted market prices. As illustrated on page 275 in Chapter 7, corporate bond prices are quoted as a *percentage* of the bond's face value or *maturity* value, which is usually $1,000. The maturity value is the amount the issuing company must pay to redeem the bond at the date it matures (becomes due). A bond quoted in the financial section of today's newspaper at *96* would therefore have a market price of $960 (96% of $1,000). Bond prices are quoted at the nearest one-eighth of a percentage point.

Types of bonds. Bonds secured by the pledge of specific assets are called *mortgage bonds.* An unsecured bond is called a *debenture bond;* its value rests upon the general credit of the corporation. A debenture bond issued by a very large and strong corporation may have a higher investment rating than a secured bond issued by a corporation in less satisfactory financial condition. For example, the $500 million of debenture bonds recently issued by IBM are rated AAA, the highest possible rating.

Some bonds have a single fixed maturity date for the entire issue. On bond issues, called *serial bonds,* provide for varying maturity dates to lessen the problem of accumulating cash for payment. For example, serial bonds in the amount of $20 million issued in 1980 might call for $2 million of bonds to *mature* in 1990, and an additional $2 million to become due in each of the succeeding nine years. Almost all bonds are *callable,* which means that the corporation has the right to pay off the bonds in advance of the scheduled maturity date. To compensate the bondholders for being forced to give up their investments, the call price is usually somewhat higher than the face value of the bonds.

Most corporation bonds issued in recent years have been *registered bonds;* that is, the name of the owner is registered with the issuing corporation. Payment of interest is made by semiannual checks mailed to the registered owners. *Coupon bonds* were more popular some years ago and many are still outstanding. Coupon bonds have interest coupons attached; each six months during the life of the bond one of these coupons becomes due. The bondholder detaches the coupon and deposits it with a bank for collection. The names of the bondholders are not registered with the corporation.

As an additional attraction to investors, corporations sometimes include a converson privilege in the bond indenture. A *convertible bond* is one which may be exchanged for common stock at the option of the bondholder. The advantages to the investor of the conversion feature in the event of increased earnings for the company were described in Chapter 11 with regard to convertible preferred stock.

Tax advantage of bond financing

Interest payments on bonds payable are deductible as an expense by the issuing company in determining the income subject to corporation income tax, but dividends paid on capital stock are not. High tax rates on corporate earnings thus encourage the use of bonds rather than capital stock to obtain long-term capital.

To illustrate the advantage of tax deductible financing costs, assume that a corporation with 1 million shares of common stock outstanding needs $10 million to finance construction of a new plant. Before considering financing costs or income taxes, the new plant is expected to add $4 million to the annual earnings of the corporation. Management is considering whether to raise the $10 million by issuing 10% preferred stock or 10% bonds. From the viewpoint of the common stockholders, which financing plan is preferable? The schedule below shows the expected increase in annual earnings per share of common stock under the two alternative financing plans.

Which financing plan is better?

	If 10% Preferred Stock Is Issued	If 10% Bonds Are Issued
Increase in annual earnings before financing costs and income taxes	$4,000,000	$4,000,000
Less: Interest on bonds (10% × $10,000,000)	–0–	1,000,000
Increase in earnings subject to income taxes	$4,000,000	$3,000,000
Less: Income taxes (assume 40% rate)	1,600,000	1,200,000
Increase in net income	$2,400,000	$1,800,000
Less: Dividends on preferred stock (10% × $10,000,000)	1,000,000	–0–
Increase in earnings applicable to common stock	$1,400,000	$1,800,000
Number of shares of common stock outstanding	1,000,000	1,000,000
Increase in earnings per share of common stock	$1.40	$1.80

At first glance, it appears that under either plan the annual financing cost is $1,000,000, whether this amount is paid out as interest or as dividends. Why, then, are the earnings applicable to common stock $400,000 greater each year if the new plant is financed by issuing bonds rather than preferred stock? The answer lies in the fact that interest payments are **deductible** in determining the earnings subject to income taxes, whereas dividend payments are not. Notice that the company will pay $400,000 **less income tax** each year if the new plant is financed by issuing bonds. In short, we might say that issuing bonds rather than stock reduces the annual **after-tax** financing cost from $1,000,000 to $600,000. This $600,000 is a net amount, represented by the $1,000,000 increase in annual interest payments offset by the $400,000 reduction in annual income tax payments.

The use of borrowed capital to enhance earnings applicable to common stock is called **leverage;** this concept is discussed further in Chapter 16.

Accounting entries for a bond issue

Assume that Wells Corporation on January 1, Year 5, after proper authorization by the board of directors and approval by the stockholders, issues $1,000,000 of 20-year, 12% bonds payable. All the bonds bear the January 1. Year 5, date, and interest is computed from this date. Interest on the bonds is payable semiannually, each July 1 and January 1. If all the bonds are sold at par value (face value), the sale will be recorded by the following entry:

Jan. 1	Cash	1,000,000	
	Bonds Payable		1,000,000
	To record issuance of 12%, 20-year bonds at 100 on the interest date.		

The first semiannual interest payment of $60,000 would be due on July 1. The computation is ($1,000,000 × .12) ÷ 2 = $60,000. The interest payment would be recorded by the following entry:

July 1   Bond Interest Expense 60,000
               Cash 60,000
          Paid semiannual interest on 12%, 20-year bonds with face
          amount of $1,000,000.

When the bonds mature 20 years later on January 1, Year 25, the entry to record payment of the principal amount will be:

Jan. 1   Bonds Payable 1,000,000
               Cash 1,000,000
          Paid face amount of bonds at maturity.

Recording the issuance of bonds between interest dates. The semiannual interest dates (such as January 1 and July 1, or April 1 and October 1) are printed on the bond certificates. However, bonds are often issued between the specified interest dates. The investor is then required to pay the interest accrued to date of issuance in addition to the stated price of the bond. This practice enables the corporation to pay a full six months' interest on all bonds outstanding at the semiannual interest payment date. The accrued interest collected from investors purchasing bonds between interest payment dates is thus returned to them on the next interest payment date. To illustrate, let us modify our present example for Wells Corporation and assume that the $1,000,000 face value of 12% bonds were issued at 100 and accrued interest, *two months after the interest date printed on the bonds.* The entry will be:

Bonds issued between interest dates   Cash 1,020,000
               Bonds Payable 1,000,000
               Bond Interest Payable 20,000
          Issued $1,000,000 face value of 12%, 20-year bonds at 100 plus
          accrued interest for two months.

Four months later on the regular semiannual interest payment date, a full six months' interest ($60 per each $1,000 bond) will be paid to all bondholders, regardless of when they purchased their bonds. The entry for the semiannual interest payment is illustrated below:

What is the net interest expense?   Bond Interest Payable 20,000
          Bond Interest Expense 40,000
               Cash 60,000
          Paid semiannual interest on $1,000,000 face value of 12% bonds.

Now consider these interest transactions from the standpoint of the investors. They paid for two months' accrued interest at the time of purchasing the bonds, and they received checks for six months' interest after holding the bonds for only four months. They have, therefore, been reimbursed properly for the use of their money for four months.

When bonds are subsequently sold by one investor to another, they sell at the quoted market price *plus accrued interest* since the last interest payment date. This practice enables the issuing corporation to pay all the interest for an interest period to the investor owning the bond at the interest date. Otherwise, the corporation would have to make partial payments to every investor who bought or sold the bond during the interest period.

The amount which investors will pay for bonds is the *present value* of the principal and interest payments they will receive. Before going further in our discussion of bonds payable, it will be helpful to review the concepts of present value and effective yield.

The concept of present value

The concept of present value is based upon the "time value" of money — the idea that receiving money today is preferable to receiving money at some later date. Assume, for example, that a bond will have a maturity value of $1,000 five years from today but will pay no interest in the meantime. Investors would not pay $1,000 for this bond today, because they would receive no return on their investment over the next five years. There are prices less than $1,000, however, at which investors would buy the bond. For example, if the bond could be purchased for $600, the investor could expect a return (interest) of $400 from the investment over the five-year period.

The *present value* of a future cash receipt is the amount that a knowledgeable investor will pay *today* for the right to receive that future payment. The exact amount of the present value depends upon (1) the amount of the future payment, (2) the length of time until the payment will be received, and (3) the rate of return required by the investor. However, the present value will always be *less* than the future amount. This is because money received today can be invested to earn interest and thereby becomes equivalent to a larger amount in the future.

The rate of interest which will cause a given present value to grow to a given future amount is caled the discount rate or *effective interest rate.* The effective interest rate required by investors at any given time is regarded as the going *market rate* of interest. The procedures for computing the present value of a future amount are illustrated in an appendix following this chapter.

The present value concept and bond prices

The price at which bonds will sell is the present value to investors of the future principal and interest payments.[2] If the bonds sell at par, the effective interest rate is equal to the *contract interest rate* (or nominal rate) printed on the bonds. The higher the effective interest rate investors require, the less they will pay for bonds with a given contract rate of interest. For example, if investors insist upon a 10% return, they will pay less than $1,000 for a 9%, $1,000 bond. Thus, if investors require an effective interest rate *greater* than the contract rate of interest for the bonds, the bonds will sell at a *discount* (price less than face value). On the other hand, if investors require an effective interest rate of *less* than the contract rate, the bonds will sell at a *premium* (price above face value).

[2] The mechanics of determining the market price of a bond issue using present value techniques are illustrated in the appendix following this chapter.

A corporation wishing to borrow money by issuing bonds must pay the going market rate of interest. Since market rates of interest are fluctuating constantly, it must be expected that the contract rate of interest may vary somewhat from the market rate at the date the bonds are issued. Thus, bonds often are issued at either a discount or a premium.

Bond prices after issuance. As stated earlier, many corporate bonds are traded daily on organized securities exchanges at quoted market prices. After bonds are issued, their market prices vary *inversely* with changes in market interest rates. As interest rates rise, investors will be willing to pay less money to own a bond that pays a given contract rate of interest. Conversely, as interest rates decline, the market prices of bonds rise.

● **CASE IN POINT** ● In October 1979, IBM sold to underwriters $500 million of $9\frac{3}{8}\%$ debenture bonds, due in 2004. The underwriters planned to sell the bonds to the public at a price of $9\frac{5}{8}$. Just as the bonds were offered for sale, however, a change in Federal Reserve credit policy started an upward surge in interest rates. The underwriters encountered great difficulty selling the bonds. Within one week, the market price of the bonds had fallen to $94\frac{1}{2}$. The underwriters dumped their unsold inventory at this price and sustained one of the largest underwriting losses in Wall Street history.

During the months ahead, interest rates soared to record levels. By the end of March 1980, the price of the bonds had fallen to $76\frac{3}{8}$. Thus, nearly one-fourth of the market value of these bonds evaporated in less than six months. The financial strength of IBM was never in question; this dramatic loss in market value was caused entirely by rising interest rates.

In addition to the current level of interest rates, the market prices of bonds are strongly influenced by the *length of time remaining until the bonds mature* — that is, are redeemed at their maturity value (par value) by the issuing corporation. As a bond nears its maturity date, its market price normally will move closer and closer to the maturity value.

● **CASE IN POINT** ● Avco Financial Services has outstanding two issues of $7\frac{7}{8}$ bonds; one issue maturing in 1989 and the other in 1992. In mid-1985, the bonds maturing in 1989 were selling at a quoted market price of 89, whereas the bonds maturing in 1992 were selling at a price of only $80\frac{1}{2}$. Both bonds pay the same amount of interest, were issued by the same company, and have identical credit ratings. Thus, the difference in the market prices is caused solely by differences in the bonds' maturity dates.

Bonds sold at a discount

To illustrate the sale of bonds at a discount, assume that a corporation plans to issue $1,000,000 face value of 9%, 10-year bonds. At the issuance date, however, the going market rate of interest is slightly above 9% and the bonds sell at a price of only 98 ($980 for each $1,000 bond). The issuance of the bonds will be recorded by the following entry:

Issuing bonds at discount

Cash	980,000	
Discount on Bonds Payable	20,000	
Bonds Payable		1,000,000
Issued $1,000,000 face value of 9%, 10-year bonds at 98.		

If a balance sheet is prepared immediately after the issuance of the bonds, the liability for bonds payable will be shown as follows:

Liability shown net of discount

Long-term liabilities:

9% bonds payable, due Dec. 31, Year 10	$1,000,000	
Less: Discount on bonds payable	20,000	$980,000

The amount of the discount is deducted from the face value of the bonds payable to show the present value or *carrying value* of the liability. At the date of issuance, the carrying value of bonds payable is equal to the amount for which the bonds were sold. In other words, the amount of the company's liability at the date of issuing the bonds is equal to the amount of money borrowed. Over the life of the bonds, however, we shall see that this carrying value gradually increases until it reaches the face value of the bonds at the maturity date.

Bond discount as part of the cost of borrowing. In Chapter 8, we illustrated two ways in which interest charges can be specified in a note payable: the interest may be stated as an annual percentage rate of the face amount of the note, or it may be included in the face amount. Bonds issued at a discount include *both* types of interest charge. The $1,000,000 bond issue in our example calls for cash interest payments of $90,000 per year ($1,000,000 × 9% contract interest rate), payable semiannually. In addition to making the semiannual interest payments, the corporation must redeem the bond issue for $1 million on December 31, Year 10. This maturity value is $20,000 greater than the $980,000 received when the bonds were issued. Thus, the $20,000 discount in the issue price may be regarded as an *interest charge included in the maturity value of the bonds.*

Although the interest charge represented by the discount will not be paid to bondholders until the bonds mature, the corporation benefits from this cost during the entire period that it has the use of the bondholders' money. Therefore, the cost represented by the discount should be allocated over the life of the bond issue. The process of allocating bond discount to interest expense is termed *amortization* of the discount.

In short, wherever bonds are issued at a discount, the total interest cost over the life of the bonds is equal to the total regular cash interest payments *plus the amount of the .discount.* For the $1 million bond issue in our example, the total interest cost over the 10-year life of the bonds is $920,000, of which $900,000 represents the 20 semiannual cash interest payments and $20,000 represents the discount. The average annual interest expense, therefore, is $92,000 ($920,000 ÷ 10 years), consisting of $90,000 paid in cash and $2,000 amortization of the bond discount. This analysis is illustrated below:

Total cash interest payments to bondholders		
($1,000,000 × 9% × 10 years)		$900,000
Add: Interest charge included in face amount of bonds:		
Maturity value of bonds	$1,000,000	
Amount borrowed	980,000	20,000
Total cost of borrowing over life of bond issue		$920,000
Average annual interest expense ($920,000 ÷ 10 years)		$ 92,000

Amortization of bond discount

The simplest method of amortizing bond discount is the ***straight-line method,*** which allocates an equal portion of the discount to Bond Interest Expense in each period.[3] In our example, the Discount on Bonds Payable account has a beginning debit balance of $20,000; each year one-tenth of this amount, or $2,000, will be amortized into Bond Interest Expense. Assuming that the interest payment dates are June 30 and December 31, the entries to be made each six months to record bond interest expense are as follows:

Payment of bond interest and straight-line amortization of bond discount

Bond Interest Expense	45,000	
Cash		45,000
Paid semiannual interest on $1,000,000 of 9%, 10-year bonds.		

Bond Interest Expense	1,000	
Discount on Bonds Payable		1,000
Amortized discount for six months on 10-year bond issue ($20,000 discount × $\frac{1}{20}$).		

The two entries shown above to record the cash payment of bond interest and to record the amortization of bond discount can conveniently be combined into one compound entry, as follows:

Bond Interest Expense	46,000	
Cash		45,000
Discount on Bonds Payable		1,000
To record payment of semiannual interest on $1,000,000 of 9%, 10-year bonds ($1,000,000 × 9% × $\frac{1}{2}$) and to amortize $\frac{1}{20}$ of the discount on the 10-year bond issue.		

Regardless of whether the cash payment of interest and the amortization of bond discount are recorded in separate entries or combined in one entry, the amount recognized as Bond Interest Expense is the same — $46,000 each six months, or a total of $92,000 a year. An alternative accounting procedure that will produce the same results is to amortize the bond discount only at year-end rather than at each interest payment date.

[3] An alternative method of amortization, called the *effective interest method,* is illustrated later in this chapter. Although the effective interest method is theoretically preferable to the straight-line method, the resulting differences generally are not material in dollar amount.

Note that the additional interest expense resulting from amortization of the discount does not require any additional cash payment. The credit portion of the entry is to the contra-liability account, Discount on Bonds Payable, rather than to the Cash account. Crediting this contra-liability account *increases the carrying value of bonds payable.* The original $20,000 discount will be completely written off by the end of the tenth year, and the net liability (carrying value will be the full face value of the bonds.

Bonds sold at a premium

Bonds will sell above par if the contract rate of interest specified on the bonds is higher than the current market rate for bonds of this grade. Let us now change our basic illustration by assuming that the $1 million issue of 9%, 10-year bonds is sold at a price of 102 ($1,020 for each $1,000 bond). The entry is shown below:

Issuing bonds at premium	Cash	1,020,000	
	Bonds Payable		1,000,000
	Premium on Bonds Payable		20,000
	Issued $1,000,000 face value of 9%, 10-year bonds at price of 102.		

If a balance sheet is prepared immediately following the sale of the bonds, the liability will be shown as follows:

Carrying value increased by premium	Long-term liabilities:		
	9% bonds payable, due Dec. 31, Year 10	$1,000,000	
	Add: Premium on bonds payable	20,000	$1,020,000

The amount of any unamortized premium is *added* to the maturity value of the bonds payable to show the current carrying value of the liability. Over the life of the bond issue, this carrying value will be reduced toward the maturity value of $1,000,000.

Bond premium as reduction in the cost of borrowing. We have illustrated how issuing bonds at a discount increases the cost of borrowing above the amount of the regular cash interest payments. Issuing bonds at a premium, on the other hand, *reduces the cost of borrowing below the amount of the regular cash interest payments.*

The amount received from issuance of the bonds is $20,000 greater than the amount which must be repaid at maturity. This $20,000 premium is not a gain but is to be offset against the periodic interest payments in determining the net cost of borrowing. Whenever bonds are issued at a premium, the total interest cost over the life of the bonds is equal to the regular cash interest payments *minus the amount of the premium.* In our example, the total interest cost over the life of the bonds is computed as $900,000 of cash interest payments minus $20,000 of premium amortized, or a net borrowing cost of $880,000. The annual interest expense will be $88,000, consisting of $90,000 paid in cash less an offsetting $2,000 transferred from the Premium on Bonds Payable account to the credit side of the Bond Interest Expense account.

The semiannual entries on June 30 and December 31 to record the payment of bond interest and amortization of bond premium are as follows:

Payment of bond interest and straight-line amortization of bond premium

Bond Interest Expense	45,000	
Cash		45,000

Paid semiannual interest on $1,000,000 of 9%, 10-year bonds.

Premium on Bonds Payable	1,000	
Bond Interest Expense		1,000

Amortized premium for six months on 10-year bond issue ($20,000 $\times \frac{1}{20}$).

Year-end adjustments for bond interest expense

In the preceding illustration, it was assumed that one of the semiannual dates for payment of bond interest coincided with the end of the company's accounting year. In most cases, however, the semiannual interest payments dates will fall during an accounting period rather than on the last day of the year.

For purposes of illustration, assume that $1 million of 12%, 10-year bonds are issued at a price of 97 on October 1, Year 1. Interest payment dates are April and October 1. The total discount to be amortized amounts to $30,000, or $1,500 in each six-months interest period. The company keeps its accounts on a calendar-year basis; consequently, the adjusting entries shown below will be necessary at December 31 for the accrued interest and the amortization of discount applicable to the three-month period since the bonds were issued.

Bond Interest Expense	30,750	
Bond Interest Payable		30,000
Discount on Bonds Payable		750

To adjust for accrued interest on bonds and to amortize discount for period from Oct. 1 to Dec. 31. Accrued interest: $1,000,000 $\times$ .12 $\times \frac{3}{12} =$ $30,000. Amortization: $30,000 $\times \frac{3}{120} =$ $750.

If the above bonds had been issued at a premium, similar entries would be made at the end of the period for any accrued interest and for amortization of premium for the fractional period from October 1 to December 31.

In the December 31, Year 1, balance sheet, the $30,000 of accrued bond interest payable will appear as a current liability; the long-term liability for bonds payable will appear as follows:

Long-term liabilities:		
12% Bonds payable, due Oct. 1, Year 11	$1,000,000	
Less: Discount on bonds payable	29,250	$970,750

When the bonds were issued on October 1, the net liability for bonds payable was $970,000. Notice that the carrying value of the bonds has *increased* over the three months by the amount of discount amortized. When the entire discount has been amortized, the carrying value of the bonds will be $1,000,000, which is equal to their maturity value.

At April 1, Year 2, it is necessary to record interest expense and discount amortization only for the three-month period since year-end. Of the semiannual $60,000 cash payment to bondholders, one-half, or $30,000, represents payment of the liability for bond interest payable recorded on December 31, Year 1. The entry on April 1 is:

Bond Interest Expense	30,750	
Bond Interest Payable	30,000	
Discount on Bonds Payable		750
Cash		60,000

To record bond interest expense and amortization of discount for three-month period since year-end and to record semiannual payment to bondholders.

Straight-line amortization: a theoretical shortcoming

Although the straight-line method of amortizing bond discount or premium recognizes the full cost of borrowing over the life of a bond issue, the method has one conceptual weakness: the same dollar amount of interest expense is recognized each year. Amortizing a discount, however, causes a gradual increase in the liability for bonds payable; amortizing a premium causes a gradual decrease in the liability. If the uniform annual interest expense is expressed as a *percentage* of either an increasing or a decreasing liability, it appears that the borrower's cost of capital is changing over the life of the bonds.

This problem can be avoided by using the *effective interest method* of amortizing bond discount or premium. The effective interest method recognizes annual interest expense equal to a *constant percentage of the carrying value of the related liability.* This percentage is the effective rate of interest incurred by the borrower. For this reason, the effective interest method of amortization is considered theoretically preferable to the straight-line method. Whenever the two methods would produce *materially different* annual results, the Financial Accounting Standards Board requires the use of the effective interest method.

Over the life of the bonds, both amortization methods recognize the same total amount of interest expense. Even on an annual basis, the results produced by the two methods usually are very similar. Consequently, either method generaly would meet the requirements of the FASB. Because of its simplicity, the straight-line methid is widely used despite the theoretical arguments favoring the effective interest method.

Effective interest method of amortization

When bonds are sold at a discount, the effective interest rate incurred by the issuing corporation is *higher* than the contract rate printed on the bonds. Conversely, when bonds are sold at a premium, the effective rate of interest is *lower* than the contract rate.

When the effective interest method is used, bond interest expense is determined by multiplying the *carrying value of the bonds* at the beginning of the period by the *effective rate of interest* for the bond issue. The amount of discount or premium to be amortized is the *difference* between the interest expense computed in this manner and the amount of interest paid (or payable) to bondholders for the period. The computation of effective interest expense and the amount of discount or premium amortization for the life of the bond issue is made in advance on a schedule called an *amortization table.*

Sale of bonds at a discount. To illustrate the effective interest method, assume that on May 1, Year 1, a corporation issues $1,000,000 face value, 9%, 10-year bonds with interest dates of November 1 and May 1. The bonds sell for $937,689, a price resulting in an effective interest rate of 10%.[4] An amortization table for this bond issue is shown below. (Amounts of interest expense have been rounded to the nearest dollar.)

Amortization Table for Bonds Sold at a Discount

($1,000,000, 10-year bonds, 9% interest payable semiannually,
sold at $937,689 to yield 10% compounded semiannually)

Six-Month Interest Period	(A) Interest Paid Semiannually ($4\frac{1}{2}$ of Face Value)	(B) Effective Semiannual Interest Expense (5% of Bond Carrying Value)	(C) Discount Amorti-zation (B − A)	(D) Bond Discount Balance	(E) Carrying Value of Bonds, End of Period ($1,000,000 − D)
Issue date				$62,311	$ 937,689
1	$45,000	$46,884	$1,884	60,427	939,573
2	45,000	46,979	1,979	58,448	941,552
3	45,000	47,078	2,078	56,370	943,630
4	45,000	47,182	2,182	54,188	945,812
5	45,000	47,291	2,291	51,897	948,103
6	45,000	47,405	2,405	49,492	950,508
7	45,000	47,525	2,525	46,967	953,033
8	45,000	47,652	2,652	44,315	955,685
9	45,000	47,784	2,784	41,531	958,469
10	45,000	47,923	2,923	38,608	961,392
11	45,000	48,070	3,070	35,538	964,462
12	45,000	48,223	3,223	32,315	967,685
13	45,000	48,384	3,384	28,931	971,069
14	45,000	48,553	3,553	25,378	974,622
15	45,000	48,731	3,731	21,647	978,353
16	45,000	48,918	3,918	17,729	982,271
17	45,000	49,114	4,114	13,615	986,385
18	45,000	49,319	4,319	9,296	990,704
19	45,000	49,535	4,535	4,761	995,239
20	45,000	49,761*	4,761	−0−	1,000,000

* In the last period, interest expense is equal to interest paid to bondholders plus the remaining balance on the bond discount. This compensates for the accumulated effects of rounding amounts.

[4] Computation of the exact effective interest rate involves mathematical techniques beyond the scope of this course. A very close estimate of the effective interest rate can be obtained by dividing the *average* annual interest expense by the *average* carrying value of the bonds. Computation of average annual interest expense was illustrated on page 541. The average carrying value of the bonds is found by adding the issue price and the maturity value of the bond issue and dividing this sum by 2. Applying these procedures to the bond issue in our example provides an estimated effective interest rate of 9.93%, computed [($900,000 interest + $62,311 discount) ÷ 10 years] divided by [($937,689 + $1,000,000) ÷ 2].

This amortization table can be used to illustrate the concepts underlying the effective interest method of determining interest expense and discount amortization. Note that the "interest periods" in the table are the ***semiannual*** (six-month) interest periods. Thus, the interest payments (column A), interest expense (column B), and discount amortization (column C) are for six-month periods. Similarly, the balance of the Discount on Bonds Payable account (column D) and the carrying value of the liability (column E) are shown as of each semiannual interest payment date.

The original issuance price of the bonds ($937,689) is entered at the top of column E. This represents the carrying value of the liability throughout the first six-month interest period. The semiannual interest payment, shown in column A, is $4\frac{1}{2}$% (one-half of the original contract rate) of the $1,000,000 face value of the bond issue. The semiannual cash interest payment does not change over the life of the bonds. The interest expense shown in column B, however, ***changes every period.*** This expense is always a ***constant percentage*** of the carrying value of the liability as of the end of the preceding period. The "constant percentage" is the effective interest rate of the bond issue. The bonds have an effective annual interest rate of 10%, indicating a semiannual rate of 5%. Thus, the effective interest expense for the first six-month period is $46,884 (5% of $937,689). This discount amortization for period 1 is the difference between this effective interest expense and the contract rate of interest paid to bondholders.

After the discount is reduced by $1,884 at the end of period 1, the carrying value of the bonds in column E ***increases*** by $1,884 (from $937,689 to $939,573). In period 2, the effective interest expense is determined by multiplying the effective semiannual interest rate of 5% by this new carrying value of $939,573 (5% × $939,573 = $46,979).

Semiannual interest expense may be recorded every perod directly from the data in the amortization table. For example, the entry to record bond interest expense at the end of the first six-month period is:

Bond Interest Expense	46,884	
Discount on Bonds Payable		1,884
Cash		45,000

To record semiannual interest payment and amortize discount for six months.

Similarly, interest expense at the end of the fifteenth six-month period would be recorded by:

Bond Interest Expense	48,731	
Discount on Bonds Payable		3,731
Cash		45,000

To record semiannual interest payment and amortize discount for six months.

When bond discount is amortized, the carrying value of the liability for bonds payable ***increases*** every period toward the maturity value. Since the effective interest expense in each period is a constant percentage of this increasing carrying value, the interest expense also increases from one period to the next. This is the basic difference between the effective interest method and straight-line amortization.

Sale of bonds at a premium. Let us now change our basic illustration by assuming that the $1,000,000 issue of 9%, 10-year bonds is sold on May 1, Year 1, at a price of $1,067,952, resulting in an effective interest rate of 8% annually (4% per six-month interest period). An amortization table for this bond issue is shown below.

Amortization Table for Bonds Sold at a Premium

($1,000,000, 10-year bonds, 9% interest payable semiannually, sold at $1,067,952 to yield 8% compounded semiannually)

Six-Month Interest Period	(A) Interest Paid Semiannually ($4\frac{1}{2}$ of Face Value)	(B) Effective Effective Semiannual Interest Expense (4% of Bond Carrying Value)	(C) Premium Amorti- zation (A − B)	(D) Bond Premium Balance	(E) Carrying Value of Bonds, End of Period ($1,000,000 + D)
Issue date				$67,952	$1,067,952
1	$45,000	$42,718	$2,282	65,670	1,065,670
2	45,000	42,627	2,373	63,297	1,063,297
3	45,000	42,532	2,468	60,829	1,060,829
4	45,000	42,433	2,567	58,262	1,058,262
5	45,000	42,330	2,670	55,592	1,055,592
6	45,000	42,224	2,776	52,816	1,052,816
7	45,000	42,113	2,887	49,929	1,049,929
8	45,000	41,997	3,003	46,926	1,046,926
9	45,000	41,877	3,123	48,803	1,043,803
10	45,000	41,752	3,248	40,555	1,040,555
11	45,000	41,622	3,378	37,177	1,037,177
12	45,000	41,487	3,513	33,664	1,033,664
13	45,000	41,347	3,653	30,011	1,030,011
14	45,000	41,200	3,800	26,211	1,026,211
15	45,000	41,048	3,952	22,259	1,022,259
16	45,000	40,890	4,110	18,149	1,018,149
17	45,000	40,726	4,274	13,875	1,013,875
18	45,000	40,555	4,445	9,430	1,009,430
19	45,000	40,377	4,623	4,807	1,004,807
20	45,000	40,193*	4,807	−0−	1,000,000

* In the last period, interest expense is equal to interest paid to bondholders minus the remaining balance of the bond premium. This compensates for the accumulated effects of rounding amounts.

In this amortization table, the interest expense for each six-month period is equal to 4% of the carrying value of the bonds at the beginning of that period. This amount of interest expense is less than the amount of cash being paid to bondholders, illustrating that the effective interest rate is less than the contract rate.

Based upon this amortization table, the entry to record the interest payment and amortization of the premium for the first six months of the bond issue is:

<table>
<tr><td>Amortization of premium decreases interest expense</td><td>Bond Interest Expense ....</td><td>42,718</td><td></td></tr>
<tr><td></td><td>Premium on Bonds Payable ....</td><td>2,282</td><td></td></tr>
<tr><td></td><td>Cash ....</td><td></td><td>45,000</td></tr>
</table>

To record semiannual interest payment and amortization of premium.

As the carrying value of the liability declines, so does the amount recognized as bond interest expense.

Year-end adjusting entries. Since the amounts recognized as interest expense change from one period to the next, we must refer to the appropriate interest period in the amortization table to obtain the dollar amounts for use in year-end adjusting entries. To illustrate, consider our example of the bonds sold at a premium on May 1, Year 1. The entry shown above records interest and amortization of the premium through November 1, Year 1. If the company keeps its accounts on a calendar-year basis, two months' interest has accrued as of December 31, Year 1, and the following adjusting entry is made at year-end:

<table>
<tr><td>Year-end adjustment</td><td>Bond Interest Expense ....</td><td>14,209</td><td></td></tr>
<tr><td></td><td>Premium on Bonds Payable ....</td><td>791</td><td></td></tr>
<tr><td></td><td>Bond Interest Payable ....</td><td></td><td>15,000</td></tr>
</table>

To record two months' accrued interest and amortize one-third of the
premium for the interest period.

This adjusting entry covers one-third (two months) of the second interest period. Consequently, the amounts shown as bond interest expense and amortization of premium are one-third of the amounts shown in the amortization table for the second interest period. Similar adjusting entries must be made at the end of every accounting period while the bonds are outstanding. The dollar amounts of these adjusting entries will vary, however, because the amounts of interest expense and premium amortization change in every interest period. The amounts applicable to any given adjusting entry will be the appropriate fraction of the amounts for the interest period then in progress.

Following the year-end adjusting entry illustrated above, the interest expense and premium amortization on May 1, Year 2, are recorded as follows:

<table>
<tr><td>Interest payment following year-end adjustment</td><td>Bond Interest Expense ....</td><td>28,418</td><td></td></tr>
<tr><td></td><td>Bond Interest Payable ....</td><td>15,000</td><td></td></tr>
<tr><td></td><td>Premium on Bonds Payable ....</td><td>1,582</td><td></td></tr>
<tr><td></td><td>Cash ....</td><td></td><td>45,000</td></tr>
</table>

To record semiannual interest payment, a portion of which had been
accrued, and amortize remainder of premium applicable to interest period.

Amortization of bond discount or premium from the investor's viewpoint

We have discussed the need for a corporation issuing bonds payable to amortize any bond discount or premium to measure correctly the bond interest expense. But what about the

purchaser of the bonds? Should an investor in bonds amortize any difference between the cost of the investment and its future maturity value in order to measure investment income correctly? The answer to this question depends upon whether the investor considers the bonds to be a ***short-term*** or a ***long-term*** investment.

A short-term investment in bonds generally is carried in the investor's accounting records at ***cost,*** and a gain or a loss is recognized when the investment is sold. Short-term investments in bonds usually will be sold before the bonds mature and the sales price will be determined by the current state of the bond market. Under these conditions, there is no assurance that amortization of premium or discount would give any more accurate measurement of investment income than would be obtained by carrying the bonds at cost.

When bonds are owned for the long term, however, it becomes more probable that the market price of the investment will move toward the maturity value of the bonds. At the maturity date the market value equals the maturity value of the bonds. Thus, companies making long-term investments in bonds ***should*** amortize over the life of the bonds any difference between the cost of the investment and its maturity value. If the effective interest method of amortization would produce results materially different from those obtained by the straight-line method, the effective interest method should be used.[5]

Retirement of bonds payable

Bonds are sometimes retired before the maturity date. The principal reason for retiring bonds early is to relieve the issuing corporation of the obligation to make future interest payments. If interest rates decline to the point that a corporation can borrow at an interest rate below that being paid on a particular bond issue, the corporation may benefit from retiring these bonds and issuing new bonds at a lower interest rate.

Most bond issues contain a call provision, permitting the corporation to redeem the bonds by paying a specified price, usually a few points above par. Even without a call provision, the corporation may retire its bonds before maturity by purchasing them in the open market. If the bonds can be purchased by the issuing corporation at less than their ***carrying value,*** a gain is realized on the retirement of the debt. If the bonds are reacquired by the issuing corporation at a price in excess of their carrying value, a loss must be recognized. The FASB has ruled that these gains and losses, if ***material*** in amount, should be shown separately in the income statement as extraordinary items.[6]

For example, assume that the Briggs Corporation has outstanding a $1 million bond issue with unamortized premium in the amount of $20,000. The bonds are callable at 105 and the company exercises the call provision on 100 of the bonds, or 10% of the issue. The entry would be as follows:

Bonds called at price above carrying value

Bonds Payable	100,000	
Premium on Bonds Payable	2,000	
Loss on Retirement of Bonds	3,000	
Cash		105,000

To record retirement of $100,000 face value of bonds called at 105.

[5] *APB Opinion No. 21,* "Interest on Receivables and Payables," AICPA (New York: 1971), p. 423.

[6] Financial Accounting Standards Board, *Statement No. 4,* "Reporting Gains and Losses from Extinguishment of Debt," FASB (Stamford, Conn.: 1975).

The carrying value of each of the 100 called bonds was $1,020, whereas the call price was $1,050. For each bond called the company incurred a loss of $30, or a total loss of $3,000. Note that when 10% of the total issue was called, 10% of the unamortized premium was written off.

If bonds remain outstanding until the maturity date, the discount or premium will have been completely amortized and the accounting entry to retire the bonds (assuming that interest is paid separately) will consist of a debit to Bonds Payable and a credit to Cash.

One year before the maturity date, the bonds payable may be reclassified from long-term debt to a current liability in the balance sheet if payment is to be made from current assets rather than from a **bond sinking fund.**

Bond sinking fund

To make a bond issue attractive to investors, a corporation may agree to create a sinking fund, exclusively for use in paying the bonds at maturity. A bond sinking fund is created by setting aside a specified amount of cash at regular intervals. The cash is usually deposited with a trustee, who invests it and adds the earnings to the amount of the sinking fund. The periodic deposits of cash plus the earnings on the sinking fund investments should cause the fund to equal approximately the amount of the bond issue by the maturity date. When the bond issue approaches maturity, the trustee sells all the securities in the fund and uses the cash proceeds to pay the holders of the bonds. Any excess cash remaining in the fund will be returned to the corporation by the trustee.

A bond sinking fund is not included in current assets because it is not available for payment of current liabilities. The cash and securities comprising the fund are usually shown as a single amount under a caption such as Long-Term Investments, which is placed just below the current asset section. Interest earned on sinking fund securities constitutes revenue to the corporation.

Conversion of bonds payable into common stock

Convertible bonds represent a popular form of financing, particularly during periods when common stock prices are rising. The conversion feature gives bondholders an opportunity to profit from a rise in the market price of the issuing company's common stock while still maintaining their status of creditors rather than stockholders. Because of this potential gain, convertible bonds generally carry lower interest rates than nonconvertible bonds.

The conversion ratio is typically set at a price above the current market price of the common stock at the date the bonds are authorized. For example, if common stock with a par value of $10 a share has a current market price of $42 a share, the **conversion price** might be set at $50 per share, thus enabling a holder of a $1,000 par value convertible bond to exchange the bond for 20 shares of common stock.[7] Let us assume that $5 million of such bonds are issued at par, and that some time later when the common stock has risen

[7] $1,000 ÷ $50 conversion price = 20 shares of common stock.

in price to $60 per share, the holders of 100 bonds decide to convert their bonds into common stock. The conversion transaction would be recorded as follows:

Conversion of bonds into common stock

Convertible Bonds Payable	100,000	
Common Stock, $10 par		20,000
Paid-in Capital in Excess of Par		80,000

To record the conversion of 100 bonds into 2,000 shares of common stock.

No gain or loss is recognized by the issuing corporation upon conversion of bonds; the carrying value of the bonds is simply assigned to the comon stock issued in exchange. If the bonds had been issued at a price above or below face value, the unamortized premium or discount relating to the bonds would be written off at the time of conversion in order to assign the carrying value of the bonds to the common stock.

Conversion of bonds from the investor's viewpoint

Investors do not always convert their investment in convertible bonds into common shares as soon as the market value of the common shares they would receive rises above the $1,000 maturity value of their bonds. As the bonds easily can be converted into common stock, their market value rises right along with that of the common stock

● **CASE IN POINT** ● Walgreen Co. has an outstanding issue of bonds payable in which each bond is convertible into 123.99 shares of the company's common stock. In April 1985, the common stock was selling for $54¼, indicating a market value for 123.99 shares of $6,726.46. The market value of the convertible bonds was quoted at 672⅝, even though the bonds mature at a price of only 100 in 1991.

In fact, there may be several good reasons for *not* converting an investment in bonds into common stock. First, the periodic interest payments received from the investment in bonds may exceed the dividends that would be received from the common shares into which the bonds could be converted. Second, an investment in bonds has less *downside risk* than an investment in common stock. (The term "downside risk" means the threat of possible loss to the investor from a drop in market price.) Bonds ultimately mature and are redeemed by the issuing corporation at their maturity value (usually $1,000 per bond). Common stock, on the other hand, has no maturity value. The price of a company's common stock may decline dramatically even though the company is not in such financial difficulty that it might default upon its obligations to bondholders.

In conclusion, when are the owners of convertible bonds likely to exchange their bonds for shares of common stock? The exchange point is reached when the dividends that would be received from the common shares *exceed the interest payments* currently being received from the investment in bonds. When the common stock dividends increase to this level, the bondholders can increase their cash receipts by converting their bonds into shares of common stock.

LEASES

A company may purchase the assets needed for use in its business or it may choose to lease them. Examples of assets often acquired by lease include buildings, office equipment, automobiles, and factory machinery. A *lease* is a contract in which the *lessor* gives the *lessee* the right to use an asset in return for periodic rental payments. The lessor is the owner of the property; the lessee is the tenant or renter. Accounting for the many forms of lease transactions and the disclosure of lease obligations by lessees are among the more important issues facing accountants today.

Operating lease

When the lessor gives the lessee the right to use the leased property for a limited period of time but retains the usual risks and rewards of ownership, the contract is known as an *operating lease.* In accounting for an operating lease, the lessor treats the monthly lease payments received as rental revenue. The lessee accounts for the lease payments as rental expense; no asset or liability (other than a short-term liability for accrued rent payable) relating to the lease is recorded in the lessee's accounts.

Capital lease

When the objectives of the lease contract are to provide financing to the lessee for the eventual purchase of the property, or for use of the property over most of its useful life, the contract is referred to as a *capital lease* (or a *financing lease*). Even though title to the leased property has not been transferred, a capital leases are regarded as *essentially equivalent to a sale* of the property by the lessor to the lessee. Thus, a capital lease should be recorded by the lessor as a *sale* of property and by the lessee as a *purchase.* In such lease agreements, an appropriate interest charge usually is added to the regular sales price of the property in determining the total amount of the lease payments.

Some manufacturing companies frequently use capital lease agreements as a means of financing the sale of their products to customers. In accounting for merchandise "sold" through a capital lease, the lessor debits Lease Payments Receivable and credits Sales for an amount equal to the *present value of the future lease payments.*[8] In most cases, the present value of these future payments is equal to the regular sales price of the merchandise. In addition, the lessor transfers the cost of the leased merchandise from the Inventory account to the Cost of Goods Sold account (assuming a perpetual inventory system is in use). When lease payments are received, the lessor should recognize an appropriate portion of the payment as representing interest revenue and the remainder as a reduction in Lease Payments Receivable.

When equipment is acquired through a capital lease, the lessee should debit an asset account, Leased Equipment, and credit a liability account, Lease Payment Obligation, for

---

[8] We have elected to record the present value of the future lease payments by a single debit entry to Lease Payments Receivable. An alternative is to debit Lease Payments Receivable for the total amount of the future payments and to credit Discount on Lease Payments Receivable, a contra-asset account, for the unearned finance charges included in the contractual amount. Either approach results in the lessor recording a net receivable equal to the present value of the future lease payments.

the present value of the future lease payments. Lease payments made by the lessee are allocated between Interest Expense and a reduction in the liability, Lease Payment Obligation. No rent expense is involved. The asset account, Leased Equipment, is depreciated over the life of the equipment rather than the life of the lease. (The journal entries used in accounting for a capital lease are illustrated on page 573 in the appendix to this chapter.)

Distinguishing between capital leases and operating leases. In *Statement No. 13,* the FASB required that a lease which meets at least one of the following criteria be accounted for as a capital lease:[9]

1 The lease transfers ownership of the property to the lessee at the end of the lease term.
2 The lease contains a "bargain purchase option."
3 The lease term is equal to 75% or more of the estimated economic life of the property.
4 The present value of the minimum lease payments is at least 90% of the fair value of the lease property.

Only those leases which meet none of the above criteria may be accounted for as operating leases.

New standards reduce off-balance-sheet financing. Prior to the issuance of *FASB Statement No. 13,* the criteria defining capital leases were much narrower. As a result, a great number of long-term leases were accounted for as operating leases by the lessees. Operating leases often are called *off-balance-sheet financing,* because the obligation for future lease payments does not appear as a liability in the balance sheet of the lessee. As a result of the criteria set forth by the FASB, the number of lease contracts qualifying as operating leases has been greatly reduced. In the opinion of the authors, accounting for long-term lease contracts as capital leases significantly improves the usefulness of the balance sheet in evaluating the resources and obligations of companies which lease substantial portions of their productive assets.

A number of more complex issues and special situations are involved in accounting for leases; these are covered in intermediate accounting.

OTHER LIABILITIES

Mortgage notes payable

Purchases of real estate and certain types of equipment often are financed by the issuance of mortgage notes payable. When a mortgage note is issued, the borrower pledges title to specific assets as collateral for the loan. If the borrower defaults on the note, the lender may foreclose upon these assets. Mortgage notes usually are payable in equal monthly installments. These monthly installments may continue until the loan is completely repaid, or the note may contain a "due date" at which the remaining unpaid balance of the loan must be repaid in a single, lump-sum payment.

[9] *FASB Statement No. 13,* "Accounting for Leases" (Stamford, Conn.: 1976), pp. 9–10.

A portion of each monthly payment represents interest on the unpaid balance of the loan and the remainder of the monthly payment reduces the amount of the unpaid balance (principal). Since the principal is being reduced each month, the portion of each successive payment representing interest will **decrease,** and the portion of the payment going toward repayment of the principal will **increase.** To illustrate, assume that on June 30 a company issues a $100,000 mortgage note to finance the purchase of a warehouse. The note requires monthly payments in the amount of $1,250 and bears interest at the annual rate of 12% (equal to 1% per month). The following partial amortization table shows the allocation of the first three monthly payments between interest and principal:

	Payment Date	(A) Monthly Payment	(B) Monthly Interest Expense (1% of Unpaid Balance)	(C) Reduction in Principal (A − B)	(D) Unpaid Principal Balance
Monthly payments on a mortgage note	June 30 — Issuance date				$100,000.00
	July 31	$1,250.00	$1,000.00	$250.00	99,750.00
	Aug. 31	1,250.00	997.50	252.50	99,497.50
	Sept. 30	1,250.00	994.98	255.02	99,242.48

The entry to record the first monthly mortgage payment on July 31 would be:

Payment is allocated between interest and principal

Interest Expense 1,000
Mortgage Payable 250
    Cash 1,250
To record interest expense and reduction in principal included in July 31 mortgage payment.

Pension plans

A **pension plan** is a contract between a company and its employees under which the company agrees to pay retirement benefits to eligible employees. An employer company usually meets its obligations under a pension plan by making regular payments to an insurance company or other outside agency. As pension obligations accrue, the employer company records them by a debit to Pension Expense and a credit to Cash. If all required payments are made promptly to the pension fund trustee, no liability need appear on the employer company's financial statements. When employees retire, their retirement benefis are paid by the insurance company. This type of arrangement is called a **funded pension plan.** Pension plans are considered in some detail in more advanced accounting courses.

Estimated liabilities

An estimated liability is one known to exist, but for which the dollar amount is uncertain. A common example is the liability of a manufacturer to honor any warranty on products sold. For example, assume that a company manufactures and sells television sets which carry a two-year warranty. To achieve the objective of offsetting current revenue with all related expenses, the liability for future warranty repairs on television sets sold during the current period should be estimated and recorded at the balance sheet date. This estimate will be based upon the company's past experience.

Loss contingencies

In Chapter 8, we discussed the **contingent liability** which arises when notes receivable are discounted at a bank. A contingent liability may be regarded as a **possible** liability, which may develop into a full-fledged liability or may be eliminated entirely by a future event. Contingent liabilities are also called **loss contingencies.** "Loss contingencies," however, is a broader term, encompassing the possible impairment of assets as well as the possible existence of liabilities.

A common loss contingency is the possibility of loss relating to a lawsuit filed against a company. Until the lawsuit is resolved, uncertainty exists as to the amount, if any, of the company's liability. Central to the definition of a loss contingency is the element of **uncertainty**—uncertainty both as to the amount of loss and whether, in fact, a loss actually has occurred.

Loss contingencies are recorded in the accounting records at estimated amounts only when both of the following criteria are met: (1) it is **probable** that a loss has been incurred, and (2) the amount of loss can be **reasonably estimated.**[10] An example of a loss contingency which meets these criteria and is recorded in the accounts is the estimated loss from doubtful accounts receivable. Loss contingencies which do not meet both of these criteria should be **disclosed in footnotes** to the financial statements whenever there is at least a **reasonable possibility** that a loss has been incurred. Pending lawsuits, for example, almost always are disclosed in footnotes, but no dollar estimate of settlement is stated. To state an amount would weaken a company's bargaining position during the litigation process. If a loss is sustained, it will be entered in the accounting records and appear in the financial statements only when the lawsuit is settled.

When loss contingencies are disclosed in footnotes to the financial statements, the footnote should describe the nature of the contingency and, if possible, provide an estimate of the amount of possible loss. If a reasonable estimate of the amount of possible loss cannot be made, the footnote should include the range of possible loss or a statement that an estimate cannot be made. The following footnote is typical of the disclosure of the loss contingency arising from pending litigation:

Footnote disclosure of a loss contingency

Note 8: Contingencies

In October of the current year, the Company was named as defendant in a lawsuit alleging patent infringement and claiming damages of $408 million. The Company denies all charges in this case and is preparing its defenses against them. The Company is advised by legal counsel that it is not possible at this time to determine the ultimate legal or financial responsibility with respect to this litigation.

Users of financial statements should pay close attention to the footnote disclosure of

---

[10] *FASB Statement No. 5,* "Accounting for Contingencies" (Stamford, Conn.: 1975).

loss contingencies. Even though no loss has been recorded in the accounting records, some loss contingencies may be so material in amount as th threaten the continued existence of the company.

● **CASE IN POINT** ● In August 1982, Manville Corp. surprised the financial community by filing for bankruptcy. Manville Corp., with its worldwide mining and manufacturing operations, had a long record of profitability and financial strength. In fact, the corporation was one of the 30 "blue chip" companies whose stock prices are used in the computation of the famous Dow-Jones Industrial Average. As late as 1981, the dollar amounts in the company's financial statements showed Manville Corp. to be both profitable and solvent.

A clue to the company's impending problems, however, could be found in the notes accompanying the statements. Beginning in 1979, the statements included a note disclosing that the company was a defendant in "numerous legal actions alleging damage to the health of persons exposed to dust from asbestos-containing products manufactured or sold by the Company. . . ." It was these pending lawsuits, which numbered over 50,000 by August of 1982, which caused the company to file for bankruptcy.

Key terms introduced or emphasized in chapter 13

Amortization of discount or premium on bonds payable. The process of systematically writing off a portion of bond discount to increase interest expense or writing off a portion of bond premium to decrease interest expense each period the bonds are outstanding.

Bond sinking fund. Cash set aside by the corporation at regular intervals (usually with a trustee) to be used to pay the bonds at maturity.

Capital lease. A lease contract which, in essence, finances the eventual purchase by the lessee of leased property. The lessor accounts for a capital lease as a sale of property; the lessee records an asset and a liability equal to the present value of the future lease payments. Also called a *financing lease.*

Contract interest rate. The contractual rate of interest printed on bonds. The contract interest rate, applied to the face value of the bonds, determines the amount of the annual cash interest payments to bondholders. Also called the *nominal interest rate.*

Debenture bond. An unsecured bond, the value of which rests on the general credit of the corporation. Not secured by pledge of specific assets.

Discount on bonds payable. Amount by which the face amount of the bond exceeds the price received by the corporation at the date of issuance. Indicates that the contractual rate of interest is lower than the market rate of interest.

Effective interest method of amortization. Discount or premium on bonds is amortized by the difference between the contractual cash interest payment each period and the amount of interest computed by applying the effective interest rate to the carrying value of the bonds at the beginning of the current interest period. Causes bond interest expense to be a constant percentage of the carrying value of the liability.

Effective interest rate. The actual rate of interest expense to the borrowing corporation, taking into account the contractual cash interest payments and the discount or premium to be amortized.

Lesee. The tenant, user, or renter of leased property.

Lessor. The owner of property leased to a lessee.

Loss contingency. A situation involving uncertainty as to whether or not a loss has occurred. The uncertainty will be resolved by a future event. An example of a loss contingency is the possible loss related to a lawsuit pending against a company. Although loss contingencies are sometimes recorded in the accounts, they are more frequently disclosed only in footnotes in the financial statements.

Maturity date. The date upon which bonds come due and are redeemed by the issuing corporation at their maturity (par) value.

Maturity value. The dollar amount at which the issuing corporation must redeem (pay off) bonds payable upon the bonds' maturity date. Maturity value generally is equal to par value.

Off-balance-sheet financing. An arrangement in which the use of resources is financed without the obligation for future payments appearing as a liability in the balance sheet. An operating lease is a common example of off-balance-sheet financing.

Operating lease. A lease contract which is in essence a rental agreement. The lesee has the use of the leased property, but the lessor retains the usual risks and rewards of ownership. The periodic lease payments are accounted for as rent expense by the lessee and as rental revenue by the lessor.

Premium on bonds payable. Amount by which the issuance price of a bond exceeds the face value. Indicates that the contractual rate of interest is higher than the market rate.

Present value of a future amount. The amount of money that an informed investor would pay today for the right to receive the future amount, based upon a specific rate of return required by the investor. Bond prices are the present value to investors of the future principal and interest payments. Capital leases are recorded as an asset and a related liability in the accounting records of the lessee at the present value of the future lease payments.

Demonstration problem

On June 30, Year 4, Laser Graphics issued $4,000,000 face value of 10-year, $9\frac{1}{2}$% bonds payable at a price of $103\frac{1}{4}$, resulting in an effective annual rate of interest of 9%. The semiannual interest payment dates are June 30 and December 31, and the bonds mature on June 30, Year 14. The company maintains its accounts on a calendar-year basis and amortizes bond premium by the effective interest method.

Instructions

a Prepare the required journal entries (with explanations) on:
   (1) June 30, Year 4, to record the sale of the bonds.
   (2) December 31, Year 4, for payment of interest and amortization of premium on bonds. (Use one compound entry.)
   (3) June 30, Year 14, for payment of interest, amortization of the remaining premium, and to retire the bonds. Assume that the carrying value of the bonds at the beginning of this last six-month interest period is $4,009,569.

b Show how the accounts, Bonds Payable and Premium on Bonds Payable, would appear on the balance sheet at December 31, Year 4.

Solution to demonstration problem

a General Journal

(1)

Year 4

June 30   Cash   4,130,000

         Bonds Payable   4,000,000

         Premium on Bonds Payable   130,000

         To record sale of $9\frac{1}{2}$%, 10-year bonds at $103\frac{1}{4}$.

(2)

Dec. 31   Bond Interest Expense   185,850

         Premium on Bonds Payable   4,150

         Cash   190,000

         To record semiannual interest payment and amortize premium:

            Interest payment ($4,000,000 \times 9\frac{1}{2}$% $\times \frac{1}{2}$ \$190,000

            Interest expense ($4,130,000 \times 9$% $\times \frac{1}{2}$ 185,850

            Premium amortization . . . .\$ 4,150

(3)

Year 14

June 30   Bond Interest Expense   180,431

         Premium on Bonds Payable   9,569

         Cash   190,000

         To record semiannual interest payment and amortize

            remaining balance of premium ($4,009,569 -

            \$4,000,000 = \$9,569$).

     30   Bonds Payable   4,000,000

         Cash   4,000,000

         To retire bonds on maturity date.

b **LASER GRAPHICS**
Partial Balance Sheet
December 31, Year 4

Long-term liabilities:

   $9\frac{1}{2}$% bonds payable, due June 30, Year 14 . . . .   \$4,000,000

   Add: Premium on bonds payable   125,850   \$4,125,850

Review questions

1 Distinguish between the two terms in each of the following pairs:

     a   Mortgage bond; debenture bond

     b   Contract (or nominal) interest rate; effective interest rate

     c   Fixed-maturity bond; serial bond

     d   Coupon bond; registered bond

e Operating lease; capital lease

f Estimated liability; contingent liability

2 K Company has decided to finance expansion by issuing $10 million of 20-year debenture bonds and will ask a number of underwriters to bid on the bond issue. Discuss the factors that will determine the amount bid by the underwriters for these bonds.

3 What is a *convertible bond?* Discuss the advantages and disadvantages of convertible bonds from the standpoint of (a) the investor and (b) the issuing corporation.

4 The Computer Sharing Co. has paid-in capital of $10 million and retained earnings of $3 million. The company has just issued $1 million in 20-year, 8% bonds. It is proposed that a policy be established of appropriating $50,000 of retained earnings each year to enable the company to retire the bonds at maturity. Evaluate the merits of this proposal in accomplishing the desired result.

5 The following excerpt is taken from an article in a leading business periodical: "In the bond market high interest rates mean low prices. Bonds pay out a fixed percentage of their face value, usually $1,000; an 8% bond, for instance, will pay $80 a year. In order for its yield to rise to 10%, its price would have to drop to $800." Give a critical evaluation of this quotation.

6 Discuss the advantages and disadvantages of a *call provision* in a bond contract from the viewpoint of (a) the bondholder and (b) the issuing corporation.

7 Many bonds now being bought and sold by investors on organized securities exchanges were issued when interest rates were much lower than they are today. Would you expect these bonds to be trading at prices above or below their face values? Explain.

8 The 6% bonds of Central Gas & Electric are selling at a market price of 72, whereas the 6% bonds of Interstate Power are selling at a price of 97. Does this mean that Interstate Power has a better credit rating than Central Gas & Electric? Explain. (Assume current long-term interest rates are in the 11 to 13% range.)

9 Explain why the effective rate of interest differs from the contract rate when bonds are issued (a) at a discount and (b) at a premium.

10 When the effective interest method is used to amortize bond discount or premium, the amount of bond interest expense will differ in each period from that of the preceding period. Explain how the amount of bond interest expense changes from one period to another when the bonds are issued (a) at a discount and (b) at a premium.

11 Explain why the effective interest method of amortizing bond discount or premium is considered to be theoretically preferable to the straight-line method.

12 John Lee buys a $1,000, 16% bond for 106, five years from the maturity date. After holding the bond for four years, he sells it for 102. Lee claims that he has a loss of $40 on the sale. A friend argues that Lee has made a gain on the sale. Explain the difference in viewpoint. With whom do you agree? Why?

13 What situation or condition is most likely to cause the holders of convertible bonds to convert their bonds into shares of common stock? (Do not assume that the bonds have been called or that they are about to mature.)

14 Explain how the lessee accounts for an operating lease and a capital lease. Why is an operating lease sometimes called *off-balance-sheet financing?*

15 A friend of yours has just purchased a house andhas incurred a $50,000, 11% mortgage, payable at $476.17 per month. After making the first monthly payment, he received a receipt from the bank stating that only $17.84 of the $476.17 had been applied to reducing the principal amount of the loan. Your friend computes that at the rate of $17.84 per month, it will take over 233 years to pay off the $50,000 mortgage. Do you agree with your friend's analysis? Explain.

16 Under what conditions are *loss contingencies* recorded at estimated amounts in the accounting records?

17 A lawsuit has been filed against Telmar Corporation alleging violations of federal antitrust laws and claiming damages which, when trebled, total $1.2 billion. Telmar Corporation denies the charges and intends to contest the suit vigorously. Legal counsel advises the company that the litigation will last for several years and that a reasonable estimate of the final outcome cannot be made at this time.

Should Telmar Corporation include in its current balance sheet a liability for the damages claimed in this lawsuit? Explain fully.

18 With reference to question 17 above, illustrate the disclosure of the pending lawsuit which should be included in the current financial statements of Telmar Corporation.

Exercises

Ex. 13-1   On March 31, Year 1, Wayne Corporation received authorization to issue $50,000,000 of 12%, 30-year debenture bonds. Interest payment dates were March 31 and September 30. The bonds were all issued at par on May 31, Year 1, two months after the interest date printed on the bonds.

Instructions

a Prepare the journal entry at May 31, Year 1, to record the sale of the bonds.

b Prepare the journal entry at September 30, Year 1, to record the semiannual bond interest payment.

c Prepare the adjusting entry at December 31, Year 1, to record bond interest accrued since September 30.

Ex. 13-2   Eastern Electric and Western Edison have the same amount of operating income (earnings before bond interest and income taxes) and the same number of outstanding sharesof common stock. However, the two companies have different capital structures. Determine the earnings per share of common stock for each of the two companies and explain the source of any difference.

	Eastern Electric	Western Edison
14% debenture bonds payable	$10,000,000	– 0 –
14% cumulative preferred stock, $10 par	– 0 –	10,000,000
Common stock, $5 par, 500,000 shares outstanding	2,500,000	2,500,000
Operating income, before interest and income taxes (assume a 40% tax rate)	7,000,000	7,000,000

Ex. 13-3   La Paloma issued $10,000,000 par value 10½% bonds on July 1, Year 5, at 98¼. Interest is due on June 30 and December 31 of each year, and the bonds mature on June 30, Year 15. The fiscal year ends on December 31; bond discount is amortized by the straight-line method. Prepare the following journal entries:

a July 1, Year 5, to record the issuance of the bonds

b December 31, Year 5, to pay interest and amortize the bond discount (two entries)

c June 30, Year 15, to pay interest, amortize the bond discount, and retire the bonds at maturity (three entries)

Ex. 13-4   North Company issued $40 million of 11%, 10-year bonds on January 1, Year 1. Interest is payable semiannually on June 30 and December 31. The bonds were sold to an underwriting group at 105.

South Company issued $40 million of 10%, 10-year bonds on January 1, Year 1. Interest is payable semiannually on June 30 and December 31. The bonds were sold to an underwriting group at 95.

Prepare journal entries to record all transactions during Year 1 for (a) the North Company bond issue and (b) the South Company bond issue. Assume that both companies amortize bond discount or premium by the straight-line method at each interest payment date.

Ex. 13-5 The following liability appears on the balance sheet of the Sunrise Company on December 31, Year 1:

Long-term liabilities:
Bonds payable, 11%, due Dec. 31, Year 15 .... $20,000,000
Premium on bonds payable ...., 420,000 $20,420,000

On January 1, Year 2, 25% of the bonds are retired at 98. Interest had been paid on December 31, Year 1.

    a Record the retirement of $5,000,000 of bonds on January 1, Year 2.
    b Record the interest payment for the six months ending December 31, Year 2, and the amortization of the premium on December 31, Year 2, assuming that amortization is recorded by the straight-line method only at the end of each year.

Ex. 13-6 On April 1, Year 1, Basin Corporation issued $1,000,000 of 10-year, 9% bonds payable and received proceeds of $937,689, resulting in an effective interest rate of 10%. Interest is payable on September 30 and March 31. The effective interest method is used to amortize bond discount; an amortization table for this bond issue is illustrated on page 545.

Instructions. Prepare the necessary journal entries (rounding all amounts to the nearest dollar) on:

    a April 1, Year 1, to record the issuance of the bonds
    b September 30, Year 1, to record the payment of interest and amortization of discount at the first semiannual interest payment date
    c December 31, Year 1, to accrue bond interest expense through year-end
    d March 31, Year 2, to record the payment of interest and amortization of bond discount at the second semiannual interest payment date

Ex. 13-7 Crown Point Corporation issued on the authorization date $1,000,000 of 10-year, 9% bonds payable and received proceeds of $1,067,952, resulting in an effective interest rate of 8%. The premium is amortized by the effective interest method; the amortization table for this bond issue is illustrated on page 547. Interest is payable semiannually.

Instructions

    a Show how the liability for the bonds would appear on a balance sheet prepared immediately after issuance of the bonds.
    b Show how the liability for the bonds would appear on a balance sheet prepared after 14 semiannual interest periods (three years prior to maturity).
    c Show the necessary calculations to determine interest expense by the effective interest method for the *second* six-month period, the premium amortized at the end of that second period, and the cash interest payment. Your calculations should include use of the effective interest rate and also the contractual rate. Round all amounts to the nearest dollar.

Ex. 13-8   Brand Corporation issued $5,000,000 of 7%, 10-year convertible bonds dated December 31, Year 1, at a price of 98. Semiannual interest payment dates were June 30 and December 31. The conversion rate was 20 shares of $1 par common stock for each $1,000 bond. Four years later on December 31, Year 5, bondholders converted $2,000,000 face value of bonds into common stock. Assume that unamortized discount on this date amounted to $60,000 for the entire bond issue. Prepare a journal entry to record the conversion of the bonds.

Problems

13-1   Accrual of bond interest (bonds issued at par)
Snow Country Resort obtained authorization to issue $12,000,000 face value of 10% 20-year bonds, dated April 30, Year 3. Interest payment dates were October 31 and April 30. Issuance of the bonds did not take place until July 31, Year 3. On this date all the bonds were sold at a price of 100 plus three months' accrued interest.

Instructions. Prepare the necessary entries in general journal form on:

a   July 31, Year 3, to record the issuance of the bonds
b   October 31, Year 3, to record the first semiannual interest payment on the bond issue
c   December 31, Year 3, to accrue bond interest expense through year-end and to close the Bond Interest Expense account
d   April 30, Year 4, to record the second semiannual interest payment

13-2   Discount and premium: straight-line amortizations
On September 1, Year 1, American Farm Equipment issued $3 million in 9% debenture bonds. Interest is payable semiannually on March 1 and September 1, and the bonds mature on September 1, Year 11. Company policy is to amortize bond discount or premium by the straight-line method at each interest payment date; the company's fiscal year ends at December 31.

Instructions

a   Make the necessary adjusting entries at December 31, Year 1, and the journal entry to record the payment of bond interest on March 1, Year 2, under each of the following assumptions:
   (1) The bonds were issued at 98.
   (2) The bonds were issued at 103.
b   Compute the net bond liability at December 31, Year 1, under assumptions (1) and (2) above.

13-3   Amortization of discount: straight-line method
The items shown below appear in the balance sheet of Napa Vineyards at December 31, Year 6:

Current liabilities:
  Bond interest payable (for three months from Sept. 30 to
    Dec. 31) .... $ 200,000
Long-term debt:
  Bonds payable, 8%, due Mar. 31, Year 17 .... $10,000,000
  Less: Discount on bonds payable 196,800   9,803,200

The bonds are callable on any interest date. On September 30, Year 7, Napa Vineyards called $2 million of the bonds at 103.

Instructions

a Prepare journal entries to record the semiannual interest payment on March 31, Year 7. Discount is amortized by the straight-line method at each interest payment date and was amortized to December 31, Year 6. Base the amortization on the 123-month period from December 31, Year 6, to March 31, Year 17.

b Prepare journal entries to record the amortization of bond discount and payment of bond interest at September 30, Yer 7, and also to record the calling of $2 million of the bonds at this date.

c Prepare a journal entry to record the accrual of interest at December 31, Year 7. Include the amortization of bond discount to the year-end.

13-4   Comprehensive problem: straight-line amortization

Country Recording Studios obtained authorization to issue $8,000,000 of 9%, 10-year bonds, dated May 1, Year 1. Interest payment dates were May 1 and November 1. Issuance of the bonds did not take place until July 1, Year 1. On this date, the entire bond issue was sold to an underwriter at a price which included the two months' accrued interest. Country Recording Studios follows the policy of amortizing bond discount or premium by the straight-line method at each interest date as well as for year-end adjusting entries at December 31.

Instructions

a Prepare all journal entries necessary to record the issuance of the bonds and bond interest expense during Yer 1, assuming that the sales price of the bonds on July 1 was $8,415,000 *including accrued interest.* (Note that the bonds will be outstanding for a period of only 9 years and 10 months.)

b Assume that the sales price of the bonds on July 1 had been $7,907,600, *including accrued interest.* Prepare journal entries for Year 1 parallel to those in part a above.

c Show the proper balance sheet presentation of the liability for bonds payable (including accrued interest) in the balance sheet prepared at December 31, *Year 6,* assuming that the original sales price of the bonds (*including accrued interest*) had been:
   (1) $8,415,000, as described in part a
   (2) $7,907,600, as described in part b

13-5   Effective interest method: bonds issued at discount

Arcades R Fun maintains its accounts on a calendar-year basis. On June 30, Year 4, the company issued $6,000,000 face value of 7.6% bonds at a price of 97¼, resulting in an effective rate of interest of 8%. Semiannual interest payment dates are June 30 and December 31. Bond discount is amortized by the effective interest method. The bonds mature on June 30, Year 14.

Instructions

a Prepare the required journal entries on:
   (1) June 30, Year 4, to record the sale of the bonds.
   (2) December 31, Year 4, to pay interest and amortize the discount using the effective interest method.
   (3) June 30, Year 14, to pay interest, amortize the discount, and retire the bonds. Assume that at the beginning of this last interest period, the carrying value of the bonds is $5,988,462. (Use a separate journal entry to show the retirement of the bonds.)

b Show how the accounts, Bonds Payable and Discount on Bonds Payable, should appear on the balance sheet at December 31, Year 4.

13-6   Amortization table: bonds issued at premium

On December 31, Year 4, Glenview Hospital sold an $8,000,000, 9½%, 12-year bond issue to an underwriter at a price of 103½. This price results in an effective annual interest rate of 9%. The bonds were dated December 31, Year 4, and the interest payment dates were June 30 and December 31. Glenview Hospital follows a policy of amortizing the bond premium by the effective interest method at each semiannual payment date.

Instructions

a Prepare an amortization table for the first two years (four interest periods) of the life of this bond issue. Round all amounts to the nearest dollar and use the following column headings:

Six-Month Interest Period	(A) Interest Paid Semi-annually ($8,000,000 × 4¾%)	(B) Effective Semi-annual Interest Expense (Carrying Value × 4½%)	(C) Premium Amortization (A − B)	(D) Bond Premium Balance	(E) Carrying Value of Bonds, End of Period ($8,000,000 + D)

b Using the information in your amortization table, prepare all journal entries necessary to record the bond issue on December 31, Year 4, and the bond interest expense during Year 5.

c Show the proper balance sheet presentation of the liability for bonds payable at December 31, Year 6.

13-7   Another amortization table: bonds issued at discount

On December 31, Year 10, Roadside Inns sold a $6,000,000 face value, 10%, 10-year bond issue to an underwriter at a price of 94. This price results in an effective annual interest rate of 11%. Interest is payable semiannually on June 30 and December 31. Roadside Inns amortizes bond discount by the effective interest method.

Instructions

a Prepare an amortization table for the first two years (four interest periods) of this bond issue. Round all amounts to the nearest dollar and use the following column headings for your table:

Six-Month Interest Period	(A) Interest Paid Semi-annually ($6,000,000 × 5%)	(B) Effective Semi-annual Interest Expense (Carrying Value × 5½%)	(C) Discount Amorti-zation (B − A)	(D) Bond Discount Balance	(E) Carrying Value of Bonds, End of Period ($6,000,000 − D)

b Using the information from your amortization table, prepare all journal entries necessary to record issuance of the bonds and bond interest for Year 11. (Use a compound entry for interest payment and amortization of bond discount at each semiannual interest payment date.)

c Show the proper balance sheet presentation of Bonds Payable and Discount on Bonds Payable at December 31, Year 12.

13-8   Comprehensive problem: effective interest method

On November 1, Year 8, Action Computers issued $11,900,000 face value of 8½% 10-year bonds with interest dates of May 1 and November 1. The bonds were purchased by an underwriter for $11,500,000, resulting in an effective interest rate to Action Computers of 9%. Company policy calls for amortizing bond discount at each interest payment date as well as for year-end adjustment of the accounts. The accounting records are maintained on a calendar-year basis.

Instructions

a Prepare the journal entries required to:
  (1) Record the sale of the bonds on November 1, Year 8.
  (2) Adjust the accounts at December 31, Year 8, for accrued bond interest and amortization of discount. (Use one compound entry.)
  (3) Record the semiannual payment of bond interest on May 1, Year 9, and amortize the bond discount. (Use one compound entry.)
b State the amounts to be reported on the financial statements at the end of Year 8 for:
  (1) Bonds payable (face amount)
  (2) Unamortized discount on bonds payable
  (3) Net amount of liability for bonds payable
  (4) Interest expense for Year 8

13-9 Capital leases: a comprehensive problem
Beach Equipment Co. frequently uses long-term contracts as a means of financing the sale of its products. On November 1, Year 1, Beach Equipment Co. leased to Star Industries a machine carried in the perpetual inventory records at a cost of $18,120. The terms of the lease called for 48 monthly payments of $650 each, beginning November 30, Year 1. The present value of these payments, after considering a built-in interest charge of 1% per month, is equal to $24,680, the regular sales price of the machine. At the end of the 48-month lease, title to the machine will transfer to Star Industries.

Instructions

a Prepare journal entries for Year 1 in the accounts of Beach Equipment Co. on:
  (1) November 1 to record the sale financed by the lease and the related cost of goods sold. (Debit Lease Payments Receivable for the $24,680 present value of the future lease payments.)
  (2) November 30, to record receipt of the first $650 monthly payment. (Prepare a compound journal entry which allocates the cash receipt between interest revenue and reduction of Lease Payments Receivable. The portion of each monthly payment recognized as interest revenue is equal to 1% of the balance of the account Lease Payments Receivable, at the beginning of that month. Round all interest computations to the nearest dollar.)
  (3) December 31, to record receipt of the second monthly payment.
b Prepare journal entries for Year 1 in the accounts of Star Industries on:
  (1) November 1, to record acquisition of the leased machine.
  (2) November 30, to record the first monthly lease payment. (Determine the portion of the payment representing interest expense in a manner parallel to that described in part a.)
  (3) December 31, to record the second monthly lease payment.
  (4) December 31, to recognize depreciation on the leased machine through year-end. Compute the depreciation expense by the straight-line method, using a 10-year service life and an estimated salvage value of $6,680.
c Compute the net carrying value of the leased machine in the balance sheet of Star Industries at December 31, Year 1.
d Compute the amount of Star Industries' lease payment obligation at December 31, Year 1.

Cases for analysis

Case 13-1   Convertible bonds: an investor's perspective

In April of a recent year, the convertible 8¼% bonds of Joseph E. Seagram & Sons, Limited, were selling at a quoted market price of 118. Each $1,000 bond was convertible into 26.49 shares of Seagram Co. Ltd. common stock, which was selling at a price of $41 per share. The common stock pays a cash dividend of $0.80 per share.

Instructions. Assume that you own 100 of Seagram's convertible bonds ($100,000 face value, in total). Under the conditions described above, would it be profitable for you to convert your 100 bonds into 2,649 shares of the company's common stock? Explain the reasons for your answer.

Case 13-2   Debt financing versus equity financing

Marvelous Mattress Co. currently earns $2 million a year before income taxes and has 400,000 shares of common stock outstanding. The company is planning to expand its plant facilities at a cost of $6 million. Management estimates that this expansion will increase annual income before income taxes by 24% of the cost of the new facilities. The company pays income taxes equal to 40% of its income before income taxes.

Two proposals are under consideration for raising the $6 million for the new plant facilities:

Stock Financing   Raise $6 million by issuing 60,000 shares of 12%, $100 par value, preferred stock.

Bond Financing   Borrow $6 million on a 20-year bond issue, with interest at 12%.

Instructions

a Prepare a schedule showing the expected earnings per share of common stock during the first year of operations following the completion of the $6 million expansion, under each of the two proposed means of financing.

b Evaluate the two proposed means of financing from the viewpoint of a common stockholder in Marvelous Mattress Co.

(13) Bonds Payable   Bk. Ex. 12-2, 5

Bk. Ex. 13-1, 2, 4, 5

14   Account Principles—
Inflation   Bk. Ex. 14-1, 3, 6

15   Changes in Financial
Position   Bk. Ex. 15-1, 2, 3   P 15-5

Tests   90 Points
Homework   6 Points
Attendance   4 Points

FORDHAM UNIVERSITY

ACCOUNTING SAC 22021 S2E

Text: Financial Accounting - Meigs & Meigs, 5th Edition
Study Guide - same author & edition

Chapter	Title		Homework		
✓ 1	Language of Business		Ce. 1-3,5,7	P 1-1,2	
✓ 2	Recording Changes	Ce. 2-3,4,8	P 2-3,5a/c		
✓ 3	Measuring Bus. Income	Ce. 3-1,2,3,8	P 3-1,4		
✓ 4	Completing Account Cycle	Ce. 4-1,4,5	P 4-6		
✓ 5	Acct. for Purchase and Sale	Ce. 5-3,5,8	P 5-1,2		
✓ 7	Cash & Marketing Sec.	Ce. 8-3,5,6	P 7-4,5		
✓ 8	Receivables & Payables	Ce. 9-2,5,7	P 8-1,2		
✓ 9	Inventories	Ce. 10-5,9,10	P 9-2		
10	Plant & Equipment	Ce. 11-4,5,6	P 10-2		
11 & 12	Forms of Business Corp.	Bk. Ex. 11-2,4,5,6			

Computer Exercises Ce. 1-3,5,7

Appendix D
Applications of present value

Several preceding chapters have included brief references to the concept of present value in discussions of the valuation of certain assets and liabilities. The purpose of this appendix is to discuss this concept more fully and also to demonstrate the use of present value tables as an aid to making present value computations. In addition, the appendix summarizes in one location the various applications of the present value concept which have been discussed throughout the book. These applications include the valuation of long-term notes receivable and payable, estimation of goodwill, computation of bond prices, and accounting for capital lease transactions.

After studying
this chapter you
should be able to:
- ✓ Explain the concept of present value.
- ✓ Identify the three factors that affect the present value of a future amount.
- ✓ Compute the present value of a future amount and of an annuity using present value tables.
- ✓ Discuss various accounting applications of the present value concept.

The concept of present value

The concept of present value has many applications in accounting, but it is most easily explained in the context of evaluating investment opportunities. In this context, the present value of an expected future cash receipt is the amount that a knowledgeable investor would pay *today* for the right to receive that future amount. The present value is always *less* than the future amount, because the investor will expect to earn a return on the investment. The amount by which the future cash receipt exceeds its present value represents the investor's profit; in short, this difference may be regarded as *interest revenue* included in the future amount.

The present value of a particular investment opportunity depends upon three factors: (1) the expected dollar amount to be received in the future, (2) the length of time until the future amount will be received, and (3) the rate of return (called the *discount rate*) required by the investor. The process of determining the present value of a future cash receipt or payment is called *discounting* the future amount.

To illustrate the present value concept, assume that a specific investment is expected to result in a $1,000 cash receipt at the end of one year. An investor requiring a 10% annual rate of return would be willing to pay $909 today (computed as $1,000 ÷ 1.10) for the right to receive this future amount. This computation may be verified as follows (amounts rounded to the nearest dollar):

Amount to be invested (present value)	$ 909
Required return on investment ($909 × 10%)	91
Amount to be received in one year (future value)	$1,000

If the $1,000 is to be received **two years** in the future, the investor would pay only $826 for the investment today [($1,000 ÷ 1.10) ÷ 1.10]. This computation may be verified as follows (amounts rounded to the nearest dollar):

Amount to be invested (present value)	$ 826
Required return on investment in first year ($826 × 10%)	83
Amount invested after one year	$ 909
Required return on investment in second year ($909 × 10%)	91
Amount to be received in two years (future value)	$1,000

The amount that our investor would pay today, $826, is the **present value** of $1,000 to be received two years later, discounted at an annual rate of 10%. The $174 difference between the $826 present value and the $1,000 future amount may be regarded as the return (interest revenue) to be earned by the investor over the two-year period.

Present value tables

Although we can compute the present value of future amounts by a series of divisions as illustrated above, a more convenient method is available. We can use a **table of present values** to find the present value of $1 at a specified discount rate and then multiply that value by the future amount. For example, in Table 1, the present value of $1 to be received in two years, discounted at an annual rate of 10%, is $0.826. If we multiply .826 by the expected future cash receipt of $1,000, we get an answer of $826, the same amount produced by the series of divisions in our previous illustration.

Selecting an appropriate discount rate

The **discount rate** may be viewed as the investor's required rate of return. All investments involve some degree of risk that actual future cash flows may turn out to be less than expected. Investors usually will expect a rate of return which justifies taking this risk. Under today's market conditions, investors require annual returns of between 8% and 12% on low-risk investments, such as government bonds and certificates of deposit. For relatively high-risk investments, such as the introduction of a new product line, investors may expect to earn an annual return of perhaps 20% or more.

In addition to the amount of risk involved, the "appropriate" discount rate for determining the present value of a specific investment depends upon the investor's cost of capital and the returns available from other investment opportunities. When a higher discount rate is used, the resulting present value will be lower and the investor, therefore, will be interested in the investment only at a lower price.

TABLE 1
Present Values of $1 Due in *n* Periods*

Number of Periods (*n*)	Discount Rate							
	1%	1½%	5%	6%	10%	12%	15%	20%
1	.990	.985	.952	.943	.909	.893	.870	.833
2	.980	.971	.907	.890	.826	.797	.756	.694
3	.971	.956	.864	.840	.751	.712	.658	.579
4	.961	.942	.823	.792	.683	.636	.572	.482
5	.951	.928	.784	.747	.621	.567	.497	.402
6	.942	.915	.746	.705	.564	.507	.432	.335
7	.933	.901	.711	.665	.513	.452	.376	.279
8	.923	.888	.677	.627	.467	.404	.327	.233
9	.914	.875	.645	.592	.424	.361	.284	.194
10	.905	.862	.614	.558	.386	.322	.247	.162
20	.820	.742	.377	.312	.149	.104	.061	.026
24	.788	.700	.310	.247	.102	.066	.035	.013

* The present value of $1 is computed by the formula $p = 1/(1 + i)^n$, where p is the present value of $1, i is the discount rate, and n is the number of periods until the future cash flow will occur. Amounts in this table have been rounded to three decimal places and are shown for a limited number of periods and discount rates.

Discounting annual cash flows

Let us now assume that an investment is expected to produce an annual net cash flow of $10,000 for each of the next three years. If Camino Company expects a 12% return on this type of investment, it may compute the present value of these cash flows as follows:

Year	Expected Net Cash Flow	×	Present Value of $1 Discounted at 12%	=	Present Value of Net Cash Flows
1	$10,000		.893		$8,930
2	10,000		.797		7,970
3	10,000		.712		7,120
Total present value of the investment					$24,020

This analysis indicates that the present value of the expected net cash flows from the investment, discounted at an annual rate of 12%, amounts to $24,020. This is the maximum amount that Camino Company could afford to pay for this investment and still expect to earn the 12% required rate of return.

In the preceding schedule, we multiplied each of the expected annual cash flows by the present value of $1 in the appropriate future period, discounted at 12% per year. The present values of the annual cash flows were than added to determine the total present value of the investment. Separately discounting each annual cash flow to its present value is necessary only when the cash flows vary in amount from one year to the next. Since the annual cash flows in our example are **uniform in amount,** there are two easier ways to compute the total present value.

One way is to add the three decimal figures representing the present value of $1 in the successive years (.893 + .797 + .712) and then to multiply this total (2.402) by the $10,000 annual cash flow. This approach produces the same result ($10,000 × 2.402 = $24,020) we obtained by determining the present value of each year's cash flow separately and adding the results.

An even easier approach to determining the present value of uniform annual cash flows is to refer to an **annuity table,** which shows the present value of $1 to be received periodically for a given number of periods. An annuity table is shown below:

TABLE 2
Present Value of $1 to Be Received Periodically for n Periods

Number of Periods (n)	Discount Rate							
	1%	1½%	5%	6%	10%	12%	15%	20%
1	0.990	0.985	0.952	0.943	0.909	0.893	0.870	0.833
2	1.970	1.956	1.859	1.833	1.736	1.690	1.626	1.528
3	2.941	2.912	2.723	2.673	2.487	2.402	2.283	2.106
4	3.902	3.854	3.546	3.465	3.170	3.037	2.855	2.589
5	4.853	4.783	4.329	4.212	3.791	3.605	3.352	2.991
6	5.795	5.697	5.076	4.917	4.355	4.111	3.784	3.326
7	6.728	6.598	5.786	5.582	4.868	4.564	4.160	3.605
8	7.652	7.486	6.463	6.210	5.335	4.968	4.487	3.837
9	8.566	8.361	7.108	6.802	5.759	5.328	4.772	4.031
10	9.471	9.222	7.722	7.360	6.145	5.650	5.019	4.192
20	18.046	17.169	12.462	11.470	8.514	7.469	6.259	4.870
24	21.243	20.030	13.799	12.550	8.985	7.784	6.434	4.937

Note that the present value of $1 to be received periodically (annually) for three years, discounted at 12% per year, is 2.402. Thus, $10,000 received annually for three years, discounted at 12%, is $24,020 ($10,000 × 2.402).

Discount periods of less than one year

The interval between regular periodic cash flows is termed the **discount period.** In our preceding examples we have assumed annual cash flows and, therefore, discount periods of one year. Often a note or a contract may call for cash payments on a more frequent basis, such as monthly, quarterly, or semiannually. The illustrated present value tables can be used with discount periods of any length, *but the discount rate must relate to the time interval of the discount period.* Thus, if we use the annuity table to find the present value of a series of monthly cash payments, the discount rate must be expressed as a monthly interest rate.

To illustrate, assume that StyleMart purchases merchandise from Western Fashions, issuing in exchange a $9,600 note payable to be paid in 24 monthly installments of $400 each. As discussed in Chapter 8, both companies should record this transaction at the present value of the note. If a reasonable *annual* interest rate for this type of note is 12%, we should discount the monthly cash payments at the *monthly* rate of 1%. The annuity table shows the present value of $1 to be received (or paid) for 24 monthly periods, discounted at 1% per month, is 21.243. Thus, the present value of the installment note issued by StyleMart is $8,497 ($400 × 21.243, rounded to the nearest dollar).

Accounting applications of the present value concept

Accounting applications of the concept of present value have been discussed at appropriate points throughout this textbook. We will now demonstrate these applications with examples which make use of our present value tables.

Valuation of long-term notes receivable and payable (Chapter 8). When a long-term note receivable or payable does not bear a realistic stated rate of interest, a portion of the face amount of the note should be regarded as representing an interest charge. The amount of this interest charge can be determined by discounting the note to its present value using as a discount rate a realistic rate of interest.

To illustrate, consider our preceding example in which StyleMart purchases merchandise from Western Fashions by issuing an installment note payable with a face amount of $9,600 and no stated rate of interest. The present value of this note, discounted at the realistic market interest rate of 1% per month, was $8,497. The difference between the $9,600 face amount of the note and its present value of $8,497 is $1,103, which represents the interest charge included in the face amount. StyleMart should use the present value of the note in determining the cost of the merchandise and the amount of the related net liability, as shown by the following entry:

Purchases	8,497	
Discount on Notes Payable	1,103	
Notes Payable		9,600

Purchased merchandise by issuing a 24-month installment note payable with a 1% monthly interest charge included in the face amount.

Assuming that StyleMart uses the effective interest method to amortize the discount on the note, the entry to record the first monthly payment and the related interest expense is as follows:

Notes Payable	400	
Interest Expense	85	
Discount on Notes Payable		85
Cash		400

To record first monthly payment on installment note payable and recognize one month's interest expense ($8,497 × 1%, rounded to nearest dollar).

Estimating the value of goodwill (Chapter 10). The asset goodwill may be defined as the present value of expected future earnings in excess of the normal return on net identifiable assets. One method of estimating goodwill is to estimate the annual amounts by which earnings are expected to exceed a normal return and then to discount these amounts to their present value.

For example, assume that John Reed is negotiating to purchase a small but very successful business. In addition to paying the fair market value of the company's net identifiable assets, Reed is willing to pay an appropriate amount for goodwill. He believes that the business will probably earn at least $40,000 in excess of "normal earnings" in each of the next five years. If Reed requires a 20% annual return on purchased goodwill, he would be willing to pay $119,640 for this expected five-year $40,000 annuity, computed as follows: $40,000 × 2.991 (from Table 2) = $119,640.

Market prices of bonds (Chapter 13). The market price of bonds may be regarded as the *present value* to bondholders of the future principal and interest payments. To illustrate, assume that a corporation issues $1,000,000 face value of 9%, 10-year bonds when the going market rate of interest is 10%. Since bond interest is paid semiannually, we must use 20 *semiannual* periods as the life of the bond issue and a 5% *semiannual* market rate of interest in our present value calculations. The expected issuance price of this bond issue may be computed as follows:

Present value of future principal payments:
  $1,000,000 due after 20 semiannual periods, discounted at 5% per period:
    $1,000,000 × .377 (from Table 1, page 569) $377,000
Present value of future interest payments:
  45,000 per period ($1,000,000 × 9% × ½) for 20 semiannual periods,
    discounted at 5%: $45,000 × 12.462 (from Table 2, page 570) 560,790
Expected issuance price of bond issue* $937,790

* **The terms of this bond issue correspond with those of the bond issue illustrated in the amortization table on page 545 in Chapter 13. In the amortization table, however, the issuance price of the bonds is $937,689, or $101 less than indicated by our computations above. The difference results from our rounding the present value of $1 to only three decimal places. Rounding to three decimal places may cause an error of up to $500 per $1 million.**

Capital leases (Chapter 13). A capital lease is regarded as a sale of the leased asset by the lessor to the lessee. At the date of this sale, the lessor recognizes sales revenue equal to the *present value* of the future lease payments receivable, discounted at a realistic rate of interest. The lessee also uses the present value of the future payments to determine the cost of the leased asset and the valuation of the related liability.

To illustrate, assume that on December 1, Kelly Grading Co. enters into a capital lease contract to finance the purchase of a bulldozer from Midwest Tractor Sales. The terms of the lease call for 24 monthly payments of $7,000 each, beginning on December 31. These lease payments include an interest charge of 1½% per month. At the end of the 24-month lease, title to the bulldozer will pass to Kelly Grading Co.

The annuity table on page 570 shows that the present value of $1 to be received monthly for 24 months, discounted at 1½% per month, is 20.030. Therefore, the present value of the 24 future lease payments is $7,000 × 20.030, or $140,210. Kelly Grading

Co. (the lessee) should use this present value in determining the cost of the bulldozer and the amount of the related liability, as shown in the following entry:

Entry by lessee

Leased Equipment 140,210
    Lease Payment Obligation 140,210
To record acquisition of bulldozer from Midwest Tractor Sales on a capital lease. Lease terms call for 24 monthly payments of $7,000, which include a 1½% monthly interest charge.

Note that the cost assigned to the leased equipment is only $140,210, even though Kelly Grading Co. must actually pay $168,000 ($7,000 × 24 payments) over the life of the lease. The difference between these two amounts, $27,790, will be recognized by Kelly Grading Co. as interest expense over the next 24 months.

    Midwest Tractor Sales (the lessor) should also use the present value of the future lease payments in determining the sales price of the bulldozer and the amount of the related receivable. Assuming that the bulldozer was carried in the perpetual inventory records at a cost of $110,000, the entry to record the sale is:

Entry by lessor

Lease Payments Receivable (net) 140,210
Cost of Goods Sold 110,000
    Inventory 110,000
    Sales 140,210
Financed sale of bulldozer to Kelly Grading Co. using a capital lease. Terms call for 24 monthly payments of $7,000 including a 1½% monthly interest charge. Gross amount of the receivable is $168,000, of which $27,790 is unearned interest.

Problems

D-1 Use of present value tables

Use the tables on pages 569 and 570 to determine the present value of the following cash flows:

a $10,000 to be paid annually for seven years, discounted at an annual rate of 12%.

b $6,300 to be received today, assuming that money can be invested to earn 15% annually.

c $600 to be paid monthly for 24 months, with an additional "balloon payment" of $15,000 due at the end of the twenty-fourth month, discounted at a monthly interest rate of 1½%.

d $40,000 to be received annually for the first three years, followed by $30,000 to be received annually for the next two years (total of five years in which payments are made), discounted at an annual rate of 15%.

D-2 Computation of bonds' market price

On June 30 of the current year, Rural Gas & Electric Co. issued $50,000,000 face value, 11%, 10-year bonds payable, with interest dates of December 31 and June 30. The bonds were issued at a discount, resulting in an effective semiannual interest rate of 6%. The company maintains its accounts on a calendar-year basis and amortizes the bond discount by the effective interest method.

Instructions

a Compute the issuance price for the bond issue which results in an effective semiannual interest rate of 6%. (Hint: Discount both the interest payments and the maturity value over 20 semian-nual periods.)

b Prepare all journal entries necessary to record the issuance of the bonds and bond interest expense during Year 1, assuming that the sales price of the bonds on June 30 was the amount you computed in part a.

D-3   Valuation of a note payable with interest in face amount

On December 1, Showcase Interiors purchased a shipment of furniture from Colonial House by paying $15,000 cash and issuing an installment note payable in the face amount of $36,000. The note is to be paid in 24 monthly installments of $1,500 each. Although the note makes no mention of an interest charge, the rate of interest usually charged to Showcase Interiors in such transactions is $1\frac{1}{2}$% per month.

Instructions

a Compute the present value of the note payable, using a discount rate of $1\frac{1}{2}$% per month.
b Prepare the journal entries in the accounts of Showcase Interiors on:
  (1) December 1, to record the purchase of the furniture (debit Purchases).
  (2) December 31, to record the first $1,500 monthly payment on the note and to recognize interest expense for one month by the effective interest method. (Round interest expense to the nearest dollar.)
c Show how the liability for this note would appear in the balance sheet at December 31. (Assume that the note is classified as a current liability.)

D-4   Discounting lease agreements to present value

Metropolitan Transit District plans to acquire a large computer system by entering into a long-term lease agreement with the computer manufacturer. The manufacturer will provide the computer system under either of the following lease agreements:

Five-year lease. MTD is to pay $2,500,000 at the beginning of the lease (delivery date) and $1,000,000 annually at the end of each of the next five years. At the end of the fifth year, MTD may take title to the system for an additional payment of $3,000,000.

Ten-year lease. MTD is to pay $2,000,000 at the beginning of the lease and $900,000 annually at the end of each of the next 10 years. At the end of the tenth year, MTD may take title for an additional payment of $1,300,000.

Under either proposal, MTD will buy the computer at the end of the lease. MTD is a governmental agency which does not seek to earn a profit and is not evaluating alternative investment opportunities. However, MTD does attempt to minimize its costs and it must borrow the money to finance either lease agreement at an annual interest rate of 12%.

Instructions

a Determine which lease proposal results in the lower cost for the computer system when the future cash outlays are discounted at an annual interest rate of 12%.
b Prepare a journal entry to record the acquisition of the computer system under the lease agreement selected in part a. This journal entry will include the initial cash payment to the computer manufacturer required at the beginning of the lease.

D-5   Valuation of note receivable with unrealistically low interest

On December 31, Year 5, Richland Farms sold a tract of land, which had cost $310,000, to Skyline

Developers in exchange for $50,000 cash and a five-year, 4%, note receivable for $300,000. Interest on the note is payable annually, and the principal amount is due on December 31, Year 10. The accountant for Richland Farms did not notice the unrealistically low interest rate on the note and made the following entry on December 31 to record this sale:

Cash	50,000	
Notes Receivable	300,000	
Land		310,000
Gain on Sale of Land		40,000

Sold land to Skyline Developers in exchange for cash and a five-year note with interest due annually.

Instructions

a Compute the present value of the note receivable from Skyline Developers, assuming that a realistic rate of interest for this transaction is 15%. (Hint: Consider both the annual interest payments and the principal amount of the note.)

b Prepare the journal entry on December 31, Year 5, to record the sale of the land correctly. Show supporting computations for (1) the gain or loss on the sale, and (2) the discount on the note receivable.

c Explain what effects the error made by Richland Farms' accountant will have upon (1) the net income for Year 5, and (2) the combined net income for Years 6 through 10. Ignore income taxes.

Part Five	Making use of accounting information
Chapter 14	Accounting principles and concepts; effects of inflation
Chapter 15	Statement of changes in financial position: cash flows
Chapter 16	Analysis and interpretation of financial statements
Chapter 17	Income taxes and business decisions

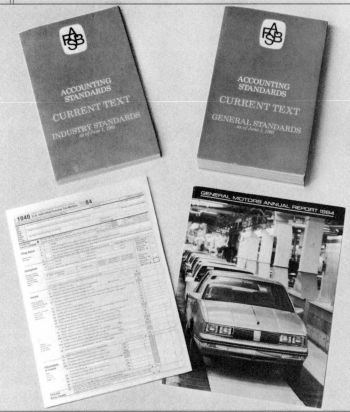

Our last four chapters cover a number of special topics relating to the use, understanding, and interpretation of accounting information. The first chapter reviews the theoretical concepts underlying financial reporting and illustrates how traditional accounting information can be adjusted for the effects of inflation. The next chapter shows how balance sheet and income statement information can be combined to form a new financial statement—the statement of changes in financial position. In the final two chapters, we discuss the analysis of financial statements by investors and the all-too-practical topic of income taxes.

Chapter 14
Accounting principles and concepts; effects of inflation

Throughout this text we try to explain the theoretical roots of each new accounting principle or standard as it first comes under consideration. In this chapter, we look back and review some of the major ideas, concepts, and traditions which form the "ground rules" for financial reporting. A second objective of the chapter is to introduce methods of adjusting accounting information for the effects of inflation. We explain and illustrate how net income can be measured under the alternative assumptions of constant dollars and current costs. Emphasis is focused upon the interpretation of income statements prepared under these assumptions.

After studying
this chapter you
should be able to:

✓ Identify the major sources of generally accepted accounting principles.
✓ Discuss the accounting principles, assumptions, and conventions presented on pages 581–589.
✓ Define an audit and discuss the nature of the auditors' report.
✓ Explain why the use of historical costs overstates profits during periods of inflation.
✓ Use a price index to restate historical costs to an equivalent number of today's dollars.
✓ Distinguish between the constant dollar and current cost approaches to measuring net income. Prepare an income statement using either approach.
✓ Explain why holding monetary items causes gains or losses in purchasing power.

Need for recognized accounting standards

The basic objective of financial statements is to provide information about a business enterprise; information that will be useful in making economic decisions. Investors, managers, economists, bankers, labor leaders, and government administrators all rely upon financial statements and other accounting reports in making the decisions which shape our economy. Therefore, it is of vital importance that the information contained in financial statements be highly reliable and clearly understood. Also, it is important for financial statements to be prepared in a manner which permits them to be compared fairly with prior years' statements and with financial statements of other companies. In short, we need a well-defined body of accounting principles or standards to guide accountants in preparing financial statements with the characteristics of *reliability, understandability,* and *comparability.*

Generally accepted accounting principles

The principles which constitute the "ground rules" for financial reporting are termed *generally accepted accounting principles.* Accounting principles are also referred to as *standards, assumptions, postulates, and concepts.* The various terms used to describe accounting principles indicate the many efforts which have been made to develop a satisfactory framework of accounting theory.[1] For example, the word *standards* was chosen rather than *principles* when the Financial Accounting Standards Board replaced the Accounting Principles Board as the top rule-making body of the accounting profession. The efforts to construct a satisfactory body of accounting theory are still in process, because accounting theory must continually change with changes in the business environment and changes in the needs of financial statement users.

Accounting principles are not rooted in laws of nature, as are the laws of the physical sciences. Rather, accounting principles are developed in relation to what we consider to be the most important objectives of financial reporting. For example, in recent years accountants as well as business executives have recognized that part of the "cost" to society of conducting certain types of economic activity includes the pollution of air and water and other damage to the environment. Research is currently being undertaken to develop accounting principles for the identification and measurement of these "social costs."

The conceptual framework project

The most recent effort to develop a comprehensive framework for financial accounting and reporting is the conceptual framework project of the Financial Accounting Standards Board. The FASB has described the conceptual framework as ". . . a coherent system of interrelated objectives and fundamentals that is expected to lead to consistent standards and that prescribes the nature, function, and limits of financial accounting and reporting."[2]

It is difficult to predict the extent to which the conceptual framework may affect the basic concepts and principles currently used in developing accounting information. Quite possibly, existing standards may not be affected at all. However, the framework should lead to internal consistency among future accounting standards developed by the FASB.

---

[1] See, for example, *Accounting Research Study No. 1,* "The Basic Postulates of Accounting," AICPA (New York: 1961); *Accounting Research Study No. 3,* "A Tentative Set of Broad Accounting Principles for Business Enterprises," AICPA (New York: 1962); and the series of *Statements of Financial Accounting Concepts* issued by the FASB.

[2] *FASB Statement of Financial Accounting Concepts No. 5,* "Recognition and Measurement in Financial Statements of Business Enterprises" (Stamford, Conn.: 1984).

Authoritative support for accounting principles

To qualify as "generally accepted," an accounting principle must usually receive "substantial authoritative support." The most influential authoritative groups in this country include (1) the American Institute of Certified Public Accountants (AICPA), (2) the Financial Accounting Standards Board (FASB), and (3) the Securities and Exchange Commission (SEC). The SEC is an agency of the federal government established to administer laws and regulations relating to the publication of financial information by large corporations. Also important in the development of accounting theory has been the American Accounting Association (AAA), an organization of accounting educators.[3]

American Institute of Certified Public Accountants (AICPA). The AICPA has long been concerned with stating and defining accounting principles because its members daily make decisions about generally accepted principles as they perform audits and other professional work. Some years ago, the AICPA established the Accounting Principles Board (APB), which issued 31 formal *Opinions* on specific accounting practices and also issued broad *Statements* designed to improve the quality of financial reporting. In 1973, the Accounting Principles Board was replaced by the Financial Accounting Standards Board. However, the Opinions and Statements of the APB *remain in effect.*

Financial Accounting Standards Board (FASB). The FASB was established by the AICPA as an independent body to assume the responsibilities of the former Accounting Principles Board. The FASB consists of seven full-time members, including representatives from public accounting, industry, government, and accounting education. Lending support to the FASB are an advisory council and a large research staff.

The FASB is authorized to issue *Statements of Financial Accounting Standards*, which represent authoritative expressions of generally accepted accounting principles. The FASB also has issued five *Statements of Financial Accounting Concepts* as part of its effort to develop a broad conceptual framework for financial accounting and reporting.

Securities and Exchange Commission (SEC). The SEC has legal authority to establish accounting principles and disclosure requirements for all large, publicly owned corporations. The views of the Commission on various accounting issues are published in the SEC's *Accounting Series Releases,* or *ASRs.* In the past, the SEC has tended to adopt or to modify the recommendations of the FASB, rather than to develop its own independent set of accounting principles.

American Accounting Association (AAA). The AAA has sponsored a number of research studies and monographs in which individual authors and Association committees attempt to summarize accounting principles. These statements have had considerable influence on the thinking of accounting theorists and practitioners. However, the AAA

---

[3] Other professional organizations which have influenced the development of accounting principles are the National Association of Accountants and the Financial Executives Institute. In addition to the SEC, the following government regulatory agencies influence financial reporting of business units falling under their jurisdiction: Federal Power Commission, Interstate Commerce Commission, and Federal Communications Commission.

lacks the power of the FASB to impose its collective view on accounting practice; it therefore exercises its influence through the prestige of its authors and the persuasiveness of their views.

In addition to the above sources, "substantial authoritative support" may include widespread use of an accounting practice within a particular industry, or general recognition of a practice in accounting literature.

Because accounting principles evolve in a constantly changing business environment, there is no complete list of generally accepted accounting principles. There is, however, a consensus among accountants and informed users of financial statements as to what these principles are. Most accounting principles are applicable to profit-making organizations of any size and form. We shall now discuss briefly the major principles that govern the accounting process and comment on some areas of controversy.

The accounting entity concept

One of the basic principles of accounting is that information is compiled for a clearly defined accounting entity. An accounting entity is any *economic unit* which controls resources and engages in economic activities. An individual is an accounting entity. So is a business enterprise, whether organized as a proprietorship, partnership, or corporation. Governmental agencies are accounting entities, as are all nonprofit clubs and organizations. An accounting entity also may be defined as an identifiable economic unit *within a larger accounting entity.* For example, the Chevrolet Division of General Motors Corporation may be viewed as an accounting entity separate from GM's other activities.

The economic unit for which accounting information is compiled also may be larger than a single corporation. *Consolidated financial statements* show the financial position and operating results of a group of affiliated corporations as though the affiliated companies were a single business organization. Consolidated financial statements were discussed in Appendix C following Chapter 12.

The basic accounting equation, Assets = Liabilities + Owners' Equity, reflects the accounting entity concept since the elements of the equation relate *to the particular entity whose economic activity is being reported in the financial statements.* Although we have considerable flexibility in defining our accounting entity, we must be careful to use the *same definition* in the measurement of assets, liabilities, owners' equity, revenue, and expense. An income statement would not make sense, for example, if it included all the revenue of General Motors Corporation but listed only the expenses of the Chevrolet Division.

The going-concern assumption

An underlying assumption in accounting is that an accounting entity will continue in operation for a period of time sufficient to carry out its existing commitments. The assumption of continuity, especially in the case of corporations, is in accord with experience in our economic system. This assumption leads to the concept of the *going concern.* In general, the going-concern concept means using cost as the basis for financial statements and ignoring liquidating values for assets and liabilities.

For example, suppose that a company has just purchased a three-year insurance policy for $5,000. If we assume that the business will continue in operation for three years or more, we will consider the $5,000 cost of the insurance as an asset which provides services (freedom from risk) to the business over a three-year period. On the other hand, if we assume that the business is likely to terminate in the near future, the insurance policy should be recorded at its cancellation value — the amount of cash which can be obtained from the insurance company as a refund on immediate cancellation of the policy, which may be, say, $4,500.

Although the assumption of a going concern is justified in most normal situations, it should be dropped when it is not in accord with the facts. Accountants are sometimes asked to prepare a statement of financial position for an enterprise that is about to liquidate. In this case the assumption of continuity is no longer valid and the accountant drops the going-concern assumption and reports assets at their current liquidating value and liabilities at the amount required to settle the debts immediately.

The time period principle

We assume an indefinite life for most accounting entities. However, accountants are asked to measure operating results and changes in economic position at relatively short time intervals during this indefinite life. Users of financial statements need yearly, quarterly, and perhaps monthly measurements for decision-making purposes.

The need for frequent measurements creates many of the accountant's most challenging problems. Dividing the life of an enterprise into time segments, such as a year or a quarter of a year, requires numerous estimates and assumptions. For example, estimates must be made of the useful lives of depreciable assets and assumptions must be made as to appropriate depreciation methods. Thus, yearly and quarterly measurements of net income and financial position are at best only informed estimates. The tentative nature of these measurements should be understood by those who rely on periodic accounting information.

The monetary principle

The monetary principle means that money is used as the basic measuring unit for financial reporting. Money is the common denominator in which accounting measurements are made and summarized. The dollar, or any other monetary unit, represents a unit of value; that is, it reflects ability to command goods and services. Implicit in the use of money as a measuring unit is the *assumption that the dollar is a stable unit of value,* just as the mile is a stable unit of distance and an acre is a stable unit of area.

Having accepted money as a measuring unit, accountants freely combine dollar measures of economic transactions that occur at various times during the life of an accounting entity. They combine, for example, a $20,000 cost of equipment purchased in 1970 and the $40,000 cost of similar equipment purchased in 1980 and report the total as a $60,000 investment in equipment.

Unlike the mile and the acre, which are stable units of distance and area, the dollar *is not a stable unit of value.* The prices of goods and services in our economy change over time. When the *general price level* (a phrase used to describe the average of all prices) increases, the value of money (that is, its ability to command goods and services) decreases.

Despite the steady erosion in the purchasing power of the dollar in the United States during the last 40 years, accountants have continued to prepare financial statements in which the value of the dollar is assumed to be stable. This unrealistic assumption is one of the reasons why financial statements are viewed by some critics as misleading. Accounting principles are currently evolving toward restatement of accounting information for the changing value of the dollar and toward the preparation of supplementary statements showing current replacement costs. The adjustment of accounting information to reflect the effects of inflation will be discussed in a subsequent section of this chapter.

The objectivity principle

The term *objective* refers to measurements that are unbiased and subject to verification by independent experts. For example, the price established in an arm's-length transaction is an objective measure of exchange value at the time of the transaction. Exchange prices established in business transactions constitute much of the raw material from which accounting information is generated. Accountants rely on various kinds of evidence to support their financial measurements, but they seek always the most objective evidence available. Invoices, contracts, paid checks, and physical counts of inventory are examples of objective evidence.

If a measurement is objective, 10 competent investigators who make the same measurement will come up with substantially identical results. However, 10 competent accountants who set out independently to measure the net income of a given business would *not* arrive at an identical result. Despite the goal of objectivity, it is not possible to insulate accounting information from opinion and personal judgment. The cost of a depreciable asset can be determined objectively but not the periodic depreciation expense. To measure the cost of the asset services that have been used up during a given period requires estimates of the residual value and service life of the asset and judgment as to the depreciation method that should be used. Such estimates and judgments can produce significant variations in net income.

Objectivity in accounting has its roots in the quest for reliability. Accountants want to make their economic measurements reliable and, at the same time, as relevant to decision makers as possible. Where to draw the line in the trade-off between *reliability* and *relevance* is one of the crucial issues in accounting theory. Thus, accountants are constantly faced with the necessity of compromising between what users of financial information would like to know and what it is possible to measure with a reasonable degree of reliability.

Asset valuation: the cost principle

Both the balance sheet and the income statement are affected by the cost principle. Assets are initially recorded in the accounts at cost, and no adjustment is made to this valuation in later periods, except to allocate a portion of the original cost to expense as the assets expire. At the time an asset is originally acquired, cost represents the "fair market value" of the goods or services exchanged, as evidenced by an arm's-length transaction. With the passage of time, however, the fair market value of such assets as land and buildings may change greatly from their historical cost. These later changes in fair market value generally have been ignored in the accounts, and the assets have continued to be valued in the balance sheet at historical cost (less the portion of that cost which has been allocated to expense).

Increasing numbers of professional accountants believe that current market values should be used as the basis for asset valuation rather than historical cost. These accountants argue that current values would result in a more meaningful balance sheet. Also, they claim that current values should be allocated to expense to represent fairly the cost to the entity of the goods or services consumed in the effort to generate revenue.

The cost principle is derived from the principle of *objectivity.* Those who support the cost principle argue that it is important that users have confidence in financial statements, and this confidence can best be maintained if accountants recognize changes in assets and liabilities only on the basis of completed transactions. Objective evidence generally exists to support cost, but evidence supporting current values may be less readily available.

Measuring revenue: the realization principle

When should revenue be recognized? Under the assumptions of accrual accounting, revenue should be recognized "when it is earned." However, the "earning" of revenue usually is an extended *economic process* and does not actually take place at a single point in time.

Some revenue, such as interest earned, is directly related to time periods. For this type of revenue, it is easy to determine how much revenue has been earned by computing how much of the earning process is complete. However, the earning process for sales revenue relates to *economic activity* rather than to a specific period of time. In a manufacturing business, for example, the earning process involves (1) acquisition of raw materials, (2) production of finished goods, (3) sale of the finished goods, and (4) collection of cash from credit customers.

In the manufacturing example, there is little objective evidence to indicate how much revenue has been earned during the first two stages of the earning process. Accountants therefore usually do not recognize revenue until the revenue has been *realized.* Revenue is realized when both of the following conditions are met: (1) the earning process is *essentially complete* and (2) *objective evidence* exists as to the amount of revenue earned.

In most cases, the realization principle indicates that revenue should be recognized *at the time of the sale of goods or the rendering of services.* Recognizing revenue at this point is logical because the firm has essentially completed the earning process and the realized value of the goods or services sold can be measured objectively in terms of the price billed to customers. At any time prior to sale, the realizable value of the goods or services being offered for sale can only be estimated. After the sale, the only step that remains is to collect from the customer, and this is usually a relatively certain event.

In Chapter 3, we described a *cash basis* of income measurement whereby revenue is recognized only when cash is collected from customers and expenses are recorded only when cash is actually paid out. Cash basis accounting *does not conform* to generally accepted accounting principles, but it is widely used by individuals in determining their *taxable* income. (Remember that the accounting methods used in income tax returns often differ from those used in financial statements.)

The installment method. Companies selling goods on the installment plan sometimes use the installment method of accounting for income tax purposes. Under the installment method, the seller recognizes the gross profit on sales gradually over an extended time span as the cash is actually collected from customers. If the gross profit rate on installment sales is 30%, then out of every dollar collected on installment receivables, the sum of 30 cents represents gross profit.

To illustrate, assume that on December 15, Year 1, a retailer sells for $400 a television set which cost $280, or 70% of the sales price. The terms of the sale call for a $100 cash down payment with the balance payable in 15 monthly installments of $20 each, beginning on January 1, Year 2. (Interest charges are ignored in this illustration.) The collections of cash and recognition of profit under the installment method are summarized below:

Installment method illustrated

Year	Cash Collected	—	Cost Recovery, 70%	=	Profit Earned, 30%
1	$100		$ 70		$ 30
2	240		168		72
3	60		42		18
Totals	$400		$280		$120

This method of profit recognition exists largely because it is allowed for income tax purposes; it postpones the payment of income taxes until cash is collected from customers. From an accounting viewpoint, there is little theoretical justification for delaying the recognition of profit beyond the point of sale. Therefore, the installment method is seldom used in financial statements.[4]

Percentage-of-completion: an exception to the realization principle. Under certain circumstances, accountants may depart from the realization principle and recognize income during the production process. An example arises in the case of long-term construction contracts, such as the building of a dam over a period of 10 years. Clearly the income statements of a company engaged in such a project would not be useful to managers or investors if no profit or loss were reported until the dam was finally completed. The accountant therefore estimates the portion of the dam completed during each accounting period, and recognizes the gross profit on the project *in proportion* to the work completed. This is known as the percentage-of-completion method of accounting for long-term contracts.

The percentage-of-completion method works as follows:

1 An estimate is made of the total costs to be incurred and the total profit to be earned over the life of the project.
2 Each period, an estimate is made of the portion of the total project completed during the period. This estimate is usually made by expressing the costs incurred during the period as a percentage of the estimated total cost of the project.
3 The percentage figure determined in step 2 is applied to the estimated total profit on

---

[4] Under generally accepted accounting principles, use of the installment method is permissible only when the amounts likely to be collected on installment sales are so uncertain that no reasonable basis exists for estimating an allowance for doubtful accounts.

the contract to compute the amount of profit applicable to the current accounting period.

4 No estimate is made of the percentage of work during the final period. In the period in which the project is completed, any remaining profit is recognized.

To illustrate, assume that Reed Construction Company enters into a contract to build an irrigation canal at a price of $5,000,000. The canal will be built over a three-year period at an estimated total cost of $4,000,000. Therefore, the estimated total profit on the project is $1,000,000. The following schedule shows the actual costs incurred and the amount of profit to be recognized in each of the three years using the percentage-of-completion method:

	(A)	(B)	(C)
		Percentage of Work	Profit Considered
	Actual Costs	Done in Year	Earned
Year	Incurred	(Column A ÷ $4,000,000)	($1,000,000 × Column B)
1	$ 600,000	15	$150,000
2	2,000,000	50	500,000
3	1,452,000	*	298,000 balance
Totals	$4,052,000		$948,000

Profit recognized as work progresses (margin note)

* Balance required to complete the contract.

The percentage of the work completed during Year 1 was estimated by dividing the actual cost incurred in the year by the estimated total cost of the project ($600,000 ÷ $4,000,000 = 15%). Because 15% of the work was done in Year 1, 15% of the estimated total profit of $1,000,000 was considered earned in that year ($1,000,000 × 15% = $150,000). Costs incurred in Year 2 amounted to 50% of the estimated total costs ($2,000,000 ÷ $4,000,000 = 50%); thus, 50% of the estimated total profit was recognized in Year 2 ($1,000,000 × 50% = $500,000). Note that no percentage of work completed figure was computed for Year 3. In Year 3, the total actual cost is known ($4,052,000), and the actual total profit on the contract is determined to be $948,000 ($5,000,000 − $4,052,000). Since profits of $650,000 were previously recognized in Years 1 and 2, the *remaining* profit ($948,000 − $650,000 = $298,000) must be recognized in Year 3.

Although an expected *profit* on a long-term construction contract is recognized in proportion to the work completed, a different treatment is accorded to an expected *loss.* If at the end of any accounting period it appears that a loss will be incurred on a contract in progress, the *entire loss should be recognized at once.*

The percentage-of-completion method should be used only when the total profit expected to be earned can be *reasonably estimated in advance.* If there are substantial uncertainties in the amount of profit which will ultimately be earned, no profit should be recognized until *production is completed.* This approach is often referred to as the *completed-contract method.* If the completed-contract method had been used in the preceding example, no profit would have been recognized in Years 1 and 2; the entire profit of $948,000 would be recorded in Year 3 when the contract was completed and actual costs known.

Measuring expenses: the matching principle

Revenue, the gross increase in net assets resulting from the production or sale of goods and services, is offset by expenses incurred in bringing the firm's output to the point of sale. Examples of expenses relating to revenue are the cost of merchandise sold, the expiration of asset services, and out-of-pocket expenditures for operating costs. The measurement of expenses occurs in two stages: (1) measuring the *cost* of goods and services that will be consumed or will expire in generating revenue and (2) determining *when* the goods and services acquired have contributed to revenue and their cost thus *becomes an expense.* The second aspect of the measurement process is often referred to as *matching costs and revenue* and is fundamental to the *accrual basis* of accounting.

Costs are matched with revenue in two major ways:

1   In relation to the product sold or service rendered. If goods or services can be related to the product or service which constitutes the output of the enterprise, their cost becomes an expense when the product is sold or the service rendered to customers. The cost of goods sold in a merchandising firm is a good example of this type of expense. Similarly, a commission paid to a real estate salesperson by a real estate brokerage office is an expense directly related to the revenue generated by the salesperson.

2   In relation to the time period during which revenue is earned. Some costs incurred by businesses cannot be directly related to the product or service output of the firm. Expired fire insurance, property taxes, depreciation on a building, the salary of the president of the company—all are examples of costs incurred in generating revenue which cannot be related to specific transactions. The accountant refers to this class of costs as *period costs,* and charges them to expense by associating them with the *period of time* during which they are incurred and presumably contribute to revenue, rather than by associating them with specific revenue-producing transactions.

The consistency principle

The principle of *consistency* implies that a particular accounting method, once adopted, will not be changed from year to year. This assumption is important because it assists users of financial statements in interpreting changes in financial position and changes in net income.

Consider the confusion which would result if a company ignored the principle of consistency and changed its method of depreciation every year. The company could cause its net income for any given year to increase or decrease merely by changing its depreciation method.

The principle of consistency does not mean that a company should *never* make a change in its accounting methods. In fact, a company *should* make a change if a proposed new accounting method will provide more useful information than does the method presently in use. But when a significant change in accounting methods does occur, the fact that a change has been made and the dollar effects of the change should be *fully disclosed* in the financial statements. In audited financial statements, the disclosure of a change in accounting method is also incorporated in the CPA's opinion on the financial statements. A typical disclosure might read as follows: "During the current year the company changed from the declining-balance method of computing depreciation to the straight-line method. This change in method had the effect of increasing net income by $210,000."

Consistency applies to a single accounting entity and increases the comparability of financial statements from period to period. Different companies, even those in the same industry, may follow different accounting methods. For this reason, it is important to determine the accounting methods used by companies whose financial statements are being compared.

The disclosure principle

Adequate disclosure means that all **material** and **relevant facts** concerning financial position and the results of operations **are communicated to users.** This can be accomplished either in the financial statements or in the notes accompanying the statements. Such disclosure should make the financial statements more useful and less subject to misinterpretation.

Adequate disclosure does not require that information be presented in great detail; it does require, however, that no important facts be witheld. For example, if a company has been named as defendant in a large lawsuit, this information must be disclosed. Other examples of information which should be disclosed in financial statements include:

1 A summary of the accounting methods used in the preparation of the statements
2 Dollar effects of any changes in these accounting methods during the current period
3 Other significant events affecting financial position, including major new contracts for sale of goods or services, labor strikes, shortages of raw materials, and pending legislation directly affecting the operations of the business
4 Identification of assets which have been pledged as collateral to secure loans
5 Terms of major borrowing arrangements and existence of large contingent liabilities
6 Contractual provisions relating to leasing arrangements, employee pension and bonus plans, and major proposed asset acquisitions

Even significant events which occur **after** the end of the accounting period but before the financial statements are issued may need to be disclosed.

Naturally, there are practical limits to the amount of disclosure that can be made in financial statements and the accompanying notes. The key point to bear in mind is that the supplementary information should be **relevant to the users** of the financial statements.

Materiality

The term **materiality** refers to the **relative importance** of an item or event. Accountants are primarily concerned with significant information and are not overly concerned with those items which have little effect on financial statements. For example, should the cost of a pencil sharpener, a wastepaper basket, or a stapler be recorded in asset accounts and depreciated over their useful lives? Even though more than one period will benefit from the use of these assets, the concept of materiality permits the immediate recognition of the cost of these items as an expense on grounds that it would be too expensive to undertake depreciation accounting for such low-cost assets and that the results would not differ significantly.

We must recognize that the materiality of an item is a relative matter; what is material for one business unit may not be material for another. Materiality of an item may depend not only on its *amount* but also on its *nature.* In summary, we can state the following rule: *An item is material if there is a reasonable expectation that knowledge of it would influence the decisions of prudent users of financial statements.*

Conservatism as a guide in resolving uncertainties

We have previously referred to the use of *conservatism* in connection with the measurement of net income and the reporting of accounts receivable and inventories in the balance sheet. Although the concept of conservatism may not qualify as an accounting principle, it has long been a powerful influence upon asset valuation and income determination. Conservatism is most useful when matters of judgment or estimates are involved. Ideally, accountants should base their estimates on sound logic and select those accounting methods which neither overstate nor understate the facts. When some doubt exists about the valuation of an asset or the realization of a gain, however, accountants traditionally select the accounting option which produces a lower net income for the current period and a less favorable financial position.

An example of conservatism is the traditional practice of pricing inventory at the lower of cost or market (replacement cost). Decreases in the market value of the inventory are recognized as a part of the cost of goods sold in the current period, but increases in market value of inventory are ignored. Failure to apply conservatism when valuations are especially uncertain may produce misleading information and result in losses to creditors and stockholders.

CPA's opinion on published financial statements

The annual financial statements of large corporations are used by great numbers of stockholders, creditors, government regulators, and members of the general public. What assurance do these people have that the information in these statements is reliable and is presented in conformity with generally accepted accounting principles? The answer is that the annual financial statements of large corporations are *audited* by independent certified public accountants (CPAs).

An audit is a thorough investigation of every item, dollar amount, and disclosure which appears in the financial statements. After completing the audit, the CPAs express their opinion as to the *fairness* of the financial statements. This opinion, called the *auditors' report,* is published with the statements in the company's annual report to its stockholders.

Considering the extensive investigation that precedes it, the audit opinion is surprisingly short. It usually consists of two brief paragraphs, unless the CPAs comment on unusual features of the financial statements. The first paragraph describes the *scope* of the auditors' examination; the second states their *opinion* of the financial statements. A report by a CPA firm might read as follows:

> We have examined the balance sheet of American Oil Corporation as of December 31, 19__, and the related statements of income, retained earnings, and the changes in financial position for the year then ended. Our examination was made in accordance with generally accepted auditing standards, and accordingly included such tests of the accounting records and such other auditing procedures as we considered necessary in the circumstances.
>
> *In our opinion*, the financial statements referred to above *present fairly* the financial position of American Oil Corporation at December 31, 19__, and the results of its operations and the changes in its financial position for the year then ended, *in conformity with generally accepted accounting principles* applied on a basis *consistent with that of the preceding year.* [Emphasis supplied.]

Over many decades, audited financial statements have developed an excellent track record of reliability. Note, however, that the CPAs *do not guarantee* the accuracy of financial statements; rather, they render their *professional opinion* as to the overall *fairness* of the statements. "Fairness," in this context, means that the financial statements are *not misleading.* However, just as a physician may make an error in the diagnosis of a particular patient, there is always a possibility that an auditor's opinion may be in error. The primary responsibility for the reliability of financial statements rests with the management of the issuing company, not with the independent CPAs.

INFLATION—THE GREATEST CHALLENGE TO ACCOUNTING

Inflation may be defined either as an increase in the general price level or as a decrease in the purchasing power of the dollar. The *general price level* is the weighted average of the prices of all goods and services in the economy. Changes in the general price level are measured by a *general price index* with a base year assigned a value of 100. The index compares the level of current prices with that of the base year. Assume, for example, that Year 1 is the base year. If prices rise by 10% during Year 2, the price index at the end of Year 2 will be 110. At the end of Year 9 the price index might be 200, indicating that the general price level had doubled since Year 1.

The most widely recognized measure of the general price level in the United States is the Consumer Price Index (CPI), published monthly by the Bureau of Labor Statistics. The base year of the Consumer Price Index is 1967. In May 1983, the CPI passed the 300 level, indicating that prices (on the average) had tripled since 1967.

We often hear statements such as "Today's dollar is worth only 33 cents." The "worth" or "value" of a dollar lies in its ability to buy goods or services. This "value" is called *purchasing power.* The reciprocal of the general price index (100 divided by the current level of the index) represents the purchasing power of the dollar in the current year *relative to that in the base year.* For example, the reciprocal of the CPI in May 1983, was $100 \div 300$, or .33⅓. Therefore, we might say that $1 in 1983 was equivalent in purchasing power to about 33 cents in 1967.

What effect do material changes in general price levels, and thus changes in the value of money, have on accounting measures? By combining transactions measured in dollars of various years, the accountant in effect ignores changes in the size of the measuring unit. For example, suppose that a company purchased land early in Year 1 for $200,000 and sold this land for $400,000 late in Year 10. Using the dollar as a measuring unit, we would recognize a gain of $200,000 ($400,000 sales price — $200,000 cost) on the sale of the land. But if prices doubled during that 10-year period and the value of money was cut in half, we might say that the company was *no better off* as a result of buying and selling this land. The $400,000 received for the land in Year 10 represents the same command over goods and services as $200,000 did when invested in the land in Year 1.

We have experienced persistent inflation in the United States for over 40 years; more importantly, the forces which have been built into our economic and political institutions almost guarantee that inflation will continue. The only question is how severe the inflationary trend will be. Our traditional accounting process is based upon the assumption of a stable dollar. This cost-based system works extremely well in periods of stable prices; it works reasonably well during prolonged but mild inflation; but it loses virtually all meaning if inflation becomes extreme. The greatest single challenge to the accounting profession today is to develop new accounting methods that will bring financial statements into accord with the economic reality of an inflationary environment.

Profits — fact or illusion?

Corporate profits are watched closely by business managers, investors, and government officials. The trend of these profits plays a significant role in the allocation of the nation's investment resources, in levels of employment, and in national economic policy. As a result of the *stable monetary assumption,* however, a strong argument may be made that much of the corporate profit reported today is an illusion.

In the measurement of business income, a distinction must be drawn between profit and the recovery of costs. A business earns a profit only when the value of goods sold and services rendered (revenue) *exceeds* the value of resources consumed in the earning process (costs and expenses). Accountants have traditionally assigned "values" to resources consumed in the earning process by using historical dollar amounts. Depreciation expense, for example, may be based upon prices paid to acquire assets 10 or 20 years ago.

When the general price level is rising rapidly, such historical costs may significantly understate the current economic value of the resources being consumed. If costs and expenses are understated, it follows that reported profits are overstated. In other words, the stable monetary assumption may lead to reporting *illusory* profits; much of the net income reported by business enterprises actually may be a return of costs.

When reported profit is actually a return of costs, what we label as income taxes is in reality a tax upon invested capital. Moreover, dividends labeled as distributions of earnings are in fact being paid from capital. The reporting of large, but fictitious, profits also leads to demands for higher wages consistent with the reported profits.

In summary, the real world is one of inflation. If we continue to measure profits on the assumption that price levels do not change, financial statements will be misleading and out of touch with reality. Several broad social consequences appear to follow. For one, corporate liquidity (debt-paying ability) may fall so low as to bring an economic crisis. Secondly, since we allocate economic resources in large part on the basis of financial statements, poor allocation of resources may be the end consequence of ignoring inflation in our financial reporting. Finally, the overstatement of profits may lead to an unrecognized failure to maintain reasonable rates of capital formation. A nation with a declining rate of capital formation will find it difficult to hold its relative position in a competitive world economy or to achieve a rising standard of living.

Two approaches to "inflation accounting"

Two alternative approaches to modifying our accounting process to cope with inflation have received much attention. These two approaches are:

1 **Constant dollar accounting.** Under this approach, historical costs in the financial statements are adjusted to the **number of current dollars representing an equivalent amount of purchasing power.** Thus, all amounts are expressed in units (current dollars) of equal purchasing power. Since a general price index is used in restating the historical costs, constant dollar accounting shows the effects of changes in the **general** price level. Constant dollar accounting is also called **general price level** accounting.

2 **Current cost accounting.** This method differs from constant dollar accounting in that assets and expenses are shown in the financial statements at the current cost to **replace** those specific resources. The **current replacement cost** of a specific asset may rise or fall at a different rate from the general price level. Thus, current cost accounting shows the effects of **specific price changes,** rather than changes in the general price level.

To illustrate these approaches to "inflation accounting," assume that in Year 1 you purchased 500 pounds of sugar for $100 when the general price index was at 100. Early in Year 2, you sold the sugar for $108 when the general price index was at 110 and the replacement cost of 500 pounds of sugar was $104. What is the amount of your profit or loss on this transaction? The amount of profit or loss determined under current accounting standards (unadjusted historical cost) and the two "inflation accounting" alternatives is shown below.

	Unadjusted Historical Cost	Adjusted for General Inflation (Constant Dollars)	Adjusted for Changes in Specific Prices (Current Costs)
Revenue	$108	$108	$108
Cost of goods sold	100	110	104
Profit (loss)	$ 8	$ (2)	$ 4

Which "cost" of goods sold is most realistic?

Under each method, an amount is deducted from revenue to provide for recovery of cost. However, the value assigned to the "cost" of goods sold differs under each of the three approaches.

Unadjusted historical cost. This method is used in current accounting practice. The use of unadjusted historical cost is based upon the assumption that the dollar is a stable unit of measure. Profit is determined by comparing sales revenue with the *historical cost* of the asset sold. In using this approach to income determination, accountants assume that a business is as well off when it has recovered its *original dollar investment,* and that it is better off whenever it recovers more than the original number of dollars invested in any given asset.

In our example of buying and selling sugar, the profit figure of $8 shows *how many dollars* you came out ahead. However, this approach ignores the fact that Year 1 dollars and Year 2 dollars are *not equivalent in terms of purchasing power.* It also ignores the fact that the $100 deduction intended to provide for the recovery of cost is not sufficient to allow you to *replace* the 500 pounds of sugar.

Constant dollar accounting. When financial statements are adjusted for changes in the general price level, historical amounts are restated as the number of current dollars *equivalent in purchasing power* to the historical cost. Profit is determined by comparing revenue with the *amount of purchasing power* (stated in current dollars) originally invested.

The general price index tells us that $110 in Year 2 is equivalent in purchasing power to the $100 invested in sugar in Year 1. But you do not have $110 in Year 2; you received only $108 dollars from the sale of the sugar. Thus, you have sustained a *$2 loss in purchasing power.*

Current cost accounting. In current cost accounting, profit is measured by comparing revenue with the *current replacement cost* of the assets consumed in the earning process. The logic of this approach lies in the concept of the going concern. What will you do with the $108 received from the sale of the sugar? If you are going to continue in the sugar business, you will have to buy more sugar. At current market prices, it will cost you $104 to replace 500 pounds of sugar; the remaining $4, therefore, is designated as profit.

Current cost accounting recognizes in the income statement the costs which a going concern actually has to pay to replace its expiring assets. The resulting profit figure, therefore, closely parallels the maximum amount which a business could distribute to its owners and still be able to maintain the present size and scale of its operations.

Which approach measures income? Which of these three approaches correctly measures income? The answer is that all three methods provide a correct measurement, but that each approach utilizes a different definition of "cost" and of "income." The real question confronting the accounting profession is which of these alternative measures of income is the *most useful to decision makers?* This question has been considered very carefully by the FASB, the SEC, and other interested parties. However, there is not yet widespread agreement as to the answer.

FASB Statement No. 33 — disclosing the effects of inflation in financial statements

Perhaps the day is coming when constant dollar or current cost information will replace the use of historical costs in financial statements. However, a change of this magnitude cannot be made without much planning and consideration of the possible consequences. Accounting information is used on a daily basis by millions of economic decision makers. A major change in the nature of this information is sure to affect the allocation of resources within our economy. Decision makers would have to learn to interpret the new information; capital would move out of some industries and into others; income tax laws and other government economic policies might change. In light of these considerations, careful experimentation with constant dollar and current cost information is needed before we abandon the use of historical costs as our basis for financial statements.

As an experimental step, the FASB issued **Statement No. 33,** which requires large corporations to include with their cost-based financial statements **supplementary schedules** showing certain constant dollar and current cost information. Note that this information is supplementary to the conventional financial statements and does not replace them.

Original disclosure requirements for constant dollars and current costs

Statement No. 33 applies only to large corporations — those with total assets of $1 billion or total inventories and plant assets (before deducting accumulated depreciation) of more than $125 million. However, the FASB also encourages (but does not require) all business organizations of every size to comply with the provisions of the *Statement.*[5]

Among the supplementary disclosures originally required by *Statement No. 33* were the following:[6]

1 Net income measured in constant dollars[7]
2 The gain or loss in purchasing power which results from holding monetary assets or having monetary liabilities
3 Net income on a current cost basis

In 1984, the FASB somewhat reduced the amount of required disclosure. However, a look at the original requirements of *Statement No. 33* will help to illustrate the basic concepts of both constant dollar and current cost accounting. The modification of these original requirements will be discussed later in this chapter.

The format used by many companies to disclose constant dollar and current cost information is illustrated below. (The three specific disclosures listed in the preceding paragraph are identified by the numbered arrows.)

---

[5] *FASB Statement No. 33,* "Financial Reporting and Changing Prices," FASB (Stamford, Conn.: 1979), par. 23–25.

[6] Other disclosure requirements of *Statement No. 33,* including changes in current costs and five-year summaries, will be discussed in an intermediate level accounting course.

[7] When a company discontinues a segment of its operations or reports an extraordinary item in its income statement, the subtotal, Income from Continuing Operations, is disclosed instead of the net income figure.

Which income figure do you think is most realistic?

Supplement to financial statements:

FLATION COMPANY
Income Statement Adjusted for Changing Prices
For Year 10

	As Reported in the Primary Statements	Adjusted for General Inflation (Constant Dollars)*	Adjusted for Changes in Specific Prices (Current Costs)
Net sales	$600,000	$600,000	$600,000
Cost and expenses:			
Cost of goods sold	$360,000	$370,000	$391,500
Depreciation expense	60,000	80,000	90,000
Other expenses	130,000	130,000	130,000
Total	$550,000	$580,000	$611,500
Net income	$ 50,000	① ⟶ $ 20,000	③ ⟶ $ (11,500)
Net gain from decline in purchasing power		②	
of net amounts owed		⟶ $ 8,000	

* Stated in dollars of average purchasing power during Year 10.

We shall now use the information in this illustration to demonstrate further the concepts of constant dollar and current cost accounting and to interpret these disclosures from the viewpoint of the financial statement user.

Net income measured in constant dollars

A basic problem with the use of historical costs for measuring income is that revenue and expenses may be stated in dollars having different amounts of purchasing power. Sales revenue, for example, is recorded in current-year dollars. Depreciation expense, on the other hand, is based upon dollars spent to acquire assets in past years. As previously emphasized, dollars in the current year and dollars of past years are not equivalent in terms of purchasing power.

In a constant dollar income statement, expenses based on "old" dollars are *restated* at the number of current dollars representing the equivalent amount of purchasing power. When all revenue and expenses are stated in units of similar purchasing power, we can see whether the business is gaining or losing in terms of the amount of purchasing power it controls.

To restate a historical amount in terms of an equivalent number of current dollars, we multiply the historical amount by the ratio of the current price level to the historical price level, as illustrated below:

Converting to current dollars

$$\text{Historical cost} \times \frac{\text{Average price index for current period}}{\text{Index at date of historical cost}} = \frac{\text{Equivalent number}}{\text{of current dollars}}$$

For example, assume that land was purchased for $100,000 when the price index stood at 100. If the price index is now 170, we may find the number of current dollars equivalent to the purchasing power originally invested in the land by multiplying the $100,000 historical cost by *170/100.* The result, $170,000 represents the number of current dollars equivalent in purchasing power to the 100,000 historical dollars.

Price index levels for our illustration. The following changes in the general price index are assumed in our Flation Company illustration:

Date	Price Index
Beginning of Year 8 (acquisition date for depreciable assets)	150
End of Year 9	180
Average price level for Year 10*	200
End of Year 10	216
Rate of inflation for Year 10†	20%

* The "average" price level for the year is computed as a monthly average and need not lie exactly halfway between the price levels at the beginning and end of the year.
† The inflation rate is computed by dividing the increase in the price index over the year by the price index at the beginning of the year: $(216 - 180) \div 180 = 20\%$.

In restating historical dollars to current dollars, we shall use the *average price level* for Year 10 (200) to represent the purchasing power of current dollars.[8]

Not all amounts are restated. Compare the constant dollar and historical cost income statements of the Flation Company for Year 10 (page 595). Note that only two items—depreciation expense and the cost of goods sold—have been restated in the constant dollar statement. Sales revenue and expenses other than depreciation consist of transactions occurring during the current year. Therefore, these amounts are *already* stated in current dollars. We need to adjust to current dollars only those expenses which are based on costs incurred in past years.

Restating depreciation expense. Assume that Flation Company's depreciation expense all relates to equipment purchased early in Year 8 when the price level was 150. The equipment cost $600,000 and is being depreciated over 10 years by the straight-line method. Since the average price level in Year 10 is 200, the purchasing power originally invested in this equipment is equivalent to $800,000 current dollars ($600,000 \times \frac{200}{150} = $800,000). Thus, the amount of purchasing power expiring in Year 10, stated in current dollars, is $80,000 ($800,000 \div 10 years).

A shortcut approach is simply to restate the historical depreciation expense, as follows:

Historical Dollars		Conversion Ratio		Equivalent Current Dollars
$60,000	×	200/150	=	$80,000

[8] An acceptable alternative is to use the year-end price level to represent the purchasing power of current dollars. However, use of the year-end price level means that all income statement amounts, including revenue and expense transactions conducted during the current year, must be restated. For this reason, the vast majority of companies presenting constant dollar information use the average price level for the current year.

Since depreciable assets are long-lived, the price level prevailing when the assets were acquired may be substantially different from the current price level. In such cases, the amount of depreciation expense recognized becomes one of the most significant differences between historical dollar and current dollar financial statements.

Restating the cost of goods sold. During Year 10, Flation Company sold merchandise with a historical cost of $360,000. Assume that $90,000 of these goods came from the beginning inventory, acquired at the end of Year 9 when the price level was 180; the remaining $270,000 of these goods were purchased during Year 10. The restatement of the cost of goods sold to average Year 10 dollars is shown below:

	Historical Dollars	Conversion Ratio	Equivalent Current Dollars
Beginning inventory	$ 90,000 ×	200/180 =	$100,000
Purchased in Year 10	270,000	*	270,000
Cost of goods sold	$360,000		$370,000

* No adjustment necessary—amount already is stated in current dollars.

Interpreting the constant dollar income statement

The basic difference between historical dollar and constant dollar income statements is the unit of measure. Historical dollar income statements use the dollar as a basic unit of measure. The unit of measure in constant dollar income statements is the *purchasing power of the current dollar.*

A conventional income statement shows how many dollars were added to owners' equity from the operation of the business. Identifying a dollar increase in owners' equity as "income" implies that owners are better off when they recover more than the original number of dollars they invested. No attention is given to the fact that a greater number of dollars may still have less purchasing power than was originally invested.

A *constant dollar* income statement shows whether the *inflow of purchasing power* from current operations is larger or smaller than the *purchasing power consumed* in the effort to generate revenue. In short, the net income figure tells us whether the amount of purchasing power controlled by the business has increased or decreased as a result of operations.

Gains and losses in purchasing power

Constant dollar accounting introduces a new consideration in measuring the effects of inflation upon a business: gains and losses in purchasing power from holding monetary items. *Monetary items* are those assets and liabilities representing claims to a *fixed number of dollars.* Examples of monetary assets are cash, notes receivable, and accounts receivable; most liabilities are monetary, including notes payable and accounts payable.

Holding monetary assets during a period of rising prices results in a loss of purchasing power because the value of the money is falling. In contrast, owing money during a period of rising prices gives rise to a gain in purchasing power because debts may be repaid using dollars of less purchasing power than those originally borrowed.

To illustrate, assume that Flation Company held $30,000 in cash throughout Year 10, while the price level rose 20% (from 180 to 216). By the end of the year, this $30,000 cash balance will have lost 20% of its purchasing power, as demonstrated by the following analysis:

Number of dollars needed at year-end to represent the same purchasing power as
$30,000 at the beginning of the year ($30,000 × 216/180) $36,000
Number of dollars actually held at year-end 30,000
Loss in purchasing power as a result of holding monetary assets .... $ 6,000

(We can also compute this $6,000 loss simply by multiplying the amount of the monetary assets held throughout the year by the 20% inflation rate: $30,000 × 20% = $6,000.)

A similar analysis is applied to any monetary liabilities. Assume, for example, that Flation Company has a $70,000 note payable outstanding throughout Year 10. The resulting gain in purchasing power is computed as follows:

Number of dollars at year-end representing the same purchasing power as $70,000
owed at the beginning of year ($70,000 × 216/180) $84,000
Number of dollars actually owed at year-end 70,000
Gain in purchasing power as a result of owing a fixed number of dollars $14,000

FASB Statement No. 33 requires disclosure of the **net gain or loss** from holding monetary assets and owing monetary liabilities. Flation Company has experienced an $8,000 net gain in purchasing power ($14,000 gain − $6,000 loss), because its monetary liabilities were greater than its monetary assets.[9] The disclosure of this net gain is illustrated in the supplementary schedule on page 595.

Interpreting the net gain or loss in purchasing power

In determining the change in the purchasing power represented by owners' equity, we must consider **both** the amount of constant dollar net income **and** the amount of any gain or loss resulting from monetary items. Thus, the purchasing power of the owners' equity in Flation Company increased by $28,000 during Year 10 ($20,000 net income + $8,000 gain in purchasing power from monetary items).

The purchasing power gain from monetary items is shown separately from the determination of net income to emphasize the special nature of this gain. The income statement shows the purchasing power created or lost **as a result of business operations.** The $8,000 net gain in purchasing power, however, is caused entirely by the **effect of inflation** upon the purchasing power of monetary assets and liabilities. A business that owns monetary assets or owes money may have a purchasing power gain or loss even if it earns no revenue and incurs no expenses.

---

[9] Some readers may notice that our net gain is stated in end-of-Year 10 dollars. To be technically consistent with the other constant dollar data on page 595, this net gain should be restated in dollars of average purchasing power for Year 10. The gain can be restated as follows: $8,000 × $\frac{200}{216}$ = $7,407. We have ignored this restatement because it is not material in dollar amount and is an unnecessary refinement for an introductory discussion.

In evaluating the effect of inflation upon a particular business, we must consider the effect of inflation upon operations and its effects upon the monetary assets and liabilities of the business. If a business must maintain high levels of cash or accounts receivable from customers, we should recognize that inflation will continually erode the purchasing power of these assets. On the other hand, if a business is able to finance its operations with borrowed capital, inflation will benefit the company by allowing it to repay smaller amounts of purchasing power than it originally borrowed.

Net income on a current cost basis

Constant dollar accounting does not abandon historical costs as the basis for measurement but simply expresses these costs in terms of the current value of money. Current cost accounting, on the other hand, does represent a departure from the historical cost concept. The term "current cost" usually refers to the **current replacement cost** of assets. In a current cost income statement, expenses are stated at the estimated cost to **replace the specific assets** sold or used up. Thus, current cost accounting involves estimates of current market values, rather than adjustments to historical costs for changes in the general price level.

Of course, the replacement cost of an asset may fluctuate during the year. Since a cost such as depreciation expense occurs continually **throughout** the year, current cost measurements are based on the **average** replacement cost during the year, not on the replacement cost at year-end.

To illustrate, assume that the replacement cost of Flation Company's equipment was estimated to be $850,000 at the beginning of Year 10 and $950,000 at year-end. Current cost depreciation expense should be based upon the $900,000 average replacement cost of the equipment during the year. Since the equipment has a 10-year life, the depreciation expense appearing in the current cost income statement (page 595) is $90,000 ($900,000 ÷ 10 years).

Now let us consider the determination of the cost of goods sold on a current cost basis. All we need to know is (1) how many units of inventory were sold during the year, and (2) the average replacement cost of these units during Year 10. If Flation Company sold 145,000 units during the year, and the average replacement cost was $2.70 per unit, the cost of goods sold would be $391,500 on a current cost basis (145,000 units × $2.70). Note that the historical cost of units in the company's beginning inventory does not enter into the current cost computation.

Interpreting a current cost income statement

A current cost income statement does **not** measure the flow of general purchasing power in and out of the business. Rather, it shows whether a company earns enough revenue to **replace** the goods and services used up in the effort to generate that revenue. The resulting net income figure closely parallels **distributable profit**—the maximum amount that the business can distribute to its owners and still maintain the present size and scale of its operations.

Unfortunately, the financial statements of large corporations show that many companies in industries vital to our economy are reporting profits measured on a historical cost basis but are incurring large *losses* according to their supplementary current cost disclosures. Companies in the oil industry and steel industry provide excellent examples. What does this mean to an informed reader of financial statements? In short, it means that these companies do not earn sufficient revenue to maintain their productive capacity. In the long run, they must either obtain capital from other sources or scale down the size of their operations.

Reduction in the amount of required disclosure

In 1984, the FASB issued *Statement No. 82,* eliminating the need for companies to include in their supplementary disclosures net income measured in constant dollars.[10] After five years of experimenting with the original disclosure requirements of *Statement No. 33,* the FASB decided that the constant dollar and current cost measurements were sufficiently similar that it is not necessary to disclose net income computed by both methods. Large companies still must disclose net income measured in current costs and the gain or loss in purchasing power resulting from holding net monetary assets or liabilities.

This change in disclosure requirements does not lessen the importance of understanding the basic concepts of constant dollar accounting. Certain financial statement disclosures which will be discussed in more advanced accounting courses continue to make use of constant dollars. Also, income tax rules are making increasing use of the concepts of constant dollar accounting. Finally, anyone who wants to interpret accounting information developed in prior years must understand the significance of changes in the general price level.

Key terms introduced or emphasized in chapter 14

Audit opinion. The report issued by a firm of certified public accountants after auditing the financial statements of a business. Expresses an opinion on the fairness of the financial statements and indicates the nature and limits of the responsibility being assumed by the independent auditors.

Conservatism. A traditional practice of resolving uncertainties by choosing an asset valuation at the lower point of the range of reasonableness. Also refers to the policy of postponing recognition of revenue to a later date when a range of reasonable choice exists. Designed to avoid overstatement of financial strength and earnings.

Consistency. An assumption that once a particular accounting method is adopted, it will not be changed from period to period. Intended to make financial statements of a given company comparable from year to year.

Constant dollar accounting. The technique of expressing all financial statement amounts in dollars of equal purchasing power. This is accomplished by restating historical costs for subsequent changes in the general price level. Also called *general price level accounting.*

Cost principle. The traditional, widely used policy of accounting for assets at their historical cost determined through arm's-length bargaining. Justified by the need for objective evidence to support the valuation of assets.

---

[10] *FASB Statement No. 82,* "Financial Reporting and Changing Prices: Elimination of Certain Disclosures," FASB (Stamford, Conn.: 1984).

Current cost accounting. The valuation of assets and measurements of income in terms of current replacement costs rather than historical costs. This approach to inflation accounting indicates the ability of a business to replace its physical capital (specific inventory and plant assets) as it is sold or used up.

Disclosure principle. Financial statements should disclose all material and relevant information about the financial position and operating results of a business. The notes accompanying financial statements are an important means of disclosure.

Entity concept. Any legal or economic unit which controls economic resources and is accountable for these resources may be considered an accounting entity. The resources and the transactions of the entity are not to be intermingled with those of its owner or owners.

General price level. The weighted-average price of all goods and services in the economy. Inflation may be defined as an increase in the general price level.

Generally accepted accounting principles. Those accounting principles which have received substantial authoritative support, such as the approval of the FASB, the AICPA, or the SEC. Often referred to by the acronym GAAP.

Going-concern assumption. An assumption that a business entity will continue in operation indefinitely and thus will carry out its existing commitments. If evidence to the contrary exists, then the assumption of liquidation would prevail and assets would be valued at their estimated liquidation values.

Installment method. An accounting method used principally in the determination of taxable income. It provides for recognition of realized profit on installment contracts in proportion to cash collected.

Matching principle. The revenue earned during an accounting period is compared or matched with the expenses incurred in generating this revenue in order to measure income. Fundamental to the accrual basis of accounting.

Materiality. The relative importance of an amount or item. An item which is not important or significant enough to influence the decisions of prudent users of financial statements is considered as *not* material. The accounting treatment of immaterial items may be guided by convenience rather than by theoretical principles. For example, purchase of 10 gallons of gasoline is treated as the incurring of an expense rather than the acquisition of an asset.

Monetary items. With respect to changes in price levels, monetary items include assets representing claims to a fixed number of dollars (such as cash and receivables) and most liabilities. Holding monetary assets during a period of rising prices results in a loss in purchasing power; conversely, owing monetary liabilities results in a gain in purchasing power.

Monetary (stable-dollar) assumption. In using money as a measuring unit and preparing financial statements expressed in dollars, accountants make the assumption that the dollar is a stable unit of measurement. This assumption is obviously faulty as a result of continued inflation, and strenuous efforts are being made to change to current cost accounting or general price-level-adjusted measurements.

Objectivity (objective evidence). The valuation of assets and the measurement of income are to be based as much as possible on objective evidence, such as exchange prices in arm's-length transactions. Objective evidence is subject to verification by independent experts.

Percentage-of-completion method. A method of accounting for long-term construction projects which recognizes revenue and profits in proportion to the work completed, based on an estimate of the portion of the project completed each accounting period.

Purchasing power. The ability of money to buy goods and services. As the general price level rises, the purchasing power of the dollar declines. Thus, in periods of inflation, an ever-increasing number of dollars is necessary to represent a given amount of purchasing power.

Realization principle. The principle of recognizing revenue in the accounts only when earned. Revenue is realized when the earning process is virtually complete, which is usually at the time of sale of goods or rendering service to customers.

Demonstration problem for your review

The accounting staff of Prescott Company has provided the following data to assist you in preparing constant dollar and current cost information to supplement the company's financial statements for the current year:

Income Statement — Historical Cost
For the Current Year

Net sales		$620,000
Cost and expenses:		
Cost of goods sold	$310,000	
Depreciation expense	50,000	
Other expenses	200,000	
Total costs and expenses		560,000
Net income		$ 60,000

Other data

(1) Changes in the general price level during the current year were as follows:

	Price Index
Beginning of year	140
Average for year	150
End of year	161
Rate of inflation [(161 − 140) ÷ 140]	15%

Amounts in the constant dollar income statement are to be stated in current-year dollars of average purchasing power.

(2) The company sells a single product and uses the first-in, first-out method to compute the cost of goods sold. The historical cost of goods sold included the following unit sales at the following costs:

	Units	×	Average Unit Costs	=	Total
From beginning inventory	14,000		$5.00		$ 70,000
From current-year purchases	40,000		6.00		240,000
Cost of goods sold	54,000		5.74		$310,000

The $70,000 beginning inventory was purchased when the general price index stood at 140. (It is not necessary to know total purchases or ending inventory for the current year.)

(3) The company's depreciable assets consist of equipment acquired four years ago when the general price index stood at 80. The equipment cost $500,000 and is being depreciated over a 10-year life by the straight line method with no estimated salvage value.

The estimated replacement cost of the equipment was $980,000 at the beginning of the current year and $1,070,000 at year-end.

(4) Throughout the current year, the company owned monetary assets of $110,000 and owed monetary liabilities of $200,000.

Intructions. Prepare a supplementary schedule in the format illustrated on page 595. Include comparative income statements prepared on the basis of historical cost, constant dollars, and current costs. Also show the net gain or loss resulting from monetary items. Show supporting computations for the (1) cost of goods sold stated in constant dollars, (2) depreciation expense stated in constant dollars, (3) net gain or loss in purchasing power from monetary items, (4) cost of goods sold measured in current costs, and (5) depreciation expense measured in current costs.

Solution to demonstration problem

PRESCOTT COMPANY
Income Statement Adjusted for Changing Prices
For the Current Year

	As Reported in The Primary Statements	Adjusted for General Inflation	Adjusted for Changes in Specific Prices
Net sales	$620,000	$620,000	$620,000
Cost and expenses:			
Costs of goods sold	$310,000	$315,000(1)	$324,000(4)
Depreciation expense	50,000	93,750(2)	102,500(5)
Other expenses	200,000	200,000	200,000
Total costs and expenses	$560,000	$608,750	$626,500
Net income (net loss)	$ 60,000	$ 11,250	$ (6,500)
Net gain from decline in purchasing power			
of net amounts owed		$ 13,500(3)	

Supporting Computations: Constant Dollar Amounts

	Historical Dollars	× Conversion Ratio =	Constant Dollars
(1) Cost of goods sold:			
From beginning inventory	$ 70,000	150/140	$ 75,000
From current year purchases	240,000	None	240,000
Cost of goods sold	$310,000		$315,000
(2) Depreciation expense	$ 50,000	150/80	$ 93,750
Alternative computation:			
Equipment	$500,000	150/80	$937,500
Depreciation expense ($937,500			
÷ 10 years)			$ 93,750

(3) Net gain or loss in purchasing power:

	Monetary Items	×	Inflation Rate	=	Gain or Loss in Purchasing Power
Average monetary assets	$110,000		15%		$16,500 L
Average monetary liabilities	200,000		15%		30,000 G
Net amount owed and net gain in purchasing power	$ 90,000				$13,500 G

Current Cost Amounts

(4) Cost of goods sold:

Number of units sold	54,000
Average replacement cost per unit	$6
Current cost of goods sold ($54,000 × $6)	$324,000

(5) Depreciation expense:

Average replacement cost of equipment ($1,070,000 + $980,000) ÷ 2	$1,025,000
Estimated useful life	10 years
Depreciation expense ($1,025,000 ÷ 10)	$ 102,500

Review questions

1 What is the basic objective of financial statements?

2 To qualify as "generally accepted," accounting principles must receive substantial authoritative support. Name three groups or organizations in the United States which have been most influential in giving substantial authoritative support to accounting principles.

3 Explain what is meant by the expression "trade-off between *reliability* and *relevance*" in connection with the preparation of financial statements.

4 Barker Company has at the end of the current period an inventory of merchandise which cost $500,000. It would cost $600,000 to replace this inventory, and it is estimated that the goods will probably be sold for a total of $700,000. If the firm were to terminate operations immediately, the inventory could probably be sold for $480,000. Discuss the relative reliability and relevance of each of these dollar measurements of the ending inventory.

5 Why is it necessary for accountants to assume the existence of a clearly defined accounting entity?

6 If it appears that the going-concern assumption is no longer valid for Company Y, should the plant assets still be valued in the balance sheet at cost less accumulated depreciation? Explain.

7 "The matching of costs and revenue is the natural extension of the time period principle." Evaluate this statement.

8 Define *objectivity, consistency, materiality,* and *conservatism.*

9 Is the assumption that the dollar is a stable unit of measure realistic? What alternative procedures would you suggest?

10 a Why is it important that any change in accounting methods from one period to the next be disclosed?

b Does the concept of consistency mean that all companies in a given industry follow similar accounting methods?

11 Briefly define the principle of **_disclosure._** List five examples of information that should be disclosed in financial statements or in notes accompanying the statements.

12 Publicly owned corporations are required to include in their annual reports a description of the accounting principles followed in the preparation of their financial statements. What advantages do you see in this practice?

13 List four stages of the productive process which might become the accountant's basis for recognizing changes in the value of a firm's output. Which stage is most commonly used as a basis for revenue recognition? Why?

14 A CPA firm's standard audit opinion consists of two major paragraphs. Describe the essential content of each paragraph.

15 Define **_monetary assets_** and indicate whether a gain or loss results from the holding of such assets during a period of rising prices.

16 Why is it advantageous to be in debt during an inflationary period?

17 Evaluate the following statement: "During a period of rising prices, the conventional income statement overstates net income because the amount of depreciation recorded is less than the value of the service potential of assets consumed."

18 How does constant dollar accounting differ from current cost accounting? For which one would the Consumer Price Index be used?

19 Alpha Company sells pocket calculators which have been decreasing in cost while the general price level has been rising. Explain why Alpha Company's cost of goods sold on a constant dollar basis and on a current cost basis would be higher or lower than on a historical cost basis.

20 The latest financial statements of Boston Manufacturing Co. indicate that income measured in terms of constant dollars is much lower than income measured in historical dollars. What is the most probable explanation for this large difference?

21 What conclusion would you draw about a company that consistently shows large net losses when its income is measured on a current cost basis?

Exercises

Ex. 14-1   Mystery Playhouse prepares monthly financial statements. At the beginning of its three-month summer season, the company has programs printed for each of its 48 upcoming performances. Under certain circumstances, either of the following accounting treatments of the costs of printing these programs would be acceptable. Justify both of the accounting treatments using accounting principles discussed in this chapter.

    a The cost of printing the programs is recorded as an asset and is allocated to expense in the month in which the programs are distributed to patrons attending performances.

    b The entire cost of printing the programs is charged to expense when the invoice is received from the printer.

Ex. 14-2   For each situation described below, indicate the principle of accounting that is being violated. You may choose from the following principles: accounting entity, disclosure, matching, materiality, objectivity, realization, and stable monetary unit.

    a The bookkeeper for a large, metropolitan auto dealership depreciates metal wastebaskets over a period of five years.

    b Upon completion of the construction of a condominium project which will soon be offered for sale, Townhome Developers increased the balance sheet valuation of the condominiums to their sales value and recognized the expected profit on the project.

c Plans to dispose of a major segment of the business are not communicated to readers of the financial statements.

d The cost of expensive, custom made machinery installed in an assembly line is charged to expense, because it is doubtful that the machinery would have any resale value if the assembly line were shut down.

e A small commuter airline recognizes no depreciation on its aircraft because the planes are maintained in "as good as new" condition.

Ex. 14-3 On September 15, Year 1, Susan Moore sold a piece of property which cost her $56,000 for $80,000, net of commissions and other selling expenses. The terms of sale were as follows: down payment, $8,000; balance, $3,000 on the fifteenth day of each month for 24 months, starting October 15, Year 1. Compute the gross profit to be recognized by Moore in Year 1, Year 2, and Year 3 (a) on the *accrual basis* of accounting and (b) on the *installment basis* of accounting. Moore uses a fiscal year ending December 31.

Ex. 14-4 The Clinton Corporation recognizes the profit on a long-term construction project as work progresses. From the information given below, compute the profit that should be recognized each year, assuming that the original cost estimate on the contract was $6,000,000 and that the contract price is $7,500,000.

Year	Costs Incurred	Profit Considered Realized
1	$1,800,000	$?
2	3,000,000	?
3	1,171,000	?
Total	$5,971,000	$1,529,000

Ex. 14-5 Empire Company paid $500,000 cash in Year 1 to acquire land as a long-term investment. At this time, the general price level stood at 100. In Year 5, the general price index stands at 140, but the price of land in the area in which Empire Company invested has doubled in value. Rental receipts for grazing and farming during the five-year period were sufficient to pay all carrying charges on the land.

Empire Company prepares a constant dollar income statement and discloses purchasing power gains and losses as supplementary information to its cost-based financial statements.

a How much, if any, of a purchasing power gain or loss relating to the land will be included in the supplementary disclosures over the five-year period? (Assume the land is still owned at the end of Year 5.)

b Assume the land is sold in Year 5 for $685,000. Compute the gain or loss on the sale on a basis of (1) historical cost and (2) constant dollars.

Ex. 14-6 Three companies started business with $600,000 at the beginning of the current year when the general price index stood at 120. The First Company invested the money in a note receivable due in four years; the Second Company invested its cash in land; and the Third Company purchased a building for $1,800,000, assuming a liability for the unpaid balance of $1,200,000. The price level stood at 140 at the end of the year. Compute the purchasing power gain or loss on monetary items for each company during the year.

Ex. 14-7   For Year 9, PhotoMart computed the cost of goods sold for the Presto, its biggest-selling camera, as follows (historical cost, fifo basis):

	Units	×	Unit Cost	=	Total
From beginning inventory	400		$40.00		$16,000
From Year 9 purchases	1,700		42.00		71,400
Cost of goods sold	2,100				$87,400

The beginning inventory of Presto cameras had been acquired when the general price index stood at 320. During Year 9, the average level of the price index was 350, and the average replacement cost of Prestos was $42.

Compute the cost of goods sold for Presto cameras during Year 9 on:

a A constant dollar basis
b A current cost basis

Ex. 14-8   Western Showcase purchased equipment for $300,000 in Year 3 when the general price index stood at 120. The company depreciates the equipment over 15 years by the straight-line method, with no estimated salvage value. In Year 7, the general price level is 180 and the estimated replacement cost of the equipment is $468,000.

Compute the amount of depreciation expense for Year 7 on:

a A historical cost basis
b A constant dollar basis
c A current cost basis

Problems

14-1   Accounting principles

Paragraphs a through e, below, describe accounting practices which ***are in accord*** with generally accepted accounting principles. From the following list of accounting principles, identify those principles which you believe justify or explain each described accounting practice. (Most of the practices are explained by a single principle; however, more than one principle may relate to a particular practice.) Briefly explain the relationship between the described accounting practice and the underlying accounting principle.

Accounting Principles

Consistency	Accounting entity
Materiality	Matching revenue with expense
Objectivity	Going-concern assumption
Realization	Adequate disclosure
Conservatism	Stable monetary unit

Accounting Practices

a The purchase of a two-year fire insurance policy is recorded by debiting an asset account even though no refund will be received if the policy is canceled.

b Hand tools with a small unit cost are charged to expense when purchased even though the individual tools have a useful life of several years.

c Although the ACRS method of depreciation is allowable for income tax purposes, it generally is not used in financial statements because it writes off an asset's cost over a period shorter than the asset's useful life.

d A lawsuit filed against a company is described in footnotes to the company's financial statements even though the lawsuit was filed with the court shortly after the company's balance sheet date.

e A real estate developer carries an unsold inventory of condominiums in its accounting records at cost rather than at estimated sales value.

14-2 A second problem on accounting principles

In each of the situations described below, indicate the accounting principle or concept, if any, that has been violated and explain briefly the nature of the violation. If you believe the treatment *is in accord with generally accepted accounting principles*, state this as your position and briefly defend it.

a The liabilities of Ellis Construction Co. are substantially in excess of the company's assets. In order to present a more impressive balance sheet for the business, Roy Ellis, the owner of the company, included in the company's balance sheet such personal assets as his savings account, automobile, and real estate investments.

b On January 9, Year 4, Gable Company's only plant was badly damaged by a tornado and will be closed for much of the coming year. No mention was made of this event in the financial statements for the year ended December 31, Year 3, as the tornado occurred after year-end.

c In prior years Regal Corporation had used the straight-line method of depreciation for both financial reporting purposes and for income tax purposes. In the current year, Regal continued to use straight-line depreciation on all assets for financial reporting purposes, but began depreciating newly acquired assets by the ACRS method for income tax purposes.

d Lakeshore Development Co. increased the carrying value of its holdings of land to current market value. The offsetting credit was made to an account entitled Gain from Appreciation of Real Estate Owned.

e Aspen Airlines follows the practice of charging the purchase of hand tools with a unit cost of less than $50 to an expense account rather than to an asset account. The average life of these tools is about three years.

14-3 Three methods of income recognition

Early in Year 1, Roadbuilders, Inc., was notified that it was the successful bidder on the construction of a section of state highway. The bid price for the project was $24 million. Construction is to begin in Year 1 and will take about 27 months to complete; the deadline for completion is in April of Year 3.

The contract calls for payments of $6 million per year to Roadbuilders, Inc., for four years, beginning in Year 1. (After the project is complete, the state will also pay a reasonable interest charge on the unpaid balance of the contract.) The company estimates that construction costs will total $16 million, of which $6 million will be incurred in Year 1, $8 million in Year 2, and $2 million in Year 3.

The controller of the company, Joe Morgan, recognizes that there are a number of ways he might account for this contract. He might recognize income at the time the contract is completed (sales method), in April of Year 3. Alternatively, he might recognize income during construction (percentage-of-completion method), in proportion to the percentage of the total cost incurred in each of

Years 1, 2, and 3. Finally, he might recognize income in proportion to the percentage of the total contract price collected in installment receipts during the four-year period (installment method).

Instructions

a Prepare a schedule (in millions of dollars) showing the profit that would be recognized on this project in each of the next four years under each of the three accounting methods being considered by the controller. Assume that the timing and construction costs go according to plan. (Ignore the interest revenue relating to the unpaid balance of the contract.)

b Explain which accounting method you consider to be most appropriate in this situation. Also explain why you consider the other two methods less appropriate.

14-4 Another problem on methods of income recognition

Nantucket Boat Works builds custom sailboats. During the first year of operations, the company built four boats for Island Charter Company. The four boats had a total cost of $216,000 and were sold for a total price of $360,000, due on an installment basis. Island Charter Company paid $120,000 of this sales price during the first year, plus an additional amount for interest charges.

At year-end, work is in progress on two other boats which are 40% complete. The contract price for these two boats totals $250,000 and costs incurred on these boats during the year total $60,000 (40% of estimated total costs of $150,000).

Instructions. Compute the gross profit for Nantucket Boat Works during its first year of operations under each of the following assumptions. (Interest earned from Island Charter Company does not enter into the computation of gross profit.)

a The entire profit is recognized on the four boats completed and profit on the two boats under construction is recognized on a percentage-of-completion basis.

b Profit on the four boats completed is recognized on the installment basis and no portion of the profit on the two boats under construction will be recognized until the boats are completed, delivered to customers, and cash is collected.

14-5 Constant dollars and current costs: a comprehensive problem

The accounting staff of Prescott Company has provided the following data to assist you in preparing constant dollar and current cost information to supplement the company's financial statements for the current year:

Income Statement — Historical Cost
For the Current Year

Net sales		$620,000
Costs and expenses:		
Cost of goods sold	$310,000	
Depreciation expense	50,000	
Other expenses	200,000	
Total costs and expenses		560,000
Net income		$ 60,000

Other data

(1) Changes in the general price level during the current year were as follows:

	Price Index
Beginning of year	140
Average for year	150
End of year	161
Rate of inflation [(161 − 140) ÷ 140]	15%

Amounts in the constant dollar income statement are to be stated in current year dollars of average purchasing power.
(2) The company sells a single product and uses the first-in, first-out method to compute the cost of goods sold. The historical cost of goods sold included the following unit sales at the following costs:

	Units	×	Average Unit Costs	=	Total
From beginning inventory	14,000		$5.00		$ 70,000
From current-year purchases	40,000		6.00		240,000
Cost of goods sold	54,000		5.74		$310,000

The $70,000 beginning inventory was purchased when the general price index stood at 140. (It is not necessary to know total purchases or ending inventory for the current year.)
(3) The company's depreciable assets consist of equipment acquired four years ago when the general price index stood at 80. The equipment cost $500,000 and is being depreciated over a 10-year life by the straight-line method with no estimated salvage value.

The estimated replacement cost of the equipment was $980,000 at the beginning of the current year and $1,070,000 at year-end.
(4) Throughout the current year, the company owned monetary assets of $110,000 and owed monetary liabilities of $200,000.

Instructions. Prepare a supplementary schedule in the format illustrated on page 595. Include comparative income statements prepared on the bases of historical cost, constant dollars, and current costs. Also show the net gain or loss resulting from monetary items. Show supporting computations for the (1) cost of goods sold stated in constant dollars, (2) depreciation expense stated in constant dollars, (3) net gain or loss in purchasing power from monetary items, (4) cost of goods sold measured in current costs, and (5) depreciation expense measured in current costs.

14-6   Constant dollars and current costs: an alternate for Problem 14-5
Sandy Malone, the president of Sandstone Art Company, has asked you to prepare constant dollar and current cost income statements to supplement the company's financial statements. The company's accountant has provided you with the following data:

Income Statement — Historical Cost
For the Current Year

Net sales		$420,000
Costs and expenses:		
Cost of goods sold	$210,000	
Depreciation expense	30,000	
Other expenses	160,000	
Total costs and expenses		400,000
Net income		$ 20,000

Other data

(1) Changes in the general price index during the current year were as follows:

	Price Index
Beginning of current year	120
Average for current year	130
End of current year	138
Rate of inflation [(138 − 120) ÷ 120]	15%

Amounts in the constant dollar income statement are to be expressed in current-year dollars of average purchasing power.

(2) The company sells a single product and uses the first-in, first-out method to compute the cost of goods sold. The historical cost of goods sold includes the following unit sales at the following costs:

	Units	×	Average Unit Costs	=	Total
From beginning inventory	10,000		$3.00		$ 30,000
From current-year purchases	56,250		3.20		180,000
Cost of goods sold	66,250		3.17		$210,000

The $30,000 beginning inventory was purchased when the general price index stood at 120. (It is not necessary to know total purchases or ending inventory for the current year.)

(3) The company's depreciable assets consist of equipment acquired five years ago when the price index stood at 75. The equipment cost $450,000 and is being depreciated over a 15-year life by the straight-line method with no estimated salvage value.

The estimated replacement cost of the equipment was $600,000 at the beginning of the current year and $630,000 at year-end.

(4) Throughout the current year, the company has owned monetary assets of $90,000 and has owed monetary liabilities of $160,000.

Instructions. Prepare a supplementary schedule in the format illustrated on page 595. Include comparative income statements prepared on the bases of historical costs, constant dollars, and current costs. Also show the net gain or loss from holding monetary items. Include supporting computations for the (1) cost of goods sold — constant dollar basis, (2) depreciation expense — constant dollar basis, (3) net gain or loss in purchasing power from holding monetary items, (4) cost of goods sold — current cost basis, and (5) depreciation expense — current cost basis.

Cases for analysis

Case 14-1 Interpretation of current cost information

Shown below is a supplementary schedule which appeared in the 1984 annual report of Chevron Corporation, formerly Standard Oil Corporation of California (in millions of dollars):

	As Reported in the Primary Statements	Current Cost
Revenues	$29,207	$29,207
Costs and Expenses		
Cost of products sold and operating expenses	21,835	22,281
Depreciation, depletion and amortization	1,388	2,630
Taxes other than on income	2,469	2,469
Interest and debt expense	961	961
Provision for taxes on income	1,020	1,020
Net Income (Loss)	$ 1,534	$ (154)

Instructions. Use this supplementary schedule to answer each of the following questions. Explain the reasoning behind your answers.

a Was Chevron's revenue sufficient to recover the original number of dollars invested in the goods and services consumed during the company's operations in 1984?

b Was Chevron's revenue sufficient to replace the goods and services consumed in the effort to generate revenue during the year?

c What do you think is the principal reason for the large difference between the amounts of net income computed under the alternative measurement techniques of historical cost and current cost?

Case 14-2 Interpretation of constant dollars and current costs

The following schedule was developed from information contained in the 1984 annual report of Ralston Purina Company, a large grocery and agricultural products company that also owns the Jack in the Box chain of restaurants:

Income Statement Adjusted for Changing Prices
(in millions of dollars)

	As Reported in the Primary Statements	Adjusted for General Inflation (Constant Dollars)	Adjusted for Changes in Specific Prices (Current Costs)
Net sales	$4,980.1	$4,980.1	$4,980.1
Costs and expenses:			
Cost of goods sold	$3,652.8	$3,664.0	$3,642.3
Depreciation expense	108.7	168.2	174.4
Other expenses	975.9	975.9	975.9
Total	$4,737.4	$4,808.1	$4,792.6
Net income (loss)	$ 242.7	$ 172.0	$ 187.5
Gain from decline in purchasing power of net amounts owed		$ 20.3	

Instructions. Use the supplementary schedule to answer each of the following questions. Explain the reasoning behind your answers.

a Was the replacement cost of the products sold by Ralston Purina rising or falling during 1984?

b Has the replacement cost of the company's depreciable assets increased faster or more slowly than the general price level since these assets were acquired?

c Were the average monetary assets held by the company during the year greater or smaller than the average monetary amounts owed?

d What was the total change in the purchasing power of the owners' equity in the business during the year?

e Assuming that this was a typical year, are the company's earnings sufficient to maintain the present size and scope of current operations on a long-term basis?

Chapter 15
Statement of changes in financial position: cash flows

This chapter is focused on a third major financial statement — the statement of changes in financial position. To make clear the purpose and importance of the funds statement, we describe and illustrate the usual sources and uses of working capital. A simple set of transactions is used to demonstrate how a statement of changes in financial position can be prepared without the use of working papers. This conceptual example is followed by a more comprehensive illustration which includes the preparation of a working paper as a preliminary step to drafting a statement of changes in financial position. The final section of the chapter deals with the related topic of cash flow statements.

After studying this chapter you should be able to:

✓ Contrast an income statement with a statement of changes in financial position, and with a cash flow statement.
✓ Explain why working capital may be viewed as a "fund" of liquid resources.
✓ Identify the principal sources and uses of working capital.
✓ Determine the amount of working capital provided by operations.
✓ Prepare a statement of changes in financial position.
✓ Convert an income statement from accrual basis to cash basis.
✓ Prepare a cash flow statement.

The business activities of a going concern may be viewed as cycles of investment, recovery of investment, and reinvestment. During the operating cycle, for example, the business acquires merchandise inventories on credit, thus creating accounts payable. These merchandise inventories are in turn sold to customers on credit. When the accounts receivable are collected from the customers, the company again has cash to apply against its debts and to begin the operating cycle anew. Thus, the current assets circulate through the business during an operating cycle. Investments in plant and equipment also must be recovered through revenue at a rate fast enough to permit replacement of these assets as they wear out or become obsolete. If a business cannot recover the cash it has invested quickly enough to pay its debts as they become due, it must borrow or obtain cash from other sources in order to survive.

The balance sheet portrays the overall financial position of the business at a specific date during these recurring cycles of investment, recovery of investment, and reinvestment. The income statement shows the dollar amount of resources generated and consumed in business operations. In a sense, the fate of any given business enterprise is read in the income statement, since it tells whether revenue is larger or smaller during any period than the cost of the resources used up in generating this revenue. In this chapter we introduce a third major financial statement, the ***statement of changes in financial position***[1] and a related summary of cash movements, the ***cash flow statement.***

STATEMENT OF CHANGES IN FINANCIAL POSITION

A statement of changes in financial position helps us to understand how and why the financial position of a business has changed during the period. This statement summarizes the long-term ***financing and investing activities*** of the business; it shows where the financial resources (funds) have come from and where they have gone. With this understanding of how funds have flowed into the business and how these funds have been used, we can begin to answer such important questions as: Do the normal operations of the business generate sufficient funds to enable the company to pay regular dividends? Has the company been forced to borrow to pay for new plant assets, or has it been able to generate the funds from current operation? Is the business becoming more solvent or less solvent. Perhaps the most puzzling question is: How can a ***profitable*** business be running low on cash and working capital? Even though a business operates profitably, its working capital may decline and the business may even become insolvent.

The statement of changes in financial position gives us answers to these questions, because it shows in detail the amount of funds received from each source and the amount of funds used for each purpose throughout the year. In fact, this financial statement used to be called a Statement of Sources and Applications of Funds. Many people still call it simply a ***Funds Statement.*** However, the name officially recommended by the FASB is the ***Statement of Changes in Financial Position.***

---

[1] In *Opinion No. 19,* "Reporting Changes in Financial Position," the Accounting Principles Board of the AICPA concluded (p. 373) that "information concerning the financing and investing activities of a business enterprise and the changes in its financial position for a period is essential for financial statement users, particularly owners and creditors, in making economic decisions. When financial statements purporting to present both financial position (balance sheet) and results of operations (statement of income and retained earnings) are issued, a statement summarizing changes in financial positions should also be presented as a basic financial statement for each period for which an income statement is presented."

"Funds" defined as working capital

In ordinary usage, the term *funds* usually means cash. Accountants and financial executives, however, think of "funds" in a broader sense. They view the funds available to a company as its *working capital* — the excess of current assets over current liabilities.

During each operating cycle, the current assets are constantly being converted into cash, a portion of which is used to pay current liabilities. That portion of the current assets not needed to pay current liabilities is viewed as liquid resources or available funds. A portion of these funds may be used to buy plant assets, to pay long-term debt, and to pay dividends. However, only a part of the liquid resources can be used for these purposes, because a major portion must be retained in circulation to meet the day-to-day needs of the next operating cycle.

If the amount of working capital increased during a given fiscal period, this means that more working capital was generated than was used for various business purposes; if a decrease in working capital occurred, the reverse is true. One of the key purposes of the statement of changes in financial position is to explain fully the increase or decrease in working capital during a fiscal period.[2] This is done by showing where working capital originated and how it was used.

Sources and uses of working capital

Any transaction that increases the amount of working capital is a *source of working capital.* For example, the sale of merchandise at a price greater than its cost is a source of working capital, because the increase in cash or receivables from the sale is greater than the decrease in inventory. Any transaction that decreases working capital is a *use of working capital.* For example, either incurring a current liability to acquire a noncurrent asset or using cash to pay expenses represents a decrease in working capital.

On the other hand, some transactions affect current assets or current liabilities but do *not* change the amount of working capital. For example, the collection of an account receivable (which increases cash and decreases an account receivable by an equal amount) is not a source of working capital. Similarly, the payment of an account payable (which decreases cash and decreases an account payable by an equal amount) does not change the amount of working capital.

The principal sources and uses of working capital are listed below:

Sources of working capital:

1 *Current operations.* If the inflow of funds from sales exceeds the outflow of funds to cover the cost of merchandise purchases and expenses of doing business, current operations will provide a net source of funds. If the inflow of funds from sales is less than these outflows, operations will result in a net use of funds. Not all expenses require the use of funds in the current period; therefore, the amount of funds

---

[2] In the preparation of a statement of changes in financial position, some companies define "funds" as cash, rather than as working capital. In these cases, the statement of changes in financial position becomes similar to the cash flow statement discussed later in this chapter. The majority of publicly owned corporations, however, use the working capital definition of "funds."

provided by operations is *not* the same as the amount of net income earned during the period. Differences between the amount of **working capital provided by operations** and the amount of net income will be discussed later in the chapter.

In the long run, operations must result in a net source of funds if the business is to survive. A business cannot obtain funds through other sources indefinitely if those funds will only be consumed by business operations.

2 **Sale of noncurrent assets.** A business may obtain working capital by selling noncurrent assets, such as plant and equipment or long-term investments, in exchange for current assets. As long as current assets are received, the sale is a source of funds **regardless of whether the noncurrent assets are sold at a gain or a loss.** For example, assume that a company sells for $500,000 cash a piece of land which had cost $600,000 a year ago. Although the land was sold at a loss, the company has increased its current assets $500,000 by selling the land. Thus the transaction is a source of working capital.

3 **Long-term borrowing.** Long-term borrowing, such as issuing bonds payable, results in an increase in current assets, thereby increasing working capital. **Short-term borrowing,** however, does *not* increase working capital. When a company borrows cash by signing a short-term note payable, working capital is unchanged because the increase in current assets is offset by an increase in current liabilities of the same amount.

4 **Sale of additional shares of stock.** The sale of capital stock results in an inflow of current assets, thereby increasing working capital. In a similar manner, additional investments of current assets by owners represent sources of funds to single proprietorships and partnerships. The issuance of capital stock in conjunction with a stock dividend or a stock split, however, does not bring any new resources into the company and is not a source of funds.

Uses of working capital:

1 **Declaration of cash dividends.** The declaration of a cash dividend results in a current liability (dividend payable) and is therefore a use of funds. Notice that it is the **declaration** of the dividend, rather than the payment of the dividend, which is the use of funds. Actual payment of the dividend reduces current assets and current liabilities by the same amount and thus has no effect upon the amount of working capital. (Stock dividends do not involve any distribution of assets and, therefore, are not a use of funds.)

2 **Purchase of noncurrent assets.** Purchases of noncurrent assets, such as plant and equipment, reduce current assets or increase current liabilities. In either case, working capital is reduced. Special situations in which noncurrent assets are acquired in exchange for other noncurrent assets or long-term liabilities are discussed later in this chapter.

3 **Repayment of long-term debt.** Working capital is decreased when current assets are used to repay long-term debt. However, repayment of short-term debt is not a use of funds, since current assets and current liabilities decrease by the same amount.

4 **Repurchase of outstanding stock.** When cash is paid out to repurchase outstanding shares of stock, working capital is reduced.

Funds flow: a simple illustration

Assume that on April 30 John Claire started a business in the form of a single proprietorship by investing $40,000 cash. The business, Claire Company, completed the transactions shown below during the month of May.

(1) Claire invested an additional $20,000 cash in the business.
(2) Purchased merchandise costing $40,000 on credit and sold three-fourths of this, also on credit, for $58,000.
(3) Collected $45,000 on receivables; paid $32,000 on accounts payable.
(4) Paid $20,500 cash for operating expenses.
(5) Purchased land for the construction of a store. Gave $30,000 cash and a six-month note for $17,000 in payment for the land.
(6) Withdrew $2,000 from the business for personal use.

The company's income statement for May and balance sheet at May 31 are shown below:

CLAIRE COMPANY
Income Statement
For the Month Ended May 31

Financial statements covering one month's operations of single proprietorship

Sales		$58,000
Cost of goods sold:		
Purchases	$40,000	
Less: Ending inventory (one-fourth of purchases)	10,000	30,000
Gross profit on sales		$28,000
Operating expenses		20,500
Net income for month of May		$ 7,500

CLAIRE COMPANY
Comparative Balance Sheet

Assets	May 31	Apr. 30
Cash	$20,500	$40,000
Accounts receivable	13,000	
Inventory	10,000	
Land	47,000	
Total assets	$90,500	$40,000

Liabilities & Owner's Equity		
Note payable	$17,000	
Accounts payable	8,000	
John Claire, capital	65,500	$40,000
Total liabilities & owner's equity	$90,500	$40,000

The working capital amounted to $40,000 (consisting entirely of cash) on April 30 but was only $18,500 ($43,500 − $25,000) on May 31, a decrease of $21,500. In analyzing the six transactions completed during the month of May, we see that working capital was increased and decreased as follows:

Transactions increasing working capital:		
Additional investment by owner		$20,000
Sale of merchandise for more than cost ($58,000 − $30,000)		28,000
Total increases in working capital		$48,000
Transactions decreasing working capital:		
Payment of operating expenses	$20,500	
Payment of cash for purchase of land	30,000	
Issuance of short-term note payable for purchase of land	17,000	
Withdrawal by owner	2,000	
Total decreases in working capital		69,500
Decrease in working capital during May		$21,500

A complete list of transactions for a fiscal period may not be readily available, and even if it were, analysis of such a list would be a laborious process. In practice, a statement of changes in financial position is prepared by analyzing the changes that occurred *in the noncurrent assets* during the fiscal period. An analysis of the comparative balance sheet for Claire Company indicates that the Land account increased by $47,000. This increase indicates that land, a noncurrent asset, was purchased during the period. Purchase of a noncurrent asset is a use of funds. Claire's capital account increased by $25,500 as a result of (1) additional investment of $20,000 (a source of funds), (2) net income of $7,500 (a source of funds), and (3) a withdrawal of $2,000 (a use of funds). We can therefore prepare the following statement of changes in financial position for the month of May, including a supporting schedule showing the changes in each element of working capital:

CLAIRE COMPANY
Statement of Changes in Financial Position
For Month of May

A simple statement of changes in financial position

Sources of working capital:		
Operations (net income)		$ 7,500
Additional investment by owner		20,000
Total sources of working capital		$27,500
Uses of working capital:		
Purchase of land	$47,000	
Withdrawal by owner	2,000	
Total uses of working capital		49,000
Decrease in working capital		$21,500

Changes in Composition of Working Capital

	End of May	End of April	Increase or (Decrease) in Working Capital
Current assets:			
Cash	$20,500	$40,000	$(19,500)
Accounts receivable	13,000	–0–	13,000
Inventory	10,000	–0–	10,000
Total current assets	$43,500	$40,000	
Current liabilities:			
Note payable	$17,000	$ –0–	(17,000)
Accounts payable	8,000	–0–	(8,000)
Total current liabilities	$25,000	$ –0–	
Working capital	$18,500	$40,000	
Decrease in working capital			$(21,500)

The differences between net income, net cash flow, and the change in working capital should be carefully noted in the foregoing example. Although Claire Company's net income for May was $7,500, its cash account *decreased* by $19,500 and its working capital *decreased* by $21,500.

Effect of transactions on working capital

In preparing a statement of changes in financial position, it is convenient to view all business transactions as falling into three categories:

1 Transactions which affect *only current asset or current liability accounts.* These transactions produce changes in working capital accounts but do not change the amount of working capital. For example, the purchase of merchandise increases inventory and accounts payable but has no effect on working capital; it may therefore be ignored in preparing a statement of changes in financial position.

2 Transactions which affect a *current asset or current liability account and a nonworking capital account.* These transactions bring about either an increase or a decrease in the amount of working capital. The issuance of long-term bonds, for example, increases current assets and increases bonds payable, a non-working capital account; therefore, the issuance of bonds payable is a source of working capital. Similarly, when the bonds approach maturity they are transferred to the current liability classification in the balance sheet. This causes a reduction (a use) of working capital. If changes in nonworking capital accounts are analyzed, these events are brought to light, and their effect on working capital will be reported in the statement of changes in financial position.

3 Transactions which affect *only noncurrent accounts* and therefore have no direct effect on the amount of working capital. The entry to record depreciation is an example of such a transaction. Other transactions in this category, such as the issuance of capital stock in exchange for plant assets, are called *exchange transac-*

tions and are viewed as *both a source and use of working capital,* but do not change the amount of working capital.

Exchange transactions. Suppose that equipment worth $200,000 is acquired in exchange for 10,000 shares of $5 par value capital stock. The entry to record this transaction would be:

<table>
<tr><td>**An exchange transaction**</td><td>Equipment ....</td><td>200,000</td><td></td></tr>
<tr><td></td><td>Capital stock ....</td><td></td><td>50,000</td></tr>
<tr><td></td><td>Paid-in Capital in Excess of Par ....</td><td></td><td>150,000</td></tr>
<tr><td></td><td colspan="3">Exchange of 10,000 shares of $5 par value capital stock for equipment worth $200,000.</td></tr>
</table>

This exchange transaction does not involve any current asset or current liability accounts and therefore has no *direct* effect upon working capital. However, the transaction may be viewed as consisting of two parts: (1) the sale of capital stock for $200,000 and (2) the use of this $200,000 to purchase equipment. Instead of being omitted from the statement of changes in financial position, an exchange transaction of this type is shown as *both a source of funds* (sale of capital stock) *and a use of funds* (purchase of equipment). This treatment is consistent with the objective of explaining in the statement of changes in financial position all the long-term financing activities of the business.

The acquisition of plant assets by issuing long-term debt and the conversion of bonds payable or preferred stock into common stock are other examples of exchange transactions which have no direct effect upon working capital. In the statement of changes in financial position, however, these transactions are shown as both a source and a use of working capital.

Most transactions affecting only long-term accounts are exchange transactions. Two exceptions, however, are stock splits and stock dividends. Stock splits and stock dividends do not involve an exchange and *do not* affect the financial position of the business. For this reason, stock splits and dividends *are not shown* in a statement of changes in financial position.

Working capital provided by operations

Working capital provided by operations is the net increase or decrease in working capital resulting from the normal business activities of earning revenue and paying expenses. There are many similarities between the providing of working capital by operations and the earning of net income. For example, earning revenue increases net income and the related inflow of cash and receivables increases working capital. However, there also are significant differences between net income and the amount of working capital provided by operations.

Some expenses do not reduce working capital. Some expenses, such as depreciation, amortization of intangible assets, and amortization of discount on bonds payable, reduce net income but have no immediate effect on the amount of working capital provided by normal operations.

To illustrate, assume that on December 31, Year 1, City Delivery Service buys two trucks at a cost of $30,000. As of January 1, Year 2, the company has no assets other than the trucks and has no liabilities. During Year 2 the company does business on a cash basis, collecting revenue of $40,000 and paying expenses of $22,000, thus showing an $18,000 increase in cash, which is its only working capital account. The company then records depreciation expense of $6,000 on its trucks, resulting in a $12,000 net income for Year 2. What is the amount of working capital provided by operations in Year 2? The recording of depreciation expense reduced net income, *but it did not reduce working capital;* working capital provided by operations remains at $18,000. The $12,000 net income figure therefore *understates* the amount of working capital provided by operations by the amount of depreciation expense recorded during the period.

One objective of the statement of changes in financial position is to explain any differences between net income and the amount of working capital provided by operations. If we are to convert the $12,000 net income of City Delivery Service to the amount of working capital provided by operations, we must *add back* the depreciation expense of $6,000. The computation of working capital provided by operations in the statement of changes in financial position of City Delivery Service for Year 2 is shown below:

Sources of working capital:
  Operations:

Net income	$12,000
Add: Depreciation expense	6,000
Working capital provided by operations	$18,000

Depreciation is not a source of funds. The addition of depreciation expense to the net income figure has led some people to view depreciation expense as a source of funds. It is important for the user of financial statements to understand that depreciation is neither a source nor a use of working capital. *No funds flow into a business as a result of recording depreciation expense.* It is shown in the statement of changes in financial position merely to explain one of the differences between the concept of net income and the concept of working capital provided by operations.

Some items which increase income do not increase working capital. We have seen that some expenses do not reduce working capital. Similarly, some items in the income statement increase net income without increasing working capital; such items must be *deducted* from net income in arriving at working capital provided by operations. An example of such an item is the amortization of premium on bonds payable, which causes annual interest expense to be less than the cash payments of interest to bondholders.[3]

Nonoperating gains and losses. Nonoperating gains and losses, if material in amount, should be eliminated from net income in order to show the working capital provided by "normal" operations.[4] For example, assume that land costing $100,000 is sold at a net gain of $50,000. In the statement of changes in financial position, the entire $150,000 in proceeds from the sale should be reported as "working capital provided by the sale of

---

[3] The treatment of this item in the working paper and in the statement of changes in financial position is illustrated in the Demonstration Problem on pages 635–638.

[4] Nonoperating gains and losses include extraordinary items, gains or losses on sales of plant assets, and other gains or losses not directly related to the company's principal business activities.

land." The $50,000 nonoperating gain, however, is included in the net income for the period. In determining the amount of working capital provided by operations, this $50,000 nonoperating gain must be **deducted** from the net income figure because the entire proceeds from the sale of the land are reported elsewhere in the statement of changes in financial position.

As a separate example, assume that the same land is sold for $70,000; then the nonoperating loss of $30,000 should be **added back** to net income to arrive at working capital provided by operations, and the working capital provided through sale of land should be reported at $70,000.

Computation of working capital provided by operations: a summary. The foregoing discussion relating to the measurement of working capital provided by operations can be summarized as follows:

Computation of Working Capital Provided by Operations

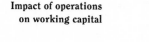

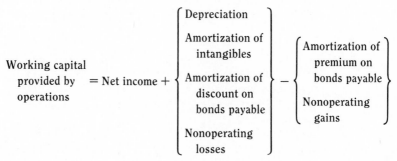

Funds flow: a comprehensive illustration

To illustrate the points just discussed, we shall prepare a statement of changes in financial position for the Allison Corporation from the comparative balance sheet and the condensed income statement shown below and on page 624. A summary of the transactions completed by Allison Corporation which resulted in changes in **noncurrent accounts** during Year 4 follows these financial statements.

ALLISON CORPORATION
Comparative Balance Sheet
At December 31

Assets	Year 4	Year 3
Current assets:		
Cash	$ 15,000	$ 35,000
Accounts receivable (net)	105,000	85,000
Inventory	200,000	120,000
Short-term prepayments	25,000	12,000
Total current assets	$ 345,000	$252,000
Land	300,000	200,000
Equipment	470,000	380,000
Less: Accumulated depreciation	(192,500)	(125,000)
Total assets	$ 922,500	$707,000

Analysis of these financial statements will explain the sources and uses of working capital

Liabilities & Stockholders' Equity

Current liabilities:		
Accounts payable	$ 145,000	$ 90,000
Accrued liabilities	22,500	42,000
Total current liabilities	$ 167,500	$132,000
Notes payable, long term	170,000	20,000
Bonds payable, due June 30, Year 20	110,000	185,000
Capital stock, $5 par	100,000	60,000
Paid-in capital in excess of par	155,000	100,000
Retained earnings	220,000	210,000
Total liabilities & stockholders' equity	$ 922,500	$707,000

ALLISON CORPORATION
Condensed Income Statement
For Year Ended December 31, Year 4

Sales (net)	$900,000
Cost of goods sold	500,000
Gross profit on sales	$400,000
Operating expenses and income taxes	340,000
Income before gain on sale of land	$ 60,000
Gain on sale of land	20,000
Net income	$ 80,000

1 *Changes in noncurrent assets:*
  a Land costing $50,000 was sold for $70,000 cash. Another parcel of land was acquired for $150,000 by issuing a long-term note payable for the entire purchase price.
  b Equipment was purchased for $90,000; the invoice was paid within 10 days.
  c Depreciation of $67,500 was recorded.

2 *Changes in noncurrent liabilities:*
  a As stated in transaction 1a, a $150,000 long-term note payable was issued in exchange for land.
  b Bonds payable of $75,000 were retired at a price equal to face value.

3 *Changes in stockholders' equity accounts:*
  a A 50% stock dividend was declared in January, requiring a transfer of $30,000 from the Retained Earnings account to the Capital Stock account.
  b In February, 2,000 shares of $5 par value stock were issued for $65,000 cash, thus increasing Capital Stock by $10,000 and Paid-in Capital in Excess of Par by $55,000.
  c Cash dividends of $40,000 were declared and paid, causing a reduction in retained earnings.
  d The net income for the year, $80,000 (including the $20,000 nonoperating gain on sale of land), was transferred to the Retained Earnings account.

From the comparative balance sheets, the income statement, and the summary of transactions affecting noncurrent accounts, we can prepare a statement of changes in financial position by completing the following three steps:

1 Compute the change in working capital during the period.
2 Prepare a working paper for analysis of changes in noncurrent accounts.
3 Prepare the statement of changes in financial position.

Computation of increase in working capital during the period. The first step in preparing a statement of changes in financial position is to determine the net increase or decrease in working capital during the period covered by the statement.

The working capital of the Allison Corporation increased by $57,500 during Year 4, determined as follows:

ALLISON CORPORATION

Computation of Increase in Working Capital during Year 4

	Dec. 31, Year 4	Dec. 31, Year 3
Current assets	$345,000	$252,000
Less: Current liabilities	167,500	132,000
Working capital	$177,500	$120,000
Increase in working capital during Year 4 ($177,500 − $120,000)		57,500
	$177,500	$177,500

Sources of working capital exceed uses by $57,500

The purpose of the statement of changes in financial position is to explain the *reasons* for the change in working capital. This is accomplished by listing the specific sources and uses of working capital during the period. Since the working capital for the Allison Corporation increased by $57,500, the sources of working capital during Year 4 exceeded the uses by this amount. But before a statement of changes in financial position can be prepared, we must analyze the changes which took place during the year in the noncurrent accounts.

Preparation of working paper for analysis of changes in noncurrent accounts. A working paper showing the analysis of changes in noncurrent accounts for the Allison Corporation is illustrated on page 626. The amount of working capital and the balances in noncurrent accounts at the beginning of the period are listed in the first column of the working paper; balances at the end of the year are listed in the last (right-hand) column. The two middle columns are used to *explain the changes* in each *noncurrent* account during the year and to indicate whether each change represents a source or a use of funds. Transactions for the year (in summary form) are recorded in these middle columns and an offsetting entry is made in the lower section of the working paper indicating the effect of each transaction upon working capital.

Explanation of entries in the middle columns. By studying the changes in the noncurrent accounts during Year 4, we are able to find the specific reasons for the $57,500

ALLISON CORPORATION
Working Paper for Statement of Changes in Financial Position
For Year Ended December 31, Year 4

Debits	Account Balances, End of Year 3	Analysis of Transactions for Year 4		Account Balances, End of Year 4
		Debit	Credit	
Working capital	120,000	(x) 57,500		177,500
Land	200,000	(6) 150,000	(5) 50,000	300,000
Equipment	380,000	(7) 90,000		470,000
Total	700,000			947,500
Credits				
Accumulated depreciation	125,000		(4) 67,500	192,500
Notes payable, long-term	20,000		(6) 150,000	170,000
Bonds payable, due June 30, Year 20	185,000	(8) 75,000		110,000
Capital stock, $5 par	60,000		(3) 30,000 (9) 10,000	100,000
Paid-in capital in excess of par	100,000		(9) 55,000	155,000
Retained earnings	210,000	(2) 40,000 (3) 30,000	(1) 80,000	220,000
Total	700,000	442,500	442,500	947,500

Sources of working capital:		Sources	Uses	
Operations — net income		(1) 80,000		(From operations, $127,500)
Add: Depreciation		(4) 67,500		
Less: Gain on sale of land			(5) 20,000	
Sale of land		(5) 70,000		
Issuance of long-term notes payable		(6) 150,000		
Sale of capital stock		(9) 65,000		
Uses of working capital:				
Cash dividends declared			(2) 40,000	
Purchase of land in exchange for long-term note payable			(6) 150,000	
Purchase of equipment			(7) 90,000	
Retirement of bonds payable			(8) 75,000	
Total sources and uses of working capital		432,500	375,000	
Increase in working capital during Year 4			(x) 57,500	
		432,500	432,500	

Explanation of transactions for Year 4:

(1) Net income, $80,000 (including nonoperating gain of $20,000 on sale of land), is transferred to Retained Earnings and is classified as a tentative source of working capital [to be adjusted by entries (4) and (5), below].

(2) Cash dividends declared, $40,000, reduce retained earnings and are a use of working capital.

(3) A 50% stock dividend had no effect on working capital.

increase in working capital. The noncurrent accounts may be analyzed in any sequence; however, we recommend the following approach:

1 Explain all transactions affecting the Retained Earnings account.
2 Complete the computation of working capital provided by operations.
3 Beginning at the top of the working paper, explain any remaining changes in noncurrent accounts.
4 Make an entry explaining the net change in working capital. This entry should bring both the upper and lower sets of middle columns into balance.

Using this approach, the entries in our illustrated working paper are explained below.

Step 1: Explain the changes in Retained Earnings

Entry

(1) Allison Corporation's net income explains an $80,000 credit change in the Retained Earnings account. In the bottom portion of the working papers, an offsetting entry is made identifying net income as a source of working capital.

(2) Cash dividends of $40,000 declared during Year 4 caused a debit change in the Retained Earnings account and were a use of funds.

(3) The 50% stock dividend caused a $30,000 debit change in the Retained Earnings account and a $30,000 credit change in the Capital Stock account. Notice that both the debit and credit portions of this entry appear in the **top portion** of the working papers. As previously stated, stock dividends (and stock splits) are an exception to the general rule that changes in noncurrent accounts represent either sources or uses of working capital. Stock dividends have **no effect** upon working capital.

With these first three entries, we have explained how the Retained Earnings account increased during Year 4 from $210,000 to its ending balance of $220,000.

Step 2: Complete the computation of working capital provided by operations

(4) The $80,000 net income figure appearing in the bottom portion of the working papers is only a tentative measure of the working capital provided by operations. Depreciation expense, for example, must be added back to this figure, because the recording of depreciation expense reduced net income but did not reduce working capital. Entry (4) shows that depreciation expense explains the $67,500 credit change in the Accumulated Depreciation account and adds this amount to net income as a step in determining working capital provided by operations.

(5) To complete the computation of working capital provided by operations, we must remove from net income the $20,000 nonoperating gain arising from the sale of

---

(4) Depreciation, $67,500, is added to net income in arriving at working capital provided by operations.
(5) Sale of land for $70,000. Explains a $50,000 credit change in the Land account. The $20,000 nonoperating gain on the sale is reclassified within the sources of working capital from the "operations" section to "sale of land."
(6) A $150,000 long-term note payable was issued (a source of funds) to acquire land (a use of funds).
(7) Working capital of $90,000 was used to purchase equipment.
(8) Working capital of $75,000 was used to retire bonds payable.
(9) Issued capital stock, increasing working capital by $65,000.
(x) Balancing figure—increase in working capital during Year 4.

land. Entry (5) removes the $20,000 gain from the "operations" section of the working paper and shows the entire $70,000 proceeds from the sale as a separate source of funds. In the top portion of the working paper, entry (5) shows that the sale of this land also caused a $50,000 credit change in the Land account.

We have now determined that working capital of $127,500 was provided by operations ($80,000 net income + $67,500 depreciation expense − $20,000 nonoperating gain).

Step 3: Explain any remaining changes in noncurrent accounts

(6) The issuance of a $150,000 long-term note payable in exchange for land is an exchange transaction, representing both a source and a use of working capital. First, an entry is made in the top portion of the working paper explaining the $150,000 increase in the Notes Payable account and an offsetting entry is made below showing a $150,000 source of funds. Next, a debit entry is made in the upper portion of the working paper explaining the $150,000 increase in the Land account, and an offsetting entry is made below showing this $150,000 use of funds.

(7) The purchase of equipment explains the $90,000 debit change in the Equipment account and is a use of working capital.

(8) During Year 4, Allison Corporation retired $75,000 of bonds payable at par. A reduction in long-term debt is a use of working capital. This transaction is recorded in the working paper by a debit to the Bonds Payable account and an offsetting entry describing the use of funds.

(9) The sale of capital stock in February for $65,000 is recorded in the upper section of the working paper by credits to Capital Stock, $10,000 (2,000 shares with a $5 par value), and to Paid-in Capital in Excess of Par, $55,000. The issuance of capital stock is a source of funds; therefore, the offsetting entry in the lower section of the working papers is entered in the Sources column.

At this point we should check carefully to determine that our entries in the Debit and Credit columns correctly explain the difference between the beginning and ending balances of each noncurrent account. If the top section of the working paper explains the change in every noncurrent account, the bottom section should include all of the sources and uses of working capital for the year.

Step 4: Record the net change in working capital

(x) We now total the Sources column ($432,500) and the Uses column ($375,000) in the bottom section of the working paper. The $57,500 difference between these column totals represents the net change in working capital during Year 4. Since working capital increased, this $57,500 is entered as a debit to Working Capital on the top line of the working paper and as the balancing figure in the Uses column at the bottom of the working paper.

Totals can now be determined for the Debit and Credit columns in the top section of the working paper. If these totals agree, we know that our analysis is correct, at least so far as the mechanics are concerned.

Preparation of statement of changes in financial position. The preceding working paper analysis explained all changes in noncurrent accounts that took place during Year 4. In making this analysis, we listed the sources and uses of working capital in the lower section of the working paper on page 626. The increase of $57,500 in working capital has been confirmed and a statement of changes in financial position, including a schedule showing the changes in the components of working capital, can now be prepared as shown below.

In published financial statements, a schedule entitled Changes in Composition of Working Capital generally accompanies the statement of changes in financial position. The purpose of this supporting schedule is to help readers of the financial statements to evaluate the *quality* of the company's working capital. Working capital that includes adequate amounts of highly liquid assets, such as cash and marketable securities, is regarded as being of higher quality than working capital that consists primarily of inventory. If the economy enters a recession, for example, a company with a large inventory may have difficulty in converting this asset into cash. Even a company with a large amount of working capital can experience at least temporary insolvency if it runs short of cash.

ALLISON CORPORATION

Statement of Changes in Financial Position

For Year Ended December 31, Year 4

Statement of changes in financial position shows sources and uses of working capital

Sources of working capital:		
Operations:		
Net income		$ 80,000
Add: Expense not requiring the use of working capital—		
depreciation	$ 67,500	
Less: Nonoperating gain on sale of land	20,000	47,500
Total working capital provided by operations		$127,500
Sale of land		70,000
Issuance of long-term notes payable		150,000
Sale of capital stock		65,000
Total sources of working capital		$412,500
Uses of working capital:		
Declaration of cash dividends	$ 40,000	
Purchase of land in exchange for long-term notes payable	150,000	
Purchase of equipment	90,000	
Retirement of bonds payable	75,000	
Total uses of working capital		355,000
Increase in working capital		$ 57,500

Changes in Composition of Working Capital

	End of Year 4	End of Year 3	Increases or (Decreases) in Working Capital
Current assets:			
Cash	$ 15,000	$ 35,000	$(20,000)
Accounts receivable (net)	105,000	85,000	20,000
Inventory	200,000	120,000	80,000
Short-term prepayments	25,000	12,000	13,000
Total current assets	$345,000	$252,000	
Current liabilities:			
Accounts payable	$145,000	$ 90,000	(55,000)
Accrued liabilities	22,500	42,000	19,500
Total current liabilities	$167,500	$132,000	
Working capital	$177,500	$120,000	
Increase in working capital			$ 57,500

This supporting schedule shows the change in each working capital account

CASH FLOW ANALYSIS

A statement of changes in financial position is designed to provide stockholders and other outsiders with an overview of the company's liquid resources. Managers, however, are often more concerned with having enough cash available to meet the company's maturing liabilities. To help managers plan and control cash balances, most companies prepare *cash flow statements.* These statements explain the change in the company's cash balance by summarizing the cash receipts and cash disbursements occurring over the accounting period.

Cash flow statements often are prepared monthly as well as annually. In addition, many companies prepare *projected* cash flow statements (called *cash budgets* or *cash forecasts*) which forecast the cash receipts and cash disbursements of future accounting periods. These forecasts enable managers to plan the company's borrowing and investment activities so as to avoid cash shortages or excessively high cash balances.

Cash flow statements usually do not appear in the annual report to stockholders and other outsiders; they are prepared only for internal use by management. However, banks often insist that a company applying for a loan include both a cash flow statement and a cash forecast with the loan application.

Preparation of a cash flow statement

The cash flow statement of Allison Corporation for Year 4 is illustrated on page 631.

ALLISON CORPORATION
Cash Flow Statement
For Year Ended December 31, Year 4

Complete summary
of cash movements
for Year 4

Cash receipts:		
Cash generated from operations (see schedule on page 634)		$ 50,000
Sale of land		70,000
Sale of capital stock		65,000
Total cash receipts		$185,000
Cash payments:		
Purchase of equipment	$90,000	
Retirement of bonds payable	75,000	
Payment of cash dividends	40,000	
Total cash payments		205,000
Decrease in cash during the year		$ 20,000

Much of this statement was developed from our preceding discussion (pages 627 – 628) of Allison Corporation's transactions in Year 4. For example, we already know that cash was received from the sale of land ($70,000) and from the sale of capital stock ($65,000). We also know that cash was paid to purchase equipment ($90,000), to retire bonds payable ($75,000), and to **pay** cash dividends ($40,000). (Notice that no cash payment occurs until a dividend is **paid**, whereas working capital is decreased as soon as a cash dividend is **declared**.) The remaining item, cash generated from operations, requires explanation and is discussed in the following paragraphs.

Cash flow from operations

Cash generated from operations is equal to the cash receipts from customers, less the cash payments for purchases of merchandise and for operating expenses and income taxes. If a company maintained its accounting records on a strict cash basis, these cash flows would appear as the balances of the revenue and expense accounts in the general ledger.[5] However, virtually all businesses maintain their accounting records on the accrual basis. To find the cash flows from operations, we must therefore **convert the accrual basis measurements of revenue and expense to the cash basis.** The conversion of net sales, cost of goods sold, and operating expenses from the accrual basis to the cash basis is illustrated in the following sections of this chapter.

Cash receipts from customers. Sales on account are an important factor in most companies. The relationship between the amount of cash collected from customers and the net

---

[5] The cash basis of accounting was explained in Chapter 3. Under the cash basis, revenue is not recorded until cash is collected from the customer; purchases of merchandise and expenses are recorded in the period in which payment is made. Under the accrual basis, on the other hand, revenue is recognized at the date of sale and expenses are recorded when the related goods or services are used.

sales reported in the income statement depends on the change in accounts receivable during the period. If accounts receivable have increased during the period, we know that credit sales are being made faster than the cash is being collected from the customers. If accounts receivable have decreased, cash is being collected faster than credit sales are being made. The relationship between net sales and cash collections from customers may be stated as follows:

Converting sales to cash basis

$$\text{Net sales} \left\{ \begin{array}{c} + \text{ decrease in accounts receivable} \\ \text{or} \\ - \text{ increase in accounts receivable} \end{array} \right\} = \begin{array}{l} \text{cash receipts from} \\ \text{customers} \end{array}$$

In the Allison Corporation example, a glance at the comparative balance sheet on page 623 tells us that net accounts receivable increased from $85,000 to $105,000 during Year 4, an increase of $20,000. Therefore, the cash receipts from customers during Year 4 can be determined as follows:

Net sales on cash basis

Net sales	$900,000
Less: Increase in net accounts receivable during the year	20,000
Cash receipts from customers	$880,000

Cash payments for purchases. The relationship between the cost of goods sold for a period and the cash payments for the purchase of merchandise depends both on the change in inventory and the change in accounts payable to merchandise suppliers during the period. The relationship may be stated, in two stages, as follows:

Converting cost of goods sold to cash basis

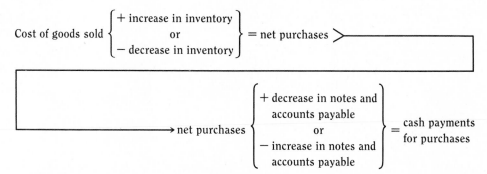

Again referring to the Allison Corporation example, we can see that the company increased its inventory by $80,000 and that accounts payable to merchandise suppliers increased by $55,000 during the year. The cash payments for purchases during Year 4 would be computed as follows:

Cost of goods sold on cash basis

Cost of goods sold	$500,000
Add: Increase in inventory	80,000
Net purchases (accrual basis)	$580,000
Less: Increase in accounts payable to suppliers	55,000
Cash payments for purchases	$525,000

Let us review the logic behind this computation. If a company is increasing its inventory, it will be buying more merchandise than it sells during the period; furthermore, if the company is increasing its account payable to merchandise creditors, it is not paying cash for all of these purchases.

Cash payments for expenses. Expenses in the income statement arise from three major sources: cash expenditures, the write-off of prepayments, and obligations incurred for accrued expenses. The relationship between operating expenses and cash payments, therefore, depends on changes in asset accounts representing the prepayment of expenses, and on change in accrued liability accounts. These relationships may be summarized as follows:

Converting an expense on accrual basis to cash basis

$$\text{Expense} \begin{cases} + \text{ increase in related} \\ \text{prepayment} \\ \text{or} \\ - \text{ decrease in related} \\ \text{prepayment} \end{cases} \text{and} \begin{cases} + \text{ decrease in related} \\ \text{accrued liability} \\ \text{or} \\ - \text{ increase in related} \\ \text{accrued liability} \end{cases} = \begin{matrix} \text{cash payments} \\ \text{for expense} \end{matrix}$$

Recording depreciation expense causes a decrease in the book value of a depreciable asset, such as buildings or equipment. This depreciable asset may be viewed as a long-term prepayment. Thus, the amount of depreciation recorded during the period must be deducted from the accrual based operating expenses as a step in computing cash payments for expense. This is consistent with the fact that recording depreciation expense does not involve any cash payment.

Using the information for the Allison Corporation, we can summarize the relationship between the operating expenses and income taxes reported in the income statement and cash payments for these expenses during Year 4 as follows:

Expenses on cash basis

Total operating expenses and income taxes in the income statement		$340,000
Add: Decrease in accrued liabilities	$19,500	
Increase in short-term prepayments	13,000	32,500
Subtotal		$372,500
Less: Decrease in long-term prepayments (depreciation)		67,500
Cash payments for operating expenses and income taxes		$305,000

Conversion of an income statement to cash basis. The differences between an accrual basis income statement and the cash generated from operations are summarized in the following schedule. Notice that this schedule includes the same adjustments to net sales, cost of goods sold, and operating expenses that were illustrated in the preceding paragraphs.

ALLISON CORPORATION
Conversion of Income Statement from Accrual to Cash Basis
For Year Ended December 31, Year 4

	Income Statement (Accrual Basis)	Add (Deduct)	Cash Basis
How much cash was generated from operations in Year 4? Net sales	$900,000		
Less: Increase in accounts receivable		$(20,000)	$880,000
Cost of goods sold	500,000		
Add: Increase in inventory		80,000	
Less: Increase in notes and accounts payable to merchandise creditors		(55,000)	525,000
Gross profit on sales	$400,000		$355,000
Operating expenses and income taxes	340,000		
Add: Decrease in accrued liabilities		19,500	
Increase in short-term prepayments		13,000	
Less: Depreciation expense		(67,500)	305,000
Income before gain on sale of land (accrual basis)	$ 60,000		
Cash generated from operations			$ 50,000

The Allison Corporation example was sufficiently simple that we could develop cash flow information from a direct inspection of the income statement and comparative balance sheets. In more complex situations, the accountant will use a working paper to convert the income statement from an accrual to a cash basis and to develop cash flow information in a systematic fashion. Familiarity with these working-paper procedures is not necessary in order to be able to understand and interpret cash flow information; therefore, discussion of this process is reserved for more advanced accounting courses.

Key terms introduced or emphasized in chapter 15

Cash basis. A method of summarizing operating results in terms of cash receipts and cash payments rather than revenue earned and expenses incurred.

Cash flow statement. A statement showing the sources of cash receipts and purposes of cash payments during an accounting period. This statement is useful for explaining changes in the balance of the Cash account, but it is not a substitute for an income statement.

Exchange transaction. In the context of a statement of changes in financial position, exchange transactions are financing or investing activities which do not directly affect working capital accounts. An example of such a transaction is the purchase of plant assets by issuing common stock. Such transactions should be shown in a funds statement as both a source and a use of working capital.

Funds. In the context of a statement of changes in financial position, "funds" are usually defined as working capital.

Noncurrent account. Any balance sheet account *other than* a current asset or a current liability. Noncurrent accounts include long-term investments, plant assets, intangible assets, long-term liabilities, and stockholders' equity accounts.

Statement of changes in financial position. A financial statement showing the sources and uses of working capital during the accounting period. In addition, this statement shows financing and investing activities, such as exchange transactions, which do not directly affect working capital.

Working capital. Current assets minus current liabilities. Working capital represents the net amount of liquid resources available to a business.

Demonstration problem for your review

Comparative financial data for Liquid Gas Company for the last two years are shown below:

	December 31	
Debits	**Year 2**	**Year 1**
Cash	$ 39,220	$ 15,800
Receivables (net of allowance for doubtful accounts)	41,400	24,000
Inventories, lower of cost or market	27,600	36,800
Short-term prepayments	4,180	4,400
Land	9,000	19,000
Buildings	270,000	250,000
Equipment	478,600	450,000
Total debits	$870,000	$800,000

Credits	**Year 2**	**Year 1**
Accumulated depreciation: buildings	$ 95,000	$ 77,000
Accumulated depreciation: equipment	153,000	120,000
Accounts payable	59,200	30,000
Accrued liabilities	20,000	10,000
Bonds payable	90,000	90,000
Premium on bonds payable	2,800	3,000
Preferred stock ($100 par)	70,000	100,000
Common stock ($25 par)	260,000	250,000
Paid-in capital in excess of par	45,000	40,000
Retained earnings	75,000	80,000
Total credits	$870,000	$800,000

Other data

(1) During Year 2, the board of directors of the company authorized a transfer of $15,000 from retained earnings to reflect a 4% stock dividend on the common stock.

(2) Cash dividends of $6,000 were paid on the preferred stock, and cash dividends of $50,000 were paid on the common stock.

(3) Three hundred shares of preferred stock were retired at par value.

(4) The only entries recorded in the Retained Earnings account were for dividends and to close the Income Summary account, which had a credit balance of $66,000 after the loss on the sale of the land.

(5) There were no sales or retirements of building and equipment during the year; land was sold for $8,000, resulting in a loss of $2,000.

Instructions

a Compute the change in working capital during Year 2. You may use totals for current assets and current liabilities.

b Prepare a working paper for a statement of changes in financial position for Year 2.

c Prepare a statement of changes in financial position for Year 2, without showing the composition of working capital.

d Prepare a cash flow statement, with a supporting schedule converting the net income from the accrual basis to the cash basis.

Solution to demonstration problem

a Computation of decrease in working capital:

	As of December 31	
	Year 2	Year 1
Current assets	$112,400	$81,000
Less: Current liabilities	79,200	40,000
Working capital	$ 33,200	$41,000
Decrease in working capital during Year 2	7,800	
	$ 41,000	$41,000

b

LIQUID GAS COMPANY

Working Paper for Statement of Changes in Financial Position

For Year 2

Debits	Account Balances, End of Year 1	Analysis of Transactions for Year 2		Account Balances, End of Year 2
		Debit	Credit	
Working capital	41,000		(x) 7,800	33,200
Land	19,000		(5) 10,000	9,000
Buildings	250,000	(6) 20,000		270,000
Equipment	450,000	(7) 28,600		478,600
Total	760,000			790,800
Credits				
Accumulated depreciation: buildings	77,000		(4) 18,000	95,000
Accumulated depreciation: equipment	120,000		(4) 33,000	153,000
Bonds payable	90,000			90,000
Premium on bonds payable	3,000	(8) 200		2,800
Preferred stock, $100 par	100,000	(9) 30,000		70,000
Common stock, $25 par	250,000		(2) 10,000	260,000
Paid-in capital excess of par	40,000		(2) 5,000	45,000
Retained earnings	80,000	(2) 15,000 (3) 56,000	(1) 66,000 }	75,000
Total	760,000	149,800	149,800	790,800

Sources of working capital:	Sources		Uses	
Operations — net income	(1)	66,000		
Add: Depreciation	(4)	51,000		(From
Loss on sale of land	(5)	2,000		operations,
Less: Amortization of premium on bonds				$118,800)
payable			(8)	200
Sale of land	(5)	8,000		
Uses of working capital:				
Payment of cash dividends			(3)	56,000
Purchase of buildings			(6)	20,000
Purchase of equipment			(7)	28,600
Retirement of preferred stock			(9)	30,000
Total sources and uses of				
working capital		127,000		134,800
Decrease in working capital	(x)	7,800		
		134,800		134,800

Explanation of transactions for Year 2:
(1) Net income, $66,000, including a loss of $2,000 on sale of land, transferred to Retained Earnings.
(2) Entry to record 4% stock dividend; no effect on working capital.
(3) Cash dividends declared, $56,000 (preferred stock, $6,000, and common, $50,000).
(4) Depreciation, $51,000, is added to net income because it is an expense which did not reduce working capital.
(5) To record sale of land for $8,000; the loss of $2,000 had no effect on working capital.
(6) To record working capital used for purchase of buildings.
(7) To record working capital used for purchase of equipment.
(8) Amortization of premium on bonds payable increased net income but had no effect on working capital.
(9) To record working capital applied to retirement of preferred stock.
(x) Balancing figure — decrease in working capital during Year 2.

c

LIQUID GAS COMPANY
Statement of Changes in Financial Position
For Year 2

Sources of working capital:
  Operations:

Net income		$ 66,000
Add: Expense not requiring the use of working capital:		
Depreciation	$51,000	
Nonoperating loss on sale of land	2,000	
Less: Increase in net income which did not provide working		
capital — amortization of premium on bonds payable ...	(200)	52,800
Total working capital provided by operations		$118,800
Sale of land		8,000
Total sources of working capital		$126,800
Uses of working capital:		
Declaration of cash dividends	$56,000	
Purchase of buildings	20,000	
Purchase of equipment	28,600	
Retirement of preferred stock	30,000	
Total uses of working capital		134,600
Decrease in working capital		$ 7,800

d

LIQUID GAS COMPANY
Cash Flow Statement
For Year 2

Cash receipts:		
Cash generated from operations (see Schedule A below)		$150,020
Sale of land		8,000
Total cash receipts		$158,020
Cash payments:		
Payment of cash dividends	$56,000	
Purchase of buildings	20,000	
Purchase of equipment	28,600	
Retirement of preferred stock	30,000	
Total cash payments		134,600
Increase in cash during the year		$ 23,420

Schedule A — Cash generated from operations:		
Working capital provided by operations — part c		$118,800
Add: Decrease in inventories	$ 9,200	
Decrease in short-term prepayments	220	
Increase in accounts payable	29,200	
Increase in accrued liabilities	10,000	48,620
Less: Increase in receivables		(17,400)
Cash generated from operations		$150,020

Review questions

1 Explain why an adequate amount of working capital is essential to the successful operation of a business.
2 What are the primary ways in which a firm generates working capital and the primary ways in which a firm uses working capital?
3 List four transactions which are neither a source nor a use of working capital and which are not disclosed in a statement of changes in financial position.
4 Sources of funds include borrowing, sale of noncurrent assets, operations, and sale of capital stock. Which of these possible sources of funds do you consider to be most important to the long-run survival of a business?
5 What information can a reader gain from a statement of changes in financial position that is not apparent from reading an income statement?
6 In preparing a statement of changes in financial position, business transactions may be classified into three categories. List three categories and indicate which category results in changes in working capital.
7 Give examples of expenses, other than depreciation expense, which reduce net income but which do not result in the use of working capital during the period.
8 Give an example of an increase in net income which does not result in an increase in working capital during the period.
9 The following quotation appeared in the annual report of a large corporation: "Depreciation,

depletion, and amortization charges provide funds which cause our working capital provided by operations to consistently exceed our net income." Evaluate this quotation.

10 Although extraordinary and nonoperating gains and losses may be included in net income, what reason can you give for excluding such gains and losses in computing the working capital provided by operations? Use the following facts to illustrate your point: Net income including gain on sale of land, $100,000; sale of land, with a book value of $70,000, for $150,000.

11 Miller Corporation acquired a building for $300,000, paying $60,000 cash and issuing a long-term note payable for the balance. What is the effect of this transaction upon the working capital of Miller Corporation? How should the transaction be shown in a statement of changes in financial position?

12 During the year, holders of $4 million of Dallas Company convertible bonds converted their bonds into shares of Dallas Company common stock. The president of Dallas Company made the following statement: "By issuing common stock to retire these bonds, the company has saved $4 million in cash. Our statement of changes in financial position will not have to show the retirement of bonds among the uses of working capital." Do you agree with this statement? Explain.

13 What is the major difference between the statement of changes in financial position and a cash flow statement?

14 Give several examples of transactions which can reduce the amount of cash generated by operations, as shown in a cash flow statement, without reducing working capital.

15 The president of Dexter Corporation was puzzled by the following statement made by the accountant: "Our working capital provided by operations amounted to $85,000 last year but our cash generated from operations was only $10,000 because of the increases in our inventory and receivables and the decrease in our accounts payable." Explain what the accountant meant.

16 An outside member of the board of directors of a small corporation made the following comment after studying the comparative financial statements for the past two years: "I have trouble understanding why our cash has increased steadily during the past two years, yet our profits have been negligible; we have paid no dividends; and inventories, receivables, payables, cost of plant and equipment, long-term debt, and capital stock have remained essentially unchanged." Write a brief statement explaining how this situation might occur.

Exercises

Ex. 15-1 You are to indicate for each of the following transactions whether it causes working capital (1) to increase, (2) to decrease, or (3) to remain unchanged:

a Collected a large past-due account receivable.

b Sold for cash a new nuclear power plant which regulatory authorities refused to license. The amount received, $30 million, was far below the $300 million book value of the plant.

c Borrowed cash by issuance of a short-term note payable to a bank.

d Split the $15 par value common stock 3 for 1; par value was reduced to $5 per share.

e Declared a cash dividend payable in the following fiscal year.

f Used cash not needed in current operations to retire a portion of a long-term mortgage payable.

g Issued 20-year, 12% bonds payable of $10 million at a price of $99.

Ex. 15-2 State the amount of the increase or decrease (if any) in working capital as a result of each of the following independent events:

a Acquisition of plant equipment with a cost of $600,000. Terms of purchase were $200,000 cash and $100,000 (plus interest) payable every six months over the next two years.

b Purchase and retirement of entire issue of bonds payable of $1,000,000 face value at price of 98. The unamortized premium on the bonds payable at date of retirement was $60,000.

c The year-end physical inventory indicated some goods in stock to be obsolete, some goods to be missing, and some to be damaged. In the aggregate, these factors caused a $60,000 write-down of inventory to a market value below cost.

d Declaration of a 40% stock dividend on $1,000,000 par value of common stock outstanding.

Ex. 15-3 Stoney Creek Corporation maintains its accounts on a calendar-year basis. Explain how each of the following events should be reported in the statement of changes in financial position for Year 8:

a On February 15 of Year 8, a cash dividend of $60,000 was paid. This dividend had been declared on December 15 of Year 7.

b Intensely competitive conditions in Year 8 caused the company to suffer its first operating loss. The loss from operations for Year 8 was $110,000.

c Depreciation of $100,000 was recorded in Year 8.

d In January of Year 8 the 20,000 shares of $15 par value stock were split 3 for 1. In March of Year 8, a 5% stock dividend was distributed. Market price of the stock at the date of the stock dividend was $30.

e A tract of land was acquired at a cost of $600,000. Payment consisted of cash of $100,000 and issuance of capital stock with a market value of $500,000.

Ex. 15-4 White Knight Corporation's annual income statement showed a net loss of $600,000. In determining this loss, the corporation included the following items among others:

Gain on sale of land	$350,000
Uninsured fire damage to building	630,000
Amortization of premium on bonds payable	90,000
Depreciation expense	460,000
Amortization of patents	150,000

Compute the amount of the working capital increase or decrease as a result of operations. Arrange your solution in the form of a schedule, beginning with "Net loss . . . $600,000" and concluding with "Working Capital provided by operations . . . $____."

Ex. 15-5 Financial information for Four Square, Inc., for Year 5 is summarized below.

	December 31 Year 5	December 31 Year 4
Working capital	$ 440,000	$ 500,000
Land	360,000	200,000
Buildings	640,000	400,000
Less: Accumulated depreciation	(160,000)	(140,000)
Totals	$1,280,000	$ 960,000
Notes payable (due in five years)	$ 280,000	$ -0-
Capital stock, no-par value	800,000	800,000
Retained earnings	200,000	160,000
Totals	$1,280,000	$ 960,000

The net income was $168,000. There were no nonoperating gains or losses during the year. Depreciation expense for the year was $20,000. A cash dividend of $128,000 was declared at the end of Year 5.

Prepare a statement of changes in financial position for Year 5 without using a working paper.

Ex. 15-6 Shown below is a comparative balance sheet for Timeflight, Inc.

TIMEFLIGHT, INC.
Comparative Balance Sheet
December 31, Year 10 and December 31, Year 9

Assets	Year 10	Year 9
Cash	$ 40,000	$ 10,000
Accounts receivable	100,000	103,000
Inventory	260,000	240,000
Land	150,000	150,000
Buildings and equipment (net)	140,000	126,000
Total assets	$690,000	$629,000

Liabilities & Stockholders' Equity		
Notes payable (short-term)	$ 70,000	$ 33,000
Accounts payable	110,000	112,000
Bonds payable (long-term)	200,000	200,000
Common stock, $10 par	100,000	100,000
Retained earnings	210,000	184,000
Total liabilities & stockholders' equity ..	$690,000	$629,000

You are to prepare a schedule of changes in composition of working capital, similar to the schedule illustrated on page 620. (Note: This exercise does not call for a statement of changes in financial position.)

Ex. 15-7 Selected information from the records of Timberline, Inc., appears below.

	End of Year	Beginning of Year
Net sales	$900,000	
Cost of goods sold	540,000	
Operating expenses (includes depreciation of $30,000)	240,000	
Accounts receivable	60,600	$ 30,600
Inventories	96,000	120,000
Prepaid expense	6,900	4,500
Accounts payable (merchandise creditors)	84,000	75,000
Accrued expenses payable	3,000	3,600

From the above information, you are to compute the following:

a Cash collected from customers during the year
b Cash paid to merchandise creditors during the year
c Cash paid for operating expenses during the year

Ex. 15-8 Comparative financial statements prepared for Surfside Corporation contain the following information:

	Year 10	Year 9
Inventory at end of year	$ 45,000	$ 84,000
Accounts receivable at end of year	27,000	36,000
Accounts payable at end of year	24,000	18,000
Depreciation expense	127,500	95,400
Net income (no extraordinary items)	180,000	111,000
Cash dividends declared in December of each year, payable		
Jan. 15 of following year	67,500	45,000

From the data above, determine the following:

a The **working capital** provided by operations in Year 10
b The **cash** generated by operations in Year 10
c **Working capital** used for dividends in Year 10

Problems

15-1 Effects of transactions on working capital and cash
Game Data, Inc., carried out the following business transactions and adjustments. For each item you are to indicate the effect first on working capital, and second on cash. In each case the possible effects are an increase, a decrease, or no change.

(1) Payment of an account payable
(2) Depreciation recorded for the period
(3) Sale of long-term investment at a loss
(4) Payment of the current year's income tax liability, which was previously recorded in the accounting records
(5) Shares of common stock issued in exchange for convertible bonds converted by bond-holders.
(6) An uncollectible account receivable written off against the Allowance for Doubtful Accounts
(7) Machinery sold for cash in excess of its carrying value
(8) Empty warehouse destroyed by fire; one-half of its carrying value covered by insurance and recorded as a receivable from the insurance company
(9) Amortization of discount on bonds payable
(10) Premium paid for a one-year insurance policy (debit to Unexpired Insurance)
(11) Declaration of a cash dividend
(12) Payment of previously declared cash dividend on common stock

Instructions

a List the numbers 1 to 12 on your answer sheet, and set up two columns headed "working capital effect" and "cash effect." For each transaction, write the words **increase, decrease,** or **no change** in the appropriate column to indicate the effect of the transaction on working capital and cash.

b Are any of the transactions listed above considered "exchange transactions" which would be listed as both a source and use of working capital in a statement of changes in financial position? Explain.

15-2 Simple statement of changes in financial position
During the year Paperback Publishers showed the following *changes* in amount for the groups of accounts listed below. For example, current assets increased by $80,000 during the year, and this amount therefore appears in the "Debit" change column.

	Changes During the Year	
	Debit	Credit
Current assets	$ 80,000	
Plant and equipment	540,000	
Accumulated depreciation		$230,000
Current liabilities		96,000
Capital stock, $10 par		90,000
Paid-in capital in excess of par		72,000
Retained earnings		132,000
Totals	$620,000	$620,000

During the year the company issued 9,000 shares of capital stock at a price of $18 per share. There were no retirements of plant and equipment during the year. Net income was $252,000 and cash dividends declared and paid during the year amounted to $120,000.

Instructions. Prepare a statement of changes in financial position for the year without using working papers.

15-3 Prepare statement of changes in financial position without working papers
Selected financial information taken from the Year 5 annual report of Nightwatch, Inc., appears below.

	End of Year 5	End of Year 4
Working capital	$125,000	$110,000
Long-term investments	48,000	60,000
Equipment	390,000	280,000
Less: Accumulated depreciation	(120,000)	(70,000)
Capital stock	150,000	150,000
Retained earnings	293,000	230,000

Depreciation for Year 5 amounted to $50,000; no equipment items were sold; investments were sold at a gain of $6,000; and net income (including the $6,000 nonoperating gain) for Year 5 was $93,000. Cash dividends of $30,000 were declared and paid.

Instructions. From the information given, prepare a statement of changes in financial position for Year 5, without using working papers.

15-4   Working papers for statement of changes in financial position

Instructions. Using the information provided in Problem 15-3, prepare a working paper for a statement of changes in financial position. (If you have already worked Problem 15-3, determine that your solutions to both problems are in agreement.)

15-5   Statement of changes in financial position: a comprehensive problem
Comparative balance sheets for Sierra Hot Tub Co. at the end of Year 1 and Year 2 are shown below:

	Year 2	Year 1
Cash	$ 35,000	$ 60,000
Accounts receivable (net)	90,000	105,000
Merchandise inventory	195,000	150,000
Land for future expansion	75,000	
Plant and equipment (see accumulated depreciation below)	500,000	375,000
Patents (net of amortization)	55,000	60,000
Totals	$950,000	$750,000
Accumulated depreciation	$157,500	$120,000
Accounts payable	61,500	45,000
Dividends payable	6,000	
Notes payable due in Year 5	45,000	
Capital stock, $10 par	650,000	525,000
Retained earnings	30,000	60,000
Totals	$950,000	$750,000

Additional data

(1) The net loss for Year 2 amounted to $24,000. (Hint: Operations result in a net **source** of working capital.)
(2) Cash dividends of $6,000 were declared.
(3) The company incurred the following expenses which did not require the use of working capital: depreciation, $37,500, and amortization of patents, $5,000.
(4) Land for future expansion was acquired at a cost of $75,000. This acquisition was financed by paying $30,000 cash and issuing a 10% note payable due in three years for the balance of the purchase price.
(5) The company issued 12,500 shares of its capital stock in exchange for equipment with a list price of $125,000. The market value of the stock was $10 per share.

Instructions

a Prepare a schedule showing the changes in the composition of working capital during Year 2. (Use the format illustrated on page 620.)
b Prepare working papers for a statement of changes in financial position for Year 2.
c Prepare a formal statement of changes in financial position for Year 2.

15-6   Working paper approach to statement of changes in financial position
Comparative after-closing trial balances for Emerging Technologies, Inc., at the ends of Years 9 and 10 are shown below:

Debits	Year 10	Year 9
Current assets	$1,380,000	$1,420,000
Land	600,000	750,000
Buildings & equipment	1,550,000	1,135,000
Goodwill	388,000	400,000
Discount on bonds payable	13,000	15,000
Totals	$3,931,000	$3,720,000

Credits	Year 10	Year 9
Current liabilities	$ 718,000	$ 720,000
Accumulated depreciation	628,000	520,000
Long-term notes payable	100,000	
Bonds payable	1,000,000	1,000,000
11% preferred stock, $100 par		300,000
Common stock, $5 par	260,000	210,000
Paid-in capital in excess of par	570,000	420,000
Retained earnings	655,000	550,000
Totals	$3,931,000	$3,720,000

Additional data

(1) Net income for Year 10 was $280,000.
(2) Cash dividends of $175,000 were declared during the year.
(3) The company incurred the following expenses which did not require the use of working capital: depreciation, $108,000; amortization of goodwill, $12,000; and amortization of discount on bonds payable, $2,000.
(4) Land with a cost of $150,000 was sold for $170,000 cash.
(5) Equipment was purchased for $415,000 by paying $315,000 in cash and issuing a 12% long-term note payable for the remaining $100,000.
(6) The company issued 10,000 shares of $5 par value common stock at a price of $20 per share. The proceeds, along with some additional cash, were used to retire the entire issue of 11% preferred stock at its par value.

Instructions

a Prepare a schedule computing the change in working capital during Year 10.
b Prepare a working paper for a statement of changes in financial position for Year 10.
c Prepare a formal statement of changes in financial position for Year 10. (Do not include the supporting schedule showing the changes in the composition of working capital.)

15-7   Working papers and statement of changes in financial position
Comparative account balances for Long Island Corporation at the end of Years 9 and 10 are listed below:

	Year 10	Year 9
Cash	$ 60,000	$ 100,000
Accounts receivable (net)	150,000	175,000
Merchandise inventory	300,000	250,000
Land for future expansion	150,000	
Plant and equipment (see accumulated depreciation below)	750,000	625,000
Patents (net of amortization)	90,000	100,000
Totals	$1,500,000	$1,250,000
Accumulated depreciation	$ 262,500	$ 200,000
Accounts payable	152,500	100,000
Dividends payable	10,000	
Notes payable due in three years	25,000	
Capital stock, $10 par	1,000,000	850,000
Retained earnings	50,000	100,000
Totals	$1,500,000	$1,250,000

The following additional information is available for your consideration:

(1) The net loss for Year 10 amounted to $40,000. (Note: Operations will be a net *source* of working capital.)
(2) Cash dividends of $10,000 were declared.
(3) The company incurred the following expenses which did not require the use of working capital: depreciation, $62,500, and amortization of patents, $10,000.
(4) The company issued 15,000 shares of its common stock at par value in exchange for land to be held for future expansion. The land was appraised at $150,000.
(5) Equipment was purchased for $125,000. The company paid $100,000 of this amount in cash and issued a 12%, three-year note payable for the balance.

Instructions

a Prepare a schedule showing the changes in the composition of working capital during Year 10. (Use the format illustrated on page 620.)
b Prepare working papers for a statement of changes in financial position for Year 10.
c Prepare a formal statement of changes in financial position for Year 10.

15-8   Accrual basis to cash basis. Cash flow statement
The financial statements shown below were presented to you by Linda Kahn, owner of Linda's Fashion Boutique, a single proprietorship.

Balance Sheet

Assets	Year 2	Year 1
Cash	$ 10,000	$ 40,000
Marketable securities	15,000	20,000
Accounts receivable (net)	100,000	35,000
Inventory	80,000	60,000
Equipment (net of accumulated depreciation)	35,000	45,000
Total assets	$240,000	$200,000

Liabilities & Owner's Equity

Accounts payable	$ 37,000	$ 40,000
Accrued liabilities	8,000	2,500
Note payable to bank (due early in Year 2)		12,500
Linda Kahn, capital	195,000	145,000
Total liabilities & owner's equity	$240,000	$200,000

Income Statement for Year 2

Sales (net)		$400,000
Cost of goods sold		300,000
Gross profit on sales		$100,000
Operating expenses (including $10,000 depreciation)	$60,000	
Loss on sale of marketable securities	500	60,500
Net income		$ 39,500
Drawings by owner		22,500
Increase in owner's equity as a result of operations		$ 17,000

Kahn is concerned over the decrease in her cash position during Year 2, especially in view of the fact that she invested an additional $33,000 in the business and had a net income of $39,500 during the year. She asks you to prepare a cash flow statement which will explain the decrease in the Cash account.

Instructions

a Prepare a schedule showing the conversion of the income statement from an accrual to a cash basis, thus determining the net cash outflow from operations. (Organize your schedule in the format illustrated on page 634.)

b Prepare a cash flow statement which explains the decrease of $30,000 in cash during Year 2.

Cases for analysis

Case 15-1   Can the past dividend policy be maintained?

Olympic Sportwear has working capital of $6,150,000 at the beginning of Year 5. Restrictions contained in bank loans require that working capital not fall below $6,000,000. The following projected information is available for Year 5:

(1) Budgeted net income (including nonoperating items) is $7,500,000. The following items were included in estimating net income: depreciation, $2,100,000; amortization of premium on bonds payable, $150,000; uncollectible accounts expense, $180,000; and income taxes, $6,300,000. The estimate of net income also included the nonoperating items described below.

(2) Sale of plant assets with a carrying value of $1,200,000 is expected to bring $1,500,000 net of income taxes.

(3) Additional plant assets costing $15,000,000 will be acquired. Payment will be as follows: 20% cash, 20% short-term note, and 60% through issuance of capital stock.

(4) Long-term investment will be sold at cost, $300,000.

(5) Bonds payable in the amount of $1,500,000, bearing interest at 11%, will be redeemed at 105

approximately 10 years prior to maturity in order to eliminate the high interest expense of $165,000 per year. The elimination of this interest and the gain or loss on the retirement of bonds payable were taken into account in estimating net income for Year 5. These bonds had been issued at par.

(6) Tentative planned cash dividend, $4,500,000.

Instructions

a Consider all the information that has been given and prepare a projected statement of changes in financial position (without showing the composition of working capital) in order to determine the estimated increase or decrease in working capital for Year 5. Some of the information given may be irrelevant.

b The planned cash dividend of $4,500,000 represents the same dividend per share as paid last year. The company would like to maintain dividends at this level. Does it appear likely that the past dividend policy can be maintained in Year 5? What factors other than working capital position should be considered in determining the level of cash dividends declared by the board of directors?

Case 15-2   Profits but no cash

When the controller of Trans-Alaska Corporation presented the following condensed comparative financial statements to the board of directors at the close of Year 2, the reaction of the board members was very favorable.

TRANS-ALASKA CORPORATION
Comparative Income Statements
(in thousands of dollars)

	Year 2	Year 1
Net sales	$ 970	$ 680
Cost of goods sold	590	480
Gross profit on sales	$ 380	$ 200
Operating expenses, including depreciation of $80 in Year 2 and $60 in Year 1	(180)	(140)
Income taxes	(90)	(25)
Net income	$ 110	$ 35

TRANS-ALASKA CORPORATION
Comparative Financial Position
As of December 31
(in thousands of dollars)

Current assets	$ 410	$395
Less: Current liabilities	200	225
Working capital	$ 210	$170
Plant and equipment (net)	970	650
Total assets minus current liabilities	$1,180	$820

Financed by following sources of long-term capital:

Long-term liabilities	$ 250	
Capital stock ($50 par value)	500	$500
Retained earnings	430	320
Total sources of long-term capital	$1,180	$820

Noting that net income rose from $3.50 per share of capital stock to $11 per share, one member of the board proposed that a substantial cash dividend be paid. "Our working capital is up by $40,000; we should be able to make a distribution to stockholders," he commented. To which the controller replied that the company's cash position was precarious and pointed out that at the end of Year 2, a cash balance of only $15,000 was on hand, a decline from $145,000 at the end of Year 1. The controller also reminded the board that the company bought $400,000 of new equipment during Year 2. When a board member asked for an explanation of the increase of $40,000 in working capital, the controller presented the following schedule (in thousands of dollars):

		Effect on Working Capital
Increase in working capital:		
Accounts receivable increased by		$ 83
Inventories increased by		45
Prepaid expenses increased by		17
Accounts payable were reduced by		62
Accrued expenses payable were reduced by		28
Total increases in working capital		$235
Decreases in working capital:		
Cash decreased by	$130	
Income tax liability increased by	65	195
Increase in working capital during Year 2		$ 40

After examining this schedule, the board member shook his head and said, "I still don't understand how our cash position can be so tight in the face of a tripling of net income and a substantial increase in working capital!"

Instructions

a Prepare a statement converting Trans-Alaska Corporation's income statement to a cash basis, determining the cash generated by operations during Year 2.

b From the information in a and an inspection of the comparative statement of financial position, prepare a cash flow statement for Year 2, explaining the $130,000 decrease in the cash balance.

c Prepare a statement accounting for the increase in working capital (statement of changes in financial position) for Trans-Alaska Corporation in a more acceptable form.

d Write a note of explanation to the board member.

Chapter 16
Analysis and interpretation of financial statements

In many of the preceding chapters we have been concerned with preparing a set of financial statements. In this chapter we start with the completed financial statements and concentrate on methods of analyzing and interpreting the information they contain. Our goal is to determine whether a company is gaining or losing ground in the unending struggle for profitability and solvency. We explore the techniques for comparing a company's present financial position with its position a year ago and for comparing this year's earnings with last year's earnings. We also compare a company's performance with that of other companies in the industry. Various types of analysis are presented to meet the special needs of common stockholders, long-term creditors, preferred stockholders, and short-term creditors.

After reading this chapter you should be able to:

✓ Put the dollar amount of a company's net income into perspective by relating it to the company's sales, assets, and stockholders' equity.
✓ Describe several sources of financial information about a business.
✓ Explain the uses and limitations of dollar and percentage changes, trend percentages, and component percentages.
✓ Compute dollar and percentage changes, trend percentages, and component percentages from a set of comparative financial statements.
✓ Compute the ratios widely used in financial statement analysis, and explain what each ratio attempts to measure.
✓ Discuss the "quality" of a company's earnings, assets, and working capital.
✓ Analyze financial statements from the viewpoints of a common stockholder, long-term creditor, preferred stockholder, and short-term creditor.

Financial statements are the instrument panel of a business enterprise. They constitute a report on managerial performance, attesting to managerial success or failure and flashing warning signals of impending difficulties. To read a complex instrument panel, one must understand the gauges and their calibration to make sense out of the array of data they convey. Similarly, one must understand the inner workings of the accounting system and the significance of various financial relationships to interpret the data appearing in financial statements. To a reader with a knowledge of accounting, a set of financial statements tells a great deal about a business enterprise.

The financial affairs of a business may be of interest to a number of different groups; management, creditors, investors, politicians, union officials, and government agencies. Each of these groups has somewhat different needs, and accordingly each tends to concentrate on particular aspects of a company's financial picture.

What is your opinion of the level of corporate profits?

As a college student who has completed (or almost completed) a course in accounting, you have a much better understanding of corporate profits than do people who have never studied accounting. The level of earnings of large corporations is a controversial topic, a favorite topic in many political speeches and at cocktail parties. Many of the statements one reads or hears from these sources are emotional rather than rational, and fiction rather than fact. Public opinion polls show that the public believes the average manufacturing company has an after-tax profit of about 30% of sales, when in fact such profit has been *about 5% of sales* in recent years. A widespread public belief that profits are six times the actual rate may lead to some unwise legislation.

An in-depth knowledge of accounting does not enable you to say at what level corporate earnings *should be;* however, a knowledge of accounting does enable you to read audited financial statements that show what the level of corporate earnings *actually is.* Moreover, you are aware that the information in published financial statements of corporations has been audited by CPA firms and has been reviewed in detail by government agencies, such as the Securities and Exchange Commission and the IRS. Consequently, you know that the profits reported in these published financial statements are reasonably reliable; they have been determined in accordance with generally accepted accounting principles and verified by independent experts.

When such troublesome problems as severe unemployment and rising prices for consumer goods and services affect so many people, it is not surprising that some political leaders look for a scapegoat to hold responsible. Often, the blame has been laid on corporate profits, which sometimes have been labeled as ''excessive,'' ''outrageous,'' and even ''obscene.'' Usually the speaker who uses these emotional adjectives cites an absolute dollar amount of profits without relating it in any way to the volume of sales or the amount of assets necessary to produce the quoted profit figure.

● **CASE IN POINT** ● General Motors in an annual report a few years ago showed a net income of $321 million. This profit may sound like a huge amount, but it was only one-half of 1% of GM's sales. Thus, of every dollar received as revenue, only $\frac{1}{2}$ cent represented profit for GM. On a $10,000 car, this was a profit of $50. Actually, earning only $321 million in a year must be regarded as very poor performance for a corporation the size of General Motors. Shortly afterward, however, GM enjoyed its best year ever, and set new records for both sales and earnings. Net income was $4.5 billion and represented about 5½ cents profit on each dollar of sales. That was a profit of $550 on a $10,000 automobile.

Some specific examples of corporate earnings . . . and losses

Not all leading corporations earn a profit every year. In one recent year, for example, General Motors incurred a net loss of more than $775 million. During a good part of the last decade, much of the airline industry operated at a loss. Net losses were incurred in one or more years by such well-known companies as American Airlines, Continental, Pan American, TWA, Western, and United Airlines.

The oil companies have been particularly subject to criticism for so-called excessive profits, so let us briefly look at the profits of Exxon, the world's largest oil company. A recent annual report of Exxon (audited by Price Waterhouse & Co.) shows that profits amounted to a little over $4 billion. Standing alone, that figure seems enormous — but we need to look a little farther. The total revenue of Exxon was over $103 billion, so net income amounted to approximately 4% of sales. On the other hand, income taxes, excise taxes, and other taxes levied upon Exxon amounted to more than $21 billion, or about 5 times as much as the company's profit. Thus, taxation represents a far greater portion of the cost of a gallon of gasoline than does the oil company's profit.

There are many ways of appraising the adequacy of corporate earnings. Certainly, earnings should be compared with total assets and with invested capital as well as with sales. In this chapter we shall look at a number of ways of evaluating corporate profits and solvency.

Sources of financial information

For the most part, our discussion will be limited to the kind of analysis that can be made by "outsiders" who do not have access to internal accounting records. Investors must rely to a considerable extent on financial statements in published annual and quarterly reports. In the case of large publicly owned corporations, additional information is filed with the Securities and Exchange Commission and is available to the public. Financial information about most large corporations is also published by Moody's Investors Service, Standard & Poor's Corporation, and stock brokerage firms.

Bankers are usually able to secure more detailed information by requesting it as a condition for granting a loan. Trade creditors may obtain financial information for businesses of almost any size from credit-rating agencies such as Dun & Bradstreet, Inc.

Comparative financial statements

Significant changes in financial data are easy to see when financial statement amounts for two or more years are placed side by side in adjacent columns. Such a statement is called a *comparative financial statement.* Both the balance sheet and the income statement are often prepared in the form of comparative statements. A highly condensed comparative income statement for three years is shown below.

BENSON CORPORATION
Comparative Income Statement
As of December 31
(in thousands of dollars)

	Year 3	Year 2	Year 1
Net sales	$600	$500	$400
Cost of goods sold	370	300	235
Gross profit	$230	$200	$165
Expenses	194	160	115
Net income	$ 36	$ 40	$ 50

Condensed three-year income statement

Tools of analysis

Few figures in a financial statement are highly significant in and of themselves. It is their relationship to other quantities, or the amount and direction of change since a previous date, that is important. Analysis is largely a matter of establishing significant relationships and pointing up changes and trends. Four widely used analytical techniques are (1) dollar and percentage changes, (2) trend percentages, (3) component percentages, and (4) ratios.

Dollar and percentage changes

The dollar amount of change from year to year is significant, but expressing the change in percentage terms adds perspective. For example, if sales this year have increased by $100,000, the fact that this is an increase of 10% over last year's sales of $1 million puts it in a different perspective than if it represented a 1% increase over sales of $10 million for the prior year.

The dollar amount of any change is the difference between the amount for a *comparison* year and for a *base* year. The percentage change is computed by dividing the amount of the change between years by the amount for the base year. This is illustrated in the tabulation below, using data from the comparative income statement above.

Dollar and percentage changes

	In Thousands			Increase or (Decrease)			
				Year 3 over Year 2		Year 2 over Year 1	
	Year 3	Year 2	Year 1	Amount	%	Amount	%
Net sales	$600	$500	$400	$100	20%	$100	25%
Net income ...	$ 36	$ 40	$ 50	$ (4)	(10%)	$ (10)	(20%)

Although net sales increased $100,000 in both Year 2 and Year 3, the percentage of change differs because of the shift in the base from Year 1 to Year 2. These calculations present no problems when the figures for the base year are positive amounts. If a negative amount or a zero amount appears in the base year, however, a percentage change cannot be computed. Thus if Benson Corporation had incurred a net loss in Year 2, the percentage change in net income from Year 2 to Year 3 could not have been calculated.

Evaluating percentage changes in sales and earnings. Computing the percentage changes in sales, gross profit, and net income from one year to the next gives insight into a company's rate of growth. If a company is experiencing growth in its economic activities, sales and earnings should increase at *more than the rate of inflation.* Assume, for example, that a company's sales increase by 6% while the general price level rises by 10%. It is probable that the entire increase in sales may be explained by inflation, rather than by an increase in sales volume. In fact, the company may well have sold fewer goods than in the preceding year.

In measuring the dollar or percentage change in *quarterly* sales or earnings, it is customary to compare the results of the current quarter with those of the *same quarter in the preceding year.* Use of the same quarter of the preceding year as the base period prevents our analysis from being distorted by seasonal fluctuations in business activity.

Percentages become misleading when the base is small. Percentage changes may create a misleading impression when the dollar amount used as a base is unusually small. Occasionally we hear a television newscaster say that a company's profits have increased by a very large percentage, such as 900%. The initial impression created by such a statement is that the company's profits must now be excessively large. But assume, for example, that a company had net income of $100,000 in Year 1; that in Year 2 net income drops to $10,000; and that in Year 3, net income returns to the $100,000 level. In Year 3, net income has increased by $90,000, representing a 900% increase over the profits of Year 2. What needs to be added is that this 900% increase *exactly offsets* the 90% decline in profits in Year 2.

Few people realize that a 90% decline in earnings must be followed by a 900% increase just to get back to the starting point.

● **CASE IN POINT** ● In the third quarter of 1979, General Motors earned $21.4 million, as compared with $527.9 million in the third quarter of 1978. This represented a 97% decline in third quarter profits, computed as follows:

Decline in profits ($527.9 − $21.4)	$506.5
Base period earnings (third quarter, 1978)	$527.9
Percentage decrease ($506.5 ÷ $527.9)	96%

How much of an increase in profits would be required in the third quarter of 1980 for profits to return to the 1978 level? Many people erroneously guess 96%. However, the correct answer is an astounding 2,367%, computed as follows:

Required increase to reach 1978 profit level (from $21.4 to $527.9)	$506.5
Base period earnings (third quarter, 1979)	$ 21.4
Required percentage increase ($506.5 ÷ $21.4)	2,367%

Unfortunately for GM, the company's 1980 profits did not return to 1978 levels. Instead, the company lost a record-setting $567 million in the third quarter of 1980.

Trend percentages

The changes in financial statement items from a base year to following years are often expressed as **trend percentages** to show the extent and direction of change. Two steps are necessary to compute trend percentages. First, a base year is selected and each item in the financial statements for the base year is given a weight of 100%. The second step is to express each item in the financial statements for following years as a percentage of its base-year amount. This computation consists of dividing an item such as Sales in the years after the base year by the amount of Sales in the base year.

For example, assume that 1980 is selected as the base year and that Sales in the base year amounted to $300,000 as shown below. The trend percentages for Sales are computed by dividing the Sales amount of each following year by $300,000. Also shown in the illustration are the yearly amounts of net income. The trend percentages for net income are computed by dividing the Net Income amount for each following year by the base-year amount of $15,000.

	1985	1984	1983	1982	1981	1980
Sales	$450,000	$360,000	$330,000	$320,000	$312,000	$300,000
Net income	22,950	14,550	21,450	19,200	15,600	15,000

When the computations described above have been made, the trend percentages will appear as shown below.

	1985	1984	1983	1982	1981	1980
Sales	150%	120%	110%	107%	104%	100%
Net income	153%	97%	143%	128%	104%	100%

The above trend percentages indicate a very modest growth in sales in the early years and accelerated growth in 1984 and 1985. Net income also shows an increasing growth trend with the exception of the year 1984, when net income declined despite a solid increase in sales. This variation could have resulted from an unfavorable change in the gross profit margin or from unusual expenses. However, the problem was overcome in 1985 with a sharp rise in net income. Overall the trend percentages give a picture of a profitable growing enterprise.

As another example, assume that sales are increasing each year, but that the cost of goods sold is increasing at a faster rate. This means that the gross profit margin is shrinking. Perhaps the increases in sales are being achieved through excessive price cutting. The company's net income may be declining even though sales are rising.

Component percentages

Component percentages indicate the **relative size** of each item included in a total. For example, each item on a balance sheet could be expressed as a percentage of total assets. This shows quickly the relative importance of current and noncurrent assets as well as the relative amount of financing obtained from current creditors, long-term creditors, and stockholders. By computing component percentages for several successive balance sheets, we can see which items are increasing in importance and which are becoming less significant.

Common size income statement. Another application of component percentages is to express all items on an income statement as a percentage of net sales. Such a statement is sometimes called a common size income statement. A condensed income statement in dollars and in common size form is illustrated below.

Income Statement

	Dollars		Component Percentages	
	Year 2	Year 1	Year 2	Year 1
Net sales	$1,000,000	$600,000	100.0%	100.0%
Cost of goods sold	700,000	360,000	70.0	60.0
Gross profit on sales	$ 300,000	$240,000	30.0%	40.0%
Expenses (including income taxes)	200,000	150,000	20.0	25.0
Net income	$ 100,000	$ 90,000	10.0%	15.0%

How successful was Year 2?

Looking only at the component percentages, we see that the decline in the gross profit rate from 40 to 30% was only partially offset by the decrease in expenses as a percentage of net sales, causing net income to decrease from 15 to 10% of net sales. The dollar amounts in the first pair of columns, however, present an entirely different picture. It is true that net sales increased faster than net income, but the dollar amount of net income did increase in Year 2, a fact not apparent from a review of component percentages alone. This points out an important limitation in the use of component percentages. Changes in the component percentage may result from a change in the component, in the total, or in both. It is important to recognize that 10% of a large total may be a greater amount than 15% of a smaller total.

Ratios

A ratio is a simple mathematical expression of the relationship of one item to another. Ratios may be stated several ways. To illustrate, let us consider the current ratio, which expresses the relationship between current assets and current liabilities. If current assets are $100,000 and current liabilities are $50,000, we may say either that the current ratio is 2 to 1 (which is written as 2 : 1), or that current assets are 200% of current liabilities. Either statement correctly summarizes the relationship — that is, that current assets are twice as large as current liabilities.

In order to compute a meaningful ratio, there must be a *significant relationship* between the two figures. A ratio focuses attention on a relationship which is significant, but a full interpretation of the ratio usually requires further investigation of the underlying data. Ratios are an aid to analysis and interpretation; they are not a substitute for sound thinking.

Comparative data in annual reports of major corporations

The annual reports of major corporations usually contain a comparative balance sheet covering two years and a comparative income statement for three years. Supplementary schedules showing sales, net income, and other key amounts are often presented for periods of five to 10 years. Shown below is a five-year summary by Sears Roebuck showing the trend of selected operating and financial data.

SEARS, ROEBUCK AND CO.
Five-Year Summary of Consolidated Financial Data
($ millions, except per common share data)

	1984	1983	1982	1981	1980
Operating results					
Revenues	$38,828	$35,883	$30,020	$27,357	$25,161
Costs and expenses	34,752	32,416	27,382	25,375	23,401
Interest	2,523	1,701	1,627	1,520	1,133
Operating income	1,553	1,766	1,011	462	627
Realized capital gains and other	349	126	71	184	62
Income taxes	458	571	232	10	99
Net income	1,455	1,342	861	650	610
Percent return on average equity	14.1	14.4	10.1	8.2	8.1
Financial position					
Investments	$17,447	$15,434	$13,497	$12,229	$11,336
Receivables	17,210	15,406	11,437	10,745	8,905
Property and equipment, net	4,361	3,938	3,396	3,312	3,153
Merchandise inventories	4,530	3,621	3,146	3,103	2,715
Total assets	57,073	46,176	36,541	34,406	28,218
Insurance reserves	6,906	6,253	5,667	5,161	4,407
Short-term borrowings	3,887	4,596	2,820	3,233	4,436
Long-term debt	9,531	7,405	5,816	5,324	2,965
Total debt	13,418	12,001	8,636	8,557	7,401
Percent of debt to equity	123	123	98	103	97
Shareholders' equity	10,911	9,787	8,812	8,269	7,665
Shareholders' common stock investment					
Book value per share (year end)	$29.48	$27.60	$25.08	$23.77	$24.32
Shareholders (Profit Sharing Fund counted as single shareholder)	340,831	339,644	350,292	354,050	349,725
Average shares outstanding (millions)	358	353	350	316	316
Net income per share	$4.01	$3.80	$2.46	$2.06	$1.93
Dividends per share	$1.76	$1.52	$1.36	$1.36	$1.36
Dividend payout percent	43.9	40.0	55.3	66.0	70.5
Market price (high-low)	$40\frac{3}{8}-29\frac{1}{2}$	$45\frac{3}{8}-27$	$32-15\frac{3}{4}$	$20\frac{3}{4}-14\frac{7}{8}$	$19\frac{1}{2}-14\frac{1}{2}$
Closing market price at year-end	$31\frac{3}{4}$	$37\frac{1}{8}$	$30\frac{1}{8}$	$16\frac{1}{8}$	$15\frac{3}{8}$
Price-earnings ratio (high-low)	10-7	12-7	13-6	10-7	10-8

Standards of comparison

In using dollar and percentage changes, trend percentages, component percentages, and ratios, financial analysts constantly search for some standard of comparison against which to judge whether the relationships that they have found are favorable or unfavorable. Two such standards are (1) the past performance of the company and (2) the performance of other companies in the same industry.

Past performance of the company. Comparing analytical data for a current period with similar computations for prior years affords some basis for judging whether the position of the business is improving or worsening. This comparison of data over time is sometimes called *horizontal* or *trend* analysis, to express the idea of reviewing data for a number of consecutive periods. It is distinguished from *vertical* or *static* analysis, which refers to the review of the financial information for only one accounting period.

In addition to determining whether the situation is improving or becoming worse, horizontal analysis may aid in making estimates of future prospects. Since changes may reverse their direction at any time, however, projecting past trends into the future is always a somewhat risky statistical pastime.

A weakness of horizontal analysis is that comparison with the past does not afford any basis for evaluation in absolute terms. The fact that net income was 2% of sales last year and is 3% of sales this year indicates improvement, but if there is evidence that net income *should be* 7% of sales, the record for both years is unfavorable.

Industry standards. The limitations of horizontal analysis may be overcome to some extent by finding some other standard of performance as a yardstick against which to measure the record of any particular firm.[1] The yardstick may be a comparable company, the average record of several companies in the same industry, or some predetermined standard.

Suppose that Y Company suffers a 5% drop in its sales during the current year. The discovery that the sales of all companies in the same industry fell an average of 20% would indicate that this was a favorable rather than an unfavorable performance. Assume further that Y Company's net income is 2% of net sales. Based on comparison with other companies in the industry, this would be substandard performance if Y Company were a manufacturer of commercial aircraft, but it would be a satisfactory record if Y Company were a grocery chain.

---

[1] For example, the Robert Morris Associates publishes *Annual Statement Studies* which contains detailed data obtained from 27,000 annual reports grouped in 223 industry classifications. Assets, liabilities, and stockholders' equity are presented as a percentage of total assets; income statement amounts are expressed as a percentage of net sales; and key ratios are given (expressed as the median for each industry, the upper quartile, and the lower quartile). Measurements, within each of the 223 industry groups, are grouped according to the size of the firm. Similarly, Dun & Bradstreet, Inc., annually publishes *Key Business Ratios* in 125 lines of business divided by retailing, wholesaling, manufacturing, and construction. A total of 14 ratios is presented for each of the 125 industry groups.

When we compare a given company with its competitors or with industry averages, our conclusions will be valid only if the companies in question are reasonably comparable. Because of the large number of diversified companies formed in recent years, the term *industry* is difficult to define, and companies that fall roughly within the same industry may not be comparable in many respects. For example, one company may engage only in the marketing of oil products; another may be a fully integrated producer from the well to the gas pump, yet both are said to be in the "oil industry."

Differences in accounting methods may lessen the comparability of financial data for two companies. For example, companies may employ different depreciation methods or estimates of the useful life of substantially similar assets; inventories may be valued by different methods; and the timing of revenue recognition may differ significantly among companies engaged in certain industries. Despite these limitations, studying comparative performances is a useful method of analysis if carefully and intelligently done.

Quality of earnings

Profits are the lifeblood of a business entity. No entity can survive for long and accomplish its other goals unless it is profitable. On the other hand, continuous losses will drain assets from the business, consume owners' equity, and leave the company at the mercy of creditors. In assessing the prospects of a company, we are interested not only in the total *amount* of earnings but also in the *rate* of earnings on sales, on total assets, and on owners' equity. In addition, we must look to the *stability* and *source* of earnings. An erratic earnings performance over a period of years, for example, is less desirable than a steady level of earnings. A history of increasing earnings is preferable to a "flat" earnings record.

A breakdown of sales and earnings by *major product lines* is useful in evaluating the future performance of a company. Publicly owned companies include with their financial statements supplementary schedules showing sales and profits by product line and by geographical area. These schedules assist financial analysts in forecasting the effect upon the company of changes in consumer demand for particular types of products.

Financial analysts often express the opinion that the earnings of one company are of higher quality than earnings of other similar companies. This concept of *quality of earnings* arises because each company management can choose from a variety of accounting principles and methods, all of which are considered generally acceptable. A company's management often is under heavy pressure to report rising earnings, and accounting policies may be tailored toward this objective. We have already pointed out the impact on current reported earnings of the choice between the lifo and fifo methods of inventory valuation and the choice of depreciation policies. In judging the quality of earnings, the financial analyst should consider whether the accounting principles and methods selected by management lead to a conservative measurement of earnings or tend to inflate reported earnings.

Quality of assets and the relative amount of debt

Although a satisfactory level of earnings may be a good indication of the company's long-run ability to pay its debts and dividends, we must also look at the composition of assets, their condition and liquidity, the relationship between current assets and current liabilities, and the total amount of debt outstanding. A company may be profitable and yet be unable to pay its liabilities on time; sales and earnings may be satisfactory but plant and equipment may be deteriorating because of poor maintenance policies; valuable patents may be expiring; substantial losses may be in prospect from slow-moving inventories and past-due receivables. Companies with large amounts of debt often are vulnerable to increases in interest rates.

● **CASE IN POINT** ● The home building industry is especially vulnerable to increases in interest rates. When interest rates rise, people stop buying new homes. In addition, most construction companies have large amounts of debt, upon which the interest charges are adjusted monthly to reflect current interest rates. Thus, when interest rates rise, these companies face large increases in their interest expense as well as declining revenue. The sustained period of high interest rates in the early 1980s caused the bankruptcy of a great many construction companies.

Impact of inflation

During a period of significant inflation, financial statements which are prepared in terms of historical costs do not reflect fully the economic resources or the *real income* (in terms of purchasing power) of a business enterprise. We discussed in Chapter 14 the requirements by the Financial Accounting Standards Board for large corporations to disclose current cost data in their annual reports. Financial analysts should therefore attempt to evaluate the impact of inflation on the financial position and operating results of the company being studied. They should raise such questions as: How much of the net income can be attributed to the increase in the general price level? Will the company lose or gain from inflation because of its holdings of monetary assets and liabilities? Will the company be able to keep its "physical capital" intact by paying the higher prices necessary to replace plant assets as they wear out? The topics of developing and interpreting accounting information designed to measure the impact of inflation were discussed in Chapter 14.

Illustrative analysis for Seacliff Company

Keep in mind the above discussion of analytical principles as you study the illustrative financial analysis which follows. The basic information for our analysis is contained in a set of condensed two-year comparative financial statements for Seacliff Company shown on the following pages. Summarized statement data, together with computations of dollar increases and decreases, and component percentages where applicable, have been compiled. For convenience in this illustration, relatively small dollar amounts have been used in the Seacliff Company financial statements.

Using the information in these statements, let us consider the kind of analysis that might be of particular interest to (1) common stockholders, (2) long-term creditors, (3) preferred stockholders, and (4) short-term creditors.

SEACLIFF COMPANY
Condensed Comparative Balance Sheet*
December 31

	Year 2	Year 1	Increase or (Decrease) Dollars	%	Percentage of Total Assets Year 2	Year 1
Assets						
Current assets	$390,000	$288,000	$102,000	35.4	41.1	33.5
Plant and equipment (net)	500,000	467,000	33,000	7.1	52.6	54.3
Other assets (loans to officers)	60,000	105,000	(45,000)	(42.9)	6.3	12.2
Total assets	$950,000	$860,000	$ 90,000	10.5	100.0	100.0
Liabilities & Stockholders' Equity						
Liabilities:						
Current liabilities	$112,000	$ 94,000	$ 18,000	(19.1)	11.8	10.9
12% long-term note payable	200,000	250,000	(50,000)	(20.0)	21.1	29.1
Total liabilities	$312,000	$344,000	$ (32,000)	(9.3)	32.9	40.0
Stockholders' equity:						
9% preferred stock, $100 par, callable at 105	$100,000	$100,000			10.5	11.6
Common stock, $50 par	250,000	200,000	$ 50,000	25.0	26.3	23.2
Paid-in capital in excess of par	70,000	40,000	30,000	75.0	7.4	4.7
Retained earnings	218,000	176,000	42,000	23.9	22.9	20.5
Total stockholders' equity	$638,000	$516,000	$122,000	23.6	67.1	60.0
Total liabilities & stockholders' equity	$950,000	$860,000	$ 90,000	10.5	100.0	100.0

* In order to focus attention on important subtotals, this statement is highly condensed and does not show individual asset and liability items. These details will be introduced as needed in the text discussion. For example, a list of Seacliff Company's current assets and current liabilities appears on page 670.

SEACLIFF COMPANY
Comparative Income Statement
Years Ended December 31

| | Year 2 | Year 1 | Increase or (Decrease) | | Percentage of Net Sales | |
			Dollars	%	Year 2	Year 1
Net sales	$900,000	$750,000	$150,000	20.0	100.0	100.0
Cost of goods sold	530,000	420,000	110,000	26.2	58.9	56.0
Gross profit on sales	$370,000	$330,000	$ 40,000	12.1	41.1	44.0
Operating expenses:						
Selling expenses	$117,000	$ 75,000	$ 42,000	56.0	13.0	10.0
Administrative expenses	126,000	95,000	31,000	32.6	14.0	12.7
Total operating expenses	$243,000	$170,000	$ 73,000	42.9	27.0	22.7
Operating income	$127,000	$160,000	$ (33,000)	(20.6)	14.1	21.3
Interest expense	24,000	30,000	(6,000)	(20.0)	2.7	4.0
Income before income taxes	$103,000	$130,000	$ (27,000)	(20.8)	11.4	17.3
Income taxes	28,000	40,000	(12,000)	(30.0)	3.1	5.3
Net income	$ 75,000	$ 90,000	$ (15,000)	(16.7)	8.3	12.0
Earnings per share of common stock (see page 663)	$13.20	$20.25	$(7.05)	(34.8)		

SEACLIFF COMPANY
Statement of Retained Earnings
Year Ended December 31

| | Year 2 | Year 1 | Increase or (Decrease) | |
			Dollars	%
Retained earnings, beginning of year	$176,000	$115,000	$61,000	53.0
Net income	75,000	90,000	(15,000)	(16.7)
	$251,000	$205,000	$46,000	22.4
Less: Dividends on common stock	$ 24,000	$ 20,000	$ 4,000	20.0
Dividends on preferred stock	9,000	9,000		
	$ 33,000	$ 29,000	$ 4,000	13.8
Retained earnings, end of year	$218,000	$176,000	$42,000	23.9

Analysis by common stockholders

Common stockholders and potential investors in common stock look first at a company's earnings record. Their investment is in shares of stock, so *earnings per share and dividends per share* are of particular interest.

Earnings per share of common stock. As indicated in Chapter 12, earnings per share of common stock are computed by dividing the income available to common stockholders by the weighted average number of shares of common stock outstanding during the year. Any preferred dividend requirements must be subtracted from net income to determine income available for common stock, as shown in the following computations for Seacliff Company:

Earnings per Share of Common Stock

		Year 2	Year 1
Net income		$75,000	$90,000
Less: Preferred dividend requirements		9,000	9,000
Income available for common stock	(a)	$66,000	$81,000
Shares of common stock outstanding, during the year	(b)	5,000	4,000
Earnings per share of common stock (a ÷ b)		$13.20	$20.25

Earnings related to number of common shares outstanding

Dividend yield and price-earnings ratio. Dividends are of prime importance to some stockholders, but a secondary factor to others. In other words, some stockholders invest primarily to receive regular cash income, while others invest in stocks principally with the hope of securing capital gains through rising market prices. If a corporation is profitable and retains its earnings for expansion of the business, the expanded operations should produce an increase in the net income of the company and thus tend to make each share of stock more valuable.

In comparing the merits of alternative investment opportunities, we should relate earnings and dividends per share to the *market value* of the stock. Dividends per share divided by market price per share determines the *yield* rate of a company's stock. Dividend yield is especially important to those investors whose objective is to maximize the dividend revenue from their investments.

Earnings performance of common stock is often expressed as a *price-earnings ratio* by dividing the market price per share by the annual earnings per share. Thus, a stock selling for $60 per share and earning $5 per share in the year just ended may be said to have a price-earnings ratio of 12 times earnings ($60 ÷ $5). The price-earnings ratio of the 30 stocks included in the Dow-Jones Industrial Average has varied widely in recent years, ranging from a low of about 6 for the group to a high of about 20.

Assume that the 1,000 additional shares of common stock issued by Seacliff on January 1, Year 2, received the full dividend of $4.80 paid in Year 2. When these new shares were issued, Seacliff Company announced that it planned to continue indefinitely the $4.80 dividend per common share currently being paid. With this assumption and the use of assumed market prices of the common stock at December 31, Year 1 and Year 2, the earnings per share and dividend yield may be summarized as follows:

Earnings and Dividends per Share of Common Stock

Earnings and
dividends related to
market price of
common stock

Date	Assumed Market Value per Share	Earnings per Share	Price-Earnings Ratio	Dividends per Share	Dividend Yield, %
Dec. 31, Year 1	$125	$20.25	6	$5.00	4.0
Dec. 31, Year 2	$100	$13.20	8	$4.80	4.8

The decline in market value during Year 2 presumably reflects the decrease in earnings per share. Investors appraising this stock at December 31, Year 2, would consider whether a price-earnings ratio of 8 and a dividend yield of 4.8% represented a satisfactory situation in the light of alternative investment opportunities. They would also place considerable weight on estimates of the company's prospective future earnings and the probable effect of such estimated earnings on the market price of the stock and on dividend payments.

Book value per share of common stock. The procedures for computing book value per share were fully described in Chapter 12 and will not be repeated here. We will, however, determine the book value per share of common stock for the Seacliff Company:

Book Value per Share of Common Stock

Why did book value
per share decrease?

		Year 2	Year 1
Total stockholders' equity		$638,000	$516,000
Less: Equity of preferred stockholders (1,000 shares at call price of $105)		105,000	105,000
Equity of common stockholders	(a)	$533,000	$411,000
Shares of common stock outstanding	(b)	5,000	4,000
Book value per share of common stock (a ÷ b)		$106.60	$102.75

Book value indicates the net assets represented by each share of stock. This statistic is often helpful in estimating a reasonable price for a company's stock, especially for small corporations whose shares are not publicly traded. However, if a company's future earnings prospects are unusually good or unusually poor, the market price of its shares may differ significantly from their book value.

Revenue and expense analysis. The trend of earnings of Seacliff Company is unfavorable and stockholders will want to know the reasons for the decline in net income. The comparative income statement on page 662 shows that despite a 20% increase in net sales, net income fell from $90,000 in Year 1 to $75,000 in Year 2, a decline of 16.7%. As a percentage of net sales, net income fell from 12% to only 8.3%. The primary causes of this decline were the increases in selling expenses (56.0%), in general and administrative expenses (32.6%), and in the cost of goods sold (26.2%), all of which exceeded the 20% increase in net sales.

Let us assume that further investigation reveals Seacliff Company decided in Year 2 to reduce its sales prices in an effort to generate greater sales volume. This would explain the decrease in gross profit rate from 44% to 41.1% of net sales. Since the dollar amount of gross profit increased $40,000 in Year 2, the strategy of reducing sales prices to increase volume would have been successful if there had been little or no increase in operating expenses. However, operating expenses rose by $73,000, resulting in a $33,000 decrease in operating income.

The next step is to find which expenses increased and why. An investor may be handicapped here, because detailed operating expenses are not usually shown in published financial statements. Some conclusions, however, can be reached on the basis of even the condensed information available in the comparative income statement for Seacliff Company shown on page 662.

The substantial increase in selling expenses presumably reflects greater selling effort during Year 2 in an attempt to improve sales volume. However, the fact that selling expenses increased $42,000 while gross profit increased only $40,000 indicates that the cost of this increased sales effort was not justified in terms of results. Even more disturbing is the increase in general and administrative expenses. Some growth in administrative expenses might be expected to accompany increased sales volume, but because some of the expenses are fixed, the growth generally should be *less than proportional* to any increase in sales. The increase in general and administrative expenses from 12.7 to 14% of sales would be of serious concern to informed investors.

Management generally has greater control over operating expenses than over revenue. The *operating expense ratio* is often used as a measure of management's ability to control its operating expenses. The unfavorable trend in this ratio for Seacliff Company is shown below:

Operating Expense Ratio

		Year 2	Year 1
Operating expenses	(a)	$243,000	$170,000
Net sales	(b)	$900,000	$750,000
Operating expense ratio (a ÷ b)		27.0%	22.7%

Does a higher operating expense ratio indicate higher net income?

If management were able to increase the sales volume while at the same time increasing the gross profit rate and decreasing the operating expense ratio, the effect on net income could be quite dramatic. For example, if in Year 3 Seacliff Company can increase its sales by 11% to $1,000,000, increase its gross profit rate from 41.1 to 44%, and reduce the operating expense ratio from 27 to 24%, its operating income will increase from $127,000 to $200,000 ($1,000,000 − $560,000 − $240,000), an increase of over 57%.

Return on investment (ROI)

The rate of return on investment (often called ROI) is a test of management's efficiency in using available resources. Regardless of the size of the organization, capital is a scarce resource and must be used efficiently. In judging the performance of branch managers or of company-wide management, it is reasonable to raise the question: What rate of return have you earned on the resources under your control? The concept of return on investment can be applied to a number of situations: for example, evaluating a branch, a total business, a product line, or an individual investment. A number of different ratios have been developed for the ROI concept, each well suited to a particular situation. We shall consider the return on total assets and the return on common stockholders' equity as examples of the return on investment concept.

Return on assets. An important test of management's ability to earn a return on funds supplied from all sources is the rate of return on total assets.

The income figure used in computing this ratio should be *operating income,* since interest expense and income taxes are determined by factors other than the efficient use of resources. Operating income is earned throughout the year and therefore should be related to the *average* investment in assets during the year. The computation of this ratio for Seacliff Company is shown below:

Percentage Return on Assets

		Year 2	Year 1
Earnings related to investment in assets Operating income	(a)	$127,000	$160,000
Total assets, beginning of year	(b)	$860,000	$820,000
Total assets, end of year	(c)	$950,000	$860,000
Average investment in assets [(b + c) ÷ 2]	(d)	$905,000	$840,000
Return on total assets (a ÷ d)		14%	19%

This ratio shows that earnings per dollar of assets invested have fallen off in Year 2. Before drawing conclusions as to the effectiveness of Seacliff's management, however, we should consider the trend in the return on assets earned by other companies of similar kind and size.

Return on common stockholders' equity. Because interest and dividends paid to creditors and preferred stockholders are fixed in amount, a company may earn a greater or smaller return on the common stockholders' equity than on its total assets. The computation of return on stockholders' equity for Seacliff Company is shown below:

Return on Common Stockholders' Equity

		Year 2	Year 1
Does the use of leverage benefit common stock- holders? Net income		$ 75,000	$ 90,000
Less: Preferred dividend requirements		9,000	9,000
Net income available for common stock	(a)	$ 66,000	$ 81,000
Common stockholders' equity, beginning of year	(b)	$416,000	$355,000
Common stockholders' equity, end of year	(c)	$538,000	$416,000
Average common stockholders' equity [(b + c) ÷ 2]	(d)	$477,000	$385,500
Return on common stockholders' equity (a ÷ d)		13.8%	21.0%

In both years, the rate of return on common stockholders' equity was higher than the rate of interest paid to long-term creditors or the dividend rate paid to preferred stockholders. This result was achieved through the favorable use of leverage.

Leverage

When the return on total assets is higher than the average cost of borrowed capital, as was the case in Seacliff Company, the common stockholders may benefit from the use of leverage. *Leverage* (or *trading on the equity*) refers to buying assets with money raised by borrowing or by issuing preferred stock. If the borrowed capital can be invested to earn a return *greater* than the cost of borrowing, then the net income and the return on common stockholders' equity will *increase.* In other words, if you can borrow money at 12% and use it to earn 20%, you will benefit by doing so. However, leverage can act as a "double-edged sword"; the effects may be favorable or unfavorable to the holders of common stock. If the return on total assets should fall *below* the average cost of borrowed capital, leverage will *reduce* net income and the return on common stockholders' equity. When this unfavorable situation occurs, one possible solution would be to pay off the loans that carry high interest rates. However, most companies do not have sufficient amounts of cash to retire long-term debt or preferred stock on short notice. Therefore, the common stockholders may become "locked in" for a long period of time to the unfavorable effects of leverage.

When the return on assets exceeds the cost of borrowed capital, the extensive use of leverage can increase dramatically the return on common stockholders' equity. However, extensive leverage also increases the *risk* to common stockholders that their return may be reduced dramatically in future years. Furthermore, if a business incurs so much debt that it becomes unable to meet the required interest and principal payments, creditors may force liquidation or reorganization of the business, to the detriment of stockholders.

In deciding how much leverage is appropriate, the common stockholders should consider the *stability* of the company's return on assets, as well as the relationship of this return to the average cost of borrowed capital. Also, they should consider the amount of risk that they are willing to accept in the effort to increase the return on their investment.

Leverage most frequently is achieved through debt financing, including both current and long-term liabilities. One advantage of debt financing is that interest payments are deductible in determining taxable income. Leverage also can be achieved through the issuance of preferred stock. Since preferred stock dividends are *not* deductible for income tax purposes, however, the advantage gained in this respect will be much smaller than in the case of debt financing.

Equity ratio. One indicator of the amount of leverage used by a business is the equity ratio. This ratio measures the proportion of the total assets financed by stockholders, as distinguished from creditors. It is computed by dividing total stockholders' equity by total assets. A *low* equity ratio indicates an extensive use of leverage, that is, a large proportion of financing provided by creditors. A high equity ratio, on the other hand, indicates that the business is making little use of leverage.

The equity ratio at year-end for Seacliff is determined as follows:

Equity Ratio

		Year 2	Year 1
Proportion of assets financed by stockholders Total stockholders' equity .... (a)		$638,000	$516,000
Total assets (or total liabilities & stockholders' equity) ...... (b)		$950,000	$860,000
Equity ratio (a ÷ b)		67.2%	60.0%

Seacliff Company has a higher equity ratio in Year 2 than in Year 1. Is this favorable or unfavorable?

From the viewpoint of the common stockholder, a low equity ratio will produce maximum benefits if management is able to earn a rate of return on assets greater than the rate of interest paid to creditors. However, a low equity ratio can be very unfavorable if the return on assets falls below the rate of interest paid to creditors. Since the return on total assets earned by Seacliff Company has declined from 19% in Year 1 to a relatively low 14% in Year 2, the common stockholders probably would *not* want to risk a low equity ratio. The action by management in Year 2 of retiring $50,000 in long-term liabilities will help to protect the common stockholders from the unfavorable effects of leverage should the return on assets continue to decline.

Analysis by long-term creditors

Bondholders and other long-term creditors are primarily interested in three factors: (1) the rate of return on their investment, (2) the firm's ability to meet its interest requirements, and (3) the firm's ability to repay the principal of the debt when it falls due.

Yield rate on bonds. The yield rate on bonds or other long-term indebtedness cannot be computed in the same manner as the yield rate on shares of stock, because bonds, unlike stocks, have a definite maturity date and amount. The ownership of a 12%, 10-year bond represents the right to receive $1,000 at the end of 10 years and the right to receive $120 per year during each of the next 10 years. If the market price of this bond is $950, the yield rate on an investment in the bond is the rate of interest that will make the present value of these two contractual rights equal to $950. *The yield rate varies inversely with changes in the market price of the bond.* If interest rates rise, the market price of existing bonds will fall; if interest rates decline, the price of bonds will rise. If the price of a bond is above maturity value, the yield rate is less than the bond interest rate; if the price of a bond is below maturity value, the yield rate is higher than the bond interest rate.

Number of times interest earned. Long-term creditors have learned from experience that one of the best indications of the safety of their investment is the fact that, over the life of the debt, the company has sufficient income to cover its interest requirements by a wide margin. A failure to cover interest requirements may have serious repercussions on the stability and solvency of the firm.

A common measure of debt safety is the ratio of income available for the payment of interest to the annual interest expense, called *number of times interest earned.* This computation for Seacliff Company would be:

Number of Times Interest Earned

		Year 2	Year 1
Operating income (before interest and income taxes)	(a)	$127,000	$160,000
Annual interest expense	(b)	$ 24,000	$ 30,000
Times interest earned (a ÷ b)		5.3	5.3

Long-term creditors watch this ratio

The ratio remained unchanged at a satisfactory level during Year 2. A ratio of 5.3 times interest earned would be considered strong in many industries. In the electric utilities industry, for example, the interest coverage ratio for the leading companies presently averages about 3, with the ratios of individual companies varying from 2 to 6.

Debt ratio. Long-term creditors are interested in the amount of debt outstanding in relation to the amount of capital contributed by stockholders. The ***debt ratio*** is computed by dividing total liabilities by total assets, shown below for Seacliff Company.

Debt Ratio

		Year 2	Year 1
Total liabilities	(a)	$312,000	$344,000
Total assets (or total liabilities & stockholders' equity)	(b)	$950,000	$860,000
Debt ratio (a ÷ b)		32.8%	40.0%

What portion of total assets is financed by debt?

From a creditor's viewpoint, the lower the debt ratio (or the higher the equity ratio) the better, since this means that stockholders have contributed the bulk of the funds to the business, and therefore the margin of protection to creditors against a shrinkage of the assets is high.

Analysis by preferred stockholders

Some preferred stocks are convertible into common stock at the option of the holder. However, many preferred stocks do not have the conversion privilege. If a preferred stock is convertible, the interests of the preferred stockholders are similar to those of common stockholders. If a preferred stock is not convertible, the interests of the preferred stockholders are more like those of long-term creditors.

Preferred stockholders are interested in the yield on their investment. The yield is computed by dividing the dividend per share by the market value per share. The dividend per share of Seacliff Company preferred stock is $9. If we assume that the market value at December 31, Year 2, is $60 per share, the yield rate at that time would be 15% ($9 ÷ $60).

The primary measurement of the safety of an investment in preferred stock is the ability of the firm to meet its preferred dividend requirements. The best test of this ability is the ratio of the net income available to pay the preferred dividend to the amount of the annual dividend, as follows:

Times Preferred Dividends Earned

		Year 2	Year 1
Net income available to pay preferred dividends	(a)	$75,000	$90,000
Annual preferred dividend requirements	(b)	$ 9,000	$ 9,000
Times dividends earned (a ÷ b)		8.3	10

Is the preferred dividend safe?

Although the margin of protection declined in Year 2, the annual preferred dividend requirement still appears well protected.

As previously discussed in Chapter 11 (pages 449–450), the market price of a preferred stock tends to vary inversely with interest rates. When interest rates are moving up, preferred stock prices tend to decline; when interest rates are dropping, preferred stock prices rise.

Analysis by short-term creditors

Bankers and other short-term creditors share the interest of stockholders and bond-holders in the profitability and long-run stability of a business. Their primary interest, however, is in the current position of the firm — its ability to generate sufficient funds (working capital) to meet current operating needs and to pay current debts promptly. Thus the analysis of financial statements by a banker considering a short-term loan, or by a trade creditor investigating the credit status of a customer, is likely to center on the working capital position of the prospective debtor.

Amount of working capital. The details of the working capital of Seacliff Company are shown below:

SEACLIFF COMPANY

Comparative Schedule of Working Capital

As of December 31

	Year 2	Year 1	Increase or (Decrease) Dollars	%	Percentage of Total Current Items Year 2	Year 1
Current assets:						
Cash	$ 38,000	$ 40,000	$ (2,000)	(5.0)	9.7	13.9
Receivables (net)	117,000	86,000	31,000	36.0	30.0	29.9
Inventories	180,000	120,000	60,000	50.0	46.2	41.6
Prepaid expenses	55,000	42,000	13,000	31.0	14.1	14.6
Total current assets	$390,000	$288,000	$102,000	35.4	100.0	100.0
Current liabilities:						
Notes payable to creditors	$ 14,600	$ 10,000	$ 4,600	46.0	13.1	10.7
Accounts payable	66,000	30,000	36,000	120.0	58.9	31.9
Accrued liabilities	31,400	54,000	(22,600)	(41.9)	28.0	57.4
Total current liabilities	$112,000	$ 94,000	$ 18,000	19.1	100.0	100.0
Working capital	$278,000	$194,000	$ 84,000	43.3		

The amount of working capital is measured by the *excess of current assets over current liabilities.* Thus, working capital represents the amount of cash, near-cash items, and cash substitutes (prepayments) on hand after providing for payment of all current liabilities.

This schedule shows that current assets increased $102,000, while current liabilities rose by only $18,000, with the result that working capital increased $84,000.

Quality of working capital. In evaluating the debt-paying ability of a business, short-term creditors should consider the quality of working capital as well as the total dollar amount. The principal factors affecting the quality of working capital are (1) the nature of the current assets comprising the working capital and (2) the length of time required to convert these assets into cash.

The preceding schedule shows an unfavorable shift in the composition of Seacliff Company's working capital during Year 2; cash decreased from 13.9 to 9.7% of current assets, while inventory rose from 41.6 to 46.2%. Inventory is a less liquid resource than cash. Therefore, the quality of working capital is not as liquid as Year 1. **Turnover ratios** may be used to assist short-term creditors in estimating the time required to turn assets such as inventories and receivables into cash.

Inventory turnover. The cost of goods sold figure on the income statement represents the total cost of all goods that have been transferred out of inventories during any given period. Therefore the relationship between cost of goods sold and the average balance of inventories maintained throughout the year indicates the number of times that inventories "turn over" and are replaced each year.

Ideally we should total the inventories at the end of each month and divide by 12 to obtain an average inventory. This information is not always available, however, and the nearest substitute is a simple average of the inventory at the beginning and at the end of the year. This tends to overstate the turnover rate, since many companies choose an accounting year that ends when inventories are at a minimum.

Assuming that only beginning and ending inventories are available, the computation of inventory turnover for Seacliff Company may be illustrated as follows:

Inventory Turnover

		Year 2	Year 1
What does inventory turnover mean? Cost of goods sold	(a)	$530,000	$420,000
Inventory, beginning of year		$120,000	$100,000
Inventory, end of year		$180,000	$120,000
Average inventory	(b)	$150,000	$110,000
Average inventory turnover per year (a ÷ b)		3.5 times	3.8 times
Average number of days to sell inventory (divide 365 days by inventory turnover)		104 days	96 days

The trend indicated by this analysis is unfavorable, since the length of time required for Seacliff Company to turn over (sell) its inventory is increasing. Furthermore, the inventory status *at the end of the year* has changed even more: At the end of Year 1 there were 104 days' sales represented in the ending inventory ($120,000/$420,000 × 365 days) compared with 124 days' sales contained in the ending inventory at the end of Year 2 ($180,000/$530,000 × 365 days).

The relation between inventory turnover and gross profit per dollar of sales may be significant. A high inventory turnover and a low gross profit rate frequently go hand in hand. This, however, is merely another way of saying that if the gross profit rate is low, a high volume of business is necessary to produce a satisfactory return on total assets. Short-term creditors generally regard a high inventory turnover as a good sign, indicating that the inventory is readily marketable.

Accounts receivable turnover. The turnover of accounts receivable is computed by dividing net credit sales by the average balance of accounts receivable. Ideally, a monthly average of receivables should be used, and only sales on credit should be included in the sales figure. For illustrative purposes, we shall assume that Seacliff Company sells entirely on credit and that only the beginning and ending balances of receivables are available:

Accounts Receivable Turnover

		Year 2	Year 1
Net sales on credit	(a)	$900,000	$750,000
Receivables, beginning of year		$ 86,000	$ 80,000
Receivables, end of year		$117,000	$ 86,000
Average receivables	(b)	$101,500	$ 83,000
Receivable turnover per year (a ÷ b)		8.9 times	9.0 times
Average number of days to collect receivables (divide 365 days by receivable turnover)		41 days	41 days

Are customers paying promptly?

There has been no significant change in the average time required to collect receivables. The interpretation of the average age of receivables would depend upon the company's credit terms and the seasonal activity immediately before year-end. If the company grants 30-day credit terms to its customers, for example, the above analysis indicates that accounts receivable collections are lagging. If the terms were for 60 days, however, there is evidence that collections are being made ahead of schedule.

In Chapter 5 we defined the term *operating cycle* as the average time period between the purchase of merchandise and the conversion of this merchandise back into cash. In other words, the merchandise acquired for inventory is gradually converted into accounts receivable by selling goods to customers on credit, and these receivables are converted into cash through the process of collection. The word *cycle* refers to the circular flow of capital from cash to inventory to receivables to cash again.

The *operating cycle* in Year 2 was approximately 145 days, computed by adding the 104 days required to turn over inventory and the average 41 days required to collect receivables. This compares to an operating cycle of only 137 days in Year 1, computed as 96 days to dispose of the inventory plus 41 days to collect the resulting receivables. From the viewpoint of short-term creditors, the shorter the operating cycle, the higher the quality of the borrower's working capital. Therefore, these creditors would regard the lengthening of Seacliff Company's operating cycle as an unfavorable trend.

Current ratio. The current ratio (current assets divided by current liabilities) is another widely used method of expressing the relationship between current assets and current liabilities. The current ratio for Seacliff Company is computed as follows:

Current Ratio

		Year 2	Year 1
Total current assets	(a)	$390,000	$288,000
Total current liabilities	(b)	$112,000	$ 94,000
Current ratio (a ÷ b)		3.5	3.1

Does this indicate satisfactory debt-paying ability?

A widely used rule of thumb is that a current ratio of 2 to 1 or better is satisfactory. By this standard, Seacliff Company's current ratio appears quite strong. As with all rules of thumb, however, this is an arbitrary standard and is subject to numerous exceptions and qualifications.

In interpreting the current ratio, a number of factors should be kept in mind:

1 Creditors tend to feel that the higher the current ratio the better, although from a managerial view there is an upper limit. Too high a current ratio may indicate that capital is not being used productively in the business.
2 Because creditors tend to stress the current ratio as an indication of short-term solvency, some firms may take conscious steps to improve this ratio just before statements are prepared at the end of a fiscal period for submission to bankers or other creditors. This may be done by postponing purchases, and by paying current liabilities.
3 The current ratio computed at the end of a fiscal year may not be representative of the current position of the company throughout the year. Since many firms arrange their fiscal year to end during a low point in the seasonal swing of business activity, the current ratio at year-end is likely to be more favorable than at any other time during the year.

Use of both the current ratio and the amount of working capital helps to place debt-paying ability in its proper perspective. For example, if Company X has current assets of $200,000 and current liabilities of $100,000 and Company Y has current assets of $2,000,000 and current liabilities of $1,900,000, each company has $100,000 of working capital, but the current position of Company X is clearly superior to that of Company Y. The current ratio for Company X is quite satisfactory at 2 to 1, but Company Y's current ratio is very low — only slightly above 1 to 1.

As another example, assume that Company A and Company B both have current ratios of 3 to 1. However, Company A has working capital of $20,000 and Company B has working capital of $200,000. Although both companies appear to be good credit risks, Company B would no doubt be able to qualify for a much *larger* bank loan than would Company A.

Adjustment for undervalued inventories. The cost of inventory is a major factor in the computation of the current ratio or the amount of working capital. If a company uses the *lifo* inventory method, the cost of inventory appearing in the balance sheet may be unrealistically low in terms of current replacement costs. In such cases, many financial analysts substitute the **current replacement cost** of inventories for the historical cost figure in computing the current ratio or amount of working capital. As explained in earlier chapters, the Financial Accounting Standards Board requires large corporations to disclose the current replacement cost of their inventories and other items as supplementary information in their financial statements.

Quick ratio. Because inventories and prepaid expenses are further removed from conversion into cash than other current assets, a statistic known as the **quick ratio** is sometimes computed as a supplement to the current ratio. The quick ratio compares the highly liquid current assets (cash, marketable securities, and receivables) with current liabilities. Seacliff Company has no marketable securities; its quick ratio is computed as follows:

Quick Ratio

		Year 2	Year 1
A measure of liquidity Quick assets (cash and receivables) .... (a)		$155,000	$126,000
Current liabilities .... (b)		$112,000	$ 94,000
Quick ratio (a ÷ b)		1.4	1.3

Here again the analysis reveals a favorable trend and a strong position. If the credit periods extended to customers and granted by creditors are roughly equal, a quick ratio of 1.0 or better is considered satisfactory.

Summary of analytical measurements

The basic ratios and other measurements discussed in this chapter and their significance are summarized below.

The student should keep in mind the fact that the full significance of any of these ratios or other measurements depends on the **direction of its trend** and its **relationship to some predetermined standard** or industry average.

Ratio or Other Measurement	Method of Computation	Significance
1 Earnings per share of common stock	$\dfrac{\text{Net income} - \text{preferred dividends}}{\text{Shares of common outstanding}}$	Gives the amount of earnings applicable to a share of common stock.
2 Dividend yield	$\dfrac{\text{Dividend per share}}{\text{Market price per share}}$	Shows the rate earned by stockholders based on current price for a share of stock.
3 Price-earnings ratio	$\dfrac{\text{Market price per share}}{\text{Earnings per share}}$	Indicates if price of stock is in line with earnings.
4 Book value per share of common stock	$\dfrac{\text{Common stockholders' equity}}{\text{Shares of common outstanding}}$	Measures the recorded value of net assets behind each share of common stock.
5 Operating expense ratio	$\dfrac{\text{Operating expenses}}{\text{Net sales}}$	Indicates management's ability to control expenses.
6 Return on assets	$\dfrac{\text{Operating Income}}{\text{Average investment in assets}}$	Measures the productivity of assets regardless of capital structures.
7 Return on common stock-holders' equity	$\dfrac{\text{Net income} - \text{preferred dividends}}{\text{Average common stockholders' equity}}$	Indicates the earning power of common stock equity.
8 Equity ratio	$\dfrac{\text{Total stockholders' equity}}{\text{Total assets}}$	Shows the protection to creditors and the extent of leverage being used.

Ratio or Other Measurement	Method of Computation	Significance
9 Number of times interest earned	$\dfrac{\text{Operating income}}{\text{Annual interest expense}}$	Measures the coverage of interest requirements, particularly on long-term debt.
10 Debt ratio	$\dfrac{\text{Total liabilities}}{\text{Total assets}}$	Indicates the percentage of assets financed through borrowing; it shows the extent of leverage being used.
11 Times preferred dividends earned	$\dfrac{\text{Net income}}{\text{Annual preferred dividends}}$	Shows the adequacy of current earnings to pay dividends on preferred stock.
12 Working capital	Current assets − current liabilities	Measures short-run debt-paying ability.
13 Inventory turnover	$\dfrac{\text{Cost of goods sold}}{\text{Average inventory}}$	Indicates marketability of inventory and reasonableness of quantity on hand.
14 Accounts receivable turnover	$\dfrac{\text{Net sales on credit}}{\text{Average receivables}}$	Indicates reasonableness of accounts receivable balance and effectiveness of collections.
15 Current ratio	$\dfrac{\text{Current assets}}{\text{Current liabilities}}$	Measures short-run debt-paying ability.
16 Quick ratio	$\dfrac{\text{Quick assets}}{\text{Current liabilities}}$	Measures the short-term liquidity of a firm.

Key terms introduced or emphasized in chapter 16

Comparative financial statements. Financial statement data for two or more successive years placed side by side in adjacent columns to facilitate study of changes.

Component percentage. The percentage relationship of any financial statement item to a total including that item. For example, each type of asset as a percentage of total assets.

Horizontal analysis. Comparison of the change in a financial statement item such as inventories during two or more accounting periods.

Leverage. Refers to the practice of financing assets with borrowed capital. Extensive leverage creates the possibility for the rate of return on common stockholders' equity to be substantially above or below the rate of return on total assets. When the rate of return on total assets exceeds the average cost of borrowed capital, leverage increases net income and the return on common stockholders' equity. However, when the return on total assets is less than the average cost of borrowed capital, leverage reduces net income and the return on common stockholders' equity. Leverage is also called *trading on the equity.*

Quality of assets. The concept that some companies have assets of better quality than others, such as well-balanced composition of assets, well-maintained plant and equipment, and receivables that are all current. A lower quality of assets might be indicated by poor maintenance of plant and equipment, slow-moving inventories with high danger of obsolescence, past-due receivables, and patents approaching an expiration date.

Quality of earnings. Earnings are said to be of high quality if they are stable, the source seems assured, and the methods used in measuring income are conservative. The existence of this concept suggests that the range of alternative but acceptable accounting principles may still be too wide to produce financial statements that are comparable.

Rate of return on investment (ROI). The overall test of management's ability to earn a satisfactory return on the assets under its control. Numerous variations of the ROI concept are used such as return on total assets, return on total equities, etc.

Ratios. See pages 674 and 675 for list of ratios, methods of computation, and significance.

Vertical analysis. Comparison of a particular financial statement item to a total including that item, such as inventories as a percentage of current assets, or operating expenses in relation to net sales.

Demonstration problem for your review

The accounting records of King Corporation showed the following balances at the end of Years 1 and 2:

	Year 2	Year 1
Cash	$ 35,000	$ 25,000
Accounts receivable (net)	91,000	90,000
Inventory	160,000	140,000
Short-term prepayments	4,000	5,000
Investment in land	90,000	100,000
Equipment	880,000	640,000
Less: Accumulated depreciation	(260,000)	(200,000)
	$1,000,000	$ 800,000
Accounts payable	$ 105,000	$ 46,000
Income taxes payable and other accrued liabilities	40,000	25,000
Bonds payable — 8%	280,000	280,000
Premium on bonds payable	3,600	4,000
Capital stock, $5 par	165,000	110,000
Retained earnings	406,400	335,000
	$1,000,000	$ 800,000
Sales (net of discounts and allowances)	$2,200,000	$1,600,000
Cost of goods sold	1,606,000	1,120,000
Gross profit on sales	$ 594,000	$ 480,000
Expenses (including $22,400 interest expense)	(330,000)	(352,000)
Income taxes	(91,000)	(48,000)
Extraordinary loss	(6,600)	– 0 –
Net income	$ 166,400	$ 80,000

Cash dividends of $40,000 were paid and a 50% stock dividend was distributed early in Year 2. All sales were made on credit at a relatively uniform rate during the year. Inventory and receivables did not fluctuate materially. The market price of the company's stock on December 31, Year 2, was $86 per share; on December 31, Year 1, it was $43.50 (before the 50% stock dividend distributed in Year 2).

Instructions. Compute the following for Year 2 and Year 1:

(1) Quick ratio
(2) Current ratio
(3) Equity ratio
(4) Debt ratio
(5) Book value per share of capital stock (based on shares outstanding after 50% stock dividend in Year 2)
(6) Earnings per share of capital stock (after extraordinary loss)
(7) Price-earnings ratio
(8) Gross profit percentage
(9) Operating expense ratio
(10) Income *before extraordinary loss* as a percentage of net sales
(11) Inventory turnover (Assume an average inventory of $150,000 for both years.)
(12) Accounts receivable turnover (Assume average accounts receivable of $90,000 for Year 1.)
(13) Times bond interest earned (before interest expense and income taxes)

Solution to demonstration problem

	Year 2		Year 1
(1) Quick ratio:			
$126,000 ÷ $145,000	.9 to 1		
$115,000 ÷ $71,000			1.6 to 1
(2) Current ratio:			
$290,000 ÷ $145,000	2 to 1		
$260,000 ÷ $71,000			3.7 to 1
(3) Equity ratio:			
$571,400 ÷ $1,000,000	57%		
$445,000 ÷ $800,000			56%
(4) Debt ratio:			
$428,600 ÷ $1,000,000	43%		
$355,000 ÷ $800,000			44%
(5) Book value per share of capital stock:			
$571,400 ÷ 33,000 shares	$17.32		
$445,000 ÷ 33,000* shares		G	$13.48
(6) Earnings per share of capital stock (including extraordinary loss of $0.20 per share in Year 2):			
$166,400 ÷ 33,000 shares	$5.04		
$80,000 ÷ 33,000* shares			$2.42

	Year 2	Year 1

(7) Price-earnings ratio:

$86 ÷ $5.04 .... 17 times

$43.50 ÷ 1.5* = $29, adjusted market price;

   $29 ÷ $2.42   12 times

(8) Gross profit percentage:

$594,000 ÷ $2,200,000 .... 27%

$480,000 ÷ $1,600,000 ....   30%

(9) Operating expense ratio:

($330,000 − $22,400) ÷ $2,200,000 .... 14%

($352,000 − $22,400) ÷ $1,600,000 ....   20.6%

(10) Income before extraordinary loss as a percentage of

   net sales:

$173,000 ÷ $2,200,000 .... 7.9%

$80,000 ÷ $1,600,000 ....   5%

(11) Inventory turnover:

$1,606,000 ÷ $150,000 .... 10.7 times

$1,120,000 ÷ $150,000 ....   7.5 times

(12) Accounts receivable turnover:

$2,200,000 ÷ $90,500 .... 24.3 times

$1,600,000 ÷ $90,000 ....   17.8 times

(13) Times bond interest earned:

($166,400 + $22,400 + $91,000) ÷ $22,400 .... 12.5 times

($80,000 + $22,400 + $48,000) ÷ $22,400 ....   6.7 times

* **Adjusted retroactively for 50% stock dividend.**

Review questions

1   a What groups are interested in the financial affairs of publicly owned corporations?
     b List some of the more important sources of financial information for investors.

2 In financial statement analysis, what is the basic objective of observing trends in data and ratios?
   Suggest some other standards of comparison.

3 In financial analysis, what information is produced by computing a ratio that is not available in a
   simple observation of the underlying data?

4 Distinguish between *trend percentages* and *component percentages.* Which would be better
   suited to analyzing the change in sales over a term of several years?

5 "Although net income declined this year as compared with last year, it increased from 3% to 5%
   of net sales." Are sales increasing or decreasing?

6 Differentiate between *horizontal* and *vertical* analysis.

7 Assume that Chemco Corporation is engaged in the manufacture and distribution of a variety of
   chemicals. In analyzing the financial statements of this corporation, why would you want to
   refer to the ratios and other measurements of companies in the chemical industry? In comparing
   the financial results of Chemco Corporation with another chemical company, why would you be
   interested in the accounting procedures used by the two companies?

8 Explain how the following accounting practices will tend to raise or lower the quality of a company's earnings. (Assume the continuance of inflation.)

    a Adoption of an accelerated depreciation method rather than straight-line depreciation.

    b Adoption of fifo rather than lifo for the valuation of inventories.

    c Adoption of a 7-year life rather than a 10-year life for the depreciation of equipment.

9 What single ratio do you think should be of greatest interest to:

    a a banker considering a short-term loan?

    b a common stockholder?

    c an insurance company considering a long-term mortgage loan?

10 Modern Company earned a 16% return on its total assets. Current liabilities are 10% of total assets. Long-term bonds carrying a 13% coupon rate are equal to 30% of total assets. There is no preferred stock. Is this application of leverage favorable or unfavorable from the viewpoint of Modern Company's stockholders?

11 In deciding whether a company's equity ratio is favorable or unfavorable, creditors and stockholders may have different views. Why?

12 Company A has a current ratio of 3 to 1. Company B has a current ratio of 2 to 1. Does this mean that A's operating cycle is longer than B's? Why?

13 An investor states, "I bought this stock for $50 several years ago and it now sells for $100. It paid $5 per share in dividends last year so I'm earning 10% on my investment." Criticize this statement.

14 Company C experiences a considerable seasonal variation in its business. The high point in the year's activity comes in November, the low point in July. During which month would you expect the company's current ratio to be higher? If the company were choosing a fiscal year for accounting purposes, how would you advise them?

15 Both the inventory turnover and accounts receivable turnover increased from 10 times to 15 times from Year 1 to Year 2, but net income decreased. Can you offer some possible reasons for this?

16 Is the rate of return on investment (ROI) intended primarily to measure liquidity, solvency, or some other aspect of business operations? Explain.

17 Mention three financial amounts to which corporate profits can logically be compared in judging their adequacy or reasonableness.

18 Under what circumstances would you consider a corporate net income of $1,000,000 for the year as being unreasonably low? Under what circumstances would you consider a corporate profit of $1,000,000 as being unreasonably high?

Exercises

Ex. 16-1   Compute **trend percentages** for the following items taken from the financial statements of Raybar, Inc., over a five-year period. Treat 1982 as the base year. State whether the trends are favorable or unfavorable.

	1986	1985	1984	1983	1982
Sales	$440,000	$380,000	$310,000	$300,000	$250,000
Cost of Goods Sold	$308,000	$247,000	$198,000	$186,000	$150,000

Ex. 16-2 Listed below are some financial items taken from the annual reports of Coast Lands, Inc., for two successive years. Compute the percentage of change from Year 1 to Year 2 whenever possible.

	Year 2	Year 1
a Sales	$960,000	$800,000
b Accounts receivable	132,000	120,000
c Notes receivable	52,200	60,000
d Retained earnings (deficit)	20,000	(40,000)
e Notes payable	50,000	–0–
f Marketable securities	–0–	20,000

Ex. 16-3 Prepare *common size* income statements for Bell Company, a single proprietorship, for the two years shown below by converting the dollar amounts into percentages. For each year, sales will appear as 100% and other items will be expressed as a percentage of sales. (Income taxes are not involved as the business is not incorporated.) Comment on whether the changes from Year 1 to Year 2 are favorable or unfavorable.

	Year 2	Year 1
Sales	$600,000	$500,000
Cost of goods sold	384,000	325,000
Gross profit	$216,000	$175,000
Operating expenses	168,000	145,000
Net income	$ 48,000	$ 30,000

Ex. 16-4 A condensed balance sheet for Magnet Corporation prepared at the end of Year 10 appears below.

Assets		Liabilities & Stockholders' Equity	
Cash	$ 26,000	Notes payable	$ 60,000
Accounts receivable	90,000	Accounts payable	100,000
Inventory	200,000	Long-term liabilities	140,000
Prepaid expenses	10,000	Capital stock, $10 par	200,000
Plant & equipment (net)	399,000	Retained earnings	250,000
Other assets	25,000		
Totals	$750,000		$750,000

During Year 10, the company earned a gross profit of $324,000 on sales of $1,080,000. Accounts receivable, inventory, and plant assets remained almost constant in amount throughout the year. From this information, compute the following:

a Current ratio
b Quick ratio
c Working capital
d Equity ratio
e Accounts receivable turnover (all sales were on credit)
f Inventory turnover
g Book value per share of capital stock.

Ex. 16-5   Selected financial data for Silverwoods, a retail store, appear below. Since monthly figures are not available, the average amounts for inventories and for accounts receivable should be based on the amounts shown for the beginning and end of Year 2.

	Year 2	Year 1
Sales (terms 2/10, n/30)	$420,000	$300,000
Cost of goods sold	315,000	225,000
Inventory at end of year	54,000	60,000
Accounts receivable at end of year	62,000	47,000

Compute the following for Year 2.

   a Gross profit percentage
   b Inventory turnover
   c Accounts receivable turnover

Ex. 16-6   Selected financial data from Rustic Products, Inc., are shown below.

	Year 2	Year 1
Total assets (40% of which are current)	$500,000	$340,000
Current liabilities	$ 90,000	$100,000
Bonds payable, 12%	150,000	65,000
Capital stock, $10 stated value	150,000	150,000
Retained earnings	110,000	25,000
Total liabilities & stockholders' equity	$500,000	$340,000

The average income tax rate is 40% and dividends of $10,000 were declared and paid in Year 2. Compute the following:

   a Current ratio for Year 2 and Year 1
   b Debt ratio for Year 2 and Year 1
   c Earnings per share for Year 2

Ex. 16-7   Selected data from the financial statements of X Company and Y Company for the year just ended are shown below. Assume that for both companies dividends declared were equal in amount to net earnings during the year and therefore stockholders' equity did not change. The two companies are in the same line of business.

	X Company	Y Company
Total liabilities	$ 400,000	$ 200,000
Total assets	1,600,000	800,000
Sales (all on credit)	3,200,000	2,400,000
Average inventory	480,000	280,000
Average receivables	400,000	200,000
Gross profit as a percentage of sales	40%	30%
Operating expenses as a percentage of sales	38%	26%
Net income as a percentage of sales	2%	4%

Compute the following for each company:

a Net income
b Net income as a percentage of stockholders' equity
c Accounts receivable turnover
d Inventory turnover

Problems

16-1   Common size income statement; interpretation of disparities

Sub Zero, Inc., manufactures camping equipment. Shown below for Year 5 are the income state-ment for the company and a common size summary for the industry in which the company operates:

	Sub Zero, Inc.	Industry Average
Sales (net)	$20,000,000	100%
Cost of goods sold	9,800,000	57
Gross profit on sales	$10,200,000	43%
Operating expenses:		
Selling	$ 4,200,000	16%
General and administrative	3,400,000	20
Total operating expenses	$ 7,600,000	36%
Operating income	$ 2,600,000	7%
Income taxes	1,200,000	3
Net income	$ 1,400,000	4%
Return on stockholders' equity	23%	14%

Instructions

a Prepare a two-column common size income statement. The first column should show for Sub Zero, Inc., all items expressed as a percentage of net sales. The second column should show as an industry average the percentage data given in the problem. The purpose of this common size statement is to compare the operating results of Sub Zero, Inc., for Year 5 with the average for the industry.

b Comment specifically on differences between Sub Zero, Inc., and the industry average with respect to gross profit on sales, selling expenses, general and administrative expenses, operat-ing income, net income, and return on stockholders' equity. Suggest possible reasons for the more important disparities.

16-2   Percentage relationships on the income statement

The following information was developed from the financial statements of Quarry Tile, Inc. At the beginning of Year 5, the company began buying its merchandise from a new supplier.

	Year 5	Year 4
Gross profit on sales	$405,000	$320,000
Income before income taxes	45,000	60,000
Net income	36,000	48,000
Net income as a percentage of net sales	4%	6%

Instructions

a Compute the net sales for each year.

b Compute the cost of goods sold in dollars and as a percentage of net sales for each year.

c Compute the operating expenses in dollars and as a percentage of net sales for each year.

d Prepare a condensed comparative income statement for Years 4 and 5. Include the following items: Net sales, cost of goods sold, gross profit, operating expenses, income before income taxes, income taxes expense, and net income. Omit earnings per share statistics.

e Comment on any significant favorable trends and unfavorable trends in the performance of Quarry Tile, Inc.

16-3   Ratios: consider advisability of incurring debt

At the end of Year 1, the following information was obtained from the accounting records of Santa Fe Boot Co.

Sales (all on credit)	$800,000
Cost of goods sold	480,000
Average inventory (fifo method)	120,000
Average accounts receivable	80,000
Interest expense	6,000
Income taxes	8,000
Net income for Year 1	36,000
Average investment in assets	500,000
Average stockholders' equity	400,000

The company declared no dividends of any kind during the year and did not issue or retire any capital stock.

Instructions. From the information given, compute the following for Year 1:

a Inventory turnover.

b Accounts receivable turnover.

c Total operating expenses. (Interest expense is a nonoperating expense.)

d Gross profit percentage.

e Return on average stockholders' equity.

f Return on average assets.

g Santa Fe Boot Co. has an opportunity to obtain a long-term loan at an annual interest rate of 12% and could use this additional capital at the same rate of profitability as indicated above. Would obtaining the loan be desirable from the viewpoint of the stockholders? Explain.

16-4   Ratios based on balance sheet and income statement data

Cyclone Corporation has issued common stock only. The company has been successful and has a gross profit rate of 25%. The information shown below was derived from the company's financial statements.

Beginning inventory	$ 700,000
Purchases	3,100,000
Ending inventory	?
Average accounts receivable	250,000
Average common stockholders' equity	1,800,000
Sales (80% on credit)	4,000,000
Net income	225,000

Instructions. On the basis of the above information, compute the following:

a Accounts receivable turnover and the average number of days required to collect the accounts receivable.

b The inventory turnover and the average number of days required to turn over the inventory.

c Return on common stockholders' equity.

16-5 Ratios: evaluation of two companies
Shown below are selected financial data for Another World, Inc., and for Imports, Inc., at the end of the current year.

	Another World, Inc.	Imports, Inc.
Net credit sales	$675,000	$560,000
Cost of goods sold	504,000	480,000
Cash	51,000	20,000
Accounts receivable (net)	75,000	70,000
Inventory	84,000	160,000
Current liabilities	105,000	100,000

Assume that the year-end balances for accounts receivable and for inventory also represent the average balances for these items throughout the year.

Instructions

a For each of the two companies, compute the following:
   (1) Working capital.
   (2) Current ratio.
   (3) Quick ratio.
   (4) Number of times inventory turned over during the year and the average number of days required to turn over the inventory. (Round computation to the nearest day.)
   (5) Number of times accounts receivable turned over during the year and the average number of days required to collect accounts receivable. (Round computation to the nearest day.)
   (6) Operating cycle.

b From the viewpoint of a short-term creditor, comment upon the relative *quality* of each company's working capital. To which company would you prefer to sell $20,000 in merchandise on a 30-day open account?

16-6 Effects of various transactions on ratios
Listed in the left-hand column below is a series of business transactions and events relating to the activities of Potomac Mills. Opposite each transaction is listed a particular ratio used in financial analysis:

Transaction	Ratio
(1) Purchased inventory on open account.	Quick ratio
(2) A larger physical volume of goods was sold at smaller unit prices.	Gross profit percentage
(3) Corporation declared a cash dividend.	Current ratio
(4) An uncollectible account receivable was written off against the allowance account	Current ratio

Transaction	Ratio
(5) Issued additional shares of common stock and used proceeds to retire long-term debt.	Debt ratio
(6) Paid stock dividend on common stock, in common stock.	Earnings per share
(7) Conversion of a portion of bonds payable into common stock. (Ignore income taxes.)	Times interest charges earned
(8) Appropriated retained earnings.	Rate of return on stockholders' equity
(9) During period of rising prices, company changed from fifo to lifo method of inventory pricing.	Inventory turnover
(10) Paid a previously declared cash dividend.	Debt ratio
(11) Purchased factory supplies on open account.	Current ratio (assume that ratio is greater than 1:1)
(12) Issued shares of capital stock in exchange for patents.	Equity ratio

Instructions. What effect would each transaction or event have on the ratio listed opposite to it; that is, as a result of this event would the ratio increase, decrease, or remain unchanged? Your answer for each of the 12 transactions should include a brief explanation.

16-7   Building financial statements from limited information, including ratios

John Gale, the accountant for Southbay Corporation, prepared the year-end financial statements, including all ratios, and agreed to bring them along on a hunting trip with the executives of the corporation. To his embarrassment, he found that only certain fragmentary information had been placed in his briefcase and the completed statements had been left in his office. One hour before Gale was to present the financial statements to the executives, he was able to come up with the following information:

SOUTHBAY CORPORATION
Balance Sheet
December 31, 19__
(in thousands of dollars)

Assets			Liabilities & Stockholders' Equity		
Current assets:			Current liabilities	$	?
Cash		?	Long-term debt, 8% interest		?
Accounts receivable (net)		?	Total liabilities	$	?
Inventory		?	Stockholder's equity:		
Total current assets	$	?	Capital stock, $5 par $300		
Plant assets:			Retained earnings 100		
Machinery and equipment . $580			Total stockholders' equity		400
Less: Accumulated					
depreciation 80		500	Total liabilities & stockholders'		
Total assets	$	?	equity	$	?

SOUTHBAY CORPORATION
Income Statement
For the Year Ended December 31, 19__
(in thousands of dollars)

Net sales	$?
Cost of goods sold	?
Gross profit on sales (25% of net sales)	$?
Operating expenses	?
Operating income (10% of net sales)	$?
Interest expense	28
Income before income taxes	$?
Income taxes — 40% of income before income taxes	?
Net income	$60

Additional information

(1) The equity ratio was 40%; the debt ratio was 60%.

(2) The only interest expense was on the long-term debt.

(3) The beginning inventory was $150,000; the inventory turnover was 4.8 times. (Inventory turnover = cost of goods sold ÷ average inventory.)

(4) The current ratio was 2 to 1; the quick ratio was 1 to 1.

(5) The beginning balance in accounts receivable was $80,000; the accounts receivable turnover for the year was 12.8 times. All sales \were made on account. (Accounts receivable turnover = net sales ÷ average accounts receivable.)

Instructions. The accountant asks you to help complete the financial statements for the Southbay Corporation, using only the information available. Present supporting computations and explanations for all amounts appearing in the balance sheet and the income statement. Hint: In completing the income statement, start with the net income figure (60% of income before income taxes) and work up.

Cases for analysis

Case 16-1   Telling it like it never was

Holiday Greeting Cards is a local company organized late in July of Year 1. The company's net income for each of its first six calendar quarters of operations is summarized below. The amounts are stated in thousands of dollars.

	Year 2	Year 1
First quarter (January through March)	$ 253	—
Second quarter (April through June)	308	—
Third quarter (July through September)	100	$ 50
Fourth quarter (October through December)	450	500
Total for the calendar year	$1,111	$550

Glen Wallace reports the business and economic news for a local radio station. On the day that Holiday Greeting Cards released the above financial information, you heard Wallace make the following statement during his broadcast: "Holiday Greeting Cards enjoyed a 350% increase in its profits for the fourth quarter, and profits for the entire year were up by over 100%."

Instructions

a Show the computations that Wallace probably made in arriving at his statistics. (Hint: Wallace did not make his computations in the manner recommended in this chapter. His figures, however, can be developed from the financial data above.)

b Do you believe that Wallace's percentage changes present a realistic impression of Holiday Greeting Cards' rate of growth in Year 2? Explain.

c What figure would you use to express the percentage change in Holiday's fourth quarter profits in Year 2? Explain why you would compute the change in this manner.

Case 16-2   Evaluation of capital structure and liquidity: two companies

Certain financial information relating to two companies. London Conspiracy and Coventry Clothiers, as of the end of the current year, is shown below. All figures (except market price per share of stock) are in *thousands of dollars.*

Assets	London Conspiracy	Coventry Clothiers
Cash	$ 126.0	$ 180.0
Marketable securities, at cost	129.0	453.0
Accounts receivable, net	145.0	167.0
Inventories	755.6	384.3
Prepaid expenses	24.4	15.7
Plant and equipment, net	1,680.0	1,570.0
Intangibles and other assets	140.0	30.0
Total assets	$3,000.0	$2,800.0

Liabilities & Stockholders' Equity		
Accounts payable	$ 344.6	$ 304.1
Accrued liabilities, including income taxes	155.4	95.9
Bonds payable, 7%, due in 10 years	200.0	500.0
Capital stock ($10 par)	1,000.0	600.0
Capital in excess of par	450.0	750.0
Retained earnings	910.0	550.0
Treasury stock (1,000 shares, at cost)	(60.0)	–0–
Total liabilities & stockholders' equity	$3,000.0	$2,800.0

Analysis of retained earnings:		
Balance, beginning of year	$ 712.0	$ 430.0
Add: Net income	297.0	240.0
Less: Dividends	(99.0)	(120.0)
Balance, end of year	$ 910.0	$ 550.0
Market price per share of stock, end of year	$50	$40

Instructions. London Conspiracy and Coventry Clothiers are generally comparable in the nature of their operations, products, and accounting procedures used. Write a short answer to each of the following questions, using whatever analytical computations you feel will best support your answer. Show the amounts used in calculating all ratios and percentages. Carry per-share computations to the nearest cent and percentages one place beyond the decimal point, for example, 9.8%.

a What is the book value per share of stock for each company?

b Prepare a four-column schedule showing for each company the component percentages represented by current liabilities, by long-term liabilities, and by stockholders' equity. Use the first two columns for London Conspiracy, showing dollar amounts in the first column and component percentages in the second column. Use the last two columns in the same way for Coventry Clothiers. On the basis of this analysis, express an opinion as to which company has a more conservative capital structure.

c Compute the price-earnings ratio and the dividend yield for each company. Use a work sheet with five money columns. Use the headings Market Price per Share, Earnings per Share, Price-Earnings Ratio, Dividends per Share, and Dividend Yield, %. Before computing the price-earnings ratio, you must compute earnings per share. Show all computations as supporting schedules.

d Compute (1) quick assets, (2) total current assets, and (3) working capital. Then compute the quick ratio and the current ratio. Finally, write a brief statement as to which company has the more liquid financial position. Base your answer on the above measurements.

Chapter 17
Income taxes and business decisions

For many college students, this chapter may be their only academic exposure to the truly remarkable system known as federal income taxes. The early part of the chapter presents a brief history and rationale of the federal tax structure. This introduction stresses the pervasive influence of income taxes upon economic activity. The next section portrays the basic process of determining taxable income and the tax liability for individual taxpayers. The income tax computations for a small corporation are also explained and illustrated. The final section of the chapter gives students an understanding of the important role that tax planning can play in the affairs of individuals and also in the decision-making of a business entity.

After studying
this chapter you
should be able to:

✓ Differentiate between tax planning and tax evasion.
✓ Explain the progressive nature of income tax rates.
✓ State the formula for determining the taxable income of an individual.
✓ Explain the income tax treatment of capital gains and losses.
✓ Distinguish between a tax deduction and a tax credit.
✓ Determine the income tax liability of an individual.
✓ Contrast the determination of taxable income for a corporation with that for an individual.
✓ Explain the concept of interperiod income tax allocation.
✓ Discuss the tax considerations in choosing a form of business entity and in designing its capital structure.

"A penny saved is a penny earned," according to an old saying credited to Benjamin Franklin. However, now that many individuals are subject to approximately a 50% income tax rate, we can modify this bit of folklore to read: "A dollar of income tax saved is worth two dollars of income earned."

In other words, almost half of what a corporation earns, and half of what some individuals earn, must be paid to the federal government as income taxes. If advance tax planning will enable an individual to avoid a dollar of income taxes, that dollar saved may be the equivalent of two dollars of before-tax earnings. Furthermore, there are a good many perfectly legal actions which can be taken to save or at least to postpone income taxes.

Tax planning versus tax evasion

Individuals who plan their business affairs in a manner that will result in the lowest possible income tax are acting rationally and legally. They are using the techniques called **tax planning.** In the words of a distinguished jurist, Judge Learned Hand:

> Over and over again courts have said that there is nothing sinister in so arranging one's affairs as to keep taxes as low as possible. Everybody does so, rich or poor; and all do right, for nobody owes any public duty to pay more than the law demands: taxes are enforced exactions, not voluntary contributions. To demand more in the name of morals is mere cant.

To reduce and to postpone income taxes are the goals of tax planning. Almost every business decision involves a choice among alternative courses of action with different tax consequences. For example, should we lease or buy business automobiles; should we obtain needed capital by issuing bonds or preferred stock; should we use straight-line depreciation or an accelerated method? Some of these alternatives will lead to much lower income taxes than others. Tax planning, therefore, means **determining in advance the income tax effect** of every proposed business action and then making business decisions which will lead to the smallest tax liability. Tax practice is an important element of the services furnished to clients by CPA firms. This service includes not only the computing of taxes and preparing of tax returns, but also tax planning.

Tax planning must begin early. Unfortunately, some wait until the end of the year and then, faced with the prospect of paying a large amount of income tax, ask their accountants what can be done to reduce the tax liability. If we are to arrange transactions in a manner that will lead to the minimum income tax liability, the tax planning must be carried out **before** the date of a transaction, not after it is an accomplished fact. Because it is important for everyone to recognize areas in which tax savings may be substantial, a few of the major opportunities for tax planning are discussed in the final section of this chapter.

Newspaper stories tell us each year of some taxpayers who have deliberately understated their taxable income by failing to report a portion of income received or by claiming fictitious deductions such as an excess number of personal exemptions. Such purposeful understatement of taxable income is called **tax evasion** and is, of course, illegal. On the other hand, **tax avoidance** (the arranging of business and financial affairs in a manner that will minimize tax liability) is entirely legal.

The critical importance of income taxes

Taxes levied by federal, state, and local governments are a significant part of the cost of operating a typical household, as well as a business enterprise. Every manager who makes business decisions, and every individual who makes personal investments, urgently needs some knowledge of income taxes. A general knowledge of income taxes will help any business manager or owner to benefit more fully from the advice of the professional tax accountant.

Some understanding of income taxes will also aid the individual citizen in voting intelligently, because a great many of the issues decided in every election have tax implications. Such issues as pollution, inflation, foreign policy, and employment are quite closely linked with income taxes. For example, the offering of special tax incentives to encourage businesses to launch massive programs to reduce pollution is one approach to protection of the environment.

In terms of revenue generated, the four most important kinds of taxes in the United States are *income taxes, sales taxes, property taxes,* and *excise taxes.* Income taxes exceed all others in terms of the amounts involved, and they also exert a pervasive influence on all types of business decisions. For this reason we shall limit our discussion to the basic federal income tax rules applicable to individuals, partnerships, and corporations.

Income taxes are usually determined from information contained in accounting records. The amount of income tax is computed by applying the appropriate tax rates (as set by federal, state, and some local governments) to *taxable income.* As explained more fully later in this chapter, *taxable income* is not necessarily the same as *accounting income* even though both are derived from the accounting records. Business managers can influence the amount of taxes they pay by their choice of form of business organization, methods of financing, and alternative accounting methods. Thus income taxes are inevitably an important factor in arriving at business decisions.

The federal income tax: history and objectives

The present federal income tax dates from the passage of the Sixteenth Amendment to the Constitution in 1913.[1] This amendment, only 30 words in length,[2] removed all questions of the constitutionality of income taxes and paved the way for the more than 50 revenue acts passed by Congress since that date. In 1939 these tax laws were first combined into what is known as the Internal Revenue Code. The administration and enforcement of the tax laws are duties of the Treasury Department, operating through a division known as the Internal Revenue Service (IRS). The Treasury Department publishes its interpretation of the tax laws in Treasury regulations; the final word in interpretation lies with the federal courts.

Originally the purpose of the federal income tax was simply to obtain revenue for the government. And at first, the tax rates were quite low — by today's standards. In 1913 a married person with taxable income of $15,000 would have been subject to a tax rate of 1%, resulting in a tax liability of $150. Today, a married person with a $15,000 taxable income (worth far less in purchasing power) would pay over $2,000 in federal income tax. The maximum federal income tax rate in 1913 was 7%. A few years ago it was 70%. Today it is 50%.

---

[1] A federal income tax was proposed as early as 1815, and an income tax law was actually passed and income taxes collected during the Civil War. This law was upheld by the Supreme Court, but it was repealed when the need for revenue subsided after the war. In 1894 a new income tax law was passed, but the Supreme Court declared this law invalid on constitutional grounds.

[2] It reads "The Congress shall have power to lay and collect taxes on incomes, from whatever source derived, without apportionment among the several States, and without regard to any census or enumeration."

The purpose of federal income tax now includes several goals apart from raising revenue. Examples of these other goals are: influencing the rate of economic growth, encouraging full employment, combatting inflation, favoring small businesses, and redistributing national income on a more equal basis.

Classes of taxpayers

In the eyes of the income tax law, there are four major classes of taxpayers: *individuals*, *corporations*, *estates*, and *trusts*. A business organized as a single proprietorship or as a partnership is not taxed as a separate entity; its income is taxed directly to the individual proprietor or partners, *whether or not the income is withdrawn from the business.* However, a partnership must file an *information return* showing the computation of total partnership net income and the allocation of this income among the partners.

A single proprietor reports his or her income from ownership of a business on an individual tax return; the members of a partnership include on their individual income tax returns their respective shares of the partnership net income. Of course, an individual's income tax return must include not only any business income from a proprietorship or partnership, but also any interest, dividends, salary, or other forms of income received.

A corporation is a separate taxable entity; it must file a corporate income tax return and pay a tax on its annual taxable income. In addition, individual stockholders must report dividends received from corporations as part of their personal taxable income. The taxing of corporate dividends has led to the charge that there is "double taxation" of corporate income — once to the corporation and again when it is distributed to stockholders. This double impact of tax is particularly apparent when a corporation is owned by one person or one family.

To illustrate, let us consider the tax impact on one dollar of corporate earnings. The *income before taxes* earned by a corporation may be subject to a federal corporate income tax rate of 46%. First, the corporation pays 46%, or 46 cents, out of the dollar to the Internal Revenue Service. That leaves 54 cents for the corporation. Next, assume that the 54 cents is distributed as dividends to individual stockholders. The dividend will be taxed to the stockholders personally at rates varying from 12 to 50%, depending on their individual tax brackets. Thus, the 54 cents of after-tax income to the corporation could be reduced by 50%, or 27 cents of individual income tax, leaving 27 cents of the original dollar for the shareholder. In summary, *federal income taxes can take as much as 73 cents out of a dollar earned by a corporation and distributed as a dividend to a shareholder.* The remaining 27 cents could be reduced further by state income taxes.

Special and complex rules apply to the determination of taxable income for estates and trusts. These rules will not be discussed in this chapter.

INCOME TAXES: INDIVIDUALS

Cash basis of accounting for income tax returns

Almost all *individual* income tax returns are prepared on the cash basis of accounting. Many small service-type business concerns and professional firms also choose to prepare their tax returns on the cash basis. Revenue is recognized when collected in cash;

expenses (except depreciation) are recognized when a cash payment is made. The cash basis (as prescribed in IRS rules) does not permit expenditures for plant and equipment to be deducted in the year of purchase. These capital expenditures are capitalized and depreciated for tax purposes, as previously discussed in Chapter 10. Also, the income tax laws do not permit use of the cash basis by companies in which inventories and the sale of merchandise are significant factors.

Although the cash basis of accounting does not measure income satisfactorily in the context of generally accepted accounting principles, it has much merit in the area of taxation. From the government's viewpoint, the logical time to collect tax on income is when the taxpayer receives the income in cash. At any earlier date, the taxpayer may not have the cash to pay income taxes; at any later date, the cash may have been used for other purposes.

The cash basis is advantageous for the individual taxpayer and for service-type businesses for several reasons. It is simple, and requires a minimum of records. The income of most individuals comes in the form of salaries, interest, and dividends. At the end of each year, an individual receives from his or her employer a W-2 form (page 346) showing the salary earned and income tax withheld during the year. This report is prepared on a cash basis without any accrual of unpaid wages. Persons receiving interest or dividends also receive from the paying companies Form 1099 summarizing amounts received for the year. Thus, most individuals are provided with reports prepared on a cash basis for use in preparing their individual tax returns.

The cash basis has other advantages for the individual taxpayer and for many professional firms and service-type businesses. It often permits tax savings by individuals who deliberately shift the timing of revenue and expense transactions from one year to another. For example, a dentist whose taxable income is higher than usual in the current year may decide in December to delay billing patients until January 1, and thus postpone the receipt of gross income to the next year. The timing of *expense payments* near year-end is also controllable by a taxpayer using the cash basis. A taxpayer who has received a bill for a deductible expense item in December may choose to pay it before or after December 31 and thereby influence the amount of taxable income in each year.

Any taxpayer who maintains a set of accounting records may *elect* to use the accrual basis in preparing a tax return, but very few taxpayers (individual or corporate) choose to do so if they are eligible to use the cash basis.

Tax rates

All taxes may be characterized as progressive, proportional, or regressive with respect to any given base. A *progressive* tax becomes a larger portion of the base as that base increases. Federal income taxes are *progressive* with respect to income, since a higher tax *rate* applies as the amount of taxable income increases. A *proportional* tax remains a constant percentage of the base no matter how that base changes. For example, a 6% sales tax remains a constant percentage of sales regardless of changes in the dollar amount of sales. A *regressive* tax becomes a smaller percentage of the base as the base increases. Regressive taxes, however, are extremely rare.

At the time this was written, the top tax rate on individuals was 50% on all types of income. The 50% maximum rate had applied to salaries for several past years, but during the 1970s the top tax rate on interest, dividends, rent, and other "unearned" income had been 70%. In the 1960s, the tax rates on individuals reached as high as 90%. When tax rates reach 70%, 80%, or 90%, the incentive to save and invest is greatly reduced. Little remains for the investor under such extreme tax rates.

Tax rate schedules

On these two facing pages we have tax rate schedules for single taxpayers and for married taxpayers filing joint returns. Tax rates for individuals at present vary from 11 to 50%, depending on the amount of income. Persons with very low incomes pay no income tax. Different tax rate schedules apply to (1) single taxpayers, (2) married taxpayers filing joint returns, (3) married taxpayers filing separate returns, and (4) single taxpayers who qualify as the head of a household. In computing the amount of the tax, the tax rates are applied to *taxable income,* a term which means gross income less certain exclusions and deductions specified in the tax law. Income tax rates are subject to *frequent revision* by Congress; in fact, a drastic revision was under consideration by Congress at the time this was written.

Single Taxpayers

Taxable Income		Tax	
Not over $2,390		-0-	
Over—	But not over—		of the amount over—
$ 2,390	$ 3,540	---------- 11%	$ 2,390
3,540	4,580	$ 126.50 + 12%	3,540
4,580	6,760	251.30 + 14%	4,580
6,760	8,850	556.50 + 15%	6,760
8,850	11,240	870.00 + 16%	8,850
11,240	13,430	1,252.40 + 18%	11,240
13,430	15,610	1,646.60 + 20%	13,430
15,610	18,940	2,082.60 + 23%	15,610
18,940	24,460	2,848.50 + 26%	18,940
24,460	29,970	4,283.70 + 30%	24,460
29,970	35,490	5,936.70 + 34%	29,970
35,490	43,190	7,813.50 + 38%	35,490
43,190	57,550	10,739.50 + 42%	43,190
57,550	85,130	16,770.70 + 48%	57,550
85,130	- - - - - -	30,009.10 + 50%	85,130

Example: Find the tax for a single person having taxable income of $22,000.

Answer: Tax on $18,940 as shown on tax rate schedule $2,848.50

   Tax on $3,060 excess at 26% 795.60

   Tax on $22,000 for a single person $3,644.10

The steeply progressive nature of income taxes

To illustrate the steeply progressive nature of income taxes, let us compare two single taxpayers, one of whom has a relatively low income and the other a relatively high income. Assume that Tom Jones has taxable income of $5,000 a year and Mary Smith has taxable income of $50,000 a year. According to the tax rate schedule on page 694, Jones would owe tax of $310.10 and Smith would owe tax of $13,599.70. The tax owed by Jones is about 6% of his total taxable income of $5,000; the tax owed by Smith is over 27% of her total taxable income of $50,000.

Married Taxpayers Filing Joint Returns			
Taxable Income		Tax	
Not over $3,540		-0-	
Over—	But not over—		of the amount over—
$ 3,540	$ 5,720	- - - - - - - - - - 11%	$ 3,540
5,720	7,910	$ 239.80 + 12%	5,720
7,910	12,390	502.60 + 14%	7,910
12,390	16,650	1,129.80 + 16%	12,390
16,650	21,020	1,811.40 + 18%	16,650
21,020	25,600	2,598.00 + 22%	21,020
25,600	31,120	3,605.60 + 25%	25,600
31,120	36,630	4,985.60 + 28%	31,120
36,630	47,670	6,528.40 + 33%	36,630
47,670	62,450	10,171.60 + 38%	47,670
62,450	89,090	15,788.00 + 42%	62,450
89,090	113,860	26,976.80 + 45%	89,090
113,860	169,020	38,123.30 + 49%	113,860
169,020	- - - - - - -	65,151.70 + 50%	169,020

Example: Find the tax for a married couple filing a joint return having a
taxable income of $50,000.

Answer: Tax on $47,670 as shown on tax rate schedule $10,171.60
Tax on $2,330 excess at 38% 885.40
Tax on $50,000 for a married couple filing a joint return $11,057.00

Next, let us consider how much additional income tax each of these two individuals would have to pay on any additional income. According to the tax rate schedules, an increase of $100 in income for Jones would be taxed at 14%. However, an increase of $100 in income for Smith would be taxed at 42%.

Supporters of a highly progressive income tax argue that the system is fair because the taxpayers most able to pay are subject to the highest rates. Critics contend that the high rates on high incomes discourage individual initiative and penalize productivity. Another criticism is that high tax rates lead to an increasing amount of violation with a significant volume of economic transactions going "underground."

Marginal tax rates compared with average tax rates

In any analysis of income taxes, it is important to distinguish the **marginal** rate of tax from the taxpayer's **average** rate. The marginal rate is the rate that will apply to the next dollar of income to be earned. For example, assume that you are an unmarried executive with a taxable income of $43,190 and are considering changing to a new job that will pay $5,000 more per year in salary. Using the tax rate schedule on page 694, your present tax is $10,739.50, an average rate of about 25%. However, your marginal tax rate on the proposed $5,000 salary increase is 42%. Your decision with respect to the new job may well be affected by the fact that you would be able to keep only slightly more than half ($2,900) of the $5,000 increase in salary.

Another way of looking at the impact of income taxes is from the viewpoint of the employer. A company that wants to increase the salary of an executive must pay about $2 for every $1 to be received by the executive in additional take-home pay.

The marginal tax rate is important in many business decisions. Often the decision is whether to invest additional money and effort in order to earn an increased amount of income. However, an increase in income will cause an increase in income taxes **at the marginal rate.** The **after-tax** result of a proposed investment must be estimated by using the marginal tax rate, and not the average tax rate. In other words, the attractiveness of an extra dollar of income depends on the marginal tax rate applicable to that particular dollar.

Income taxes and inflation

As salaries and prices in general have risen sharply in recent years, people find themselves in higher income tax brackets even though their higher salaries represent no increase in purchasing power. Because income tax rates are steeply progressive, this means that many people must pay a **higher percentage** of their earnings as income taxes solely as a result of inflation. Thus, income taxes are actually being increased in each year of inflation even though the schedule of tax rates remains unchanged. A $20,000 salary may buy no more today than a $10,000 salary some years ago, but a $20,000 salary is taxed at a much higher rate.

A few years ago Congress passed **indexing** legislation designed to prevent tax increases based solely on inflation. This law provided that beginning in 1985, the tax brackets, personal exemption, and the zero bracket amount (see page 700) will be increased to reflect annual changes in the Consumer Price Index.

Income tax formula for individuals

The federal government supplies standard income tax forms on which taxpayers are guided to a proper computation of their taxable income and the amount of the tax. It is helpful to visualize the computation in terms of an income tax formula. The general formula for the determination of taxable income for individual taxpayers is outlined on the next page.

The actual sequence and presentation of material on income tax forms differs somewhat from the arrangement in this formula. However, it is easier to understand the structure and logic of the federal income tax and to analyze tax rules and their effect by referring to the tax formula.

Total income and gross income

Total income as defined for tax purposes is a very broad concept that includes in the words of the law, "all income from whatever source derived." **Gross income** is computed by deducting from total income certain items excluded by the tax laws, as for example, interest received on state and municipal bonds. A concise definition of gross income is "all income not excluded by law." Gross income therefore includes salaries, commissions, bonuses, dividends, interest, rent, and gains from sale of securities, real estate, and other property. To determine whether any given income item is included in gross income, one must ask, "Is there a provision in the tax law excluding this item of income from gross income?" Among the items **currently excluded from gross income** by statute are interest on state and municipal bonds, gifts and inheritances, life insurance proceeds, workmen's compensation, social security benefits (subject to certain limits), the portion of receipts from annuities that represents return of cost, pensions to veterans, compensation for actual damages, and the first $100 of dividends received ($200 on a joint tax return).

Among the items of miscellaneous income which must be **included** in gross income are prizes and awards won, tips received, and gains from sale of personal property. The fact that income arises from an illegal transaction does not keep it from being taxable.

Deductions to arrive at adjusted gross income

Some of the more common deductions from **gross income** allowed in computing **adjusted gross income** are discussed below.

1 **Business expenses of a single proprietorship.** These include all ordinary and necessary expenses of carrying on a trade, business, or profession (other than as an employee). For the actual tax computation, business expenses are deducted from business revenue, and net business income is then included in adjusted gross income on the proprietor's tax return.

2 **Business expenses of an employee.** Some expenses incurred by employees in connection with their employment are allowed as a deduction if the employees are not reimbursed by the employer. These include, for example, travel and transportation as part of employee's duties, expenses of "outside salespersons," and certain moving expenses. The costs of commuting between home and work are not deductible.

3 **Expenses attributable to rental properties.** The owner of rental property, such as an apartment building, incurs a variety of operating expenses. Depreciation, property taxes, repairs, maintenance, interest on indebtedness related to property, and any other expenses incurred in connection with the earning of rental income are

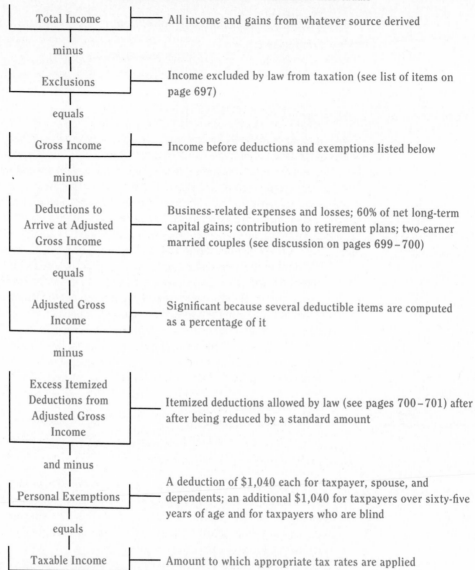

General Federal Income Tax Formula for Individuals

Use this formula to compute taxable income for individuals

Total Income ———— All income and gains from whatever source derived

minus

Exclusions ———— Income excluded by law from taxation (see list of items on page 697)

equals

Gross Income ———— Income before deductions and exemptions listed below

minus

Deductions to Arrive at Adjusted Gross Income ———— Business-related expenses and losses; 60% of net long-term capital gains; contribution to retirement plans; two-earner married couples (see discussion on pages 699–700)

equals

Adjusted Gross Income ———— Significant because several deductible items are computed as a percentage of it

minus

Excess Itemized Deductions from Adjusted Gross Income ———— Itemized deductions allowed by law (see pages 700–701) after after being reduced by a standard amount

and minus

Personal Exemptions ———— A deduction of $1,040 each for taxpayer, spouse, and dependents; an additional $1,040 for taxpayers over sixty-five years of age and for taxpayers who are blind

equals

Taxable Income ———— Amount to which appropriate tax rates are applied

allowed as a deduction. This means that only the *net income* derived from rental property is included in adjusted gross income.

4 *Losses from the sale of property used in business.* Any loss resulting from the sale of property used in a trade or business may be deducted against other items of gross income.[3]

---

[3] Losses arising from the sale of personal property, such as a home or personal automobile, are not deductible. On the other hand, gains from the sale of personal property are taxable. This appears inconsistent, until one realizes that a loss on the sale of personal property usually reflects depreciation through use, which is a personal expense.

5 *Net capital losses.* Up to $3,000 of net capital losses may be deducted to arrive at adjusted gross income. Capital gains and losses are discussed on pages 702–704.

6 *Long-term capital gain deduction.* Sixty percent of the excess of net long-term capital gains over net short-term capital losses is a deduction to arrive at adjusted gross income. In other words, only 40% of a long-term capital gain is taxable.

7 *Net operating loss carry-over.* Taxable income may be either positive or negative. If positive income were taxed and no allowance made for operating losses, a tax-payer whose yearly business income fluctuated between profitable years and loss years would pay a relatively higher tax than one having a steady income averaging the same amount. Therefore, the tax law allows the carry-back and carry-over of net operating losses as an offset against the income of other years. At the present time a loss may be carried back against the income of the three preceding years, and then forward against the income of the next seven years.

8 *Contributions to retirement plans: IRA and Keogh plans.* A retirement plan known as *IRA* (Independent Retirement Arrangement) offers tax advantages and is available to anyone who receives earned income. Both employees and self-employed persons are eligible. This plan permits anyone with earned income to contribute to the plan and to deduct from gross income as much as $2,000 a year of compensation received. Thus, an individual in, say, the 40% tax bracket, can save $800 in taxes by investing $2,000 in this type of retirement plan. Since the interest or dividends earned on an IRA plan are also free from tax, the investment grows much more rapidly than investments yielding taxable income.

Another type of retirement plan, often referred to as a *Keogh H.R.10 plan,* offers larger deductions for self-employed persons. Individuals who are *self-employed* are permitted to deduct from gross income the amounts they contribute to a Keogh plan. The present limit on such contributions is the lower of $15,000 or 15% of the self-employed person's annual earnings. By taking a deduction for this contribution, a self-employed person earning $100,000 or more can reduce adjusted gross income by $15,000 each year. The amounts contributed plus earnings on the fund are taxable when the taxpayer retires and begins making withdrawals from the fund. The Keogh plan is intended to provide self-employed persons with opportunities similar to those of persons employed by organizations with pension or retirement plans. A self-employed person may contribute to both an IRA and a Keogh plan.

9 *Deduction for two-earner married couples.* Under the tax rate schedules in effect before 1982, a two-earner married couple was subject to a higher tax than would have been imposed if they were single and the lower-earning spouse provided at least 20% of the combined incomes. This aspect of the tax laws was referred to as the "marriage penalty" and was subject to much criticism. New legislation has now provided some relief through a new deduction in computing adjusted gross income for a married couple when both work. The deduction is limited to 10% of the lower-earning spouse's earned income up to $30,000; thus the maximum deduction is $3,000 a year.

In identifying the lower of the two incomes, a first step is to reduce each income by any payments that individual made to an IRA or Keogh retirement plan and by the amount of any employee business expenses. For example, John earns a salary of $20,000 and incurs $6,000 of employee business expenses. Mary earns a salary of

$17,000 and contributes $2,000 to an IRA. John's qualified earned income would be $14,000 and Mary's would be $15,000. Since the lower of the two spouses' qualified earnings is $14,000, a deduction of $1,400 (10% of $14,000) could be taken on a joint tax return.

10 *Other deductions to arrive at adjusted gross income.* Among other deductions are moving expenses caused by change of jobs, alimony paid, and penalty on early withdrawals from long-term savings deposits.

Adjusted gross income. By deducting from gross income the various items described in the preceding section, we arrive at a very significant subtotal called *adjusted gross income.* This amount is significant because several deductible items, such as contributions, are limited to a percentage of the taxpayer's adjusted gross income.

Deductions from adjusted gross income (itemized deductions)

Remember that there are two basic groups of deductions for individuals: (1) items deductible from gross income to arrive at adjusted gross income and (2) items deductible from adjusted gross income to arrive at taxable income. We will now consider the second group of items (such as charitable contributions, interest on home mortgage, and sales taxes) which an individual may deduct *from* adjusted gross income. These items are referred to as *itemized deductions.*

The importance of itemizing deductions lies in the fact that every deduction reduces the income subject to tax. The taxpayer should retain documentary evidence supporting the deductions claimed.

Zero bracket amount. For many years taxpayers were permitted to take a standard deduction computed as a percentage of adjusted gross income. This standard deduction was based on the concept that all taxpayers could be expected to claim some deductions, such as interest expense and charitable contributions. As an alternative to taking the standard deduction, taxpayers could *itemize* their deductions. The extra work to itemize deductions was worthwhile if the total was more than the standard deduction. In recent years the tax laws have been changed to provide a new *zero bracket amount* which replaced the standard deduction. This zero bracket amount was built into the tax tables in order to simplify the computation of tax liability. The result is to assure a given amount of tax-free income to all taxpayers. At present, the zero bracket amount is $2,390 for single taxpayers and $3,540 for married taxpayers filing a joint return. In effect, the law is assuming that every taxpayer could claim at least $2,390 of deductions ($3,540 if married); therefore the proof of those amounts need not be submitted. The zero bracket amount automatically allows for them.

Excess itemized deductions. We have seen that the zero bracket amount is the equivalent of a standard deduction from adjusted gross income. The amount of income subject to tax can be reduced further by single taxpayers who itemize deductions in excess of $2,390 and by married taxpayers filing a joint return who itemize deductions in excess of $3,540. In other words, a reduction in tax is possible if a taxpayer has relatively large amounts of such items as contributions, interest, state income taxes, and property taxes, and the combined amount of these itemized deductions is in excess of the zero bracket amount. The term **excess itemized deductions** means the excess of itemized deductions over the zero bracket amount.

The major categories of itemized deductions allowable under the law are described below and on the following page.

1 *Interest.* Interest on any indebtedness, within certain limits.
2 *Taxes.* State and local real and personal property taxes, state income taxes, and all sales taxes are deductible by the person on whom they are imposed. No federal taxes qualify as itemized deductions.
3 *Contributions.* Contributions by individuals to charitable, religious, educational, and certain other nonprofit organizations are deductible, within certain limits. Gifts to friends, relatives, or other persons are not deductible.
4 *Medical expenses.* Medical and dental expenses of the taxpayer and his or her family are deductible to the extent that they exceed 5% of adjusted gross income, subject to certain maximum limits.
5 *Casualty losses.* Losses in excess of $100 from any fire, storm, earthquake, theft, or other sudden, unexpected, or unusual causes are deductible only to the extent that they exceed 10% of adjusted gross income. For example, assume that a taxpayer with adjusted gross income of $45,000 sustains an uninsured fire loss of $10,100. First, we eliminate $100 of the loss, leaving the amount of $10,000. Next, we reduce the loss by 10% of the adjusted gross income of $45,000, a reduction of $4,500. This leaves $5,500 as the net deduction from adjusted gross income in arriving at the amount subject to tax.
6 *Expenses related to the production of income.* In this category are included any necessary expenses in producing income or for the management of income-producing property, other than those deductible to arrive at adjusted gross income. Some examples of **miscellaneous deductible expenses** are union dues, work clothes, professional dues, subscriptions to professional periodicals, investment advisers' fees, legal fees relating to investments, fees paid to employment agencies to get a job, and fees for income tax advice and for preparation of tax returns. Examples of **miscellaneous nondeductible expenses** are the cost of going to and from work, gifts to needy friends, most living expenses, babysitting expenses, gasoline taxes, the cost of school tuition, and gambling losses in excess of gambling winnings.

Personal exemptions

In addition to itemized deductions, a deduction from adjusted gross income is allowed for **personal exemptions.** One exemption each is allowed for the taxpayer, the taxpayer's spouse, and each person who qualifies as a dependent of the taxpayer. At present the amount of each personal exemption is $1,040, however, the indexing plan which became effective in 1985 provides for an annual inflation adjustment based on the Consumer Price Index.

The term **dependent** means a person who (1) receives over one-half of his or her support from the taxpayer, (2) is either closely related to the taxpayer or lives in the taxpayer's home, and (3) has gross income during the year of less than the current exemption amount unless he or she is a child of the taxpayer and is under nineteen years of age or is a full-time student.[4] A taxpayer and spouse may each claim an additional personal exemption if sixty-five years of age or over, and another exemption if blind. These additional exemptions do not apply to dependents.

Taxable income — individuals

We have now traced the steps required to determine the taxable income of an individual. In brief, this process includes:

1 Computation of total income
2 Exclusion of certain items specified by law to determine gross income
3 Deduction of business-related expenses to arrive at adjusted gross income
4 Deduction of excess itemized deductions and personal exemptions to arrive at the key figure of taxable income.

The concept of taxable income is most important because it is the amount to which the appropriate tax rate is applied to determine the tax liability.

Capital gains and losses

Fortunate is the taxpayer who derives most of his or her income from long-term capital gains. The tax on such gains is only 40% as high as the tax on an equal amount of income from other sources, such as salaries or interest received. Our starting point in studying this important tax-saving area is the nature of the transactions which qualify for favored tax treatment.

Certain kinds of property are defined under the tax laws as **capital assets.**[5] Common examples are investments in securities and real estate (including a personal residence). Gains and losses from the sale of such assets are granted special favorable treatment for income tax purposes. From the standpoint of tax planning, this situation calls for taxpayers to invest in properties that offer the possibility of capital gains.

The rationale underlying special treatment of capital gains is to strengthen the economy by encouraging long-term investment in equities by individuals and by business concerns. If our future economy is to be strong and healthy, investment capital must flow into new growth industries. New growth industries are speculative. They do not offer investors assured low-risk income, but do offer the possibility of capital appreciation. Our tax laws can provide an incentive for risk-taking by investors, if capital gains are taxed at

---

[4] A child under nineteen or a full-time student who qualifies as a dependent in all other respects but who earns over the current exemption amount in any one year has, in effect, two personal exemptions. One may be taken by the taxpayer who claims him or her as a dependent; the other he will claim for himself on his own personal income tax return.

[5] The Internal Revenue Code defines capital assets to include all items of property except: (a) business inventories; (b) accounts and notes receivable; (c) plant and equipment used in a business; (d) intangible assets such as copyrights and artistic compositions; and (e) government bonds and notes issued at a discount and due within one year.

much lower rates than low-risk income such as interest on bonds and insured bank deposits.

Amount of gain or loss. A gain from the sale of a capital asset occurs if the sales price exceeds the *basis* of the property sold. A loss occurs if the sales price is less than the basis of the asset. In general, the basis of purchased property is its *cost* reduced by the accumulated depreciation allowed or allowable in computing taxable income. The detailed rules for determining the basis of property are quite complex and will not be considered here. These rules depend in part on how the property was acquired (purchase, gift, or inheritance), whether it is personal or business property, and whether it is sold at a gain or a loss.

Long-term versus short-term. Long-term capital gains (or losses) result from the sale of capital assets held *for more than six months;* short-term capital gains and losses result when capital assets are held six months or less.

The term *net short-term gain* means short-term gains in excess of short-term losses. Net short-term gains must be reported in full and are taxed as ordinary income. *Net long-term capital gains* means the excess of long-term gains over long-term losses. Only 40% of net long-term gains, reduced by any net short-term loss, are included in adjusted gross income.

Remember that long-term capital gains are the ones that receive favorable tax treatment; short-term capital gains are taxed as ordinary income. If an individual invests in a capital asset which rises greatly in market price, the classic mistake would be to sell it one day short of the holding period required to qualify the gain as long-term. That one-day error in timing would more than double the tax on the capital gain. To illustrate the importance of timing of capital gains transactions, consider the following set of facts.

John Riley, M.D., is a successful doctor with a marginal tax bracket of 50%. On July 6, Year 1, Riley invested $98,000 to acquire a large but run-down house in an excellent neighborhood. During the next few months, Riley spent $42,000 improving the house, bringing his total investment to $140,000. On December 23, Year 1, Riley sold the house for $210,000, and recognized a short-term capital gain of $70,000. This gain increased Riley's Year 1 income taxes by $35,000 ($70,000 gain × 50% tax rate). From a tax-planning viewpoint, Riley sold his investment too soon. If he had held the property until January or just two more weeks — his $70,000 profit would have become a long-term capital gain and the related tax would have been only $14,000 ($70,000 × 40% taxable portion × 50% tax rate). Not only could Riley have saved $21,000 in income taxes, but delaying the sale of the house would have made the gain taxable in Year 2 rather than Year 1. This would substantially postpone the date upon which Riley must pay the tax.

Limited deductibility of capital losses. In general, capital *losses,* either long-term or short-term, are deductible only against capital gains. If total capital losses exceed gains, however, individual taxpayers (but not corporations) may deduct capital losses against other gross income up to a maximum of $3,000 a year. For example, if an individual incurred a capital loss of $100,000 but also had a salary of $50,000, he or she would have adjusted gross income of $47,000. The unused capital loss could be carried forward and offset against capital gains, if any, in future years, or against other income at the rate of

$3,000 a year. Thus, a great many years would be required to offset the $100,000 capital loss against other income.

Only 50% of a net long-term capital loss can be used in arriving at the maximum which can be offset against other income in a single year. In other words, a net long-term capital loss of $4,000 would be required to entitle the taxpayer to take a $2,000 deduction. Although capital losses not deductible in any given year may be carried forward to future tax years, it is apparent that a large capital loss, as in the preceding example, probably will not be utilized fully in future years unless the taxpayer is fortunate enough to have a large capital gain.

Wash sales. When the prices of stocks or bonds drop sharply, some taxpayers may be inclined to sell their holdings in order to get the tax advantage of a capital loss to offset against other income. If a sale is made, the seller must not repurchase identical securities within 30 days or the capital loss will not be deductible. The IRS considers a "wash sale" to have occurred if substantially identical securities are purchased within 30 days before or after a sale.

Business plant and equipment. Buildings, machinery, and other depreciable property used in a trade or business are not capital assets under the tax law. This means that a net loss realized on the sale or disposal of such business property is fully deductible. However, under certain circumstances, a gain on the sale of such property held more than one year may be treated as a capital gain.

The tax liability

After determining the amount of taxable income, we can compute the **gross tax liability** by using the tax rate schedule on page 694 or 695. This gross amount of tax owed is then reduced by subtracting any tax credits and tax prepayments. Notice the difference between tax credits and the deductions previously discussed. A tax credit is subtracted directly from the tax owed, whereas a deduction, such as charitable contributions, is subtracted from adusted gross income and thus leads to a smaller amount of taxable income to which the tax rate is applied. Thus, a tax credit of, say, $500, is worth much more to the taxpayer than a $500 deduction. If we assume a marginal tax rate of 30%, an additional $500 tax deduction would decrease the tax liability by $150 ($500 × 30%), but a tax credit of $500 would reduce the tax liability by the full $500.

One of the most important tax credits is the **investment tax credit** arising from purchase of depreciable business property. The investment tax credit is an example of efforts to provide tax incentives as a means of stimulating business investment and thus increasing the level of economic activity. When a business buys new long-lived assets such as office equipment or machinery, it can take a credit of 10% of the cost of the property as a deduction from the income tax for the year. The use of an investment credit does not affect the depreciation of the asset.

The variety of tax credits currently available indicates the continuing efforts by government to use the tax laws to achieve various social goals. A few examples are the residential energy credit, the alcohol fuel credit, credit for the elderly, credit for increasing research activities, and credit for political contributions.

Tax prepayments. We have seen that the gross tax liability is reduced by subtracting any available tax credits. Most taxpayers can also subtract prepayments of tax in the form of income taxes withheld from salary or estimated tax paid in advance on dividend or interest income not subject to withholding. To summarize, the gross tax liability is reduced dollar for dollar by subtracting tax credits and tax prepayments. The remaining amount is the *net tax liability*—the amount to be paid with the tax return.

Quarterly payments of estimated tax

The federal income tax law stresses a pay-as-you-go system for all taxpayers. The tax must be paid as the taxpayer receives income during the year. There are two methods of carrying out the pay-as-you-go principle: one is *withholding* and the other is payment of *estimated taxes* on a current basis.

Income in the form of salaries has long been subject to withholding. However, for self-employed persons, such as doctors, dentists, and owners of small unincorporated business concerns, there is no salary and no withholding. Other examples of income on which no withholding occurs are interest, dividends, rental income, and capital gains.

To equalize the treatment of self-employed persons and salaried employees, the tax law requires persons having taxable income not subject to withholding to pay *estimated taxes* in advance quarterly installments. One-quarter of the current year's estimated income tax must be paid by April 15 and the remainder in three equal quarterly installments. Thus, a self-employed person may write two checks to the IRS on April 15; one for any balance due with last year's tax return and one for one-quarter of the estimated tax for the current year.

Although salaried employees are subject to withholding, many have other income such as capital gains or rent which are not subject to withholding. These persons must therefore make quarterly payments of estimated tax if the income not subject to withholding is substantial. Both estimated tax payments and the amounts of income tax withheld are treated as tax prepayments to be deducted at year-end in determining the taxpayer's remaining tax liability or the amount of a tax refund.

Tax returns, tax refunds, and payment of the tax

Whether you must file a tax return depends upon the amount of your income and your filing status. At present, a single person with income of $3,430 or more (the personal exemption plus the zero bracket amount) must file a return. A married couple filing jointly and having income of $5,620 or more must file. However, for a self-employed person, net earnings from self-employment of as little as $400 impose a requirement to file a return. These dollar limits, along with tax rates, are likely to be changed from year to year. The tax return must be filed within $3\frac{1}{2}$ months after the close of the taxable year. Most taxpayers are on a calendar-year basis; therefore, the deadline for filing is April 15.

Withholding makes the system work. Without the withholding feature, the present income tax system would probably be unworkable. The high rate of income taxes would pose an impossible collection problem if employees received their total earnings in cash and were later called upon at the end of the year to pay the government a major portion of a year's salary.

The amounts withheld from an employee's salary for income tax can be considered as payments on account. If the amount of income tax as computed by preparing a tax return at the end of the year is less than the amount withheld during the year; the taxpayer is entitled to a refund. On the other hand, if the tax as computed at year-end is more than the amount withheld, the additional amount must be paid with the tax return. Persons who are entitled to a refund because withholdings or payments of estimated tax exceed the tax liability will of course file a tax return to obtain a refund, even though they might not have sufficient income to make the filing of a tax return compulsory.

The deceptive lure of a tax refund check. Most American taxpayers receive tax refunds each year. Apparently these 60 million or more persons so enjoy receiving a refund check that they are willing to have the government withhold excessive amounts of tax from their paychecks throughout the year. The IRS reports that millions of individual taxpayers declare fewer personal exemptions than they expect to claim at year-end. The result is over-withholding of billions of dollars on which the government pays no interest. It seems strange during a period of inflation and high interest rates that American taxpayers would choose to have the government hold their money throughout the year with no interest in order to be paid back at year-end in dollars worth less in purchasing power than when earned.

Tax tables

Earlier in this chapter we considered the *tax rate schedules* (pages 694–695) used by all taxpayers with incomes of $50,000 or more. However, most taxpayers with income below this level compute their tax liability by using *tax tables* provided by the IRS. Our interest is in the basic concepts of the income tax structure rather than in the mechanics of filling out tax returns; consequently, these lengthy tax tables are not illustrated. The tax tables are derived from the tax rate schedules. The taxpayer calculates his or her *taxable income* and looks through the tax tables to determine the income tax liability.

Computation of individual income tax illustrated

The computation of the federal income tax for Mary and John Reed is illustrated below.

In this example it is assumed that the Reeds provide over one-half the support of their two children. John Reed is a practicing attorney who received $81,000 in gross fees from his law practice and incurred $32,000 of business expenses. Mary Reed earned $24,400 during the year as a CPA working for a national firm of accountants. During the year, $4,000 was withheld from her salary for federal income taxes. Just before the end of the year, John Reed contributed $3,000 to a Keogh H.R.10 retirement plan. The Reeds received $700 interest on municipal bonds, and $1,120 interest on savings accounts. Dividends received on stock jointly owned amounted to $7,440. During the year, stock purchased several years ago by John Reed for $2,600 was sold for $3,600, net of brokerage fees, thus producing a $1,000 long-term capital gain.

The Reeds have total itemized deductions (contributions, interest expense, taxes, medical costs, etc.) of $17,100. They paid a total of $8,000 on their declaration of estimated tax during the year. John Reed is entitled to an investment credit of $1,000 on $10,000 worth of office equipment purchased during the year.

MARY AND JOHN REED
Illustrative Federal Income Tax Computation
For the Year 198X

Gross income (excluding $700 interest on municipal bonds):			
Gross fees from John Reed's law practice	$81,000		
Less: Expenses incurred in law practice	32,000	$49,000	
Salary received by Mary Reed		24,400	
Dividends received, $7,440 (less exclusion of $200)		7,240	
Interest received		1,120	
Long-term capital gain on stock held over one year		1,000	$82,760
Deductions to arrive at adjusted gross income:			
Long-term capital gain deduction (60% of $1,000)		$ 600	
Deduction for contribution to Keogh retirement plan		3,000	
Deduction for two-earner married couple		2,440	6,040
Adjusted gross income			$76,720
Deductions from adjusted gross income:			
Excess itemized deductions (itemized deductions, $17,100, minus			
$3,540 zero bracket amount)		$13,560	
Personal exemptions (4 × $1,040)		4,160	17,720
Taxable income			$59,000
Computation of tax (using tax rate schedule on page 695)			
Tax on $47,670 (joint return)		$10,172	
Tax on $11,330 at 38%		4,305	$14,477
Less: Investment tax credit (10% of $10,000)			1,000
Total tax			$13,477
Less: Advance payments and amounts withheld:			
Payments by Reeds on declaration of estimated tax		$ 8,000	
Tax withheld from Mary Reed's salary		4,000	12,000
Amount of tax remaining to be paid with return			$ 1,477

On the basis of these facts, the taxable income for the Reeds is shown to be $59,000. Since they file a joint return, the tax on this amount of taxable income may be computed from the tax rate schedule for married couples filing jointly and is $14,477. This tax is reduced by the $1,000 investment credit, producing a tax liability of $13,477. Taking withholdings and payments on declared estimated tax into account, the Reeds have already paid income taxes of $12,000 and thus owe $1,477 at the time of filing their tax return.

Partnerships

Partnerships are not taxable entities. Under the federal income tax law, a partnership is treated as a conduit through which taxable income flows to the partners. Although a partnership pays no income tax, it must file an *information return* showing the computation of net income or loss and the share of net income or loss allocable to each partner. The partners must include in their personal tax returns their respective shares of the net income or loss of the partnership.

INCOME TAXES: CORPORATIONS

Taxation of corporations

A corporation is a separate taxable entity. Our discussion is focused on the general business corporation and does not cover certain other types of corporations for which special tax treatment applies. Every corporation, unless specifically exempt from taxation, must file an income tax return whether or not it has taxable income or owes any tax.

The earning of taxable income inevitably creates a liability to pay income taxes. This liability and the related charge to expense must be entered in the accounting records before financial statements are prepared. The following journal entry is typical:

```
Income Taxes Expense  .........................................  60,000
    Income Taxes Payable  ....................................             60,000
To record corporate income taxes for the current period.
```

Corporation tax rates

Tax rates for corporations are in a graduated five-step structure, shown below. Legislation to reduce the number of brackets is presently being considered by Congress.

Corporate Income Tax Rates

Taxable Income	Rates
Up to $25,000	15%
Over $25,000 but not over $50,000	18%
Over $50,000 but not over $75,000	30%
Over $75,000 but not over $100,000	40%
Over $100,000	46%

Note that above $100,000 the income tax on corporations is not progressive. No matter how large taxable income may be, the rate remains the same for amounts above $100,000.

Computation of taxable income of corporations

The taxable income of corporations is computed in much the same way as for individuals: that is, by deducting ordinary business expenses from gross income. However, the following major differences from taxation of individuals must be considered:

1. *Dividends received.* The dividends received by a corporation on its investments in stocks of other corporations are included in gross income, but 85% of such dividends can be deducted from gross income. The net result is that only 15% of dividend income is taxable to the receiving corporation. Corporations are not entitled to the dividend exclusion of $100 allowed to individual taxpayers.
2. *Capital gains and losses.* Net long-term capital gains of corporations are subject to a maximum tax of 28%. A corporation is not entitled to the 60% long-term capital gain deduction as is an individual. If a corporation's taxable income (including any long-term capital gain) is below $50,000, the corporation pays only the regular rates of tax on the long-term capital gain rather than the 28% maximum capital gain tax rate.

The dividing line between long-term and short-term capital gains and losses is six months — the same as for individuals. Corporations may deduct capital losses only to the extent of capital gains. However, if capital losses exceed capital gains, the net loss may be offset against any capital gains of the three preceding years (carry-back) or the following five years (carry-forward).

3 *Other variations from taxation of individuals.* The concept of adjusted gross income is not applicable to a corporation. There is no deduction for personal exemptions and no zero bracket amount. *Gross income* minus the deductions allowed to corporations equals *taxable income.*

Illustrative tax computation for corporation

Shown below is an income statement for Stone Corporation, along with a separate supporting schedule for the tax computation. In this supporting schedule, we compute the amount of income taxes to appear in the income statement and also show the payments of estimated tax, thus arriving at the amount of tax payable with the tax return.

STONE CORPORATION
Income Statement
For the Year Ended December 31, 19__

Revenue:		
Sales		$800,000
Dividends received from domestic corporations		20,000
Total revenue		$820,000
Expenses:		
Cost of goods sold	$536,000	
Other expenses (includes capital loss of $13,000)	100,000	636,000
Income before income taxes		$184,000
Income taxes expense		62,550
Net income		$121,450

SCHEDULE A
Computation of Income Tax

Income before income taxes		$184,000
Add back: Items not deductible for tax purposes:		
Capital loss deducted as part of operating expenses		13,000
Subtotal		$197,000
Deduct: Dividends received credit ($20,000 × 85%)		17,000
Taxable income		$180,000
Income tax:		
15% of first $25,000	$ 3,750	
18% of second $25,000	4,500	
30% of third $25,000	7,500	
40% of fourth $25,000	10,000	
46% of $80,000 (taxable income above $100,000)	36,800	
Total income tax		$ 62,550
Deduct: Quarterly payments of estimated tax		60,000
Balance of tax payable with tax return		$ 2,550

A shortcut method of computing the tax for a corporation with taxable income above $100,000 consists of multiplying the **entire amount** of taxable income by 46% and then subtracting $20,250. The $20,250 figure is the excess of 46% of $100,000 over the tax computed by applying the several rates of 15%, 18%, 30%, and 40% to the four $25,000 segments of the first $100,000.

For example, the shortcut method of computing the tax owed by Stone Corporation on its taxable income of $180,000 is as follows:

$180,000 × 46%	$82,800
Deduct	20,250
Total income tax	$62,550

Accounting income versus taxable income

In the determination of **accounting income,** the objective is to measure business operating results as accurately as possible in accordance with the generally accepted accounting principles summarized in Chapter 14. **Taxable income,** on the other hand, is a legal concept governed by statute and subject to sudden and frequent change by Congress. In setting the rules for determining taxable income, Congress is interested not only in meeting the revenue needs of government but in achieving certain public policy objectives. Since accounting income and taxable income are determined with different purposes in mind, it is not surprising that they often differ by material amounts.

Differences between taxable income and accounting income may result from special tax rules which are unrelated to accounting principles.

1 Some items included in accounting income are not taxable. For example, interest on state or municipal bonds is excluded from taxable income.
2 Some business expenses are not deductible. For example, goodwill is amortized in determining accounting income, but for income tax purposes goodwill is considered to have an indefinite life and amortization is not a deductible expense.
3 Special deductions in excess of actual business expenses are allowed some taxpayers. For example, depletion deductions in excess of actual cost are allowed taxpayers in some mining industries. However, the **statutory depletion** (or **percentage depletion**) allowance which formerly existed for income derived from oil and gas operations has been eliminated.

In addition, the **timing** of the recognition of certain revenue and expenses under tax rules differs from that under accounting principles. Some items of income received in advance may be taxed in the year of receipt while certain accrued expenses may not be deductible for income tax purposes until they are actually paid in cash.

Alternative accounting methods offering possible tax advantages

There are many examples of elective methods which postpone income taxes. Companies which sell merchandise on the installment basis may elect to report income on their tax returns in proportion to the cash received on the installment contracts rather than at the time of the sale of the merchandise. Taxpayers engaged in exploration for oil may charge the cost of drilling oil wells to expense as incurred rather than capitalizing these costs for later depreciation. Ranchers may treat the cost of cattle feed as expense in the year of purchase rather than in the year the feed is consumed. However, the tax laws require that a business electing the lifo method of inventory valuation to determine taxable income must also use this method for financial reporting.

The accelerated cost recovery system (ACRS) created by Congress in 1981 replaced for tax purposes the useful-life depreciation concept which had been followed since the beginning of the federal income tax. For units of plant and equipment acquired in 1981 or later, depreciation under ACRS is based on a recovery period shorter than useful life. This arbitrary shorter recovery period is not in accordance with generally accepted accounting principles; consequently a different amount of depreciation expense based on useful life will appear in financial statements. Thus, another factor exists to cause taxable income to differ from accounting income. Under present tax laws, taxpayers have the option of using straight-line depreciation rather than the rapid write-off provided by ACRS. However, taxpayers generally choose for income tax purposes those accounting methods which cause expenses to be recognized as soon as possible and revenue to be recognized as late as possible.

Interperiod income tax allocation

We have seen that differences between generally accepted accounting principles and income tax rules can be material. Some businesses might consider it more convenient to maintain their accounting records in conformity with the tax rules, but the result would be to distort financial statements. It is clearly preferable to maintain accounting records by the principles that produce relevant information about business operations. The data contained in the records can then be adjusted by use of work sheets to arrive at taxable income.

When a corporation follows one method in its accounting records and financial statements but uses a different method for its income tax return, a financial reporting problem arises. The difference in method will usually have the effect of postponing the recognition of income on the tax return (either because an expense deduction is accelerated or because revenue recognition is postponed). The question is whether the income tax expense should be accrued when the income is recognized in the accounting records, or when it is actually subject to taxation.

To illustrate the problem, let us consider a very simple case. Suppose the Pryor Company has before-tax accounting income of $200,000 in each of two years. However, the company takes as a tax deduction in Year 1 an expense of $80,000 which is reported for accounting purposes in Year 2. The company's accounting and taxable income, and the actual income taxes due (assuming for convenience an average tax rate of 40%) are shown below:

	Year 1	Year 2
Accounting income (before income taxes)	$200,000	$200,000
Taxable income	120,000	280,000
Actual income taxes due each year, at assumed rate of 40% of		
taxable income	48,000	112,000

Let us assume the Pryor Company reports as an expense in its income statement each year the amount of income taxes due for that year. The effect on reported net income as shown in the company's financial statements would be as follows:

	Year 1	Year 2
Accounting income (before income taxes)	$200,000	$200,000
Income taxes expense (amount actually due)	48,000	112,000
Net income	$152,000	$ 88,000

Company reports actual taxes

The readers of Pryor Company's income statement might well wonder why the same $200,000 accounting income before income taxes in the two years produced such widely varying amounts of tax expense and net income.

To deal with this distortion between pretax income and after-tax income, an accounting policy known as **interperiod income tax allocation** is required for financial reporting purposes.[6] Briefly, the objective of income tax allocation is to accrue income taxes in relation to accounting income, whenever differences between accounting and taxable income are caused by differences in the **timing** of revenue or expenses. In the Pryor Company example, this means we would report in the Year 1 income statement a tax expense based on $200,000 of accounting income even though a portion of this income ($80,000) will not be subject to income tax until Year 2. The effect of this accounting procedure is demonstrated by the following journal entries to record the income tax expense in each of the two years:

Entries to record income tax allocation

Year 1 Income Taxes Expense	80,000	
Current Income Tax Liability		48,000
Deferred Income Tax Liability		32,000
To record current and deferred income taxes at 40% of accounting income of $200,000.		

Year 2 Income Taxes Expenses	80,000	
Deferred Income Tax Liability	32,000	
Current Income Tax Liability		112,000
To record income taxes of 40% of accounting income of $200,000 and to record actual income taxes due.		

Using tax allocation procedures, Pryor Company's financial statements would report net income during the two-year period as follows:

	Year 1	Year 2
Income before income taxes	$200,000	$200,000
Income taxes expense (tax allocation basis)	80,000	80,000
Net income	$120,000	$120,000

Company uses tax allocation procedure

[6] For a more complete discussion of tax allocation procedures, see *APB Opinion No. 11*, "Accounting for Income Taxes," AICPA (New York: 1967).

In this example, the difference between taxable income and accounting income (caused by the accelerated deduction of an expense) was fully offset in a period of two years. In practice, differences between accounting and taxable income may persist over extended time periods and deferred tax liabilities may accumulate to significant amounts. For example, in a recent balance sheet of Sears, Roebuck and Co., deferred taxes of more than $1.5 billion were reported. This huge deferral of tax payments resulted from the use of the installment sales method for income tax purposes while reporting net income in financial statements by the usual accrual method.

In contrast to the example for the Pryor Company in which income taxes were deferred, income taxes *may be prepaid* when taxable income exceeds accounting income because of timing differences. The portion of taxes paid on income deferred for accounting purposes would be reported as prepaid taxes in the balance sheet. When the income is reported as earned for accounting purposes in a later period, the *prepaid taxes are recognized as tax expense* applicable to the income currently reported but *taxed in an earlier period.*[7]

TAX PLANNING

Federal income tax laws have become so complex that detailed tax planning is now a way of life for most business firms. Almost all companies today engage professional tax specialists to review the tax aspects of major business decisions and to develop plans for legally minimizing income taxes. We will now consider some areas in which tax planning may offer substantial benefits.

Form of business organization

Tax factors should be carefully considered at the time a business is organized. As a single proprietor or partner, a business owner will pay taxes at individual rates, ranging currently from 11 to 50%, on the business income earned in any year *whether or not it is withdrawn from the business.* Corporations, on the other hand, are taxed on earnings at rates varying from 15 to 46%. In determining taxable income, corporations deduct salaries paid to owners for services but cannot deduct dividends paid to stockholders. Both *salaries and dividends* are taxable income to the persons receiving them.

These factors must be weighed in deciding in any given situation whether the corporate or noncorporate form of business organization is preferable. There is no simple rule of thumb, even considering only these basic differences. To illustrate, suppose that Able, a married man, starts a business which he expects will produce, before any compensation to himself and before income taxes, an average annual income of $80,000. Able plans to withdraw $20,000 yearly from the business. The combined corporate and individual taxes under the corporate and single proprietorship form of business organization are summarized below.

---

[7] A good example of this treatment is found in the annual report of the Ford Motor Company. A recent balance sheet showed "Income Taxes Allocable to the Following Year," $206.5 million, as a current asset. This large prepaid tax came about as a result of estimated car warranty expense being deducted from revenue in the period in which cars were sold; for income tax purposes, this expense is deductible only when it is actually incurred.

Form of Business Organization

Which form of
business organiza-
tion produces a
lower tax?

		Corporation	Single Proprietorship
Business income		$80,000	$80,000
Salary to Able		20,000	
Taxable income		$60,000	$80,000
Corporate tax:			
15% of first $25,000	$3,750		
18% of next $25,000	4,500		
30% on excess of $10,000	3,000	11,250	
Net income		$48,750	$80,000
Combined corporate and individual tax:			
Corporate tax on $60,000 income (above) ...		$11,250	
Individual tax — joint return:*			
On Able's $20,000 salary		2,414	
On Able's $80,000 share of business income			$23,159
Total tax on business income		$13,664	$23,159

* Able's personal exemptions and deductions have been ignored, on the assumption that his other income equals personal exemptions and deductions. For convenience, we have used the tax rate schedule on page 695 to compute Able's personal tax rather than the tax tables. We have rounded amounts to the nearest dollar.

Under these assumptions, the formation of a corporation is favorable from an income tax viewpoint. If the business is incorporated, the combined tax on the corporation and on Able personally will be $13,664. If the business is not incorporated, the tax will be $23,159, or almost twice as much. The key to the advantage indicated for choosing the corporate form of organization is that Able did not take much of the earnings out of the corporation.

If Able decides to operate as a corporation, the $48,750 of net income retained in the corporation will be taxed to Able as ordinary income *when and if* it is distributed as dividends. In other words, Able cannot get the money out of the corporation without paying personal income tax on it. An advantage of the corporation as a form of business organization is that Able can *postpone* payment of a significant amount of tax as long as the earnings remain invested in the business.

If all earnings of the business are to be withdrawn. Now let us change one of our basic assumptions and say that Able plans to withdraw all net income from the business each year. Under this assumption the single proprietorship form of organization would be better than a corporation from an income tax standpoint. If the business is incorporated and Able again is to receive a $20,000 salary plus dividends equal to the $48,750 of corporate net income, the total tax will be much higher. The corporate tax of $11,250 plus personal tax of $18,434 (based on $20,000 salary and $48,750 in dividends) would amount to $29,684. This is considerably higher than the $23,159 which we previously computed as the tax liability if the business operated as a proprietorship.

We have purposely kept our example as short as possible. You can imagine some variations which would produce different results. Perhaps Able might incorporate and set his salary at, say, $75,000 instead of $20,000. If this salary were considered reasonable by the IRS, the corporation's taxable income would drop to $5,000 rather than the $60,000 used in our illustration. This and other possible assumptions should make clear that the choice between a corporation and a single proprietorship requires careful consideration of a number of factors in each individual case. Both the marginal rate of tax to which individual business owners are subject and the extent to which profits are to be withdrawn are always basic issues in studying the relative advantages of one form of business organization over another.

Under certain conditions, small, closely held corporations may elect to be Subchapter S corporations, in which case the corporation pays no tax but the individual shareholders are taxed directly on the corporation's earnings.

Tax planning in the choice of financial structure

In deciding upon the best means of raising capital to start or expand a business, consideration should be given to income taxes. Different forms of business financing produce different amounts of tax expense. Interest on debt, for example, is *fully deductible* in computing taxable income, but dividends on preferred or common stock are not. This factor operates as a strong incentive to finance expansion by borrowing.

Let us suppose that a corporation subject to a 46% marginal tax rate needs $100,000 to invest in productive assets on which it can earn a 20% annual return. If the company obtains the needed money by issuing $100,000 in 14% preferred stock, it will earn *after taxes* only $10,800, which is not even enough to cover the $14,000 preferred dividend. (This after-tax amount is computed as $20,000 income less taxes at 46% of $20,000.)

Now let us assume on the other hand that the company borrowed $100,000 at 14% interest. The additional gross income would be $20,000 but interest expense of $14,000 would be deducted, leaving taxable income of $6,000. The tax on the $6,000 at 46% would be $2,760, leaving after-tax income of $3,240. Analysis along these lines is also needed in choosing between debt financing and financing by issuing common stock.

The choice of financial structure should be considered from the viewpoint of investors, especially in the case of a small, closely held corporation.

● **CASE IN POINT** ● The owners of a small incorporated business decided to invest an additional $100,000 in the business to finance expanding operations. They were undecided whether to make a $100,000 loan to the corporation or to purchase $100,000 worth of additional capital stock. Finally, the owners turned to a CPA firm for advice. The CPAs suggested that the loan would be better because the $100,000 cash invested could be returned by the corporation at the maturity date of the loan without imposing any individual income tax on the owners. The loan could be arranged to mature in installments or at a single fixed date. Renewal of the note could be easily arranged if desired.

On the other hand, if the $100,000 investment were made by purchase of additional shares of capital stock, the return of these funds to the owners would be more difficult. If the $100,000 came back to the owners in the form of dividends, a considerable portion would be consumed by individual income taxes. If the corporation repurchased $100,000 worth of its stock from the owners, the retained earnings account would become restricted by this amount. In summary, the CPAs pointed out that it is easier for persons in control of a small corporation to get their money back if the investment takes the form of a loan rather than the purchase of additional capital stock.

Tax shelters

A tax shelter is an investment which produces a loss for tax purposes in the near term but hopefully proves profitable in the long run. Near the close of each year, many newspaper advertisements offer an opportunity to invest in a program which promises to reduce the investor's present tax liability yet produce future profits. These programs have a particular appeal to persons in very high tax brackets who face the prospect of paying much of a year's net income as taxes.

A limited partnership organization is often used for tax shelter ventures, so that each investor may claim his or her share of the immediate losses. Typical of the types of ventures are oil and gas drilling programs and real estate investments offering high leverage and accelerated depreciation. Unfortunately, many so-called tax shelters have proved to be merely unprofitable investments, in which the investors saved taxes but lost larger amounts of capital. A sound approach to tax shelters should probably be based on the premise that if an investment does not appear ***worthwhile without the promised tax benefits, it should be avoided.***

Some tax shelters, on the other hand, are not of a high-risk nature. State and municipal bonds offer a modest rate of interest which is tax exempt. Investment in real estate with deductions for mortgage interest, property taxes, and depreciation will often show losses which offset other taxable income, yet eventually prove profitable because of rising market value, especially in periods of inflation.

Key terms introduced or emphasized in chapter 17

Accelerated cost recovery system (ACRS). An accelerated depreciation method for income tax purposes for depreciable assets acquired after 1980. Such assets are depreciated over a period of 3, 5, 10, or 18 years. This method is used in income tax returns but not in financial statements prepared in accordance with generally accepted accounting principles.

Adjusted gross income. A subtotal in an individual's tax return computed by deducting from gross income any business-related expenses and other deductions authorized by law. A key figure to which many measurements are linked.

Capital asset. Stocks, bonds, and real estate not used in a trade or business.

Capital gain or loss. The difference between the cost basis of a capital asset and the amount received from its sale.

Cash basis of accounting. Revenue is recorded when received in cash and expenses are recorded in the period in which payment is made. Widely used for individual tax returns and for tax returns of professional firms and service-type businesses. Gives taxpayers a degree of control over taxable income by deliberate timing of collections and payments. Not used in most financial statements because it fails to match revenue with related expenses.

Declaration of estimated tax. Self-employed persons and others with income not subject to withholding must file by April 15 each year a declaration of estimated tax for the current year and must make quarterly payments of such tax.

Excess itemized deductions. The excess of itemized deductions over the zero bracket amount.

Gross income. All income and gains from whatever source derived unless specifically excluded by law, such as interest on state and municipal bonds.

Interperiod tax allocation. Allocation of income tax expense among accounting periods because of timing differences between accounting income and taxable income. Causes income tax expense reported in financial statements to be in logical relationship to accounting income.

Itemized deductions. Personal expenses deductible from adjusted gross income, such as interest, taxes, contributions, medical expenses, casualty losses, and expenses incurred in production of income.

Long-term capital gains and losses. Gains and losses resulting from sale of capital assets owned for more than a specified period (currently six months). A net long-term capital gain qualifies for a special lower tax rate.

Marginal tax rate. The rate to which a taxpayer is subject on the top dollar of income received.

Personal exemption. A deduction (currently $1,040) from adjusted gross income for the taxpayer, the taxpayer's spouse, and each dependent.

Tax credit. An amount to be subtracted from the tax itself. Examples are investment credit, residential energy credit, and credit for wages paid in work incentive programs.

Tax planning. A systematic process of minimizing income taxes by considering in advance the tax consequences of alternative business or investment actions. A major factor in choosing the form of business organization and capital structure, in lease-or-buy decisions, and in timing of transactions.

Tax shelters. Investment programs designed to show losses in the short term to be offset against other taxable income, but offering the hope of long-run profits.

Taxable income. The computed amount to which the appropriate tax rate is to be applied to arrive at the tax liability.

Zero bracket amount. A specified amount of income not subject to individual income tax. Currently $2,390 for single taxpayers and $3,540 for married taxpayers filing jointly. Replaced the standard deduction.

Demonstration problem for your review

Robert and Helen Sands have been engaged in various businesses for many years and have always prepared their own joint income tax return. In Year 11 the Sands decided to ask a certified public accountant to prepare their income tax returns.

Early in Year 12, the Sands presented the following tax information for Year 11 to the CPA:

Personal revenue:

Salary from Sands Construction Company, after withholding of $3,168 federal income taxes and social security taxes of $1,140	$ 14,692
Dividends from Sands Construction Company (jointly owned)	16,675
Drawings from Northwest Lumber Company	6,000
Drawings from S & S Business Advisers	9,600
Interest income — City of Norwalk bonds	800
Interest income — savings account	1,150
Proceeds on sale of stock:	
Sale of stock acquired two years ago for $6,200	14,200
Sale of stock held for three months, cost $4,100	3,400
Sale of stock held for over six years, cost $3,500	1,800

Personal expenses:

Contribution to St. Jerome's Church	$ 610
Interest on mortgage, $2,996; on personal note, $400	3,396
Property taxes	3,480
Sales taxes, including $580 paid on purchase of new automobile for personal use	850
Income taxes paid to state	2,100
Medical expenses	1,100
Subscription to investment advisory service	385

Single proprietorship—wholesale lumber, doing business as Northwest Lumber Company:

Sales	118,000
Cost of goods sold	82,000
Operating expenses	38,800
Drawings by Sands	6,000

Partnership—engaged in business consulting under the name of S & S Business Advisers:

Fees earned	76,300
Gain on sale of vacant lot acquired four years ago	4,400
Salaries paid to employees	32,400
Supplies expense	3,500
Contributions to charity	1,000
Rent expense	4,800
Miscellaneous business expenses	7,100
Drawings (Sands, $9,600 and Sims, $6,400)	16,000

Corporation—engaged in construction under the name of Sands Construction Company:

Customer billings	230,000
Materials used	70,000
Construction labor	60,000
Officers' salaries expense	25,000
Legal and professional expense	3,500
Advertising expense	2,000
Other business expenses	19,800
Loss on sale of equipment	4,200
Cash dividends paid	22,500

The Sands have a 60% share in the profits of S & S Business Advisers and John Sims has a 40% share. The Sands own 75% of the stock of Sands Construction Company. Because of their controlling interest, they have assumed responsibility for the preparation of the income tax returns for these organizations.

The Sands are married, have three children, and support Robert's seventy-nine-year-old mother. Robert is fifty-five years old and Helen is younger but declines to give her date of birth. The oldest child, Bill, is twenty years old and attends school full time. The Sands provide all of their son's support, even though Bill earns approximately $1,400 per year from odd jobs and from investments inherited from his grandfather.

In April of Year 11, the Sands paid the $3,100 balance due on their federal income tax return for

Year 10. In addition to the income taxes withheld by the Sands Construction Company, Robert and Helen Sands made four quarterly payments of $1,200 each on their estimated tax for Year 11.

Instructions. Using the tax rate schedule on page 695, prepare the joint return for Robert and Helen Sands for Year 11, showing the amount of tax due (or refund coming). (Round amounts to the nearest dollar.) You should also prepare in summary form the information for the partnership tax return for S & S Business Advisers and the corporation income tax return for the Sands Construction Company. Assume that a personal exemption is $1,040, that the corporate tax rate is 15% on the first $25,000 of taxable income and 18% on the next $25,000, and that Sands Construction Company has not paid any part of its income tax for Year 11.

Solution to demonstration problem

S & S BUSINESS ADVISERS (a partnership)
Computation of Ordinary Income
For Year Ended December 31, Year 11

Fees earned		$76,300
Operating expenses:		
Salaries paid to employees	$32,400	
Supplies expense	3,500	
Rent expense	4,800	
Miscellaneous business expenses	7,100	47,800
Ordinary income		$28,500

Ordinary income and other items are to be included in partners' individual tax returns as follows:

	Sands (60%)	Sims (40%)
Ordinary income, $28,500	$17,100	$11,400
Gain on sale of vacant lot, long-term capital gain, $4,400	2,640	1,760
Contributions to charity, $1,000	600	400

SANDS CONSTRUCTION COMPANY
Income Tax Return
For Year Ended December 31, Year 11

Customer billings		$230,000
Operating expenses:		
Materials used	$70,000	
Construction labor	60,000	
Officers' salaries expense	25,000	
Legal and professional expenses	3,500	
Advertising expense	2,000	
Other business expenses	19,800	
Loss on sale of equipment	4,200	184,500
Taxable income		$ 45,500
Total income tax: 15% of $25,000	$ 3,750	
18% of 20,500	3,690	$ 7,440

ROBERT AND HELEN SANDS
Joint Income Tax Return
For Year 11

Gross Income:

Salary from Sands Construction Company ($14,692 + $3,168 + $1,140)		$19,000	
Dividends from Sands Construction Company (less $200 exclusion)		16,475	
Interest on savings account		1,150	
Income from S & S Business Advisers, a partnership		17,100	
Net long-term capital gain:			
Stock acquired two years ago	$8,000		
Stock held over six years	(1,700)		
Gain on sale of vacant lot — from partnership return	2,640		
Total long-term capital gain	$8,940		
Less: Short-term loss on stock held for three months	700	8,240	$61,965

Deductions to arrive at adjusted gross income:

Loss incurred by Northwest Lumber Company, a single proprietorship ($118,000 − $82,000 − $38,800)		$2,800	
Long-term capital gain deduction (60% of $8,240)		4,944	7,744
Adjusted gross income			$54,221

Deductions from adjusted gross income:

Itemized deductions:

Contributions ($600 from partnership return and $610 to St. Jerome's Church)	$ 1,210	
Interest paid	3,396	
Property taxes	3,480	
Sales taxes	850	
Income taxes paid to state	2,100	
Subscription to investment advisory service	385	
Total itemized deductions	$11,421	
Less: Zero bracket amount	3,540	
Excess itemized deductions	$ 7,881	
Personal exemptions (6 × $1,040)	6,240	14,121
Taxable income for Year 11		$40,100

Computation of tax for Year 11:

Tax on $36,630 on joint return (see page 695)	$ 6,528	
Tax on $3,470 excess at 33%	1,145	$ 7,673
Deduct:		
Tax withheld from salary	$ 3,168	
Payments on declaration of estimated tax ($1,200 × 4)	4,800	7,968
Amount to be refunded		$ 295

Notes applicable to income tax return on page 720

(1) The loss from the single proprietorship is properly deducted in arriving at adjusted gross income despite the fact that the Sands withdrew $6,000 from the business.

(2) The Sands' share of ordinary income from the partnership (S & S Business Advisers), $17,100, is fully taxable despite the fact that they withdrew only $9,600 from the partnership.

(3) The salary from the Sands Construction Company is included in gross income as $19,000, the gross salary before any deductions.

(4) The ordinary income for the partnership is determined without taking into account the contribution to charity of $1,000 or the long-term capital gain of $4,400. These items are reported by the partners on their personal income tax return on the basis of the profit- and loss-sharing ratio agreed upon by the partners.

(5) Medical expenses are less than 5% of adjusted gross income, and therefore none is deductible.

(6) The oldest son, Bill, qualifies as a dependent even though he earned $1,400, because he is a full-time student.

(7) Interest on City of Norwalk bonds, $800, is not taxable.

Review questions

1 Some of the decisions that business owners must make in the organization and operation of a business will affect the amount of income taxes to be paid. List some of these decisions which affect the amount of income taxes legally payable.

2 What is meant by the expression "tax planning"?

3 What are the four major classes of taxpayers under the federal income tax law?

4 It has been claimed that corporate income is subject to "double taxation." Explain the meaning of this expression.

5 Taxes are characterized as *progressive, proportional,* or *regressive* with respect to any given base. Describe an income tax rate structure that would fit each of these characterizations.

6 State whether you agree with the following statements and explain your reasoning:

   a A person in a very high tax bracket who makes a cash contribution to a college will reduce his or her tax liability by more than the amount of the gift.

   b A decision as to whether a person is willing to undertake additional work in order to obtain additional income should be influenced more by a person's *marginal* tax rate than by his or her *average* tax rate.

7 State in equation form the federal income tax formula for individuals, beginning with total income and ending with taxable income.

8 List some differences between the tax rules for corporations and the tax rules for individuals.

9 What are some objectives of the federal income tax structure other than providing revenue for the government?

10 Explain the difference between *tax avoidance* and *tax evasion,* and give an example of each.

11 Peggy Bame, M.D., files her income tax return on a cash basis. During the current year she collected $12,600 from patients for medical services rendered in prior years, and billed patients $77,000 for services rendered this year. She has accounts receivable of $16,400 relating to this year's billings at the end of the year. What amount of gross income from her practice should Bame report on her tax return?

12 Joe Gilmore, a single man, files his income tax return on a cash basis. During the current year $800 of interest was credited to him on his savings account; he withdrew his interest on January 18 of the following year. No other interest and no dividends were received by Gilmore.

In December of the current year Gilmore purchased some business equipment having an estimated service life of 10 years. He also paid a year's rent in advance on certain business property on December 29 of the current year. Explain how these items would be treated on Gilmore's income tax return for the current year.

13 Which of the following is not a capital asset according to the Internal Revenue Code? (a) an investment in General Motors stock; (b) a personal residence; (c) equipment used in the operation of a business; (d) an investment in Krugerrands (gold coins).

14 An individual with a yearly salary of $20,000 had a capital loss of $25,000. To what extent, if any, could this capital loss be offset against the salary in computing taxable income? Explain.

15 Even when a taxpayer uses the accrual method of accounting, taxable income may differ from accounting income. Give four examples of differences between the tax treatment and accounting treatment of items that are included in the determination of income.

16 Under what circumstances is the accounting procedure known as *income tax allocation* appropriate? Explain the purpose of this procedure.

17 List some tax factors to be considered in deciding whether to organize a new business as a corporation or as a partnership.

18 Explain how the corporate income tax makes debt financing in general more attractive than financing through the issuance of preferred stock.

19 The depreciation expense computed by Zane Company under the accelerated cost recovery system (ACRS) appeared in the tax return as $150,000. In the accounting records and financial statements. Zane's depreciation was computed on the straight-line basis and amounted to $100,000. Under interperiod tax allocation procedures, would Zane Company's balance sheet show prepaid income taxes or deferred income taxes? Explain.

Exercises

Ex. 17-1   You are to consider the income tax status of each of the items listed below. List the numbers 1 to 15 on your answer sheet. For each item state whether it is *included in gross income* or *excluded from gross income* for federal income tax on individuals. Add explanatory comments if needed.

(1) Trip to Hawaii received by employee as reward for outstanding service.
(2) Pension received by veteran from U.S. Government for military service.
(3) Gain on sale of Bart Corporation capital stock, held for five months.
(4) Salary received from a corporation by a stockholder who owns directly or indirectly all the shares of the company's outstanding stock.
(5) Amount received as damages for injury in automobile accident.
(6) Share of income from partnership in excess of drawings.
(7) Rent received on personal residence while on extended vacation trip.
(8) Value of U.S. Treasury bonds received as a gift.
(9) Tips received by a waitress.
(10) Proceeds of life insurance policy received on death of husband.
(11) Interest received on River City municipal bonds.
(12) Inheritance received on death of a distant relative.
(13) Gain on the sale of an original painting purchased 10 years ago.
(14) Value of a color TV set won as a prize in a quiz contest.
(15) Cash dividends of $500 received on stock of American Oil Company. (Assume taxpayer had no other dividend income.)

Ex. 17-2   You are to determine the deductibility status, for federal income tax purposes, of each of the items listed below. List the numbers 1 to 10 on your answer sheet. For each item state whether the item *is* *deducted to arrive at adjusted gross income; deducted from adjusted gross income;* or *not deductible.*

(1) Interest paid on mortgage covering personal residence.
(2) Carry-forward of an unused operating loss from previous year.
(3) Capital loss on the sale of securities.
(4) Damage in storm to motorboat used for pleasure.
(5) State sales tax paid on purchase of personal automobile.
(6) Contribution to a Keogh H.R.10 plan.
(7) Travel expense incurred by an employee in performance of duties; not reimbursed by employer.
(8) Cost of traveling between home and place of employment.
(9) Fee paid to accountant for assistance in preparation of income tax return.
(10) Payment to an IRA.

Ex. 17-3   You are to compute the taxable income for Roger and Judy Collins, a married couple filing a joint return. Use only the relevant items from the following list.

Total income, including gifts, inheritances, interest on municipal bonds, etc.	$54,320
Exclusions (gifts, inheritances, interest on municipal bonds, etc.)	8,100
Deductions to arrive at adjusted gross income	1,500
Itemized deductions (assume zero bracket amount of $3,540)	4,600
Personal exemptions ($1,040 each)	4,160
Income taxes withheld from salary	6,710

Ex. 17-4   Refer to the tax rate schedules on pages 694–695 and compute the tax for each of the following.

	Taxable Income
a Single taxpayer	$ 17,000
b Single taxpayer	130,000
c Married couple filing joint return	17,000
d Married couple filing joint return	130,000

Ex. 17-5   Tom and Susan are planning to be married. Tom is single and earns $20,000 a year. Susan is single and earns $19,000 a year. Each has one personal exemption and no excess itemized deductions. Refer to the tax rate schedules on pages 694–695 and compute how much tax Tom and Susan currently pay as single taxpayers. If Tom and Susan get married and file a joint return, will their combined tax go up or down? By how much? (Assume that the two-earner married couple deduction is limited to 10% of the lower-earning spouse's earned income up to $30,000. Assume also that the personal exemption is $1,040.)

Ex. 17-6   James Smith purchased a small office building as an investment at a price of $200,000. The terms of purchase were $50,000 cash down and a 12% note payable in installments over a period of 20 years. Five years later Smith sold the building for cash at a price of $300,000. Depreciation recognized by Smith during the five years he owned the building amounted to $40,000.

a What was the tax basis of the property to Smith at the time he sold it?
b Is the entire amount of the gain taxable (included in adjusted gross income)? Explain.
c Compute the capital gain on the sale of the property by Smith.

Ex. 17-7 John and Kay Martin, a married couple filing a joint return, had a capital gain of $9,000 from the sale of an investment in shares of IBM stock. Use the tax rate schedule on page 695 to compute the federal income tax the Martins will have to pay on this capital gain under each of the independent assumptions listed below. Round answers to the nearest dollar. You are not required to compute the total tax payable, only the tax applicable to the capital gain. Note that this exercise focuses on the distinction between long- and short-term capital gains and the marginal tax rate.

    a The Martins had owned the IBM shares for several years. Their only other taxable income for the current year consisted of salaries and dividends totaling $25,600.

    b The Martins had owned the IBM shares for 18 months. Their other taxable income was derived from their accounting practice and amounted to $175,000.

    c The Martins had owned the IBM shares for three months. Their other taxable income amounted to $175,000.

    d The Martins had owned the IBM shares for 18 months. Their only other income for the current year consisted of dividends of $12,400 and social security payments received of $12,000.

    e The Martins had owned the IBM shares for two months and had received no dividends. Their only other income consisted of $14,000 interest on municipal bonds.

Ex. 17-8 La Costa Corporation reports the following income for the year:

Operating income (taxable at regular rates)	$750,000
Long-term capital gain	250,000
Extraordinary item:	
Loss (fully deductible from operating income)	100,000

Assume that corporate tax rates are as follows:

On first $25,000 of taxable income	15%
On second $25,000 of taxable income	18%
On third $25,000 of taxable income	30%
On fourth $25,000 of taxable income	40%
On taxable income over $100,000	46%
On long-term capital gains	28%

Compute the total tax liability for La Costa Corporation for the year.

Ex. 17-9 Mission Bay Corporation deducted on its tax return for Year 5 an expense of $100,000 which was not recognized as an expense for accounting purposes until Year 6. The corporation's accounting income before income taxes in each of the two years was $425,000. The company uses tax allocation procedures.

    a Prepare the journal entries required at the end of Year 5 and Year 6 to record income tax expense. Use the shortcut method of computing tax as illustrated on page 710; multiply the entire amount of taxable income by 46% and then subtract $20,250.

    b Prepare a two-column schedule showing the net income to appear on the financial statements for Years 5 and 6, assuming tax allocation procedures are used. Also prepare a similar schedule on the assumption that tax allocation procedures are *not* used.

Problems

17-1   Computation of tax: joint return

Linda and Gary Klein are married and file a joint tax return. They claim one personal exemption each, plus an exemption for their young daughter. Since both Linda and Gary are employed in full-time positions, the "deduction for a married couple when both work" is available to them. Gary's salary for the year was $20,000 and he contributed $2,000 to an IRA. Linda's salary was $22,000 and she incurred $800 of deductible business expenses as an employee.

Assume that a personal exemption is $1,040, that the zero bracket amount for a joint return is $3,540, and that the deduction for a married couple when both work is 10% of the income of the lower-earning spouse (minus any employee business expense and minus any payments to an IRA).

The Kleins have compiled the following information as a preliminary step toward preparing their joint tax return:

Total income (including $42,000 salaries, $600 in municipal bond interest, and $6,000 income from other sources)	$48,600
Federal income taxes withheld from salaries	5,000
Payments of estimated tax	2,000
Employee business expenses (Linda)	800
Itemized deductions (remember zero bracket amount)	4,040
Payment to an IRA (Gary)	2,000

Instructions

a Compute gross income.

b Compute adjusted gross income.

c Compute taxable income.

d Compute the amount of tax remaining to be paid. (Use the tax rate schedule for married individuals filing joint returns, page 695).

17-2   Capital gains and losses: individual

During Year 8, Gary Lopez earned a salary of $21,000 and also had the following sales transactions involving capital gains or losses in the common stocks of four companies.

Description	Date of Sale	Date of Purchase	Cost	Sales Proceeds
Young Company	Aug. 10, Year 8	Apr. 10, Year 8	$ 8,600	$ 7,000
Davis Company	Oct. 1, Year 8	Oct. 1, Year 6	9,000	15,400
Ames Company	Nov. 15, Year 8	Aug. 15, Year 8	5,000	5,700
Tell Company	Dec. 20, Year 8	Dec. 1, Year 1	13,500	12,000

Instructions

a Compute the net long-term capital gain or loss. (List securities by name and show the sales proceeds, cost, and gain or loss on each.)

b Compute the net short-term capital gain or loss.

c Compute the long-term capital gain deduction.

d Compute Lopez's adjusted gross income. Start with salary, then include a section for capital gains and losses, showing separately the net long-term and net short-term gain or loss, the computation of the capital gain deduction, the net gain from sale of capital assets (after the capital gain deduction), and the adjusted gross income.

17-3   Adjusted gross income and taxable income
The following two cases are independent of each other. See the instructions following the second case.

Case A. The following information related to the income tax situation of Rick Jones, an unmarried taxpayer, for the current year:

Total income	$96,000
Personal exemptions	1,040
Deductions to arrive at adjusted gross income	7,680
Itemized deductions	13,090
Exclusions from gross income	1,920

Case B. Jill Friday, a psychiatrist, uses the accrual basis of accounting in maintaining accounting records for her business and in preparing financial statements, but uses cash basis accounting in determining her income subject to federal income tax. For the current year, her business net income (computed on an accrual basis) was $90,480. A comparison of the current balance sheet for the business with a balance sheet prepared a year earlier showed an increase of $14,400 in accounts receivable from clients during the current year. Current liabilities for rent, salaries owed to employees, and other operating expenses were $8,160 less at year-end than they were one year ago. The business income of $90,480 included $1,440 of interest received on municipal bonds.

Apart from the business, Friday has a personal savings account to which $864 of interest was credited during the year, none of which was withdrawn. During the year Friday contributed $8,000 to a Keogh plan and $2,000 to an IRA. She has one personal exemption of $1,040 and her itemized deductions are $11,090.

Instructions. For each of the situations described above, determine the amount of the taxpayer's adjusted gross income and the taxable income for the year. Assume a zero bracket amount of $2,390 in each case.

17-4   Joint return: a comprehensive problem
Ralph and Jennifer Lane own a hardware store and an apartment building. They file a joint income tax return. For the purpose of computing the deduction for a married couple when both work, assume that the net income from the hardware store is self-employment income divided equally between Ralph and Jennifer. (Income from the apartment building is considered investment income rather than earned income.)

The Lanes furnish over one-half the support of their son who attends college and who earned $2,560 in part-time jobs and summer employment. They also support Ralph's father, who is eighty years old and has no taxable income of his own.

The depreciation basis of the apartment building is $160,000; depreciation is recorded at the rate of 4% per year on a straight-line basis. During the current year, the Lanes had the following cash receipts and cash expenditures applicable to the hardware business, the apartment building, other investments, and personal activities.

Cash receipts:

Cash withdrawn from hardware business (net income, $48,000) $36,000
Gross rentals from apartment building 28,800
Cash dividends on stock owned jointly 2,960
Interest on River City bonds 976
Received from sale of stock purchased two years ago for $10,000 16,000
Received from sale of stock purchased four months previously for $6,600 4,600
Received from sale of motorboat purchased three years ago for $4,792 and used
    entirely for pleasure 2,712

Cash expenditures:

Expenditures relating to apartment building:

Interest on mortgage 7,200
Property taxes 4,720
Insurance (one year) 560
Utilities 2,368
Repairs and maintenance 3,872
Gardening 640

Other cash expenditures:

Mortgage interest on residence 3,800
Property taxes on residence 1,700
Insurance on residence 400
State income tax paid 1,900
State sales taxes 700
Charitable contributions 1,200
Medical expenses 1,376
Payment by Ralph to a Keogh H.R.10 plan 3,000
Payment by Jennifer to an IRA 2,000
Payments on declaration of estimated tax for current year 7,000

Instructions

a Determine the amount of taxable income Ralph and Jennifer Lane would report on their federal
income tax return for the current year. In your computation of taxable income, first list the net
income of the hardware business. Second, show the revenue and expenses of the apartment
building and the amount of net income from this source. Third, show the data for dividends and
capital gains. After combining the above amounts and appropriate deductions to determine
adjusted gross income, list the itemized deductions and personal exemptions to arrive at
taxable income. Assume that the zero bracket amount is $3,540 and that the personal exemp-
tion is $1,040 each.

b Compute the income tax liability for Ralph and Jennifer Lane using the tax rate schedule on
page 695. Indicate the amount of tax due (or refund to be received).

17-5   Corporation return: accounting methods to reduce tax
Ward Corporation is completing its first year of operation. The company has been successful and a
tentative estimate by the controller indicates an income before taxes of $250,000 for the year.
Among the items entering into the calculation of the taxable income were the following:

(1) Inventories were reported on a first-in, first-out basis and amounted to $132,500 at year-end.

(2) Accounts receivable of $3,250 considered to be worthless were written off (direct charge-off method) and recorded as uncollectible accounts expense.

(3) Depreciation of $15,000 was recorded using the straight-line method.

Officers of the corporation are concerned over the large amount of income taxes to be paid and decide to change accounting methods for both financial reporting and tax purposes as follows:

(1) Inventories on a last-in, first-out basis would amount to $100,000.

(2) An acceptable allowance for doubtful accounts, after the write-off of $3,250 mentioned above, would be $10,000.

(3) Use of the ACRS method of depreciation would increase depreciation expense from $15,000 to $28,750.

Instructions

a Determine the **taxable income** of Ward Corporation on the revised basis.

b Assume that the tax rates on corporations are 15% on the first $25,000; 18% on the second $25,000; 30% on the third $25,000; 40% on the fourth $25,000; and 46% on taxable income in excess of $100,000. Compute the income tax liability for Ward Corporation (1) before the accounting changes, and (2) after the accounting changes. Also compute the reduction in the current year's income tax liability resulting from the accounting changes.

17-6   Corporation income statement and computation of tax

Dayton Corporation had total revenue for Year 10 of $940,000, consisting of sales of $900,000 and dividends of $40,000 received from domestic corporations. During the year, the corporation made four quarterly payments of estimated tax in the amount of $9,000 each. Expenses (other than income taxes) were as follows for the year.

Advertising expense	$ 80,000
Depreciation expense	65,000
Interest expense	45,000
Other expense (including a capital loss of $28,000)	35,000
Rent expense	150,000
Salaries expense	355,000
Telephone expense	40,000
Utilities expense	30,000

Instructions

a Prepare an income statement in a format similar to that illustrated on page 709. Reference the amount for "Income tax expense" to Schedule A, a separate supporting schedule (see b below) showing the computation of income tax expense. (Suggestion: First, prepare the upper part of the income statement from "Revenue" down through "Income before income taxes"; next, prepare Schedule A, Computation of Income Tax; and finally complete the income statement, using the amount of total income tax computed in Schedule A.)

b Compute Dayton Corporation's total income tax for the year in a schedule which begins with "Income before Income Taxes" (as shown in the income statement) and shows all details of the tax computation. Include in this schedule the payments of estimated tax and the balance remaining to be paid with the tax return.

17-7   Corporation: evaluation of proposed transaction

Riverbend Corporation had total revenue for the year of $304,000. Included in this amount were dividends of $6,000 received from domestic corporations. Expenses of the company for the year were as follows:

Advertising expense	$ 18,800
Depreciation expense	6,400
Property taxes expense	4,500
Rent expense	34,000
Salaries expense	110,000
Travel expense	8,400
Utilities expense	6,900

Instructions

a Prepare an income statement for the corporation. Show Dividends Received as a separate item following Income from Operations. Reference the amount for Income Tax Expense to a separate supporting schedule as called for in b below.

b Compute Riverbend's total income tax for the year in a schedule which begins with "Income before income taxes," and shows all details of the tax computation.

c At a meeting of the board of directors of Riverbend Corporation late in December, the controller outlined the financial results for the year as shown above. A member of the board then offered the following suggestion.

"As I recall, the Corporation has an investment in General Motors stock which is worth about $15,000 less than we paid for it. Why don't we sell that stock on December 31 and buy back the same number of shares on the first business day in January? That will give us a capital loss this year, which will put us in a lower tax bracket and save several thousand dollars of income tax. By buying the stock back on January 2, we will maintan our investment position so if the stock goes up next year we won't have missed the boat."

Evaluate the director's suggestion from an income tax viewpoint.

17-8 Corporation: tax allocation

The following summary amounts reflect the operations of Dunleer Corporation for Year 10:

Net sales	$985,000
Cost of goods sold	630,000
Selling expenses	100,000
Administrative expenses	50,000

In addition to the selling expenses shown above, Dunleer Corporation incurred a cost of $65,000 during the year for a sales promotion campaign for a new line of products. The $65,000 cost of this sales campaign will be deducted in computing taxable income for Year 10, but the company has chosen to defer this $65,000 expenditure for accounting purposes so that it may be charged against revenue during Year 11 when sales of the new product line will be reflected in revenue. The company will follow tax allocation procedures in reporting the income taxes expense in the income statement during Year 10.

In Year 11, revenue was $1,200,000. The total of cost of goods sold and expenses (including the $65,000 of sales promotion cost deferred from Year 10) amounted to $1,000,000.

Instructions

a Prepare an income statement for Dunleer Corporation for Year 10. In a separate supporting schedule, show your computation of the provision for federal income taxes for Year 10. In computing the tax, use the short-cut method of multiplying the entire taxable income by 46% and then subtracting $20,250.

b Prepare the journal entry which should be made to record Dunleer's current income taxes expense, the current income tax liability, and the deferred income tax liability at the end of Year 10.

c Prepare the journal entry needed at December 31, Year 11, to record the company's current income taxes expense for Year 11. (Again, use the short-cut method to compute income tax expense.)

Cases for analysis

Case 17-1   Investors choose between debt and equity

Bill and Hannah Bailey own a successful small company, Bailey Corporation. The outstanding capital stock consists of 1,000 shares of $100 par value, of which 400 shares are owned by Bill and 600 by Hannah. In order to finance a new branch operation, the corporation needs an additional $100,000 in cash. Bill and Hannah have this amount on deposit with a savings and loan association and intend to put these personal funds into the corporation in order to establish the new branch. They will either arrange for the corporation to issue to them at par an additional 1,000 shares of stock, or they will make a loan to the corporation at an interest rate of 12%.

Income before taxes of the corporation has been consistently averaging $150,000 a year, and annual dividends of $64,000 have been paid regularly. It is expected that the new branch will cause *income before taxes* to increase by $30,000. If new common stock is issued to finance the expansion, the total annual dividend of $64,000 will be continued unchanged. If a loan of $100,000 is arranged, the dividend will be reduced by $12,000, the amount of annual interest on the loan.

Instructions

a From the standpoint of the individual income tax return which Bill and Hannah file jointly, would there be any savings as between the stock issuance and the loan? Explain.

b From the standpoint of getting their money out of the corporation (assuming that the new branch is profitable), should Bill and Hannah choose capital stock or a loan for the infusion of new funds to the corporation?

c Prepare a two-column schedule, with one column headed If New Stock Is Used and the other headed If Loan Is Used. For each of these proposed methods of financing, show (1) the present corporate income *before taxes;* (2) the corporate income *before taxes* after the expansion; (3) the corporate income taxes after the expansion; and (4) the corporate net income after the expansion.

Case 17-2   Tax advantages and disadvantages of incorporating

Gary and Joy Allen, a married couple, are in the process of organizing a business which is expected to produce, before any compensation to the Allens and before income taxes, an income of $72,000 per year. In deciding whether to operate as a single proprietorship or as a corporation, the Allens are willing to make the choice on the basis of the relative income tax advantage under either form of organization.

The Allens file a joint return, have no other dependents, and have itemized deductions that average around $8,800 per year.

If the business is operated as a single proprietorship, the Allens expect to withdraw the entire income of $72,000 each year. Of this $72,000 total, the amount of $42,000 is considered a fair payment for the personal services rendered by the Allens, that is, $21,000 each. (Calculate the deduction for two-earner married couples as 10% of $21,000, or $2,100.)

If the business is operated as a corporation, the Allens will own all the shares; they will pay themselves salaries of $21,000 each and will withdraw as dividends the entire amount of the corporation's net income after income taxes. In computing adjusted gross income, again assume that the deduction for two-earner married couples is 10% of $21,000, or $2,100.

It may be assumed that the accounting income and the taxable income for the corporation would be the same and that the personal exemption is $1,040. Mr. and Mrs. Allen have only minor amounts of nonbusiness income, which may be ignored.

Instructions. Determine the relative income tax advantage to the Allens of operating either as a single proprietorship or as a corporation, and make a recommendation as to the form of organization they should adopt. Use the individual (joint return) and corporate tax rate schedules given on pages 695 and 708.

To provide a basis for this recommendation, you should prepare two schedules: one for operation as a single proprietorship, and one for operation as a corporation.

In the first schedule, compute the total income tax on the Allens' joint personal return when the business is operated as a proprietorship. Also show the Allens' disposable income, that is, the amount withdrawn minus personal income tax.

In the second schedule, compute the corporate income tax and the amount remaining for dividends. Also compute the Allens' *personal* income tax if the corporate form of business entity is used. From these two steps, you can determine the Allens' disposable income under the corporate form of operation.

Appendix E
Financial statements of a publicly owned company

The financial statements of American Home Products Corporation, a company listed on the New York Stock Exchange, are presented on the following pages. These financial statements have been audited by Arthur Andersen & Co., an international firm of certified public accountants. The audit report is attached. This particular company was selected because its financial statements provide realistic illustrations of many of the financial reporting issues discussed in this book.

Notice that several pages of explanatory notes are included with the basic financial statements. These explanatory notes supplement the condensed information in the financial statements and are designed to carry out the disclosure principle discussed in Chapter 14 of this book. As indicated in Chapter 14, the disclosure principle means that all material and relevant facts should be communicated to the users of financial statements.

Consolidated Balance Sheets
American Home Products Corporation and Subsidiaries

December 31,		**1984**		1983
Assets		*(In thousands)*		
Cash and cash equivalents	$	**767,980**	$	612,559
Accounts receivable less allowances (1984—$20,070 and 1983—$25,619).		**641,147**		561,889
Inventories		**529,391**		501,673
Deferred taxes and other current assets		**89,624**		96,826
Net current assets of businesses sold and deconsolidated		**—**		167,259
Total current assets		**2,028,142**		1,940,206
Investments (market value, 1984—$20,219 and 1983—$9,562)		**17,464**		5,871
Property, plant and equipment:				
Land		**29,248**		29,757
Buildings		**427,704**		418,468
Machinery and equipment		**778,308**		705,333
		1,235,260		1,153,558
Less accumulated depreciation		**465,637**		421,508
		769,623		732,050
Intangibles		**182,851**		193,861
Deferred taxes and other assets		**34,503**		31,392
Net noncurrent assets of businesses sold and deconsolidated		**—**		78,081
	$	**3,032,583**	$	2,981,461
Liabilities				
Loans payable to banks	$	**9,885**	$	9,862
Accounts payable and accrued expenses		**526,825**		512,968
Accrued federal and foreign taxes on income		**51,719**		59,445
Total current liabilities		**588,429**		582,275
Deferred compensation payable under Management Incentive Plan		**70,526**		71,748
Other noncurrent liabilities		**285,044**		278,549
Stockholders' Equity				
$2 convertible preferred stock, par value $2.50 per share		**280**		326
Common stock, par value $.33¹/₃ per share		**50,667**		51,957
Additional paid-in capital		**187,338**		155,684
Retained earnings		**1,959,723**		1,933,968
Currency translation adjustments		**(109,424)**		(93,046)
Total stockholders' equity		**2,088,584**		2,048,889
	$	**3,032,583**	$	2,981,461

Consolidated Statements of Income

American Home Products Corporation and Subsidiaries

Years Ended December 31,	1984	1983	1982
	(In thousands except per share amounts)		
Net sales	$ 4,485,470	$ 4,273,299	$ 3,972,673
Other income, net	82,936	56,707	53,119
	4,568,406	4,330,006	4,025,792
Cost of goods sold	1,799,537	1,759,095	1,696,276
Selling, administrative and general expense	1,594,404	1,491,204	1,343,572
	3,393,941	3,250,299	3,039,848
Income before federal and foreign taxes on income ...	1,174,465	1,079,707	985,944
Provision for taxes on income:			
Federal	394,259	358,829	317,957
Foreign	124,378	130,032	131,747
	518,637	488,861	449,704
Income from continuing operations	655,828	590,846	536,240
Businesses sold			
Income, net of taxes	19,754	36,387	23,863
Gain on sales, net of taxes	56,500	—	—
	76,254	36,387	23,863
Provision for impairment of investments in certain foreign locations	(50,000)	—	—
Net income....................................	$ 682,082	$ 627,233	$ 560,103
Net income per share of common stock:			
Continuing operations	$ 4.26	$ 3.77	$ 3.44
Businesses sold	.13	.23	.15
Gain on sales.................................	.37	—	—
Provision for impairment of investments in certain foreign locations	(.33)	—	—
Net income per share..........................	$ 4.43	$ 4.00	$ 3.59

Consolidated Statements
American Home Products Corporation and Subsidiaries

Years Ended December 31,		1984		1983		1982
Retained Earnings			*(In thousands)*			
Balance, beginning of year	$	1,933,968	$	1,746,610	$	1,542,560
Net income		682,082		627,233		560,103
		2,616,050		2,373,843		2,102,663
Cash dividends declared:						
$2 convertible preferred stock		237		277		320
Common stock		406,181		374,814		334,029
		406,418		375,091		334,349
Cost of treasury stock acquired, less amounts charged to capital		249,909		64,784		21,704
		656,327		439,875		356,053
Balance, end of year	$	1,959,723	$	1,933,968	$	1,746,610
Additional Paid-in Capital						
Balance, beginning of year	$	155,684	$	104,417	$	59,782
Excess over par value of common stock issued		40,198		46,766		40,786
Miscellaneous, net		(8,544)		4,501		3,849
Balance, end of year	$	187,338	$	155,684	$	104,417
Currency Translation Adjustments						
Balance, beginning of year	$	93,046	$	59,732	$	15,977
Aggregate translation adjustments for the year		49,349		33,314		43,755
Cumulative translation adjustments related to businesses sold		(17,786)		—		—
Cumulative translation adjustments related to foreign investments deconsolidated		(15,185)		—		—
Balance, end of year	$	109,424	$	93,046	$	59,732

Consolidated Statements of Changes in Working Capital
American Home Products Corporation and Subsidiaries

Years Ended December 31,	1984	1983	1982
Sources of Working Capital:		*(In thousands)*	
Income from continuing operations	$ 655,828	$ 590,846	$ 536,240
Items not affecting working capital:			
Depreciation and amortization	93,614	82,537	66,225
Other expenses and income	46,985	51,640	34,819
Working capital provided from continuing operations	796,427	725,023	637,284
Income from businesses sold including items not affecting working capital ...	26,850	45,321	34,725
Cash proceeds from sales of businesses, net of taxes of $46,500	291,700	—	—
Working capital of businesses sold......................	(147,350)	—	—
Working capital of deconsolidated companies	(29,450)	—	—
Proceeds from Industrial Revenue Bonds	—	40,000	—
Exercise of stock options	28,750	27,190	26,744
Sale of investment and reclassification to current assets	—	23,801	—
Sale of property, plant and equipment	6,319	14,612	9,061
	973,246	875,947	707,814
Uses of Working Capital:			
Dividends declared	406,418	375,091	334,349
Purchase of property, plant and equipment	141,891	187,593	134,717
Effect of exchange rates on working capital	31,163	19,587	28,444
Purchase of treasury stock........................	269,125	69,143	22,983
Purchase of Sherwood Medical Group	—	—	427,368
Working capital provided by acquisition of Sherwood Medical Group	—	—	(71,729)
Other items, net	42,867	2,834	34,465
	891,464	654,248	910,597
Net increase (decrease) in working capital	81,782	221,699	(202,783)
Working capital, beginning of year.....................	1,357,931	1,136,232	1,339,015
Working capital, end of year	$ 1,439,713	$ 1,357,931	$ 1,136,232
Net increase (decrease) in working capital is represented by the following:			
Increase (decrease) in current assets—			
Cash and cash equivalents	$ 155,421	$ 159,953	$ (262,200)
Accounts receivable less allowances	79,258	42,186	80,064
Inventories	27,718	27,020	62,599
Deferred taxes and other current assets	(7,202)	769	3,226
Net current assets of businesses sold and deconsolidated..............	(167,259)	(7,741)	(26,507)
	87,936	222,187	(142,818)
Less:			
Increase (decrease) in current liabilities—			
Loans payable to banks	23	(343)	1,035
Accounts payable and accrued expenses	13,857	21,549	76,733
Accrued federal and foreign taxes on income	(7,726)	(20,718)	(17,803)
	6,154	488	59,965
Net increase (decrease) in working capital	$ 81,782	$ 221,699	$ (202,783)

Notes to Consolidated Financial Statements

1. Summary of Significant Accounting Policies:

Principles of consolidation: The accompanying consolidated financial statements include the accounts of the Company and its subsidiaries with the exception of those subsidiaries described in Note 3 which are accounted for on a cash basis.

Inventories are valued at the lower of cost or market. Inventories valued under the last-in, first-out (LIFO) method amounted to $281,437,000 at December 31, 1984 and $269,434,000 at December 31, 1983. Current value exceeded LIFO value by $67,618,000 and $55,283,000 at the 1984 and 1983 year-ends. The remaining inventories continue to be valued under the first-in, first-out (FIFO) or average method.

Inventories at December 31 consist of:

	1984	1983
	(In thousands)	
Finished goods	$ 262,739	$ 251,616
Work in process	73,548	78,583
Materials and supplies	193,104	171,474
	$ 529,391	$ 501,673

Property, plant and equipment is carried at cost. Depreciation is provided over the estimated useful lives of the related assets, principally on the straight-line method.

Intangible assets at December 31, 1984 consist of $98,089,000 of goodwill being amortized over a 40-year period; $43,157,000 of patent rights and trademarks being amortized over periods ranging from 5 to 40 years; and goodwill of $41,605,000 relating to acquisitions initiated prior to October 31, 1970, which is not being amortized since the Company believes there has been no diminution in value.

Research and development costs from continuing operations amounted to $183,733,000 in 1984, $158,780,000 in 1983 and $134,874,000 in 1982.

Income Taxes: The effective tax rates for continuing operations were 44.2%, 45.3% and 45.6% for 1984, 1983 and 1982. In all years the effective tax rate was increased due to non-deductible foreign currency adjustments which were offset by other items which lowered the effective tax rate. Deferred taxes are provided for certain items of revenue and expense when the timing of their recognition for financial statement and income tax purposes differs. The net result of these timing differences is such that taxes currently payable were $33,488,000, $31,100,000 and $7,746,000 less than the provisions for federal and foreign taxes on income in 1984, 1983, and 1982 respectively. Net deferred tax benefits in the accompanying balance sheets amounted to $49,632,000 and $83,120,000 at December 31, 1984 and 1983, respectively, of

which $62,027,000 and $70,827,000 were classified as current assets. The benefits represent the net cumulative amounts by which future provisions for federal and foreign taxes on income will exceed income taxes actually payable. Income taxes payable upon distribution of accumulated earnings of foreign subsidiaries and affiliates are not significant. Investment tax credits, which are not material, are accounted for as a reduction of income tax expense in the year the related assets are placed in service.

2. Businesses Sold:
In 1984, the Company completed the sales of its Ekco Housewares Division, Ekco Canada Inc., E-Z Por Corp., Ekco Products Inc., Dupli-Color and its majority interest in The Prestige Group PLC. The aggregate proceeds on these sales were $338,200,000 in cash and notes and convertible preferred stock valued at $10,000,000. The results of operations have been restated to report businesses sold as a separate component in 1984, 1983 and 1982. Net sales of these businesses were $318,829,000, $482,357,000 and $486,109,000 in 1984, 1983 and 1982. Net income of $19,754,000, $36,387,000 and $23,863,000 was net of taxes of $14,669,000, $25,367,000 and $28,528,000.

3. Provision for Impairment of Investment in Certain Foreign Locations:
In the fourth quarter, the Company recorded a charge of $50,000,000 recognizing the impairment of its investment in its subsidiaries in South America, except for its investment in Brazil. The provision was made after determining that the continued imposition of constraints such as dividend restrictions, exchange controls, price controls and import restrictions in these countries so severely impede management's control of the economic performance of the businesses that continued inclusion of these subsidiaries in the consolidated financial statements is inappropriate. Net sales from continuing operations have been restated to exclude sales from these countries of $95,084,000, $100,845,000 and $123,314,000 in 1984, 1983 and 1982, respectively.

Net income of these subsidiaries included in the financial statements was approximately $2,000,000 for 1984 and 1983 and approximately $7,000,000 in 1982. The Company intends to continue operating these subsidiaries, which for the most part are self-sufficient; however, the subsidiaries have been deconsolidated and earnings will be recorded only as dividends or other cash remittances are received.

4. Other Noncurrent Liabilities include provisions for loss contingencies relating to taxes, general and product liability and worker's compensation claims. Also included under this caption are provisions for severance payments to foreign employees, foreign income taxes payable after one year, and noncurrent debt which includes $40,000,000 of privately placed Adjustable Rate Industrial Revenue Bonds 1983 Series A due December 1, 2018. The effective annual interest rate on the bonds is 8.21% per annum through November 30, 1988 after which date the rate will be reset annually unless the Company elects to establish a fixed rate to be paid for the remaining term of the bonds.

5. Capital Stock: There were 210,000,000 shares of common stock and 5,000,000 shares of preferred stock authorized at December 31, 1984. Of the authorized preferred shares, there is a series of 126,320 shares which is designated as $2 convertible preferred stock. Each share of the $2 series is convertible at the option of the holder into four and one-half shares of common stock. This series may be called for redemption at $60 per share plus accrued dividends if the market price of the common stock is at least $13.33 per share. In the event of involuntary liquidation, the liquidation value of this series would exceed its par value by $50 per share ($57.50 in voluntary liquidation).

Changes in outstanding common shares during 1984, 1983 and 1982 are summarized as follows:

	1984	1983	1982
	(In thousands)		
Balance beginning of year.	155,870	155,858	155,069
Issued for stock options and deferred compensation	1,175	1,373	1,335
Conversion of preferred stock (19,000 shares in 1984, 21,000 in 1983 and 25,000 in 1982)	84	94	111
Purchase of shares for Treasury	(5,127)	(1,512)	(657)
Issued for acquisition of businesses . . .	—	57	—
Balance end of year (excludes treasury shares—16,858,000 in 1984, 12,905,000 in 1983 and 12,824,000 in 1982).	152,002	155,870	155,858

6. Stock Options: The Company has, at the present, three Stock Option Plans—1980, 1978 and 1972. Under the 1980 Plan, a maximum of 7,000,000 shares and under the 1978 and 1972 Plans, a maximum of 3,000,000 shares may be sold at prices not less than 100 percent of the fair market value at the date of option grant. The 1980 and 1978 Plans provide for the granting of incentive stock options as defined under the Economic Recovery Tax Act of 1981. Under the Plans, grants may be made to selected officers and employees of non-qualified options with a ten-year term or incentive stock options with a term not exceeding ten years.

The Stock Option Plans provide for the granting of Stock Appreciation Rights (SAR's) subject to certain conditions and limitations to holders of options under these plans. SAR's permit the optionee to surrender an exercisable option for an amount equal to the excess of the market price of the common stock over the option price when the right is exercised. Transactions involving the Plans are summarized as follows:

	1984	1983
Option Shares		
Outstanding January 1	3,554,221	3,876,308
Granted	2,825,160	827,750
Cancelled	(183,742)	(163,350)
Exercised and surrendered for SAR's (1984— $24.75 to $46.06 per share).	(948,187)	(986,487)
Outstanding December 31	5,247,452	3,554,221
Exercisable December 31 (1984—$27.25 to $52.88 per share)	2,516,452	2,454,806

	1984	1983
Stock Appreciation Rights		
Outstanding January 1	433,750	617,250
Granted	405,000	12,500
Cancelled	(12,800)	(7,600)
Exercised (1984—$29.75 to $38.00 per share) .	(127,600)	(188,400)
Outstanding December 31	698,350	433,750
Exercisable December 31 (1984—$29.88 to $38.00 per share)	285,850	411,250

At December 31, 1984, 1,754,849 shares were available for future grants under the 1980 and 1978 plans.

7. Management Incentive Plan: The Company's Management Incentive Plan provides for cash and deferred contingent common stock awards to key employees. The maximum shares issuable under the plan are 6,000,000 common shares of which 3,359,611 shares have been awarded through December 31, 1984. Deferred contingent common stock awards plus accrued dividends for a total of 1,682,507 shares were outstanding at December 31, 1984. Awards for 1984 amounted to $12,676,000 which included deferred contingent common stock of $7,530,000 (147,060 shares). Awards for 1983 amounted to $13,724,000 which included deferred contingent common stock of $8,260,000 (165,282 shares). Awards for 1982 amounted to $13,756,000 which included deferred contingent common stock of $8,329,000 (183,524 shares).

8. Pension Plans: The Company and its subsidiaries sponsor various retirement plans for most full-time employees. Total pension expense for continuing operations for 1984, 1983 and 1982 was $20,775,000, $16,833,000 and $21,712,000. It has been the policy to fund all current and prior service costs under these retirement plans, and all liabilities for accrued vested and unvested benefits have been fully funded. All such liabilities under the United States and major foreign plans have been guaranteed by financial institutions.

9. Postretirement Benefits: The Company provides post-retirement health care and life insurance benefits to most full-time employees. All costs are funded by insurance policies. The cost of these programs amounted to $3,796,000 in 1984.

10. Net Income Per Share of common stock is based on the average number of common shares and common share equivalents outstanding during the year: 154,057,000 shares in 1984, 156,684,000 shares in 1983 and 156,039,000 shares in 1982.

11. Company Data by Industry Segment*

	Prescription Drugs & Medical Supplies	Packaged Medicines	Food & Household Products	Corporate	Consolidated Totals
			(Millions of dollars)		
Net sales to customers					
1984	$2,416.8	$598.8	$1,469.9	—	$4,485.5
1983	2,278.1	584.0	1,411.2	—	4,273.3
1982	2,075.4	550.5	1,346.8	—	3,972.7
Operating income before taxes					
1984	$ 765.5	$142.0	$ 207.4	$ 59.6	$1,174.5
1983	713.9	151.4	187.0	27.4	1,079.7
1982	647.3	129.4	176.8	32.4	985.9
Total assets at December 31,					
1984	$1,519.1	$158.6	$ 472.5	$882.4	$3,032.6
1983	1,418.8	151.1	453.5	712.7	2,736.1
1982	1,309.2	155.5	399.5	608.7	2,472.9
Depreciation expense					
1984	$ 55.6	$ 5.3	$ 17.9	$ .9	$ 79.7
1983	51.5	4.6	16.1	.9	73.1
1982	40.3	4.3	13.9	.9	59.4
Capital expenditures					
1984	$ 100.0	$ 13.1	$ 28.5	$ .3	$ 141.9
1983	134.8	13.2	39.4	.2	187.6
1982	93.0	9.3	32.2	.2	134.7

Company Data by Geographic Segment*

	United States	Canada & Latin America	Europe & Africa	Other Foreign	Consolidated Totals
			(Millions of dollars)		
Net sales to customers					
1984	$3,435.9	$366.7	$ 537.0	$145.9	$4,485.5
1983	3,178.3	399.1	558.6	137.3	4,273.3
1982	2,871.0	419.5	556.2	126.0	3,972.7
Operating income before taxes					
1984	$ 931.6	$ 97.4	$ 121.9	$ 23.6	$1,174.5
1983	828.2	100.4	130.3	20.8	1,079.7
1982	744.0	89.9	131.3	20.7	985.9
Total assets at December 31,					
1984	$2,459.8	$183.4	$ 289.9	$ 99.5	$3,032.6
1983	2,131.6	205.1	297.4	102.0	2,736.1
1982	1,962.7	186.7	236.9	86.6	2,472.9

Transactions between industry and geographic segments are not material. Foreign exchange adjustments, which are included in Operating income before taxes in this note and in Other income, net, in the Consolidated Statements of Income on page 31 resulted in net charges to income of $16.1 million in 1984, $22.9 million in 1983 and $31.0 million in 1982. For a description of the products in each industry segment, see pages 7 to 27 herein.

*Amounts for years prior to 1984 have been restated for the effects of businesses sold and deconsolidated.

Auditors' Report

To the Board of Directors and Shareholders of
American Home Products Corporation:

We have examined the consolidated balance sheets of American
Home Products Corporation (a Delaware corporation) and subsidiaries as of December 31, 1984 and 1983, and the related consolidated statements of income, retained earnings, additional paid-in
capital, currency translation adjustments and changes in working
capital for each of the three years in the period ended December
31, 1984. Our examinations were made in accordance with generally accepted auditing standards and, accordingly, included such
tests of the accounting records and such other auditing procedures as we considered necessary in the circumstances.

In our opinion, the consolidated financial statements referred to
above present fairly the financial position of American Home
Products Corporation and subsidiaries as of December 31, 1984
and 1983, and the results of their operations and changes in working capital for each of the three years in the period ended December 31, 1984, in conformity with generally accepted accounting
principles applied on a consistent basis.

New York, N.Y.,   Arthur Andersen & Co.
January 21, 1985.

Inflation Information

The following Consolidated Supplementary Inflation-Adjusted
Income Statement reflects the effect on income from continuing
operations of restating (1) cost of goods sold to cost of inventories
at the time of sale and (2) depreciation expense based on the average of asset replacement costs at the beginning and end of the year.

Consolidated Supplementary Inflation-Adjusted Income Statement

Year Ended December 31, 1984	As Reported in the Primary Statements	Adjusted for Changes in Specific Prices (Current Cost)
	(In thousands except per share amounts)	
Net sales and other operating revenues	$ 4,568,406	$ 4,568,406
Cost of goods sold	1,799,537	1,816,767
Selling, administrative and general expense	1,594,404	1,601,635
Provision for income taxes	518,637	518,637
Income from continuing operations	$ 655,828	$ 631,367
Income per common share of stock from continuing operations	$4.26	$4.10
Depreciation expense included in cost of goods sold and selling, administrative and general expense	$ 79,724	$ 103,625

Five-Year Comparison of Selected Supplementary
Financial Data Adjusted for the Effects of Changing Prices (Average 1984 Dollars)

Years Ended December 31,	1984	1983	1982	1981	1980
	(Dollars in thousands except per share amounts)				
Net sales and other operating revenues from continuing operations	**$4,568,406**	$4,514,292	$4,332,148	$4,066,541	$4,055,796
Current cost information:					
Net income from continuing operations	**631,367**	595,551	534,416	499,692	478,822
Net income per common share from continuing operations.	**4.10**	3.81	3.42	3.20	3.04
Increase (decrease) in specific prices net of changes in general price level	**4,599**	15,484	50,256	(37,823)	(43,731)
Net assets at year-end.	**2,397,042**	2,512,264	2,380,443	2,236,633	2,228,043
Cumulative translation adjustment.	**139,387**	125,452	76,054	—	—
Loss from decline in purchasing power of net monetary assets held	**21,391**	16,063	12,973	50,876	61,678
Cash dividends declared per common share	**2.64**	2.50	2.31	2.17	2.15
Market price per common share at year-end	**49.98**	50.99	47.60	40.35	33.87
Average consumer price index.	**311.1**	298.4	289.1	272.4	246.8

Other 1984 Inflation-Adjusted Data

	(In thousands)
Loss from decline in purchasing power of net monetary assets held	$ 21,391
Increase in specific prices (current cost) of inventories and property, plant, and equipment held during the year[1].	$ 67,111
Effect of increase in general price level	62,512
Increase in specific prices net of changes in general price level	$ 4,599[2]
Translation adjustment	$58,392[3]

The above data are based on the translate-restate method (that is, after translation and based on the U.S. C.P.I.-U.).

[1]At December 31, 1984 current cost of inventories was $576,300 and current cost of property, plant and equipment, net of accumulated depreciation, was $1,053,907.

[2]The increase in specific prices (current cost) restated in average 1984 dollars to eliminate the effect of inflation as measured by the U.S. Consumer Price Index for all Urban Consumers.

[3]The effect of changes in exchange rates during the year on equity of foreign hard currency companies measured in current cost at average 1984 dollars.

Ten-Year Selected Financial Data*

American Home Products Corporation and Subsidiaries

Years Ended December 31,	1984	1983	1982
Summary of Earnings	*(Dollars in thousands except per share amounts)*		
Net Sales.	**$4,485,470**	$4,273,299	$3,972,673
Other Income, Net	**82,936**	56,707	53,119
Income from Continuing Operations	**655,828**	590,846	536,240
Net Income** .	**682,082**	627,233	560,103
Per Common Share:			
Continuing Operations	**4.26**	3.77	3.44
Net Income**	**4.43**	4.00	3.59
Dividends Per Common Share	**2.64**	2.40	2.15
Average Stockholders' Equity	**2,068,737**	1,946,258	1,749,050
Return on Average Stockholders' Equity	**33.0%**	32.2%	32.0%
Year-End Financial Position			
Current Assets	**$2,028,142**	$1,940,206	$1,718,019
Current Liabilities	**588,429**	582,275	581,787
Ratio of Current Assets to Current Liabilities	**3.45 to 1**	3.33 to 1	2.95 to 1
Total Assets	**3,032,583**	2,981,461	2,726,710
Stockholders—Outstanding Shares			
Number of Common Stockholders	**79,541**	80,578	75,351
Number of Preferred Stockholders	**1,975**	2,131	2,215
Average Number of Common Shares Outstanding (in thousands and assuming conversion of Preferred Stock)	**154,057**	156,684	156,039
Preferred Shares Outstanding at Year-End (in thousands)	**112**	131	151
Employment Data			
Number of Employees at Year-End	**47,298**	47,447	46,798
Wages and Salaries	**$ 839,794**	$ 836,253	$ 779,747
Benefits (including Social Security Taxes)	**$ 148,160**	$ 139,042	$ 134,650

*Restated as appropriate, see Notes to Consolidated Financial Statements.
**Net Income in 1984 includes a Gain on Sales of Businesses of $56,500 ($.37 per share) and a Provision for Impairment of Investments in Certain Foreign Locations of $50,000 ($.33 per share).

1981	1980	1979	1978	1977	1976	1975
$3,471,381	$3,146,277	$2,839,226	$2,573,443	$2,234,833	$2,071,752	$1,902,808
89,293	71,243	40,043	37,973	22,684	20,077	36,931
474,201	413,521	364,479	324,624	282,875	259,231	234,268
497,332	445,889	396,039	348,422	306,167	277,931	250,689
3.03	2.63	2.31	2.06	1.79	1.63	1.47
3.18	2.84	2.51	2.21	1.94	1.75	1.58
1.90	1.70	1.50	1.325	1.15	1.00	.90
1,563,623	1,397,393	1,249,984	1,108,113	1,014,876	945,247	849,694
31.8%	31.9%	31.7%	31.4%	30.2%	29.4%	29.5%
$1,944,318	$1,761,840	$1,524,683	$1,347,150	$1,114,184	$1,030,590	$ 926,773
605,303	586,650	484,375	444,869	353,839	316,280	298,341
3.21 to 1	3.00 to 1	3.15 to 1	3.03 to 1	3.15 to 1	3.26 to 1	3.11 to 1
2,588,538	2,370,262	2,090,674	1,862,181	1,611,305	1,510,862	1,390,712
75,523	77,181	75,613	77,241	78,396	77,122	75,441
2,297	2,609	2,923	3,209	3,518	3,846	4,202
156,261	156,988	157,995	157,834	158,141	159,182	159,088
176	205	244	278	325	371	427
40,819	40,563	40,583	39,930	39,421	37,846	36,799
$ 659,400	$ 592,768	$ 552,683	$ 493,715	$ 443,853	$ 404,871	$ 365,621
$ 109,907	$ 96,025	$ 84,821	$ 72,200	$ 59,055	$ 55,330	$ 52,261

Quarterly Financial Data

	First Quarter 1984	Second Quarter 1984	Third Quarter 1984	Fourth Quarter 1984
	(Thousands of dollars and cents per share)			
Continuing Operations:				
Net Sales	$1,138,696	$1,073,157	$1,167,885	$1,105,732
Gross Profit	673,688	653,935	703,221	655,089
Income	164,754	151,505	173,059	166,510
Businesses Sold:				
Operations	8,098	6,761	4,037	858
Gain on Sales	—	—	—	56,500
Provision for Impairment of Investment in Certain Foreign Locations	—	—	—	(50,000)
Net Income	$ 172,852	$ 158,266	$ 177,096	$ 173,868
Net Income Per Share:				
Continuing Operations	$1.06	$ .98	$1.13	$1.09
Businesses Sold	.05	.04	.03	.01
Gain on Sales	—	—	—	.37
Provision for Impairment of Investment in Certain Foreign Locations	—	—	—	(.33)
Net Income per Share	$1.11	$1.02	$1.16	$1.14

	First Quarter 1983	Second Quarter 1983	Third Quarter 1983	Fourth Quarter 1983
Continuing Operations:				
Net Sales	$1,081,823	$1,033,969	$1,094,012	$1,063,495
Gross Profit	629,757	615,372	643,207	625,868
Income	149,982	137,635	155,696	147,533
Businesses Sold:				
Operations	7,159	5,297	8,344	15,587
Gain on Sales	—	—	—	—
Provision for Impairment of Investment in Certain Foreign Locations	—	—	—	—
Net Income	$ 157,141	$ 142,932	$ 164,040	$ 163,120
Net Income Per Share:				
Continuing Operations	$ .95	$ .88	$1.00	$ .94
Businesses Sold	.05	.03	.05	.10
Gain on Sales	—	—	—	—
Provision for Impairment of Investment in Certain Foreign Locations	—	—	—	—
Net Income per Share	$1.00	$ .91	$1.05	$1.04

Market Prices of Common Stock and Dividends

	1984 Range of Prices* High	1984 Range of Prices* Low	Dividends Per Share	1983 Range of Prices* High	1983 Range of Prices* Low	Dividends Per Share
First Quarter	$54.75	$48.63	$.66	$50.25	$41.75	$.60
Second Quarter	55.75	51.75	.66	52.25	42.88	.60
Third Quarter	53.63	48.13	.66	49.13	43.63	.60
Fourth Quarter	52.50	46.75	.66	54.25	48.13	.60

*Prices are those of the New York Stock Exchange—Composite Transactions.

Management's Discussion and Analysis of Financial Condition and Results of Operations

The following comments should be read in conjunction with the Chairman's Report to Shareholders on pages 2 to 6, the consolidated financial statements on pages 30 to 33, Note 11 to consolidated financial statements on page 36 and data on pages 37 and 38 with respect to the effects of inflation.

Results of Continuing Operations

Net sales in 1984 increased 5% over 1983. Sales in 1983 increased 8% over 1982. For 1984 and 1983, sales increased in all segments. For 1984, domestic sales of each segment increased while foreign sales, measured in U.S. dollars, declined.

Domestically, net sales of prescription drugs and medical supplies increased 9%, led by increases in our major pharmaceutical divisions, Wyeth and Ayerst. Wyeth's sales benefited from a 30% increase in sales of *Ativan*, a tranquilizer and a 10% increase in sales of oral contraceptives. In addition infant formula sales increased 20% domestically. Ayerst's domestic sales increase was led by a 25% increase in sales of hormonal products and a 17% increase in sales of cardiovascular drugs led by *Inderal* and *Inderide*.

Domestic sales of packaged medicines increased 10% paced by the successful introduction of *Advil*, a new analgesic product.

Domestic sales of food and household products increased by 6% for the year with sales of Brach's candy increasing by 13% led by *Pick-a-Mix* and several new products introduced in 1984. Domestic sales of American Home Foods increased by 6% while sales of Household products were flat.

Overall total domestic sales increased 8% for the year. For 1983, domestic net sales increased 11% overall.

Foreign sales of prescription drugs and medical supplies declined by 1% in 1984 while foreign sales of packaged medicines declined 16%, and food and household products declined 6%. Overall, foreign sales declined by 4% in 1984. Foreign sales in 1983 decreased by 1% over 1982. The foreign sales declines in 1984 were principally due to the continued strength of the U.S. dollar. Foreign sales measured in local currencies recorded gains in most major markets.

All industry segments recorded unit sales growth in 1984 over 1983 both in the U.S. and abroad except for a slight decline in unit sales of the foreign operations of the packaged medicines segment. Price increases also contributed to the sales growth in each of the segments; (however, the rate of price increases has declined with the decline in inflation). All industry segments recorded unit sales growth in 1983 over 1982 both in the U.S. and abroad.

The cost of goods sold as a percentage of net sales declined in both 1984 and 1983 versus the previous year, as a result of continued savings in certain raw material costs, and selling price increases.

Selling, administrative and general expenses increased in 1984 over 1983 primarily because of increased expenditures for research and development and increased promotional expenditures.

The increase in other income, net in 1984 was mainly attributable to an increase in interest income due to a larger portfolio and higher interest rates, on average, during the year and also to a decrease in foreign exchange losses. For 1983, the increase in other income, net was due to a gain from the sale of a portion of the investment in the common stock of the Wm. Wrigley Jr. Company.

Income before taxes increased 9% in 1984 over 1983 while income from continuing operations increased 11% due to a slightly lower effective tax rate (44.2% vs. 45.3%) mainly the result of increased investment tax credits and research credits. In 1983 income before taxes and income from continuing operations each increased by 10% over 1982. Net income per share from continuing operations increased 13% in 1984 over 1983 reflecting in part the effect of the repurchase by the Company of 5 million shares of its common stock during the year. Net income per share from continuing operations in 1983 increased by 10% over 1982.

Financial Condition

The Consolidated Balance Sheets and Consolidated Statements of Changes in Working Capital continue to reflect the Company's strong financial position. During 1984 the Company's current position was enhanced by cash generated from continuing operations and the proceeds on the sale of the housewares segment of the business notwithstanding the repurchase of more than 5 million shares of its common stock and an increase of $31 million in dividends paid on common and preferred stock. In view of its continuing liquid position, ability to generate cash and virtually debt-free balance sheet, the Company foresees no difficulty in financing its future needs.

Index

Accelerated Cost Recovery System (ACRS), 402–403, 414, 711, 716
Accelerated depreciation methods, 398–400
Account, 41–42, 61
  (*See also* Accounts)
Accountants(s):
  certified public, 9, 28, 275–276
  controller as, 10
  opinion on financial statements, 9, 589–590, 740
  tax services of, 9–10
Accounting:
  accrual basis of, 103, 130
  as basis for business decisions, 13
  cash basis of, 103
  cost, 10, 28
  defined, 4
  financial, 7–8
  governmental, 11–12
  as language of business, 4
  management, 11, 29
  primary business objectives and, 12–13
  private, 10–11
  purpose and nature of, 4, 28
Accounting applications of the computer, 238–239
Accounting cycle, 58–59, 61, 101–102, 143–144, 148
  diagram of, 145
Accounting entity concept, 581
Accounting equation, 21–22, 25–26, 28
Accounting information, 4–7
  classifying, 5
  communicating, 6–7
  recording, 5
  user-oriented character of, 6–7
  using, 8
Accounting period, 79, 103, 120
Accounting principles, 579–589
  authoritative support for, 580
  conceptual framework project for, 579
  generally accepted, 7–8, 529–530, 579

Accounting principles (*Cont.*):
  international, the quest for uniformity, 529
  need for, 578–579
Accounting Principles Board (APB), 579, 580
  APB Opinion No. 19, "Reporting Changes in Financial Position," 615
Accounting procedures:
  in a computer-based system, 102
  in a manual system, 101–102
Accounting Series Releases, 580
Accounting standards, 12
  need for, 578–579
Accounting systems:
  computer-based, 59–60
  design of, 10
  diagram of, 6
  EDP as (*see* Electronic data processing)
  manual (*see* Manual accounting systems)
Accounts:
  chart of, 49
  contra, 299, 324
  contra-asset, 91, 104, 299, 324
  contra-liability, 318, 542
  controlling, 216–218
  drawing, 431, 434–435
  financial statement order, 88
  ledger (*see* Ledger accounts)
  noncurrent, 625, 634
  sequence of, 88
  valuation, 299, 324
  (*See also* Account)
Accounts payable:
  classification of, in balance sheet, 185
  defined, 19
  subsidiary ledger for, 220–221, 240
Accounts receivable, 297–308
  aging of, 301–302
  analysis of, 308
  on balance sheet, classification of, 298–300, 315

Accounts receivable (*Cont.*):
  credit balances in, 307–308
  internal controls, 308
  subsidiary ledger for, 216–217, 241
  turnover in, 671–672
  uncollectible (*see* Uncollectible accounts)
Accrual of interest, 127–128
Accrual basis of accounting, 103, 130
Accrued expenses:
  adjusting entries for, 126–129
  defined, 148
Accrued revenue:
  adjusting entries for, 129–130
  defined, 148
Accumulated depreciation, 90–91, 103, 124–125
  not a fund of cash, 396
Acid-test ratio, 673, 675
ACRS (Accelerated Cost Recovery System), 402–403, 414, 711, 716
Adjusted gross income, 697–700, 716
Adjusted trial balance, 91–92, 103
Adjusting entries:
  for accrued expenses, 126–129
  for accrued revenue, 129–130
  defined, 103
  for depreciation, 91, 103
  four main types of, 121–122
  reason for, 121
  from work sheet, 140–141
After-closing trial balance, 101, 103, 144
Aging of accounts receivable, 301–302
AICPA (American Institute of Certified Public Accountants), 9, 12
  and generally accepted accounting principles, 580
Allowance for Doubtful Accounts, 299, 324
American Accounting Association, 12, 589
American Airlines, 468, 652
American Express credit card, 306
American Institute of Certified Public Accountants (AICPA), 9, 12, 580

American Telephone & Telegraph
Company (AT&T), 275
Amortization:
of bond premium or discount,
541–548, 556
defined, 540–541, 556
effective interest method, 544–548,
556
effective interest rate, 544, 557
from investor's viewpoint, 548–549
straight-line method, 541–544
theoretical considerations on, 544
of discount on notes payable, 318–319
of intangible assets, 410, 413, 415
Analysis of financial statements,
650–675
accounts receivable turnover,
671–672, 675
book value per share of common
stock, 664, 674
common size income statement, 656
by common stockholders, 663–668
comparative data in annual reports of
major corporations, 656–657
comparative financial statements,
652–653, 656–657, 675
component percentages in, 655, 675
dividend yield and price-earnings
ratio, 663–664
dollar and percentage changes in,
653–654
evaluating percentage changes in sales
and earnings, 654
illustrative analysis of, 660–674
impact of inflation on, 660
industry standards for, 658
inventory turnover, 671, 675
leverage, 667–668
by long-term creditors, 668–669
percentages misleading when base is
small, 654
by preferred stockholders, 669
quality of assets in, 660, 676
quality of earnings in, 659
quick ratio, 673, 675
ratios in, 656
return on investment (ROI), 665–666,
676
revenue and expense analysis,
664–665
by short-term creditors, 670–674
sources of financial information, 653
standards of comparison for, 658–659
summary of analytical measurements
used in, 674–675
times interest earned, 668–669, 675

Analysis of financial statements (*Cont.*):
tools of, 653
trend percentages, 655
working capital, amount and quality,
670–671, 675
APB (*see* Accounting Principles Board)
Articles of incorporation, 441
Assets:
capital stock issuance for, other than
cash, 450–451
current, 184–185, 197
defined, 17, 28
fixed (*see* Plant and equipment)
intangible (*see* Intangible assets)
quality of, 660, 676
rules of debit and credit, 43
tangible, 391
treasury stock not an asset, 486
valuation of, 17, 583–584
(*See also specific types of assets*)
Audit report, 9, 28
Auditing:
of corporations, 9, 28, 275–276, 740
internal, 11
Auditors' report on financial statements,
589–590, 740
Avco Financial Services, 539
Average-cost method of inventory
valuation, 359–360, 375
Avon Products, 444

Bad debts (*see* Uncollectible accounts)
Balance sheet:
account form, 94
analysis of (*see* Analysis of financial
statements)
classification, 183–186
comparative, 656–657, 661
consolidated, 509, 733
corporation, illustrated, 455
defined, 15–16, 28
effects of business transactions upon,
22–25
nature and purpose of, 15–16
report form, 94, 104
stockholders' equity section on, 455
Bank checking accounts:
control features of, 268
miscellaneous charges on, 270
NSF checks and, 271, 282
reconciliation of, 271–274, 282
service charges for, 270
statement of, 268–269
Bank of America, 519
Bank reconciliation, 271–274, 282

Bankers, 27
Batch processing, 238
Beginning inventory, 171–172
Board of directors, 442–443, 455
Bond premium and discount, 275,
539–549, 556, 557
amortization of (*see* Amortization, of
bond premium or discount)
Bonds:
authorization of, 534
callable, 535
characteristics of, 535
contract interest rate, 538, 556
convertible, 535, 551
coupon, 535
debenture, 535, 556
defined, 282
effect of bond financing on holders of
capital stock, 535–536
income on investments in, 277
interest on: entries to record earned,
277
payment of, 276–277
purchase of bonds between interest
dates, 277
maturity value of, 278, 282, 557
mortgage, 535
present value concept and, 538–539
quoted market prices of, 275, 535,
538–539
registered, 535
serial, 535
sinking fund, 550, 556
tax advantage of bond financing,
535–536
transferability of, 534–535
and trustee, 534
underwriter of, 534
yield rate on, 668
Bonds payable, 533–551
accounting entries for, 536–538
amortization of discount or premium
for, 541–542, 544–548
carrying value of, 544
conversion of, into common stock,
550–551
defined, 533–534
discount on, 539–542, 556
effective interest method of
amortization, discount or
premium, 544–548
issuance of: at discount, 539–542
between interest dates, 537–538
at premium, 542–543
recording issuance of bonds between
interest dates, 537–538

Bonds payable (*Cont.*):
  retirement of, 549–550
  straight-line amortization, discount or
    premium, 541–544
  and year-end adjustments for interest
    expense, 543–544, 548–549
Book value:
  defined, 125, 148, 487
  per share of common stock, 487, 489,
    664, 674
  of plant and equipment, 395, 415
  when both preferred and common
    stock outstanding, 488–489
Bookkeeping, 9
Books of original entry (*see* Journals)
British Petroleum, 520
Buildings, 393
Business combinations, purchase
    method and pooling-of-interests
    method, 513–514
Business decisions, accounting as basis
    for, 13
Business entity, 16, 28
Business objectives, 12–13
Bylaws, 441

Call provision:
  for bonds, 535
  for preferred stock, 448, 454
Capital account:
  in partnership, 434–435
  in single proprietorship, 430
Capital asset, 702, 716
Capital expenditures, 393, 415
Capital gains and losses, 702–704,
    717
Capital leases, 552–553, 556
Capital stock, 443–453
  authorization of, 443–444
  defined, 20–21
  effects of bond financing on holders
    of, 535–536
  issuance of, 443–445
    for assets other than cash, 450–451
  no-par, 445, 456
  par value of, 444–445, 456
  and stated capital, 445, 456
  subscriptions to, 451–452, 456
  underwriting of, 450, 456
  (*See also* Common stock; Preferred
    stock)
Carrying value:
  of bonds payable, 544
  of plant and equipment, 125
Carte Blanche credit card, 306

CASE IN POINT, 79, 236, 237, 260–261,
    263, 371, 372, 394, 450, 539, 551,
    556, 654, 660, 715–716
Cash:
  in balance sheet presentation, 259
  and cash registers, 260–261
  defined, 258
  disbursements of, 262–268
  dividends in, 82, 475–476
  internal control over, 259–260
  issuance of capital stock for assets
    other than, 450–451
  management responsibilities over, 259
  over and short, 261–262
  petty (*see* Petty cash fund)
  and prenumbered sales tickets, 261
  received in mail, 261
Cash basis of accounting, 103, 631–634,
    692–693, 716
Cash discounts, 169–170, 195–197
Cash flow from operations, 631–634
  and conversion of income statement
    to cash basis, 633–634
  payments for expenses, 633
  payments for purchases, 632–633
  from customers, 631–632
Cash flow analysis, 630
Cash flow statement, 630–631, 634
Cash over and short, 261–262
Cash payments journal, 223–225
Cash receipts, 260–262
Cash receipts journal, 220–223
Cash registers, 260–261
Certificate in Management Accounting,
    11, 28
Certified public accountant (CPA), 9, 28,
    275–276
Chart of accounts, 49
Check register, 264, 282
Check-signing machines, 263
Checking accounts (*see* Bank checking
    accounts)
Classification:
  of balance sheet, 183–186
  of income statement, 186–187
Classified financial statements, 182–187
Closing entries:
  defined, 95–96, 103
  of dividends accounts, 99–100
  of expense accounts, 96–97, 181
  illustrative diagram of, 100
  for Income Summary account, 97,
    181
  of inventory accounts, 180–181
  in merchandising business, 180–182
  in partnerships, 435–436

Closing entries (*Cont.*):
  reasons for, 95–96
  for revenue accounts, 96–97, 181
  summary of procedures for, 100–
    101
  from work sheet, 140–142
Coca-Cola Company, 413, 520
Common size income statement, 656
Common stock:
  book value per share of, 487, 489,
    664, 674
  converting bonds payable into, 535,
    551
  defined, 445–446
  earnings per share of, 472–475, 490,
    663, 674
  market price of, 450
  ownership rights, 442
  (*See also* Capital stock)
Common stockholders, financial
    statement analysis by, 663–668
Comparative financial statements,
    652–653
Component percentages, 655
Compound journal entry, 97
Computer-based accounting systems,
    59–60, 102, 143, 235–240
  advantages of, 235–236
  input controls, 238
  internal control and the computer,
    236
  journals and ledgers, 240
  on-line, real-time (OLRT) system,
    236, 238, 241
  organizational controls, 236–237
  payrolls, 239–240
  point-of-sale terminal, 235, 241
  program controls, 238
  retail sales, 239
  security controls, 237
  work sheets in, 143
Computer fraud, 236, 237
Conceptual framework project,
    579
Conservatism, 82, 104, 300, 589
Consistency in valuation of inventories,
    363, 375
Consistency principle, 587–588
Consolidated accounting entity, 506
Consolidated balance sheet, 509
Consolidated financial statements,
    505–515
  when to prepare, 514–515
Consolidated income statement, 512
Consolidation of foreign subsidiaries,
    528–530

Constant-dollar financial statements:
  defined, 592
  distinguished from current cost, 592
  income statement and, 595, 597
  monetary items in, 597–598, 601
  purchasing power gains and losses,
    597–599
Construction contracts, long-term,
  585–586, 601
Consumer Price Index (CPI), 590
Continental Airlines, 652
Contingent liabilities, 315
Continuing operations, 470
Contra-asset account, 91, 104, 299, 324
Contra-liability account, 318, 542
Controller, 10, 443
Controlling accounts, 216–218
Conversion feature:
  of bonds, 535, 551
  of preferred stock, 448, 449
Convertible preferred stock, 448–449
Copyrights, 413–414
Corporate earnings, rate of, 468,
  651–652
  specific examples of, 652
Corporations:
  advantages of the corporate form, 440
  articles of incorporation, 441
  audits of, 9, 28
  balance sheet, illustrated, 455, 509,
    733
  board of directors, 442–443, 454
  business combination and, 513
  bylaws of, 441
  capital stock of (*see* Capital stock)
  charter of, 441
  closely held, 454
  common stock of (*see* Common
    stock)
  controller of, 443
  defined, 14–15, 28, 440
  disadvantages of the corporate form,
    441
  formation of, 441–443
  income statement, illustrated, 93,
    139, 175, 474, 484, 734
  listed, 275–276, 440, 453
  minutes book, 443
  officer functions in, 443
  organization chart, 443
  organization costs of, 441–442, 456
  paid-in capital, 441, 443–444, 453, 455
  proxy statements of, 442
  publicly owned, 440
  (*See also* Stockholders; *specific
    types of stock*)

Corporations (*Cont.*):
  rights of stockholders, 442
  secretary of, 443
  stockholders' records, 452–453
  (*See also entries beginning with the
    term:* Stock)
Cost of goods sold:
  for merchandising firm, 170, 197
  restating, for price-level changes,
    597
Cost accounting, 10, 28
  (*See also* Current-cost accounting)
Cost depletion, 409
Cost principle, 17, 28, 583–584
Counterbalancing errors in inventory,
  354
Coupon bonds, 535
CPA (certified public accountant), 9, 28,
  275–276, 740
  report of, on financial statements,
    275–276, 589–590, 740
CPA certificate, 9
Credit, 42, 62
  (*See also* Debit and credit)
Credit balance(s), 42, 62
  in accounts receivable, 307–308
Credit card sales, 306–307
  bank credit cards, 306
  entry to record sale on, 307
  other credit cards, 306
Credit department, 298
Credit memoranda, 195, 197
Credit terms, 169
Creditors, 18, 28
  financial analysis statement by: long-
    term creditors, 668–669
    short-term creditors, 670–674
Currency fluctuations, 526–528
Current assets, 184–185, 197
Current-cost accounting, 592–600
  defined, 592, 593, 601
  distinguished from general price level,
    592–593
  (*See also* Replacement costs)
Current liabilities, 185, 197, 315–316
Current ratio, 185, 197, 672–673, 675

Data base, 60, 62
Data processing (*see* Electronic data
  processing)
Date of declaration (of dividend), 476
Date of payment (of dividend), 477
Date of record (of dividend), 476, 489
Debenture bonds, 535, 556
Debit, 42, 62

Debit and credit:
  defined, 42
  equality of, 43
  rules of, 43, 82
Debit balance, 42–43, 62
Debit memoranda, 195
Debt ratio, 669, 675
Debt securities, 533–535
Debts (*see* Liabilities)
Declining-balance depreciation,
  398–399, 415
Deductions:
  employee earnings, 343–345
  income tax, 697–701
    from adjusted gross income,
      700–701
    to arrive at adjusted gross income,
      697–700
    and excess itemized deductions,
      700–701, 717
    itemized deductions, 701
Deferred charges, 414, 415
Deferred revenue, 125–126
Deficit, 454, 455
Dependents, 701–702
Depletion of natural resources, 408–409,
  415
Deposits in transit, 271, 282
Depreciation:
  accelerated, 398–400, 415
  Accelerated Cost of Recovery System
    (ACRS), 402–403
  accumulated, 90–91, 103, 124–125,
    402
  adjusting entry for, 91
  allocation of cost, 395
  of assets related to natural resources,
    409
  causes of, 396
  defined, 89–90, 104, 395, 415
  for fractional periods, 400–401
  half-year convention on, 400–401,
    415
  historical cost versus replacement
    cost, 404
  inadequacy as cause of, 396
  and income taxes, 401–402
  and inflation, 403–404
  methods of computing, 396–401
    declining-balance, 398–399, 415
    straight-line, 396–398, 415
    sum-of-the-years'-digits, 399–400,
      415
    units-of-output, 398, 415
  not a process of valuation, 395
  not a store of cash, 396, 622

Depreciation (*Cont.*):
  obsolescence as cause of, 396
  physical deterioration as cause of, 396
  residual value, 397
  restating in constant dollars, 596–597
  revision of rates, 401
  salvage value, 397–400, 415
Diners' Club credit cards, 306
Direct charge-off method, 305–306, 324
Direct posting from invoices, 233
Directors, 442–443, 454
Disclosing the effects of inflation, 365–366
Disclosure of inventory profits, 364–366
Disclosure principle, 588, 601
Discontinued operations, 469–471, 490
Discount:
  on notes payable, 318–319, 322, 324
  on notes receivable, 322, 324
  purchase, 172–173
  of short-term notes, 317–319
  (*See also* Bond premium and discount; Cash discounts)
Discounting notes receivable, 313–314
Disposal of plant and equipment, 404–408
Dividends:
  in arrears, 447–448
  cash, 82, 475–476
  dates, 476–477
  declaration and payment of, 102–103
  defined, 20, 28, 82, 104
  entries for, 82, 85, 99–100, 277, 477
  liquidating, 477
  preferred, 446–447
  property, 477
  receipt of dividend, entry for, 277
  requirements for paying, 447, 476
  stock (*see* Stock dividends)
  times preferred dividends earned, 669
  yield of, 674
Dollar and percentage changes, 653–654
Dollar signs, 58
Donated capital, 452
Double-entry system, 44, 62
Double taxation of dividends, 441
Doubtful accounts (*see* Uncollectible accounts)
Dow-Jones Industrial Average, 556
Drawing accounts, 431, 434–435
Dun & Bradstreet, Inc., 298

Earned surplus (*see* Retained earnings; *specific sources of earnings*)

Earnings per share, 472–475, 663, 674
  defined, 472, 490
  in income statement presentation, 473–474
  interpreting per-share amounts, 474–475
  and preferred dividends, 473
  primary and fully diluted, 475, 490
  and stock dividends and splits, 480–481
  (*See also* Weighted-average shares outstanding)
EDP (*see* Electronic data processing)
Effective interest rate, 321, 544–548
Electronic cash registers, 236, 260–261
Electronic data processing (EDP):
  applications of, 238–240
    in accounting, 59–61, 102
    electronic cash registers, 236
    for journals and ledgers, 59–61, 240
    payroll, 239–244
  control totals, 238
  input controls, 238
  internal control, 236
  limit test 238
  organizational controls, 236–237
  program controls, 238, 241
  security controls, 237
Electronic scanning equipment, 260–261
Entity concept, 581, 601
Environment of inflation, 364
Equation, fundamental accounting, 21–22, 25–26, 28
Equipment (*see* Plant and equipment)
Equity:
  stockholders', on balance sheet, 19–21, 733
  (*See also* Owners' equity)
Equity method, 504–505, 512
Equity ratio, 667–668, 674
Equity securities, 278
Estimated liabilities, 316
Estimated tax payments, 705, 716
Excess itemized deductions, 700–701, 717
Exchange rates, foreign currencies and, 520–523
  strategies to avoid loss from rate fluctuations, 527
Excise tax, 700–701, 717
Ex-dividend date, 476–477, 490
Expenditures:
  capital, 393–394, 415
  indirect, inventory valuation and, 357
  revenue, 393–394, 415

Expenses:
  analysis of, 664–665
  defined, 81, 104
  expense transactions, illustrated, 83–85
  ledger accounts for, 82–83
  operating expense ratio, 665
  payments for, 124
  prepaid, 123–124
  rules of debit and credit, 82
  unrecorded, 126–129
  (*See also* Accrued expenses; Expenditures)
Extraordinary items, 471–472, 490
Exxon Corporation, 520, 652

FASB (*see* Financial Accounting Standards Board)
Federal income tax [*see* Income tax (federal)]
Federal Insurance Contributions Act (FICA) tax, 343–347
Federal Unemployment Tax Act (FUTA), 346–347
FICA (Federal Insurance Contributions Act) tax, 343–347
Fifo (first-in, first-out) method, 360, 375
Financial accounting, 7–8
Financial Accounting Standards Board (FASB), 12, 29, 579, 580
  Statement No. 12, 276
  Statement No. 13, 553
  Statement No. 17, 410
  Statement No. 33, 594
  Statement No. 82, 600
Financial forecast, 10, 192, 197
Financial information, sources of, 652
Financial statement order, 88–89, 104
Financial statements:
  analysis of (*see* Analysis of financial statements)
  classified, 182–187
  comparative, 652–653
  consolidated, 505–515
  constant-dollar (*see* Constant-dollar financial statements)
  defined, 15, 29
  interim, 144, 148
  marketable securities in, 281–282
  monthly, 144
  opinion on, 9, 589–590, 740
  prepared from work sheet, 179
  uncollectible accounts in, 298–299
  use of, by outsiders, 27
  (*See also* Income statement)

First-in, first-out (fifo) method, 360, 375
Fiscal year, 79–80, 104
Fixed assets (*see* Plant and equipment)
F.O.B. destination, 356, 375
F.O.B. shipping point, 356, 375
F.O.B. shipments, 174
Footing, 42, 62
Ford Motor Company, 713
Forecasting, 10, 192, 197
Foreign Corrupt Practices Act, 188
Foreign currencies and exchange rates, 520–523, 527
Foreign currency translation:
    cumulative translation adjustment, 528–529
    exchange rates, 520–523
    translating financial statement amounts, 528–529
Franchises, 413
Fraud:
    computer, 236, 237
    defined, 197
    prevention of, 191–192
Fully diluted earnings per share, 475, 490
Fundamental accounting equation, 21–22, 25–26, 28
Funds, defined as working capital, 616, 634
Funds flow:
    a comprehensive illustration, 623–630
    a simple illustration, 618–620
FUTA (Federal Unemployment Tax Act), 346–347

Gains and losses:
    capital, 702–704, 717
    on equipment sales, 405–406
    on marketable securities sales, 278
    nonoperating, 471–472
    in purchasing power, 597–599, 601
    (*See also* Losses; Profits; Uncollectible accounts)
General journal, 50–52, 226–227
General ledger, 41, 62, 228–230
General Motors Corporation, 446, 651–652, 654
General price index, 590
General price level, 590, 601
General price-level financial statements (*see* Constant-dollar financial statements)
Generally accepted accounting principles (GAAP), 7–8, 29, 529–530, 579, 601
    accounting entity concept, 581, 601

Generally accepted accounting principles (GAAP) (*Cont.*):
    authoritative support for, 580
    conservatism as a guide in resolving uncertainties, 589
    consistency principle, 587–588
    cost principle, 583–584
    CPAs' opinion on financial statements, 589–590
    disclosure principle, 588
    going-concern assumption, 17, 29, 581–582, 601
    matching principle, 587, 601
    materiality principle, 588–589, 601
    monetary principle, 582–583, 601
    objectivity principle, 583, 601
    realization principle, 584, 601
    time period principle, 582
Getty, J. Paul, 79
Goodwill:
    in business combinations, 513–514
    defined, 410–411, 415
    estimating, 411–412
    recording, in accounting records, 412, 513–514
Governmental accounting, 11–12
Gross income [*see* Income tax (federal)]
Gross profit on sales, 167, 176, 197
Gross profit method, 368–369, 375
Gross profit rate, 176–177

Hedging, currency fluctuations, 527–528
Historical cost, 404
Horizontal analysis, 658, 675

IBM Corporation, 520, 535, 539
Income:
    gross, 697, 717
    measurement of, 76–77
    net, 78–80, 104
        in constant dollars, 595–597
        on current cost basis, 599
    taxable, 702–704, 717
    (*See also specific sources of income*)
Income statement:
    analysis of, 663–665
    common size of, 656, 657
    comparative, 652–653, 662
    consolidated, 512, 734
    constant-dollar financial statement and, 595, 597
    and conversion to cash basis, 633–634
    for corporation, illustrated, 79, 175, 471, 474, 734
    earnings per share in, 473–475

Income statement (*Cont.*):
    interim, 144, 148
    for merchandising business, 174–176
    multiple-step, 186
    nature and purpose of, 92–93, 104
    of partnerships, 436
    single-step, 186–187
    statement of retained earnings combined with, 484
Income Summary account, 96–99, 180
Income tax (federal), 689–716
    Accelerated Cost Recovery System (ACRS), 402–403, 414, 711
    accounting versus taxable income and, 710
    adjusted gross income, 697–700, 716
    allocation of: between continuing and discontinuing operations, 469–471
        between regular operations and extraordinary items, 471–472
    alternative accounting methods for, 710–711
    capital asset, 702, 716
    capital gains and losses and, 702–704, 716, 717
    cash basis versus accrual basis for income tax returns, 103, 631–634, 692–693, 716
    and classes of taxpayers, 692
    computing corporate, illustrated, 708–710
    computing individual, illustrated, 706–707
    corporations, 708–713
    declaration of estimated tax, 705, 716
    deductions from adjusted gross income, 700–701
    deductions to arrive at adjusted gross income, 697–700
    dependents and, 701–702
    excess itemized deductions, 700–701, 717
    exclusions from gross income and, 697
    and financial structure, 715
    and form of business organization, 713–715
    gross income, 697, 717
    history and objectives of, 691–692
    importance of, 690–691
    individuals, 692–707
    and inflation, 696
    installment sales and, 324, 325
    interperiod income tax allocation, 711–713

Income tax (federal) (*Cont.*):
  IRA plan, 699
  itemized deductions (deductions from adjusted gross income), 700–701, 717
  marginal tax rates compared with average tax rates, 696, 717
  and marketable securities, 281
  and partnerships, 707
  payment of, 705–706
  personal exemptions, 701–702, 717
  planning, 713–717
  progressive nature of, 695
  quarterly payments of estimated tax, 705
  rates of tax: corporation, 708
    individuals, 693–694
  and tax formula for individuals, 696–698
  tax rate schedules, 694–695
  tax returns, tax refunds, and payment of the tax, 705–706
  tax shelters, 716, 717
  taxable income, individuals, 702–704, 717
  total income and gross income, 697
  wash sales, 704
  withholding makes the system work, 705–706
  zero bracket amount, 700, 717
  [*See also* Deductions, income tax; Tax(es); *entries beginning with the term:* Tax]
Independent auditors' report on financial statements, 9, 589–590, 741
Inflation:
  accounting for, 18
  and constant dollar accounting, 592, 600
  constant dollar income statement, 597
  and current cost accounting, 592, 600
  current cost income statement, 599
  defined, 590
  FASB Statement No. 33, disclosing the effects of inflation in financial statements, 594
  and GAAP, the greatest challenge to accounting, 590–591
  gains and losses in purchasing power, 597–599
  impact of inflation on financial statements, 660
  and inventories: disclosing the effects of inflation, 365–366
    the environment of inflation, 364–365

Inflation (*Cont.*):
  inventory profits, 364–365
  net income on a current cost basis, 599
  net income measured in constant dollars, 595–597
  original disclosure requirements for constant dollars and current costs, 594–595
  profits, fact or illusion, 591
  reduction in the amount of required disclosure, 600
  restating cost of goods sold for price-level changes, 596–597
  restating depreciation expense for price-level changes, 596–597
  two approaches to inflation accounting, 592
Insolvent company, 13
Installment method, 585, 601
Installment receivables, 323–324
Installment sales, 324, 325
Insurance, adjusting entries for insurance premiums, 123
Intangible asets:
  amortization of, 410
  characteristics of, 409–410
  copyrights, 413–414
  deferred charges, 414, 415
  franchises, 413
  goodwill, 410–412, 415, 513–514
  operating expenses versus, 410
  patents, 413
  trademarks, 413
Intercompany debt, elimination of, in consolidated financial statements, 509
Intercompany eliminations, 508–509
Intercompany revenue and expense, elimination of, in consolidated financial statements, 512
Intercompany stock ownership, elimination of, in consolidated financial statements, 508–509
Intercompany transactions, 507
Interest:
  accrual of, 127–128
  on bonds (*see* Bonds, interest on)
  computing, 309–311
  nature of, 309, 325
  rates of: effective, 321
    prevailing, 310–311
  times interest earned, 668–669, 675
Interest dates:
  issuance of bonds payable between, 537–538
  purchase of bonds between, 277

Interim financial statements, 144, 148
Internal auditing, 11, 191, 197
Internal control:
  accounting controls, 188
  accounts receivable, 308
  administrative controls, 188
  over cash, 259–260
  over cash payments, 262–268
  over cash receipts, 260–262
  and computers, 236
  defined, 14, 29, 187, 197
  and financial forecasts, 192
  Foreign Corrupt Practices Act and, 188
  and internal auditing, 191
  legal requirements and, 188
  limitations of, 192
  and organization plan, 188–191
  and perpetual inventory system, 370–371
  prevention of fraud with, 191
  over sales and purchases, 192–196
  and separation of accounting from custody of assets, 189–191
  with serially numbered documents, 192
  and subdivision of duties, 189
  of transactions, 189
Internal Revenue Code, 691
Internal Revenue Service, 11–12, 371, 691
International accounting and foreign currency translation, 519–530
International investors, 530
Interperiod income tax allocation, 711–713
Inventories:
  average-cost method, 359–360, 375
  beginning and ending, 171–172, 197
  consistency in valuation of, 363, 375
  counterbalancing errors in, 354
  defined, 170, 197, 351
  disclosing the effects of inflation, 365–366
  entry to close, 181
  entry to record, 181
  estimating: by gross-profit method, 368–369
    by retail method, 369–370
  and fictitious profits, 364–365
  first-in, first-out (fifo) method, 360, 375
  goods in transit, 356
  importance of accurate valuation of, 352–353
  and income measurement, 352

Inventories (*Cont.*):
  and inflation, 364
  and inventory profits, 364–365
  last-in, first-out (lifo) method,
    360–361, 375
  lower-of-cost-or-market rule and,
    366–367, 375
    application of, 367
  of manufacturing business, 351
  net realizable value of, 367
  passage of title and, 356
  periodic system of, 171, 197, 351
  perpetual system of, 351
    advantages of 374–375
    defined, 170–171, 197, 375
    general ledger entries for, 373–374
    and internal control, 370–371
  physical count of, 355, 375
  planning of, 355
  pricing of, 356–357
  replacement cost of, 365
  retail method of, 369–370, 375
  specific identification method,
    358–359, 375
  taking, 355–356
  theft and other losses and, 174
  turnover in, 671
  valuation of: consistency of, 363
    cost basis for, 357–358
    and indirect expenditures, 357
    and measurement of income, 352
  valuation errors and:
    counterbalancing errrors, 354
    effects of, 353–354
    relation of, to net income, 355
  valuation methods for: average-cost
    method, 359–360, 375
    compared, 361–362
    fifo, 360, 375
    lifo, 360–361, 375
    specific identification, 358–359, 375
  on work sheet, 177–178
Inventory profits, 364–365, 375
Inventory turnover, 671
Investments:
  rate of return on, 276–277
  (*See also specific types of
    investments*)
Invoices:
  defined, 194, 197
  direct posting from, 233
  illustration of, 194
  purchase, 194–195
  recording, at net price, 195–196
  sales, 194–195
  verification of, 195
Itemized deductions, 700–701, 717

Johnson & Johnson, 489
Journals, 49–54, 62, 214–227
  cash payments, 223–225
  cash receipts, 220–223
  defined, 49–50, 62
  general, 50–52, 226–227
  posting from, 52–54
  purchase, 218–220
  sales, 214–218
  special, 214

Land, 392–393
Land improvements, 393
Last-in, first-out (lifo) method, 360–361,
  375
Leases:
  capital, 552–553
  defined, 552
  off-balance-sheet financing of, 553
  operating, 553
Ledger:
  general, 41, 62
  subsidiary, 216–218, 220, 227,
    232–233, 241
Ledger accounts:
  defined, 41, 61
  financial statement order for, 88–89
  footings of, 42
  form of, 41
  general, 228–232
  illustrated, 45–48
  normal balance of, 42–43, 48
  numbering of, 49
  proving, 232–233
  for recording transactions, 45–47
  for revenue and expense, 82–83, 88
  running balance form of, 48
  sequence of, 49, 88
  subsidiary, 231–233
  T account form and, 41–42
Lessee, 552, 557
Lessor, 552, 557
Leverage, 667–668
Liabilities:
  contingent, 315
  contra-liability, 318, 542
  current, 185, 197, 315–316
  defined, 18–19, 29
  estimated, 316
  intercompany, 509
  long-term, 319–320, 533–534,
    668–669
  rules of debit and credit, 43
Lifo (last-in, first-out) method, 360–361,
  375
Limited partnership, 434, 455

Liquidating dividends, 477
Listed corporations, 275–276
Long-term capital gains and losses,
  703
Long-term construction contracts,
  accounting for, 585–586, 601
Long-term creditors, financial statement
  analysis by, 668–669
Long-term investments, 504
Loss contingencies, 555–557
Losses:
  inventory theft and other losses, 174
  on investments in marketable
    securities, 278–280
  and loss contingencies, 555–557
  unrealized, 279–280, 282
  (*See also* Gains and losses)
Lower-of-cost-or-market rule:
  for inventory, 366, 375
    application of, 367
  for marketable securities, 279–282

Maker of promissory note, 309, 325
Management accounting, 11, 29
Management advisory services, 10
Manual accounting systems, 214–235
  cash payments journals in, 223–225,
    241
  cash receipts journals in, 220–223,
    227–233, 241
  comparison with computer-based
    systems, 59
  controlling accounts and subsidiary
    ledgers in, 216–218, 241
  direct posting from invoices in, 233
  general journal in, 226–227
  ledger accounts in (*see* Ledger
    accounts)
  purchases journal in, 218–220, 241
  sales journal in, 214–218, 241
  unit record for transactions in, 235
Manufacturing business, inventory of,
  351
Manville Corporation, 556
Market price:
  of bonds and marketable securities,
    275
  of common stock, 275
Marketable securities:
  accounting for investments in,
    276–277
  as current assets, 276
  defined, 274, 282
  determining cost of, 278–281
  in financial statements, 281–282
  gains and losses on sale of, 278

Marketable securities (*Cont.*):
    income on investments in bonds and
        stocks, 277
    income tax rules on, 281
    portfolio of, 274
    quoted market prices for, 275
    reasons for investing in, 274
    valuation of, 278–281
        account for, 279–280
        debt securities, 278
        equity securities, 278–279
        lower-of-cost-or-market, 279–280
        market, 281
MasterCard credit card, 306
Matching principle, 81, 104, 587, 601
Materiality principle, 588–589, 601
Maturity date of note, 310, 325
Maturity value:
    bonds, 278
    notes receivable, 310, 325
Merchandise, 167
Merchandising business, 167–187
    balance sheet, 180
    income statement for, 174–176
    statement of retained earnings, 179
    transactions and related accounting
        entries in, 172–173
    work sheet for, 177–179
Minority interest, 512
Minutes book, 443
Monetary items, 597–598, 601
Monetary principle, 582–583, 601
Monthly financial statements, 144
Moody's Investors Service, 652
Mortgage bonds, 535
Mortgage notes payable, 553–554
Multiple-step income statement, 186,
    197
Mutual agency in partnerships, 433, 456

Natural resources:
    accounting for, 408–409
    depletion of, 408–409
        depreciation of related assets, 409
        percentage versus cost, 409
    nature of, 408, 415
Nestles, 520
Net identifiable assets, 411
Net income (*see* Income, net)
Net price method of recording purchase
    invoices, 195–197
Net sales, 167–168, 176–177, 197
Net worth (*see* Owners' equity)
New York Stock Exchange, 274–275,
    440, 453
Noncumulative stock, 448

Noncurrent accounts, 625, 634
Nonoperating gains and losses, 471–472
No-par capital stock, 445
Notes payable:
    amortization of discount, 318–319
    comparison of two forms of, 319–320
    defined, 19, 29, 325
    discount on, 318
    with interest in face amount, 317–318
    issued to banks, 316–317
    present value applied to, 319–321
        illustrated, 321–323
Notes receivable, 309–315
    accounting for, 311–313
    adjustments for interest on, 311–312
    classification of, in balance sheet, 315
    computing interest on, 309–310
    contingent liabilities and, 315
    defaults, 312–313
    defined, 309, 325
    discounting, 313–314
    illustrative entries for, 311–313
    installment receivables, 323–324
    maker, 309
    maturity value, 310
    payee, 309, 325
    present value applied to, 319–321
        illustrated, 321–323

Objectivity principle, 17–18, 583, 601
Off-balance-sheet financing, 553, 557
Office supplies, accounting for, 123–124
On-line, real-time (OLRT) system, 236,
    238, 241
Operating cycle, 184, 197
Operating expense ratio, 665, 674
Operating lease, 552, 557
Organization chart, 443
Organization costs, 441–442, 456
Outstanding checks, 270–271, 273, 282
Owners, use of financial statements by,
    27
Owners' equity:
    in corporations (*see* Corporations)
    decreases in, 20
    defined, 19, 29
    increases in, 20
    for partnership (*see* Partnerships)
    rules of debit and credit, 43
    in single proprietorship, 20

Paid-in capital, 441, 443–444, 453, 455
Pan American, 468, 682
Par value, 444–445, 456
Parent and subsidiary companies,
    505–506

Participating preferred stock, 449
Partnerships:
    accounting for, 434–437
    additional investments in, 435
    advantages and disadvantages of, 433
    capital accounts, 434–435
    closing entries, 435–436
    contract of, 434
    co-ownership of property profits, 433
    defined, 14, 29
    dividing partnership income, 437–439
    features of, 432–433
    formation of, 432, 434–435
    income dividing methods in, 437–439
    income statement, 436
    income tax of partners, 437
    initial investments in, 434–435
    liability of partners in, 433
    limited, 434, 455
    mutual agency, 433, 456
    opening the accounts of a new
        partnership, 434–435
    statement of partners' capitals, 437,
        456
    unlimited liability, 433
    withdrawals from, 435
Patents, 413
Payee of promissory note, 309, 325
Payroll accounting:
    computerized, 239–240
    [*See also* Tax(es), payroll]
Pension plans, 554
Percentage-of-completion method,
    585–586, 601
Percentage changes and dollar, 653–654
Percentage depletion, 409, 415
Periodic inventory system, 171, 197
Perpetual inventory system:
    advantages of, 374–375
    defined, 170–171, 197, 375
    general ledger entries for, 373–374
    records for, 372–373
Personal exemptions, 701–702, 717
Petty cash fund, 267–268, 282
Philadelphia Electric, 450
Physical inventory, 197, 371–375
Plant and equipment:
    amortization of intangibles, 410
    apportionment of lump sum purchase,
        393
    book value of, 395, 415
    buildings as, 393
    capital and revenue expenditures,
        393–394, 415
    carrying value of, 395, 415
    categories of, 391
    defined, 390–391

Plant and equipment (*Cont.*):
depreciation of (*see* Depreciation)
determining cost of, 391–393
disposal of, 404–408
FASB Statement No. 33 and, 404
gains and losses: on disposal of plant
and equipment, 405–406
for income tax purposes, 406–407
historical versus replacement cost of,
404
intangible assets, 409–415
land, 392
land improvements, 393
natural resources and (*see* Natural
resources)
replacement cost, 403–404, 415
disclosure of, 404
residual value of, 397–400, 415
as a stream of services, 391
trade-in of, 407–408
Point-of-sale terminal, 235, 241
Polaroid Corporation, 444
Pooling-of-interests method, 513–514
Portfolio (of securities), 274, 282
Posting:
the cash payments journal, 225
the cash receipts journal, 221–223
to controlling accounts, 217–218,
220, 222–223, 225–226
defined, 52, 62
directly from invoices, 233
illustration of, 53
procedure for, 52–54
to subsidiary ledgers, 218, 220, 222,
225
Predictive information, 468–469
Preemptive right of corporations, 442
Preferred stock:
callable, 448, 455
characteristics of, 446
convertible, 448–449
cumulative, 447–448
market price of, 449–450
noncumulative, 448
participating, 449
preferred as to assets, 448
preferred as to dividends, 446–447
(*See also* Capital stock)
Preferred stockholders, financial analysis
by, 669
Premium (*see* Bond premium and
discount)
Prenumbered sales tickets, 261
Prepaid expenses, 123, 148
Present value:
accounting applications of the present
value concept, 571–573

Present value (*Cont.*):
applied to long-term notes, 319–323,
571
applied to notes payable, 321–322,
571
illustrated, 321–323
applied to notes receivable, 322–324,
571
illustrated, 321–323
and bond prices, 538, 557, 572
concept of, 319–321, 325, 538, 567
discount periods of less than one year,
570–571
discounting annual cash flows,
569–570
effective rate of interest, 321
and estimating the value of goodwill,
572
of future cash receipts, 321, 325, 567
and installment sales, 323–324
and leases, 572–573
selecting an appropriate discount rate,
568–569
tables, 568–570
Price-earnings ratio, 472, 490, 663–664,
674
Price level, changes in, 590–591
Price Waterhouse & Co., 652
Primary earnings per share, 475
Principal amount, 316, 325
Principles of accounting (*see* Accounting
principles)
Prior period adjustments, 481–482, 490
Private accounting, 10–11
Proceeds from sale of note receivable,
313–314, 325
Profit and loss statement (*see* Income
statement)
Profits:
corporate, level of, 468, 651–652
defined, 77
economic function of, 77–78
fact or illusion, 591–592
inventory, 364–365
public opinion polls on, 468, 651
(*See also specific sources of profit*)
Program, 237, 241
Program controls, 238, 241
Promissory notes, 127, 148
maker of, 309, 325
payee of, 309, 325
Property, plant and equipment (*see*
Plant and equipment)
Property dividends, 477
Proxy statements, 442
Publicly owned corporations, 440
(*See also* Stockholders)

Purchase method in business
combinations, 513–514
Purchase orders, 193–194
Purchases:
account, 172
cash flow statement and, 632–633
discount on, 172–173
freight charges on, 173–174
internal control on, 192–196
invoice for, 194–195
journal of, 218–220
orders for, 193–194
returns and allowances on, 173
Purchases journal, 218–220
Purchasing power:
defined, 590–591, 601
gains and losses in, 597–599

Quality of assets, 660, 676
Quality of earnings, 659, 676
Quick ratio, 673, 675

R & D (research and development)
costs, 414
Rate of corporate earnings, 468
Rate of return on investment (ROI),
665–666, 676
Ratios, 656
Realization principle, 80, 104, 280, 282,
584, 601
Receiving reports, 193, 198
Reconciling the bank account, 270–274
Reconciling subsidiary ledgers and
controlling accounts, 232–233
Recording prepayments directly in
expense accounts, 124
Registered bonds, 535
Regulatory agencies, reports to, 8
Replacement costs:
for inventories, 365
for plant and equipment, 403–404,
415
disclosure of, 404
Report form balance sheet, 94, 104
Research and development (R & D)
costs, 414
Residual value of plant and equipment,
397–400, 415
Restrictions of retained earnings, 485,
490
Retail method of inventory, 369–370,
375
Retained earnings:
appropriations and restrictions of,
484–485, 490

Retained earnings (*Cont.*):
  deficit and, 453–454
  defined, 20, 29, 78, 104
  prior period adjustments, 481, 490
  statement of (*see* Statement of
    retained earnings)
Return:
  on common stockholders' equity, 666,
    674
  on investment (ROI), 665–666
  on total assets, 666, 674
  (*See also* Profits)
Revenue:
  closing entries for revenue accounts,
    96–97, 181
  collected in advance, 125–126
  defined, 80, 104
  and expense analysis, 664–665
  illustrative transactions, 83–85
  ledger accounts for, 80
  revenue expenditures, 393–394
  rules of debit and credit, 82
  (*See also* Accrued revenue)
Reversing entries, 144–148
  in a computer-based system, 147–
    148
  which adjusting entries should be
    reversed, 147
Revision of depreciation rates, 401
ROI (rate of return on investment),
    665–666, 676

Salaries:
  accrual of, 128–129
  reversing entries for, 146–147
Sales:
  credit terms, 169
  defined, 167–168
  discounts, 169–170
  entries to record, 168
  of equipment, 404–408
  installment, 324, 325
  internal controls, 192–196
  invoices, 194–195
  journal, 214–218
  of marketable securities, 278
  returns and allowances on, 168–169
  uncollectible accounts as percentages
    of, 302–303
  wash, 704
Sales journal, 214–218
Sales taxes, 182
Salvage value of plant and equipment,
    397–400, 415
Scrapping fully depreciated assets, 405
Sears, Roebuck & Co., 444, 657
Secretary of corporation, 443

Securities (*see specific types of*
    securities)
Securities and Exchange Commission
    (SEC), 12, 29, 580
Securities exchanges, 274–275
Segment of a business, 469
Service businesses, 167
Service charges by bank, 270
Short-term capital gains and losses, 703
Short-term creditors, financial
    statement analysis by, 670–674
Short-term notes, amortization of
    discount on, 318–319
Singer Company, The, 534
Single proprietorship, 430–432, 456
  capital account in, 20, 430
  closing the accounts in, 431
  defined, 14, 29, 430, 456
  drawing account in, 431
  financial statements of, 431–432
Single-step income statement, 186–187
Sinking fund bonds, 550, 556
Social security tax (FICA), 343–347
Solvency, 12, 29
Sony Corporation, 520
Special journals:
  four main types of, 214
  variations in, 223
Standard & Poor's Corporation, 652
Standard Oil Company of California, 478
State unemployment compensation tax,
    346–347
Stated capital, 445, 456
Statement of changes in financial
    position:
  comprehensive illustration of,
    623–630
  exchange transactions in, 621, 634
  nonoperating gains and losses in,
    622–623
  purpose of, 615, 635
  simple illustration of, 618–620
  working capital, 616–617
    effects of depreciation and, 622
    effects of transactions on, 620–621
    provided by operations, 621–623
    sources and uses of, 616–617
  working papers for, 625–628
Statement of retained earnings, 93–95,
    482–483, 490
  combined with income statement, 484
  defined, 93–94, 104
  prior period adjustments, treatment
    of, 483
  from work sheet, 139
Stock (*see* Common stock; Preferred
    stock; Treasury stock)

Stock certificate, 452, 456
Stock dividends:
  defined, 477, 490
  distinguished from stock splits, 480
  earnings per share and (*see* Earnings
    per share)
  effect of, on financial position, 478
  entries to record, 479–480
  from investor's viewpoint, 480–481
  memorandum entry for, 481
  reasons for, 478
Stock registrar, 453, 456
Stock splits, 480, 490
  distinguished from large stock
    dividend, 480
  memorandum entry, 481
Stock transfer agent, 453, 456
Stockholders:
  equity of, on balance sheet, 19–20,
    29, 489
  financial statment analysis by,
    663–669
  ledger of, 452–453, 456
  records of, 452–453
  rights of, 442
  (*See also specific types of stock*)
Straight-line amortization of bond
    discount, 541–544
Straight-line depreciation, 396–398, 415
Subscriptions to capital stock, 451–452
Subsidiary company, 505–506
  acquiring stock of, 510–511
  minority interest, 572
Subsidiary ledgers, 231–233
Sum-of-the-years'-digits depreciation,
    399–400, 415

T accounts, 41–42
Tangible assets, 391
Tax(es):
  avoidance, 690
  evasion, 690
  federal and state unemployment,
    346–347
  federal income [*see* Income tax
    (federal)]
  interperiod allocation of, 711–713
  payroll: employee deductions, 343
    on employer, 346–347
    employer's responsibility for
      amounts withheld, 345
    entries for, 346–347
  planning, 690, 713–717
  sales, 182
  social security, 343–347
  withholding, 705–706
  withholding statement, 346

Tax credits, 704
Tax planning, 690, 713–717
Tax rate schedules, 694–695
Tax rates, 693–695
  marginal versus average, 696
Tax returns, 705–706, 708
Tax services of accountants, 9–10, 690
Tax shelters, 716, 717
Tax tables, 706
Temporary owners' equity accounts, 95, 104
Theft of inventory, 174
Time period principle, 582
Times interest earned, 668–669, 675
Times preferred dividends earned, 675
Title, passage of, 356
Trademarks, 413
Trading in used assets on new, 407–408
Transactions:
  defined, 5, 29
  effects of: on accounting equation, 25–26
    on balance sheet, 22–25
  with foreign countries, 523–528
  intercompany, 507–509
  internal controls, 189
  recording, 45–47
  unit record for, 235
  (See also Purchases; Sales)
Translation adjustment, foreign currencies, 528–529
Transportation-in, 173–174
Treasurer, 443
Treasury stock:
  on balance sheet, 486
  defined, 485, 490
  entries to record purchase and reissuance of, 485–486
  not an asset, 486
  reissuance of, 486–487
  and restriction of retained earnings, 487
Trend percentages, 655
Trial balance:
  after-closing, 101, 103, 144
  illustrated, 56, 89
  sources of errors in, 57–58
  uses and limitations of, 56–57

Trustees, bonds, 534
TWA, 468, 652

Uncollectible accounts:
  adjusting entry, 302, 303
  aging of accounts receivable, 301–302, 324
  Allowance for Doubtful Accounts, 299–324
  balance sheet approach, 300–301
  conservatism as a factor in valuing accounts receivable, 300
  direct charge-off method for, 305–306, 324
  estimating, 298–302
  in financial statements, 298–299
  income statement approach, 302–303
  as percentage of sales, 302–303
  recovery of, 305
  writing off, 303–305
Underwriters:
  of bonds, 534
  of stock issues, 450
Unearned revenue, 125–126, 148
Unemployment compensation tax, 346–347
Unexpired insurance, 123
United Airlines, 489, 652
United States Steel, 489
Units-of-output depreciation, 398, 415
Unlimited liability in partnership, 433
Unrealized losses and gains, 279–280, 282
Unrecorded expenses, 126–127
Unrecorded revenue, 129–130

Valuation:
  of assets, 17, 583–584
  inventory (see Inventories, valuation of)
  of marketable securities (see Marketable securities, valuation of)
Valuation Allowance for Marketable Securities, 279–280, 282
Vertical analysis, 658, 676

Visa credit card, 306
Volkswagen, 520
Voucher, 264–265, 283
Voucher register, 264, 283
Voucher system, 263–267
  flow chart, 266
  preparing a voucher, 264

Wage and Tax Statement (Form W-2), 346
Walgreen Co., 551
Wasting assets (see Natural resources)
Weighted-average shares outstanding, 472–473
Western Air Lines, 652
Withdrawals by single proprietor or partner, 431, 435
Work sheet:
  adjusting entries from, 140–141
  closing entries from, 140, 142
  in computer-based systems, 143
  defined, 130–131, 148
  illustrated, 132–134, 136, 138
  for merchandising business, 177–179
  purpose of, 130–131
  self-balancing nature of, 137
  sequence of procedures, 131–137
  for service-type business, 130–138
  uses of, 137–142
Working capital, 615–617
  analysis of changes in (see Statement of changes in financial position, working capital)
  defined, 185–186, 635
  effect of transactions on, 620–621
  provided by operations, 621–623
  sources and uses of, 616–617
Write-off of uncollectible accounts receivable, 303–305

Yield rate:
  on bonds, 668
  on dividends, 663–664

Zero bracket amount, 700, 717